PAGE 52

ON THE ROAD

YOUR COMPLETE DESTINATION GUIDE
In-depth reviews, detailed listings and insider tips

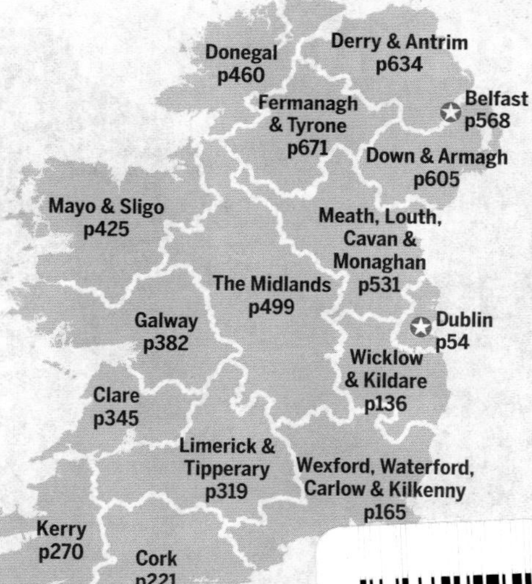

PAGE 725

SURVIVAL GUIDE

VITAL PRACTICAL INFORMATION TO HELP YOU HAVE A SMOOTH TRIP

THIS EDITION WRITTEN AND RESEARCHED BY

Fionn Davenport, Catherine Le Nevez, Etain O'Carroll, Ryan Ver Berkmoes, Neil Wilson

welcome to Ireland

Ireland of the Postcard

Yes, it exists. Along the peninsulas of the southwest, the brooding loneliness of Connemara and the dramatic wildness of County Donegal. You'll also find it in the lakelands of Counties Leitrim and Roscommon and the undulating hills of the sunny southeast ('sunny' of course being a relative term). Ireland has modernised dramatically, but some things never change. Brave the raging Atlantic on a crossing to Skellig Michael or spend a summer's evening in the yard of a thatched-cottage pub and you'll experience an Ireland that has changed little in generations, and is likely the Ireland you most came to see.

Tread Carefully...

...for you tread on history. Everywhere you go Ireland's history presents itself, from the breathtaking monuments of prehistoric Ireland at Brú na Bóinne to the fabulous ruins of Ireland's rich monastic past at Glendalough and Clonmacnoise. More recent history is visible in the famine museum in Cobh to the interactive displays of Vinegar Hill in County Wexford. And there's history so young that it's still considered the present, best experienced on a black-taxi tour of West Belfast or an examination of Derry's astonishingly colourful political murals.

GARETH MCCORMACK/LONELY PLANET IMAGES ©

A small country with a big reputation, helped along by a timeless, age-caressed landscape and a fascinating, friendly people, whose lyrical nature is expressed in the warmth of their welcome.

(left) Evening at the Giant's Causeway (p658)
(below) Enjoying the craic in the Market Bar (p110), Dublin

JONATHAN SMITH/LONELY PLANET IMAGES ©

A Cultural Well

Ireland operates an astonishing cultural surplus. Throughout your travels you will be overwhelmed by the choices on offer – a play by one of the theatrical greats in Dublin, a traditional music 'session' in a west-Ireland pub or a rock gig in a Limerick saloon. The Irish summer is awash with all manner of festivals, celebrating everything from flowers in bloom to high literature.

Tá Fáilte Romhat

(Taw fall-cha row-at) – 'You're very welcome'. Or, more famously, *céad míle fáilte* – a hundred thousand welcomes. Why a hundred thousand when one is perfectly adequate everywhere else? Irish friendliness is a tired cliché, an over-simplification of a character that is infinitely complex, but there's no denying that the Irish are warm and welcoming, if a little reserved at first. Wherever you meet them – the shop, the bar, the bank queue – there's a good chance a conversation will be struck up, pleasantries exchanged and, should you be a stranger in town, the offer of a helping hand extended. But, lest you think this is merely an act of unfettered altruism, rest assured that the comfort they seek is actually their own, for the Irish cannot be at ease in the company of those who aren't. A hundred thousand welcomes. It seems excessive, but in Ireland, excess is fine, so long as it's practised in moderation. Friendly but never fawning.

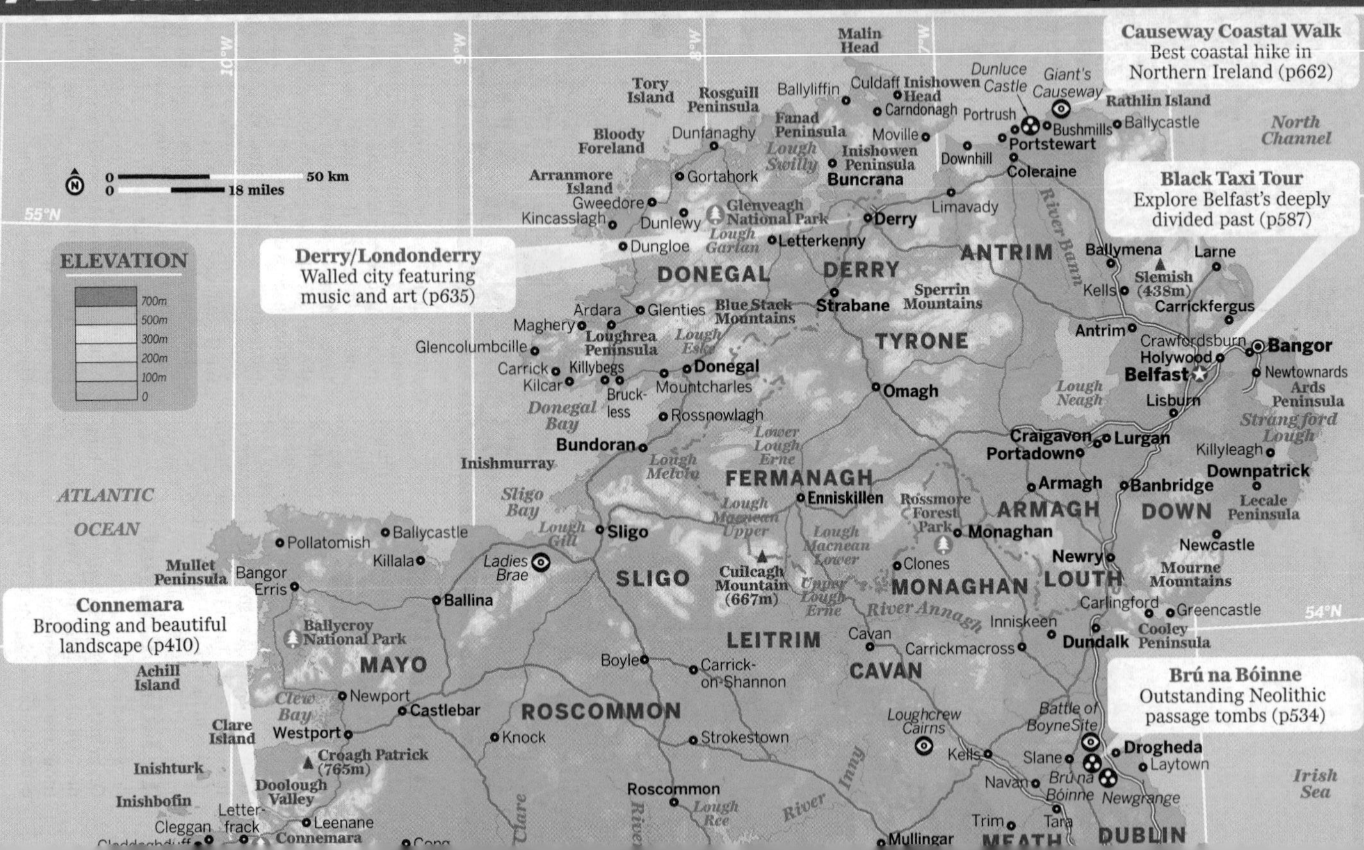
Causeway Coastal Walk
Best coastal hike in Northern Ireland (p662)
Black Taxi Tour
Explore Belfast's deeply divided past (p587)
Derry/Londonderry
Walled city featuring music and art (p635)
Connemara
Brooding and beautiful landscape (p410)
Brú na Bóinne
Outstanding Neolithic passage tombs (p534)
ELEVATION
700m
500m
300m
200m
100m
0
0
50 km
0
18 miles
55°N
54°N
10°W
9°W
8°W
7°W
ATLANTIC
OCEAN
North Channel
Irish Sea
Malin Head
Tory Island
Rosguill Peninsula
Ballyliffin
Culdaff
Inishowen Head
Carndonagh
Dunluce Castle
Giant's Causeway
Rathlin Island
Ballycastle
Portrush
Bushmills
Portstewart
Downhill
Coleraine
Bloody Foreland
Dunfanaghy
Fanad Peninsula
Lough Swilly
Moville
Inishowen Peninsula
Buncrana
Arranmore Island
Gortahork
Gweedore
Kincasslagh
Dunlewy
Glenveagh National Park
Lough Gartan
Derry
Limavady
Dungloe
Letterkenny
DONEGAL
DERRY
ANTRIM
River Bann
Ballymena
Larne
Slemish (438m)
Kells
Carrickfergus
Ardara
Glenties
Blue Stack Mountains
Strabane
Sperrin Mountains
Maghery
Loughrea Peninsula
Lough Eske
TYRONE
Antrim
Crawfordsburn
Bangor
Holywood
Belfast
Newtownards
Ards Peninsula
Glencolumbcille
Carrick
Killybegs
Kilcar
Donegal
Bruck-less
Mountcharles
Omagh
Lough Neagh
Lisburn
Donegal Bay
Rossnowlagh
Strangford Lough
Bundoran
Lower Lough Erne
Craigavon
Lurgan
Portadown
Killyleagh
Inishmurray
Lough Melvin
FERMANAGH
Downpatrick
Armagh
Banbridge
Sligo Bay
Enniskillen
Rossmore Forest Park
ARMAGH
DOWN
Lecale Peninsula
Lough Gill
Sligo
Lough Macnean Upper
Lough Macnean Lower
Monaghan
Pollatomish
Ballycastle
Killala
Ladies Brae
Newry
Newcastle
Mullet Peninsula
Bangor Erris
SLIGO
Cuilcagh Mountain (667m)
Clones
MONAGHAN
LOUTH
Mourne Mountains
Ballina
Upper Lough Erne
River Annagh
Carlingford
Greencastle
Ballycroy National Park
LEITRIM
Cavan
Inniskeen
Dundalk
Cooley Peninsula
MAYO
Boyle
Carrick-on-Shannon
Carrickmacross
CAVAN
Achill Island
Clew Bay
Newport
Castlebar
ROSCOMMON
Loughcrew Cairns
Battle of Boyne Site
Clare Island
Westport
Knock
Strokestown
Kells
Slane
Drogheda
Laytown
Croagh Patrick (765m)
Inny
Brú na Bóinne
Newgrange
Inishturk
Navan
Doolough Valley
Roscommon
Lough Ree
River
Inishbofin
Letter-frack
Leenane
Trim
Tara
Cleggan
Connemara
Mullingar
MEATH
DUBLIN
Clare
River

Clonmacnoise
Ancient monastic city overlooking the Shannon (p509)
Galway Festivals
Irish hedonism epitomised (p395)
Clare Coastal Walk
Cliffs and coastal splendours (p364)
Dingle
Beautiful, Irish-speaking fishing town (p299)
Ring of Kerry
Ireland's most famous panoramic loop (p284)
Cork
Superb restaurants in Ireland's second city (p223)
Rock of Cashel
Breathtaking ancient fortress atop rock (p335)
Kilkenny
Regal medieval city (p203)
Glendalough
Ancient monastic site in stunning setting (p142)
Dublin
Pulsating and friendly capital city (p54)
GALWAY
KILDARE
OFFALY
LAOIS
CARLOW
KILKENNY
WICKLOW
WEXFORD
TIPPERARY
CLARE
LIMERICK
KERRY
CORK
WATERFORD
DUBLIN
Howth
Dalkey
Maynooth
Straffan
Newbridge
Kildare
Athlone
Kilbeggan
Ballinasloe
Clonmacnoise
Durrow Abbey
Shannonbridge
Tullamore
Athenry
Galway
Clarinbridge
Kilcolgan
Loughrea
Banagher
Portarlington
Donnelly's Hollow
Mountmellick
Birr
Kinnitty
Portumna
Slieve Bloom Mountains
Rock of Dunamaise
Glendalough
Wicklow Mountains
River Avoca
Wicklow
Mizen Head
Roscrea
Timahoe
Mountshannon
Nenagh
Donaghmore
Abbeyleix
Castledermot
Durrow
Carlow
Ballina
Killaloe
Ballon
Bunratty
Shannon Airport
Limerick
Kilkenny
Ballingarry
Dungarvan
Borris
Mt Leinster (796m)
Ferns
Wexford Bay
Kells
Enniscorthy
Cashel
St Mullins
Fethard
River Barrow
Tipperary
Glen of Aherlow
Cahir
Clonmel
Carrick-on-Suir
River Suir
New Ross
Wexford
Curracloe Beach
Galtee Mountains
Newcastle
Mitchelstown Caves
Curraghmore Estate
Waterford
Rosslare Strand
Rosslare Harbour
Tramore
Hook Peninsula
Dunmore East
Kilmore Quay
Saltee Islands
River Blackwater
Lismore
Cappoquin
Dungarvan
Ring Peninsula
Mallow
Fota Wildlife Park
Youghal
Ardmore
Youghal Bay
Cork
Cobh
Kinsale
Clonakilty
Skibbereen
Castletownshend
Baltimore
Clear Island
Schull
Mizen Head Peninsula
Sheep's Head Peninsula
Bantry
Glengarriff
Beara Peninsula
Dursey Island
Gougane Barra Forest Park
Kenmare
Killarney
Killarney National Park
Kerry Bog Village Museum
Killorglin
Castlemaine
Tralee
Listowel
Ballingarry
Adare
Ballybunion
Tarbert
Mouth of the Shannon
Loop Head
Scattery Island
Kilrush
Kilkee
Miltown Malbay
Ennis
Ennistymon
Liscannor
Hag's Head
Cliffs of Moher
Corofin
Kilfenora
Lisdoonvarna
Doolin
Inisheer
Inishmaan
Inishmór
Aran Islands
Fanore
Burren
Black Head
Ballyvaughan
Kinvara
Gort
Mace Head
Omey Island
Cashel
Roundstone
Oughterard
Dingle Peninsula
Connor Pass
Annascaul
Inch
Dingle
Rossbeigh Strand
Kells
Caherciveen
Ring of Kerry
Valentia Island
Portmagee
Sneem
Waterville
Caherdaniel
Skellig Islands
Skellig Ring
St George's Channel
53°N
52°N
9°W
8°W
7°W
6°W

21 TOP EXPERIENCES

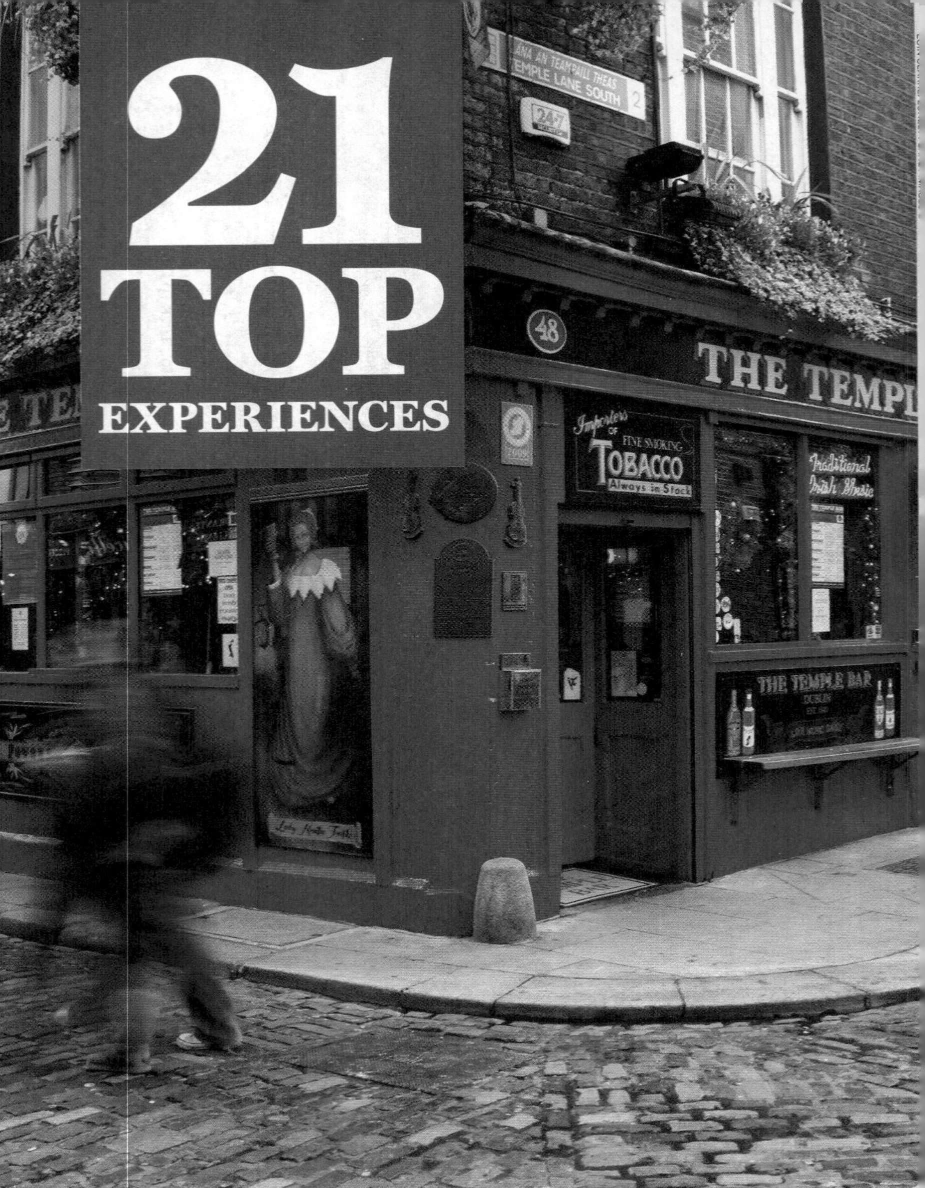

The Pub

1 Every town and hamlet has at least one: no matter where you go, you'll find that the social heart of the country beats loudest in the pub, still the best place to discover what makes the country tick. In suitable surroundings – whether a quiet traditional pub with flagstone floors and a large peat fire or a more modern bar with flashing lights and music – take a moment or an evening to listen for that beating heart…and drink some decent beer in the process. Pub in Temple Bar, Dublin, above

Dublin

2 Ireland's capital (p54) and largest city by some stretch is the main gateway into the country, but it has enough distractions to keep visitors mesmerised for at least a few days. From world-class museums and entertainment, superb dining and top-grade hotels, Dublin has all the baubles of a major international metropolis. But the real clinchers are Dubliners themselves, who are friendlier, more easy-going and welcoming than the burghers of virtually any other European capital. And it's the home of Guinness. O'Connell Bridge and O'Connell St, below

Connemara, County Galway

3 A filigreed coast of tiny coves and beaches is the Connemara Peninsula's (p410) beautiful border with the wild waters of the Atlantic. Wandering characterful roads bring you from one village to another, each with trad pubs and restaurants serving seafood chowder cooked from recipes that are family secrets. Inland, the scenic drama is even greater. In fantastically desolate valleys, green hills, yellow wildflowers and wild streams reflecting the blue sky provide elemental beauty. Rambles take you far from others, back to a simpler time. Clifden and Connemara mountains, right

Traditional Music

4 Western Europe's most vibrant folk music is Irish traditional music (p712), which may have earned worldwide fame thanks to the likes of Riverdance but is best expressed in a more sedate setting, usually an old-fashioned pub. The west of Ireland is particularly musical: from Donegal down to Kerry there are centres of musical excellence, none more so than Doolin (p311) in County Clare, the unofficial capital of Irish music. It's unlikely you'll be asked to join in, but there's nothing stopping your foot from tapping and your hands from clapping. Playing Celtic music at a céilidh, left

Glendalough, County Wicklow

5 St Kevin knew a thing or two about magical locations. When he chose a remote cave on a glacial lake nestled at the base of a forested valley as his monastic retreat, he inadvertently founded a settlement (p142) that would later prove to be one of Ireland's most dynamic universities and, in our time, one of the country's most beautiful ruined sites. The remains of the settlement (including an intact round tower), coupled with the stunning scenery, are unforgettable. St Kevin's Kitchen, Glendalough, right

Galway City

7 One word to describe Galway city (p384)? Craic! Ireland's liveliest city literally hums through the night at music-filled pubs where you can hear three old guys playing spoons and fiddles or a hot, young band. Join the locals as they bounce from place to place, never knowing what fun lies ahead but certain of the possibility. Add in local bounty such as the famous oysters and nearby adventure in the Connemara Peninsula and the Aran Islands and the fun never ends. Galway City harbour, below

Dingle, County Kerry

6 Dingle is the name of both the picturesque peninsula (p297) jutting into the Atlantic from County Kerry, strewn with ancient ruins, and its delightful main town (p299), the peninsula's beating heart. Fishing boats unload fish and shellfish that couldn't be any fresher if you caught it yourself, many pubs are untouched since their earlier incarnations as old-fashioned shops, artists sell their creations (including beautiful jewellery with Irish designs) at intriguing boutiques, and toe-tapping trad sessions take place around roaring pub fires. Slea Head, Dingle Peninsula, above

Walking & Hiking

8 Yes, you can visit the country easily enough by car, but Ireland is best explored on foot, whether you opt for a gentle afternoon stroll along a canal towpath or take on the challenge of any of the 31 waymarked long-distance routes. There are coastal walks and mountain hikes; you can explore towns and villages along the way or steer clear of civilisation by traipsing along lonely moorland and across barren bogs. All you'll need is a decent pair of boots and, inevitably, a rain jacket. Diamond Hill, Connemara National Park, below

Brú na Bóinne, County Meath

9 Looking at once ancient and yet eerily futuristic, Newgrange's immense, round, white stone walls topped by a grass dome is one of the most extraordinary sights you'll ever see. Part of the vast Neolithic necropolis Brú na Bóinne (the Boyne Palace; p534), it contains Ireland's finest Stone Age passage tomb, predating the Pyramids by some six centuries. Most extraordinary of all is the tomb's precise alignment with the sun at the time of the winter solstice. Early engineering at its finest. Passage tomb, Newgrange, below

JOHN ELK III/LONELY PLANET IMAGES ©

Rock of Cashel, County Tipperary

10 Soaring up from the green Tipperary pastures, this ancient fortress (p335) takes your breath away at first sight. The seat of kings and churchmen who ruled over the region for more than a thousand years, it rivalled Tara as a centre of power in Ireland for 400 years. Entered through the 15th-century Hall of the Vicars Choral, its impervious walls guard an awesome enclosure with a complete round tower, a 13th-century Gothic cathedral and the most magnificent 12th-century Romanesque chapel in Ireland. Cathedral, Rock of Cashel, left

Links Golf

11 If Scotland is the home of golf, then Ireland is where golf goes on holiday. And the best vacation spots are along the sea, where the country's collection of seaside links are dotted in a steady string along virtually the entire Irish coastline, each more revealed than carved in the undulating, marram-grass-covered landscapes. Some of the world's best-known courses share spectacular scenery with lesser-known gems, and each offers the golfer the opportunity to test their skills against the raw materials provided by Mother Nature.

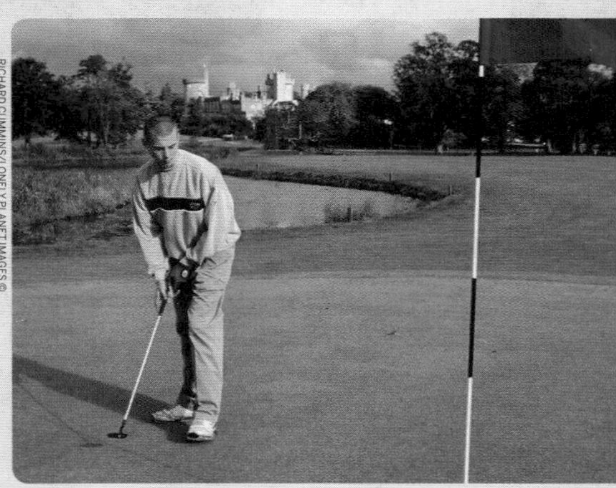
RICHARD CUMMINS/LONELY PLANET IMAGES ©

RICHARD CUMMINS/LONELY PLANET IMAGES ©

Cork City

12 The Republic's second city (p223) is second only in terms of size – in every other respect it will bear no competition. A tidy, compact city centre is home to an enticing collection of art galleries, museums and – most especially – places to eat. From cheap cafes to top-end gourmet restaurants, Cork City excels, although it's hardly a surprise given the county's exceptional foodie reputation. At the heart of it is the simply wonderful English Market, a covered produce market that is an attraction unto itself. St Fin Barre's Cathedral and the River Lee, Cork City, left

Ring of Kerry

13 Driving around the Ring of Kerry (p284) is an unforgettable experience in itself, but you don't need to limit yourself to the main route. Along this 179km loop around the Iveragh Peninsula there are countless opportunities for detours. Near Killorglin, it's a short hop up to the beautiful, little-known Cromane Peninsula. Between Portmagee and Waterville, you can explore the Skellig Ring. The peninsula's interior offers mesmerising mountain views. And that's just for starters. Wherever your travels take you, remember to charge your camera!

JOHN ELK III/LONELY PLANET IMAGES ©

DAMIAN TULLY/ALAMY ©

Black Taxi Tour, Belfast

14 No trip to Northern Ireland is complete without visiting the Republican and Loyalist murals (p584) of Belfast's Falls and Shankhill districts. But for an outsider, the city's bitterly divided society can be hard to get your head around. Without a local guide to provide some background and explanation, the murals can be just so much garish paint. Belfast's black taxi tours are justifiably famous because they provide that context, with drivers who are both insightful and darkly humorous without making light of a serious and often tragic situation. Republican murals along Falls Rd, left

Kilkenny City

15 From its regal castle to its soaring medieval cathedral, Kilkenny (p203) exudes a permanence and culture that have made it an unmissable stop on journeys to the south and west. Its namesake county boasts scores of artisans and craftspeople and you can browse their wares at Kilkenny's classy shops and boutiques. Chefs eschew Dublin in order to be close to the source of Kilkenny's wonderful produce and you can enjoy the local brewery's namesake brew at scores of delightful pubs. Houses along the River Nore, Kilkenny City, left

Causeway Coastal Walk

16 Put on your walking boots and rucksack and set off along one of Ireland's finest coastal walks, stretching for 16 scenic kilometres between the swaying rope bridge of Carrick-a-Rede (p659) and the geological flourish of the Giant's Causeway (p658). This is coastal hiking at its best, offering an ever-changing vista of cliffs and islands, sandy beaches and ruined castles, framed by scenic, seabird-haunted Rathlin Island at one end and the cheering prospect of a dram or two at the Old Bushmills Distillery at the other. Carrick-a-Rede rope bridge, County Antrim, right

Castles & Stately Homes

17 The Anglo-Normans left an indelible stamp on Ireland, best seen in the country's collection of handsome homes and impressive castles, built to reflect the power, glory and wealth of their respective owners. Although some have fallen into ruin, many have been meticulously maintained, including the superb country piles designed in the Georgian (or Palladian) style, found in pastoral settings around Dublin. Others have been converted from homes to luxury hotels and are memorable overnight experiences. Powerscourt Estate, County Wicklow, left

Clonmacnoise, County Offaly

18 One of Ireland's most important ancient monastic cities, Clonmacnoise (p509) was founded by St Ciarán in the 6th century and soon became an unrivalled bastion of religion, literature and art. Attracting monks and lay people from all over Europe, it helped earn Ireland the title of the 'land of saints and scholars'. Most of what remains of the magnificent ecclesiastical city dates from the 10th to 12th centuries and is in remarkably good condition with numerous early churches, high crosses, round towers and graves overlooking the River Shannon. Monastic site, Clomacnoise, below

Derry/Londonderry

19 History runs deep in Northern Ireland's second city (p635). The symbols of the country's sectarian past are evident, from the 17th-century city walls built to protect Protestant settlers, to the bipartite Republican/Loyalist name, Derry/Londonderry. But the new bridge that spans the River Foyle provides another symbol – of an attempt to bridge that divide and to look to the future as a city filled with a restless creative energy, expressed in its powerful murals, vibrant music scene and numerous art galleries, and now nominated as UK City of Culture 2013. Maurice Harron's Hands Across the Divide Peace Monument, Derry/Londonderry, below

A Gaelic Football or Hurling Match

20 It depends on whether you're in a football or hurling stronghold (some, like County Cork, are both) but attending a match of the county's chosen sport (p722) is not just a unique Irish experience but also a key to unlocking local passions and understanding one of the cultural pillars of Ireland. Whether you attend a club football match in County Galway or an intercounty hurling battle between old foes like Kilkenny and Tipperary, you cannot but be swept up in the emotion of it all. Kilmacud Crokes v Cuala hurling match, left

Clare Coast

21 Bathed in the golden glow of the late afternoon sun, the iconic Cliffs of Moher (p368) are but one of the splendours of County Clare. From a boat bobbing below, the towering stone faces have a jaw-dropping dramatic beauty that's enlivened by scores of sea birds, including cute little puffins. Down south in Loop Head, pillars of rock towering above the sea have abandoned stone cottages whose very existence is inexplicable. All along the coast are cute little villages like trad-session-filled Ennistymon and the surfer mecca of Lahinch. Cliffs of Moher, the Burren, above

need to know

Currency

» Euro (€) – Republic of Ireland

» Pound Sterling (£) – Northern Ireland

Language

» English and Irish

When to Go

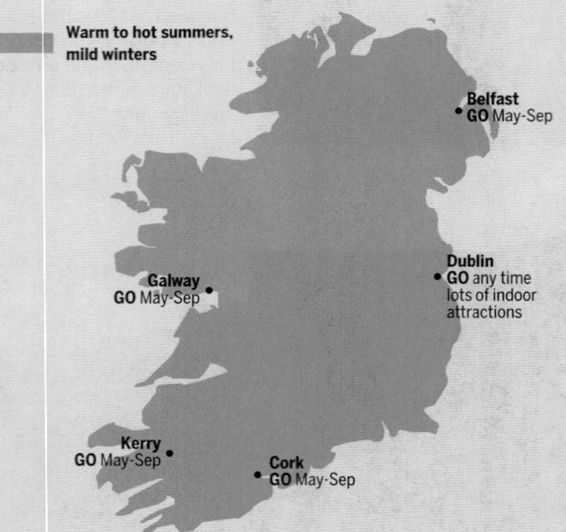

High Season

(Jun–Aug)

» Weather at its best.

» Accommodation rates at their highest (especially August).

» Tourist peak in Dublin, Kerry, southern and western coasts.

Shoulder

(Easter to end May, mid-Sep to end Oct)

» Weather often good, sun and rain in May. 'Indian summers' and often warm in September.

» Crowds and accommodation rates drop off.

Low Season

(Nov–Feb)

» Reduced opening hours from October to Easter; some destinations shut down.

» Cold and wet weather throughout the country; fog can reduce visibility.

» Big city attractions operate as normal.

Your Daily Budget

Budget less than

€60

» Dorm beds €12–20

» Cheap meals in cafes and pubs €6–12

» Inter-city bus travel €12–25 for 200km trip

» Pint €4.50

Midrange

€60-120

» Midrange hotel or B&B €40–100 (more in Dublin) per double room

» Main course in midrange restaurant €10–18

» Car rental from €40 per day

» Three-hour train journey €65

Top End over

€120

» Four-star hotel stay from €150

» Three-course meal in good restaurant around €50 per person

» Top round of golf from €80 midweek

Money

» Change bureaus and ATMs widely available, especially in cities and major towns. Credit cards accepted in all hotels, many B&Bs and most restaurants.

Visas

» Not required by most citizens of Europe, Australia, NZ, USA and Canada.

Mobile Phones

» Phones from most other countries work in Ireland, but attract roaming charges. Local SIM cards cost from €10; SIM and basic handset around €40.

Driving

» Drive on left. Steering wheels on right. Most hire (rental) cars have manual gears (stick shift).

Websites

» **Entertainment Ireland** (www.entertainment.ie) Countrywide listings for every kind of entertainment

» **Failte Ireland** (www.discoverireland.ie) Official tourist board site – practical info and a huge accommodation database

» **Lonely Planet** (www.lonelyplanet.com) Destination information, hotel bookings, traveller forums and more

» **Northern Ireland Tourist Board** (www.nitb.com) Official tourist site

Exchange Rates

Australia	A$1	€0.75
Canada	C$1	€0.73
Japan	Y100	€0.95
New Zealand	NZ$1	€0.60
UK	£1	€1.15
USA	US$1	€0.73

For current exchange rates see www.xe.com

Important Numbers

Include code only when outside area or from a mobile phone. Drop initial 0 when abroad.

Country Code	☎+353 Republic ☎+44 Northern Ireland
International Access Code	☎00
Emergency (police, fire, ambulance)	☎999

Arriving in Ireland

» **Dublin Airport**

Private coach – every 15 minutes to city centre (€7)

Taxi – 30–45 minutes to city centre (€20–25)

» **Dun Laoghaire Ferry Port**

Bus – Public bus about 45 minutes to city centre

DART (suburban rail) – about 25 minutes to city centre

» **Dublin Port Terminal**

Bus – timed to coincide with arrivals & departures (€2.50)

Measuring Up

The measures might have the same name, but they're a little bit different. With drinks, bear in mind that the Irish (or imperial) pint is bigger than the US one, and that Irish bartenders serve a smaller measure of spirits than their counterparts elsewhere.

ITEM	US SIZE	EUROPEAN SIZE	IRISH/UK SIZE
Dress (Women)	6	34	8
Pint (1)		473mL	568mL
Shoes (Men)	9	41	8
Shoes (Women)	6	38	4
Shirts (Men)	14	36	14
Spirits	59mL	50mL	35.5mL
Suits (Men)	40	50	40

first time

Everyone needs a helping hand when they visit a country for the first time. There are phrases to learn, customs to get used to and etiquette to understand. The following section will help demystify Ireland so your first trip goes as smoothly as your fifth.

Top Tips for Your Trip

» Quality rather than quantity should be your goal: instead of a hair-raising race to see everything, pick a handful of destinations and give yourself time to linger. The most memorable experiences in Ireland are often the ones where you're doing very little at all.

» If you're driving, get off the main roads when you can: some of the country's most stunning scenery is best enjoyed on secondary or tertiary roads that wind their narrow way through standout photo ops.

» Make the effort to greet the locals: the best experiences of Ireland are to be had courtesy of the Irish themselves, whose helpfulness, friendliness and fun has not been overexaggerated.

Booking Ahead

If you're planning to visit in the high season, the sooner you book your accommodation the better – up to two months in advance for a July visit. Activities should also be booked now – cooking courses, organised tours, etc.

A month before you travel book your hire car and reserve a table in whatever top-end restaurant you plan to dine in. Now is also the time to make theatre reservations, especially for new productions.

Two weeks before you arrive, check attraction opening hours and prices. A week before, get the weather forecast. Then ignore it.

What to Wear

Ireland is a fairly casual destination and you can wear pretty much whatever you like all the time. For fancy dinners, smart casual is all that's required – no restaurant will insist on jackets or ties, as won't any theatre or concert hall.

Ireland's youth have become far more comfortable with their bodies than the generations that preceded them, so summer wear has seen hemlines rise and necklines plunge. Summers, however, are warm but rarely hot, so you'll always want something around your legs and shoulders when the inevitable cool sets in.

In the end, the factor that will determine your outfits the most is the weather, which also means that a light, waterproof jacket should always be close at hand, preferably one that you can fold and keep in a shoulder bag.

What to Pack

» Good walking shoes, as Ireland is best appreciated on foot

» Raincoat – you will undoubtedly need it

» UK/Ireland electrical adapter

» A finely honed sense of humour

» A hollow leg – all that beer has to go somewhere

» Irish-themed MP3 playlist

Checklist

» Make sure your passport is valid for at least six months past your arrival date

» Make all necessary bookings (for accommodation, events and travel)

» Check the airline baggage restrictions

» Inform your debit-/credit-card company

» Arrange for appropriate travel insurance (see p729)

» Check if you can use your mobile/cell phone (p731)

Etiquette

Although largely informal in their everyday dealings, the Irish do observe some (unspoken) rules of etiquette.

» Greetings
Shake hands with men, women and children when meeting for the first time and when saying goodbye. Irish expect a firm handshake with eye contact. Female friends are greeted with a single (air) kiss.

» Conversation
Generally friendly but often reserved, the Irish avoid conversations that might embarrass. They are deeply mistrustful of 'oversharers'.

» Language
The Irish speak English quickly and strong accents can often be indecipherable. Don't take offence at indiscriminate bad language; many Irish unconsciously pepper their speech with curse words, which are intended only to be emphatic.

» Round System
The Irish generally take it in turns to buy a 'round' of drinks for the whole group and everyone is expected to take part. The next round should always be bought before the first round is drunk.

Tipping

» Hotels
One euro per bag is standard; gratuity for cleaning staff completely at your discretion.

» Pubs
Not expected unless table service is provided, then €1/£1 for a round of drinks.

» Restaurants
For decent service 10%, up to 15% in more expensive places.

» Taxis
Tip 10% of fare, or rounded up to nearest euro/pound.

» Toilet Attendants
Only loose change, no more than 50c/50p.

Money

ATMs can generally be found throughout Ireland; even in the smallest villages chances are a shop will have one. All ATMs are linked to the main international money systems, so you should have no issue withdrawing money with your bank's own card – but be sure to check with your bank before you travel.

Credit and debit cards can be used almost everywhere except for some rural B&Bs that only accept cash. Make sure bars or restaurants will accept cards before you order – some don't. The most popular cards are Visa and MasterCard; American Express is only accepted by the major chains, and virtually no one will accept Diners or JCB. Chip-and-PIN is the norm for card transactions – only a few places will accept a signature.

If you don't want to rely on plastic, banks, post offices and some of the larger hotels will change cash and travellers cheques.

what's new

For this new edition of Ireland, our authors have hunted down the fresh, the revamped, the transformed, the hot and the happening. These are some of our favourites. For up-to-the-minute reviews and recommendations, see lonelyplanet.com/ireland.

National Museum of Ireland – Natural History

1 Following the collapse of its central staircase, the 150-year-old 'Dead Zoo' was forced to close for a major revamp. Thankfully, it has now reopened and once again we can gawk admiringly at the two-million-odd exhibits from all over the world in a grand old building that doesn't seem to have changed much since Dr Livingstone cut the ribbon in 1857 (p75).

Titanic Quarter

2 The long overdue construction of the 'iconic visitor attraction' centred on the construction of the world's most famous sunken ship is scheduled for completion in April 2012 (p578).

Waterford Museum of Treasures

3 The interactive museum detailing Waterford's thousand-year history moved to the newly renovated Bishop's Palace, an 18th-century stunner on the Mall (p183).

Peace Bridge

4 An elegant new footbridge is but the most visible sign of Derry City's makeover, just in time for its starring role as UK City of Culture in 2013 (p635).

Little Museum of Dublin

5 Excellent new museum that aims to serve as a 'biography of the city' and whose myriad exhibits have all been donated by Dubliners (p79).

Foxford Woollen Mill

6 A sparkling new visitor centre in an old (but still functioning) woollen mill built to ease post-Famine suffering by offering much-needed work to locals (p445).

Carlow County Museum

7 The dust has been blown off this small museum housed in an old convent; it's now one of the highlights of a visit to Carlow Town (p198).

Model

8 Sligo's top art gallery – home to the excellent Niland Collection – has been expanded to accommodate new galleries and a permanent performance space (p447).

Temple House Festival

9 A three-day festival featuring an eclectic line up of music, arts, workshops and woodland crafts is the west's answer to Electric Picnic (p447).

Rowan Tree Hostel

10 An 18th-century gentlemen's club has been successfully converted into a fab new hostel overlooking the River Fergus. Excellent common areas and all the rooms have balconies (p347).

if you like...

Tracing Your Roots

Roughly 80 million people worldwide can claim to be part of, or descended from, the Irish diaspora, with about 41 million of those in the US alone. Most major towns have a heritage centre with a genealogical service.

Genealogical Office Based in the National Library in Dublin, this is the place to start your search for your Irish ancestors (p75)

PRONI (Public Record Office of Northern Ireland) Belfast's purpose-built centre in the Titanic Quarter is the place to go to track down your Ulster family history (p592)

Dún na Sí Heritage Centre A folk park 16km east of Athlone with an associated genealogical centre attached (p525)

Ulster-American Folk Park Ulster's rich links with the US explored in one of Northern Ireland's best museums (p687)

Literary Corners

Four Nobel laureates for literature are just the highlight of a rich literary tradition. Ireland is one of the English-speaking world's most notable heavyweights of the written word, a tradition that continues to thrive through contemporary writers and literary festivals.

Cape Clear Island International Storytelling Festival The storytelling tradition is kept alive by tales tall and long from all over the world (p256)

Cúirt International Festival of Literature Galway attracts writers from all over the world to its April literary showcase (p395)

Dublin Literary Tours No city of comparable size has been more written about or produced as many great authors as the capital, so take one of its many literary tours to find out more (p94)

Listowel Writers Week The Irish literary festival, held in June in the hometown of John B Keane (p317)

Traditional Pubs

Everybody's got their favourite, so picking the best ones is a futile exercise. What can be done, however, is to select a handful that won't disappoint you, especially if you're looking for a traditional pub in the classic mould.

Blake's of the Hollow, Enniskillen Ulster's best pint of Guinness in a Victorian classic (p676)

John Benny's, Dingle Stone slab floor, memorabilia on the walls and rocking trad sessions most nights (p306)

McCarthy's, Fethard A pub, restaurant and undertakers, all in one (p342)

Morrissey's, Abbeyleix Half-pub, half-shop, it's one of the best drinking establishments on the whole island (p502)

Séhan Ua Neáchtain, Galway One of Ireland's best-known traditional pubs (p393)

Stag's Head, Dublin Beloved by students, auteurs and boozers alike, a Victorian classic with beautiful stained-glass windows (p113)

Vaughan's Pub, Kilfenora Superb bar with outstanding reputation for traditional music (p376)

GARETH MCCORMACK/LONELY PLANET IMAGES ©

» Clew Bay beneath Croagh Patrick (p432), County Mayo

Great Views

Irish scenery is among the most spectacular in Europe, with breathtaking views and stunning landscapes throughout the whole country. There are the famous spots, of course, but they're not alone.

Binevenagh Lake Spectacular view over Lough Foyle, Donegal and the Sperrin Mountains from the cliff top at the height of the Bishop's Rd (p650)

Clew Bay The 365 islands of this County Mayo bay are best viewed from the top of Croagh Patrick (p432)

Kilkee Cliffs Jaw-dropping views of soaring cliffs that *aren't* the Cliffs of Moher (p364)

Scarriff Inn Stunning views of Kenmare Bay and Bantry Bay from the windows of this Kerry restaurant (p294)

Poisoned Glen The views down this Donegal valley are breathtaking; the final touch is the ruined church at the foot of the glen (p480)

Irish Cooking Schools

The renaissance of Irish cuisine has been spearheaded by a visionary gang of Irish chefs and producers, many of whom have dedicated themselves to passing on their secrets by setting up a cookery school.

Ballymaloe The most famous cooking school in the country run by its best-known chef, Darina Allen (p236)

Belle Isle School of Cookery A reputable school at the north end of Upper Lough Erne (p677)

Ghan House This cookery school specialising in classic cuisine is attached to a beautiful 18th-century Georgian house (p558)

Source A small cookery school atop a restaurant that covers the full range of Irish traditional cooking, from farm to fork (p449)

Tannery Cookery School Well-known chef Paul Flynn runs a successful school at the back of his excellent restaurant (p191)

A Good Walk

From afternoon ambles to week-long hikes, Ireland offers plenty of opportunities to stretch your legs. You don't have to follow a waymarked way, but there are 31 of them in the country should you prefer a signposted hike.

Ardmore Cliff Walk Marvellous 5km walk from an ancient Christian well across sea cliffs to Ardmore town (p195)

Burren Way Any portion of this 123km marked way is rewarding (p370)

Causeway Coast Way The best section is the 16.5km hike between Carrick-a-Rede and the Giant's Causeway (p662)

Doolough Valley History and scenery combine on this route between Leenane and Westport (p430)

River Barrow Towpath A beautiful path along the Barrow between Graiguenamanagh in County Kilkenny and St Mullins in County Carlow (p201)

Ross Castle A 3km stroll through Killarney National Park (p279)

If you like...hang-gliding and paragliding, some of the finest airwaves can be found at Mt Leinster (p181) in Carlow, the Great Sugarloaf Mountain (p152) in Wicklow and Benone and Magilligan Beaches (p650) in Derry.

Traditional Music

Western Europe's most vibrant folk music is kept alive by musicians who ply their craft (and are plied with drink) in impromptu and organised sessions in pubs and music houses throughout the country; even the 'strictly for tourists' stuff will feature excellent performances.

An Droichead Excellent music sessions at an arts centre dedicated to Irish culture (p599)

Leo's Tavern Live nightly sessions in summer in a pub owned by Enya's parents (p480)

Matt Molloy's The Chieftain's fife player owns this pub where the live *céilidh* (session of traditional music and dancing) kick off at 9pm nightly (p436)

Miltown Malbay Every pub in this County Clare town features outstanding Irish trad sessions (p365)

Tig Cóilí Galway's best trad sessions in the pub whose name means 'house of music' (p393)

Marine Bar Wonderful music nightly during summer months at this 200-year-old pub (p193)

Ancient Ruins

Thanks to the pre-Celts, Celts and early Christians, ancient and monastic sites are a feature of the Irish landscape. Thanks to the Vikings and Henry VIII, many of these are ruins, but no less impressive.

Askeaton Evocative 14th-century ruins of a castle, monastery and a church (p330)

Brú na Bóinne Europe's most impressive Neolithic burial site (p534)

Carrowkeel Megalithic cemetery and majestic views (p453)

Clonmacnoise Ireland's finest monastic site (p509)

Devenish Island Ruins of an Augustinian monastery and near-perfect round tower on the biggest island in Lough Erne (p679)

Dún Aengus Stunning Stone Age fort perched perilously on Inishmór's cliffs (p400)

Glendalough Ruins of a once-powerful monastic city in stunning surroundings (p142)

Bookshops

Ireland's long and wonderful relationship with the written word has resulted in some marvellously atmospheric bookshops where you can while away an hour or three and perhaps even pick up a rare copy of your favourite Irish book.

An Café Liteártha This specialist bookstore sells Irish-interest books and there's an idyllic little café at the back; settle in with a book and a scone (p306).

An Cló Ceart Irish-language books, traditional music and other examples of fine Irish culture, including woodwork and other crafts (p647)

Cathach Books Dublin's best second-hand bookstore specialises in Irish-interest books and some outstanding first editions, including ones by Ireland's literary giants (p123)

Charlie Byrne's Rambling rooms hold a treasure trove of new, second-hand and hard-to-find books (p394)

month by month

Top Events

1 **St Patrick's Day,** March

2 **Galway Arts Festival,** July

3 **Willie Clancy Summer School,** July

4 **Féile An Phobail,** August

5 **All-Ireland Finals,** September

February

Bad weather makes February the perfect month for indoor activities. Some museums launch new exhibits, and it's a good time to visit the major towns and cities.

Dublin International Film Festival

Sponsored by Jameson, the island's biggest film festival (www.jdiff.com) runs during the last two weeks of February, offering a mix of local flicks, arty international films and advance releases of mainstream movies.

March

Spring is in the air, and the whole country is getting ready for arguably the world's most famous parade. Dublin's is the biggest, but every town in Ireland holds one.

St Patrick's Day

Ireland erupts into one giant celebration on 17 March (www.stpatricksday.ie), but Dublin throws a five-day party around the parade (attended by 600,000), with gigs and festivities that leave the city with a giant hangover.

April

The weather is getting better, the flowers are beginning to bloom and the festival season begins anew. Seasonal attractions start to open up around the middle of the month or at Easter.

Circuit of Ireland International Rally

Northern Ireland's most prestigious rally race – known locally as the 'Circuit' (www.circuitofireland.net) – sees over 130 competitors throttle and turn through some 550km (342 miles) of Northern Ireland and parts of the Republic over two days at Easter.

Irish Grand National

Ireland loves horse racing, and the race they love the most is the Grand National (www.fairyhouse.ie), the showcase of the national hunt season that takes place at Fairyhouse in County Meath on Easter Monday.

World Irish Dancing Championships

There's far more to Irish dancing than Riverdance. Every April, some 4500 competitors from all over the world gather to test their steps and skills against the very best. The location varies from year to year; see www.worldirishdancing.com for details.

May

The May Bank Holiday (on the first Monday) sees the first of the busy summer weekends as the Irish take to the roads to enjoy the budding good weather.

Cork International Choral Festival

One of Europe's premier choral festivals (www.corkchoral.ie), with the winners going on to the Fleischmann International Trophy Competition; held over four days from the first Monday of May.

North West 200

Ireland's most famous road race (www.northwest200.org) is also the country's biggest

DOUG MCKINLAY/LONELY PLANET IMAGES ©

(above) Irish musician playing in a Doolin pub
(below) St Patrick's Day celebrations

MUSTANG79/DREAMSTIME.COM ©

outdoor sporting event; 150,000-plus people line the triangular route to cheer on some of the biggest names in motorcycle racing. Held in mid-May.

☆ Fleadh Nua

The third week of May sees the cream of the traditional music crop come to Ennis, County Clare, for one of the country's most important festivals (www.comhaltas.ie).

June

The bank holiday at the beginning of the month sees the country spoilt for choice as to what to do. Weekend traffic is getting busier, the weather gets better.

☆ Cat Laughs

Kilkenny gets very, very funny in early June with the country's premier comedy festival (www.thecatlaughs.com), which draws comedians both known and unknown from the four corners of the globe.

☆ Irish Derby

Wallets are packed and fancy hats donned for the best flat-race festival in the country (www.curragh.ie), run during the first week of the month.

☆ Bloomsday

Edwardian dress and breakfast of 'the inner organs of beast and fowl' are but two of the elements of the Dublin festival celebrating 16 June, the day on which Joyce's *Ulysses* takes place; the real highlight is retracing Leopold Bloom's daily steps (p99).

July

There isn't a weekend in the month that a major festival doesn't take place, while visitors to Galway will find that the city is in full swing for the entire month.

Willie Clancy Summer School

Inaugurated to celebrate the memory of a famed local piper, this exceptional festival of traditional music sees the world's best players show up for gigs, pub sessions and workshops over 10 days in Miltown Malbay, County Clare (p366).

Galway Arts Festival

Music, drama and a host of artistic endeavours are on the menu at the most important arts festival in the country, which sees Galway go merriment mad for the last two weeks of the month (p395).

Galway Film Fleadh

Irish and international releases make up the program at one of the country's premier film festivals, held in early July (p395).

Oxegen

Ireland's answer to Glastonbury is a three-day supergig (www.oxegen.ie) in mid-July at Punchestown Racecourse in County Kildare, featuring some of the big names in rock and pop (p97).

Killarney Summerfest

From kayaking to street theatre to gigs by international artists, this week-long extravaganza (www.killarneysummerfest.com) in late July has something for everybody.

August

Schools are closed, the sun is shining (or not!) and Ireland is in holiday mood. Seaside towns and tourist centres are at their busiest as the country looks to make the most of its time off.

Féile An Phobail

The name translates simply as the 'people's festival' and it is just that: Europe's largest community arts festival takes place on the Falls Rd in West Belfast over two weeks (p589).

Fleadh Cheoil nah Éireann

The mother of all Irish music festivals (www.comhaltas.ie; usually at the end of the month) attracts in excess of 250,000 music-lovers and revellers to whichever town is playing host – there's some great music amid the drinking.

Galway Race Week

The biggest horse-racing festival west of the Shannon is not just about the horses, it's also a celebration of Irish culture, sporting gambles and elaborate hats (p395).

Mary From Dungloe

Ireland's second-most important beauty pageant takes place in Dungloe, County Donegal, at the beginning of the month – although it's an excuse for a giant party, the young women really do want to be crowned the year's 'Mary'.

Puck Fair

Ireland's quirkiest premise for a festival: crown a goat king and celebrate for three days. Quirky idea, brilliant festival that takes place in Killorglin in mid-August (p285).

Rose of Tralee

The Irish beauty pageant (www.roseoftralee.ie) sees wannabe Roses plucked from Irish communities throughout the world competing for the ultimate prize. For everyone else, it's a big party (p313).

September

Summer may be over, but September weather can be surprisingly good, so it's often the ideal time to enjoy the last vestiges of the sun as the crowds dwindle.

Galway International Oyster Festival

Galway kicks off its oyster season with a festival (www.galwayoysterfest.com) celebrating the local catch. Music and beer have been the accompaniment since its inception in 1953.

Dublin Fringe Festival

Upwards of 100 different performances take the stage, the street, the bar and the car in the fringe festival (www.fringefest.com) that is unquestionably more innovative than the main theatre festival that follows it.

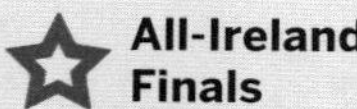

All-Ireland Finals

The second and fourth Sundays of the month see the finals of the hurling and Gaelic football championships respectively, with 80,000-plus crowds thronging into Dublin's Croke Park for the biggest sporting days of the year.

October

The weather starts to turn cold, so it's time to move the fun indoors again. The calendar is still packed with activities and distractions, especially over the last weekend of the month.

Dublin Theatre Festival

The most prestigious theatre festival in the country (www.dublintheatrefestival.com) sees new work and new versions of old work staged in theatres and venues throughout the capital.

Wexford Opera Festival

Opera fans gather in the atmospheric grounds of Johnstown Castle to enjoy Ireland's premier festival of opera (www.wexfordopera.com), which eschews the big hits in favour of lesser-known works (p170).

Cork Jazz Festival

Ireland's best-known jazz festival (www.corkjazzfestival.com) sees Cork taken over by over a thousand musicians and their multitude of fans during the last weekend of the month.

Belfast Festival at Queen's

Northern Ireland's top arts festival (www.belfastfestival.com) attracts performers from all over the world for the second half of the month; on offer is everything from visual arts to dance.

December

Christmas dominates the calendar as the country prepares for the feast with frenzied shopping and after-work drinks with friends and family arrived home from abroad. On Christmas Day nothing is open.

Christmas

This is a quiet affair in the countryside, though on 26 December (St Stephen's Day) the ancient custom of Wren Boys is re-enacted, most notably in Dingle, County Kerry, when groups of children dress up and go about singing hymns.

itineraries

Whether you've got six days or 60, these itineraries provide a starting point for the trip of a lifetime. Want more inspiration? Head online to lonelyplanet.com/thorntree to chat with other travellers.

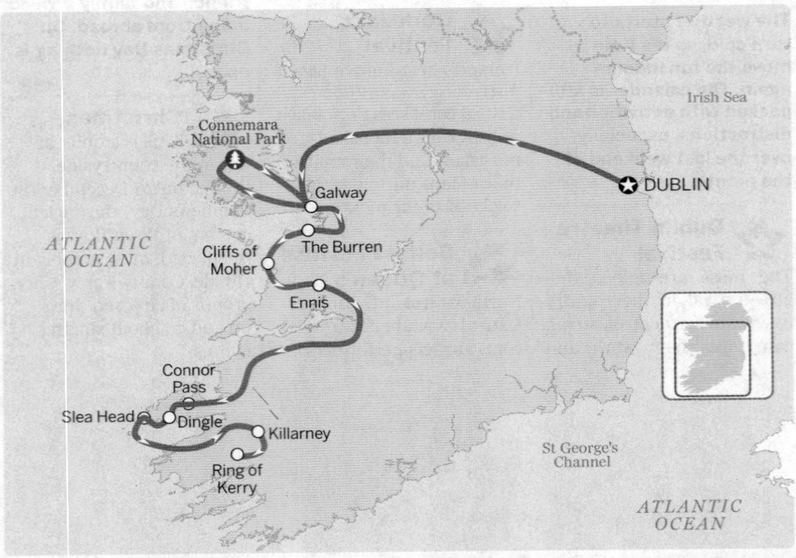

One Week
Ireland Highlights

This tourist trail takes you past some of Ireland's most famous attractions and through spectacular countryside. It's only about 300km so you could manage it in three days, but what's the point? Start with a whistle-stop tour of **Dublin**, including visits to Trinity College and the Book of Kells as well as a sample of Guinness in its hometown. The next day, head west to **Galway**, from which you should take a drive through stunning, brooding **Connemara** (which can be driven in a nice loop) before heading southward through the moonlike landscape of the **Burren**. Take a detour to the **Cliffs of Moher**, then head to **Ennis**, a good spot to enjoy a bit of traditional Irish music. Keep going south through the **Connor Pass** into County Kerry, stopping for a half-day in **Dingle** before setting out to visit its peninsula, particularly the views and prehistoric monuments of **Slea Head**. Continue on to **Killarney**, which will be the perfect base from which to explore the famous **Ring of Kerry**, a much-trafficked loop around the Iveragh Peninsula. The drive back to Dublin should provide enough time to plan your return visit.

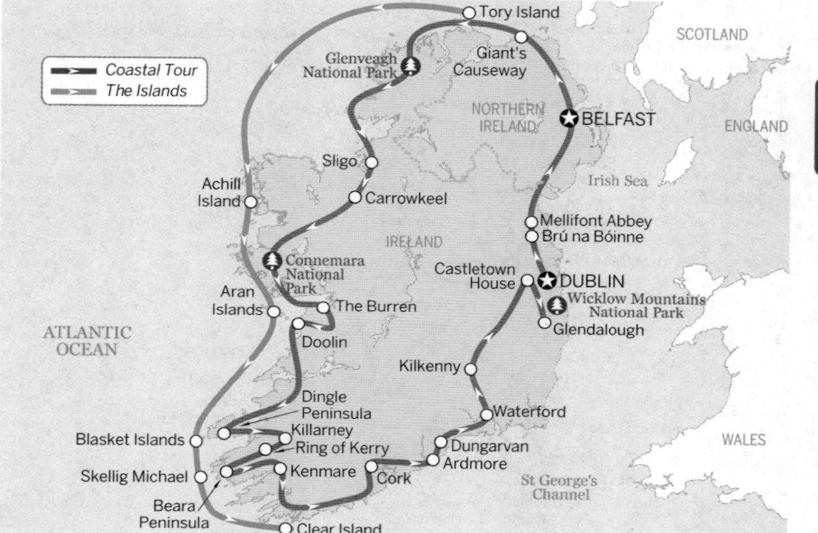

Three Weeks
The Islands

Start at the remote, Irish-speaking **Tory Island** in Donegal, a wonderful bird-watching spot. Joined to the mainland by a bridge, **Achill Island**, in County Mayo, is renowned for its dramatic cliffs, water sports and deserted famine village. Off the coast of Galway, the three Aran Islands are probably Ireland's most visited. The largest, **Inishmór**, has some fine archaeological remains, including the magical fort of Dún Aengus. The middle island, **Inishmaan**, favourite of the writer JM Synge, is a pleasure to walk around, with its stone walls and tiny fields. The smallest and least visited, **Inisheer**, best accessed from Doolin in County Clare, has some wonderful wild walks. Some other very special islands to visit are Europe's most westerly. Uninhabited since 1953, the **Blasket Islands**, off the Kerry coast, offer the chance to spot puffins, seals and porpoises. **Skellig Michael**, off Cahersiveen in Kerry, is a Unesco World Heritage site and home to a 7th-century monastery – it's a breathtaking, spiritual place and a highlight of any trip to Ireland. Ornithologists and orators alike will enjoy **Clear Island**, off the western coast of Cork, famous for its Manx shearwaters and its lively Storytelling Festival in September.

Three Weeks
Coastal Tour

Start in **Dublin** then head north to the Neolithic necropolis at **Brú Na Bóinne**. Continue north to **Mellifont Abbey** before crossing the border into Northern Ireland and **Belfast**. Go northwest along the Antrim coast to the **Giant's Causeway**. Continue around the coastline of north Donegal, stopping at **Glenveagh National Park**. Head south into **Sligo** and climb the Stone Age passage grave at **Carrowkeel** for views of Lough Arrow. Make your way to the southwest via **Connemara**. Wonder at the **Burren** and check out traditional music in **Doolin** before crossing into County Kerry and exploring the **Dingle Peninsula**. Go through **Killarney** on your way round the **Ring of Kerry**. Camp in **Kenmare** and explore the **Beara Peninsula**, then Ireland's second city, **Cork**. Explore County Waterford from seaside **Ardmore**. Visit **Dungarvan** and its castle, and the Waterford Museum of Treasures in **Waterford**. Go northwards through Thomastown and to St Canice's Cathedral in **Kilkenny** before exploring the city's medieval core. Visit **Castletown House** in County Kildare, then cut east to **Glendalough** in the **Wicklow Mountains National Park**. Head back to Dublin.

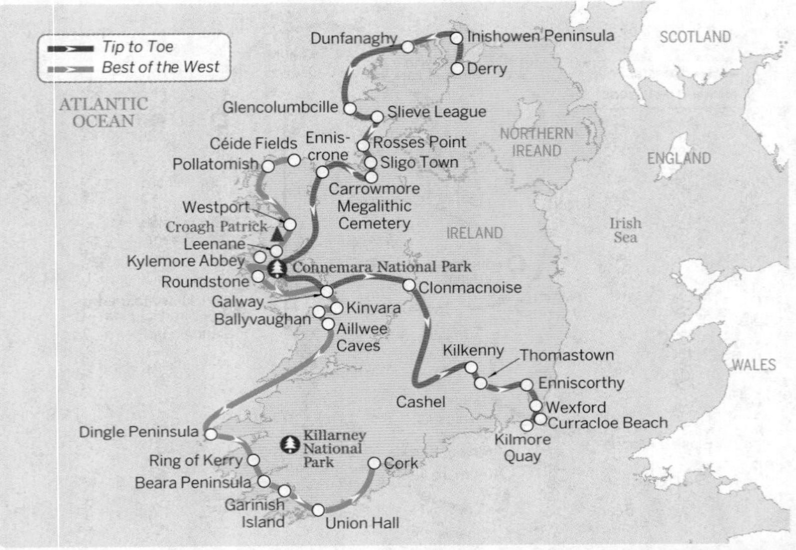

One Week
Best of the West

The west of Ireland is rightly at the top of most people's must-visit lists. Begin at the excavated **Céide Fields** in Mayo. Wind your way round the coast, stopping at some of Ireland's wildest beaches, to the pretty village of **Pollatomish**. Head to the pub-packed heritage town of **Westport**, continuing past (and perhaps climbing) **Croagh Patrick** and through **Leenane** – situated on Ireland's only fjord – to **Connemara National Park**. Take the beautiful coastal route, passing **Kylemore Abbey** and Clifden's scenic **Sky Road** through pretty **Roundstone**, or else try the stunning wilderness of the inland route through Maam Cross to **Galway**. Move on to the fishing villages of **Kinvara** and **Ballyvaughan** in the heart of the **Burren** and visit the ancient **Aillwee Caves**. Explore the **Dingle Peninsula** before following the **Ring of Kerry**, ending in **Killarney National Park**. Continue down the **Beara Peninsula** to the Italianate **Garinish Island**, with its exotic flowers. Follow the coast to **Cork** through Castletownshend and the fishing village of **Union Hall**.

Two Weeks
Tip to Toe

Begin in Northern Ireland's second city, **Derry**, by walking the city walls and exploring the Bogside neighbourhood. On day two, cross into County Donegal and explore the **Inishowen Peninsula** before spending the night in **Dunfanaghy**. As you move down Donegal's coastline, check out the monastic ruins of **Glencolumbcille** and the sea cliffs at **Slieve League**. Cross into County Sligo and visit the **Carrowmore Megalithic Cemetery** before checking in to your **Sligo Town** hotel. The next day, treat yourself to a round of golf at the County Sligo Golf Club at **Rosses Point** or a seaweed bath in **Enniscrone**. You'll skirt **Connemara's** eastern edge as you travel southward to **Galway**, from where you should strike out for **Clonmacnoise**. From here, move through the heart of the Midlands and head for another monastic gem, **Cashel**, in County Tipperary. Medieval **Kilkenny** is only an hour away. Visit the city's stunning castle before exploring nearby **Thomastown** and Jerpoint Abbey. Using **Wexford Town** as a base, explore **Curracloe Beach** and visit **Enniscorthy** and the excellent National 1798 Rebellion Centre. Or you could chill out and watch the fishermen draw in their lines in **Kilmore Quay**.

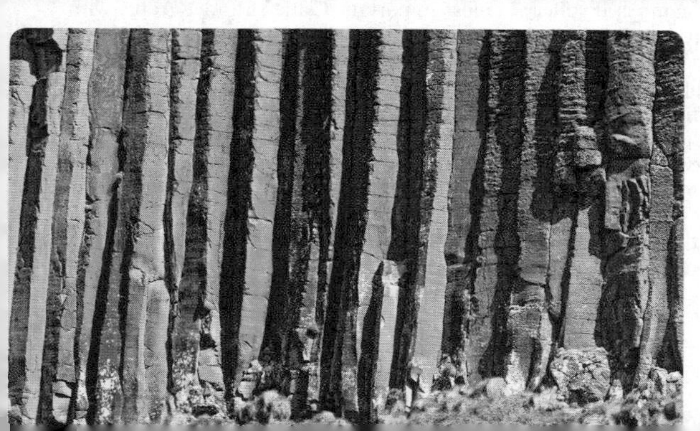

» (above) Stone stairway leading to monastic settlement, Skellig Michael (p291)

» (left) Giant's Causeway (p658), County Antrim

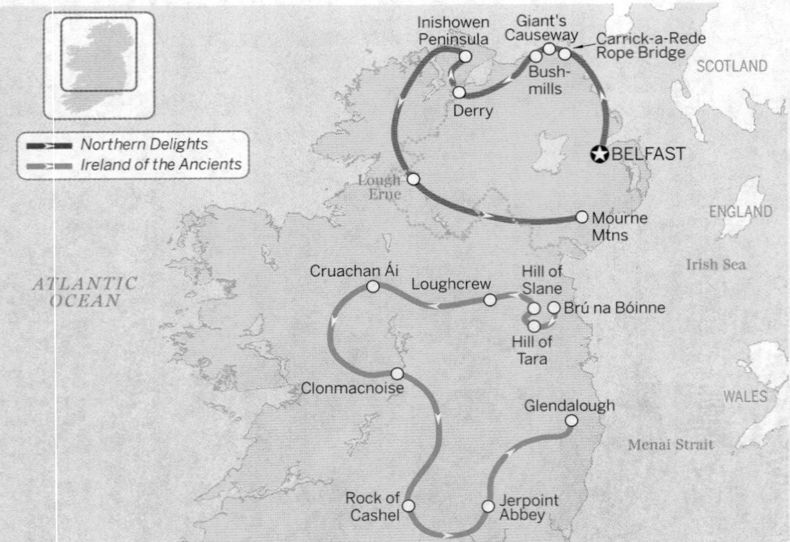

10 Days
Northern Delights

One of the many benefits to a more peaceful Northern Ireland has been the ability of the province to showcase its outstanding visitor attractions and superb scenery. Start in **Belfast**, where you should take a black taxi tour and/or visit the docks on a boat tour, before heading north toward the Antrim coast and the **Carrick-a-Rede** Rope Bridge – it's a short but brave walk across the bridge but the views are worth it. Nearby is the Unesco World Heritage **Giant's Causeway** that shouldn't be missed by any visitor to Northern Ireland and, just beyond it, the fascinating village of **Bushmills**, home to the famous distillery. **Derry City** is worth a day – walk the city's walls and explore its more recent past in the Bogside and then cross the invisible border into the Republic by visiting the **Inishowen Peninsula** in Donegal. Back in the North, go southeast to **Lough Erne**, taking in both **White Island** and the carved stones of **Devenish Island**, before heading east to the famed **Mourne Mountains**, where you can hike along ancient smugglers' trails – or just admire the fabulous views before heading back to Belfast.

One Week
Ireland of the Ancients

Begin at the stunning Neolithic tombs of **Newgrange** and **Knowth** in County Meath, in the heart of **Brú na Bóinne**. Nearby, stand at the top of the celebrated **Hill of Tara**, a site of immense folkloric significance and seat of the high kings of Ireland until the 11th century. Across the plain is the **Hill of Slane**, where St Patrick lit a fire in 433 to proclaim Christianity throughout the land. To the west is the Neolithic monument of **Loughcrew** – a quieter alternative to Brú na Bóinne. Keep going west to County Roscommon. Just outside Tulsk village is **Cruachan Aí**, the most important Celtic site in Europe, with 60 scattered megalithic tombs and burial sites. Head south to **Clonmacnoise Abbey**, the 6th-century monastic site in County Offaly. Continue south through the heart of the country to the impressive **Rock of Cashel** in County Tipperary. Turn east and head through County Kilkenny, stopping at the Cistercian **Jerpoint Abbey**, at the pretty village of Thomastown. From here, travel northeast to Wicklow and magnificent **Glendalough**, where the substantial remains of a monastic settlement linger by two beautiful lakes.

The Great Outdoors

Best Long-Distance Routes

Wicklow Way, County Wicklow Ireland's most popular waymarked way (p148)
Beara Way, County Cork Non-strenuous 196km loop over historic tracks (p264)
Dingle Way, County Derry 168km walk around stunning peninsula (p305)
Kerry Way, County Kerry 214km around the Ring of Kerry (p277)

Best for Short Walks

Glendalough, County Wicklow Range of short walks around monastic site (p147)
Connemara, County Galway Scenic Sky Road around Clifden (p416)
Lough Key, County Roscommon Forested walks around lake in Roscommon (p516)
Antrim Coast, County Antrim Rocky trails above the coast (p662)

Best Surf Spots

Bundoran, County Donegal Host of two European Surfing Championships (p467)
Easkey, County Sligo Two top-grade intermediate surf breaks (p454)
Mullaghmore, County Sligo Big wave for experienced surfers (p458)
Rossnowlagh, Co Donegal Best beach for beginners (p467)

It may not always have full cooperation from the weather, but Ireland is a country best appreciated out of doors. Whether you're a hiker, a cyclist, a surfer or an angler, it's merely a question of donning the right gear and going for it: there is something extraordinarily invigorating – never mind refreshing – about hiking in a summer storm or cycling into the teeth of a blowing gale. Then the clouds break and the sun appears, and you can while away an evening with a roach pole by the banks of a river or catch a tidy late wave when the rest of Europe has turned in for the evening.

Walking

There is simply no better way of experiencing this wildly beautiful country than on foot or on two wheels – and the rewards can be spectacular. From rolling hills of green to lush riparian woods; from rugged limestone escarpments to broad sandy beaches; and from dramatic sea cliffs to blankets of bog stretching as far as the eye can see, Ireland's landscapes will never disappoint.

There are, however, some issues that have made what should be some of the best walking in Europe a frustrating or even disappointing experience. Some trails run through kilometres of tedious forestry tracks and bitumen roads. The ways are marked with signposts showing the standard yellow arrow and hiker – in theory at least: waymarking is often variable and in some cases totally nonexistent. Ireland has a tradition

MORE WALKS IN IRELAND

- » The Great Sugarloaf, County Wicklow (p153)
- » Mt Seefin, County Cork (p263)
- » Reeks Ridge, County Kerry (p283)
- » Tipperary Heritage Trail, County Tipperary (p340)
- » Killary Harbour, County Galway (p420)
- » Inisheer, County Galway (p407)
- » Slieve Donard, County Down (p622)
- » Fair Head, County Antrim (p665)
- » The Cliffs of Magho, County Fermanagh (p681)
- » Cuilcagh Mountain via the Legnabrocky Trail, County Fermanagh (p685)

of relatively free access to open country, but the growth in the number of walkers and the carelessness of a few have made some farmers less obliging. Unfortunately, it's not uncommon to find unofficial signs on gateways barring access or physical barriers blocking ways. If you come across this problem, refer to the local tourist office.

The maintenance and development of the ways is administered in the Republic by the **National Trails Office** (☎01-860 8800; www.walkireland.ie) and in the North by **Countryside Access & Activities Network** (CAAN; ☎9030 3930; www.countrysiderecreation.com).

If you don't have a travelling companion you could consider joining an organised walking group:

Go Ireland (☎066-976 2094; www.goactivities.com; Old Orchard House, Killorglin, Co Kerry) Offers walking tours of the west.

South West Walks Ireland (☎066-712 8733; www.southwestwalksireland.com; 6 Church St, Tralee, Co Kerry) Provides a series of guided and self-guided walking programs around the southwest, northwest and Wicklow.

Where to Walk

For a small country, Ireland is packed with choice – from seaside ambles to long-distance treks in mountain ranges. Here's our favourite selection:

Day Walks

In just about any part of Ireland you can take a leisurely day hike.

» **Barrow Towpath** Along the River Barrow in Counties Kilkenny and Carlow, perfectly pleasant walks can be had along the towpath from Borris (p201) to Graiguenamanagh (p218).

» **Glendalough** The wooded trails around this ancient monastic in County Wicklow lure many a traveller from nearby Dublin for a few hours rambling (p147).

» **Lough Key** The woods around this lake in County Roscommon have a wonderful canopied trail (p516).

» **Sky Road** In County Galway, Clifden's Sky Road yields views of the Connemara coast; it's suitable for walking or cycling (p416).

» **South Leinster Way** The prettiest section of this waymarked way is a 13km hike between the charming villages of Graiguenamanagh and Inistioge in County Kilkenny (p220).

Coastal Walks

Ireland's coastlines are naturally conducive to long and reflective walks with or without shoes on. If that sounds like your particular nirvana, the coast of County Galway's Connemara and the pristine beaches of Counties Mayo and Sligo beckon. Some coastal walks, however, present unexpected challenges:

» **Causeway Coast Way** County Antrim is rife with rocky trails above the surf. Particularly spectacular is the final 16.5km of this waymarked way, starting from Carrick-a-Rede (p662).

» **Wexford Coastal Walk** Following 221km of trails overlooking the bones of old shipwrecks (p182).

Mountain Hikes

Ireland's mountain ranges aren't as magnificent as the Alps, but they do offer gratifying hill-walking opportunities, many of which can be done in a day.

» **Blue Stack Mountains** Range in County Donegal that encompasses varied terrain and dramatic peaks (p465).

» **Brandon Way** Not to be confused with Mt Brandon in County Kerry, the smaller Brandon Hill (516m) in County Kilkenny has a path that wends up to the summit from woodlands and moorlands along the River Barrow (p220).

» **Killarney National Park** Superb and challenging routes for the walker. The top walk, of course, is up Mt Carrantuohil (1039m; p278), the highest peak in all Ireland.

» (above) Killarney National Park (p278)
» (left) Hikers on the Beara Way (p264)

» **Mourne Mountains** You'll find Northern Ireland's best hill-walking in the mountains of County Down. In this range, Northern Ireland's highest peak, Slieve Donard (853m), is within reach on a day's walk from the town of Newcastle (p622).

» **Mt Leinster** This County Wexford peak affords views of five counties from its 796m summit (p181).

» **Mt Brandon** The highest peak (951m) on the Dingle Peninsula has spectacularly rugged trails that yield jaw-dropping views (p310).

Waymarked Ways

The country's network of 31 long-distance 'waymarked ways' can keep a traveller walking for a week or longer. Though many of these run on for several hundred kilometres, you can jump in or jump out as you see fit.

» **Beara Way** A non-strenuous loop of 196km that follows historic routes and tracks on a stunning peninsula in West Cork (p264).

» **Burren Way** At only 35km, this shortish walk takes in County Clare's unique, rocky landscape, the Cliffs of Moher and the musical town of Doolin (p370).

» **Cavan Way** Impressive topographic variety packed into its short 26km route, taking in bogs, Stone Age monuments and the source of the River Shannon (p560).

» **Dingle Way** A popular 168km route in County Kerry that loops round one of Ireland's most beautiful peninsulas (p305).

» **East Munster Way** Starting in County Tipperary and ending up in County Waterford, a 70km walk through forest and open moorland, and along the towpath of the River Suir (p343).

» **Kerry Way** A 214km route that takes in the spectacular Macgillycuddy's Reeks and the Ring of Kerry coast (p277).

» **Ulster Way** A footpath totalling 900km, making a circuit around the six counties of Northern Ireland and Donegal. It can easily be broken down into smaller sections (p679).

» **Wicklow Way** Ireland's most popular walking trail is this 132km route, which starts in southern Dublin and ends in Clonegal in County Carlow (p148).

Cycling

Cyclists, alas, will have to share the road with the motorised bully, but they can find solace in scenic routes through sparsely populated countryside or along rugged coasts. The tourist boards can supply you with a list of operators who organise cycling holidays. For more on the practicalities of travelling around Ireland with a bike, see p736.

For organised cycling tours, you can try:

Go Ireland (066-976 2094; www.goactivities.com; Old Orchard House, Killorglin, Co Kerry)

Irish Cycling Safaris (01-260 0749; www.cyclingsafaris.com; Belfield Bike Shop, UCD, Dublin)

Where to Cycle

You can cycle the length and breadth of the country if you like, but you'll spend most of the time fighting off traffic and concrete views. There are, however, some stunning cycleways.

» **West Clare Cycleway** This 70km-long, signposted cycleway stretches from Killimer on the Shannon Estuary (where you can get the Shannon Ferry to Tarbert in County Kerry, p318) to Lahinch in County Clare (p366). For more information, check out www.shannonregiontourism.ie/west_clare_cycleway.

» **Killarney National Park** The park has an adventurous 55km bike route that takes a scenic

KNOWING THE WAY

For comprehensive coverage of a selection of long and short walking routes, we (naturally) recommend Lonely Planet's very own *Walking in Ireland*, which also covers places to stay and eat along the way. There are a host of other good walking guides for Ireland; recommended are Michael Fewer's *Irish Long-Distance Walks* and *Best Irish Walks* by Joss Lynam.

EastWest Mapping (053-937 7835; www.eastwestmapping.ie) has good maps of long-distance walks in the Republic and the North. Tim Robinson of **Folding Landscapes** (095-35886; www.foldinglandscapes.com) produces superbly detailed maps of the Burren, the Aran Islands and Connemara. His and Joss Lynam's *Mountains of Connemara: A Hill Walker's Guide* contains a useful detailed map.

route via the lakes past Kate Kearney's Cottage to Lord Brandon's Cottage (p278).

» **Kingfisher Trail** A waymarked, long-distance cycling trail stretching some 370km along the back roads of Counties Fermanagh, Leitrim, Cavan and Monaghan (p673).

Horse Riding

Whether it's a gentle hack or a gallop across a wild beach, riding is one of Ireland's most beloved pastimes, and there's something for riders of every level. There are hundreds of centres throughout Ireland, offering possibilities ranging from a one-hour walk (adult/child from €25/15) to fully packaged, residential equestrian holidays.

Surprisingly, there is no legislation governing the set-up and conduct of horse yards, but the **Association of Irish Riding Establishments** (AIRE; ☎045-850800; www.aire.ie; Beech House, Millennium Park, Naas, Co Kildare) has over 200 member schools and centres spread throughout the country: being AIRE-approved means that the yard has qualified instructors, a resident first-aider, child-protection schemes, are insurance certified and, crucially, all of the horses are maintained according to an acceptable standard of care. We recommend that you stick to AIRE-approved centres.

Watersports

Ireland has 3100km of coastline and numerous rivers and lakes, so no matter where in the country you may be, you're never far from a place to surf, windsurf, scuba dive, paddle a canoe, swim or simply cast a line into a cool stream ribboned with salmon. Outfitters and information sources abound.

Surfing & Windsurfing

Surfing is all the rage on the coast, especially in the west. The most popular spots include:

» **County Donegal** The unofficial capital of Irish surfing, Bundoran (p467), hosts the Irish national championships in April. Along the coast there are at least a half dozen top-rated spots for beginners and advanced surfers to test their skills. Windsurfing and kite-surfing are equally popular around Port-na-Blagh (p484).

» **County Sligo** Easkey (p454) and Strandhill (p451) are famous for their year-round surf, and have facilities for travellers who seek room and board (with the room being optional).

» **County Clare** Has nice breaks at Kilkee (p362), Lahinch (p366) and Fanore (p379).

» **County Waterford** Tramore Beach (p189) is a coastal resort that's home to Ireland's largest surf school.

» **County Wexford** Surfing and windsurfing are popular in the shallow waters off Rosslare Strand (p172).

» **County Antrim** The beaches around Portrush (p653) afford good surfing and body-surfing. The swells are highest and the water warmest in September and October.

TOP ADVENTURE CENTRES

Adventure centres can be found around Ireland, especially near the coast. These centres make it easy for a traveller to indulge in such activities as canoeing, surfing, kayaking, orienteering, hiking, climbing and other sports. Some also provide accommodation. Here's a select list:

» Killary Adventure Centre, County Galway (p421)

» Delphi Mountain Resort, County Mayo(p430)

» Dunmore East Adventure Centre, County Waterford (p188)

» Donegal Adventure Centre, County Donegal (p467)

» Carlingford Adventure Centre (p557)

Sailing

There is a long history of sailing in Ireland and the country has more than 120 yacht and sailing clubs. The most popular areas for sailing are the southwestern coast, especially between Cork Harbour and the Dingle Peninsula; the coast of Antrim; along the sheltered coast north and south of Dublin; and some of the larger lakes such as Loughs Derg, Erne and Gill.

The **Irish Association for Sail Training** (☎01-605 1621; www.irishmarinefederation.com) watches over professional schools; the national governing body is the **Irish Sailing Association** (☎01-280 0239; www.sailing.ie). A recommended publication, available from most booksellers, is *Irish Cruising Club*

GARETH MCCORMACK/LONELY PLANET IMAGES ©

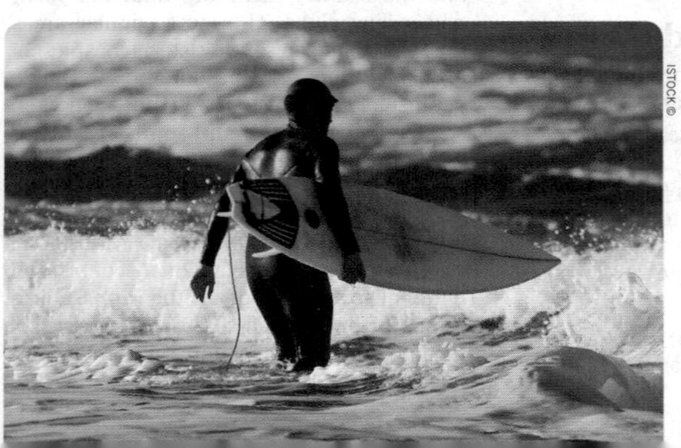

ISTOCK ©

» (above) Hiker, Mourne Mountains (p623), County Down
» (left) Surfer at Bundoran (p467), County Donegal

Sailing Directions. It contains details of port facilities, harbour plans and coast and tidal information.

Scuba Diving

With little sewage from cities to obscure the waters, Ireland's west coast has some of the best scuba diving in Europe. The offshore islands and rocks host especially rich underwater life. The best period for diving is roughly March to October. Visibility averages more than 12m, but can increase to 30m on good days.

For more details about scuba diving in Ireland, contact Comhairle Fó-Thuinn (CFT), also known as the **Irish Underwater Council** (☎01-284 4601; www.cft.ie); Ireland's diving regulatory body, it publishes the dive magazine *SubSea* (also available online).

Fishing

The watery sport for which Ireland is best known is the traditional pastime of fishing, be it from a boat on the deep seas or on a quiet spot along a river. Ireland is justly famous for its (generally no-fee) coarse fishing, e.g. bream, pike, perch, roach, rudd, tench, carp and eel. The killing of pike over 6.6lb (3kg) in weight is prohibited, so anglers are limited to one pike; the killing of coarse fish is frowned upon and anglers are encouraged to return coarse fish to the water alive. Freshwater game fish available here include salmon, sea trout and brown trout. Some managed fisheries also stock rainbow trout.

The enormous Shannon and Erne river systems, stretching southwards from Counties Leitrim and Fermanagh, are prime angling spots, and Cavan (p559), the 'Lake County', is a favourite with hardcore fishers. In the west, the great lakes of Corrib (p412) and Conn (p444) have plenty of lakeshore B&Bs, good sturdy boats and knowledgeable boaters.

While Ireland is a land of opportunity for the angler, intensive agriculture and the growth of towns have brought about a general reduction in water quality in many areas, markedly so in some. Fáilte Ireland and the NITB produce several information leaflets on fishing, accommodation, events and licences required.

Rock Climbing

Ireland's mountain ranges aren't high – Mt Carrantuohil in Kerry's Macgillycuddy's Reeks is the tallest mountain in Ireland at only 1039m – but they're often beautiful and offer some excellent climbing possibilities (see p283). The highest mountains are in the southwest.

Adventure centres around the country run courses and organise climbing trips. For further information contact the **Mountaineering Council of Ireland** (☎01-625 1115; www.mountaineering.ie), which also publishes climbing guides and the quarterly magazine *Irish Mountain Log*, or check the forums on **Irish Climbing Online** (www.climbing.ie).

Watching Wildlife

Spotting animals in the wild is often a highlight on a walk through Ireland's diverse natural settings. The country's forests, lakes, bogs, wetlands and coastal islands are rife with birds, furtive furry creatures and sea mammals. In many parts of the country your chance of spotting wildlife is quite high.

A LICENCE TO FISH

While no licence is needed for trout, pike and coarse fishing in the Republic of Ireland, a rod licence is required in Northern Ireland. You need a licence for salmon and sea trout fishing in both jurisdictions.

Licences in the Republic are available from the local tackle shop or direct from the **Central Fisheries Board** (☎01-884 2600; www.fishinginireland.info). In the North, rod licences for coarse and game fishing are obtainable from the **Foyle, Carlingford & Irish Lights Commission** (☎7134 2100; www.loughs-agency.org) for the Foyle and Carlingford areas, and from the **Fisheries Conservancy Board** (☎3833 4666; www.fcbni.com) for all other regions. You also require a permit from the owner, which is usually the **Department of Culture, Arts & Leisure, Inland Waterways & Inland Fisheries Branch** (☎9025 8825; www.dcalni.gov.uk).

FOR THE BIRDS

Some useful publications on birdwatching are Dominic Couzens' *Collins Birds of Britain and Ireland* and the slightly out-of-date *Where to Watch Birds in Ireland* by Clive Hutchinson.

More information on birdwatching can be obtained from the tourist boards and from the following organisations:

» **Birds of Ireland News Service** (☎01-830 7364; www.birdsireland.com)

» **BirdWatch Ireland** (☎01-281 9878; www.birdwatchireland.ie) Runs birdwatching field courses, all of which take place on Cape Clear Island in County Cork.

» **National Parks & Wildlife Service** (☎01-888 2000; www.npws.ie)

» **Royal Society for the Protection of Birds** (RSPB; ☎9049 1547; www.rspb.org.uk; Belvoir Park Forest, Belfast)

Land Mammals

Killarney National Park, in County Kerry, has been designated a Unesco Biosphere Reserve for its bounty of intriguing plant and animal species. It is home to the only wild herd of red deer, Ireland's most magnificent native mammal. Steely-nerved hares are commonly observed along many of Ireland's rural walkways.

Water Mammals

Aquatic mammals are commonly spotted around Ireland's periphery, as well in some of its streams. Whales, including fin whales, humpbacks and minke whales, are often spotted off the coast of West Cork during summer, when they come to feed offshore. Dolphins and porpoises are year-round residents of Irish waters, particularly favouring the natural harbours of Counties Kerry and Cork.

Seals live all around Ireland's perimeter. You're likely to encounter them on the island of Inishbofin (p418) off the coast of Galway; near Portaferry (p611) in County Down; on Rathlin Island (p663) off the Antrim coast; and around Greencastle (p497) in Donegal's Inishowen Peninsula. One of Ireland's prized animals is the river otter, which has survived here long after disappearing from much of the rest of Europe. They are extremely shy, but a sharp-eyed walker may be lucky along the streams of Connemara (p410) in County Galway. Some otters have been known to leave the water to search for food in boglands in the west of Ireland. You're more likely to spot scratched markings left on turf piles, or tiny otter footprints.

Birds

Ireland is a stopover for migrating birds, many of them from the Arctic, Africa and North America. Additionally, irregular winds frequently deliver exotic blowovers rarely seen in Western Europe. Birders on Ireland's coasts and islands are always on the lookout for breeding sea birds such as the gannet, kittiwake, cormorant and heron. The rare corncrake often appears along the west coast. Large colonies of puffins inhabit coastal cliffs, particularly on islands off Donegal and Northern Ireland. Peregrine falcons, long ago hunted out, were reintroduced to Donegal's Glenveagh National Park (p487) in 2001, and since then the species has shown signs that it will re-establish itself in Ireland.

The birding is good just about everywhere in Ireland. There are more than 70 reserves and sanctuaries in Ireland, many of them open to the public. Good places to go include:

» **Inishowen Peninsula** in County Donegal (p491)

» **Skellig Islands** off the coast of County Kerry (p293)

» **Cooley Birdwatching Trail** in County Louth (p557)

» **Castle Espie** in County Down (p614)

At the Irish Table

Finding the Best Irish Food & Drink

www.bestofbridgestone.com Extensive coverage of artisan producers and the best restaurants serving their produce.

www.bordbia.ie Irish Food Board website, with a few local producers listed, as well as a comprehensive list of farmers markets.

Good Food in Cork Excellent annual booklet detailing artisan producers in Cork, established by Myrtle Allen; pick it up from the Farmgate Café (p230) in Cork city; also available online at www.corkfreechoice.com.

www.irishcheese.ie The Association of Irish Farmhouse Cheesemakers, with every small dairy covered.

www.slowfoodireland.com Organisation supporting small producers, with social events across Ireland.

Ireland's recently acquired reputation as a gourmet destination is thoroughly deserved. A host of chefs and producers are leading a foodie revolution that, at its heart, is about bringing to the table the kind of meals that have long been taken for granted on well-run Irish farms.

Coupled with the growing sophistication of the Irish palate – by now well used to the varied flavours of worldwide cuisines – it's relatively easy to eat well on all budgets. Needless to say, this has been a boon to the tourist industry, who no longer have to explain why so many Irish meals are so memorable – for the completely wrong reasons.

A Plate for Every Season

January–March

The coldest time of the year is perfect for a cooked Irish breakfast. This is also the perfect season for stew: the **Só Sligo Festival** (www.sosligo.com) in mid-March sees professional chefs from around the world compete in the **World Irish Stew Championship** (there's also an amateur category open to all).

April–June

The budding of spring sees freshly picked fruit and vegetables, such as asparagus and rhubarb, make an appearance.

Spring food festivals include the following:

» **Waterford Festival of Food** (www.waterfordfestivaloffood.com) Three days of local produce and fine food in Dungarvan in mid-April, including a seaside BBQ and a craft beer garden.

» **Taste of Dublin** (www.tastefestivals.ie) The capital's best restaurants combine to serve up sample platters of their best dishes amid music and other entertainment.

July–September

In July, the first of the season's new potatoes appear, along with jams and berry pies with gooseberries, blackberries and loganberries. Culinary celebrations take place all over the country, and include the following:

» **Belfast Taste & Music Festival** (www.belfasttasteandmusicfest.com) On the Great Lawn of the Botanic Gardens during the first week of August, this is Northern Ireland's top foodie event.

» **Carlingford Oyster Festival** (www.carlingford.ie) Oysters come early in this County Louth town and the season is marked with a small festival in mid-August.

» **Clarenbridge Oyster Festival** (www.clarenbridge.com) A long-established festival in the South Galway town takes place in the first week of September.

» **Hillsborough Oyster Festival** (www.hillsboroughoysterfestival.com) Some 12,000 people from all over the world gather over the first weekend of September to sample the region's best and to take part in the World Oyster Eating Championships.

VEGETARIANS & VEGANS

Ireland has come a long, long way since the days when vegetarians were looked upon as odd creatures; nowadays, even the most militant vegan will barely cause a ruffle in all but the most basic of kitchens. Which isn't to say that travellers with plant-based diets are going to find the most imaginative range of options on menus outside the bigger towns and cities – or in the plethora of modern restaurants that have opened in the last few years – but you can rest assured that the overall quality of the homegrown vegetable is top-notch and most places will have at least one dish that you can tuck into comfortably.

» **Taste of West Cork Food Festival** (www.atasteofwestcork.com) Skibbereen brings together its best producers to put on this week-long festival in mid-September

» **Waterford Harvest Food Festival** (www.waterfordharvestfestival.ie) A 10-day festival in mid-September with food markets, taste workshops, celebrity-chef clinics and open-air picnics.

» **Midleton Food & Drink Festival** (www.midletonfoodfestival.ie) In mid-September, this County Cork town hosts cookery demos, wine tastings and over 50 stalls featuring the best of local produce.

» **Galway International Oyster Festival** (www.galwayoysterfest.com) Last weekend in September sees plenty of oysters, washed down with lashings of Guinness.

October–December

October is apple-picking month. The main potato crop is dug up. It is the end of the food-festival season, but it goes out with a bang, with the **Kinsale Gourmet Festival** (www.kinsalerestaurants.com): the unofficial gourmet capital of Ireland struts its culinary stuff over three days in early October.

Local Specialities

To Eat...

» **Potatoes** It's a wonder the Irish retain their good humour amid the perpetual potato-baiting they endure. But, despite the stereotyping, and however much we'd like to disprove it, potatoes are still paramount here and you'll see lots of them on your travels. The mashed potato dishes colcannon and champ (with cabbage and spring onion, respectively) are two of the tastiest recipes in the country.

» **Meat & Seafood** Irish meals are usually meat-based, with beef, lamb and pork common options. Seafood, long neglected, is finding a place on the table in Irish homes. It's widely available in restaurants and is often excellent, especially in the west. Oysters, trout and salmon are delicious, particularly if they're direct from the sea or a river rather than a fish farm. The famous Dublin Bay prawn isn't actually a prawn but a lobster. At its best, it's superlative, but it's priced accordingly. If you're going to splurge, do so here – but make sure you choose live Dublin Bay prawns because once these fellas die, they quickly lose their flavour.

OLIVER STREWE/LONELY PLANET IMAGES ©

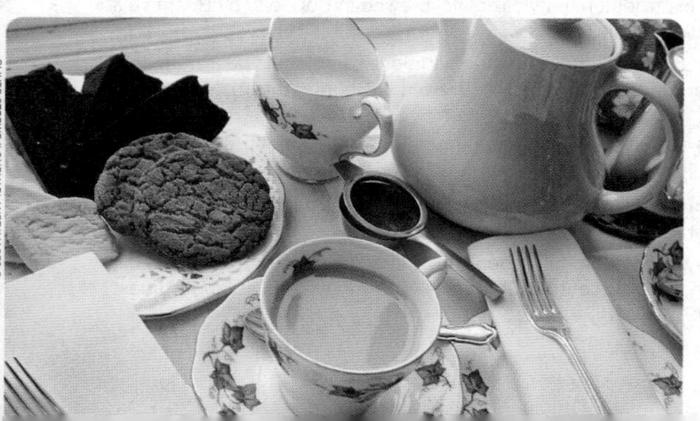

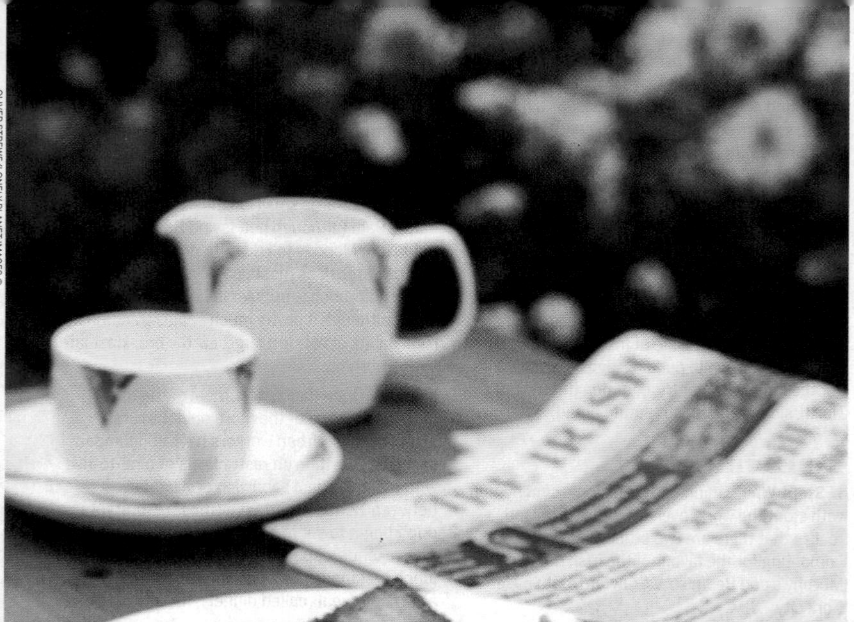

OLIVER STREWE/LONELY PLANET IMAGES ©

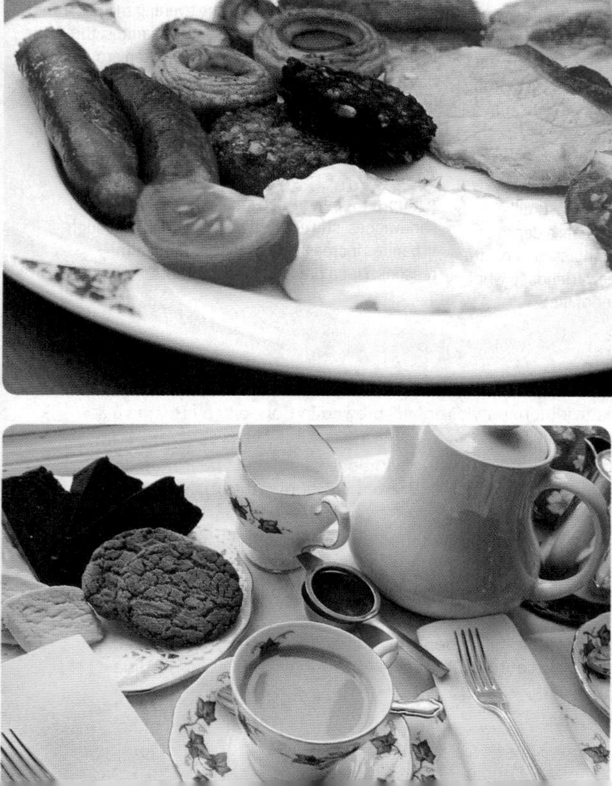

» (above) A full Irish breakfast
» (left) An Irish favourite – a cup of tea and biscuits

» **Soda Bread** The most famous Irish bread, and one of the signature tastes of Ireland. Irish flour is soft and doesn't take well to yeast as a raising agent, so Irish bakers of the 19th century leavened their bread with bicarbonate of soda. Combined with buttermilk, it makes a superbly tasty bread, and is often on the breakfast menus at B&Bs.

» **The Fry** Perhaps the most feared Irish speciality is the fry – the heart attack on a plate that is the second part of so many B&B deals. In spite of hysterical health fears, the fry is still one of the most common traditional meals in the country. Who can say no to a plate of fried bacon, sausages, black pudding, white pudding, eggs and tomatoes? For the famous Ulster fry, common throughout the North, simply add fadge (potato bread).

To Drink...

» **Stout** While Guinness has become synonymous with stout the world over, few outside Ireland realise that there are two other major producers competing for the favour of the Irish drinker: Murphy's and Beamish & Crawford, both based in Cork city.

» **Tea** The Irish drink more tea, per capita, than any other nation in the world and you'll be offered a cup as soon as you cross the threshold of any Irish home. Taken with milk (and sugar, if you want) rather than lemon, preferred blends are very strong, and nothing like the namby-pamby versions that pass for Irish breakfast tea elsewhere.

» **Whiskey** At last count, there were almost 100 different types of Irish whiskey, brewed by only three distilleries – Jameson's, Bushmills and Cooley's. A visit to Ireland reveals a depth of excellence that will make the connoisseur's palate spin while winning over many new friends to what the Irish call *uisce beatha* (water of life).

When to Eat

Irish eating habits have changed over the last couple of decades, and there are differences between urban and rural practices.

» **Breakfast** An important meal given the Irish tendency towards small lunches. Usually eaten before 9am (although hotels and B&Bs will serve until 11am Monday to Friday, to noon at weekends in urban areas), as most people rush off to work. Weekend brunch is popular in bigger towns and cities, although it pretty much copies traditional rural habits of eating a large, earthy breakfast late in the morning.

» **Lunch** Once the biggest meal of the day, lunch is now one of the more obvious rural/urban divides. Urban workers have succumbed to the eat-on-the-run restrictions of nine-to-five, with most eating a sandwich or a light meal between 12.30pm and 2pm (most restaurants don't begin to serve lunch until at least midday). At weekends, especially Sunday, the midday lunch is skipped in favour of a substantial mid-afternoon meal (called dinner), usually between 2pm and 4pm.

» **Tea** No, not the drink, but the evening meal – also confusingly called dinner. For urbanites, this is the main meal of the day, usually eaten around 6.30pm. Rural communities eat at the same time but with a more traditional tea of bread, cold cuts and, yes, tea. Restaurants follow international habits, with most diners not eating until at least 7.30pm.

» **Supper** A before-bed snack of tea and toast or sandwiches, still enjoyed by many Irish, although urbanites increasingly eschew it for health reasons. Not a practice in restaurants.

OTHER IRISH BEERS

» **Beamish Red Ale** This traditional-style red ale, brewed in Cork city by Beamish & Crawford, is sweet and palatable.

» **Caffrey's Irish Ale** One of the most exciting additions to Ireland's beer map, this creamy ale has been around only since 1994. Brewed in County Antrim, it's a robust cross between a stout and an ale.

» **Kinsale Irish Lager** Brewed in the eponymous County Cork town, this golden-coloured lager has a slightly bitter taste that fades after a few sips.

» **McCardles Traditional Ale** This wholesome, dark, nutty ale is hard to come by but worthy of an exploration.

» **Smithwick's** A lovely, refreshing, full scoop with a charming history. It's brewed in Kilkenny, on the site of the 14th-century St Francis Abbey in what is Ireland's oldest working brewery (p209).

Choosing Your Eatery

Restaurants From cheap 'n' cheerful to Michelin-starred, Ireland has something for every palate and budget.

Cafes Ireland is awash with cafes of every description, many of which are perfect for a quick, tasty bite.

Hotels Even if you're not a guest, most hotel restaurants cater to outside diners. Top hotels usually feature good restaurants with prices to match.

Pubs Pub grub is ubiquitous, mostly of the toasted-sandwich variety. However, a large number also have full menu service, with some of them being as good as any top restaurant.

Dining Etiquette

The Irish aren't big on restrictive etiquette, preferring friendly informality to any kind of stuffy to-dos. Still, the following are a few tips to dining with the Irish:

Children All restaurants welcome kids up to 7pm, but pubs and some smarter restaurants don't allow them in the evening. Family restaurants have children's menus, others have reduced portions of regular menu items.

Returning a dish If the food is not to your satisfaction, it's best to politely explain what's wrong with it as soon as you can; any respectable restaurant will endeavour to replace the dish immediately.

Paying the bill If you insist on paying the bill for everyone, be prepared for a first, second and even third refusal to countenance such an exorbitant act of generosity. But don't be fooled: the Irish will refuse something several times even if they're delighted with it. Insist gently but firmly and you'll get your way!

Food Experiences

Meals of a Lifetime

Restaurant Patrick Guilbaud Two Michelin stars makes this elegant French eatery in Dublin the best restaurant in Ireland (p106).

THE BEST IRISH CHEESES

» **Ardrahan** Flavoursome farmhouse creation with a rich, nutty taste.

» **Corleggy** Subtle, pasteurised goats cheese from County Cavan

» **Durrus** A creamy, fruity cheese, beloved of fine-food fans (p260).

» **Cashel Blue** Creamy blue cheese from Tipperary.

» **Cooleeney** Award-winning Camembert-style cheese.

Fishy Fishy Café, Kinsale, Country Cork (p242)

Castle Murray, Dunkineely, County Donegal (p472)

Jacks Coastguard Restaurant, Cromane Peninsula, Country Kerry (p285)

Dare to Try

Ironically, while the Irish palate has become more adventurous, it is the old-fashioned Irish menu that features some fairly challenging dishes. Dare to try the following:

Black pudding Made from congealed pork blood, suet and other fillings; a ubiquitous part of an Irish cooked breakfast.

Boxty A Northern Irish starchy potato cake made with a half-and-half mix of cooked mashed potatoes and grated, strained raw potato.

Carrageen The typical Irish seaweed that can be found in dishes as diverse as salad and ice cream.

Corned Beef Tongue Usually accompanied by cabbage, this dish is still found on a traditional Irish menu.

Lough Neagh Eel A speciality of Northern Ireland, typically eaten around Halloween; it's usually served in chunks and with a white onion sauce.

Poitín It's rare enough for you to be offered a drop of the 'cratur', as illegally distilled whiskey (made from malted grain or potatoes) is called here. Still, there are pockets of the country with secret stills – in Donegal, Connemara and West Cork.

regions at a glance

Dublin

Museums ✓✓✓
Entertainment ✓✓✓
History ✓✓✓

Museums
Dublin's small but impressive collection of museums includes some world-class institutions. The National Museum is home to the world's best collection of Celtic and pre-Celtic art, and the city's galleries range from the Renaissance to the contemporary with elegant ease; and then there's the Chester Beatty Library, whose unrivalled collection of Islamic books, ancient texts and scrolls is the best you'll find anywhere.

Entertainment
With a thousand-odd pubs to choose from, there is plenty of choice when deciding where to enjoy a pint of Dublin's most celebrated produce. But beyond Guinness and pub chatter there is theatre old and new, concerts fine and frenzied, and all manner of sporting distractions, from an afternoon in the country's largest stadium to a night at the dogs – with dinner and betting slip served at your table.

History
Virtually every Dublin street is lined with monuments to its storied history, from the cobbled grounds of Trinity College to the bloodied walls of Kilmainham Gaol. Its finest buildings and most elegant streets belong to its golden Georgian age, when Dublin was the second city of the empire. But even the most innocuous alley and unassuming house has a story to tell, and Dubliners are only too keen to tell it, although given the fractious nature of the city's history, you're not always guaranteed to hear the same version of the same story!

p54

Counties Wicklow & Kildare

Scenery ✓✓✓
Monastic Ruins ✓✓
Activities ✓✓

Scenery
There are splendid views pretty much everywhere in the Wicklow Mountains, especially at the top of the passes that cut through the range; on a clear day you can see five counties in some spots. In Kildare, the fecund Bog of Allen offers another classic Irish landscape.

Monastic Ruins
Not only are the ruins of Glendalough utterly absorbing, but also their location, at the bottom of a glacial valley by two lakes, is absolutely enchanting and well worth the visit alone.

Activities
Ireland's most popular walking trail, the Wicklow Way, cuts through the county north to south. Kildare is horse-breeding country, where the walking paths are a little bit gentler but no less enjoyable.

p136

Counties Wexford, Waterford, Carlow & Kilkenny

Scenery ✓✓
History ✓✓✓
Food ✓✓

Scenery
Iconic emerald-green fields above ragged ebony cliffs that end in a cerulean sea: you will never tire of the vista. Should you need a break, perfect pockets of sand dot the coast, while Wexford's beaches stretch beyond the horizon. Inland, rural Ireland includes wild rivers and bucolic farms.

History
You half expect to encounter a Viking as you wander the streets of Waterford and Wexford, where traces of the Middle Ages are all around you. Kilkenny's medieval past is impossible to miss, from its soaring cathedral to its great castle.

Food
Head to Dungarvan to enjoy Irish cooking at its best, and enjoy the region's wonderful produce in all towns, big and small.

p165

County Cork

Food ✓✓✓
Scenery ✓✓✓
History ✓✓

Food
County Cork is the unofficial gourmet heartland of Ireland, from the fabulous eateries of Cork City to the wealth of local producers and foodie artisans of West Cork, where you can buy directly at source and eat like a lord.

Scenery
The county's three western peninsulas – Mizen Head, Sheep's Head and Beara – have it all: mountain passes, lonely windswept hills, beautiful beaches and views that will stay with you long after you've left for home.

History
The Rebel County wears its history with pride, even the sorrowful kind. You can explore it all, from famine memorials and scenes of 17th-century battles to the powerful tribute to its more recent fallen heroes.

p221

County Kerry

Scenery ✓✓✓
Seafood ✓✓✓
Traditional Music ✓✓✓

Scenery
County Kerry is the very definition of scenic Ireland – the Connor Pass, the Dingle Peninsula and, particularly, the Ring of Kerry are the gold standard by which Irish landscapes are judged. Judge for yourself by picking up a postcard.

Seafood
Kerry's intimate relationship with the sea means that the fresh catch of the day is exactly that: throughout the Dingle Peninsula you can eat fish fresh off the boat you've just watched land.

Traditional Music
No Kerry town or village is complete without at least one pub featuring traditional music, played by musicians schooled in the respective styles of their region. It's the proper accompaniment to a visit to the county.

p270

Counties Limerick & Tipperary

Walking ✓✓✓
History ✓✓
Scenery ✓✓

Walking

It's a long way to Tipperary, but keep going once you get there, tramping through the chequered Glen of Aherlow and the more challenging Tipperary Heritage Trail, a 55km walk through beautiful river valleys dotted with ancient ruins.

History

From the mighty monastic city of Cashel in County Tipperary to the impressive fortifications of King John's Castle in Limerick City, the varied fortunes of the region's history are easily discernible throughout the two counties.

Scenery

At its broadest point, the mighty Shannon makes for some beautiful vistas, while the rolling hills and farmland of County Tipperary, peppered with ancient ruins, offer the kind of views for which Ireland is known throughout the world.

p319

County Clare

Scenery ✓✓✓
Music ✓✓✓
Pubs ✓✓

Scenery

Rising from the stormy Atlantic in all their sheer dramatic glory, the Cliffs of Moher are an arresting sight not to be missed. The rest of Clare's coast holds additional beauty, especially in the south where mysterious stone columns rise high above the waters. The Burren offers a landscape that's at once mysterious and alien.

Music

Clare plays Ireland's most traditional music, with few modern influences. At festivals, in pubs or even just around any corner, you can hear brilliant trad sessions by the county's surfeit of musicians.

Pubs

There is *no* town in Clare that doesn't have at least one wonderful old pub where the Guinness is ready, the peat is lit and the craic never ends.

p345

County Galway

Scenery ✓✓✓
Food ✓✓
Culture ✓✓✓

Scenery

Hundreds of years of ceaseless toil have brought green accents to the otherwise barren rocks of the Aran Islands. The results are gorgeous, and a walk around these windswept and intriguing islands is one of Ireland's great highlights. In spring, when the gorse blooms in brilliant yellow, the Connemara Peninsula's beauty astounds.

Food

Even as you read this, millions of succulent oysters are growing to the perfect size out in the tidal waters of Galway Bay. Local chefs excel at creating taste treats with the water's bounty.

Culture

On any given night, Galway city's pubs and clubs hum with trad sessions, brilliant rock and tomorrow's next big band. It's a feast for the ears.

p382

Counties Mayo & Sligo

Islands ✓✓
Megalithic Remains ✓✓✓
Yeats Country ✓✓

Islands
There are reputed to be 365 islands in Clew Bay, including one once owned by John Lennon. There's also Craggy Island, which isn't the island of Father Ted fame but rather the home of the notorious pirate queen, Granuaile.

Megalithic Remains
From the world's most extensive Stone Age monument at Céide Fields to the Megalithic cemeteries at Carrowmore and Carrowkeel, the environs of Ballycastle are a step back into prehistory.

Yeats Country
County Sligo is Yeats country: he's buried in the church at Drumcliff, in the shadow of Ben Bulben; and throughout the county you'll find tributes to him in museums and heritage centres, while the landscapes are reflected in his poetry.

p425

County Donegal

Wild Landscapes ✓✓✓
Pristine Beaches ✓✓✓
Surfing ✓✓✓

Wild Landscapes
Untamed and almost impossibly wild, Donegal is the ultimate frontier country, from the wave- and wind-lashed cliffs and beaches of the coast to the mountainous interior, as brooding as it is beautiful.

Pristine Beaches
The county with the second-longest coastline has the country's best beaches, including surf-friendly Rossnowlagh, unspoilt Tramore and the red-tinged sands of Malinbeg. The multitude of coves hide an astonishing number of sandy hideaways.

Surfing
In Donegal you can learn to surf as well as take on some of the world's toughest breaks – the county is arguably the best place in the country to ride the waves due to its great mix of beaches and abundance of surf centres.

p460

The Midlands

Traditional Pubs ✓✓✓
Shannon Cruise ✓✓
Ecclesiastical Remains ✓✓

Traditional Pubs
Spread almost innocuously across the Midlands are some of the most atmospheric pubs in the country, from Morrissey's of Abbeyleix in County Laois to MJ Henry's in Cootehall, County Roscommon; all authentic boozers with ne'er a whiff of fakery.

Shannon Cruise
What better to way to explore the length and breadth of the country's belly than by cruiser along Ireland's longest river? See the sights and stop off along the way to eat in the river-bank restaurants that have sprouted for that purpose.

Ecclesiastical Remains
The top monastic site in Ireland is Clonmacnoise, perched on the edge of the Shannon in County Offaly. Within its walled enclosure you'll find early churches, high crosses, round towers and graves in astonishingly good condition.

p499

Counties Meath, Louth, Cavan & Monaghan

History ✓✓✓
Fishing ✓✓✓
Scenery ✓✓

History

Irish history was lived and written across these counties, at the Hill of Tara, the Neolithic monuments of Brú na Bóinne and Loughcrew, in the magnificent abbeys of Mellifont and Monasterboice, and in towns like Drogheda.

Fishing

County Cavan's myriad lakes are famed for coarse fishing. County Monaghan isn't far behind, and if you fancy a little sea angling, towns like Clogherhead and Carlingford in County Louth are the places to go.

Scenery

These counties offer all kinds of scenery, from the lakelands of Cavan and Monaghan to the fecund hills of County Meath. There are beautiful seaside views too, along the Louth coast as far up as scenic Carlingford.

p531

Belfast

History ✓✓✓
Pubs ✓✓✓
Music ✓✓

History

There's nowhere in Europe where you can get as close to recent history as you can in West Belfast, which has turned the trauma of the Troubles into one of the most interesting tourist attractions in Ireland.

Pubs

The Victorian classics of the city centre are Belfast's most beloved treasure – the Crown might be the most famous, but equally beautiful are the John Hewitt and the Garrick, while older taverns like White's and Kelly's have even more atmosphere.

Music

From DJs spinning tunes in the Eglington to sell-out gigs at the Odyssey, Belfast's music scene is top notch. Best of the lot is probably the Belfast Empire, which features new bands and established acts nightly.

p568

Counties Down & Armagh

Activities ✓✓
Wildlife ✓✓✓
Food ✓✓

Activities

With an impressive calendar of yearly events including birdwatching meets, walking festivals and more strenuous activities like rock climbing and canoeing, there's enough to do here to keep you busy for every day of the year.

Wildlife

The bird-filled mudflats of Castle Espie in County Down are home to a wildfowl and wetlands centre that will entice even the most indifferent of ornithologists, while large colonies of grey seals are but the most obvious of visitors to Strangford Lough in County Armagh.

Food

You'll find top-notch dining in the restaurants and gastropubs of Hillsborough, Bangor and Warrenpoint, all in County Down, plus wonderful spots in the unlikeliest of places, like the marvellous bistro at the back of Ireland's oldest pub in Donaghadee, on the Ards Peninsula.

p605

Counties Derry & Antrim

History ✓✓
Scenery ✓✓✓
Walking ✓✓✓

History

Derry, Ireland's only walled city, has a rich historical past, poignantly told along the walls that withstood a siege in 1688–89, its storied museums and, most tellingly, in the political murals of the Bogside, where history was played out on its very streets.

Scenery

Virtually the entire length of the Antrim coast is scenic gold, but the real stars are the southern section around Carnlough Bay and the North's most outstanding tourist attraction, the surreal geological formations of the Giant's Causeway.

Walking

The Causeway Coast Way stretches 53km between from Portstewart to Ballycastle, but the most scenic section – the 16.5km between Carrick-a-Rede and the Giant's Causeway – can be done in a day and offers one of the finest coastal walks in Ireland.

p634

Counties Fermanagh & Tyrone

Activities ✓✓✓
Scenery ✓✓✓
History ✓✓

Activities

Need something to do? How about fishing in the waters of County Fermanagh, or taking part in the Ulster American Folk Park's annual Appalachian and bluegrass festival? Or, for something more spiritual, why not climb to the summit of Mullaghcarn along with other pilgrims?

Scenery

Whether you're boating on Lough Erne, staring out the windows at the top of the round tower on Devenish Island or hiking across the broad range of the Sperrin Mountains, the scenery is beguiling, especially if you have any kind of decent weather.

History

The towns of Omagh and Enniskillen speak volumes about the atrocities of violence, but Northern Ireland's history isn't just one of conflict: the Ulster American Folk Park expertly tells the story of the province's strong links with the United States.

p671

Look out for these icons:

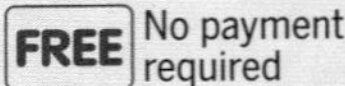

See the Index for a full list of destinations covered in this book.

On the Road

Dublin

POPULATION 1.3 MILLION / AREA 921 SQ KM

Includes »

Best Places to Eat

» Chapter One (p110)
» Coppinger Row (p105)
» Green Nineteen (p105)
» Honest to Goodness (p106)
» Juniors (p112)

Best Places to Stay

» Gibson Hotel (p103)
» Isaacs Hostel (p102)
» Merrion Hotel (p99)
» Number 31 (p98)
» Pembroke Townhouse (p104)

Why Go?

Form is temporary, but class is permanent: the good times may have gone, but Dublin still knows how to have a good time. From its music, art and literature to the legendary nightlife that has inspired those same musicians, artists and writers, Dublin has always known how to have fun and does it with deadly seriousness. As you'll soon find out.

There are world-class museums, superb restaurants and the best collection of entertainment in the country: from rock music to classical concerts there's always something on, and should there not be, you'll always have its thousand or so pubs to while away an evening. And should you wish to get away from it all, the city has a handful of seaside towns at its edges that make for wonderful day trips.

When to Go

March brings the marvellous mayhem of St Patrick's Festival, with 600,000 parade viewers. The world's most popular women's mini-marathon is held in June, with over 40,000 participants. In August the Dun Laoghaire Festival of World Cultures brings musicians and artists from all over the world.

History

Dublin's been making noise since around 500 BC, when a bunch of intrepid Celts camped at a ford over the River Liffey, which is the provenance of the city's tough-to-pronounce Irish name, Baile Átha Cliath (Town of the Hurdle Ford). The Celts went about their merry way for a thousand years or so, but it wasn't until the Vikings showed up that Dublin was urbanised in any significant way. By the 9th century raids from the north had become a fact of Irish life, and some of the fierce Danes chose to stay rather than simply rape, pillage and depart. They intermarried with the Irish and established a vigorous trading port at the point where the River Poddle joined the Liffey in a *dubh linn* (black pool). Today there's little trace of the Poddle, which has been channelled underground and flows under St Patrick's Cathedral to dribble into the Liffey by the Capel St (Grattan) Bridge.

Fast-forward another thousand years, past the arrival of the Normans in the 12th century and the slow process of subjugating Ireland to Anglo-Norman (then British) rule, during which Dublin generally played the role of bandleader. Stop at the beginning of the 18th century, when the squalid city packed with poor Catholics hardly reflected the imperial pretensions of its Anglophile burghers. The great and the good – aka the Protestant Ascendancy – wanted big improvements, and they set about transforming what was in essence still a medieval town into a modern, Anglo-Irish metropolis. Roads were widened, landscaped squares laid out and new town houses were built, all in a proto-Palladian style that soon became known as Georgian after the kings then on the English throne. For a time, Dublin was the second-largest city in the British Empire and all was very, very good – unless you were part of the poor, mostly Catholic masses living in the city's ever-developing slums.

The Georgian boom came to a sudden and dramatic halt after the Act of Union in 1801, when Ireland was formally united with Britain and its separate parliament closed down. Dublin went from being the belle of the imperial ball to the annoying cousin who just wouldn't take the hint, and slid quickly into economic turmoil and social unrest. During the Potato Famine (1845–51), the city's population was swollen by the arrival of tens of thousands of starving refugees from the west, who joined the ranks of an already downtrodden working class. As Dublin entered the 20th century, it was a dispirited place plagued by poverty,

DUBLIN IN...

Two Days

If you've only got two days (whatever is taking you away better be worth it!), start with **Trinity College** and the **Book of Kells** before venturing into the Georgian heartland – amble through **St Stephen's Green** and **Merrion Square**, but be sure to visit both the **National Museum** and the **National Gallery**. In the evening, try an authentic Dublin pub – **Kehoe's** off Grafton St will do nicely. The next day go west, stopping at the **Chester Beatty Library** on your way to the **Guinness Storehouse**; if you still have legs for it, the **Irish Museum of Modern Art** and **Kilmainham Gaol** will round off your day perfectly. Take in a traditional Irish music session at the **Cobblestone**.

Four Days

Follow the two-day itinerary, but stretch it out between refuelling stops at some of the city's better pubs. Visit **Glasnevin Cemetery** and the **Dublin City Gallery – Hugh Lane**. Become a whiskey expert at the **Old Jameson Distillery** and a literary (or beer) one with a **Dublin Literary Pub Crawl**. Take a DART out to **Howth**, walk the headland and try some of the fabulous fish restaurants. Oh, and don't forget **Temple Bar** – there are distractions there for every taste.

One Week

As above, but add a day for the southern suburbs of **Dalkey** and **Sandycove**; a visit to the **Phoenix Park** and exploration of the **Docklands**; there might even be someone you'd love to see performing at the **Grand Canal Theatre**. Alternatively, attend a play at either the **Abbey** or the **Gate**.

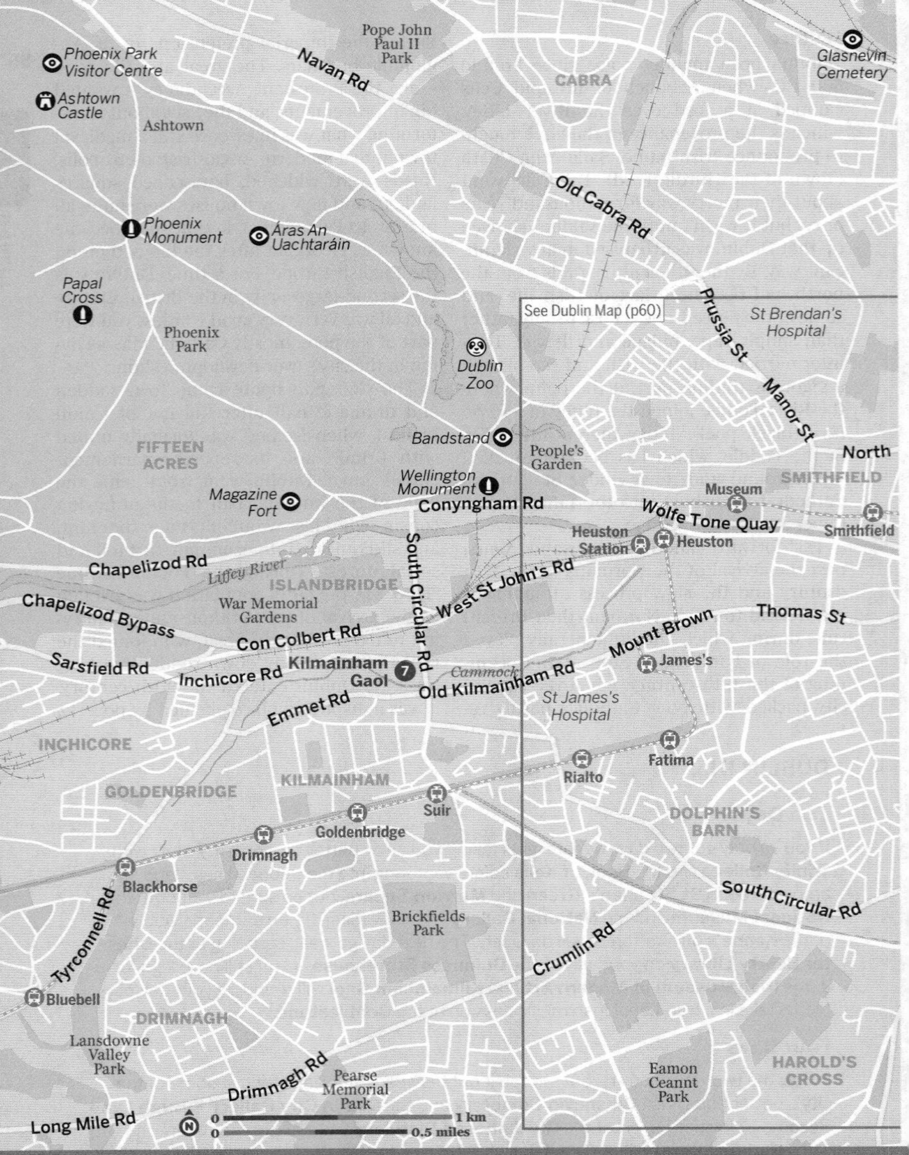

Dublin Highlights

1 Stroll the Elizabethan cobbled grounds of **Trinity College** (p59)

2 Pore over ancient books and other printed wonders from all around the world in the **Chester Beatty Library** (p68)

3 Explore your thespian side by taking in a play at one of Dublin's **theatres** (p121)

4 Get to grips with Ireland's historic treasures and ancient past with a visit to the **National Museum** (p69)

5 Tap into your inner Victorian botanist (and watch the kids go 'wow') with a visit to the 'dead zoo', the **Museum of Natural History** (p75)

6 Enjoy Georgian gems surrounding the landscaped **Merrion Square** (p80) and **St Stephen's Green** (p75)

7 See the past up close and personal at **Kilmainham Gaol** (p84)

8 Quaff a pint or five in one of Dublin's many **pubs** (p113)

disease and more social problems than anyone cared to mention. It's hardly surprising that the majority of Dublin's citizenry were disgruntled and eager for change.

The first fusillade of transformation came during the Easter Rising of 1916, which caused considerable damage to the city centre. At first, Dubliners weren't too enamoured of the rebels, who caused more chaos and disruption than most locals were willing to put up with, but they soon changed their tune when the leaders were executed – Dubliners being natural defenders of the underdog.

County Dublin

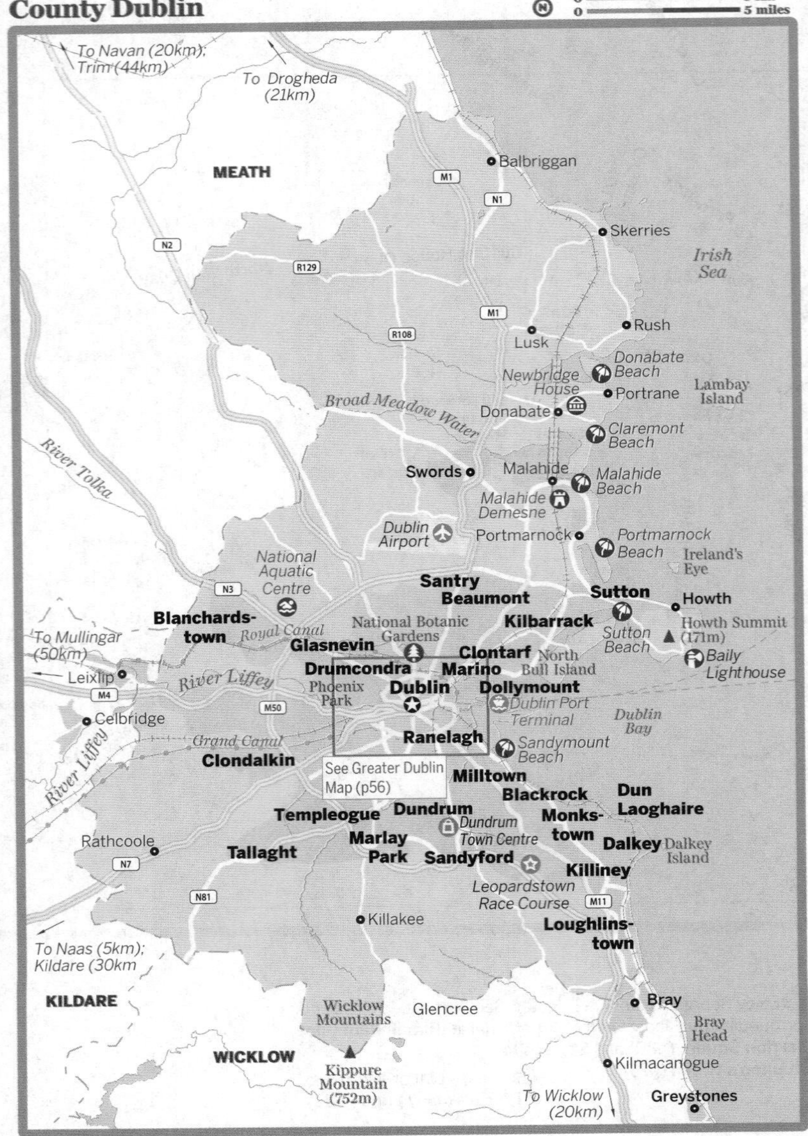

As the whole country lurched radically towards full-scale war with Britain, Dublin was, surprisingly, not part of the main theatre of events. In fact, although there was an increased military presence, the odd shooting in the capital and the blowing up of some notable buildings – such as the Custom House in 1921 – it was business as usual for much of the War of Independence.

A year later, Ireland – minus its northern bit – was independent, but it then tumbled into the Civil War, which led to the burning of more notable buildings, this time the Four Courts in 1922. Ironically, the war among the Irish was more brutal than the struggle for independence – O'Connell St became 'sniper row' and the violence left deep scars that took most of the 20th century to heal.

When the new state finally started doing business, Dublin was an exhausted capital. Despite slow and steady improvements, the city – like the rest of Ireland – continued to be plagued by rising unemployment, high emigration rates and a general stagnation that hung about like an impenetrable cloud. Dubliners made the most of the little they had, but times were tough.

Then, in the 1960s, a silver lining appeared in the shape of an economic boom: Dublin went suburban and began the outward expansion that continues unabated today.

A boom ain't a miracle, however, and Dublin trudged along for another couple of decades with pretty much the same age-old problems (high unemployment, emigration) and some new ones (drug addiction, gangland criminality) before everything began to change in 1994 and a terrible beauty known as the Celtic Tiger was born.

Nearly two decades later, Dublin may be once again facing some tough times, but it is a place transformed, a capital in more than name and a city that has finally taken its rightful place as one of the most vibrant in Europe.

Sights

GRAFTON STREET & AROUND

Dublin's most celebrated shopping street is the elegant, pedestrianised spine of the southern city centre: at its northern end is Trinity College, the country's oldest and most beautiful university, which stretches its leafy self across a healthy chunk of south-city real estate. A few steps northwest is Temple Bar, where bacchanalia and bohemia scrap it out for supremacy – when the sun sets, Bacchus is king. Grafton St's southern end runs into the main entrance to St Stephen's Green, Dublin's perennially popular green lung; surrounding and beyond it is the capital's exquisite Georgian heritage, a collection of galleries, museums, and private and public buildings as handsome as any you'll see in Europe.

Trinity College HISTORIC BUILDING

(Map p64; walking tours 01-896 1827; www.tcd.ie; tour €10; tours every 30min 10.15am-3.40pm Mon-Sat, 10.15am-3pm Sun mid-May–Sep) On a summer's evening, when the bustling crowds have gone for the day, there's hardly a more delightful place in Dublin than the grounds of Ireland's most prestigious **university**, a masterpiece of architecture and landscaping beautifully preserved in Georgian aspic. Not only is this Dublin's most attractive bit of historic real estate, but it's also home to one of the world's most famous – and most beautiful – books, the gloriously illuminated Book of Kells. There is no charge to wander around the gardens on your own between 8am and 10pm.

Officially, the university's name is the University of Dublin, but Trinity is its sole college. Its charter was granted by Elizabeth I in 1592 – on grounds confiscated from an Augustinian priory that was dissolved in 1537 – with the hope that young Dubliners would desist from skipping across to Continental Europe for their education and becoming 'infected with popery'. The 16-hectare site is now in the centre of the city, but when it was founded it was described as 'near Dublin' and was bordered on two sides by the estuary of the River Liffey. Nothing now remains of the original Elizabethan college, which was replaced in the Georgian building frenzy of the 18th century. The most significant change, however, is the student population: the university was exclusively Protestant until 1793, but today most of its 17,000-odd students are Catholic (although until 1970 their own church forbade them from attending on pain of excommunication). All of this would surely have horrified Archbishop Ussher, one of the college's founders, whose greatest scientific feat was the precise dating of the act of creation to 4004 BC. (Darwin, Schmarwin.)

Facing College Green, the Front Gate (Regent House entrance) to the college grounds was built between 1752 and 1759 and is guarded by **statues** of the poet

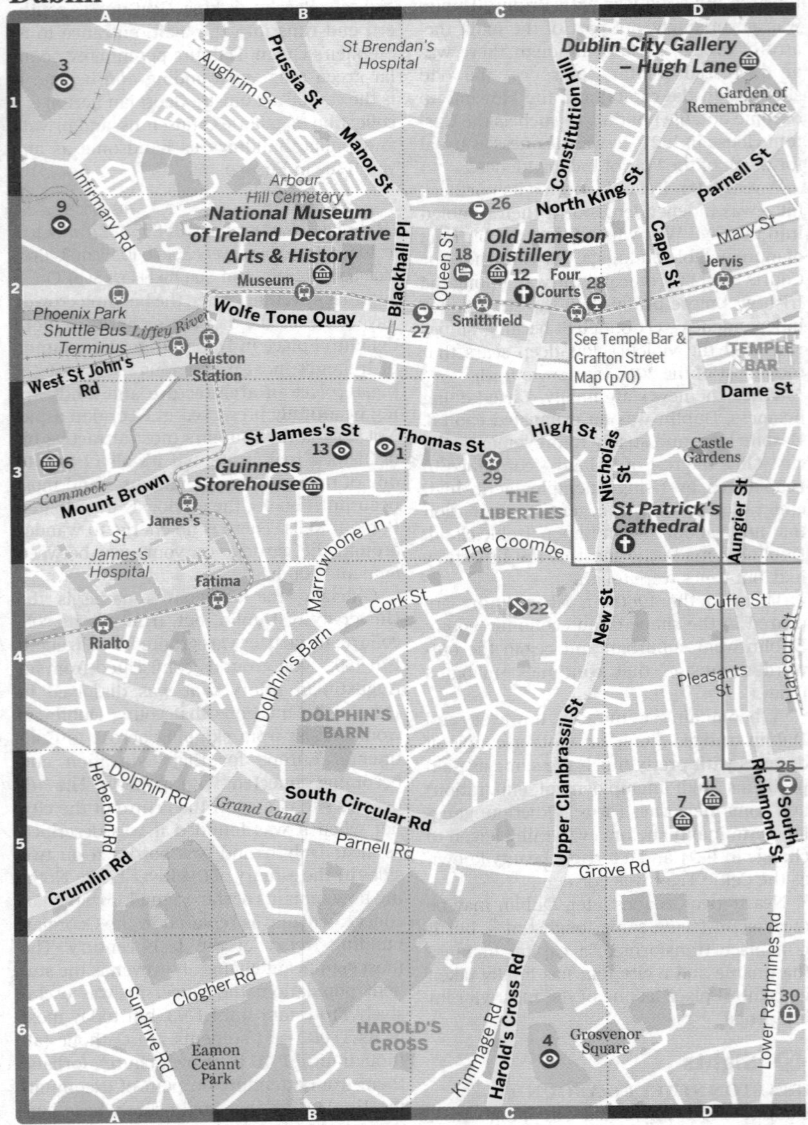

Oliver Goldsmith (1730–74) and the orator Edmund Burke (1729–97). The summer walking tours of the college depart from here.

The open area reached from Regent House is divided into Front Sq, Parliament Sq and Library Sq. The area is dominated by the 30m-high **Campanile**, designed by Charles Lanyon and erected between 1852 and 1853 on what was believed to be the centre of the monastery that preceded the college. To the north of the Campanile is a

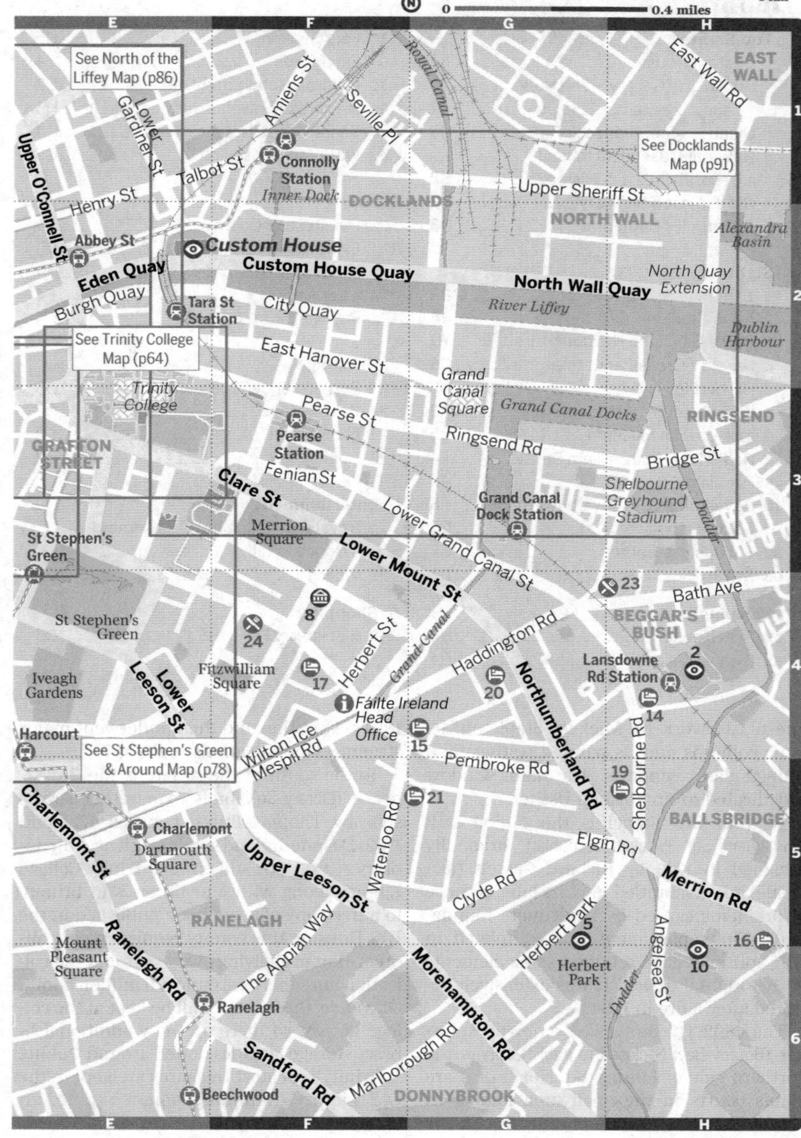

statue of George Salmon, college provost from 1888 to 1904, who fought bitterly to keep women out of the college. He carried out his threat to permit them 'over my dead body' by promptly dropping dead when the worst came to pass.

Clockwise round Front Sq from the Front Gate, the first building is the **chapel** (Front Sq; admission free), built in 1798 to plans made in 1777 by the architect Sir William Chambers (1723–96) and, since 1972, open to all denominations. It's noted for its extremely

Dublin

Top Sights

Custom House E2
Dublin City Gallery – The Hugh Lane D1
Guinness Storehouse B3
National Museum of Ireland – Decorative Arts & History B2
Old Jameson Distillery C2
St Patrick's Cathedral D3

Sights

1 1 Thomas St B3
2 Aviva Stadium H4
3 Garda Síochána Headquarters A1
4 Harold's Cross Park C6
5 Herbert Park G5
6 Irish Museum of Modern Art A3
7 Irish-Jewish Museum D5
8 No 29 Lower Fitzwilliam St F4
9 People's Garden A2
10 Royal Dublin Society Showground H6
11 Shaw Birthplace D5
12 St Michan's Church C2
13 St Patrick's Tower B3

Sleeping

14 Ariel House H4
15 Dylan G4
16 Four Seasons H5
17 Latchfords F4
18 Maldron Hotel Smithfield C2
19 Pembroke Townhouse H5
20 Schoolhouse Hotel G4
21 Waterloo House G5

Eating

22 Dublin Food Co-op C4
Expresso Bar .... (see 15)
23 Juniors H4
24 L'Ecrivain F4
Paulie's Pizza .... (see 23)

Drinking

25 Bernard Shaw D5
26 Cobblestone C2
27 Dice Bar C2
28 Hughes' Bar C2

Entertainment

Royal Dublin Society Showground Concert Hall .... (see 10)
29 Vicar St C3

Shopping

30 Blackberry Fair D6

fine plasterwork by Michael Stapleton, its Ionic columns and its painted (rather than stained-glass) windows. The main window is dedicated to Archbishop Ussher.

Next to the chapel is the **dining hall** (Parliament Sq; closed to public), originally designed in 1743 by Richard Cassels (aka Castle) but dismantled 15 years later because of problems caused by inadequate foundations. The replacement was completed in 1761 and may have retained some elements of the original design. It was extensively restored after a fire in 1984.

The 1892 **Graduates' Memorial Building** (Botany Bay; closed to public) forms the northern side of Library Sq. North of it are tennis courts in the open area known as Botany Bay. The legend behind this name is that the unruly students housed around the square were suitable candidates for the British penal colony at Botany Bay in Australia.

At the eastern side of Library Sq, the redbrick **Rubrics Building** dates from around 1690, making it the oldest building in the college. It was extensively altered in an 1894 restoration and then underwent major structural modifications in the 1970s.

To the south of the square is the **Old Library** (Library Sq), built in a rather severe style by Thomas Burgh between 1712 and 1732. Despite Ireland's independence, the Library Act of 1801 still entitles Trinity College Library, along with four libraries in Britain, to a free copy of every book published in the UK. Housing this bounty requires nearly another 1km of shelving every year and the collection amounts to around 4.5 million books. Of course, these cannot all be kept at the college library, so there are now additional library storage facilities dotted around Dublin.

Trinity's greatest treasures are kept in the Old Library's stunning 65m **Long Room** (East Pavilion, Library Colonnades; adult/student/child €9/8/free; 9.30am-5pm Mon-Sat year-round, noon-4.30pm Sun Oct-Apr, 9.30am-4.30pm Sun May-Sep), which houses about 250,000 of the library's oldest volumes, including the breathtaking **Book of Kells** (see the boxed text, p63). Your entry ticket includes admission to temporary exhibitions on display in the East Pavilion. The ground-floor Colonnades was originally an open arcade, but was enclosed in 1892 to increase the storage area. A previous attempt to increase the room's storage capacity had been made in 1853, when the Long Room ceiling was raised. Other displays include a rare copy of the Proclamation of the Irish Republic, which was read out by Pádraig Pearse at the beginning of the Easter Rising in 1916. Also here is the so-called **harp of Brian Ború**, which was definitely not in use when the army of this early Irish hero defeated the Danes at the Battle of Clontarf in 1014. It does, however, date from around 1400, making it one of the oldest harps in Ireland.

Continuing clockwise around the Campanile, there's the **1937 Reading Room** and the **Exam Hall** (Public Theatre), which dates from 1779 to 1791. Like the chapel, it was the work of William Chambers and also has plasterwork by Michael Stapleton. The Exam Hall has an oak chandelier rescued from the Houses of Parliament (now the Bank of Ireland) across College Green, and an organ supposedly salvaged from a Spanish ship in 1702, though evidence indicates otherwise.

Behind the Exam Hall is the 1760 **Provost's House**, a very fine Georgian house where the provost (college head) still resides. The house and its adjacent garden are not open to the public.

To one side of the Old Library is Paul Koralek's 1967 **Berkeley Library** (Fellows' Sq; ⏲closed to public). This solid, square, brutalist-style building has been hailed as the best example of modern architecture in Ireland, though it has to be admitted the competition isn't great. It's fronted by Arnaldo Pomodoro's 1982 sculpture **Sphere Within Sphere**. George Berkeley was born in Kilkenny in 1685, studied at Trinity when he was only 15 years old and went on to a distinguished career in many fields, particularly philosophy. His influence spread to the new colonies in North America where, among other things, he helped to found the University of Pennsylvania. Berkeley, California, and its namesake university are named after him.

South of the Old Library is the 1978 **Arts & Social Science Building**, which backs on to Nassau St and forms the alternative entrance to the college. Like the Berkeley

THE PAGE OF KELLS

More than half a million visitors stop in each year to see Trinity's top show-stopper, the world-famous **Book of Kells**. This illuminated manuscript, dating from around AD 800 and therefore one of the oldest books in the world, was probably produced by monks at St Colmcille's Monastery on the remote island of Iona, off the western coast of Scotland. Repeated looting by marauding Vikings forced the monks to flee to the temporary safety of Kells, County Meath, in AD 806, along with their masterpiece. Around 850 years later, the book was brought to the college for safekeeping and has remained here since.

The Book of Kells contains the four Gospels of the New Testament, written in Latin, as well as prefaces, summaries and other text. If it were merely words, the Book of Kells would simply be a very old book – it's the extensive and amazingly complex illustrations that make it so wonderful. The superbly decorated opening initials are only part of the story, for the book has smaller illustrations between the lines.

And here the problems begin. Of the 680 pages, only two are on display – one showing an illumination, the other showing text – which has led to it being dubbed the *page* of Kells. No getting around that one, though: you can hardly expect the right to thumb through a priceless treasure at random. No, the real problem is its immense popularity, which makes viewing it a rather unsatisfactory pleasure. Punters are herded through the specially constructed viewing room at near lightning pace, making for a there-you-see-it, there-you-don't kind of experience.

To really appreciate the book, you can buy your own reproduction copy for a mere €22,000. Failing that, the library bookshop stocks a plethora of souvenirs and other memorabilia, including Otto Simm's excellent *Exploring the Book of Kells* (€12.95), a thorough guide with attractive colour plates, and a popular DVD-ROM (€31.95) showing all 800 pages. Kids looking for something a little less stuffy might enjoy the animated *Secret of Kells* (2009), which is more fun than accurate in its portrayal of how the gospel was actually put together.

Trinity College

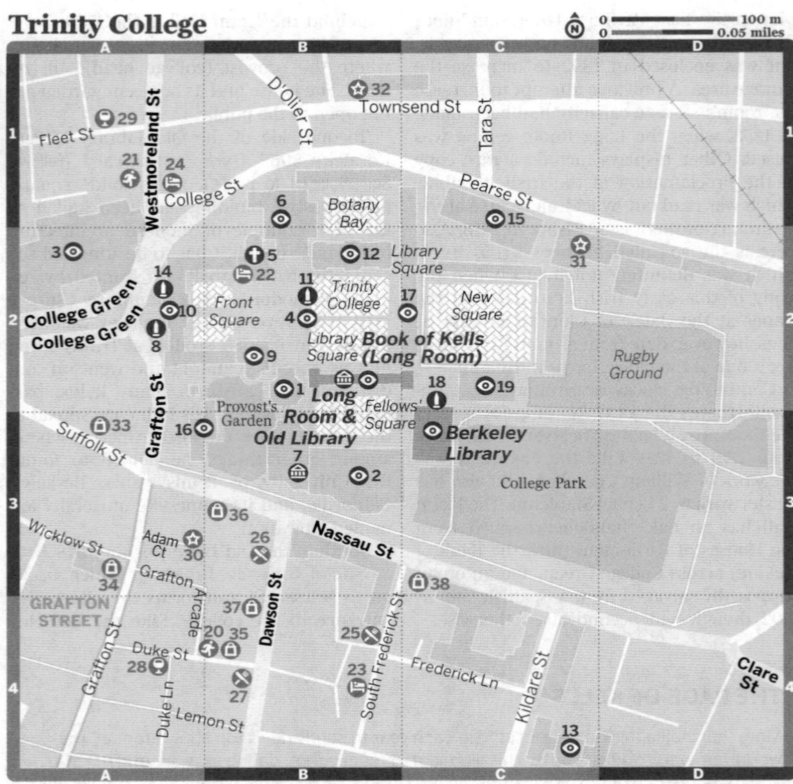

Library, it was designed by Paul Koralek; it also houses the **Douglas Hyde Gallery of Modern Art** (www.douglashydegallery.ie; admission free; ⏲11am-6pm Mon-Wed & Fri, 11am-7pm Thu, 11am-4.45pm Sat).

Trinity's newest attraction is the **Science Gallery** (Map p91; www.sciencegallery.ie; Pearse St; admission free; ⏲exhibitions usually noon-8pm Tue-Fri, noon-6pm Sat & Sun, cafe 8am-8pm Tue-Fri, noon-6pm Sat & Sun), a refreshingly lively and informative exploration of the relationship between science, art and the world we live in. Past exhibits have touched on a range of fascinating topics, including how memory works and how humans may evolve in the future. The ground-floor Flux Café, bathed in floor-to-ceiling light, is a pretty good spot to take a load off.

Behind the Rubrics Building, at the eastern end of Library Sq, is New Sq. The highly ornate **Victorian Museum Building** (☎01-896 1477; New Sq; admission free; ⏲by prior arrangement), built from 1853 to 1857, has the skeletons of two enormous Giant Deer just inside the entrance, and the **Geological Museum** upstairs.

The 1734 **Printing House**, designed by Richard Cassels to resemble a Doric temple, and now used for the microelectronics and electrical engineering departments, is on the northern side of New Sq.

At the eastern end of the college grounds are the rugby ground and College Park, where cricket is played. There are a number of science buildings here also. The **Lincoln Place Gate** (Map p91) at this end is usually open and makes a good entrance or exit from the college, especially if you're on a bicycle.

Temple Bar NEIGHBOURHOOD

Many a wild night has been had within the cobbled precincts of Temple Bar (Map p70), Dublin's most visited neighbourhood, a maze of streets and alleys sandwiched be-

Trinity College

Top Sights

	Berkeley Library	C3
	Book of Kells (Long Room)	B2
	Long Room & Old Library	B2

Sights

1	1937 Reading Room	B2
2	Arts & Social Science Building	B3
3	Bank of Ireland	A2
4	Campanile	B2
5	Chapel	B2
6	Dining Hall	B1
7	Douglas Hyde Gallery of Modern Art	B3
8	Edmund Burke Statue	A2
9	Exam Hall	B2
10	Front Gate	A2
	Genealogical Office	(see 13)
11	George Salmon Statue	B2
12	Graduates' Memorial Building	B2
13	National Library	C4
14	Oliver Goldsmith Statue	A2
15	Printing House	C1
16	Provost's House	A3
17	Rubrics Building	C2
18	Sphere within Sphere	C2
19	Victorian Museum Building	C2

Activities, Courses & Tours

20	Dublin Literary Pub Crawl	B4
21	Dublin Rock'n'Roll Writers Bus Tour Stop	A1

Sleeping

22	Accommodations Office	B2
23	Trinity Lodge	B4
24	Westin Dublin	A1

Eating

	Avoca	(see 33)
25	Dunne & Crescenzi	B4
26	Lemon	B3
27	Marco Pierre White Steakhouse & Grill	B4

Drinking

28	Davy Byrne's	A4
29	Palace Bar	A1

Entertainment

30	Lillie's Bordello	A3
31	Players' Theatre	C2
32	Screen	B1

Shopping

33	Avoca Handweavers	A3
34	Brown Thomas	A3
35	Cathach Books	B4
36	DesignYard	B3
37	Hodges Figgis	B4
38	Kilkenny Shop	C3

tween Dame St and the Liffey, running from Trinity College to Christ Church Cathedral. But it's not all booze and infamy: you can browse for vintage clothes, check out the latest art installations, get your nipples pierced and nibble on Mongolian barbecue. In good weather you can watch outdoor movies in one square or join in a pulsating drum circle in another – just another slice of life in the city's most popular neighbourhood.

During the day and on weekday nights Temple Bar does have something of a bohemian bent about it – if you ignore the crappy tourist shops and dreadful restaurants serving bland, overpriced food – but at weekends, when the party really gets going, it can get very sloppy. The huge, characterless bars crank up the sounds and throw their doors open to the tens of thousands of punters looking to drink and score like the end of the world is nigh. By 3am, the only culture on display is in the pools of vomit and urine that give the whole area the aroma of a sewer – welcome to Temple Barf.

Temple Bar Information Centre (Map p70; ☎01-677 2255; www.templebar.ie, www.visit-templebar.ie; 12 East Essex St; ⏰9am-5.30pm Mon-Fri) publishes the TASCQ cultural guide to Temple Bar, which gives information on attractions and restaurants in the area. It's available from the information centre or at businesses around Temple Bar. It's best to check the websites for details of events.

Meeting House Square (Map p70) is one of the real success stories of Temple Bar. On one side is the excellent **Gallery of Photography** (Map p70; admission free; ⏰11am-6pm Mon-Sat), hosting temporary exhibitions of contemporary local and international photographers. Staying with the photography theme, the other side of the square is home to the **National Photographic Archive** (Map p70; admission free; ⏰11am-6pm Mon-Sat, 2-6pm Sun), a magnificent resource for

Trinity College, Dublin

STEP INTO THE PAST

Ireland's most prestigious university, founded on the order of Queen Elizabeth I in 1592, is an architectural masterpiece, a cordial retreat from the bustle of modern life in the middle of the city. Step through its main entrance and you step back in time, the cobbled stones transporting you to another era, when the elite discussed philosophy and argued passionately in favour of empire. Standing in Front Square, the 30m-high **Campanile** 1 is directly in front of you with the **Dining Hall** 2 to your left. On the far side of the square is the Old Library building, the centrepiece of which is the magnificent **Long Room** 3, which was the inspiration for the computer generated imagery of the Jedi Archive in *Star Wars Episode II: Attack of the Clones*. Here you'll find the university's greatest treasure, the **Book of Kells** 4. You'll probably have to queue to see this masterpiece, and then only for a brief visit, but it's very much worth it. Just beyond the Old Library is the very modern **Berkeley Library** 5, which nevertheless fits perfectly into the campus' overall aesthetic: directly in front of it is the distinctive **Sphere Within a Sphere** 6, the most elegant of the university's sculptures.

DON'T MISS

» Douglas Hyde Gallery, the campus' designated modern art museum

» Cricket match on pitch, the most elegant of pastimes

» Pint in the Pavilion Bar, preferably while watching the cricket

» Visit to the Science Gallery, where science is made completely relevant

Campanile
Trinity College's most iconic bit of masonry was designed in the mid-19th century by Sir Charles Lanyon; the attached sculptures were created by Thomas Kirk.

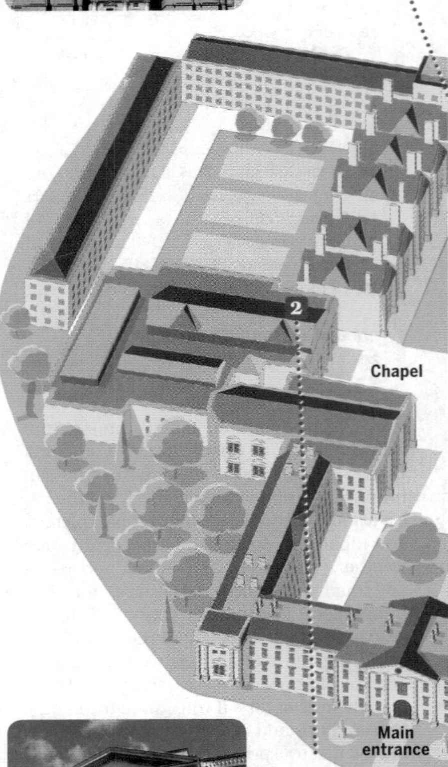

Dining Hall
Richard Cassels' original building was designed to mirror the Examination Hall directly opposite on Front Square: the hall collapsed twice and was rebuilt from scratch in 1761.

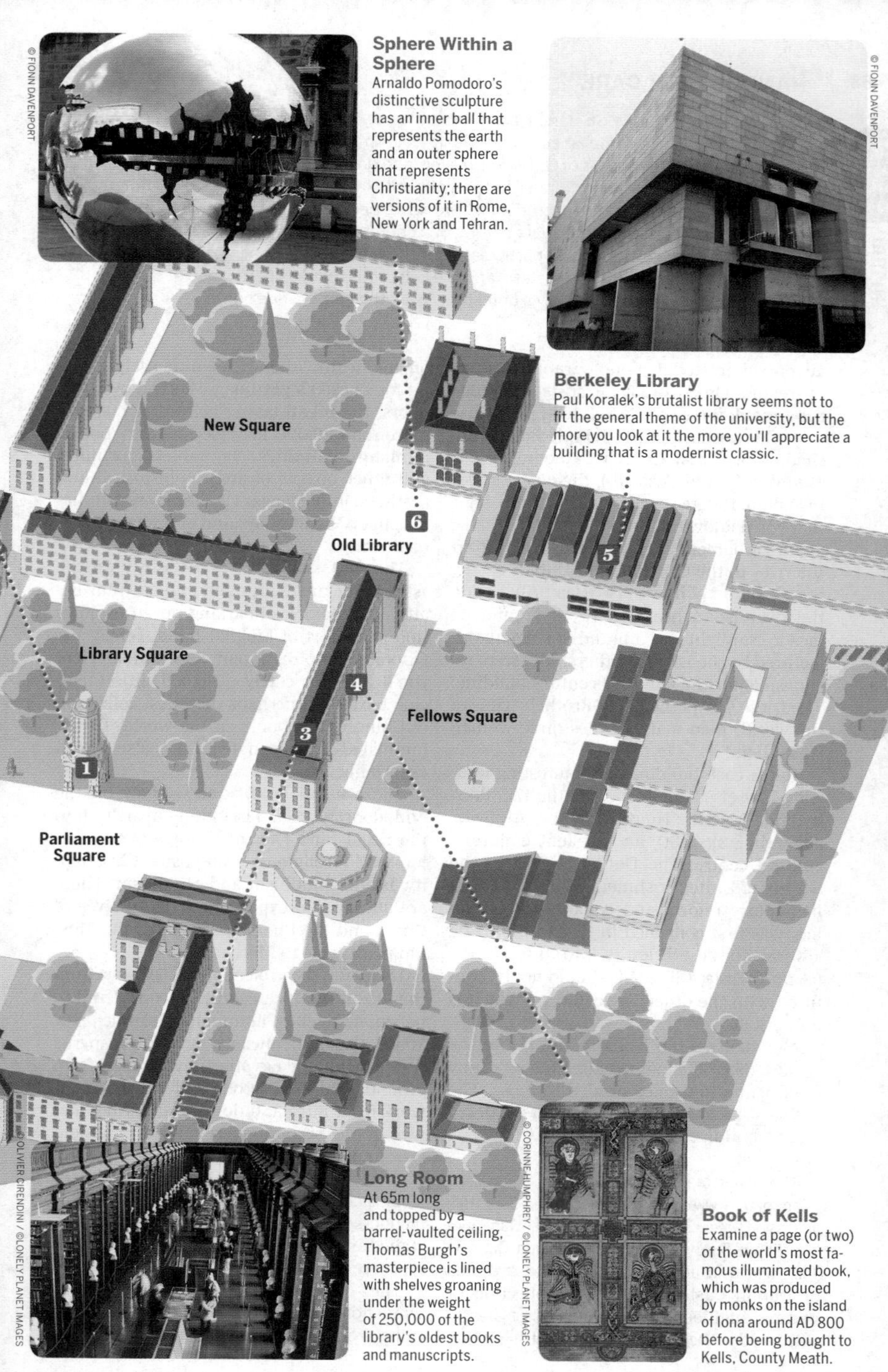

Sphere Within a Sphere

Arnaldo Pomodoro's distinctive sculpture has an inner ball that represents the earth and an outer sphere that represents Christianity; there are versions of it in Rome, New York and Tehran.

Berkeley Library

Paul Koralek's brutalist library seems not to fit the general theme of the university, but the more you look at it the more you'll appreciate a building that is a modernist classic.

Long Room

At 65m long and topped by a barrel-vaulted ceiling, Thomas Burgh's masterpiece is lined with shelves groaning under the weight of 250,000 of the library's oldest books and manuscripts.

Book of Kells

Examine a page (or two) of the world's most famous illuminated book, which was produced by monks on the island of Iona around AD 800 before being brought to Kells, County Meath.

HANDEL WITH CARE

In 1742 the nearly broke GF Handel conducted the very first performance of his epic work *Messiah* in the since demolished Dublin Music Hall, on the city's oldest street, Fishamble St. Jonathan Swift – author of *Gulliver's Travels* and dean of St Patrick's Cathedral – had suggested that his own and Christ Church's choirs take part, but revoked his invitation when he discovered that the sacred music would be performed in a common music hall rather than in the more appropriate setting of a church, and vowed to 'punish such vicars [who allowed their choristers to participate] for their rebellion, disobedience and perfidy'. The concert went ahead nonetheless, and the celebrated work is performed at the original spot in Dublin annually – now a hotel that bears the composer's name.

anyone interested in a photographic history of Ireland. On Saturdays it hosts a popular **food market** (see the boxed text, p108).

At the western end of Temple Bar, in the shadow of Christ Church Cathedral, is **Fishamble Street** (Map p70), the oldest street in Dublin. It dates back to Viking times – not that you'd know that to see it now.

On Parliament St, which runs south from the river to the City Hall and Dublin Castle, the **Sunlight Chambers** (Map p70) beside the river has a beautiful frieze around its facade. Sunlight was a brand of soap manufactured by the Lever Brothers, who were responsible for the late-19th-century building. The frieze shows the Lever Brothers' view of the world: men make clothes dirty, women wash them!

To the east, buildings on interesting **Eustace Street** (Map p70) include the 1715 Presbyterian Meeting House, now the **Ark** (www.ark.ie; 11A Eustace St), an excellent children's cultural centre. The Dublin branch of the Society of United Irishmen, who sought Parliamentary reform and equality for Catholics, was first convened in 1791 in the Eagle Tavern, now the **Friends' Meeting House** (Map p70; Eustace St). (This should not be confused with the other Eagle Tavern, which is on Cork St.)

Merchant's Arch leads to the **Ha'penny Bridge** (Map p86), named after the ha'penny (half-penny) toll once needed to cross. The **Stock Exchange** (Map p64) is on Anglesea St, in a building dating from 1878.

TOP CHOICE **Chester Beatty Library** MUSEUM

(Map p70; www.cbl.ie; Dublin Castle, Cork Hill; admission free; ⏲10am-5pm Mon-Fri, 11am-5pm Sat, 1-5pm Sun year-round, closed Mon Oct-Apr) The world-famous library, in the grounds of Dublin Castle, houses the collection of mining engineer Sir Alfred Chester Beatty (1875–1968), bequeathed to the Irish State on his death. And we're immensely grateful for Chester's patronage: spread over two floors, the breathtaking collection includes more than 20,000 manuscripts, rare books, miniature paintings, clay tablets, costumes and other objects of artistic, historical and aesthetic importance. The library runs tours at 1pm on Wednesdays and at 3pm and 4pm on Sundays.

The **Artistic Traditions Gallery** on the 1st floor begins with memorabilia from Beatty's life, before embarking on an exploration of the art of Mughal India, Persia, the Ottoman empire, Japan and China. Here you'll find intricately designed little medicine boxes and perhaps the finest collection of Chinese jade books in the world. The illuminated European texts are also worth examining.

The **Sacred Traditions Gallery** on the 2nd floor gives a fascinating insight into the rituals and rites of passage of the major world religions – Judaism, Christianity, Islam, Buddhism and Hinduism. There are audiovisual explorations of the lives of Christ and the Buddha, as well as the Muslim pilgrimage to Mecca.

Head for the collection of Qu'rans from the 9th to the 19th centuries, considered to be among the best illuminated Islamic texts. You'll also find ancient Egyptian papyrus texts (including Egyptian love poems from around 1100 BC), scrolls and exquisite artwork from Burma, Indonesia and Tibet – as well as the second-oldest biblical fragment ever found (after the Dead Sea Scrolls).

The comprehensive **Reference Library** (⏲by appointment only), complete with a finely lacquered ceiling that Beatty himself had installed in his own London home, is a great resource for artists or students.

The library regularly holds specialist workshops, exhibitions and talks on everything from origami to calligraphy, and admission is free. It's easy to escape from the rigours of Western life on the serene rooftop **Japanese garden** or at the Silk Road Cafe on the ground floor, which serves delicious Middle Eastern cuisine.

Dublin Castle HISTORIC BUILDING

(Map p70; www.heritageireland.ie; Cork Hill; adult/concession €4.50/3.50; ⏲10am-4.45pm Mon-Fri, 2-4.45pm Sat & Sun; 🚌50, 54, 56a, 77, 77a) If you're looking for a medieval castle straight out of central casting you'll be disappointed; the stronghold of British power in Ireland for 700 years is principally an 18th-century creation that is more hotch-potch palace than turreted castle. Only the Record Tower, completed in 1258, survives from the original Anglo-Norman fortress commissioned by King John from 1204.

It was officially handed over to Michael Collins on behalf of the Irish Free State in 1922, when the British viceroy is reported to have rebuked Collins on being seven minutes late. Collins replied, 'We've been waiting 700 years, you can wait seven minutes.' The castle is now used by the Irish government for meetings and functions, and can be visited only on a guided tour of the State Apartments and excavations of the former Powder Tower.

As you walk into the grounds from the main Dame St entrance, there's a good example of the evolution of Irish architecture. On your left is the Victorian **Chapel Royal** (occasionally part of the Dublin Castle tours), decorated with more than 90 heads of various Irish personages and saints carved out of Tullamore limestone. Beside this is the Norman **Record Tower** (Map p70), which has 5m-thick walls and now houses the **Garda Museum** (admission free), which follows the history of the Irish police force. It doesn't have all that much worth protecting, but the views are fab (ring the bell for entry). On your right is the Georgian **Treasury Building**, the oldest office block in Dublin, and behind you, yikes, is the uglier-than-sin **Revenue Commissioners Building** of 1960.

Heading away from that eyesore, you ascend to the Upper Yard. On your right is a figure of Justice with her back turned to the city, an appropriate symbol for British justice, reckoned Dubliners. Next to it is the 18th-century **Bedford Tower** (Map p70), from which the Irish Crown Jewels were stolen in 1907 and never recovered. Opposite is the entrance to the tours.

The 45-minute guided tours (departing every 20 to 30 minutes, depending on numbers) are pretty dry, but they're included in the entry fee. You get to visit the State Apartments, many of which are decorated in dubious taste. You will also see St Patrick's Hall, where Irish presidents are inaugurated and foreign dignitaries toasted, and the room in which the wounded James Connolly was tied to a chair while convalescing after the 1916 Easter Rising – brought back to health to be executed by firing squad.

The highlight is a visit to the subterranean excavations of the old castle, discovered by accident in 1986. They include foundations built by the Vikings (whose long-lasting mortar was made of ox blood, egg shells and horse hair), the hand-polished exterior of the castle walls that prevented attackers from climbing them, the steps leading down to the moat and the trickle of the historic River Poddle, which once filled the moat on its way to join the Liffey.

FREE **National Museum of Ireland – Archaeology & History** MUSEUM

(Map p78; www.museum.ie; Kildare St; admission free; ⏲10am-5pm Tue-Sat, 2-5pm Sun) Designed by Sir Thomas Newenham Deane and completed in 1890, the star attraction of this branch of the **National Museum of Ireland** is the Treasury, home to the finest collection of Bronze Age and Iron Age gold artefacts in the world, and the world's most complete collection of medieval Celtic metalwork.

The centrepieces of the Treasury's unique collection are Ireland's most famous crafted artefacts, the **Ardagh Chalice** and the **Tara Brooch**. Measuring 17.8cm high and 24.2cm in diameter, the 12th-century Ardagh Chalice is made up of gold, silver, bronze, brass,

DUBLIN PASS

If you're planning some heavy-duty sightseeing, you'll save a packet by investing in the **Dublin Pass** (adult/child 1-day €35/19, 2-day €55/31, 3-day €65/39, 6-day €95/49). Not only do you gain free entry to 32 attractions but you also can skip whatever queue there is by presenting your card; it also includes free transfer to and from the airport on the Aircoach (see p130). The Dublin Pass is available from any of the Dublin Tourism offices (p129).

Temple Bar & Grafton Street

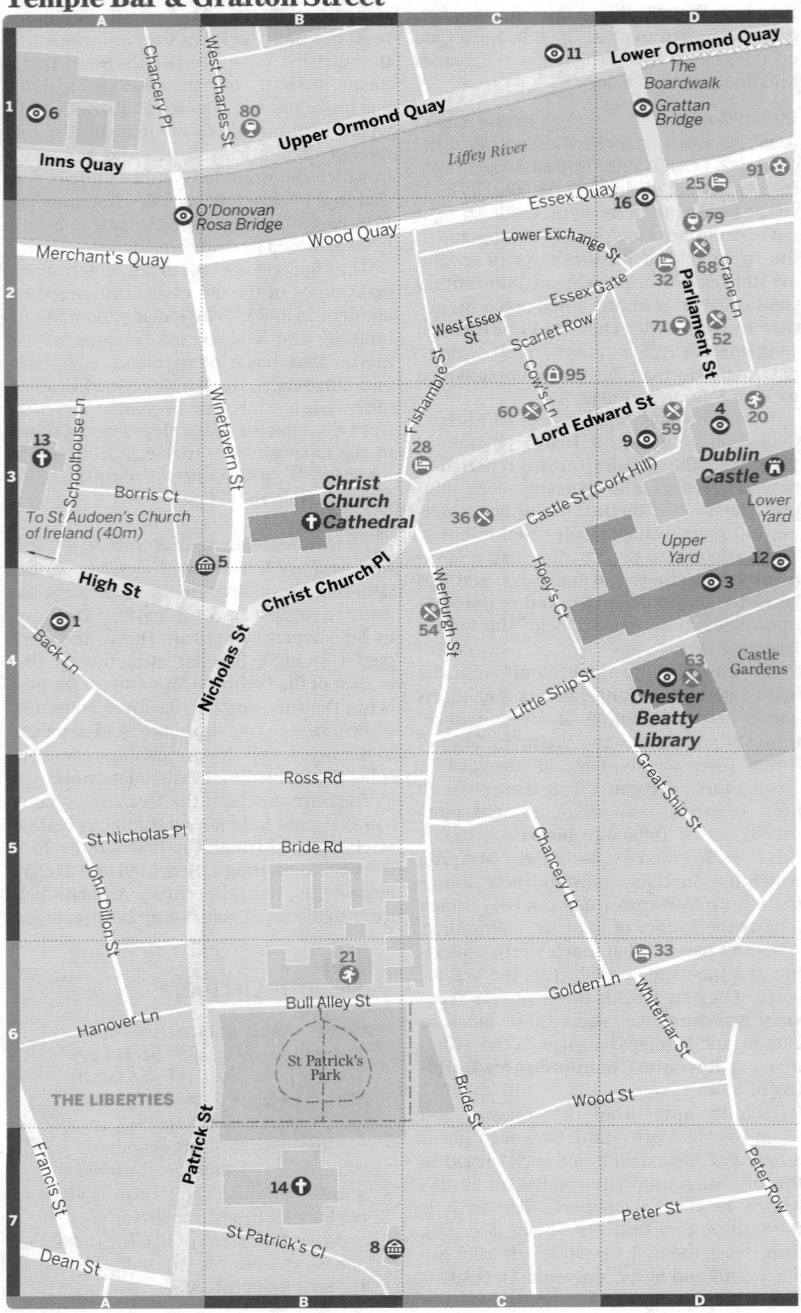

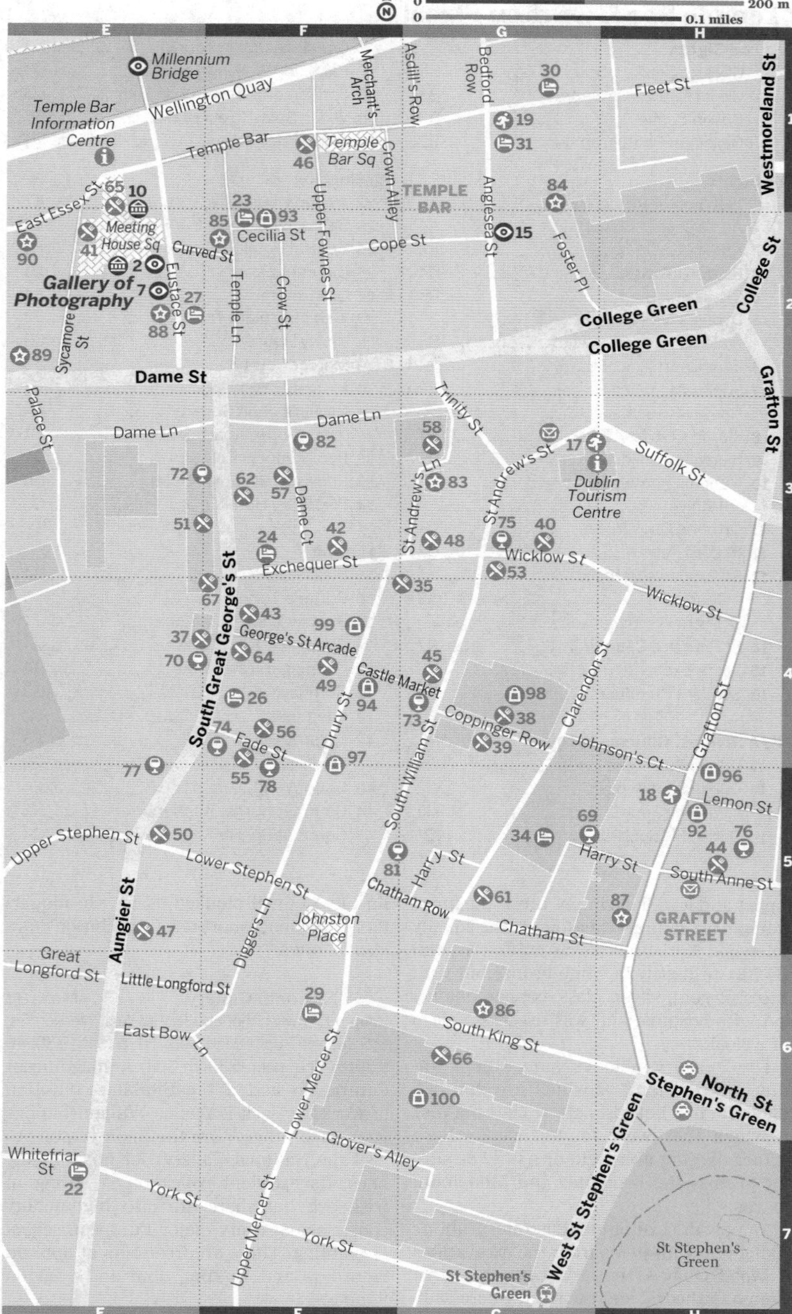
0 200 m
0 0.1 miles
Millennium Bridge
Temple Bar Information Centre
Wellington Quay
Temple Bar
Temple Bar Sq
Merchant's Arch
Asdill's Row
Bedford Row
Fleet St
Westmoreland St
Crown Alley
Upper Fownes St
TEMPLE BAR
Anglesea St
Foster Pl
East Essex St
Meeting House Sq
Curved St
Cecilia St
Cope St
Gallery of Photography
Eustace St
Temple Ln
Crow St
Sycamore St
College Green
College St
Dame St
Grafton St
Palace St
Dame Ln
Trinity St
St Andrew's St
Suffolk St
Dublin Tourism Centre
St Andrew's Ln
Dame Ct
Exchequer St
Wicklow St
South Great George's St
George's St Arcade
Castle Market
Drury St
South William St
Coppinger Row
Clarendon St
Johnson's Ct
Fade St
Lemon St
Upper Stephen St
Lower Stephen St
Harry St
South Anne St
Chatham Row
Chatham St
Johnston Place
GRAFTON STREET
Aungier St
Diggers Ln
Great Longford St
Little Longford St
East Bow Ln
Lower Mercer St
South King St
North St Stephen's Green
West St Stephen's Green
Glover's Alley
Whitefriar St
York St
Upper Mercer St
St Stephen's Green

Temple Bar & Grafton Street

Top Sights

	Chester Beatty Library	D4
	Christ Church Cathedral	B3
	Dublin Castle	D3
	Gallery of Photography	E2

Sights

	1916 Easter Rising Walk	(see 75)
1	An Taisce	A4
2	Ark	E2
3	Bedford Tower	D4
4	City Hall	D3
5	Dvblinia & The Viking World	B3
6	Four Courts	A1
7	Friends' Meeting House	E2
	Garda Musuem	(see 12)
8	Marsh's Library	B7
9	Municipal Buildings	D3
10	National Photographic Archive	E2
11	Ormond Quay Hotel	C1
12	Record Tower	D3
13	St Audoen's Catholic Church	A3
	St Michael's Tower	(see 12)
14	St Patrick's Cathedral	B7
15	Stock Exchange	G2
16	Sunlight Chambers	D2

Activities, Courses & Tours

17	Dublin Bus Tours	G3
18	Dublin Footsteps Walking Tour	H5
19	Dublin Musical Pub Crawl	G1
	Gray Line Dublin Tour	(see 17)
	Pat Liddy Walking Tours	(see 17)
20	Sandeman's New Dublin Tour	D3
21	Viking Splash Tours	B6
	Wild Wicklow Tour	(see 17)

Sleeping

22	Avalon House	E7
23	Barnacles Temple Bar House	F2
24	Central Hotel	F3
25	Clarence Hotel	D1
26	Grafton House	F4
27	Irish Landmark Trust	E2
28	Kinlay House	C3
29	Mercer Court	F6
30	Morgan Hotel	G1
31	Oliver St John Gogarty's Penthouse Apartments	G1
32	Paramount Hotel	D2
33	Radisson Blu Royal Hotel	D6
34	Westbury Hotel	G5

Eating

35	Blazing Salads	G4
36	Bottega Toffoli	C3
37	Brasserie Sixty6	E4
38	Coppinger Row Market	G4
39	Coppinger Row Market	G4
40	Cornucopia	G3
41	Eden	E2
42	Fallon & Byrne	F3
	Fresh	(see 98)
43	Good World	F4
44	Gourmet Burger Kitchen	H5
45	Gourmet Burger Kitchen	G4

copper and lead. Put simply, this is the finest example of Celtic art ever found. The equally renowned Tara Brooch was crafted around AD 700, primarily in white bronze but with traces of gold, silver, glass, copper, enamel and wire beading, and was used as a clasp for a cloak.

The Treasury includes many other stunning pieces, many of which are grouped together in 'hoards', after the manner in which they were found, usually by a farmer digging up a field or a bog. Be sure not to miss the Broighter and Mooghaun hoards.

An upstairs exhibition illustrates Dublin's Viking era, with items from the excavations at Wood Quay – the area between Christ Church Cathedral and the river, where Dublin City Council plonked its new headquarters. Frequent short-term exhibitions are also on offer.

FREE National Gallery ART GALLERY

(Map p91; www.nationalgallery.ie; West Merrion Sq; 9.30am-5.30pm Mon-Wed, Fri & Sat, 9.30am-8.30pm Thu, noon-5.30pm Sun) A magnificent Caravaggio and a breathtaking collection of works by Jack B Yeats – William Butler's younger brother – are the main reasons to visit the National Gallery, but not the only ones. Its excellent collection is strong in Irish art, but there are also high-quality collections of every major European school of painting. There are free tours at 3pm on Saturdays and at 2pm, 3pm and 4pm on Sundays.

46 Gourmet Burger Kitchen F1
47 Govinda's E5
48 Green Hen G3
49 Honest to Goodness F4
50 Jaipur E5
51 Juice E3
52 Larder D2
53 Lemon G3
54 Leo Burdock's C4
55 L'Gueuleton F4
56 Market Bar F4
57 Odessa F3
Pepperpot .... (see 98)
58 Pichet G3
59 Queen of Tarts D3
60 Queen of Tarts C3
61 Saba G5
62 Shebeen Chic F3
63 Silk Road Café D4
64 Simon's Place F4
65 Temple Bar Farmers Market E1
66 Wagamama G6
67 Yamamori F4
68 Zaytoon D2

Drinking

69 Bruxelles G5
70 Dragon E4
71 Front Lounge D2
72 George E3
73 Grogan's Castle Lounge G4
74 Hogan's F4
75 International Bar G3
76 Kehoe's H5
77 Long Hall E5
Market Bar .... (see 56)
78 No Name Bar F5
Oliver St John Gogarty's .... (see 31)
79 Porterhouse D2
80 Sin É B1
81 South William F5
82 Stag's Head F3

Entertainment

83 Andrew's Lane Theatre G3
Ark .... (see 2)
84 Bank of Ireland Arts Centre G1
85 Button Factory F2
86 Gaiety Theatre G6
87 HMV H5
International Bar .... (see 75)
88 Irish Film Institute (IFI) E2
89 Olympia Theatre E2
90 Project Arts Centre E2
91 Workman's Club D1

Shopping

Bow Boutique .... (see 98)
92 BT2 .... H5
93 Claddagh Records F2
94 Costume F4
95 Cow's Lane Designer Mart C2
96 Dubray Books H5
George's St Arcade .... (see 49)
97 Jenny Vander F4
98 Powerscourt Townhouse Shopping Centre G4
99 Smock F4
100 St Stephen's Green Shopping Centre G6

The gallery has four wings: the original Dargan Wing, the Milltown Rooms, the North Wing and the impressive Millennium Wing. On the ground floor of the **Dargan Wing** (named after railway magnate and art lover William Dargan, whose statue graces the front lawn) is the imposing **Shaw Room** (named after writer George Bernard, another great benefactor; his bronze statue keeps Dargan company outside), lined with full-length portraits and illuminated by a series of spectacular Waterford crystal chandeliers. Upstairs, a series of rooms is dedicated to the early and high Italian Renaissance, 16th-century northern Italian art, and 17th- and 18th-century Italian art. Fra Angelico, Titian and Tintoretto are among the artists represented, but the highlight is undoubtedly Caravaggio's *Taking of Christ* (1602), which lay for over 60 years in a Jesuit house in Leeson St and was accidentally discovered by chief curator Sergio Benedetti.

The central **Milltown Rooms** were added between 1899 and 1903 to hold Russborough House's art collection, which was presented to the gallery in 1902. The ground floor displays the gallery's fine Irish collection, plus a smaller British collection, with works by Reynolds, Hogarth, Gainsborough, Landseer and Turner. Absolutely unmissable is the **Yeats Collection** at the back of the gallery, displaying more than 30 works by Irish impressionist Jack B Yeats (1871–1957), Ireland's most important 20th-century painter.

Upstairs are works from Germany, the Netherlands and Spain. There are rooms full of works by Rembrandt and his circle, and by the Spanish artists of Seville. The Spanish collection also features works by El Greco, Goya and Picasso.

The **North Wing** was added only between 1964 and 1968, but has already undergone extensive refurbishment. It houses works by British and European artists.

With its light-filled, modern design, the **Millennium Wing** can also be entered from Clare St. It houses a small collection of 20th-century Irish art, high-profile visiting collections (for which there are admission charges), an art reference library, a lecture theatre, a good bookshop and Fitzer's Café.

FREE **Leinster House** NOTABLE BUILDING
(Map p78; ☎tour information 01-618 3271; www.oireachtas.ie; Kildare St; ⏲observation gallery 2.30-8.30pm Tue, 10.30am-8.30pm Wed, 10.30am-5.30pm Thu Nov-May, tours 10.30am, 11.30am, 2.30pm & 3.30pm Mon-Fri when parliament is not in session) Dublin's grandest Georgian home, built by Richard Cassels between 1745 and 1748 for the very grand James Fitzgerald, Earl of Kildare, is now the seat of both houses of the Oireachtas na Éireann (Irish Parliament) – the Dáil (Lower House) and Seanad (Upper House). Originally called Kildare House, it was changed to Leinster House after the earl assumed the title of Duke of Leinster in 1766.

Leinster House's Kildare St frontage was designed by Richard Cassels to look like a town house, whereas the Merrion Sq frontage was made to look like a country house. Hard to imagine it now, but when Cassels built the house it was in the wild expanses south of the Liffey, far from the genteel northern neighbourhoods where Dublin's aristocracy lived. Never short of confidence, the earl dismissed his critics, declaring, 'Where I go, society will follow.' There's no doubt about it: Jimmy Fitz had a nose for real estate.

The Dublin Society, later named the Royal Dublin Society, bought the building in 1814 but moved out in stages between 1922 and 1925, when the first government of an independent Ireland decided to establish Parliament here. The obelisk in front of the building is dedicated to Arthur Griffith, Michael Collins and Kevin O'Higgins – the architects of independent Ireland.

The Seanad meets in the north-wing saloon, while the Dáil meets in a less interesting room, originally a lecture theatre, which was added to the original building in 1897. When Parliament is sitting, visitors are admitted to an observation gallery. You'll get an entry ticket from the Kildare St entrance on production of some identification. Bags can't be taken in, nor can notes or photographs be taken. Free guided tours are available (by appointment) on weekdays when parliament is not in session.

LOCAL KNOWLEDGE

CATHY KELLY: MY DUBLIN

Belfast-born but Dublin-raised, Cathy Kelly is the bestselling author of 13 novels of 'female fiction' – beginning in 1997 with *Woman to Woman* and most recently with *Homecoming* (2010).

Best Way to Experience Dublin?

Get walking. One of Dublin's joys is that it is a compact city and, weather permitting, you can walk to most places.

Recommended Tour?

The Viking Splash Tour (p97). It's like being on a school tour again and with a mad hat on, a latent childishness comes out and you can yell to your heart's content, as well as travel around the city yelling at Celts and seeing the main historic sights from your growly vehicle. But if you go in winter, wear lots of warm clothes. Those things are freezing!

Favourite Museum?

The National Gallery (p72). Just dip in for an hour and stand in front of a few paintings to ground yourself. I can't even say what I love most: sometimes it's the pure energy of the [works of] Jack B Yeats, and other times I want to marvel at the fire inside Caravaggio's *Taking of Christ*.

FREE **National Museum of Ireland – Natural History** MUSEUM

(Map p78; www.museum.ie; Merrion St; ⏲10am-5pm Tue-Sat, 2-5pm Sun) Dusty, weird and utterly compelling, this window into Victorian times has barely changed since Scottish explorer Dr David Livingstone opened it in 1857 – before disappearing into the African jungle for a meeting with Henry Stanley. Which was perfectly fine until July 2007 when a large section of the original stone staircase collapsed, injuring 10 people and forcing the closure of one of the city's most beloved museums for a major restoration. It reopened in 2010, once again allowing us into explore its (slightly less) creaking interior crammed with some two million stuffed animals, skeletons and other specimens from around the world, ranging from West African apes to pickled insects in jars. Some are freestanding, others behind glass, but everywhere you turn the animals of the 'dead zoo' are still and staring.

Compared to the multimedia, interactive this and that of virtually every modern museum, this is a beautifully preserved example of Victorian charm and scientific wonderment. It is usually full of fascinated kids, but it's the adults who seem to make the most noise as they ricochet like pinballs between displays. The **Irish Room** on the ground floor is filled with mammals, sea creatures, birds and some butterflies all found in Ireland at some point, including the skeletons of three 10,000-year-old Irish elk that greet you as you enter. The **World Animals Collection**, spread across three levels, has as its centrepiece the skeleton of a 20m-long fin whale found beached in County Sligo. Evolutionists will love the line-up of orang-utan, chimpanzee, gorilla and human skeletons on the 1st floor. A new addition here is the **Discovery Zone**, where visitors can do some firsthand exploring of their own, handling taxidermy and opening drawers. Other notables include the extinct Australian marsupial the Tasmanian tiger (mislabelled as a Tasmanian wolf), a giant panda from China, and several African and Asian rhinoceroses. The wonderful **Blaschka Collection** comprises finely detailed glass models of marine creatures whose zoological accuracy is incomparable.

FREE **National Library** HISTORIC BUILDING

(Map p64; www.nli.ie; Kildare St; ⏲9.30am-9pm Mon-Wed, 10am-5pm Thu & Fri, 10am-1pm Sat) Flanking the Kildare St entrance to Leinster House is this library, built between 1884 and 1890 by Sir Thomas Newenham Deane and his son Sir Thomas Manly Deane, at the same time and to a similar design as the National Museum. Leinster House, the library and museum were all part of the Royal Dublin Society (formed in 1731), which aimed to improve conditions for the poor and to promote the arts and sciences. The library's extensive collection has many valuable early manuscripts, first editions, maps and other items; its reading room was featured in James Joyce's *Ulysses*. Temporary displays are often held in the entrance area.

On the 2nd floor is the **Genealogical Office** (☎603 0200; 2nd fl, National Library, Kildare St; ⏲9.30am-5pm Mon-Fri, 9.30am-1pm Sat), where you can obtain information on how best to trace your Irish roots. A genealogist can do the trace for you (at a fee dependent on research) or simply point you in the right direction (for free).

A WORD IN YOUR EAR

If you fancy a go-it-alone guided walk, why not download one of Pat Liddy's excellent **iWalks** (www.visitdublin.com/iwalks), which you can play on your MP3 player. You can download them from the website or subscribe to them via iTunes. The 12 walks range from tours of the city's different districts to walks tailored to historical, architectural and activity themes.

St Stephen's Green & Around PARK

(Map p78; admission free; ⏲dawn-dusk) While enjoying the nine gorgeous, landscaped hectares of Dublin's most popular square, consider that once upon a time it was an open common used for public whippings, beatings and hangings. Activities in the green have quieted since then and are generally confined to the lunchtime picnic-and-stroll variety. Still, on a summer's day it is the favourite retreat of office workers, lovers and visitors alike, who come to breathe a little fresh air, feed the ducks and cuddle on the grass.

Although a stone wall was erected in the 17th century when Dublin Corporation sold off the surrounding land to property developers, railings and locked gates were added only in 1814, when an annual fee of one guinea was charged to use the green –

National Museum of Ireland

NATIONAL TREASURES

Ireland's most important cultural institution is the National Museum, and its most important branch is the original one, housed in this fine neoclassical (or Victorian Palladian) building designed by Sir Thomas Newenham Deane and finished in 1890. Squeezed in between the rear entrance of Leinster House – the Irish parliament – and a nondescript building from the 1960s, it's easy to pass by the museum. But within its fairly cramped confines you'll find the most extensive collection of Bronze and Iron Age gold artefacts in Europe and the extraordinary collection of the Treasury. This includes the stunning **Ardagh Chalice** 1 and the delicately crafted **Tara Brooch** 2. Amid all the lustre, look out for the **Broighter Gold Collar** 3 and the impressively crafted **Loughnashade War Trumpet** 4, both extraordinary examples of Celtic art. Finally, pay a visit to the exquisite **Cross of Cong** 5, which was created after the other pieces but is just as beautiful.

As you visit these treasures – all created after the arrival of Christianity in the 5th century – bear in mind that they were produced with the most rudimentary of instruments.

VIKING DUBLIN

Archaeological excavations in Dublin between 1961 and 1981 unearthed evidence of a Viking town and cemeteries along the banks of the River Liffey. The graves contained weapons such as swords and spears, together with jewellery and personal items. Craftsmen's tools, weights and scales, silver ingots and coins show that the Vikings, as well as marauding and raiding, were also engaged in commercial activities. The Viking artefacts are now part of the National Museum's collection.

Lunch Break

Enjoy homemade pasta along with a nice glass of Italian red at the very authentic Dunne & Crescenzi (14-16 South Frederick St), or a pancake on the go from Lemon (Dawson St).

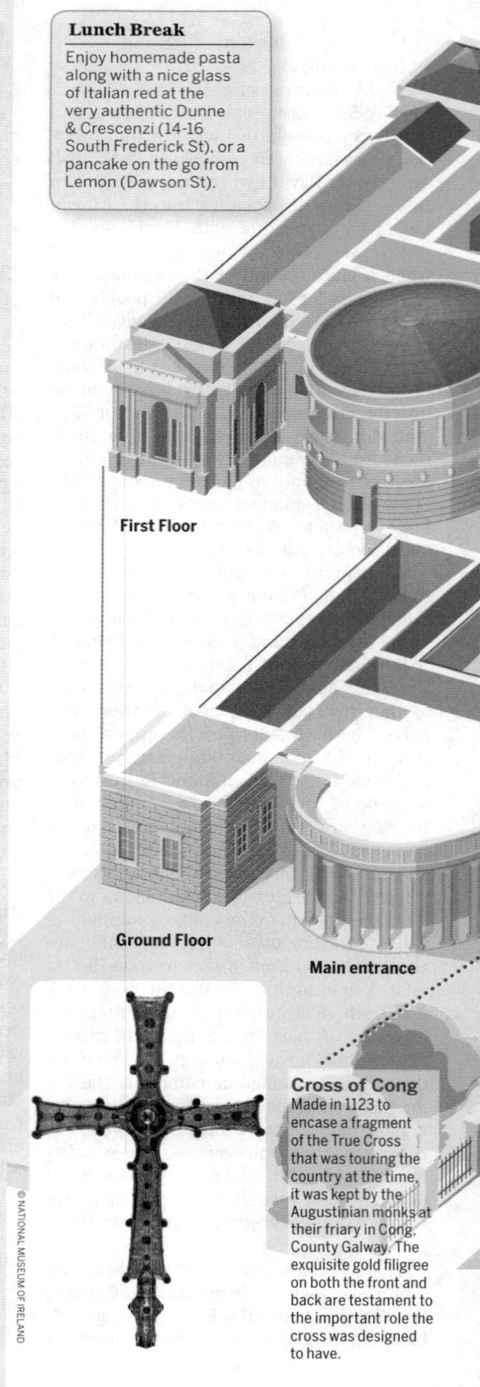

Cross of Cong

Made in 1123 to encase a fragment of the True Cross that was touring the country at the time, it was kept by the Augustinian monks at their friary in Cong, County Galway. The exquisite gold filigree on both the front and back are testament to the important role the cross was designed to have.

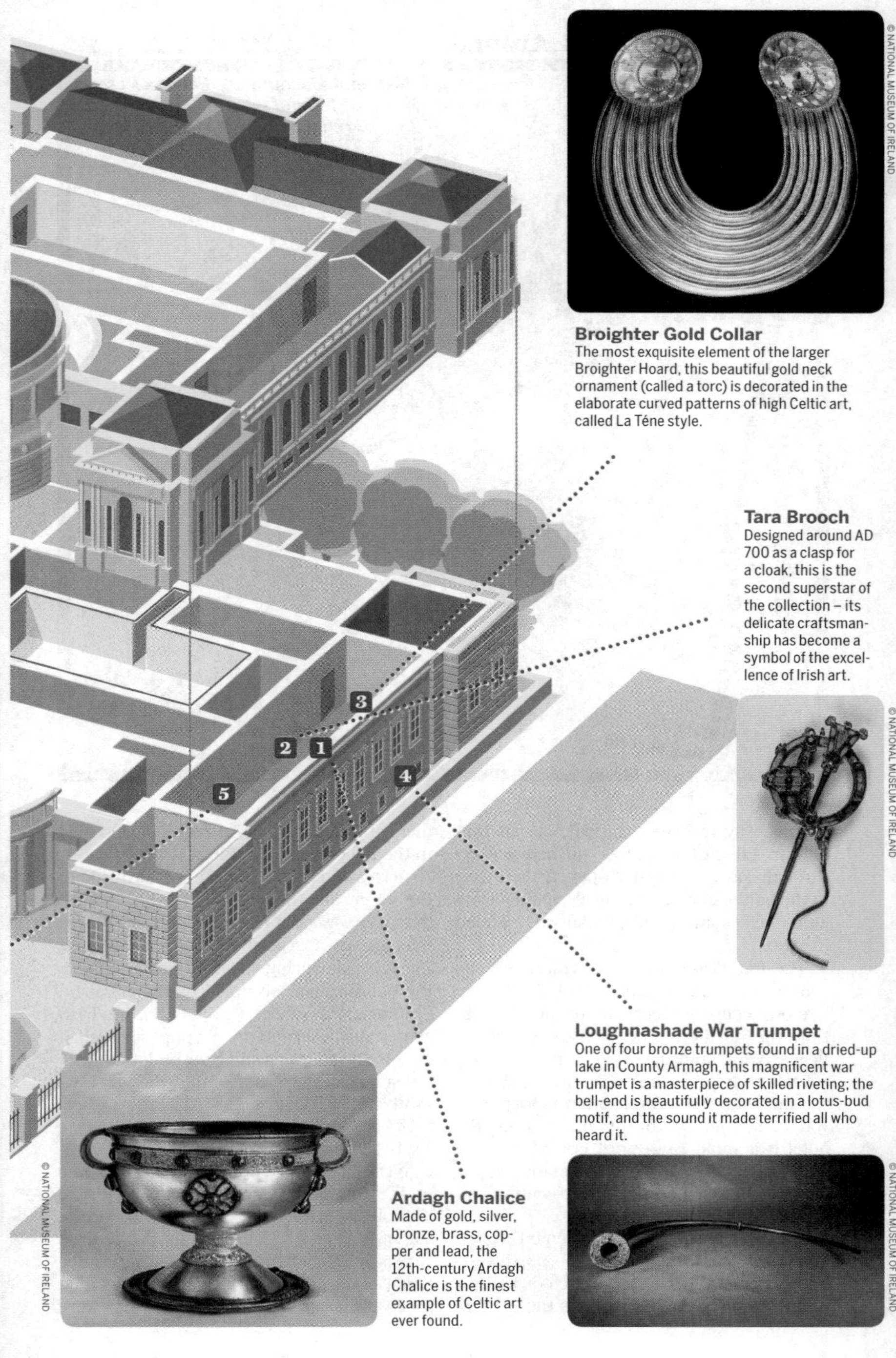

Broighter Gold Collar
The most exquisite element of the larger Broighter Hoard, this beautiful gold neck ornament (called a torc) is decorated in the elaborate curved patterns of high Celtic art, called La Téne style.

Tara Brooch
Designed around AD 700 as a clasp for a cloak, this is the second superstar of the collection – its delicate craftsmanship has become a symbol of the excellence of Irish art.

Loughnashade War Trumpet
One of four bronze trumpets found in a dried-up lake in County Armagh, this magnificent war trumpet is a masterpiece of skilled riveting; the bell-end is beautifully decorated in a lotus-bud motif, and the sound it made terrified all who heard it.

Ardagh Chalice
Made of gold, silver, bronze, brass, copper and lead, the 12th-century Ardagh Chalice is the finest example of Celtic art ever found.

St Stephen's Green & Around

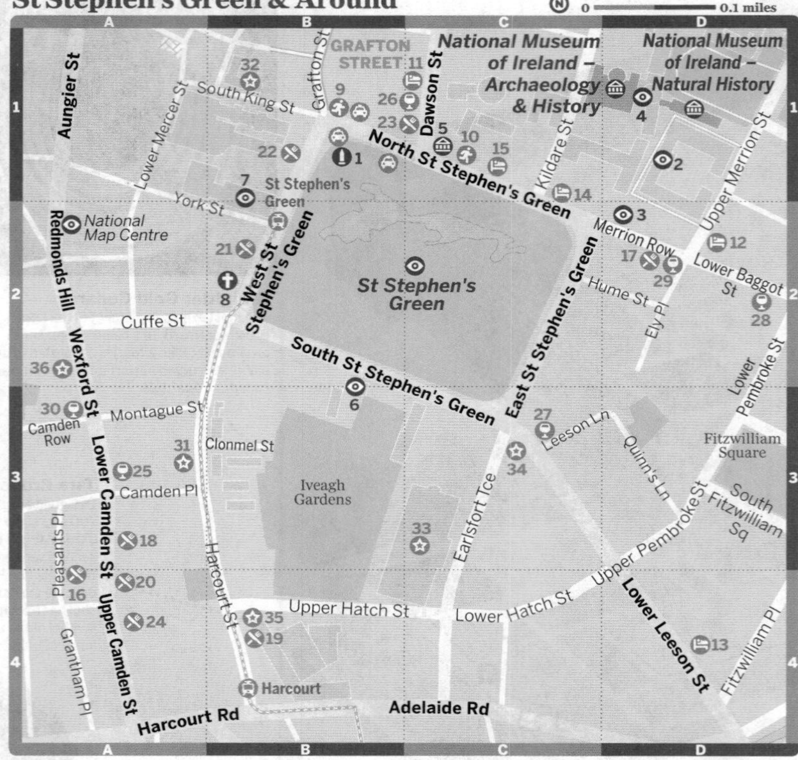

a great way to keep the poor out. In 1877 Arthur Edward Guinness pushed an act through Parliament that opened the green to the public once again. He also paid for the green's lakes and ponds, which were added in 1880.

The fine Georgian buildings around the square date mainly from Dublin's mid- to late-18th-century Georgian prime. At that time the northern side was known as the Beaux Walk and it's still a pretty fancy stretch of real estate; drop in for tea at the imposing 1867 **Shelbourne Hotel** and you'll see what we mean. Just beyond the hotel is a small **Huguenot cemetery** (Map p78) dating from 1693, when many French Huguenots fled here from persecution under Louis XIV.

The main entrance to the green is through **Fusiliers' Arch** (Map p78) at the northwestern corner. Modelled on the Arch of Titus in Rome, the arch commemorates the 212 soldiers of the Royal Dublin Fusiliers who died in the Boer War (1899–1902).

Across the road from the western side of the green are the 1863 **Unitarian Church** (Map p78; worship 7am-5pm) and the **Royal College of Surgeons** (Map p78), with a fine facade. During the 1916 Easter Rising, the building was occupied by the colourful Countess Markievicz (1868–1927), an Irish Nationalist married to a supposed Polish count. The columns still bear bullet marks.

On the southern side of the green is **Newman House** (Map p78; 85-86 St Stephen's Green; adult/child €6/5; tours noon, 2pm, 3pm & 4pm Tue-Fri Jun-Aug), now part of University College Dublin. These two buildings have some of the finest plasterwork in the city. The Catholic University of Ireland, predecessor of University College Dublin, acquired No 85 in 1865, then passed it to the Jesuits. Some of the plasterwork was too detailed for Jesuit tastes, however, so cover-ups were

St Stephen's Green & Around

Top Sights

National Museum of Ireland – Archaeology & History D1
National Museum of Ireland – Natural History D1
St Stephen's Green C2

Sights

1 Fusiliers' Arch B1
2 Government Buildings D1
3 Huguenot Cemetery D2
4 Leinster House D1
5 Little Museum of Dublin C1
6 Newman House B3
7 Royal College of Surgeons B1
8 Unitarian Church B2

Activities, Courses & Tours

9 Carriage Tours B1
10 Viking Splash Tours C1

Sleeping

11 La Stampa C1
12 Merrion D2
13 Number 31 .... D4
14 Shelbourne C1
15 The Cliff Townhouse C1

Eating

Bentley's Oyster Bar & Grill .... (see 15)
16 Cake Café A4
17 Govinda's D2
18 Green Nineteen A3
19 Harcourt St Market B4
20 Listons A4
Restaurant Patrick Guilbaud .... (see 12)
21 Shanahan's on the Green B2
The Cliff Townhouse .... (see 15)
22 Thornton's B1
23 Town Bar & Grill C1
24 Zaytoon A4

Drinking

25 Anseo A3
26 Dawson Lounge C1
27 Hartigan's C3
28 James Toner's D2
29 O'Donoghue's D2
Village .... (see 36)
30 Whelan's A3

Entertainment

31 Copper Face Jack's A3
Crawdaddy .... (see 35)
32 Gaiety Theatre B1
33 National Concert Hall C3
34 Sugar Club C3
35 Tripod B4
36 Village A2

prescribed. On the ceiling of the upstairs saloon, previously naked female figures were clothed in what can best be described as furry swimsuits. One survived the restoration process.

Attached to Newman University Church is the **Newman Chapel**, built between 1854 and 1856 with a colourful neo-Byzantine interior that attracted a great deal of criticism at the time. Today it's one of the most fashionable churches in Dublin for weddings.

One of Dublin's most beautiful parks is the landscaped **Iveagh Gardens** (Map p78; admission free; ⏲dawn-dusk year-round), directly behind Newman House and reached via Clonmel St, just off Harcourt St. The imposing walls give the impression that they are private gardens, but they are one of the nicest places to relax on a summer's day or before a show in the National Concert Hall.

Little Museum of Dublin MUSEUM

(Map p78; (☎661 1000; www.littlemuseum.ie; 15 St Stephen's Green N; admission €6.95; ⏲10am-5pm Mon-Fri) The idea is ingeniously simple: a museum, spread across two rooms of an elegant Georgian building, devoted to the history of Dublin in the 20th century, made up of memorabilia contributed by the general public. Open only since summer 2011, the contributions have been impressive – amid the nostalgic posters, timeworn bric-a-brac and wonderful photographs of personages and cityscapes of yesteryear are some extraordinary finds, including an original copy of the fateful letter given to the Irish envoys to the treaty negotiations of 1921, whose contradictory instructions were at the heart of the split that resulted in the Civil War. But you don't need to know anything about Irish history or Dublin to appreciate it: visits are by guided tour and everyone is presented with a handsome booklet on the history of the city.

WORTH A TRIP

PORTOBELLO MUSEUMS

Just north of the Grand Canal, in the warren of streets of the handsome Portobello neighbourhood, are two worthwhile museums that are often overlooked.

Shaw Birthplace (Map p60; 33 Synge St; adult/child/student €6/4/5; ⏲10am-1pm & 2-5pm Mon-Sat year-round, plus 11am-1pm & 2-5pm Sun May-Sep) Birthplace of the noted playwright, this house has been preserved in all its muted Victorian elegance.

Irish-Jewish Museum (Map p60; 4 Walworth Rd; ⏲11am-3.30pm Tue, Thu & Sun May-Sep, 10.30am-2.30pm Sun only Oct-Apr) Just around the corner, this was once a synagogue but is now a museum dedicated to the city's small but culturally important Jewish population.

Merrion Square PARK

(Map p60; admission free; ⏲dawn-dusk) St Stephen's Green may win the popularity contest, but this tranquil square is our choice for favourite city park. Surrounding the well-kept lawns and beautifully tended flower beds are some of Dublin's most exceptional Georgian frontages, with fine doors, peacock fanlights, ornate door knockers and foot scrapers (used by gentlemen to scrape mud from their boots before venturing indoors).

Despite the air of affluent calm, life around here hasn't always been a well-pruned bed of roses. During the Famine, the lawns of the square teemed with destitute rural refugees who lived off the soup kitchen organised here. The British embassy was located at 39 Merrion Sq East until 1972, when it was burnt out in protest against the killing of 13 innocent civilians in Derry on Bloody Sunday.

That same side of Merrion Sq once continued into Lower Fitzwilliam St in the longest unbroken series of Georgian houses anywhere in Europe, but in 1961 the Electricity Supply Board (ESB), in a myopic crime against history and aesthetics, knocked down 26 of the houses in order to build an ugly office block.

Enthusiasts should visit the **Oscar Wilde statue** (Map p91)at the northwestern corner of the square, as it is adorned with the witty one-liners for which Wilde was famous.

Just to prove that it was not entirely unmindful of Dublin's priceless architectural heritage, the ESB had the decency to preserve one fine old Georgian house, **No 29 Lower Fitzwilliam St** (Map p60; www.esb.ie/education; 29 Lower Fitzwilliam St; adult/student/child €6/3/free; ⏲10am-5pm Tue-Sat, 1-5pm Sun, closed late Dec) at the southeastern corner of Merrion Sq. It has been restored to give a good impression of genteel home life in Dublin between 1790 and 1820. A short film on its history is followed by a 30-minute guided tour for groups of up to nine.

Bank of Ireland NOTABLE BUILDING

(Map p64; College Green; admission free; ⏲10am-4pm Mon-Wed & Fri, 10am-5pm Thu) This imposing bank, directly opposite Trinity College, was originally built by Sir Edward Lovett Pearce in 1729 to house the Irish Parliament. When the Parliament voted itself out of existence by the Act of Union in 1801, it became a building without a role. It was sold in 1803 with instructions that the interior be altered to prevent its being used as a debating chamber in the future; consequently, the large central House of Commons was remodelled, but the smaller chamber of the House of Lords survived. After independence the Irish government chose to make Leinster House the new parliamentary building and ignored the possibility of restoring this fine building to its original use.

City Hall MUSEUM

(Map p70; www.dublincity.ie; Cork Hill; adult/student/child €4/2/1.50; ⏲10am-5.15pm Mon-Sat, 11am-5pm Sun) Fronting Dublin Castle on Lord Edward St, City Hall was built by Thomas Cooley between 1769 and 1779 as the Royal Exchange, and later became the offices of Dublin Corporation (now called Dublin City Council). It's on the site of the Lucas Coffee House and the Eagle Tavern, in which Dublin's infamous Hell Fire Club was established in 1735. Founded by Richard Parsons, Earl of Rosse, it was one of a number of gentlemen's clubs in Dublin where less-than-gentlemanly conduct took place. It gained a reputation for debauchery and black magic, but there's no evidence that such things took place.

The Story of the Capital is a multimedia exhibition in the basement, tracing the history of Dublin from its earliest beginnings.

The 1781 **Municipal Buildings**, just west of the City Hall, were built by Thomas Ivory (1720–86), who was also responsible for Bedford Tower in Dublin Castle.

Government Buildings NOTABLE BUILDINGS
(Map p78; www.taoiseach.gov.ie; Upper Merrion St; admission free; ⏲tours 10.30am-1.30pm Sat) Dublin's domed Government Buildings were opened for business in 1911. Architecturally, they are a rather heavy-handed Edwardian interpretation of the Georgian style. Each free, 40-minute tour accommodates about 15 people, so you may have to wait a while for a big enough group to assemble. Tours can't be booked in advance, but if you go in on Saturday morning you can put your name down for one later in the day. You get to see the office of the Taoiseach (prime minister), the cabinet room, the grand ceremonial stair case – with a stunning stained-glass window designed by Evie Hone (1894–1955) for the 1939 New York Trade Fair – and innumerable fine examples of modern Irish arts and crafts. Tickets for the tours are available from the ticket office of the **National Gallery** (Map p91; ☎01-661 5133; www.nationalgallery.ie; West Merrion Sq; ⏲9.30am-5.30pm Mon-Wed, Fri & Sat, 9.30am-8.30pm Thu, noon-5.30pm Sun).

THE LIBERTIES & KILMAINHAM

At the top of a small hill, just west of Dublin Castle, is the most impressive monument of medieval Dublin, Christ Church Cathedral. It stood firmly inside the city walls, whereas that other great place of worship, St Patrick's, lay just outside them: today there's nothing between them but a couple of buildings and the expanse of a garden. To the west of both is the Liberties, Dublin's oldest surviving neighbourhood. The western end of the Liberties has a curious aroma in the air: it is the smell of roasting hops, used in the production of Guinness – Dublin's black gold and, for many visitors, the epitome of all things Irish. Further along St James's St is Kilmainham, home to the old prison that was central to the struggle for Irish independence (now a city highlight) and an ancient soldiers' hospital, now the country's most important modern art museum.

Guinness Storehouse BREWERY/MUSEUM
(Map p60; www.guinness-storehouse.com; St James's Gate Brewery; admission €15/11, under 6yr free, discounts apply for online bookings; ⏲9.30am-5pm Sep-Jun, 9.30am-7pm Jul-Aug; 🚌21a, 51b, 78, 78a or 123 from Fleet St); 🚊St James's) The most popular visit in town is the beer-lover's Disneyland, a multimedia bells-and-whistles homage to the country's most famous export and the city's most enduring symbol. The old grain storehouse, the only part of the massive, 26-hectare St James's Gate Brewery open to the public, is a suitable cathedral in which to worship the black gold; shaped like a giant pint of Guinness, it rises seven impressive storeys high around a stunning central atrium. At the top is the head, represented by the **Gravity Bar**, with a panoramic view of Dublin.

From the time Arthur Guinness (1725–1803) founded the brewery in 1759, the operation has expanded down to the Liffey and across both sides of the street; at one point, it had its own railway and there was a giant gate stretching across St James's St, hence the brewery's proper name. At its apogee in the 1930s, it employed over 5000 workers, making it the largest employer in the city. Increased automation has reduced the workforce to around 600, but it still produces 2.5 million pints of stout *every day*.

You'll get to drink one of those pints at the end of your tour, but not before you have walked through the extravaganza that is the Guinness floor show, spread across 1.6

LITERARY ADDRESSES

Merrion Sq has long been the favoured address of Dublin's affluent intelligentsia. Playwright Oscar Wilde (1854–1900) spent much of his youth at 1 North Merrion Sq. Poet WB Yeats (1865–1939) lived at 52 East Merrion Sq and later, between 1922 and 1928, at 82 South Merrion Sq. George ('AE') Russell (1867–1935), the self-proclaimed 'poet, mystic, painter and cooperator', worked at No 84. Political leader Daniel O'Connell (1775–1847) was a resident of No 58 in his later years. The Austrian Erwin Schrödinger (1887–1961), co-winner of the 1933 Nobel Prize for Physics, lived at No 65 between 1940 and 1956. Dublin also seems to attract writers of horror stories: Joseph Sheridan Le Fanu (1814–73), who penned the vampire classic *Carmilla*, was a resident of No 70.

hectares and involving an array of audiovisual, interactive displays that cover pretty much all aspects of the brewery's history and the brewing process. It's slick and sophisticated, but you can't ignore the man behind the curtain: the extensive exhibit on the company's incredibly successful history of advertising is a reminder that for all the talk of mysticism and magic, it's all really about marketing and manipulation.

The point is made deliciously moot when you finally get a pint in your hand and let the cream pass your lips in the vertiginous heights of the Gravity Bar. It's the best pint of Guinness in the world, claim the cognoscenti (while there's no arguing with how good it tastes, give us a pint among friends in a spit-and-sawdust pub closer to the ground any day of the week).

Around the corner at **1 Thomas St** (Map p60; ⏲closed to public) a plaque marks the house where Arthur Guinness lived. In a yard across the road stands **St Patrick's Tower** (Map p60; ⏲closed to public), Europe's tallest smock windmill (with a revolving top), which was built around 1757.

St Patrick's Cathedral CHURCH

(Map p70; www.stpatrickscathedral.ie; St Patrick's Close; adult/senior & student/child €5.50/4.50/free; ⏲9am-6pm Mon-Sat, 9-11am, 12.45-3pm & 4.15-6pm Sun Mar-Oct, 9am-6pm Mon-Fri, 9am-5pm Sat, 10-11am & 12.45-3pm Sun Nov-Feb; 🚌50, 50A or 56A from Aston Quay or 54 or 54A from Burgh Quay) It was at this cathedral, reputedly, that St Paddy himself dunked the Irish heathens into the waters of a well, so the church that bears his name stands on one of the earliest Christian sites in the city and a pretty sacred piece of turf. Although there's been a church here since the 5th century, the present building dates from 1190 or 1225 (opinions differ) and it has been altered several times, most notably in 1864 when the flying buttresses were added, thanks to the neo-Gothic craze that swept the nation. **St Patrick's Park**, the expanse of green beside the cathedral, was a crowded slum until it was cleared and its residents evicted in the early 20th century.

Like Christ Church Cathedral, the building has suffered a rather dramatic history of storm and fire damage. Oliver Cromwell, during his 1649 visit to Ireland, converted St Patrick's to a stable for his army's horses, an indignity to which he also subjected numerous other Irish churches. Jonathan Swift, author of *Gulliver's Travels,* was the dean of the cathedral from 1713 to 1745, but prior to its restoration it was very neglected.

Entering the cathedral from the southwestern porch you come almost immediately, on your right, to the graves of Swift and his longtime companion Esther Johnson, aka Stella. On the wall nearby are Swift's own Latin epitaphs to the two of them, and a bust of Swift.

The huge, dusty **Boyle Monument** to the left was erected in 1632 by Richard Boyle, Earl of Cork, and is decorated with numerous painted figures of members of his family. The figure in the centre on the bottom level is the earl's five-year-old son Robert Boyle (1627–91), who grew up to become a noted scientist. His contributions to physics include Boyle's Law, which relates the pressure and volume of gases.

Marsh's Library HISTORIC BUILDING

(Map p70; www.marshlibrary.ie; St Patrick's Close; adult/child/student €2.50/free/1.50; ⏲10am-1pm & 2-5pm Mon & Wed-Fri, 10.30am-1pm Sat; 🚌50, 50A or 56A from Aston Quay or 54 or 54A from Burgh Quay) One of the city's most beautiful open secrets is Marsh's Library, a barely visited antique library with a look and atmosphere that has hardly changed since it opened its doors to awkward scholars in 1707. It's just around the corner from St Patrick's Cathedral.

Crammed into its elaborately carved oak bookcases are over 25,000 books dating from the 16th to early 18th centuries, as well as maps, numerous manuscripts and a collection of incunabula (books printed before 1500). One of the oldest and finest tomes in the collection is a volume of Cicero's *Letters to His Friends* printed in Milan in 1472.

The building was commissioned by Archbishop Narcissus March (1638–1713) and designed by Sir William Robinson, the creator of the Royal Hospital Kilmainham (now the Irish Museum of Modern Art; today it is one of the few 18th-century buildings in Dublin still used for the purpose for which it was built. In short, it's a bloody gorgeous place and you'd be mad not to visit.

Christ Church Cathedral CHURCH

(Church of the Holy Trinity; Map p70; www.cccdub.ie; Christ Church Pl; adult/senior/student €6/4/3; ⏲9.45am-4.15pm Mon-Sat, 12.30-2.30pm Sun Sep-May, 9.45am-6.15pm Mon-Tue & Fri, to 4.15pm Wed-Thu & Sat, 12.30-2.30pm & 4.30-6.15pm Sun Jun–mid-Jul, 9.45am-6.15pm Mon-Fri, to 4.15pm Sat, 12.30-2.30pm & 4.30-6.15pm Sun mid-Jul-

EVENSONG AT THE CATHEDRALS

In a rare coming together, the choirs of St Patrick's Cathedral and Christ Church Cathedral both participated in the first-ever performance of Handel's *Messiah* in nearby Fishamble St in 1742, conducted by the great composer himself. Both houses of worship carry on their proud choral traditions, and visits to the cathedrals during evensong will provide enchanting and atmospheric memories. The choir performs evensong in St Patrick's at 5.45pm Monday to Friday (not on Wednesday in July and August), while the Christ Church choir competes at 5.30pm on Sunday, 6pm on Wednesday and Thursday, and 5pm Saturday. If you're going to be in Dublin around Christmas, do not miss the carols at St Patrick's; call ahead for the hard-to-get tickets on ☎01-453 9472.

Aug; 🚌50, 50A or 56A from Aston Quay or 54 or 54A from Burgh Quay) Its hilltop location and eye-catching flying buttresses make this the most photogenic by far of Dublin's three cathedrals as well as one of the capital's most recognisable symbols.

It was founded in 1030 on what was then the southern edge of Dublin's Viking settlement. It was later smack in the middle of medieval Dublin: Dublin Castle, the Tholsel (Town Hall; demolished in 1809) and the original Four Courts (demolished in 1796) were all close by. Nearby, on Back Lane, is the only remaining guildhall in Dublin. The 1706 Tailors Hall was due for demolition in the 1960s, but survived to become the office of **An Taisce** (National Trust for Ireland).

The original wooden church in this spot wasn't really a keeper, so the Normans rebuilt the lot in stone from 1172, mostly under the impetus of Richard de Clare, Earl of Pembroke (better known as Strongbow), the Anglo-Norman noble who invaded Ireland in 1170.

Throughout much of its history, Christ Church vied for supremacy with nearby St Patrick's Cathedral but it also fell on hard times in the 18th and 19th centuries – earlier, the nave had been used as a market and the crypt had housed taverns – and was virtually derelict by the time restoration took place. Today, both Church of Ireland cathedrals are outsiders in a largely Catholic nation.

From the southeastern entrance to the churchyard, walk past ruins of the chapter house, which dates from 1230. The entrance to the cathedral is at the southwestern corner and as you enter you face the northern wall. This survived the collapse of its southern counterpart but has also suffered from subsiding foundations.

The southern aisle has a monument to the legendary Strongbow. The armoured figure on the tomb is unlikely to be Strongbow (it's more probably the Earl of Drogheda), but his internal organs may have been buried here. A popular legend relates that the half figure beside the tomb is Strongbow's son, who was cut in two by his father when his bravery in battle was suspect.

The southern transept contains the superb baroque tomb of the 19th Earl of Kildare (died 1734). His grandson, Lord Edward Fitzgerald, was a member of the United Irishmen and died in the abortive 1798 Rising.

An entrance just by the southern transept descends to the unusually large arched crypt, which dates back to the original Viking church. Curiosities in the crypt include a glass display case housing a mummified cat chasing a mummified mouse, which were trapped inside an organ pipe in the 1860s! From the main entrance, a bridge, part of the 1871–78 restoration, leads to Dvblinia.

Dvblinia & the Viking World MUSEUM

(Map p70; www.dublinia.ie; adult/student/child €6.95/5.95/4.95; ⌚10am-5pm Apr-Sep, 10am-4.30pm Oct-Mar) A must for the kids, the old Synod Hall attached to Christ Church Cathedral is home to the seemingly perennial Dvblinia, a kitschy and lively attempt to bring medieval Dublin to life. Models, streetscapes and somewhat old-fashioned interactive displays do a fairly decent job of it, at least for kids. The model of a medieval quayside and a cobbler's shop are both excellent, as is the scale model of the medieval city. The Viking World tells the story of Dublin's 9th- and 10th-century Scandinavian invaders and the city they built – but the real treat is finding out what life was like aboard their longboats and why they pillaged so many monasteries. Finally, you can climb neighbouring **St Michael's Tower** for views over the city to the Dublin Hills.

Your ticket gets you into Christ Church Cathedral for free (via the link bridge).

Kilmainham Gaol MUSEUM

(Map p56; www.heritageireland.com; Inchicore Rd; adult/student/child €6/2/2; ⌚9.30am-5pm Apr-Oct, 9.30am-4pm Mon-Sat, 10am-4pm Sun Nov-Mar; 🚌23, 51, 51A, 78 or 79 from Aston Quay) If you have *any* desire to understand Irish history – especially the juicy bits about resistance to English rule – then a visit to this former prison is an absolute must. This threatening grey building, built between 1792 and 1795, has played a role in virtually every act of Ireland's painful path to independence.

The uprisings of 1798, 1803, 1848, 1867 and 1916 ended with the leaders' confinement here. Robert Emmet, Thomas Francis Meagher, Charles Stewart Parnell and the 1916 Easter Rising leaders were all visitors, but it was the executions in 1916 that most deeply etched the jail's name into the Irish consciousness. Of the 15 executions that took place between 3 May and 12 May after the revolt, 14 were conducted here. As a finale, prisoners from the Civil War were held here from 1922. The jail closed in 1924.

An excellent audiovisual introduction to the building is followed by a thought-provoking tour of the eerie prison, the largest unoccupied building of its kind in Europe. Sitting incongruously outside in the yard is the *Asgard*, the ship that successfully ran the British blockade to deliver arms to Nationalist forces in 1914. The tour finishes in the gloomy yard where the 1916 executions took place.

FREE Irish Museum of Modern Art ART GALLERY

(IMMA; Map p60; www.imma.ie; Military Rd; ⌚10am-5.30pm Tue-Sat, noon-5.30pm Sun; 🚊Heuston) Ireland's most important collection of modern and contemporary Irish art is housed in the elegant, airy expanse of the Royal Hospital at Kilmainham, which in 1991 became a magnificent exhibition space.

The Royal Hospital Kilmainham was designed by William Robinson (who also designed Marsh's Library), and was built between 1680 and 1687 as a home for retired soldiers. It fulfilled this role until 1928, after which it languished for nearly 50 years until a 1980s restoration. At the time of its construction, it was one of the finest buildings in Ireland and there were mutterings that it was altogether too good a place for its residents.

The blend of old and new works wonderfully, and you'll find such contemporary Irish artists as Louis Le Brocquy, Sean Scully, Barry Flanagan, Kathy Prendergrass and Dorothy Cross featured here, as is a film installation by Neil Jordan. The permanent exhibition also features paintings from heavy hitters Pablo Picasso and Joan Miró, and is topped up by regular temporary exhibitions. There's a good cafe and bookshop on the grounds.

There are free guided tours (2.30pm Wednesday, Friday and Sunday) of the museum's exhibits throughout the year, but we strongly recommend the free seasonal heritage **tours** (50 min; ⌚hourly 11am-4pm Tue-Sat, 1-4pm Sun Jun-Sep) of the building itself, which run from July to September.

St Audoen's Churches CHURCHES

The more interesting of the two adjacent churches named after St Audoen, the 7th-century bishop of Rouen (and patron saint of Normandy) is the smaller **Church of Ireland** (Map p70; Cornmarket, High St; admission free; ⌚9.30am-4.45pm Jun-Sep), the only surviving medieval parish church still in use in Dublin. It was built between 1181 and 1212, though recent excavations unearthed a 9th-century burial slab, suggesting that it was built on top of an even older church. Its tower and door date from the 12th century and the aisle from the 15th century, but the church today is mainly a 19th-century restoration.

As part of the tour, you can explore the ruins, as well as the present church and the visitor centre in **St Anne's Chapel**, which houses a number of tombstones of leading members of Dublin society from the 16th to the 18th centuries. At the top of the chapel is the tower, which houses the three oldest bells in Ireland, dating from 1423. Although the church's exhibits are hardly spectacular, the building itself is very beautiful and a genuine slice of medieval Dublin.

The church is entered from the north through an arch off High St. Part of the old city wall, this arch was built in 1240 and is the only surviving reminder of the city gates.

Joined onto the older Protestant St Audoen's is the newer and larger **St Audoen's Catholic Church** (Map p70; Cornmarket, High St; admission free; ⌚9.30am-5.30pm Jun-Sep, 10am-4.30pm Oct-May), a large church that is home to the Polish chaplaincy in Ireland.

War Memorial Gardens PARK

(Map p56; www.heritageireland.ie; South Circular Rd, Islandbridge; admission free; ⏲8am-dusk Mon-Fri, from 10am Sat & Sun; 🚌25, 25A, 26, 68 or 69 from city centre) By our reckoning, the most beautiful patch of landscaped greenery in Dublin is these gardens, if only because they're as tranquil a spot as any you'll find in the city. Designed by Sir Edwin Lutyens, they commemorate the 49,400 Irish soldiers who died during WWI; their names are inscribed in the two huge granite bookrooms that stand at one end. A beautiful spot and a bit of history to boot.

NORTH OF THE LIFFEY

What does a northsider use for protection? A bus shelter. Boom boom. Northsider/southsider jokes are a permanent fixture of the city's canon of humour, mostly because they highlight the perceived gap between the city's two halves, with the north side generally coming off second-best in all things save social ills and – as northsiders will happily tell you – true Dublin character. What does a southsider use for protection? Personality.

As gritty as the southside is glitzy, the northside is as much home to 'real Dubs' as it is the heart of the city's newer, multicultural identity: mixed in among the impressive relics of the city's storied past is a bustling Babel of exotic activity with traders from Africa, Asia and Eastern Europe selling everything from hair extensions to tinned caviar.

Running through the heart of it is O'Connell St, Dublin's grandest thoroughfare, which has in recent years rediscovered much of its 18th-century glory. Its most dominating feature is the **Spire** (Map p86), a narrow metal column built in 2001 that tapers 120m into the sky. To the west is Quartier Bloom – a small-but-vibrant Italian corner – and, beyond it, Smithfield (Map p86), the heart of which is a cobbled square that has been home to a horse market since the 17th century. Although largely gentrified, here you'll find some of the city's most worthwhile pit stops – from great pubs to top-class museums.

TOP CHOICE **Dublin City Gallery – Hugh Lane** ART GALLERY

(Map p86; www.hughlane.ie; 22 North Parnell Sq; admission free; ⏲10am-6pm Tue-Thu, 10am-5pm Fri & Sat, 11am-5pm Sun) Whatever reputation Dublin has as a repository of world-class art has a lot to do with the simply stunning collection housed within this exquisite gallery, which is not only home to works by some of the brightest stars in the modern and contemporary art world both foreign and domestic, but also where you'll find one of the most singular exhibitions to be seen anywhere: the actual studio of one of the 20th century's truly iconic artists, Francis Bacon.

It's all contained within the fabulous confines of the 18th-century **Charlemont House** and a recent modernist extension that has more than doubled the gallery's capacity. The new building, based in the old **National Ballroom**, spans three floors and includes 13 bright galleries showing works from the 1950s onwards, a specialist bookshop and chic restaurant in the basement. The gallery's remit neatly spans the gap between the old masters of the National Gallery and the contemporary works exhibited in the Irish Museum of Modern Art.

All the big names of French Impressionism and early 20th-century Irish art are here. Sculptures by Rodin and Degas and paintings by Corot, Courbet, Manet and Monet sit alongside works by Irish greats Jack B Yeats, William Leech and Nathaniel Hone.

The gallery's **Francis Bacon Studio** was painstakingly moved, in all its shambolic mess, from 7 Reece Mews, London, where the Dublin-born artist lived for 31 years. Bacon, who claimed that chaos suggested art to him and famously hated Ireland, would no doubt have found it amusing that a team of conservators spent years cataloguing scraps of newspaper, horse whips, old socks, dirty rags, jars of pickle and mouse droppings, to reverently reassemble it all in Dublin.

DUBLIN BY APP

Visit Dublin's **Official Mobile Guide** (www.visitdublin.com; free) is an iPhone and Android app that uses GPS and compass technology to identify where you are and guide you in the direction you want to go. The information – a quarterly update of the tourist office's own database – is cached, which means there are no roaming charges for its basic use, which includes comprehensive listings of sights, attractions, hotels and places to eat. It is also available from the app store.

North of the Liffey

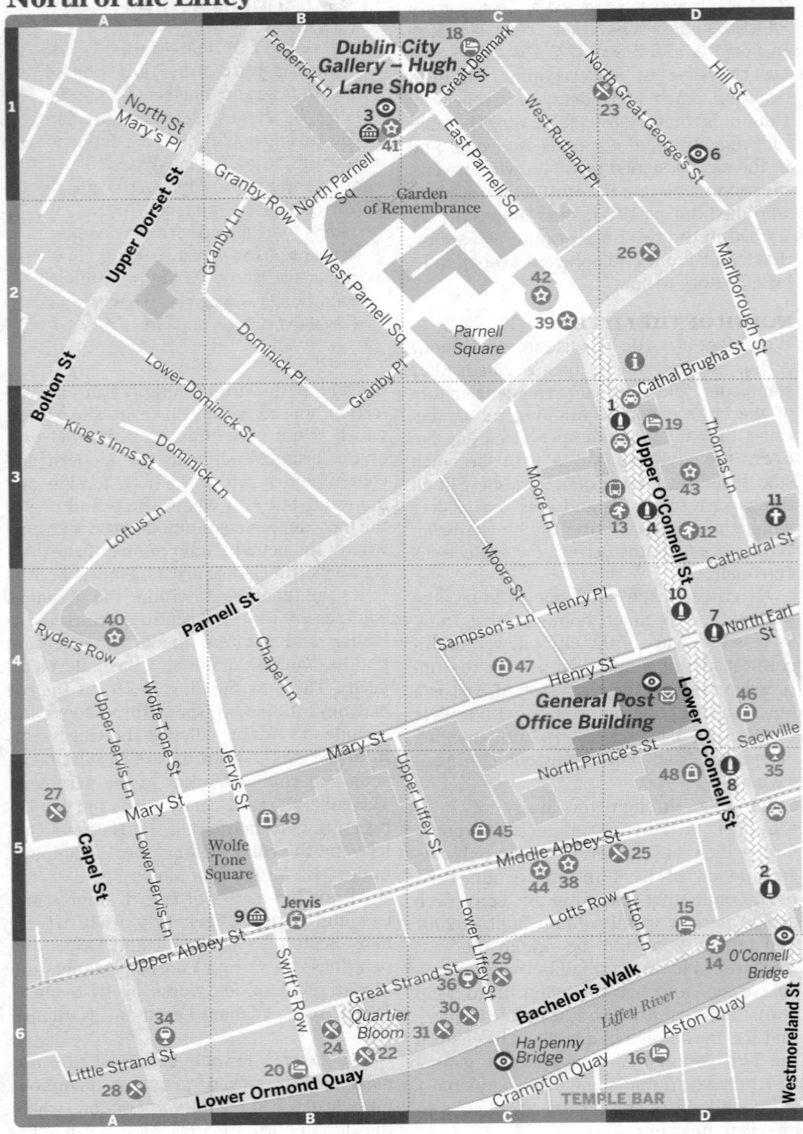

The gallery was founded in 1908 by wealthy art dealer Sir Hugh Lane, who died in 1915 on the *Lusitania* after that ship was torpedoed by a German U-boat. Following his death, a bitter row erupted between the National Gallery in London and the Hugh Lane Gallery over the jewels of his collection; even now, after years of wrangling, half of the works are displayed in Dublin and half in London on a rotating basis, but for the time being the Hugh Lane will hold on to its most prized possession, Renoir's *Les Parapluies*.

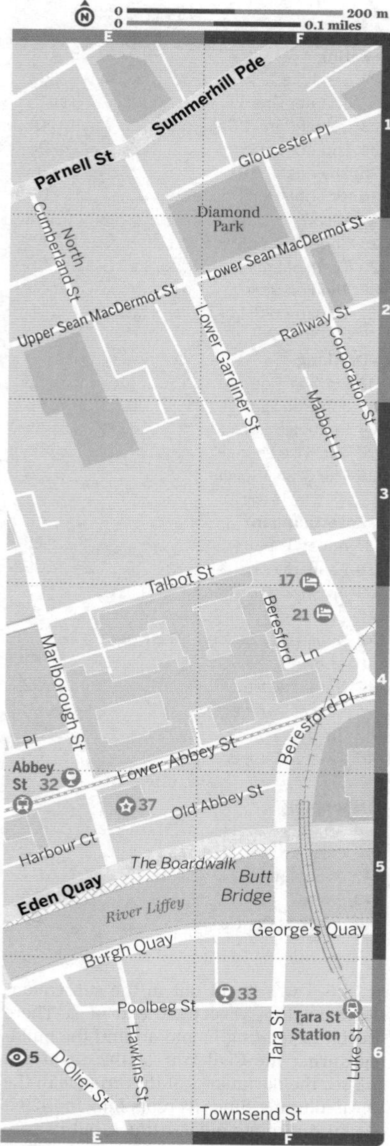

Old Jameson Distillery MUSEUM
(Map p60; www.jamesonwhiskey.com; Bow St; adult/child/student €13.50/8/11; ⌚tours every 35min 9am-5.30pm) Smithfield's biggest draw is this converted distillery, now a huge museum devoted to *uisce beatha* (the water of life). Beginning with a short film, the tour runs through the whole process of distilling, from grain to bottle. There are plenty of interesting titbits, such as what makes a single malt, where whiskey gets its colour and bouquet, and what the difference is between Irish whiskey and Scotch (other than the spelling, which prompted one Scot to comment that the Irish thought of everything: they even put an 'e' in 'whisky').

Then it's straight to the bar for a drop of the subject matter; eager drinkers can volunteer for the tasting tour, where you get to sample whiskies from all over the world and learn about their differences. Finally, you head to the almighty shop. If you're buying whiskey, go for the stuff you can't buy at home, such as the excellent Red Breast or the super-exclusive Midleton, a very limited reserve that is appropriately expensive.

FREE **National Museum of Ireland – Decorative Arts & History** MUSEUM
(Map p60; www.museum.ie; Benburb St; ⌚10am-5pm Tue-Sat, 2-5pm Sun) Known colloquially as Collins Barracks, the decorative arts and history annexe of the National Museum of Ireland is housed in one of the most beautiful buildings in the whole city, built in 1704 on the orders of Queen Anne and at one time the largest military barracks in the world. At its heart is the huge central square surrounded by arcaded colonnades and blocks linked by walking bridges. While wandering about the plaza, imagine it holding up to six regiments in formation. The whole shebang is the work of Thomas Burgh (1670–1730), who also designed the Old Library in Trinity College and St Michan's Church.

Inside the imposing exterior lies a treasure trove of artefacts ranging from silver, ceramics and glassware to weaponry, furniture and folk-life displays. Some of the best pieces are gathered in the 'Curator's Choice' exhibition, a collection of 25 objects handpicked by different curators, and displayed with an account of why they were chosen.

The museum offers a glimpse of Ireland's social, economic and military history over the last millennium. It's a big ask – too big, say its critics – but well-designed displays, interactive multimedia and a dizzying array of disparate artefacts make for an interesting and valiant effort. On the 1st floor is the museum's **Irish silver collection**, one of the largest collections of silver in the world; on the 2nd floor you'll find **Irish period**

North of the Liffey

Top Sights

- Dublin City Gallery – Hugh Lane Shop B1
- General Post Office Building D4

Sights

1 Charles Stewart Parnell Statue D3
2 Daniel O'Connell Statue D5
3 Dublin Writers Museum B1
4 Father Theobald Mathew Statue D3
5 Harrisons E6
6 James Joyce Cultural Centre D1
7 James Joyce Statue D4
8 Jim Larkin Statue D5
9 National Leprechaun Museum B5
10 Spire D4
11 St Mary's Pro-Cathedral D3

Activities, Courses & Tours

12 City Sightseeing D3
13 Dublin Bus Tours D3
Gray Line Tours .... (see 19)
James Joyce Walking Tour .... (see 6)
14 River Liffey Cruises D6

Sleeping

15 Abbey Court Hostel D5
16 Abigail's Hostel D6
17 Anchor Guesthouse F3
18 Castle Hotel C1
Globetrotter Tourist Hostel .... (see 21)
19 Gresham Hotel D3
20 Morrison Hotel B6
21 Townhouse F4

Eating

22 Bar Italia B6
Chapter One .... (see 3)
23 Cobalt Café & Gallery D1
24 Enoteca Langhe B6
25 Govinda's D5
26 Kim Chi/Hop House D2
27 Melody A5
28 Soup Dragon A6
29 Taste of Emilia C6
30 Winding Stair C6
31 Yamamori Sushi C6

Drinking

32 Flowing Tide E5
33 John Mulligan's F6
34 Pantibar A6
35 Sackville Lounge D5
36 The Grand Social C6

Entertainment

37 Abbey Theatre E5
38 Academy C5
39 Ambassador Theatre C2
40 Cineworld A4
41 Dublin City Gallery – The Hugh Lane B1
42 Gate Theatre C2
Peacock Theatre .... (see 37)
43 Savoy D3
44 Twisted Pepper C5

Shopping

45 Arnott's C5
46 Clery's & Co D4
47 Debenham's C4
48 Eason D5
49 Jervis St Centre B5

furniture and **scientific instruments**, while the 3rd floor has simple and sturdy **Irish country furniture**.

General Post Office HISTORIC BUILDING
(Map p86; www.anpost.ie; O'Connell St; ⏲8am-8pm Mon-Sat) Talk about going postal. The country's most important post office will forever be linked to the dramatic and tragic events of Easter Week 1916, when Pádraig Pearse, James Connolly and the other leaders of the Easter Rising read their proclamation from the front steps and made the building their headquarters. The building – a neoclassical masterpiece designed by Francis Johnston in 1818 – was burnt out in the subsequent siege, but that wasn't the end of it. There was bitter fighting in and around the building during the Civil War of 1922; you can still see the pockmarks of the struggle in the Doric columns. Since its reopening in 1929 it has lived through quieter times, but its central role in the history of independent Ireland has made it a prime site for everything from official parades to personal protests.

Dublin Writers Museum MUSEUM
(Map p86; www.writersmuseum.com; 18 North Parnell Sq; adult/child/student €7.50/4.70/6.30; ⏲10am-5pm Mon-Sat Sep-May, to 6pm Jun-Aug,

11am-5pm Sun year-round) You'd think that Dublin's rich literary tradition would ensure that a museum devoted to Ireland's greatest scribblers would be a real treat. But somehow this museum is something of a damp squib, and the collection of vaguely literary ephemera associated with some of the city's most recognisable names (Samuel Beckett's phone; Brendan Behan's union card) is diminished by the museum's decision to omit *living* writers from its purview.

If you plan to visit the **James Joyce Museum** (boxed text, p133) and the **Shaw Birthplace** (boxed text, p104), bear in mind that a **combined ticket** (adult/student/child €11.50/9.50/7.50) is cheaper than three separate ones.

FREE **Four Courts** HISTORIC BUILDINGS

(Map p70; Inns Quay; ⌚9am-5pm Mon-Fri) Appellants quake and the accused may shiver, but visitors are only likely to be amazed by James Gandon's imposing Four Courts, Ireland's uppermost courts of law. Gandon's Georgian masterpiece is a mammoth structure incorporating a 130m-long facade and a collection of statuary. The Corinthian-columned central block, connected to flanking wings with enclosed quadrangles, was begun in 1786 and not completed until 1802. The original four courts (Exchequer, Common Pleas, King's Bench and Chancery) all branch off the central rotunda.

The Four Courts played a brief role in the 1916 Easter Rising without suffering damage, but the events of 1922 were not so kind. When anti-Treaty forces seized the building and refused to leave, it was shelled from across the river. As the occupiers retreated, the building was set on fire and many irreplaceable early records were burned – an event that sparked off the Civil War. The building wasn't restored until 1932.

Visitors are allowed to wander through the building, but not to enter courts or other restricted areas. In the lobby of the central rotunda you'll see bewigged barristers conferring and police officers handcuffed to their charges.

St Mary's Pro-Cathedral CHURCH

(Map p86; Marlborough St; admission free; ⌚8am-6.30pm) Dublin's most important Catholic church is not quite the showcase you might expect. For one, it's in a cramped street rather than in its intended spot on O'Connell St, where the GPO Building is now located: the city's Protestants had a fit and insisted that it be built on a less conspicuous side street. And less conspicuous it certainly was, unless you were looking for purveyors of the world's oldest profession. Then you were smack in the middle of Monto – as Marlborough St was then known – the busiest red-light district in Europe, thanks to the British army stationed here. After independence and the departure of the British, Monto became plain old Marlborough St and the only enduring evidence is in the writings of James Joyce, who referred to the area where he lost his virginity as 'Nighttown'.

The area mightn't be the hot spot it used to be, but at least you won't be distracted while admiring the six Doric columns of the cathedral, built between 1816 and 1825 and

O'CONNELL STREET STATUARY

Although overshadowed by the Spire, O'Connell St is lined with statues of Irish history's good and great. The big daddy of them all is the 'Liberator' himself, **Daniel O'Connell** (Map p86), whose massive bronze bulk soars high above the street at the bridge end. The four winged figures at his feet represent O'Connell's supposed virtues: patriotism, courage, fidelity and eloquence.

O'Connell is rivalled for drama by the spread-armed figure of trade-union leader **Jim Larkin** (1876–1947; Map p86), just south of the General Post Office; you can almost hear the eloquent tirade.

Looking on with a bemused air from the corner of pedestrianised North Earl St is a small statue of **James Joyce** (Map p86), whom wagsters like to refer to as 'the Prick with the Stick'. Joyce would have loved the vulgar rhyme.

Further north is the statue of **Father Theobald Mathew** (1790–1856; Map p86), the 'Apostle of Temperance' – a hopeless role in Ireland. This quixotic task, however, also resulted in a Liffey bridge bearing his name. The northern end of the street is completed by the imposing statue of **Charles Stewart Parnell** (1846–91; Map p86), Home Rule advocate and victim of Irish morality.

modelled on the Temple of Theseus in Athens. The best time to visit is Sunday at 11am for the Latin Mass sung by the Palestrina Choir, the very choir in which Count John McCormack, Ireland's greatest singing export (sorry, Bono), began his career in 1904.

Finally, a word about the term 'pro' in the title. It roughly means 'unofficial cathedral', due to the fact that church leaders saw this building as an interim cathedral that would do until funds were found to build a much grander one. This has never happened, leaving this most Catholic of cities with two incredible but underused Protestant cathedrals and one fairly ordinary Catholic one. Irony, one; piety, nil.

National Leprechaun Museum MUSEUM

(Map p86; www.leprechaunmuseum.ie; Twilfit House, Jervis St; adult/child & student €10/8.50; ⏲9.30am-6.30pm Mon-Sat, from 10.30am Sun; Jervis) It's meant to be a folklore museum, but with a bit fun thrown in. It's neither. What you get is an introductory glimpse at the leprechaun story, told from the (largely American) image of a gold-burying, good-luck-bringing Lucky Charms–type figure to the far more ominous creature associated with the mythical Tuatha dé Danann people that preceded the Celts. The vaguely interactive displays are strictly for the little 'uns; for the rest, this is just a bad invitation to read more about Irish mythology.

St Michan's Church CHURCH

(Map p60; Lower Church St; adult/child/student €4/3/3.50; ⏲10am-12.45pm & 2-4.45pm Mon-Fri, 10am-12.45pm Sat May-Oct, 12.30-3.30pm Mon-Fri Nov-Apr; Smithfield) The macabre remains of the ancient dead are the attraction at this old church near the Four Courts, founded by the Danes in 1095 and named after one of their saints. Incredibly, it was the *only* church on the north side of the Liffey until 1686. The original church has largely disappeared beneath several additions, most dating from the 17th century (except for the battlement tower, which dates from the 15th century). It was considerably restored in the early 19th century and again after the Civil War, during which it had been damaged.

The very unchurchlike interior – it looks a bit like a courtroom – contains an organ from 1724 that Handel may have played for the first performance of his *Messiah*. A skull on the floor on one side of the altar is said to represent Oliver Cromwell. On the opposite side, a penitent's chair was where 'open and notoriously naughty livers' did public penance.

The big draw is the tour of the subterranean crypt, where you'll see bodies between 400 and 800 years old, preserved not by mummification but by the constant dry atmosphere. Tours are organised on an ad hoc basis depending on how many people there are.

James Joyce Cultural Centre CULTURAL CENTRE

(Map p86; www.jamesjoyce.ie; 35 North Great George's St; adult/child/student €5/free/4; ⏲10am-5pm Tue-Sat) Denis Maginni, the exuberant, flamboyant dance instructor immortalised by James Joyce in *Ulysses,* taught in this house. In 1982 Senator David Norris, a renowned Joycean scholar and leading gay-rights activist, bought the run-down house and restored it before opening it as a cultural centre for the study of Joyce and his books, as well as a small museum devoted to the author and his times.

There isn't much period stuff, but its absence is more than made up for by the superb interactive displays, which include three documentary films on various aspects of Joyce's life and work and – the centre's highlight – computers that allow you to explore the content of *Ulysses* episode by episode and Joyce's life year by year. It's enough to demolish the myth that Joyce's works are an impenetrable mystery and render him as he should be to the contemporary reader: a writer of enormous talent who sought to challenge and entertain his audience with his breathtaking wit and use of language.

Some of the fine plaster ceilings are restored originals, others careful reproductions of Michael Stapleton's designs. For information on a James Joyce-related walking tour departing from the centre, see p97.

DOCKLANDS

It's a cardinal rule of any program of urban development: if your city is at the mouth of the sea, you cannot modernise without giving the docklands a revamp. And so it was with Dublin: the eastern banks north and south of the Liffey – aka 'Canary Dwarf' – have been given a major makeover and now sport an impressive array of contemporary office blocks, fancy apartments and snazzy public buildings, including Kevin Roche's angled, tubelike **National Convention Centre** (Map p91) and Daniel Liebeskind's marvellous **Grand Canal Theatre** (p119).

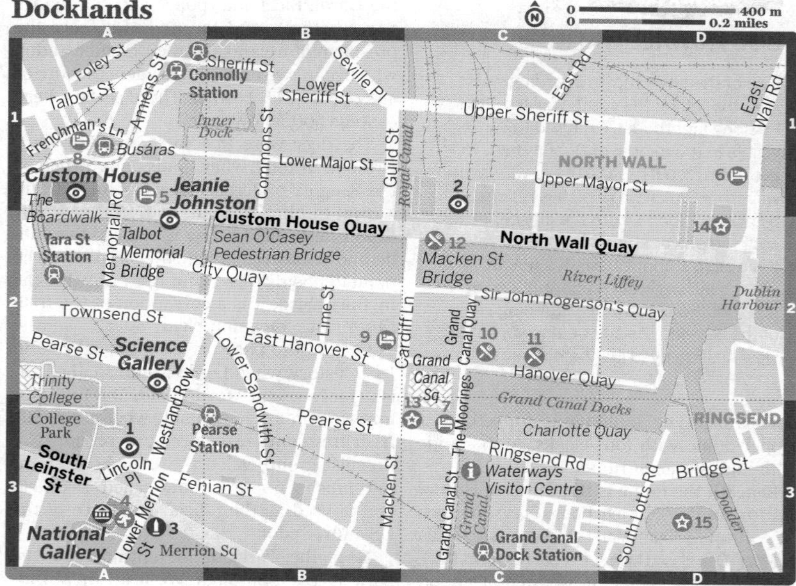

Docklands

Top Sights

Custom House A1
Jeanie Johnston A2
National Gallery A3
Science Gallery A2

Sights

1 Lincoln Place Gate A3
2 National Convention Centre C1
3 Oscar Wilde Statue A3

Activities, Courses & Tours

4 Dublin By Bike Tour A3

Sleeping

5 Clarion Hotel IFSC A1
6 Gibson Hotel D1
7 Home from Home Apartments C3
8 Isaacs Hostel A1
9 Maldron Hotel Cardiff Lane B2

Eating

10 Ely HQ C2
11 herbstreet C2
12 Quay 16 ...... C2

Entertainment

13 Grand Canal Theatre C3
14 O2 ...... D2
15 Shelbourne Park Greyhound Stadium D3

Custom House MUSEUM

(Map p91) James Gandon (1743–1823) announced his arrival on the Dublin scene with the stunning, glistening white building that is the Custom House, one of the city's finest Georgian monuments. It was constructed between 1781 and 1791, in spite of opposition from city merchants and dockers at the original Custom House, upriver in Temple Bar.

In 1921, during the independence struggle, the Custom House was set alight and completely gutted in a fire that burned for five days. The interior was later extensively redesigned, and a further major renovation took place between 1986 and 1988.

The best complete view of a building that stretches 114m along the Liffey is obtained from across the river, though a close-up inspection of its many fine details is also

WORTH A TRIP

SOUTH WALL WALK

One of the city's most rewarding walks is a stroll along the south wall to the Poolbeg Lighthouse (that red tower visible in the middle of Dublin Bay). To get there, you'll have to make your own way from Ringsend (which is reachable by buses 1, 2 or 3 from the city centre), past the power station to the start of the wall (it's about 1km). It's not an especially long walk – about 800m or so – but it will give you a stunning view of the bay and the city behind you, a view best enjoyed just before sunset.

worthwhile. The building is topped by a copper dome with four clocks. Atop stands a 5m-high statue of Hope.

Beneath the dome is the **Custom House Visitor Centre** (Custom House Quay; admission €1; ⏲10am-12.30pm Mon-Fri, 2-5pm Sat & Sun mid-Mar–Oct, closed Mon-Tue & Sat Nov–mid-Mar), which features a small museum on Gandon himself, as well as information on the history of the building.

Jeanie Johnston MUSEUM/SHIP

(Map p91; www.jeaniejohnston.ie; Custom House Quay; adult/child €8.50/4.50; ⏲tours hourly 11am-noon & 2-4pm) One of the city's most original tourist attractions is an exact working replica of a 19th-century 'coffin ship', as the sailing boats which transported starving emigrants away from Ireland during the Famine were gruesomely known. The good news is that this three-masted barque, originally built in Quebec in 1847, made 16 transatlantic voyages carrying more than 2500 people and never suffered a single death. A small museum on board details the harrowing plight of a typical journey, which usually took around 47 days.

PHOENIX PARK

Measuring 709 glorious hectares, the **Phoenix Park** (Map p56; admission free) is Europe's largest city park: a green lung that is more than double the size of New York's Central Park (a paltry 337 hectares), and larger than all of London's major parks put together. Here you'll find gardens and lakes; pitches for all kinds of British sports from soccer to cricket to polo (the dry original one, with horses); the second-oldest zoo in Europe; a castle and visitor centre; the headquarters of the Garda Síochána (police); the Ordnance Survey offices; and the homes of both the president of Ireland and the US ambassador, who live in two exquisite residences more or less opposite each other. There's even a herd of some 500 fallow deer.

The deer were first introduced by Lord Ormond in 1662, when lands once owned by the Knights of Jerusalem were turned into a royal hunting ground. In 1745 the viceroy Lord Chesterfield threw it open to the public and it has remained so ever since. (The name 'Phoenix' has nothing to do with the mythical bird; it is a corruption of the Irish *fionn uisce,* meaning 'clear water'.)

In 1882 the park played a crucial role in Irish history, when Lord Cavendish, the British chief secretary for Ireland, and his assistant were murdered outside what is now the Irish president's residence by an obscure Nationalist group called the Invincibles. Lord Cavendish's home is now called Deerfield and is used as the official residence of the US ambassador.

Near the Parkgate St entrance to the park is the 63m-high **Wellington Monument**. This took from 1817 to 1861 to build, mainly because the Duke of Wellington fell from public favour during its construction. Nearby is the **People's Garden**, dating from 1864, and the **bandstand** in the Hollow.

The large Victorian building behind the zoo, on the edge of the park, is the 19th-century **Garda Síochána Headquarters**, designed by Benjamin Woodward (also author of the Old Library in Trinity College).

In the centre of the park, the **Papal Cross** marks the site where Pope John Paul II preached to 1.25 million people in 1979. The **Phoenix Monument**, erected by Lord Chesterfield in 1747, looks very un-phoenix-like and is often referred to as the Eagle Monument. The southern part of the park is a 200-acre stretch (about 81 hectares) known as the **Fifteen Acres** (don't ask, nobody knows), which is given over to a large number of football pitches – winter Sunday mornings are the time to come and watch. To the west, the rural-looking **Glen Pond** corner of the park is extremely attractive.

Back towards the Parkgate entrance is **Magazine Fort** on Thomas' Hill. Built at a snail's pace between 1734 and 1801, the fort has served as an occasional arms depot for the British and, later, the Irish armies. It was a target during the 1916 Easter Rising and again in 1940, when the IRA made off with the entire ammunitions reserve of the Irish army (they retrieved it after a few weeks).

To get to Dublin's beloved playground, take bus 10 from O'Connell St or bus 25 or 26 from Middle Abbey St. The best way to get around the park is to hop on the **Phoenix Park Shuttle Bus** (Map p60; adult/child €2/1; ⏲hourly 7am-5pm Mon-Fri, 10am-5pm Sat & Sun), which goes from just outside the main gate on Parkgate St and loops around to the visitor centre.

Dublin Zoo ZOO

(Map p56; www.dublinzoo.ie; Phoenix Park; adult/child/family €14/9.50/40; ⏲9.30am-6pm Mar-Sep, 9.30am-dusk Oct-Feb; 🚌10 from O'Connell St or 25 & 26 from Middle Abbey St) Established in 1830, the 12-hectare Dublin Zoo just north of the Hollow is one of the oldest in the world, and as thrilling or depressing as any other old zoo trying to drag itself into the 21st century. The zoo is well known for its lion-breeding program, which dates back to 1857, and includes among its offspring the lion that roars at the start of MGM films. You'll see these tough cats, from a distance, on the 'African Plains', which were added a few years ago, doubling the size of the zoo and making it a much nicer place to stroll around.

Áras an Uachtaráin HISTORIC BUILDING

(Map p56; Phoenix Park; admission free; ⏲guided tours hourly 10.30am-4.30pm Sat) The residence of the Irish president is a Palladian lodge that was built in 1751 and enlarged a couple of times since, most recently in 1816. It was home to the British viceroys from 1782 to 1922, and then to the governors general until Ireland cut ties with the British Crown and created the office of president in 1937. Queen Victoria stayed here during her visit in 1849, when she appeared not to even notice the Famine. The candle burning in the window is an old Irish tradition, to guide 'the Irish diaspora' home.

Tickets for the free one-hour **tours** (hourly 10am to 4pm Saturday) can be collected from the **Phoenix Park Visitor Centre** (admission free; ⏲10am-5.45pm Mar-Sep, 9.30-5.30pm Wed-Sun Oct-Feb), the converted former stables of the papal nunciate, where you'll see a 10-minute introductory video before being shuttled to the Áras itself to inspect five state rooms and the president's study. If you can't make it on a Saturday, just become elected president of your own country or become a Nobel laureate or something, and then wrangle a personal invite.

Next door is the restored four-storey **Ashtown Castle**, a 17th-century tower house 'discovered' inside the 18th-century nuncio's mansion when the latter was demolished in 1986 due to dry rot. You can visit the castle only on a guided tour from the visitor centre.

BEYOND THE ROYAL CANAL

Beyond the Royal Canal lie the suburbs and an authentic slice of north city life. There are also some beautiful gardens, the country's biggest stadium, a historic cemetery and one of the most interesting buildings in all of Dublin.

Glasnevin Cemetery CEMETERY, MUSEUM

(Map p56; www.glasnevin-cemetery.ie; Finglas Rd; admission free; ⏲24hr, tours 2.30pm Wed & Fri; 🚌40, 40A or 40B from Parnell St) Ireland's largest and most historically important burial site (aka Prospect Cemetery) was established in 1832 by Daniel O'Connell as a burial ground for people of all faiths, a high-moral-ground response to Protestant cemeteries' refusal to bury Catholics.

The tombstones read like a 'who's who' of Irish history: a modern replica of a round tower acts as a handy landmark for locating the tomb of O'Connell, who died in 1847 and was reinterred here in 1869 when the tower was completed. Charles Stewart Parnell's tomb is topped with a huge granite rock. Other notable people buried here include Sir Roger Casement, executed for treason by the British in 1916; the Republican leader Michael Collins, who died in the Civil War; the docker and trade unionist Jim Larkin, a prime force in the 1913 general strike; and the poet Gerard Manley Hopkins.

The history of the cemetery is told in wonderful, award-winning detail in the new **museum** (admission €6; ⏲10am-5pm Mon-Fri, 11am-6pm Sat & Sun), which tells the social and political story of Ireland through the lives of the people known and unknown that are buried in the cemetery. The City of the Dead covers the burial practice and religious beliefs of the roughly 1.5m people whose final resting place is here, while the Milestone Gallery features a 10m-long digitally interactive timeline outlining the lives and links of the cemetery's most famous residents.

The best way to visit the cemetery is to take one of the daily **tours** (€5; ⏲11.30am, 12.30pm & 2.30pm) which will (ahem) bring to life the rich and important stories of those buried in what is jokingly referred to by Dubs as 'Croak Park'.

Croke Park STADIUM

(Map p56; Clonliffe Rd; 3, 11, 11A, 16, 16A or 123 from O'Connell St) It's a magnificent stadium (if you're impressed by them) that is Ireland's largest and the fourth largest in Europe, but Croke Park is about much more than 82,000-plus sporting butts on plastic seats. No, Croker – as it's lovingly known in Dublin – is the fabulous fortress that protects the sanctity and spirit of Gaelic games in Ireland, as well as the administrative HQ of the Gaelic Athletic Association (GAA), the body that governs them. Sound a little hyperbolic? Well, the GAA considers itself not just the governing body of a bunch of Irish games but also the stout defender of a cultural identity that is ingrained in Ireland's sense of self. To get an idea of just how important the GAA is here, a visit to the **Croke Park Experience** (www.gaa.ie; New Stand, Croke Park, Clonliffe Rd; adult/child/student museum €6/4/4.50, museum & tour €11/7.50/8.50; 9.30am-5pm Mon-Sat, noon-5pm Sun Apr-Oct, 10am-5pm Tue-Sat, noon-4pm Sun Nov-Mar) is a must, though it will help if you're any kind of sporting enthusiast. The twice-daily tours (except match days) of the impressive stadium are excellent.

FREE **National Botanic Gardens** GARDEN

(Map p58; Botanic Rd, Glasnevin; 9am-6pm Mon-Sat, 11am-6pm Sun Apr-Oct, 10am-4.30pm Mon-Sat, 11am-4.30pm Sun Nov-Mar; 13, 13A or 19 from O'Connell St, or bus 34 or 34A from Middle Abbey St) Founded in 1795, the 19.5-hectare botanic gardens are home to a series of curvilinear glasshouses, dating from 1843 to 1869, created by Richard Turner, who was also responsible for the glasshouse at Belfast Botanic Gardens and the Palm House in London's Kew Gardens. Within these Victorian masterpieces you will find the latest in botanical technology, including a series of computer-controlled climates reproducing environments of different parts of the world. Among the pioneering botanical work conducted here was the first attempt to raise orchids from seed, back in 1844.

Casino at Marino MUSEUM

(Map p56; www.heritageireland.ie; Malahide Rd; adult/child/senior €3/1/2; 10am-5pm May-Sep; 20A, 20B, 27, 27B, 42, 42C or 123 from city centre) It's not the roulette-wheel kind of casino but the original Italian kind, the one that means 'summer home' (it literally means 'small house'), and this particular casino is one of the most enchanting constructions in all of Ireland. Entrance is by guided tour only; the last tour is 45 minutes before closing.

It was built in the mid-18th century for the Earl of Charlemont, who returned from his grand tour of Europe with more art than he could store in his own home, Marino House, which was on the same grounds but was demolished in the 1920s. He also came home with a big love of the Palladian style – hence the architecture of this wonderful folly.

The exterior of the building, with a huge entrance doorway, and 12 Tuscan columns forming a templelike facade, creates the expectation that its interior will be a simple single open space. But instead it is an extravagant convoluted maze: flights of fancy include chimneys for the central heating that are disguised as roof urns, downpipes hidden in columns, carved draperies, ornate fireplaces, beautiful parquet floors constructed of rare woods, and a spacious wine cellar. A variety of statuary adorns the outside but it's the amusing fakes that are most enjoyable. The towering front door is a sham – a much smaller panel opens to reveal the secret interior. The windows have blacked-out panels to hide the fact that the interior is a complex of rooms, not a single chamber.

Tours

A plethora of tours offer a range of exploring options; you can walk (or crawl, if you opt for a drinking tour), get a bus or hop aboard an amphibious vehicle. There are lots of themed tours too, while some companies will combine a city tour with trips further afield. You'll save a few euro booking online.

City Sightseeing BUS TOURS

(Map p86; www.city-sightseeing.com; Dublin Tourism, 14 Upper O'Connell St; adult/child/family €16/7/38; every 8-15min 9am-6pm) City Sightseeing's time-tested hop-on, hop-off open-top tours. Allow 1½ hours.

Dublin Bus Tours BUS TOURS

(www.dublinbus.ie; tours €16-26; tours daily) O'Connell St (Map p86; 01-872 0000; 59 Upper O'Connell St); Suffolk St (Map p70; Dublin Tourism Centre, St Andrew's Church, 2 Suffolk St) Offers a variety of tours, including Dublin City Tour, Ghost Bus Tour, Coast and Castles Tour, and South Coast and Gardens Tour.

Dublin Rock'n'Roll Writers Bus Tour BUS TOURS

(Map p64; 01-620 3929; www.dublinrocktour.ie; 3 Westmoreland St; tours €15; noon, 2pm,

DUBLIN FOR CHILDREN

Dublin has some good activities that parents and children can enjoy together, including Dvblinia (p83), the Natural History Museum (p75) and the National Leprechaun Museum (p90). The National Museum (p69 and p87) and the Irish Museum of Modern Art (p84) run fun, educational programs for children at weekends.

The **Ark** (Map p70; 01-670 7788; www.ark.ie; 11A Eustace St) is a children's cultural centre that organises plays, exhibitions and workshops for four-to-14-year-olds. You need to book in advance for events.

A real treat is a puppet show at the **Lambert Puppet Theatre** (01-280 0974; www.lambertpuppettheatre.com; Clifton Lane, Monkstown; 7, 7A, 8, 46A, 46X or 746 from city centre) which stages puppet shows for the over-threes in Monkstown, 10km south of the city centre. The kids can also get their splash on in the **National Aquatic Centre** (Map p58; www.nationalaquaticcentre.ie; Snugborough Rd, Blanchardstown; adult/child & student €14/12; 6am-10pm Mon-Fri, 9am-8pm Sat & Sun; 38A from Hawkins St), 8km northwest of the city centre. A nice spot for a picnic is **Newbridge House** (Map p58; www.newbridgehouseandfarm.com; Donabate; adult/child €4/3; 10am-5pm Tue-Sat, 2-6pm Sun Apr-Sep, 2-5pm Sat & Sun Oct-Mar; from Connolly or Pearse St), with its large traditional farm, which has cows, pigs and chickens, a large park and an adventure playground. It's northeast of Swords at Donabate, 19km from the centre.

All but a few hotels will provide cots and most top-range hotels have baby-sitting services (€8 to €15 per hour). Restaurants are generally accommodating until 6pm, after which things can get difficult, especially for babies: check while making a booking.

4pm & 6pm) Dublin's rich rock legacy is explored audiovisually from the comfort of a kitted-out tour bus. The bus stop is outside O'Brien's sandwich shop on Westmoreland St; the tour lasts about 90 minutes.

Gray Line Dublin Tour BUS TOURS
(01-872 9010; www.irishcitytours.com; adult/child/student/family €16/free/14/38; every 15min 9.30am-5.30pm, to 6.30pm Jul & Aug) Bachelor's Walk (Map p86; 33 Bachelor's Walk); Suffolk St (Map p70; Dublin Tourism Centre, St Andrew's Church, 2 Suffolk St) This is another hop-on, hop-off tour (1½ hours) of the city's primary attractions.

Dublin by Bike CYCLING TOURS
(Map p91; 01-280 1899; www.dublinbybike.ie; Merrion Sq West; €28, twilight tour €15; 10.30am, twilight tour 5.30pm) A great way to see the city, these three-hour tours start from the National Gallery and take in all the sights; the bikes are the small-wheeled kind, helmets are provided and the guides fun and informative. They also run a 90-minute twilight tour.

Wild Wicklow Tour BUS TOURS
(Map p70; 01-280 1899; www.discoverdublin.ie; Dublin Tourism Centre, St Andrew's Church, 2 Suffolk St; adult/child €28/25; 9.10am) Award-winning and lots of fun, this top 8½-hour tour leaves from Dublin Tourism Centre and does a quick city run before heading down the coast to Avoca Handweavers, Glendalough and the Sally Gap.

1916 Easter Rising Walk WALKING TOURS
(Map p70; 01-676 2493; www.1916rising.com; International Bar, 23 Wicklow St; adult/child €12/free; 11.30am Mon-Sat, 1pm Sun Mar-Oct) A recommended two-hour tour run by graduates of Trinity College, it takes in parts of Dublin that were directly involved in the Easter Rising. Leaves from the International Bar.

Dublin Footsteps Walking Tours WALKING TOURS
(Map p70; 01-496 0641; Bewley's Bldg, Grafton St; adult €11; 10.30am Mon, Wed, Fri & Sat Jun-Sep) Departing from Bewley's on Grafton St, these excellent two-hour tours weave Georgian, literary and architectural Dublin into a fascinating walk.

Dublin Literary Pub Crawl WALKING TOURS
(Map p64; 01-670 5602; www.dublinpubcrawl.com; the Duke, 9 Duke St; adult/student €12/10; 7.30pm Mon-Sat, noon & 7.30pm Sun Apr-Nov, 7.30pm Thu-Sun Dec-Mar) An award-winning 2½-hour walk-and-performance tour led by two actors, exploring pubs with literary connections. There's plenty of drink taken, which makes it all the more popular; get to the Duke pub by 7pm to reserve a spot.

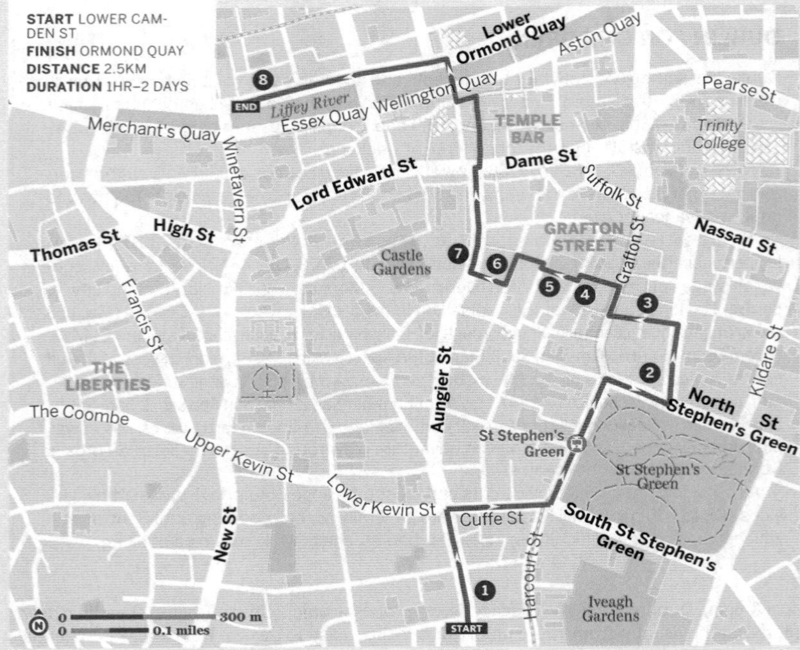

Walking Tour

Dublin Crawl

Dubliners of old would assure their 'bitter halves' that they were 'going to see a man about a dog' before beating a retreat to the nearest watering hole. Visiting barflies need no excuse to enjoy the social and cultural education – ahem – of a tour of Dublin's finest, most charming and most hard-core bars.

Start in the always excellent 1 **Anseo** on Camden St, where hipsters rub shoulders with the hoi polloi and everyone toe-taps to the great bag of DJ tunes. Head deep into the city centre and stop for one at Dublin's smallest pub, the 2 **Dawson Lounge**, before sinking a pint of plain in the snug at South Anne St's 3 **Kehoe's**, one of the city centre's most atmospheric bars. Find a spot out front of 4 **Bruxelle's**: the bronze statue of Thin Lizzy's Phil Lynott outside is testament to the bar's reputation as a great spot for rock music, even if it's just on the stereo. Discuss the merits of that unwritten masterpiece with a clutch of frustrated writers and artists in 5 **Grogan's Castle Lounge** on Castle Market, a traditional haunt that admirably refuses to modernise. A couple of streets away is one of the latest contenders for coolest bar in town, the appropriately named 6 **No Name Bar**; there's no sign but it's up the stairs from the doorway next door to L'Gueuleton restaurant. If it's more conversation you require, make your way to the 7 **Long Hall**, where the vicissitudes of life are discussed in a sombre Victorian setting.

Cross the Liffey and make a beeline for Ormond Quay and 8 **Sin É**, a small bar with a big reputation for top-class music and a terrific night out. If you've followed the tour correctly, it's unlikely that you'd now be referring to this guide. How many fingers?

Dublin Musical Pub Crawl WALKING TOURS
(Map p70; ☎01-478 0193; www.discoverdublin.ie; Oliver St John Gogarty's, 58-59 Fleet St; adult/student €12/10; ⏰7.30pm Apr-Oct, 7.30pm Thu-Sat Nov-Mar) The story of Irish traditional music and its influence on contemporary styles is explained and demonstrated by two expert musicians in a number of Temple Bar pubs. Tours meet upstairs at Oliver St John Gogarty's and take 2½ hours.

James Joyce Walking Tour WALKING TOURS
(Map p86; ☎01-878 8547; James Joyce Cultural Centre, 35 North Great George's St; adult/student €10/8; ⏰2pm Tue, Thu & Sat) Excellent 1¼-hour walking tours of northside attractions associated with James Joyce, departing from James Joyce Cultural Centre.

Pat Liddy Walking Tours WALKING TOURS
(Map p70; ☎01-831 1109; www.walkingtours.ie; Dublin Tourism Centre, St Andrew's Church, 2 Suffolk St; adult €6-22, child €5-20) Award-winning themed tours of the city by well-known Dublin historian Pat Liddy, ranging from the 75-minute Dublin Experience to the two-hour Great Guinness Walk, which includes a queue-skipping tour of the Guinness Storehouse. Check the website for details of tour options and times. All tours depart from the Dublin Tourism Centre.

FREE **Sandeman's New Dublin Tour** WALKING TOURS
(Map p70; ☎01-878 8547; www.newdublintours.com; City Hall; ⏰11am) A high-energy and thoroughly enjoyable three-hour walking tour of the city's greatest hits – and it's free: tip only if you enjoyed the tour. Spanish-language tours are also available.

River Liffey Cruises BOAT TOURS
(Map p86; ☎01-473 4082; www.liffeyvoyage.ie; Bachelor's Walk; adult/student/child €14/12/8; ⏰9am-5.30pm Mar-Oct) Experience the city from the river aboard the (all-important) all-weather *Spirit of the Docklands*. The history of Dublin is told from a watery point of view, from the Vikings to the recent developments of the Docklands.

Viking Splash Tours AMPHIBIOUS VEHICLE TOURS
(☎01-707 6000; www.vikingsplash.ie; adult/child/family from €20/10/60; ⏰9am-5.30pm Mar-Oct, 10am-4pm Tue-Sun Nov, 10am-4pm Wed-Sun Feb) Patrick St (Map p70; 64-65 Patrick St); St Stephen's Green (Map p78; North St Stephen's Green) It's hard not to feel a little cheesy with a plastic Viking helmet on your head, but the punters get a real kick out of these amphibious 1¼-hour tours that end up in the Grand Canal Dock.

Festivals & Events

Temple Bar Trad Festival MUSIC FESTIVAL
(www.templebartrad.com) Traditional music festival in the bars of the cultural quarter over the last weekend in January.

Jameson Dublin International Film Festival FILM FESTIVAL
(www.dubliniff.com) Local flicks, arty international films and advance releases of mainstream movies make up the menu of the city's film festival, which runs over two weeks in mid-February.

St Patrick's Festival PARADE FESTIVAL
(www.stpatricksfestival.ie) The mother of all festivals; 600,000-odd gather to 'honour' St Patrick over four days around 17 March on city streets and in venues.

Dublin Writers Festival WRITERS FESTIVAL
(www.dublinwritersfestival.com) Four-day literature festival in early June that attracts Irish and international writers to its readings, performances and talks.

Diversions ARTS FESTIVAL
(www.templebar.ie) Free outdoor music, children's and film events at weekends from June to September in Temple Bar's Meeting House Sq.

Oxegen MUSIC FESTIVAL
(www.oxegen.ie) Three-day mega-music festival in mid-July at Punchestown Racecourse, featuring heavyweight pop, rock and dance acts.

Dun Laoghaire Festival of World Cultures ETHNIC FESTIVAL
(www.festivalofworldcultures.com) Colourful multicultural music, art and theatre festival on the last weekend of August.

Dublin Theatre Festival THEATRE FESTIVAL
(www.dublintheatrefestival.com) Established international theatre festival held over a fortnight in late September/early October.

Dublin Fringe Festival THEATRE FESTIVAL
(www.fringefest.com) Comedy and alternative fringe theatre from late September to early October.

Women's Mini-Marathon RACE
(www.womensminimarathon.ie) This 10km road race for charity (on the second Sunday in June) – the largest of its kind in the world – attracts around 40,000 runners each year.

Taste of Dublin FOOD
(www.tastefestivals.ie) Over a weekend in mid-June, the Iveagh Gardens hosts a gourmet extravaganza as restaurants from all over the city offer up sample versions of their best dishes. There's lots of music and entertainment.

Liffey Swim SWIM
(☎833 2434) Five hundred lunatics swim 2.5km from Rory O'More Bridge to the Custom House in late July – one can't but admire their steel will.

Sleeping

Dublin gets busy in summer and it can be tough to get a central bed from around May to September. The south/north divide is also a constant, and you're more likely to get better value for money north of the Liffey – a large-roomed comfortable B&B in the northside suburbs may cost you as little as €50 per person, but the owners of a small, mediocre guesthouse within walking distance of St Stephen's Green won't balk at asking €100 for a room barely bigger than a shoebox. Still, some of the city's most characteristic properties are in the leafy suburbs directly south of the city centre, which is pretty accessible by cab or by public transportation (if you don't fancy a longish walk).

You can pay anything from €80 to €200 for a quality guesthouse or midrange hotel, while the city's top digs usually start their rates at €200; at the other end of the scale, a hostel bed will cost anything from €10 to as much as €34. (Note that hostel rates don't include breakfast; exceptions are noted.)

Always check online (see the boxed text, p101) and query the rack rate: discounts are more available now than ever before.

GRAFTON STREET & AROUND

You can't get more central than the relatively small patch of real estate just south of the Liffey, which has a good mix of options ranging from backpacker hostels to the fanciest hotels. Bear in mind that the location comes with a price.

TOP CHOICE **Number 31** GUESTHOUSE €€
(Map p78; ☎01-676 5011; www.number31.ie; 31 Leeson Close; s/d/tr from €100/140/240; wifi) This elegant slice of accommodation paradise, designed for his own use by modernist architect Sam Stephenson (of Central Bank fame – or infamy), is unquestionably the most distinctive of Dublin's hotels. Separated by a beautiful garden, its 21 bedrooms are split between the chichi coach house and the more gracious Georgian house, where rooms are individually furnished with French antiques and big beds. Gourmet breakfasts are served in the conservatory. Children under 10 are not permitted.

Radisson Blu Royal Hotel HOTEL €€
(Map p70; ☎01-898 2900; www.radissonblu.ie/royalhotel-dublin; Golden Lane; r €160-220; P ❄ wifi) The stunning Dublin flagship of this well-respected Scandinavian group is an excellent example of how sleek lines and muted colours can combine beautifully with luxury to make for a memorable night's stay: from the hugely impressive public areas (the bar alone is worth the visit) to the sophisticated bedrooms – each with flat-screen digital TVs embedded in the wall – this is bound to be one of the most popular options for the business traveller, or anyone looking for an elegant contemporary bed.

Irish Landmark Trust SELF-CATERING €€
(Map p70; ☎01-670 4733; www.irishlandmark.com; 25 Eustace St; 1 night/week €300/1800) If you're travelling in a group, instead of renting a bunch of doubles in a hotel that you'll barely remember a week after you've gone home, why not go for this fabulous 18th-century heritage house, gloriously restored to the highest standard by the Irish Landmark Trust? You'll have this unique house all to yourselves. It sleeps up to seven in its double, twin and triple bedrooms. Furnished with tasteful antiques, authentic furniture and fittings (including a grand piano in the drawing room), this kind of period rental accommodation is something really special. A €7 daily contribution to offset energy costs is included in the price.

Cliff Townhouse GUESTHOUSE €€
(Map p78; ☎01-638 3939; www.theclifftownhouse.com; 22 North St Stephen's Green; s/d from €145/155; @ wifi) As *pied-à-terres* go, this is a doozy: the sister property to the much-heralded Cliff House in Ardmore, County Waterford, there are 10 exquisitely appoint-

BLOOMSDAY

It's 16 June. There's a bunch of weirdos wandering around the city dressed in Edwardian gear and talking nonsense in dramatic tones. They're not mad – at least not clinically; they're only Bloomsdayers committed to commemorating James Joyce's epic *Ulysses*, which anyone familiar with the book will tell you (and that doesn't necessarily mean that they've *read* the bloody thing) takes place over the course of one day. What they mightn't be able to tell you is that Leopold Bloom's latter-day odyssey takes place on 16 June 1904 because it was on that day that Joyce first 'stepped out' with Nora Barnacle, the woman he had met six days earlier and with whom he would spend the rest of his life. (When James' father heard about this new love he commented that with a name like that she would surely stick to him.)

Although Ireland treated Joyce like a literary pornographer while he was alive, the country (and especially Dublin) can't get enough of him today. Bloomsday is a slightly gimmicky and touristy phenomenon that appeals almost exclusively to Joyce fanatics and tourists, but it's plenty of fun and a great way to lay the groundwork for actually reading what could be the second-hardest book written in the 20th century (the hardest, of course, being Joyce's follow-up blockbuster *Finnegan's Wake*, the greatest book *never* to be read).

In general, events are designed to follow Bloom's progress around town, and in recent years festivities have expanded to continue over four days around 16 June. On Bloomsday proper you can kick things off with breakfast at the **James Joyce Cultural Centre** (p90), where the 'inner organs of beast and fowl' come accompanied by celebratory readings.

In the morning, guided tours of Joycean sites usually leave from the General Post Office and the James Joyce Cultural Centre. Lunchtime activity focuses on **Davy Byrne's** (Map p64; Duke St), Joyce's 'moral pub', where Bloom paused to dine on a glass of burgundy and a slice of gorgonzola. Street entertainers are likely to keep you amused through the afternoon as you take guided walks and watch animated readings from *Ulysses* and Joyce's other books; there's a reading at **Ormond Quay Hotel** (Map p70; Ormond Quay) at 4pm and **Harrisons** (Map p86; Westmoreland St) in the late afternoon.

Events also take place in the days leading up to and following Bloomsday. The best source of information about what's on in any particular year is likely to be the James Joyce Cultural Centre, close to the date.

ed bedrooms spread across a wonderful Georgian property whose best views overlook St Stephen's Green. Downstairs is Sean Smith's superb restaurant, Cliff Townhouse.

Trinity Lodge GUESTHOUSE €€
(Map p64; ☎01-617 0900; www.trinitylodge.com; 12 South Frederick St; s/d from €130/170;) Martin Sheen's grin greets you on entering this cosy, award-winning guesthouse. Not that he's ditched movies for hospitality: he just enjoyed his stay (and full Irish breakfast, presumably) at this classically refurbished Georgian pad so much that he let them take a mugshot. Room 2 has a lovely bay window.

Grafton House GUESTHOUSE €€
(Map p70; ☎01-679 2041; www.graftonguesthouse.com; 26-27 South Great George's St; s/d from €60/100;) This slightly offbeat guesthouse in a Gothic-style building gets the nod in all three key categories: location, price and style. Just next to George's St Arcade, the Grafton offers the traditional friendly features of a B&B (including a terrific breakfast), coupled with a funky design – check out the psychedelic wallpaper. Hard to beat at this price, especially off-season weekdays, when the deals are at their most interesting.

Merrion HOTEL €€€
(Map p78; ☎01-603 0600; www.merrionhotel.com; Upper Merrion St; r from €455; P@) This is a resplendent five-star hotel set in a terrace of beautifully restored Georgian town houses. Try to get a room in the old house (which has the largest private art collection in the city) – rather than the newer wing – to sample the hotel's truly elegant comforts. Located opposite government buildings, its marble corridors are patronised by visiting dignitaries and the odd celeb. Even if you don't stay, come for the superb afternoon tea

GAY & LESBIAN DUBLIN

Dublin's not a bad place to be gay. Most people in the city centre wouldn't bat an eyelid at cross-dressing or public displays of affection between same-sex couples, but discretion is advised in the suburbs.

FESTIVALS & EVENTS

International Dublin Gay Theatre Festival (www.gaytheatre.ie) The only event of its kind anywhere in the world, with more than 30 gay- and lesbian-themed productions over two weeks in May.

Mardi Gras (www.dublinpride.org) Not the traditional feast that precedes the Catholic Lent but a week-long festival of theatre, performance, music, readings and – inevitably – a high-energy, colourful parade through the city centre for the city's queers, dykes, bis and fetishists. Usually held the last week in June.

Gaze International Lesbian & Gay Film Festival (www.gaze.ie) An international film and documentary festival held at the Irish Film Institute in August.

DRINKING

Dragon (Map p70; 64-65 South Great George's St) High-concept, high-octane and loaded with attitude, the Dragon is the slightly trendier alternative to the long-established George down the street (George and the Dragon; get it?). It's more popular with guys than gals, and even then with a certain type of guy – young, brash and unafraid to express themselves...on the dancefloor or in the arms of another.

George (Map p70; 89 South Great George's St) The purple mother of Dublin's gay bars is a long-standing institution, having lived through the years when it was the only place in town where the gay crowd could, well, be gay. There are other places to go, but the George remains the best, if only for tradition's sake. Shirley's legendary Sunday night bingo is as popular as ever.

Front Lounge (Map p70; 33 Parliament St) The unofficially gay 'Flounge' is a sophisticated and friendly bar that is quieter and more demure than other gay joints, and popular with a mixed crowd. Sexual orientation here is secondary to having a drink and a laugh with friends, even though the 'Back Lounge' towards the back of the bar is traditionally predominantly gay.

Pantibar (Map p86; www.pantibar.com; 7-8 Capel St) Pantibar is bold and brash, mostly because its owner, the eponymous Panti, is an outrageous entertainer who makes sure that a night in *her* bar is one to remember. The floor shows – both on and off the stage – are fabulous. It's open late Friday and Saturday.

INFORMATION

Gay & Lesbian Garda Liaison Officer (☎01-666 9000) If you encounter any sort of trouble on the streets, don't hesitate to call. (For sexual assaults, contact the Sexual Assault Unit.)

Gay Community News (www.gcn.ie) A useful nationwide news- and issues-based monthly paper. The glossy *Q-Life* and *Free!* are entertainment guides that can be found in Temple Bar businesses and the Irish Film Institute (p120).

Gay Switchboard Dublin (☎01-872 1055; www.gayswitchboard.ie) A friendly and useful voluntary service that provides information ranging from where to find accommodation to legal issues.

Outhouse (☎01-873 4932; www.outhouse.ie; 105 Capel St) Top gay, lesbian and bisexual resource centre. Great stop-off point to see what's on, check notice boards and meet people. It publishes the free *Ireland's Pink Pages*, a directory of gay-centric services, which is also accessible on the website.

Sexual Assault Unit (☎01-666 6000) Call or visit the Garda Station on Pearse St (Map p60).

(€36), with endless cups of tea served out of silver pots near a raging fire.

Avalon House HOSTEL €

(Map p70; ☎01-475 0001; www.avalon-house.ie; 55 Aungier St; dm/s/d €10/34/54; wi-fi) Before there was tourism, this hostel in a gorgeous Victorian building catered to the thin trickle of adventurers who landed in Dublin. They flood in these days – book ahead – but Avalon still takes good care of them, whether they're young backpackers or families. The lounges are great for hanging out, the Bald Barista serves a sublime cappuccino and there's free wi-fi.

Paramount Hotel HOTEL €€

(Map p70; ☎01-417 9900; www.paramounthotel.ie; cnr Parliament St & Essex Gate; s/d €85/170; wi-fi) Behind the Victorian facade, the Paramount's lobby is a faithful recreation of a 1930s hotel, complete with dark wood floors, leather chesterfield couches and heavy velvet drapes. The 70-odd rooms don't quite bring *The Maltese Falcon* to mind, but they're handsomely furnished and very comfortable.

Central Hotel HOTEL €€

(Map p70; ☎01-679 7302; www.centralhoteldublin.com; 1-5 Exchequer St; s/d from €65/100; wi-fi) The rooms are a little snug for the grand Edwardian-style decor, but it's still a classy joint – no more so than in the wonderful 1st-floor Library Bar: all leather armchairs and sofas, and nothing short of one of the finest spots for an afternoon drink in the whole city. Location-wise, the name says it all.

Westbury Hotel HOTEL €€€

(Map p70; ☎01-679 1122; www.doylecollection.com; Grafton St; s/d from €218/245; P @ wi-fi) The Westbury sits snugly on a small street just off Grafton St, which suits the high-powered business people and visiting celebs who favour the hotel's finer suites, where they can watch TV from the Jacuzzi before retiring to a four-poster bed. Mere mortals tend to make do with the standard rooms, which are perfectly appointed but lack the sophisticated grandeur promised by the luxurious public spaces.

Morgan Hotel HOTEL €€

(Map p64; ☎01-679 3939; www.themorgan.com; 10 Fleet St; r from €90; @ wi-fi) Designer cool isn't really part of the Temple Bar zeitgeist, but the cream-leather look of this place works surprisingly well considering that fake tan can leave some nasty marks. It might be popular with wannabe WAGs and their gelled-up partners, but the facilities here are top-notch. Aromatherapy treatments and massages are extra, as is breakfast (€17).

Westin Dublin HOTEL €€€

(Map p64; ☎01-645 1000; www.westin.com; Westmoreland St; s/d €210/260; P @ wi-fi) Formerly a grand branch of the Allied Irish Bank, this fine old building was gutted and reborn as a stylish upmarket hotel. The rooms, many of which overlook a beautiful atrium, are decorated in elegant mahogany and soft colours: you will sleep on 10 layers of the Westin's own (trademarked) Heavenly Bed, which is damn comfortable indeed. The hotel's most elegant room is the former banking hall, complete with gold-leaf plasterwork on the ceiling, now used for banquets. Breakfast will set you back €27.

La Stampa HOTEL €€

(Map p78; ☎01-677 4444; www.lastampa.ie; 35 Dawson St; r weekday/weekend €120/240; @ wi-fi) La Stampa is an atmospheric little hotel on trendy Dawson St, with 29 Asian-influenced rooms in white decorated with rattan furniture and exotic velvet throws. The Ayurvedic spa is a nice treat, but to fully benefit from your restorative treatments ask for a top-floor bedroom away from the revelling at SamSara bar, located below.

BOOKING SERVICES

Your best bet for booking accommodation is using Dublin Tourism's computerised booking system (see p129). Alternatively, you can go it alone online using one of these competitive internet booking sites:

All Dublin Hotels (www.irelandhotels.com/hotels/dublin)

Dublin City Centre Hotels (http://dublin.city-centre-hotels.com)

Dublin Hotels (www.dublinhotels.com)

Go Ireland (www.goireland.com)

Hostel Dublin (www.hosteldublin.com)

See the Directory, p726, for more options, or try www.lonelyplanet.com/hotels.

Shelbourne HOTEL €€€
(Map p78; ☎01-676 6471; www.theshelbourne.ie; 27 North St Stephen's Green; r from €200; P@wi-fi) Dublin's most iconic hotel has long been the best address in town – it was good enough for the framers of the Irish Constitution – but since a major refurbishment and its acquisition by the Marriott group there has been steady grumbling that the hotel is not quite at the top of its five-star game. It *looks* pretty impressive, especially the Lord Mayor's Lounge, where afternoon tea is still one of the best experiences in town.

Clarence Hotel HOTEL €€€
(Map p70; ☎01-407 0800; www.theclarence.ie; 6-8 Wellington Quay; r €390-440, ste €780-2800; @wi-fi) Dublin's coolest hotel is synonymous with its rock-star owners, Bono and the Edge, so it's hardly surprising that they're used to dealing with celebrity heavyweights. The 50-odd rooms aren't short on contemporary style, but they lack that grandeur you would expect from a top hotel. The hotel was slated to get a megabucks makeover, but the economic downturn has put that on ice for the foreseeable future.

Abigail's Hostel HOSTEL €
(Map p86; ☎01-677 9300; www.abigailshostel.com; 7-9 Aston Quay; dm/d from €9/24; wi-fi) The dorms at this hostel (converted from an unremarkable hotel) aren't especially big – the eight-bed one is particularly cosy – but they're modern, sunny and well-appointed with all-pine furniture. All rooms have private bathrooms.

Barnacles Temple Bar House HOSTEL €
(Map p70; ☎01-671 6277; www.barnacles.ie; 19 Lower Temple Lane; dm/d from €10/30; wi-fi) Bright, spacious and set in the heart of Temple Bar, this hostel is immaculately clean, and has nicely laid-out dorms with private bathrooms and doubles with in-room storage and bathroom. Because of its location, rooms are quieter towards the back. Top facilities, a comfy lounge, and linen and towels are provided – as is breakfast.

Kinlay House HOSTEL €
(Map p70; ☎01-679 6644; www.kinlaydublin.ie; 2-12 Lord Edward St; dm/d from €15/30; @wi-fi) A former boarding house for boys, this busy hostel has some massive, 24-bed mixed dorms, as well as smaller rooms. Not for the faint-hearted – the hostel has a reputation for being a bit of a party spot. There's a nice TV lounge and a continental breakfast is included. There's free wi-fi throughout.

NORTH OF THE LIFFEY

There are a few classy digs around O'Connell St, but the real draw round these parts is just to the east on Gardiner St, Dublin's B&B row. *Caveat emptor:* the further north you go along Gardiner St the dodgier the lodgings and the neighbourhood get, so we've kept our inclusions to the southern end of the street, below Mountjoy Sq.

TOP CHOICE **Isaacs Hostel** HOSTEL €
(Map p91; ☎01-855 6215; www.isaacs.ie; 2-5 Frenchman's Lane; dm/d from €10/55; wi-fi) Located in a 200-year-old wine vault, this popular, grungy hostel with loads of character is the place to head if you want one of the cheapest beds in town – without sacrificing the basics of health and hygiene. The lounge area is where it all happens, from summer BBQs to live music, and the easygoing staff is on hand 24/7 for advice and help. Global nomads will feel right at home.

Morrison Hotel HOTEL €€€
(Map p86; ☎01-887 2400; www.morrisonhotel.ie; Lower Ormond Quay; r from €195, ste from €255; @) Fashion designer John Rocha's loosely Oriental style is evident in the zenlike contemporary furnishings and exclusive use of muted earth colours. There's little doubt this place is cool and sophisticated, but it's starting to wear a little around the edges, a fact that no amount of iMac computers and iPod docking stations can hide. The rooms in the newer wing are by far your best option: the seven studio rooms have plenty of space and even a balcony. A great hotel that needs a once-over.

Maldron Hotel Smithfield HOTEL €€
(Map p60; ☎01-485 0900; www.maldronhotels.com; Smithfield Village; r €140; @wi-fi, family) This modern hotel, with big bedrooms and plenty of earth tones to soften the contemporary edges, is your best bet in this part of town. We loved the floor-to-ceiling windows – great for checking out what's going on below in the square.

Gresham Hotel HOTEL €€€
(Map p86; ☎01-874 6881; www.gresham-hotels.com; Upper O'Connell St; r from €200, ste €450-2500; @wi-fi) A city landmark and one of Dublin's oldest hotels, the Gresham shed its traditional granny's parlour look with a major overhaul some years ago. Despite its

UNIVERSITY ACCOMMODATION

From mid-June to late September, you can stay in accommodation provided by the city's universities. Be sure to book well in advance.

Trinity College (Map p64; ☎01-896 1177; www.tcd.ie; Accommodations Office, Trinity College; s/d from €60/81; P@📶) Comfortable rooms ranging from basic to those with private bathrooms in one of the most atmospheric settings in Dublin.

Mercer Court (Map p70; ☎01-478 2179; www.mercercourt.ie; Lower Mercer St; r from €70; @📶) Owned and run by the Royal College of Surgeons, Mercer Court has modern rooms that are up to hotel standard.

brighter, smarter, modern appearance and a fabulous open-plan foyer, its loyal clientele – elderly groups on shopping breaks to the capital and well-heeled Americans – has stuck firmly. Rooms are spacious and well serviced, though the decor is a little brash.

Anchor Guesthouse INN €
(Map p86; ☎01-878 6913; www.anchorguesthouse.com; 49 Lower Gardiner St; s/d from €55/75) Most B&Bs round these parts offer pretty much the same sort of thing: TVs, tea- and coffee-making facilities, a half-decent shower and clean linen. The Anchor does all of that, but it has an elegance you won't find in many of the other B&Bs along this stretch. This lovely Georgian guesthouse, with its delicious wholesome breakfasts, comes highly recommended by readers. They're dead right.

Globetrotter Tourist Hostel HOSTEL €
(Map p86; ☎01-878 8088; www.globetrottersdublin.com; 46-48 Lower Gardiner St; dm/d €20/60; 📶) This is a really friendly place with 94 beds in a variety of dorms, all with bathrooms and under-bed storage. The funky decor is due to the fact that it shares the same artistic ethos (and dining room) as the Townhouse next door. There's a little patio garden to the rear for that elusive sunny day.

Abbey Court Hostel HOSTEL €
(Map p86; ☎01-878 0700; www.abbey-court.com; 29 Bachelor's Walk; dm/d €18/79; @) Spread over two buildings on the Liffey quays, this large, well-run hostel has 33 clean dorms with good storage. Doubles with private bathrooms are in the newer building, where a light breakfast is also provided in the cafe.

Castle Hotel HOTEL €€
(Map p86; ☎01-874 6949; www.castle-hotel.ie; 3-4 Great Denmark St; r from €99) In business since 1809, the Castle is one of the most pleasant hotels this side of the Liffey. The fabulous palazzo-style grand staircase leads to the 50-odd bedrooms, whose furnishings are tidy if a little unspectacular; check out the original Georgian cornicing around the high ceilings.

Townhouse INN €€
(Map p86; ☎01-878 8808; www.townhouseofdublin.com; 47-48 Lower Gardiner St; s/d/tr from €60/80/120; 📶) The ghostly writing of Irish-Japanese author Lafcadio Hearn may have influenced the Gothic-style interior of his former home. A dark-walled, gilt-framed foyer with a jingling chandelier leads into 82 individually designed, comfy rooms. Some rooms in the new wing at the back are larger, with balconies overlooking the small Japanese garden.

DOCKLANDS

As a hive of activity, the Docklands isn't quite what the planners had hoped it would be, which means that you'll still be making your way west along the quays to get to the action. Still, the hotels here are all good in their respective categories.

Gibson Hotel HOTEL €€
(Map p91; ☎01-618 5000; www.gibsonhotel.ie; Point Village; r from €99; Grand Canal Dock, 151 from city centre; P@📶) A sleek, brand-new hotel with 250-odd rooms all decked out in snazzy Respa beds, flat-screen TVs and internet work stations is the ideal stopping point for the business traveller looking to press the flesh in the Docklands – and for the performers playing at the O2 Arena next door. The hotel is owned by the same folks who own the arena, so there are some great deals if you're looking for tickets to a show and a bed for the night.

Maldron Hotel Cardiff Lane HOTEL €€
(Map p91; ☎01-643 9500; www.maldronhotels.com; Cardiff Lane; r/ste from €99/179; @📶) On the south side of the Liffey a short walk away from the Grand Canal Dock, this is one of the best midrange options in the city. The

HOME AWAY FROM HOME

Self-catering apartments are a good option for visitors staying a few days, for groups of friends, or families with kids. Apartments range from one-room studios to two-bedroom flats with lounge areas, and include bathrooms and kitchenettes. A decent two-bedroom apartment will cost about €100 to €150 per night. Good, central places include the following:

Premier Suites (Map p60; ☎01-638 1111; www.premierapartments.com; 14-17 Lower Leeson St) Deluxe studios and suites, with in-room safe, fax, modem facilities and CD player.

Home from Home Apartments (Map p91; ☎01-678 1100; www.yourhomefromhome.com; The Moorings, Fitzwilliam Quay) Deluxe one- to three-bedroom apartments in the southside city centre.

Latchfords (Map p60; ☎01-676 0784; www.latchfords.ie; 99-100 Lower Baggot St) Studios and two-bedroom flats in a Georgian town house.

Oliver St John Gogarty's Penthouse Apartments (Map p64; ☎01-671 1822; www.gogartys.ie; 18-21 Anglesea St) Perched high atop the pub of the same name, these one- to three-bedroom places have views of Temple Bar.

rooms are large and extremely comfortable, but the real catch is the amenities: two restaurants, a top-class fitness centre complete with sauna and a 22m swimming pool, the largest hotel pool in town.

Clarion Hotel IFSC HOTEL €€€
(Map p91; ☎01-433 8800; www.clarionhotelifsc.com; Custom House Quay; r from €160, ste €395-1000; P❄@📶🏊) This swanky business hotel in the heart of the Irish Financial Services Centre has beautiful rooms decorated in contemporary light oak furnishings and a blue-and-taupe colour scheme that is supposed to relax the mind after a long day of meetings. We prefer to relax with a swim in the Sanovitae health club downstairs.

BEYOND THE GRAND CANAL

You'll get more for your euro in the largely stylish digs dotted throughout the southern city suburb of Ballsbridge, 3km south of the city centre. You'll be rubbing shoulders with the jet set and embassy crowd.

TOP CHOICE **Pembroke Townhouse** INN €€
(Map p60; ☎01-660 0277; www.pembroketownhouse.ie; 90 Pembroke Rd; s €90-195, d €115-290; 🚌5, 7, 7A, 8, 18 or 45 from city centre; P📶👪) This superluxurious town house is a perfect example of what happens when traditional and modern combine to great effect. A classical Georgian house has been transformed into a superb boutique hotel, with each room carefully crafted and appointed to reflect the best of contemporary design and style, right down to the modern art on the walls and the handy lift to the upper floors. May we borrow your designer?

Schoolhouse Hotel BOUTIQUE HOTEL €€
(Map p60; ☎01-667 5014; www.schoolhousehotel.com; 2-8 Northumberland Rd; s/d from €99/199; 🚌5, 7, 7A, 8, 18, 27X or 44 from city centre; P📶👪) A Victorian schoolhouse dating from 1861, this beautiful building has been successfully converted into an exquisite boutique hotel that is (ahem) ahead of its class. Its 31 cosy bedrooms, named after famous Irish people, all have king-sized beds, big white duvets and loudly patterned headboards. The Canteen bar and patio bustles with local business folk in summer.

Ariel House INN €€
(Map p60; ☎01-668 5512; www.ariel-house.net; 52 Lansdowne Rd; s/d €70/140; 🚌5, 7, 7A, 8, 18 or 45 from city centre; P📶) Somewhere between a boutique hotel and a luxury B&B, this highly rated Victorian-era property has 28 rooms with private bathrooms, all individually decorated in period furniture, which lends the place an air of genuine luxury. A far better choice than most hotels.

Four Seasons HOTEL €€€
(Map p60; ☎01-665 4000; www.fourseasons.com; Simmonscourt Rd; r from €225; 🚌5, 7, 7A, 8, 18 or 45 from city centre; P@📶🏊) Like Alexis Carrington gliding down the stairs in *Dynasty*, you know you're in the presence of a diva when you step inside the grand lobby of this enormous hotel. To some, the effect is a little garish, a bit like Joan Collins herself – but to others, the combination of marble, chande-

liers and marvellous bedrooms scream luxury. Whatever your take, there's no denying the quality of the service, which is as good as you'll find anywhere in Ireland. It's in the grounds of the Royal Dublin Showgrounds.

Dylan HOTEL **€€€**
(Map p60; ☎01-660 3001; www.dylan.ie; Eastmoreland Pl; r from €200; 🚌5, 7, 7A, 8, 18, 27X or 44 from city centre; ❄@📶) A genuine contender for favourite celebrity stopover, the Dylan's designer OTT look – baroque meets Scandinavian sleek by way of neo-art nouveau and glammed-up 1940s art deco – has nevertheless been a big hit, a reflection perhaps of a time when too much was barely enough for the glitterati who signed contracts over cocktails before retiring to the crisp Frette linen sheets in the snazzily appointed rooms upstairs.

Waterloo House INN **€€**
(Map p60; ☎01-660 1888; www.waterloohouse.ie; 8-10 Waterloo Rd; s/d €89/139; 🚌5, 7, 7A, 8, 18 or 45 from city centre; P📶) A short walk from St Stephen's Green, this lovely guesthouse is spread over two ivy-clad Georgian houses off Baggot St. Rooms are tastefully decorated with high-quality furnishings in authentic Farrow & Ball Georgian colours, and all have cable TV and kettles. Home-cooked breakfast is served in the conservatory or in the garden on sunny days.

Eating

Of all of the transformations brought on by prosperity, none has been so dramatic, so downright revolutionary, as how Dubliners deal with grub. Gone are the days when food was nothing more than a biological necessity to be endured: today, the city is brimming with self-appointed gourmands who know their tagines from their terrines.

Making a decent fist of the restaurant business is tough enough at the best of times, but since the crash it's become an exercise in blind optimism, as a bunch of the city's best-known restaurants have closed, with most others facing an uncertain future – there's a chance that some of those listed below mightn't be around when you visit. We've done our best to include only those that stand a better-than-even shot of making it through these difficult times.

But it's not all bad news, for diners at least. Restaurateurs have rolled their sleeves up and have reimagined their menus to suit the shrinking budgets of their punters. Prices have come down, but the real difference is in the menu itself, which has lots of enticing recession-buster specials now available to ensure that you will keep coming back.

The most concentrated restaurant area is Temple Bar but, apart from a handful of good places, the bulk of eateries offer bland, unimaginative fodder and cheap set menus for tourists. Better food and service can usually be found on either side of Grafton St, while the top-end restaurants are clustered around Merrion Sq and Fitzwilliam Sq. Fast-food chains dominate the northside, though some fine cafes and eateries are finally appearing there too. The area around Parnell St, in particular, is worth checking out for the spate of new exotic restaurants – a reflection of the increasingly diverse ethnic communities that have settled in the area.

For many restaurants, particularly those in the centre, it's worth booking for Friday or Saturday nights to ensure a table.

GRAFTON STREET & AROUND

If you spent your whole time in this area you would eat pretty well; the south city centre is the hub of the best the city has to offer.

Green Nineteen IRISH **€€**
(Map p78; ☎01-478 9626; 19 Lower Camden St; mains €10-12; ⏰10am-11pm Mon-Sat, noon-6pm Sun) Proof that good food doesn't have to be expensive resides in this sleek restaurant that specialises in locally sourced, organic grub. Braised lamb chump, corned beef, pot-roast chicken and the ubiquitous burger are but the meaty part of the menu which also includes salads and vegie options. We love it, but so does everybody else: book ahead.

Coppinger Row MEDITERRANEAN **€€**
(Map p70; www.coppingerrown.com; Coppinger Row; mains €12-17; ⏰noon-10pm; 👪) The South William boys have applied their criteria of cool to this new eatery just around the corner and come up trumps – the chefs have combined to create a tasty, unfussy menu of Mediterranean treats, to be enjoyed as main courses or as bar bites. We like the roast guinea fowl with borlotti beans but will settle for the meatball linguini.

Silk Road Café MIDDLE EASTERN **€€**
(Map p70; Chester Beatty Library, Dublin Castle; mains around €11; ⏰11am-4pm Mon-Fri) Museum cafes don't often make you salivate, but this vaguely Middle Eastern–North African–Mediterranean gem is the exception. On the

ground floor of the Chester Beatty Library, it is the culinary extension of the superb collection upstairs, gathering together exotic flavours into one outstanding menu that is about two-thirds vegie. Complementing the house specialities like Greek moussaka and spinach lasagne are daily specials like *djaj mehshi* (chicken stuffed with spices, rice, dried fruit, almonds and pine nuts and served with okra and Greek yoghurt). For dessert, there's Lebanese baklava and coconut kataif, or you could opt for the juiciest dates this side of Tyre. All dishes are halal and kosher.

Town Bar & Grill FRENCH €€€

(Map p78; ☎01-662 4724; 21 Kildare St; mains €22-29; ⏲noon-11pm Mon-Sat, to 10pm Sun) One of our favourite restaurants in town came within a hair's breadth of closing in 2010 due to the credit crunch, but it was rescued by one of its regular clientele of affluent and influential people. Thank goodness for that – otherwise we'd no longer be able to treat ourselves to the simply mouth-watering food, which ranges from basics like lambs' liver to slow-roasted rabbit or sweet pepper-stuffed lamb.

Dunne & Crescenzi ITALIAN €€

(Map p64; 14-16 South Frederick St; mains €9-20; ⏲9am-7pm Mon & Tue, to 10pm Wed-Sat) This exceptional Italian eatery delights its regulars with a basic menu of rustic pleasures: panini, a single pasta dish and a superb plate of mixed antipasti drizzled in olive oil. The shelves are stacked with wine, the coffee is perfect and the desserts are sinfully good.

Bottega Toffoli ITALIAN €€

(Map p70; 34 Castle St; sandwiches & salads €9-12; ⏲8am-4pm Tue-Wed, 8am-9pm Thu-Fri, 11am-8pm Sat, 1-8pm Sun) Tucked away in the city centre (to the point where you would never find it unless you actually looked for it) is this superb Italian cafe, home of one of the best sandwiches you'll eat in town: beautifully cut prosciutto, baby tomatoes and rocket salad drizzled with imported olive oil, all on homemade *piadina* bread that is just too good to be true.

Green Hen FRENCH €€

(Map p70; 33 Exchequer St; mains €11-15; ⏲lunch & dinner Mon-Fri, brunch & dinner Sat & Sun) Borrowing a page out of New York's book on how to successfully reimagine the French brasserie, the Green Hen is Dublin's version of a buzzing, stylish Soho eatery. Elegance and economy live side by side here, so if you don't fancy gorging on oysters or tucking into a divine Irish Hereford rib eye, you can opt for the plat du jour or avail yourself of the early bird menus, but watch out for their killer cocktails.

Honest to Goodness CAFE €

(Map p70; George's St Arcade; mains €6.95; ⏲9am-6pm Mon-Sat, noon-4pm Sun) Wholesome sandwiches (made with freshly baked bread), tasty soups and a near-legendary Sloppy Joe, all made on the premises using produce sourced from local farmers, have earned this lovely spot in George's St Arcade a bevy of loyal fans who want to keep it all to themselves.

Restaurant Patrick Guilbaud FRENCH €€€

(Map p78; ☎01-676 4192; www.restaurantpatrickguilbaud.ie; 21 Upper Merrion St; 2-/3-course set lunch €38/50, dinner mains €38-56; ⏲12.30-2.30pm & 7.30-10.30pm Tue-Sat) Handing out the title of 'Best in the Country' involves some amount of personal choice, but few disagree that this exceptional restaurant is a leading candidate, not least those good people at Michelin, who have put two stars in its crown. The reasons are self-evident: the service is formal but surprisingly friendly, the setting elegant but not stuffy, the wine list simply awesome and head chef Guillaume Lebrun's *haute cuisine* proudly French. The food is innovative without being fiddly, just beautifully cooked and superbly presented. The lunch menu is an absolute steal, at least in this stratosphere.

L'Ecrivain FRENCH €€€

(Map p60; ☎01-661 1919; www.lecrivain.com; 109A Lower Baggot St; 3-course lunch menu €25/35/45, dinner menu €65, mains €40-47; ⏲closed Sun & lunch Sat) A firm favourite with the bulk of the city's foodies, L'Ecrivain trundles along with just one Michelin star to its name, but the plaudits just keep coming. Head chef Derry Clarke is considered a gourmet god for the exquisite simplicity of his creations, which put the emphasis on flavour and the use of the best local ingredients – all given the French once-over and turned into something that approaches divine dining.

L'Gueuleton FRENCH €€

(Map p70; 1 Fade St; mains €12-25; ⏲noon-3pm & 6-11.30pm Mon-Sat) Dubliners have a devil of a time pronouncing the name (which means 'the Gluttonous Feast') and have had their patience tested with the no-reservations, get-in-line-and-wait policy, but they just can't get enough of the restaurant's take on French rustic cuisine, which makes twisted tongues and sore feet a small price to pay. The steak is sensational, but the Toulouse sausages with *choucroute* (sauerkraut) and Lyonnaise potatoes is a timely reminder that when it comes to the pleasures of the palate, the French really know what they're doing.

Pichet FRENCH €€

(Map p70; ☎01-677 1060; www.pichet-restaurant.com; 14-15 Trinity St; mains €16-26; ⊙lunch & dinner) It's not the most obvious spot to open a fancy new restaurant, but that didn't stop Nick Munier, made famous by the English TV show *Hell's Kitchen,* and Stephen Gibson, formerly of L'Ecrivain, who've brought their version of modern French cuisine to this elongated dining room replete with blue leather chairs and lots of windows to stare out of. The result is pretty good indeed, the food excellent (we expected nothing less) and the service impeccable. Sit down the back – the atmosphere is better.

Lemon FAST FOOD €

(pancakes from €4.25; ⊙9am-7pm Mon-Sat, 10am-6pm Sun) South William St (Map p64; 66 South William St); Dawson St (Map p64; 61 Dawson St) Dublin's best pancake joint is staffed by a terrific bunch who like their music loud and their pancakes good: proper paper-thin sweet and savoury crepes smothered, stuffed and sprinkled with a variety of toppings, fillings and sauces. There's a second branch on nearby Dawson St.

Jaipur INDIAN €€

(Map p70; www.jaipur.ie; 41 South Great George's St; mains €19-23; ⊙noon-10pm) A stylish and contemporary room sets the scene for some of the best Indian cuisine in town. Critics rave about the subtle and varied flavours produced by Jaipur's kitchen, which is down to its refusal to skimp on even the smallest dash of spice; what you get here is as close to the real deal as you'll get anywhere outside India.

Pepperpot CAFE €

(Map p70; www.thepepperpot.ie; Powerscourt Townhouse; mains €5-8; ⊙10am-6pm Mon-Wed & Fri, to 8pm Thu, 9am-6pm Sat & noon-6pm Sun) Everything is baked and made daily at the lovely cafe on the 1st-floor balcony of the Powerscourt Townhouse. The salads with homemade brown bread are delicious but the real treat is the soup of the day (€4.50) – the ideal liquid lunch.

Simon's Place CAFE €

(Map p70; George's St Arcade, South Great George's St; mains from €4; ⊙9am-5.30pm Mon-Sat) Simon hasn't had to change the menu of sandwiches with thick-cut bread and wholesome vegetarian soups since he first opened shop two decades ago – and why should he? His grub is as heartening and legendary as he is. It's a great place to sip a coffee and watch life go by in the old-fashioned arcade.

Yamamori JAPANESE €€

(Map p70; ☎01-475 5001; 71 South Great George's St; mains €16-25, lunch bento €9.95; ⊙12.30-11pm) Hip, inexpensive and generally pretty good, Yamamori rarely disappoints with its bubbly service and vivacious cooking that swoops from sushi and sashimi to whopping great plates of noodles, with plenty in between. It's a great spot for a sociable group – including vegetarians – although you'll have to book at the weekend to be one of the happy campers. The lunch bento is one of the best deals in town. There's another branch north of the river (p111).

Listons SANDWICH SHOP €

(Map p78; www.listonsfoodstore.ie; 25 Camden St; lunch €5-12; ⊙8.30am-7.30pm Mon-Thu, to 6.30pm Fri, 10am-6pm Sat) Lunchtime queues out the door testify that Listons is undoubtedly the best deli in Dublin. Its sandwiches with delicious fillings, roasted vegetable quiches, rosemary potato cakes and sublime salads will have you coming back again and again. The only problem is there's too much to choose from. On fine days it's great to retreat to the solitude of the nearby Iveagh Gardens with your gourmet picnic.

Shanahan's on the Green STEAKHOUSE €€€

(Map p78; ☎01-407 0939; www.shanahans.ie; 119 West St Stephen's Green; mains €36-52; ⊙from 6pm Mon-Thu & Sat & Sun, from noon Fri) 'American-style steakhouse' hardly does justice to this elegant restaurant where JR Ewing and his cronies would happily have done business. Spread across three floors of a stunning Georgian building are four elegant dining areas, where impeccable service and a courteous bonhomie attract the great, the good and the not-so-good to its well-laid-out tables. Although the menu features seafood, this place is all about meat, notably the best cuts of impossibly juicy and tender Irish Angus beef you'll find anywhere on the island.

The mountainous onion rings are the perfect accompaniment, while the sommeliers are among the best in the business.

Gourmet Burger Kitchen BURGERS €€
(www.gbkinfo.com; burgers €9-13) South William St (Map p70; 14 South William St; ⏲noon-10pm Sun-Wed, noon-11pm Thu-Sat); South Anne St (Map p70; 5 South Anne St; ⏲noon-10pm Sun-Wed, noon-11pm Thu-Sat); Temple Bar (Map p70; Unit 1, Temple Bar Sq; ⏲noon-11pm Mon-Sat, noon-10pm Sun) Burgers are back, and they don't get any better than the ones served at the three city-centre branches of this restaurant. The menu has a big range of choice, from your straight-up beef burger with cheese to something a little more adventurous: how about a Kiwi-burger topped with beetroot, egg, pineapple, cheese, salad and relish? They also have decent vegie options.

Odessa MEDITERRANEAN €€
(Map p70; ☎01-670 7634; 13 Dame Ct; mains €13-26; lunch & dinner Wed-Sun; ♿) Odessa's lounge atmosphere, with comfy sofas and retro standard lamps, has long attracted the city's hipsters, who flock here for homemade burgers, steaks or daily fish specials. You may not escape the sofa after you've quaffed a few of Odessa's renowned cocktails while playing a game of backgammon. Weekend brunch is *extremely* popular.

Shebeen Chic IRISH €€
(Map p70; 5 South Great George's St; mains €10-15; ⏲noon-10pm Sun-Wed, to 11pm Thu-Sat) Cracked chandeliers, paintings hung at odd angles and ne'er a matching table-and-chair set create the suitably ramshackle tone for a restaurant whose name comes from the Irish word for 'illegal drinking establishment'. The menu reads like it was written by Tom Waits: 'spudballs with broccoli, mushrooms and auld cheddar', or 'leek, spud and maybe mud' are representatives of a cuisine best described as 'Irish with attitude'. In the basement is a bar with a speakeasy vibe.

Larder FUSION €€
(Map p70; 8 Parliament St; mains €6-10; ⏲8am-6pm) This welcoming cafe-restaurant has a positively organic vibe to it, what with its wholesome porridge breakfasts, gourmet sandwiches such as *serrano* ham, gruyère and rocket (arugula), and speciality Suki teas (try the Gunpowder Green Tea). It's confident about its food – we like the fact that it lists suppliers – and so are we.

Avoca CAFE €€
(Map p64; www.avoca.ie; 11-13 Suffolk St; mains €11-14) The waiters are easy on the eye for a reason: the upstairs cafe of the city's best designer crafts store has long been the favourite spot of the Ladies Who Lunch. Designer bags can get very heavy, so there's nothing better to restore flagging energy than the simple, rustic delights on offer: organic shepherd's pie, roast lamb with couscous, or sumptuous salads from the Avoca kitchen. There's also a takeaway salad bar and hot counter in the basement. For more information on the handicrafts, see p122.

FARMERS & ORGANIC MARKETS

Dublin Food Co-op (Map p60; www.dublinfoodcoop.com; 12 Newmarket; ⏲2-8pm Thu, 9.30am-4.30pm Sat) A buzzing community market specialising in organic veg, homemade cheeses and organic wines; there's also a bakery and even baby-changing facilities.

Coppinger Row Market (Map p70; Coppinger Row; ⏲9am-7pm Thu) It's small – only a handful of stalls – but it packs a proper organic punch, attracting punters with the waft of freshly baked breads, delicious hummus and other goodies.

Harcourt St Food Market (Map p78; www.irishfarmersmarkets.ie; Park Pl, Station Bldgs, Upper Hatch St; ⏲10am-4pm Thu) Organic vegies, cheeses, olives and meats made into dishes from all over the world.

Temple Bar Farmers Market (Map p70; Meeting House Sq; ⏲9am-4.30pm Sat) This great little market is a fabulous place to while away a Saturday morning, sampling and munching on organic gourmet goodies bound by the market's only rule: local producers only. From cured meats to wildflowers, you could fill an entire pantry with their selection of delights.

For more info on local markets, check out www.irishfarmersmarkets.ie, www.irishvillagemarkets.com or local county council sites such as www.dlrcoco.ie/markets.

Thornton's FRENCH €€€

(Map p78; ☎01-478 7000; www.thorntonsrestaurant.com; 128 St Stephen's Green; midweek 2-/3-course lunch €25/49, dinner tasting menus €79-125; ⏰12.30-2pm & 7-10pm Tue-Sat) Kevin Thornton shrugged his shoulders when Michelin saw fit to strip him of one of his two stars, and replied by ordering a refurb of his über-trendy room on the 1st floor of the Fitzwilliam Hotel overlooking St Stephen's Green. The food – a mouth-watering Irish interpretation of new French cuisine – remains as good as ever, offering a mix of succulent seafood and gamey dishes like roast woodcock. A nice touch is Kevin himself making a round of the tables, answering questions and explaining the dishes. He also offers an all-day masterclass (€200) on how to recreate his cuisine.

Marco Pierre White Steakhouse & Grill STEAKHOUSE €€€

(Map p64; www.marcopierrewhite.ie; 51 Dawson St; mains €26-35; ⏰noon-11pm) Bad boy chef Marco Pierre White (he who once made Gordon Ramsay cry) lent his name and designed the menu at this casual but upmarket steakhouse, where cuts of beef (and hunks of fish) are the fare, presented with a minimum of fuss but with plenty of taste.

Cake Café CAFE €

(Map p78; Pleasant Pl; mains €2-8; ⏰10am-6pm; 👪) Dublin's best-kept pastry secret is this great little cafe in a tough-to-find lane just off Lower Camden St. The easiest way in is through Daintree stationery shop (61 Camden St); through the back of the Daintree is the self-contained yard, which in good weather is the best spot to enjoy a coffee and a homemade cake.

Queen of Tarts CAFE €

(Map p70; snacks from €4) Cork Hill (4 Cork Hill; ⏰7.30am-6pm Mon-Fri); Cow's Lane (Map p70; 3-4 Cow's Lane; ⏰7.30am-6pm) Pocket-sized Queen of Tarts, with its mouth-watering array of savoury tarts and filled focaccias, fruit crumbles and wicked pastries, was so popular that they opened a bigger version around the corner on Cow's Lane. Either is perfect for breakfast or lunch.

Wagamama JAPANESE €€

(Map p70; South King St; mains €11-18; ⏰11am-11pm) There's ne'er a trace of raw fish to be seen, but this popular chain dishes up some terrific Japanese food nonetheless. Production-line rice and noodle dishes served pronto at canteen-style tables mightn't seem like the most inviting way to dine, but boy this food is good, and the basement it's served up in is surprisingly light and airy – for a place with absolutely no natural light.

Saba ASIAN FUSION €€

(Map p70; ☎01-679 2000; www.sabadublin.com; 26-28 Clarendon St; mains €12-23; ⏰lunch & dinner) The name means 'happy meeting place' and so far this Thai–Vietnamese fusion restaurant has proven to be just that, packed virtually every night with all sorts tucking into the extensive Southeast Asian menu amid the kind of contemporary decor that screams designer cool. We thought both the menu and the look were good without being exceptional, but it's really popular, so what the hell do we know?

Cliff Townhouse IRISH €€€

(Map p78; ☎01-638 3939; www.bentleysdublin.com; 22 North St Stephen's Green; mains €19-35; ⏰noon-2.30pm & 6-11pm Mon-Sat, noon-4pm & 6-10pm Sun) Emboldened by the Michelin star awarded to its sister property in Ardmore (p195), Sean Smith's menu is a confident expression of the very best of Irish cuisine – Warrenpoint fish pie, organic fillet of pork and a loin of venison share the menu with a masterful fish and chips.

Brasserie Sixty6 FUSION €€

(Map p70; www.brasseriesixty6.com; 66 South Great George's St; mains €12-20; ⏰8am-11.30pm Mon-Sat, from 11am Sun) This New York–style brasserie does a mean rotisserie chicken, four different ways at any given time. Besides its signature dish, the meat-heavy menu features things like lamb shank and a particularly good bit of liver. For that special occasion, there's a whole roast pig, but you need to order seven days in advance and be in a group of eight.

Eden FUSION €€€

(Map p70; ☎01-670 5372; www.edenrestaurant.ie; Meeting House Sq; mains €15-28; ⏰noon-2.30pm & 6-10.30pm Mon-Fri, noon-3pm & 6-11pm Sat & Sun; 👪) The epitome of Temple Bar chic, Eden's minimalist look – designed to look something like the interior of an (empty) swimming pool – and contemporary European menu has earned plenty of kudos over the last decade. The menu, which offers dishes as diverse as braised lamb shank with Moroccan spices and organic beef and Guinness stew, is generally excellent, but we enjoy it best at brunch on the much-sought-after ground-floor terrace. Try to avoid the upstairs dining room, which can get very hot.

Zaytoon MIDDLE EASTERN €
(shish kebab meal €11; ⌚noon-4am) Temple Bar (Map p70; 14-15 Parliament St); Camden St (Map p78; 44-55 Upper Camden St) If at the end of the night you need something to absorb the booze, then the Middle Eastern delights at this joint are the thing for you. Just don't expect anything more than what makes up a kebab.

Fallon & Byrne DELICATESSEN & BRASSERIE €€
(Map p70; Exchequer St; deli mains €6-9, brasserie mains €18-27; ⌚deli 9am-8pm Mon-Sat, 11am-6pm Sun, brasserie noon-4.30pm & 6.30-10.30pm Mon-Wed, to 11.30pm Thu-Sat, 11am-4pm Sun) Dublin's answer to New York's much-loved upmarket grocery store Dean & Deluca is this food hall, wine cellar and restaurant. The queues for the delicious deli counter are constant, even if the chic brasserie upstairs isn't quite the gastronomic feast you'd expect. For wine and nibbles, go downstairs to the well-stocked cave, pick your tipple from the hundreds on offer and while away an evening.

Good World CHINESE €€
(Map p70; 18 South Great George's St; dim sum €4-6, mains €11-18; ⌚12.30pm-2.30am) A hands-down winner of our 'best Chinese restaurant' competition, the Good World has two menus, but to really get the most out of this terrific spot, steer well clear of the Western menu and its unimaginative fare. With listings in two languages, the Chinese menu is packed with dishes and delicacies that keep us coming back for more.

Market Bar TAPAS €€
(Map p70; Fade St; mains €8.50-14; ⌚noon-11pm) This one-time sausage factory, now a trendy bar, also has a super kitchen knocking out Spanish tapas and other Iberian-influenced bites. Dishes come in half and full portions, so you can mix and match your dishes and not pig out. Proof that the carvery lunch isn't the height of pub dining.

Juice VEGETARIAN €€
(Map p70; 73 South Great George's St; mains €11-16; ⌚noon-10pm Mon-Thu, noon-11pm Fri & Sat, 10am-10pm Sun) Lighten up, folks, it's just food! If the staff at this trendy, self-conscious vegetarian restaurant lost some of their attitude and smiled occasionally, we might actually forget the cool-out and focus on the terrific Pacific Rim–style cuisine, as well as tasty stir-fries, soups, wraps, soya desserts, organic wines and, of course, delicious fresh juices and smoothies. Isn't yoga supposed to be *relaxing*?

THE LIBERTIES & KILMAINHAM

Fast-food outlets and greasy-spoon diners still dominate the food map in this part of the city, but there's one spot that rises out of the boiling oil and batter-in-a-bucket and takes its place among the legends.

Leo Burdock's FISH & CHIPS €
(Map p70; 2 Werburgh St; cod & chips €8.50; ⌚noon-midnight Mon-Sat, 4pm-midnight Sun) You will often hear that you haven't eaten in Dublin until you've queued in the cold for a cod and chips wrapped in paper from the city's most famous chipper. Total codswallop, of course, but there's something about sitting on the street, balancing the bag on your lap and trying to eat the chips quickly before they go cold and horrible that smacks of Dublin in a bygone age. It's nice to revisit the past, especially if you don't have to get stuck there.

NORTH OF THE LIFFEY

Bar a couple of classy restaurants and one simply outstanding one, the northside's greatest contribution to the city's restaurant map has been in ethnic cuisine: Parnell St and Capel St particularly abound with Chinese, Korean and African eateries; you can spot the good ones by how popular they are with the local immigrant communities.

TOP CHOICE **Chapter One** MODERN IRISH €€€
(Map p86; ☎01-873 2266; www.chapteronerestaurant.com; 18 North Parnell Sq; mains €32-72; ⌚12.30-2pm Tue-Fri, 6-11pm Tue-Sat) One of the best restaurants in Dublin, this venerable old trooper in the vaulted basement of the Dublin Writers Museum sets its ambitions no further than modern Irish cuisine, which it has realised so brilliantly that those Michelin lads saw fit to throw one of their sought-after stars its way. Menus change regularly but the dishes are always top-notch, the service first class and the atmosphere reassuringly reserved – although its success means that you have to book well in advance to land a table. Get there between 6pm and 7.40pm for the three-course pre-theatre special (€37.50).

Winding Stair MODERN IRISH €€€

(Map p86; ☎01-873 7320; 40 Lower Ormond Quay; mains €21-27; ⊙noon-4pm & 6-10pm Tue-Sat, 1-10pm Sun) Housed within a beautiful Georgian building that was once home to the city's most beloved bookshop (the ground floor still is one), the conversion to elegant restaurant has been faultless. The wonderful Irish menu – creamy fish pie, bacon and organic cabbage, steamed mussels and Irish farmyard cheeses – coupled with an excellent wine list make for a memorable meal.

Taste of Emilia ITALIAN €

(Map p86; 28 Lower Liffey St; mains €4-10; ⊙7.30am-7pm Mon-Wed & Fri & Sat, to 9.30pm Thu) Half bar, half Italian deli, this warm, buzzing locale does a wonderful trade in cured meats and cheeses from all over Italy, paying particular attention to the produce of the true heartland of Italian cuisine, Emilia-Romagna. The sandwiches are made with homemade *piadina* bread or *tigelle,* and you can wash it down with a light sparkling wine from Northern Italy. Italians love the joint, and it's no wonder.

Yamamori Sushi JAPANESE €€

(Map p86; www.yamamorinoodles.ie; 38-39 Lower Ormond Quay; sushi €3-3.50, mains €16-35; ⊙lunch & dinner Sun-Wed, dinner Thu-Sat) Sushi arrives on the northside and immediately proves successful, but that's hardly surprising considering that its southside sister has been doing the Japanese thang with great aplomb for a very long time. The menus in both are largely the same, but we prefer this newer location – right on the river – because it's just that little bit more airy and spacious. The bento boxes are a popular choice – especially at lunchtime – but we really just can't get enough of the Nami Moriawase (€25).

Enoteca delle Langhe ITALIAN €

(Map p86; Bloom's Lane; mains €8-10; ⊙lunch & dinner) Developer, Italophile and recently elected parliamentarian Mick Wallace's Italian Quarter – as the lane between Ormond Quay and Great Strand St is known – has a trio of eateries that serve simple pastas, antipasti and cheeses. It also has an excellent selection of Piedmontese wines.

Bar Italia ITALIAN €€

(Map p86; 28 Lower Ormond Quay; mains €9-15; ⊙10.30am-11pm Mon-Sat, 1-9pm Sun) A well-established and authentic Italian restaurant that specialises in ever-changing pasta dishes, homemade risottos and excellent Palombini coffee.

Kim Chi/Hop House ASIAN €€

(Map p86; www.hophouse.ie; 160 Parnell St; buffet €8-13; ⊙closed lunch Sun) Two distinct halves – one strictly Korean, the other very Irish – make up this buzzy eatery on one of Dublin's most ethnically diverse streets. The food – a mixture of Korean with the odd Japanese bento thrown in for good measure – is served in kimchi (which refers to a pickled vegetable ever-present in Korean cuisine), while just across the room is the Hop House, Korea's version of an Irish bar, where you can wash it all down with a beer, local or imported.

Soup Dragon SOUP BAR €

(Map p86; 168 Capel St; soups €5-10; ⊙8am-5.30pm Mon-Fri, 11am-5pm Sat) Eat in or take away one of 12 tasty varieties of homemade soups, including shepherd's pie or spicy vegetable gumbo. Bowls come in three different sizes, and prices include fresh bread and a piece of fruit. Kick-start your day (or afternoon) with a healthy all-day breakfast selection: try fresh smoothies or the generous bowls of yoghurt, fruit and muesli.

Melody CHINESE €€

(Map p86; ☎01-878 8988; 122 Capel St; buffet €10-18, karaoke rooms €25-60; ⊙5.30pm-midnight) Lots of red lacquer, black marble, a couple of fish tanks and the biggest TV we've ever seen are clear evidence that this place was designed to suit the sensibilities of the city's substantial Chinese community, but it works for the Irish, too: they come, preferably in big groups, and tuck into the fairly standard Chinese fare. Downstairs, a warren of tunnels leads to the karaoke dining rooms – probably the real reason this place is so popular.

Cobalt Café & Gallery CAFE €

(Map p86; ☎01-873 0313; 16 North Great George's St; mains €6-10; ⊙10am-4.30pm Mon-Fri) This elegant cafe in a bright and airy Georgian drawing room is a must if you're in the 'hood. Almost opposite the James Joyce Cultural Centre, Cobalt has a simple menu, but you can enjoy hearty soups by a roaring fire in winter, or fresh sandwiches in the garden on warmer days.

VEGIE BITES

Blazing Salads (Map p70; 42 Drury St; mains €4-9; ⌚10am-6pm Mon-Sat, to 8pm Thu) Organic breads (many suitable for special diets), Californian-style salads, smoothies and pizza slices can all be taken away from this delicious vegetarian deli.

Fresh (Map p70; top fl, Powerscourt Townhouse Shopping Centre, 59 South William St; lunch €6-12; ⌚9.30am-6pm Mon-Sat, 10am-5pm Sun) This long-standing vegetarian restaurant serves a variety of salads and filling, hot daily specials. Many dishes are dairy- and gluten-free without compromising taste. The baked potato topped with organic cheese (€5.50) comes with two salads and is a hearty meal in itself.

Cornucopia (Map p64; 19 Wicklow St; mains from €6; ⌚9am-7pm Mon-Wed & Fri & Sat, to 9pm Thu) For those escaping the Irish cholesterol habit, Cornucopia is a popular wholefood cafe turning out healthy goodies. There's even a hot vegetarian breakfast as an alternative to muesli.

Govinda's (www.govindas.ie; mains €7-11) Aungier St (Map p70; 4 Aungier St; ⌚noon-9pm Mon-Sat); Merrion Row (Map p78; 18 Merrion Row; ⌚noon-9pm Mon-Sat); Middle Abbey St (Map p86; 83 Middle Abbey St; ⌚noon-9pm Mon-Sat, to 7pm Sun) Authentic beans-and-pulses vegetarian place run by the Hare Krishna, now with branches on both sides of the river. The cheap, wholesome mix of salads and Indian-influenced hot daily specials are filling and tasty.

DOCKLANDS

Although the crash has put paid to some of the grander plans for restaurant openings in the Docklands, there are a couple of good options that reflect the best of new dining in the city.

Ely CHQ Bar & Brasserie FUSIO €€
(Map p91; www.elywinebar.ie; Custom House Quay; mains €15-24; ⌚noon-3pm & 6-10pm Mon-Fri, 1-4pm & 6-10pm Sat;) Scrummy homemade burgers, bangers and mash, and wild smoked salmon salad are some of the meals you'll find in this restaurant contained within a converted tobacco warehouse in the heart of the International Financial Services Centre (IFSC). Dishes are prepared with organic and free-range produce from the owner's family farm in County Clare, so you can rest assured of the quality. There's a large wine list to choose from, with over 70 sold by the glass. There's another branch, **Ely HQ** (Map p91; Hanover Quay; ⌚lunch & dinner Mon-Sun) on the other side of the river by Grand Canal Sq, which has been branded a gastro-pub.

herbstreet FUSION €€
(Map p91; www.herbstreet.ie; Hanover Quay; mains €13-19; ⌚lunch & dinner Mon-Fri, dinner only Sat) The hand-driers use low power, the LED lighting uses 1 watt per bulb, the chairs date from 1956 and the wines are European only: this eatery is taking its green responsibilities seriously by making sure its carbon footprint is as shallow as possible. The fish is farmed locally and all of the other dishes – nothing too radical, just fine, delicious portions of sandwiches, burgers, salads – are sourced as close to the restaurant as they can.

Quay 16 FUSION €€€
(Map p91; ☎01-817 8760; www.mvcillairne.com; MV Cill Airne, North Wall Quay; bar food €12-16, mains €19.50-32; ⌚noon-3pm Mon-Fri, 6-10pm Mon-Sat) MV *Cill Airne,* commissioned in 1961 as a passenger liner tender, is now permanently docked along the north quays, where it serves the public as a bar, bistro and fine restaurant. The food in the restaurant is surprisingly good – dishes like monkfish on saffron risotto and seared beef fillet are expertly done and served with an excellent choice of wines.

BEYOND THE GRAND CANAL

It's hardly surprising that the chichi southern suburbs would have their fair share of decent eateries – it's where the city's privileged classes can turn their collars up and unwind after a hard day of making money. If you're in Ranelagh or Ballsbridge, there's always somewhere to get a decent bite.

Juniors ITALIAN €€
(Map p60; ☎01-664 3648; www.juniors.ie; 2 Bath Ave, Sandymount; mains €15-24; ⌚lunch & dinner) Cramped and easily mistaken for any old cafe, Juniors is anything but ordinary:

designed to imitate a New York deli, the food (Italian-influenced, all locally sourced produce) is delicious, the atmosphere always buzzing (it's often hard to get a table) and the ethos top-notch, which is down to the two brothers who run the place.

Paulie's Pizza ITALIAN €€
(Map p60; www.juniors.ie; 58 Upper Grand Canal St; pizzas €12-16; ⌚closed dinner Mon & lunch Sat & Sun) In July 2010 the brothers who created Juniors (just around the corner) imported a traditional Neapolitan pizza oven and set about introducing Dubliners to proper, thin-crusted pizza from the city of its birthplace. Margheritas, biancas (no tomato sauce), calzone and other Neapolitan specialities are the real treat, but there's also room for a classic New York slice as well as a few local creations.

Expresso Bar CONTINENTAL €€
(Map p60; ☎01-660 0585; 1 St Mary's Rd, Ballsbridge; mains €9-17; ⌚7.30am-9.15pm Mon-Fri, 9am-9.15pm Sat & 10am-5pm Sun) Just across the street from the Dylan hotel, this bright and cheery spot does a roaring trade for Sunday brunch – and you've a good chance to spot an Irish celeb or two. The eggs Benedict are excellent.

Drinking

Come hell or high water, Dubliners will always take a drink, and if you don't join them for at least one you will never crack the social code that makes this city tick – and you'll run the risk of being dismissed as a dry shite who really doesn't know how to enjoy themselves. No pressure, then.

It'll hardly come as a surprise that there are some good pubs in Dublin – it's probably one of the main reasons you came here in the first place – but first-time visitors may be taken aback by the protagonist's role the pub has in virtually every Dubliner's social life. The pub is a meeting point for friends and strangers alike, a place to mark a moment and pass the time, a forum for discourse and a temple of silent contemplation. It is where Dubliners are at their friendly and convivial best – and at their drunken and belligerent worst.

There are pubs for every taste and sensibility, although the *truly* traditional haunts populated by flat-capped pensioners bursting with insightful anecdotes are about as rare as hen's teeth: the city has been overwhelmed by designer bars and themed locales that could be found pretty much anywhere else in the world. But despair not, for it is not the spit or sawdust that makes a great Dublin pub (although it can help with the setting) but the patrons themselves.

Last orders are at 11.30pm Monday to Thursday, 12.30am Friday and Saturday and 11pm on Sunday, with 30 minutes' drinking-up time each night. However, many central pubs have licences to serve until 1.30am or 2.30am.

For gay and lesbian bars, see the boxed text, p100.

GRAFTON STREET & AROUND

TOP CHOICE Stag's Head PUB
(Map p70; 1 Dame Ct) The Stag's Head was built in 1770, remodelled in 1895 and thankfully not changed a bit since then. It's a superb pub: so picturesque that it often appears in films and also featured in a postage-stamp series on Irish bars. It's probable that some of the fitters who worked on this pub would have also worked on churches in the area, so the stained-wood-and-polished-brass similarities are no accident.

Anseo BAR
(Map p78; 28 Lower Camden St) Unpretentious, unaffected and incredibly popular, this cosy alternative bar is a favourite with those who live by the credo that to try too hard is far worse than not trying at all. Wearing cool like a loose garment, the punters thrive on the mix of chat and terrific music.

Kehoe's PUB
(Map p70; 9 South Anne St) This is one of the most atmospheric pubs in the city centre and a real favourite with all kinds of Dubliners. It has a beautiful Victorian bar, a wonderful snug, and plenty of other little nooks and crannies. Upstairs, drinks are served in what was once the publican's living room. And it looks it!

Whelan's BAR
(Map p78; www.whelanslive.com; 25 Wexford St) The bar of one of the city's most beloved live music venues is always full of earnest young things on a good night out. The bar is done up like a traditional pub, the crowd are fun and the music is all kinds of rock, folk and contemporary.

Long Hall PUB
(Map p70; 51 South Great George's St) Luxuriating in full Victorian splendour, this is one of the city's most beautiful and best-loved

1

5

4

1. St Stephen's Green (p75)
Enjoy a stroll and feed the ducks in Dublin's green heart.

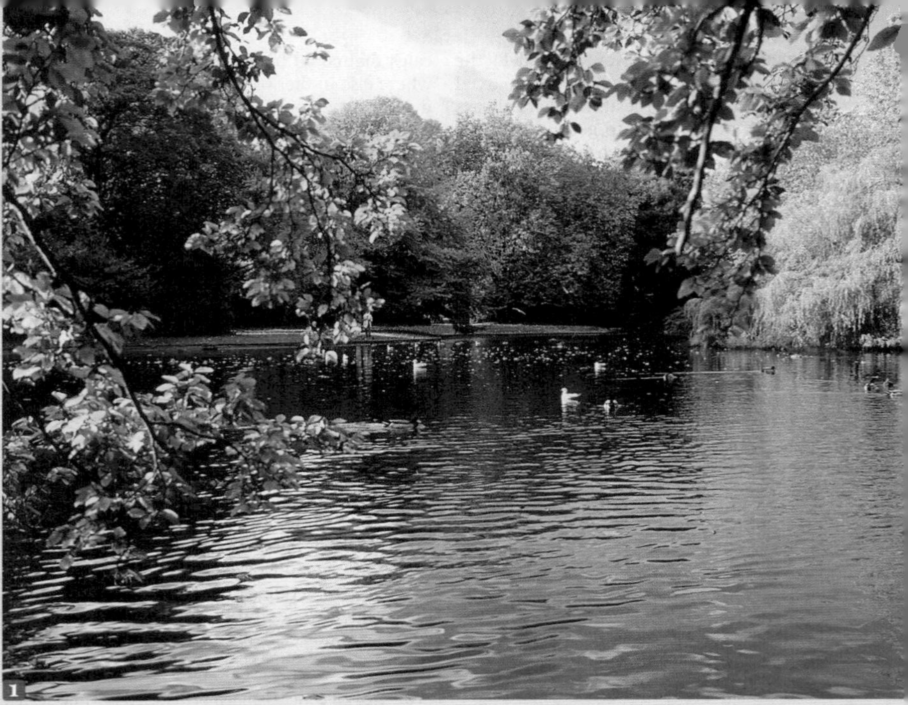

2. Temple Bar (p64)
Kick up your heels in the cobbled maze of Temple Bar.

EOIN CLARKE/LONELYPLANETIMAGES ©

2

3. Spire (p85)
The 120m-tall Spire dominates O'Connell St.

4. Ha'penny Bridge (p68)
A ha'penny toll was once needed to cross this bridge over the River Liffey.

5. Temple Bar (p64)
Street musician strumming in Temple Bar.

3

RICHARD I'ANSON/LONELYPLANETIMAGES ©

pubs. Check out the elegant chandeliers and the ornate carvings in the woodwork behind the bar. The bartenders are experts at their craft – an increasingly rare experience in Dublin these days.

Dawson Lounge PUB
(Map p78; 25 Dawson St) To see the smallest bar in Dublin, go through a small doorway, down a narrow flight of steps and into two tiny rooms that always seem to be filled with a couple of bedraggled drunks who look like they're hiding. Psst, here's a secret: a certain sunglassed lead singer of a certain ginormous Irish band is said to love unwinding in here from time to time.

No Name Bar BAR
(Map p70; 3 Fade St) A low-key entrance just next to L'Gueuleton leads upstairs to one of the nicest bar spaces in town – three huge rooms in a restored Victorian town house plus a sizeable heated patio area for smokers. It gets its name from not having one.

John Mulligan's PUB
(Map p86; 8 Poolbeg St) Outside the eastern boundary of Temple Bar, John Mulligan's is another pub that has scarcely changed over the years. It featured as the local in the film *My Left Foot* and is also popular with journalists from the nearby newspaper offices. Mulligan's was established in 1782 and was long reputed to have the best Guinness in town, as well as a wonderfully varied collection of regulars.

South William DJ BAR
(Map p70; South William St) Its star doesn't shine quite as brightly as it did a few years ago when it opened, but this remains one of the hippest bars in town. Behind the glass frontage you'll get top-class music, great DJs and a downstairs club.

Grogan's Castle Lounge PUB
(Map p70; 15 South William St) A city-centre institution, Grogan's has long been a favourite haunt of Dublin's writers and painters, as well as others from the bohemian, alternative set. An odd quirk of the pub is that drinks are marginally cheaper in the stone-floor bar than the carpeted lounge, even though they are served by the same bar!

Hogan's BAR
(Map p70; 35 South Great George's St) Hogan's is a gigantic boozer spread across two floors. A popular hang-out for young professionals, it gets very full at the weekend with folks eager to take advantage of its late licence.

Bernard Shaw BAR
(Map p60; www.bodytonicmusic.com; 11-12 South Richmond St) This old-style pub was taken over a couple of years ago by the Bodytonic production crew and restyled as one of the hippest joints in town. There are DJs nightly, playing anything from dub reggae to ambient electronica.

Market Bar BAR
(Map p70; Fade St) This fashionable watering hole is run by the same guys as the Globe around the corner. Little would you know this beautiful, airy Victorian space was a sausage factory in a former life.

James Toner's PUB
(Map p78; 139 Lower Baggot St) With its stone floor, Toner's is almost a country pub in the heart of the city, and the shelves and drawers are reminders that it once doubled as a grocery store. Not that its suit-wearing business crowd would ever have shopped here…

Hartigan's PUB
(Map p78; 100 Lower Leeson St) This is about as spartan a bar as you'll find in the city, and it's the daytime home to some serious drinkers, who appreciate the quiet, no-frills surroundings. In the evening it's popular with students from the medical faculty of University College Dublin.

O'Donoghue's PUB
(Map p78; 15 Merrion Row) Still the most famous traditional music bar in Dublin, O'Donoghue's is where world-famous folk group the Dubliners started off in the 1960s. On summer evenings a young, international crowd spills out into the courtyard beside the pub.

Porterhouse BAR
(Map p70; 16-18 Parliament St) Dublin's first microbrewery is our favourite Temple Bar watering hole. Especially popular with foreign residents and visitors, the Porterhouse sells only its own stouts and beers – and they're all excellent.

Bruxelles PUB
(Map p70; 7-8 Harry St) This place has weekly live rock music, perhaps the only link the now trendy pub has to its heavy-metal past.

International Bar PUB
(Map p70; 23 Wicklow St) The International has live jazz and blues most nights.

Oliver St John Gogarty's PUB
(Map p64; 58-59 Fleet St) There's live traditional music nightly at this busy Temple Bar pub, catering to a mostly tourist crowd.

NORTH OF THE LIFFEY

Sin É BAR
(Map p70; 14-15 Upper Ormond Quay) This excellent quayside bar is proof that the most important quality for any pub is ambience. There's no real decor to speak of, but this place buzzes almost nightly with a terrific mix of students and professionals, the hip and the uncool. It helps that the DJs here are all uniformly excellent.

Cobblestone PUB
(Map p60; North King St) This pub is on the main square in Smithfield, an old northside marketplace. There's a great atmosphere in the cosy upstairs bar, where the nightly music sessions – both traditional and up-and-coming folk and singer-songwriter acts – are superb.

The Grand Social BAR
(Map p86; www.thegrandsocial.ie; 35 Lower Liffey St) This new multi-purpose venue hosts club nights, comedy and live music gigs as well as being a decent bar for a drink. It's spread across three floors, each of which has a different theme: The Parlour downstairs; the mid-level Ballroom (where the dancing is) and the upstairs Loft, which hosts a variety of events.

Dice Bar BAR
(Map p60; 79 Queen St) Co-owned by singer Huey from the band Fun Lovin' Criminals, the Dice Bar looks like something you'd find on New York's Lower East Side. Its black-and-red-painted interior, dripping candles and distressed seating, combined with rocking DJs most nights, make this place a magnet for Dublin's beatnik crowds.

Hughes' Bar PUB
(Map p60; 19 Chancery St) Directly behind the Four Courts, this bar has nightly, if impromptu, sessions that often result in a closed door – that is, they go on long past official closing time. The pub is also a popular lunchtime spot with barristers working nearby.

Flowing Tide PUB
(Map p86; 9 Lower Abbey St) This beautiful and atmospheric old pub is directly opposite the Abbey Theatre and is predictably very popular with theatre-goers – it can get swamped around 11pm, after the curtain comes down. They blend in with some no-bullshit locals who give the place a vital edge and make it a great place for a drink and a natter.

Palace Bar PUB
(Map p64; 21 Fleet St) With its mirrors and wooden niches, Palace Bar is often said to be the perfect example of an old Dublin pub. It's within Temple Bar and is popular with journalists from the nearby *Irish Times*.

Sackville Lounge PUB
(Map p86; Sackville Pl) This tiny one-room, wood-panelled 19th-century bar is discreetly located just off O'Connell St, which perhaps explains why it's so popular with actors, theatregoers and anyone who appreciates a nice pint in a gorgeous old-style bar.

☆ Entertainment

From period drama to dog racing, Dublin's range of amusements is enough to satisfy *almost* all desires. For entertainment information, pick up a copy of the *Dublin Event Guide* (www.dublineventguide.com), a bimonthly freebie available at many locations, including bars, cafes and hostels or the fortnightly music-review *Hot Press* (www.hotpress.com). Friday's *Irish Times* has a pull-out entertainment section called the *Ticket*, which has comprehensive listings of clubs and gigs; the *Irish Independent's* version, also out on Friday, is called *Day & Night*.

Rock & Pop

Dublin's love affair with popular music has made it one of the preferred touring stops for all kinds of musicians, who seem to relish the unfettered manner in which audiences embrace their favourite artists. There are venues of every size; bookings can be made either directly at the venues or through **HMV** (Map p70; ☎01-679 5334; 65 Grafton St) or **Ticketmaster** (☎0818 719 300, 01-456 9569; www.ticketmaster.ie), but they charge between 9% and 12.5% service charge *per ticket*, not per booking, on credit-card bookings.

Workman's Club LIVE MUSIC
(Map p70; ☎01-670 6692; www.theworkmansclub.com; 10 Wellington Quay) A 300-capacity venue and bar in the former workingmen's club of Dublin, this new spot puts the emphasis on

keeping away from the mainstream, which means a broad range of performers, from singer-songwriters to electronic cabaret.

Button Factory NIGHTCLUB
(Map p70; ☎01-670 9202; www.buttonfactory.ie; Curved St) A top-class sound system, a carpeted back bar and a big main stage make this an excellent venue to hear some of the more interesting visiting and local acts.

Vicar Street LIVE MUSIC
(Map p60; ☎01-454 5533; www.vicarstreet.com; 58-59 Thomas St) Smaller performances take place at this intimate venue, near Christ Church Cathedral. It has a capacity of 1000, spread between table-serviced group seating downstairs and a theatre-style balcony. It has a varied program of performers, with a strong emphasis on folk and jazz.

O2 LIVE MUSIC
(Map p91; ☎01-819 8888; www.theo2.ie; East Link Bridge, North Wall Quay) The premier indoor venue in the city has a capacity of around 10,000 and plays host to the very brightest stars in the firmament: Rihanna, Bryan Adams and the cast of Glee are just some of the acts that have brought their magic to its superb stage.

Whelan's LIVE MUSIC
(Map p78; ☎01-478 0766; www.whelanslive.com; 25 Wexford St) Whelan's near-legendary status as the home of the sensitive, soul-searching singer – and where gigs are treated like semi-mystical experiences by their devoted fans – is inevitably the cause of much derision in some Dublin quarters, but there's no denying the venue's special place in the Dublin musical scene. It's a pretty intimate space, perfect if you're looking to 'connect' with your favourite artists, who will most likely be cadging drinks off fans in the bar afterwards.

Crawdaddy LIVE MUSIC
(Map p78; ☎01-478 0225; www.pod.ie; 35A Harcourt St) Named after the London club where the Stones launched their professional careers in 1963, Crawdaddy is an intimate bar/venue that specialises in putting on rootsy performers, from African drum bands to avant-garde jazz artists and flamenco guitarists. It's attached to the nightclub Tripod.

DUBLIN BY SONG

Dublin is one of the most musical cities in Europe, so it stands to reason that there are a few worthwhile songs that sing its praises – and its faults. Here's our pick of tracks to download to your MP3 to enrich your Dublin saunter:

» **Running to Stand Still** (U2) A poignant portrayal of the 1980s heroin epidemic; the 'seven towers' of the song refer to a (now demolished) notorious flat complex in the north city suburb of Ballymun.

» **Old Town** (Philip Lynott) If you want to see what Dublin looked like at the end of '80s, check out the video for this fabulous tune on You Tube.

» **Summer in Dublin** (Bagatelle) A nostalgic, singalong pop tune that was the band's biggest hit and the city's favourite song about itself.

» **City of Screams** (Paranoid Visions) Dublin in the 1980s, as imagined in all its anger and ugliness by the city's foremost '80s punk band

» **Phil Lynott** (Jape) Captures the essence of the city today – without naming any locations.

The city's most famous folk band, the Dubliners, have a bunch of songs about the capital – these are our favourites:

» **Auld Triangle** Taken from Brendan Behan's play *The Quare Fellow*, this poignant tune is about being imprisoned in Mountjoy Prison.

» **Raglan Road** Patrick Kavanagh's poem given music, life and profound meaning by Luke Kelly.

» **Rocky Road to Dublin** A traditional 19th-century tune about a difficult journey to Dublin.

» **Take Her up to Monto** A charming traditional ditty about taking a girl up to the city's one-time notorious red-light district.

Village LIVE MUSIC
(Map p78; ☎01-475 8555; www.thevillagevenue.com; 26 Wexford St) An attractive midsize venue that is a popular stop for acts on the way up and down, the Village has gigs virtually every night of the week, featuring a diverse range of rock bands and solo performers. It's also a good showcase for local singer-songwriters.

Ambassador Theatre THEATRE
(Map p86; ☎1890 925 100; O'Connell St) The Ambassador started life as a theatre and then became a cinema. Not much has changed inside, making it a cool retro place to see visiting and local rock acts perform.

Gaiety Theatre THEATRE
(Map p78; ☎01-677 1717; www.gaietytheatre.com; South King St; ⏰to 4am) This old Victorian theatre is an atmospheric place to come and listen to late-night jazz, rock or blues on the weekend.

Olympia Theatre THEATRE
(Map p70; ☎01-677 7744; Dame St) This pleasantly tatty place features everything from disco to country on Friday nights; the eclectic 'Midnight at the Olympia' runs from midnight to 2am on Friday.

Sugar Club LIVE MUSIC
(Map p78; ☎01-678 7188; 8 Lower Leeson St) There's live jazz, cabaret and soul music at weekends in this comfortable new theatre-style venue on the corner of St Stephen's Green.

Classical

Classical music concerts and opera take place in a number of city-centre venues. There are also occasional performances in churches; check the press for details.

Grand Canal Theatre THEATRE
(Map p91; ☎01-677 7999; www.grandcanaltheatre.ie; Grand Canal Sq) Daniel Liebeskind's masterful design is a three-tiered, 2000-capacity auditorium where you're as likely to be entertained by the Bolshoi or a touring state opera as you are to see Disney on Ice or Barbra Streisand. It's a magnificent venue – designed for classical, paid for by the classics.

National Concert Hall LIVE MUSIC
(Map p78; ☎01-417 0000; www.nch.ie; Earlsfort Tce) Ireland's premier orchestral hall hosts a variety of concerts year-round, including a series of lunchtime concerts from 1.05pm to 2pm on Tuesdays, June to August.

Gaiety Theatre THEATRE
(Map p78; ☎01-677 1717; www.gaietytheatre.com; South King St) This popular Dublin theatre hosts a program of classical concerts and opera.

Bank of Ireland Arts Centre LIVE MUSIC
(Map p64; ☎01-671 1488; Foster Pl) The arts centre hosts a free, regular, midweek lunchtime recital beginning at 1.15pm, as well as an occasional evening program of concerts. Call for details.

Dublin City Gallery – the Hugh Lane LIVE MUSIC
(Map p86; ☎01-874 1903; www.hughlane.ie; Charlemont House, Parnell Sq) At noon on Sunday, from September to June, the art gallery hosts up to 30 concerts of contemporary classical music.

Nightclubs

Dublin's nightclub scene just doesn't compare to other European capitals. Restrictive opening hours, the proliferation of late-night bars and the squeeze of the musical mainstream have resulted in a fairly tepid scene, although this is often offset by the clubbers themselves, who love to dance and will not let the total absence of rhythm or style get in the way of getting down – a lack of inhibition brought on by a long night's drinking.

The seemingly endless list of what's on is constantly changing, so check out the (by no means exhaustive) listings in the *Event Guide* and *In Dublin*. Most clubs open just after pubs close (11.30pm to midnight) and close at 2.30am or 3am. Admission varies widely, although it's usually cheaper to arrive early (before 11.30pm).

Twisted Pepper NIGHTCLUB
(Map p86; ☎01-873 4800; www.bodytonicmusic.com; 54 Middle Abbey St; ⏰8am-midnight Mon-Wed, 10am-2.30am Thu-Sat) Dublin's coolest new venue comes in four parts: the basement is where you can hear some of the best DJs in town, the stage is for live acts, the mezzanine is a secluded bar area above the stage and the cafe serves Irish breakfast all day. All run by the Bodytonic crew, one of the most exciting music and production crowds in town. What more could you want?

Academy NIGHTCLUB
(Map p86; ☎01-877 9999; 57 Middle Abbey St; admission €6-10; ⏰10.30pm-3am Fri & Sat) A terrific mid-size venue, the Academy's music

policy runs the gamut from disco and R&B to alternative rock and hard dance...whatever keeps them dancing, so long as it's not sellout commercial.

Tripod NIGHTCLUB
(Map p78; ☎01-478 0025; www.pod.ie; 35 Harcourt St; admission €5-20; ⌚Mon-Sat) Launched in late 2006 on the site of former club PoD in the atmospheric old Harcourt St station, Tripod now integrates three venues (geddit?): a state-of-the-art, 1300-capacity live rock and pop venue, a smaller dance club and the intimate live venue Crawdaddy.

Village NIGHTCLUB
(Map p78; ☎01-475 8555; www.thevillagevenue.com; 26 Wexford St; admission €5-11; ⌚Thu-Sat) When the live music ends at the Village, the club music kicks off, taking 600-odd groovers through a consistent mix of new and old tunes, dancefloor classics and whatever else will shake that booty. A great venue, an eager crowd and an overall top night out.

Andrew's Lane Theatre NIGHTCLUB
(Map p70; ☎01-478 0766; St Andrew's Lane; admission €6-12; ⌚10.30pm-3am Thu-Sun) Recently converted from a much-loved theatre, ALT's stripped-down look will please club purists: a huge dancefloor, an amazing sound system and a bar are the essentials to a good night. Add a couple of regular nights (Sunday's Italian Factory is a banging night of European hard house), a regular menu of visiting DJs and live gigs and you've got the makings of a *great* night.

Copper Face Jacks NIGHTCLUB
(Map p78; ☎01-475 8777; Jackson Court Hotel, 29-30 Harcourt St; admission €6-12; ⌚10.30pm-3am) Chart hits and established favourites provide the musical backdrop in Dublin's favourite meat-market, the nightclub of choice for country lads and lasses, nurses, the odd GAA star and even off-duty cops, who are often the biggest miscreants of the lot.

Lillie's Bordello NIGHTCLUB
(Map p64; ☎01-679 9204; www.lilliesbordello.ie; Adam Ct; admission €10-20; ⌚11pm-3am) Lillie's is strictly for big hairs, wannabes and visiting rock stars. Don't think you'll get to rub shoulders with celebs, though, as they'll be whisked out of view and into the VIP room in a flash. As you might expect, the music is mostly safe and commercial.

Cinemas

Ireland boasts the highest attendances in Europe of young filmgoers. Consequently it's best to book in advance by credit card, or be prepared to queue for up to half an hour for tickets at night-time screenings. Dublin's cinemas are more heavily concentrated on the northern side of the Liffey. Admission prices are generally €6 for early afternoon shows and around €9 for the rest of the day.

Irish Film Institute CINEMA
(Map p70; ☎01-679 5744; 6 Eustace St) The multiscreen cinema shows classics and arthouse films. The complex also has a bar, a cafe and a bookshop.

Savoy CINEMA
(Map p86; ☎01-874 6000; Upper O'Connell St; ⌚from 2pm) A traditional four-screen first-run cinema, Savoy has late-night shows at weekends.

Screen CINEMA
(Map p64; ☎01-671 4988; 2 Townsend St; ⌚from 2pm) Between Trinity College and O'Connell Bridge, the Screen shows new independent and smaller commercial films on its three screens.

Cineworld CINEMA
(Map p86; ☎01-872 8400; Parnell Centre, Parnell St; ⌚from 10am) This multiscreen cinema is where you'll get all the mainstream releases.

Sport

Aviva Stadium SPORTS
(Map p56; ☎01-647 3800; www.avivastadium.ie; 11-12 Lansdowne Rd) Gleaming, new 50,000-capacity ground with an eye-catching curvilinear stand in the swanky neighbourhood of Donnybrook. Home to Irish rugby and football internationals.

Croke Park SPORTS
(Map p56; ☎01-836 3222; www.crokepark.ie; Clonliffe Rd; 🚌19 or 19A from city centre) Hurling and Gaelic football games are held from February to November at Europe's fourth-largest stadium (capacity around 82,000), north of the Royal Canal in Drumcondra; see www.gaa.ie for schedules.

Harold's Cross Park SPORTS
(Map p56; ☎01-497 1081; www.igb.ie; 151 Harold's Cross Rd; adult/child €10/6; ⌚6.30-10.30pm Mon, Tue & Fri; 🚌16 or 16A from city centre) This greyhound track is close to the city centre and offers a great night out for a fraction of what it would cost to go to the horses.

Leopardstown Race Course SPORTS
(Map p58; ☎01-289 3607; www.leopardstown.com; Foxrock; 🚌special from Eden Quay) The Irish love of horse racing can be observed about 10km south of the city centre in Foxrock. Special buses depart from the city centre on race days; call the racecourse for details.

Shelbourne Park Greyhound Stadium SPORTS
(Map p91; ☎01-668 3502, on race nights 01-202 6601; www.igb.ie; Bridge Town Rd, Ringsend; adult/child €10/6; ⏰7-10.30pm Wed, Thu & Sat; 🚌3, 7, 7A, 8, 45 or 84 from city centre) A top-class dog track with terrific vantage points from the glassed-in restaurant, where you can eat, bet and watch without leaving your seat.

Theatre

Dublin's theatre scene is small but busy. Bookings can usually be made by quoting a credit-card number over the phone and tickets collected just before the performance.

Gate Theatre THEATRE
(Map p86; ☎01-874 4045; www.gatetheatre.ie; 1 Cavendish Row) To the north of the Liffey, the Gate Theatre specialises in international classics and older Irish works with a touch of comedy by playwrights such as Oscar Wilde, George Bernard Shaw and Oliver Goldsmith, although newer plays are sometimes staged too. Prices vary according to what's on, but they're usually around €20.

Abbey Theatre THEATRE
(Map p86; ☎01-878 7222; www.abbeytheatre.ie; Lower Abbey St) Ireland's national theatre resides in a large concrete box by the river. It puts on new Irish works, as well as revivals of classic Irish plays by writers such as WB Yeats, JM Synge, Sean O'Casey, Brendan Behan and Samuel Beckett. Tickets for evening performances cost up to €25, except on Monday, when they're cheaper. The smaller **Peacock Theatre** (Map p86; ☎01-878 7222) is part of the same complex and stages more fringe work.

Gaiety Theatre THEATRE
(Map p78; ☎01-677 1717; www.gaietytheatre.com; South King St) Opened in 1871, this theatre is used for modern plays, TV shows, musical comedies and revues.

Helix THEATRE
(☎01-700 7000; www.thehelix.ie; Collins Ave, Glasnevin) The Helix, Dublin City University's new theatre venue in Glasnevin (Map p58), has already established its reputation as a serious theatre with its mix of accessible and challenging productions. To get here, take bus 11, 13, 13A or 19A from O'Connell St.

International Bar THEATRE
(Map p64; ☎01-677 9250; 23 Wicklow St) This is one of several pubs that host theatrical performances; it also hosts comedy on Wednesday evening at 9.30pm (admission €9).

Olympia Theatre THEATRE
(Map p70; ☎01-677 7744; 72 Dame St) This theatre specialises in light plays and, at Christmastime, pantomimes.

Players' Theatre THEATRE
(Map p64; ☎01-677 2941, ext 1239; Regent House, Trinity College) The Trinity College Players' Theatre hosts student productions throughout the academic year, as well as the most prestigious plays from the Dublin Theatre Festival in October.

Project Arts Centre THEATRE
(Map p70; ☎1850 260 027; www.project.ie; 39 East Essex St) This art gallery centre puts on excellent productions of experimental plays by up-and-coming Irish and foreign writers.

Shopping

Whether they have cash or are relying on an ever-tightening credit line, Dubliners like to shop. And if they're not shopping, they're browsing.

British and US chains dominate the high street and major shopping centres but there are also numerous small, independent shops selling high-quality, locally made goods. Irish designer clothing and streetwear, hand made jewellery, unusual homewares and crafts, and cheeses to die for are readily available if you know where to look.

While souvenir hunters can still buy toy sheep, Guinness magnets and shamrock tea towels, a new breed of craft shop offers one-off or limited-edition crafts and art. Traditional Irish products such as crystal and knitwear remain popular choices, and you can increasingly find innovative modern takes on the classics.

Grafton St is the city's most prestigious shopping thoroughfare, but it's largely the domain of the British-style high-street shop, as is busy Henry St, just off O'Connell St. In the warren of streets between Grafton St and South Great George's St, you'll find a plethora of Irish-owned fashion outlets, jewellers and secondhand stores. Francis St in the Liberties is great for antiques and art.

THE DUBLIN TEE-ATER

Although all major towns and cities have a theatrical reputation, none can hold a candle to the capital's long tradition with the stage, which has long attracted aficionados from every social milieu. Dublin's first theatre was founded in Werburgh St in 1637, although it was closed only four years later by the Puritans. Another theatre, named the Smock Alley Playhouse or Theatre Royal, opened in 1661 and continued to stage plays for more than a century. The literary revival of the late 19th century resulted in the establishment of Dublin's Abbey Theatre, now Ireland's national theatre. Its role is to present works by historical greats such as WB Yeats (1865-1939), George Bernard Shaw (1856–1950), JM Synge (1871–1909) and Sean O'Casey (1880–1964), as well as to promote modern Irish dramatists. The Gate Theatre produces classics and comedies, while the Gaiety and Olympia Theatres present a range of productions. Dublin's Project Arts Centre offers a more experimental program.

Under pressure to justify itself as a going concern, Irish theatre has subconsciously turned more and more towards the fizz-bang-wallop of spectacle, often at the expense of quality. Some of the most successful plays of recent years seem obsessed with recreating the high-paced neurotic energy of the action thriller on the stage, as though the audience isn't patient enough to be engrossed by the slow build-up usually associated with theatrical drama. More noise, more guns and sharp dialogue out of an American pulp novel might keep the audience laughing, but it doesn't make for lasting, quality theatre.

Theatre's tattered flag is still kept flying, however, by some excellent writers and companies. Brian Friel (b 1929) and Tom Murphy (b 1935) are the country's leading established playwrights, but the future has been enlivened by a bunch of new writers, including Michael Collins, John Comiskey, Oonagh Kearney, Gina Moxley and Arthur Riordan, playwrights who have been helped on to the stage by innovative production companies like Rough Magic.

The present is also pretty shiny for the likes of Enda Walsh, author of *Disco Pigs* (1996; made into a film starring Cillian Murphy in 2001) – he's written 11 plays since then, the most recent of which is *The Man in the Moon* (2009). Mark O'Rowe, who presented an electrifying picture of gangland Dublin in his award-winning *Howie the Rookie* (1999) and followed it with *Made in China* (2001) and *Crestfall* (2003), is one of the very hot names in the contemporary scene, but he too has made the move into film writing, co-scripting *Intermission* (2003); his latest play, *Terminus* (2007), was very well received. Conor McPherson, who made his name with the excellent film *I Went Down*, cemented his reputation as a dramatist with a series of plays that explore dysfunctional relationships and the importance of traditional folklore, like *The Weir* (1997) and *The Seafarer* (2006).

Citizens of non-EU countries can reclaim the VAT paid on purchases made at stores that display a cash-back sticker; ask for details.

Most department stores and shopping centres are open from 9.30am to 6pm Monday to Saturday (open to 8pm Thursday) and noon to 6pm Sunday.

GRAFTON STREET & AROUND

Avoca Handweavers IRISH CRAFTS

(Map p64; ☎01-677 4215; 11-13 Suffolk St) This contemporary craft shop is a treasure trove of interesting Irish and foreign products. The colourful shop is chock-a-block with woollen knits, ceramics, handcrafted gadgets and a wonderful toy selection – and not a tweed cap in sight.

Powerscourt Townhouse Shopping Centre SHOPPING MALL

(Map p70; ☎01-679 4144; 59 South William St) This absolutely gorgeous and stylish centre is in a carefully refurbished Georgian town house, originally built between 1741 and 1744. These days it's best known for its cafes and restaurants but it still does a top-end, selective trade in high fashion, art, exquisite handicrafts and other chichi sundries.

George's St Arcade ARCADE

(Map p70; www.georgesstreetarcade.ie; btwn South Great George's St & Drury St; ⌚9am-6.30pm Mon-Sat, to 8pm Thu; noon-6pm Sun) Dublin's best nonfood market (there's sadly not much competition) is sheltered within an elegant Victorian Gothic arcade. Apart from the shops and stalls selling new and old clothes, second-hand books, hats, posters, jewellery and records, there's a fortune teller, some gourmet nibbles and a fish-and-chipper who does a roaring trade.

DesignYard IRISH CRAFTS
(Map p64; ☎01-474 1011; 48-49 Nassau St) A high-end craft-as-art shop where everything you see – be it glass, batik, sculpture, painting – is one-off and handmade in Ireland. It also showcases contemporary jewellery from young international designers in its exhibition space.

Kilkenny Shop IRISH CRAFTS
(Map p64; ☎01-677 7066; 6 Nassau St) This shop has a wonderful selection of finely made Irish crafts, featuring clothing, glassware, pottery, jewellery, crystal and silver from some of Ireland's best designers.

Brown Thomas DEPARTMENT STORE
(Map p64; ☎01-605 6666; 92 Grafton St) This is Dublin's most expensive department store, suitably stocked to cater for the city's more moneyed shoppers. You'll find every top label represented here. The 3rd-floor Bottom Drawer outlet stocks the finest Irish linen you'll find anywhere.

Costume CLOTHING
(Map p70; ☎01-679 5200; 10 Castle Market) From casuals to sparkly full-length dresses, Costume specialises in stylish contemporary women's wear from young European designers. Its own Costume label sits alongside pieces by Isabel Marant, Roland Mouret and Proenza Schouler.

Bow Boutique CLOTHING
(Map p70; ☎01-707 1763; Powerscourt Townhouse) A collaborative effort by four top-rated Irish designers – Eilis Boyle, Wendy Crawford, Matt Doody and Margaret O'Rourke – Bow is a superb, independently owned shop that features the work not just of its owners but of a range of Irish fashionistas.

Hodges Figgis BOOKSTORE
(Map p64; ☎01-677 4754; 56-58 Dawson St) Dublin's largest bookshop, with the widest selection of titles spread across three roomy floors.

St Stephen's Green Shopping Centre SHOPPING MALL
(Map p70; ☎01-478 0888; St Stephen's Green) Inside this flash shopping centre you will discover a diverse mixture of chain stores and individual shops.

Smock CLOTHING
(Map p70; ☎01-613 9000; 31 Drury St) This elegant designer shop sells cutting-edge international women's wear from classy 'investment labels' Easton Pearson, Veronique Branquinho and AF Vandevorft, as well as a small range of interesting jewellery and lingerie.

BT2 CLOTHING
(Map p70; ☎01-679 5666; 88 Grafton St) This is Brown Thomas' young and funky offshoot, with high-end casuals for men and women and a juice bar upstairs overlooking Grafton St. Brands include DKNY, Custom, Diesel, Ted Baker and Tommy Hilfiger.

Jenny Vander CLOTHING
(Map p70; ☎01-677 0406; 50 Drury St) A visit to Jenny Vander is like walking into an exotic 1940s boudoir. The selection of vintage and antique clothing, hats and jewellery is pretty wild, although you won't find many bargains.

Claddagh Records MUSIC STORE
(Map p70; ☎01-677 0262; 2 Cecilia St) This shop sells a wide range of Irish traditional and folk music.

Dubray Books BOOKSTORE
(Map p70; ☎01-677 5568; 36 Grafton St) Three roomy floors devoted to bestsellers, recent releases, coffee-table books and a huge travel section make this one of the better bookshops in town.

Cathach Books BOOKSTORE
(Map p64; ☎01-671 8676; www.rarebooks.ie; 10 Duke St) A rich and remarkable collection of rare and secondhand Irish-interest books, including first editions.

NORTH OF THE LIFFEY

Arnott's DEPARTMENT STORE
(Map p86; ☎01-805 0400; 12 Henry St) Occupying a huge block with entrances on Henry, Liffey and Abbey Sts, this formerly mediocre department store has been completely overhauled and is now probably Dublin's best. It stocks virtually everything you could possibly want to buy, from garden furniture to high fashion, and everything is relatively affordable.

Eason BOOKSTORE
(Map p86; ☎01-873 3811; www.easons.ie; 40 Lower O'Connell St) Large Irish-owned chain with one of the biggest magazine inventories in Ireland.

(Continued on page 128)

Literary Dublin

Is there a city of comparable size anywhere in the world that can hold a candle to Dublin as a literary heavyweight? It's not just the Nobel Prize winners — it's the host of other scribes, writing in every conceivable genre, for every conceivable taste.

Marsh's Library

1 Dublin's oldest working library (p82) is an early 18th-century classic, packed with ancient books and manuscripts including some of the world's rarest.

Samuel Beckett

2 Like his great mentor Joyce, Beckett (p715) left Dublin for Paris, where he produced his finest work, including the watershed *Waiting For Godot*, a Modernist classic. A memorial bridge dedicated to Beckett, designed by architect Santiago Calatrava, was opened in Dublin in 2009.

James Joyce

3 Ireland's most famous literary export, Joyce (p89) devoted virtually his entire career to writing about one subject: Dublin. His book of short stories, *Dubliners*, remains one of the must-reads on the capital.

Clockwise from top left
1. Books at Marsh's Library **2.** Samuel Beckett Bridge over the River Liffey **3.** Marjorie Fitzgibbon's statue of James Joyce, North Earl St

ROMA
ROMA
2

Dublin Writers Museum

4 A collection of memorabilia associated with Dublin's rich literary past, including Brendan Behan's union card and Samuel Beckett's phone (p88).

Trinity College Library

5 Two super-highlights: the breathtaking 65m Long Room (p62), the most beautiful library in Ireland, and the Book of Kells, the most famous illustrated Gospels in the world.

Oscar Wilde

6 Outstanding playwright, thoughtful poet, writer of children's literature and famous wit, Oscar Wilde (p80) is one of Dublin's most beloved literary progeny.

Clockwise from top left

1. Dublin Writers Museum, North Parnell Sq **2.** Examining a book in the Long Room, Trinity College **3.** Interior of the Long Room, Trinity College **4.** Danny Osborne's Oscar Wilde statue, Merrion Sq

2

3

DOUG MCKINLAY/LONELY PLANET IMAGES ©

(Continued from page 123)

Clery's & Co DEPARTMENT STORE
(Map p86; ☎01-878 6000; O'Connell St) This graceful shop is a Dublin classic. Recently restored to its elegant best, it caters to the more conservative Dublin shopper.

Jervis St Centre SHOPPING MALL
(Map p86; ☎01-878 1323; Jervis St) Just north of the Capel St Bridge, this is an ultramodern mall with dozens of outlets.

Debenham's DEPARTMENT STORE
(Map p86; ☎01-873 0044; Henry St) This UK giant hit these shores in 2006; it's bold and glass-fronted on the outside and holds street-smart fashion labels such as Zara, Warehouse and G-Star on the inside, as well as the obligatory homewares and electrical sections.

BEYOND THE GRAND CANAL

Dundrum Town Centre SHOPPING MALL
(Map p58; ☎01-299 1700; Sandyford Rd, Dundrum; ⏲9am-9pm Mon-Fri, 8.30am-7pm Sat, 10am-7pm Sun) Modern Ireland's grandest cathedral is this huge shopping and entertainment complex in the southern suburb of Dundrum. Over 100 retail outlets are represented. To get here, take the Luas to Ballaly, or catch bus 17, 44C, 48A or 75 from the city centre.

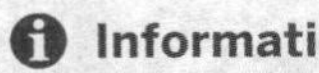

Information

Dangers & Annoyances

Dublin is generally quite a safe city, although petty crime of the bag-snatching, car break-in variety can be a low-level irritant. Be sensible: guard your belongings, don't leave anything in your car and consider the use of supervised car parks for overnight parking. Remember also that insurance policies often don't cover losses from cars.

The only consistent trouble in Dublin is alcohol-related: where there are pubs and clubs there are worse-for-wear revellers looking to get home and/or get laid, and sometimes the frustrations of getting neither can result in a trip to the casualty department of the nearest hospital – hospitals are clogged to bursting with drink-related cases throughout the weekend.

When using ATMs, guard your PIN details carefully. Don't use one that looks like it's been tampered with as card cloning is a growing problem.

The area north of Gardiner St, O'Connell St and Mountjoy Sq is not especially salubrious – gangs of disaffected youths and drug addicts on the make are a recipe for trouble and sometimes violence.

Emergency

For national emergency numbers, see the inside front cover.

Drugs Advisory & Treatment Centre (☎01-677 1122; Trinity Ct, 30-31 Pearse St)

Police/Fire/Ambulance (☎01-999)

Rape Crisis Centre (☎1800 778 888, 01-661 4911; 70 Lower Leeson St)

Internet Access

Global Internet Café (8 Lower O'Connell St; per hr €5; ⏲8am-11pm Mon-Fri, from 9am Sat, from 10am Sun)

Internet Exchange (3 Cecilia St, Temple Bar; per hr €5; ⏲8am-2am Mon-Fri, 10am-midnight Sat & Sun)

Internet resources include:

Dublin City Council (www.dublincity.ie)

Dublin Tourism (www.visitdublin.com)

Entertainment.ie (www.entertainment.ie)

Nialler9 (www.nialler9.com) Great music and gig blog.

Overheard in Dublin (www.overheardindublin.com)

Totally Dublin (www.totallydublin.ie)

DUBLIN MARKETS

Blackberry Fair (Map p60; Lower Rathmines Rd; ⏲10am-5pm Sat & Sun) You'll have to rummage through a lot of junk to find a gem in this charmingly run-down weekend market that stocks furniture, records and a few clothes stalls. It's cheap, though.

Blackrock Market (Main St, Blackrock; ⏲11am-5.30pm Sat & Sun; 🚉Blackrock) This long-running market, in an old merchant house and yard in the seaside village of Blackrock (Map p58), south of Dublin, has all manner of stalls selling everything from New Age crystals to futons.

Cow's Lane Designer Mart (Map p70; Cow's Lane; ⏲10am-5pm Sat) For the best in new Irish design, artwork and clothing, you'll find everything here, including yarn spun right in front of you and Ireland's only bone jeweller.

Media

The *Evening Herald* (€1) is a tabloid with all the latest news, the more salacious the better. All of the national dailies have plenty of Dublin coverage.

Medical Services

Should you experience an immediate health problem, contact the casualty section (emergency room) of the nearest public hospital; in an emergency, call an ambulance (☎01-999). There are no 24-hour pharmacies in Dublin; the latest any stay open is 10pm.

Baggot St Hospital (☎01-668 1577; 18 Upper Baggot St; ⏰7.30am-4.30pm Mon-Fri) Southside city centre.

Caredoc (☎1850 334 999; www.caredoc.ie; ⏰24hr) Doctors on call; available only out of regular surgery hours.

City Pharmacy (☎01-670 4523; 14 Dame St; ⏰9am-10pm)

Dental Hospital (☎01-612 7200; 20 Lincoln Pl; ⏰9am-5pm Mon-Fri, from 8am for prebooked appointments)

Grafton Medical Centre (☎01-671 2122; www.graftonmedical.ie; 34 Grafton St; ⏰8.30am-6.30pm Mon-Thu, to 6pm Fri) One-stop shop with male and female doctors and physio therapists.

Health Service Executive (☎01-679 0700, 1800 520 520; www.hse.ie; Dr Steevens' Hospital, Steeven's Lane; ⏰9.30am-5.30pm Mon-Fri) Central health authority with Choice of Doctor Scheme, which can advise you on a suitable GP from 9am to 5pm Monday to Friday. Information services for those with physical and mental disabilities.

Mater Misericordiae Hospital (☎01-830 1122; Eccles St) Northside city centre, off Lower Dorset St.

O'Connell's Pharmacy Grafton St (☎01-679 0467; 21 Grafton St; ⏰9am-10pm); O'Connell St (☎01-873 0427; 55-56 Upper O'Connell St; ⏰9am-10pm)

St James's Hospital (Map p60; ☎01-453 7941; James's St) Southside.

Well Woman Centre Lower Liffey St (☎01-872 8051; www.wellwomancentre.ie; 35 Lower Liffey St; ⏰9.30am-7.30pm Mon, Thu & Fri, 8am-7.30pm Tue & Wed, 10am-4pm Sat & 1-4pm Sun); Pembroke Rd (☎01-660 9860; 67 Pembroke Rd, Ballsbridge; ⏰10am-7.30pm Mon-Wed, 8am-7.30pm Thu & Fri, 10am-4pm Sat) For female health issues. Supplies contraceptives, including the morning-after pill (€65).

Money

There are currency-exchange counters at Dublin airport in the baggage-collection area, and on the arrival and departure floors. The counters are open 5.30am to 11pm.

There are numerous banks around the city centre with exchange facilities, open during regular bank hours.

First Rate (1 Westmoreland St; ⏰8am-9pm Mon-Fri, 9am-9pm Sat, 10am-9pm Sun Jun-Sep, 9am-6pm Mon-Sat Oct-May)

Post

The most convenient post offices in the city centre are the **General Post Office** (Map p86; ☎01-705 7000; O'Connell St; ⏰8am-8pm Mon-Sat) on the northside and **Andrew's St post office** (Map p64; ☎01-705 8206; www.anpost.ie; St Andrew's St) on the southside.

Tourist Information

No tourist information offices in Dublin provide any information over the phone – they're exclusively walk-in services.

You can book accommodation via www.visitdublin.ie or www.gulliver.ie, or via telephone: in Ireland call ☎1800 668 668; from Britain call ☎00800 6686 6866; from the rest of the world call ☎66-979 2030.

Dublin Tourism (Map p70; ☎01-605 7700; www.visitdublin.com; St Andrew's Church, 2 Suffolk St; ⏰9am-7pm Mon-Sat, 10.30am-3pm Sun Jul & Aug, 9am-5.30pm Mon-Sat Sep-Jun) is the main tourist office. There's a booking fee of €5 for serviced accommodation or €7 for self-catering accommodation, and a 10% deposit that is refunded through your hotel bill. There are branches at **Dublin Airport** (arrivals hall; ⏰8am-10pm), **Dun Laoghaire** (Dun Laoghaire ferry terminal; ⏰10am-1pm & 2-6pm Mon-Sat), **O'Connell Street** (Map p86; 14 Upper O'Connell St; ⏰9am-5pm Mon-Sat) and **Wilton Terrace** (Map p60; Wilton Tce; ⏰9.30am-noon & 12.30-5.15pm Mon-Fri).

Fáilte Ireland head office (Map p60; ☎1850 230 330; www.ireland.ie; Wilton Tce; ⏰9am-5.15pm Mon-Fri)

Getting There & Away

Air

Dublin Airport (Map p58; ☎01-814 1111; www.dublinairport.com), 13km north of the centre, is Ireland's major international gateway airport, with direct flights from Europe, North America and Asia. For information on who flies in and out of here, see p734.

Boat

Dublin has two ferry ports: the **Dun Laoghaire ferry terminal** (☎01-280 1905; Dun Laoghaire), 13km southeast of the city, serves Holyhead in Wales and can be reached by DART to Dun Laoghaire, or bus 7, 7A or 8 from Burgh Quay or bus 46A from Trinity College; and the **Dublin Port**

terminal (Map p58; ☎01-855 2222; Alexandra Rd), 3km northeast of the city centre, serves Holyhead and Liverpool.

Buses from Busáras (p130) are timed to coincide with arrivals and departures: for the 9.45am ferry departure from Dublin Port, buses leave Busáras at 8.30am. For the 9.45pm departure, buses depart from Busáras at 8.30pm. For the 1am sailing to Liverpool, the bus departs from Busáras at 11.45pm. All bus trips cost adult/child €2.50/1.25.

See p734 for details of ferry journeys.

Bus

Busáras (Map p91; ☎01-836 6111; www.buseireann.ie; Store St), the main bus station, is just north of the river behind Custom House, and serves as the main city stop for **Bus Éireann** (www.buseireann.ie).

For information on fares, frequencies and durations to various destinations in the Republic and Northern Ireland, see p736.

Car & Motorcycle

The main rental agencies, which also have offices at the airport, include the following:

Avis Rent-a-Car (☎01-605 7500; www.avis.ie; 35-29 Old Kilmainham Rd, Dublin 8)

Budget Rent-a-Car (☎01-837 9611, airport 01-844 5150; www.budget.ie; 151 Lower Drumcondra Rd, Dublin 7)

Europcar (☎01-648 5900, airport 01-844 4179; www.europcar.com; 29 Parkgate St, Dublin 7)

Hertz Rent-a-Car (☎01-709 3060, airport 844 5466; www.hertz.com; 151 South Circular Rd, Dublin 8)

Thrifty (☎01-844 1944, airport 840 0800; www.thrifty.ie; 26 Lombard St East, Dublin 2)

Train

For general train information, contact **Iarnród Éireann Travel Centre** (☎01-836 6222; www.irishrail.ie; 35 Lower Abbey St; ⏲9am-5pm Mon-Fri, 9am-1pm Sat). **Connolly Station** (Map p91; ☎01-836 3333), just north of the Liffey and the city centre, serves the north and northwest (including Belfast, Derry and Sligo). **Heuston Station** (Map p60; ☎01-836 5421), just south of the Liffey and west of the centre, serves all destinations to the south and west including Cork, Galway, Killarney, Limerick, Wexford and Waterford. See p739 for more information.

ℹ Getting Around

To/From the Airport

There is no train service to/from the airport, but there are bus and taxi options.

BUS

Aircoach (☎01-844 7118; www.aircoach.ie; one way/return €7/12) Private coach service with two routes from the airport to 18 destinations throughout the city, including the main streets of the city centre. Coaches run every 10 to 15 minutes between 6am and midnight, then hourly from midnight until 6am.

Airlink Express Coach (☎01-872 0000, 01-873 4222; www.dublinbus.ie; adult/child €6/3) Bus 747 runs every 10 to 20 minutes from 5.45am to 11.30pm between the airport, the central bus station (Busáras) and the Dublin Bus office on Upper O'Connell St; bus 748 runs every 15 to 30 minutes from 6.50am to 10.05pm between the airport and Heuston and Connolly Stations.

Dublin Bus (Map p60; ☎01-872 0000; www.dublinbus.ie; 59 Upper O'Connell St; adult/child €2.20/1) A number of buses serve the airport from various points in Dublin, including buses 16A (Rathfarnham), 746 (Dun Laoghaire) and 230 (Portmarnock); all cross the city centre on their way to the airport.

TAXI

There is a taxi rank directly outside the arrivals concourse. A taxi should cost about €20 from the airport to the city centre, including a supplementary charge of €2.50 (not applied going to the airport). Make sure the meter is switched on.

Bicycle

Dublin is pretty flat and the traffic can be awful, so getting around on a bike can make life a lot easier. Still, though Dublin has an increasing number of rust-red cycle lanes, cyclists share them with drivers who are indifferent to the line markings, making cycling a little more of a challenge than it really ought to be.

The blue bikes of **Dublinbikes** (www.dublinbikes.ie) have become a ubiquitous presence around the city centre, making this scheme one of the most successful transport initiatives of recent years. The pay-as-you-go service is straightforward: cyclists purchase a €10 Smart Card (as well as pay a credit card deposit of €150) – either online or at any of the 40 stations throughout the city centre – before 'freeing' a bike for use, which is then free for the first 30 minutes and 50c for each half hour thereafter.

Car & Motorcycle

Traffic in Dublin is a nightmare and parking is an expensive headache. There are no free spots to park anywhere in the city centre during business hours (7am to 7pm Monday to Saturday), but there are plenty of parking meters, 'pay and display' spots (€2.70 to €5.20 per hour), and over a dozen sheltered and supervised car parks (around €5 per hour).

Clamping of illegally parked cars is thoroughly enforced, with an €80 charge for removal. Parking is free after 7pm Monday to Saturday and all day Sunday in all metered spots and on single yellow lines.

Car theft and break-ins are a problem, and the police advise visitors to park in a supervised car park. Cars with foreign number plates are prime targets; never leave your valuables behind. When booking accommodation, enquire about parking facilities.

Public Transport

BUS

The office of **Dublin Bus** (Map p60; ☎01-872 0000; www.dublinbus.ie; 59 Upper O'Connell St; ⏰9am-5.30pm Mon-Fri, 9am-2pm Sat) has free single-route timetables of all its services.

Buses run from around 6am (some start at 5.30am) to 11.30pm. Travel within the city centre bus corridor (roughly between Parnell Sq to the north and St Stephen's Green to the south) costs €0.50; all other fares are calculated according to stages: 1–3 (€1.20), 4–7 (€1.65), 8–13 (€1.85) and 14–23 (€2.30).

You must use exact change for tickets when boarding buses; anything more and you will be given a receipt for reimbursement, which is possible only at the Dublin Bus main office. Avoid this by using a smartcard ticket, available at most Spar or Centra shops.

LUAS

The **Luas** (www.luas.ie; ⏰5.30am-12.30am Mon-Fri, from 6.30am Sat, 7am-11.30pm Sun) light-rail system has two lines: the Green Line (trains run every five to 15 minutes), which connects St Stephen's Green with Sandyford in south Dublin via Ranelagh and Dundrum; and the Red Line (trains run every 20 minutes), which runs from the Point Village in the Docklands to Tallaght via the north quays and Heuston Station. There are ticket machines at every stop or you can buy tickets from newsagencies throughout the city centre; a typical short-hop fare will cost you €1.80. Smartcard tickets can also be used.

NITELINK

These late-night buses run from the College St, Westmoreland St and D'Olier St triangle (at Trinity College's northwest corner), covering most of Dublin's suburbs. Buses leave at 12.30am and 2am Monday to Wednesday, and every 20 minutes between 12.30am and 3.30am Thursday to Saturday. Tickets start at €4.

TRAIN

The **Dublin Area Rapid Transport** (DART; ☎01-836 6222; www.irishrail.ie) provides quick train access to the coast as far north as Howth (about 30 minutes) and as far south as Greystones in County Wicklow. Pearse Station (Map p91) is convenient for central Dublin south of the Liffey, and Connolly Station (Map p91) for north of the Liffey. There are services every 10 to 20 minutes, sometimes even more frequently, from around 6.30am to midnight Monday to Saturday; services are less frequent on Sunday. Dublin to Dun Laoghaire takes about 15 to 20 minutes. A one-way DART ticket from Dublin to Dun Laoghaire or Howth costs €2.30; to Bray it's €2.75.

There are also suburban rail services north as far as Dundalk, inland to Mullingar and south past Bray to Arklow.

TAXI

From 8am to 10pm, taxi fares begin with a flagfall of €4.10, followed by around €1 per kilometre thereafter; from 10pm to 8am, it's €4.45 flagfall and €1.35 per kilometre. Extra charges include €1 for each extra passenger and €2 for telephone bookings; there is no charge for luggage.

Taxis can be hailed on the street and found at taxi ranks around the city, including O'Connell St, College Green (in front of Trinity College) and St Stephen's Green at the end of Grafton St. There are numerous taxi companies that will dispatch taxis by radio. Some options:

City Cabs (☎01-872 2688)

National Radio Cabs (☎01-677 2222)

Phone the **Garda Carriage Office** (☎01-475 5888) if you have any complaints about taxis or queries regarding lost property.

FARE SAVER PASSES

The increasingly integrated public transport system offers a range of fare-saver passes, available from Dublin Bus and the tourist office. These include:

Freedom Pass (adult/child €26/10) offers three days of unlimited travel on all Dublin Bus services, including its Airlink, Xpresso and hop-on, hop-off tourist bus.

Rambler 1 Day Family (€10.50) One day unlimited travel for two adults and two children on all Dublin Bus services, including Airlink and Xpresso.

Family 1 Day Short Hop (€15.75) One day unlimited travel for two adults and two children on all Dublin Bus services, including Xpresso, DART and suburban rail services.

AROUND DUBLIN

Without even the smallest hint of irony Dubliners will happily tell you that one of the city's best features is how easy it is to get out of it, and they do, whenever they can. But they don't go especially far: for many the destination is one of the small seaside villages that surround the capital. To the north are the lovely villages of Howth and Malahide – slowly and reluctantly being sucked into the Dublin conglomeration – while to the south is Dalkey, which has long since given up the fight but has managed to retain that village vibe.

Dalkey

Dublin's most important medieval port has long since settled into its role as an elegant dormitory village, but there are some revealing vestiges of its illustrious past, most notably the remains of three of the eight castles that once lorded over the area. Facing each other on Castle St are the 15th-century Archibold's Castle and Goat Castle. The latter (aka the Towerhouse), along with the adjoining St Begnet's Church, has been converted into the **Dalkey Castle & Heritage Centre** (☎01-285 8366; www.dalkeycastle.com; Castle St; adult/child/student/family €6/4/5/16; ⏲10am-6pm Mon & Wed-Sun May-Aug, 9.30am-5pm Mon & Wed-Fri, 11am-5pm Sat & Sun Sep-Apr), where models, displays and exhibitions are but the backdrop to the 'Medieval Experience', a live show every 30 minutes by actors from the Deilg Inis Living History Theatre.

Overlooking Bullock Harbour are the remains of Bulloch Castle, built by the monks of St Mary's Abbey in Dublin around 1150.

A few hundred metres offshore is Dalkey Island, home to **St Begnet's Holy Well** (admission free; boat from Coliemore Harbour per hr €25), the most important of Dalkey's so-called holy wells. This one is reputed to cure rheumatism, making the island a popular destination for tourists and the faithful alike. The island is easily accessible by boat from Coliemore Harbour; you can't book a boat, so just show up. The waters around the island are popular with scuba divers; qualified divers can rent gear in Dun Laoghaire, further north, from **Ocean Divers** (☎01-280 1083; www.oceandivers.ie; West Pier; half-day dive with full equipment & boat €59).

To the south there are good views from the small park at Sorrento Point and from Killiney Hill. A number of rocky swimming pools are also found along the Dalkey coast.

About 1km south of Dalkey is the super-affluent seaside suburb of **Killiney**, home to some of Ireland's wealthiest people and a handful of celebrities, including Bono, Enya and filmmaker Neil Jordan. The attraction is self-evident, from the long, curving sandy beach of Killiney Bay (which 19th-century residents felt resembled Naples' Sorrento Bay, hence the Italian names of all the local roads) to the gorse-covered hills behind it, which make for a great walk. Alas, for most of us, Killiney will always remain a place to visit; on the rare occasion that a house comes on the market, it would take a cool €5 million to get the seller to bite.

Eating

Guinea Pig SEAFOOD **€€€**
(☎01-285 9055; 17 Railway Rd; mains €19-35; ⏲dinner only) Despite the name, is this the best seafood restaurant in Dublin? Many a food critic seems to think so.

Caviston's Seafood Restaurant SEAFOOD **€€€**
(☎01-280 9245; Glasthule Rd, Sandycove; mains €18-27; ⏲noon-5pm Tue-Thu, noon-midnight Fri & Sat) All self-respecting crustacean lovers should make the 1km trip to Caviston's for a seafood meal to remember.

Getting There & Away

Dalkey is 8km south of the city centre along the coast. It is best reached by DART from Connolly or Pearse Stations or, for a slower journey, you can catch bus 8 from Burgh Quay. Both cost €2.20.

Howth

Tidily positioned at the foot of a bulbous peninsula, the pretty port village of Howth (the name rhymes with 'both') is a major fishing centre, yachting harbour and one of the most sought-after addresses in town, with the best properties discreetly spread atop the gorse-rich hill that dominates the peninsula – spectacular views of Dublin Bay are standard. Dubliners who can't afford to live here make do with a weekend excursion – there are beautiful walks around Howth Head and a popular farmers market at the seafront.

WORTH A TRIP

SANDYCOVE & JAMES JOYCE MUSEUM

About 1km north of Dalkey is **Sandycove**, with a pretty little beach and a **Martello tower** – built by British forces to keep an eye out for a Napoleonic invasion – now housing the **James Joyce Museum** (☎01-280 9265; www.visitdublin.com; Joyce Tower, Sandycove; adult/child/student €6/4/5; ⏲10am-1pm & 2-5pm Tue-Sat, 2-6pm Sun Apr-Aug, by appointment only Sep-Mar). This is where the action begins in James Joyce's epic novel *Ulysses*. The museum was opened in 1962 by Sylvia Beach, the Paris-based publisher who first dared to put *Ulysses* into print, and has photographs, letters, documents, various editions of Joyce's work and two death masks of Joyce on display.

Below the Martello tower is the **Forty Foot Pool**, an open-air, sea-water bathing pool that took its name from the army regiment, the Fortieth Foot, that was stationed at the tower until the regiment was disbanded in 1904. At the close of the first chapter of *Ulysses*, Buck Mulligan heads off to the Forty Foot Pool for a morning swim. A morning wake-up here is still a local tradition, winter or summer. In fact, a winter dip isn't much braver than a summer one since the water temperature varies by only about 5°C (9°F). Basically, it's always bloody cold.

Pressure from female bathers eventually opened this public stretch of water – originally nudist and for men only – to both sexes, despite strong opposition from the 'forty foot gentlemen'. They eventually compromised with the ruling that a 'Togs Must Be Worn' sign would apply after 9am. Prior to that time nudity prevails and swimmers are still predominantly male.

Sights

Howth Castle CASTLE

Most of the town backs onto the extensive grounds of Howth Castle, built in 1564 but much changed over the years, most recently in 1910 when Sir Edwin Lutyens gave it a modernist make-over. Today the castle is divided into four very posh and private residences. The original estate was acquired in 1177 by the Norman noble Sir Almeric Tristram, who changed his surname to St Lawrence after winning a battle at the behest (or so he believed) of his favourite saint. The family has owned the land ever since, though the unbroken chain of male succession came to an end in 1909.

On the grounds are the ruins of the 16th-century **Corr Castle** and an ancient dolmen (tomb chamber or portal tomb made of vertical stones topped by a huge capstone) known as **Aideen's Grave**. Legend has it that Aideen died of a broken heart after her husband was killed at the Battle of Gavra near Tara in AD 184, but the legend is rubbish because the dolmen is at least 300 years older than that.

The **castle gardens** (admission free; ⏲24hr) are worth visiting, as they're noted for their rhododendrons (which bloom in May and June), azaleas and a long, 10m-high beech hedge planted in 1710.

Also within the grounds are the ruins of **St Mary's Abbey** (Abbey St, Howth Castle; admission free), originally founded in 1042 by the Viking King Sitric, who also founded the original church on the site of Christ Church Cathedral. The abbey was amalgamated with the monastery on Ireland's Eye (see the boxed text, p134) in 1235. Some parts of the ruins date from that time, but most are from the 15th and 16th centuries. The tomb of Christopher St Lawrence (Lord Howth), in the southeastern corner, dates from around 1470. See the caretaker or read instructions on the gate for opening times.

Howth Summit VIEWPOINT

Howth is essentially a very large hill surrounded by cliffs, and Howth Summit (171m) has excellent views across Dublin Bay right down to County Wicklow. From the Summit you can walk to the top of the Ben of Howth, a headland near the village, which has a cairn said to mark a 2000-year-old Celtic **royal grave**. The 1814 **Baily Lighthouse** at the southeastern corner is on the site of an old stone fort and can be reached by a dramatic clifftop walk. There was an earlier hilltop beacon here in 1670.

WORTH A TRIP

IRELAND'S EYE

A short distance offshore from Howth is Ireland's Eye (Map p58), a rocky sea-bird sanctuary with the ruins of a 6th-century monastery. There's a Martello tower at the northwestern end of the island, where boats from Howth land, while a spectacularly sheer rock face plummets into the sea at the eastern end. As well as the sea birds overhead, you can see young birds on the ground during the nesting season. Seals can also be spotted around the island.

Doyle & Sons (☎01-831 4200; return €14) takes boats out to the island from the East Pier of Howth Harbour during the summer, usually on weekend afternoons. Don't wear shorts if you're planning to visit the monastery ruins because they're surrounded by a thicket of stinging nettles. And please bring all your rubbish back with you – far too many island visitors don't.

Further north from Ireland's Eye is **Lambay Island**, an important sea-bird sanctuary that cannot be visited.

Eating

TOP CHOICE House IRISH €€

(☎01-839 6388; www.thehouse.ie; 4 Main St; mains €16-22; ⏰9am-3pm Mon-Fri, 11.30am-3pm & 6pm-11pm Sat & Sun) Wonderful spot on the main street leading away from the harbour where you can feast on dishes like crunchy Bellingham blue cheese polenta or wild Wicklow venison stew as well as a fine selection of fish.

Howth Fishermen's & Farmer's Market FARMERS MARKET €

(☎01-611 5016; www.irishfarmersmarkets.ie; West Pier, Howth Harbour; ⏰10am-5pm Sun & bank holidays) One of the best in Dublin, this is the place to come for fresh fish (obviously) but also for organic meat, veg and homemade everything else, including jams, cakes and breads. A great option for Sunday lunch.

Oar House SEAFOOD €€

(☎01-839 4562; www.oarhouse.ie; 8 West Pier; tapas €5-12, mains €12-24; ⏰12.30-10pm) A feast-o-fish is what the menu is all about at this newish restaurant – particularly the locally caught variety. Par for the course in a fishing village, but this place stands out both for the way the fish is prepared and because you can get everything on the menu in smaller, tapas-style portions as well as mains.

Getting There & Away

The easiest and quickest way to get to Howth from Dublin is on the DART, which whisks you there in just over 20 minutes for a fare of €2.20. For the same fare, buses 31 and 31A from Lower Abbey St in the city centre run as far as the Summit, 5km to the southeast of Howth.

Malahide

Malahide (Mullach Íde) was once a small village with its own harbour, a long way from the urban jungle of Dublin. The only thing protecting it from the northwards expansion of Dublin's suburbs is Malahide Demesne, 101 well-tended hectares of parkland dominated by a castle once owned by the powerful Talbot family. The handsome village remains relatively intact, but the once-quiet marina has been massively developed and is now a bustling centre with a pleasant promenade and plenty of restaurants and shops.

Sights

Malahide Castle CASTLE

(☎01-846 2184; www.malahidecastle.com; adult/child/student/family €7.50/4.70/6.30/18; ⏰10am-5pm Mon-Sat, 11am-6pm Sun Apr-Oct, 11am-5pm Sat & Sun Nov-Mar) Despite the vicissitudes of Irish history, the Talbot family managed to keep the castle under its control from 1185 to 1976, apart from a brief Cromwellian interlude (1649–60). It's now owned by Dublin County Council. The castle is the usual hotchpotch of additions and renovations; the oldest part is a three-storey 12th-century tower house. The facade is flanked by circular towers that were tacked on in 1765.

The castle is packed with furniture and paintings; highlights are a 16th-century oak room with decorative carvings, and the medieval Great Hall, which has family portraits, a minstrel's gallery and a painting of the Battle of the Boyne. Puck, the Talbot family ghost, is said to have last appeared in 1975.

The **parkland** (admission free; ⏰10am-9pm Apr-Oct, 10am-5pm Nov-Mar) around the castle is a good place for a picnic and, on a fine day, the best part of a visit.

Eating

Chez Sara FRENCH €€
(☎01-845 1882; 3 Old St; mains €18-26; ⏰dinner only Mon-Fri, lunch & dinner Sat & Sun) Irish lamb, red snapper and a beautifully cooked steak are just three of the highlights of this cosy French restaurant in the middle of the village.

Sale e Pepe INTERNATIONAL €€
(☎01-845 4600; www.saleepepe.ie; The Diamond, Main St; mains €17-29; ⏰dinner only) Despite the name, there's only a handful of Italian dishes on a menu that emphasises well-prepared steaks, fish and chips, and homemade organic burgers.

Getting There & Away

Malahide is 13km north of Dublin. Bus 42 (€2.30) from Talbot St takes around 45 minutes. The DART stops in Malahide (€2.50), but be sure to get on the right train (it's marked on the front carriage) since the line splits at Howth Junction.

Counties Wicklow & Kildare

POPULATION: 345,000 / AREA: 3718 SQ KM

Includes »

Best Places to Eat

» Ballyknocken House (p155)

» Emilia's Restaurant (p141)

» Tinakilly Country House & Restaurant (p154)

» Grangecon Café (p151)

» Poppies Country Cooking (p141)

Best Places to Stay

» Brook Lodge & Wells Spa (p156)

» Rathsallagh House & Country Club (p156)

» Hunter's Hotel (p152)

» Sheepwalk House & Cottages (p157)

Why Go?

Wicklow and Kildare may be neighbours and have a boundary with Dublin in common, but that's where the similarities end.

South of the capital is scenic, wild Wicklow. Its most imposing natural feature is a gorse-and-bracken mountain spine that is home to one of Ireland's most stunning landscapes, replete with dramatic glacial valleys, soaring mountain passes and important archaeological treasures – from breathtaking early-Christian sites to the elegant country homes of the wealthiest of Ireland's 18th-century nobility.

To the west, Kildare is far more sedate but one of the country's most prosperous farming counties. It is also where you'll find some of the most lucrative thoroughbred stud farms in the world, many with links to the horse-breeding centre of Kentucky in the US. Horse breeding is a big deal in Ireland, but in Kildare it's the very lifeblood of the county, generating many millions of tax-free euro.

When to Go

Summer – June to September – is the best time to visit Wicklow, especially if you're going to walk the Wicklow Way or do a little green thumb exploring, as the Wicklow Gardens Festival runs from Easter to late August and the Wicklow Arts Festival takes place in May. The Irish Derby – the most prestigious flat race in the Irish racing calendar – is run in late June at the Curragh in County Kildare, but there are meets there right up to October.

COUNTY WICKLOW

Just south of Dublin, Wicklow (Cill Mhantáin) is the capital's favourite playground, a wild pleasure garden of coastline, woodland and a daunting mountain range through which runs the country's most popular walking trail.

Stretching 132km from Dublin's southern suburbs to the rolling fields of County Carlow, the Wicklow Way leads walkers along disused military supply lines, old bog roads and nature trails. Along the way you can explore monastic ruins, handsome gardens and some magnificent 18th-century mansions.

National Parks

Wicklow Mountains National Park covers just over 200 sq km of mountainous blanket bogs and woodland. Within the boundaries of the protected area are two nature reserves, owned and managed by the Heritage Service and legally protected by the Wildlife Act 1976. The larger reserve, west of the Glendalough Visitor Centre, conserves the extensive heath and bog of the Glendalough Valley plus the Upper Lake and valley slopes on either side. The second, Glendalough Wood Nature Reserve, conserves oak woods stretching from the Upper Lake as far as the Rathdrum road to the east.

Most of Ireland's native mammal species can be found within the confines of the park. Large herds of deer roam on the open hill areas, though these were introduced in the 20th century as the native red-deer population became extinct during the first half of the 18th century. The uplands are the preserve of foxes, badgers and hares. Red squirrels are usually found in the pine woodlands – look out for them around the Upper Lake.

The bird population of the park is plentiful. Birds of prey abound, the most common being peregrine falcons, marlins, kestrels, hawks and sparrowhawks. Hen harriers are a rarer sight, though they too live in the park. Moorland birds found in the area include meadow pipits and skylarks. Less common birds such as whinchats, ring ouzels and dippers can be spotted, as can red grouse, whose numbers are quickly disappearing in other parts of Ireland. For information, call in or contact the **National Park Information Point** (Map p146; ☎0404-45425; www.wicklownationalpark.ie; Bolger's Cottage, Miners' Rd, Upper Lake, Glendalough; ⏲10am-6pm May-Sep, to dusk Sat & Sun Oct-Apr), off the Green Rd that runs by the Upper Lake, about 2km from the Glendalough Visitor Centre. There's usually someone on hand to help, but if you find it closed the staff may be out running guided walks. *Exploring the Glendalough Valley* (Heritage Service; €2) is a good booklet on the trails in the area.

Getting There & Away

Wicklow is relatively easy to get around.

CAR The main routes are the N11 (M11), which runs north-south through the county from Dublin to Wexford, and the N81, which runs down the western spine of the Wicklow Mountains through Blessington into County Carlow.

BUS St Kevin's Bus runs twice daily from Dublin and Bray to Roundwood and Glendalough. Dublin Bus 65 runs regularly as far as Blessington.

TRAIN The Dublin Area Rapid Transport (DART) suburban rail line runs southward from Dublin as far as Bray, and there are regular train and bus connections from the capital to Wicklow town and Arklow.

For more details, see the Getting There & Away section for each town.

Wicklow Mountains

As you leave Dublin and cross into Wicklow, the landscape changes dramatically. From Killakee, still in Dublin, the Military Rd begins a 30km southward journey across vast sweeps of gorse-, bracken- and heather-clad moors, bogs and mountains dotted with small corrie lakes.

The numbers and statistics aren't all that impressive. The highest peak in the range, Lugnaquilla (924m), is really more of a very large hill, but that hardly matters here. This vast granite intrusion, a welling-up of hot igneous rock that solidified some 400 million years ago, was shaped during the Ice Ages into the schist-capped mountains visible today. The peaks are marvellously desolate and as raw as only nature can be. Between the mountains are a number of deep glacial valleys, most notably Glenmacnass, Glen malure and Glendalough; while corrie lakes such as Lough Bray Upper and Lower, gouged by ice at the head of the glaciers, complete the wild topography.

The narrow Military Rd winds its way through the most remote parts of the mountains, offering some extraordinary views of the surrounding countryside. The best place

Counties Wicklow & Kildare Highlights

1 Go back in time at the evocative ruins and the marvellous slopes and forests of gorgeous **Glendalough** (p142)

2 Explore County Kildare's huge tracks of fecund land at the **Bog of Allen** (p160)

3 Walk at least part of Ireland's most popular hiking trail, the **Wicklow Way** (p148)

4 Examine the art and atmosphere of magnificent **Russborough House** (p150)

5 Admire the gorgeous Italianate gardens and impressive waterfall at **Powerscourt Estate** (p140)

6 Take the tour at Ireland's most impressive Palladian mansion, **Castletown House** (p158), once owned by the country's richest man

7 Contemplate your spiritual health with an overnight stay in one of the **Glendalough Hermitages** (p148)

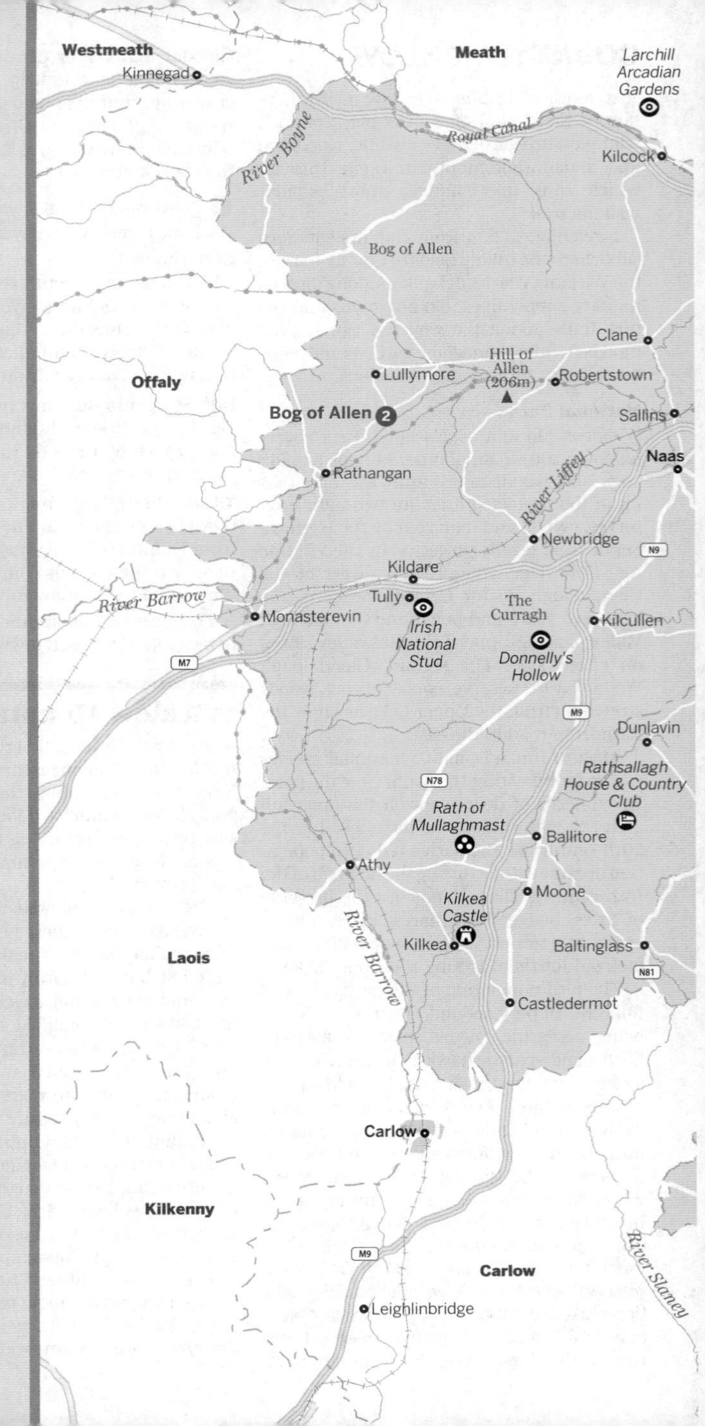

Swords
Irish Sea
Howth
To Dublin (summer only)
Howth Peninsula
North Bull Island
Maynooth
Leixlip
M4
River Liffey
6 Castletown House
Celbridge
Dublin
Dublin Bay
Dun Laoghaire
Straffan
Sandycove
Dalkey
Dalkey Island
Rathcoole
Grand Canal
Killiney
M7
Kill
Loughlinstown
Kippure Mountain (752m)
Glencree
Bray
Kilbride
Powerscourt Estate
Enniskerry
N81
R759
Bray Head
Kilmacanogue
Blessington
Powerscourt Waterfall
M11
Great Sugarloaf Mtn (503m)
Greystones
River Liffey
Ballymore Eustace
Russborough House
Sally Gap
Poulaphouca Reservoir
Mt Mullagh-cleevaun (848m)
Kilpedder
Kilcoole
Military Rd
Lough Tay
Luggala Estate
Vartry Reservoir
Valleymount
River Glenmacnass
Sraghmore
Wicklow Mountains
Hollywood
Lough Dan
Roundwood
Mt Tonelagee (816m)
Vartry Reservoir
Devil's Glen
Table Mountain (700m)
Wicklow Gap
N11
Camaderry Mtn (700m)
Annamoe
Donard
Glendalough
Ashford
Lugduff (652m)
Laragh
Ballinclea
Turlough Hill
Spink Mtn (550m)
Rathnew
Wicklow
Knockanarrigan
River Avonmore
Ballyknocken House
Glenmalure
Mullacor (657m)
Glenealy
Wicklow Head
Lugnaquilla Mtn (924m)
Glen of Imaal
Drumgoff
Derrynamuck
River Avonbeg
Vale of Clara
Rathdrum
Silver Strand
Slieve Maan (550m)
Greenane
Avondale House
Ardmore Point
Rathdangan
Redcross
Aghavannagh
R754
Carrickashane Mtn (508m)
Meeting of the Waters
Brittas Bay
Vale of Avoca
Wicklow Way
River Ow
Avoca
Mizen Head
St George's Channel
Maheramore
Aughrim
River Avoca
Woodenbridge
Clogga Beach
Tinahely
Arklow
River Bann
N11
Shillelagh
Kilmichael Point
Carnew
Wexford
M11
0
15 km
0
10 miles

to join it is at Glencree (from Enniskerry). It then runs south through the Sally Gap, Glenmacnass Valley and Laragh, then on to Glenmalure Valley and Aghavannagh.

On the trip south you can divert east at the Sally Gap to look at Lough Tay and Lough Dan. Further south you pass the great waterfall at Glenmacnass before dropping down into Laragh, with the magnificent monastic ruins of Glendalough nearby. Continue south through the valley of Glenmalure and, if you're fit enough, climb Lugnaquilla.

ENNISKERRY & POWERSCOURT ESTATE

POP 2672

At the top of the '21 Bends', as the winding R117 from Dublin is known, the handsome village of Enniskerry is home to art galleries and the kind of all-organic gourmet cafes that would treat you as a criminal if you admitted to eating battery eggs. Such preening self-regard is a far cry from the village's origins, when Richard Wingfield, Earl of nearby Powerscourt, commissioned a row of terraced cottages for his labourers in 1760. These days, you'd want to have laboured pretty successfully to get your hands on one of them.

The village is lovely, but the main reason for its popularity is the magnificent 64-sq-km **Powerscourt Estate** (☎01-204 6000; www.powerscourt.ie; adult/child/student €8/5/7; ⏲9.30am-5.30pm Feb-Oct, to 4.30pm Nov-Jan), which gives contemporary observers a true insight into the style of the 18th-century super-rich. The main entrance is 500m south of the village square.

The estate has existed more or less since 1300, when the LePoer (later anglicised to Power) family built themselves a castle here. The property changed Anglo-Norman hands a few times before coming into the possession of Richard Wingfield, newly appointed Marshall of Ireland, in 1603. His descendants were to live here for the next 350 years. In 1731 the Georgian wunderkind Richard Cassels (or Castle) was given the job of building a Palladian-style mansion around the core of the old castle. He finished the job in 1743, but an extra storey was added in 1787 and other alterations were made in the 19th century.

The Wingfields left during the 1950s, after which the house had a massive restoration. Then, on the eve of its opening to the public in 1974, a fire gutted the whole building. The estate was eventually bought by the Slazenger sporting-goods family who have overseen a second restoration, as well as the addition of two golf courses, a cafe, a huge garden centre and a bunch of cutesy little retail outlets as well as a small exhibition on the house's history.

Basically, it's all intended to draw in the punters and wring as many euros out of their pockets as possible in order to finish the huge restoration job and make the estate a kind of profitable wonderland. If you can deal with the crowds (summer weekends are the worst) or, better still, avoid the worst of them and visit midweek, you're in for a real treat. Easily the biggest drawcards of the whole pile are the simply magnificent 20-hectare formal gardens and the breathtaking views that accompany them.

Originally laid out in the 1740s, the gardens were redesigned in the 19th century by Daniel Robinson, who had as much fondness for the booze as he did for horticultural pursuits: he liked (needed?) to be wheeled around in a wheelbarrow after a certain point in the day. Perhaps this influenced his largely informal style, which resulted in a magnificent blend of landscaped gardens, sweeping terraces, statuary, ornamental lakes, secret hollows, rambling walks and walled enclosures replete with more than 200 types of trees and shrubs, all beneath the stunning natural backdrop of the Great Sugarloaf Mountain to the southeast. Tickets come with a map laying out 40-minute and hour-long tours of the gardens. Don't miss the exquisite Japanese Gardens or the Pepperpot Tower, modelled on a three-inch actual pepperpot owned by Lady Wingfield. Our own favourite, however, is the animal cemetery, final resting place of the Wingfield pets and even some of their favourite milking cows. Some of the epitaphs are astonishingly personal.

A 7km walk to a separate part of the estate takes you to the 130m **Powerscourt Waterfall** (adult/child/student €5/3.50/4.50; ⏲9.30am-7pm May-Aug, 10.30am-5.30pm Mar-Apr & Sep-Oct, to 4.30pm Nov-Jan). It's the highest waterfall in Britain and Ireland, and is most impressive after heavy rain. You can also get to the falls by road, following the signs from the estate. A nature trail has been laid out around the base of the waterfall, taking you past giant redwoods, ancient oaks, beech, birch and rowan trees. There are plenty of birds in the vicinity, including the chaffinch, cuckoo, chiffchaff, raven and willow warbler.

Tours

All tours that take in Powerscourt start in Dublin.

Bus Éireann BUS TOUR
(01-836 6111; www.buseireann.ie; Busáras; adult/child/student €28/22/25; 10am mid-Mar–Oct) A whole-day tour that takes in Powerscourt and Glendalough (all admissions included), departing from Busáras (Map p60).

Dublin Bus Tours BUS TOUR
(Map p60; 01-872 0000; www.dublinbus.ie; 59 Upper O'Connell St; adult/child €28/14; 11am) A visit to Powerscourt is included in the four-hour South Coast & Gardens tour, which takes in the stretch of coastline between Dun Laoghaire and Killiney before turning inland to Wicklow and on to Enniskerry. Admission to the gardens is included.

Irish Sightseeing Tours BUS TOUR
(Map p60; 01-872 9010; www.irishcitytours.com; Gresham Hotel, O'Connell St; adult/student/child €32/30/25; 10am Fri-Sun) Wicklow's big hits – Powerscourt, Glendalough and the lakes and a stop at Avoca, then Dun Laoghaire and Dalkey (includes admission to Glendalough visitor centre and Powerscourt, but not coffee).

Sleeping & Eating

Summerhill House Hotel HOTEL €€
(01-286 7928; www.summerhillhousehotel.com; r from €90; P) A truly superb country mansion about 700m south of town just off the N11 is the best place around to lay your head, on soft cotton pillows surrounded by delicate antiques and pastoral views in oils. Everything about the place – including the top-notch breakfast – is memorable.

Coolakay House B&B €€
(01-286 2423; www.coolakayhouse.com; Waterfall Rd, Coolakay; r €75; P) A modern working farm about 3km south of Enniskerry (it is signposted along the road), this is a great option for walkers along the Wicklow Way. The four bedrooms are all very comfortable and have terrific views, but the real draw is the restaurant, which does a roaring trade in snacks and full meals (mains around €11).

Emilia's Ristorante ITALIAN €€
(01-276 1834; Clock Tower, The Square; mains €12-16; 5-10.45pm Mon-Sat, noon-9.30pm Sun) A lovely 1st-floor restaurant to satisfy even the most ardent craving for thin-crust pizzas. Emilia's does everything else just right too, from the organic soups to the perfect steaks down to the gorgeous meringue desserts.

Poppies Country Cooking CAFE €
(01-282 8869; The Square; mains around €9; 8.30am-6pm) If the service wasn't so slow and the organisation so frustratingly haphazard, this poky little cafe on the main square would be one of the best spots in Wicklow. The food – when you finally get a chance to eat it – is sensational: wholesome salads, filling sandwiches on doorstop-cut bread and award-winning ice cream will leave you plenty satisfied.

Johnnie Fox SEAFOOD €€
(01-295 5647; www.jfp.ie; Glencullen; seafood platter €29.95; noon-10pm) Busloads of tourists fill the place nightly throughout the summer, mostly for the knees-up, faux-Irish floorshow of music and dancing. But there's nothing contrived about the seafood, which is so damn good we'd happily sit through yet another chorus of *Danny Boy* and even consider joining in the jig. The pub is 3km northwest of Enniskerry in Glencullen.

WICKLOW GARDENS FESTIVAL

If you want unfettered access to more than 40 of Wicklow's famed public and private gardens, visit during the yearly **Wicklow Gardens Festival** (20070; www.visitwicklow.ie), which runs from Easter roughly through to the end of August. The obvious advantage for green thumbs and other garden enthusiasts is access to beautiful gardens that would ordinarily be closed to the public. Some of the larger gardens are open throughout the festival, while other smaller ones open only at specific times; call or check the website for details of entrants, openings and special events, including all manner of horticultural courses.

Getting There & Away

Enniskerry is 18km south of Dublin, just 3km west of the M11 along the R117. Getting to Powerscourt House under your own steam is not a problem (it's 500m from the town), but getting to the waterfall is tricky.

Dublin Bus (01-872 0000, 01-873 4222) Service 44 (€2.40, every 20 minutes) takes about 1¼ hours to get to Enniskerry from Hawkins St in Dublin. Alternatively, you can take the DART train to Bray (€2.90) and catch bus 185 (€1.60, hourly) from the station, which takes an extra 40 minutes.

Alpine Coaches (01-286 2547; www.alpinecoaches.ie) Runs a shuttle service between the DART station in Bray, Powerscourt Waterfall (€6 return) and the house (€4.50). Shuttles leave Bray at 11.05am (11.30am July and August), 12.30pm, 1.30pm (and 3.30pm September to June) Monday to Saturday, and 11am, noon and 1pm Sunday. The last departure from Powerscourt House is at 5.30pm.

ROUNDWOOD

POP 589

Unspectacular but useful to walkers along the Wicklow Way (which runs past the town 3km to the west), Roundwood is reputedly Ireland's highest village – although at 238m that's hardly too impressive. Still, it's a handy spot for a stopover and a decent meal.

Activities

Footfalls Walking Holidays (0404-45152; www.walkinghikingireland.com; Trooperstown, Roundwood) Guided or self-guided tour options up to eight days in Wicklow (and plenty of other spots in Ireland): a six-day trek through the Wicklow Mountains complete with full bed and board will cost €730.

WORTH A TRIP

SALLY GAP

One of the two main east–west passes across the Wicklow Mountains, the Sally Gap is surrounded by some spectacular countryside. From the turn-off on the lower road (R755) between Roundwood and Kilmacanogue near Bray, the narrow road (R759) passes above the dark and dramatic Lough Tay, whose scree slopes slide into **Luggala** (Fancy Mountain). This almost fairy-tale estate is owned by one Garech de Brún, member of the Guinness family and founder of Claddagh Records, a leading producer of Irish traditional and folk music. The small River Cloghoge links Lough Tay with Lough Dan just to the south. It then heads up to the Sally Gap crossroads, where it cuts across the Military Rd and heads northwest for Kilbride and the N81, following the young River Liffey, still only a stream.

Sleeping & Eating

Roundwood Caravan & Camping Park CAMPING €
(01-281 8163; www.dublinwicklowcamping.com; campsites per adult/child €8/4; Apr-Sep;) Top-notch facilities, including a kitchen, dining area and TV lounge, make this one of the best camping grounds in all of Wicklow. It is about 500m south of the village and is served by the daily St Kevin's Bus service between Dublin and Glendalough.

Roundwood Inn INTERNATIONAL €€
(01-281 8107; Main St; bar food €10-16, mains €16-32; bar noon-9pm, restaurant 7.30-9.30pm Fri & Sat, 1-3pm Sun) This 17th-century German-owned house has a gorgeous bar with a snug open fire, in front of which you can sample bar food with a difference: on the menu are dishes such as Hungarian goulash and Irish stew with a German twist. The more formal restaurant is the best in town, and has earned praise for its hearty, delicious cuisine. The menu favours meat dishes, including seasonal game, Wicklow rack of lamb and a particularly good roast suckling pig. Reservations are required.

Getting There & Away

St Kevin's Bus (01-281 8119; www.glendaloughbus.com) passes through Roundwood on its twice-daily jaunt between Dublin and Glendalough (one way/return €8/14, 1¼ hours).

WICKLOW GAP

Between Mt Tonelagee (816m) to the north and Table Mountain (700m) to the southwest, the Wicklow Gap is the second major pass over the mountains. The eastern end of the road begins just to the north of Glendalough and climbs through some lovely scenery northwestwards up along the Glendassan Valley. It passes the remains of some old lead and zinc workings before meeting a side road that leads south and up Turlough Hill, the location of Ireland's only pumped-storage power station. You can walk up the hill for a look over the Upper Lake.

GLENDALOUGH

POP 280

If you've come to Wicklow, chances are that a visit to Glendalough (Gleann dá Loch, 'Valley of the Two Lakes') is one of your main reasons for being here. And you're not wrong, for this is one of the most beautiful corners of the whole country and the epitome of the kind of rugged, romantic Ireland that probably drew you to the island in the first place.

The substantial remains of this important monastic settlement are certainly impressive, but the real draw is the splendid setting: two dark and mysterious lakes tucked into a deep valley covered in forest. It is, despite its immense popularity, a deeply tranquil and spiritual place, and you will have little difficulty in understanding why those solitude-seeking monks came here in the first place.

History

In AD 498 a young monk named Kevin arrived in the valley looking for somewhere to kick back, meditate and be at one with nature. He pitched up in what had been a Bronze Age tomb on the southern side of the Upper Lake and for the next seven years slept on stones, wore animal skins, maintained a near-starvation diet and – according to the legend – became bosom buddies with the birds and animals. Kevin's ecofriendly lifestyle soon attracted a bunch of disciples, all seemingly unaware of the irony that they were flocking to hang out with a hermit who wanted to live as far away from other people as possible. Over the next couple of centuries his one-man operation mushroomed into a proper settlement and by the 9th century Glendalough rivalled Clonmacnoise (p509) as the island's premier monastic city. Thousands of students studied and lived in a thriving community that was spread over a considerable area.

Inevitably, Glendalough's success made it a key target for Viking raiders, who sacked the monastery at least four times between 775 and 1071. The final blow came in 1398, when English forces from Dublin almost destroyed it. Efforts were made to rebuild and some life lingered on here as late as the 17th century when, under renewed repression, the monastery finally died.

Sights

UPPER LAKE

The original site of St Kevin's settlement, **Teampall na Skellig** is at the base of the cliffs towering over the southern side of the Upper Lake and is accessible only by boat; unfortunately, there's no boat service to the site and you'll have to settle for looking at it across the lake. The terraced shelf has the reconstructed ruins of a church and early graveyard. Rough wattle huts once stood on the raised ground nearby. Scattered around are some early grave slabs and simple stone crosses.

Just east of here and 10m above the lake waters is the 2m-deep artificial cave called **St Kevin's Bed**, said to be where Kevin lived. The earliest human habitation of the cave was long before St Kevin's era – there's evidence that people lived in the valley for thousands of years before the monks arrived. In the green area just south of the car park is a large circular wall thought to be the remains of an early Christian **stone fort** *(caher)*.

Follow the lakeshore path southwest of the car park until you come to the considerable remains of **Reefert Church** above the tiny River Poulanass. It's a small, plain, 11th-century Romanesque nave-and-chancel church with some reassembled arches and walls. Traditionally, Reefert (literally 'Royal Burial Place') was the burial site of the chiefs of the local O'Toole family. The surrounding graveyard contains a number of rough stone crosses and slabs, most made of shiny mica schist.

Climb the steps at the back of the churchyard and follow the path to the west and you'll find, at the top of a rise overlooking the lake, the scant remains of **St Kevin's Cell**, a small beehive hut.

LOWER LAKE

While the Upper Lake has the best scenery, the most fascinating buildings lie in the lower part of the valley east of the Lower Lake,

WORTH A TRIP

GLENMACNASS

Desolate and utterly deserted, the Glenmacnass valley, a stretch of wild bogland between the Sally Gap crossroads and Laragh, is one of the most beautiful parts of the mountains, although the sense of isolation is quite dramatic.

The highest mountain to the west is Mt Mullaghcleevaun (848m), and River Glenmacnass flows south and tumbles over the edge of the mountain plateau in a great foaming cascade. There's a car park near the top of the waterfall. Be careful when walking on rocks near **Glenmacnass Waterfall** as a few people have slipped to their deaths. There are fine walks up Mt Mullaghcleevaun or in the hills to the east of the car park.

Glendalough

WALKING TOUR

A visit to Glendalough is a trip through ancient history and a refreshing hike in the hills. The ancient monastic settlement founded by St Kevin in the 5th century grew to be quite powerful by the 9th century, but it started falling into ruin from 1398 onwards. Still, you won't find more evocative clumps of stones anywhere.

Start at the **Main Gateway** 1 to the monastic city, where you will find a cluster of important ruins, including the (nearly perfect) 10th-century **Round Tower** 2, the **Cathedral** 3 dedicated to **Sts Peter and Paul**, and **St Kevin's Kitchen** 4, which is really a church. Cross the stream past the famous **Deer Stone** 5, where Kevin was supposed to have milked a doe, and turn west along the path. It's a 1.5km walk to the **Upper Lake** 6. On the lake's southern shore is another cluster of sites, including the **Reefert Church** 7, a plain 11th-century Romanesque church where the powerful O'Toole family buried their kin, and **St Kevin's Cell** 8, the remains of a beehive hut where Kevin is said to have lived.

ST KEVIN

St Kevin came to the valley as a young monk in AD 498, in search of a peaceful retreat. He was reportedly led by an angel to a Bronze Age tomb now known as St Kevin's Bed. For seven years he slept on stones, wore animal skins, survived on nettles and herbs and – according to legend – developed an affinity with the birds and animals. One legend has it that, when Kevin needed milk for two orphaned babies, a doe stood waiting at the Deer Stone to be milked.

Kevin soon attracted a group of disciples and the monastic settlement grew, until by the 9th century Glendalough rivalled Clomacnoise as Ireland's premier monastic city. According to legend Kevin lived to the age of 120. He was canonised in 1903.

St Kevin's Cell
This beehive hut is reputedly where St Kevin would go for prayer and meditation; not to be confused with St Kevin's Bed, a cave where he used to sleep.

Deer Stone
The spot where St Kevin is said to have truly become one with the animals is really just a large mortar called a *bullaun*, used for grinding food and medicine.

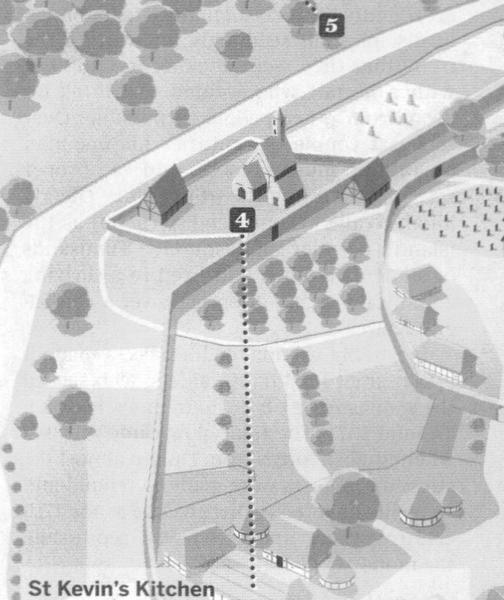

St Kevin's Kitchen
This small church (called the Priests' House) is unusual in that it has a round tower sticking out of the roof – it looks like a chimney, hence the church's nickname.

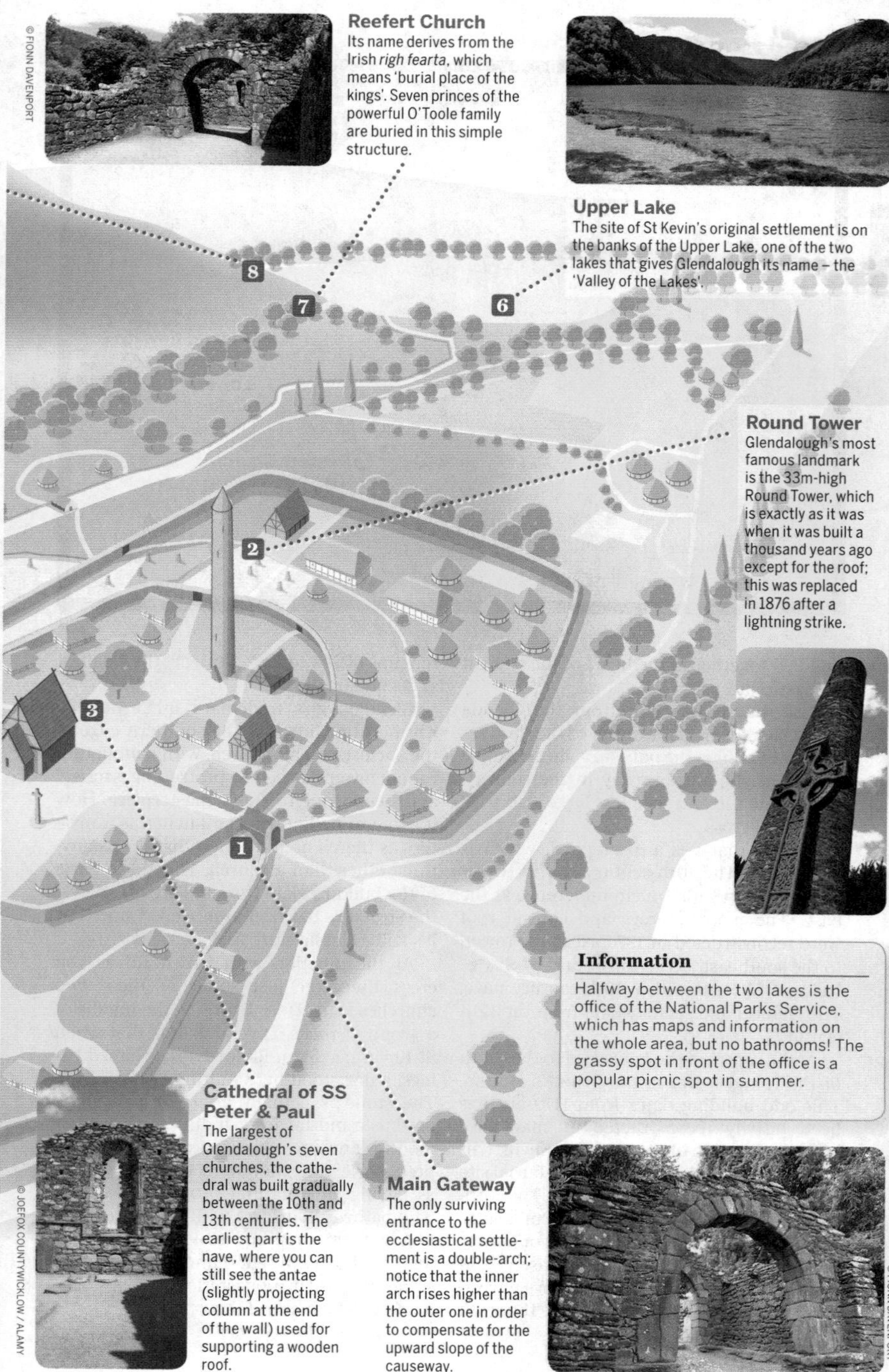
© FIONN DAVENPORT
Reefert Church
Its name derives from the Irish righ fearta, which means 'burial place of the kings'. Seven princes of the powerful O'Toole family are buried in this simple structure.
© FIONN DAVENPORT
Upper Lake
The site of St Kevin's original settlement is on the banks of the Upper Lake, one of the two lakes that gives Glendalough its name – the 'Valley of the Lakes'.
8
7
6
Round Tower
Glendalough's most famous landmark is the 33m-high Round Tower, which is exactly as it was when it was built a thousand years ago except for the roof; this was replaced in 1876 after a lightning strike.
2
© FIONN DAVENPORT
3
1
Information
Halfway between the two lakes is the office of the National Parks Service, which has maps and information on the whole area, but no bathrooms! The grassy spot in front of the office is a popular picnic spot in summer.
Cathedral of SS Peter & Paul
The largest of Glendalough's seven churches, the cathedral was built gradually between the 10th and 13th centuries. The earliest part is the nave, where you can still see the antae (slightly projecting column at the end of the wall) used for supporting a wooden roof.
© JOEFOX COUNTYWICKLOW / ALAMY
Main Gateway
The only surviving entrance to the ecclesiastical settlement is a double-arch; notice that the inner arch rises higher than the outer one in order to compensate for the upward slope of the causeway.
© FIONN DAVENPORT

Glendalough

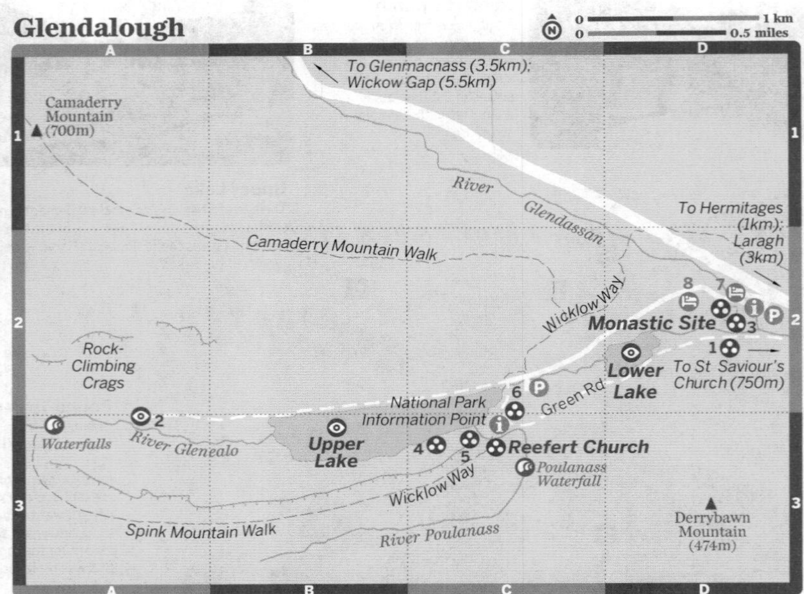

huddled together in the heart of the ancient monastic site.

Just round the bend from the Glenda lough Hotel is the stone arch of the **monastery gatehouse**, the only surviving example of a monastic entranceway in the country. Just inside the entrance is a large slab with an incised cross.

Beyond that lies a **graveyard**, which is still in use. The 10th-century **round tower** is 33m tall and 16m in circumference at the base. The upper storeys and conical roof were reconstructed in 1876. Near the tower, to the southeast, is the **Cathedral of St Peter and St Paul** with a 10th-century nave. The chancel and sacristy date from the 12th century.

At the centre of the graveyard to the south of the round tower is the **Priest's House**. This odd building dates from 1170 but has been heavily reconstructed. It may have been the location of shrines of St Kevin. Later, during penal times, it became a burial site for local priests – hence the name. The 10th-century **St Mary's Church**, 140m southwest of the round tower, probably originally stood outside the walls of the monastery and belonged to local nuns. It has a lovely western doorway. A little to the east are the scant remains of **St Kieran's Church**, the smallest at Glendalough.

Glendalough's trademark is **St Kevin's Kitchen** or Church at the southern edge of the enclosure. This church, with a miniature round towerlike belfry, protruding sacristy and steep stone roof, is a masterpiece. How it came to be known as a kitchen is a mystery as there's no indication that it was anything other than a church. The oldest parts of the building date from the 11th century – the structure has been remodelled since but it's still a classic early Irish church.

At the junction with Green Rd as you cross the river just south of these two churches is the **Deer Stone** in the middle of a group of rocks. Legend claims that when St Kevin needed milk for two orphaned babies, a doe stood here waiting to be milked. The stone is actually a *bullaun* (a stone used as a mortar for grinding medicines or food). Many such stones are thought to be prehistoric, and they were widely regarded as having supernatural properties: women who bathed their faces with water from the hollow were supposed to keep their looks forever. The early churchmen brought the stones into their monasteries, perhaps hoping to inherit some of their powers.

Glendalough

Top Sights

	Lower Lake	D2
	Monastic Site	D2
	Reefert Church	C3
	Upper Lake	B3

Sights

	Cathedral of St Peter & Paul	(see 3)
1	Deer Stone	D2
2	Mine Workings	A3
	Priest's House	(see 3)
3	Round Tower	D2
4	St Kevin's Bed	C3
5	St Kevin's Cell	C3
	St Kieran's Church	(see 3)
	St Mary's Church	(see 3)
6	Stone Fort	C2
	Teampall na Skellig	(see 4)

Sleeping

7	Glendalough Hotel	D2
8	Glendalough International Hostel	D2

Eating

	Glendalough Hotel	(see 7)

The road east leads to **St Saviour's Church**, with its detailed Romanesque carvings. To the west, a nice woodland trail leads up the valley past the Lower Lake to the Upper Lake.

Activities

The Glendalough Valley is all about **walking** and clambering. There are nine marked ways in the valley, the longest of which is about 10km, or about four hours walking. Before you set off, drop by the **National Park Information Point** (0404-45425; 10am-6pm daily May-Sep, to dusk Sat & Sun Oct-Apr) and pick up the relevant leaflet and trail map (all around €0.50) or, if you're solo, arrange for walking partners. It also has a number of excellent guides for sale – you won't go far wrong with Joss Lynam's *Easy Walks Near Dublin* (€7.99). A word of warning: don't be fooled by the relative gentleness of the surrounding countryside or the fact that the Wicklow Mountains are really no taller than big hills. The weather can be merciless here, so be sure to take the usual precautions, have the right equipment and tell someone where you're going and when you should be back. For Mountain Rescue call 999.

The easiest and most popular walk is the gentle hike along the northern shore of the Upper Lake to the lead and zinc **mine workings**, which date from 1800. The better route is along the lakeshore rather than on the road (which runs 30m in from the shore), a distance of about 2.5km one way from the Glendalough Visitor Centre. Continue on up the head of the valley if you wish.

Alternatively, you can walk up the **Spink** (from the Irish for 'pointed hill'; 380m), the steep ridge with vertical cliffs running along the southern flanks of the Upper Lake. You can go part of the way and turn back, or complete a circuit of the Upper Lake by following the top of the cliff, eventually coming down by the mine workings and going back along the northern shore. The circuit is about 6km long and takes about three hours – if you feel like going on, check out the boxed text, p148.

The third option is a hike up **Camaderry Mountain** (700m), hidden behind the hills that flank the northern side of the valley. The walk starts on the road just 50m back towards Glendalough from the entrance to the Upper Lake car park. Head straight up the steep hill to the north and you come out on open mountains with sweeping views in all directions. You can then continue up Camaderry to the northwest or just follow the ridge west looking over the Upper Lake. To the top of Camaderry and back is about 7.5km and takes about four hours.

Tours

A couple of bus tours depart Dublin if you don't want to explore Glendalough under your own steam:

Bus Éireann BUS TOUR
(Map p60; 01-836 6111; www.buseireann.ie; Busáras; adult/child/student €29/23/25; departs 10am mid-Mar–Oct) Includes admission to the visitor centre and a visit to Powerscourt Estate in this whole-day tour, which returns to Dublin at about 5.45pm. The guides are good but impersonal.

Wild Wicklow Tour BUS TOUR
(01-280 1899; www.discoverdublin.ie; adult/student & child €28/25; departs 9am) Award-winning tours of Glendalough, Avoca and the Sally Gap that never fail to generate rave reviews for atmosphere and all-round fun, but so much craic has made a casualty of informative depth. The first pick-up is at the Dublin Tourism office, but there are a variety of pick-up points throughout Dublin;

check the point nearest you when booking. The tour returns to Dublin about 5.30pm.

Sleeping

Most B&Bs are in or around Laragh, a village 3km east of Glendalough, or on the way there from Glendalough.

TOP CHOICE **Glendalough Hermitages** HERMITAGE €
(☎0404-45140, for bookings 45777; www.hermitage.dublindiocese.ie; St Kevin's Parish Church, Glendalough; s/d €50/75) In an effort to recreate something of the contemplative spirit of Kevin's early years in the valley, St Kevin's

WALK: THE WICKLOW WAY – GLENDALOUGH TO AUGHRIM

The Wicklow Way is one of Ireland's most popular long-distance walks because of its remarkable scenery and its relatively fluid and accessible starting and finishing points – there are plenty of half- and full day options along the way.

This section is 40km long and takes you through some of the more remote parts of the Wicklow Mountains and down into the southeastern foothills. There's relatively little road walking but the greater part of the day is through conifer plantations. The walk should take between 7½ and eight hours, with an ascent of 1035m.

From the **National Park Information Point** on the southern side of the Upper Lake, turn left and ascend beside Lugduff Brook and **Poulanass Waterfall**. Veer left when you meet a forest track, then left again at a junction and cross two bridges. The Way leads northeast for about 600m then, from a tight right bend, heads almost directly southwards (via a series of clearly marked junctions), up through the conifer plantations, across Lugduff Brook again and beside a tributary, to open ground on the saddle between **Mullacor** (657m) and **Lugduff** (652m; 1¾ hours from Glendalough). From here on a good day, massive Lugnaquilla sprawls across the view to the southwest; in the opposite direction is Camaderry's long ridge above Glendalough, framed against the bulk of Tonelagee. Follow the raised boardwalk down, contour above a plantation and drop into it where a steep muddy and rocky path descends to a forest road; turn left.

If you're planning to stay at Glenmalure Hostel (see p150), rather than go all the way down to the crossroads in Glenmalure, follow the Way from the left turn for about 1km southwards. At an oblique junction where the Way turns southeast, bear left in a westerly direction and descend steeply to the road in Glenmalure. The hostel is about 2km northwest.

To continue straight on along the Way from the left turn, follow forest roads south then southeast for 1.6km to a wide zigzag above open ground, then contour the steep slope, swing northeast and drop down to a minor road beside two bridges. Continue down to an intersection and Glenmalure; it's about 1¼ hours from the saddle.

The Way presses straight on (south) through the crossroads for 500m, across the River Avonbeg and past silent **Drumgoff Barracks**, built in 1803 but long since derelict, then right along a forest track. Keep left past a ruined cottage and start to gain height in two fairly long reaches; go through two left turns then it's down and across a stream. About 800m further on, turn right along a path to start the long ascent almost to the top of **Slieve Maan** (550m) via four track junctions, maintaining a southwesterly to south-southwesterly direction. Back on a forest track, the Way turns left (southeast) close to unforested ground to the west. With a few more convoluted turns, you're out of the trees and on a path between the plantation and the road (mapped as the Military Rd). The Way eventually meets the latter beside a small tributary of the River Aghavannagh (two hours from Glenmalure).

Walk down the road for about 250m, then turn off left along a forest track, shortly bearing left to gain height steadily on a wide path over **Carrickashane Mountain** (508m). Descend steeply to a wide forest road and continue down for about 1km. Bear right to reach a minor road and turn right. Leave the road 500m further on and drop down to another road – Iron Bridge is just to the right (an hour from Military Rd).

Walk 150m up to a road and turn left; follow this road down the valley of the River Ow for 7.5km to a junction – Aughrim is to the left, another 500m. Buses along the Dublin to Wexford line stop here.

Parish Church rents out five *cillíns* (hermitages) for folks looking to take time out from the bustle of daily life and reflect on more spiritual matters. In keeping with modern needs, however, there are a few more facilities than were present in Kevin's cave. Each hermitage is a bungalow consisting of a bedroom, a bathroom, a small kitchen area and an open fire supplemented by a storage heating facility. The whole venture is managed by the local parish, and while there is a strong spiritual emphasis here, it is not necessarily a Catholic one. Visitors of all denominations and creeds are welcome, so long as their intentions are reflective and meditative; backpackers looking for a cheap place to bed down are not. The hermitages are in a field next to St Kevin's Parish Church, about 1km east of Glendalough on the R756 to Laragh.

Glendalough Hotel HOTEL €€
(☎0404-45135; www.glendaloughhotel.com; s/d €110/150; P@⌔ⓘ) There's no mistaking Glendalough's best hotel, conveniently located next door to the visitor centre. There is no shortage of takers for its 44 fairly luxurious bedrooms.

Glendale B&B €€
(☎0404-45410; www.glendale-glendalough.com; Laragh East; r €72, cottage per week €355-755; P⌔) This is an immaculately modern and tidy B&B with large, comfortable rooms. Also available are five modern self-catering cottages that sleep six. Every cottage has all the mod cons, from TV and video to a fully equipped kitchen complete with microwave, dishwasher and washer-dryer. The owners will also drop you off in Glendalough if you don't fancy the walk.

Glendalough International Hostel HOSTEL €
(☎0404-45342; www.anoige.ie; The Lodge; dm/d €24/50; @⌔) Conveniently, this modern hostel is situated near the round tower, set within the deeply wooded glacial area that makes up the Glendalough Valley. All dorms have en-suite bathrooms and there's a decent cafeteria on the premises.

Eating

Laragh's the place for a bit of grub, as only the Glendalough Hotel serves food near the site.

Wicklow Heather Restaurant INTERNATIONAL €€
(☎0404-45157; www.thewicklowheather.com; Main St, Laragh; mains €16-26; ⊙noon-8.30pm) This is the best place for anything substantial. The menu offers Wicklow lamb, wild venison, Irish beef and fresh fish (the trout is excellent) – most of it sourced locally and all of it traceable from farm to fork.

Information

At the valley entrance, before the Glendalough Hotel, is **Glendalough Visitor Centre** (☎0404-45325; www.heritageireland.ie; adult/child & student €3/2; ⊙9.30am-6pm mid-Mar–Oct, to 5pm Nov–mid-Mar). It has a high-quality 17-minute audiovisual presentation called *Ireland of the Monasteries*, which does exactly what it says on the tin.

Getting There & Away

St Kevin's Bus (☎01-281 8119; www.glendaloughbus.com) departs from outside the Mansion House on Dawson St in Dublin at 11.30am and 6pm Monday to Saturday, and 11.30am and 7pm Sunday (one way/return €13/20, 1½ hours). It also stops at the Town Hall in Bray. Departures from Glendalough are at 7.15am and 4.30pm Monday to Saturday. During the week in July and August the later bus runs at 5.30pm, and there is an additional service at 9.45am.

GLENMALURE

As you go deeper into the mountains southwest of Glendalough near the southern end of the Military Rd, everything gets a bit wilder and more remote. Beneath the western slopes of Wicklow's highest peak, Lugnaquilla, is Glenmalure, a dark and sombre blind valley flanked by scree slopes of loose boulders. After coming over the mountains into Glen malure you turn northwest at the Drumgoff bridge. From there it's about 6km up the road beside the River Avonbeg to a car park where trails lead off in various directions.

Glenmalure figures prominently in the national tale of resistance against the British. The valley was a clan stronghold and in 1580 the redoubtable chieftain Fiach Mac Hugh O'Byrne (1544–97) and his band of merry men actually managed to defeat an army of 1000 English soldiers; the battle cost the lives of 800 men and drove Queen Elizabeth into an apoplectic rage. In 1597 the English avenged the disaster when they captured O'Byrne and impaled his head on the gates of Dublin Castle.

Sights & Activities

Near Drumgoff is Dwyer's or **Cullen's Rock**, which commemorates both the Glenmalure battle and Michael Dwyer, a member of the United Irishmen who fought unsuccessfully against the English in the Rising of 1798 (see also p698) and holed up here. Men were hanged from the rock during the Rising.

You can walk up Lugnaquilla Mountain or head up the blind Fraughan Rock Glen east of the car park. Alternatively, you can go straight up Glenmalure Valley passing the small, seasonal An Óige Glenmalure Hostel, after which the trail divides – heading northeast, the trail takes you over the hills to Glendalough, while going northwest brings you into the Glen of Imaal (p151).

The head of Glenmalure and parts of the neighbouring Glen of Imaal are off-limits. It's military land, well posted with warning signs.

Sleeping

Glenmalure Hostel HOSTEL €
(01-830 4555; www.anoige.ie; Greenane; dm €15; Jun-Aug, Sat only Sep-May) No telephone, no electricity (lighting is by gas), just a rustic two-storey cottage with 19 beds and running water. This place has a couple of heavyweight literary links: it was once owned by WB Yeats' femme fatale, Maud Gonne, and was also the setting for JM Synge's play, *Shadow of a Gunman*. It's isolated, but is beautifully situated beneath Lugnaquilla.

Glenmalure Log Cabin SELF-CATERING €€
(01-269 6979; www.glenmalure.com; 11 Glen malure Pines, Greenane; 2 nights €200-290, 3 nights €350-550;) In the heart of Glenmalure, this modern, Scandinavian-style lodge has two rooms with private bathrooms, a fully equipped kitchen and a living room kitted out with all kinds of electronic amusements, including your very own DVD library. Hopefully, though, you'll spend much of your time here enjoying the panorama from the sun deck. There's a two-night minimum stay, except for July and August when it's seven days.

Western Wicklow

As you go west through the county, the landscape gets less rugged and more rural, especially towards the borders of Kildare and Carlow. The wild terrain gives way to rich pastures; east of Blessington the countryside is dotted with private stud farms where some of the world's most expensive horses are trained in jealously guarded secrecy.

The main attraction in this part of Wicklow is the magnificent Palladian pile at Russborough House, just outside Blessington, but if it's more wild scenery you're after, you'll find it around Kilbride and the upper reaches of the River Liffey, as well as further south in the Glen of Imaal.

BLESSINGTON

POP 4018

There's little to see in Blessington; it's basically made up of a long row of pubs, shops and 17th- and 18th-century town houses. It's the main town in the area and as such makes a decent exploring base. Just outside Blessington is the Poulaphouca Reservoir, created in 1940 to drive the turbines of the local power station to the east of town and to supply Dublin with water.

The **tourist office** (045-865 850; Blessington Craft Centre, Main St; 9.30am-4pm Mon-Fri) is across the road from the Downshire House Hotel.

Sights

Russborough House HISTORIC BUILDING
(045-865 239; www.russborough.ie; Blessington; adult/child/student €10/5/8; 10am-6pm May-Sep, Sun & bank holidays only Apr & Oct) Magnificent Russborough House is one of Ireland's finest stately homes, a Palladian pleasure palace built for Joseph Leeson (1705–83), later the first Earl of Milltown and, later still, Lord Russborough. It was built between 1741 and 1751 to the design of Richard Cassels, who was at the height of his fame as an architect. Poor old Richard didn't live to see it finished, but the job was well executed by Francis Bindon. Now, let's get down to the juicy bits.

The house has always attracted unwelcome attention, beginning in 1798 when Irish forces took hold of the place during the Rising; they were soon turfed out by the British army who got so used to the comforts of the place that they didn't leave until 1801, and then only after a raging Lord Russborough challenged their commander, Lord Tyrawley, to a duel 'with blunderbusses and slugs in a sawpit'. Miaow.

The house remained in the Leeson family until 1931. In 1952 it was sold to Sir Alfred Beit, the eponymous nephew of the co-founder of the de Beers diamond-mining company. Uncle Alfred was an obsessive art collector, and when he died his impressive haul – which includes works by Velázquez, Vermeer, Goya and Rubens – was passed on to his nephew, who brought it to Russborough House. The collection was to attract the interest of more than just art lovers.

In 1974 the IRA decided to get into the art business by stealing 16 of the paintings. They were eventually all recovered, but 10 years later the notorious Dublin criminal Martin Cahill (aka the General) masterminded another robbery, this time for Loyalist paramilitaries. On this occasion, however, only some of the works were recovered and of those, several were damaged beyond repair – a good thief does not a gentle curator make. In 1988 Beit got the picture and decided to hand over the most valuable of the paintings to the National Gallery; in return for the gift, the gallery agreed to lend other paintings to the collection as temporary exhibits. The sorry story didn't conclude there. In 2001 two thieves took the direct approach and drove a jeep through the front doors, making off with two paintings worth nearly €4 million, including a Gainsborough that had been stolen, and recovered, twice before. And then, to add abuse to the insult already added to injury, the house was broken into again in 2002, with the thieves taking five more paintings, including two by Rubens. Incredibly, however, both hauls were quickly recovered.

The admission price includes a 45-minute tour of the house, decorated in typical Georgian style, and all the important paintings, which, given the history, is a monumental exercise in staying positive. Whatever you do, make no sudden moves.

Activities

Rathsallagh Golf Club GOLF
(☎045-403 316; www.rathsallaghhousehotel.com; green fees hotel guest/visitor from €60/65) This golf club is known – somewhat optimistically – as 'Augusta without the Azaleas', but it is still one of the best parkland courses in Ireland, stretching over 6.5km amid mature trees, small lakes and shallow streams.

Sleeping & Eating

TOP CHOICE **Rathsallagh House & Country Club** HOTEL €€€
(☎045-403 112; www.rathsallaghhousehotel.com; Dunlavin; mains €33-42, s/d from €135/260) About 20km south of Blessington, this fabulous country manor, converted from Queen Anne stables in 1798, is more than just a fancy hotel. Luxury is par for the course here, from the splendidly appointed rooms to the exquisite country-house dining (the food here is some of the best you'll eat anywhere in Ireland) and the marvellous golf course that surrounds the estate. Even the breakfast is extraordinary: it has won the National Breakfast Award three times. Is there anything Irish tourism doesn't have an award for?

Haylands House B&B €€
(☎045-865 183; haylands@eircom.net; Dublin Rd; s/d from €40/70; P) We highly recommend this modern bungalow for its lovely rooms (all with en-suite bathrooms), warm welcome and excellent breakfast. It's only 500m out of town on the main Dublin road. As it's popular, book early if you can.

Grangecon Café INTERNATIONAL €€
(☎045-857 892; Tullow Rd; mains €11-18; ⏲10am-5pm Tue-Sat) Salads, home-baked dishes and a full menu of Irish cheeses are the staples at this tiny, terrific cafe in a converted schoolhouse. Everything here – from the pasta to the delicious apple juice – is made on the premises and many of the ingredients are organic. A short but solid menu represents the best of Irish cooking.

Russborough House hosts a monthly **farmers market** (☎087-611 5016; ⏲10am-4pm, first Sun of the month) that goes indoors during the winter months.

Getting There & Away

Blessington is 35km southwest of Dublin on the N81. There are regular daily services by **Dublin Bus** (☎01-872 0000, 01-873 4222); catch bus 65 from Eden Quay in Dublin (€4.70, 1½ hours, every 1½ hours). **Bus Éireann** (☎01-836 6111; www.buseireann.ie) operates express bus 005 to and from Waterford, with stops in Blessington two or three times daily; from Dublin it's pick-up only and from Waterford drop-off only.

GLEN OF IMAAL

About 7km southeast of Donard, the lovely Glen of Imaal is about the only scenery of consequence on the western flanks of the Wicklow Mountains. It's named after Mal, brother of the 2nd-century king of Ireland, Cathal Mór. Unfortunately, the glen's northeastern slopes are mostly cordoned off as an army firing range and for manoeuvres. Look out for red danger signs.

The area's most famous son was Michael Dwyer, who led rebel forces during the 1798 Rising and held out for five years in the local hills and glens. On the southeastern side of the glen at Derrynamuck is a small whitewashed, thatched cottage where Dwyer and three friends were surrounded by 100 English soldiers. One of Dwyer's companions, Samuel McAllister, ran out the front, drawing fire and meeting his death, while Dwyer escaped into the night. He was eventually deported in 1803 and jailed on Norfolk Island, off the eastern coast of Australia. He became chief constable of Liverpool, near Sydney, before he died in 1825. The cottage is now a small **folk museum** (☎0404-45325; Derrynamuck; admission free; ⏰2-6pm mid-Jun–Sep) located on the Knockanarrigan–Rathdangan road.

The Coast

Wicklow's coastline is not nearly as scenic or dramatic as its mountains and inland marvels: its largely unassuming towns and small coastal resorts have a subtle kind of charm that isn't immediately apparent and virtually disappears on a rainy day. Most attractive of all are the fine beaches of Brittas Bay, a wide lazy arc of coastline immediately south of Wicklow Town. Running alongside it is the N11 (M11) from Dublin to Wexford, a busy road that cuts through a great glacial rift, the **Glen of the Downs**, carved out of an Ice Age lake by floodwaters. There's a forest walk up to a ruined teahouse on top of the ridge to the east.

If you're looking for quieter and more scenic coastal byways, we recommend the coastal route through Greystones, Kilcoole and then along country lanes to Rathnew.

KILMACANOGUE & THE GREAT SUGARLOAF

POP 839

At 503m, it's not even Wicklow's highest mountain, but the Great Sugarloaf is one of the most distinctive peaks in Ireland, its conical tip visible for many miles around. The mountain towers over the small village of Kilmacanogue, on the N11 about 4km south of Bray, which would barely merit a passing nod were it not for the presence of the mother of all Irish craft shops just across the road from the village.

Avoca Handweavers (☎01-286 7466; www.avoca.ie; Main St) is one hell of an operation, with seven branches nationwide and an even more widespread reputation for adding elegance and style to traditional rural handicrafts. Operational HQ is in a 19th-century arboretum, and its showroom will leave you in no doubt as to the company's incredible success.

Shopping for pashminas and placemats can put a fierce hunger on you and there's no better place to satisfy it than at the shop's huge and always-busy **restaurant** (mains €12-18; ⏰9.30am-5.30pm), which puts a premium on sourcing the very best ingredients for its dishes. It is best known for its beef-and-Guinness casserole, but vegetarians are very well catered for, too. Many of the recipes are available in the three volumes of the *Avoca Cookbook*, available as a package for €45.

Getting There & Away

Bus Éireann (☎01-836 6111; www.buseireann.ie) operates bus 133 from Dublin to Wicklow town and Arklow, with stops in Kilmacanogue (one way/return €3.80/6, 30 minutes, 10 daily).

GREYSTONES TO WICKLOW

The resort of Greystones, 8km south of Bray, was once a charming fishing village, and the seafront around the little harbour is idyllic. In summer, the bay is dotted with dinghies and windsurfers. Sadly, the surrounding countryside is vanishing beneath housing developments.

Sights

Horticulturalists from around the world can be found salivating and muttering in approval as they walk around the 8-hectare **Mt Usher Gardens** (☎0404-40116; www.mountushergardens.ie; adult/child/student €7.50/3/6; ⏰10.30am-6pm mid-Apr-Oct), just outside the unremarkable town of Ashford, about 10km south of Greystones on the N11. OK, not really, but the gardens are pretty special, with trees, shrubs and herbaceous plants from around the world laid out in Robinsonian style – ie according to the naturalist principles of famous Irish gardener William Robinson (1838-1935) – rather than the formalist style of preceding gardens.

Sleeping & Eating

TOP CHOICE **Hunter's Hotel** HOTEL €€

(☎0404-40106; www.hunters.ie; Newrath Bridge, Rathnew; s/d €80/130; P) This exquisite property just outside Rathnew on the R761 is an absolute find, with 16 stunning rooms, each decorated with unerringly good taste. The house, one of Ireland's oldest coaching inns, is surrounded by an award-winning garden that is part of the Wicklow Gardens Festival (see the boxed text, p141).

WALK: THE GREAT SUGARLOAF

Before you attack the 7km, moderately difficult walk to the summit, we recommend that you get the *Wicklow Trail Sheet No 4* (€1.50) from the tourist office in Bray.

Start your walk by taking the small road opposite **St Mochonog's Church** (named after the missionary who administered the last rites to St Kevin). Ignore the left turn and continue round the bend until you get to a small bridge on your right. To your right, you'll see the expanse of the **Rocky Valley** below, a defile eroded by water escaping from a glacial lake that developed during the last Ice Age, about 10,000 years ago. Continue on the path until you reach a fork: the lower road to the right continues round the mountain, while the left turn will take you up to the summit. As you reach the top, the track starts to drop; turn left and scramble up the rocky gully to the top. Return by the same path and continue southwards until you reach a large grassy area. Cross it, keeping to your left until you reach a gate. With the fence on your right, go downhill until you reach a path of grass and stones. This path takes you around the southern side of the mountain, where you will eventually pass a small wood on your right. Immediately afterwards you will see, on your left, a sports pitch known as the Quill. Beyond it is Kilmacanogue.

Three Q's INTERNATIONAL €€
(01-287 5477; Church Rd; mains €14-20; 9am-10pm Tue-Fri, to 3pm Sat & Sun) You'll find a smart menu at this elegant restaurant, with dishes like wood pigeon and duck sharing the space with North African delicacies like baked Moroccan fish with chickpeas, tomato and coriander.

Hungry Monk IRISH €€€
(01-287 5759; Church Rd; mains €19-28; 7-11pm Wed-Sat, 12.30-9pm Sun;) An excellent 1st-floor restaurant on Greystones' main street. The blackboard specials are the real treat, with dishes like suckling pig with prune and apricot stuffing to complement the fixed menu's classic choices – fresh seafood, Wicklow rack of lamb, bangers and mash and so forth. This is one of the better places to get a bite along the whole of the Wicklow coast.

Getting There & Away

Bus Éireann (01-836 6111; www.buseireann.ie) operates bus 133 from Dublin to Wicklow town and Arklow with stops outside Ashford House, in Ashford (one way/return €5.70/8.10, one hour, 10 daily).

WICKLOW TOWN

POP 6930

Busy Wicklow town has a fine harbour and a commanding position on the crescent curve of a wide bay, which stretches north for about 12km and includes a long pebble beach that makes for a fine walk. One top-notch attraction aside, this is not really a big tourist town and, unless you have your own transport, it doesn't make an especially good base for exploring inland.

The **tourist office** (0404-69117; www.wicklow.ie; Fitzwilliam Sq; 9.30am-6pm Jun-Sep, 9am-1pm & 2-5pm Oct-May, closed Sun) is in the heart of town.

Sights

Wicklow's Historic Gaol HISTORIC BUILDING
(0404-61599; www.wicklowshistoricgaol.com; Kilmantin Hill; adult/child/student incl tour €7.30/4.50/6; 10.30am-4.30pm Mon-Sat, from 11.30am Sun, Apr-Oct) Wicklow's infamous **jail**, opened in 1702 to deal with prisoners sentenced under the repressive Penal Laws, was renowned throughout Ireland for the brutality of its keepers and the harsh conditions suffered by its inmates. The smells, vicious beatings, shocking food and disease-ridden air have long since gone, but adults and children alike can experience a sanitised version of what the prison was like – and stimulate the secret sadist buried deep within – in the highly entertaining tour of the prison, now one of Wicklow's most popular tourist attractions. Actors play the roles of the various jailers and prisoners, adding to the sense of drama already heightened by the various exhibits on show, including a life-size treadmill that prisoners would have to turn for hours on end as punishment, and the gruesome dungeon.

On the 2nd floor is a model of HMS *Hercules*, a convict ship that was used to

WORTH A TRIP

TINAKILLY COUNTRY HOUSE & RESTAURANT

Wicklow has no shortage of fine country homes converted into luxury manor hotels, but **Tinakilly Country House & Restaurant** (☎0404-69274; www.tinakilly.ie; Rathnew; r €115-200, dinner mains €22-29), a magnificent Victorian Italianate house just outside Rathnew (about 5km west of Wicklow town) stands out for sheer elegance. The guest rooms are divided between the period rooms in the west wing, decked out in original antiques, four-poster and half-tester canopy beds, and the shockingly sumptuous suites in the east wing, which have gorgeous views of either the richly colourful garden or the Irish Sea, albeit somewhere in the distance. And then there's the restaurant, which takes country-house cuisine to a whole new level of sophistication.

transport convicts to New South Wales under the captaincy of the psychotic Luckyn Betts: six months under his iron rule and most began to see death as a form of mercy. The top floor is devoted to the stories of the prisoners once they arrived in Australia. Tours are every 10 minutes except between 1pm and 2pm; on the last Friday of every month there are **adult-only tours** (⊙every 30 min, 7-9pm; €15) of the prison, complete with ghouls, finger food and a glass of wine.

The few remaining fragments of the **Black Castle** are on the shore at the southern end of town, with pleasant views up and down the coast. The castle was built in 1169 by the Fitzgeralds from Wales after they were granted land in the area by the Anglo-Norman conqueror, Strongbow. It used to be linked to the mainland by a drawbridge, and rumour has it that an escape tunnel ran from the sea cave underneath up into the town. At low tide you can swim or snorkel into the cave.

The walk south of town along the cliffs to **Wicklow Head** offers great views of the Wicklow Mountains. A string of **beaches** – Silver Strand, Brittas Bay and Maheramore – start 16km south of Wicklow. With high dunes, safe bathing and powdery sand, the beaches attract droves of Dubliners in good weather.

Festivals

Wicklow Arts Festival (☎086-033 3906; www.wicklowartsfestival.ie) A five-day extrav aganza of music, poetry, comedy and workshops that usually takes place in mid to late May.

Wicklow Regatta Festival (☎0404-68354; www.wicklowregatta.com) Held every year for 10 days from late July into early August. The extensive program of events and activities includes swimming, rowing, sailing and raft races, singing competitions, concerts and the Festival Queen Ball.

Sleeping & Eating

Town lodgings are not that great, so if you are planning on staying in the area, you're better off staying in one of the beautiful country homes within a few kilometres of town.

Grand Hotel HOTEL €€
(☎0404-67337; www.grandhotel.ie; Abbey St; s/d from €80/130; P📶) Wicklow town's best accommodation is this mock-Tudor hotel which is quite a bit short of 'grand', but it's a handsome, comfortable place nonetheless. The rooms are immaculate and the smallish size of the place assures a personalised, friendly service.

Halpin's Bridge Cafe CAFE €
(☎0404-32677; www.halpinscafe.com; Bridge St; mains €6-9; ⊙8.30am-6.30pm Mon-Sat, to 4pm Sun) An award-winning cafe serving delicious salads, homemade wraps, soups and an ever-changing special of the day. Eat in or take away.

Donelli's INTERNATIONAL €€
(☎0404-61333; www.donellis.ie; Market Sq; mains €17-24; ⊙9am-3pm Mon-Wed, to midnight Thu-Sat) From great coffee and cakes to an excellent menu of inviting dishes – including the likes of Penang chicken, vegetarian curry and Asian marinated salmon – this is a wonderful place to eat or linger in.

A **farmers market** (⊙10am-3pm Sat) is held weekly on Market Square, just off Main St.

Getting There & Around

Bus Éireann (01-836 6111; www.buseireann.ie) Runs bus 133, serving Wicklow town from Dublin (€8, 1½ hours, 10 daily); Wicklow town is also served by express bus 2 running between Dublin (one hour, 12 daily) and Rosslare Harbour (€16, 1½ hours).

Iarnród Éireann (Irish Rail; 01-836 6222) Serves Wicklow town from Dublin on the main Dublin to Rosslare Harbour line (one way/return €13/16, one hour, five daily). The station is a 10-minute walk north of the town centre.

Wicklow Cabs (0404-66888; Main St) Usually sends a few cabs to meet the evening trains from Dublin. The fare to anywhere in town should be no more than €6.

Southern Wicklow

South of Wicklow town, the landscape gives way to rolling hills and valleys cut through by rustling rivers and dotted with lovely little hamlets, including the especially beautiful Vale of Avoca, favoured by song and busloads of tourists.

RATHDRUM

POP 2123

The quiet village of Rathdrum at the foot of the Vale of Clara comprises little more than a few old houses and shops, but in the late 19th century it had a healthy flannel industry and a poorhouse. It's not what's in the town that's of interest to visitors, however, but what's just outside it.

The small **tourist office** (0404-46262; 29 Main St; 9am-5.30pm Mon-Fri) has leaflets and information on the town and surrounding area, including the Wicklow Way.

Sights

'Woe be to the man by whom the scandal cometh...It would be better for him that a millstone were tied about his neck and that he were cast into the depth of the sea rather than he should scandalise one of these, my least little ones.'

James Joyce, *A Portrait of the Artist as a Young Man*

Joyce's fictional dinner-table argument wasn't about a murderer or any such criminal, but about Charles Stewart Parnell (1846–91), the 'uncrowned king of Ireland' and unquestionably one of the key figures in the Irish independence movement.

Avondale House (0404-46111; adult/student & child €7/6.50; 11am-6pm May-Aug, Sat & Sun only Apr, by appointment only rest of year), a fine Palladian mansion surrounded by a marvellous 209-hectare estate, was the birthplace and Irish headquarters of Charles Stewart Parnell. Designed by James Wyatt in 1779, the house's many highlights include a stunning vermilion-hued library (Parnell's favourite room) and beautiful dining room.

From 1880 to 1890 Avondale was synonymous with the fight for Home Rule, which was brilliantly led by Parnell until 1890, when a member of his own Irish Parliamentary Party, Captain William O'Shea, sued his wife Kitty for divorce and named Parnell as co-respondent. Parnell's affair with Kitty O'Shea scandalised this 'priest-ridden' nation, and the ultraconservative clergy declared that Parnell was 'unfit to lead' – despite the fact that as soon as the divorce was granted the two lovers were quickly married. Parnell resigned as leader of the party and withdrew in despair to Avondale, where he died the following year.

WORTH A TRIP

BALLYKNOCKEN HOUSE

As fine a country home as you could ever hope to find, **Ballyknocken House & Cookery School** (0404-44627; www.ballyknocken.com; Glenealy, Ashford; s/d €90/110, 3-/4-course dinner €35/45;) is a beautiful ivy-clad Victorian home, 5km south of Ashford on the R752 to Glenealy. Each of the bedrooms is carefully appointed with original furnishings and have en-suite bathrooms, some with stencilled Victorian claw-foot tubs, which lends the whole place an air of timeless elegance that is becoming increasingly difficult to find. The old milking parlour on the farm grounds has been converted into a tidy two-bedroom loft that sleeps up to six people. Besides the home itself, the big draw is Catherine Fulvio's **cooking classes** (www.thecookeryschool.ie; €110), which run throughout the year; she also runs kids courses for junior chefs.

Surrounding the house are 200 hectares of forest and parkland, where the first silvicultural experiments by the Irish Forestry Service (Coillte) were conceived, after the purchase of the house by the state in 1904. These plots, about half a hectare in size, are still visible today, flanking what many consider to be the best of Avondale's many walking trails, the Great Ride. You can visit the park during daylight hours year-round.

Sleeping

Old Presbytery Hostel HOSTEL €
(☎0404-46930; www.hostels-ireland.com; The Fairgreen, Rathdrum; dm/d €16/45; P) This modern, centrally located IHH hostel looks more like campus accommodation. There is a mix of large, comfy dorms and well-appointed doubles with en-suite bathrooms, as well as family rooms. A laundry and a TV room round off the facilities. You can also camp in the grounds.

Getting There & Away

Bus Éireann (☎01-836 6111; www.buseireann.ie) Service 133 goes to Rathdrum from Dublin (one way/return €7/9.70, 1¾ hours, 10 daily) on its way to Arklow.

Iarnród Éireann (☎01-836 6222) Trains serve Rathdrum from Dublin on the main Dublin to Rosslare Harbour line (one way/return €16.20/20.40, 1½ hours, five daily).

VALE OF AVOCA

In summer, tour buses and other interested parties clog the road through the scenic Vale of Avoca on their way to the renowned mills in the eponymous village. En route, tourists *ooh* and *aah* at the gorgeous scenery of the darkly wooded valley that begins where the Rivers Avonbeg and Avonmore come together to form the River Avoca. This is a lovely spot suitably named the **Meeting of the Waters**, made famous by Thomas Moore's 1808 poem of the same name.

The Meeting of the Waters is marked by a pub called the **Meetings** (☎0402-35226; www.themeetingsavoca.com; ⊙noon-9pm), which serves food (mains €10 to €15) and has music at weekends year-round. There are *céilidh* (traditional music and dancing sessions) between 4pm and 6pm Sunday, April to October. There's also a guesthouse attached (known as Robin's Nest) with decent, clean rooms (single/double €45/75). Buses to Avoca from Dublin stop at the Meetings, or you could walk from Avoca, 3km south of here.

AVOCA

POP 570

The tiny village of Avoca (Abhóca) still trades on being the setting for the now-defunct BBC TV series *Ballykissangel,* but the main reason to visit is to amble about – and hopefully spend loads of money in – the birthplace of the superstar of all Irish cottage industries, **Avoca Handweavers** (☎0402-35105; www.avoca.ie; Old Mill, Main St; ⊙9am-6pm May-Sep, 9.30am-5.30pm Oct-Apr), housed in Ireland's oldest working mill.

It's been turning out linens, wools and other fabrics since 1723, and a lot of Avoca's much-admired line is produced here. You are free to wander in and out of the weaving sheds.

Just in case you might want some local info, the **tourist office** (☎0402-35022; Old Courthouse; ⊙10am-5pm Mon-Sat) is in the library.

WORTH A TRIP

IN THE LAP OF LUXURY

Brook Lodge & Wells Spa (☎0402-36444; www.brooklodge.com; Macreddin; r/ste from €260/330; P 📶) is one of Ireland's fanciest boltholes. It's a fine country house about 3km west of Rathdrum in the village of Macreddin. The 39 standard rooms set a pretty high tone, with four-poster and sleigh beds dressed in crisp Frette linen. But the suites sing an altogether more harmonious tune, each a minimalist marvel that wouldn't seem out of place in a New York boutique hotel – massive beds, flat-screen plasma TVs, top-of-the-range sound system and every other style sundry. The accommodation is pure luxury, but it's the outstanding spa that keeps guests coming back for more. Mud and flotation chambers, Finnish and aroma baths, *hammam* (Turkish bath) massages and a full range of Decléor and Carita treatments make this one of the top spas in the country. Your credit card will never have nestled in softer hands.

An **organic market** (⊙10am-5pm Sun, Apr-Oct) is held in Macreddin on the first Sunday of each month during summer.

Sleeping

TOP CHOICE Sheepwalk House & Cottages B&B €€

(☎0402-35189; www.sheepwalk.com; Arklow Rd; s/d €60/90, cottages per week €250-420; 📶) Built in 1727 for the Earl of Wicklow, this is our favourite place to stay in Avoca (although it's 2km out of town). The main house is splendid, with beautifully appointed rooms, while the converted outbuildings – complete with beamed ceilings, fireplaces and flagstone floors – are a wonderful option for groups of four or six.

River Valley Park CAMPING €

(☎0402-41647; www.rivervalleypark.com; campsites €12, mobile homes €475-620 per week; 👪) This well-equipped campsite is about 1km south of the village of Redcross, 7km northeast of Avoca on the R754 country road. It has mobile homes for rent that sleep up to six, and also includes a Secret Garden on the grounds for adults only.

Koliba B&B €€

(☎/fax 0402-32737; www.koliba.com; Beech Rd; s/d €40/65; ⏲Apr-Oct; 📶👪) A thoroughly modern bungalow with comfortable, well-appointed rooms (all with en-suite bathrooms). Koliba is 3km out of Avoca on the Arklow road.

Getting There & Away

Bus Éireann (☎01-836 6111; www.buseireann.ie) operates bus 133 from Dublin, which serves Avoca via Bray, Wicklow and Rathdrum on its way to Arklow (one way/return €10.80/14.50, two hours, 10 daily).

COUNTY KILDARE

Once a backwater from Dublin, the lush green pastures of County Kildare (Cill Dara) are prime suburbia, and charming towns like Maynooth and Kildare have become commuter bedrooms, a reality reflected in the ever-expanding motorway network that seeks to ease the traffic burden.

Still, the county has some of the best farmland in Ireland and is home to some of the country's most prestigious stud farms, many surrounding the sweeping grasslands of the Curragh. The northwest of the county is dominated by a vast swathe of bog. The county isn't especially stuffed with must-see attractions, but there are enough diversions to justify a day trip from the capital or a stop on your way out west.

Maynooth

POP 10,715

Much of Maynooth's (Maigh Nuad) life comes from the university (National University of Ireland Maynooth; NUIM), which gives this tree-lined town with stone-fronted houses and shops a dynamism that belies its country-town appearance. It's within easy reach of Dublin by public transport, thanks as much to the university as to the legions of barristers and other swells who make the town their home. Main St and Leinster St join and run east–west, while Parson St runs south to the canal and the train station (accessed via a couple of footbridges) and Straffan Rd runs south to the M4.

Sights

St Patrick's College UNIVERSITY

(☎01-628 5222; www.maynoothcollege.ie; Main St) Turning out Catholic priests since 1795, **St Patrick's College & Seminary** was founded to ensure that aspiring priests wouldn't skip off to seminary school in France and get infected with strains of republicanism and revolution. It became a Pontifical University in 1898 (granting control of the college's theological courses to the Holy See) but in 1910 it joined the newly established National University of Ireland (NUI), which governed the university's non-theological studies. Nevertheless, the student body remained exclusively clerical until 1966, when lay students were finally admitted. A restructuring of the NUI in 1997 made St Patrick's College independent of the bigger university, which now has more than 6500 students; there are only a few dozen studying for the priesthood.

The college buildings are impressive – Gothic architect Augustus Pugin had a hand in designing them – and well worth an hour's ramble. You enter the college via Georgian Stoyte House, where the **accommodation office** (☎01-708 3576; ⏲8.30am-5.30pm & 8-11pm Mon-Fri, 8.30am-12.30pm & 1.30-11pm Sat & Sun) sells booklets (€5) for guiding yourself around. In summer there's also a **visitor centre** (⏲11am-5pm Mon-Fri, 2-6pm Sat & Sun May-Sep) and a small **science museum** (admission by donation; ⏲2-4pm Tue & Thu, to 6pm Sun May-Sep). The college grounds contain a number of lofty Georgian and neo-Gothic buildings, gardens and squares, but the highlight of the tour has to be the **College Chapel**. Pull open the squeaky door and you enter the world's largest choir chapel, with

WORTH A TRIP

CASTLETOWN HOUSE

The magnificent **Castletown House** (☎01-628 8252; www.castletownhouse.ie; Celbridge; adult/child €4.50/3.50; ⏲10am-4.45pm Tue-Sun Easter-Oct) simply has no peer. It is Ireland's largest and most imposing Georgian estate, and a testament to the vast wealth enjoyed by the Anglo-Irish gentry during the 18th century.

The house was built between the years 1722 and 1732 for William Conolly (1662–1729), speaker of the Irish House of Commons and, at the time, Ireland's richest man. Born into relatively humble circumstances in Ballyshannon, County Donegal, Conolly made his fortune through land transactions in the uncertain aftermath of the Battle of the Boyne (1690; see p698).

The original '16th-century Italian palazzo' design of the house was by the Italian architect Alessandro Galilei (1691–1737) in 1718. In 1724 the project was entrusted to Sir Edward Lovett Pearce (1699–1733).

Inspired by the work of Andrea Palladio, Pearce enlarged the original design of the house and added the colonnades and the terminating pavilions. A highlight of the opulent interior is the Long Gallery, replete with family portraits and exquisite stucco work by the Francini brothers. (In the US, Thomas Jefferson became a Palladian acolyte and much of official Washington DC is in this style.)

Conolly didn't live to see the completion of his wonder-palace. His widow, Katherine, continued to live at the unfinished house after his death in 1729, and instigated many improvements. Her main architectural contribution was the curious 42.6m **obelisk**, known locally as the Conolly Folly. Her other offering is the Heath Robinson-esque (or Rube Goldberg-esque, if you prefer) **Wonderful Barn**, six teetering storeys wrapped by an exterior spiral staircase, on private property just outside Leixlip.

Castletown House remained in the family's hands until 1965, when it was purchased by Desmond Guinness, who restored the house to its original splendour. His investment was continued from 1979 by the Castletown Foundation. In 1994 Castletown House was transferred to state care and today it is managed by the Heritage Service.

Buses 120 and 123 run from Dublin to Celbridge (€3.50; 30 minutes; every half-hour Monday to Friday, hourly Saturday, six buses Sunday).

stalls for more than 450 choristers and some magnificent ornamentation.

FREE **Maynooth Castle** CASTLE
(☎01-628 6744; ⏲10am-6pm Mon-Fri, 1-6pm Sat & Sun Jun-Sep, 1-5pm Sun Oct) Near the entrance to St Patrick's College you can see the ruined gatehouse, keep and great hall of this 13th-century castle, home of the Fitzgerald family. The castle was dismantled in Cromwellian times, when the Fitzgeralds moved to Kilkea Castle (now closed). Entry is by a 45-minute guided tour only; there's a small exhibition on the castle's history in the keep.

Activities

Canoeing

Leixlip, on the River Liffey between Maynooth and Dublin, is an important **canoeing** centre and the starting point of the annual 28km **International Liffey Descent Race** (www.liffeydescent.com). Usually held in early September, the race attracts more than 1000 competitors. For more information on canoeing in Ireland, try **Canoeing Ireland** (www.canoe.ie).

Golf

On the edge of town, **Carton House** (☎01-651 7720; www.cartonhousegolf.com; green fees €75 Mon-Thu, €85 Fri-Sun) is home to two outstanding 18-hole championship courses designed by Colin Montgomery and Mark O'Meara respectively. See the following Carton House sleeping review for details of the attached hotel.

Sleeping

Carton House HOTEL €€€
(☎01-505 2000; www.cartonhouse.com; r from €145; P@≋🛜) It really doesn't get any grander than this vast, early 19th-century estate set on over 1000 acres of lavish grounds. The interiors belie the Palladian exterior and are stylishly minimalist. As you'd expect, the

beautiful rooms come equipped with all the latest high-tech gadgetry. To reach the hotel, follow the R148 east towards Leixlip along the Royal Canal.

NUI Maynooth UNIVERSITY €
(01-708 6200; www.maynoothcampus.com; s €25-100, d €40-126;) The university campus can accommodate 1000 guests in seven types of room, ranging from a traditional college room to doubles in an apartment in the purpose-built university village. Most are in the mid-1970s North Campus, but rooms are better in the South Campus, where the accommodation office is. These are strewn around the courts and gardens of atmospheric St Patrick's College (p157). Availability is best in the summer months.

Glenroyal Hotel & Leisure Club HOTEL €€
(01-629 0909; www.glenroyal.ie; Straffan Rd; r from €75;) This modern 113-room hotel is tailored to business travellers and weddings. The design is bog standard but the rooms are spacious and spotless, with high-speed internet, and there are *two* swimming pools.

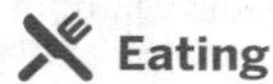

Eating

Mohana INDIAN €€
(01-505 4868; Main St; mains €13-17; noon-2.30pm & 5-11pm) Several cuts above the usual curry joint, Mohana has a wide range of excellent South Asian dishes. The dining room has a gracious air and it's a floor above the street. For a kick in the old masala, try the chicken chilli version.

Avenue INTERNATIONAL €
(01-628 5003; www.avenuecafe.ie; Main St; meals €6-10; 8am-4pm Mon-Sat;) The menu at this cafe is designed for broadest appeal: steaks, bangers and mash and a particularly good fish and chips share space with a variety of salads and burgers to keep everyone happy.

Getting There & Away

Dublin Bus (01-873 4222; www.dublinbus.ie) runs a service to Maynooth (€3.50, one hour) leaving several times an hour from Pearse St in Dublin.

Maynooth is on the main Dublin–Sligo line, with regular trains in each direction: to Dublin (€2.70, 35 minutes, one to four per hour); to Sligo (€35, two hours 40 minutes, four per day).

Straffan

POP 439

Teeny Straffan has a few small attractions for the young (or at least the young at heart), and one huge one for golf enthusiasts.

Sights & Activities

Mechanical fanatics worship at the **Steam Museum & Lodge Park Walled Garden** (01-627 3155; www.steam-museum.com; adult/concession €7.50/5; 2-6pm Wed-Sun Jun-Aug), located in an old church, which traces the history of steam power and the Industrial Revolution. The collection includes working steam engines from breweries, distilleries, factories and ships. Next door, the 18th-century walled garden has traditional fruits, flowers and formal plantings.

Just down the road at the **Straffan Butterfly Farm** (01-627 1109; www.straffanbutterflyfarm.com; Ovidstown; adult/child €8/5; noon-5.30pm Jun-Aug), you can wander through a tropical greenhouse full of enormous exotic butterflies, or commune with critters like Larry, the leopard gecko.

Two of Ireland's top golf courses can be found at the **K Club** (Kildare Hotel & Country Club; 01-601 7200; www.kclub.ie; Straffan; r from €200;), a Georgian estate and golfers' paradise. Inside there are 92 well-appointed rooms and lots of public spaces for having a drink and lying about your exploits outside. There are two golf courses: one, with Arnold Palmer's design imprimatur, is one of the best in Ireland; the second course opened in 2003. Green fees range from €85 to €295, depending on which course you play and at what time of year.

Bus Éireann (01-836 6111; www.buseireann.ie) runs buses from Dublin (one way/return €4/5.90, 30 minutes, every half hour, six buses Sunday).

Along the Grand Canal

Heading west from Straffan, there are some interesting sites as you follow the banks of the Grand Canal, which flows gently from Dublin to tiny, tranquil **Robertstown**, just past Clane and well worth a detour. This picturesque village has remained largely untouched and is dominated by the now-dilapidated Grand Canal Hotel, built in 1801. It's a good place to start a canal walk (see the boxed text, p161).

Just southwest of Robertstown and at the centre of the Kildare flatlands, the **Hill of Allen** (206m) was a strategic spot through the centuries due to its 360-degree view. Today the top is marked by a 19th-century folly and the ruins of some Iron Age fortifications said to mark the home of Fionn McCumhaill.

Further west you'll find the wonderfully interpretive **Bog of Allen Nature Centre** (045-860 133; www.ipcc.ie; R414, Lullymore; adult/child €6/free; 9.30am-5pm Mon-Fri), a fascinating institution run by the nonprofit Irish Peatland Conservation Council. The centre traces the history of bogs and peat production, and has the largest carnivorous plant collection in Ireland, including sundews, butterwort and other bog-native protein-eaters. Much funding comes from the Netherlands, where the historic bogs are all gone. It's common to find dewy-eyed Dutch volunteers assisting in the ongoing renovations. In an effort to bring the science of the bog to bear for Irish students, 2008 saw the opening of a dipping pond for freshwater invertebrates and facilities for observing how bog 'grows'. A nearby boardwalk extends into the Bog of Allen.

A rather mangy rabbit mascot greets visitors to the cheerful **Lullymore Heritage & Discovery Park** (045-870 238; www.lullymoreheritagepark.com; Lullymore; admission €9; 10am-6pm Mon-Sat, from 11am Sun Easter-Oct, 11am-6pm Sat & Sun Nov-Easter), about 1km north of the Bog of Allen Nature Centre. Aimed right at kids, a woodland trail leads you past various dwellings (including Neolithic huts, a not-so-festive Famine-era house and an enchanting fairy village), and there's crazy golf and a road train. Should the unthinkable happen and it rains, the Funky Forest is a vast indoor playground.

For information on hiring narrow boats on the canal, see the boxed text, p505.

Newbridge & the Curragh

POP 17,042

The fairly unremarkable town of Newbridge (Droichead Nua) is near the junction of the M7 and M9. Many tourists flock to the **Newbridge Silverware Visitor Centre** (045-431 301; www.newbridgecutlery.com), a purely commercial venture that trades on the area's metalwork heritage as it peddles vast quantities of silver-plated spoons, forks and whatnots. At the back of the showroom is the totally out-of-place **Museum of Style Icons** (admission free; 9am-6pm Mon-Sat, 11am-6pm Sun), which displays an ever-changing range of star-studded memorabilia, including clothing belonging to Princess Diana, Audrey Hepburn, Marilyn Monroe and Grace Kelly; very popular in 2011 was an exhibit of Michael Jackson's personal effects, including his diamond-encrusted glove, the suit he wore in the 'Thriller' video and his 'famous' black Fedora hat.

Odd museums and silverware aside, the town is more famous as the gateway to the Curragh, one of the country's largest pieces of unfenced fertile land and the centre of the Irish horse industry. It's renowned for its **racecourse** (045-441 205; www.curragh.ie; admission €15-60; mid-Apr–Oct), the oldest and most prestigious in the country, which in 2010 got a substantial spruce-up thanks in large part to the generosity of one of its best known patrons, the Aga Khan. Even if you're not a horsey type, it's well worth experiencing the passion, atmosphere and general craic of a day at the races, which can verge on mass hysteria. If you miss the chance to hear the hooves, you can still see some action: if you get up early or pass by in the late evening, you'll see the thoroughbreds exercising on the wide-open spaces surrounding the racecourse.

The M7 runs through the Curragh (exit 12) and Newbridge from Dublin. There is

BOG OF ALLEN

Stretching like a brown, moist desert through nine counties, including Kildare, Laois and Offaly, the Bog of Allen is Ireland's best-known raised bog, and once covered much of the midlands. Unfortunately, in a pattern repeated across Ireland, the peat is rapidly being turned into potting compost and fuel. Once Ireland had almost 17% of its land covered in bogs; today it's less than 2%. Bogs are home to a wide range of plants and animals, including cranberries, insect-eating sundews, all manner of frogs and butterflies. For more information on ways to discover this rich land, enquire at the Bog of Allen Nature Centre (see above), found right along the Grand Canal.

frequent Bus Éireann service between Dublin's Busáras bus station and Newbridge (€7.90, 90 minutes). From Newbridge, buses continue to the Curragh racecourse (€1.60, 10 minutes) and Kildare town. There are extra buses on race days.

Getting There & Away

The Dublin–Kildare **train** (☎01-836 6222) runs from Heuston train station and stops in Newbridge (€13, 30 minutes, hourly). Check the timetable for trains that stop at the racecourse.

South Kildare Community Transport (☎045-871 916; www.skct.ie) runs a local bus service on two routes that serve Athy, Ballitore, Castledermot, Kildare town and Moone and Newbridge among others (five times daily).

Kildare Town

POP 7538

Built around a compact, triangular square fronting its impressive cathedral, Kildare is a busy enough place, even if there aren't a lot of attractions within the town itself. It is closely associated with Ireland's second-most important saint, Brigid.

Sights

St Brigid's Cathedral CATHEDRAL

(☎045-521 229; Market Sq; admission by donation; ⏱10am-1pm & 2-5pm Mon-Sat, 2-5pm Sun May-Sep) The solid presence of 13th-century **St Brigid's Cathedral** looms over Kildare Sq. Look out for a fine stained-glass window inside that depicts the three main saints of Ireland: Patrick, Brigid and Colmcille. The church also contains the restored tomb of Walter Wellesley, Bishop of Kildare, which disappeared soon after his death in 1539 and was only found again in 1971. One of its carved figures has been variously interpreted as an acrobat or a sheila-na-gig (a carved female figure with exaggerated genitalia).

The 10th-century **round tower** (admission €5) in the grounds is Ireland's second highest at 32.9m, and one of the few that you can climb, provided the guardian is around. Its original conical roof has been replaced with an unusual Norman battlement. Near the tower is a **wishing stone** – put your arm through the hole and touch your shoulder and your wish will be granted. On the north side of the cathedral are the heavily restored foundations of an ancient **fire temple** (see the boxed text, p162).

> **WALKING THE TOWPATH**
>
> The Grand Canal towpath is ideal for leisurely walkers and there are numerous access points, none better than Robertstown if you fancy a long-distance ramble. The village is the hub of the Kildare Way and River Barrow towpath trails, the latter stretching all the way to St Mullin's, 95km south in County Carlow. From there it's possible to connect with the South Leinster Way (p220) at Graiguenamanagh, or the southern end of the Wicklow Way (p137) at Clonegal, north of Mt Leinster.
>
> A variety of leaflets detailing the paths can be picked up at most regional tourist offices. **Waterways Ireland** (www.waterwaysireland.org) is also a good source.

Irish National Stud & Gardens STUD, GARDENS

(☎045-521 617; www.irish-national-stud.ie; Tully; adult/child €10.50/5.50; ⏱9.30am-6pm mid-Feb–Dec, last admission 5pm) With highlights like the 'Teasing Shed', the Irish National Stud, about 3km south of town, is the big attraction in the locality – horse-mad Queen Elizabeth II dropped in during her historic 2011 visit. The stud was founded by Colonel Hall Walker (of Johnnie Walker whiskey fame) in 1900. He was remarkably successful with his horses, but his eccentric breeding technique relied heavily on astrology: the fate of a foal was decided by its horoscope and the roofs of the stallion boxes opened on auspicious occasions to reveal the heavens and duly influence the horses' fortunes. Today the immaculately kept centre is owned and managed by the Irish government. It breeds high-quality stallions to mate with mares from all over the world.

There are **guided tours** (many of the guides have a real palaver) of the stud every hour on the hour, with access to the intensive-care unit for newborn foals. If you visit between February and June, you might even see a foal being born. Alternatively, the foaling unit shows a 10-minute video with all the action. You can wander the stalls and go eye-to-eye with famous stallions. Given that most are now geldings, they probably have dim memories of their time in the aforementioned Teasing Shed, the place where stallions are stimulated for mating, while

ST BRIGID

Along with St Patrick, St Brigid is one of Ireland's most important saints, hailed as an early feminist but also known for her compassion, generosity and special ways with barnyard animals. Stories about her are both many and mythical. All agree that she was a strong-willed character: according to one legend, when her father chose her an unwanted suitor, she pulled out her own eye to prove her resolve never to wed. After she had taken her vows, and was mistakenly ordained a bishop rather than a nun, her beauty was restored. Another has her being shipped off to a convent after she compulsively gave away the family's wealth to the poor. One tale even has Brigid being spirited to Ireland from Portugal by pirates.

Brigid founded a monastery in Kildare in the 5th century for both nuns and monks, which was unusual at the time. One lurid account says it had a perpetual fire tended by 20 virgins that burned continuously until 1220 when the Bishop of Dublin stopped the tradition, citing it as 'un-Christian'. The supposed fire pit can be seen in the grounds of St Brigid's Cathedral where a fire is lit on 1 February, St Brigid's feast day. Nonvirgins are welcome.

Brigid was a tireless traveller and, as word of her many miracles spread, her influence stretched across Europe. Yet another legend claims that the medieval Knights of Chivalry chose St Brigid as their patron and that it was they who first chose to call their wives 'brides'.

Brigid is remembered by a simple reed cross first woven by her to explain the redemp tion to a dying chief. The cross, said to protect and bless a household, is still found in many rural homes. She is also the patron of travellers, chicken farms and seamen, among others.

dozens look on. The cost: tens of thousands of euros for a top horse.

After the thrill of seeing such prized stallions up close, the revamped **Irish Horse Museum** is quite disappointing; its celebration of championship horses and the history of horse racing is one step above what you'd expect to see from a really good school project.

Also disappointing are the much-vaunted **Japanese Gardens** (part of the complex), considered to be the best of their kind in Europe – which doesn't say much for other contenders. Created between 1906 and 1910, they trace the journey from birth to death through 20 landmarks, including the Tunnel of Ignorance, the Hill of Ambition and the Chair of Old Age. When in bloom the flowers are beautiful, but the gardens are too small and bitty to really impress.

St Fiachra's Garden is another bucolic feature, with a mixture of bog oak, gushing water, replica monastic cells and an underground crystal garden of dubious distinction. Both gardens are great for a relaxing stroll, though.

The large **visitor centre** houses the obligatory cafe, shop and children's play area. A tour of the stud and gardens takes about two hours.

Lying outside the site, behind the museum, are the ruins of a 12th-century **Black Abbey**; and just off the road back to Kildare is **St Brigid's Well**, where five stones represent different aspects of Brigid's life.

Sleeping & Eating

Martinstown House HOTEL €€

(☎045-441 269; www.martinstownhouse.com; The Curragh; s/d from €95/150; ⊙mid-Jan–mid-Dec; P) This beautiful 18th-century country manor is built in the frilly Strawberry Hill Gothic style and set in a 170-acre estate and farm surrounded by trees. The house has four rooms filled with antiques; children are banned – darn. You can arrange for memorable dinners in advance (€55); ingredients are drawn from the kitchen garden.

Derby House Hotel HOTEL €€

(☎045-522 144; www.derbyhousehotel.ie; s/d €35/70; P) This old hotel has 20 decent rooms right in the centre of town. It's an easy walk from here to bars, restaurants and all the St Brigid lore you could hope for.

Agape CAFE €
(☎045-533 711; Station Rd; meals €5-10; ⊙9am-6pm Mon-Sat) Just off Market Sq, this trendy little cafe has a fine range of homemade food. There's a full coffee bar and a menu of salads, soups, sandwiches and tasty hot specials.

ℹ Information

The **Tourist Office & Heritage Centre** (☎045-521 240; www.kildare.ie; Market House, Market Sq; ⊙9.30am-1pm & 2-5.30pm Mon-Sat May-Sep) has an **exhibition** (admission free) outlining Kildare's history. There's also local art for sale.

ℹ Getting There & Away

There is frequent Bus Éireann service between Dublin Busáras and Kildare (€10.70, 1¾ hours). Buses continue to Limerick (€10.20, 2½ hours, four daily). Some Dublin buses also service the Stud.

The Dublin–Kildare **train** (☎01-836 6222) runs from Heuston train station and stops in Kildare (€14.50, 35 minutes, one to four per hour). This is a major junction and trains continue to numerous places including Ballina, Galway, Limerick and Waterford.

See p161 for information on local bus service provided by South Kildare Community Transport.

Donnelly's Hollow to Castledermot

This 25km stretch south towards Carlow contains some interesting detours to tiny towns bypassed by the speedy but unlovely N9.

See p161 for information on local bus service provided by South Kildare Community Transport.

DONNELLY'S HOLLOW

Dan Donnelly (1788–1820) is revered as Ireland's greatest bare-knuckle fighter of the 19th century. He's also the stuff of legend – his arms were so long he could supposedly tie his shoelaces without having to bend down. This spot, 4km west of Kilcullen on the R413, was his favourite battleground, and the obelisk at the centre of the hollow details his glorious career.

BALLITORE

POP 338

Low-key Ballitore is the only planned and permanent Quaker settlement in Ireland. It was founded by incomers from Yorkshire in the early 18th century. A small **Quaker Museum** (☎059-862 3344; Mary Leadbeater House,

CHRISTY MOORE: A NEW TRADITION FOR TRADITIONAL MUSIC

A native of Newbridge, County Kildare, Christy Moore is one of Ireland's best-known, and certainly best-loved, traditional singers. Combining a ready wit and puckish charm, he has produced more than 23 solo albums of songs that are easy on the ear if not the mind.

The causes he has championed – Travellers, antinuclear protests, South Africa, Northern Ireland – might give one the wrong impression: Christy is equally at home singing tender love songs ('Nancy Spain'), haunting ballads ('Ride On'), comic ditties ('Lisdoonvarna') and bizarre flights of lyrical fancy ('Reel in the Flickering Light'). He was also influential as a member of Planxty and Moving Hearts, as Ireland experimented during the 1970s and 1980s with its traditional musical forms to combine folk, rock and jazz in a heady and vibrant fusion.

Born in 1945, Moore grew up the son of a grocer and was influenced early in his musical career by a Traveller, John Riley. He was denied the musical opportunities he craved in Ireland and left in 1966 for England, where he quickly became popular on the British folk scene in Manchester and West Yorkshire.

Moore's first big break came with *Prosperous* (named after the Kildare town), on which he teamed up with the legendary Donal Lunny, Andy Irvine and Liam O'Flynn. They went on to form Planxty and recorded three ground-breaking albums.

Moore has done much to breathe life into traditional music. His work is always entertaining but, like any good pub ballad, there's far more to his lyrics than you might first suspect. He's passionate, provocative and distinctive; you'll hear the influences of others as diverse as Jackson Browne and Van Morrison.

Certainly, even as he curtails his live performances to write, he is an iconic figure among Irish trad musicians and fans. He has built an international reputation as a writer and interpreter of a living tradition, at the head of the table of Irish traditional music.

Recommended listening: *The Christy Moore Collection, 1981-1991*.

Main St; admission by donation; ⏰noon-5pm Tue-Sat year-round, 2-6pm Sun Jun-Sep), in a tiny restored house, documents the lives of the community (including the namesake former owner who was known for her aversion to war). There's a Quaker cemetery and Meeting House, and a modern **Shaker Store** (☎059-862 3372; www.shakerstore.ie; Main St; ⏰10am-6pm Mon-Fri, from 2pm Sat & Sun), which sells delightfully humble wooden toys and furniture. It also has a tearoom.

About 2km west is **Rath of Mullaghmast**, an Iron Age hill fort and standing stone where Daniel O'Connell, champion of Catholic emancipation, held one of his 'monster rallies' in 1843.

MOONE

POP 380

Just south of Ballitore, the unassuming village of Moone is home to one of Ireland's most magnificent high crosses. The unusually tall and slender **Moone High Cross** is an 8th- or 9th-century masterpiece, which displays its carved biblical scenes with the confidence and exuberance of a comic strip. The cross can be found 1km west of Moone village and the N9 in an atmospheric early Christian churchyard. Old stone ruins add to the mood of the drive.

The solid, stone 18th-century **Moone High Cross Inn** (☎059-862 4112; www.moonehighcrossinnonline.com; Bolton Hill; s/d from €50/80; P), 2km south of Moone, has five rooms decorated in quaint country-house style. The delightful bar downstairs serves good pub lunches and there's a proper **restaurant** (mains €12-19; ⏰6-8.30pm), which uses local and organic ingredients. The inn revolves around a Celtic theme, celebrating pagan festivals and hoarding healing stones, lucky charms and even a 'love stone' in the outside courtyards.

CASTLEDERMOT

POP 1160

Castledermot was once home to a vast ecclesiastical settlement, but all that remains of St Diarmuid's 9th-century **monastery** is a 20m round tower topped with a medieval battlement. Nearby are two well-preserved, carved, 10th-century granite high crosses; a 12th-century Romanesque doorway; and a medieval Scandinavian 'hogback' gravestone, the only one in Ireland. Reach the ruins by entering the rusty gate on all-too-busy Main St (N9), then walking up the tree-lined avenue to St James' church. At the southern end of town, the ruins of an early 14th-century **Franciscan friary** can be seen alongside the road.

Counties Wexford, Waterford, Carlow & Kilkenny

POPULATION 507,000 / AREA 7193 SQ KM

Includes »

Best Places to Eat

- » Tannery (p192)
- » Lennons (p199)
- » Campagne (p211)
- » Cafe Nutshell (p178)

Best Places to Stay

- » Waterford Castle (p184)
- » Butler House (p210)
- » Richmond House (p196)
- » Powersfield House (p192)

Why Go?

Counties Wexford, Waterford, Carlow and Kilkenny are (along with the southern chunk of Tipperary) collectively referred to as the 'sunny southeast'. This being Ireland the term is, of course, relative. But due to the moderating effect of the Gulf Stream, it *is* the country's warmest, driest region.

Wexford and Waterford are wreathed with wide, sandy beaches, along with thatched fishing villages, genteel seaside towns and remote, windswept peninsulas littered by wrecks – as well as a swashbuckling history of marauding Vikings, lighthouse-keeping monks and shadowy knights' sects.

Deeper inland, the meandering River Barrow separates the verdant counties of Carlow and Kilkenny. County Carlow offers farm-filled spaces, country lodgings and flowering estates. County Kilkenny's namesake city is the urban star with a castle, cathedral, medieval lanes, cracking pubs and hip eateries, making it one of Ireland's top destinations.

When to Go

During summer, the long, craggy coast of Counties Wexford and Waterford is alive with holidaymakers enjoying the long days on the countless beaches, seaside seafood cafes and music-filled pubs. Outside of this time, the scenery will be grey and windswept. Towns and cities like Waterford, Dungarvan and Kilkenny have indoor pleasures year-round. However if you're a foodie, you may find that the non-winter months offer up the greatest range of the bounty for which the four counties are famous. Hardy walkers can enjoy trails during all but the winter months.

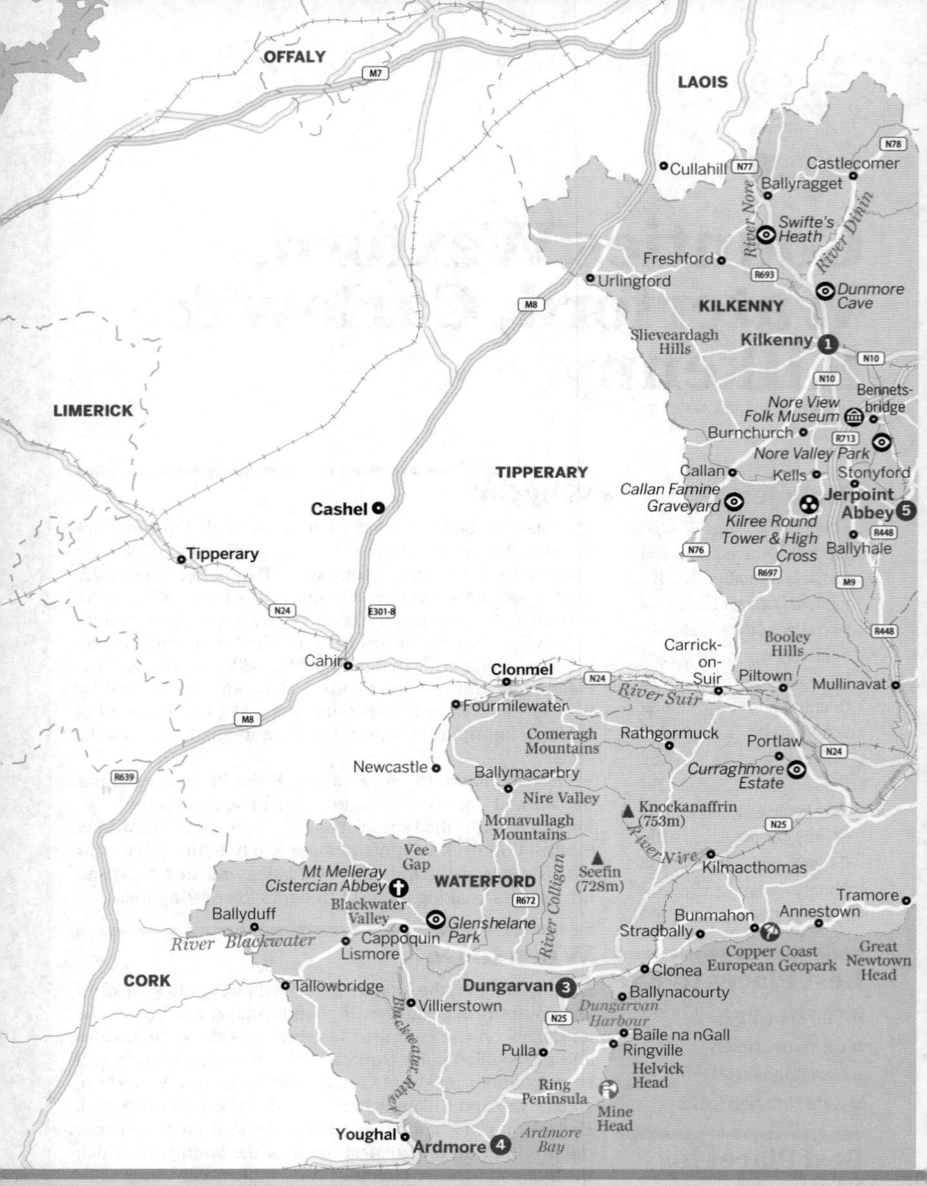

Counties Wexford, Waterford, Carlow & Kilkenny Highlights

1 Revel in the urban pleasures of **Kilkenny** (p203), one of Ireland's most vibrant cities

2 Learn about Ireland's poignant history aboard the Famine ship in **New Ross** (p178)

3 Gobble your way into foodie heaven at **Dungarvan** (p191), where top chefs ply their trade

4 Immerse yourself in County Waterford's coastal beauty including hidden cove beaches in and around historic **Ardmore** (p194)

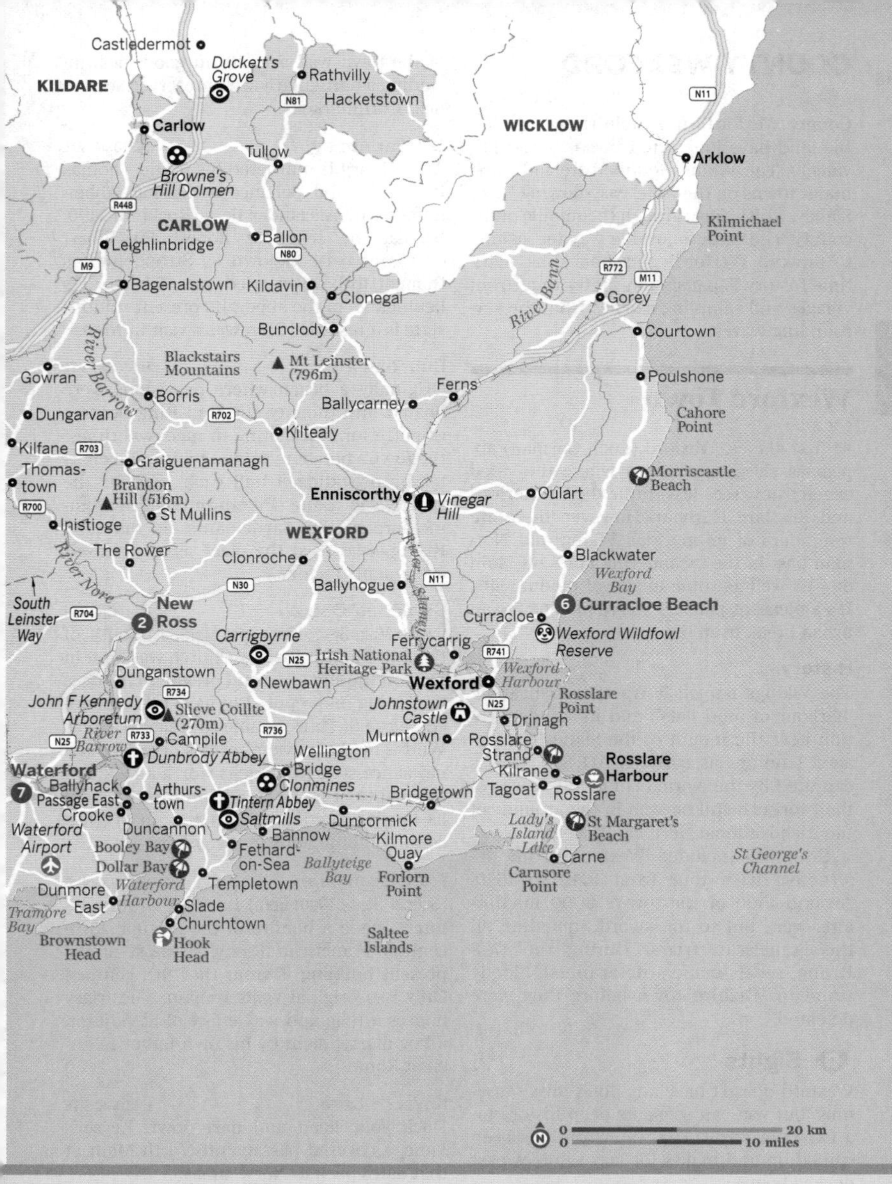

5 Feel like a monk at the moody and evocative ruins of **Jerpoint Abbey** (p217) in County Kilkenny

6 Walk to the end of **Curracloe Beach** (p172) near Wexford, a nearly endless vision of white powder

7 Relive the days of the Normans in the museums and narrow streets of **Waterford** (p182)

COUNTY WEXFORD

POP 145,000

County Wexford's navigable rivers and fertile land have long lured invaders and privateers. The Vikings founded Ireland's first major towns on the wide, easy-flowing River Slaney, which cuts through the middle of the county. The most enjoyable way for visitors to unwrap Wexford's swashbuckling maritime history is pausing in pretty waterfront villages and sampling catches from the surrounding waves.

Wexford Town

POP 8700

At first glance, Wexford (Loch Garman) appears a sleepy port town where the silted estuary now sees less traffic than Waterford and Rosslare Harbour. However, there are reminders of its glorious Viking and Norman past in the meandering lanes off Main St – as well as some medieval monuments. It's a pleasant pause if you're looking for an urban break from the coast.

History

The Vikings named it Waesfjord (meaning 'harbour of mud flats') and its handy location near the mouth of the Slaney encouraged landings as early as AD 850. It was captured by the Normans in 1169; traces of their fort can still be seen in the grounds of the Irish National Heritage Park.

Cromwell included Wexford in his destructive Irish tour from 1649 to 1650. Around 1500 of the town's 2000 inhabitants were put to the sword, including all the Franciscan friars. During the 1798 Rising, rebels made a determined, bloody stand in Wexford town before they were defeated.

Sights

Wexford doesn't have any don't miss museums, but you can sense its deep history on a two-hour stroll. The waterfront has been spiffed up and makes for lazy rambles past docked boats.

Westgate LANDMARK

The only survivor of the six original town gates is the 14th-century Westgate. It was originally a tollgate, and the recesses used by the toll collectors are still intact, as is the lockup used to incarcerate 'runagates' – those who tried to avoid paying. Some stretches of the town wall are also in good nick, including a particularly well-preserved section near Cornmarket.

Selskar Abbey HISTORIC SITE

After Henry II murdered his friend Thomas Becket, he did penance at Selskar Abbey, founded by Alexander de la Roche in 1190. Basilia, the sister of Robert FitzGilbert de Clare (better known as Strongbow), is thought to have married one of Henry II's lieutenants in the abbey. Its present ruinous state is a result of Cromwell's visit in 1649.

Bull Ring HISTORIC SITE

Originally a beach where provisions were boated into the city, the Bull Ring became a centre for bull baiting in medieval times: the town's butchers gained their guild charter by providing a bull each year for the sport. The **Lone Pikeman statue** commemorates the participants in the 1798 Rising, who used the place as an open-air armaments factory.

St Iberius' Church CHURCH

(North Main St; ⏲10am-3pm Mon-Sat) South of the Bull Ring, St Iberius' Church was built in 1760 on the site of several previous churches (including one reputed to have been founded before St Patrick came to Ireland). Oscar Wilde's forebears were rectors here. The Renaissance-style frontage is worth a look, but the real treat is the **Georgian interior** with its finely crafted altar rails and set of 18th-century monuments in the gallery.

Franciscan Friary HISTORIC BUILDING

(School St; ⏲10am-6pm) In 1649 Cromwell's forces made a bonfire of the original 13th-century Franciscan Friary, so most of the present building is from the 19th century. Only two original walls remain. The friary houses a relic and wax effigy of St Adjutor, a boy martyr slain by his own father in ancient Rome.

Keyser's Lane HISTORIC SITE

Duck your head and dart down Keyser's Lane, a covered passage off North Main St that dates back to Norse times.

Tours

TOP CHOICE **Walking tours** (www.wexfordwalkingtours.com; tour €4; ⏲11am Mar-Oct) of Wexford are the best way to understand its complicated past and confusing remains. The 90-minute walks depart from the tourist office.

Wexford

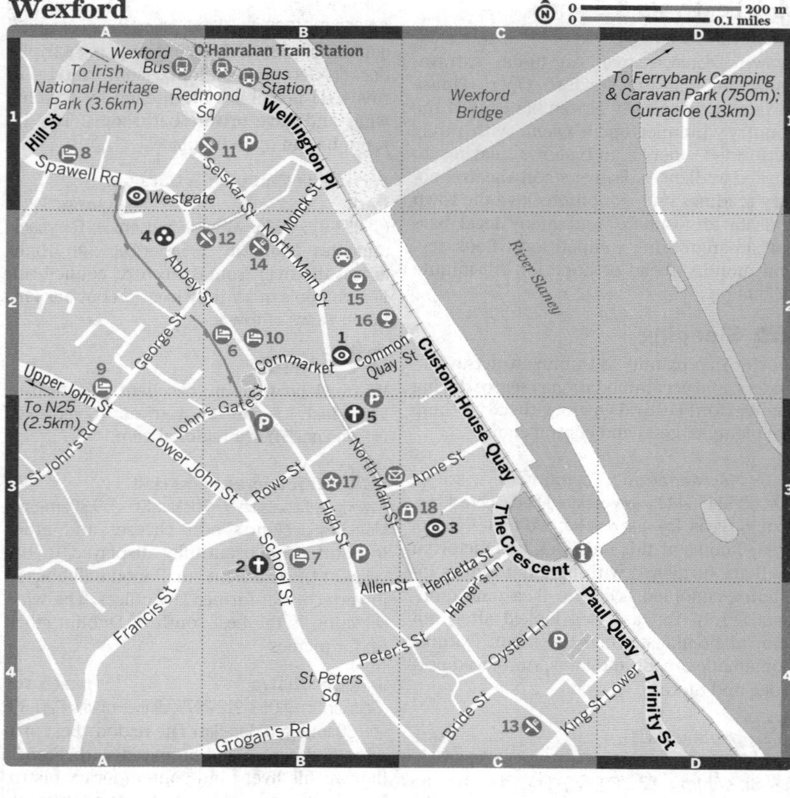

COUNTIES WEXFORD, WATERFORD, CARLOW & KILKENNY WEXFORD TOWN

Wexford

Sights
- 1 Bull Ring B2
- 2 Franciscan Friary B3
- 3 Keyser's Lane C3
- Lone Pikeman Statue .... (see 1)
- 4 Selskar Abbey A2
- 5 St Iberius' Church B3

Sleeping
- 6 Abbey B&B B2
- 7 Kirwan House B3
- 8 McMenamin's Townhouse A1
- 9 St George Guest House A2
- 10 Whites of Wexford B2

Eating
- Farmers Market .... (see 1)
- 11 Greenacres Food Hall B1
- Jacques Bistro .... (see 11)
- 12 La Dolce Vita B2
- 13 Le Tire Bouchon C4
- SkyView Cafe .... (see 17)
- 14 Yard B2

Drinking
- 15 Centenary Stores B2
- 16 Chaz Bar B2
- Sky & the Ground .... (see 13)

Entertainment
- 17 Wexford Opera House B3

Shopping
- 18 Wexford Book Centre C3

Festivals & Events

Wexford Festival Opera OPERA FESTIVAL
(wwww.wexfordopera.com) An 18-day extravaganza held at the Wexford Opera House in late October/early November, this is the country's premier opera event, with rarely performed operas and shows playing to packed audiences. Fringe street theatre, poetry readings and exhibitions give the town a fiesta atmosphere, and many local bars run amateur song competitions. Book several months ahead or hope for last-minute tickets.

Sleeping

Wexford's proximity to Dublin attracts weekenders, and accommodation is scarce during the Wexford Festival Opera. Otherwise there are plenty of good and central choices.

TOP CHOICE **McMenamin's Townhouse** B&B €€
(☎053-914 6442; www.wexford-bedandbreakfast.com; 6 Glena Tce, Spawell Rd; s/d from €65/90; P) Rooms at this red-brick late-Victorian B&B are furnished with period antiques including canopied beds (no Ikea pine numbers here!). You are well looked after, not least at breakfast when the menu features homemade breads and jams, rum-laced porridge and more.

TOP CHOICE **Abbey B&B** B&B €
(☎053-912 4408; www.abbeyhouse.ie; 34-36 Abbey St; s/d from €35/60;) Dwarfed by the enormous Whites hotel across the street, this cute, black-and-white B&B blazes with window boxes trailing red blooms in summer. Its seven rooms all have private bathrooms and fresh floral decor. The owners are total charmers.

Whites of Wexford HOTEL €€
(☎053-912 2311; www.whitesofwexford.ie; Abbey St; r €100-200; P) With its bars, restaurants and hi-tech spa, Whites is a contemporary colossus. The 157 rooms are all metal right-angles, tech touches and glass. Many have views gazing across the estuary to Curracloe Beach. Service is polished.

St George Guest House B&B €€
(☎053-914 3474; www.stgeorgeguesthouse.com; Upper George St; s/d from €40/70; P) Close to the centre, this well-run B&B has a small parking area and is always tidy. Rooms are standard; some have skylights in the bathrooms. A classic no-fuss choice.

Kirwan House HOSTEL €
(☎053-9121208; www.wexfordhostel.com; 3 Mary St; dm/s/d from €21/40/55;) Occupying a triple-decker Georgian building, some rooms in this IHH hostel are brightened by sky-blue walls and have private bathrooms. The TV room has an open fireplace.

Ferrybank Camping & Caravan Park CAMPGROUND €
(☎053-916 6926; www.wexfordcorp.ie; Ferrybank; campsites from €15; Easter-Sep; P) Right across the river from the centre, council-run Ferrybank is in a windy location but has fantastic views of town.

Eating

Wexford boats some excellent restaurants. The lush **farmers market** (Cornmarket; 9am-2pm Fri) is a regional gem.

TOP CHOICE **Greenacres Food Hall** DELI
(www.greenacres.ie; 7 Selskar St; 9.30am-6pm Mon-Sat) Ireland's best cheeses and other foodstuffs are beautifully displayed in the cases at the excellent small food hall housed in very correct former law offices. The wine selection is the best south of Dublin; stock up for picnics.

Jacques Bistro FRENCH €€€
(Selskar St; ☎053-912 2975; dinner mains €20-30; 9.30am-10pm Mon-Sat) The region's best produce and seafood is prepared with French flair at this lively and contemporary bistro. By day you can enjoy a coffee at a table outside or a lunch special. At night the kitchen prepares dishes such as luscious local crab claws, cassoulet and more.

SkyView Cafe CAFE €
(Wexford Opera House, High St; dishes €5-10; 10am-4pm Mon-Sat;) Whisk up to the 3rd floor of Wexford's snazzy opera house for salad bowls, brilliant sandwiches, muffins and many specials. Or just sneak up for tasty tea and amazing cake, accompanied by panoramic waterfront views.

La Dolce Vita ITALIAN €€
(6-7 Trimmers Lane; mains €10-22; 9am-5pm Mon-Thu, until 9pm Fri & Sat) You can always settle down with a perfect Italian coffee under the tricoloured awnings outside. Or have a perfect little plate of pasta. But on weekend nights you can fully enjoy the talents of Roberto Pons, who prepares exquisite little dishes that transport you to Tuscany.

Le Tire Bouchon FRENCH €€€
(☎053-9124877; www.letirebouchon.ie; 112-113 South Main St; mains €17-30; ⏰dinner) Above the Sky & the Ground pub, the 'Corkscrew' serves dishes direct from the cordon bleu school of cooking. No trace of the gregarious pub makes its way upstairs to a mannered dining room that oozes simple elegance. Irish meats and seafood are the basis for rich and flavourful dishes.

Yard MODERN IRISH €€
(www.theyard.ie; 3 Lower George St; lunch mains €8-12, dinner mains €18.50-26.50; ⏰cafe 9am-6pm, restaurant lunch & dinner) This intimate low-lit restaurant opens to an elegant courtyard beneath a canopy of fairy lights. Adventurous contemporary cuisine changes with the season – the emphasis is on fresh and unfussy.

Drinking & Entertainment

Wexford is a regional centre for frivolity and pubs abound, especially on Monck St and Cornmarket.

Centenary Stores PUB/NIGHTCLUB
(Charlotte St) One of Wexford's livelier spots, this former warehouse is a mix of old and new, with friezes on the ceiling and a nightclub that's full even on Sundays. Enjoy the Sunday lunchtime trad music sessions.

Chaz Bar PUB
(Commercial Quay) Across from the gentrified waterfront, this throwback pub hides behind a modest green facade. There's good live local music most nights in summer and the owner is a fount of local info.

Sky & the Ground PUB
(112-113 South Main St) A longstanding Wexford favourite, the Sky & the Ground's decor is classic, with enamel signage and a roaring fire. Trad music sessions frequently take place on weeknights.

Wexford Opera House LIVE MUSIC/THEATRE
(www.wexfordoperahouse.ie; High St) Recently opened, Wexford's gleaming opera house packs more architectural punch inside than out. In addition to opera, it stages drama and concerts by local and touring artists.

Shopping

Wexford Book Centre BOOKSTORE
(5 South Main St; ⏰9am-6pm Mon-Sat, 1-5pm Sun) Lots of worthwhile Irish titles plus local guides and maps.

Information

Main post office (Anne St)

Tourist office (Quayfront; ⏰9am-6pm Mon-Sat Apr-Oct plus 11am-1pm & 2-5pm Sun Jul & Aug, 9.15am-1pm & 2-5pm Mon-Sat Nov-Mar)

Getting There & Around

Bus

Bus Éireann (www.buseireann.ie) buses leave from O'Hanrahan train station on Redmond Sq and travel to Rosslare Harbour (€5, 30 minutes, at least nine daily), Waterford (€8, one hour, six daily) and Dublin (€14, three hours, at least nine daily), normally via Enniscorthy (€6, 25 minutes). Tickets are available across the street at the Mace newsagency.

Wexford Bus (www.wexfordbus.com) operates to/from Dublin airport (€19, 2¾ hours, seven daily) via Enniscorthy, Ferns and Dublin.

Taxi

Wexford Cabs (☎053-912 3123; 3 Charlotte St)

Train

O'Hanrahan Station (☎053-912 2522; Redmond Sq) is small and lacks lockers. Wexford is on the Dublin Connolly (€24, 2½ hours) to Rosslare Europort (€5, 25 minutes) line (via Enniscorthy and Rosslare Strand), served by three trains daily in each direction.

Around Wexford Town

Sights

Irish National Heritage Park MUSEUM/PARK
(www.inhp.com; Ferrycarrig; adult/child €8/4; ⏰9.30am-6.30pm Apr-Sep, 9.30am-5.30pm Oct-Mar) Over 9000 years of Irish history up to the Normans are squashed together at this recreated open-air museum. Costumed actors guide you past a recreated Neolithic farmstead, stone circle, ring fort, monastery, *crannóg* (artificial island), Viking shipyard and Norman castle. Your love of the place will likely be in inverse proportion to your age. The park is 3.5km northwest of Wexford town off the N25. A taxi from Wexford town costs about €8.

Johnstown Castle & Gardens CASTLE, GARDEN
(per car €6; ⏰9am-4.30pm) Parading peacocks guard this splendid 19th-century castellated house, the former home of the once-mighty Fitzgerald and Esmonde families. The empty castle overlooks a small lake and is surrounded by 20 hectares of beautiful wooded gardens.

DON'T MISS

CURRACLOE BEACH

Gorgeous white powdery sand, gentle surf and a lack of development are but some of the superlatives for 11km-long, Blue Flag–rated Curracloe Beach. On sunny days when the temp cracks 20°C (68°F) families flock here, but due to the size you can easily find a half-acre to call your own. Walks on the strand and among the dunes go on and on. There are scattered parking sites and toilets. If you're discreet you can pitch a tent in the sheltered dunes.

The opening carnage of *Saving Private Ryan* (1997) wasn't filmed in Normandy, but here. Many of the birds found at the **Wexford Wildfowl Reserve** can also be seen at Curracloe's **Raven Nature Reserve**. It's signposted 13km northeast of Wexford (from Wexford, take the R741).

In the castle outbuildings, the **Irish Agricultural Museum** (www.irishagrimuseum.ie; adult/child €6/4; ⌚9am-5pm Mon-Fri, 11am-4.30pm Sat & Sun Apr-Oct, 9am-5pm Mon-Fri Nov-Mar) has a bounty of items that will excite the tractor set.

The castle is 7km southwest of Wexford town en route to Murntown.

FREE **Wexford Wildfowl Reserve** NATURE RESERVE

(North Slob; guided tours on request; ⌚9am-5pm) Sitting below sea level and protected by dikes, a la Holland, this vast natural area protects a bird habitat and has an observation tower, assorted hides and a visitor centre with detailed exhibits. The name Slobs may not sound inspiring (the name derives from the Irish *slab,* meaning 'mud, mire or a soft-fleshed person'), but the reserve inspires awe among birdwatchers. Each winter, it's home to one-third of the world's population of Greenland white-fronted geese – some 10,000 in total. Winter is also a good time to spot the brent goose from Arctic Canada.

From Wexford, head north for 3km on the R741 towards Dublin and take the signposted right-hand turn; the visitor centre is another 2km along the lane. Trivia buffs may also know the Slobs and its birds as the inspiration for the *Guinness Book of World Records* – see the boxed text, p171.

Rosslare Strand

POP 1300

Surrounded by suburban-style homes, Rosslare (Ros Láir) town, 12km northwest of Rosslare Harbour, is rather soulless but opens onto a glorious Blue Flag beach. In summer, the beach is the habitat of hordes of ice cream–fuelled children. In winter, the empty sands billow at the feet of the occasional solitary walker.

The long shallow bay is perfect for windsurfing. During the summer months, gear hire for windsurfing, kayaking, sailing and more is available at **Rosslare Watersports Centre** (www.rosslareholidayresort.ie).

Sleeping & Eating

B&Bs and pubs with fish and chips are as common as driftwood on the beach after a storm.

TOP CHOICE **Kelly's Resort Hotel** HOTEL €€€

(☎053-913 2114; www.kellys.ie; Strand Rd; s/d from €90/180; P@≋) Established in 1895 and run by the fourth generation of the same family, this seaside family resort is an Irish institution. While the service remains delightfully old-fashioned and personal, the property is continually updated, with bright, contemporary rooms and oodles of facilities, including tennis, crazy golf, snooker, badminton, yoga, croquet, restaurants, bars and a spa.

Killiane Castle INN €€

(☎053-915 8885; www.killianecastle.com; Drinagh; s/d from €75/100; P) Sleep in a castle! This farmhouse lodge is in a 17th-century house attached to a 13th-century Norman fort – guests can climb its tower for panoramas of the surrounding countryside and coastline. Self-catering apartments are set in the leafy grounds, which also accommodate a golf range, tennis court, croquet lawn and nature trails. It's northeast of the N25 en route to Wexford.

La Marine FRENCH €€

(☎053-32114; lunch mains €11-16, dinner mains €18-25; ⌚noon-10pm) The wonderful Gallic bistro-bar at Kelly's has the most sophisticated menu south of Wexford city. Preparations have earned the kitchen great renown.

Getting There & Away

Wexford Bus (053-914 2742; www.wexfordbus.com) runs four buses a day to Wexford (€4, 40 minutes).

On the main Dublin-Wexford-Rosslare Harbour line, three trains per day in each direction call at Rosslare Strand (from Dublin €23, three hours; from Wexford €5, 20 minutes; from Rosslare Europort €5, 10 minutes).

Rosslare Harbour

POP 1000

Busy, functional Rosslare Harbour has connections to Wales and France from the concrete Europort ferry terminal, where you will also find Rosslare Europort train station. A road leading uphill from the harbour becomes the N25 and should be your first choice on arrival as the only reason to stay here is if you have an early ferry out.

Sleeping & Eating

St Martin's Rd is lined with B&Bs that cater for ferry-catchers with early breakfasts. There are plenty of pubs with standard fare.

TOP CHOICE **O'Leary's Farmhouse B&B** B&B €€
(053-913 3134; www.olearysfarm.com; Killilane, Kilrane; s/d from €40/80; P) Not a ba-a-a-d place to stay. The O'Leary family have been raising rare breeds of sheep and cattle at this working organic farm since the 1800s, and have eight airy, whitewashed guest rooms with hardwood floors and crisp linens. Breakfast includes vegan options. Turn off the N25 onto the road separating Kilrane's pair of pubs, the Kilrane Inn and Culleton's Pub, from where it's a clearly signposted 3km.

Harbour View Hotel HOTEL €
(053-916 1450; www.harbourviewhotel.ie; s/d from €45/60; P) Service at this buttercup-yellow hotel melts away the Europort's hulking presence, as do its sprightly, colourful rooms.

Churchtown House B&B €€
(053-913 2555; www.churchtownhouse.com; Tagoat; s/d €75/90; Mar-Nov; P) Set back from the R736 on 3 hectares of farmland, this 17th-century manor house has uncluttered, flowing guest rooms decorated in autumn hues.

Getting There & Away

Buses and trains depart from the Rosslare Europort station, located at the ferry terminal.

Boat

Rosslare ferries link Ireland to Wales and France. For more information see p734.

Irish Ferries (www.irishferries.com) Sails to Pembroke in Wales (foot passenger adult/child €28/17, bicycle €9, motorbike and driver from €51, car and driver from €69, four hours, two daily). Also has ferries to Cherbourg, France (foot passenger €64, bicycle €10, motorbike and driver from €80, car and driver from €100, 19½ hours, up to three weekly mid-February to mid-December); and with similar fares to Roscoff, France (18 hours, up to three weekly mid-May to September).

Stena Line (www.stenaline.ie) Sails to Fishguard in Wales (foot passenger adult/child €30/15, bicycle €8, motorbike and driver from €55, car and driver from €85, two to five sailings per day). The crossing takes two to 3½ hours.

Bus

Bus Éireann (053-912 2522) Services to numerous Irish towns and cities, including Dublin (€18, three hours, at least nine daily) via Wexford (€5, 30 minutes), and Cork (€22, four hours, three to five daily) via Waterford (€15, 1½ hours).

Car

Budget (www.budget.ie) Has an outlet in the ferry terminal.

Train

Three trains daily operate on the Rosslare Europort-Wexford-Dublin route (to Wexford €5, 25 minutes; to Dublin Connolly Station €22.50, three hours).

THIRST FOR KNOWLEDGE

During a hunting trip to the Slobs near Wexford in the 1950s, the Guinness Brewery's managing director, Sir Hugh Beaver, shot at but missed a golden plover. A spirited debate ensued among his hunting party over whether it, or the red grouse, was Europe's fastest game bird. Sir Hugh realised similar debates regularly cropped up in pubs, and that publishing definitive answers could resolve them (over pints of Guinness, of course). He was right on that score (today the *Guinness Book of World Records* is a record-holder itself, as the biggest-selling copyrighted book in the world), but wrong about Europe's fastest game bird (it's the spur-wing goose).

South of Rosslare Harbour

The village of Carne has a few pretty, whitewashed, thatched cottages and a fine beach. It's lovely to ride or drive these beachy back roads.

TOP CHOICE **Lobster Pot** (Carne; lunch mains €8-12, dinner mains €20-35; ⏲restaurant dinner Tue-Sun, bar food noon-7.30pm Tue-Sun, closed Jan) packs in locals and visitors in summer (at which time it doesn't take bookings), but it's worth the squeeze to get at the fab fresh seafood. The chowder – brimming with cockles, mussels, prawns, salmon, crab and cod – is among the best anywhere. Sunny tables outside are the pick, although the woody interior has its charms.

Heading back up the road takes you past Lady's Island Lake containing Our Lady's Island, site of an early Augustinian priory and still a centre of devotion. Fervent pilgrims used to crawl round the island; people still walk it barefoot. Look out for the stump of the Norman tower, which tilts more than the Leaning Tower of Pisa. When it's not waterlogged, you can drive out to the castle on the island and walk a 2km circuit taking in the shrine.

St Margaret's Beach Caravan & Camping Park (☎053-913 1169; www.campingstmargarets.ie; St Margaret's Beach; campsites €17-25, caravan rental per day from €50; ⏲mid-Mar–Sep; 📶) is a well-equipped campground 500m from the beach. It also has small caravans you can sleep in.

Kilmore Quay

POP 400

Dotted with thatched cottages, Kilmore Quay is a small, working fishing village whose harbour is the jumping-off point for Ireland's largest bird sanctuary, the Saltee Islands, which are clearly visible out to sea. It is one of the busiest fishing ports in the southeast; the cry of gulls and smell of the sea provide atmosphere for fine fish and chips shops.

Sights & Activities

Sandy beaches stretch northwest and northeast from Forlorn Point (Crossfarnoge). There are some signposted walking trails behind the peaceful dunes, circled by serenading skylarks. Look out for St Patrick's Bridge causeway, which stretches towards Little Saltee. The fishing harbour is always fascinating for a stroll.

Wrecks like SS *Isolde* and SS *Ardmore*, both dating back to the 1940s, and extraordinary marine life keep divers occupied. Contact Wexford Sub Aqua Club (www.divewexford.org) for info.

The local website, www.kilmorequayweb.com, has links to local activities such as fishing boat charters.

Ballycross Apple Farm FARM
(☎053-913 5160; www.ballycross.com; Bridgetown; ⏲2-6pm Sat & Sun mid-Aug–Mar) About 9km north of Kilmore Quay, Ballycross sells its apples, apple juices, chutneys and jams direct to the public.

Festivals & Events

Seafood Festival SEAFOOD FESTIVAL
(www.kilmorequayseafoodfestival.com) Mussel in on the four-day festival in July for music, dancing and, of course, tastings.

Sleeping & Eating

Mill Road Farm B&B €€
(☎053-912 9633; www.millroadfarm.com; R739; s/d €45/70; ⏲closed late Dec; P📶) About 2km northeast of Kilmore Quay on the R739, this working dairy farm offers simple rooms and breakfasts featuring homemade bread and free-range eggs.

Hotel Saltees HOTEL €€
(☎053-912 9601; www.hotelsaltees.ie; Kilmore Quay; s/d from €55/90; P) Although rooms here are typical motel-style, they're generously sized and enlivened by painterly canvases and fresh colours.

Silver Fox Seafood Restaurant SEAFOOD €€€
(www.thesilverfox.ie; Kilmore Quay; mains €18-32; ⏲noon-10pm May-Sep, reduced hours other times) Just back from the quay, the Silver Fox's fresh-from-the-ocean offerings include a creamy fisherman's pie filled with prawns, monkfish, salmon and cod plus all manner of specials depending on what arrives at the docks.

Crazy Crab SEAFOOD €€
(Kilmore Quay; mains €10-20; ⏲noon-8pm) Nab a table on the patio and you can enjoy views of the sea beyond the playground across the way. All manner of fresh seafood is on offer – from classic fish and chips to fancier bistro fare.

PRINCE OF THE SALTEES

The Saltees were bought in 1943 by Michael Neale, who immediately proclaimed himself 'Prince of the Saltees'. Something of a strange one, he erected a throne and obelisk in his own honour on Great Saltee, and had a full-blown coronation ceremony there in 1956. Although the College of Arms in London refuted Neale's claim to blue blood, he won a small victory when Wexford County Council began addressing letters to 'Prince Michael Neale'.

The prince broadcast his intention to turn Great Saltee into a second Monte Carlo, but was distracted by a war right on his doorstep. In an escalation of hostilities, he released two ferrets, then a dozen foxes, then 46 cats onto the island to kill the rabbits that he hated so. He died in 1998.

Kehoe's PUB €€

(Kilmore Quay) Decorated with nautical equipment, right down to the beer garden built from a trawler mast and boom, this inviting pub just up the hill has live music at weekends.

Getting There & Away

Wexford Bus (www.wexfordbus.com) Runs to/from Wexford up to four times daily (€6, 45 minutes).

Saltee Islands

Once the haunt of privateers, smugglers and 'dyvars pyrates', the **Saltee Islands** (www.salteeislands.info; open for visits 11.30am-4pm) now have a peaceful existence as one of Europe's most important bird sanctuaries. Over 375 recorded species make their home here, 4km offshore from Kilmore Quay, principally the gannet, guillemot, cormorant, kittiwake, puffin, aux and Manx shearwater. The best time to visit is the spring and early summer nesting season. The birds leave once the chicks can fly, and by early August it's eerily quiet.

The two islands are privately owned. The 90-hectare **Great Saltee** and the 40-hectare **Little Saltee** (closed to visits) were inhabited as long ago as 3500 to 2000 BC. From the 13th century until the dissolution of the monasteries, they were the property of Tintern Abbey, after which various owners were granted the land.

Two of the Wexford rebel leaders, Bagenal Harvey and John Colclough, hid here after the failed 1798 Rising. They were betrayed by a paid informer, tracked down in a six-hour manhunt, taken to Wexford, hanged, and their heads stuck on spikes.

Boats make the trip from Kilmore Quay harbour, but docking depends on the wind direction and is often impossible. Contact **Declan Bates** (053-912 9684, 087 252 9736; day trip €30); book in advance.

Hook Peninsula & Around

The road shadowing the long, tapering finger of the Hook Peninsula is signposted as the **Ring of Hook coastal drive**. Around every other bend is a quiet beach, a crumbling fortress, a stately abbey or a seafood restaurant, and the world's oldest working lighthouse is flung out at its tip.

Strongbow (Robert FitzGilbert de Clare, Earl of Pembroke) landed here on his way to capture Waterford in 1170, reputedly instructing his men to land 'by Hook or by Crooke', the latter referring to the nearby settlement of Crooke in County Waterford across the harbour.

DUNCORMICK TO WELLINGTON BRIDGE

The promontory east of the Hook Peninsula, signposted as the **Bannow Drive**, is littered with Norman ruins. The invaders founded a town at **Bannow**, yet nothing of it remains other than a ruined church. Enthusiastic historians, eyeing the uneven ground in front of the church and the shifting sands of the estuary, speak of the 'buried city of Bannow'.

Bannow Bay is a sanctuary for wildfowl including brent geese, redshank, wigeon and teal, and is also a cultivation site for Irish oysters. The remains of the medieval village of **Clonmines**, which fell into decline when its estuary silted up, are southwest of Wellington Bridge. The ruins are on private land, but there's a good view just south of the bridge as you head north into town.

TINTERN ABBEY

In better structural condition than its Welsh counterpart, from where its first monks hailed, Ireland's moody **Tintern Abbey** (Salt mills;

adult/child €3/1; ⏲10am-6pm mid-May–Sep) is secluded amid 40 hectares of woodland. William Marshal, Earl of Pembroke, founded the Cistercian abbey in the early 13th century after he nearly perished at sea and swore to establish a church if he made it ashore.

The abbey sits amid wooded trails, lakes and idyllic streams. The grounds are always open, and a walk here is worth the trip at any time.

FETHARD-ON-SEA

POP 325

Continuing south towards the Head, Fethard is the largest village in the area. It's home to the scant ruins of 9th-century church **St Mogue's** and the unstable ruins of a 15th-century **castle**, which belonged to the bishop of Ferns. The small **harbour** is worth a visit for its views.

Southeast Ireland has many good **dive sites**, especially around Hook Head and **surfing** is hugely popular. **Scuba South East** (☎087 094 5771; www.scubasoutheast.ie; Fethard-on-Sea) is an excellent resource. **Monkey's Rock Surf Shop** (☎087 647 2068; Main St, Fethard-on-Sea) and **Freedom Surf School** (☎086 391 4908; www.freedomsurfschool.com) have surf gear and info.

The short main drag has cafes, pubs and there are B&Bs all around. The community-run **tourist office** (☎051-397 502; www.hooktourism.com; Wheelhouse Cafe, Main St; ⏲10am-6pm May-Sep) covers the region.

HOOK HEAD & AROUND

The journey from Fethard to Hook Head takes in a hypnotic stretch of horizon, with few houses between the flat, open fields on the tapering peninsula. Views extend across Waterford Harbour and, on a clear day, as far as the Comeragh and Galtee Mountains.

This is prime day-trip country from either Wexford or Waterford. Villages like **Slade**, where the most activity is in the swirl of seagulls above the ruined castle and harbour, beguile. Beaches include the wonderfully secluded **Dollar Bay** and **Booley Bay** just beyond Templetown en route to Duncannon.

Sights

TOP CHOICE Hook Head Lighthouse HISTORIC SITE
(www.hookheritage.ie; adult/child €6/3.50; ⏲9.30am-6pm Jun-Aug, 9.30am-5pm other times) On its southern tip, Hook Head is capped by the world's oldest working lighthouse. It's said that monks first lit a beacon on the head from the 5th century and that the first Viking invaders were so happy to have a guiding light that they left them alone. In the early 13th century William Marshal erected a more permanent structure, which is still standing today under its black and white exterior. Access is by half-hour guided tour which includes a climb up the 115 steps for great views; the visitor centre has a simple cafe. The grassy grounds and surrounding shore are popular for **picnics** and **walks**.

Loftus Hall HISTORIC BUILDING
About 5km northeast of the Hook Head lighthouse, this ghostly manor house (closed to the public) gazes across the estuary at Dunmore East. It was built by the Marquis of Ely in the 1870s. The English-owned Loftus estate once covered much of the peninsula.

Medieval Church HISTORIC BUILDING
(Templetown) In 1172 Henry II granted land hereabouts to the Knights Templar; they made nearby Templetown their headquarters and built various churches. The 13th-century structure they built here was later added to by the Knights Hospitaller and the Loftus estate. On the ground to the left of the church, a stone slab bears a Templar seal: a lamb and crucifix. It is on the road south from Duncannon to Hook Head. The ruins are beside the road and you can wander about them.

Activities

There are brilliant, blustery **walks** on both sides of Hook Head. Poke around the tide pools while watching for surprise showers from blowholes on the western side of the peninsula. The rocks around the shore are Carboniferous limestone, rich in **fossils**. Search carefully and you may find 350-million-year-old shells and tiny disclike pieces of crinoids, a type of starfish. A good place to hunt is **Patrick's Bay**, on the southeast of the peninsula.

At low tide, there's a good walk between **Grange and Carnivan beaches**, past caves, rock pools and **Baginbun Head**, which, surmounted by a 19th-century **Martello tower**, is where the Normans first landed (1169) for their conquest of Ireland. It's a good vantage point for **birdwatching**: over 200 species have been recorded passing through. You might even spot dolphins or whales in the estuary, particularly between December and February.

Eating

Templars Inn PUB €€
(Templetown; mains €10-22; restaurant 12.30-8.30pm Mar-Oct, pub noon-late daily) This very inviting place opens to a panoramic outdoor terrace overlooking the ruins of the medieval church, fields and ocean beyond. Inside, the dark-timber interior looks like a wayfarers' tavern, but is a cosy place for a steak or seafood.

DUNCANNON & AROUND

POP 280

The small, dusty holiday town of Duncannon slopes down to a sandy beach that's transformed into a surrealist canvas during August's **Duncannon International Sand Sculpting Festival**.

Just west of the village, star-shaped **Duncannon Fort** (www.duncannonfort.com; adult/child with tour €5/3; tours 10am-5.30pm daily Jun–mid-Sep, site 10am-4.30pm Mon-Fri other times) was used as a set for *The Count of Monte Cristo* starring Richard Harris and Guy Pearce (2001). The fort was built in 1588 to stave off a feared attack by the Spanish Armada, and later used by the Irish army as a WWI training base (it mostly reflects buildings dating from this period). There's a small **maritime museum** and a cafe, a small moat and an **art gallery**.

About 4km northwest of Duncannon is pretty **Ballyhack**, from where a **car ferry** travels to Passage East in County Waterford. It's dominated by the 15th-century **Ballyhack Castle** (www.heritageireland.ie; admission free; 10am-6pm mid-Jun–late Aug), a Knights Hospitallers tower house, containing a small exhibition on the Crusades.

Beside the R733, some 9km north of Duncannon, the ruined **Dunbrody Abbey** (www.dunbrodyabbey.com; Campile; adult/child €2/1; 11am-5pm May–mid-Sep) is a remarkably intact Cistercian abbey founded by Strongbow in 1170 and completed in 1220. A combined ticket (adult/child €4/2) includes a **museum** with a huge doll's house, minigolf, and a very fun yew-hedge **maze** made up of over 1500 trees.

Sleeping & Eating

The Duncannon area boasts some lovely country estates in addition to simple beachside B&Bs.

TOP CHOICE **Aldridge Lodge Restaurant & Guesthouse** INN €€
(051-389 116; www.aldridgelodge.com; Duncannon; s/d from €55/100; dinner Tue-Sun; P) In a windblown spot on open fields above Duncannon, Aldridge takes a bit of finding, but it's worth it for its elegant, contemporary guest rooms and fresh local seafood like Hook Head crab claws or Kilmore cod (dinner €39). Two caveats: book in advance, and kids under seven aren't allowed.

Dunbrody Country House Hotel, Restaurant & Cookery School HOTEL €€€
(051-389 600; www.dunbrodyhouse.com; Arthurstown; s/d €140/225; multicourse meals from €60; P) Chef Kevin Dundon is a familiar face on Irish TV, and the author of cookbooks *Full On Irish* and *Great Family Food*. His spa hotel, in a period-decorated 1830s Georgian manor on 120-hectare grounds, is the stuff of foodies' fantasies, with a gourmet restaurant and cookery school (one-day courses from €175).

Glendine Country House INN €€
(051-389 500; www.glendinehouse.com; Arthurstown; s/d from €65/110; P) This vine-covered 1830s-built former dower house is wonderfully homey. Bay windows overlook the estuary and grounds populated by deer, cattle and sheep. The Crosbie family lay on a vast and mostly organic breakfast. The rooms are a mix of traditional in the original house and stylish in a modern wing.

Sqigl Restaurant & Roche's Bar MODERN IRISH €€
(051-389 188; www.sqiglrestaurant.com; Quay Rd, Duncannon; restaurant mains €19.50-23.50; bar 10.30am-10pm daily, restaurant dinner Wed-Sat) Local produce is the mainstay of Sqigl, where dishes range from spring lamb to local seafood (bookings essential). Roche's Bar adjoins and has excellent bar food daily. It's adorned with vintage advertising posters and seamen's knots. Trad music sessions take place many nights.

Getting There & Away

There's limited public transport as far as Fethard, but none to Hook Head.

Bus

Bus Éireann (www.buseireann.ie) Rte 370 runs between Waterford, New Ross, Duncannon, Templetown and Fethard. The entire journey takes over two hours and there is only one bus in each direction each day Monday to Saturday.

Ferry

If you're travelling directly to Waterford city, the Ballyhack-Passage East car ferry (see the boxed text, p188) saves detouring via New Ross.

New Ross

POP 4600

The big attraction at New Ross (Rhos Mhic Triúin), 34km west of Wexford town, is the opportunity to board a 19th-century Famine ship. But New Ross' historical links stretch back much further – to the 12th century, when it developed as a Norman port on the River Barrow. A group of rebels tried to seize the town during the 1798 Rising. They were repelled by the defending garrison, leaving 3000 dead and much of the place in tatters. Today its eastern bank retains some intriguing steep, narrow streets and the impressive ruins of a medieval abbey.

Sights & Activities

TOP CHOICE Dunbrody Famine Ship MUSEUM

(051-425 239; www.dunbrody.com; The Quay; adult/child €7.50/4.50; 10am-6pm Apr-Sep, 10am-5pm Oct-Mar) Called 'coffin ships' due to the fatality rate of their passengers, the leaky, smelly boats that hauled a generation of Irish to America are recalled at this replica ship on the waterfront. The emigrants' sorrowful yet often-inspiring stories (they paid an average of £7 for the voyage) are brought to life by docents during 30-minute tours. A 10-minute **film** gives you background on the original three-masted barque and the construction of the new one. Admission includes access to the on-site **database** of Irish emigration to America from 1845 to 1875, containing over two million records.

Ros Tapestry MUSEUM

(www.rostapestry.com; The Quay; adult/child €6/4; 10am-5pm Tue-Sun) The Normans' influence on 13th-century Ireland (up to 400 boats with goods for trade would be in port at New Ross) is recalled via 15 tapestry panels created by volunteer embroiderers. There are audioguides and a shop. It's close to the Famine ship.

St Mary's Abbey CHURCH

(Church Lane) One of the largest medieval churches in Ireland, St Mary's was founded by Isabella of Leinster and her husband William in the 13th century. Ask at the tourist office for access.

Sleeping & Eating

New Ross has an excellent **farmers market** (The Quay; 9am-2pm Sat).

MacMurrough Farm Hostel HOSTEL €

(051-421 383; www.macmurrough.com; MacMurrough, New Ross; dm €15-22, d €30-44, 2-person cottage per night €60-70; mid-Mar–Oct; P) A strutting rooster serves as an alarm clock at Brian and Jenny's remote hilltop IHH hostel. The farm's cheery bedrooms and stove-warmed common area have a rustic charm, as does the two-person self-catering cottage in the old stables. There's also a family-size cottage (ask for prices). Follow the hand-painted signs up a series of tracks 3.5km northeast of town. A cosy old pub and a market are not far.

Brandon House Hotel HOTEL €€

(051-421 703; www.brandonhousehotel.ie; New Ross; s/d from €105/140; P@) This 1865-built red-brick manor certainly lives up to its reputation as family friendly, with kids happily bounding around the place. Winning elements include river views, open log fires, a library bar and large rooms, as well as a spa. It's up a steep driveway 2km south of New Ross.

TOP CHOICE Cafe Nutshell IRISH €€

(8 South St; mains €10-16; 9am-5.30pm Tue-Sat) It's a shame that Nutshell closes of an evening, as New Ross' town centre is short on places of this calibre. Scones, breads and buns are all baked on the premises, hot lunch specials utilise local produce and there's a great range of smoothies, juices and organic wines. Mains come with an array of fresh salads. The shop in the front, In a Nutshell, is the perfect place for picnic provisions.

Information

Tourist office (www.newrosstourism.com; The Quay; 9am-6pm Apr-Sep, 9am-5pm Oct-Mar) In the flash new building that doubles as the ticket office for the Dunbrody Famine Ship.

Getting There & Away

Bus Éireann (www.buseireann.ie) Buses depart from Dunbrody Inn on the Quay and travel to Waterford (€6, 30 minutes, seven to 11 daily), Wexford (€7, 40 minutes, three to four daily) and Dublin (€14, three hours, four daily).

Enniscorthy

POP 3200

County Wexford's second-largest town, Enniscorthy (Inis Coirthaidh), has a warren of steep streets descending from Augustus Pugin's cathedral to the Norman castle and the River Slaney. Enniscorthy is inextricably linked to some of the fiercest fighting of the 1798 Rising, when rebels captured the town and set up camp at Vinegar Hill.

Sights

FREE Enniscorthy Castle HISTORIC BUILDING

(Castle Hill; ⏲10am-5pm) During the 1798 Rising, rebels used this castle as a prison. The stout, four-towered keep was built by the Normans; Queen Elizabeth I awarded its lease to the poet Edmund Spenser for the flattering things he said about her in his epic *The Faerie Queene*. Rather ungratefully, he sold it to a local landlord. Like everything else in these parts, the castle was attacked by Cromwell in 1649. It now houses a good local **museum** which includes displays showing how the town grew and a spectacular rooftop deck.

National 1798 Rebellion Centre MUSEUM

(www.1798centre.ie; Mill Park Rd; adult/child €6/3.50; ⏲same hours as tourist office) A visit here before climbing Vinegar Hill greatly enhances its impact. The centre's exhibits cover the French and American revolutions that sparked Wexford's abortive uprising against British rule in Ireland, before chronicling what was one of the most bloodthirsty battles of the 1798 Rebellion, and a turning point in the struggle. A month later, English troops attacked and forced the rebels to retreat, massacring hundreds of women and children in the 'follow-up' operation. Interactive displays include a chessboard with pieces representing key figures in the Rising, and a multiscreen recreation of the finale atop a virtual Vinegar Hill. From Abbey Sq walk out of town along Mill Park Rd or south along the river.

Vinegar Hill HISTORIC SITE

To visit the scene of the 1798 events, get a map from the tourist office and look for signs. It's a 2km drive or about a 45-minute walk from Templeshannon on the eastern side of the river. At the summit there's a memorial to the uprising, explanatory signs and views across the county.

WORTH A TRIP

WEXFORD & THE KENNEDYS

In 1848 Patrick Kennedy left the horrible conditions in County Wexford aboard a boat like the Famine ship in New Ross. Hoping to find something better in America, he succeeded beyond his wildest dreams (a US president, senators and rum-runners are just some of his progeny). You can recall the family's Irish roots at two sites near New Ross.

Kennedy Homestead (☎051-388 264; www.kennedyhomestead.com; Dunganstown; adult/child €5/2.50; ⏲10am-5pm Jul & Aug, 11.30am-4.30pm Mon-Fri May, Jun & Sep, by appointment rest of year) The birthplace of Patrick Kennedy, great-grandfather of John F Kennedy, is a farm that still looks – and smells – much as it must have 160 years ago. When JFK visited the farm in 1963 and hugged the current owner's grandmother, it was his first public display of affection, according to his sister Jean. The outbuildings have been turned into a recently expanded museum that examines the Irish-American dynasty's history on both sides of the Atlantic. It's about 7km south of New Ross along a very narrow but beautifully overgrown road.

John F Kennedy Arboretum (www.heritageireland.ie; adult/child €3/1; ⏲10am-8pm May-Aug, 10am-6.30pm Apr & Sep, 10am-5pm Oct-Mar) On a sunny day, this place is so nice for families that it could be called Camelot. The park, 2km southeast of the Kennedy Homestead, has a small visitor centre, tearooms and a picnic area; a miniature train tootles around in the summer months. It has 4500 species of trees and shrubs in 252 hectares of woodlands and gardens. **Slieve Coillte** (270m), opposite the park entrance, has a viewing point from where you can see the arboretum and six counties on a clear day.

St Aidan's Cathedral CHURCH
(Church St) Restored to its original glory (check out the star-spangled roof), the dazzling Roman Catholic cathedral (1846) was designed by Augustus Pugin, the architect behind the Houses of Parliament in London. It's near the castle.

Activities

You can take an excellent 2km **walk** if you do a looping route on a visit to the rebellion centre that includes the promenade along the River Slaney. Including Vinegar Hill is best reserved for those ready to climb hills.

Festivals & Events

Strawberry Fest STRAWBERRY FESTIVAL
(www.strawberryfest.ie) Enniscorthy holds this weekend festival in late June, when pubs extend their hours, bands are booked, and strawberries and cream are laid on heavily.

Sleeping

The lush, rolling hills in this part of County Wexford shelter some lovely country houses.

Woodbrook House INN €€
(053-925 5114; www.woodbrookhouse.ie; Killanne; s/d from €95/150;) Damaged in the 1798 rebellion, this glorious country estate is now a three-room guesthouse. The entry features a gravity-defying spiral staircase that amazes now just as it did over 200 years ago. Green practices are used throughout and you can make arrangements for dinner (organic, of course). It is 13km west of Enniscorthy.

Old Bridge House B&B €
(053-923 4222; www.oldbridgehouse.com; Slaney Pl; s/d from €35/60;) Overlooking the Slaney, the Redmonds' comfortable guesthouse, with bohemian artefacts, arty prints and a personable welcome, is the perfect antidote to big-hotel blandness and B&B tweeness. The River Slaney passes by the breakfast windows and Vinegar Hill is but a 15-minute jaunt.

Salville House B&B €€
(053-923 5252; www.salvillehouse.com; s/d from €60/100; P) The views across the great lawn and through the birch trees to the River Slaney are reason enough to stay at this small country estate, which boasts five bedrooms. Three of the rooms have their own bathrooms, the other two are in a self-contained apartment. Dinner (€40) features four courses of seasonal, organic fare. It's about 2km south of town.

Treacy's Hotel HOTEL €€
(053-923 7798; www.treacyshotel.com; Templeshannon; s/d from €50/70; P) With spruced-up rooms in streamlined, woodsy colours, Treacy's is a large hotel with two bars, two restaurants (one international, one Thai) and a nightclub. Entertainment includes live bands and Irish dancing, and guests can use the leisure centre opposite for free.

Monart HOTEL €€€
(053-923 8999; www.monart.ie; The Still; s/d from €135/180; P) Hidden in woodland 2km west of Enniscorthy, the 68 rooms at this discreet, adults-only spa resort surround a pond. Modern touches such as a glass walkway have been added to the main house without lessening its stately grandeur.

Eating & Drinking

Enniscorthy's **farmers market** (Abbey Sq; 9am-2pm Sat) sells local and organic goods and prepared foods. Look for Carrigbyrne cheese. Pedestrianised Slaney St is a good place to start your pub crawl, which owing to its steepness may literally be a crawl.

Galo Chargrill Restaurant PORTUGUESE €€
(19 Main St; mains €10-20; lunch & dinner Tue-Sun) The spicy chargrills like double chicken fillets with chilli are a burst of sunshine at this small Portuguese restaurant with a big reputation. On balmy days the front opens up like the lid on a can of anchovies.

Toffee & Thyme CAFE €
(24 Rafter St; dishes €6-12; 8am-5pm Mon-Sat) A stylish cafe with good dishes created from regional produce. There are many daily specials, from sandwiches and salads to savoury soups and hot meals.

Bailey IRISH €€
(www.thebailey.ie; Barrack St; lunch mains €9-14, dinner mains €13-26.50; 10am-10pm) Leather armchairs lurk between Jurassic potted plants in this converted riverside grain store. Dishes span the gamut of pub fare. There's live music and comedy some nights and a tiny terrace outside.

Antique Tavern PUB
(14 Slaney St) Slanted on the side of a hill, this creaky black-and-white pub is somewhere between twee and rustic. It has traditional live music most weekends in summer.

Shopping

Kiltrea Bridge Pottery IRISH CRAFTS
(www.kiltreapottery.com; ⏲10am-1pm & 2-5.30pm Mon-Sat) The Enniscorthy area has been a centre of pottery since the 17th century. Continuing the tradition, Kiltrea creates hand-thrown terracotta pots including some stunning oversized conversation pieces. It's 6.5km west of Enniscorthy off the Kiltealy Rd (R702).

Information

Tourist office (☎053-923 4699; Mill Park Rd; ⏲9.30am-5pm Mon-Fri, noon-5pm Sat & Sun Apr-Sep, 9.30am-4pm Mon-Fri Oct-Mar) In the centre inside Enniscorthy castle.

Getting There & Away

Bus

Bus Éireann (www.buseireann.ie) stops on the Shannon Quay on the eastern bank of the river, outside the **Bus Stop Shop** (⏲9am-10pm) where you can buy tickets. There are nine daily buses to Dublin (€11, 2½ hours), and eight to Rosslare Harbour (€10, one hour) via Wexford (€6, 25 minutes).

Train

The **train station** (Templeshannon) is on the eastern bank of the river. Trains serve Dublin Connolly station (€24, 2¼ hours) and Wexford (€7, 25 minutes) three times daily.

Ferns

POP 950

It's hard to believe that this workaday village was once the powerhouse of the kings of Leinster, in particular Dermot MacMurrough (1110–71), who is forever associated with bringing the Normans to Ireland. The Normans left behind a cathedral and a doughty castle, later smashed to pieces by Cromwell. Today, you can see these sights in an hour's walk.

Sights

FREE **Ferns Castle** HISTORIC SITE
(www.heritageireland.ie; ⏲visitor centre 10am-6pm Jun-Sep) The castle was built around 1220. A couple of walls and part of the moat survive ignominiously in the middle of town; you can climb to the top of the one complete tower. Parliamentarians destroyed the castle and executed most of the local population in 1649. The ruins are thought to stand on the site of Dermot MacMurrough's old fortress. There is access to the site all year.

St Edan's Cathedral CHURCH
At the eastern end of the main street is the cathedral, built in early Gothic style in 1817. Its graveyard contains a ruined **high cross**, said to mark the resting place of Dermot MacMurrough.

Medieval Ruins HISTORIC SITE
Behind the cathedral are two medieval ruins sitting in lonely isolation surrounded by grass: the Norman-built **Ferns Cathedral** and, with an unusual square-based round tower, **St Mary's Abbey**. Dermot MacMurrough founded it in 1158, inviting Augustinian monks to run a monastery here. An earlier Christian settlement founded here by St Aedan (also known as St Mogue) in 600 was destroyed by the Vikings.

St Peter's Church CHURCH
Further out of town is St Peter's, which was built from stones taken magpie-like from Ferns Cathedral and St Mary's Abbey.

Getting There & Away

Ferns is an easy 12km drive northeast of Enniscorthy on the N11. Buses between Dublin and Wexford all stop here.

Mt Leinster

The highest peak in the Blackstairs Mountains, Mt Leinster (796m) has magnificent views of Counties Waterford, Carlow, Kilkenny and Wicklow from the top. It's home to some of Ireland's best hang-gliding: contact the **Irish Hang Gliding & Paragliding Association** (www.ihpa.ie) for further information.

The car park at the foot of the mountain is signposted from Bunclody, 16km northwest of Ferns. From here, it's a steep 1½-hour return walk. See p201 if you're coming from the western side of the mountains. Ordnance Survey's Discovery map number 68 covers the Blackstairs Mountains region.

COUNTY WATERFORD

POP 67,000

Diverse County Waterford harbours gorgeous seaside scenery, craggy beaches and villages like Dungarvan along its beautiful coast; a warren of walking trails in the beautiful Nire Valley, concealed by the Comeragh and Monavullagh Mountains; and lively Waterford city, with its winding medieval lanes and well-preserved Georgian architecture.

Waterford City

POP 47,000

Ireland's oldest city, Waterford (Port Láirge), is first and foremost a busy port. It lies on the tidal reach of the River Suir, 16km from the coast. Some parts of the city still feel almost medieval, though, with narrow alleyways leading off larger streets. An ongoing revitalisation campaign is polishing up one block after another. New and existing museums tell the story of Ireland's Middle Ages better than any other city in the country.

History

In the 8th century Vikings settled at Port Láirge, which they renamed Vadrafjord and turned into a booming trading post. Their ferocity made Waterford the most powerful and feared settlement in the country. Local tribes paid a tribute known as *Airgead Sróine* (nose money), and defaulters had their noses cut off.

Anglo-Normans attacked the strategically situated town in 1170, defeating a combined Irish-Viking army and hurling 70 prominent citizens to their deaths off Baginbun Head. Strongbow (the Earl of Pembroke) then finished the takeover with 200 soldiers and 1000 archers, and married local chief Dermot MacMurrough's daughter.

King John extended the original Viking city walls in 1210 and Waterford became Ireland's most powerful city. In the 15th century it resisted the forces of two pretenders to the English Crown, Lambert Simnel and Perkin Warbeck, earning the motto *Urbs Intacta Manet Waterfordia* (Waterford city remains unconquered). The city defied Cromwell in 1649, but in 1650 his forces returned and Waterford surrendered. Although the town escaped the customary slaughter, Catholics were either exiled to the west or shipped as slaves to the Caribbean, and the population declined.

Sights & Activities

The ancient streets northwest of The Mall are getting a burnish with new museums and attractions that highlight the city's rich past.

Waterford Museum of Treasures MUSEUM
(www.waterfordtreasures.com) This is the umbrella name for three excellent museums which cover 1000 years of local history and shouldn't be missed.

TOP CHOICE **Reginald's Tower** HISTORIC BUILDING
(The Quay; adult/child €3/1; 10am-5pm daily Easter-Oct, to 6pm Jun-mid-Sep, 10am-5pm Wed-Sun Oct-Easter) The oldest complete building in Ireland and the first to use mortar, 12th-century Reginald's Tower is an outstanding example of medieval defences and was the city's key fortification. The Normans built its 3m- to 4m-thick walls on the site of a Viking wooden tower. Over the years, the building served as an arsenal, a prison and a mint. The exhibits relating to the latter role are interesting: medieval silver coins, a wooden 'tally stick' with notches indicating the amount owed, a 12th-century piggy bank (smashed) and a coin balance used to determine weight and bullion value. Architectural oddities include the toilet that drained halfway up the building.

Behind the tower, a section of the old wall is incorporated into the Bowery bar. The

> **WALKS: COUNTIES WEXFORD & WATERFORD**
>
> Counties Wexford and Waterford have plenty of opportunities to stretch your legs, both inland and beside the sea. Among the best:
>
> » **Wexford Coastal Walk** – signposted 221km walk along Wexford's wreck-littered coastline.
>
> » **Mt Leinster** (p181) – views of five counties from its 796m summit.
>
> » **St Declan's Way** (p195) – 94km pilgrim route via Lismore Castle.
>
> » **Comeragh Mountains** (p197) – glacial moraine and Stone Age remains.

two arches were sally ports, to let boats 'sally forth' into the inlet.

TOP CHOICE **Bishop's Palace** MUSEUM
(Bishop's Palace, The Mall; adult/child €5/2; ⌚9am-6pm Mon-Sat, from 11am Sun Jun-Aug, to 5pm Sep-May) This interactive museum detailing Waterford's long history is in the newly renovated Bishop's Palace (1741). It has dazzling displays covering Waterford's history from 1700 to 1970 and includes treasures from the city's collection, such as golden Viking brooches, jewel-encrusted Norman crosses and 18th-century church silver.

Chorister's Hall MUSEUM
(Greyfriar's St) Set to open in 2012, this new museum traces the city's rich medieval past and covers all the steamy and stinky details of local life until 1700. It's located in the renovated 12th century Undercrofts. The star attraction will be the magnificent 1372 4m-long **Great Charter Roll** which shows portraits of five medieval kings of England.

Edmund Rice International Heritage Centre MUSEUM
(www.edmundrice.ie; Barrack St; adult/child €5/2; ⌚9am-5pm Mon-Fri, 10am-2pm Sat) Edmund Ignatius Rice, founder of the Christian Brothers, established his first school at Mt Sion on Barrack St. A whiz-bang interactive museum recreates life in 18th-century Waterford. It incorporates a chapel, where Edmund Rice's **tomb** takes pride of place, awaiting the anticipated canonisation of its occupant.

Christ Church Cathedral CHURCH
(www.waterford-cathedral.com; Cathedral Sq; ⌚10am-6pm Mon-Fri, 10am-4pm Sat) Christ Church Cathedral is Europe's only neoclassical Georgian cathedral. Designed by local architect John Roberts, it was built on the site of an 11th-century Viking church, also the site where the 12th-century marriage of Strongbow and Aiofe took place. The highlight is the 15th-century **tomb of James Rice**, seven times lord mayor of Waterford: sculpted worms and frogs crawl out of the statue of his decaying body. Guided tours (adult/child €6/5) take place at 11.30am and 3.30pm. The cathedral also acts as a **concert venue** with wonderful acoustics – its broad program of performances features everything from choirs to pop quartets.

Holy Trinity Cathedral CHURCH
(Barronstrand St) The sumptuous interior of this Catholic cathedral boasts a carved-oak baroque pulpit, painted pillars with Corinthian capitals and 10 **Waterford Crystal chandeliers**. It was built between 1792 and 1796 by John Roberts, who, unusually, also designed the Protestant Christ Church Cathedral.

French Church CHURCH
(Greyfriar's Church, Greyfriar's St) The elegant ruin of the stone French Church is announced by a statue of Luke Wadding, the Waterford-born Franciscan friar who persuaded the Pope to negotiate with Charles I on behalf of Irish Catholics. Hugh Purcell gave the church to the Franciscans in 1240, asking them in return to pray for him once a day. The church became a hospital after the dissolution of the monasteries, and was then occupied by French Huguenot refugees between 1693 and 1815. John Roberts is buried here. Ask the staff at Reginald's Tower to let you in.

Historic Buildings HISTORIC BUILDINGS
The Mall, a wide 18th-century street built on reclaimed land, was once a tidal inlet. From the river end, its stateliest buildings are John Roberts' **City Hall** (1788) and beautifully refurbished **Theatre Royal**, arguably Ireland's most intact 18th-century theatre.

Crumbling fragments of the old city wall include **Beach Tower** at the top of Jenkin's Lane and **Half Moon Tower** (both are just off Patrick St). One impossible-to-miss building in Waterford is its landmark 1860s **clock tower**.

House of Waterford Crystal TOURIST ATTRACTION
(www.waterfordvisitorcentre.com; The Mall; adult/child €12/4; ⌚9am-5pm) The city's famed Waterford Crystal is almost an icon in name only. A symbol of Irish success during boom times in the 1980s and 1990s, the company fell on hard times after a disastrous series of ownership changes and management decisions that saw debt piled on amid unwise expansion. (The first Waterford glass factory was established at the western end of the riverside quays in 1783 but closed 68 years later because of punitive taxes imposed by the British before its revival last century. It was reconstituted in the 1940s.) In 2009 the company's operations in Waterford County were suddenly closed – as many as

Waterford

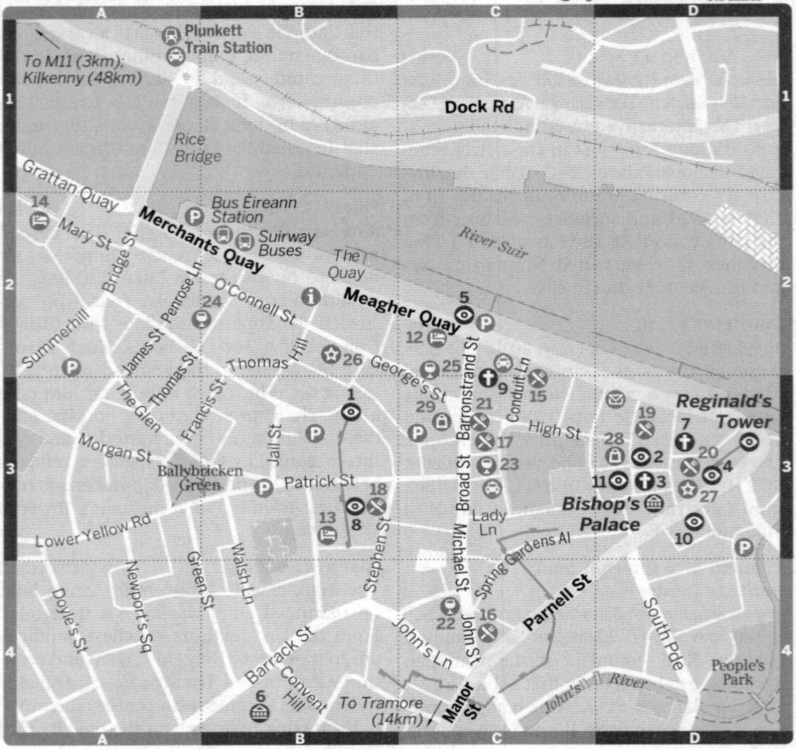

N
0 200 m
0 0.1 miles
A
B
C
D
1
2
3
4
Plunkett Train Station
To M11 (3km); Kilkenny (48km)
Dock Rd
Rice Bridge
Grattan Quay
Bus Éireann Station
Suirway Buses
Merchants Quay
Mary St
Bridge St
Penrose Ln
O'Connell St
The Quay
River Suir
Meagher Quay
Summerhill
James St
Thomas St
Thomas Hill
George's St
Barronstrand St
Conduit Ln
Reginald's Tower
The Glen
Francis St
Jail St
High St
Morgan St
Ballybricken Green
Patrick St
Broad St
Bishop's Palace
Lower Yellow Rd
Lady Ln
Spring Gardens Al
Stephen St
Walsh Ln
Green St
Newport's Sq
Doyle's St
Michael St
Parnell St
South Pde
John St
John's Ln
Barrack St
Convent Hill
To Tramore (14km)
Manor St
John's River
People's Park
1
2
3
4
5
6
7
8
9
10
11
12
13
14
15
16
17
18
19
20
21
22
23
24
25
26
27
28
29

3000 skilled workers had been employed just a few years before. An American investment firm came in and bought the brand and a few assets. Today the flashy centre on The Mall offers a tour showing how crystal is produced, but in the vast company store you can search for a long time before you find any crystal bearing the label 'Made in Ireland'.

Tours

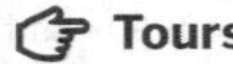

TOP CHOICE Jack Burtchaell's Guided Walking Tour WALKING TOUR
(☎051-873 711; tour €7; ⊙11.45am & 1.45pm) Jack's 'gift of the gab' brings Waterford's nooks and crannies alive, effortlessly squeezing 1000 years of history into one hour. Tours leave from near the tourist office (confirm the exact location there), picking up walkers from the Granville Hotel en route.

Festivals & Events

Waterford International Festival of Music MUSIC FESTIVAL
(www.waterfordintlmusicfestival.com; ⊙Nov) Now over 50 years old, the Waterford Music Festival focuses on light opera with a seasoning of gospel and other styles.

Sleeping

Waterford's centre is not overstocked with places to stay.

TOP CHOICE Waterford Castle HOTEL €€€
(☎051-878 203; www.waterfordcastle.com; The Island, Ballinakill; s €90-150, d €120-240; P@) Getting away from it all is an understatement at this mid-19th-century turreted castle, which is located on its own 124-hectare island roamed by deer. A free, private car ferry signposted just east of the Waterford Regional Hospital provides round-the-clock access. All 19 castle rooms have clawfoot

Waterford

baths, and some have poster beds. There are also 48 contemporary self-catering cottages on the island. Breakfast is available for €18 to €22, and both guests and nonguests can dine on organic fare in chef Michael Quinn's sublime oak-panelled restaurant (menus from €65), or play a round of golf.

Coach House at Butlerstown Castle B&B €€
(051-384 656; www.butlerstowncastle.com; Butlerstown; r €80-150; P) A 10-minute drive from town, this 19th-century stone B&B is as appealing inside as it is out, with deep, studded leather armchairs to sink into, toasty open fires to warm up by, canopied beds to drift off in, and pancakes to wake up to. It has 17 rooms and is 5km west of town off the N25.

Granville Hotel HOTEL €€
(051-305 555; www.granville-hotel.ie; Meagher Quay; s/d from €80/100; P) The floodlit 18th-century building overlooking the waterfront is the Granville, one of Ireland's oldest hotels. Brocaded bedrooms maintain a touch of Georgian elegance, as do the public areas, including a fine restaurant and bar. The hotel's had its share of famous guests: Charles Stewart Parnell gave a speech from a 1st-floor window.

Belmont House B&B €€
(051-850 282; www.marytritschler.com; Kings Channel; s/d €70/100; P@) Artist Mary Tritschler and her architect husband Martin showcase their creativity in their stylish, elegant yet artfully informal house with a pool.It's near the river and just beyond the hospital, going west of town on the Dunmore Rd.

Portree Guesthouse B&B €€
(051-874 574; www.portreeguesthouse.ie; Mary St; s/d from €60/90; P) This large, 24-room Georgian B&B is on a quiet street – a bonus in noisy Waterford. It is well-run and definitely not fancy but you'll find everything you need, including a laundry. Reserve ahead as it's popular with groups.

Mayor's Walk House B&B €
(051-855 427; www.mayorswalk.com; 12 Mayor's Walk; s/d from €30/50) This respectable four-room B&B is in a tall, thin building. The landing bathrooms are shared, but the large (if dated) rooms have washbasins.

Eating

Waterford has a big range of food on offer.

TOP CHOICE L'Atmosphere FRENCH €€
(051-858 426; 19 Henrietta St; mains €12-25; ⌚lunch Mon-Fri, dinner daily; 📶) Always crowded, this rollicking bistro has an energy most places in Paris wish they could import. Classic French dishes with modern Irish flair (and Waterford produce) are served with élan. Perhaps hard to imagine, but you really will need to try to save room for dessert – they're superb.

TOP CHOICE Harlequin ITALIAN €€
(37 Stephen St; lunch mains €8-12, dinner mains €10-14; ⌚8.30am-8.30pm Mon-Wed, 8.30am-10.30pm Thu & Fri, 9.30am-10.30pm Sat; 📶) Run by young, charismatic Italian duo Simone and Alessandro, this authentic little trattoria morphs throughout the day from a coffee and pastry stop to a busy dining spot to a candlelit wine bar. House speciality antipasti platters are laden with cheeses, marinated vegetables and/or finely sliced cured meats.

TOP CHOICE Saturday Market MARKET
(John Roberts Sq; ⌚10am-4pm Sat) An excellent market featuring many prepared foods. Watch for the irresistible baked goods by Mary Doherty of Granny Maddock's Pantry.

Ardkeen Food Store DELI/GROCERY
(www.ardkeen.com; Dunmore Rd; ⌚8am-9pm Mon-Sat, 9am-6pm Sun) Some of the region's best foods are sold here, 3km southeast of the centre. On the second and fourth Sunday of each month, there's a mouth-watering **farmers market** (⌚9.30am-2pm) outside.

Bodéga! MEDITERRANEAN €€
(www.bodegawaterford.com; 54 John St; mains €7-25; ⌚lunch Mon-Fri, dinner Mon-Sat) The exclamation mark in the name clues you in to the effusive nature of this Mediterranean cantina. Sun-inspired, seasonally changing dishes are drawn from the region's seafood, produce and meats. The bar buzzes with people enjoying glasses from the great wine list.

RAYMOND CHANDLER & WATERFORD

Could Philip Marlowe have been spawned in the old medieval streets of Waterford? Author **Raymond Chandler** lived here for a time as a child with his mother and bachelor uncle after her marriage collapsed in the US in 1895. Look for blue markers on the side of an austere building on Peter St.

Near the end of his life Chandler said he had an idea for a story in which a vacationing Marlowe gets caught up in a Waterford murder. He never wrote it.

Berfranks CAFE €
(86 The Quay; meals €5-10; ⌚8am-5pm Mon-Sat) Irish artisan foods line the shelves in the deli section while mouth-watering creations line the menu on the cafe side. This is an ideal place for a pit stop while you unravel Waterford's medieval past.

Munster Bar PUB €€
(Bailey's New St; mains €8-16; ⌚noon-10pm) Dating from 1822, this wonderful old pub has long been a cosy spot for a pint by its roaring open fire. It's especially liked for its upscale pub food: gourmet burgers, steaks, pasta and more. It's the perfect casual end to a long day touring.

Cafe Lucia CAFE €
(2 Arundel Lane; mains €8-11; ⌚9.30am-5pm Mon-Sat) This bright, funky cafe dishes up homemade soups, salads, sandwiches in many flavours, daily hot specials and more. It's beloved for its succulent desserts.

Drinking

TOP CHOICE Henry Downes Bar PUB
(Thomas St; ⌚from 5pm) For a change from stout, drop into Downes, which has been brewing its No 9 Irish whiskey for over two centuries. Have a dram in its series of character-filled rooms, or buy a bottle to take away.

Geoff's PUB
(9 John St) This cavernous local with creaky wooden floors and rock music pumping from the speakers is a home away from home for Wexford's alternative crowd.

T&H Doolan's PUB
(32 George's St) A licensed establishment for over 300 years, Doolan's hosts traditional music every night of the week.

Gingerman PUB
(6/7 Arundel Lane) A genial pub on a narrow lane right in the centre, it is run by a caring owner who keeps the beer selection interesting.

Entertainment

The town's nightlife relies heavily on the students at the Waterford Institute of Technology, many of whom disappear home at weekends. Clubs concentrate around the Apple Market area. The best are Ruby's and Kazbar, both on John St.

Garter Lane Arts Centre MUSIC/CINEMA/THEATRE
(www.garterlane.ie; 22a O'Connell St) This much-complimented theatre stages art-house films, music, dance and plays in an atmospheric 18th-century building.

Theatre Royal THEATRE
(www.theatreroyal.ie; The Mall) Beautifully refurbished, Waterford's flagship theatre stages plays, musicals and dance.

Shopping

The main shopping street runs directly south from the Suir, beginning as Barronstrand St and passing through John Roberts Sq before becoming Broad St, Michael St and John St, which intersects with Parnell St; this then runs northeast back up to the quay-lined river, becoming The Mall on the way. Most shops lie within this triangle.

TOP CHOICE **Kite Design Studios** ART/CRAFTS
(11 Henrietta St) Some of Waterford's best artists and craftspeople have space in this combination studio and shop. Anne McDonnell's prints are a highlight.

Sean Egan Art Glass GLASSWARE
(seaneganartglass.com) One of the finest designers at the 'old' Waterford crystal factory, Egan didn't take getting sacked in 2009 sitting down. He has a full-blown crystal studio here and is busy through the day making exquisite items.

Waterford Book Centre BOOKSTORE
(25 John Roberts Sq; 9am-6pm Mon-Thu & Sat, 9am-9pm Fri, 1-5pm Sun) Three floors of books – with an excellent selection of Irish classics – and a cafe.

Information

Left luggage (items stored from €3; 8am-7pm) The sweet shop inside the bus station stores luggage.

Post office (Parade Quay)

Waterford city tourist office (www.discoverwaterfordcity.ie; Merchants Quay; 9am-6pm Mon-Sat, 11am-5pm Sun Jul & Aug, shorter hours other times)

Waterford Regional Hospital (051-848 000; Dunmore Rd)

FINDING WATERFORD'S ARTISANS

Crystal aside, Waterford has a wealth of local craftspeople creating textiles, paintings, jewellery, pottery, papier-mâché, candles, and furniture built from recycled materials. The website www.waterforddesignermakers.com maintains an updated list, including contact details to arrange appointments.

Getting There & Away

Air

Waterford Airport (www.flywaterford.com) The airport is 9km south of the city centre at Killowen. Primarily has flights to London Luton, Manchester and Birmingham.

Bus

Bus Éireann (www.buseireann.ie; Merchant's Quay) Frequent services to Tramore (€3, 30 minutes); Dublin (€13, three hours) via Enniscorthy or Carlow; Wexford (€8, one hour); Cork (€18, 2¼ hours); and Dungarvan (€11, 50 minutes).

Train

Plunkett train station (051-873 401) North of the river. Up to eight services to/from Dublin's Heuston Station (from €20, two to 2½ hours) and Kilkenny (from €10, 40 minutes).

Getting Around

There is no public transport to the airport. A **taxi** (051-858 585, 051-77710) costs around €15. There are taxi ranks at Plunkett train station, Dunnes Stores and Coal Quay.

Altitude (051-870 356; www.altitude.ie; 22 Ballybricken; 9.30am-6pm Mon-Fri, 9.30am-5.30pm Sat) Rents bicycles for €15 per day.

Curraghmore Estate

Lord and Lady Waterford dwell at the 1000-hectare **Curraghmore Estate** (www.curraghmorehouse.ie; Portlaw; admission €5; 1-5pm Thu Easter–mid-Oct), which has belonged to the family since the 12th century. Its lavish **gardens** incorporate the whimsical **shell house** built by Catherine Countess of Tyrone in 1754, who arranged for sea captains docking at Wexford's port to bring her seashells from distant shores. By prior appointment, the fine Georgian house (admission €15; ⌚9am-1pm Mon-Fri Feb & May-Jul, plus 1st & 3rd Sun of month May-Jul), containing some superior plaster work, is open to visitors.

Curraghmore is 14km northwest of Waterford town, 3.5km northwest of the pretty village of Portlaw. **Suirway** (☎051-382 209; www.suirway.com) buses from Waterford can drop you 1km from the estate entrance.

Southeast County Waterford

This hidden corner of the county makes an easy day trip from Waterford city or as a lovely detour on an onward journey. The waters are tidal and have numerous personalities through the day.

Less than 14km east of Waterford is the estuary village of **Passage East**, from where car ferries yo-yo to Ballyhack in County Wexford. A pretty little fishing village, it's also lined with thatched cottages surrounding its neat harbour.

A little-travelled 11km-long **coast road** wiggles south between Passage East and Dunmore East. At times single-vehicle-width and steep, it offers mesmerising views of the ocean and undulating fields that you won't see from the main thoroughfares. On a bike it is a thrill.

Getting There & Away

Suirway (www.suirway.com; adult/child €4/2) buses connect Waterford with Passage East seven to eight times daily.

> **WATERFORD–WEXFORD FERRY**
>
> If you're going to travel between Counties Waterford and Wexford along the coast, you can cut out a long detour around Waterford Harbour and the River Barrow by taking the five-minute **car ferry** (www.passageferry.ie; ⌚7am-10pm Mon-Sat, 9.30am-10pm Sun Apr-Sep, 7am-8pm Mon-Sat, 9.30am-8pm Oct-Mar) between Passage East and Ballyhack in County Wexford. Single/return tickets for pedestrians or cyclists cost €2/3 and for cars €8/12.

Dunmore East

POP 800

Some 19km southeast of Waterford, Dunmore East (Dún Mór) is strung out along a coastline of red sandstone cliffs full of screaming kittiwakes and concealed coves. In the 19th century, the town was a station for the steam packets that carried mail between England and the south of Ireland. Legacies left from the era include thatched cottages lining the main street and an unusual Doric **lighthouse** (1825) overlooking the working harbour.

Sights & Activities

The area slumbers in winter but wakes up in summer when bathers head to a series of tiny cove beaches along the cliffs. Among them, **Counsellor's Beach** is near good pubs and cafes while **Ladies Cove** is close to a pretty park. At the first sign of sun and temps above 20°C (68°F) families flock to the narrow strips of sand.

Going west, the 16.5km **scenic drive** to the seaside frivolities of **Tramore** is packed with enough natural thrills (rolling green hills, soaring coastal vistas, cows etc) to make the carnival attractions of Tramore pale.

Dunmore East Adventure Centre ADVENTURE ACTIVITIES
(www.dunmoreadventure.com; Stoney Cove) Hires out equipment for kayaking, surfing and snorkelling, and also runs sailing courses and land-based activities like archery and rock climbing.

Festivals & Events

Bluegrass Festival MUSIC FESTIVAL
Each August the air thrums with the beat of banjos.

Sleeping

Haven Hotel HOTEL €€
(☎051-383 150; www.thehavenhotel.com; s/d from €60/100; ⌚restaurant dinner daily, brunch Sun, hotel open Mar-Oct; P) Built in the 1860s as a summer house for the Malcolmson family, whose coat of arms can still be seen on the fireplaces, the Haven is now run by the Kelly family and remains an elegant retreat with wood-panelled bathrooms and, in two rooms, four-poster beds. Local produce underpins dishes in the casual restaurant (mains €12 to €20) and the low-lit crimson-toned bar.

Avon Lodge B&B B&B €€
(☎051-385 775; www.avonlodgebandb.com; r from €60; P) Although the exterior of this large suburban-style house looks rather bland, it's in a great location near Ladies Beach. Run by traditional musician Richie Roberts, homey rooms are clean, comfortable and brightened by beachy colour schemes.

Eating & Drinking

TOP CHOICE **Spinnaker Bar** SEAFOOD €€
(www.thespinnakerbar.com; mains €8-20; food noon-9pm) Eat at sidewalk tables watching beachgoers pass, inside amid nautical knick-knacks or out back in the sheltered beer garden. Wherever you choose, you'll enjoy top-notch casual seafood fare. Chowders, fish and chips, salads and fresh specials are expertly prepared. There's live music on summer weekends.

TOP CHOICE **Lemon Tree Cafe** MODERN IRISH €€
(www.lemontreecatering.ie; mains €8-20; 10am-6pm Tue-Sun, dinner Fri & Sat Jun-Aug) Organic coffees and delectable baked goods hold the fort through much of the day. At lunch there's a long list of ever-changing sandwiches, soups and hot specials. It's pedal to the metal for summer dinners with a wide range of fresh and creative dishes.

Bay Cafe CAFE €
(Dock Rd; mains €7-11; 9am-6pm) With harbour views so good there's a whale-watching guide stuck to the window, this artsy cafe serves interesting twists on casual cafe fare. The open-faced sandwiches are made with local seafood.

Power's Bar PUB
(Dock Rd) Toe-tapping trad sessions take place on Tuesday nights year-round at this butter-yellow corner pub. It's nicknamed 'the Butcher's' after its former incarnation as a meat and grocery store.

Information

Information on the area is available at www.discoverdunmore.com.

Getting There & Away

Suirway (www.suirway.com; adult/child €4/2) buses connect Waterford with Dunmore East seven to eight times daily.

Tramore

POP 9200

In summer the seafront spread out below the steep town of Tramore (Trá Mhór in Irish, meaning 'big beach') is a whirl of fairground rides, amusement arcades and all the other tack of an old-style beach town. (In winter, it's considerably quieter.) Come here for cotton candy and arcade games, or escape for more natural seashores nearby.

Sights

Tramore Bay is hemmed in by **Great Newtown Head** to the southwest and **Brownstown Head** to the southeast. Their 20m-high concrete pillars were erected by Lloyds of London in 1816 after a shipping tragedy: 363 lives were lost when the *Seahorse* mistook Tramore Bay for Waterford Harbour and was wrecked.

Some of the best views of the heads extend from the delightful, sheltered swimming spot, **Guillamene Cove**, where an obsolete sign dating back over 60 years decrees that the beach is for 'men only'.

Atop Great Newtown Head is the inaccessible **Metal Man**, a 12ft sailor made from iron in 1819. In white breeches and blue jacket, he points dramatically seawards as a warning to approaching ships. Legend has it that if a girl hops around the base of the statue three times on one leg, she will be married within a year.

Activities

Tramore's eponymous wide, 5km-long **beach** is capped by 30m-high sand dunes at the eastern end, and is a premier **surfing** spot. Its break is great for surfers of all levels, including beginners, thanks to slow-forming waves. The town has year-round surf schools which also offer **eco-walks** around the Back Strand, one of Europe's largest intertidal lagoons, and various other activities.

Surfing lessons cost around €45 for a group class and €90 for private tuition. Equipment hire is around €25 for two hours including wetsuits and (much-needed) boots, gloves and hoods during winter.

Oceanics SURFING
(☎051-390 944; www.oceanics.ie; Red Cottage, Riverstown) Besides lessons, it organises surf parties.

T-Bay Surf & Wildlife Centre SURFING
(051-391 297; www.tbaysurf.com) Ireland's largest.

Freedom Surf School SURFING
(086 391 4908; www.freedomsurfschool.com; The Gap, Riverstown) Also runs lessons in 'blokarting' (sail-powered beach buggying).

Lake Tour Stable HORSE RIDING
(051-381 958; www.laketourstables.ie; treks from adult/child €25/20) To saddle up, contact Tramore's pony trekking and riding centre.

Festivals & Events

Tramore Racecourse Meeting HORSE RACING
(www.tramore-racecourse.com; Graun Hill) The first European horserace meeting of the year takes place on 1 January at Tramore Racecourse, and is one of many events throughout the year.

Sleeping

Newtown Caravan & Camping Park CAMPGROUND €
(051-381 979; www.newtowncove.com; Dungarvan Coast Rd; campsites €8-20; Easter-Sep;) About 2km out of town, this family-run affair is the best local campground.

Beach Haven House B&B & Hostel B&B/HOSTEL €
(051-390 208; www.beachhavenhouse.com; Waterford Rd; dm €18-30, s/d from €40/60, studio €70-90; P) One of the few B&Bs in town to open year-round. Californian Avery and his Irish wife Niamh's B&B has eight, cream-coloured rooms with skylights, private bathrooms and seashell decorations. Next door, their well-equipped hostel has spotless rooms and dorms and a common area opening onto a BBQ patio. They also have six stylish studio apartments with kitchenettes.

O'Shea's Hotel HOTEL €€
(051-381 246; www.osheas-hotel.com; Strand St; s/d from €50/100) O'Shea's rooms are not as classy as the flower-emblazoned, black-and-white exterior suggests. Still, this family-run hotel offers good value and a coveted location close to the beach. They get points for acknowledging that some rooms are hit by bar noises at weekends.

Eating & Drinking

If it's fried you'll find it on a Tramore menu. At weekends the pubs draw raucous crowds from the region, especially on long summer evenings.

Seahorse Tavern MODERN IRISH €€
(3 Strand St; mains €15-25; 9am-9pm) The Seahorse pushes the 'gastropub' concept hard, but why not? It does have food better than most of the town's chippers and judging by the crowds, the masses are onboard. Breakfasts and sandwiches by day morph into steaks and seafood at night. The bar is one of Tramore's calmer spots for a pint.

Vee Bistro MODERN IRISH €€
(1 Lower Main St; mains €10-28; breakfast, lunch & dinner daily, hours reduced outside summer) In a port-wine-coloured building with tribal art and abstract canvases on the walls, the Vee's French-accent is most apparent at night when the menu really is bistro-derived. By day, expect competent cafe food: fry-ups in the am, lunch specials in the pm.

Getting There & Away

Bus Éireann (www.buseireann.ie) runs frequent buses daily between Waterford and Tramore (€3, 30 minutes). The main bus stop is opposite the Majestic Hotel.

The Copper Coast

Cerulean skies, azure waters, impossibly green hills and ebony cliff faces provide a vibrant palette of colour on the beautiful **Copper Coast** drive west of Tramore to Dungarvan. The R675 winds its way from one stunning vista to another.

Annestown has a couple of cute cafes and is a good place to stop, especially if you are still unsettled by the carnival barking charms of Tramore. At **Dunabrattin Head** watch for a little **cove beach** just west. It's wide and inviting yet there's almost no development and seldom any others to share your good karma.

At 25km west of Tramore, the rugged coastline of the **Copper Coast European Geopark** (www.coppercoastgeopark.com; park office 9.30am-5pm Mon-Fri) takes its name from the 19th-century copper mines outside Bunmahon. Among the area's scalloped coves and beaches are geological formations dating back 460 million years, including quartz blocks, fossils and former volcanoes. Free one-hour guided **walks** are available in summer or download a walking guide from the website. A visitor centre is slowly being developed in a deconsecrated church in Knockmahon.

To explore the Copper Coast's caves, coves and cliffs in sea kayaks, contact **Sea Paddling** (051-393 314; www.seapaddling.com; tours from €50). Tours last from a few hours to a few days and cover various parts of Waterford's coast.

Before you reach Dungarvan, on the north side of the harbour near Ballynacourty, is **Clonea Strand**, a beautiful patch of pristine beach.

Dungarvan

POP 7800

With its pastel-shaded buildings ringing the picturesque bay where the River Colligan meets the sea, beguiling Dungarvan (Dún Garbhán) resembles Galway in miniature. St Garvan founded a monastery here in the 7th century, but most of the centre dates from the early 19th century when the Duke of Devonshire rebuilt the streets around Grattan Sq. Overlooking the bay are a dramatic ruined castle and an Augustinian abbey, as well as lively pubs. Dungarvan is also renowned for its cuisine, with outstanding restaurants, a famous cooking school and the annual Waterford Festival of Food.

Sights

The colourful 18th-century **Davitt's Quay** is an idyllic spot to grab a pint and watch the boats sail in. **Grattan Square** is a good anchor for wanders along the town's lively streets.

TOP CHOICE Dungarvan Castle HISTORIC BUILDING
(www.heritageireland.ie; 10am-6pm Jun-Sep) Renovation is restoring this stone fortress to its former Norman glory. Once inhabited by King John's constable Thomas Fitz Anthony, the oldest part of the castle is the unusual 12th-century shell keep, built to defend the mouth of the river. The 18th-century British army barracks house a visitor centre with various exhibits. Admission is by guided tour only.

FREE Waterford County Museum MUSEUM
(www.waterfordcountymuseum.org; St Augustine St; 9am-5pm Mon-Fri, 2-5pm Sat Jun-Sep) Small but nicely presented, this museum covers maritime history (with relics from shipwrecks), Famine history, local personalities and various other titbits, all displayed in a former wine store.

St Augustine's Church CHURCH
On the east side of the bridge overlooking Dungarvan Harbour, this solitary church was built in 1832 and once had a thatched roof. There are features incorporated from the original 13th-century abbey, including a well-preserved tower and nave. The abbey was destroyed during the Cromwellian occupation of the town, but the church remains in use today.

Old Market House Arts Centre ART GALLERY
(Lower Main St; admission free; 11am-5pm Tue-Sat) A building dating to 1641 hosts regularly changing local exhibitions.

Activities

TOP CHOICE Tannery Cookery School COOKING COURSE
(058-45420; www.tannery.ie; 10 Quay St; courses €50-200) Looking like a futuristic kitchen showroom, best-selling author and chef Paul Flynn's cookery school adjoins a fruit, vegetable and herb garden. Some courses include foraging for ingredients, while others cover market gardening. Other topics include seafood, advanced topics and France.

Festivals & Events

TOP CHOICE Waterford Festival of Food FOOD FESTIVAL
(www.waterfordfestivaloffood.com; mid-Apr) The area's abundant fresh produce is celebrated at this hugely popular festival that features cooking workshops and demonstrations, talks by local producers at their farms, and a food fair. A new craft brew beer garden is an excellent addition.

Féile na nDéise MUSIC FESTIVAL
(www.feilenandeise.com; 1st May bank holiday weekend) Local pubs and hotels host a lively traditional music and dance festival that attracts around 200 musicians.

Sleeping

In keeping with Dungarvan's foodie street cred, breakfasts at B&Bs are often minor spectacles of intriguing dishes and prepared foods sourced from the owner's gardens.

TOP CHOICE Powersfield House B&B €€

(☎058-45594; www.powersfield.com; Ballinamuck West; s/d from €60/90; P 📶) Energetic chef and Tannery cookery instructor Eunice Power lives in one half of this Georgian home with her family, and has opened six beautifully decorated rooms in the other for guests. Breakfast is a veritable feast of Eunice's baked goods, jams, chutneys and delicacies from her garden. It's a five-minute drive north of town on the road to Clonmel.

TOP CHOICE Mountain View House INN €€

(☎058-42588; www.mountainviewhse.com; O'Connell St; s/d from €45/70; P 📶) This beautiful Georgian house, built in 1815 and set in walled grounds, has great high-ceilinged rooms and views of the Comeragh Mountains. Rates drop if you forego breakfast (though with choices like porridge drizzled with warm honey on the menu, you may not want to). It's a five-minute walk down O'Connell St from Grattan Sq.

Tannery Townhouse INN €€

(☎058-45420; www.tannery.ie; Church St; s/d €65/110; ⏲Feb-Dec; P 📶) Just around the corner from the Tannery Restaurant is this boutique guesthouse, which spans two buildings in the town centre. Its 14 rooms are modern and stylish, and have fridges stacked with juices, fruit and muffins so you can enjoy a continental breakfast on your own schedule. An honour bar and snacks ease the transition from afternoon to evening.

Cairbre House B&B €€

(☎058-42338; www.cairbrehouse.com; Abbeyside; s/d from €45/80; ⏲closed mid-Dec–mid-Jan; P 📶) Blazing with red flowers in summer, this oft-recommended four-room B&B is set on a half-hectare of riverside gardens a 1km stroll from the town centre. The gardens come into their own at breakfast, providing many of the ingredients including fragrant herbs.

Lawlor's Hotel HOTEL €€

(☎058-41122; www.lawlorshotel.com; TF Meagher St; s €60-80, d €90-150; P 📶) Across the road from the tourist office, the landmark, lemon-yellow Lawlor's was praised by William Makepeace Thackeray in 1843 as a 'very neat and comfortable inn'. Today, its latest swish incarnation extends from its intimate, artfully lit restaurant and bar to its 94 contemporary, creamy-toned bedrooms, many of which have harbour views.

Seahorse Suites INN €€

(☎058-41153; www.seahorsesuites.com; 4/5 Grattan Sq; r from €120; 📶) Overlooking the action on Grattan Sq, these three apartments are equipped with kitchenettes. Each occupies a whole floor: two have two double beds, and one a single and a double. Expect lots of exposed brick and stone walls and dormer windows with views.

Eating

As you'd expect, Dungarvan's **farmers market** (www.dungarvanfarmersmarket.com; Grattan Sq; ⏲9am-2pm Thu) is a minor festival of breads, cheeses, chocolate, produce and hot food. It's also a community gathering.

TOP CHOICE Tannery MODERN IRISH €€€

(☎058-45420; www.tannery.ie; 10 Quay St; mains €18-29; ⏲12.30-2.30pm Fri & Sun, 6-9.30pm Tue-Sat, also Sun Jul & Aug) An old leather tannery houses this innovative and much-lauded restaurant, where Paul Flynn creates seasonally changing dishes that focus on just a few flavours and celebrates them through preparations that are at once comforting yet surprising. There's intimate seating downstairs or tables in the buzzing, loftlike room upstairs. Service is excellent. Book so you don't miss out.

TOP CHOICE Nude Food MODERN IRISH €€

(www.nudefood.ie; 86 O'Connell St; mains €8-16; ⏲9am-6pm Mon-Wed, 9am-9.30pm Thu-Sat) When you've gained fame for a market cart called Naked Lunch, naming your next venture is easy. The only thing bare here is the plates after diners finish. From carefully crafted coffees to a beautiful selection of deli items, this cafe stands out. But save yourself for the lunch and dinner menus which feature top Waterford ingredients in sandwiches, salads, starters and hot mains that are hearty, honest and flavourful.

Quealy's MODERN IRISH €€

(82 O'Connell St; mains €12-22; ⏲lunch & dinner Wed-Mon) It's comfort food with a modern twist at this stylish bistro. Staples like seafood chowder, fish pie, pork belly and fish and chips are given a dash of energy and

a brimming ladle of goodness. The staff is young and cheery. The wine and beer selection is affordable and diverse.

Mill Restaurant SEAFOOD
(058-45488; Davitt's Quay; mains €8-20; from 5pm Wed-Sat, from 3pm Sun) From the moment you walk in the door, you feel at ease: staff are patient with kids, the place is smart but relaxed, and it's clear everyone's having a good time. Seafood, such as pistachio- encrusted cod, is the main speciality, but it also serves succulent steaks and crispy pizzas.

Drinking

The Tannery and Quealy's offer sophisticated drinking in their small bar areas. Look for Dungarvan Brewing's locally produced microbrews, which include the crisp and hoppy Helvick Gold Blonde Ale.

Moorings PUB
(Davitt's Quay) Beautiful original timber cabinetry and a snug are the main features of the creaky original room at this waterfront bar. Outside there's a vast new beer garden that has potions covered for three-season joy. Dungarvan beers are on tap.

Kiely's PUB
(O'Connell St) A neighbourhood pub in the centre, half-timbered Kiely's has frequent trad sessions that pull in the entire bar.

Bridie Dee's PUB
(Mary St) Almost eternally burning turf fires, codgers trading lies at the bar and a little beer garden out back add up to an unbeatable combination. Frequent trad sessions.

Information

Dungarvan has a handful of ATMs but by Sunday they may be as empty inside as the wallets of the weekend partiers who drained them.

Tourist office (www.dungarvantourism.com; Courthouse Bldg, TF Meagher St; 9.30am-5pm Mon-Fri year-round, plus 10am-5pm Sat May-Sep)

Getting There & Away

Bus Éireann (www.buseireann.ie) buses pick up and drop off on Davitt's Quay on the way to and from Waterford (€12, one hour, 12 daily) and Cork (€16, 1½ hours, 12 daily).

Ring Peninsula

POP 390

Just 15 minutes' drive from Dungarvan, the Ring Peninsula (An Rinn, meaning 'the headland') is one of Ireland's best-known Gaeltacht (Irish speaking) areas. En route, views of the Comeragh Mountains, Dungarvan Bay and the Copper Coast drift away to the northeast. At the peninsula's tip, the small working harbour in Helvick Head has a stoic **monument** to the crew of *Erin's Hope*. The crew brought guns from New York in 1867, intending to start a Fenian uprising, but were arrested when they landed here. Follow signs to An Rinn then Cé Heilbhic, passing Baíle na nGall ('village of strangers'; it was founded by fishermen from elsewhere).

You can easily spend a day exploring quiet country lanes here, with the promise of a hidden beach or fine old trad pub around the next bend in the road.

Ex-Waterford Crystal worker Eamonn Terry returned home to the peninsula to set up his own workshop, **Criostal na Rinne** (058-46174; www.criostal.com; by appointment), where you can buy deep-prismatic-cut, full-lead crystal vases, bowls, clocks, jewellery and even chandeliers.

Sleeping & Eating

Seaview B&B €€
(058-41583; www.seaviewdungarvan.com; Pulla; s/d from €45/70; P) Handy for the wonderful An Seanachaí and the Marine Bar, this light-filled pink-hued guesthouse has eight comfy rooms and sweeping views of Dungarvan and the Comeragh Mountains. Good walks begin at the front door.

Dún Ard B&B €€
(058-46782; www.ringbedandbreakfast.ie; Gaotha, Dungarvan; s/d from €50/80; P) Perched high above Dungarvan Bay, this sophisticated B&B has four cool, contemporary rooms and exceptionally helpful hosts. It is close to a fine old pub.

TOP CHOICE **Marine Bar** PUB €€
(www.marinebar.com; Pulla; mains €10-20; kitchen noon-9pm) Sure, there's good traditional food at this two-century-old pub, but the real reason to stop by is the craic (fun). Year-round, traditional sessions rock the place on Monday and Saturday nights, while locals contest the traditional Irish

WATERFORD FARMSTAYS

If you're beguiled by the beautiful Waterford countryside, why not bed down in the middle of it, with only the sound of a distant snoring cow to break the silence? **Waterford Farm Accommodation** (www.waterfordfarms.com) arranges stays on local farms near towns such as Dungarvan, Ardmore and Ring. Don't expect to sleep in a hayloft, however – accommodation is in rooms done up to a high B&B standard with private bathrooms and averages €40 to €45 per person per night.

card game '45' on Wednesday evenings (anyone can join in). There's music most nights in summer. A monument to the Daley clan – who followed the Kennedys to America and formed their own political dynasty – is nearby.

An Seanachaí PUB €€

(☎058-46755; www.seanachai.ie; Pulla; mains €12-20; ⏰kitchen 11am-9pm Mon-Sat, 12.30-9pm Sun) The rough-hewn walls of the 'Old Storyteller' could certainly tell a few stories of their own. Parts of this thatched-roof pub date back to the 14th century from its earliest incarnation as a farm. It's an atmospheric spot for a pint, a meal (try the house-speciality fish pie) or regular live music. On the grounds, a dozen self-catering cottages are available for multi-day rentals.

Getting There & Around

Pubs, accommodation and shops are scattered along the peninsula; you really need a car or bicycle to get around.

Bus Éireann (www.buseireann.ie) Stops in Ring en route between Ardmore (30 minutes) and Waterford (1¼ hours) via Dungarvan. But frequency is seldom: once daily in summer, much less often other times.

Ardmore

POP 410

The enticing seaside village of Ardmore may look quiet these days, but it's claimed that St Declan set up shop here between 350 and 420. This brought Christianity to southeast Ireland long before St Patrick arrived from Britain. Today's visitors come for its beautiful strand, watersports, ancient buildings and good places to eat and/or sleep. A winning combination!

Sights & Activities

Plan on spending a day on rambles about the town, ancient sites, coast and countryside.

TOP CHOICE St Declan's Church HISTORIC SITE

In a striking position on a hill above town, the ruins of St Declan's Church stand on the site of St Declan's original monastery alongside an impressive cone-roofed, 29m-high, 12th-century **round tower**, one of the best examples of these structures in Ireland.

On the outer western gable wall of the 13th-century church, weathered 9th-century carvings set in unusual arched panels show the Archangel Michael weighing souls, the adoration of the Magi, Adam and Eve, and a clear depiction of the judgement of Solomon. Inside the church are two Ogham stones featuring the earliest form of writing in Ireland, one with the longest such inscription in the country. Local lore claims St Declan was buried in the 8th-century Oratory (Beannachán), which was re-roofed and modernised in 1716. Inside is an empty pit beneath a missing flagstone, the result of centuries of relic collection. The site was leased to Sir Walter Raleigh in 1591 after the dissolution of the monasteries. In 1642 the building was occupied by Royalist troops, 117 of whom were hanged here.

St Declan's Well HISTORIC SITE

Pilgrims once washed in these waters, which are located in front of the ruins of Dysert Church, behind the hotel development above Ardmore Pottery.

St Declan's Stone LANDMARK

Different geologically from other rocks in the area, this stone steeped in lore is at the southern end of the beach. It was perhaps brought by glacier from the Comeragh Mountains but, according to legend, St Declan's bell, which he is often pictured with in his hand, drifted across the sea from Wales on the stone after his servant forgot to pack it. He decreed that wherever the stone came to rest would be the place of his resurrection.

TOP CHOICE Ballyquin Beach SECLUDED BEACH

Tide pools, fascinating rocks and sheltered sand are just some of the appeals of this beautiful beach. It's 1km off the R673 4km northeast of Ardmore. Look for the small sign.

Ardmore Pottery POTTERY
(www.ardmorepottery.com; ⏲10am-6pm Mon-Sat, 2-6pm Sun May-Oct) Near the start of the cliff walk, this cosy little house sells beautiful pottery, many in lovely shades of blue and cream. Other locally produced goods include warm hand-knitted socks. This is a good source of tourist info for the area.

Walks WALKING
A 5km, cobweb-banishing **cliff walk** leads from St Declan's Well. On the one-hour round trip you'll pass the wreck of a crane ship that was blown ashore in 1987 on its way from Liverpool to Malta. The 94km **St Declan's Way** mostly traces an old pilgrimage route from Ardmore to the Rock of Cashel (County Tipperary) via Lismore. Catholic pilgrims walk along it on St Declan's Day (24 July).

Ardmore Adventures WATER TOURS
(www.ardmoreadventures.ie; Main St) There's always something going on at this action-packed place: kayak tours of the coast (€45), surfing, climbing and more.

Phil's Walking Tours of Ardmore WALKING TOURS
(☎087 952 6288; mchugh.phil@gmail.com; tours from €10; ⏲noon) Tours led by an archaeologist explore ruins in and around town.

Sleeping & Eating

Cliff House Hotel HOTEL €€€
(☎024-87800; www.thecliffhousehotel.com; r €225-450; P@🛜🏊) Built into the cliff-face, all guest rooms at this cutting-edge edifice overlook the bay, and most have balconies or terraces. Some suites even have two-person floor-to-ceiling glass showers (strategically frosted in places) so you don't miss those sea views. There are also sea views from the indoor swimming pool, outdoor Jacuzzi and spa, the bar and the much-lauded modern Irish restaurant (menu from €60). Service is discreet but anticipatory.

Newtown Farm Guesthouse B&B €€
(☎024-94143; www.newtownfarm.com; Grange; s/d from €45/72; P🛜) Fresh eggs, homemade scones, local cheeses and smoked salmon are on the breakfast menu at this stylish B&B on a working sheep farm. Coming from Dungarvan on the N25, go *past* the Ardmore turn-off and take the next left 1km further on, from where it's 100m up the road.

TOP CHOICE **White Horses** IRISH €€
(☎024-94040; Main St; lunch mains €8-13, dinner mains €13-24; ⏲11am-late Tue-Sun May-Sep, Fri-Sun other times) Energetically run by three sisters, this tasty bistro serves nourishing fare like fresh seafood chowder or locally caught seafood on plates handmade in the village. Enjoy a drink on the bench out front or a meal at a sunny lawn table out back.

Ardmore Gallery & Tearoom CAFE €
(Main St; dishes €5-12; ⏲9.30am-6pm daily Apr-Sep, weekends Oct-Mar) Displays of cute, luscious cakes pull you in. Displays of local art keep you interested and the coffees and sandwiches keep you fuelled. If you feel a creative urge, you can arrange for painting lessons.

Getting There & Away

Bus Éireann (www.buseireann.ie) operates one to three buses daily west to Cork (€15, 1¾ hours); connections east to Dungarvan and beyond range from one daily in summer to seldom other times.

Cappoquin & Around

POP 740

Slinking up a steep hillside, the small market town of Cappoquin sits at the foot of the rounded, heathery Knockmealdown Mountains. To the west lies the picturesque Blackwater Valley, where traces of the earliest Irish peoples have been discovered, dating back over 9000 years.

The **Dromana Drive** to Cappoquin from Villierstown (An Baile Nua), 6km south, traces the River Blackwater through the Dromana Forest. At the bridge over the River Finisk is a remarkable **Hindu-Gothic gate**, inspired by the Brighton Pavilion in England and unique to Ireland.

The beautiful 19th-century **Mt Melleray Cistercian Abbey** (www.mountmellerayabbey.org; admission free; ⏲7am-7pm) is a fully functioning monastery with two dozen Trappist monks, but welcomes visitors wishing 'to take time for quiet contemplation'. There are tearooms (closed Monday) and a heritage centre. It's signposted 6km north from Cappoquin in the Knockmealdown foothills.

Turn right off the road to Mt Melleray for the forest walks and picnic spots at **Glenshelane Park**.

Cappoquin House and Gardens (house €5, garden €5; ⏲9am-1pm Mon-Sat Apr-Jul, by appointment rest of year) is a magnificent 1779-built Georgian mansion and 2 hectares of formal gardens overlooking the River Blackwater. It's the private residence of the Keane family who've lived here for 200 years. The entrance to the house is just north of the centre of Cappoquin; look for a set of huge black iron gates.

TOP CHOICE **Richmond House** (☎058-54278; www.richmondhouse.net; N72; s/d from €70/120; ⏲restaurant dinner nightly Apr-May, Tue-Sat Oct-Mar; P 📶), which dates back even further to 1704, was built by the Earl of Cork, and is set on 5.5 hectares of woodlands. All the same, its 10 guest rooms – furnished with countrified plaids, prints and mahogany – are cosy rather than imposing, and service is genuinely friendly. Nonguests are welcome at its modern Irish restaurant, where local produce includes West Waterford lamb and Helvick monkfish (five-course menu €55).

Barron's Bakery (The Square; dishes €3-8, ⏲8.30am-5.30pm Mon-Sat) has used the same Scotch brick ovens since 1887. Sandwiches, light meals and a mouth-watering selection of cakes and buns baked on the premises are available in its spearmint-green-painted cafe, while its breads are also sold throughout the area.

Getting There & Away

Bus Éireann (www.buseireann.ie) services stop in Cappoquin en route to Lismore (€3) and Dungarvan (€5, 20 minutes) on Monday, Thursday and Saturday. Buses to Waterford and Cork run once or twice a week.

Lismore

POP 750

Today, Lismore's enormous 19th-century castle seems out of proportion to this quiet, elegant town on the River Blackwater. Most of its existing buildings date from the early 19th century, but Lismore once had over 20 churches – many of which were destroyed during 9th- and 10th-century Viking raids. Over the centuries, statesmen and luminaries have streamed through Lismore, the location of a great monastic university founded by St Carthage in the 7th century. King Alfred of Wessex attended the university, Henry II visited the papal legate Bishop Christian O'Conarchy (Gilla Crist Ua Connairche) here in 1171, and even Fred Astaire dropped by when his sister Adele married into the Cavendish family, who own the castle.

Sights

Between doses of history and legend at the castle and cathedral, you can picnic in the **Millennium Gardens**, beside the castle car park, or take a 20-minute riverside stroll along **Lady Louisa's Walk** to the cathedral with its Edward Burne-Jones window.

Lismore Castle HISTORIC SITE

(www.lismorecastlearts.ie, www.lismorecastle.com; gardens adult/child €8/4; ⏲11am-4.45pm mid-Mar–Sep) From the Cappoquin road there are stunning glimpses of the riverside 'castle', which has lots of windows that would undercut any efforts at defence. While you can't get inside the four impressive walls of the main, crenulated building (unless you're looking to rent it for a group event), you can visit the 3 hectares of ornate and manicured **gardens**. Thought to be the oldest in Ireland, they are divided into the walled Jacobean upper garden and less formal lower garden. There are brilliant herbaceous borders, magnolias and camellias, and a splendid **yew walk** where Edmund Spenser is said to have written *The Faerie Queen*. There are contemporary sculptures in the gardens and a contemporary **art gallery** in the west wing of the castle.

The original castle was erected by Prince John, lord of Ireland, in 1185, although most of what you see now is from the early 19th century. After a stint as the local bishop's residence, it was presented to Sir Walter Raleigh in 1589 along with 200 sq km of the surrounding countryside.

St Carthage's Cathedral CHURCH

'One of the neatest and prettiest edifices I have seen', commented William Thackeray in 1842 about the striking 1679 cathedral. And that was before the addition of the Edward Burne-Jones **stained-glass window**, which features all the Pre-Raphaelite hallmarks: an effeminate knight and a pensive maiden against a sensuous background of deep-blue velvet and intertwining flowers. Justice, with sword and scales, and Humility, holding a lamb, honour Francis Currey, who helped to relieve the suffering of the poor during the Famine. Among the cathedral's oddities and wonders are some noteworthy **tombs**, including the elaborately carved MacGrath family crypt dating from 1557 and fossils in the pulpit.

Lismore Heritage Centre MUSEUM
(Main St; adult/child €5/3.50; ⏲9.30am-5.30pm Mon-Fri, 10am-5.30pm Sat, noon-5.30pm Sun mid-Mar–Christmas) Features a 30-minute audio-visual presentation taking you from the arrival of St Carthage in AD 636 to the present day via the discovery of the *Book of Lismore* behind a wall in the castle in 1814 and John F Kennedy's visit in 1947.

Sleeping & Eating

Glencairn Inn & Pastis Bistro B&B €€
(☎058-56232; www.glencairninn.com; Glencairn, Lismore; s/d from €60/95; ⏲restaurant dinner Thu-Sat, lunch Sun, inn & restaurant closed mid-Nov–mid-Jan; P 📶) Painted the colour of churned butter, this south-of-France-style country inn has four rooms with brass beds, classic French cuisine (mains €20 to €30), and a quintessentially Provençal pétanque pitch. Follow the signposts 4km west of town.

Lismore House Hotel HOTEL €€
(☎058-72966; www.lismorehousehotel.com; Main St; r €55-100; P 📶) Directly opposite the Heritage Centre, Ireland's oldest purpose-built hotel was built in 1797 by the Duke of Devonshire. He'd still recognise the exterior, but inside rooms have had a contemporary makeover with sleek dark timber furniture and cream-and-gold fabrics. Breakfast is extra. Book online for deals.

TOP CHOICE **O'Brien Chophouse** MODERN IRISH €€
(☎058-53810; www.obrienchophouse.ie; Main St; mains €14-28; ⏲lunch & dinner Wed-Sun; 📶) Up here in Waterford's hills the sea seems distant which makes the menu of steaks and chops all the more appropriate at this bastion of traditional cooking. But there's modern flair in the kitchen and always a surprise or two on the specials board. The Victorian decor of this old pub has been beautifully restored.

TOP CHOICE **Lismore Farmers Market** MARKET €
(Castle Ave; ⏲10am-4pm Sun) The upscale surrounds attract a fab collection of vendors including Dungarvan's Naked Lunch, whose tasty sandwiches you can enjoy in the park or at tables set up on the gravel path.

Foley's IRISH €€
(Main St; mains €10-24; ⏲9am-9pm) This inviting trad pub serves good steaks, fish and burgers in its interior replete with peacock wallpaper, leather-backed benches and an open fire, or in a beer garden out back.

Information

Tourist office (www.discoverlismore.com; Main St; ⏲9.30am-5.30pm Mon-Fri, 10am-5.30pm Sat, noon-5.30pm Sun mid-Mar–Christmas) Inside the Lismore Heritage Centre; pick up the info-packed *Lismore Walking Tour Guide* (€3).

Getting There & Around

Bus Éireann (www.buseireann.ie) service serves Cappoquin (€3) and Dungarvan (€5, 20 minutes) on Monday, Thursday and Saturday. Buses to Waterford and Cork run once or twice a week.

Lismore Cycling Holidays (☎087 935 6610; www.cyclingholidays.ie; rentals per day from €23) Hires out bikes and delivers them throughout the region.

Northern County Waterford

Some of the most scenic parts of County Waterford are in the north around Ballymacarbry and in the Nire Valley, which runs between the Comeragh and Monavullagh Mountains. While not as rugged as the west of Ireland, this mountain scenery has a stark beauty and doesn't attract much tourist traffic. It's a place of long walks and country stays.

Sights & Activities

Rolling hills and woodland stuffed with megalithic remains make the county's north a superb area for walkers. The Comeragh Mountains, where there are ridges to trace and loughs to circle, are named after their many *coums* (valleys, often of glacial origin). Coumshingaun and Coum Iarthair – next to Crotty's Lough, and named after an outlaw who lay low in a cave there – are some of Ireland's finest.

Stop for a pint and panini in **Melody's Nire View** (Ballymacarbry), where the genial folk have info on local walks and activities.

Otherwise make sure you're around for the **Nire Valley Walking Festival** (www.nirevalley.com), which takes place on the second weekend in October, with guided walks and traditional music in the pubs.

The **East Munster Way** (see the boxed text, p343) walking trail covers some 70km between Carrick-on-Suir in County Tipperary and the northern slopes of the

Knockmealdown Mountains. Access is at Fourmilewater, about 10km northwest of Ballymacarbry.

Sleeping

TOP CHOICE Hanora's Cottage B&B €€

(☎052-36134; www.hanorascottage.com; Nire Valley, Ballymacarbry; s/d from €80/150; ⊙restaurant dinner Mon-Sat; P) This 19th-century ancestral home next to Nire Church houses one of the country's best B&Bs. All 10 posh rooms have Jacuzzis (try for one overlooking the River Nire). Note that it's kid-free. Everything in the gourmet restaurant is made on the premises (dinner €40 to €50); they'll even pack you a walking lunch. Take the road east from Ballymacarbry, opposite Melody's; it's signposted 5km further on.

Powers the Pot CAMPGROUND €

(☎052-23085; www.powersthepot.com; Harney's Cross; campsites €13; ⊙May-Sep) An intimate little camping ground run by an archaeology and hiking buff. There is a kitchen and a thatched bar that has great acoustics for musicians to jam around the peat fire. It's in the hills 9km southeast of Clonmel in County Tipperary, signposted from the road to Rathgormuck.

Glasha Farmhouse B&B B&B €€

(☎052-36108; www.glashafarmhouse.com; Ballymacarbry; s/d from €60/100; P) Olive O'Gorman takes meticulous pride in maintaining the plaid- and brocade-decorated bedrooms at her working dairy farm. Some wonderful loop walks fan out around the farm; afterwards, reward yourself with dinner (arrange in advance) served by candlelight (€35 to €45) served in a glass conservatory. The farm is signposted 2km northwest of Ballymacarbry.

Getting There & Away

Bus service is very limited; this region is best done by car, bike or foot.

COUNTY CARLOW

POP 55,000

Strings of quietly picturesque villages wind through Carlow (Ceatharlach), Ireland's second-smallest county after Louth. The scenic Blackstairs Mountains dominate the southeast, while the region's most dramatic chunk of history is Europe's biggest dolmen, just outside quiet Carlow town. A ruined Gothic mansion and a reputedly haunted castle form the backdrop to two of the county's best flower-filled gardens – see p200 for more blooming information.

Carlow Town

POP 13,500

The narrow streets and lanes of Carlow have some heritage diversions plus a good museum and gallery to keep you wandering for an afternoon. An increasingly popular dormitory for commuters to Dublin, it is less than an hour's drive away on the M9 motorway. It's a good base for explorations of the county's real attractions: the countryside gardens.

Sights

Carlow town's main sights are all in a compact zone you can walk in under an hour.

TOP CHOICE Carlow County Museum MUSEUM

(www.carlowcountymuseum.com; cnr College & Tullow Sts) The musty, fusty displays of old are, well, history. This new incarnation of the local museum focuses on the lives of people in the county through the ages. It's thoroughly engaging. Look for ancient treasures, which were often uncovered through the generations by Carlow's toiling farmers. The museum is housed within the solid grey stone walls of an old convent. The museum got a refit in 2011 with pricing and hours not decided at the time of research.

Visual Centre for Contemporary Art ART GALLERY

(www.visualcarlow.ie; Old Dublin Rd; ⊙vary by exhibit) Opened in 2009, this glowing opaque-white cubelike space on the grounds of St Patrick's College is the county's cultural hub. British architect Terry Pawson scooped the international competition for the purpose-built centre with his factory-inspired industrial design of concrete, steel and glass. Known simply as Visual, its five separate galleries include the 'cathedral', the largest single exhibition space in Ireland. Rotating exhibits highlight local artists. It also houses the **George Bernard Shaw Theatre.**

Carlow Castle HISTORIC BUILDING

(Castle Hill) Built by William de Marshall on the site of an earlier Norman motte-and-bailey fort, this soaring 13-century castle survived Cromwell's attentions. It later succumbed to the grand plans of a certain Dr Middleton, who decided to convert it into a lunatic asylum. Proving the cliché about the lunatics running the asylum, he blew up much of the castle in 1814 in order to 'remodel' it. The evocative portion that survives is a part of the keep flanked by two towers.

Cathedral of the Assumption CHURCH
(College St) Between the county museum and the college is this elegant Regency Gothic cathedral, which dates from 1833. It was the brainchild of Bishop Doyle, a staunch supporter of Catholic emancipation. His statue inside includes a woman said to represent Ireland rising up against her oppressors. The church also has an elaborate pulpit and some fine stained-glass windows.

St Patrick's College NOTABLE BUILDING
(www.carlowcollege.ie; College St) Officially known as Carlow College, the main building opened as one of Ireland's first seminaries in 1793. Today it specialises in humanities and social studies and has a student body of 800. The wide grounds, which also front Visual, have a sort of regal, grassy elegance and are dotted with modern sculptures.

Festivals & Events

Éigse Carlow Arts Festival ARTS FESTIVAL
(www.eigsecarlow.ie; mid-Jun) Musicians, writers, actors and street performers take over the town.

Garden Festival GARDEN FESTIVAL
(www.carlowfloralfestival.com; late Aug) Talks by Irish gardening personalities and tours.

Sleeping

Diminutive County Carlow's abundance of charming inns means it's easy to stay out in the bucolic countryside (see listings throughout the County Carlow section) and pop into town for food and culture. There are some worthwhile options in the centre.

TOP CHOICE **Red Setter Guest House** B&B €€
(059-914 1848; www.redsetterguesthouse.ie; 14 Dublin St; s/d from €40/70; P wi-fi) Great attention to detail and extra touches like gorgeous bouquets of fresh flowers make this otherwise humble B&B the winning in-town choice. Breakfasts are grand and the owners can't do enough to be helpful.

Barrowville Townhouse INN €€
(059-914 3324; www.barrowville.com; Kilkenny Rd; s/d from €45/80; P wi-fi) This whitewashed 18th-century town house has been meticulously converted into a classy B&B, under five minutes' walk south of town. The seven rooms vary in size, but are all perfectly atmospheric for curling up with a book. Enjoy local free-range eggs for breakfast in the airy conservatory.

Eating & Drinking

The town is the nightlife hub for those out in the sticks; there's a squadron of large pubs at the east end of Tullow St. Excellent restaurants make use of the county's bounty. Look for O'Hara beers, including a fine India Pale Ale. They are brewed nearby in Borris.

TOP CHOICE **Lennons** MODERN IRISH €€
(www.lennons.ie; Visual, off College St; mains €8-18; lunch daily, dinner Thu-Sat) Carlow's best dining is found amid the artsy surrounds of Visual. It's a sleek and appropriately stylish space, with a wide patio outside where you can see sculpture on the college's grassy grounds. Lunch features creative sandwiches, salads and hot specials. Dinner is more refined with a seasonal menu that emphasises the organic. Excellent wine list and a chic bar area.

TOP CHOICE **Farmers Market** MARKET €
(9am-2pm Sat) Fittingly held on the Potato Market – look out for Tom Malone's mouth-watering freshly made jams and juices as well as Hennessy's baked goods and much, much more.

Caffe Formenti CAFE €€
(20 Dublin St; mains €9-14; 8am-6pm) This buzzing cafe combines the talents of an Irish-Italian husband-and-wife team. In addition to daily lunch specials and wholesome soups, there's a tempting selection of Italian pastries, freshly made gelati (yum!) and aromatic coffees.

Hennessy's Fine Foods DELI €€
(059-913 2849; 26 Dublin St; dishes €10-12; 8am-3pm Mon-Sat) A worthy stop for a meal or a gourmet grocery picnic (local cheeses, red onion marmalade, chilli jam, red pepper pesto and so on). The vast range of savoury baked goods are filling treats.

Information

Post office (cnr Kennedy Ave & Dublin St)

Tourist office (www.carlowtourism.com; cnr Tullow & College Sts; 9.30am-1pm & 2-5.30pm Mon-Fri) A useful source of county-wide information. It is at the entrance to the county museum.

Getting There & Away

Bus

Buses leave from the bus station at the eastern end of Kennedy Ave.

Bus Éireann (www.buseireann.ie) goes to Dublin (€12, two hours, nine daily), Cork (€22, 3½ hours, one daily), Kilkenny (€9, 35 minutes, three daily) and Waterford (€10, 1½ hours, seven daily), while **JJ Kavanagh & Sons** (www.jjkavanagh.ie) goes to Dublin (€12, two hours, 12 daily) and Dublin Airport (€12, three hours).

Taxi

Carlow Cabs (059-914 0000)

Train

The **train station** (www.irishrail.ie; Station Rd) is to the northeast of town. Carlow is located on the Dublin Heuston (from €10, 70 minutes) to Waterford line (€16, 80 minutes) via Kilkenny. There are eight to 10 trains each way daily.

Around Carlow Town

Although the entire county is a day trip from Carlow, the following sights are very close.

Sights

TOP CHOICE **Delta Sensory Gardens** GARDEN
(www.deltasensorygardens.com; Strawhall Estate, Cannery Rd; adult/child €5/free; 9am-5pm Mon-Fri, 11am-5pm Sat & Sun) Some 16 interconnecting, themed gardens cover one hectare and span the five senses – from sculpture garden to a formal rose garden, water and woodland garden, willow garden and a musical garden with mechanical fountains. Admission proceeds benefit the adjoining Delta Centre, which provides services and respite for adults with learning disabilities. Find the gardens incongruously hidden in an industrial estate on the northern edge of Carlow.

Browne's Hill Dolmen LANDMARK
This 5000-year-old granite monster is Europe's largest portal dolmen (tomb chamber) and one of Ireland's most famous. The capstone alone weighs well over 100 tonnes. It's signposted 3km east of Carlow on the R726; a 300m path leads round the field to the dolmen.

TOP CHOICE **Duckett's Grove** HISTORIC BUILDING
(admission free; 10am-5.30pm Apr-Oct, 10am-4pm Nov-Mar) Adjoining a foreboding ruined Gothic mansion, the original high brick garden walls of this estate frame two sprawling, interconnected formal gardens. Filled with the scents of lavender and fruit blossom in spring and summer, they border a shaded woodland area, covering some 4.5 hectares. Check with Carlow's tourist office for the gardens' program of events. There's no public transport; the gardens are 12.5km northeast of Carlow off the R726.

Killeshin Church HISTORIC SITE
Once the site of an important monastery with one of the finest round towers in the country, this medieval marvel was destroyed early in the 18th century by a philistine farmer worried that it might collapse and kill his cows. The **ruins** of a 12th-century church remain, including a remarkable **Romanesque doorway** dat-

CARLOW IN BLOOM

County Carlow is renowned for its gardens, 16 of which form part of Ireland's first dedicated **garden trail** (www.carlowgardentrail.com). Most tourist offices will have a copy of the invaluable (and free) guide *Carlow Garden Trail*.

Our top five gardens:

» **Delta Sensory Gardens** – a multisensory, fountain-filled oasis.

» **Huntington Castle and Gardens** (p202) – rambling, overgrown grounds in the shadow of a haunted castle, incorporating a canopy of yew trees planted by monks over 700 years ago.

» **Duckett's Grove** – restored walled gardens behind a ruined Gothic mansion.

» **Kilgraney House Herb Gardens** (p201) – aromatic gardens filled with medicinal and kitchen plants.

» **Altamont Gardens** (p201) – Heritage-listed Victorian splendour, hosting a weeklong Snowdrop Festival in February.

Flower fans shouldn't miss County Carlow's summertime **Garden Festival** (p199).

ing from the 5th century. Look for the wonderful bearded face on the capstone. Killeshin is 5km west of Carlow on the R430.

Ballon

POP 600

Grand estates and gardens envelop the small village of Ballon on the N80 and N81.

Sights

TOP CHOICE **Altamont Gardens** GARDEN

(www.heritageireland.ie; admission free; ⏲10am-7pm daily summer, to 5pm other times, Mon-Fri only Dec) One of Ireland's most magnificent old walled formal gardens, this 16-hectare garden has a design dating to Victorian times. It emphasises carefully selected plantings arranged in naturalistic, idealised settings. The gardens are 5km east of Ballon.

Sleeping & Eating

TOP CHOICE **Sherwood Park House** INN €€

(☎059-915 9117; www.sherwoodparkhouse.ie; Kilbride, Ballon; s/d from €60/100; P) Inside a greystone Georgian manor dating from 1730, the five rooms here are huge and boast such period niceties as satin- and velvet-adorned four-poster beds. You can make arrangements for dinner (€40 per person; BYO wine). This is prime walking country; Altamont Gardens are just 600m south.

TOP CHOICE **Forge Restaurant** IRISH €€

(Kilbride Cross, Ballon; dishes €5-11; ⏲9.30am-5.30pm Mon-Sat, 11am-6pm Sun) Mary Jordan cooks up steaming soups and hot lunches, as well as baked goods to take away at this hugely popular roadside inn near Altamont Gardens. Local produce is used. A shop sells local art and crafts. There's often a wait for a table at weekends.

Borris & Around

POP 600

This seemingly untouched hillside Georgian village has a dramatic mountain backdrop and traditional main street. A huge stone railway viaduct on the edge of town has been disused since the line closures of the 1950s.

Borris is full of character, with plenty of atmospheric bars hosting summertime trad music.

Sights & Activities

Borris is strung out like a string bean down the side of a hill. It's a pleasant place to begin a long stroll amid the modest yet solid buildings lining the street.

Borris is a starting point for the 13km **Mt Leinster Scenic Drive** (it can also be walked) and is also on the South Leinster Way (see the boxed text, p220). To reach the mighty mountain (p181) from Borris, follow the Mt Leinster Scenic Drive signposts 13km towards Bunclody in County Wexford. The last few kilometres are on narrow, exposed roads with steep fall-offs. It takes a good two hours on foot or 20 minutes by car. On the northern slopes of Mt Leinster, the tiny village of Kildavin is the starting point of the South Leinster Way.

Alternatively, there's a lovely 10km walk along the **River Barrow towpath** to picturesque Graiguenamanagh (County Kilkenny) and on to St Mullins.

Heading north from Borris, the R705 follows the scenic **River Barrow Valley** for 12km to Bagenalstown.

TOP CHOICE **Kilgraney House Herb Gardens**

(www.kilgraneyhouse.com; Bagenalstown; admission €5; ⏲2-5pm Thu-Sun May-Sep) boasts a heady cocktail of medicinal and kitchen plants. Herbs as you've never seen them grow in orderly profusion in this garden which also serves as a source of food for the inn and restaurant here. The recreated medieval monastic herb garden is a favourite. It's off the R705 halfway between Borris and Bagenalstown.

Carlow Brewing Company BREWERY

(☎059-913 4356; www.carlowbrewing.com; Royal Oak Rd, Bagenalstown; tours by reservation €11) The popular microbrewery offers tours of its O'Hara's brand beers. Its award-winning Irish Stout bursts with flavour and certainly holds its own against that *other* Irish stout.

Sleeping & Eating

TOP CHOICE **Step House Hotel** HOTEL €€

(☎059-977 3209; www.stephousehotel.ie; 66 Main St, Borris; s/d from €65/130; P 📶) At the top end of town, this Georgian home has undergone a stunning makeover in elegant shades of pistachio green. Its 23 rooms boast balconies and have a clever opulence. Views are framed by Mt Leinster. Tables in the Cellar Restaurant are tucked in romantic corners beneath vaulted ceilings. The woodsy bar is

WORTH A TRIP

CLONEGAL

The idyllic village of Clonegal has a tiny little centre out of a nursery rhyme with an arched stone bridge over a river that boasts both swans and water flowers.

It is the southern terminus of Ireland's inaugural long-distance walking trail, the **Wicklow Way**. Nonhikers can reach it by driving along a series of signposted winding local roads 5km east of Kildavin and the N80.

Huntington Castle (www.huntingtoncastle.com; Clonegal; castle & gardens tour adult/child €8/5, gardens only €5/3; ⏲house 2-6pm Jun-Aug, by appointment rest of year, gardens 10am-6pm May-Sep) is a spooky, dusty old keep built in 1625 by the Durdin-Robertson family, who still own it and live here today. The family conduct hour-long tours of the property, which, they claim, is haunted by two ghosts: Bishop Leslie (a former bishop of Limerick) and Ailish O'Flaherty (the granddaughter of Grace O'Malley, the Pirate Queen). Descending to the castle's basement brings you to the Temple of Isis, where the Fellowship of Isis, worshipping the ancient Egyptian goddess, was founded by the family in 1963. The gardens combine the formal with rural fantasy. It's accessed by a long driveway off Clonegal's main street.

Sha-Roe Bistro (☎053-937 5636; Main St; mains €18-25; ⏲lunch Sun, dinner Wed-Sat), tucked inside an 18th-century building, serves standout modern Irish cuisine that draws on the bounty of the region. The menu lists local suppliers who provide ingredients fresh from the surrounding orchards and farms. Book at least two weeks ahead.

A traditional stop for Wicklow Way walkers, **Osborne's pub** (Main St) is slightly eerie thanks to its bar made from coffin lids.

the perfect place for a boozy respite after a day walking.

Lorum Old Rectory B&B **€€**
(☎059-977 5282; www.lorum.com; s/d from €95/150; ⏲Mar-Nov; Ⓟ) Halfway between Borris and Bagenalstown off the R705, this historic manor house sits on a prominent knoll east of the road. The gardens stretch in all directions, offering peaceful views from each of the five rooms. The largely organic cooking here is renowned; confirm dining arrangements when you book.

Kilgraney Country House INN **€€€**
(☎059-977 5283; www.kilgraneyhouse.com; s/d from €120/170; ⏲Mar-Nov; Ⓟ) The River Barrow burbles down the shallow valley from this six-room Georgian manor. The owners, veteran travellers, have created a fabulous interior with artefacts collected from far-away places like the Philippines. Unwind in the spa, the famous herb gardens or over a six-course meal (from €50). It's off the R705 halfway between Borris and Bagenalstown.

M O'Shea PUB
(Main St) Surprises abound in this tidy warren of rooms that combines a general store, modern grocery store and old-fashioned pub where spare parts and bits of machinery still hang from the ceiling.

ℹ Getting There & Away

Borris is on the east–west R702, which links the M9 with the N11 in County Wexford.

Eight to 10 trains a day travel between Carlow town and Bagenalstown (€7, 15 minutes) en route to/from Kilkenny (€7, 20 minutes).

St Mullins

Tranquil little St Mullins sits 6km downstream from Graiguenamanagh, which is in County Kilkenny. The village is the maternal home of Michael Flatley of *Riverdance* fame. Sure enough, the river snakes through here in the shadow of Brandon Hill, as does the River Barrow towpath from Borris. From the river, a trail winds uphill to the ruined hulk of an old **monastery** surrounded by the graves of 1798 rebels. A 9th-century Celtic cross, badly worn down over the centuries, still stands beside the monastery. Nearby, **St Moling's Well** is a holy well that seems to attract spare change.

Overlooking the weir at the river's edge, Martin and Emer O'Brien have eschewed corporate life to convert St Mullins' **Old Grain Store** (☎051-424 4440; www.oldgrainstorecottages.ie; cottages per week €300-480; ⏲cafe 11am-6pm Tue-Sun summer, other times varies) into a fabulous cafe serving fresh meals, and three self-catering cottages sleeping two to four people, set in the coach house, the forge and the stables. The cottages' interiors are stylish yet homey, with shelves of books and wood-burning stoves. Shorter stays are sometimes possible on request. Martin and Emer also lend guests bikes and kayaks.

Just up the hill from the river, **Mulvarra House** (☎051-424 936; www.mulvarra.com; s/d from €40/70; P) is a modern, comfortable B&B with guest rooms opening to balconies taking in the glorious setting. Dinner (€30) is available by arrangement, and you can also indulge in spa treatments.

COUNTY KILKENNY

POP 95,000

County Kilkenny's centrepiece is, of course, its namesake city. An enduring gift of the Normans, it mesmerises visitors with its medieval alleys that wind past its castle, cathedral, ruined abbeys and dynamic modern-day nightlife.

But the appeal of the county as a whole shouldn't be underestimated. It's a place of rolling hills, where you'll soon run out of adjectives for green. Tiny roads navigate the valleys alongside swirling rivers, moss-covered stone walls and relics of centuries of Irish religious history. Wanderers and ramblers are rewarded by characterful pubs and fine restaurants. Shamrock-cute Inistioge village may be star of many movies, but it's the real deal, as are towns like Graiguenamanagh, Bennettsbridge and Thomastown, where you'll find skilled artists and craftspeople busy creating in their studios.

Kilkenny City

POP 8900

Kilkenny (Cill Chainnigh) is the Ireland of many visitors' imaginations. Its majestic riverside castle, tangle of 17th-century passageways, rows of colourful, old-fashioned shopfronts and centuries-old pubs with traditional live music all have a timeless appeal, as does its splendid medieval cathedral. But Kilkenny is also awash with contemporary eateries and is a hotbed of arts, crafts and cultural life.

Kilkenny's architectural charm owes a huge debt to the Middle Ages, when the city was a seat of political power. It's also sometimes called the 'marble city' because of the local black limestone, which resembles a slate-coloured marble and is used on floors and in decorative trim all over town.

To avoid the crowds, try to visit on a weekday or sometime out of summer, when you're better able to appreciate the elegance and vibrancy that give the town (oops, locals insist on 'city') a timeless appeal. You can cover pretty much everything on foot in half a day, but sampling its many delights will take much longer.

History

In the 5th century, St Kieran is said to have visited Kilkenny and, on the site of the present Kilkenny Castle, challenged the chieftains of Ossory to accept the Christian faith. Subsequently, St Canice established his monastery here. Kilkenny consolidated its importance in the 13th century under William Marshall, the Earl of Pembroke and son-in-law of the Anglo-Norman conqueror Strongbow. Kilkenny Castle was built to secure a crossing point on the River Nore.

In the Middle Ages, Kilkenny was intermittently the unofficial capital of Ireland, with its own Anglo-Norman parliament. In 1366 the parliament passed the so-called Statutes of Kilkenny aimed at preventing the assimilation of Anglo-Normans into Irish society. Anglo-Normans were prohibited from marrying the native Irish, taking part in Irish sports, speaking or dressing like the Irish or playing any Irish music. Although the laws remained theoretically for over 200 years, they were never enforced with any great effect and did little to halt the absorption of the Anglo-Normans into Irish culture.

During the 1640s Kilkenny sided with the Catholic royalists in the English Civil War. The 1641 Confederation of Kilkenny, an uneasy alliance of native Irish and Anglo-Normans, aimed to bring about the return of land and power to Catholics. After Charles I's execution, Cromwell besieged Kilkenny for five days, destroying much of the southern wall of the castle before the ruling Ormonde family surrendered. The defeat signalled a permanent end to Kilkenny's political influence over Irish affairs.

Today, tourism is Kilkenny's main economic focus, but it's also the regional centre for more traditional pursuits like agriculture – you'll see farmers on tractors stoically dodging tour buses.

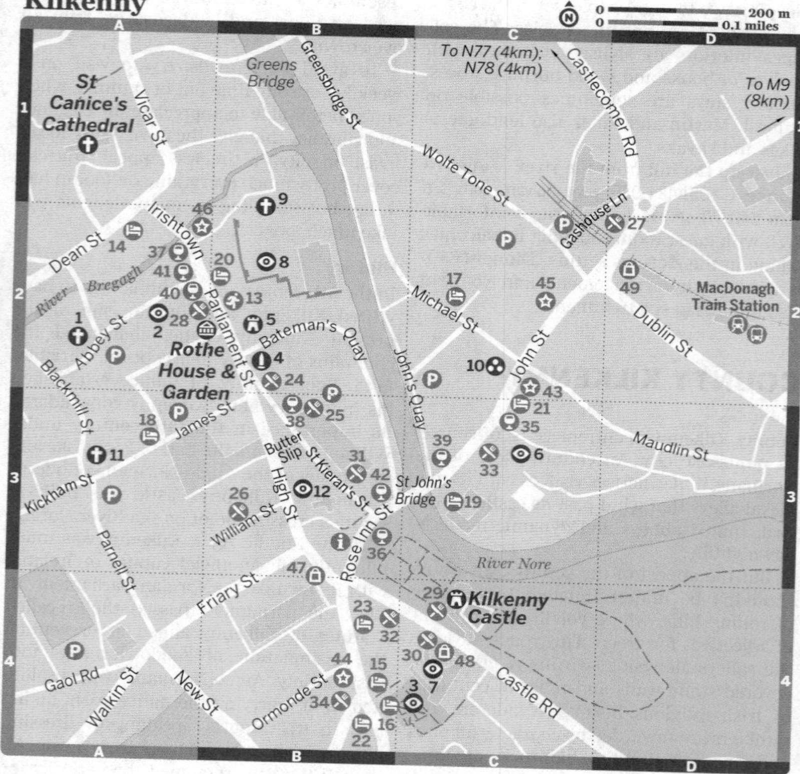

Sights

TOP CHOICE **Kilkenny Castle** HISTORIC BUILDING

(www.kilkennycastle.ie; adult/child €6/2.50; ⌚9am-5.30pm Mar-Sep, 9.30am-4.30pm Oct-Feb) Rising above the Nore, Kilkenny Castle is one of Ireland's most visited heritage sites. The first structure on this strategic site was a wooden tower built in 1172 by Richard de Clare, the Anglo-Norman conqueror of Ireland better known as Strongbow. In 1192, Strongbow's son-in-law, William Marshall, erected a stone castle with four towers, three of which survive. The castle was bought by the powerful Butler family in 1391, and their descendants continued to live there until 1935. Maintaining such a structure became a big financial strain and most of the furnishings were sold at auction. The castle was handed over to the city in 1967 for the princely sum of £50.

One glance tells you that the castle has been modified through the centuries. First of all it's missing a wall – a key defensive deficiency. Second, there are all those windows – perfect targets, say, for a catapult. Most of the changes visible today date from the 19th century when efforts were made to banish the gloom and bring in the cheer. By then the only real defensive worry was a peasant flinging a rotten potato.

Regular 40-minute guided tours focus on the **Long Gallery**, in the wing of the castle nearest the river. The gallery, which showcases stuffy portraits of the Butler family members over the centuries, is an impressive hall with high ceilings vividly painted with Celtic and Pre-Raphaelite motifs.

The castle basement is also home to the **Butler Gallery** (www.butlergallery.com; admission free), one of the country's most impor-

Kilkenny

Top Sights

Sights

Activities, Courses & Tours

Sleeping

Eating

Drinking

Entertainment

Shopping

tant art galleries outside Dublin. Small exhibitions featuring the work of contemporary artists are held throughout the year. Also in the basement, the castle kitchen houses a popular summertime cafe. You can access the Butler Gallery and the cafe without paying admission.

About 20 hectares of **parkland** (admission free; daylight hours) are a refuge from city nuttiness. The grounds echo with chirping birds and extend to the southeast, with a Celtic cross-shaped **rose garden**, a fountain to the northern end and a children's playground to the south. There are many good views of the river. The castle's former stables are now home to the **Kilkenny Design Centre**.

TOP CHOICE **St Canice's Cathedral** CHURCH

(www.stcanicescathedral.ie; St Canice's Pl; adult/child €4/3; 9am-6pm Mon-Sat, 2-6pm Sun Jun-Aug, 10am-1pm & 2-5pm Mon-Sat, 2-5pm Sun Apr-May & Sep, until 4pm other times) Soaring over the north end of the centre is Ireland's second-largest medieval cathedral (after St Patrick's in Dublin). This Gothic edifice with its iconic round tower has had a long and fascinating history. Legend has it that the first monastery was built here in the 6th century by St Canice, Kilkenny's patron saint. Records show that a wooden church on the site was burned down in 1087.

The existing structure was raised between 1202 and 1285, but then endured a series of catastrophes and resurrections. The first disaster, the collapse of the church tower

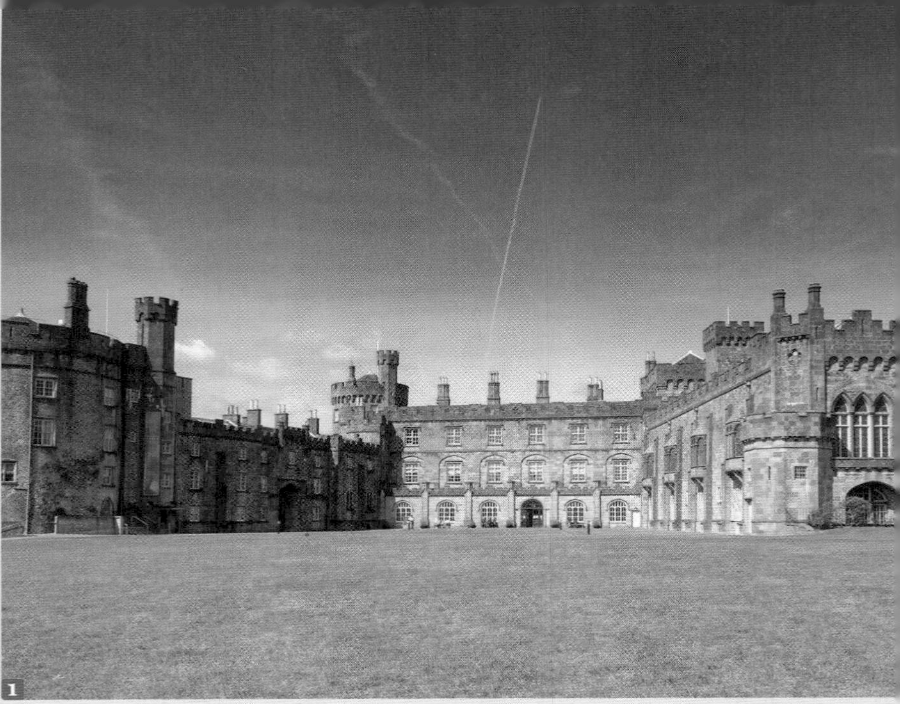

1

5

4

1. Kilkenny Castle (p204)
Kilkenny Castle, which includes 20 hectares of parkland, is one of Ireland's most visited heritage sites.

2. Long Gallery, Kilkenny Castle (p204)
The gallery showcases portraits of the powerful Butler family, who lived in the castle from 1391 to 1935.

2

3. Medieval Room, Kilkenny Castle (p204)
Stone face carving in the castle's Medieval Room.

4. Great Hall, Kilkenny Castle (p204)
Exterior of the castle's Great Hall.

5. Butler Gallery, Kilkenny Castle (p204)
Statue outside Butler Gallery, one of the country's most important art galleries outside Dublin.

3

in 1332, was the consequence of Dame Alice Kyteler's conviction for witchcraft. Her maid was also convicted, and her nephew, William Outlawe, was implicated. The unfortunate maid was burned at the stake, but Dame Alice escaped to London and William spared himself by offering to re-roof part of St Canice's Cathedral with lead tiles. His new roof proved too heavy, however, bringing the church tower down with it.

In 1650 Cromwell's forces defaced and damaged the church, using it to stable their horses. Repairs began in 1661 and are still ongoing. The beautiful roof in the nave was completed in 1863. Also worth a look is a model of Kilkenny as it was in 1642 – things haven't changed that much.

Inside, highly polished ancient **grave slabs** are set on the walls and the floor. On the northern wall, opposite the entrance, a slab inscribed in Norman French commemorates Jose de Keteller, who died in 1280; despite the difference in spelling he was probably the father of Alice Kyteler. The stone chair of St Kieran embedded in the wall dates from the 13th century. The fine 1596 monument to Honorina Grace at the western end of the southern aisle is made of beautiful local black limestone. In the southern transept, a handsome **black tomb** has effigies of Piers Butler, who died in 1539, and his wife, Margaret Fitzgerald. Tombs and monuments (listed on a board in the southern aisle) to other notable Butlers crowd this corner of the church.

Outside the cathedral, a 30m-high **round tower** (adult/12-18 years €3/2.50; ⏲Apr-Oct) rises amid an odd array of ancient tombstones and is the oldest structure within the grounds. It was built sometime between AD 700 and 1000 on the site of an earlier Christian cemetery. Apart from missing its crown, the round tower is in excellent condition and those aged over 12 can admire a fine view from the top. It's a tight squeeze and you'll need both hands to climb the 100 steps up steep ladders.

The approach to the cathedral on foot from Parliament St leads you over Irishtown Bridge and up **St Canice's Steps**, which date from 1614; the wall at the top contains fragmentary medieval carvings. The leaning tombstones scattered about the grounds prompt you to look at the very least for a black cat.

Rothe House & Garden HISTORIC BUILDING

(www.rothehouse.com; Parliament St; adult/child €5/4; ⏲10.30am-5pm Mon-Sat year-round, 2-6pm Sun Apr-Oct) Ireland's best surviving example of a 16th-century merchant's house is the Tudor Rothe House. Built around a series of courtyards, it now houses a **museum** with local artefacts including a well-used Viking sword found nearby and a grinning head sculpted from a stone by a Celtic artist. The king-post roof of the 2nd floor is a meticulous reconstruction. Recent changes include new exhibits about the Rothe family and ongoing restorations of the urban gardens out back.

In the 1640s the wealthy Rothe family played a part in the Confederation of Kilkenny, and Peter Rothe, son of the original builder, had all his property confiscated. His sister was able to reclaim it, but just before the Battle of the Boyne (1690) the family supported James II and so lost the house permanently. In 1850 a Confederation banner was discovered in the house; it's now in the National Museum in Dublin.

National Craft Gallery & Kilkenny Design Centre ART GALLERY

(www.ccoi.ie; Castle Yard; ⏲10am-5.30pm Tue-Sat) Contemporary Irish crafts are showcased at this imaginative gallery in the former castle stables that also house the shops of the Kilkenny Design Centre. Ceramics dominate, but exhibits often feature furniture, jewellery and weaving from the members of the Crafts Council of Ireland. There are regular classes in pottery and jewellery making.

Behind the complex, look for the walkway that extends into the beautiful **Butler House gardens** of, with an unusual water feature constructed from remnants of the British-built Nelson Column, blown up by nationalists in Dublin around a century ago.

Black Abbey CHURCH

(Abbey St; ⏲open daily for Mass) This Dominican abbey was founded in 1225 by William Marshall and takes its name from the monks' black habits. In 1543, six years after Henry VIII's dissolution of the monasteries, it was turned into a courthouse. Following Cromwell's visit in 1650, it remained a roofless ruin until restoration in 1866. Much of what survives dates from the 18th and 19th centuries, but remnants of more ancient archways are still evident within the newer stonework. Look for the 13th-century coffins near the entrance.

Tholsel HISTORIC SITE
The (City Hall) on High St was built in 1761 on the spot where Dame Alice Kyteler's maid, Petronella, was burned at the stake in 1324.

Butter Slip HISTORIC SITE
With its arched entry and stone steps, Butter Slip, a narrow and dark walkway connecting High St with St Kieran's St (previously called Low Lane) is the most picturesque of Kilkenny's many narrow medieval corridors. It was built in 1616 and once was lined with the stalls of butter vendors.

Black Freren Gate HISTORIC SITE
(Abbey St) This is the only gate from the old Norman city walls still standing, albeit with the help of metal bracing to ensure the safety of those who pass through. Crumbling sections of the old walls remain throughout the central city.

Confederation Hall Monument HISTORIC SITE
On the corner of Parliament St and the road leading down to Bateman's Quay, this monument (really just a fragment) built into the Bank of Ireland marks the site where the national Parliament met from 1642 to 1649. Nearby is the carefully restored **Grace's Castle**, originally built in 1210, but lost to the family and converted into a prison in 1568, and then in 1794 into a courthouse, which it remains today. Rebels from the 1798 Rising were executed here.

St Mary's Cathedral CHURCH
The 19th-century cathedral is visible from most parts of town. A plaque at the entrance notes: 'The construction of the cathedral began in 1843 and continued during the Famine years, the years of emigration, coffin ships, starvation, and even despair because of the many thousands of our people who died of hunger and disease..', before going on to list yet more tribulations.

St John's Priory HISTORIC SITE
Across the river stand the ruins of this priory, which was founded in 1200 and was noted for its many beautiful windows until Cromwell's visit. Nearby **Kilkenny College** (John St) dates from 1666. Its students included Jonathan Swift and the philosopher George Berkeley, but it now houses Kilkenny's county hall.

Tours

Kilkenny Cycling Tours BIKE TOURS
(☎086 895 4961; www.kilkennycyclingtours.com; adult/child from €14/10) Explore the city and surrounds on a bike over a 2½-hour tour that can include a lunch option.

Tynan Tours WALKING TOURS
(☎087 265 1745; adult/student €6/5.50; ⏲2-4 tours daily mid-Mar–Oct) Entertaining, informative hour-long walking tours that meander Kilkenny's narrow lanes, steps and pedestrian passageways. Meet at the tourist office.

Festivals & Events

Kilkenny hosts several world-class events throughout the year that attract revellers in the thousands.

Kilkenny Rhythm & Roots MUSIC FESTIVAL
(www.kilkennyroots.com; ⏲early May) Over 30 pubs and other venues participate in hosting

LOCAL BREWS GOOD & BAD, ER BUD

John Smithwick opened the **brewery** in Kilkenny city in 1710 on the site of the 13th-century **St Francis Abbey** (the abbey's ruins remain within the complex). But it wasn't until the 1980s that it started selling the beer overseas. The Kilkenny name was chosen, as the export version was stronger than the Smithwick's original. Today 'Kilkenny' refers to a similar yet distinctly different beer – it is more bitter and has a creamy, Guinnesslike head (Smithwick's retains a thinner head and smoother taste). Both are sold locally.

Ireland's oldest working brewery, Smithwick's is now owned by drinks giant Diageo (Guinness, Harp et al), and primarily brews Budweiser and, shudder, Bud Lite under licence. As a brewer there told us: 'Any port in a storm', when asked about the watery American brands. Although, like an especially bad hangover rumours of the brewery's closure never go away, its future seems assured for now.

After a hiatus of many years, **Smithwick's Brewery Tours** (Parliament St; admission €10; ⏲12.30-3.30pm Tue-Sat) are again on offer. You learn about the brewing process, history of the brewery, visit the abbey and do some tasting during the 90-minute tour. Be sure to ask them how they get the flavour *out* of the Bud.

Ireland's biggest music festival, with an emphasis on country and 'old-timey' American roots music.

Cat Laughs Comedy Festival COMEDY
(www.thecatlaughs.com; ⌚late May-early Jun) Acclaimed gathering of world-class comedians in Kilkenny's hotels and pubs.

Kilkenny Arts Festival ARTS
(www.kilkennyarts.ie; ⌚mid-Aug) The city comes alive with theatre, cinema, music, literature, visual arts, children's events and street spectacles for 10 action-packed days.

Kilkenny Celtic Festival CULTURAL
(www.celticfestival.ie; ⌚late Sep-early Oct) A week-long celebration of all things trad Irish, especially the language, spanning performances, exhibits, seminars and more.

Sleeping

If you're arriving in town with no room booked (an unwise move at weekends, in summer and during festivals), the tourist office runs an efficient accommodation booking service (€4). Otherwise you'll find lodging at all prices throughout town.

TOP CHOICE **Butler House** HOTEL €€
(☎056-772 2828; www.butler.ie; 16 Patrick St; s €60-120, d €100-180; P@) You can't stay in Kilkenny Castle, but this historic mansion is surely the next best thing. Once the home of the earls of Ormonde, who built the castle, these days it houses a boutique hotel with aristocratic trappings including sweeping staircases, marble fireplaces, an art collection and impeccably trimmed gardens. The 13 generously sized rooms are individually decorated. Just to remind you you're staying in history, the floors creak.

Pembroke Hotel HOTEL €€€
(☎056-778 3500; www.pembrokekilkenny.com; Patrick St; r €120-200; P) Wake up to castle views (from some of the 74 rooms) at this stylish, modern epicentral hotel. Deluxe rooms feature balconies, a rarity in Ireland (along with the air-con). There's a leather-sofa-filled bar on-site and use of swimming and leisure facilities just around the corner.

Celtic House B&B €€
(☎056-776 2249; www.celtic-house-bandb.com; 18 Michael St; r €70-90; P@) Artist Angela Byrne extends one of Ireland's warmest welcomes at her spick-and-span B&B. Some of the bright rooms have sky-lit bathrooms, others have views of the castle, and Angela's landscapes adorn many of the walls. Book ahead.

Butler Court INN €€
(☎056-776 1178; www.butlercourt.com; Patrick St; r €80-130; @) Not to be confused with the grand Butler House a few doors uphill, this was originally the mail coach yard for Kilkenny Castle. Wrapping around a flower-filled courtyard, contemporary rooms have Canadian-cherry parquet floors and king-size beds. A continental breakfast, including fresh fruit and filtered coffee, is stocked in your in-room fridge.

Kilkenny River Court HOTEL €€€
(☎056-772 3388; www.rivercourthotel.com; John St; r €95-200; P@) When not unwinding in your nicely appointed modern room, you can dine at the respected restaurant, swim laps in the award-winning health club's sunlit indoor pool, or sip a cocktail on the cobblestone terrace of the wraparound bar overlooking the bridge and castle. Staff are consistently helpful.

Bregagh House B&B €€
(☎056-772 2315; www.bregaghhouse.com; Dean St; s/d from €50/70; P) If you want the cosiness that comes with staying in a family home, this B&B is a good bet for its convenient location opposite the cathedral, friendly hosts, and filling hot breakfasts. There's ample on-site parking and a pretty back garden that features kid-friendly pet rabbits.

Kilkenny Tourist Hostel HOSTEL €
(☎056-776 3541; www.kilkennyhostel.ie; 35 Parliament St; dm €14-20, d €36-42; @) Inside an ivy-covered 1770s Georgian town house, this cosy, 60-bed IHH hostel has a sitting room warmed by an open fireplace, and a timber- and leadlight-panelled dining room adjoining the self-catering kitchen. Most pubs are within stumbling distance.

O'Malley's B&B B&B €
(☎056-777 1003; www.omalleysguesthouse.com; Ormonde Rd; s/d from €40/60; P) Close to the centre, this three-storey rowhouse has basic but comfortable rooms. For once the maroon colours of half of Ireland's B&Bs are missing, replaced by a palette of lettuce and mustard.

Langton House Hotel HOTEL €€
(☎056-776 5133; www.langtons.ie; 67 John St; s €65-100, d €100-150; P@) In the same family since the 1930s, but constantly evolving, this Kilkenny icon has some 34 rooms of

varying styles – from clubby, leather-upholstered affairs to dramatically decorated ones with colours that pop off the wall and showers that need control panels. There's also a fine restaurant (Edward Langton's) and a popular pub.

Kilford Arms Hotel HOTEL €€
(☎056-776 1018; www.kilfordarms.ie; John St; s/d from €50/90; P @) Mounted in the lobby, a stuffed 150-year-old Bengal tiger (somewhat mangy, but in better shape than the Celtic Tiger) sets the tone at this hotel, which is also home to high-profile bars. The 60 rooms are generic albeit with quirks: some have sweeping city views obscured by frosted windows, others are vulnerable to raucous pub noise.

Darcy's Guesthouse B&B €€
(☎056-777 0219, 056-777 0087; James St; s/d from €50/90; P) Ideally located, this guesthouse is a cheery B&B that flies flags from its facade. The 11 rooms come in a variety of pastel combos, all with twee little cushioned headboards.

Tree Grove Caravan & Camping Park CAMPGROUND €
(☎056-777 0302; www.treegrovecamping.com; New Ross Rd; campsites €15-25; Mar–mid-Nov) This camping ground in a small park is 1.5km south of Kilkenny off the R700. Bike hire can be arranged.

Eating

Kilkenny's restaurants are among the best in the southeast. See the range of local produce and prepared foods available at the **farmers market** (Mayors Walk, The Parade; 9am-2pm Thu).

TOP CHOICE **Campagne** MODERN IRISH €€€
(☎056-777 2858; www.campagne.ie; The Arches, 5 Gashouse Lane; lunch 2-/3-course set menu €24/29, dinner mains €25-30; lunch Fri-Sun, dinner Tue-Sat) Chef Garrett Byrne who gained fame and Michelin stars in Dublin is the genius behind this bold, stylish restaurant in his native Kilkenny. He's passionate about supporting local and artisan producers and he takes the goods and produces ever-changing, ever-memorable meals. There's a French accent to everything he does.

TOP CHOICE **Blueberry** CAFE/DELI €€
Cafe (www.blueberrykilkenny.com; Winston's, 8 Parliament St; dishes €7-9; 9am-5pm Mon-Sat) Deli (2 Market Yard; 8.30am-6pm Mon-Sat) On the top floor of the posh Winston's department store, there is a stunning cafe run by the long-running deli. Choose from coffees, juices and teas. Enjoy sandwiches, hot specials, cakes and more out on the spectacular rooftop terrace. The original deli is still the place for picnic supplies.

TOP CHOICE **Cafe Sol** MODERN IRISH €€
(☎056-776 4987; William St; lunch mains €9-15, dinner mains €17-25; lunch & dinner) Leisurely lunches stretch until 5pm at this much-loved restaurant. Local organic produce is featured in dishes that emphasise what's fresh each season. The flavours are frequently bold and have global influences. Service albeit casual is excellent.

Kilkenny Design Centre Cafe CAFE €€
(Castle Yard; dishes €8-13; 10am-7pm) Upstairs from the craft shops, this arty, organic-oriented cafe is one of the best places in town for home-baked breads and scones, salads in a vast variety, sandwiches made with local salmon, numerous hot specials, and sumptuous desserts. It's cafeteria style so you can ponder your choices in detail.

Two Dames CAFE €
(80 John St; dishes €4-8; 8.30am-5pm Tue-Sat) Organic porridge, granola with organic yoghurt and 'CYO' (create your own) sandwiches are just a few of the reasons locals squeeze into this hole-in-the-wall cafe. The owners have great personalities and you feel like a regular from the time you enter. Breakfast is served until noon.

Chez Pierre FRENCH €€
(17 Parliament St; mains €6-20; 10am-5pm Mon-Sat, plus dinner Thu-Sat) This sunny-sweet French spot does great *tartines* (open-faced sandwiches), soups and sweets plus blackboard specials at lunch. Breakfast is served until noon; dinner fixed menus start at €22.

Rinuccini ITALIAN €€
(☎056-776 1575; www.rinuccini.com; 1 The Parade; lunch mains €10-20, dinner mains €19-30; lunch & dinner) Follow a short flight of steps down to a candlelit basement to bliss out on Antonio Cavaliere's classical Italian cuisine, including his sublime *spaghetti al astice* (lobster tossed with pasta, shallots, cream, brandy and black truffle, doused with fresh parmesan, and served in the shell). There's a cute and romantic table in front under an atrium. Service wins plaudits.

Kilkenny City

Whether it's strolling around Kilkenny's medieval quarters, lazing away the day on the banks of the River Nore or pub-hopping from one trad session to the next, you can't go out in this town and not find pleasure.

Traditional Pubs

1 You'll always find a pub with a song in its heart in Kilkenny (p214). On boards battered by generations of drinkers, musicians perform impromptu trad sessions. Modern bands can be heard in one great setting after another on weekends.

Shopping

2 Shopping (p215) is greatly rewarding in Kilkenny, and not just for the shopkeeper. The county is loaded with artisans and craftspeople who sell their wares at shops and boutiques in the streets around the castle.

River Nore

3 Flowing through the centre of Kilkenny, the inky waters of the River Nore (p203) reflect the city's stone-built beauty. A walk along its banks or a pause on a bench are the perfect breaks from touring the surrounding streets.

St Canice's Cathedral

4 The soaring spire of St Canice's Cathedral (p205) looms large over much of the city and has since the 13th century. Despite the efforts of Cromwell and the forces of nature through the years, it still stands proud.

Kilkenny Kitchen

5 County Kilkenny offers a bounty of produce and local chefs are up to the task. From modern Irish creativity to classic seafood goodness, restaurants and cafes (p211) excel.

PHOTOLIBRARY ©

1

3

RICHARD CUMMINS/LONELY PLANET IMAGES ©

Clockwise from top left

1. Exterior of Matt the Millers pub **2.** Facade of old-fashioned grocer's shop **3.** John's Quay, River Nore

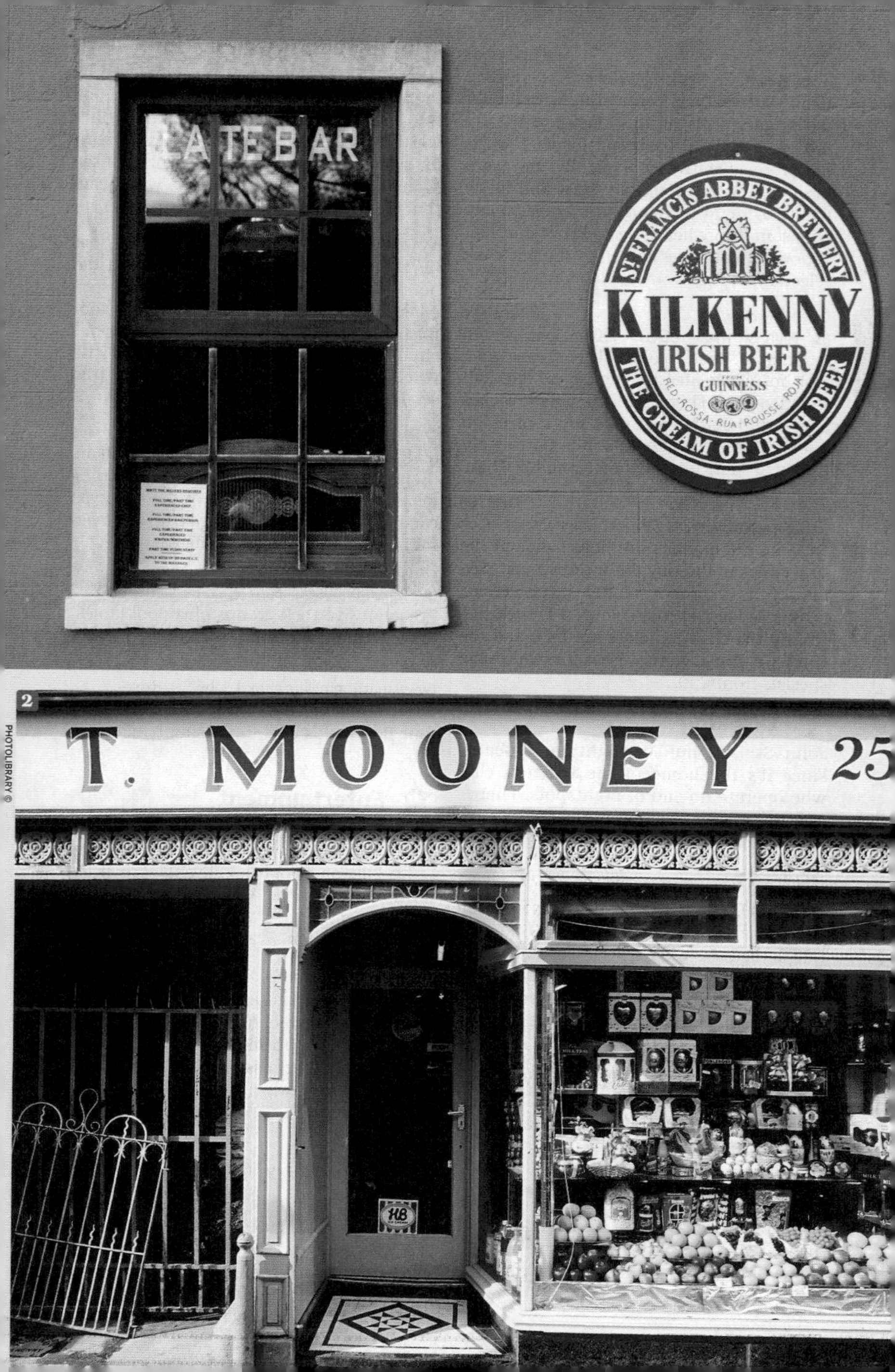

2

PHOTOLIBRARY ©

Zuni CAFE, TAPAS €€
(www.zuni.ie; 26 Patrick St; dishes €7-15; ⊙8am-11pm) Dark leathers contrasting with lighter tables and walls at this one-time theatre provide a stylised backdrop for chef Maria Rafferty's inventive cooking. By day it's a posh cafe with a long breakfast and lunch menu, by night there's a varied tapas menu with some more hearty seafood options. Linger over small plates and enjoy the fine wine selection.

Café Mocha CAFE €
(84 High St; meals €6-10; ⊙10am-5pm;) All manner of juices, coffee drinks, teas and, yes, hot chocolates are served at this kid-friendly cafe. There are a few sandwiches and tarts but the real food joy centres on a long dessert list. Look for the narrow entrance to stairs on the main shopping drag.

Lautrec's Brasserie FRENCH €€
(9 St Kieran's St; mains €16-26; ⊙dinner daily, lunch Sat & Sun) Romantics can hold hands at the tiny tables in the tiny dining room and partake of the disproportionate wine selections at this seductive, rose-coloured French bistro. All the classic choices are here and the frites are thin and crisp. Look for two-course specials from €20.

Drinking

John St is a hub of nightlife, probably since it's the home of the Langton clan who operate no end of nightspots. There's another clutch of no-nonsense trad pubs on Parliament St.

TOP CHOICE **Tynan's Bridge House** PUB
(St John's Bridge) Looking like it might fall down at any moment, this wonky Georgian pub is the best trad bar in town. To be sure, the 300-year-old building has settled a bit over the years, but then so have many of the customers.

John Cleere PUB
(22 Parliament St) One of Kilkenny's finest venues for live music, this long bar has blues, jazz and rock, as well as trad music sessions.

Grapevine WINE BAR
(6 Rose Inn St) If yet another pint in an atmospheric pub is just one too many, take refuge at this smart wine bar. There's also a stellar range of craft beers and a fine selection of tapas.

Bridie's General Store PUB, DELI
(John St) Top design talent was employed by the Langton's empire to create the fictional trad grocery-cum-pub. But the results are worth it. The baked goods and deli items for sale in front are top-notch. Through the swinging doors is a new/old pub with beautiful tiles. In back is a classy beer garden.

Kyteler's Inn PUB
(27 St Kieran's St) Dame Alice Kyteler's old house was built back in 1224 and has seen its share of history: the Dame had four husbands, all of whom died in suspicious circumstances, and she was charged with witchcraft in 1323. Today you can enjoy trad sessions in the basement and courtyard.

O'Riada PUB
(25 Parliament St) The lowest-key bar in Kilkenny gets pretty lively when there's a hurling match screening. But most of the time you can ponder your pint and strike up a conversation with anyone – including yourself.

Pumphouse BAR
(www.pumphousekilkenny.ie; 26 Parliament St) Frequent live rock groups plus pool tables, big TVs and a rooftop terrace.

Matt the Millers BAR
(www.mattthemillers.com; 1 John St) Rose-coloured medieval mill with four bars over four floors plus crowd-pleasing bands and DJs.

Entertainment

For information on local events, check out the weekly *Kilkenny People* newspaper (www.kilkennypeople.ie). Events are listed on the tourist office website, and on www.whazon.com.

Theatre

Watergate Theatre THEATRE
(www.watergatetheatre.com; Parliament St) The top theatre venue hosts drama, comedy and musical performances. If you're wondering why intermission lasts 18 minutes, it's so patrons can nip into John Cleere's pub for a pint.

Nightclubs

Clubs are mostly open 10pm to 2am weekends.

O'Faolain's & Club 51 NIGHTCLUB
(Kilford Arms Hotel, John St) Built on three levels around a 16th-century stone church that was brought over in crates from Wales and painstakingly rebuilt here, numbered stone

by numbered stone, O'Faolain's is a lively night-time spot year-round. Between Easter and October, Club 51 (admission free to €10), in a strobe-lit space out back, sees dancers getting sweaty on Saturday nights.

Morrison's Bar NIGHTCLUB
(1 Ormonde St) In the belle-époque cellar of the Hibernian Hotel, DJs spin an eclectic mix for an upmarket crowd that actually cares about getting spilled on.

67 Club NIGHTCLUB
(67 John St; cover varies; ⏲Tue, Thu & Sat) The pubs at Langton's morph into a lively club three nights a week. There's live music, DJs and sometimes comedy.

Sport

Nowlan Park SPORTS
(www.kilkennygaa.ie; O'Loughlin Rd) One of the unique pleasures of a trip to Ireland is catching a game of hurling at the Kilkenny Cats' hallowed home stadium.

Shopping

An interesting mix of local stores concentrates on High St. The most-exclusive shops are found on The Parade and Patrick St. In parts of the old train station, the chain-store-filled shopping mall MacDonagh Junction is the largest in the region.

TOP CHOICE **Kilkenny Design Centre** ARTS & CRAFTS
(☎056-772 2118; www.kilkennydesign.com; Castle Yard) Top-end Irish crafts and artwork for sale include items by artisans county-wide. Look for John Hanly wool blankets, Cushendale woollen goods, Foxford scarves and Bunbury cutting boards.

Kilkenny Book Centre BOOKSTORE
(10 High St) The largest bookshop in town, stocking plenty of Irish-interest fiction and nonfiction, periodicals and a big range of maps. There's a good cafe upstairs.

Information

Police (☎056-22222; Dominic St)

Bretts Launderette (Michael St; per small/large load €18-24; ⏲8.30am-7pm Mon-Sat)

Sam McCauley Pharmacy (33 High St) The largest of High St's many pharmacies.

St Luke's Hospital (☎056-778 5000; Freshford Rd)

Tourist office (www.discoverireland.ie; Rose Inn St; ⏲9am-7pm Mon-Sat, 11am-5pm Sun Jul & Aug, 9.15am-1pm & 2-5pm Mon-Sat Sep-Jun) County Kilkenny's only tourist office, stocking excellent guides and walking maps.It's in Shee Alms House, built in local stone in 1582 by local benefactor Sir Richard Shee to help the poor.

Getting There & Away

Bus

Bus Éireann (www.buseireann.ie) Operates from a shelter about 200m east of John St adjacent to the train station. Patrick St in the centre of town is also a stop. Services: Carlow (€9, 35 minutes, three daily), Cork (€18, three hours, two daily), Dublin (€12, 2¼ hours, five daily) and Waterford (€10, one hour, two daily).

JJ Kavanagh & Sons (www.jjkavanagh.ie; stop at Ormonde Rd) Dublin airport (€12, three hours, six daily).

Train

Trains (www.irishrail.ie) Eight times daily to/from Dublin's Heuston Station (from €10, 1¾ hours) and Waterford (from €10, 50 minutes). MacDonagh train station, on the eastern side of the shopping mall, has no lockers.

Getting Around

There are large car parks off both sides of High St, and numerous others throughout the city.

Kilkenny Cabs (☎056-775 2000)

Kilkenny Cycling Tours (☎086 895 4961; www.kilkennycyclingtours.com; per day €15) Rents bikes and delivers to hotels etc.

Central Kilkenny

The area south – and notably southeast – of Kilkenny city is laced with country roads and dotted with cute villages overlooking the rich, green Barrow and Nore Valleys. This is fine walking country and is home to some of the county's most notable craftspeople, whose workshops can be visited.

Much of the area is easily visited on a day trip from the city, but you really need your own wheels, as public transport is limited.

KELLS & AROUND

Kells (not to be confused with Kells in County Meath) is a mere hamlet with a fine stone bridge on a tributary of the Nore. However, in **Kells Priory**, the village has one of Ireland's most impressive and romantic monastic sites. The village is 13km south of Kilkenny city on the R697.

Sights

TOP CHOICE **Kells Priory** HISTORIC SITE
This is the best sort of ruin, where visitors can amble about whenever they like, with

no tour guides, tours, set hours or fees. At dusk on a vaguely sunny day the old priory is simply beautiful. Most days you stand a chance of exploring the site alone (apart from bleating and pooping sheep).

The earliest remains of this gorgeous monastic site date from the late 12th century, while the bulk of the present ruins are from the 15th century. In a sea of rich farmland, a carefully restored protective wall connects seven dwelling towers. Inside the walls are the remains of an **Augustinian abbey** and the foundations of some chapels and houses. It's unusually well fortified for a monastery and the heavy curtain walls hint at a troubled history. Indeed, within a single century from 1250, the abbey was twice fought over and burned down by squabbling warlords. It slid into permanent decline beginning when it was suppressed in 1540.

The ruins are 500m east of Kells on the Stonyford road. There are signs showing an excellent 3km **walk** around the ruins, river and village.

Kilree Round Tower & High Cross HISTORIC SITE

About 2km south of Kells (signposted from the priory car park) there's a 29m-high round tower and a simple early high cross, which is said to mark the grave of a 9th-century Irish high king, Niall Caille. He's said to have drowned in the King's River at Callan some time in the 840s while attempting to save a servant, and his body washed up near Kells. His final resting place lies beyond the church grounds because he wasn't a Christian.

Callan Famine Graveyard HISTORIC SITE

West of Kilree, and signposted 2km off the R698 about 2km south of Callan, is a cemetery where the local victims of the Great Famine are buried. Park at the sign and then follow a farmers lane for 300m. It isn't much to look at, but the unmarked mass grave is a poignant reminder of the anonymity of starvation.

CRAFTY KILKENNY

At least 130 full-time craftspeople and artists work commercially in Kilkenny County – one of the highest concentrations in Ireland – thanks to its fine raw materials and inspirational scenery.

Among the best places to see their work are:

» **Bennettsbridge** Several craft studios are located in and around the village.

» **Graiguenamanagh** Wool and crystal studios operate near the centre.

» **Kilkenny city** Kilkenny Design Centre has works by more than a dozen local crafts people.

» **Stonyford** A famous glass studio and a shop with locally produced foods.

Also, pick up the excellent free **craft trail brochure** from the Kilkenny tourist office or crafts shops.

BENNETTSBRIDGE & AROUND

POP 680

Just 7km south of Kilkenny city on the R700, Bennettsbridge is an arts-and-crafts treasure chest, although these treasures are scattered throughout the town, rather than within a concentrated area.

Sights & Activities

Nore View Folk Museum MUSEUM

(056-27749; Danesfort Rd; adult/child €5/2; varies, often 10am-6pm) On a small road above Nicholas Mosse, this is not your average museum. Seamus Lawlor is a passionate chronicler of Irish life and is full of fascinating facts about his private collection of local items, including farming tools, kitchen utensils and other wonderful old bric-a-brac.

Nore Valley Park FARM

(www.norevalleypark.com; Annamult; day admission €6, campsites from €12; park 9am-6pm Mon-Sat Mar-Oct, campground Mar-Oct;) A 2-hectare farm where you can also camp. Kids can caress goats, cuddle rabbits, navigate a maze and jump on a straw bounce. There's a tearoom and picnic area. If you're coming into Bennettsbridge from Kilkenny along the R700, turn right just before the bridge.

Shopping

Nicholas Mosse Irish Country Shop CRAFTS

(www.nicholasmosse.com; 10am-6pm Mon-Sat, 1.30-5pm Sun) In a big mill by the river west of town, this pottery shop specialises in handmade spongeware – creamy-brown pottery decorated with sponged patterns. It also sells linens and other handmade craft items (although some hail from lands of

DON'T MISS

JERPOINT ABBEY

One of Ireland's finest Cistercian ruins, **Jerpoint Abbey** (☎056-24623; www.heritageireland.ie; Hwy R448, Thomastown; adult/child €3/1; ⏲9am-5.30pm Mar-Oct, check hours Nov-Feb) is about 2.5km southwest of Thomastown. It was established in the 12th century and has been partially restored. The tower and cloister are late 14th or early 15th century. Look for the series of often amusing figures carved on the cloister pillars, including a knight. There are also stone carvings on the church walls and in the tombs of members of the Butler and Walshe families. Faint traces of a 15th- or 16th-century painting remain on the northern wall of the church. This chancel area also contains a tomb thought to belong to hard-headed Felix O'Dulany, Jerpoint's first abbot and bishop of Ossory, who died in 1202. The excellent 45-minute tours happen throughout the day. Set yourself apart in the remains of the cloisters and see if you can hear the faint echo of a chant.

According to local legend, St Nicholas (or Santa Claus) is buried near the abbey. While retreating in the Crusades, the knights of Jerpoint removed his body from Myra in modern-day Turkey and reburied him in the **Church of St Nicholas** to the west of the abbey. The grave is marked by a broken slab decorated with a carving of a monk.

cheap labour far from Ireland). A seconds shop yields huge savings. Its cafe is the best choice locally for lunch, with a creative line-up of soups, sandwiches, hot dishes and its renowned scones.

Keith Mosse Bespoke CRAFTS
(☎056-772 7948; www.keithmosse.com; ⏲11am-6pm Wed-Sat, noon-6pm Sun) Signposted up the road, Keith Mosse Bespoke is home to the eponymous craftsman, who takes fine woods from five continents and turns them into elegant furniture and decorator items.

Moth to a Flame CRAFTS
(www.mothtoaflamecandles.com; ⏲9am-6pm Mon-Sat year-round, plus noon-6pm Sun May-Dec) Another few hundred metres away, by the bridge, this place creates elaborate candles.

Chesneau CRAFTS
(☎056-772 7456; www.chesneaudesign.com; ⏲9am-6pm Mon-Fri, 10am-6pm Sat, noon-6pm Sun) For fine leather designs, check out this factory boutique in the village centre. Stylish bags and accessories are on offer in a rainbow of colours – emerald-green numbers are big sellers. Most of the designs are created locally and sold internationally.

THOMASTOWN

POP 1800

This small market town has a serenity it hasn't known in decades now that the M9 has diverted Dublin traffic away. The centre makes for an interesting, short stroll. Named after Welsh mercenary Thomas de Cantwell, Thomastown has fragments of medieval and, down by the river, **Mullin's Castle**, sole survivor of the 14 castles that once stood here.

Like the rest of Kilkenny, the area has a vibrant craft scene. Look out for **Clay Creations** (Low St; ⏲10am-5pm Wed-Sat) displaying the quixotic ceramics and sculptures of local artist Brid Lyons.

Just 4km southwest of Thomastown, high-fliers tee off at the Jack Nicklaus–blessed **Mount Juliet** (www.mountjuliet.ie; green fees from €100). Set over 600 wooded hectares, it also has its own equestrian centre, a gym and spa, two restaurants, wine master-classes, and posh rooms catering to every whim, right down to the pillow menu (accommodation from €120).

Eating

TOP CHOICE **Blackberry Cafe** CAFE €
(Market St; dishes €4.50-7.50, ⏲9.30am-5.30pm Mon-Fri, 10am-5.30pm Sat) Superb thick-cut sandwiches and warming soups are served with pumpkin-seed-speckled soda bread here. Much is organic and the tarts and cakes are baked daily. Between noon and 2pm, great-value multicourse hot lunches see the place squeezed to bursting. It's right in town.

Sol Bistro MODERN IRISH €€
(Low St; mains €12-25; ⏲lunch & dinner) Kilkenny's modern Irish cafe has a branch in Thomastown's centre. It's a small cafe in a tidy old storefront and combines the best local ingredients for Irish classics with a twist.

Getting There & Away

Trains on the Dublin to Waterford route via Kilkenny stop eight times daily in each direction in Thomastown. The station is 1km west of town.

AROUND THOMASTOWN

STONYFORD

Only 6km west of Thomastown is the small village of Stonyford. The local highlight, the nationally renowned **Jerpoint Glass Studio** (www.jerpointglass.com; shop 10am-6pm Mon-Sat, noon-5pm Sun), is housed in a rural stone-walled farm building 1km south of town where you can watch workers craft molten glass into exquisite artistic and practical items.

TOP CHOICE **Knockdrinna Farm Shop** (www.knockdrinna.com; meals from €5; 9am-6pm Tue-Fri, 10am-6pm Sat, noon-6pm Sun) is right in town and is a tour de force of local foods. From the house-made cheese to cured meats, smoked fish, salads, coffees and much more you can assemble a meal that may outclass your previous best picnic. Or settle in at the tables here.

KILFANE

The village of Kilfane, 3km north of Thomastown on the R448, has a small, ruined **13th-century church** and **Norman tower**, 50m off the road and signposted. The church has a remarkable stone carving of Thomas de Cantwell called the Cantwell Fada or Long Cantwell. It depicts a tall, thin knight in detailed chain-mail armour brandishing a shield decorated with the Cantwell coat of arms.

INISTIOGE

POP 260

The little village of Inistioge (*in*-ish-teeg) is a picture. Its 18th-century, 10-arch **stone bridge** spans the River Nore and vintage shops face its tranquil square. Somewhere so inviting could hardly hope to escape the attention of movie-location scouts: Inistioge's film credits include *Widow's Peak* (1993), *Circle of Friends* (1994) and *Where the Sun is King* (1996). If a future production needs a crowd scene, all they need do is shoot on a weekend: day-trippers abound.

Escape the mobs on a **river walk** heading south from town.

With a scenic stretch of the South Leinster Way coursing through town, this is a good base for exploring the region. The R700 from Thomastown makes for a lovely **scenic drive** through the river valley, which features views of the ruined 13th-century **Grennan Castle**. Better yet, try the **hiking trails** that follow the river and side trails leading up into the hills.

Approximately 500m south, on Mt Alto, is the heavily forested **Woodstock Gardens** (www.woodstock.ie; parking in coins €4; 9am-7pm Apr-Sep, 10am-4pm Oct-Mar), a beauty of a park with expansive 19th-century gardens, picnic areas and trails. The panorama of the valley and village below is spectacular. Coming from town, follow the signs for Woodstock Estate and enter the large gates (despite appearances, it's a public road) then continue along the road for about 1km until you reach the car park.

Sleeping & Eating

Several cafes dot the centre and offer up chow to the undiscerning masses.

TOP CHOICE **Bassetts at Woodstock** MODERN IRISH €€€
(056-775 8820; www.bassetts.ie; mains €10-28; lunch Wed-Sun, dinner Wed-Sat) Adjacent to Woodstock Gardens, John Bassett has turned his family home into an inspired dining experience. Saturday nights feature tasting menus (€9.50 per course) paired with wines (from €5 per glass) served at set intervals from 7.30pm. It's a great way to spend an evening with a table of friends. The food is fresh, local and inventive. Future meals graze right outside the door.

Woodstock Arms B&B/PUB €€
(056-775 8440; www.woodstockarms.com; s/d from €45/70) This friendly pub has tables outside overlooking the square and seven simple rooms that are squeaky clean. The triples are particularly spacious. Breakfast is served in a pretty little room out back with wooden tables and blue-and-white china.

GRAIGUENAMANAGH

POP 1300

Graiguenamanagh (greg-*na*-muh-na; known locally simply as Graigue) is the kind of place where you could easily find yourself staying longer than planned. Spanning the Barrow, an ancient six-arch stone bridge is illuminated at night and connects the village with the smaller township of Tinnahinch on the County Carlow side of the river (look for the darker stones on the Carlow side – a legacy from being blown up during the 1798 rebellion).

Sights & Activities

Some picturesque **walks** pass through and near town – see the boxed text, p220.

Duiske Abbey CHURCH

(8am-6pm) This was once Ireland's largest Cistercian abbey. What you see today is the result of 800 years of additions and changes and it is very much a working parish. The simple exterior and whitewashed interior only hint at its long history. To the right of the entrance look for the **Knight of Duiske**, a 14th-century, high-relief carving of a knight in chain mail who's reaching for his sword. On the floor nearby, a glass panel reveals some of the original 13th-century floor tiles, now 2m below the present floor level. In the grounds stand two early **high crosses** (7th century and 9th century), brought here for protection in the last century. The smaller Ballyogan Cross has panels on the eastern side depicting the crucifixion, Adam and Eve, Abraham's sacrifice of Isaac, and David playing the harp. The western side shows the massacre of the innocents.

Around the corner, the **Abbey Centre** (varies) houses a small exhibition of Christian art, plus pictures of the abbey in its unrestored state.

Festivals & Events

Town of Books Festival BOOK FESTIVAL

(www.booktownireland.com) Graiguenamanagh's narrow streets spill over in mid-September with booksellers, authors and bibliophiles during the three-day Town of Books Festival. Plans are under way for Graiguenamanagh to become a year-round 'book town' in the same vein as Wales' Hay-on-Wye. Meanwhile, there are a couple of good used and antiquarian bookshops.

Sleeping & Eating

Waterside INN €€

(059-972 4246; www.watersideguesthouse.com; The Quay; s/d from €55/80; restaurant lunch Sun year-round, dinner Mon-Sat Apr-Sep, dinner Fri & Sat only Oct-Mar) Down by the boats tied up along the river, this inviting guesthouse and restaurant occupies a converted solid granite 19th-century corn store. Its 10 renovated rooms have exposed timber beams. Hosts Brian and Brigid Roberts can point out the village's hidden nooks and crannies. The restaurant is well regarded for its interesting modern Irish menu (mains €18 to €26) and its regular 'After Dinner Live' music acts featuring anything from jazz to bluegrass.

Boats Bistro MODERN IRISH €€

(www.boatsbistro.com; The Quay; mains €10-20; lunch Fri-Sun, dinner Fri & Sat mid-Mar–Oct) Cheerful is the perfect word for this unpretentious cafe right on the water. At tables outside or in the light and airy dining room you can enjoy dishes sourced locally. The menu emphasises seafood from the southeast and old faves like seafood chowder and fish pie reach new heights.

Drinking

One of Graiguenamanagh's hidden treasures is its pair of unchanged-in-generations old pubs, **Mick Doyle's** (Abbey St) and **Mick Ryan's** (Abbey St). The former still has its sheep-dipping sign and sells a range of hardware; the latter has an equally untouched timber snug.

Murray's PUB

On the corner of the Quay and Abbey St, this is another cosy, old-time pub. It's the life and soul of the village during its Sunday evening trad sessions; listen out for songs featuring local landmarks.

Shopping

TOP CHOICE **Cushendale Woollen Mill** WOOL SHOP

(www.cushendale.ie; 8.30am-12.30pm & 1.30-5.30pm Mon-Fri, 10am-1pm Sat) Produces knitting yarns, blankets, tweed and winter woollies; ask for an informal, behind-the-scenes peek at the mill's century-old machinery in action.

Duiske Glass CRYSTAL SHOP

(www.duiskeglass.ie; 9am-5pm Mon-Sat) This small studio creates contemporary and traditional crystal. It's in the village centre.

Getting There & Away

Graiguenamanagh is 23km southeast of Kilkenny city on the R703. **Kilbride Coaches** (www.kilbridecoaches.com) runs two buses Monday to Saturday to/from Kilkenny bus station (€5, one hour).

WALKS: COUNTIES CARLOW & KILKENNY

The **South Leinster Way** slices through the hilly southern part of County Kilkenny, from Graiguenamanagh through Inistioge, down to Mullinavat and westward to Piltown. By far the prettiest part, a stretch of some 13km, begins on the River Barrow. It links Graiguenamanagh and Inistioge, two charming villages with amenities for travellers. In either village you can reward yourself with a top-notch meal.

Alternatively, along this path, you can branch off onto **Brandon Way** (4km south of Graiguenamanagh), which scales **Brandon Hill** (516m). The broad moorland summit is easily reached and affords a lovely view of the Blackstairs Mountains and Mt Leinster to the east. A return trip from Graigue is a fairly relaxed 12km walk.

The trail down **River Barrow** from Graiguenamanagh to St Mullins in County Carlow is equally beautiful, with a firm path wending past canals and through some wooded country and pleasant grassy picnic areas.

Northern Kilkenny

The rolling green hills of northern County Kilkenny are idyllic for leisurely drives along the back roads with the makings of a picnic stowed in the boot. There's not a whole lot going on in this part of the county; it's best enjoyed by simply taking in the scenery and discovering peaceful little villages.

CASTLECOMER & AROUND

POP 1500

Castlecomer is on the gentle River Dinin, some 18km north of Kilkenny. The town became a centre for anthracite mining after the fuel was discovered nearby in 1636; the mines closed for good in the mid-1960s. The anthracite, a very hard form of coal, contains very little sulphur and produces almost no smoke.

Coal-mining exhibits are set among lush woodlands at the **Castlecomer Discovery Park** (www.discoverypark.ie; Estate Yard; adult/child €8/5; ⌚9.30am-6pm May-Aug, 10am-5pm Sep-Oct & Mar-Apr, 10.30am-4.30pm Nov-Feb), including some **ancient fossils** predating dinosaurs found here.

About 10km southwest of Castlecomer is **Swifte's Heath**, home to Jonathan Swift during his school years in Kilkenny. The 'e' was evidently dropped from the name before the satirist gained notoriety as the author of *Gulliver's Travels* and *A Modest Proposal*.

Bus Éireann (☎056-64933) has five buses daily to Kilkenny (€5, 20 minutes).

DUNMORE CAVE

Striking calcite formations enliven **Dunmore Cave** (☎056-776 7726; www.heritageireland.ie; Ballyfoyle; adult/child €3/1; ⌚9.30am-6.30pm Jun-Sep, 9.30am-5pm Mar-May & Sep-Oct, 9.30am-5pm Wed-Sun Nov-Mar), some 6km north of Kilkenny on the Castlecomer road (N78). In 928 marauding Vikings killed 1000 people at two ring forts near here. When survivors hid in the caverns, the Vikings tried to smoke them out by lighting fires at the entrance. It's thought that they then dragged off the men as slaves and left the women and children to suffocate. Excavations in 1973 uncovered the skeletons of at least 44 people, mostly women and children. They also found coins dating from the 10th century. One theory suggests that the coins were dropped by the Vikings (who often carried them under the arms, secured with wax) while engaged in the slaughter. However, there are few marks of violence on the skeletons, lending weight to the theory that suffocation was the cause of death.

Admission to the cave is via a compulsory but highly worthwhile guided tour. After a steep descent you enter caverns full of stalactites, stalagmites and columns, including the 7m **Market Cross**, Europe's largest free-standing stalagmite. Although well lit and spacious, it's damp and cold; bring warm clothes.

Contact the cave office for details on the bus service.

County Cork

POPULATION: 518,000 / AREA: 7508 SQ KM

Includes »

Best Places to Eat

- » Fishy Fishy Cafe (p242)
- » Jim Edwards (p242)
- » Market Lane (p228)
- » Cafe Paradiso (p228)
- » Farmgate Café (p230)

Best Places to Stay

- » Garnish House (p228)
- » Ballymaloe House (p236)
- » Bridge House (p253)
- » Blair's Cove House (p260)
- » Imperial Hotel (p225)

Why Go?

Everything good about Ireland can be found in County Cork. Surrounding the country's second city – a thriving metropolis made glorious by location and its almost Rabelaisian devotion to the finer things of life – is a lush landscape dotted with villages that offer up days of languor and idyll.

Cork City's understated confidence is easily understood given its plethora of markets and ever-changing cast of creative eateries, while its selection of pubs, entertainment and cultural pursuits provide a depth of fun.

Further afield, you'll want to do just that: go further afield, past the inlets of the eroded coasts and its multitude of perfectly charming old fishing towns and villages, such as Kinsale, Clonakilty and Baltimore.

And don't forget the scenery: in West Cork, it's every bit as enchanting as the best bits of Ireland. The thumb of the bunch, the Beara Peninsula, is the place to settle in. Tackle mountain passes and touch Ireland's ancient past.

When to Go

Although the summer months promise the best weather, the shoulder seasons are festival times – in May, there's the seafood and jazz festival in Baltimore, while autumn sees the rest of West Cork go food crazy. This is especially so in the gourmet capital of Kinsale, which has two excellent gourmet festivals in October. Late October is the perennially popular jazz festival in Cork City.

County Cork Highlights

1. Revel in buzzing Cork city (p223), with its intriguing selection of restaurants, pubs, music and theatres
2. Drive or cycle along the stunning Beara Peninsula coastal road around **Allihies** (p267)
3. Explore the medieval streets, mammoth forts, shoreline walks and lovely seafood pubs in **Kinsale** (p239)
4. Relive the age of ocean liners, good and bad, in **Cobh** (p234)
5. Discover unspoilt fishing villages, including **Union Hall** and **Glandore** (p251), **Castletownshend** (p252), **Castletownbere** (p266) and **Baltimore** (p254)

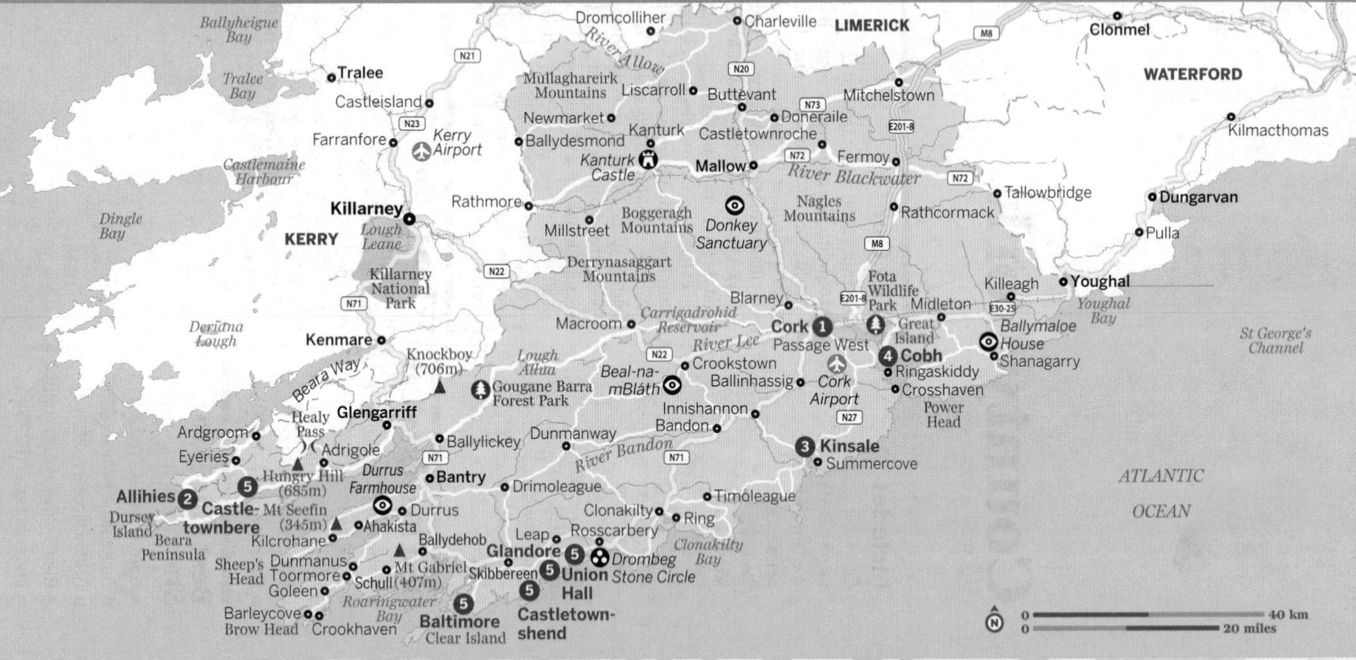

CORK CITY

POP 120,000

Ireland's second city is first in every important respect, at least according to the locals, who cheerfully refer to it as the 'real capital of Ireland.' The compact city centre is surrounded by interesting waterways and is chock full of great restaurants fed by arguably the best foodie scene in the country. Its location is also something of a blessing, on the doorstep of the scenic mecca that is the southwest but also within easy reach of lesser known idylls in East Cork and West Waterford.

The River Lee flows around the centre, an island packed with grand Georgian parades, cramped 17th-century alleys and modern masterpieces such as the opera house. St Patrick's St runs from St Patrick's Bridge on the North Channel of the Lee, through the city's main shopping and commercial area, to the Georgian Grand Parade, which leads to the river's South Channel. North and south of St Patrick's St lie the city's most entertaining quarters: webs of narrow streets crammed with pubs, cafes, restaurants and shops.

A flurry of urban renewal has resulted in new buildings, bars and arts centres as well as a general tidy-up of the main thoroughfares. The best of the city is still happily traditional, though – snug pubs with live music sessions most of the week, excellent local produce in an ever-expanding list of restaurants and a genuinely proud welcome from the locals.

History

Cork has a long and bruising history, inextricably linked with Ireland's struggle for nationhood.

The story begins in the 7th century, when St Finbarre (also spelt Finbarr and Fin Barre) founded a monastery on a *corcach* (marshy place). By the 12th century the settlement had become the chief city of the Kingdom of South Munster, having survived raids and sporadic settlement by Norsemen. Irish rule was short-lived and by 1185 Cork was under English rule. Thereafter it changed hands regularly during the relentless struggle between Irish and Crown forces. It survived a Cromwellian assault only to fall to that merciless champion of Protestantism, William of Orange.

During the 18th century Cork prospered, with butter, beef, beer and whiskey exported round the world from its port. A mere century later famine devastated both county and city, and robbed Cork of tens of thousands (and Ireland of millions) of its inhabitants by death or emigration.

The 'Rebel City's' deep-seated Irishness ensured that it played a key role in Ireland's struggle for independence. Mayor Thomas MacCurtain was killed by the Black and Tans (British auxilliary troops, so-named because their uniforms were a mixture of army khaki and police black) in 1920. His successor, Terence MacSwiney, died in London's Brixton prison after a hunger strike. The British were at their most brutally repressive in Cork – much of the centre, including St Patrick's St, the City Hall and the Public Library, was burned down. Cork was also a regional focus of Ireland's Civil War in 1922–23.

Sights

The best sight in Cork is the city itself as you wander its streets. Note that the once hugely popular **former Beamish & Crawford Brewery** was closed by owners Heineken in 2009. The fate of the beautiful half-timbered headhouse is uncertain.

FREE **Crawford Municipal Art Gallery** ART GALLERY
(☎021-490 7855; www.crawfordartgallery.ie; Emmet Pl; ⏲10am-5pm Mon-Sat, to 8pm Thu) Cork's public gallery houses a small but excellent permanent collection covering the 17th century to the modern day. Highlights include works by Sir John Lavery, Jack B Yeats, Nathaniel Hone and a room devoted to Irish women artists from 1886 to 1978 – don't miss the works by Mainie Jellet and Evie Hone.

The Sculpture Galleries contain snow-white plaster casts of Roman and Greek statues, given to King George IV by the pope in 1822. George didn't like the gift and stuck the sculptures in the cellar until someone suggested that Cork might appreciate them.

The downstairs exhibition hall hosts superior temporary displays.

St Fin Barre's Cathedral CATHEDRAL
(☎021-496 3387; www.cathedral.cork.anglican.org; Bishop St; adult/child €4/2; ⏲9.30am-5.30pm Mon-Sat & 12.30-5pm Sun) Spiky spires, gurning gargoyles and rich sculpture make up the exterior of Cork's Protestant cathedral, an attention-grabbing mixture of French Gothic and medieval whimsy. Local legend says that the golden angel on the eastern

side will blow its horn when the Apocalypse is due to start… Yikes!

The grandeur continues inside, with marble floor **mosaics**, a colourful chancel ceiling and a huge pulpit and bishop's throne. Quirky items on display include a cannonball blasted into an earlier medieval spire during the Siege of Cork (1690).

Most of the ostentation is the result of a competition, held in 1863, to choose an architect for the building. William Burges was the hands-down winner, and once victory was assured he promptly redrew all his plans – with an extra choir bay and taller towers – and his £15,000 budget went out the window. Luckily, the bishop understood such perfectionism and spent the rest of his life fundraising for the project.

The cathedral sits about 500m south of the centre, on the spot where Cork's patron saint, Finbarre, founded his monastery in the 7th century.

Lewis Glucksman Gallery ART GALLERY

(☎021-490 2760; www.glucksman.org; University College Cork; suggested donation €5; ⌚10am-5pm Tue-Sat, noon-5pm Sun) This award-winning gallery in the grounds of University College Cork (UCC) is a startling limestone, steel and timber construction that was the most visible symbol of Corkonian optimism when it opened in 2004. Not even severe flood damage to its basement storage rooms in November 2009 has dampened its sense of purpose, which is to display the best in both national and international contemporary art and installation. If you're in town, don't miss the free fortnightly curatorial tours; the website has details. The gallery's situation in the university grounds means it's always buzzing with people coming to attend lectures, view the artwork or procrastinate in the cafe (see p230).

Cork City Gaol MUSEUM

(☎021-430 5022; www.corkcitygaol.com; Convent Ave, Sunday's Well; adult/child €7/4; ⌚9.30am-5pm) Faint-hearted souls may find this imposing former prison a little grim, but it's certainly worth a visit, if only to get a sense of how crap life was for prisoners a century ago. An audio tour guides you around the restored cells, which feature models of suffering prisoners and sadistic-looking guards. It's very moving, bringing home the harshness of the 19th-century penal system. The most common crime was that of poverty; many of the inmates were sentenced to hard labour for stealing loaves of bread.

The prison closed in 1923, reopening in 1927 as a radio station, so the Governor's House has been converted into the **Radio Museum Experience**. Alongside collections of beautiful old radios you can hear the story of Guglielmo Marconi's conquest of the airwaves.

To get there, walk from the city centre, or take bus 8 from the bus station to the UCC; walk north across Fitzgerald Park, over Mardyke Bridge, along the Banks of the River Lee Walkway and follow the signs up the hill.

Shandon NEIGHBOURHOOD

Perched on a hillside overlooking the city centre from the north, Shandon is a great spot for the views alone, but you'll also find **galleries**, **antique shops** and **cafes** along its old lanes and squares. Those tiny old row houses, where generations of workers raised huge families in very basic conditions, are now sought-after urban pieds-à-terre.

Shandon is dominated by the 1722 **St Anne's Church** (☎021-450 5906; www.shandonbells.org; John Redmond St; ⌚10am-5pm Mon-Sat), aka the 'Four-Faced Liar', so called as each of the tower's four clocks used to tell a different time. Wannabe campanologists can ring the **bells** (adult/child €6/5) on the 1st floor of the 1750 Italianate tower and continue the 132 steps up to the top for 360-degree views of the city.

Cork has a long tradition of butter manufacturing (in the 1860s it was the world's largest butter market, exporting butter all over the then-British Empire) and its history is told through displays and dioramas in the **Cork Butter Museum** (☎021-430 0600; www.corkbutter.museum; O'Connell Sq; adult/child €4/3; ⌚10am-5pm Mar-Jun & Sep-Oct, 10am-6pm Jul & Aug). The square in front of the museum – with its butter-coloured walls – is dominated by the striking **Firkin Crane**, a round building that was central to the old butter market and which now houses a dance centre (p231).

☞ Tours

Cork City Tour BUS TOUR

(☎021-430 9090; www.corkcitytour.com; adult/student/child €14/12/5; ⌚10am-5.30pm Apr-Oct, last bus starts at 4pm) Hop-on-hop-off open-top bus linking the city's main areas of interest. The Outer Limits Tour takes you outside the centre.

THE BOOZE BUSTER

The imposing **statue** on St Patrick's St, just south of the River Lee North Channel, is of Father Theobald Mathew, the 'Apostle of Temperance,' who crusaded against the ills of alcohol in the 1830s and 1840s with such success that a quarter of a million people took the 'pledge' and whiskey production was cut in half. The **Holy Trinity Church** (Fr Mathew Quay) was designed by the Pain brothers in 1834 in his honour, and the Father Mathew Bingo Hall around the corner also celebrates his memory.

Cork Historic Walking Tours WALKING TOUR
(☎085 100 7300; www.walkcork.ie; adult/child €10/5; ⏲10am & 2pm Mon-Fri Apr-Sep) Runs 90-minute tours from the tourist office.

Cork Literary Tour SELF-GUIDED TOUR
A free audio walking tour of Cork; pick up a copy or download one onto your MP3 player at the **Cork City Library** (☎021-492 4900; www.corkcity libraries.ie; 57-61 Grand Pde; ⏲10am-5.30pm Mon-Sat).

Cork Walks SELF-GUIDED TOUR
Cork City Council's two free self-guided tours cover the South Parish and Shandon. Pick up the guide and map at the tourist office (p233).

Festivals & Events

Book well in advance, particularly for the October jazz and film festivals.

Cork World Book Festival (www.cometo cork.ie) A huge book festival with loads of authors in late April; sponsored by the Cork City Library.

International Choral Festival (www. corkchoral.ie) A major event held from late April to early May in the City Hall and other venues.

Cork Pride (www.corkpride.com) Week-long gay pride celebrations in May/June.

Guinness Jazz Festival (www.corkjazzfes tival.com) All-star line-up in venues across town for Cork's biggest festival, held in October.

Cork Film Festival (www.corkfilmfest.org) Eclectic week-long program of international films held in October/November.

Sleeping

City Centre

Whether you stay on the main island or to the north, across St Patrick's Bridge in Shandon or around MacCurtain St, you're right in the heart of the action.

Imperial Hotel HOTEL €€
(☎021-427 4040; www.flynnhotels.com; South Mall; r €90-220; P@) Fast approaching her bicentenary, the Imperial knows how to age gracefully. Public spaces resonate with opulent period detail such as marble floors, elaborate floral bouquets and more. The 130 rooms are of four-star hotel standard: and include writing desks, restrained decor and modern touches, like a digital music library. A posh Aveda spa is a recent addition – something unheard of when Charles Dickens stayed here.

Brú Bar & Hostel HOSTEL €
(☎021-455 9667; www.bruhostel.com; 57 MacCurtain St; dm €12-24, tr from €50; P@) This buzzing hostel has its own internet cafe, with free web access for guests, and a fantastic bar, popular with backpackers and locals alike. The dorms (each with a bathroom) have four to six beds and are both clean and stylish – ask for one on the upper floors to avoid bar noise. Breakfast is free.

Emerson House B&B €€
(☎021-450 3647; www.emersonhousecork.com; 2 Clarence Tce, North Summer Hill; s/d from €60/80; P) Near the top of busy Summer Hill is this gay and lesbian B&B tucked away on a quiet terrace. The accommodation, in a Georgian house retaining many original features, is comfortably elegant, and host Cyril is a mine of information on the area.

Auburn House B&B €€
(☎021-450 8555; www.auburnguesthouse.com; 3 Garfield Tce, Wellington Rd; s/d €58/80; P) There's a warm family welcome at this neat B&B, which has smallish but well-kept rooms brightened by window boxes. Try to bag one of the back rooms, which have sweeping views over the city. Breakfast has vegetarian choices; the location near the fun of MacCurtain St is a plus.

Sheila's Hostel HOSTEL €
(☎021-450 5562; www.sheilashostel.ie; 4 Belgrave Pl, Wellington Rd; dm €14-19, d €46-54; P@) Sheila's heaves with young travellers, and it's

Cork

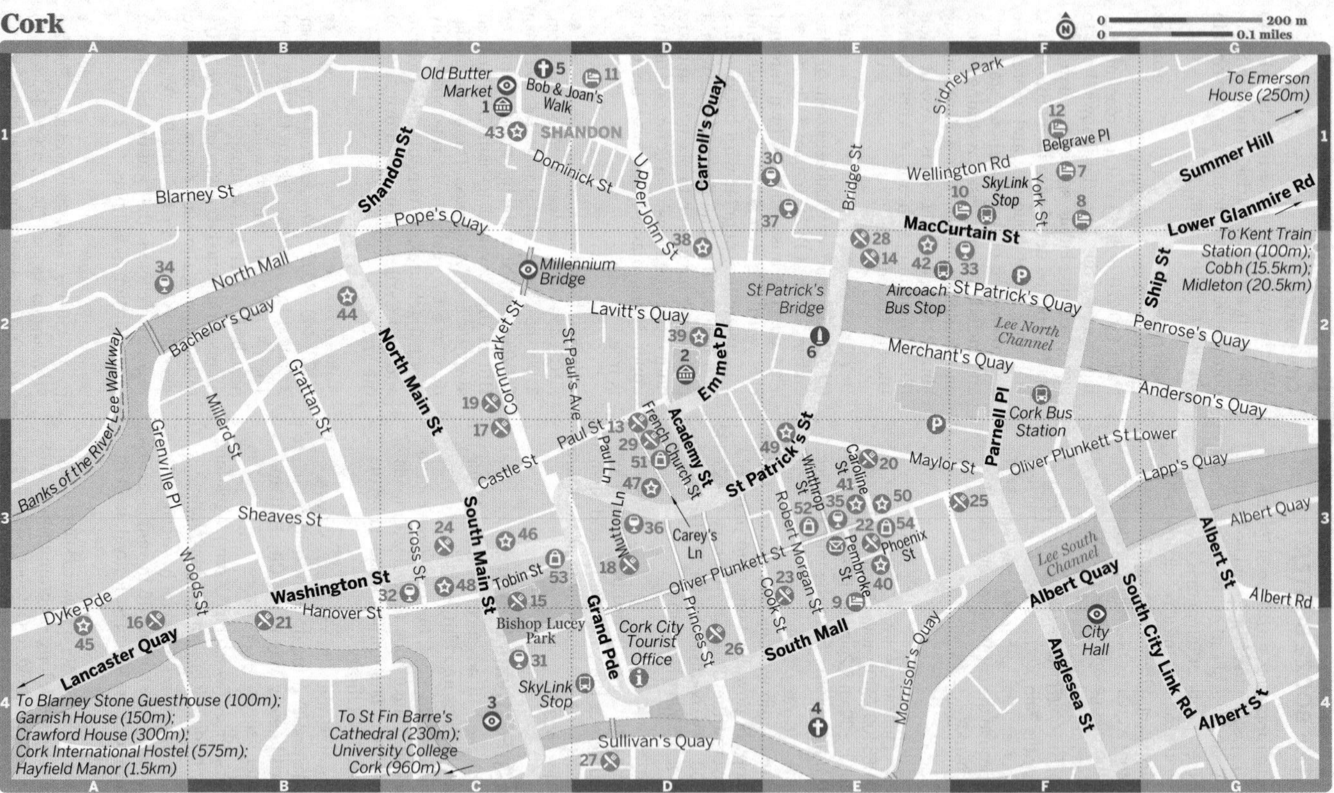
Old Butter Market
Bob & Joan's Walk
SHANDON
Dominick St
Upper John St
Carroll's Quay
Sidney Park
To Emerson House (250m)
Belgrave Pl
Wellington Rd
SkyLink Stop
York St
Summer Hill
Lower Glanmire Rd
To Kent Train Station (100m); Cobh (15.5km); Midleton (20.5km)
Blarney St
Shandon St
Pope's Quay
Bridge St
MacCurtain St
Ship St
North Mall
Millennium Bridge
St Patrick's Bridge
Aircoach Bus Stop
St Patrick's Quay
Lee North Channel
Penrose's Quay
Bachelor's Quay
Lavitt's Quay
Cornmarket St
St Paul's Ave
Emmet Pl
Merchant's Quay
Anderson's Quay
Banks of the River Lee Walkway
Millerd St
Grattan St
North Main St
Parnell Pl
Cork Bus Station
Grenville Pl
Paul St
Paul Ln
French Church St
Academy St
St Patrick's St
Winthrop St
Caroline St
Maylor St
Oliver Plunkett St Lower
Lapp's Quay
Castle St
Sheaves St
Mutton Ln
Carey's Ln
Robert Morgan St
Pembroke St
Phoenix St
Albert Quay
Cross St
South Main St
Tobin St
Oliver Plunkett St
Lee South Channel
Albert St
Woods St
Washington St
Hanover St
Cook St
Albert Rd
Dyke Pde
Bishop Lucey Park
Grand Pde
Cork City Tourist Office
Princes St
South Mall
Morrison's Quay
Albert Quay
City Hall
South City Link Rd
Anglesea St
Lancaster Quay
SkyLink Stop
To Blarney Stone Guesthouse (100m); Garnish House (150m); Crawford House (300m); Cork International Hostel (575m); Hayfield Manor (1.5km)
To St Fin Barre's Cathedral (230m); University College Cork (960m)
Sullivan's Quay
Albert St
200 m
0.1 miles

Cork

Sights

1 Cork Butter Museum ... C1
2 Crawford Municipal Art Gallery ... D2
Firkin Crane ... (see 43)
3 Former Beamish & Crawford Brewery ... C4
4 Holy Trinity Church ... E4
5 St Anne's Church ... C1
6 Statue of Father Mathew ... E2

Sleeping

7 Auburn House ... F1
8 Brú Bar & Hostel ... F1
9 Imperial Hotel ... E3
10 Isaac's Hotel ... F1
11 Kinlay House ... D1
12 Sheila's Hostel ... F1

Eating

13 Amicus Café & Restaurant ... D3
14 Boqueria ... E2
15 Cafe Antigua ... C3
16 Café Paradiso ... A4
17 Cornstore ... C3
18 English Market ... D3
19 Farmers Market ... C2
Farmgate Café ... (see 18)
20 Idaho Café ... E3
21 Indigo ... B4
22 Jacques Restaurant ... E3
Joup ... (see 18)
23 Les Gourmandises ... E3
24 Liberty Grill ... C3
25 Market Lane ... F3
26 Nash 19 ... D4
On the Pigs Back ... (see 18)
27 Quay Co-op ... D4
Quay Co-op Organic & Wholefood Shop ... (see 27)
Sandwich Stall ... (see 18)
28 Star Anise ... E2
29 Strasbourg Goose ... D3

Drinking

30 Abbot's Ale House ... E1
31 An Spailpín Fánac ... C4
32 Chambers ... C3
Cornstore ... (see 17)
Crane Lane Theatre ... (see 40)
33 Dan Lowry's ... F2
34 Franciscan Well Brewery ... A2
35 Long Valley ... E3
36 Mutton Lane Inn ... D3
37 Sin É ... E1

Entertainment

38 Cork Arts Theatre ... D2
39 Cork Opera House ... D2
40 Crane Lane Theatre ... E3
41 Cyprus Avenue ... E3
42 Everyman Palace Theatre ... E2
43 Firkin Crane ... C1
Flux! ... (see 8)
44 Gate Multiplex ... B2
45 Granary ... A4
Half Moon Theatre ... (see 39)
46 Other Place ... C3
47 Pavilion ... D3
48 Ruby's ... C3
49 Savoy ... E3
50 Scotts ... E3
Triskel Arts Centre ... (see 15)

Shopping

51 O'Connaill ... D3
52 P Cashell ... E3
53 Plugd Records ... C3
54 Pro Musica ... E3

no wonder given its excellent central location. Facilities include a sauna, free internet access, a pool table and barbecue. Staff can arrange bicycle and car hire. Breakfast is €3 extra.

Kinlay House HOSTEL €
(☎021-450 8966; www.kinlayhousecork.ie; Bob & Joan's Walk; dm €15-18, d €48-70; @☜) This labyrinthine hostel is in a bucolic spot near St Anne's Church in Shandon. It has a fun, laid-back atmosphere; services include bureau de change, laundry and luggage storage. Guests can use the next-door gym at a discount.

Isaac's Hotel HOTEL €€
(☎021-450 0011; www.isaacs.ie; 48 MacCurtain St; r €60-160; @☜) Location is the real selling point at this grand old hotel housed in what once was a Victorian furniture warehouse. The 47 rooms are decorated in a faded salmon-rust scheme and service can be a bit spotty. Also, be sure to get a room away from the busy street. Rooms without a fan can get steamy on sunny days, no matter what you get up to...

EATING IN THE HUGUENOT QUARTER

The narrow, nearly lightless pedestrianised streets north of St Patrick's St throng with cafes and restaurants, and the place hops day and night. A plethora of options await – all have outside tables and many serve till late, so the best advice is go for a wander and find somewhere that suits your mood and budget. Among the best picks:

» **Amicus Café & Restaurant** (021-427 6455; 23 Paul St Plaza) Bistro fare overlooking a small and vibrant square, where Cork's fresh-faced goths gather on Saturdays.

» **Strasbourg Goose** (021-427 9534; 17-18 French Church St) Excellent food, although the French accent is illusory: prime Irish sirloin?

Western Rd & Around

Western Rd runs southwest from the city centre to the large UCC campus; it has the city's biggest choice of B&Bs. Take bus No 8 or walk, preferably along the less busy Dyke Parade.

TOP CHOICE **Garnish House** B&B €€
(021-427 5111; www.garnish.ie; Western Rd; s/d €75/80; P) Every attention is lavished upon guests at this award-winning B&B. The legendary breakfast menu (30 choices!) includes fresh fish, French toast, omelettes and a whole lot more. Typical of the touches here is the freshly cooked porridge, which comes with creamed honey and your choice of whiskey or Baileys. Enjoy it out on the garden terrace. The 14 rooms are very comfortable; reception is open 24 hours.

Hayfield Manor HOTEL €€€
(021-484 9500; www.hayfieldmanor.ie; Perrott Ave, College Rd; r €180-350; P@) Roll out the red carpet and pour yourself a sherry for *you have arrived.* A kilometer and a half from the city centre but with all the ambience of a country house, Hayfield combines the luxury and facilities of a big hotel with the informality and welcome of a small one. The 88 beautiful bedrooms (choose from traditional or contemporary styling) enjoy 24-hour room service, although you may want to idle the hours away in the library.

Blarney Stone Guesthouse B&B €€
(021-427 0083; www.blarneystoneguesthouse.ie; Western Rd; s/d €59/89; P@) A standout from this close-knit row of B&Bs – if for no other reason than its brilliant white paint scheme out front – the Blarney Stone will make you want to kiss something after you settle into one of its eight rooms. Decor is lavish in a way that harks back to the time when vinyl roofs were popular on cars; there's lots of frill and curlicues.

Crawford House B&B €€
(021-427 9000; www.crawfordguesthouse.com; Western Rd; r €60-90; P@) You'll have no problem getting wet at Crawford House, a luxurious B&B: power showers and large spa baths feature in the 12 rooms, which include king-size beds and gracious yet restrained wooden furnishings. The standard is that of a contemporary hotel (24-hour reception); the atmosphere, that of a family home.

Cork International Hostel HOSTEL €
(021-454 3289; www.anoige.ie; 1 & 2 Redclyffe, Western Rd; dm €15, d €55; P@) Housed in an attractive, Victorian red-brick building near the university, this 98-bed An Óige hostel has bright dorms and cheerful staff, who do a great job coping with the constant stream of guests. The drawback is the 2km walk (or bus 8 ride) to the centre along a busy road.

Eating

Cork's food scene is reason enough to visit. The English Market (see p230) is a local – no, make that national – treasure.

TOP CHOICE **Market Lane** INTERNATIONAL €€
(021-427 4710; www.market lane.ie; 5 Oliver Plunkett St; mains €10-26; noon-late Mon-Sat, 1-9pm Sun) It's always hopping at this bright corner bistro with an open kitchen. Service is quick and attentive, but you may want to pause at the long wooden bar anyway. The menu is broad, and changes often to reflect what's fresh: how about braised ox cheekstew to challenge the palate? Steaks come with awesome aioli. The €10 lunch menu, with half a sandwich, soup and tea or coffee, is a steal. Lots of wines by the glass.

Cafe Paradiso VEGETARIAN €€€
(021-427 7939; www.cafeparadiso.ie; 16 Lancaster Quay; mains €23-25; noon-3pm & 6-10.30pm Tue-Sat) A contender for best eatery in town, this down-to-earth vegetarian restaurant serves

a superb range of dishes, including vegan fare: how about sweet chilli-glazed panfried tofu with asian greens in a coconut and lemongrass broth, soba noodles and a gingered aduki bean wonton; or spring cabbage dolma of roast squash, caramelised onion & hazelnut with cardamom yoghurt, harissa sauce, broad beans and saffron-crushed potatoes? Reservations are essential.

Nash 19 INTERNATIONAL €€
(☎021-427 0880; www.nash19.com; Princes St; mains €8-18; ⏰7.30am-5pm Mon-Fri) A sensational bistro with a small market inside; local foods are honoured from breakfast to lunch and on to tea. Fresh scones draw in the crowds early; daily fresh specials (soups, salads, desserts, etc) and an incredible burger keep them coming through the rest of the day.

Jacques Restaurant MODERN IRISH €€€
(☎021-427 7387; www.jacquesrestaurant.ie; 9 Phoenix St; mains €22-27; ⏰6-10pm Mon-Sat) With almost three decades in the business, Jacqueline and Eithne Barry have built up a terrific network of local suppliers to help them realise their culinary ambitions – the freshest Cork food cooked simply. The menu, served in an elegant dining room, changes daily: we loved the fennel risotto with beef short ribs. Clattering dishes in the upstairs kitchen echo down this spot's tiny lane.

Les Gourmandises FRENCH €€€
(☎021-425 1959; www.les gourmandises.ie; 17 Cook St; mains €20-30; ⏰6-9.30pm Tue-Sat) Remember those beautiful fresh fish you saw in the English Market? Many of them end up at this cute little restaurant that reminds you of that perfect place you stumbled upon in Paris once... The talented kitchen turns out an array of local fish, and meats also get their due: the rack of lamb is a perennial fave. Service is gracious and calm.

Boqueria TAPAS €€
(☎021-455 9049; www.boqueria.ie; 6 Bridge St; tapas €6-8; ⏰noon-late Mon-Sat & 5pm-late Sun) The flavours of Spain shine (even if the sun doesn't) at this ever-popular tapas bar. In addition to the usual onion-garlic-tomato combinations, the chefs use local creations, such as sourdough, Gubbeen cheese and salmon, to create tasty Irishified tapas. It's a dusky, intimate spot, favoured by couples in the evenings, and at lunch by friends seeking a civilised glass of wine.

Star Anise MODERN EUROPEAN €€€
(☎021-455 1635; 4 Bridge St; mains €19-27; ⏰lunch & dinner Mon-Sat) Fresh and creative cooking is the hallmark at this narrow little shopfront bistro. There are steaks for the masses but also treats like tiger prawns on chickpea salad and a killer vegetarian lasagne. The wine list is both superb and affordable. Three-course dinner specials are a fine deal at €29.

Cornstore MODERN EUROPEAN €€€
(☎021-427 4777; www.cornstorecork.com; 40A Cornmarket St; mains €23-29; ⏰noon-11pm) Bustling and buzzy day and night, this modern restaurant has a swish bar, where you can enjoy creative cocktails while waiting for a table. Some tables are minute, but if you're having the amazing house special of lobster hold out for a large one so your elbows and shells can fly. There's also excellent fresh fish, steaks and pasta.

Indigo BRASSERIE €€
(☎021-427 9556; 16 Washington St; mains €7.50-13; ⏰lunch & dinner Mon-Sat) A table on the fabulous riverside deck overlooking the Lee is the ideal spot at this relatively new brasserie, but should you be forced inside you'll find consolation in the menu, which offers up excellent burgers, steak sandwiches, salads and sandwiches, all made with locally sourced ingredients. They have a pretty decent wine list too.

Idaho Café CAFE €
(☎021-427 6376; 19 Caroline St; dishes €7-12; ⏰8.30am-5pm) It looks like a traditional old caff from the outside, but take a gander at the menu and you'll find all sorts of creative takes on Irish standards. The tea selection includes scads of herbal numbers and there's a good per-glass wine menu. Tight seating means nothing is private. Idaho Café makes a good place to regroup while touring or shopping.

Liberty Grill DINER €€
(☎021-427 1049; www.libertygrillcork.com; 32 Washington St; mains €7-20; ⏰8am-10pm) A gleaming white outpost on an otherwise faded street of brick facades, the Liberty Grill is popular for its locally sourced menu of crowd pleasers, like traditional breakfasts, burgers, sandwiches, salads and slightly more ambitious dinner fare. Think of it as a diner for foodies.

DON'T MISS

THE ENGLISH MARKET

It could just as easily be called the Victorian Market for its ornate vaulted ceilings and columns, but the **English Market** (Princes St; ⌚9am-5.30pm Mon-Sat) is a true gem, no matter what you name it. Scores of vendors sell some of the very best local produce, meats, cheeses and takeaway food in the region. On decent days, take your lunch to nearby Bishop Lucey Park, a popular alfresco eating spot. A few favourites:

» **Joup** (☎021-422 6017) Has a range of soups and Med-flavoured salads, plus sandwiches on a variety of homemade breads.

» **On the Pig's Back** (☎021-427 0232) Boasts house-made sausages and incredible cheeses, many ready to munch.

» **Sandwich Stall** Has a drool-worthy display of remarkable and creative sandwiches.

On a mezzanine overlooking part of the market is one of Cork's best eateries. **Farmgate Café** (☎021-427 8134; English Market; lunch €4-13, dinner €18-30; ⌚8.30am-10pm Mon-Sat) is an unmissable experience. Like its sister restaurant in Midleton, this cafe has mastered the magic art of producing delicious meals without fuss or faddism. The food, from rock oysters to the lamb for an Irish stew, is sourced from the market below. There are tables but the best seats are at the balcony counter, where you can ponder the passing parade of shoppers. We still have memories of the seafood chowder and the raspberry crumble.

Fresco INTERNATIONAL €
(☎021-490 1848; www.glucksman.org; Lewis Glucksman Gallery, University College Cork; dishes €4-8; ⌚10am-4pm Mon-Sat & noon-4pm Sun) This above-par museum cafe has sweeping views of the university grounds and a broad range of dishes on its menu – from burgers to burritos, salads, pastas and a pretty tasty club sandwich, it's all freshly made and served with style.

Quay Co-op CAFE €
(☎021-431 7026; www.quaycoop.com; 24 Sullivan's Quay; mains €10; ⌚9am-9pm Mon-Sat) A gathering spot for the People's Republic of Cork proletariat, this nonflash cafe offers a range of self-service vegie options (all organic), including big breakfasts, hearty soups and casseroles. There's daily specials; dishes cater for gluten-, dairy- and wheat-free needs. The bulletin board has news for and of the masses.

Drinking

In Cork pubs, drink Guinness at your own peril, even though Heineken now owns both of the local stout legends, Murphy's and Beamish (and closed down the latter's brewery). Cork's microbrewery, the Franciscan Well Brewery, makes quality beers, including Friar Weisse, popular in summer.

An Spailpín Fánac PUB
(South Main St) 'The Wandering Labourer' really hangs on to its character, with exposed brickwork, stone-flagged floors, snug corners and open fires. There are good trad music sessions most nights.

Sin É PUB
(Coburg St) You could easily while away an entire day at this great old place, which is every thing a craic-filled pub should be. There are no frills or fuss here – just a comfy, sociable pub, long on atmosphere and short on pretension. There's music most nights, much of it traditional, but with the odd surprise.

Dan Lowry's PUB
(13 MacCurtain St) Genial is the word as you first enter this timeless family pub and are greeted by the generations of regulars. It's cosy in more ways than one; you can often get a seat on a Saturday night and enjoy an intimate chat.

Mutton Lane Inn PUB
(Mutton Lane) Tucked down the tiniest of laneways off St Patrick's St, this inviting pub, lit by candles and fairy lights, is one of Cork's most intimate drinking holes. It's minuscule and much admired, so try to get in early to bag the snug, or join the smokers perched on beer kegs outside.

Long Valley PUB
(Winthrop St) A Cork institution that dates from the mid-19th century and is still going strong. Some of the furnishings hail from White Star Line ocean liners that used to call at Cobh.

Franciscan Well Brewery PUB
(www.franciscanwellbrewery.com; 14 North Mall) The copper vats gleaming behind the bar give the game away: the Franciscan Well brews its own beer. The best place to enjoy it is in the enormous beer garden at the back. The pub holds regular beer festivals with other small (and often underappreciated) Irish breweries – check the website for details.

Abbot's Ale House PUB
(Devonshire St) A low-key 1st-floor pub, whose small size contrasts with a huge beer list. There are always several on tap and another 300 in bottles. Good for preclubbing.

Pubs are Cork's best asset but, if you hanker after a cocktail, there's a booming bar scene, too:

Chambers BAR
(Washington St; ⏲late Thu-Sun) A haberdasher swallowed a copy of *Wallpaper,* and Chambers was born.

Cornstore BISTRO
(see p229) The buzzy bistro's bar is a swishy place for a cocktail.

Crane Lane Theatre THEATRE BAR
(see p232) Their courtyard beer garden is a central Cork oasis.

☆ Entertainment

For listings of Cork's vibrant scene, pick up a copy of the free *WhazOn?* (www.whazon.com).

Theatre

Cork's cultural life is as fine as any in Ireland and attracts numerous internationally renowned performers.

Cork Arts Theatre THEATRE
(☎021-450 5624; www.corkartstheatre.com; Camden Court, Carroll's Quay) An excellent theatre putting on thought-provoking drama and new works.

Cork Opera House OPERA HOUSE
(☎021-427 0022; www.corkopera house.ie; Emmet Pl; ⏲box office 9am-8.30pm, to 5.30pm non performance nights) This leading venue has been entertaining the city for more than 150 years with everything from opera and ballet to stand-up and puppet shows. Performances are as varied as *Carmen,* Brian Kennedy and *Jane Eyre.*

Everyman Palace Theatre THEATRE
(☎021-450 1673; www.everymanpalace.com; 15 MacCurtain St; ⏲box office 10am-7.30pm Mon-Sat, to 6pm nonperformance nights) Acclaimed musical and dramatic productions are the main bill of fare here, but there's also the occasional band, comedy act, etc.

Firkin Crane THEATRE
(☎021-450 7487; www.firkincrane.ie; Shandon) One of Ireland's premier centres for modern dance. Located in part of the old butter market (see p224).

Granary THEATRE
(☎021-490 4275; www.granary.ie; Dyke Pde) Contemporary and experimental works are staged at the Granary by the University College Cork drama group and visiting companies.

Half Moon Theatre THEATRE
(☎021-427 0022; www.halfmoontheatre.ie; Emmet Pl) One of Cork's best venues for live theatre, comedy and music. It's at the back of the Cork Opera House.

Triskel Arts Centre ARTS CENTRE
(☎021-472 2022; www.triskelart.com; Tobin St; tickets around €15) Expect a varied program of live music, installation art, photography and theatre at this intimate venue. There's also a great cafe.

Cinemas

Gate Multiplex CINEMA
(☎021-427 9595; www.corkcinemas.com; North Main St) Multiscreen cinema showing mainstream films.

Live Music

Cork's musical credentials are impeccable. Besides the pubs that feature live music, the following places are either dedicated music venues or bars known particularly for their live events. For full listings, refer to *WhazOn?,* PLUGD Records (p232) and www.corkgigs.com. Buy tickets at the venues themselves or from PLUGD.

Cyprus Avenue MUSIC VENUE
(☎021-427 6165; www.cyprusavenue.ie; Caroline St; ⏲7.30pm-late) A mid-sized venue that is probably the best spot in town to see all kinds of gigs, from heartfelt singer-songwriters to

WORTH A TRIP

GONE TO THE DOGS

If you tire of the pubs, the live music and the theatre, there's always the dogs. Greyhound racing is big news in Ireland, particularly with families, and **Curraheen Greyhound Park** (☎]021-454 3095; www.igb.ie/cork; Curraheen Park; adult/child €10/5; ⏲from 6.45pm, days vary) is one of the country's poshest stadiums. There are 10 races a night, plus a restaurant, bar and live music to keep you entertained in between. Curraheen is 5.5km from the centre; to get there, take bus 8. A free bus drops you back between 10.30pm and 12.30am.

excellent bands on their way to fame (or on their way down from it).

Everyman Palace Theatre THEATRE
(☎021-450 1673; www.everymanpalace.com; 15 MacCurtain St; ⏲box office 10am-7.30pm Mon-Sat, to 6pm nonperformance nights) Musicians with a decent following will inevitably find themselves performing on the stage of the Everyman, which is a great venue for gigs that require a little bit of respectful silence.

Pavilion CAFE, LIVE MUSIC
(☎021-427 6230; www.pavilioncork.com; 13 Carey's Lane; ⏲noon-late) This modern-day coffee house has java by day, which you can enjoy at long tables. By night it has one of Cork's best mixes of bands, musicians and vocalists. Jazz, blues, rock, alternative and more are on the line-up.

Savoy THEATRE
(☎021-422 3910; www.savoytheatre.ie; St Patrick's St) A multi-purpose theatre with a pretty decent gig list, mostly of the mid-level chart variety – this is the place to see the latest UK R'n'B star strut their funky stuff.

An Cruiscín Lán PUB
(☎021-484 0941; www.cruiscinlive.com; Douglas St) Trad bands and world, blues and pop musicians all play at this acclaimed bar south of the river.

Crane Lane Theatre THEATRE
(☎021-427 8487; www.cranelanetheatre.com; Phoenix St) An excellent venue for live music, Crane Lane also has a great beer garden during the day.

Nightclubs

With such a big student population, the city's small selection of nightclubs do a thriving trade, mostly with pissed students and 20-somethings on the pull. Entry ranges from free to €15 and most are open until 2am on Friday and Saturday.

Savoy THEATRE, NIGHTCLUB
(☎021-422 3910; www.savoytheatre.ie; Patrick St; ⏲Thu-Sun) The city's best DJs (and a changing menu of visiting ones) usually show their skills in the Savoy's weekend club nights.

Scotts BAR
(☎021-422 2779; www.scotts.ie; Caroline St; ⏲Fri & Sat) This scenester venue, all dark wood and moody lighting, has a fine restaurant downstairs and an upstairs club featuring mainstream floor fillers for well-groomed over-20s.

Shopping

St Patrick's St is the retail heart of Cork, housing all the major department stores and malls. But pedestrianised Oliver Plunkett St is the retail spine; it and nearby narrow lanes are lined with interesting small shops.

O'Connaill CHOCOLATE
(☎021-437 3407; 16B French Church St) Don't leave Cork without sampling the Chocolatier's Hot Chocolate (€4) at O'Connaill confectioners' tiny counter. The foolhardy can stagger away with 2.5kg slabs of chocolate, but there are subtler concoctions on offer.

P Cashell ANTIQUES
(☎021-427 5824; 13 Winthrop St) A timeless and jammed antique and curio shop that seems entirely out of place amid the glitz of central Cork. It's like a treasure hunt.

PLUGD Records RECORD STORE
(☎021-472 2022; www.triskelart.com; Tobin St) Saved from closure by the Triskel Arts Centre, this newly relocated record store is the best in town for all kinds of music as well as the place to buy gig tickets and keep up with the ever-changing club scene.

Pro Musica MUSICAL INSTRUMENTS
(☎021-427 1659; Oliver Plunkett St) The heart of Cork's world for musicians: sheet music,

instruments and a notice board with ads by and for musicians.

Information

Emergency

Mercy University Hospital (☎021-427 1971; www.muh.ie; Grenville Pl)

Internet Access

Webworkhouse.com (☎021-427 3090; www.webworkhouse.com; 8A Winthrop St; per hr €1.50-3; ⌚24hr) Also offers low-cost international phone calls.

Post

General Post Office (☎021-485 1042; Oliver Plunkett St; ⌚9am-5.30pm Mon-Sat)

Tourist Information

Cork City Tourist Office (☎021-425 5100; www.cometocork.com; Grand Pde; ⌚9am-6pm Mon-Sat, 10am-5pm Sun Jul & Aug, 9.15am-5pm Mon-Fri & 9.30am-4.30pm Sat Sep-Jun) Souvenir shop and information desk with plenty of brochures and books about the city and county, as well as Ordnance Survey maps. **Stena Line** (see p735) ferries has a desk here.

People's Republic of Cork (www.peoplesrepublicofcork.com) Picking up on the popular nickname for this liberal-leaning city, this indie website has excellent info.

Getting There & Away

Air

Cork Airport (ORT; ☎021-431 3131; www.cork-airport.com) is 8km south of the city on the N27. Facilities include ATMs and car-hire desks for all the main companies. Airlines servicing the airport include Aer Lingus, BMI, Ryanair and Wizz. There are flights to Dublin, London Heathrow and a few cities in Europe.

Boat

Brittany Ferries (☎021-427 7801; www.brittanyferries.ie; 42 Grand Pde) sails to Roscoff (France) weekly from the end of March to October. The crossing takes 15 hours and fares are widely variable. The ferry terminal is at Ringaskiddy.

Bus

Aircoach (☎01-844 7118; www.aircoach.ie) serves Dublin Airport and Dublin city centre from St Patrick's Quay (€18; 4¼ hours; every two hours 7am to 7pm).

Bus Éireann (☎021-450 8188; www.buseireann.ie) operates from the bus station on the corner of Merchant's Quay and Parnell Pl. You can get to most places in Ireland from Cork, including Dublin (€11.70, 3 hours, six daily), Killarney (€15.30, 1¾ hours, 14 daily), Kilkenny (€16.65, two hours, three daily) and Waterford (€17.10, 2¾ hours, 14 daily).

Citylink (☎1890 280 808; www.citylink.ie) operates services to Galway (3¼ hours) and Limerick (2¼ hours). Buses are frequent and fares are as low as €10.

Train

Kent Train Station (☎021-450 4777) is north of the River Lee on Lower Glanmire Rd. Bus 5 runs into the centre (€1.80) and a taxi costs from €9 to €10.

The train line goes through Mallow, where you can change for the line to Tralee, and Limerick Junction, for the line to Ennis (and the new extension to Galway), then on to Dublin (€38, three hours, 16 daily).

Getting Around

To/From the Airport

SkyLink (☎021-432 1020; www.skylinkcork.com; adult/child €5/2.50; ⌚hourly) buses pick up around central Cork and take up to 30 minutes.

A taxi to/from town costs €15 to €20.

To/From the Ferry Terminal

The ferry terminal is at Ringaskiddy, 15 minutes by car southeast of the city centre along the N28. Taxis cost €28 to €35. Bus Éireann runs a service from the bus station to link up with departures (bus 223; adult/child €5.30/3.20, 50 minutes). Confirm times. There's also a service to Rosslare Harbour (bus 40, adult/child €23.70/16.70, four to five hours).

GAY & LESBIAN CORK

» **Cork Pride** (www.corkpride.com) Week-long festival every May/June, with events throughout the city.

» **Emerson House** Gay and lesbian B&B (see p225).

» **Gay Cork** (www.gaycork.com) What's-on listings and directory.

» **L.inC** (☎021-480 8600; www.linc.ie; 11A White St) Excellent resource centre for lesbians and bisexual women.

» **Other Place** (☎021-427 8470; www.gayprojectcork.com; 8 South Main St) Affiliated with the Southern Gay Health Project (www.gayhealthproject.com); has a bookstore and a cafe-bar (noon to 8pm Tue-Sat).

Bus

Most places are within easy walking distance of the centre. A single bus ticket costs €1.60. A day pass is €4.40.

Car

PARKING

Streetside parking requires scratch-card parking discs (€2 per hour), obtained from the tourist office and some newsagencies. Be warned – the traffic wardens are ferociously efficient and the cost of retrieving your vehicle is hefty. There are several signposted car parks around the central area, with charges of €2 per hour and €12 overnight.

Taxi

For taxi hire, try **Cork Taxi Co-op** (021-427 2222) or **Shandon Cabs** (021-450 2255).

AROUND CORK CITY

Blarney Castle

If you need proof of the power of a good yarn, then join the queue to get into this 15th-century **castle** (021-438 5252; www.blarneycastle.ie; Blarney; adult/student/child €10/8/3.50; 9am-7pm Mon-Sat & 9am-5.30pm Sun Jun-Aug, 9am-6.30pm Mon-Sat & 9.30am-5.30pm Sun May & Sep, 9am-sundown Sun Oct-Apr), one of Ireland's most inexplicably popular tourist attractions.

They're here, of course, to plant their lips on the **Blarney Stone**, a cliché that has entered every lexicon and tour route. The object of their affections is perched at the top of a steep climb up slippery spiral staircases. On the battlements, you bend backwards over a long, long drop (with safety grill and attendant to prevent tragedy) to kiss the stone; as your shirt rides up, coach loads of onlookers stare up your nose. Once you're upright, don't forget to admire the stunning views before descending. Try not to think of the local lore about all the fluids that drench the stone *other* than saliva. Better yet, just don't do it.

The custom of kissing the stone (which supposedly gives one the gift of gab – if not other things) is a relatively modern one, but Blarney's association with smooth talking goes back a long time. Queen Elizabeth I is said to have invented the term 'to talk blarney' out of exasperation with Lord Blarney's ability to talk endlessly without ever actually agreeing to her demands.

Be warned: this place gets mobbed. If it all gets too much, vanish into the **Rock Close**, part of the beautiful and often ignored **gardens**. And a hint: Barryscourt Castle (p236), east of Cork, is more impressive and much less crowded.

Blarney is 8km northwest of Cork and buses run frequently from Cork bus station (adult/child €3.30/2, 30 minutes).

Fota

Fota Wildlife Park (021-481 2678; www.fotawildlife.ie; Carrigtwohill; adult/child €14/9; 10am-6pm Mon-Sat & 11am-6pm Sun, last admission 1hr before closing) is a huge outdoor zoo, where animals roam without a cage or fence in sight. Here you can see kangaroos bound past; monkeys and gibbons leap and scream on wooded islands; and cheetahs run.

A **tour train** runs a circuit round the park every 15 minutes in high season (one way/return €1/2), but the 2km **circular walk** offers a more close-up experience.

From the wildlife park, you can take a stroll down to the Regency-style **Fota House** (021-481 5543; www.fotahouse.com; Carrigtwohill; adult/child €6/3; 10am-5pm Mon-Sat, from 11am Sun Apr-Oct). The mostly barren interior contains a fine kitchen and ornate plasterwork ceilings; interactive displays bring the rooms to life.

Attached to the house is the 150-year-old **arboretum**, which has a Victorian fernery, a magnolia walk and some beautiful trees, including giant redwoods and a Chinese ghost tree.

Fota is 10km east of Cork. The hourly Cork-Fota train (€3.20, 13 minutes) goes on to Cobh. A car park (€3.50) is shared by the park and the house.

Cobh

POP 6800

If you're looking for a palpable sense of the tragedy that was the Famine, go no further than the port of Cobh (pronounced 'cove'), from where 2.5 million people emigrated in order to escape the ravages of starvation. They left Ireland through the glistening estuary, although these days this handsome hill town, speckled with brightly coloured houses and overlooked by a splendid cathedral, is popular with Corkonians looking for a spot of R&R.

Cobh is on the south side of Great Island, one of three islands that fill Cork Harbour. The other two (visible from the waterfront) are Haulbowline Island (once the base of the Irish Naval Service) and the greener Spike Island (which housed a prison).

The Old Yacht Club is home to the **tourist office** (☎021-481 3301; www.cobhharbourchamber.ie; ⊙9.30am-5.30pm Mon-Fri, 1-5pm Sat & Sun) and an arts centre.

History

For many years Cobh was the port of Cork, and it has always had a strong connection with Atlantic crossings, including many fateful ones. In 1838 the *Sirius,* the first steamship to cross the Atlantic, sailed from Cobh. The *Titanic* made its last stop here before its fateful journey in 1912, and, when the *Lusitania* was torpedoed off the coast of Kinsale in 1915, it was here that many of the survivors were brought and the dead buried. Cobh was also the last glimpse of Ireland for the people who emigrated during the Famine.

In 1849 Cobh was renamed Queenstown after Queen Victoria paid a visit. The name lasted until Irish independence in 1921 when, unsurprisingly, the local council reverted to the Irish original.

The world's first yacht club, the Royal Cork Yacht Club, was founded here in 1720, but now operates from Crosshaven on the other side of Cork Harbour.

Sights

TOP CHOICE Cobh, The Queenstown Story MUSEUM

(☎021-481 3591; www.cobhheritage.com; adult/child €8/4; ⊙10am-6pm, last admission 1hr before closing) The howl of storms almost blows your hair, there's a bit of fake vomit and the people in the pictures all look pretty miserable. That's just one room at **Cobh Heritage Centre**. Housed in the old train station, this interactive museum is far above average. The room described above deals with the mass Famine emigrations across the Atlantic: trips where the people were green – and not with envy. Displays show how conditions improved – except for the *Titanic* or *Lusitania,* which have fateful links to Cobh.

There's also some shocking stuff on the fate of convicts, shipped to Australia in transport 'so airless that candles could not burn'. Scenes of sea travel in the 1950s, however, might actually make you wistful for a more gracious way of transiting the world. There's a genealogy centre attached and an adjoining café.

St Colman's Cathedral CATHEDRAL

(☎021-481 3222; Cathedral Pl; admission by donation) Standing dramatically above Cobh on a hillside terrace, this massive French Gothic Cathedral is out of all proportion to the unassuming town. Its most exceptional feature is the 47-bell carillon, the largest in Ireland, with a range of four octaves. The biggest bell weighs a stonking 3440kg – about as much as a full-grown elephant! You can hear carillon recitals at 4.30pm on Sundays between May and September.

The cathedral, designed by EW Pugin, was begun in 1868 but not completed until 1915. Much of the funding was raised by nostalgic Irish communities in Australia and the USA.

Cobh Museum MUSEUM

(☎021-481 4240; www.cobhmuseum.com; High Rd; adult/child €4/2; ⊙11am-1pm Mon-Sat & 2-5.30pm daily Apr-Oct) A small but lively museum is housed in the 19th-century Scottish Presbyterian church overlooking the train station. It holds model ships, paintings, photographs and curious artefacts tracing Cobh's history.

Tours

Marine Transport Services BOAT TOUR

(☎021-481 1485; www.scottcobh.ie; adult/child €8/4) One-hour boat tours of the harbour.

Titanic Trail WALKING TOUR

(☎021-481 5211; www.titanic-trail.com; adult/child €9.50/4.75; ⊙11am year-round, 2pm Jun-Aug) Michael Martin's 1¼-hour guided walk leaves from the Commodore Hotel on Westbourne Pl, with a free sampling of stout at the end. Martin also runs a ghoulish **Ghost Walk** (€15).

Sleeping & Eating

Knockeven House B&B €€

(☎021-481 1778; www.knockevenhouse.com; Rushbrooke; s/d €65/90) Knockeven is a splendid, relaxed Victorian house with huge bedrooms done out with period furniture and overlooking a magnificent garden full of magnolias and camellias. Breakfasts are great too – homemade breads and fresh fruit – and are served in the sumptuous dining room. The decor takes you back to 1st-class passage on a vintage liner. It is 1.5km north of Cobh.

Commodore Hotel HOTEL €€
(☎021-481 1277; www.commodorehotel.ie; Westbourne Pl; s/d €60/100; @🛜🏊) A classic seaside hotel with soaring chandeliered hallways and 42 well-appointed rooms (it's worth paying extra for one with a sea view). The pool is indoors and a roof garden offers yet more views.

Eleven West INTERNATIONAL €€
(☎021-481 6020; www.elevenwest.ie; 11 West Beach St; mains €15-23; ⏲9am-10pm) A buzzing restaurant on the waterfront that serves up a broad range of dishes such as steaks, curries and a particularly good rack of lamb.

Kelly's PUB €
(☎021-481 1994; Westbourne Pl; meals €7-12) Sunny Kelly's is filled with sociable punters day and night. The pub's two rooms are decked out with pew-style seating, chunky wooden furniture, a wood-burning stove and, curiously, a stag's head. Seating outside is good for a pint and a sandwich.

A **farmers market** is held on the seafront every Friday from 10am to 1pm.

Drinking

Jack Doyles PUB
(☎021-420 1932; Midleton St) Named for a famous local boxer *and* tenor, this sports-mad pub, a short walk uphill from the cathedral, is a fine place to meet residents of Cobh.

Getting There & Away

Cobh is 15km southeast of Cork, off the main N25 Cork-Rosslare road; Great Island is linked to the mainland via a causeway. Hourly trains connect it with Cork (€3.70, 25 minutes).

Barryscourt Castle

Immigrants from Wales in the 12th century, the Barry family quickly began intermarrying with important Irish families of the time. Soon they had huge tracts of land and real wealth. In order to protect their fortune, the clan began building a vast fortification in the 15th century.

FREE **Barryscourt Castle** (☎021-488 3864; www.heritageireland.ie; admission free; ⏲10am-6pm Jun-Sep) survives in remarkably good condition (albeit with a lot of restoration). An authentic 16th-century kitchen and decorative gardens have been recreated.

The castle is just off the N25, 2km east of the turn-off to Cobh and near Carrigtwohill.

Midleton & Around

POP 3900

Aficionados of a particularly fine Irish whiskey will recognise the name and the main reason to linger in this bustling market town is to visit the old whiskey distillery. However, the surrounding region is full of pretty villages, craggy coastline and some heavenly rural hotels – precisely why you should visit the town but stay elsewhere.

The **tourist office** (☎021-461 3702; www.eastcorktourism.com; ⏲9.30am-1pm & 2-5.15pm Mon-Sat May-Sep) is by the entrance gate to the distillery.

WORTH A TRIP

THE GOURMET HEARTLAND OF BALLYMALOE

Drawing up at wisteria-clad **Ballymaloe House** (☎021-465 2531; www.ballymaloe.ie; Shanagarry; s/d from €130/260; 🏊🛜), you know you've arrived somewhere special. The Allen family has been running this superb hotel and restaurant in the old family home for more than 40 years now; Myrtle is a living legend, acclaimed internationally for her near single-handed creation of fine Irish cooking. The rooms have been individually decorated with period furnishings and are a pleasing mass of different shapes and sizes. Guests enjoy beautiful grounds and amenities, which include a tennis court, a swimming pool, a shop, minigolf and public rooms. And don't forget the celebrated **restaurant**, whose menu is drawn up daily to reflect the availability of produce from Ballymaloe's extensive farms and other local sources. The hotel also runs wine and gardening weekends; check the website for details.

A few kilometres down the road on the R628, TV personality Darina Allen runs a famous **cookery school** (☎021-464 6785; www.cookingisfun.ie). Lessons, from half-day sessions (€75 to €115) to 12-week certificate courses (€10,295), are often booked well in advance. There are pretty **cottages** amid the 100 acres of grounds for overnight students.

Sights

The big attraction in town is the **Jameson Experience** (☎021-461 3594; www.jamesonwhiskey.com; Old Distillery Walk; tours adult/student/child €13.50/11/8; ⊙shop 9am-6.30pm, tour times vary). Coachloads pour in to tour the restored 200-year-old building and purchase bottles from the gift shop. Exhibits and tours explain the process of taking barley and creating whiskey (Jameson is today made in a modern factory in Cork).

Sleeping & Eating

Midleton has several attractive cafes in its centre, making it worth wandering in off the bypass. The **farmers market** is one of Cork's best markets, with bushels of local produce on offer and producers who are happy to chat. It's on every Saturday morning behind the courthouse on Main St.

Loughcarrig House B&B €€
(☎021-463 1952; www.loughcarrig.com; Ballinacurra; s/d €50/80) Right on Cork Harbour, this gracious old Georgian house has four rooms available, ideal for those looking for a restful country retreat. Walks and birdwatching on the beautiful land here are prime activities. The owners can also set you up for some angling in the fish-filled waters. Breakfasts are suitably hearty.

TOP CHOICE **Farmgate Restaurant** RESTAURANT/BAKERY €€
(☎021-463 2771; www.farmgate.ie; The Coolbawn; restaurant mains around €18; ⊙coffee & snacks 9am-5.30pm, lunch noon-3.30pm Mon-Sat, dinner 6.30-9.30pm Thu-Sat) The original and sister establishment to Cork's Farmgate Café (p230), the Midleton restaurant offers the same superb blend of traditional and modern Irish in its approach to cooking. In the front is a shop selling amazing baked goods and local produce, including organic fruit and vegetables, cheeses and preserves. Behind is the farmhouse-style cafe-restaurant, where you'll eat as well as anywhere in Ireland.

Getting There & Away

Midleton is 20km east of Cork. There are buses every 30 minutes from Monday to Saturday (hourly on Sunday) from Cork bus station (€6.40, 25 minutes). There are no buses between Cobh and Midleton, and you'll need a car to explore the surrounding area.

WORTH A TRIP

SMOKIN'

Two kilometres out of Midleton on the N25 towards Fota, the effervescent Frank Hederman runs **Belvelly** (☎021-481 1089; www.frankhederman.com), the oldest natural smoke house in Ireland – and indeed the only one. Seafood and cheese are smoked here, but the speciality is fish – in particular, salmon. In a traditional process that takes 24 hours from start to finish, the fish is filleted and cured before being hung in the tiny smoke house to smoke over beech woodchips. No trip to Cork is complete without a visit to an artisan food producer, and Frank is more than happy to show you around; phone or email to arrange. Or stop by his booth at the Midleton farmers market.

Youghal

POP 6500

The ancient seaport of Youghal (Eochaill; pronounced yawl), at the mouth of the River Blackwater, has a rich history that may not be instantly apparent, especially if you coast past on the N25. In fact, even if you stop, it may just seem like a humdrum Irish market town. But take a little time and you'll sniff out some of its once-walled past and enjoy views of the wide River Blackwater estuary.

The town was a hotbed of rebellion against the English in the 16th century, and Oliver Cromwell wintered here in 1649 as he sought to drum up support for his war in England and quell insurgence from the pesky Irish. Youghal was granted to Sir Walter Raleigh during the Elizabethan Plantation of Munster, and he spent brief spells living here in his house, Myrtle Grove.

Sights & Activities

In 1956 the harbour stood in for New Bedford, Massachusetts, in the US for the filming of *Moby Dick,* starring Gregory Peck in one of his best roles. Today it is very quiet.

Youghal has two Blue Flag **beaches**, ideal for building sandcastles modelled after the Clock Gate. Claycastle (2km) and Front Strand (1km) are both within walking distance of town, off the N25. Claycastle has summer lifeguards.

WALKING TOUR

Youghal's history is best understood through its landmarks. Heading through town from south to north, this tour details the more prominent sights.

The curious **Clock Gate** was built in 1777, and served as a clock tower and jail concurrently; several prisoners taken in the 1798 Rising were hanged from its windows.

The beautifully proportioned brick **Red House**, on North Main St, was designed in 1706 by the Dutch architect Leuventhen, and features some Dutch Renaissance details. Main St has an interesting curve that follows the original shore; many of the shopfronts are from the 19th century. A few doors further up the street are six **almshouses** built by Englishman Richard Boyle, who bought Raleigh's Irish estates and became the first Earl of Cork in 1616 in recognition of his work in creating 'a very excellent colony'. The almshouses were given to ex-soldiers, along with an annual pension of £5.

Across the road is the 15th-century tower house **Tynte's Castle** (www.tyntescastle.com), which originally had a defensive riverfront position. When the River Blackwater silted up and changed course in the 17th and 18th centuries, the castle was left high and dry. It's currently under renovation.

Built in 1220, **St Mary's Collegiate Church** incorporates elements of an earlier Danish church dating back to the 11th century. Inside there's a monument to Richard Boyle, portrayed with his wife and 16 kids. The Earl of Desmond and his troops, rebelling against English rule, demolished the chancel roof in the 16th century; Cromwell is believed to have given a funerary speech inside for a fallen general in 1650. The churchyard is bounded by a fine stretch of the 13th-century **town wall** and one of the remaining turrets.

Beside the church, **Myrtle Grove** is the former home of Sir Walter Raleigh. Local tradition claims that he smoked the first cigarette and planted the first potatoes here, but historians (the spoilsports) tend to disagree. His **gardens**, on the other side of St Mary's, have recently been restored and are open to the public.

Whale of a Time (☎086 328 3256; www.whaleofatime.ie; adult/child €20/15) runs sea and river cruises, including whale-watching trips.

Dinky **Fox's Lane Folk Museum** (☎024-20170, 024-91145; www.tyntescastle.com/fox; North Cross Lane; adult/child €4/2; ⊙10am-1pm & 2-6pm Tue-Sat Jul & Aug) contains more than 600 household gadgets, dating from 1850 to 1950, and a Victorian kitchen.

Sleeping

Aherne's B&B €€

(☎024-92424; www.ahernes.net; 163 North Main St; s/d from €130/150; @ 🛜) The 12 rooms above the popular restaurant are extremely well appointed; larger ones have small balconies, where you can get a whiff of the sea air.

Roseville B&B €€

(☎024-92571; www.rosevillebb.com; New Catherine St; r €55-72; 🛜) In the heart of Youghal, deep-red Roseville, with its own walled garden, has the mood of a country house. The rooms have big comfy beds and are decorated in restful shades of beige. The garden is a fine place for lounging on a summer evening.

Avonmore House B&B €€

(☎024-92617; www.avonmoreyoughal.com; South Abbey; s/d €55/100) This grand Georgian house near the clock tower was built in 1752 on the site of a Franciscan abbey destroyed by Cromwellian troops. Avonmore belonged to the earls of Cork before passing into private hands in 1826. Rooms are basic and multicoloured.

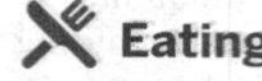

Eating

You'll find a few cafes and pubs in the centre near the Clock Gate.

Aherne's Seafood Bar & Restaurant (☎024-92424; 163 North Main St; bar food €10-18, dinner €24-40; ⊙bar food noon-10pm, dinner 6.30-9.30pm) Three generations of the same family have run Aherne's, an award-winning restaurant, justifiably famous for its terrific menu. Besides the restaurant there is a stylish, cosy bar and a much larger one popular with locals. The pub food is excellent.

Drinking

For an end-of-day pint and traditional live music, nowhere beats **Treacy's** (The Nook; 20 North Main St), Youghal's oldest boozer, aka The Nook.

Information

Youghal Visitor Centre (☎024-20170; www.eastcorktourism.com; Market Sq; ⏲9am-5.30pm Mon-Fri, 10am-5pm Sat & Sun), housed in an attractive old market house on the waterfront, contains a small **heritage centre**. Pick up the free leaflet *Youghal Town Map* or the excellent booklet *Youghal: Historic Walled Port* (€5) to learn more.

Getting There & Away

Bus Éireann (☎021-450 8188; www.buseireann.ie) runs services to Cork (€10.25, 50 minutes, 14 daily) and Waterford (€17.10, 1½ hours, 11 daily).

WESTERN CORK

The Irish coast begins the slow build of beauty that culminates in counties even further west and north, but what you find here in Cork is already quite lovely. Kinsale is a superb little waterside town and there are many smaller ones almost as charming along the craggy coast to the Ring of Beara. It's perfect for aimless wandering as roads criss-cross the area like lace made by a deranged person.

Kinsale

POP 4100

Narrow winding streets lined with artsy little shops and a handsome harbour full of bobbing fishing boats and pleasure yachts make Kinsale (Cionn tSáile) one of Ireland's favourite mid-sized towns; its superb foodie reputation is just another reason to visit. Its sheltered bay is guarded by a huge and engrossing fort, just outside the town at Summercove.

Most of Kinsale's hotels and restaurants are situated near the harbour and within easy walking distance of the town centre; Scilly, a peninsula to the southeast, is barely a 10-minute walk away. A path continues from there to Summercove and Charles Fort.

History

In September 1601 a Spanish fleet anchored at Kinsale was besieged by the English. An Irish army from the north, which had appealed to the Spanish king to help it against the English, marched the length of the country to liberate the ships, but was defeated in battle outside the town on Christmas Eve. For the Catholics, the immediate consequence was that they were banned from Kinsale; it would be another 100 years before they were allowed back in. Historians now cite 1601 as the beginning of the end of Gaelic Ireland.

After 1601 the town developed as a shipbuilding port. In the early 18th century, Alexander Selkirk left Kinsale Harbour on a voyage that left him stranded on a desert island, providing Daniel Defoe with the idea for *Robinson Crusoe*.

Sights

Charles Fort FORTRESS
(☎021-477 2263; www.heritageireland.ie; adult/child €4/2; ⏲10am-6pm mid-Mar-Oct) One of the best-preserved 17th-century star-shaped forts in Europe, this wonderful fortress would be worth a visit for its spectacular views alone. But there's much more here: ruins inside the vast site date from the 18th and 19th centuries and make for some fascinating wandering. Displays explain the typically tough lives led by the soldiers who served here and the comparatively comfortable lives of the officers. Built in the 1670s to guard Kinsale Harbour, the fort was in use until 1921, when much of it was destroyed as the British withdrew. The best way to get here is to walk – follow the signs on the lovely walk around the bay from Scilly to Summercove, 3km east of Kinsale.

Regional Museum MUSEUM
(☎021-477 7930; Market Sq; adult/concession €3/1.50; ⏲10am-5pm Wed-Sat, 2-5pm Sun) This nifty museum is based in the 17th-century courthouse that was used for the inquest into the sinking of the *Lusitania* in 1915. The museum contains information on the disaster, as well as curiosities as diverse as Michael Collins' hurley and shoes belonging to the eight-foot-tall Kinsale Giant.

Desmond Castle CASTLE
(☎021-477 4855; www.heritageireland.ie; Cork St; adult/child €3/1; ⏲10am-6pm Tue-Sun Easter-Sep, last admission 45min before closing) Kinsale's roots with the old wine trade are on display at this early 16th-century fortified house that was occupied by the Spanish in 1601. Since then it has served as a customs house,

Kinsale

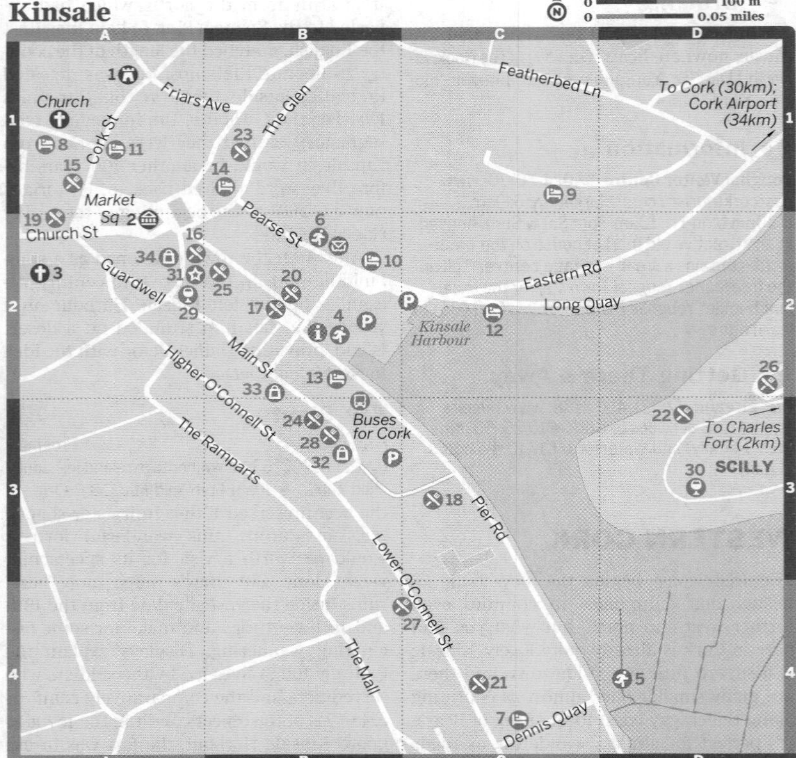

as a prison for French and American captives and as a workhouse during the Famine. There are lively exhibits detailing its history and a small **wine museum** (www.winegeese.ie) that tells the story of the Irish wine-trading families, including names like Hennessy (of brandy fame), who fled to France because of British rule.

St Multose Church CHURCH
(Church of Ireland Church; ☎rectory 021-477 2220; Church St) This is one of Ireland's oldest Church of Ireland churches, built around 1190 by the Normans on the site of a 6th-century church. Not much of the interior is original but the exterior is preserved beautifully. The **graveyard** has some interesting large family tombs, and several victims of the *Lusitania* sinking are also buried there. Inside, a flat stone carved with a round-handed figure was traditionally rubbed by fishermen's wives to bring their husbands home safe from the sea.

Activities

For sailings to Charles Fort, James Cove and up the River Bandon, you can phone **Kinsale Harbour Cruises** (☎021-477 8946, 086 250 5456; www.kinsaleharbourcruises.com; adult/child €12.50/6). Departure times vary throughout the year and are weather dependent; check the website or with the tourist office for details. The boats leave from near Vista Wine Bar on Pier Rd towards the marina.

Whale of a Time (☎086 328 3250; www.whaleofatime.ie) offers coastal cruises and whale-watching trips from €35 per person for 90 minutes on fast speedboats.

For those interested in fishing, tackle can be hired at **Mylie Murphy's** (☎021-477 2703; 14 Pearse St) for €12 per day. For those hooked on fishing trips, contact **Kinsale Angling Co-op** (☎021-477 4946; www.kinsale-angling.com).

Kinsale

Sights

1 Desmond Castle.... A1
2 Regional Museum.... A2
3 St Multose Church.... A2
Wine Museum.... (see 1)

Activities, Courses & Tours

4 Dermot Ryan's Heritage Town Walks.... B2
Don & Barry's Historic Stroll.... (see 4)
5 Kinsale Harbour Cruises.... D4
6 Mylie Murphy's.... B2

Sleeping

7 Chart House.... C4
8 Cloisters B&B.... A1
9 Danabel.... C1
10 Old Bank House.... B2
11 Old Presbytery.... A1
12 Perryville House.... C2
13 Pier House.... B2
14 White House.... B1

Eating

15 Crackpots.... A1
16 Cucina.... A2
17 Farmers Market.... B2
18 Fishy Fishy Cafe.... C3
19 Fishy Fishy Shop & Chippie.... A2
20 Jim Edwards.... B2
21 Jola's.... C4
22 Man Friday.... D3
23 Market Garden.... B1
24 Max's Wine Bar.... B3
25 Quay Food Co.... B2
26 Spaniard Bar & Restaurant.... D2
27 Stolen Pizza.... C4
28 Tom's Artisan Bakery.... B3

Drinking

29 De Teac.... A2
30 Harbour Bar.... D3

Entertainment

31 An Seanachai.... A2
Spaniard Bar & Restaurant.... (see 26)

Shopping

32 Giles Norman Gallery.... B3
33 Granny's Bottom Drawer.... B2
34 Kinsale Crystal.... A2

Tours

Dermot Ryan's Heritage Town Walks WALKING TOUR
(021-477 2729; www.kinsaleheritage.com; 1 hr tour adult/child €5/free; 10.30am & 3pm) Depart from the tourist office.

Don & Barry's Historic Stroll WALKING TOUR
(021-477 2873; www.historicstrollkinsale.com; 90-min tour adult/child €6/1; 9.15am & 11.15am May-Sep, 11.15am Oct-Apr) Depart from the tourist office.

Festivals & Events

Gourmet Festival (www.kinsalerestaurants.com) Tastings, meals and harbour cruises in early October add to the town's foodie reputation.

Kinsale Jazz Festival (www.kinsale.ie) Chilled-out entertainment over the late-October bank-holiday weekend.

Sleeping

Pier House B&B €€
(021-477 4475; www.pierhousekinsale.com; Pier Rd; r €80-140; P) This superb guesthouse, set back from the road in a sheltered garden, is a lovely place to rest your head. Pristine rooms, decorated with shell-and-driftwood sculptures, and have black-granite bathrooms with power showers and underfloor heating. Four of the rooms also have balconies and views of the milling mobs outside.

Old Bank House HOTEL €€€
(021-477 4075; www.oldbankhousekinsale.com; 11 Pearse St; r €130-220; @) Georgian elegance and style give a timeless quality to this top-of-the-range 18-room hotel. Beautiful objets d'art and paintings grace the walls, and the luxurious public rooms add a country-house ambience. Although room decor is lavish, it manages to avoid pretension through subtle whimsy. Breakfasts, with homemade breads (from the bakery downstairs) and jams, are superb.

Old Presbytery B&B €€
(021-477 2027; www.oldpres.com; Cork St; s €90, d €110-170; closed Jan–mid-Feb;) The Old Presbytery has gracefully moved into the 21st century with a careful refurbishment that maintains its character without pushing it into the 'batty old dowager' category.

The timeless pine furniture contrasts with the refitted bathrooms. Stay in room 6 only if you have plans to see nothing of Kinsale: with its sunroom and balcony, you'll never want to leave. The breakfasts, cooked by landlord and former chef Phillip, are the stuff of legend.

Perryville House BOUTIQUE HOTEL €€
(021-477 2731; www.perryvillehouse.com; Long Quay; r €110-250; P) It's top-to- bottom grandeur at family-run Perryville, whether you're pulling up outside its imposing wrought-iron-clad facade or taking afternoon tea in the drawing room. All the 26 rooms exude comfort; move up the rate card and the beds go from queen to king, while balconies and sea views appear. Bathrooms are huge. Eggs at breakfast are laid by a staff member's chickens.

White House B&B €€
(021-477 2125; www.whitehouse-kinsale.com; Pearse St; s/d from €65/100; P@) In the heart of town, this stylish inn has 10 large, modern rooms attached that are the height of comfort – not quite presidential, but fit for a cabinet secretary.

Cloisters B&B B&B €€
(021-470 0680; www.cloisterskinsale.com; Friars St; s €60, d €70-110) Little touches make the difference at this delightful B&B near Desmond Castle. Inside the vermilion walls, chocolates await your arrival, and the orthopaedic mattresses are so comfy that only the creative breakfasts will tempt you out of bed. It's right across from St John the Baptist Church.

Danabel B&B €€
(021-477 4087; www.danabel.com; Sleaveen; s/d from €45/70; P) Just off Featherbed Lane (we're not making this up), this modern home has comfortable rooms with large private bathrooms and nice hardwood floors; some have views of the harbour. It's a brief walk to the centre.

Chart House B&B €€
(021-477 4568; www.charthouse-kinsale.com; 6 Dennis Quay; s/d from €80/110; P) There's a relaxed elegance about this Georgian town house; the four rooms have period pieces but not the fussiness that often accompanies them. The large dining room is so nice for breakfast you might want to stay for lunch.

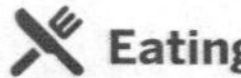

Eating

You're in for a treat. Kinsale fully deserves its billing as a foodie haven and you can eat wonderfully on every budget. Surf – brought in by the busy fishing fleet – is the specialty, but most restaurants will serve up some turf too.

TOP CHOICE **Fishy Fishy Cafe** SEAFOOD €€
(021-470 0415; www.fishyfishy.ie; Crowley's Quay; mains €13-34; noon-4pm Mon-Fri, noon-4.30pm Sat & Sun) Arguably the best seafood restaurant in the country has a wonderful setting, with stark white walls splashed with bright artwork and a terrific decked terrace at the front. All the fish is caught locally; have the cold seafood platter, a tasty spectacle that's a concert of what's fresh. Scallops are dollops of goodness. Front-of-house staff are charmers, but waitstaff can look tired. The Fishy Fishy empire also includes a superb fish 'n' chip shop.

Jim Edwards SEAFOOD €€
(021-477 2541; www.jimedwardskinsale.com; Market Quay; bar meals €7-20, restaurant meals €15-30; bar 12.30-10pm, restaurant 6-10pm) If Fishy Fishy has a serious rival, it's 200m away in this unassuming pub, where the bar food is way above standard and the restaurant exceptional. A very traditional ambience belies the high quality of the menu, which doffs a cap to meat-eaters but specialises mostly in all kinds of locally caught fish.

Bulman Bar & Toddies SEAFOOD €€
(021-477 2131; Summercove; mains €16-21; 12.30-9.30pm) This is seaside eating at its best. Escape from central Kinsale to this gastro pub in an unspoilt harbourside venue, where salty informality is a style in its own right. Seafood excels here, whether swimming in chowder or laid out seductively on a platter. Much of everything is sourced locally; herbs are right from the kitchen garden. The more formal restaurant **Toddies** (dinner only Wed-Sat) serves an excellent range of beautifully prepared seafood – the lobster risotto (€18.95) is recommended.

Spaniard Bar & Restaurant INTERNATIONAL €€
(021-477 2436; www.thespaniard.ie; Scilly; bar meals €4-14; restaurant mains €14-24) This is a classic pub on Scilly, with low ceilings and a peat fire, so why not crack open some crab claws or settle for a sandwich at the bar. Prices for most dishes at the bar are

around €10; there's a pricier restaurant upstairs, which serves more or less the same food as downstairs but doesn't have half the atmosphere.

Jola's MODERN IRISH €€€
(☎021-477 3322; www.jolasrestaurant.com; 18-19 Lower O'Connell St; mains €20-29; ⊙dinner only Wed-Sat & Bank Holidays) With double-height ceilings, exposed brick walls and a stunning chandelier, Jola Wojtowicz's restaurant brings a dash of metropolitan style to Kinsale. The food is equally adept, confidently marrying Eastern European and Irish cuisine. The *pierogi* (dumplings) made with Clonakilty black pudding are divine, but are merely preparation for the mouth-watering mains, which include a particularly lovely dish of lamb cutlets with basil and walnut pesto.

Man Friday MODERN IRISH €€€
(☎021-477 2260; www.manfridaykinsale.ie; cnr River & High Rds, Scilly; mains €23-29; ⊙dinner only) Around the harbour walk in relaxing Scilly, this veteran seafood restaurant has outdoor seating with views back across the harbour to Kinsale. Book if you want a terrace table on balmy evenings. Just the walk down to the entrance is magical.

Cucina CAFE €
(☎021-470 0707; www.cucina.ie; 9 Market St; meals €5-14; ⊙9am-5pm Mon-Sat, last orders 4pm) Laid-back jazz sets the mood at this modern little cafe. Healthy bruschetta, salads and soups, and not-so-healthy but very delicious cup cakes are served in a simple setting.

Fishy Fishy Shop & Chippie FISH & CHIPS €
(☎021-477 4453; Guardwell; meals €8-15; ⊙noon-9pm Apr-Oct) The casual retail outlet for the vaunted restaurant, you can pause here on your Kinsale ramble for *just* a superb coffee but, really, you'll want some of the best fish and chips in town, or one of the other treats. Tables are located both inside and out.

Crackpots MODERN IRISH €€
(☎021-477 2847; www.crackpots.ie; 3 Cork St; mains €14-28; ⊙lunch & dinner Mon-Sat, lunch only Sun) The title 'ceramic restaurant' over the front door refers to the fact that all the crockery in use here was made…here. Normally, when you combine art workshop and food something will give, but in this instance it's certainly not the grub, which relies on locally sourced meats, fresh catch from the sea and organically grown veg. Owner Carole Norman has recently given over her walls to local artists – you can peruse the art for sale while you dine.

Stolen Pizza ITALIAN €€
(☎021-470 0488; 66 Lower O'Connell St; mains €10-16; ⊙noon-9pm) An old neighbourhood pub has been reborn and has a welcoming dinner menu of Italian classics. It's great for when you want to say no to mussels and say yes to spaghetti and meatballs. There's excellent pizza and, in a nod to local tradition, fine seafood ravioli. By day this charmer is good for a coffee and a pause along the gentrifying street.

Max's Wine Bar MODERN IRISH €€
(☎021-477 2443; 48 Main St; 2/3-course evening menu €24/30; ⊙noon-2pm & 6-10pm Tue-Sun, shorter hours in winter) Behind the brilliant red traditional wooden facade is a restaurant popular with locals that combines French influences with the best Irish produce and seafood. The menu changes regularly but the wine list doesn't (at least in concept): it's always vast and alluring.

Drinking & Entertainment

Harbour Bar PUB
(Scilly; ⊙from 6pm) Romping home in Kinsale's 'most unusual bar' stakes, this is like being in someone's front room. Battered old sofas, a fire stoked in the hearth, characters in every corner and benches with water views in the garden are all part of the charm.

Spaniard Bar & Restaurant PUB
(☎021-477 2436; www.thespaniard.ie; Scilly) The food is good, but the real appeal of this old pub (it feels like it dates back to the Armada)

DIY DINNER

The **Quay Food Co** (☎021-477 4000; www.quayfood.com; Market Quay; sandwiches €4-6; ⊙9am-6pm daily) is good for local produce and little luxuries. Also good for picnickers is **Market Garden** (☎021-477 574; The Glen; 9am-7pm Mon-Sat), a low-ceilinged warren of organic and local fruit and veg. Window displays at **Tom's Artisan Bakery** (☎021-477 3561; 46 Main St; ⊙8am-5pm Mon-Sat) are suitably artful. There's a weekly **farmers market** (Short Quay; ⊙9.30am-1.30pm Tue) in front of Jim Edwards' restaurant.

1

1. Toddie's Restaurant, Kinsale (p242)
Presenting a plate at Toddie's restaurant.

2. Fresh Bread (p44)
Try Ireland's famous soda bread or fadge (potato bread).

3. Irish Cheese (p45)
Sample rich, nutty Ardrahan cheese.

4. Kinsale Restaurants (p242)
Enjoy fine dining on the best local produce.

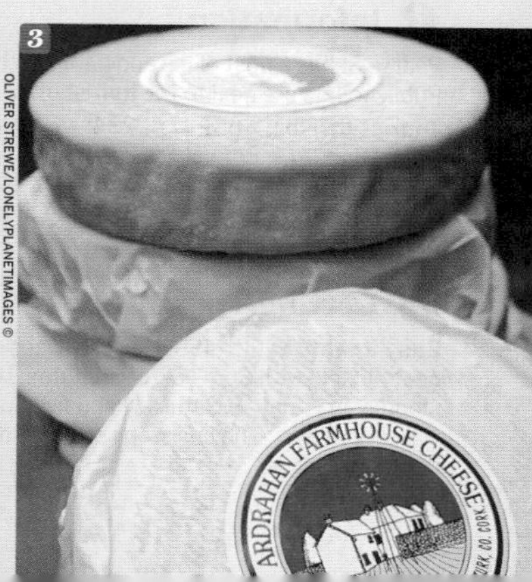

lies in the quiet corners, where you can smell the peat fire and catch fragments of hushed conversations that could be about smuggling but are likely to be about sport.

De Teac PUB
(☎021-477 4602; 1 Main St) The pub menu has gone a hair upmarket, but this is still a rollicking local boozer, where locals prance in and out as if it were their living room (actually it is) and the regulars all their family.

An Seanachai PUB
(☎021-477 7077; 6 Market St) This cavernous, barnlike pub has traditional music sessions most nights.

Bulman PUB
(☎021-477 2131; Summercove) Always worth the stroll, the pub matches the restaurant (p242) in salt-tinged allure.

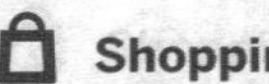

Shopping

Giles Norman Gallery PHOTOGRAPHY
(☎021-477 4373; 45 Main St) There's a big selection of evocative black-and-white imagery of Ireland here, from a master of the genre. Prints start at €30 (unframed) and €45 (framed).

Granny's Bottom Drawer IRISH CRAFTS
(☎021-477 4839; 53 Main St) A great range of exquisite Irish linen, damask and vintage-style homewares is sold at this cheerful shop with the perfect name.

Kinsale Crystal CRYSTAL
(☎021-477 4493; Market St) Sells exquisite work by an ex-Waterford craftsman who stands by the traditional 'deep-cutting, high-angle style'. A million tiny sparkles greet you as you enter.

Information

Pearse St has a post office and banks with ATMs. Public toilets are next to the tourist office.

Tourist office (☎021-477 2234; www.kinsale.ie; cnr Pier Rd & Emmet Pl; ⏲9.15am-5pm Tue-Sat Nov-Mar, Mon Apr-Jun, Sep & Oct, 10am-5pm Sun Jul & Aug) Has a good map detailing walks in and around Kinsale.

Getting There & Away

Bus Éireann (☎021-450 8188) services connect Kinsale with Cork (€7, 50 minutes, 14 daily Monday to Friday, 11 Saturday and five Sunday) via Cork airport. The bus stops on Pier Rd, near the tourist office.

Getting Around

Kinsale Cabs (☎021-477 2642)

Clonakilty

POP 4200

Cheerful, brightly coloured Clonakilty is a bustling market town that serves as a hub for the scores of beguiling little coastal towns that surround it. You'll find smart B&Bs, top restaurants and cosy pubs alive with music. Little waterways coursing through add a drop of charm.

Clonakilty is famous for two things: it's the birthplace of Michael Collins (see the boxed text, p252), embodied in a large **statue** on the corner of Emmet Sq; and it's the home of the most famous black pudding in the country.

Roads converge on Asna Sq, dominated by a **1798 Rising monument** commemorating the event. Also in the square is the **Kilty Stone**, a piece of the original castle that gave Clonakilty (Clogh na Kylte in Irish, meaning 'castle of the woods') its name.

Sights & Activities

Wandering the centre is good for a couple of hours; Georgian **Emmet Square** attests to the area's traditional wealth. **Spillers Lane** has nifty little shops.

Of the more than 30,000 ring forts scattered across Ireland, **Lisnagun** (Lios na gCon; ☎023-883 2565; www.liosnagcon.com; adult/child €5/3; ⏲tours noon-4pm summer) is the only one that's been reconstructed on its original site. Complete with souterrain and central thatched hut, it gives a vivid impression of life in a 10th- century farmstead. To get there, take the turn signposted to Bay View House B&B at the roundabout at the end of Strand Rd. Follow the road uphill to the T-junction, turn right, then continue for about 800m before turning right again (signposted).

You can't help but smile at the **West Cork Model Railway Village** (☎023-883 3224; www.modelvillage.ie; Inchydoney Rd; adult/child €8/4.25; ⏲11am-5pm Sep-Jun, 10am-5pm Jul & Aug). It features a vast outdoor recreation of the West Cork Railway as it was during the 1940s and superb miniature models of the main towns in western Cork. Less fun, the **road train** (adult/child incl admission to Railway Village €12/6.25; ⏲daily summer, weekends winter) leaves from the Railway Village on a 20-min-

Clonakilty

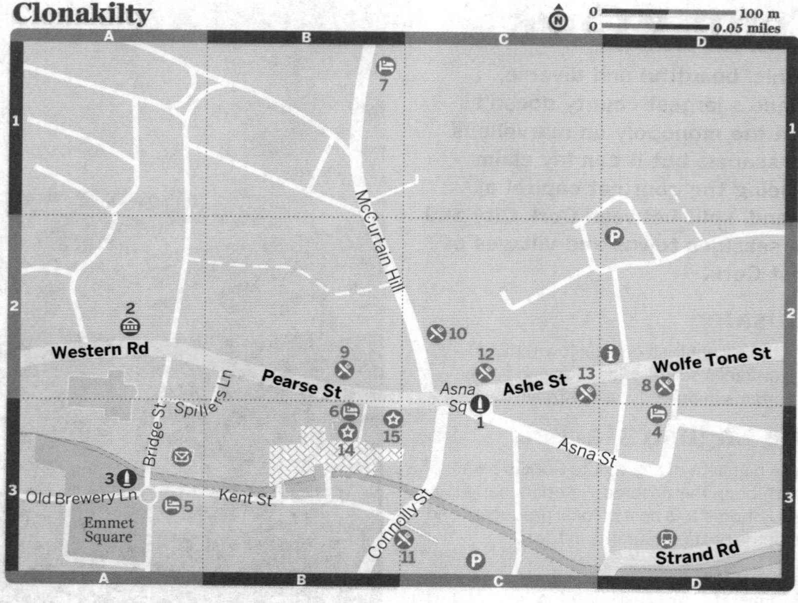

Clonakilty

Sights
1 1798 Rising Monument C3
2 Clonakilty Museum A2
Kilty Stone .... (see 1)
3 Statue of Michael Collins A3

Sleeping
4 An Súgán B&B D3
5 Emmet Hotel A3
6 O'Donovan's Hotel B3
7 Tudor Lodge B1

Eating
8 An Súgán D2
9 Edward Twomey B2
10 Farmers Market C2
11 Gleesons C3
12 Harts C2
13 Malt House Granary C2

Entertainment
14 An Teach Beag B3
15 De Barra's B3

ute circuit of Clonakilty. It's good if you like being cooped up and stared at.

The bay is good for **swimming**, albeit in a bracing sort of way. The sandy Blue Flag **beach** at Inchydoney Island, 4km from town, is good, too, but watch out for the dangerous rip tide; when lifeguards are on duty, a red flag indicates danger. The **West Cork Surf School** (☎086 869 5396; www.westcorksurfing.com) is riding the wave of Irish surfing's recent popularity. A two-hour lesson will set you back €40. In town, **Jellyfish Surf Co** (☎023-883 5890; Spillers Lane) can advise surfers where to go locally.

Sleeping

With one major exception, your best bet is to stay as close to the centre as possible, near the action.

Inchydoney Island Lodge & Spa RESORT HOTEL €€€
(☎023-883 3143; www.inchydoneyisland.com; Inchydoney Island; r mid-week/weekend €190/250;) A superb spa is at the heart of this plush resort hotel, where the service is outstanding, the food delicious and the décor... well, they could do with updating the chic 70s look, but that's a minor quibble with

County Cork

Scenic, beautiful and diverse, Ireland's largest county doesn't have the monopoly on marvellous landscapes, but it can lay claim to being the gourmet capital of Ireland, split between Cork City and the seasides towns and villages of West Cork.

Kinsale

1 The perfect Irish coastal town (p239) combines scenery, location and terrific restaurants in one tidy, alley-strewn package.

The English Market

2 A highlight of any visit to Cork is a walk through this covered Victorian market (p230), home to a host of local producers and one of the best restaurants in town.

Clonakilty

3 A bustling market town (p246) with good B&Bs, great restaurants and top-class pubs featuring great traditional music.

Baltimore

4 The West Cork village of Baltimore (p254) is a mariner's dream, with a cluster of colourful houses gathered around the busy fishing port and pleasure-sailing marina.

PHOTOLIBRARY ©

1

ISTOCK ©

3

Clockwise from top left
1. Bay view, Kinsale 2. Fresh fish at the English Market, Cork City 3. Boats near Clonakilty

2

OLIVER STREWE / LONELY PLANET IMAGES ©

what is otherwise a top class resort, 5km south of Clonakilty.

Emmet Hotel HOTEL €€
(☎023-883 3394; www.emmethotel.com; Emmet Sq; r €65-120; 📶) This lovely Georgian accommodation option on the elegant square happily mixes period charm and old-world service with the perks of a modern hotel. The 20 rooms are large and plush; O'Keeffe's restaurant on site serves up tasty Irish food made from organic and local ingredients.

Bay View House B&B €€
(☎023-883 3539; www.bayviewclonakilty.com; Old Timoleague Rd; s/d €50/80; 📶) This frothy pink house offers immaculate B&B standards, a genial welcome and great breakfasts. Rooms 5 and 6 and the cosy landing lounge offer fantastic views over the fields that slope down to Clonakilty Bay. It is 300m east of the town centre, just off the main N71 roundabout into town.

O'Donovan's Hotel HOTEL €€
(☎023-883 3250; www.odonovanshotel.com; Pearse St; s/d €45/90; 📶) Behind the vintage vivid-red exterior beats the heart of a classic old hotel. Service is simple but friendly. Rooms are straightforward and you can't beat the central location. A WWII plaque out front will intrigue Americans.

Tudor Lodge B&B €€
(☎023-883 3046; www.tudorlodgecork.com; McCurtain Hill; s/d €50/80; 📶) A modern, mock-Tudor family home sitting pleasantly above it all a short walk from the town centre. Standards are kept up to scratch in impeccably smart, peaceful rooms.

An Súgán B&B B&B €€
(☎023-883 3719; www.ansugan.com; Sand Quay; r €50-80; ⊙mid-Mar–Oct) There are few frills at this central B&B, but you do get a relaxed atmosphere and enormous rooms in a great location a couple of doors down from An Súgán restaurant.

Eating

Try to pay a visit to the twice-weekly **farmers market** (McCurtain Hill; ⊙10am-2pm Thu & Sat).

An Súgán MODERN IRISH €€€
(☎023-883 3719; www.ansugan.com; 41 Wolfe Tone St; bar menu €5-25, dinner mains €14-28; ⊙noon-10pm) A traditional bar with a national reputation for excellent seafood. You dine in a room crammed with knick-knacks – jugs dangle from the ceiling, patrons' business cards are stuffed beneath the rafters, and lanterns and even ancient fire-extinguishers dot the walls. But there's nothing idiosyncratic about the food – the seafood chowder is great for a light meal, the crab cakes are memorable and there's a choice of around 10 different kinds of fish, depending on the daily catch.

Malt House Granary MODERN IRISH €€€
(☎023-883 4355; 30 Ashe St; mains €18-25; ⊙5-10pm Mon-Sat) You'll be able to check out the Clonakilty black pudding, Boilie goat's cheese, Gubbeen chorizo and Bantry Bay mussels among other ingredients on the menu at the Malt House, as everything on your plate originates from West Cork. The interior design is a hotchpotch of stylish and kitsch. The seafood platter is a classic.

Harts CAFE €
(☎023-883 5583; 8 Ashe St; meals €5-10; ⊙10am-5pm Mon-Sat) Always busy, this classic city-centre caff surprises with creative takes on standards. Ciabatta sandwiches, fine baked goods, local cheese plates and homemade preserves set the tone.

Gleesons MODERN IRISH €€
(☎023-882 1834; www.gleesons.ie; 3-4 Connolly St; mains €14-22; ⊙6.30-9.30pm Mon-Fri, 6-10pm Sat) Gleesons is a temple of fine dining that melds Irish produce with continental technique. The surrounds are nicely understated, with a wood and slate decor. The seafood, not surprisingly, is tasty. Early diners can enjoy a good value three-course set menu (€35).

Entertainment

TOP CHOICE **De Barra's** PUB
(www.debarra.ie; 55 Pearse St) A marvellous atmosphere, walls splattered with photos, press cuttings, masks and musical instruments, plus the cream of live music every night of the week (starting around 9.30pm) make this a busy pub.

An Teach Beag PUB
(5 Recorder's Alley) This intriguing pub, out back from O'Donovan's Hotel, has all the atmosphere necessary for good traditional music sessions. You might even catch a *scríocht* (a session by storytellers and poets) in full flow. There's music nightly during July and August, and on weekends for

the rest of the year. Check out the historical plaque at the start of the alley – times have changed…

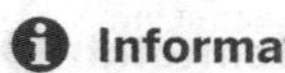

Information

There are public toilets on the corner of Connolly and Kent Sts.

Tourist office (☎023-883 3226; www.clonakilty.ie; Ashe St; ⏲9.30am-5.30pm Mon-Sat Sep-Jun, 9am-7pm Mon-Sat & 10am-5pm Sun Jul & Aug) Has a good, free map.

Post Office In the old Presbyterian chapel on Bridge St.

AIB Bank (cnr Pearse & Bridge Sts) Has an ATM.

Clon Business Solutions (☎023-883 4515; 32 Pearse St; per hr €6; ⏲9am-6pm Mon-Fri, 10am-5pm Sat) Internet access.

Getting There & Away

There are eight daily buses Monday to Saturday and seven Sunday to Cork (€11.50, 65 minutes) and Skibbereen (€8, 40 minutes). Buses stop across from Harte's Spar shop on the bypass going to Cork. Note the alternative way to Kinsale is on the R600.

Getting Around

MTM Cycles (☎023-883 3584; 33 Ashe St) hires bikes for €12 per day. A nice ride is to Duneen Beach, about 13km south of town.

Clonakilty to Skibbereen

Picturesque villages, a fine stone circle and calming coastal scenery mark the less-taken route from Clonakilty to Skibbereen. Rather than follow the main N71 all the way, when you get to Rosscarbery, turn left onto the R597 at the far end of the causeway (signposted Glandore); or, even better, take twice as long and freelance your way along narrow roads near the water the entire way.

DROMBEG STONE CIRCLE

On an exposed hillside, with fields sweeping away towards the coast and bothered cattle braying in the distance, the Drombeg Stone Circle is superbly atmospheric. Its 17 uprights once guarded the cremated bones of an adolescent, discovered during a 1960s excavation. The 9m-diameter circle probably dates from the 5th century AD, representing a sophisticated Iron Age update of an earlier Bronze Age monument.

Just beyond the stones are the remains of a hut and an Iron Age cooking pit, known as a *fulachta fiadh*. Experiments have shown that its heated rocks would boil water and keep it hot for nearly three hours – enough time to cook hunks of meat. Generally quiet, there's usually a few vestiges of private rituals held here.

To get there, take the signposted left turn off the R597, approximately 4km west of Rosscarbery.

> **DON'T MISS**
>
> **THE BEST BLACK PUDDING**
>
> Clonakilty's most treasured export is its black pudding, the blood sausage that features on most local restaurant menus. The best place to buy it is **Edward Twomey** (☎023-883 3733; www.clonakiltyblackpudding.ie; 16 Pearse St; puddings from €2.75), where you can buy different varieties based on the original recipe, formulated in the 1880s.

GLANDORE & UNION HALL

POP 250

The pretty waterside villages of Glandore (Cuan Dor) and Union Hall burst into life in summer when fleets of yachts tack into the shelter of the Glandore Harbour inlet. A tangle of back roads meander across the area; you should, too.

Union Hall, accessible from Glandore via a long narrow causeway over the estuary, was named after the 1800 Act of Union, which abolished the separate Irish parliament. The 1994 film *War of the Buttons*, about two battling gangs of youngsters, was filmed here.

There's an ATM, post office and general store in Union Hall and food is available in both villages. Union Hall has the most choice, with a deli, coffee shop and several pubs, two of which have fantastic waterside terraces.

Sights & Activities

Delightful Theresa O'Mahoney runs the **Ceim Hill Museum** (☎028-36280; adult/child €4/2; ⏲10am-7pm) from her farmhouse off Castletownshend Rd. The small collection of Iron Age bits in the 'Independence' room are worth a glance if you're passing.

You can splash round the coast with **Atlantic Sea Kayaking** (☎028-21058; www.atlanticseakayaking.com; Union Hall; half-day trip €50; ⏲year-round), which offers many tours and classes, including nighttime paddles.

MICHAEL COLLINS – THE 'BIG FELLA'

Born on a farm just outside Clonakilty, Michael Collins is one of County Cork's most famous and beloved sons, the commander-in-chief of the army of the Irish Free State that won independence from Britain in 1922.

He became a key figure in Irish nationalism after the Easter Rising of 1916, revolutionising the way Irish rebels fought by organising them into guerrilla-style 'flying columns' that proved especially effective against the much larger but less mobile British forces ranged against him. His political acumen landed him the job as main negotiator of the 1921 Anglo-Irish Treaty; forced to make major concessions, including the partition of the country, he signed reluctantly, famously declaring that he was signing his own death warrant.

He was tragically correct, as Civil War broke out in the aftermath of the treaty and during a tour of western Cork, Collins was ambushed and killed by anti-Treaty forces on 22 August 1922 at Beal-na-mBláth, near Macroom. Each year, a commemorative service is held on the anniversary of the killing. To visit the site, follow the N22 west from Cork for about 20km, then take the left turn (R590) to Crookstown. From there turn right onto the R585 to Béal-na-mBláth. The ambush site is on the left after 4km.

The useful map and leaflet *In Search of Michael Collins* (€4.50) is available at the Clonakilty tourist office, outlining places in the district associated with him. A visit to the **Michael Collins Centre** (☎023-884 6107; www.michaelcollinscentre.com; adult/child €6/3; ⏲10.30am-5pm Mon-Fri, 11am-2pm Sat mid-Jun-Sep) is an excellent way to make sense of his life and that period of Ireland's history. A tour reveals photos, letters and a reconstruction of the 1920s country lane where Collins was killed, complete with armoured vehicle. The centre runs occasional tours of the crucial locations in Collins' life. It is signposted off the R600 between Timoleague and Clonakilty.

The **Clonakilty Museum** (Western Rd; admission €3; ⏲Jun-Sep) has some more memorabilia, including Collins' weapons and uniform. The museum is run on a voluntary basis; contact the tourist office for exact opening hours.

Two outfits offer whale and dolphin tours year-round from Reen Pier, about 3km beyond Union Hall. Prices average €50/30 per adult/child for half-day cruises.

Whale Watch West Cork WHALE WATCHING
(☎028-33357; www.whalewatchwestcork.com)

Whale Watch with Colin Barnes WHALE WATCHING
(☎086 327 3226; www.whalewatchwithcolinbarnes.com)

Sleeping & Eating

Bay View House B&B €€
(☎028-33115; Glandore; s/d €50/80) The truth: Bay View House has *spectacular* views across the bay. Try to snag Room 1 for the best view of all. Bright citrus colours, tidy pine furniture and gleaming bathrooms add to the appeal. Local pubs are a stumble away.

Meadow Camping Park CAMPSITE €
(☎028-33280; meadowcamping@eircom.net; Rosscarbery Rd, Glandore; campsites €20; ⏲Easter & May–mid-Sep) This small idyllic site, in a garden filled with trees and flowers, is 2km east of Glandore on the R597 to Rosscarbery.

Shearwater B&B B&B €€
(☎028-33178; www.shearwaterbandb.com; Union Hall; s/d €50/70; ⏲Apr-Oct) On a small hill about 500m from the centre of Union Hall, rooms are comfy and there is a large terrace with killer views.

Hayes Bar PUB €€
(☎028-33214; The Square, Glandore; meals €8-20; ⏲kitchen noon-9pm) The food – and the decor – at this perfect portside pub will put you in the pink. Soups, tapas, sandwiches and more are best enjoyed at the picnic tables outside.

Getting There & Away

Buses stop in nearby Leap (3km north), from where most B&B owners will pick you up if you arrange it in advance.

CASTLETOWNSHEND

POP 160

With its grand houses and higgledy-piggledy stone cottages dating back to the 17th and 18th centuries tumbling down the precipitously steep main street, Castletownshend is one of Ireland's most enigmatic villages. At the bottom of the hill is a small quayside and the castle (really a crenellated mansion) after which the village is named. Once you've seen these, you can just put your feet up and relax: you've ticked all the boxes.

The **castle** (☎028-36100; www.castle-townshend.com; r €90-170), sitting imposingly on the waterfront, is a rocky fantasy. Huge mullioned windows obviate any authenticity of the decorative defensive touches. The seven guest rooms range from one with an old four-poster, where you can play 'royal and consort' games, to small but bright rooms, some with terraces and views.

The only way here is by car down the R596 for 8km. A **taxi** (☎028-21258) from Skibbereen costs about €15.

Skibbereen

POP 2300

The busy market town of Skibbereen (Sciobairín) is as close to glitzy as West Cork gets, as the weekending swells and yachties from Dublin descend upon the town with bulging wallets. A far cry from the Famine, when Skib was hit perhaps harder than any other town in Ireland, with huge numbers of the local population emigrating or dying of starvation or disease. 'The accounts are not exaggerated – they cannot be exaggerated – nothing more frightful can be conceived.' So wrote Lord Dufferin and GF Boyle, who journeyed from Oxford to Skibbereen in February 1847 to see if reports of the Famine were true. Their eyewitness account makes horrific reading; Dufferin was so appalled by what he saw that he contributed £1000 (about €100,000 in today's money) to the relief effort.

The main landmark in town is a statue in the central square, dedicated to heroes of Irish rebellions against the British.

Sights

Constructed on the site of the town's old gasworks, the **Skibbereen Heritage Centre** (☎028-40900; www.skibbheritage.com; Old Gasworks Bldg, Upper Bridge St; adult/child €6/3; ⏲10am-6pm) houses a haunting exhibition about the Famine, with actors reading heartbreaking contemporary accounts. A visit here puts Irish history into harrowing perspective. There's also a smaller exhibition about nearby Lough Hyne, the first marine nature reserve in Ireland, and a genealogical centre.

Guided evening **historical walks** (adult/child €5/2.50), lasting 1½ hours, leave from the Heritage Centre. Call ahead to confirm times.

The **Abbeystrewery Cemetery** is a 1km walk east of the centre, on the N71 to Schull, and holds the mass graves of 8000 to 10,000 local people who died during the Famine.

A beautiful and disused **old railway bridge** crosses the river near Ilen St. A **cattle market** on Fridays at the showgrounds is a frenetic, smelly glimpse of rural life.

Sleeping

TOP CHOICE **Bridge House** B&B €€

(☎028-21273; www.bridgehouseskibbereen.com; Bridge St; s/d €40/70; Wi-Fi) Mona Best has turned her entire house into a work of art, filling the rooms with fabulous Victorian tableaux and period memorabilia. The whole place bursts at the seams with cherished clutter, crazed carvings, dressed-up dummies and fragrant fresh flowers. Guests can request black satin sheets.

West Cork Hotel HOTEL €€

(☎028-21277; www.westcorkhotel.com; Ilen St; r €55-150; Wi-Fi) This stolid veteran has 30 comfortable and recently redone rooms next to the river and old railway bridge. The bar is a good retreat; rooms at the back have pastoral views.

Eating

There's a **county market** (⏲12.30-2.30pm) every Friday and a **farmers market** (⏲10am-1.30pm) every Saturday on Old Market Sq. If you're in town in mid-September, don't miss the **Taste of West Cork Food Festival** (www.atasteofwestcork.com), with a lively market and events at local restaurants.

Kalbo's Bistro INTERNATIONAL €€

(☎028-21515; 26 North St; breakfast & lunch €4-11, dinner €17-30; ⏲9am-9pm Mon-Sat year-round, plus 5.30-9.30pm Sun Jul & Aug; family-friendly) This local favourite recently downsized to give the owners a slight break for their well-deserved popularity. But the simply prepared classic meals continue. Locally sourced produce and a deft hand in the kitchen mean that pancakes in the morning and bacon sandwiches at lunch are tops. Dinners are creative.

Over the Moon MODERN IRISH €€

(☎028-22100; 46 Bridge St; lunch €8-14, dinner mains €16-25; ⏲lunch & dinner Wed-Mon, dinner only Sun) The classic deep-blue and white exterior plus the beguiling logo make you want to walk inside; you should. Locally sourced foods (purveyors are listed) star on a creative and changing menu of fresh fare.

Information

Tourist office (☎028-21766; www.skibbereen.ie; North St; ⊙10am-5pm Mon-Fri Sep-May, Sat & Sun Jun-Aug)

Skibbereen Business Services (☎028-23287; 27A Main St; per 10 min €1; ⊙9.30am-6pm Mon-Fri, 10am-5pm Sat) Internet facilities available.

Getting There & Away

Bus Éireann (☎021-450 8188; www.buseireann.ie) runs buses to Cork nine times daily Monday to Saturday, and five on Sunday (€15, 1¾ hours); and to Schull eight times daily Monday to Saturday and six times Sunday (€6, 30 minutes) from outside the former Eldon Hotel on Main St.

Baltimore

POP 400

Crusty old seadog Baltimore is a classic maritime village, its busy little port full of fishing trawlers and pleasure boats. Away from its central terrace overlooking the port are the multitude of holiday cottages that cater to the summer swell that brings sailing folk, anglers, divers and visitors to nearby Sherkin and Clear Islands.

All a far cry from June 20, 1631, when Barbary pirates attacked the village and made off with 108 townspeople, who were sold into slavery in North Africa; only three made it back to Ireland again.

There's an information board at the harbour, or check out www.baltimore.ie. The nearest ATM is in Skibbereen. There's internet access (€4 per hour) at Casey's hotel (see p254).

Sights & Activities

Besides the remains of the **Dun na Sead** (Fort of the Jewels; ☎028-20735; adult/child €3/free; ⊙11am-6pm Jun-Sep), which overlooks the harbour, Baltimore is all about the sea.

There's some excellent **diving** to be had on the reefs around Fastnet Rock; the waters are warmed by the Gulf Stream and a number of shipwrecks lie nearby. **Aquaventures Dive Centre** (☎028-20511; www.aquaventures.ie; Stonehouse B&B, Lifeboat Rd) charges €85 for a full day's diving, and also offers diving and accommodation packages in the attached B&B; contact the centre for prices.

Baltimore Sailing School (☎028-20141; www.baltimoresailingschool.com) provides courses (five days for €340) from May to September for beginners and advanced sailors.

For a shorter taste of the sea, set sail with **Baltimore Yacht Charters** (☎028-20160; www.baltimoreyachtcharters.com), which has a variety of cruises starting at €50. Also leaving from the harbour, **Baltimore Sea Safari** (☎028-20753) has various sailing adventures starting at €30 for 1½ hours.

Information about other diving, sailing and angling operators is posted by the harbour.

A white-painted landmark beacon (aka Lot's Wife) stands on the western headland of the peninsula and makes for a pleasant **walk**, especially at sunset.

Ten kilometres from Baltimore, on the R585 towards Skibbereen, there's good **walking** around **Lough Hyne** and the **Knockamagh Wood Nature Reserve**. Well-marked trails lead around the lake and up a steep hill through the forest. You're rewarded with stunning views at the top.

Festivals & Events

The town goes nuts in May.

Fiddle Fair (www.fiddlefair.com) The second weekend of May, with sessions from international and local musicians.

Walking Festival (www.westcork.ie) Guided walks of Balitmore and the region in mid-May.

Seafood Festival (www.baltimore.ie) Over the last full weekend of May, jazz bands perform and pubs bring out the mussels and prawns; wooden boats parade.

Sleeping

Rolf's Country House GUESTHOUSE €€
(☎028-20289; www.rolfscountryhouse.eu; Baltimore Hill; s/d €50/100; @📶) Upmarket Rolf's, in a much-restored old farmhouse in restful gardens on the outskirts of town, does the lot: there are 14 smartly decorated private rooms, self-catering cottages (from €500 per week), helpful staff and a charming restaurant.

Waterfront HOTEL €€
(☎028-20600; www.water fronthotel.ie; r €50-120; @📶) Smack in the middle of town is this 13-room hotel with small but tidy rooms. Ask for one with a view of the sea.

Casey's of Baltimore HOTEL €€
(☎028-20197; www.caseysofbaltimore.com; Skibbereen Rd; s/d €80/150; @🛜) Ten of the 14 bedrooms here have estuary views and spiffy rooms with huge beds. Eating is a delight as well. The hotel is right at the entrance to town.

Top of the Hill Hostel HOSTEL €
(☎028-20094; www.topofthehillhostel.ie; dm/d €15/44) Everything, from the exterior to the duvets, is white at this beautiful hostel, which is exactly where you'd think but still close to the centre. Sleep securely on sturdy steel bunks. The communal areas consist of a lounge, dining room and kitchen, and there's a lovely garden to the side.

Eating

Glebe Gardens & Café MODERN IRISH €€
(☎028-20232; www.glebegardens.com; meals €15-30; ⏲10am-10pm Wed-Sat, 10am-6pm Sun Apr-Oct) The beautiful gardens here are an attraction in themselves; lavender and herbs add fragrant aromas that waft over the tables inside and out. Food is simple and fresh, sourced from the gardens and a list of local purveyors.

La Jolie Brise INTERNATIONAL €€
(☎028-20600; mains €12-20; ⏲10am-10pm) Part of the Youen Jacob empire that also owns the Waterfront next door, this casual restaurant does excellent food. Enjoy meals (delicious thin-crust pizza and fish and chips) at the plethora of picnic tables on the square in front of the Waterfront guesthouse.

Casey's of Baltimore SEAFOOD €€
(☎028-20197; lunches €4-10, mains €14-28; ⏲12.30-3pm & 6.30-9pm, bar meals all day) At Casey's your food comes with fantastic views, whether you call in for breakfast, sandwiches or a tasty dinner. Seafood includes mussels fresh from the hotel's own shellfish farm in Roaringwater Bay, and the hotel specialty, crab claws in garlic butter.

Chez Youen SEAFOOD €€
(☎028-20136; The Quay; dinner from €30; ⏲6-10pm, closed Nov & Feb) This Breton-inspired restaurant was the town's gourmet pioneer and it's still as good as ever. The luscious shellfish platter (€50), containing lobster, prawns, brown crab, velvet crab, shrimps and oysters, offers the chance to sample shellfish at its unadorned best.

Drinking

Bushe's Bar PUB
(www.bushesbar.com; The Quay) Seafaring paraphernalia literally drips from the ceiling at this genuinely character-filled old bar. The benches outside on the main square are the best spots in town for a sundowner and you can watch sailors get misty at the nautical views. Famous crab sandwiches are served at times.

Getting There & Away

There are four daily buses weekdays and three times over the weekend between Skibbereen and Baltimore (€3.70, 20 minutes).

Cape Clear Island

POP 150

With its lonely inlets, pebbly beaches, gorse- and heather-covered cliffs, Cape Clear Island (Oileán Chléire; Cape Clear Island) is an escapist's heaven – albeit one that is only 5km long and just over 1.5km wide at its broadest point. But that's just as well, as you'll want time to appreciate this small, rugged Gaeltacht (Irish-speaking) area, the southernmost inhabited island in the country. It's a place for quiet walks, hunting down standing stones and birdwatching. Soon you'll catch the alternative, independent vibe of the place.

Facilities are few, but there are a couple of B&Bs, one shop and three pubs.

Sights

The small **heritage centre** (☎028-39119; admission €3; ⏲2.30-5pm Jun-Aug) has exhibits on the island's history and culture, and fine views north across the water to Mizen Head.

The ruins of 14th-century **Dunamore Castle**, the stronghold of the O'Driscoll clan, can be seen perched on a rock on the northwestern side of the island (follow the track from the harbour). The great hall lives up to its name and is sometimes open for tours (€3) when visitors turn up.

Activities

Birdwatching

Cape Clear is one of the top birdwatching spots in Ireland, particularly known for sea birds, including Manx shearwater, gannet, fulmar and kittiwake. Guillemot breed on the island, but other birds head to and fro on hunting trips from the rocky outposts of the western peninsulas. Tens of thousands of birds can pass hourly, especially in the early morning and at dusk. The best time of year for twitching here is October.

The white-fronted **bird observatory** is by the harbour (turn right at the end of the pier and it's 100m along). It's worth calling in to ask about any planned birdwatching trips.

Walking

There are marked trails all over the island, and B&Bs and the tourist information post can advise on other walks. For **guided walks** covering historical, archaeological or ecological aspects of the island, phone 028-39157 (during summer); for walks focused on literature and culture, phone 028-39190.

Courses

Once you're this isolated, you might as well learn something.

Ionad Foghlama Chléire (Cape Clear Island Language Services; 028-39190; www.cleire.com) runs Irish-language programs for adults.

Besides running the bird observatory, **BirdWatch Ireland** (www.birdwatchireland.ie) runs birdwatching field courses to Cape Clear. Details are on the website and the group has a small house so birdwatchers can stay the night.

For everything you need to know about goat husbandry, contact Ed Harper at **Chléire Goats** (028-39126; www.oilean-chleire.ie/english/goats.htm), based at a farm west of the church. He makes ice cream and cottage cheese, available for tastings, and runs half-day (€35) to week-long (€155) courses on goat keeping.

Festivals & Events

The **Cape Clear Island International Storytelling Festival** (028-39157; www.capeclearstorytelling.com; weekend ticket €65) brings hundreds of people to Cape Clear Island for storytelling, workshops and walks, as summer wanes in early September.

Sleeping & Eating

Accommodation on the island is satisfyingly unfancy. Book ahead, especially between May and September. Ask for directions to all of the following:

Chléire Haven CAMPSITE €
(028-39119; www.yurt-holidays-ireland.com; per person €10; Jun-Sep) There's campsites here and also yurts and tepees. The latter require multiple-day stays (a good thing) and start at €190 for two nights in high season.

Cluain Mara B&B €€
(028-39153, 028-39172; www.capeclearisland.com; North Harbour; r €54-70;) There are self-catering cottages here at the isolated end of the already isolated island. The pub does home-cooked meals (€8 to €12) throughout the year.

Cape Clear Island Hostel HOSTEL €
(028-41968; www.mamut.net/anoigecapeclear; Old Coastguard Station, South Harbour; dm from €20; @) In a large white building at the south harbour, amid lovely gardens.

Ard Na Gaoithe B&B €€
(028-39160; www.oilean-chleire.ie/english/leonard.htm; The Glen; r from €70) Has restful rooms in a simple sturdy house.

Information

Tourist information post (028-39100; 11am-1pm & 3-6pm May-Aug) Beyond the pier, next to the coffee shop.

Internet resource (www.oilean-chleire.ie) Good links to a surprising number of books written about the island.

Getting There & Away

From Baltimore, the ferry **Naomh Ciarán II** (028-39153; www.capeclearferry.com; adult/child return €16/8) takes 45 minutes to cover the 11km journey to Clear Island and it's a stunning trip on a clear day. There are four sailings daily from June to mid-September, with the earliest leaving at 11am and the latest returning at 7pm, and at least two per day the rest of the year. Bicycles travel free.

From Schull, the **Cape Clear Island ferry** (028-28278; www.capeclearferries.com; 10.30am, 2.30pm & 4.30pm Jun-Aug, 2.30pm Sep; adult/child return €14/7) leaves from the pier. The trip takes 45 minutes.

Gougane Barra Forest Park

Gougane Barra (www.gouganebarra.com) is a truly magical part of inland County Cork. It's almost alpine in feel, with spectacular vistas of craggy mountains, silver streams and pine forests sweeping down to a mountain lake, the source of the River Lee. St Finbarre, the founder of Cork, established a monastery here in the 6th century. He had a hermitage on the island in **Gougane Barra Lake** (Lough an Ghugain), which is now approached by a short causeway. The small **chapel** on the island has fine stained-glass representations of obscure Celtic saints. A road runs through the park in a loop, but you're better off slowing down and walking the well-marked network of paths and **nature trails** through the forest.

The area cries out for a hostel, but the only place to air your hiking boots is the **Gougane Barra Hotel** (☎026-47069; www.gouganebarrahotel.com; r from €99). There's an on-site restaurant (serving a hearty dinner for €42), a cafe and a pub next door. The hotel runs a summer theatre festival.

Getting There & Away

Bus connections to the park will make you feel like an explorer. Call the hotel for details and possible pick-up part way.

The Macroom **tourist office** (☎026-43280; ⏲summer only) can help with accommodation in town if needed. Alternatively, take a **taxi** (☎026-41152) from Macroom for around €35, or possibly organise a tour from Bantry.

The park is signposted on the R584 after Ballingeary. Returning to the main road afterwards and continuing west, you'll travel over the Pass of Keimaneigh and emerge on the N71 at Ballylickey, midway between the Beara Peninsula and the Sheep's Head Peninsula

MIZEN HEAD PENINSULA

From Skibbereen the road rolls west through Ballydehob, the gateway to the Mizen, and then on to the pretty village of Schull. Travelling on into the undulating countryside takes you through ever-smaller settlements to the village of Goleen.

Even here the Mizen isn't done. Increasingly narrow roads head further west to spectacular Mizen Head itself and to the hidden delights of Barleycove Beach and Crookhaven. Without a decent map you may well reach the same crossroads several times.

Heading back from Goleen, you can bear north to join the scenic coast road that follows the edge of Dunmanus Bay for most of the way to Durrus. At Durrus, one road heads for Bantry while the other turns west to Sheep's Head Peninsula.

Schull

POP 700

The boating and creative crowd (often the same folk) have turned the small fishing village of Schull (pronounced 'skull') into a buzzing little metropolis, even if the regular townsfolk still go about their business as before, when the busy harbour was the main focus of their attentions. Today, a cluster of vessels keep the port alive, but there are also craft shops and art galleries to distract the visitor. It's particularly crowded during Calves Week, a sailing regatta usually held after the August bank holiday.

Schull also has a popular **Sunday Country Market** (www.schullmarket.com; Pier Car Park; ⏲Easter-Dec), which draws producers and purveyors from around the region.

Sights & Activities

Founded by a German visitor who fell in love with Schull, the Republic's only **planetarium** (☎028-28552; www.schullcommunitycollege.com; Colla Rd; adult/child €5/3.50; Jun-Sep) is on the grounds of Schull Community College. A 45-minute **star show** starts at 4pm or 8pm during the rather complex opening hours; call to confirm times.

The planetarium is at the Goleen end of the village on Colla Rd. You can also reach it by walking along the foreshore path from the pier.

There are a number of **walks** in the area, including a 13km return trip up **Mt Gabriel** (407m). It was once mined for copper, and there are Bronze Age remains and 19th-century mine shafts and chimneys. For a gentler stroll try the short 2km foreshore path from the pier out to **Roaringwater Bay** and a view of the nearby islands. These and other walking routes are outlined in *Schull Visitor's Guide*.

The **Schull Watersport Centre** (☎028-28554; The Pier) hires out sailing dinghies (€65 per half-day) and snorkelling gear (€15 per day), and can arrange sea-kayaking sessions (a two-hour session costs €35) plus other activities, like sailing lessons.

In addition to running courses and dives to wreck and reef sites, **Divecology** (☎028-28943; www.divecology.com; Cooradarrigan) offers guided walks along the shore looking for spiny critters. Check around the dock for charter boats going out fishing.

Horse- and pony-trekking and trap rides are available at the **Ballycumisk Riding School** (☎028-37246, 087 961 6969; Ballycumisk), outside Schull on the way to Ballydehob, for €30 per hour.

Sleeping & Eating

Grove House B&B €€
(☎028-28067; www.grovehouseschull.com; Colla Rd; s/d €75/100;) This beautifully restored ivy-covered mansion has lovely pine floors and is exquisitely decorated in an easygoing antiques-and-homemade-rugs style. It also has a terrific **restaurant** (mains €15-24; ⊙Wed-Mon Jul & Aug, Thu-Sat Sep-Jun) that is open to non-guests where Swedish influences combine with Irish staples and a substantial wine list to make for a memorable dining experience.

Corthna-Lodge Guesthouse B&B €€
(☎028-28517; www.corthna-lodge.net; Airhill; s/d from €65/90;) The pleasures come aplenty at this rambling modern home just outside the centre. There's an outdoor hot tub, sauna house and gym. Should you just need to pass out, the seven rooms have a sprightly decor and attractive furniture that will help you reawaken.

TOP CHOICE **Hackett's** MODERN IRISH €€
(Main St; ⊙lunch daily year-round, dinner Wed & Thu Jul & Aug, Fri & Sat year-round; bar meals €4-9, dinner €15-20) The town's social hub, Hackett's rises above the norm with a creative pub menu of organic dishes prepared from scratch. Black-and-white photos and tin signs adorn the pub's crooked walls and there's a mishmash of old kitchen tables and benches on the worn stone floor. It's a democratic place, where swells mingle with crusty locals inside or out front on the sunny benches.

Newman's West PUB FOOD €
(☎028-27776; www.tjnewmans.com; Main St; dishes €6-15; ⊙9am-11pm;) This sailor-filled wine bar (with many good choices by the glass) and art gallery serves soup and salads and enormous chunky sandwiches filled with local cheese and salami. The daily Western Seaboard specials might include Bantry Bay mussels and chowder. The original pub, TJ Newman's, is a charmer.

Information

Allied Irish Bank (Main St) ATM and bureau de change.

@Your Service (☎028-28600; Main St; per 30/60min €3/6; ⊙10am-10pm summer, shorter hr winter) Internet access and tourist info.

Internet resource (www.schull.ie)

Getting There & Away

There are two buses daily from Cork to Schull (€17.30, 2½ hours), via Clonakilty and Skibbereen.

Getting Around

Betty Johnson's Bus Hire (☎028-28410, 086 265 6078) Bus and taxi service

West of Schull to Mizen Head

If you're driving or cycling, take the undulating coastal route from Schull to Goleen. On a clear day there are great views out to Clear Island and the Fastnet lighthouse. The landscape becomes wilder around the hamlet of Toormore. From Goleen, roads run out to thrilling Mizen Head and to the picturesque harbour village of Crookhaven.

Take time to admire the old local houses that are made of stone, many now derelict in fields. While there's obviously no shortage of materials, building these houses to withstand Atlantic gales required enormous amounts of labour on the part of locals, already challenged by the unreliable fertility of the land.

GOLEEN

Tourism in the Goleen area is handled well by the local community, with the intriguing **Mizen Head Signal Station** (p260) being a token of their commitment and imagination. In summer it hums with holidaymakers.

Sleeping & Eating

Fortview House B&B €€
(☎028-35324; www.fortviewhouse.ie; Gurtyowen, Toormore; s/d €50/100; ⊙Apr-Oct) Out on its own, in terms of location, warmth *and* quality, this lovely house has five antique-filled, flower-themed bedrooms. Hospitable hostess Violet has the most infectious laugh ever, and her breakfast choice is gourmet standard, with eggs from cheerfully clucking hens in the garden. To get there, head along the road that turns off the R592 for Durrus about 1km northeast of Goleen.

Rock Cottage B&B €€
(☎028-35538; www.rockcottage.ie; Barnatonicane, Schull; s/d €100/140) This slate-clad Georgian hunting lodge has three rooms, which stylishly mix antique furniture and modern textiles for an elegant yet cheery effect. Rock Cottage is also a working 17-acre farm (you can commune with a sheep) and many of the ingredients on the evening set menu (€52) come from the surrounding fields. To find it, continue 1km up the road from Fortview House and go through the gate on your left.

Heron's Cove B&B, RESTAURANT €€
(☎028-35225; www.heronscove.com; Goleen; s/d €40/80) A delightful location, on the shores of the tidal inlet of Goleen Harbour, makes this fine restaurant and B&B a top choice. Rooms have been refurbished to a restful style and several have balconies overlooking the inlet. The small restaurant has an excellent menu of organic and local food. It's open for dinner April to October (and year-round for guests staying at the Heron's Cove). Mains are between €16 and €25. Book in summer.

Getting There & Away

Bus Éireann (www.buseireann.ie) has two buses a day from Skibbereen (€10, 70 minutes) via Schull. Goleen is the end of the line for bus service on the peninsula.

CROOKHAVEN

Onwards from Goleen, the westerly outpost of Crookhaven feels so remote that you imagine it's more easily reached by boat than by road. And so it is for some people – in summer there's a big yachting presence and Crookhaven bustles with life. Off season it's quiet.

In its heyday Crookhaven's natural harbour was an important anchorage. Mail from America was collected here, and sailing ships and fishing vessels found ready shelter. On the opposite shore the gaunt remains of quarry buildings, closed in 1939, lie embedded in the hillside, and are the source of many dubious yarns by locals in response to curious questions from visitors.

Sleeping & Eating

Pints in the sunshine are the reward for venturing out on the crooked road to Crookhaven. (If it's raining, make that 'Pints by the fireplace...').

Galley Cove House B&B €€
(☎028-35137; www.galleycovehouse.com; s/d €55/90) A cheerful welcome complements the secluded location of this modern home, 2km from Crookhaven and with terrific views across the ocean. It's handy for Barleycove Beach, and the pine-floored rooms are clean, airy and filled with light.

Crookhaven Inn PUB FOOD €€
(☎028-35309; mains €5-20; ⏲12.30-8pm Apr-Oct) Set discreetly back from the water, this stone cottage of a pub also has a bulwark of picnic tables outside. The food here is an ambitious take on pub grub; seafood, of course, is tops. In summer there are trad music sessions many nights.

O'Sullivan's Bar PUB FOOD €
(☎028-35319; meals €5-15; ⏲kitchen noon-8pm) A timeless building right on the harbour. Several generations' of picnic tables draw several generations of punters when there's even a hint of sun. Pub food like seafood chowder and fried shrimp is popular – and good.

BROW HEAD

This is the southernmost point on the Irish mainland and is well worth the walk. As you leave Crookhaven, you'll notice a turn-off to the left marked 'Brow Head'. If travelling by car, park at the bottom of the hill – the track is very narrow and there's nowhere to pull over should you meet a tractor coming the other way. After 1km the road ends. Continue on a path to Brow Head where you'll see an **observation tower**, from which Guglielmo Marconi transmitted his first radio message (to Cornwall) that received a reply.

BARLEYCOVE

Vast sand dunes hemmed in by two long bluffs dissolve into the surf, forming western Cork's finest beach. Rarely crowded, it's a great place for youngsters, with gorgeous stretches of golden sand, a safe bathing area where a stream flows down to the sea, lifeguards in July and August, and a Blue Flag award marking the cleanliness of the water. Access is via a long boardwalk and pontoon, which protect the surrounding wetlands from the impact of visitors' feet. There's a car park at the edge of the beach, on the south side of the causeway on the road to Crookhaven.

Barleycove Beach Hotel (☎028-35234; www.barleycovebeachhotel.com; Barleycove; r from €65, 2-bedroom self-catering per week €420) The only thing interrupting the view is this

WORTH A TRIP

DURRUS CHEESE

Durrus has earned an international reputation for its marvellous cheese, thanks to the likes of **Durrus Farmhouse** (027-61100; Coomkeen, Durrus; 10.30am-12pm Thu-Fri), whose produce is sold all over Ireland, the UK and even the United States. You can't visit the production area, so you'll have to make do with an informal presentation by Jeffa Gill that lasts about 10 minutes. You can, however, buy all the cheese you want. To get to the farm, go 900m out of Durrus along the Ahakista road, turn right at St James' Church and continue for 3km until you see the sign for the farm.

modern aberration, from whose broad terrace you can sit and admire the view! A mere 200m away from the sand, the rooms are simply finished, with beach views, and there's a bar-restaurant with outdoor seating. Bring ear plugs – the bedroom walls are thin.

Near the beach on the other side of the bay, **Barleycove Holiday Park** (028-35302; Barleycove; campsite €18; mid-Apr–mid-Sep;) is an ideally located camping ground with bike rental, shop and children's club.

MIZEN HEAD SIGNAL STATION

Ireland's most southwesterly point is dominated by this **signal station** (028-35225/115; www.mizenhead.ie; Mizen Head; adult/child €6/3.50; 10am-6pm), a complex completed in 1909 to help warn ships off the rocks, which appear in the water around here like crushed ice in a cola.

Like many Victorian-era public works, it exudes the pride of the builders. From the visitors centre, you can take various pathways out to the station, culminating in the crossing of a spectacular **arched bridge** that spans a vast gulf in the cliffs. The views are simply stunning, with spurting plumes of white water in every direction.

The station is beyond the bridge, at the far point of the outer rock island, and contains the **keeper's quarters**, **engine room** and **radio room**: you can see how the keepers lived and how the station worked (until its automation in 1993), but the real rush (even among crowds on a busy day) is the sense of so much Atlantic beneath vast skies.

Back at the visitors centre is **Fastnet Hall**, with plenty of information about local ecology, history and the namesake lighthouse. There's also a modest **cafe**.

Northside of the Peninsula

Although the landscape is less dramatic on this side of the peninsula, it's well worth driving along the coast road here for the great views out to Sheep's Head Peninsula and beyond to the magnificent Beara Peninsula.

DURRUS

POP 900

This perky little crossroads at the head of Dunmanus Bay has become something of a gourmet hot spot in recent years as well as serving as the access point for both the Mizen Head and Sheep's Head peninsulas.

Travel a world of plants at **Kilravock Garden** (027-61111; Ahakista Rd; adult/child €6/3; 10am-6.30pm Mon-Sat May-Sep;), which has been transformed over two decades from a field of scrag and stone to a feast of exotic plants by one green-fingered couple.

Sleeping & Eating

TOP CHOICE **Blair's Cove House** B&B €€€
(027-61127; www.blairscove.ie; r €120-260; Mar-Jan) Set in five acres of land, this magnificent Georgian country house looks like it belongs in a style magazine. Centred around an exquisite courtyard are superbly appointed rooms and a self-catering apartment dripping with elegance. The **restaurant** (dinner Tue-Sat, lunch Sunday Mar-Oct), in a chandeliered hall, offers a superb set three-course dinner (€58) with local produce given international treatment. Booking is advised.

TOP CHOICE **Good Things Café** MODERN IRISH €€
(027-61426; www.thegoodthingscafe.com; Ahakista Rd; lunch mains €10-20, dinner mains €21-38; 12.30-3pm & 7-9pm Thu-Mon mid-Jun–Dec) This foodie haven right on Dunmanus Bay serves great contemporary dishes made with organic, locally sourced ingredients; think everything from a fluffy omelette with locally smoked haddock, to grilled lobster. Tables on a vast terrace have views of nervous sheep. Popular cooking courses include a two-day Kitchen Miracle program (€375) for those whose cooking skills stop after reading the microwave directions on the frozen meal.

Bantry

POP 3300

Framed by the craggy Caha Mountains, vast, magnificent Bantry Bay is one of the country's most attractive inlets and a worthwhile stop on any West Cork itinerary. Pride of place goes to Bantry House, the former home of one Richard White, who earned his place in history when in 1798 he warned authorities of the imminent landing of patriot Wolfe Tone and his French fleet in their effort to join the countrywide rebellion of the United Irishmen (see p698). In the end storms prevented the fleet from landing and the course of Irish history was definitively altered – all Wolfe Tone got for his troubles was a square and a statue bearing his name.

Bantry struggled through the 19th century due to famine, poverty and mass emigration but today it's a prosperous town thanks to commerce and the bay: you'll see Bantry oysters and mussels on menus throughout County Cork.

Sights

With its melancholic air of faded gentility, 18th-century **Bantry House** (☎027-50047; www.bantryhouse.com; Bantry Bay; adult/child €10/3; ⊙10am-6pm mid-Mar–Oct) makes for an intriguing visit. The house has belonged to the White family since 1729 and every room brims with treasures brought back from each generation's travels since then. The entrance is paved with mosaics from Pompeii, French and Flemish tapestries adorn the walls, and Japanese chests sit next to Russian shrines. Upstairs, worn bedrooms look out wanly over an astounding view of the bay – the 18th-century Whites had ringside seats to the French armada. Experienced pianists are invited to tinkle the ivories of the ancient piano in the library. It's possible to stay the night in the wings.

The **gardens** of Bantry House are its great glory. Lawns sweep down from the front of the house towards the sea, and the formal Italian garden has an enormous 'stairway to the sky', offering spectacular views.

In the former stables you'll find the **1796 French Armada Exhibition Centre**, with its powerful account of the doomed French invasion of Ireland. The fleet was torn apart by storms; one frigate, *La Surveillante,* was scuttled by its own crew and today lies 30m down at the bottom of the bay.

Bantry House is 1km southwest of the town centre on the N71.

Festivals & Events

West Cork Chamber Music Festival

(www.westcork music.ie) Held at Bantry House for a week in June/July, when the house closes to the public. The garden, craft shop and tearoom remain open.

Sleeping

Ballylickey House B&B €€

(☎027-50071; www.ballylickeymanorhouse.com; Ballylickey; r €90-180; ⊙Mar-Nov;) Possessing a name that rolls off the tongue, Ballylickey is a beautiful manor house with manicured lawns overlooking the bay. There are two choices for the night: rooms in the house or cute cottages set round a swimming pool. All are spacious and comfortably furnished.

Bantry House MANOR HOUSE €€€

(☎027-50047; www.bantryhouse.com; Bantry Bay; r €180-250; ⊙Mar-Oct;) Bantry House's guest rooms, decorated in pale hues and a mixture of antiques and contemporary furnishings, are luxurious places to while away the hours. Rooms 22 and 25 are double winners, with views of both the garden and the bay. Enhance the dream by playing croquet, lawn tennis or billiards and lounging in the house's library once the doors are shut to the public. And if you see French ships offshore, tell absolutely nobody – White's actions may have earned him English kudos, but the Irish weren't overly impressed!

Sea View House Hotel HOTEL €€

(☎027-50073; www.seaviewhousehotel.com; Ballylickey; s €85-95, r €100-205;) You'll find everything you'd expect from a luxury hotel here: country-house ambience, tastefully decorated public rooms, expansive service and 25 cosy, posh bedrooms. The hotel is on the N71, 5km northeast of Bantry.

Eagle Point Camping CAMPSITE €

(☎027-50630; www.eaglepointcamping.com; Glengarriff Rd, Ballylickey; campsites from €29; ⊙May-Sep) An enviable location at the end of a filigreed promontory 6km north of Bantry makes this a popular site. Most of the 125 spots have sea views, and there's direct access to the pebbly beaches nearby.

Mill B&B B&B €€
(☎027-50278; Glengarriff Rd; www.the-mill.net; r from €75; ⊙Easter-Oct) This modern house, on the immediate outskirts of town, oozes individuality. The irrepressible landlady, Tosca, is just part of it. The rooms are a riot of knick-knacks, and the spacious dining room has a wonderful collection of Indonesian puppets and Tosca's art to accompany solid breakfasts.

Bantry Bay Hotel HOTEL €€
(☎027-50062; www.bantrybayhotel.ie; Wolfe Tone Sq; r €60-140; @📶) Most of the 14 rooms overlook the square, with glimpses of the bay. Nothing about the decor will surprise and, in fact, there's nothing to keep you in your room and forgo local explorations. The bar's maritime theme may put you in the mood to hoist the mizzen-mast.

Eating

Wolfe Tone Sq takes on a heady mix of aromas for the **Friday Market**, which draws in the masses – both vendors and shoppers – from a wide area.

TOP CHOICE **Fish Kitchen** MODERN IRISH €€
(☎027-56651; New St; mains €8-20; ⊙noon-9pm Tue-Sat) This outstanding little restaurant above a fish shop does seafood to perfection, from the local oysters (served with lemon and tabasco sauce) to a particularly fine dish of pan-seared scallops. But if for some reason you don't fancy sea fare, it does a juicy steak too. Friendly, unfussy and absolutely delicious.

Stuffed Olive DELI €
(☎027-55883; New St; meals €4-7; ⊙8am-5pm Mon-Sat) This exquisite bakery and deli has a fine coffee bar and stools along a narrow counter in the sunny front window. Luscious baked goods are displayed like, well, a bunch of tarts. Find your picnic lunch here and nab one of the excellent bottles of wine.

Organico DELI, VEGETARIAN €€
(☎027-51391; 2 Glengariff Rd; lunch €8-15; ⊙9.30am-5.30pm Mon-Sat; 📶) The milk in the organic latte here is fairtrade – just one example of the green ethos prevalent throughout this very attractive bakery-deli-cafe. Enjoy fine baked goods throughout the day; at lunch there's an array of daily specials. The soups are hearty and fresh, the salads innovative. Everything is meat-free but not dairy-free: cheese lovers, enjoy!

Drinking & Entertainment

Crowley's PUB
(Wolfe Tone Sq) One of the best bars for music, Crowley's has traditional bands on Wednesday nights.

Anchor Tavern PUB
(New St) Old salts literally anchor the bar; enjoy a pint and ponder the many old nautical instruments on display – although they may not help you get home after a few.

Information

Tourist office (☎027-50229; Wolfe Tone Sq; ⊙9.15am-5pm Mon-Sat Apr-Oct) In the old courthouse.

Post office (Blackrock Rd)

Allied Irish Bank (Wolfe Tone Sq) ATM

Fast.Net Business Services (☎027-51624; Bridge St; per 10/60 min €1/5; ⊙9am-6pm Mon-Fri, 10am-5pm Sat)

Getting There & Away

Bus Éireann (www.buseireann.ie) has eight buses daily Monday to Saturday (four on Sunday) between Bantry and Cork (€15.50, two hours). There's one or two daily to Glengarriff. Heading

SHIPLAKE MOUNTAIN HOSTEL

Far up a twisting track lies one of Cork's most unusual hostels. The IHH-affiliated **Shiplake Mountain Hostel** (☎023-884 5750; www.shiplakemountainhostel.com; Dunmanway; campsite €7, dm €18, d €45-50; ⊙Apr-Oct; 📶) consists of three brightly coloured gypsy caravans (each with a double bed squeezed in), two dorms in an old stone cottage and a traditional farmhouse that sleeps up to four. The owners take their environmental responsibility seriously – the showers use local spring water and you can have the hostel's own duck eggs for breakfast. They can pick you up from nearby Dunmanway, which has an ATM and grocery shops. Once here, chase the ducks, go for walks (scads of maps and advice available), borrow a bike (free) or gather round the stove in the common room for a good yarn.

WORTH A TRIP

WALK: MT SEEFIN

Make time for an exhilarating 1km stride to the summit of Mt Seefin (345m). It's not challenging, but this is open country, where mist can easily descend, so go properly equipped. There's a path, but it fades out in places.

The ascent begins at the top of the Goat's Path Rd, halfway (about 2km from each) between Gortnakilly and Kilcrohane. On the roadside is an out-of-place imitation of Michelangelo's *Pietà* – follow the track that starts opposite the parking area on the south side of the sculpture. Keep to the path along the rocky spine of the hill until you reach a depression. Follow a path up a short gully to the right of a small cliff and then continue, again on the rocky spine of the broad ridge, to a trig point on the summit. Retracing your steps can be challenging. From the trig point it's best to keep high along the broad ridge and not drift too far to the left.

north to the Ring of Beara, Kenmare and Killarney requires backtracking through Cork.

Bantry Rural Transport (☎027-52727; www.ruraltransport.ie; 5 Main St) runs a useful series of circular routes to Dunmanway, Durrus, Goleen, Schull, Skibbereen and outlying villages. There's a set price of €4/6 one-way/return. Service is not frequent; check the website for details.

Getting Around

Bicycles can be hired at **Nigel's Bicycle Shop** (☎027-52657; Glengarriff Rd; per day/week €15/60).

SHEEP'S HEAD PENINSULA

The least visited of Cork's three peninsulas, Sheep's Head Peninsula has a charm all its own – and plenty of sheep. There are good seascapes to appreciate from the loop road running along most of its length. A good link road with terrific views, called the Goat's Path Rd, runs between Gortnakilly and Kilcrohane (on the north and south coasts respectively), over the western flank of Mt Seefin.

Ahakista (Atha an Chiste) consists of a couple of pubs and a few houses stretched out along the R591. An ancient **stone circle** is signposted at the southern end of Ahakista; access is via a short pathway. The peninsula's other village is **Kilcrohane**, 6km to the southwest, beside a fine **beach**. You can get pub food in both villages.

For more information about the area, take a look at the **website** (www.thesheepshead.com).

Walking & Cycling

Walkers and cyclists will relish the chance to stretch their legs and enjoy the windswept **moors**, wild gorse, foxgloves and fuchsias in beautiful solitude. On the Goat's Path Rd, the steep Bantry-Kilcrohane section requires firm thighs; the Ahakista-Durrus stretch is more gentle. Bantry's tourist office (see p262) can book accommodation along the Sheep's Head Way, has lots of info on the peninsula and sells a map and guide (€12.50).

The **Sheep's Head Way** is an 88km-long walking route around the peninsula, on roads and tracks where possible. Use Ordnance Survey maps 85 and 88 to navigate your way around (see www.osi.ie to purchase maps). There are no campsites on Sheep's Head Peninsula; camping along the route is allowed with permission from the landowner.

The 120km **Sheep's Head Cycle Route** runs anticlockwise from Ballylickey, round the coastline of Sheep's Head Peninsula, back onto the mainland and down to Ballydehob. There are opportunities to take short cuts or alternative routes (eg over the Goat's Path Rd, or along the coast from Ahakista to Durrus). The widely available brochure, *The Sheep's Head Cycle Route*, has full details.

Getting There & Away

Bantry Rural Transport (☎027-52727; www.ruraltransport.ie; 5 Main St, Bantry) buses run a circular route on various days, going via the Goat's Path Rd to Kilcrohane and Durrus (one-way/return €4/6; nine daily).

BEARA PENINSULA (RING OF BEARA)

The Beara Peninsula is the third major 'ring' (circular road around a peninsula) in the west. Dingle and Kerry are comfortably in the number one and two spots respectively, leaving Beara in third place, which is just about right. A small part of the peninsula lies in Kerry, but is covered here for the convenience of people travelling the Ring of Beara. Castletownbere in Cork and Kenmare in Kerry make good bases for exploring the area.

You can easily drive the 137km around the coast in one day, but you would miss the spectacular **Healy Pass Road** (R574), which cuts across the peninsula from Cork to Kerry. In fact, if pressed for time, skip the rest and do the pass.

The south side, along Bantry Bay, is a series of interesting working fishing villages and scenery that's mild on the eyes. The north side, in contrast, is often a stunner, with craggy drives in and out of the nooks and crannies of the peninsula. A plus is that many of these roads are off the tourist trail.

Other highlights include a thrillingly wobbly **cable car** at the tip of the peninsula, which takes you and the sheep out to tiny **Dursey Island** and exhilarating hill walking requiring some skill and commitment, as well as proper clothing and navigational experience.

The 196km **Beara Way** is a signposted walk linking Glengarriff with Kenmare (in Kerry) via Castletownbere, Bere Island, Dursey Island and the north side of the peninsula; for more details, see p264. The 138km **Beara Way Cycle Route** takes a similar direction, passing through all the villages on Beara via small lanes.

The following towns are described in a route that assumes you're starting from Glengarriff and working your way clockwise to Kenmare.

Glengarriff

POP 1100

Hidden deep in the Bantry Bay area, Glengarriff (Gleann Garbh) is an attractive village that snares plenty of passers-by in need of sweaters.

The rough, rocky **Caha Mountains** make for good hill walking. There are plenty of gentler strolls, too, in mature oak woodlands and through the coastal Blue Pool Amenity Area, where seals, perched on submerged rocks, appear to levitate on the water.

In the second half of the 19th century, Glengarriff became a popular retreat for prosperous Victorians, who sailed from England, took the train to Bantry, then chugged over to the village in a paddle steamer. By 1850 the road to Kenmare had been blasted through the mountains and the link with Killarney was established. Today Glengarriff lies on the main Cork to Killarney road (N71).

Sights

If you're becalmed in town, wander down past the Blue Ferry pier and enjoy good **nature walks** along the coast. Signs with maps show you your options. Try to spot a seal.

Garinish (Ilnacullin) Island GARDENS

(☎027-63040; www.heritageireland.ie; adult/senior & child €4/3; ⏲10am-6.30pm, from 11am Sun Jun-Sep, to 4pm Oct, last admission 1hr before closing) The magical **Italianate garden** on Garinish Island is the top sight in Glengarriff. Subtropical plants flourish in the rich soil and warm climate. The camellias, magnolias and rhododendrons especially provide a seasonal blaze of colour. There are good views from a **Grecian temple** at the end of a cypress avenue, and a spectacular panorama from the top of the 19th-century **Martello tower**, built to watch out for a possible Napoleonic invasion.

This little miracle of a place was created in the early 20th century, when the island's owner, Annan Bryce, commissioned the English architect Harold Peto to design him a garden on the then-barren outcrop.

Garinish Island is reached by taking a 10-minute boat trip past islands and colonies of basking seals. The ferry companies leave every 20 to 30 minutes when the garden is open. The return boat fare (adult €12, child €6) doesn't include entry to the gardens.

Blue Pool Ferry FERRY

(☎027-63333) From a little cove near the centre of the village.

Harbour Queen Ferries FERRY

(☎027-63116, 087 234 5861; www.harbourqueenferry.com) From the pier opposite the Eccles Hotel.

Bamboo Park GARDENS

(☎027-63570; www.bamboo-park.com; adult/child €5/free; ⏲9am-7pm) Glengarriff's mild,

Beara Peninsula (Ring of Beara)

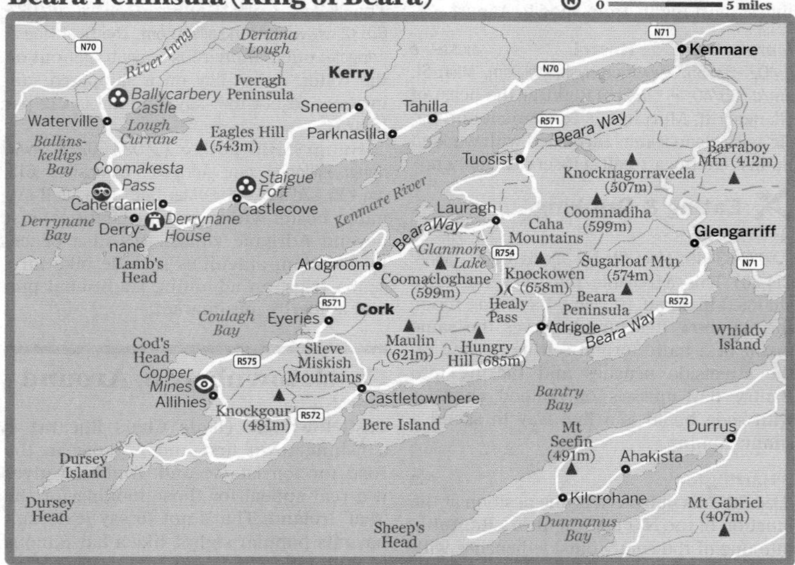

frost-free climate allows this small 12-hectare **park** to flourish. It has a variety of exotic plants, including palm trees and tree ferns, as well as coastal woodland walks.

Glengarriff Woods Nature Reserve NATURE RESERVE
(☎027-63636; www.glengarriffnaturereserve.ie; admission free) The 300-hectare ancient **woodland** lining Glengarriff's glacial valley was owned by the White family of Bantry House in the 18th century. The thick tree cover maintains humid conditions that allow ferns and mosses to flourish.

The woodlands and bogs are also home to Ireland's only arboreal ant and the rare and protected Kerry slug. If you're lucky (have camera ready so you can share your slug with friends and family), you'll see these spotty cream-coloured gastropods on the lichen carpet munching after rainfall.

There are four marked **trails** through the reserve, separately covering woodland, mountain, river and meadow, and you can combine them to form one big walk (8.5km, three to four hours).

To get to the woods, leave Glengarriff on the N71 towards Kenmare. The entrance is about 1km along on the west.

Sleeping

Casey's Hotel HOTEL €€
(☎027-63010; www.caseyshotelglengarriff.ie; Main St; r from €69; @) Old-fashioned Casey's has been welcoming guests since 1884 and is proud of such past visitors as Éamon de Valera. The 19 rooms have been modernised a bit but are still small. It's got gobs of atmosphere though, and the vast terrace is a treat.

Eccles Hotel HOTEL €€
(☎027-63003; www.eccleshotel.com; Glengarriff Harbour; r €100-140; @) Just east of the centre, the Eccles has a long and distinguished history (since 1745), counting the British War Office, Thackeray, George Bernard Shaw and WB Yeats as former occupants. The decor is an attempt to combine 19th-century grandeur with early 1990s style, but the 66 rooms are big and bright. Ask for a bayside room on the 4th floor.

Dowlings Caravan & Camping Park CAMPSITE €
(☎027-63154; glengarriffccp@gmail.com; Castletownbere Rd; campsites from €10; Apr-Oct) This well-set-up park, 4km west of Glengarriff on the road to Castletownbere, enjoys a woodland setting. Amenities include a games

room and a licensed bar staging traditional music most nights from June to August.

Murphy's Village Hostel HOSTEL €
(☎027-63555; www.murphyshostel.com; Main St; dm/d €15/40; ⊙Jun-Sep) Right at the heart of Glengarriff, Murphy's is convenient and basic, with clean rooms furnished with wooden bunks. There's a small self-service kitchen.

Eating & Drinking

Hawthorne Bar PUB €€
(☎027-63440; Main St; bar meals €5-10, dinner €14-20) This agreeable pub may not have changed in about 40 years. Its dining room, the Rainbow Restaurant, serves the same menu in a more formal setting. Sitting on the streetside benches and tucking into Bantry Bay mussels or seafood chowder with soda bread is a fine way to spend a sunny evening.

P Harrington's PUB
(Main St) This pub has a prime position at the junction of the N71 and the Beara Rd. Settle into one of the comfy outside benches with a pint.

Information

There's a **Fáilte Ireland tourist office** (☎027-63084; Main St; ⊙9.30am-1pm & 2-5pm Jun-Aug) and a privately run **tourist office** (⊙10am-1pm & 2-6pm Mon-Sat Jun-Aug) beside the Blue Pool Ferry ticket booth. See www.glengarriff.ie for more local info.

Getting There & Away

Bus Éireann (www.buseireann.ie) has up to three buses daily to Bantry and on to Cork (€16, 2½ hours).

Glengarriff to Castletownbere

The striations of the peninsula's underlying bedrock become evident as you drive west from Glengarriff towards Castletownbere. On the highest hills, Sugarloaf Mountain and Hungry Hill, rock walls known as 'benches' snake backwards and forwards across the slopes. They can make walking on these mountains quite challenging, and dangerous in fog. Take a map (Ordnance Survey Discovery series 84 and 85 cover the area) and compass if venturing into the hills, and seek local advice.

Adrigole is a scattered strip of houses. The **West Cork Sailing Centre** (☎027-60132; www.westcorksailing.com; The Boat House, Adrigole) offers numerous ways to get out on the water. A half-day on a skippered sailing boat costs €160; kayak rental is €12 per hour.

Hungry Hill Lodge (☎027-60228; www.hungryhilllodge.com; Adrigole; campsites €15, dm €15, s/d €25/44; ⊙Mar-Dec) is a well-situated hostel with excellent facilities, just beyond Adrigole village. It's in a peaceful location; amenities include bike hire, scuba trips, an adjoining traditional pub and a nearby minimarket.

Castletownbere & Around

POP 850

Castletownbere (Baile Chais Bhéara) is a fishing town first and a pause in the road for tourists second. And that gives it a real appeal for those looking for the 'real' Ireland. That's not to say it doesn't have its popular sights, like a bar famous to millions.

On Main St and The Square, you'll find ATMs as well as cafes, pubs and grocery stores.

Sights

On a lonely hill 2km from Castletownbere, the impressive **Derreenataggart Stone Circle**, consisting of 10 stones, can be found close to the roadside. It's signposted at a turn-off to the right at the western end of town. There are a number of other standing stones in the surrounding area.

Looming offshore, **Bere Island** is a place that makes Castletownbere seem like the big city. Only 12km by 7km, it has a couple of hundred permanent residents but attracts scores more to summer holiday homes. There are bits of old ruins and some craggy coves good for swimming. A **ferry** (☎027-75009; www.bereislandferries.com; passenger/car return €8/25; ⊙every 90 mins Mon-Sat Jun-Aug, less often Sun & Sep-May) leaves from town.

Sleeping & Eating

Rodeen B&B B&B €€
(☎027-70158; www.rodeencountryhouse.com; s/d €40/76; ⊙Mar-Oct) A delightful six-room haven, tucked away above the eastern approach to town. The musical-instrument-filled house has stunning sea views and is

surrounded by gardens full of crumbling Delphic columns. Flowers from the garden grace the breakfast table, and there are home-baked scones with honey from landlady Ellen's bees.

Olde Bakery MODERN IRISH €€
(☎027-70869; www.oldebakery.com; Castletown House; mains €13-21; ⏰5.30-9.30pm daily, plus noon-4.30pm Sun) One of the best restaurants in town, the Olde Bakery serves hearty portions of top regional seafood to locals who won't settle for seconds – unless it's a second helping. A few tables out front are just the place to be on a long evening.

Taste DELICATESSEN €
(☎027-71842; Main St; ⏰9.30am-6pm Mon-Fri, 10am-5pm Sat) A wide range of local foods, including creamy Milleens cheese, are on offer. There are creative sandwiches to take away from this inviting shop just off The Square.

Jack Patrick's INTERNATIONAL €€
(☎027-70319; Main St; mains €10-16; ⏰noon-3pm) Run by one of the top local butchers – the shop is next door – this simple restaurant is just the choice if you want to get out of your shell and have some meat. Steaks and chops and other meaty mains, like bacon and cabbage, are on offer here.

Drinking

TOP CHOICE **McCarthy's Bar** PUB
(Main St) If you're carrying an original copy of the late Pete McCarthy's bestseller, *McCarthy's Bar*, you'll be excited to see the front-cover photo sitting in three dimensions on Main St. McCarthy's is a grocery as well as a pub, so if you fancy a tin of peaches and a can of corn to go with your Beamish, you've come to the right place. There's frequent live music and a wicked wee snug inside the door.

Information

Tourist office (☎027-70054; www.bearatourism.com; Main St; ⏰Tue-Sat) Just outside the Church of Ireland.

Getting There & Away

Bus Éireann (www.buseireann.ie) has up to three buses daily to Bantry and on to Cork (€18; 3¼ hours). Check signage at the bus stop on The Square for occasional private buses along the peninsula or ask at the tourist office.

Dursey Island

POP 60

Tiny Dursey Island, at the end of the peninsula, is reached by Ireland's only **cable car** (adult/child return €4/1; ⏰9-11am, 2.30-5pm & 7-8pm Mon-Sat, 9-10am, 1-2.30pm & 7-7.30pm Sun year-round, plus 4-5pm Sun Jun-Aug), which sways 30m above Dursey Sound. In a perfect photo op, livestock take precedence over humans in the queue. The later times shown above are for returning only; bikes are not allowed.

The island, just 6.6km long by 1.5km wide, is a wild bird and whale **sanctuary**, and dolphins can sometimes be seen swimming in the waters around it. There's no accommodation, but it's easy to find somewhere to camp. **Camping** is legal, so long as you respect the common rules and clean up after yourself.

The **Beara Way** loops round the island for 11km, and the signal tower is an obvious destination for a short walk.

Northside of the Beara

The entire north side is the scenic highlight of the Beara Peninsula. A series of roads, some single-lane tracks, snake around the ins and outs of the weathered, rugged coast. Boulder-strewn fields tumble dramatically towards the ocean and it's blissfully remote – your only company along some stretches are flocks of sheep and the odd sheepdog.

ALLIHIES

The edge-of-the-world village of Allihies (Na hAilichí) has dramatic vistas, plenty of walks and a long history of mining.

Copper-ore deposits were first identified on the far Beara in 1810. While mining quickly brought wealth to the Puxley family who owned the land, it brought low wages and dangerous, unhealthy working conditions for the labour force, which at one time numbered 1300. Experienced Cornish miners were brought into the area, and the dramatic ruins of engine houses replicate those of Cornwall's coastal tin mines. As late as the 1930s, more than 30,000 tonnes of pure copper were exported annually, but by 1962 the last mine was closed.

You'll see the most **mine ruins** along the R575 north of the village; signs mark the spots. In town the **Allihies Copper Mine Museum** (☎027-73218; adult/child €5/3;

BEARA WAY

This moderately easy, 196km walk forms a loop around the Beara Peninsula. The peninsula is relatively unused to mass tourism and makes a pleasant contrast with the Iveragh Peninsula to the north.

Part of the walk, between Castletownbere and Glengarriff, follows the route taken by Donal O'Sullivan and his band after the English took his castle following an 11-day siege in 1602. At Glengarriff, O'Sullivan met up with other families and set out on a journey north, hoping to reunite with other remaining pockets of Gaelic resistance. Of the 1000 or so men who set out that winter, only 30 completed the trek. Bundle up.

The Beara Way mostly follows old roads and tracks and rarely rises above 340m. There's no official start or finish point and the route can be walked in either direction. It could easily be reduced to seven days by skipping Bere and Dursey Islands and, if you start at Castletownbere, you could reach Kenmare in five days or less.

There's a good downloadable guide to the walk (and the peninsula itself) at **Beara Tourism** (www.bearatourism.com).

10am-5pm daily May-Sep, Sat & Sun Oct-Apr) is the result of years of work by the community and has engaging exhibits plus a summer cafe housed in an old wooden church.

There are inviting pubs and B&Bs in Allihies and a small tourist information kiosk, beside the church, opens in summer.

Sleeping & Eating

Allihies Village Hostel HOSTEL €
(027-73107; www.allihieshostel.net; dm/d €18/50) A modest hostel run by a father-and-daughter team has smart wood-floored dorms and public areas, a courtyard and a barbecue area. Michael is a mine of information on the area and can advise on local walks and pony trekking.

Sea View B&B B&B €€
(027-73004; www.seaviewallihies.com; s/d €45/75) Clean, tidy and basic, the 10 rooms in this two-storey yellow building have an abundance of pine; some have views north over the waters. The spread at breakfast will help fuel your rambles.

O'Neill's PUB €€
(027-73008; meals €7-15; kitchen noon-9pm) The most appealing pub in town, with a tidy red and blue facade and some polished wooden benches and picnic tables out the front for enjoying the views. Pub food intermingles with fresh local seafood.

EYERIES TO LAURAGH

Heading north and east from Allihies, the beautiful **coastal road** (R575), with hedges of fuchsias and rhododendrons, twists and turns for about 12km to **Eyeries**. This cluster of brightly coloured houses overlooking Coulagh Bay is often used as a film set. The town is also home to **Milleens cheese** (027-74079; www.milleenscheese.com), from pioneering producer Veronica Steele. She welcomes visitors to her farm; phone ahead.

From Eyeries, forsake the R571 for the even smaller coast roads (lanes really) to the north and east. This is the Beara at its most spectacular – and intimate. Tiny coves are like pearls in a sea of rocks and the views of the Ring of Kerry to the north sublime.

Rejoin the R571 at the crossroads of **Ardgroom** (Ard Dhór). As you head east towards Lauragh, look for signs pointing to the Ardgroom **stone circle**, an unusual Bronze Age monument with nine tall, thin uprights. There's muddy parking at the end of a 500m-long narrow approach lane. The circle is visible about 200m away and a path leads to it across bogland. A crude sign says simply 'money' and a US dollar under a rock gives a hint.

Lauragh (Laith Reach), situated northeast of Ardgroom, is in County Kerry. It's home to the **Derreen Gardens** (064-83103; adult/child €6/3; 10am-6pm Apr-Oct), planted by the fifth Lord Lansdowne around the turn of the 20th century. Mossy paths weave through an abundance of interesting plants, including spectacular New Zealand tree ferns and red cedars, and you may see seals on the shore.

From Lauragh, a serpentine road travels 11km south across the other-worldly **Healy Pass** and down to Adrigole, offering spectacular views of the rocky inland scenery. About 1km west of Lauragh, along the R571, is a road to **Glanmore Lake**, with the remains of an old hermitage on a tiny island in the middle. There are walking opportunities in the area, but gaining access can be problematic: ask locally for advice.

Sleeping & Eating

The small road just west of Lauragh off the R575 leads into a lovely valley along Glanmore Lake.

Glanmore Lake Hostel HOSTEL €
(☎064-83181; www.anoige.ie; Glanmore Lake; dm adult/child from €17/14; ⊙end-May–end-Sep) A rural atmosphere and an engaging location at the heart of Glanmore make this remote An Óige hostel an appealing place. It's in Glanmore's old boarding school, 5km from the R571.

Josie's Lakeview House MODERN IRISH €€
(☎064-83155; Glanmore Lake; lunch €6-15, dinner mains €15-25) Captivating lake views accompany your food. Josie's sits on a hill overlooking Glanmore Lake. Choose from salads and sandwiches for lunch, cakes at tea or heartier rack of lamb and local seafood specials at night. Josie's is 4km from the R571; follow the signs.

Getting There & Away

The bus service in this area is limited. Contact **Bus Éireann** (☎021-450 8188; www.buseireann.ie) for times and prices of the summer services between Kenmare and Castletownbere via Lauragh.

LAURAGH TO KENMARE

Leaving Lauragh, take the R573, which hugs the coast, rejoining the more no-nonsense R571 at Tuosist for the 16km run east to Kenmare in Kerry.

NORTHERN CORK

Northern Cork lacks the glamour and romance of the county's coastal regions, but the area's towns and villages have a refreshing rural integrity.

Donkey Sanctuary

The **Donkey Sanctuary** (☎022-48398; www.thedonkeysanctuary.ie; Liscarroll; admission free; ⊙9am-4.30pm Mon-Fri, 10am-5pm Sat & Sun) is a wonderful nonprofit institution dedicated to Ireland's iconic beasts of burden. Naturally bedraggled looking, the small, sturdy steeds of the Irish countryside are also often abused by thoughtless owners either out of meanness or simply because economic conditions have made it too hard to care for them properly.

At this large farm, abandoned and abused donkeys are given a home for life. There are pastures, food, medical care and virtually no demands on them. It's a splendid operation and one most visitors end up supporting – especially after they've seen one of the winsome critters up close through the self-guided tour of the pastures and barns.

The sanctuary is in the small town of Liscarroll, which is on the R522, 13km west of Buttevant on the main N20 highway to Cork. There are some scenic **ruins** of a castle close to the sanctuary.

Mallow

Mallow (Mala) is a prosperous town located in the Blackwater Valley on the main N20 highway. Visitors to its spa in the 19th century christened it the 'Bath of Ireland'. The comparison is far-fetched these days, though the architecture in the town centre hints at its former grandeur.

The **tourist office** (☎022-42222; www.eastcorktourism.com; ⊙9.30am-1pm & 2-5.30pm Mon-Fri) can help with accommodation and activities.

In the town itself, you can spot white fallow deer around the imposing ruins of **Mallow Castle** (Bridge St), which dates back to 1585. Also look out for the distinctive **Clock House** (Bridge St), designed by an amateur architect after an Alpine holiday – you'd never guess.

Around Mallow

At Buttevant, about 20km north of Mallow on the N20, are the ruins of a 13th- century **Franciscan abbey**. Between Mallow and Killarney, you might want to divert to see the well-preserved remains of 17th-century **Kanturk Castle**. Inhabited only by crows these days, the castle acted as both fortification and country house from the early 17th century to 1906.

Red deer scamper around the 400 acres of landscaped gardens at **Doneraile Park** (⊙dawn-8pm), 13km northeast of Mallow. There are woodland walkways, cascades and playgrounds to keep the kids happy.

County Kerry

POPULATION: 145,000 / AREA: 4746 SQ KM

Includes »

Best Places to Eat

» Jacks Coastguard Restaurant (p285)

» Out of the Blue (p306)

» Bianconi (p285)

» Chapter 40 (p275)

» Truffle Pig (p296)

Best Places to Stay

» Aghadoe Heights Hotel (p282)

» Pax House (p304)

» Harbour House (p311)

» Parknasilla Resort & Spa (p294)

» Crystal Springs B&B (p272)

Why Go?

County Kerry contains some of Ireland's most iconic scenery: impossibly crenulated coastlines, endless green fields crisscrossed by tumbledown stone walls, and mist-shrouded mountain peaks and bogs.

With one of the country's finest national parks as its backyard, the lively tourism hub of Killarney spills over with colourful shops, restaurants and pubs with spirited trad sessions. Killarney is the jumping-off point for Kerry's two famed loop drives. The larger Ring of Kerry skirts the Iveragh Peninsula, fringed by islands scattered offshore. The compact Dingle Peninsula is like a condensed version of its southern neighbour, with ancient sites, sandy beaches and glimpses of a hard, unforgiving land.

Kerry's exquisite beauty makes it one of Ireland's most popular tourist destinations. But if you need to escape from the crowds, there's always a mountain pass, an isolated cove or an untrodden trail to discover.

When to Go?

Scads of festivals take place during the warmer months, particularly June to August (when you'll need to book accommodation well ahead). Highlights on Kerry's calendar include Listowel's Writers' Week in early June; Dingle town's races and regatta, both in August; and Killorglin's Puck Festival, also in August, which dates back at least as far as the 17th century. And even in the depths of winter, you'll find storytellers and musicians taking part in impromptu sessions in pubs throughout the county.

County Kerry Highlights

1. Drink in 'Ireland's finest view' across the rugged coastline over a pint on the **Ring of Kerry** (p294)
2. Savour seafood straight off the boats on the enchanting **Dingle Peninsula** (p297)
3. Cycle through the dramatic **Gap of Dunloe** (p282)
4. Sail on the Upper Lake in **Killarney National Park** (p278)
5. Clip-clop around **Killarney** in a horse-drawn jaunting car (p277)
6. Island-hop around the rocky **Skelligs** (p291) and evacuated **Blaskets** (p308)
7. Groove to old-school funk at the hippest little bar in **Tralee** (p314)
8. Scuba-dive the crystal-clear waters around **Castlegregory** (p311)

KILLARNEY

POP 16,900

In a town that's been practising the tourism game for over 250 years, Killarney is a well-oiled machine in the middle of the sublime scenery of its namesake national park. Beyond the obvious proximity to lakes, waterfalls, woodland and moors dwarfed by 1000m-plus peaks, it has many charms of its own. Competition keeps standards high, and no matter your budget, you can expect to find good restaurants, fine pubs and plenty of accommodation.

Killarney and its surrounds have been inhabited probably since the Neolithic period and were certainly important Bronze Age settlements, based on the copper ore mined on Ross Island. Killarney changed hands between warring tribes, the most notable of which were the Fir Bolg ('bag men'), expert stonemasons who built forts and devised Ogham script. It wasn't until much later, in the 17th century, that Viscount Kenmare developed the town as an Irish version of England's Lake District. Among its many notable 19th-century tourists were Queen Victoria and the Romantic poet Percy Bysshe Shelley, who began *Queen Mab* here.

Mobbed in summer, Killarney is perhaps at its best in the late spring and early autumn when you can enjoy its outdoor pursuits and the crowds are manageable.

Sights & Activities

Killarney's biggest attraction, in every sense, is Killarney National Park – see p278. The town itself can easily be explored on foot in an hour or two.

See p283 for details of tour operators in the surrounding area, including tours of the Ring of Kerry and Dingle Peninsula.

St Mary's Cathedral CATHEDRAL
(Map p274; Cathedral Pl) Built between 1842 and 1855, St Mary's Cathedral is a superb example of neo-Gothic revival architecture. Designed by Augustus Pugin, the cruciform building was inspired by Ardfert Cathedral, near Tralee.

Franciscan Friary FRIARY
(Map p274; Fair Hill) This 1860s Franciscan friary displays an ornate Flemish-style altarpiece, some impressive tile work and most notably stained-glass windows by Harry Clarke. The Dublin artist's organic style was influenced by art nouveau, art deco and symbolism.

Fishing FISHING
Fishing for brown trout in Killarney National Park's lakes is free. You can fish for trout and salmon in the Rivers Flesk (per day €10) and Laune (per day €25); a state salmon licence is required (€46 for three weeks). **O'Neill's** (Map p274; www.fishingkillarney.com; 6 Plunkett St), which looks like a gift shop but is a long-established fishing centre, has information, permits and licences and rents equipment.

Festivals & Events

Rally of the Lakes CAR RALLY
(www.rallyofthelakes.com; late Apr/early May) Drivers take death-defying twists and turns around the lakes and mountains over the May bank holiday weekend. (Take care: cars often hoon around Killarney's streets after the official stages.)

Killarney Summerfest OUTDOOR ACTIVITIES
(www.killarneysummerfest.com; late Jul) Horse riding, canoeing, kayaking and walking are part of this family-oriented festival, in addition to art workshops and street performers.

Sleeping

You'll find numerous B&Bs just outside the centre on Rock, Lewis and Muckross Rds. The latter also has scores of generic hotels aimed at tour groups. Many places offer bike hire (around €12 per day) and discounted tours. Book ahead everywhere in summer.

See the Around Killarney section for more options in the surrounding area.

TOP CHOICE **Crystal Springs** B&B €€
(Map p278; 064-663 3272; www.crystalspringsbb.com; Ballycasheen; d €80-110; P) You can cast a line from the timber deck of this wonderfully relaxing riverside B&B or just laze about on the adjacent lawn. Rooms are richly furnished with patterned wallpapers and walnut timber; en suite bathrooms (most with spa baths) are larger than many Irish hotel rooms. The glass-enclosed breakfast room also overlooks the fast-flowing River Flesk. It's about a 15-minute stroll to town.

The Fairview INN €€
(Map p274; 064-663 4164; www.fairviewkillarney.com; College St; d from €110; P) Done out in beautiful timbers, the individually decorated rooms (some with classical printed wallpaper, some with contemporary sofas and glass) at this boutique guesthouse offer bet-

ter bang for your buck than bigger, less personal places around town. A veritable feast is laid on at breakfast; the elegant onsite restaurant is a winner come evening.

Killarney Plaza Hotel HOTEL €€€
(Map p274; ☎064-662 1100; www.killarneyplaza.com; Kenmare Pl; s/d from €115/238; P@≈ᯤ👪) Dominating the view of the south end of Main St, on the edge of Killarney National Park, this large, 198-room hotel is built in a brilliant white traditional style. Classically furnished guestrooms and public facilities are in keeping with its class; besides the marble lobby and lavishly tiled indoor pool, there's a sauna, steam room and spa, and three restaurants.

Railway Hostel HOSTEL €
(Map p274; ☎064-663 5299; www.killarneyhostel.com; Fair Hill; dm €16-22, s/d from €45/54; P@ᯤ) Fronted by a terrace with picnic tables, this tucked-away place near the train station is about as inviting as hostels get, with bunks nestling in nooks, and maps and cycling itineraries on the walls. Private rooms have en suite bathrooms; prices include continental breakfast.

Murphy's of Killarney INN €€
(Map p274; ☎064-663 1294; www.murphysofkillarney.com; College St; s/d €59-85; ᯤ) A great midrange option close to the action, Murphy's 20 rooms have been stylishly refurbished – ask for one overlooking the street. If it's lashing rain, you won't have to leave as there's a highly respected restaurant and pub onsite. Wi-fi is available in public areas.

Chelmsford House B&B €€
(off Map p274; ☎064-663 6402; www.chelmsfordguesthouse.com; Muckross View, Countess Grove; d €60; P@👪) Overlooking the lake and the mountains, gardens frame the entrance of this friendly B&B. Rooms with private bathrooms are bright and airy, with timber floors and a minimum of frills. It's a 10-minute stroll into town.

Neptune's Killarney Town Hostel HOSTEL €
(Map p274; ☎064-663 5255; www.neptuneshostel.com; Bishop's Lane, New St; dm €16-20, d €40-50; @ᯤ) Neptune's dorms can sleep over 150, but this central hostel feels much smaller thanks to the roaring fire in reception and the staff's unfailing helpfulness. There's a laundry service; rates include breakfast.

Súgán Hostel HOSTEL €
(Map p274; ☎064-663 3104; www.killarneysuganhostel.com; Lewis Rd; dm €15-17, d €40; ᯤ) Behind its publike front, 250-year-old Súgán is an amiably eccentric hostel with an open fire in the cosy common room, low, crazy-cornered ceilings and hardwood floors. Note that it's an alcohol-free zone, which is either a good thing or a bad thing, depending on your point of view.

Kingfisher Lodge B&B €€
(Map p274; ☎064-663 7131; www.kingfisherlodgekillarney.com; Lewis Rd; s €60-70, d €86-100; P@ᯤ) Lovely back gardens are a highlight at this immaculate B&B, whose 11 rooms are done out in vivid yellows, reds and pinks. Owner Donal Carroll is a certified walking guide with a wealth of knowledge on hiking in the area.

Malton HOTEL €€€
(Map p274; ☎064-663 8000; www.themalton.com; s/d from €100-150; P@ᯤ≈👪) So commanding it doesn't need an address, the pillared, ivy-covered Malton in the centre of town is a throwback to Victorian elegance – at least from the outside – with pompous service to match. Inside it's had a thorough strip-and-refit; of the 172 rooms, the pick are those in the 1852 wing, which have retained their period opulence. There are several stunning restaurants and a spa and leisure centre with a 17m swimming pool, gym and two tennis courts.

Algret House B&B €€
(off Map p274; ☎064-663 2337; www.algret.com; Countess Grove; s/d €35/65; Pᯤ👪) Knotted pine dominates the decor of this light, bright B&B a five minute walk from the centre.

Killarney Haven APARTMENTS €
(Map p274; ☎064-663 3570; www.killarney-selfcatering.com; High St; apt per week from €340; P👪) Great central base. Contemporary apartments open onto balconies and have full kitchens.

Killarney Flesk Caravan & Camping Park CAMPGROUND €
(Map p278; ☎064-663 1704; www.killarneyfleskcamping.com; Muckross Rd; campsites from €10; ⏲Jun-Sep; Pᯤ👪) About 1.3km south of town on the N71, this well-tended park is surrounded by woods and has majestic mountain views. Facilities include bike hire, a supermarket, cafe and bar.

Killarney

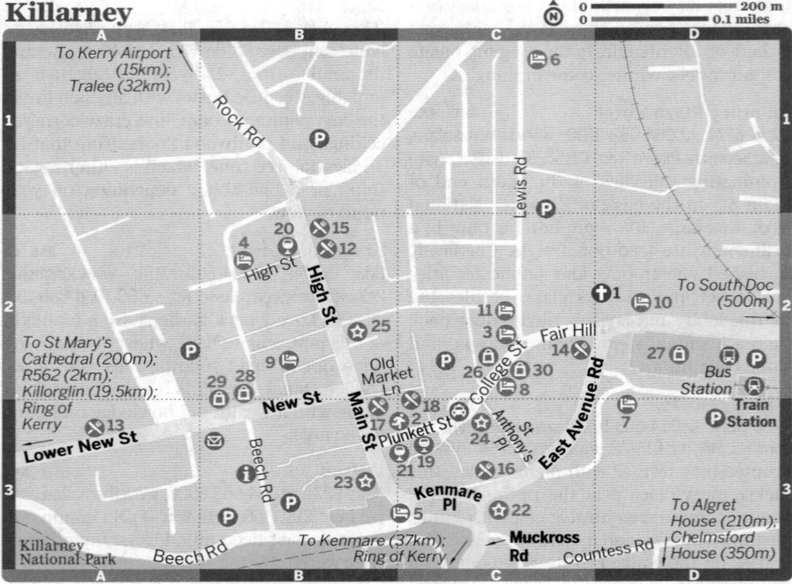

Killarney

Sights
1 Franciscan Friary ... D2

Activities, Courses & Tours
2 O'Neill's ... C3

Sleeping
3 Fairview ... C2
4 Killarney Haven ... B2
5 Killarney Plaza Hotel ... C3
6 Kingfisher Lodge ... C1
7 Malton ... D3
8 Murphy's of Killarney ... C2
9 Neptune's Killarney Town Hostel ... B2
10 Railway Hostel ... D2
11 Súgán Hostel ... C2

Eating
12 Brícín ... B2
13 Chapter 40 ... A3
14 Farmers Market ... C2
15 Gaby's Seafood Restaurant ... B2
16 Lir Café ... C3
17 Murphy's Ice Cream ... B3
Smoke House ... (see 25)
18 Vanilla Pod ... C3

Drinking
19 Courtney's ... C3
20 Hussy's ... B2
21 Tatler Jack's ... C3

Entertainment
22 Killarney Cineplex ... C3
23 Killarney Grand ... B3
24 McSorley's ... C3
25 O'Connor's ... B2

Shopping
Brícín ... (see 12)
26 Dungeon Bookshop ... C2
27 Killarney Outlet Centre ... D2
28 O'Sullivan's Outdoor Store ... B2
29 Pages Bookstore ... B2
30 Variety Sounds ... C2

FOOTBALL FEVER

Gaelic football clubs are as common in Ireland as green fields and pub signs bearing the 'G' word. However, among Kerrymen, the obsession with the sport reaches fever pitch.

Run by the GAA (Gaelic Athletic Association), the 15-a-side game is played with a heavy leather ball on a rectangular grass pitch with H-shaped, net-backed goals. Teams score through a confusing combination of kicking, carrying, hand-passing and *soloing* (dropping and toe-kicking the ball into the hands). See p722 for an explanation of the rules. The game, which closely resembles Australian Rules football, dates back to the 16th century, but took its current form in the 19th century.

If you'd like to watch Gaelic football and you're in town during the season (February to September), head to the **Fossa GAA Ground** in Fossa (map p278). To learn about the game from some lifelong pub commentators, have a drink at GAA bars such as **Tatler Jack's** (p276).

Eating

Many of Killarney's hotels have excellent restaurants – see the Sleeping section for more options. As elsewhere in Kerry, fresh seafood stars on many menus.

TOP CHOICE Chapter 40 IRISH €€
(Map p274; ☎064-667 1833; www.chapter40.ie; Lower New St; mains €22.50-28.50; ⊙dinner Tue-Sat) Popular with Killarney's stylish bounders (and chefs on their nights off), this beautiful dining room is all polished wood and cream leather. Starters like grilled polenta with wild mushrooms are followed by classy mains such as pork Wellington with pea and crab salsa. The wines by the glass show a deft hand in the cellar.

The Smoke House BISTRO €€
(Map p274; ☎064-662 0801; www.thesmokehouse.ie; High St; mains €13-34; ⊙breakfast, lunch & dinner) One of Killarney's newest and busiest ventures, this tiled bistro is the first establishment in Ireland to cook with a Josper (Spanish charcoal oven). Stylish salads include Norwegian king crab; its Kerry surf 'n turf burger – with gambas tails and house-made barbecue sauce – has a local following.

Gaby's Seafood Restaurant SEAFOOD €€
(Map p274; ☎064-663 2519; www.gabysireland.com; 27 High St; mains €22-50; ⊙dinner Mon-Sat) Gaby's is a refined dining experience for those who want superb seafood served in a traditional manner. Peruse the menu by the fire before drifting past the wine cellar to the low-lit dining room to savour exquisite Gallic dishes such as lobster in cognac and cream. The wine list is long and the advice unerring.

Brícín INTERNATIONAL €€
(Map p274; ☎064-663 4902; www.bricin.com; 26 High St; mains €19-26; ⊙dinner Tue-Sat) Decorated with fittings from a convent, an orphanage and a school, this Celtic deco restaurant doubles as the town museum, with Jonathan Fisher's 18th-century views of the national park taking pride of place. Try the house speciality, boxty (potato pancake).

Vanilla Pod IRISH €€
(Map p274; ☎064-662 6559; www.thevanillapodrestaurants.com; Old Market Lane; mains €18-27; ⊙breakfast, lunch & dinner) By day, Gavin Gleeson's gem of a cafe serves dishes like beer-battered salmon and salads such as almond-crusted goats' cheese with raspberry dressing. Dinner, offering mains like maple-glazed pork, is a more upmarket affair.

Lir Café CAFE €
(Map p274; Kenmare Pl; www.lircafe.com; dishes €2-5; ⊙breakfast, lunch & dinner;) Food is limited to cakes, biscuits and the real treat, handmade chocolates, including Bailey's truffles. Great coffee, hip atmosphere.

Farmers Market MARKET €
(Map p274; Scott's St; ⊙10am-2pm Fri) Fruit, vegetables, cakes, cheeses and more is sold at Killarney's farmers market, along with crafts. For details of farmers markets throughout County Kerry, visit www.kerryfarmersmarkets.com.

Murphy's Ice Cream ICE CREAM €
(Map p274; www.murphysicecream.ie; 37 Main St; ⊙11am-6pm) The Killarney branch of this superlative Dingle ice cream maker (p306), with wonderfully thick hot chocolates including chilli.

Drinking & Entertainment

Most pubs put on live music, and most nights are lively here – even early in the week, when many of the town's hospitality staff are released to the fun side of the bar. Plunkett and College Sts are lined with pubs. The tourist office has a handy night-by-night listing of sessions.

O'Connor's PUB
(Map p274; High St) This tiny traditional pub with leaded glass doors is one of Killarney's most popular haunts. Live music plays every night; good bar food is served daily at lunch and dinner. In warmer weather, the crowds spill out onto the adjacent laneway.

Courtney's PUB
(Map p274; www.courtneysbar.com; Plunkett St) Inconspicuous on the outside, inside this timeless trad pub bursts at the seams with traditional music sessions many nights year-round. This is where locals come to see their old mates perform and to kick off a night on the town.

Hussy's PUB
(Map p274; High St) Escape the tourist mobs and muse over a pint in this small pub retaining a snug at the entrance.

Tatler Jack's PUB
(Map p274; www.tatlerjack.com; Plunkett St) Photos of proud local sports teams line the walls at this surprisingly large pub, which features pool tables, the comfiest stools in town and merciless craic.

McSorley's BAR, NIGHTCLUB
(Map p274; www.mcsorleyskillarney.com; College St) A local favourite for its big beer garden and nightclub with a decently sized dance floor. Trad sessions take place from early evening to 10pm, with live bands from 11.30pm. Admission to the main bar is free.

Killarney Grand BAR, NIGHTCLUB
(Map p274; www.killarneygrand.com; Main St) There's traditional live music from 9pm to 11pm, bands from 11.30pm to 1.30am and a disco from 11pm at this Killarney institution. Entry is free before 11pm.

Killarney Cineplex CINEMA
(Map p274; www.killarneycineplex.ie; Kenmare Pl) Screens current releases.

Shopping

Variety Sounds MUSIC
(Map p274; College St) Eclectic music shop with a good range of traditional music, instruments, sheet music and hard-to-find CDs.

Killarney Outlet Centre FASHION
(Map p274; www.killarneyoutletcentre.com; Fair Hill) This mall in renovated old train sheds has a number of shops including Nike and Blarney Woollen Mills, selling discounted brand-name goods.

O'Sullivan's Outdoor Store OUTDOOR GEAR
(Map p274; www.killarneyrentabike.com; New St) Crams a vast amount of activity gear into a small space.

Brícín CRAFTS
(Map p274; www.bricin.com; 26 High St) Interesting local craftwork, including jewellery and pottery, alongside touristy wares, plus a restaurant (p275).

The Dungeon Bookshop BOOKS
(Map p274; College St) Excellent second-hand bookshop hidden above a newsagent (take the stairs at the back of the shop).

Pages Bookstore BOOKS
(Map p274; www.pagesbookstore.net; 20 New St) Lots of new titles and classics, including Irish literature.

Information

The website www.killarney.ie has lots of tourism links.

Internet Access

Killarney Library (www.kerrylibrary.ie; Rock Rd; ⏲10am-5pm Mon, Wed, Fri & Sat, 10am-8pm Tue & Thu) Free access.

Leaders (Beech Rd; per 30 min €2; ⏲9.30am-1.30pm & 2-6pm Mon-Sat)

Rí Rá (☎064-663 8729; Plunkett St; per 30 min €2.50; ⏲10.30am-8pm Mon-Sat, noon-8pm Sun)

Medical Services

The closest accident and emergency unit is at Tralee General Hospital (p315).

SouthDoc (off Map p274; ☎1850-335 999; Upper Park Rd) Doctors outside surgery hours; 500m east of the centre.

Money

Many banks have a bureau de change, an ATM, or both.

Post

Killarney Post Office (Map p274; New St)

Tourist Information

Tourist office (Map p274; ☎064-663 1633; www.corkkerry.ie; Beech Rd; ⏱9am-8pm Jun-Aug, 9.15am-5pm Sep-May) Can handle almost any query, especially dealing with transport intricacies.

Getting There & Away

Air

Kerry Airport (KIR; www.kerryairport.com; 📶) is at Farranfore, about 15km north of Killarney along the N22, then a further 1.5km along the N23. **Ryanair** (www.ryanair.com) rules the roost with daily flights to Dublin and London's Luton and Stansted airports, and less frequent services to Hahn, Germany, Faro, Portugal and Alicante, Spain. **Aer Arann** (www.aerarann.com) has four flights a week to Manchester.

The small airport has a restaurant, bar, bureau de change and ATM. Virtually all the major car-hire firms have desks at the airport.

Bus

Bus Éireann (☎064-663 0011; www.buseireann.ie) operates from the east end of the Killarney Outlet Centre, offering regular links to destinations including Cork (€17, two hours, 15 daily); Dublin (€25.50, six hours, six daily); Galway (€23.50, seven hours, seven daily) via Limerick (€18, 2¼ hours); Tralee (€8.70, 40 minutes, hourly); and Waterford (€23.50, 4½ hours, hourly).

Train

Killarney's train station is behind the Malton Hotel, just east of the centre. **Irish Rail** (☎064-6631067; www.irishrail.ie) has up to three direct trains a day to Cork (€20, 1½ hours) and nine to Tralee (€9.50, 45 minutes). There are some direct trains to Dublin (from €26.40, 3½ hours), but you usually have to change at Mallow.

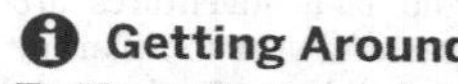

Getting Around

To/From the Airport

Bus Éireann has six to seven services daily between Killarney and Kerry Airport (€4.50, 20 minutes).

A taxi to Killarney costs about €35.

Bicycle

Bicycles are ideal for exploring the scattered sights of the Killarney area, many of which are accessible only by bike or on foot.

O'Sullivan's Bike Hire (Map p274; www.killarneyrentabike.com; per day €15) has branches on New St, opposite the cathedral, and on Beech Rd, opposite the tourist office.

Car

The centre of Killarney can be thick with traffic at times. **Budget** (☎064-663 4341; Kenmare Pl) is the only car-hire outfit with an office in town. Otherwise contact the companies at the airport.

There is a sizeable, free car park next to St Mary's Cathedral.

Jaunting Car

Killarney's traditional transport is the horse-drawn **jaunting car** (☎064-663 3358; www.killarneyjauntingcars.com), also known as a trap, which comes with a driver known as a jarvey. The pick-up point, nicknamed 'the Ha Ha' or 'the Block', is on Kenmare Pl. Trips cost €30 to €70, depending on distance; traps officially carry four people. Jaunting cars also congregate in the N71 car park for Muckross House and Abbey, and at the Gap of Dunloe.

Taxi

The town taxi rank is on College St. Taxi companies include **Killarney Taxi & Tours** (☎086 389 5144; www.killarneytaxi.com).

KERRY WAY

The 214km **Kerry Way** (www.kerryway.net) is the Republic's longest way-marked footpath and is usually walked anticlockwise. Starting and ending in Killarney, it stays inland for the first three days, winding through the spectacular Macgillycuddy's Reeks and past 1039m Mt Carrantuohil, Ireland's highest mountain, before continuing around the Ring of Kerry coast through Cahirciveen, Waterville, Caherdaniel, Sneem and Kenmare.

You could complete the walk in about 10 days, provided you're up to a good 20km per day. With less time it's worth walking the first three days, as far as Glenbeigh, from where a bus or a lift could return you to Killarney.

Accommodation isn't a problem, but places to eat are few; consider carrying your own food. Ordnance Survey Discovery Series maps 78, 83 and 84 cover the walk. **Go Ireland** (www.govisitireland.com) offer seven- and 11-day self-guided walks from €675/980 including pre-booked accommodation, route maps and luggage transfers.

AROUND KILLARNEY

Castles, gardens and lake adventures are among the highlights of a visit to Killarney National Park, immediately south of the city. Just beyond, there's rugged scenery including the too-gorgeous-for-words Gap of Dunloe, with its rocky terrain, babbling brooks and alpine lakes.

Killarney National Park

You can escape Killarney for the surrounding wilderness surprisingly quickly. Buses rumble up to Ross Castle and Muckross House, but it's possible to find your own refuge in the 10,236 hectares of **Killarney National Park** (www.killarneynationalpark.ie) among Ireland's only wild herd of native red deer, the country's largest area of ancient oak woods and views of most of its major mountains.

The glacial **Lough Leane** (the Lower Lake or 'Lake of Learning'), **Muckross Lake** and the **Upper Lake** make up about a quarter of the park. Their peaty waters are as rich in wildlife as the surrounding soil: cormorants skim across the surface, deer swim out to graze on the islands, and salmon, trout and perch prosper in a pike-free environment. Lough Leane has vistas of reeds and swans.

Designated a Unesco Biosphere Reserve in 1982, the park extends to the southwest of town. There are pedestrian entrances opposite St Mary's Cathedral in Killarney, with other entrances for drivers off the N71.

Killarney's tourist office stocks walking guides and the map (Ordnance Survey Map Discovery Series No 78) for several mountains, including Carrantuohil (1039m), Ireland's highest peak, within the Macgillycuddy's Reeks range.

Around Killarney

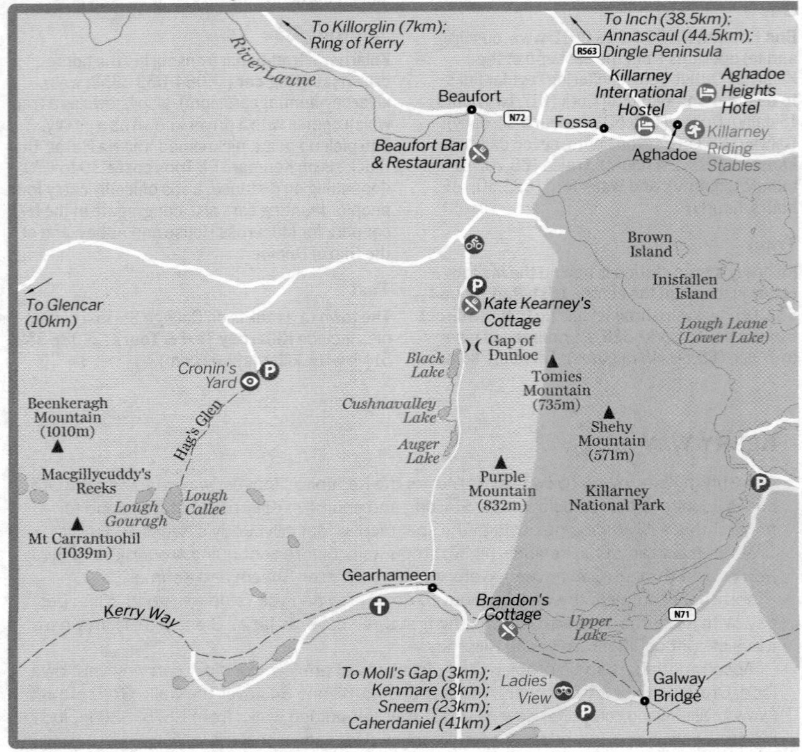

KNOCKREER HOUSE & GARDENS

Near the St Mary's Cathedral entrance to the park stands Knockreer House, with gardens featuring a terraced lawn and a summer-house. The original 1870s structure burned down; the present incarnation dates from 1958. The house isn't open to the public, but its **gardens** have magnificent views across the lakes to the mountains.

From the St Mary's Cathedral entrance, follow the path immediately to your right uphill for about 500m to reach the gardens.

ROSS CASTLE

Restored by Dúchas, **Ross Castle** (Map p278; ☎064-663 5851; www.heritageireland.ie; Ross Rd; adult/child €6/2; ⏱9am-5.45pm Apr-Sep, 9.30am-5.45pm Oct & mid-late Mar) dates back to the 15th century, when it was a residence of the O'Donoghues. It was the last place in Munster to succumb to Cromwell's forces, thanks partly to its cunning spiral staircase, every step of which is a different height in order to break an attacker's stride.

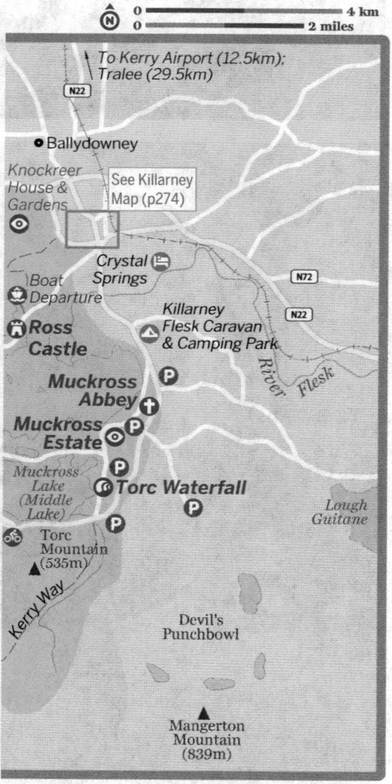

The castle is a lovely 3km walk from the St Mary's Cathedral pedestrian park entrance; you may well see deer. If you're driving from Killarney, turn right opposite the petrol station at the start of Muckross Rd. Access is by guided tour only.

See p283 for boat tours departing from Ross Castle.

INISFALLEN ISLAND

The first monastery on Inisfallen Island (at 22 acres, the largest of the national park's 26 islands) is said to have been founded by St Finian the Leper in the 7th century. The island's fame dates from the early 13th century when the Annals of Inisfallen were written here. Now in the Bodleian Library at Oxford, they remain a vital source of information on early Munster history. On Inisfallen are the ruins of a 12th-century **oratory** with a carved Romanesque doorway and a **monastery** on the site of St Finian's original.

You can hire boats (around €5) from Ross Castle to row to the island.

MUCKROSS ESTATE

The core of Killarney National Park is the Muckross Estate, donated to the state by Arthur Bourn Vincent in 1932. **Muckross House** (Map p278; ☎064-667 0144; www.muckross-house.ie; adult/child €7/3, combined ticket with farms €12/6; ⏱9am-7pm Jul & Aug, to 5.30pm Sep-Jun) is a 19th-century mansion, restored to its former glory and packed with contemporaneous fittings. Entrance is by guided tour.

The beautiful **gardens** slope down, and a block behind the house contains a restaurant, craft shop and **studios** where you can see potters, weavers and bookbinders at work. Jaunting cars wait to run you through deer parks and woodland to **Torc Waterfall** and **Muckross Abbey** (about €20 each return; haggling can reap discounts). The visitor centre has an excellent cafe.

Immediately east of Muckross House are the **Muckross Traditional Farms** (☎064-663 1440; adult/child €7.50/4, combined ticket with Muckross House €12/6; ⏱10am-6pm Jun-Aug, 1-6pm May & Sep, 1-6pm Sat, Sun & public holidays Apr & Oct). These reproductions of 1930s Kerry farms, complete with chickens, pigs, cattle and horses, show farming and living conditions when people had to live off the land.

Wildlife Watching in Killarney National Park

Although Killarney is one of southwestern Ireland's liveliest urban centres, a plethora of wildlife lives right on its doorstep, with pedestrian entrances to the national park (p278) right in the town centre.

The park's mountains, lakes and woodlands sprawl over 10,236 hectares. And while its proximity to Killarney and high visitor numbers are an ongoing risk, it's an important conservation area for many rare species. The park's upland areas are home to Ireland's only remaining wild herd of native red deer (around 700), which has lived here continuously for 12,000 years.

Fish in the park's waterways include brown trout and salmon (see p272 for fishing information), as well as rare Arctic char and Killarney shad.

Keep your eyes peeled too for the park's smallest residents, its insects, including the northern emerald dragonfly, which isn't normally found this far south in Europe and is believed to have been marooned here after the last ice age.

Birdlife abounds throughout the park. With a bit of luck, you might see white tailed sea eagles, whose 2.5m wingspan soars overhead. The eagles were reintroduced here in 2007 after more than 100 years of extinction. There are now over 50 in the park and they're starting to settle in Ireland's rivers, lakes and coastal regions. And like Killarney itself, the park is also home to plenty of summer visitors, including migratory cuckoos, swallows and swifts.

Clockwise from top left

1. Long-eared owl **2.** Bridge over rushing stream **3.** Rhododendrons in green fields **4.** Red deer – doe with fawn

RICHARD CUMMINS/LONELY PLANET IMAGES ©

2

DAVID TIPLING/LONELY PLANET IMAGES ©

3

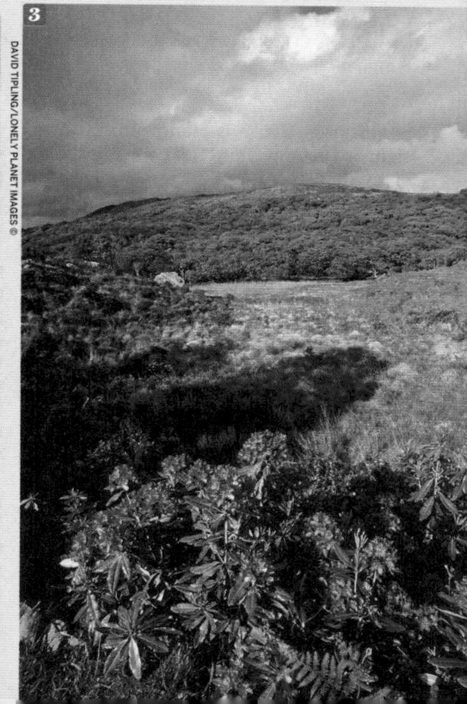

WORTH A TRIP

AGHADOE

On a hilltop just 5km west of town, Aghadoe's sweeping views of Killarney, the lakes and Inisfallen Island have made jaws drop for centuries. At the eastern end of the meadow are the ruins of a **Romanesque church** and the 13th-century **Parkavonear Castle**. Parkavonear's keep, still standing, is one of the few cylindrical rather than rectangular keeps built by the Normans in Ireland. Unsurprisingly, its name translates as 'field of the meadow'.

The ruins lie in front of Killarney's best luxury hotel.

Aghadoe Heights Hotel (Map p278; ☎064-31766; www.aghadoeheights.com; Aghadoe; d €200, ste €300; P@) A huge, glassed-in swimming pool overlooking the lakes is the centrepiece of this stunning contemporary hotel, but you can also soak up the views from the **bar** (mains €12-23; ⊙lunch & dinner) and **Lake Room Restaurant** (mains €18-38; ⊙dinner), both of which are open to nonguests, as is the decadent spa, with 11 treatment rooms and four-chamber thermal suite. Heavenly beds have memory foam mattresses. Kids get their own menus (with dishes such as Marge Simpson's beef burger and Nemo's battered fish fingers) and colouring-in books. There are board games for rainy days and a tennis court.

At the other end of the budget spectrum, **Killarney International Hostel** (Map p278; ☎064-663 1240; www.anoige.ie; Aghadoe House, Fossa; dm €20, tw54; P@) occupies the Headley barons' former residence, built in the 18th century and set in 75 acres of woodland. It's the regal quarters for a 170-bed An Óige hostel. Common areas have open fires and a piano; there's a laundry room and a free bus to/from town (June to September). Continental breakfast costs €3.

If you're driving from Killarney, turn right off the N72 after the turn for **Killarney Riding Stables** (Map p278; ☎064-663 1686; www.killarney-riding-stables.com; Ballydowney), 1.5km west of the centre on the N72, which offers short rides (from €35 for one hour) as well as two- and five-day rides through the Iveragh Peninsula for more experienced riders.

Between Monday and Saturday, June to September, four daily buses link Killarney and Aghadoe. Some tours stop here.

Muckross House is 5km south of town, signposted from the N71. If you're walking or cycling, there's a cycle track alongside the Kenmare road for most of the first 2km. A path then turns right into Killarney National Park. Following this path, after 1km you'll come to **Muckross Abbey**, which was founded in 1448 and burned by Cromwell's troops in 1652. William Thackeray called it 'the prettiest little bijou of a ruined abbey ever seen'. Muckross House is another 1.5km from the abbey ruins.

Cycling around Muckross Lake (Middle Lake) is easier and more scenic in an anticlockwise direction.

GAP OF DUNLOE

Geographically, the Gap of Dunloe is outside the Killarney National Park, but most people include it in their visit to the park. The land is ruggedly beautiful, and fast-changing weather conditions add drama.

In the winter, it's an awe-inspiring mountain pass, overshadowed by Purple Mountain and Macgillycuddy's Reeks. In high summer, though, it's a bottleneck for the tourist trade, with buses ferrying countless visitors for horse-and-trap rides through the Gap.

In the south, surrounded by lush, green pastures, **Brandon's Cottage** (Map p278; dishes €3-6; ⊙breakfast & lunch Apr-Oct) is a simple old 19th-century hunting lodge with an open-air cafe and a dock for boats crossing the Upper Lake. From here a narrow road weaves up the hill to the Gap. Heading down towards the north the scenery is a fantasy of rocky bridges over clear mountain streams and lakes.

Eventually you reach the 19th-century pub **Kate Kearney's Cottage** (Map p278; ☎064-664 4146; www.katekearneyscottage.com; mains €8.50-19.50; ⊙lunch & dinner), where many drivers park in order to walk up to the Gap. You can also rent ponies and jaunting cars here (bring cash).

Beaufort Bar & Restaurant (Map p278; ☎064-664 4032; www.beaufortbar.com; Beaufort; mains €16-22; ⊙lunch Sun, dinner Fri & Sat) Continuing north to the N72, you'll reach this charming 1851 stone pub. Upstairs, its exceptional restaurant utilises local produce in starters such as Aghadoe black pudding and mains based on Kerry lamb. The gleaming timber dining room is refined, intimate and relaxed.

See p284 for tips on exploring the Gap, and see Tours for more information.

MACGILLYCUDDY'S REEKS

Ascending **Macgillycuddy's Reeks** and their neighbours (Purple, Tomies and Shehy mountains, between the Gap of Dunloe and Lough Leane, and Torc and Mangerton mountains, southeast of Muckross Lake) should never be attempted without a map and compass (and knowing how to use them). Weatherproof and waterproof footwear and clothing are essential at all times of the year. Seek advice locally before attempting mountain walks.

There are several ways up **Carrantuohil**, the country's highest peak, in the Macgillycuddy's Reeks range. Some require reasonable hill-walking ability, others are serious scrambling or rock-climbing routes. Get a taste of the Reeks at close quarters by walking up **Hag's Glen**, the beautiful approach valley that leads to the Callee and Gouragh lakes below the north face of Carrantuohil.

The best approach is from **Cronin's Yard** (☎064-662 4044; www.croninsyard.com; Mealis, Beaufort), where there's a **tearoom**, showers and toilets, a public telephone and packed lunches available on request. It's at the road's end (OS ref 836873), reached from the N72 via Beaufort, west of Killarney. You may be asked to pay a small fee for using the car park. From here, the way lies alongside the River Gaddagh, which you need to ford in places; great care is required if it's in flood. It's just over 3km to the lakes.

The popular but hair-raising way to summit Carrantuohil from the lakes is via **Devil's Ladder**, a gruelling trudge up a badly eroded gully path, southwest of the lakes. The ground is loose in places, and in wet conditions the way becomes muddy. It takes six hours return from Cronin's Yard.

Tours

Killarney Guided Walks WALKS
(☎087 639 4362; www.killarneyguidedwalks.com; adult/child €9/5) Guided two-hour national park walks leave at 11am daily from opposite St Mary's Cathedral at the western end of New St. Tours meander through Knockreer gardens, then to spots where Charles de Gaulle holidayed, David Lean filmed *Ryan's Daughter* and Brother Cudda slept for 200 years. Trips are available at other times on request.

Ross Castle Open Boats BOAT
(☎087 689 9241) The open boats you can charter at Ross Castle offer more appealing trips with boatmen who define 'character'. It normally costs €10 from Ross Castle to the Muckross (Middle) Lake and back; €15 for a tour of all three lakes.

Gap of Dunloe Tours BUS, BOAT
(☎064-663 0200; www.gapofdunloetours.com) Runs Gap of Dunloe bus and boat tours (from €30), with the option of jaunting car (extra €20), or pony (extra €30) rides. Ask about bike-on-boat tours.

Killarney Day Tour BOAT, WALKS
(☎064-663 1068; www.killarneydaytour.com) Offers bus and boat tours (€30) and boat-only tours (€15) from Ross Castle. Also arranges guided walks for all levels.

Corcoran's BUS
(☎064-663 6666; www.corcorantours.com) Runs Gap of Dunloe (€27), Ring of Kerry (€18) and Dingle and Slea Head (€22) tours, as well as tours around Killarney (€15).

Dero's Tours BUS
(☎064-663 1251; www.derostours.com) Gap of Dunloe (€27), Ring of Kerry (€18) and Dingle and Slea Head (€22) tours.

O'Connor Autotours BUS
(☎064-663 4833; www.oconnorautotours.ie) Ring of Kerry tours (from €22).

Killarney Lake Tours BOAT, JAUNTING CAR
(☎087 257 1492; www.killarneylaketours.ie) Has a range of boat and jaunting car tours, plus combination tours.

Outdoors Ireland OUTDOOR ACTIVITIES
(☎086 860 45 63; www.outdoorsireland.com) Kayaking (including sunset kayak trips), walking and rock and mountain climbing.

Hidden Ireland Adventures WALKS
(☎087 221 4002; www.hiddenirelandadventures.com) Twice-weekly guided ascents of Macgillycuddy's Reeks (€75) and customised walks.

Killarney to Kenmare

The vista-crazy N71 to Kenmare (32km) winds between rock and lake, with plenty of lay-bys to stop and admire the views (and recover from the switchback bends). Watch out for the buses squeezing along the road.

About 2km south of the entrance to Muckross House, a path leads 200m to the pretty **Torc Waterfall**. After another 8km on the N71 you come to **Ladies' View**, where the fine views along Upper Lake were much enjoyed by Queen Victoria's ladies-in-waiting. A further 5km on **Moll's Gap** is worth a stop for great views and food – and not necessarily in that order.

 **Avoca Cafe** (www.avoca.ie; mains €9-13; ⊙lunch) has jaw-dropping panoramas and delicious fare like smoked salmon salad, pistachio-studded pork terrine and decadent cakes.

RING OF KERRY

The Ring of Kerry is the longest and the most diverse of Ireland's big circle drives, combining jaw-dropping coastal scenery with emerald pastures and villages.

The 179km circuit winds past pristine beaches, the island-dotted Atlantic, medieval ruins, mountains and loughs (lakes). The coastline is at its most rugged between Waterville and Caherdaniel in the southwest of the peninsula. It can get crowded in summer, but even then, the remote Skellig Ring can be uncrowded and serene – and starkly beautiful.

The Ring of Kerry can easily be done as a day trip, but if you want to stretch it out, places to stay are scattered along the route. Killorglin and Kenmare have the best dining options, with some excellent restaurants; elsewhere, basic (sometimes very basic) pub fare is the norm.

Getting Around

Although you can tour it in one day by car or three days by bicycle, the more time you take, the more you'll enjoy it.

Tour buses travel the Ring in an anticlockwise direction. Getting stuck behind one is tedious, so consider driving clockwise; just watch out on blind corners. There's little traffic on the **Ballaghbeama Gap**, which cuts across the peninsula's central highlands with some spectacular views: it's perfect for a long cycle, as is the longer **Ballaghisheen Pass** to Waterville.

The 214km Kerry Way (p277) starts and ends in Killarney.

Between mid-June and mid-September, **Bus Éireann** (☎064-663 0011; www.buseireann.ie) circumnavigates the Ring of Kerry daily (Killarney to Killarney €25.50, seven hours). Stops include Killorglin, Glenbeigh, Caherciveen, Waterville (stopping for one hour) and Caherdaniel. Outside summer, transport on the Ring is not good.

A number of Killarney tour companies run daily bus trips around the Ring – see p283.

EXPLORING THE GAP OF DUNLOE

The best way to see the Gap is to hire a bike in Killarney and cycle to Ross Castle. Arrive before 11am to catch a boat up the lakes to Brandon's Cottage, then cycle through the Gap and back to Kilkenny via the N72 and a path through the golf course (bike hire and boat trip about €30).

The 1½-hour boat ride alone justifies the trip. It crosses all the lakes, passing islands and bridges and winding between the second two lakes via Meeting of the Waters and the Long Range.

On land, walking, pony or four-person trap can be substituted for cycling. The Gap pony men charge €50 per hour or €80 for the two-hour trip between Brandon's Cottage and Kate Kearney's Cottage. Note that it's hard to do the Gap as part of a walking loop. You can get as far as Kate Kearney's, from where your best bet would be to call a cab, as it's a long slog back to Killarney on busy roads.

You can also drive this route, but really only outside summer and even then walkers and cyclists have the right of way, and the blind hairpin bends are nerve testing. To reach Brandon's Cottage by car you have to drive a long, scenic detour on the N71 to the R568 and then come back down a gorgeous rugged valley. It takes about 45 minutes.

See p283 for tours of the Gap.

WORTH A TRIP

CROMANE PENINSULA

The Cromane Peninsula is the kind of place you have to hear about, because you wouldn't chance upon it otherwise. A five-minute drive off the N70 from both Killorglin and Glenbeigh, its tiny namesake village sits at the base of a narrow shingle spit. Mercifully, it all but escaped the wrath of the Celtic Tiger, with few garish new builds and/or unfinished dwellings. Instead, open fields give way to spectacular water vistas and multihued sunsets.

Cromane's exceptional restaurant is a local secret and justifies the trip.

Jacks Coastguard Restaurant (☎066-976 9102; www.jackscromane.com; mains €16.50-27; ⏲dinner Thu-Sat, lunch & dinner Sun) Entering this 1866-built coastguard station feels like arriving at a low-key village pub. But a narrow doorway at the back of the bar leads to a striking, whitewashed contemporary space with lights glittering from midnight-blue ceiling panels, stained-glass and metallic fish sculptures, a pianist, and huge picture windows overlooking the water. Menu standouts include chicken liver and aged pork pâté, followed by oven-roasted hake with wild mushroom risotto and black truffle oil, as well as a shellfish paella, accompanied by heavenly homemade bread.

For more info on the area, visit www.cromane.net.

Cromane is 9km from Killorglin. Heading southwest from Killorglin along the N70, take the second right and continue straight ahead until you get to the crossroads. Turn right; Jacks Coastguard Station restaurant is on your left.

Killorglin

3900

Travelling anticlockwise from Killarney, the first town on the Ring is Killorglin (Cill Orglan), 23km northwest. The town is quieter than the waters of the River Laune that lap against the eight-arched bridge, built in 1885. In August, there's an explosion of time-honoured ceremonies at the famous pagan festival, the Puck Fair. A statue of King Puck (a goat) peers out from the Killarney side of the river. Author Blake Morrison documents his mother's childhood here in *Things My Mother Never Told Me*.

Festivals & Events

Puck Fair Festival HISTORIC

(Aonach an Phuic; www.puckfair.ie; ⏲mid-Aug) First recorded in 1603, with hazy origins, this lively festival is based around the custom of installing a billy goat (a poc, or puck), the symbol of mountainous Kerry, on a pedestal in the town, its horns festooned with ribbons. Other entertainment ranges from a horse fair and bonny baby competition to street theatre, concerts and fireworks; the pubs stay open until 3am.

Sleeping & Eating

A bunch of old-boozer-style pubs line Upper Bridge St.

TOP CHOICE Bianconi INN €€

(☎066-976 1146; www.bianconi.ie; Bridge St; s/d €60/90, mains €12.50-25; ⏲restaurant lunch & dinner Mon-Sat) Bang in the centre of town, this low-lit inn has a classy ambience and cooked-to-perfection Modern Irish fare like sage-stuffed roast chicken with cranberry sauce. Its spectacular salads, such as Cashel blue cheese, apple, toasted almonds and chorizo, are a meal in themselves. Guestrooms were undergoing refurbishment at the time of writing – check for updates.

Coffey's River's Edge B&B €€

(☎066-976 1750; www.coffeysriversedge.com; the Bridge; s/d €50/70; P🛜) Next to the bridge, you can sit out on the balcony overlooking the river at this contemporary B&B, with spotless spring-toned rooms and hardwood floors. It's a short stroll uphill to the centre of town.

Giovannelli ITALIAN €€

(☎087 123 1353; Lower Bridge St; mains €15-30; ⏲lunch & dinner Tue-Sat) Northern Italian native Daniele Giovannelli makes all of his pasta by hand at this simple but intimate little restaurant. Highlights of the blackboard menu might include seafood linguine with mussels in shells, and beef ravioli.

Ring of Kerry

Windswept beaches, Atlantic waves crashing against rugged cliffs and islands, medieval ruins, soaring mountains and glinting loughs are some of the stunning distractions along the twisting 179km Ring of Kerry circle drive around the Iveragh Peninsula.

Killorglin

1 Even if you're racing around the ring, don't miss its first town (heading anticlockwise). The riverside village of Killorglin (p285) is home to a salmon smokehouse, some standout restaurants and, in August, the historic Puck Fair Festival (p285).

Kenmare

2 A fitting last (or first) stop on the ring, Kenmare (p295) sums up its greatest charms. A beautiful location on the bay (from where boat trips depart), colourful shops and gracious architecture are cornerstones of this classic Irish town.

Skellig Ring

3 A ring within the ring, this 18km loop (p292) off the main route offers an escape from the crowds. The wild, scenic drive links Portmagee and Waterville via a Gaeltacht (Irish-speaking) area centred on Ballinskelligs (Baile an Sceilg).

Valentia Island

4 Islands are a scenic highlight on the ring. Some are accessible by boat, but picturesque Valentia Island (p290) is even easier to reach, via a short bridge. There's also a summer car-ferry service departing just south of Caherciveen (p289).

Caherdaniel

5 The ring's scenery is at its most rugged around Caherdaniel (p293). Highlights here include the Derrynane National Historic Park (p293) with its stately house and palm-filled gardens, horse riding, a Blue Flag beach and water sports galore.

1

4

Clockwise from top left
1. Local farmer at the Puck Fair, Killorglin 2. Traditional shop front, Kenmare 3. Hikers ascending steps, Skellig Michael 4. Farmhouse on Valentia Island

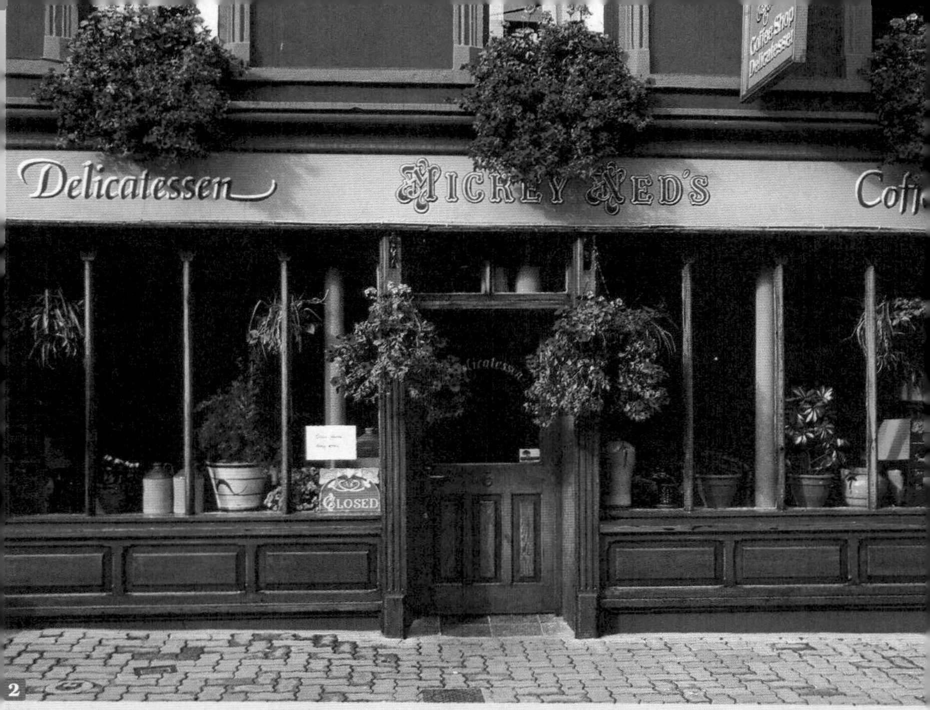

2

GARETH MCCORMACK/LONELY PLANET IMAGES ©

3

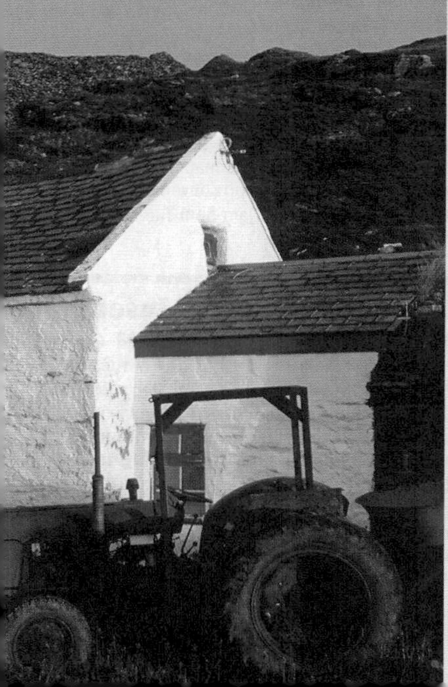

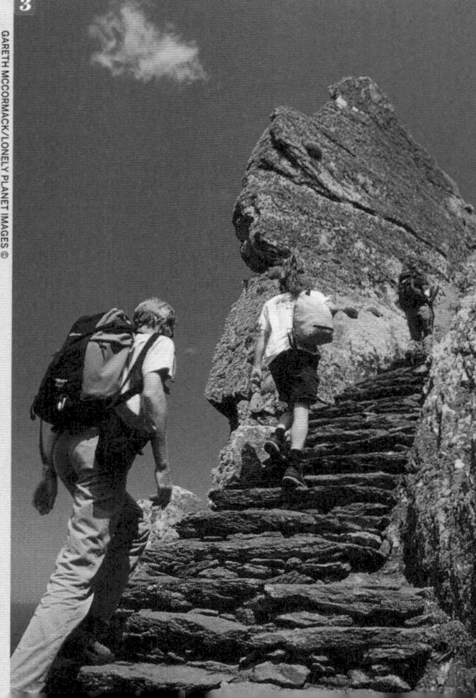

Ring of Kerry

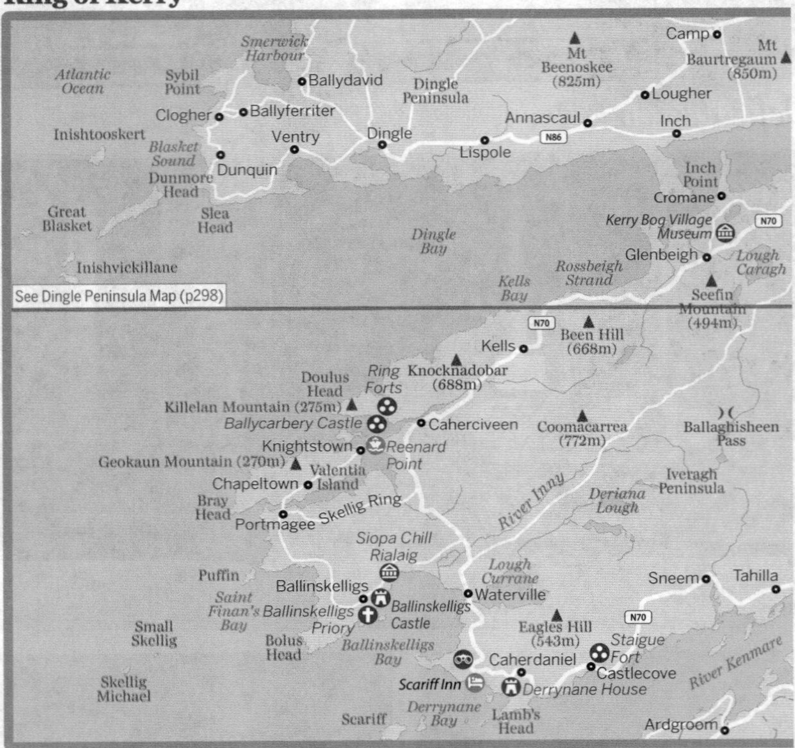

Sol Y Sombra TAPAS €€
(☎066-976 2347; www.solysombra.ie; Lower Bridge St; tapas €6.50-12, mains €15-20; ⏰dinner Wed-Sun) Set in a beautifully renovated 1816 church, Sol Y Sombra transports you to Mediterranean soil with its tapas and larger *raciones* dishes for sharing, such as grilled squid, marinated anchovy fillets and an array of tostadas. Bands often play.

Jack's Bakery BAKERY €
(Lower Bidge St) Jack Healy bakes amazing breads and also makes patés and beautiful sandwiches.

KRD Fisheries SEAFOOD €
(www.krdfisheries.com; the Bridge; ⏰9am-5pm Mon-Fri, 9am-1pm Sat, 9am-11am Sun) Across the bridge from Coffey's River's Edge B&B, you can buy this smokery's salmon direct from the premises.

Information

Tourist office (☎066-976 1451; Library Pl; ⏰10am-3pm Mon-Fri) Sells maps, walking guides, fishing licences and souvenirs.

Library (Library Pl; ⏰10am-5pm Tue-Sat) Free internet access.

Kerry Bog Village Museum

On the N70 between Killorglin and Glenbeigh, the **Kerry Bog Village Museum** (Map p288; www.kerrybogvillage.ie; admission €5; ⏰8.30am-6pm) recreates a 19th-century bog village, typical of the small communities that carved out a precarious living in the harsh environment of Ireland's ubiquitous peat bogs. You'll see the thatched homes of the turfcutter, blacksmith, thatcher and labourer, as well as a dairy, and meet rare Kerry Bog ponies.

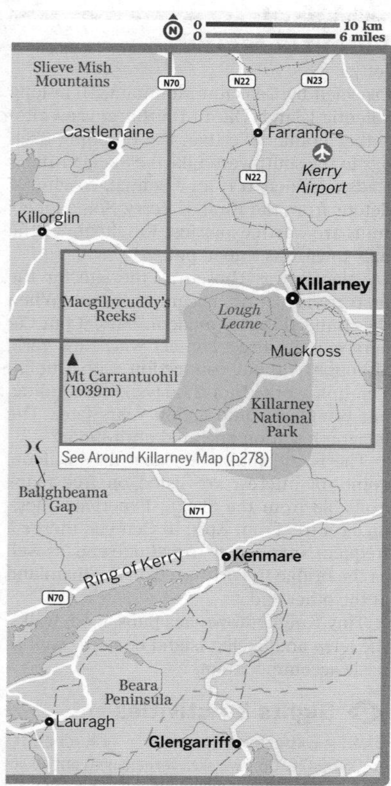

Rossbeigh Strand

This unusual **beach**, 1.6km west of Glenbeigh, is a tendril of sand protruding into Dingle Bay, with views of Inch Point and the Dingle Peninsula. On one side the sea is ruffled by Atlantic winds; on the other it's sheltered and calm.

Burke's Activity Centre (☎087 237 9110; www.burkesactivitycentre.ie; Rossbeigh; admission €6) offers crazy golf, a hedge maze and a working farm, as well as horse trekking (beach rides per hour from €25). Call for seasonal opening hours.

Caherciveen

POP 1300

Caherciveen's population, over 30,000 in 1841, was decimated by the Great Famine and emigration to the New World. A sleepy outpost remains, overshadowed by the 688m peak of **Knocknadobar**. It looks rather dour compared with the peninsula's other settlements, but in many ways this village does more to recall the tough 1930s in Ireland than any other you'll see in Kerry. It's close to a cool castle and some good accommodation.

Sights

Paths along the river have information boards on the area's wildlife.

Ballycarbery Castle & Ring Forts CASTLE, FORTS

(Map p288;) The best attraction locally is the ruins of 16th-century Ballycarbery Castle, 2.4km along the road to White Strand Beach from the barracks. The atmospheric remains are surrounded by green pastures inhabited by cows who like to get in the pictures.

Along the same road are two stone ring forts. **Cahergall**, the larger one, dates from the 10th century and has stairways on the inside walls, a *clochán* (beehive hut), and the remains of a house. The smaller, 9th-century **Leacanabuile** has the entrance to an underground passage. Their inner walls and chambers give a strong sense of what life was like in a ring fort. If driving leave your car in the parking area next to a stone wall and walk up the footpaths.

Barracks HERITAGE CENTRE

(☎066-947 2777; www.theoldbarracks.com; off Main St; adult/child €4/2; ⏲10am-4.30pm Mon-Fri, 11.30am-4.30pm Sat, 1-5pm Sun) The Old Barracks Heritage Centre is housed in a tower of the former Royal Irish Constabulary (RIC). The barracks were burnt down in 1922 by anti-Treaty forces. Today it looks over-restored, like an oddball confection.

Topped by a spiral staircase ascending to a lookout (best suited for those who don't care to see anything), the museum covers the Fenian Rising, Daniel O'Connell and Caherciveen's other great son, Gaelic football star Jack O'Shea. There are recreations of a local dwelling at the time of the Famine and of the barracks during the 1916 Easter Rising.

O'Connell's Birthplace RUINS

The ruined cottage on the eastern bank of the Carhan River, on the left as you cross the bridge en route from Kells, is the humble birthplace of Daniel O'Connell, 'the

Great Liberator' (see p699). On the opposite bank there's a stolid bust of O'Connell.

Activities

Local walks include the 5½-hour **Killelan Mountain circuit** and the less strenuous **foreshore walk** to the castle and ring forts. Ask at the tourist office for info on local guided walks and boat rides.

Festivals & Events

Caherciveen Festival of Music & the Arts MUSIC
(www.celticmusicfestival.com; late Jul/early Aug) Celtic bands, busking competitions and set dancing star at this family-friendly festival held over the August bank holiday weekend.

Sleeping & Eating

B&Bs are scattered around the area. Trad music sessions regularly take place in the town's pubs.

TOP CHOICE **Mannix Point Camping & Caravan Park** CAMPGROUND €
(066-947 2806; www.campinginkerry.com; Mannix Point; campsites from €8.50; Mar-Oct; P) Mortimer Moriarty's award-winning coastal site has an inviting kitchen, campers' sitting room with a turf fire (no TV but regular music sessions), a barbecue area and even a birdwatching platform.

Petit Delice PATISSERIE €
(http://ringofkerrypatisserie.com; Main St; dishes €4.50-10; lunch Mon-Sat;) Scrumptious range of homemade chocolates, ice creams and sorbets, and a counter full of freshly baked cakes, patisseries and breads. Lunchtime dishes include quiches, soups and filled baguettes.

The Thatch Restaurant IRISH €€
(www.thethatchrestaurant.com; Strands End; 2-course menus €19-22; lunch Sun, dinner Thu-Sun;) Inside a cute butter-coloured thatched cottage on the northern edge of Caherciveen, you can tuck into hearty Irish standards over a pint.

Information

Caherciveen has a **post office** and banks with **ATMs**.

AIB has a bureau de change.

The **Barracks Heritage Centre** off Main St is the best place for tourist information.

Valentia Island

POP 720

Crowned by Geokaun Mountain, 11km-long Valentia Island (Oileán Dairbhre) is an altogether homier isle than the brooding Skelligs to the southwest. Like the Skellig Ring it leads to, Valentia is an essential, coach-free detour from the Ring of Kerry. Some lonely ruins are worth exploring. Knightstown, the only town, has a good pub.

Valentia was chosen as the site for the first transatlantic telegraph cable. When the connection was made in 1858, it put Caherciveen in direct contact with New York, although without connection with Dublin. The link worked for 27 days before failing, but went back into action years later. The telegraph station operated until 1966.

The island makes an ideal driving loop. Points of interest are listed on free maps available from the Skellig Experience heritage centre. From April to October, there's a frequent, quick ferry trip at one end, as well as the bridge to Portmagee on the mainland at the other end.

Tiny **Knightstown** has pubs, food, walks, the ferry and Skellig Island boats, as well as basic accommodation.

Sights & Activities

Skellig Experience HERITAGE CENTRE
(066-947 6306; www.skelligexperience.com; adult/child €5/3; 10am-7pm Jul & Aug, to 6pm May, Jun & Sep) Immediately across the bridge from Portmagee, this distinctive building with turf-covered barrel roofs contains exhibitions on the life and times of the Skellig Michael monks, the history of the island's lighthouses and the wildlife. From April to September, it also runs two-hour **cruises** (adult/child €27.50/14.50, incl Skellig Experience entry) around the islands. If the weather's bad, there's often the option of a 90-minute **minicruise** (€22/11 incl entry) in the harbour and channel.

In March, April, October and November the centre is open from 10am to 5pm five days a week, but the exact days change each year – check ahead.

St Brendan's Well HISTORIC SITE
Out in the boggy west, with its lonely vistas worthy of some lost world, look for signs for this ancient religious site that still attracts a smattering of pilgrims. Legend has it that St Brendan sailed here from Dingle, scaled the cliffs (in the 5th century), found a couple of dying pagans and anointed them.

Getting There & Away

A bridge links Valentia Island with Portmagee. From April to September, there is a **ferry service** (☎087 241 8973) to Knightstown on Valentia Island from Reenard Point, 5km southwest of Caherciveen. The five-minute crossing costs one way/return €5/8 for a car, €2/3 for a cyclist and €1.50/2 for a pedestrian. It departs every 10 minutes between 7.45am (9am Sunday) and 9.30pm (10pm in July and August).

Portmagee

POP 375

Portmagee overlooks the south side of Valentia Island from the mainland. Its single street is a rainbow of colourful houses and is much photographed. On summer mornings, the small pier comes to life with boats embarking on the choppy crossing to the Skellig Islands.

Portmagee holds **set-dancing workshops** (www.moorings.ie) over the May bank holiday weekend, with plenty of stomping practice sessions in the town's **Bridge Bar** (bar food €10-22), a friendly local gathering point, which itself is good for impromptu music by locals year-round and more formal sessions in summer.

The Bridge Bar neighbours the **Moorings** (☎066-947 7108; www.moorings.ie; s €70-100, d €100-140; Ⓟ), with 16 rooms split between modern sea-view choices and simpler – and cheaper – options, most refreshingly white. The nautical-themed **restaurant** (mains €18-37; dinner Tue-Sun Apr-Oct) specialises in seafood (including hot seafood platters) and its own pâté.

Perfect for hanging around waiting for the weather to clear for the Skelligs, **Portmagee Hostel** (☎066-948 0018; www.portmageehostel.com; dm €15, d €46-52; wi-fi) is a sociable, no-frills place that's also a good hub for walking. Double rooms at the upper end of the price scale have en suite bathrooms.

Skellig Islands

GANNET POP 45,000

The Skellig Islands (Oileáin na Scealaga) are impervious to the ever-pounding Atlantic. George Bernard Shaw said Skellig Michael was 'the most fantastic and impossible rock in the world'.

You'll need to do your best grisly sea-dog impression ('argh!') on the 12km crossing, which can be rough. There are no toilets or shelter on Skellig Michael, the only island visitors are permitted to land on. Bring something to eat and drink and wear stout shoes and weatherproof clothing. Due to the steep (and often slippery) terrain and sudden wind gusts, it's not suitable for young children or people with limited mobility.

The Skelligs are a **birdwatching** paradise. During the boat trip you may spot diminutive storm petrels (also known as Mother Carey's chickens) darting above the water like swallows. Gannets are unmistakable with their savage beaks, imperious eyes, yellow caps and 100cm-plus wing spans. Kittiwakes – small, dainty seabirds with black-tipped wings – are easy to see and hear around Skellig Michael's covered walkway as you step off the boat. They winter at sea then land in their thousands to breed between March and August.

Further up the rock you'll see stubby-winged fulmars, with distinctive bony 'nostrils' from which they eject an evil-smelling green liquid if you get too close. In May, puffins come ashore to lay a solitary egg at the far end of a burrow, and parent birds can be seen guarding their nests. Puffins stay only until the first weeks of August.

SKELLIG MICHAEL

The jagged, 217m-high rock of **Skellig Michael** (Archangel Michael's Rock; like St Michael's Mount in Cornwall and Mont Saint Michel in Normandy) is the larger of the two islands and a Unesco World Heritage site. It looks like the last place on earth where anyone would try to land, let alone establish a community, yet early Christian monks survived here from the 6th until the 12th or 13th century. Influenced by the Coptic Church (founded by St Anthony in the deserts of Egypt and Libya), their determined quest for ultimate solitude led them to this remote, windblown edge of Europe.

The **monastic buildings** perch on a saddle in the rock, some 150m above sea level, reached by 600 steep steps cut into the rock face. The astounding 6th-century oratories and beehive cells vary in size; the largest cell has a floor space of 4.5m by 3.6m. You can see the monks' south-facing vegetable garden and their cistern for collecting rainwater. The most impressive structural achievements are the settlement's foundations – platforms built on the steep slope using nothing more than earth and drystone walls.

Not much is known about the life of the monastery, but there are records of Viking raids in AD 812 and 823. Monks were kidnapped or killed, but the community recovered and carried on. In the 11th century a rectangular oratory was added to the site, but although it was expanded in the 12th century, the monks abandoned the rock around this time.

After the introduction of the Gregorian calendar in 1582, Skellig Michael became a popular spot for weddings. Marriages were forbidden during Lent, but since Skellig used the old Julian calendar, a trip to the islands allowed those unable to wait for Easter to tie the knot.

In the 1820s two **lighthouses** were built on Skellig Michael, together with the road that runs around the base.

There are no toilets on the island.

SMALL SKELLIG

While Skellig Michael looks like two triangles linked by a spur, Small Skellig is longer, lower and much craggier. From a distance it looks as if someone battered it with a feather pillow that burst. Close up you realise you're looking at a colony of over 20,000 pairs of breeding gannets, the second-largest breeding colony in the world. Most boats circle the island so you can see the gannets and you may see basking seals as well. Small Skellig is a bird sanctuary; no landing is permitted.

Getting There & Away

Skellig Michael's fragility places limits on the number of daily visitors. The 15 boats are licensed to carry no more than 12 passengers each, for a maximum of 180 people at any one time. It's wise to book ahead in July and August, bearing in mind that if the weather's bad the boats may not sail (about two days out of seven). Trips usually run from Easter until September, depending, again, on weather.

Boats leave around 10am and return at 3pm, and cost about €45 per person. You can depart from Portmagee, Ballinskelligs or Derrynane. Boat owners generally restrict you to two hours on the island, which is the bare minimum to see the monastery, look at the birds and have a picnic. The crossing takes about 1½ hours from Portmagee, 35 minutes to one hour from Ballinskelligs and 1¾ hours from Derrynane. Services sometimes run from Knightstown; check with the Skellig Experience heritage centre for updates.

Local pubs and B&Bs will point you in the direction of boat operators, including the following:

Ballinskelligs Boats (☎086-417 6612; http://bestskelligtrips.com; Ballinskelligs)

Casey's (☎066-947 2437; www.skelligislands.com; Portmagee)

John O'Shea (☎087 689 8431; www.skelligtours.com; Derrynane)

Seanie Murphy (☎066-947 6214; www.skelligsrock.com; Reenard Point, Valentia Island)

If you just want to see the islands up close and avoid actually having to clamber out of the boat, you could consider a cruise with Skellig Experience (p290).

Skellig Ring

This fascinating and little-travelled 18km detour from the Ring of Kerry (N70) links Portmagee and Waterville via a Gaeltacht (Irish-speaking) area centred on Ballinskelligs (Baile an Sceilg). Ballinskelligs' name translates as 'town of the crag', which may elicit sniggers from fans of *Father Ted* and his Craggy Island pals (see p404). The area is as wild and beautiful as anything on Ted's fictional isle, with the ragged outline of Skellig Michael never far from view.

Sights

Siopa Chill Rialaig ART GALLERY

(Map p288; ☎066-947 9277; crsiopa@gmail.com; Dun Geagan; ⏰11am-6pm Jul-Aug, by reservation rest of yr) On the site of a village abandoned during the Famine, this contemporary art gallery is packed with work by local artists and talent from around Ireland and the world. It is the shop window of the Cill Rialaig Project, which provides a retreat for creative people who pay for their stay with art.

The gallery is by the R566 at the north-eastern end of Ballinskelligs. You'll spot its circular, thatched roofs and the sculpture that resembles a hallucinogenic mushroom. There's a **cafe** inside.

Ballinskelligs Priory & Bay RUINS, BEACH

The sea and salty air are eating away at the atmospheric ruins of this **medieval priory** (Map p288), a monastic settlement that was probably built by the Skellig Michael monks after they fled their isolated outpost in the 12th century. To reach it, follow the sign to the pier at the western end of town and you will see it on the left.

Another sign points to the fine little blue flag **beach**. At the western end of the beach are the last remnants of the 16th-century **castle** stronghold of the McCarthys, built on the isthmus as a defence against pirates.

Activities

St Finian's Bay is good for surfing. **Ballinskelligs Watersports** (☎086 389 4849; www.skelligsurf.com) hires out surfboards, kayaks and windsurfers, and gives lessons (surfing/windsurfing per two hours €35/€45).

Sleeping & Eating

The Old School House B&B €€
(☎066-947 9340; www.rascalstheoldschoolhouse.com; Cloon; d €69; P 📶 👪) Colourful checked fabrics, rustic prints and painted architraves brighten the rooms of this charmer of a B&B. Pancakes with berries and cream are among the tempting breakfast choices.

Caifé Cois Trá CAFE €
(☎066-947 9323; snacks €2-3.50; ⏲breakfast & lunch) At the Ballinskelligs strand car park, locals flock to this beach-hut cafe and craft shop for their morning caffeine jolt.

Waterville

POP 550

Waterville, a line of colourful houses strung on the N72 between Lough Currane and Ballinskelligs Bay, is charm-challenged in the way of many such mass-consumption beach resorts. A statue of its most famous guest, Charlie Chaplin, beams out from the seafront. The **Charlie Chaplin Comedy Film Festival** (charliechaplincomedyfilmfestival.com) takes place in late August.

Sights in the town itself are few, but at the north end of Lough Currane, **Church Island** has the ruins of a medieval church and beehive cell reputedly founded as a monastic settlement by St Finian in the 6th century.

Mór Active (☎066-947 8857; www.activityireland.ie) rents bikes (per day €15), body boards (€35 including wetsuits), and canoes and kayaks (€50); they can also arrange instruction.

The pick of Waterville's B&Bs is **Brookhaven House** (☎066-947 4431; www.brookhavenhouse.com; New Line; d €90-110; P 📶 👪), a stylish contemporary house run by a friendly family, with spick-and-span rooms and comfy beds. Piping-hot breakfasts are dished up with sea views in the sunny dining room.

Backpackers should head to **Silver Sands** (☎066-947 8788; silversandshostel@gmail.com; Main St; dm €14, d €30; @ 📶), a sociable spot on the seafront with musical instruments for jam sessions. Doubles have en suite bathrooms; avoid the dark downstairs room and go for one upstairs.

A smattering of restaurants and bars are on or just off the main street.

Waterville Craft Market (☎066-947 4212; craftmarket@eircom.net; ⏲9am-6pm) has tourist information in addition to quality Irish jewellery, homewares, clothing and more.

Caherdaniel

POP 350

Hiding between Derrynane Bay and the foothills of Eagles Hill, Caherdaniel barely qualifies as a tiny hamlet. Businesses are scattered about the undergrowth like smugglers, fitting since this was once a haven for the same.

This is the ancestral home of Daniel O'Connell, 'the Liberator' (see p699), whose family made money smuggling from their base by the dunes. The area boasts a blue flag beach, plenty of activities, good hikes and some pubs where you may be tempted to break into pirate talk. Lines of wind-gnarled trees add to the wild air.

Sights

Derrynane National Historic Park HISTORIC SITE
(Map p288; ☎066-947 5113; www.heritageireland.ie; Derrynane; adult/child €3/1; ⏲10.30am-6pm Apr-Sep, 10.30am-5pm Wed-Sun Oct-late Nov) **Derrynane House** is the family home of Daniel O'Connell, the campaigner for Catholic emancipation. His ancestors bought the house and surrounding parkland, having grown rich on smuggling with France and Spain. It's largely furnished with O'Connell memorabilia, including the restored triumphal chariot in which he lapped Dublin after his release from prison in 1844.

The **gardens**, warmed by the Gulf Stream, hold palms, 4m-high tree ferns, gunnera ('giant rhubarb') and other South American species. A **walking track** through them leads to wetlands, beaches and clifftops. You can spot wild pheasants and other birds, whose musical calls add a note of contrast to the dull roar of the surf. The **chapel**, which O'Connell added to Derrynane House in 1844, is a copy of the ruined one on **Abbey Island**, which can usually be reached on foot across the sand.

Look out for the **Ogham stone** on the left of the road to the house. With its carved

DON'T MISS

IRELAND'S FINEST VIEW

Midway between Waterville and Sneem, the **Scarriff Inn** (☎066 947 5132; http://scarriffinn.com; Caherdaniel; d €70, mains €16-24; ⏲restaurant lunch & dinner; P) claims to have 'Ireland's finest view'. And, even in such a scenic country, they might just be right. The Scarriff's wall-to-wall windows frame stupendous views across the rocky coastline and scattered islands to Kenmare Bay and Bantry Bay. Drink them in over a snack, steak or seafood (call ahead to confirm seasonal kitchen hours) or just a pint. Or wake up to them from one of its six airy rooms with private bathrooms at its neighbouring B&B, which can also organise dive trips and fishing gear.

notches representing the simple Ogham alphabet of the ancient Irish, the stone has several missing letters, but is thought to represent the name of a local chieftain.

Activities

Most of the activity here centres on the beach. The Kerry Way (p277) passes through here and continues on to a megalithic tomb at the base of Farraniaragh Mountain, 248m above sea level.

Derrynane Sea Sports WATER SPORTS
(☎087 908 1208; www.derrynaneseasports.com) Organises sailing, canoeing, windsurfing and waterskiing for all levels, operating from the beach.

Eagle Rock Equestrian Centre HORSE RIDING
(☎066-947 5145; www.eaglerockcentre.com) Offers beach, mountain and woodland treks for all levels from €30 per hour.

Sleeping & Eating

Olde Forge B&B €
(☎066-947 5140; www.theoldeforge.com; d €60; 📶) Fantastic views of Kenmare Bay and the Beara Peninsula unfold from this B&B, which has six streamlined, comfortable rooms. If you want to base yourself here for some R&R, it also has two self-catering cottages (from €400 per week). It's 1.2km southeast of town on the N70.

Wave Crest CAMPGROUND €
(☎066-947 5188; www.wavecrestcamping.com; campsites from €21; P@) Just 1.6km southeast of Caherdaniel, this cliffside park has a superb setting and well-kept facilities. Book ahead during high season.

Blind Piper PUB €€
(☎066-947 5126; mains €12-17; ⏲lunch & dinner) This local institution with tables outside is a great family pub during the day, serving expensive but quality grub. Deep-fried monkfish gives the idea that they're striving for more here. After dark, locals and visitors crowd inside, and music sessions strike up.

Sneem

Halfway between Caherdaniel and Kenmare, Sneem (An tSnaidhm) is a good place to pause, especially if you're travelling anticlockwise, as for the remaining 27km to Kenmare the N70 drifts away from the water and coasts along under a canopy of trees.

The village's Gaeilge name translates as 'the knot', which is thought to refer to the River Sneem that swirls, knot-like, into nearby Kenmare Bay. Sneem is nicknamed 'the knot in the Ring of Kerry'. Other local puns include one about Charles de Gaulle, who holidayed here when Paris was burning in 1968. The statue commemorating this is called 'Le Gallstone'.

Take a gander at the town's two cute squares, then pop into the **Blue Bull** (South Square; mains €12-22; ⏲lunch & dinner), a perfect little old stone pub where you can probably learn more local puns.

The area is home to one of the finest castle hotels in the country.

TOP CHOICE **Parknasilla Resort & Spa** HOTEL €€€
(☎064-667 5600; www.parknasillahotel.ie; d from €180; P@≋📶) This hotel has been wowing guests (including one George Bernard Shaw) since 1895 with its 500 acres of pristine resort on the edge of the village of Sneem with the broad expanse of the Kenmare River separating it from the Beara Peninsula to the south (oh, the views!). From the modern, luxuriously appointed bedrooms to the top-grade spa (which includes a lap pool) and the elegant restaurant serving superb modern Irish cuisine, everything here is done just right: the service is friendly and professional without ever becoming fussy or overly obsequious. Irish hospitality at its very best.

Kenmare

POP 2500

The copper-covered limestone spire of Holy Cross Church, drawing the eye to the wooded hills above town, may make you forget for a split second that Kenmare is a seaside town. But with rivers named Finnihy, Roughty and Sheen emptying into Kenmare Bay, you couldn't be anywhere other than southwest Ireland.

In the 18th century, Kenmare was laid out on an X-plan, with a triangular market square in the centre. Today the inverted V to the south is the focus. Kenmare Bay stretches out to the southwest, and there are glorious views of the mountains.

Sights

FREE Kenmare Heritage Centre HERITAGE CENTRE

(064-664 1233; kenmaretio@eircom.net; the Square; vary) Reached through the tourist office, Kenmare's heritage centre tells the history of the town from its founding as Neidín by the swashbuckling Sir William Petty in 1670. The centre also relates the story of the Poor Clare Convent, founded in 1861, which is still standing behind Holy Cross Church.

Local women were taught needlepoint lace-making at the convent and their lacework catapulted Kenmare to international fame. Upstairs from the Heritage Centre, the **Kenmare Lace and Design Centre** (www.kenmarelace.ie) has displays including designs for 'the most important piece of lace ever made in Ireland' (in a 19th-century critic's opinion).

It's generally open Monday to Wednesday and Friday to Saturday from 9.15am to 5pm from Easter to October but hours can vary.

Stone Circle STONE CIRCLE

Signposted southwest of the Square is an early Bronze Age stone circle, one of the biggest in southwest Ireland. Fifteen stones ring a boulder dolmen, a burial monument rarely found outside this part of the country.

Holy Cross Church CHURCH

(Old Killarney Rd) Built in 1862, this church has a splendid wooden roof with 14 angel carvings. Intricate **mosaics** adorn the aisle arches and edges of the stained-glass window over the altar. The architect was Charles Hansom, collaborator and brother-in-law of Augustus Pugin (the architect behind London's Houses of Parliament).

Activities

The tourist office has details of **walks** around Kenmare Bay and into the hills, on sections of the Kerry Way (p277) and Beara Way (p264).

Star Sailing WATER SPORTS

(064-664 1222; www.staroutdoors.ie; R571, Dauros) Offers activities including sailing (per hour from €65 for up to six people; you'll need some prior experience), sea kayaking (single/double per hour €18/32) and hillwalking for all levels.

Seafari BOAT TRIPS

(064-664 2059; www.seafariireland.com; Kenmare Pier; adult/child €20/12.50; Apr-Oct) Warm yourself on tea, coffee, rum and the captain's sea shanties on an entertaining two-hour spotting voyage to see Ireland's biggest seal colony and other marine life; binoculars (and lollipops!) are provided.

Sleeping

B&Bs abound, especially on Henry St.

TOP CHOICE Virginia's Guesthouse B&B €€

(064-664 1021; www.virginias-kenmare.com; Henry St; s/d €60/80;) You can't get more central than this award-winning B&B, whose creative breakfasts celebrate organic local produce (rhubarb and blueberries in season, for example, as well as fresh-squeezed OJ and porridge with whiskey). Its eight rooms are super comfy without being fussy. Outstanding value.

Sheen Falls Lodge BOUTIQUE HOTEL €€€

(064-664 1600; www.sheenfallslodge.ie; d €115-230; Feb-Dec;) The Marquis of Landsdowne's former summer residence still feels like an aristocrats' playground, with a spa and 66 rooms with DVD players and Italian marble bathrooms, and views of the falls and across Kenmare Bay to Carrantuohil. Amenities are many (clay-pigeon shooting, anyone?).

Hawthorn House B&B €€

(064-664 1035; www.hawthornhousekenmare.com; Shelbourne St; d €80-90;) This stylish house has eight spacious rooms, including a majestic family room, all named after local towns and decked out with fresh flowers. It's set back from busy Shelbourne St behind a low wall.

Whispering Pines B&B €€
(☎064-664 1194; wpines@eircom.net; Glengarrif Rd; s/d €45/80; ⊙Easter-Nov; 📶) In a quiet spot near the pier, this homey B&B has four immaculate rooms and a cheerful welcome. The location out here near the brine is fantastic; town is less than five minutes' stroll away.

Rose Cottage B&B €€
(☎064-664 1330; The Square; d €60-70; 📶👪) Opposite the park on the central square, amid beautiful gardens, this stone-fronted building has three rooms with private bathrooms. The Poor Clare nuns stayed here when they arrived in Kenmare, then had to leave just as the apples were ripening in the orchard.

Greenville B&B B&B €€
(☎064-664 1769; Killowen Rd; d €70) Just 100m east of Main St, this modern house has hedged cottage gardens and ancient stone walls, as well as four comfy bedrooms with en suite bathrooms. Breakfasts are hearty and the bucolic scene is enhanced by views of the golf course.

Eating

TOP CHOICE Horseshoe PUB €€
(☎064-664 1553; www.thehorseshoekenmare.com; 3 Main St; mains €14.50-26.50; ⊙lunch & dinner) Ivy frames the entrance to this gastropub, which has a short but excellent menu that runs from Kenmare Bay mussels in creamy apple cider sauce to local lamb on mustard mash and Kerry's best burgers. Vegetarian specials appear daily.

D'Arcy's Oyster Bar and Grill IRISH €€
(☎064-664 1589; www.darcyskenmare.com, mains €14.50-25.50, d €50; ⊙dinner; 📶) Local purveyors supply the best in organic produce, cheeses and fresh seafood, all served in modern, low-key surrounds. The raw oysters capture the scent of the bay; the hazelnut-crusted, twice-baked crab and prawn soufflé is divine. Guests staying in its antique-adorned rooms get discounted evening meals.

The Bread Crumb BAKERY, CAFE €
(www.thebreadcrumb.com; New Rd; dishes €4-8; ⊙breakfast & lunch) Not only does this bakery have a tantalising selection of freshly baked breads, its vegetarian cafe has blackboard specials like rice slices with roast pepper, spinach and blue cheese, and spelt pancakes with sun-dried tomatoes.

Mulcahys Restaurant IRISH €€
(☎064-42383; 36 Henry St; mains €18.50-29.50; ⊙dinner Thu-Sun) Creative twists on local seafood, such as cod with pomme purée, and pan-seared scallops with caper and raisin dressing, are the pick of the menu here, but Mulcahys also serves meat-based classics like beef Wellington.

Prego IRISH, ITALIAN €
(☎064-664 2350; Henry St; mains €7.50-11; ⊙breakfast, lunch & dinner; 👪) Prego's breakfast menu is long and varied, and the antidote to the black pudding you've avoided on your B&B plate (the crispy bacon sandwiches are a winner). Other specialities include great-value pizza and pasta.

PF McCarthy's PUB €€
(☎064-664 1516; 14 Main St; dinner €14-24.50; ⊙lunch Mon-Sat, dinner Tue-Sat) Proudly boasting 'no fried food', this mannered spot serves meals well above the pub-grub norm.

Truffle Pig DELI €
(⊙Mon-Sat) Fine meats, farmhouse cheeses and a treasure trove of other deli items from the region.

Farmers Market MARKET €
(⊙10am-4pm Wed) On the Square.

Drinking & Entertainment

Crowley's PUB
(Henry St) Traditional pub with good trad sessions.

Florry Batt's PUB
(Henry St) Draws a cheerful crowd and occasional singalongs.

PF McCarthy's LIVE MUSIC
(14 Main St) A wide range of acts perform from Thursday to Saturday.

Shopping

Kenmare has many quality craft shops. On 15 August every year, marketers from throughout Ireland descend on the town with crafts, local produce, ponies, cattle, sheep and bric-a-brac.

PFK Gold & Silversmith JEWELLERY
(www.pfk.ie; 18 Henry St) Minimalist jewellery by Paul Kelly and contemporary Irish designers. Kelly also takes commissions.

Soundz of Muzic MUSIC
(www.soundzofmuzic.ie; 9 Henry St) Great selection of instruments and Irish and contemporary music.

Information

The website www.kenmare.com is crammed with tourist information. Banks and ATMs are common.

Post office (cnr Henry & Shelbourne Sts)

Tourist office (☎064-663 1633; The Square; ⏰9am-5pm Easter-Oct) Pick up free maps detailing a heritage trail around town and longer walks of up to 13km.

Getting There & Away

The twisting, 32km-long drive on the N71 from Killarney is surprisingly dramatic with tunnels and stark mountain vistas.

Twice-daily buses serve Killarney (€8.82, 50 minutes), with additional services in summer. Buses stop outside Roughty Bar (Main St).

Finnegan's Coach & Cab (☎064-664 1491; www.kenmarecoachandcab.com) Runs a variety of tours including the Ring of Kerry.

Getting Around

Finnegan's Cycle Centre (☎064-664 1083; Shelbourne St) Rents bikes for €15/85 per day/week.

DINGLE PENINSULA

Unlike the Ring of Kerry, where the cliffs tend to dominate the ocean, it's the ocean that dominates the smaller Dingle Peninsula. The opal-blue waters surrounding the promontory's multihued landscape of green hills and golden sands give rise to aquatic adventures and to fishing fleets that haul in impossibly fresh seafood that appears on the menus of some of the county's finest restaurants.

Dingle Peninsula culminates in Europe's westernmost point, gazing across the sound at the ghost town on Great Blasket Island. Mt Brandon, the Connor Pass and other mountainous areas add drama, as do a high concentration of ring forts and other ancient ruins. But it's where the land meets the ocean, at whitewater-pounded rocks or secluded coves, that Dingle's beauty is unforgettable.

Centred on charming Dingle town, there's an alternative way of life here, lived by artisans and idiosyncratic characters and found at trad sessions and folkloric festivals across Dingle's tiny settlements.

The classic loop drive around Slea Head from Dingle town is 50km, but allow a day to take it all in – longer if you have time to stay overnight in Dingle town. The main road to Dingle town is the N86 via Tralee but the coast road is far more beautiful and shouldn't be missed.

The following section follows a figure eight, starting from the southwestern end nearest Killarney and following the scenic coast road to Dingle town, looping around Slea Head and passing back through Dingle town before traversing the Connor Pass to the northern side of the peninsula, from where you can rejoin the N86 to Tralee and Killarney.

Tours

A number of Killarney companies run daily day trips by bus around the Dingle Peninsula (see p283). Alternatively, Dingle-based companies operate guided minibus tours of the peninsula daily from May to September.

O'Connor's Slea Head Tours HISTORIC
(☎087 248 0008; www.dingletourskerry.com; €10 per person, per hr; ⏰11am & 2pm daily) Mainly covers the coast, with a focus on forts and other ancient sites. Tours last approximately three to four hours, departing from Dingle town's tourist office.

Getting Around

Regular buses serve Dingle town from Killarney and Tralee (see p307), but service to the rest of the peninsula is limited to community buses running once or twice a week. Your own wheels (two or four) are the best way to explore the peninsula; alternatively you can join a tour leaving from Dingle town or Killarney.

For drivers, the N86 from Tralee to Dingle town has little to recommend it other than being faster than the Connor Pass route. By bike it's less demanding.

On foot, the Dingle Way (p305) runs near the road for the first three days. The thicket of lanes on the north side of the Dingle Peninsula is matched only by the even thicker network of walking paths. Get the Ordnance Survey Discovery series no 70, which shows every path on the peninsula in exhaustive detail.

Killarney to Dingle Town via Castlemaine

The quickest route from Killarney to Dingle passes through Killorglin and Castlemaine. At Castlemaine, head west on the R561. You'll soon meet the coast, then pass through the beachy seaside town of Inch before joining the N86 to Dingle.

Dingle Peninsula

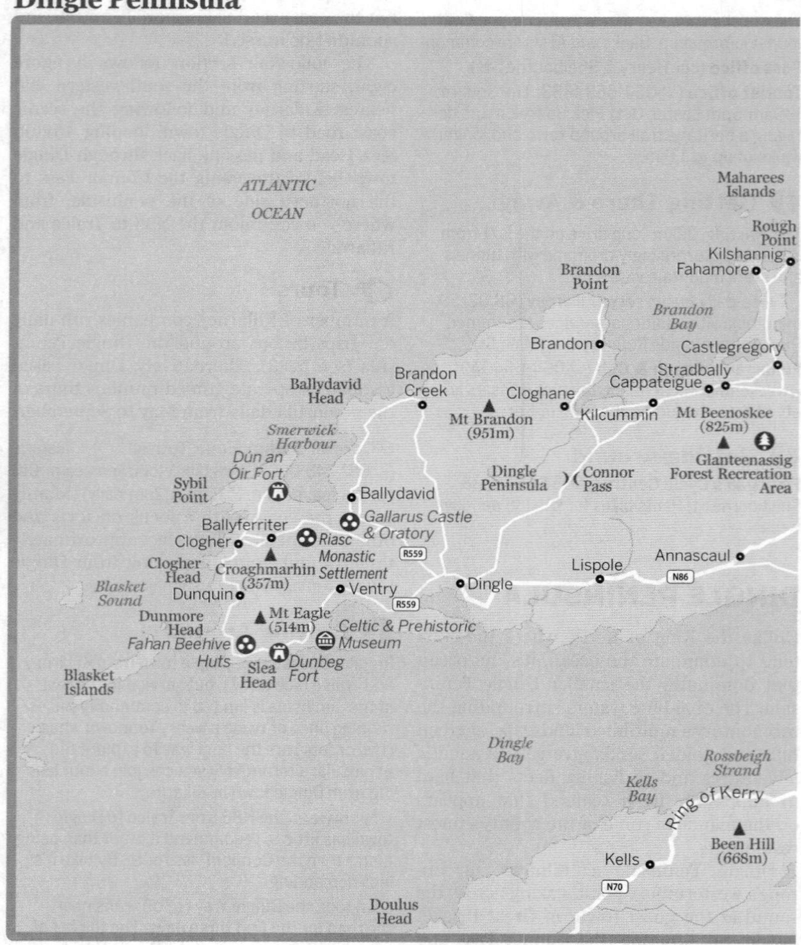

Phoenix Vegetarian Restaurant & Accommodation (066-976 6284; www.thephoenixorganic.com; Shanahill East, Castlemaine; campsites €12, s €52.50, d €70, mains €14-23; lunch & dinner Easter-Oct) The owner of this colourful place runs a dance centre here and there's a film club, music and various theme nights. The restaurant specialises in vegetarian dishes using produce from the organic gardens. Rooms are quirkily interesting, but be sure to inspect the gypsy caravans and toilets before you commit. It's 1.5km west of Boolteens village, which is just over 4km west of Castlemaine.

Castlemaine is well connected with Tralee, Killorglin, and Limerick via Killarney, but there are no buses from Castlemaine to Annascaul via Inch.

INCH

Inch's 5km-long **sand spit** was a location for both *Ryan's Daughter* and *Playboy of the Western World*. Sarah Miles, love interest in the former film, described her stay here as 'brief but bonny'.

The dunes are certainly bonny, scattered with the remains of **shipwrecks** and **Stone Age and Iron Age settlements**. The west-

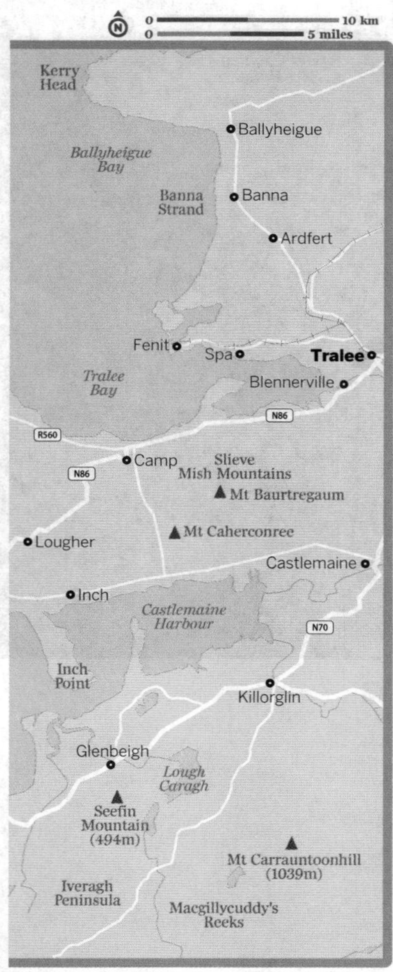

facing beach is also a hot surfing spot; waves average 1m to 3m. Learn to ride them with **Westcoast Surf School** (☎086 836 0271; www.westcoastsurfschool.ie), which offers lessons starting from €30/20 per adult/child for a two-hour group class.

Cars are allowed on the beach, but don't end up providing others with nonstop laughs by getting stuck.

Sammy's (☎066-915 8118; mains €12.50-19; ⏲lunch & dinner; @ 📶 👪), at the entrance to the beach, is the nerve centre of the village. The beach-facing bar-restaurant serves a vast range of dishes from sandwiches and pasta to fresh oysters and mussels. There's a shop, tourist information and trad sessions during the summer. Camping is offered in a field above the beach – at the time of research there were no amenities (and none planned), making pitching up free.

Chic and contemporary, **Inch Beach Guest House** (☎066-915 8333; www.inchbeachguesthouse.com; d from €70; P @ 👪) is more like a boutique hotel than a guesthouse: all skylights and sea views. Airy, neutral-toned rooms come with king-size beds. For longer stays, ask about its spectacularly sited self-catering cottages.

Annascaul

POP 271

The main reason to pause in Annascaul (Abhainn an Scáil), also spelled Anascaul, is to visit the **South Pole Inn** (☎066-915 7388; Main St; mains €12.50-18; ⏲lunch & dinner). Antarctic explorer Tom Crean ran this big blue pub in his retirement. Now it's a regular Crean **museum** and **gift shop**, as well as a cracking pub serving hearty dishes worthy of an explorer. It's signposted from the coast road; buses stop here on the Dingle to Tralee run.

Dingle Town

POP 1800

Framed by its fishing port, the peninsula's charming little 'capital' is quaint without even trying. Dingle is one of Ireland's largest Gaeltacht towns; many pubs double as shops, so you can enjoy Guinness and a singalong among screws and nails, wellies and horseshoes. It has long drawn runaways from across the world, making it a surprisingly cosmopolitan, creative place. In summer its hilly streets can be clogged with visitors, there's no way around it; in other seasons its authentic charms are yours for the savouring.

Although this is Gaeltacht country, the locals have voted to retain the name Dingle rather than go by the officially sanctioned – and dictated – An Daingean.

Sights

Dingle is one of those towns whose very fabric is its attraction. Wander up and down the streets, poke around back alleys, head off across the docks and amble into quality shops and pubs and see what you find.

Dingle Peninsula

The enchanting Dingle Peninsula distils County Kerry's best attractions into an eminently manageable day trip. But, like the many artisans who now call it home, the longer you spend here, the more likely it is you'll never want to leave – or at least return at the first opportunity.

Slea Head

1 The Dingle Peninsula's piéce de résistance is Slea Head (p308), which has the greatest concentration of ancient sites in Kerry. In between them – and the camera-craving scenery – illuminating stops include the quirky Celtic & Prehistoric Museum (p308).

Castlegregory

2 On the northern side of the Dingle Peninsula, Castlegregory (p311) is the gateway to its water sports playground. Diving is the number one attraction; there are also magical woodlands to wander.

Connor Pass

3 There are quicker routes across the Dingle Peninsula's interior, but none as scenic as Connor Pass (p310). As Ireland's highest mountain pass, at 456m, it has captivating views across the peninsula.

Inch Beach

4 Perfect breakers, a wide, sandy shore and a brilliant pub/restaurant/cafe, Sammy's (p299), make Inch Beach an essential stop. Sign up for surf lessons or take blustery walks along the 5km-long sand spit.

Dingle Town

5 The peninsula's namesake 'capital' (p299) fulfils every notion of an Irish seaside village: antique pubs still doubling as grocery stores, higgledy-piggledy streets, trad music sessions and a harbour unloading fresh seafood.

Clockwise from top left

1. Wild iris at Slea Head **2.** View of Scariff island and Castlegregory cliffs **3.** Waterfall, Connor Pass **4.** Inch beach at sunset

1

4

2

3

Dingle Town

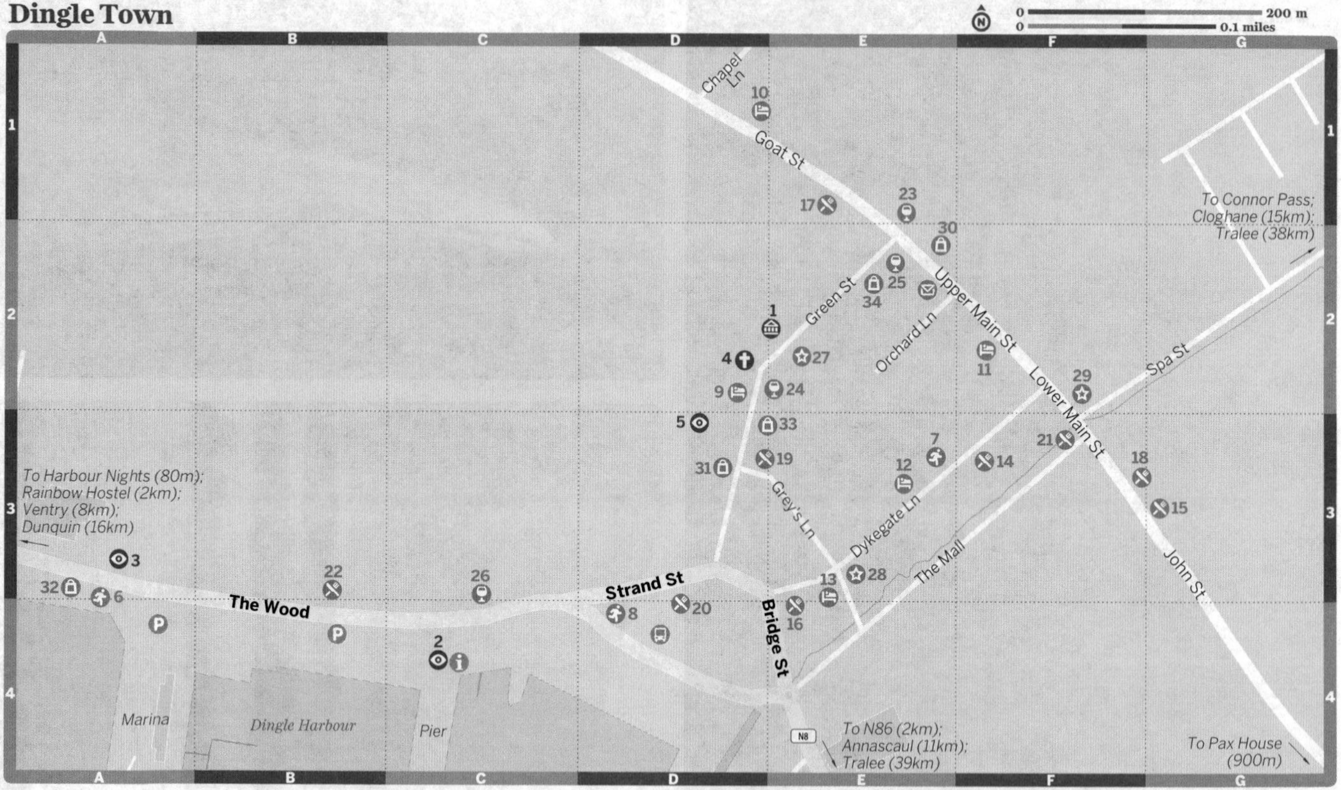

0 200 m
0 0.1 miles
To Connor Pass; Cloghane (15km); Tralee (38km)
To Harbour Nights (80m); Rainbow Hostel (2km); Ventry (8km); Dunquin (16km)
To N86 (2km); Annascaul (11km); Tralee (39km)
To Pax House (900m)
Chapel Ln
Goat St
Green St
Upper Main St
Orchard Ln
Lower Main St
Spa St
John St
Grey's Ln
Dykegate Ln
The Mall
Strand St
Bridge St
The Wood
N8
Marina
Dingle Harbour
Pier

Dingle Town

Sights
1 An Díseart ... E2
2 Dingle Boatmen's Association ... C4
3 Dingle Oceanworld ... A3
4 St Mary's Church ... D2
5 Trinity Tree ... D3

Activities, Courses & Tours
6 Dingle Marina Diving Centre ... A3
7 Dingle Music School ... E3
8 Mountain Man Outdoor Shop ... D4

Sleeping
9 An Capall Dubh ... D2
10 Barr Na Sráide Inn ... D1
11 Dingle Benner's Hotel ... F2
12 Hideout Hostel ... E3
13 Kirrary ... E3

Eating
14 An Café Liteártha ... F3
15 Doyles ... G3
16 Farmers Market ... E4
17 Goat Street Cafe ... E1
18 Half Door ... F3
John Benny's ... (see 26)
19 Little Cheese Shop ... D3
20 Murphy's ... D4
21 Old Smokehouse ... F3
22 Out of the Blue ... B3

Drinking
23 Curran's ... E1
24 Dick Mack's ... E2
25 Foxy John's ... E2
26 John Benny's ... C3

Entertainment
27 Blue Zone ... E2
MacCarthy's ... (see 17)
28 Phoenix Dingle ... E3
29 Small Bridge Bar ... F2

Shopping
30 An Gailearaí Beag ... E2
31 Brian de Staic ... D3
32 Brian de Staic Workshop ... A3
Dingle Record Shop ... (see 27)
33 Lisbeth Mulcahy ... D3
34 NU Goldsmith ... E2

Dingle Marine & Leisure runs boat trips to the Blasket Islands from the marina – see p308.

Fungie the Dolphin BOAT TRIP
(Map p302; ☎066-915 2626; www.dingledolphin.com; The Pier; adult/child €16/8) Boats run by the Dingle Boatmen's Association cooperative leave the pier daily for one-hour dolphin-spotting trips of Dingle's most famous resident, Fungie (see p304). It's free if Fungie doesn't show, but he usually does.

In the warmer months, the association also runs a daily two-hour boat trip when you can **swim with Fungie** (☎066-915 1146; per person €25, plus wetsuit hire €20; 8am or 9am Apr–mid-Sep). Advance bookings are essential.

Dingle Oceanworld AQUARIUM
(Map p302;☎066-915 2111; www.dingle-oceanworld.ie; Dingle Harbour; adult/child/€13/7.50; 10am-5pm;) Dingle's aquarium is a lot of fun. Psychedelic fish glide through tanks that recreate such environments as Lake Malawi, the River Congo and the piranha-filled Amazon. Reef sharks and stingrays cruise the shark tank; water is pumped from the harbour for the spectacularly ugly wreck fish. There's a walk-through tunnel and a touch pool.

An Díseart CULTURAL CENTRE
(Map p302; ☎066-915 2476; www.diseart.ie; adult/family €2/5; 9-5pm Mon-Sat) In a magnificent neo-Gothic former convent, this Celtic culture centre has stained-glass windows by Harry Clarke depicting 12 scenes from the life of Christ. Admission includes a 15-minute guided tour.

Trinity Tree SCULPTURE
(Map p302; Green St) Close to **St Mary's Church**, the Trinity Tree sculpture, representing the Holy Trinity, is made from an unusual three-trunked sycamore. Its carved faces make it look like something out of a fairytale.

Activities

Irish Adventures WATER SPORTS
(☎066-915 2400; www.irishadventures.net; Strand St) The **Mountain Man Outdoor Shop** is a shopfront for Irish Adventures, which offers guided trips including rock climbing, mountain climbing, biking, and kayaking with Fungie (half-day or sunset trip €50).

Dingle Jaunting CARRIAGE TOURS
(☎086 177 1117; www.dinglejaunting.com; per person €10) Horse-drawn jaunting cars depart on the hour from the harbour car park for a 40-minute trip around Dingle. At Christmas there are 'jingle jaunts'.

Dingle Marina Diving Centre DIVING
(Map p302; ☎066-915 2789, 915 2422; www.divingdingle.ie; The Wood; s-tank dive incl gear €75, introductory dive €99) Arranges snorkelling and scuba diving trips in Dingle Bay and around the Blasket Islands, as well as courses and wreck dives.

Dingle Hill Walking Club WALKS
(www.dinglehillwalkingclub.com) Great local club that welcomes visitors for regular half-day guided hill walks (many of them free) and full-day eco tours (€50 including packed lunch).

Dingle Music School MUSIC LESSONS
(Map p302; ☎086 319 0438; www.dinglemusicschool.com; Wren's Nest Cafe, Dykegate Lane; per hr €30) John Ryan offers bodhrán and tin whistle workshops for beginners through to experienced players – lessons can be arranged for early morning or evening. Instruments are supplied.

Festivals & Events

Check upcoming events and gigs online at www.dinglenews.com/events.

Dingle Film Festival FILM
(www.dinglefilmfestival.com; mid-Mar) Shorts, feature-length films and documentaries, as well as question and answer sessions and visual art.

Dingle Food & Wine Festival FOOD, WINE
(www.dinglefood.com; early Oct) Fabulous foodie fest featuring a 'taste trail' with cheap-as-chips sampling at over 40 locations around town, plus a market, cooking demonstrations, workshops, and a foraging walk.

Dingle Races HORSE RACES
(www.dingleraces.ie; mid-August) Held every second weekend in August, Dingle's races bring crowds from far and wide. The racetrack is 1.6km east of town on the N86.

Dingle Regatta BOAT RACES
(late Aug) This harbour race in traditional Irish *currach* (or *naomhóg*) canoes is County Kerry's largest event of its kind and inspired the trad song of the same name.

Sleeping

This tourist town has loads of midrange B&Bs. A number of pubs also offer accommodation.

TOP CHOICE **Pax House** B&B €€
(off Map p302; ☎066-915 1518; www.pax-house.com; Upper John St; s/d from €90/120; P@) From its highly individual decor (including contemporary paintings) to the outstanding

FUNGIE THE DOLPHIN: DINGLE'S TOURISM PATRON

In 1984 a bottlenose dolphin swam into Dingle Bay and local tourism hasn't been the same since. Showing an unnatural affinity for humans, it swam around with the local fishing fleet. Eventually somebody got the idea of charging tourists to go out on boats and see the friendly dolphin. Today up to 12 boats at a time and over 1000 tourists a day ply the waters with Dingle's mascot, the cornerstone of the local economy.

A few Fungie facts:

» **His name** One of the first fishermen to take an interest in Fungie was nicknamed Fungie because his efforts to grow a beard looked like fungus. His name became the dolphin's name.

» **His nature** Bottlenose dolphins are migratory, Fungie isn't. Some suspect he escaped from a dolphin show and made Dingle Bay his new home.

» **His sex** Fungie is a boy. There are loads of stories told in local pubs about a friend's cousin who swam with Fungie and found him to be very much a him and *very* friendly.

» **His powers** Promoters arrived in the early 1990s claiming that swimming with Fungie would produce miraculous health benefits, not unlike a trip to Lourdes.

» **His future** Bottlenose dolphins have an average lifespan of 25 years, which is longer than Fungie's been in Dingle. (Uh-oh.)

views over the estuary from room balconies and the terrace, Pax House is a treat. Choose from cheaper hill-facing rooms, rooms that overlook the estuary, and two-room family suites opening to the terrace. Wi-fi is available in the lounge. It's 1km from the town centre.

Hideout Hostel HOSTEL €
(Map p302; ☎066-915 0559; www.thehideouthostel.com; Dykegate Ln; dm €18, d €50; P@🛜) Converted from a former guesthouse, Dingle's newest and best hostel has inherited bathrooms in all rooms. Top-notch facilities include two lounges with groovy furnishings, bike storage and a well-equipped kitchen. Rates include light breakfast (tea, coffee, toast, cereal). Switched-on owner Mícheál is a fount of local info.

Dingle Skellig Hotel HOTEL €€€
(☎066-915 0200; www.dingleskellig.com; d €130-248; P@🛜) An ocean-like swimming pool and a spa with an outdoor hot tub are the highlights of these luxurious digs down near the water, just off the N86. Rooms are rich in chocolate-box-like creams, caramels, hazelnuts and dark browns. There are interconnecting rooms for families, plus a crèche and kids club, as well as a restaurant and several bars.

Kirrary B&B €€
(Map p302; ☎066-915 1606; collinskirrary@eircom.net; Avondale; d €66; P🛜) You'll get plenty of info and chat from the hosts of this cheerful place with decently sized rooms with private bathrooms. Enjoy tea and refreshments in the flowering garden, screened by a hedge.

Harbour Nights B&B €€
(off Map p302; ☎066-915 2499; www.dinglebandb.com; the Wood; d €70-80; P@🛜) Right on the waterfront, away from the hustle and bustle, yet less than five minutes' walk from town, all 14 rooms at this roomy B&B have stunning views of Dingle's harbour, as does the upstairs sitting room, which opens to a terrace.

Dingle Benner's Hotel HOTEL €€€
(Map p302; ☎066-915 1638; www.dinglebenners.com; Main St; s €97-127, d €144-204; P🛜) A Dingle institution, melding old-world elegance, local touches and modern comforts in the quiet rooms, lounge, library and refurbished, very popular Mrs Benners Bar. Rooms in the 300-year-old wing have the most character; those in the new parts are quieter. Wi-fi is available in the bar and is planned for the rest of the building.

DINGLE WAY

This 168km walk loops around the peninsula. It takes eight days to complete, beginning and ending in Tralee, with an average daily distance of 21km. The first three days offer the easiest walking but the first day, from Tralee to Camp, is the least interesting; it could be skipped by taking the bus to Camp. Ordnance Survey Discovery Series map 70 covers the peninsula. **Go Ireland** (www.govisitireland.com) offers seven- and 10-day self-guided walks from €675/885, including pre-booked accommodation, route maps and luggage transfers.

An Capall Dubh B&B €€
(Map p302; ☎066-915 1105; www.ancapalldubh.com; Green St; d €70-80; P🛜) Entered via a 19th-century coach entrance into a cobbled courtyard, this airy B&B is furnished with light timbers and checked fabrics. Ask about its self-catering townhouses, which sleep up to six people.

Barr Na Sráide Inn INN €€
(Map p302; ☎066-915 1331; www.barrnasraide.ie; Upper Main St; s €50-55, d €80-110; P@🛜) The bar by the entrance has a style that only beautifies the crusty regulars and their hearts of gold. One of the best amenities is up on the 3rd floor: a guest self-serve laundry. Parts of the building have wi-fi.

Rainbow Hostel HOSTEL €
(Map p302; ☎066-915 1044; www.rainbowhosteldingle.com; campsite per person €9, dm/d €15/40; P🛜) While this rural, houselike hostel is some 1.5km west of Dingle town centre, there's a free shuttle service and bike hire. It's a good choice when the in-town budget places are packed out or you want to wake up to the scents of nature.

Eating

In a county famed for its seafood, Dingle still stands out. There are some superb restaurants and cafes, as well as excellent pub fare, particularly at John Benny's (p306).

TOP CHOICE **Out of the Blue** SEAFOOD €€€
(Map p302; ☎066-915 0811; The Wood; lunch €10-20, mains €15-30; ⊙dinner daily, lunch Sun) 'No chips', reads the menu of this funky blue-and-yellow, fishing-shack-style restaurant on the waterfront. Despite its rustic surrounds, this is Dingle's best restaurant, with an intense devotion to fresh local seafood; if they don't like the catch, they don't open. Creative dishes change nightly, but might include steamed crab claws in garlic butter or pan-seared scallops flambéed in Calvados. Who needs chips?

Doyle's SEAFOOD €€€
(Map p302; ☎066-915 2674; www.doylesofdingle.ie; 4 John St; mains €25-30; ⊙dinner daily) Recently reopened, the scarlet-fronted Doyle's has reconfirmed its reputation for serving some of the best seafood in the area (which in these parts is really saying something). Starters such as tempura of fish, seafood risotto and seafood pie team up with mains like warm shellfish salad, seafood linguine and lobster.

Old Smokehouse IRISH €€
(Map p302; ☎066-915 1061; http://oldsmokehousedingle.com; Lower Main St; mains €16-29; ⊙lunch daily, dinner Mon-Sat;) Garrett Bradshaw, the new owner and chef of this stone-fronted building, has a small farm, so – in addition to seafood – meat and poultry also figure on the menu, as does basil, which appears in virtually every dish. Combinations include herb-marinated chargrilled sirloin with tiger prawns. Arrive early to grab a table in the conservatory overlooking the stream.

Half Door SEAFOOD €€€
(Map p302; ☎066-915 1600; John St; mains €26-32; ⊙lunch & dinner Mon-Sat) Seafood is superbly presented at this dignified, genteel seafood restaurant. Fish and shellfish are delivered daily fresh from the docks; the local prawns and larger crustaceans are especially good here.

An Café Liteártha CAFE, BOOKSHOP €
(Map p302; Dykegate Ln; snacks €3-6; ⊙9am-6pm Mon-Sat) Curl up with a book, a cup of tea and a scone or a warming soup at this delightful cafe at the back of this bookshop specialising in Irish history, and soak up the spirit of literary Dingle.

Goat Street Cafe CAFE €
(Map p302; www.thegoatstreetcafe.com; Goat St; dishes €5-13; ⊙breakfast & lunch Mon-Sat) With its own photographic gallery, polished hardwood surfaces and sophisticated furnishings, this is one of Dingle's most popular cafes for international fare – from lamb tajines to Thai green curries, ginger stir-fries and Mediterranean casseroles.

Farmers Market MARKET €
(Map p302; cnr Bridge St & Dykegate Ln; ⊙9am-3pm Fri) Fresh produce and homemade goodies galore.

Little Cheese Shop CHEESE €
(Map p302; www.thelittlecheeseshop.net; Grey's Ln; ⊙9.30am-3.30pm Mon-Fri, 10am-5pm Sat) Swiss-trained cheesemaker Maja Binder's tiny shop overflows with aromatic cheeses including her own.

Murphy's ICE CREAM €
(Map p302; www.murphysicecream.ie; Strand St; cones from €3.50; ⊙11.30am-6pm;) Made in Dingle, with branches in Killarney and Dublin, amazing ice cream flavours include Guinness, Kilbeggan whiskey, brown bread, sea salt, honeycomb and cooling mint.

Drinking & Entertainment

Dingle has literally dozens of pubs, many with entertainment. Gigs are listed in the free *West Kerry Live* magazine, widely available around town, and online at www.dinglenews.com.

TOP CHOICE **John Benny's** PUB
(Map p302; www.johnbennyspub.com; Strand St; mains €10-19; ⊙lunch & dinner) A toasty cast iron woodstove, stone slab floor, memorabilia on the walls, great staff and no intrusive TV make this one of Dingle's most enjoyable traditional pubs. An influx of local musos pours in most nights for rockin' trad sessions. The **bar menu**, including creamy seafood chowder, is hands-down the best in town.

Dick Mack's PUB
(Map p302; http://dickmacks.homestead.com; Green St) Announced by stars in the pavement bearing the names of its celebrity customers, Dick Mack's has an irrepressible sense of self. Ancient wood and ancient snugs dominate the interior, which is lit like the inside of a whiskey bottle. Out the back there's a warren of tables, chairs and characters.

Shop pubs PUBS

A number of Dingle's pubs are mongrel affairs that still have vestiges of their lives as shops. Two untouched examples are **Foxy John's** (Map p302; Main St) and **Curran's** (Map p302; Main St), which respectively have old stock of hardware and outdoor clothing lying about. Don't expect an exuberant welcome from the flinty-eyed locals.

MacCarthy's PUB

(Map p302; www.maccarthyspub.com; Goat St) Former bakery containing one of Ireland's smallest venues. There's often music at the weekends.

Small Bridge Bar LIVE MUSIC

(Map p302; An Droichead Beag; Lower Main St) Traditional music kicks off at 9.30pm nightly at this raucous pub by the bridge.

Blue Zone JAZZ, PIZZA

(Map p302; Green St; ⏲from 5.30pm, closed Mon in winter) Great late-night hangout that's part jazz venue, part pizza restaurant and part wine bar, with moody blue and red surrounds.

Phoenix Dingle CINEMA

(Map p302; Dykegate Ln; www.phoenixdingle.net) Cosy family-run cinema screening first releases and art house films.

Shopping

Amid Fungie flotsam you'll find shops with beautiful goods by local artisans.

Lisbeth Mulcahy FASHION, HOMEWARES

(Map p302; www.lisbethmulachy.com; Green St) Beautiful scarves, rugs and wall hangings are created on a 150-year-old loom by this long-established designer. Also sold here are ceramics by her husband, who has a workshop at Louis Mulcahy Pottery (p309), west of Dingle.

An Gailearaí Beag ART, CRAFTS

(Map p302; http://gailearaibeag.blogspot.com; Main St) Often staffed by the artists themselves, this little gallery is a showcase for the work of the West Kerry Craft Guild, selling ceramics, paintings, wood carvings, photography, batik, jewellery, stained glass and much more.

Brian de Staic JEWELLERY

(Map p302; www.briandestaic.com; Green St) This renowned local designer's exquisite modern Celtic work includes symbols such as the Hill of Tara, crosses and standing stones, as well as jewellery inscribed with Ogham script. All of de Staic's jewellery is individually handcrafted. De Staic's **Dingle workshop** (Map p302; The Wood) also has a retail store; there's a handful of other branches around the country.

Dingle Record Shop MUSIC

(Map p302; www.dinglerecordshop.com; Green St) Tucked under jazz venue Blue Zone, this jammed music hub has all the good stuff you can't download yet. Podcasts recorded in-store are available online.

NU Goldsmith JEWELLERY

(Map p302; www.nugoldsmith.com; Green St ⏲Tue-Sat) Original jewellery by Niamh Utsch is on display at this pricey but stylish little gallery.

Information

The banks on Main St have ATMs and bureaux de change. The post office is off Lower Main St. Parking is free throughout town, with metered parking at the harbour.

Tourist office (Map p302; ☎066-915 1188; www.dingle-peninsula.ie; The Pier; ⏲9.15am-5pm Mon-Sat) Busy but helpful, this place has maps, guides and plenty of information on the entire peninsula. It books accommodation for a €5 fee.

Getting There & Away

Bus Éireann (www.buseireann.ie) buses stop outside the car park behind the supermarket. Up to six buses a day serve Killarney (€12.87, 80 minutes) via Tralee (€10.53, 45 minutes), where you can connect across Ireland or hop on the train.

Getting Around

Dingle is easily covered on foot. Taxi company **Dingle Co-op Cabs** (☎087 222 5777) can also arrange private tours of the peninsula.

Bike-hire places include **Foxy John's** (Map p302; ☎066-915 1316; Main St; per day €12), where you can abandon your energetic ideas and simply have a pint.

West of Dingle

At the tip of the peninsula is the Slea Head drive along the R559. It has the greatest concentration of ancient sites in Kerry, if not the whole of Ireland. Specialist guides on sale in An Café Liteártha (p306) and the tourist office in Dingle list the most interesting and accessible sites.

The landscape is dramatic, especially in shifting mist, although full-on sea fog obliterates everything. For the best views, follow the Slea Head drive in a clockwise direction. Although a mere 50km in length, doing this drive justice requires a full day, at least.

VENTRY & AROUND

POP 410

The village of Ventry (Ceann Trá), 6km west of Dingle town, is idyllically set next to a wide sandy bay. It's a departure point for the wild Blasket Islands – see p308 for boats.

An ideal base for exploring the area is **Ceann Trá Heights** (066-915 9866; www.iol.ie/~ventry; s €45-55, d €60-76; Mar-Oct; P), a comfortable, modern five-room guesthouse overlooking Ventry Harbour (rooms 1 and 2 have stunning water views). An open fire warms the cosy sitting room.

Near Ceann Trá Heights is **Long's Riding Stables** (066-915 9723; www.longsriding.com; 1hr/day rides from €30/130), which offers mountain and beach treks, as well as lessons (per hour from €25).

About 3km west of the village, the **Celtic & Prehistoric Museum** (Map p298; 087-770 3280; www.celticmuseum.com; Kilvicadownig, Ventry; admission €5; 10am-5.30pm mid-Mar–Oct) squeezes in an astonishing collection of Celtic and prehistoric artefacts. Among its 500-plus pieces are the largest woolly mammoth skull and tusks in the world, as well as a 40,000-year-old cave bear skeleton, Viking horse-bone ice skates, stone battle-axes, flint daggers and jewellery. It started as the private collection of owner Harry Moore, a US expat musician (ask him to strike up a Celtic tune). The gift shop stocks 'weird stuff', including fossils.

SLEA HEAD & DUNMORE HEAD

Overlooking the mouth of Dingle Bay, Mt Eagle and the Blasket Islands, Slea Head has fine **beaches**, good walks and superbly preserved structures from Dingle's ancient past including **beehive huts**, forts, inscribed stones and church sites. Dunmore Head is the westernmost point on the Irish mainland and the site of the wreckage in 1588 of two Spanish Armada ships.

The Iron Age **Dunbeg Fort** (Map p298) is a dramatic example of a promontory fortification, perched atop a sheer sea cliff about 7km southwest of Ventry on the road to Slea Head. The fort has four outer walls of stone. Inside are the remains of a house and a beehive hut, as well as an underground passage.

The **Fahan beehive huts** (Map p298), including two fully intact huts, are 500m west of Dunbeg Fort on the inland side of the road.

When the kiosks are open in summer, expect to be charged about €2 to €3 for entrance to the sights.

DUNQUIN

Yet another pause on a road of scenic pauses, Dunquin is a scattered village beneath Mt Eagle and Croaghmarhin. It's a hub for all things Blasket. The local website (www.dunchaoin.com) notes that it is the next parish to America.

The **Blasket Centre** (Ionad an Bhlascaoid Mhóir; 066-915 6444; www.heritageireland.ie; adult/child €4/2; 10am-6pm Apr-Oct) is a wonderful interpretive centre in a long, white hall ending in a wall-to-ceiling window overlooking the islands. Great Blasket's rich community of storytellers and musicians is profiled along with its literary visitors like John Millington Synge, writer of *Playboy of the Western World*. The more prosaic practicalities of island life are covered by exhibits on shipbuilding and fishing. There's a cafe with Blasket views and a bookshop.

Europe's westernmost hostel, **Dunquin Hostel** (066-915 6121; www.anoige.ie; dm €15-18.50, tw €42; Mar-Oct; P), has a terrific location near the Blasket Centre, not far from Dunquin Pier, with awesome views. Private rooms and smaller dorms have en suite bathrooms.

Mustard-coloured **De Mórdha B&B** (066-915 6276; www.demordha.com; d from €60;) is a pleasant little B&B with mod cons and great views. The pub is under a 1km walk away. Check for seasonal closures.

An Portán (066-915 6212; www.anportan.com; mains €12-25; Easter-Sep) serves traditional Irish meals with an international flavour. It has a separate guesthouse with 14 modern, large and fairly unadorned rooms.

BLASKET ISLANDS

The Blasket Islands (Na Blascaodaí), 5km out into the Atlantic, are the most westerly islands in the country. At 6km by 1.2km, **Great Blasket** (An Blascaod Mór) is the largest and most visited, and mountainous enough for strenuous **walks**, including a good one detailed in Kevin Corcoran's *Kerry Walks*. All of the Blaskets were inhabited at one time or another; there is evidence of Great Blasket being inhabited during the Iron Age and early Christian times. The last islanders left for the mainland in 1953 after they and the government agreed that it was no longer feasible to live in such isolated and harsh conditions, although today a few people make their home out here for part of the year.

There are no camping facilities on the islands.

Boats trips generally run from Easter to September, but even then weather can cause boat cancellations – call for seasonal sailing times.

Blasket Island Ferries (☎066-915 1344, 066-915 6422; www.blasketisland.com; adult/child €20/10) Boats depart from Dunquin Harbour and take 20 minutes; add €15 for an ecotour of the island.

Blasket Islands Eco Marine Tours (☎066-915 4864, 087 231 6131; www.marinetours.ie; morning/afternoon/day tour €25/35/40) Eco-oriented tours departing from Ventry Harbour.

Dingle Marine & Leisure (☎066-915 1344, 087 672 6100; www.dinglebaycharters.com; ferry adult/child return €30/15, 3hr island tour €40/15) Ferries take 45 minutes from Dingle town's marina.

CLOGHER HEAD & BALLYFERRITER

Continuing north from Dunquin, stop at **Clogher Head**, where a short walk takes you out to the head with views down to a perfect little beach at Clogher. It's a prime resting spot for **seals** and other mammals with thick layers of insulating blubber not affected by the frigid waters.

Follow the road another 500m around to the crossroads at **Clogher**. Leave the loop road here and follow a narrow paved track down to the **beach**. The rugged surf is intoxicating, ceaselessly pounding this perfect crescent of sand.

Back on the loop road, follow the road as it turns inland to reach **Ballyferriter** (Baile an Fheirtearaigh). It's named after Piaras Ferriter, a poet and soldier who emerged as a local leader in the 1641 rebellion and was the last Kerry commander to submit to Cromwell's army. The entire landscape is a rocky patchwork of varying shades of green, delineated by miles and miles of ancient stone walls.

In the tiny village itself, the **Dingle Peninsula Museum** (Músaem Chorca Dhuibhne; ☎066-915 6100; www.westkerrymuseum.com; admission €3.50; ⌚10am-5pm Jun-Sep, by appointment rest of year) is housed in the 19th-century schoolhouse, with displays on the archaeology and ecology of the peninsula. Across the street there's a lonely, lichen-covered church.

Louis Mulcahy Pottery (☎066-915 6229; Clogher; ⌚9am-5.30pm Mon-Fri, 10am-5.30pm Sat & Sun) has contemporary clay creations and a workshop where you can see how they're made and have a spin yourself on a pottery wheel (book ahead). Upstairs, its **cafe** (dishes €3-10) serves open sandwiches topped with organic smoked salmon and Dingle cheeses.

About 2.5km northeast of is **Dún an Óir Fort** (Map p298; Fort of Gold), the scene of a hideous massacre during the 1580 Irish rebellion against English rule. The fort was held by Sir James Fitzmaurice, who commanded an international brigade of Italians, Spaniards and Basques. On 7 November English troops under Lord Grey attacked the fort; within three days the defenders surrendered. All that remains of the fort is a network of grassy ridges, but it's a pretty spot overlooking Smerwick Harbour, which has relatively sheltered waters that lack the sense of impending doom of those facing due west. The fort is about 2.5km north of Ballyferriter, near the Beal Bán beach.

The remains of the 5th- or 6th-century **Riasc Monastic Settlement** (Map p302) are one of the peninsula's more impressive and haunting sites, particularly the pillar with beautiful Celtic designs. Excavations have also revealed the foundations of an oratory first built with wood and later stone, a kiln for drying corn and a cemetery. The ruins are signposted as 'Mainistir Riaisc' along a narrow lane off the R559, about 2km east of Ballyferriter.

If you're not ready to do the Slea Head loop in a day, or you just want a fine base for explorations on foot, **An Speice** (☎066-915 6254; www.anspeice.com; Ballyferriter; s/d 40/66; P 🛜; ⌚Feb-Nov) has four sunny rooms furnished in an attractive modern style that would flummox most Irish B&B owners: where are the garish patterns? The mismatched linen? The colours usually seen these days only on rusting '70s appliances?

Free camping is possible near Ferriter's Cove but there are no facilities; ask locally before pitching.

GALLARUS CASTLE & ORATORY

One of the Dingle Peninsula's few surviving castles, **Gallarus Castle** (☎087 249 7034; www.heritageireland.ie; adult/child €3/free; ⌚10am-6pm Jun-Aug) was built by the FitzGeralds around the 15th century. Guided tours can be arranged by phoning in advance. There's no parking next to the castle.

The dry-stone Gallarus Oratory (☎066-915 6444; www.heritageireland.ie; admission free; ⊙10am-6pm Jun-Aug) is quite a sight, standing in its lonely spot beneath the brown hills as it has done for some 1200 years. It has withstood the elements perfectly, apart from a slight sagging in the roof. Traces of mortar suggest that the interior and exterior walls may have been plastered. Shaped like an upturned boat, it has a doorway on the western side and a round-headed window on the eastern side. Inside the doorway are two projecting stones with holes that once supported the door.

Parking by the oratory is extremely limited and tends to become a mess in summer. There is a nearby private parking area at the visitor centre (☎066-915 5333; adult/child €3/free; ⊙9am-9pm Jun-Aug, 10am-6pm Feb-May & Sep-10 Nov) that shows a 15-minute audiovisual display.

The castle and oratory are signposted off the R559, about 2km further on from the Riasc Monastic Settlement turn-off.

BALLYDAVID

About 2km from Gallarus Castle and Oratory, this little settlement has a fine setting on a sheltered cove and old coastguard breakwater. Europe's westernmost camping ground, Oratory House Camping (Campaíl Teach An Aragail; ☎066-915 5143; www.dingleactivities.com; Gallarus; campsites from €18; ⊙Apr-mid-Sep; P), is nearby. It's a source of much local information on a mass of activities, especially walking.

The pub, Tigh TP (☎066-915 5300; www.tigh-tp.ie; mains €8-15), is a good place for a waterside pint. Next door to it is the Coast Guard Lodge (d €75), which has six rooms with private bathrooms that sleep three to four people each in military comfort for €75 (or €50 for more than one night) per room, and a self-catering kitchen.

Connor Pass

At 456m, the Connor (or Conor) Pass is Ireland's highest mountain pass. On a foggy day you'll see nothing but the road just in front of you, but in fine weather it offers phenomenal views of Dingle Harbour to the south and Mt Brandon to the north. The road is in good shape, despite being very narrow and *very* steep (large signs portend doom for buses and trucks).

The summit car park yields views down to two lakes in the rock-strewn valley below plus the remains of walls and huts where people once lived impossibly hard lives. When visibility is good, the 10-minute climb to the summit is well worthwhile for the kind of vistas that inspire mountain-climbers.

If you're cycling, the pass is best approached from the northeast heading southwest, as you'll get the narrowest and steepest section over with early in the ride and can coast down the (relatively) gentler gradient and wider road towards Dingle town.

North Side of the Peninsula

At Kilcummin, a road heads west to the quiet villages of Cloghane and Brandon, and finally to Brandon Point overlooking Brandon Bay.

CLOGHANE & AROUND

POP 280

Cloghane (An Clochán) is another little piece of peninsula beauty. The village's friendly pubs and accommodation nestle between Mt Brandon and Brandon Bay, with views across the water to the Stradbally Mountains.

Sights & Activities

For walkers, the main goal is scaling 951m-high Mt Brandon (Cnoc Bhréannain), Ireland's eighth-highest peak. If that sounds too energetic, there are plenty of coastal strolls.

Brandon's Point VIEWING POINT

The 5km drive out to Brandon's Point from Cloghane follows ever-narrower single-track roads, culminating in cliffs with fantastic views north and east. Sheep wander the constantly eroding rocks oblivious to their tenuous positions.

St Brendan's Church CHURCH

This vacuum-silent church has a stained-glass window showing the Gallarus Oratory and Ardfert Cathedral.

Festivals & Events

Lughnasa HARVEST FESTIVAL

(⊙late Jul) On the last weekend in July, Cloghane celebrates the ancient Celtic harvest festival Lughnasa with events – especially bonfires – both in the village and atop Mt Brandon.

Brandon Regatta BOAT RACE

(⊙late Aug) Traditional *currach* canoe race.

Sleeping & Eating

Mount Brandon Hostel HOSTEL €
(☎066-713 8299; www.mountbrandonhostel.com; dm/s/tw €17/30/36; ⏰Mar-Jan; P@♿) A small, simple hostel with scrubbed wooden floors and furniture, and a patio overlooking the bay. Most rooms have en suite bathrooms; an apartment sleeping up to four people is also available for a minimum of two nights. Kid-friendly facilities include cots and high chairs. Neighbouring the hostel is the cherry-coloured traditional pub, **O'Donnell's**.

O'Connors PUB, B&B €€
(☎066-713 8113; www.cloghane.com; s/d €45/80; @📶) Book ahead to bag a room or a table in this welcoming village pub, which serves evening **meals** (mains €14-21; ⏰dinner) made with local produce, ranging from salmon to steak. Landlord Michael has loads of local info and can also explain why there's an aeroplane engine out the front.

Information

Pick up tourist info, including local walking and hiking guides, from the shop and post office near the hostel and pub.

CASTLEGREGORY & AROUND

POP 950

Castlegregory (Caislean an Ghriare), which once rivalled Tralee as a busy local centre, is a quiet village, with a highlight being views back to the often snowy hills to the south (a lowlight is the sprawl of philistine holiday homes).

However, things change when you drive up the sandstrewn road along the Rough Point peninsula, the broad spit of land between Tralee Bay and Brandon Bay. Up here, it's a playground. Not content with being a prime **windsurfing** location, the peninsula sees new sports like wave-sailing and kitesurfing, while divers can glimpse pilot whales, orcas, sunfish and dolphins.

Activities

Wind and/or water sports abound, and great underwater visibility makes this one of Ireland's best **diving** areas. Nearby, there are lakes and woodlands to explore.

FREE **Glanteenassig Forest Recreation Area** LAKES, WOODS
(www.coillte.ie; ⏰7am-10pm May-Aug, 9am-6pm Sep-Apr) East of Castlegregory, these 450 hectares of woodland, mountain, lake and bog are a magical, little-visited treasure. There are two **lakes**; you can drive right up to the higher lake, which is encircled by a plank boardwalk, though it's too narrow for wheelchairs or prams. Make sure you're out before closing, or you'll have to pay a call-out fee to have the gates unlocked. It's signposted 7km south of Castlegregory, and also 7km west of the village of Aughacasla on the northern coast road (the R560), which links up with the N86 to Tralee.

Waterworld DIVING
(☎066-713 9292; www.waterworld.ie; s-tank dive incl gear €45) Professional dive shop based at Harbour House (p311).

Jamie Knox Watersports WATER SPORTS
(☎066-713 9411; www.jamieknox.com; Brandon Bay) Offers surf, windsurf, kitesurf, canoe and pedalo hire and lessons. Surf lessons start from €45 for a 'taster'. Look for the garish yellow trailers.

Sleeping & Eating

TOP CHOICE **Harbour House** HOTEL €€
(☎066-713 9292; www.maharees.ie; Scraggane Pier; s/d from €40/80; P🏊📶♿) In a stunning position overlooking the Maharees Islands, this superb family-run establishment has the intimate feel of a B&B, with 15 comfortable, contemporary rooms and a gorgeous mascot, Lucy the dog. The leisure centre is home to Waterworld dive centre (the pool is also used for diver training). Its **Islands Seafood Restaurant** (mains €6-15; ⏰dinner) is excellent and astonishingly well priced; the family have their own fishing boat, bringing catches 'from the tide to the table', with vegetables grown in the garden out the back. Harbour House is 5km north of Castlegregory near the end of the peninsula.

Seven Hogs IRISH €€
(☎066-713 9719; www.sevenhogs.ie; Aughacasla; mains €15-20; s/d €40/50; ⏰lunch & dinner; 📶♿) Set up above the R560 northern coast road, this apricot-painted place has an open-plan interior with a stone fireplace and book-filled shelves running the full width of the walls. In-the-know locals head here for its gourmet burgers with handcut chips, but there are also some inspired seafood options. There are cosy B&B rooms onsite.

O'Donnell's Old Ship Inn PUB €€
(☎087 143 8011; W Main St, Castlegregory; d €80; P📶) An old pub has had a swab of the poop deck and emerged shipshape. B&B rooms have a modern, elegant style (lots of glossy timber), while the gastropub **restaurant**

(mains €15-24; ⌚dinner) has simple preparations of local seafood and meats, though the handwritten menu takes some deciphering. The bar is ideal for a cultured pint.

Spillane's SEAFOOD €€
(☎066-713 9125; www.spillanesbar.com; Fahamore; bar mains €7.50-14.50, mains €11.50-23.50; ⌚dinner;) Outside tables overlook the beach, bay and mountains at this relaxing spot. Seafood is a speciality, but the bar menu is great for pizza and burgers (with a pint, of course).

NORTHERN KERRY

The landscape of Northern Kerry is often dull compared with the glories of the Ring of Kerry and the Dingle Peninsula, Killarney and Kenmare. But there are some interesting places that should give you pause on your drive. Tralee has a great museum while Ballybunion and the blustery beaches south of the Shannon estuary are worth a look.

Tralee

POP 22,100

Although it's the county town, Tralee is often dismissed elsewhere in Kerry as an overflow valve for Limerick and its social problems. While that's unfair – there are some good restaurants and bars and a great museum – it's certainly down-to-earth and more engaged with the business of everyday life than the tourist trade. Stop in for a stroll of an Irish town where you *might* have a hard time buying a shamrock-clutching leprechaun.

Founded by the Normans in 1216, Tralee has a long history of rebellion. In the 16th century the last ruling earl of the Desmonds was captured and executed here. His head was sent to Elizabeth I, who spiked it on London Bridge. The Desmond castle once stood at the junction of Denny St and the Mall, but any trace of medieval Tralee that survived the Desmond Wars was razed during the Cromwellian period.

Elegant Denny St and Day Pl are the oldest parts of town, with 18th-century buildings, while the Square, just south of the Mall, is a pleasant open space with a contemporary style.

Sights & Activities

Kerry County Museum MUSEUM
(Map p313; ☎066-712 7777; Denny St; adult/child €5/free; ⌚9.30am-5.30pm) An absolute treat, Kerry's county museum has excellent interpretive displays on Irish historical events and trends, with an emphasis on County Kerry. The **Medieval Experience** re-creates life (smells and all) in Tralee in 1450. Check out the deranged nights, a vision of horror right out of Monty Python. Children will love strolling the medieval streets and there's a commentary in various languages. The **Tom Crean Room** celebrates the local hero, an early-20th-century explorer who accompanied both Scott and Shackleton on epic Antarctic expeditions. It's housed in the neoclassical Ashe Memorial Hall.

Blennerville Windmill & Visitor Centre WINDMILL
(Map p313; Visitor Centre ☎066-712 1064; adult/child €5/3; ⌚9am-6pm Jun-Aug, 9.30am-5.30pm Apr-May & Sep-Oct) Blennerville, just over 1km southwest of central Tralee on the N86 to Dingle, used to be the city's chief port, though the harbour has long since silted in. A 19th-century flour **windmill** here has been restored and is the largest working mill in Ireland and Britain. Its modern **visitor centre** houses an exhibition on grain-milling, and on the thousands of emigrants who boarded 'coffin ships' from what was then Kerry's largest embarkation point. There's also a database of the Irish émigrés who flocked to America. Admission includes a 30-minute guided tour of the windmill.

Steam Railway & Lee Valley Eco Park RAILWAY, PARK
Between 1891 and 1953 a narrow-gauge steam railway connected Tralee with Dingle. A 3km Tralee-Blennerville section has been restored and will run through the new, 25-acre Lee Valley Eco Park, which was being developed at the time of research, and will have walking and cycling trails, a wildlife area, fish-stocked lake and an ecoconscious visitor centre. The railway is expected to reopen in mid-2012 – check with the tourist office for updates.

Hibernia Adventures OUTDOOR ACTIVITIES
(☎066-713 6300; www.hiberniaadventures.com) In the summer months (usually July and August) Hibernia runs guided tours departing from Tralee and Killarney to the Dingle Peninsula and Ring of Kerry with various

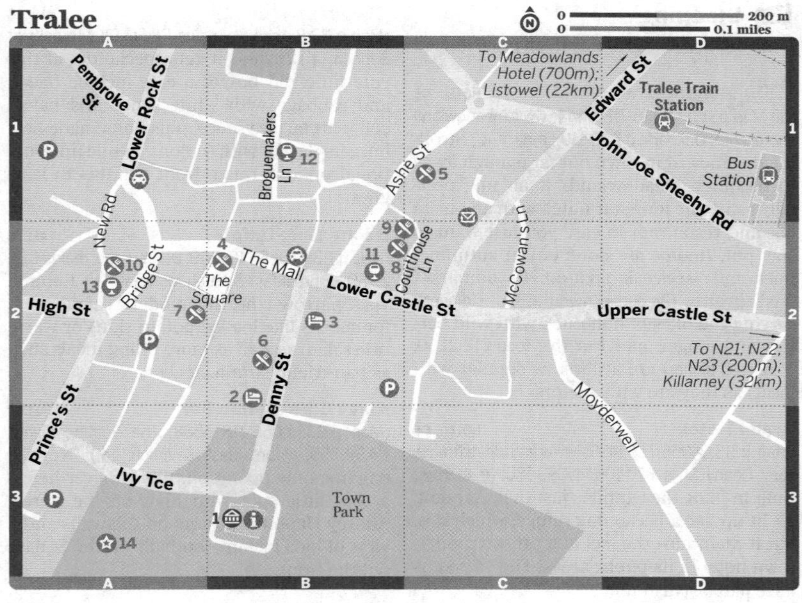

Tralee

Sights

1 Kerry County Museum B3

Sleeping

2 Finnegan's Holiday Hostel B2
3 Grand Hotel B2

Eating

4 Aines Café & Wine Bar B2
5 Chopin's Café C1
6 Denny Lane Café B2
7 Farmers Market A2
8 French Flair B2
9 Genting Thai C2
10 Manna Organic Store A2

Drinking

11 Baily's Corner B2
12 Roundy's B1
13 Séan Óg's A2

Entertainment

14 Siamsa Tíre A3

adrenalin-charged options like high-speed rib boat rides, rock climbing, mountain biking, horse trekking and kayaking. Trips start from €95.

Festivals & Events

Rose of Tralee BEAUTY PAGEANT

(www.roseoftralee.ie; Aug) In Ireland and beyond, Tralee is synonymous with the Rose of Tralee, a beauty pageant open to Irish women and women of Irish descent from around the world (the 'roses'). They're accompanied by unmarried men (known as 'escorts'), who also undergo a selection process. More than just a beauty contest, it's a five-day-long festival bookended by a gala ball and a 'midnight madness' parade led by the newly crowned Rose of Tralee, followed by a fireworks display. Other highlights include a fashion show. If you fancy your chances of becoming a rose or an escort, application forms are available online.

Kerry Film Festival FILM

(www.kerryfilmfestival.com; late Oct/early Nov) Eight-day festival organised by local arts group **Samhlaiocht** (www.samhlaiocht.com), which also stages exhibitions.

Sleeping

Denny St has places to stay in all price ranges.

TOP CHOICE **Meadowlands Hotel** HOTEL €€
(off Map p313; ☎066-718 0444; www.meadowlandshotel.com; Oakpark; d €90-110; P@🛜👶) Strolling distance from town but far enough away to be quiet, Meadowlands is an unexpectedly romantic four-star hotel, with an onsite bar and restaurant in case you just want to stay put. Rooms are done out in autumnal hues and service is spot-on. Its upmarket **restaurant** (3-course menu €32; ⊙dinner), serving the likes of half-duck with wild berries and ginger, and **bar** (bar food €12-21.50; ⊙lunch & dinner) are at least as popular with locals as they are with visitors.

Grand Hotel HOTEL €€
(Map p313; ☎066-712 1499; www.grandhoteltralee.com; Denny St; s €70-105, d €99-180; P@🛜👶) Built in 1928, the Grand is just that. At night, it's lit up like a beckoning refuge, which it is, but it maintains the feel of a proper county-town hotel in its public areas. The 44 rooms have had a stylish refit.

Finnegan's Holiday Hostel HOSTEL, B&B €
(Map p313; ☎066-712 7610; www.finneganshostel.com; 17 Denny St; dm/d from €12/40; @🛜) An elegant Georgian facade fronts this friendly hostel and B&B. The grandeur has faded, but there are a sizeable kitchen and lounge. The dorms, named after Irish scribblers, have their own bathrooms as do the private rooms. Breakfast is available for €5.

Eating

TOP CHOICE **French Flair** FRENCH €€
(Map p313; ☎066-711 8315; 6 Courthouse Lane; meals €4-10; ⊙breakfast & lunch Mon-Sat, dinner Thu-Sat) Crispy crêpes, melt-in-your-mouth quiche and *tartiflette* (traditional potato, bacon and melted reblochon cheese dish from the French Alps) are among the dishes that almost convince you that you've arrived in France, and its charming decor does nothing to dissuade you from the illusion.

Genting Thai THAI €€
(Map p313; ☎066-719 4285; 11 Courthouse Lane; mains €8-14; ⊙dinner Mon-Sat, lunch & dinner Sun) It's the real deal here at this little bistro. The menu is actually Thai (without a lot of interloping Chinese dishes) and is both perfectly spiced and often spicy: if your tongue's deadened by Irish cooking, you'll love the many dishes rated with three chillies on the menu.

Chopin's Cafe CAFE €
(Map p313; 8 Ashe St; mains €8.50-12; ⊙breakfast & lunch; 👶) Irish-as-it-gets specialities at this cute little red box of a cafe include bacon and cabbage with white sauce and baked cod with tartare sauce, plus homemade beef burgers laced with onions, while international options range from frittatas to lasagnes.

Denny Lane Cafe CAFE €
(Map p313; ☎066-719 4319; Denny Lane; mains €13-23.50; ⊙breakfast & lunch Mon-Sat; 👶) Entered via a narrow lane, this modern cafe is great for snacks like loaded potato skins or warm brie salad, as well as more filling meals such as pan-friend sirloin steaks.

Aines Cafe & Wine Bar CAFE €
(Map p313; ☎066-718 5388; The Square; dishes €4.50-7.50; ⊙breakfast & lunch; 👶) Now a daytime-only operation, this is nevertheless a cosy little spot with Elvis on the stereo, Audrey Hepburn posters on the walls and a view of kids kicking footballs on the Square out the front.

Farmers Market MARKET €
(Map p313; The Square; ⊙10am-4pm Sat) Tralee's farmers market sprawls across the main square. Days vary, but it's usually busiest on Saturdays.

Manna Organic Store ORGANIC €
(Map p313; ☎066-711 8501; New Rd; ⊙8am-6pm Mon-Sat) Organic produce, groceries and various feel-good potions and lotions. Wheatgrass grows in the window.

Drinking & Entertainment

Castle St is thick with mass-market pubs, many of them offering live entertainment. There are some reasonable cafe-bars on the Square where you could easily pass an afternoon watching Tralee coming and going.

TOP CHOICE **Roundy's** BAR
(Map p313; 5 Broguemakers Lane; ⊙from 5pm) Ingeniously converted from a terrace house (with a tree still growing right through the courtyard garden-turned-interior), this funky little bar has hip iPod tunes, regular DJs spinning old school funk and live bands, plus free *aperitivi*-style finger food on the bar. Very cool.

Baily's Corner PUB
(Map p313; Lower Castle St) Deservedly popular for its traditional sessions, with local

TRACING YOUR ANCESTORS

County Kerry currently has no genealogy centre, but some church records are available free of charge on the **Irish Genealogy** (www.irishgenealogy.ie) website.

musicians performing original material most weeknights during summer and at least a couple of nights a week the rest of the year.

Seán Óg's PUB
(Map p313;Bridge St) Fair diddling trad music is on at this rambling and raucous bar from Sunday to Thursday in summer and up to a couple of times a week outside season.

Siamsa Tíre THEATRE
(Map p313; 066-712 3055; www.siamsatire.com; Town Park; shows per person €15-30; booking office 9am-6pm Mon-Sat) Siamsa Tíre, the National Folk Theatre of Ireland, re-creates dynamic aspects of Gaelic culture through song, dance, drama and mime. There are several shows a week from May to September at 8.30pm. Winter shows range from dance to drama and mainstream musicals.

Information

Castle St has banks with ATMs and bureaux de change.

Post office (Edward St)

Tourist office (066-712 1288; Denny St; 8am-6pm Jul & Aug, 9am-5pm Mon-Sat Sep-Jun) Below Kerry County Museum.

Tralee General Hospital (066-712 6222; Boherbee) Has an accident and emergency unit.

Getting There & Away

Bus Éireann (066-716 4700; www.buseireann.ie) has buses from the **bus station** next to the train station, east of the town centre. Eight daily services run to Dublin (€22.95, six hours), going via Listowel (€6.84, 30 minutes) and changing in Limerick (€15.75, two hours). There are hourly buses to Waterford (€22.95, 5½ hours), Killarney (€7.83, 40 minutes) and Cork (€16.65, 2½ hours).

Irish Rail (066-712 3522; www.irishrail.ie) has services including three direct daily services to Cork (€26.50, 2¼ hours), nine to Killarney (€9.50, 45 minutes) and one direct to Dublin (€37, four hours) and others requiring a change in Mallow.

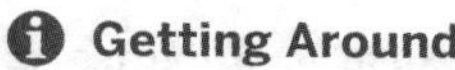

Getting Around

There's a taxi rank on the Mall, or try **Jackie Power Tours & Cabs** (066-712 6300; 2 Lower Rock St). **Tralee Gas & Bicycle Supplies** (066-712 2018; Strand St) hires out bikes (€15 per day).

Around Tralee

East of town you'll find one of the country's finest caves. Heading west takes you past the tiny township of Spa to the fishing port of Fenit. Travelling northeast of here takes you to Ardfert's medieval cathedral.

CRAG CAVE

This **cave** (066-714 1244; www.cragcave.com; Castleisland; adult/child €12/5; 10am-6.30pm Jul & Aug, 10am-6pm Thu-Tue Mar-Jun, 10am-6pm Sep-Dec, call for tour times Jan & Feb) was discovered in 1983, when problems with water pollution led to a search for the source of the local river. In 1989, 300m of the 4km-long cave were opened to the public; admission is by 30-minute guided tour. The remarkable rock formations include a stalagmite shaped like a statue of the Madonna (at least to some). There are play areas for kids, as well as a restaurant and, of course, a gift shop.

The cave is 18km east of Tralee, signposted from both Castleisland and the Abbeyfeale-Castleisland stretch of the N21. Castleisland is well connected with both Tralee and Killarney by bus.

SPA & FENIT

POP 435

Due west of Tralee, it's about 7km to the small settlement of Spa (sometimes referred to on maps as 'The Spa') and another 6km on to Fenit.

Fenit's Irish name, An Fhianait, translates as 'the Wild Place', and although the remote village itself is tiny, its position on the Atlantic has given rise to a sizeable fishing port and marina, and some sublime seafood restaurants in the area.

West End Bar & Bistro SEAFOOD €€
(066-713 6246; Fenit; www.westendfenit.ie; Fenit; d €60-70, mains €10-20; restaurant lunch & dinner; P) A local icon, this fifth-generation whitewashed bar has a mouthwatering lineup of seafood, including baguettes filled with Tralee Bay crab, plus plenty of locally sourced meat dishes. Rates for its 10 rooms with private bathrooms include hearty breakfasts.

Spa Seafoods Cafe DELI, CAFE €€

(☎066-713 6164; Spa; mains €5.50-15; ⊙breakfast & lunch Tue-Sun) Opposite the Oyster Tavern, a contemporary glass building houses a scrumptious deli selling fresh seafood and condiments that self-caterers will find irresistible, and a smart cafe. The short but stellar menu includes home-smoked haddock and spinach tart and sautéed clams with Spanish sherry and Iberico ham.

Oyster Tavern SEAFOOD €€€

(☎066-713 6102; Spa; mains €14-28; ⊙dinner daily, lunch Sun;) Grilled Atlantic salmon, pan-fried Kerry Head crab claws, Dingle Bay prawn scampi and lobster in season star at this classy restaurant, but carnivores and vegetarians aren't forgotten, with plenty of inventive options. There's a cheaper bar menu.

The Tankard SEAFOOD €€€

(☎066-713 6164; Kilfenora, Fenit; mains €15-27; ⊙dinner Mon-Sat, lunch Sun) The menu of this bright-yellow pub/restaurant brims with local catches served in classical styles – pan fried, deep fried, and mornays including a luscious scallop mornay with piped potato crust.

ARDFERT

POP 950

Ardfert (Ard Fhearta), about 10km northwest of Tralee on the Ballyheigue road, is most notable for the soaring **Ardfert Cathedral** (☎066-713 4711; www.heritageireland.ie; adult/child €3/1; ⊙10am-6pm Easter-Sep). Most of the building dates back to the 13th century, but it incorporates elements of an 11th-century church. Set into one of the interior walls is an effigy, said to be of St Brendan the Navigator, who was educated in Ardfert and founded a monastery here. The grounds contain the ruins of two other churches, 12th-century Templenahoe and 15th-century Templenagriffin.

Turning right in front of the cathedral and going 500m down the road brings you to the extensive remains of a **Franciscan friary**, dating from the 13th century, but with 15th-century cloisters.

KERRY HEAD

Jutting out into the Atlantic, the loop drive encircling Kerry Head looks promising on the map, especially given the stunning scenery of the Dingle and Ring of Kerry peninsulas to the south. However, that's where the similarity ends: this flat, windswept stretch of coastline is littered with new-build bungalows, including countless unfinished dwellings with tarpaulins flapping in the wind and forsaken 'for sale' signs.

Perhaps in the years to come, Kerry Head will offer what many people visit Ireland for today – relics and ruins dotting the landscape (in this case, circa Celtic Tiger). For now, you're not missing out if you scratch it from your itinerary.

Listowel

POP 3900

The late writer Bryan MacMahon said of Listowel: 'I harbour the absurd notion of motivating a small town in Ireland, a speck on the map, to become a centre of the imagination.' Listowel certainly has more literary credentials than your average provincial town, with connections to such accomplished scribes as John B Keane, Maurice Walsh, George Fitzmaurice and Brendan Kennelly.

Outside these connections and a few venues, however, the town is little more than some tidy Georgian streets arranged around a main square with the St John's Theatre and Arts Centre, formerly St John's Church, and a park running along the edge of the River Feale, which can be reached down a road alongside the castle.

There's metered parking in the main square and free parking downhill to the right of the castle.

Sights & Activities

Kerry Literary & Cultural Centre CULTURAL CENTRE

(Seanchaí; ☎068-22212; www.kerrywritersmuseum.com; 24 the Square; adult/child €5/3; ⊙9.30am-5.30pm daily Jun-Sep, 1-4pm Mon-Fri Oct-May) The audiovisual Writers' Exhibition at this gem of a cultural centre gives due prominence to Listowel's heritage of literary observers of Irish life. Rooms are devoted to local greats such as John B Keane and Bryan MacMahon, with simple, haunting tableaux narrating their lives and recordings of them reading their work. There is a cafe and a performance space where events are sometimes staged.

Keane is remembered with a **statue** on the opposite side of the square, in which he seems to be hailing a cab. He wrote with wry humour about subjects ranging from

Limerick's beggars to the perils of giving up porter as a New Year's resolution.

On Church St, opposite the police station, a **literary mural** depicts the local writers and their pronouncements.

Listowel Castle CASTLE
(☎086 385 7201; www.heritageireland.ie; admission free; ⏰9.30am-5.30pm late May-Aug) Behind the Kerry Literary & Cultural Centre, this 12th-century castle was once the stronghold of the Fitzmaurices, the Anglo-Norman lords of Kerry. It was the last castle in Ireland to succumb to the Elizabethan attacks during the Desmond revolt. What remains of the castle has been thoroughly restored.

Lartigue Monorailway RAILWAY
(☎068-24393; www.lartiguemonorail.com; John B Keane Rd; adult/child €6/3; ⏰1-4.30pm May-Sep) Designed by Frenchman Charles Lartigue, this unique survivor of Victorian railway engineering operated between the town and Ballybunion on the coast. Although it no longer travels as far as Ballybunion, the renovated section of line is short (less than a kilometre) but fascinating, with manual turntables at either end for swinging the train around.

Childers Park PARK
About 300 metres east of the Square, Childers Park spreads out to the east. Within the park is the **Garden of Europe**, opened in 1995. Its 12 sections represent the 12 members of the EU of the day. There's a bust of the poet Schiller and, strikingly, Ireland's only public monument to those who died in the Holocaust, and to all victims of injustice.

St Mary's Church CHURCH
(The Square) Built in 1829 in the neo-Gothic style, this church has some lovely mosaic work over the altar and a vaulted roof with timber beams.

St John's Theatre & Arts Centre ARTS CENTRE
(☎068-22566; www.stjohnstheatrelistowel.com; The Square) Located in a former church and now hosting art exhibitions as well as drama, music and dance events.

Walking WALKS
The tourist office has leaflets on walks such as the 3.5km **river walk** and the 10km **Sive walk**, which takes in John B Keane Rd, a disused railway track and a bog.

Festivals & Events

Writers' Week LITERARY
(www.writersweek.ie) Each year during the first weekend in June, bibliophiles flock to Listowel for readings, poetry, music, drama, seminars, storytelling and many other events held at various places around town. The festival attracts an impressive list of writers, which have included Booker Prize-winning Colm Tóibín, John Montague, Jung Chang, Damon Galgut, Rebecca Miller and Terry Jones.

Listowel Races HORSE RACING
(www.listowelraces.ie) Races take place over Whit weekend in June and for a week during mid-September.

Sleeping & Eating

Listowel Arms Hotel HOTEL €€
(☎068-21500; The Square; www.listowelarms.com; s €75-115, d €120-180; P@) Listowel's only full-service hotel is a family-run affair in a Georgian building that balances touches of grandeur with country charm. Furnished with antiques and marble sinks, the 42 rooms overlook the river and the racecourse. The **Writers Bar** (wi-fi) is a good place to find music in the summer; while the **Georgian Restaurant** (mains €23-27; ⏰dinner) serves refined fare like honey-roasted duck on parsnip mash.

Billeragh House Hostel HOSTEL €
(☎068-40321; billeraghhousehostel@yahoo.com; dm/d from €20/50; P) This peaceful 36-bed hostel is housed in a heritage-listed, ivy-clad Georgian hall 3.5km south of Listowel on the N69 amid farmland. Facilities include private bathrooms in all rooms, a kitchen, dining room and laundry. Call ahead to confirm your arrival time.

Allo's INTERNATIONAL €€
(☎068-22880; Church St; d from €70, mains €24.50-28.50; ⏰lunch & dinner Tue-Sat; wi-fi) This popular spot is best known for its bar/bistro, whose interior of reused architectural items and wood create a traditional feel. Global influences range from tempura of oysters with coconut and lemongrass to tandoori- and coriander-marinated cod. The wine list is excellent. Three comfy rooms with private bathrooms are tucked upstairs.

Grape & Grain CAFE €€
(Church St; dishes €4-10.50; ⏰breakfast & lunch Mon-Sat; child-friendly) In addition to coffee and cake,

perennial cafe fare at this stylish, burgundy- and green-coloured place includes big salads served with garlic bread and sandwiches with salad, nachos and dip.

Farmers Market MARKET
(⏲9am-2pm Fri) Held on the Square, as markets have been for centuries.

Drinking

Woulfe's Horseshoe Bar PUB
(14 Lower William St) The food (daily roasts, battered fish et al) is nothing to write home about, nor is the service. Still, this pub just off the Square is a cosy spot for a pint.

John B Keane PUB
(37 William St) Once run by the late writer himself, this small, unassuming bar is swathed in Keane memorabilia.

Information

Bank of Ireland (The Square) Has an ATM and bureau de change.

Post office (William St) At the northern end of the street.

Tourist office (☎068-22212; www.listowel.ie; ⏲9am-5pm Tue-Sun Jun-Sep) Seasonally opening office housed in the Kerry Literary & Cultural Centre.

Getting There & Away

Frequent daily buses serve both Tralee (€8.84, 40 minutes) and Limerick (€15.75, 1½ hours).

Around Listowel

BALLYBUNION

There are a surprising number of reasons to visit this one-seahorse beach town 15km northeast of Listowel on the R553. Beyond the statue of a club-swinging Bill Clinton, commemorating his visit to the **Ballybunion Golf Club** (☎068-27146; www.ballybuniongolfclub.ie; green fees €65-180; ⏲tee times by reservation) in 1998, reputed as one of the finest links courses in the world, there are two blue flag **beaches**.

Overlooking the southern beach are the remains of **Ballybunion Castle**, the 16th-century seat of the Fitzmaurices. There's an underground passage leading from the castle to the cliff.

Horse treks offered by **Moonshine Lodge Equestrian Centre** (☎087-689 3568; www.horsetrekking.ie; rides from €25 per person, per hr) include picnic rides (May to August) and pub rides (year round).

The **Ballybunion Bachelor Festival** takes place in June. The event sees 15 tuxedo-clad bachelors from across Ireland vying to impress the judges, while the town enjoys a long weekend of street entertainment and celebrations.

One bus (two in summer) runs from Listowel to Ballybunion Monday to Saturday (€3.15, 25 minutes).

TARBERT

POP 810

Tarbert is 16km north of Listowel on the N69. **Shannon Ferry Limited** (☎068-905 3124; www.shannonferries.com; one way/return bicycle & foot passengers €5/7, motorcycles €9/14, cars €18/28; ⏲7.30am-9.30pm Jun-Aug, to 7.30pm Sep-May, from 9.30am Sun year-round) runs a half-hourly ferry between Tarbert and Killimer in County Clare, skipping the traffic congestion around Limerick city. The ferry dock is clearly signposted 2.2km west of Tarbert. If you do go through Limerick city from here, the N69 (p330) is the most scenic route.

Before you hop on the ferry, it's worth visiting the renovated **Tarbert Bridewell Jail & Courthouse** (http://tarbertbridewell.com/museum.html; adult/child €5/2.50; ⏲10am-6pm Apr-Oct), which has exhibits (including stoic mannequins) on the rough social and political conditions of the 19th century. From the jail, the 6.1km **John F Leslie Woodland Walk** runs along Tarbert Bay towards the mouth of the Shannon.

If you want to stay overnight, the colourfully renovated 18th-century **Ferry House Hostel** (☎068-36555; www.ferryhousehostel.com; The Square; dm €15-20, d without/with private bathroom €44/50; P 📶), bang in the centre of town, is run by a well-travelled family and has clean, airy dorms and private rooms and a cute onsite cafe. Wi-fi is available in parts of the historic stone building.

In July and August, buses serve Limerick (€13.80, 1¼ hours).

Counties Limerick & Tipperary

POPULATION: 350,000 / AREA: 6989 SQ KM

Includes »

Best Places to Eat

» Wild Geese (p332)
» The Mustard Seed at Echo Lodge (p333)
» Market Square Brasserie (p325)
» Cafe Hans (p337)
» Country Choice (p344)

Best Places to Stay

» Adare Manor (p332)
» The Boutique Hotel (p325)
» Aherlow House Hotel (p334)
» Dunraven Arms (p332)
» Apple Caravan & Camping Park (p339)

Why Go?

From marching ditties to rhyming puns, the names Tipperary and Limerick are part of the lexicon, but both are relatively unexplored by visitors.

County Limerick is closely tied to its namesake city, which has a history as dramatic as Ireland's. In a nation of hard knocks, it seems to have had more than its fair share. The city's streets have tangible links to the past and a gritty, honest vibrancy, and treasures abound in its lush, green country side.

In contrast, Tipperary town is minor. But amid the county's rolling hills, rich farmland and deep valleys bordered by soaring mountains, it's a peaceful place that's perfect for following a river to its source or climbing a stile to see a lonely ruin.

In both counties, ancient Celtic sites, medieval abbeys and other relics endure in solitude, awaiting discovery. And even Limerick and Tipperary's best-known sights retain a rough, inspiring dignity.

When to Go

As the third-largest city in Ireland, with a sizeable student population, Limerick city bustles year-round, but is at its liveliest during the warmer months, from around April to October. These are also the best months to explore the rural villages, towns and countryside of both counties, when opening hours for attractions are longest and the weather is at its best. It's also when you'll encounter most of the counties' festivities, including wonderful walking festivals in the Glen of Aherlow.

Counties Limerick & Tipperary Highlights

1 Discover another side to hardscrabble **Limerick city** (p322) in its sophisticated cafe culture, art galleries and waterfront bars

2 Take in the Shannon water vistas while wandering Limerick's back roads via the centuries-old ruins at **Askeaton** (p330) and the flying boat museum at **Foynes** (p330)

3 Tramp in the wilds of Tipperary, from the **Glen of Aherlow** (p334) to the **River Suir Valley** (p340)

4 Walk the walls and keep of the wonderfully preserved castle in **Cahir** (p338)

5 Gaze out over County Tipperary from the soaring **Rock of Cashel** (p335)

6 Deliberate over mouthwatering restaurant menus in the thatched heritage town of **Adare** (p332)

7 Spend a day at the races at **Tipperary** (p333), one of the country's finest tracks

8 Chat to locals over a pint in the historic village of **Fethard** (p342)

COUNTY LIMERICK

Limerick's low-lying farmland is framed on its southern and eastern boundaries by swelling uplands and mountains. Limerick city is boisterously urban in contrast and has enough historic and cultural attractions for a day's diversion. About 15km south of the city are the haunting archaeological sites around Lough Gur, while about the same distance southwest of the city is the charming thatched village of Adare.

Limerick City

POP 57,000

Limerick city straddles the Shannon's broadening tidal stream, where the river swings west to join the Shannon Estuary. Despite some unexpected glitz and gloss, it remains an unflinchingly honest town that doesn't shy away from a tough past as portrayed in Frank McCourt's *Angela's Ashes*.

Limerick has an intriguing castle, a lively art museum and contemporary cafe culture to go with its uncompromised pubs, as well as locals who go out of their way to welcome you.

The city is compact enough to get around on foot or by bike. To walk across town from St Mary's Cathedral to the train station takes about 15 minutes.

History

Viking adventurers established a settlement on an island in the River Shannon in the 9th century. They fought with the native Irish for control of the site until Brian Ború's forces drove them out in 968 and established Limerick as the royal seat of the O'Brien kings. Brian Ború finally destroyed Viking power and presence in Ireland at the Battle of Clontarf in 1014. By the late 12th century, invading Normans had supplanted the Irish as the town's rulers. Throughout the Middle Ages the two groups remained divided, with the oppressed Irish clustering to the south of the River Abbey in Irishtown and the Anglo-Normans walling themselves in to the north, in Englishtown.

From 1690 to 1691, Limerick acquired heroic status in the saga of Ireland's struggle against occupation by the English. After their defeat in the Battle of the Boyne in 1690, Jacobite forces withdrew west behind the famously strong walls of Limerick town. Months of bombardment followed and eventually the Irish Jacobite leader Patrick Sarsfield sued for peace. The terms of the Treaty of Limerick (1691) were then agreed and Sarsfield and 14,000 soldiers were allowed to leave the city for France. The treaty guaranteed religious freedom for Catholics, but the English later reneged and enforced fierce anti-Catholic legislation, an act of betrayal that came to symbolise the injustice of British rule.

During the 18th century, the old walls of Limerick were demolished and a well-planned and prosperous Georgian town developed. Such prosperity had waned by the early 20th century, as traditional industries fell on hard times. Several high-profile nationalists hailed from here, including Éamon de Valera. These days, technological and service industries are major employers.

Sights

You'll find the main places of interest clustered to the north on King's Island (the oldest part of Limerick and once part of Englishtown), to the south around the Crescent and Pery Sq (the city's noteworthy Georgian area) and all along the riverbanks.

King John's Castle CASTLE
(www.shannonheritage.com; Nicholas St; adult/child €9/5.50; ⌚10am-5pm Mon-Fri, till 5.30pm Sat & Sun) The massive curtain walls and towers of Limerick's showpiece castle are best viewed from the west bank of the River Shannon. The castle was built by King John of England between 1200 and 1212 on the site of an earlier fortification. It served as the military and administrative centre of the rich Shannon region.

Inside there are recreations of brutal medieval weapons like the trebuchet, as well as excavated Viking sites, reconstructed Norman features and other artefacts. Walk the walls and imagine you're carrying a bucket of boiling oil.

Across medieval Thomond Bridge, on the other side of the river, the **Treaty Stone** marks the spot on the riverbank where the Treaty of Limerick was signed. Before you cross the bridge, look out for the 18th-century **Bishop's Palace** (Church St; ⌚10am-1pm & 2-4.30pm Mon-Fri) and the ancient **toll gate**.

Hunt Museum MUSEUM
(www.huntmuseum.com; Palladian Custom House, Rutland St; adult/child €8/4.25; ⌚10am-5pm

Mon-Sat, 2-5pm Sun;) Although named for its benefactors, this museum might well be named for a treasure hunt. Visitors are encouraged to open drawers and otherwise poke around the finest collection of Bronze Age, Iron Age and medieval treasures outside Dublin. The 2000-plus items are from the private collection of the late John and Gertrude Hunt, antique dealers and consultants, who championed historic preservation throughout the region. Look out for a tiny but exquisite bronze horse by da Vinci, and a Syracusan coin thought to have been one of the 30 pieces of silver paid to Judas for his betrayal of Christ. Cycladic sculptures, a Giacometti drawing and paintings by Renoir, Picasso and Jack B Yeats add to the feast. Guided tours from the dedicated and colourful volunteers are available. The museum has an excellent in-house restaurant.

Georgian House & Garden HISTORIC SITE
(www.georgianhouseandgarden.ie; 2 Pery Sq; adult/child €6/4; 9.30am-4.30pm Mon-Fri) There's an engaging eeriness about the lofty, echoing rooms of the restored Georgian House, a re creation showing how Limerick's swells once lived. Lavish marble, stucco and wall decorations adorn the main rooms, while things are decidedly downscale when you reach the bare boards and dusty furnishings of the servants' quarters. The hackneyed but entertaining limericks on various wall plaques are a treat. Out back, the restored garden is an antidote – and beautiful contrast – to the plain fronts on the street. It leads to a coach house that contains a photographic memoir of Limerick.

FREE **Limerick City Gallery of Art** GALLERY
(www.limerickcitygallery.ie; Carnegie Bldg, Pery Sq; 9.30am-5.30pm Mon-Fri) Limerick's excellent gallery was undergoing refurbishments at the time of writing, but should have reopened in all its glory by the time you're reading this. Among its permanent collection of traditional paintings from the last 300 years are works by Sean Keating and Jack B Yeats. Check out Keating's atmos pheric *Kelp Burners* and Sir John Lavery's *Stars in Sunlight;* both infuse their subjects with inner light and a certain joy. The gallery also stages changing exhibitions of often pseudo-scandalous works and is the home of **ev+a** (www.eva.ie), a long-running city-wide contemporary annual art exhibition. Check the website for dates.

The gallery is beside the peaceful **People's Park**, at the heart of Georgian Limerick.

St Mary's Cathedral CATHEDRAL
(061-310 293; www.cathedral.limerick.anglican.org; Bridge St; admission €2 donation; vary) Limerick's ancient cathedral was founded in 1168 by Donal Mór O'Brien, king of Munster. Parts of the 12th-century Romanesque western doorway, nave and aisles survive, and there are splendid 15th-century black-oak misericords (support ledges for choristers), unique examples of their kind in Ireland. Call ahead to confirm opening hours and to check if there are any musical events scheduled.

FREE **Limerick City Museum** MUSEUM
(www.limerickcity.ie; Castle Lane; admission free; 10am-1pm & 2.15-5pm Tue-Sat) This small museum is beside King John's Castle. Exhibits include Stone Age and Bronze Age artefacts, the civic sword, Limerick silverwork, and examples of Limerick's lace and kid-glove manufacturing. Tough times in the late 19th century are also covered.

Thomond Park Stadium STADIUM
From 1995 until 2007, the **Munster rugby team** (www.munsterrugby.ie) was undefeated in this legendary stadium, which was massively rebuilt in 2008, the year they won the Heineken European Cup for the second time. **Tours** (adult/child €10/8, €3/2 on match days) of the hallowed ground include its memorabilia-filled museum. It's an easy 1km walk northwest of the centre along High St.

Tours

Walking Tour WALKING
(087 235 1339; €10) Noel Curtain runs entertaining and informative 90-minute walking tours of the city.

Red Viking BUS
(061-334 920; http://redvikingtours.com; adult/child €10/5; Mar-Oct) One-hour open-top bus tours depart from in front of the Court House on Merchant's Quay.

Sleeping

Try to find a place to stay near the city centre, so you can walk around and enjoy the nightlife. Otherwise you'll be on or near approach roads, in which case you might prefer to opt for something further afield that will be more bucolic.

Limerick

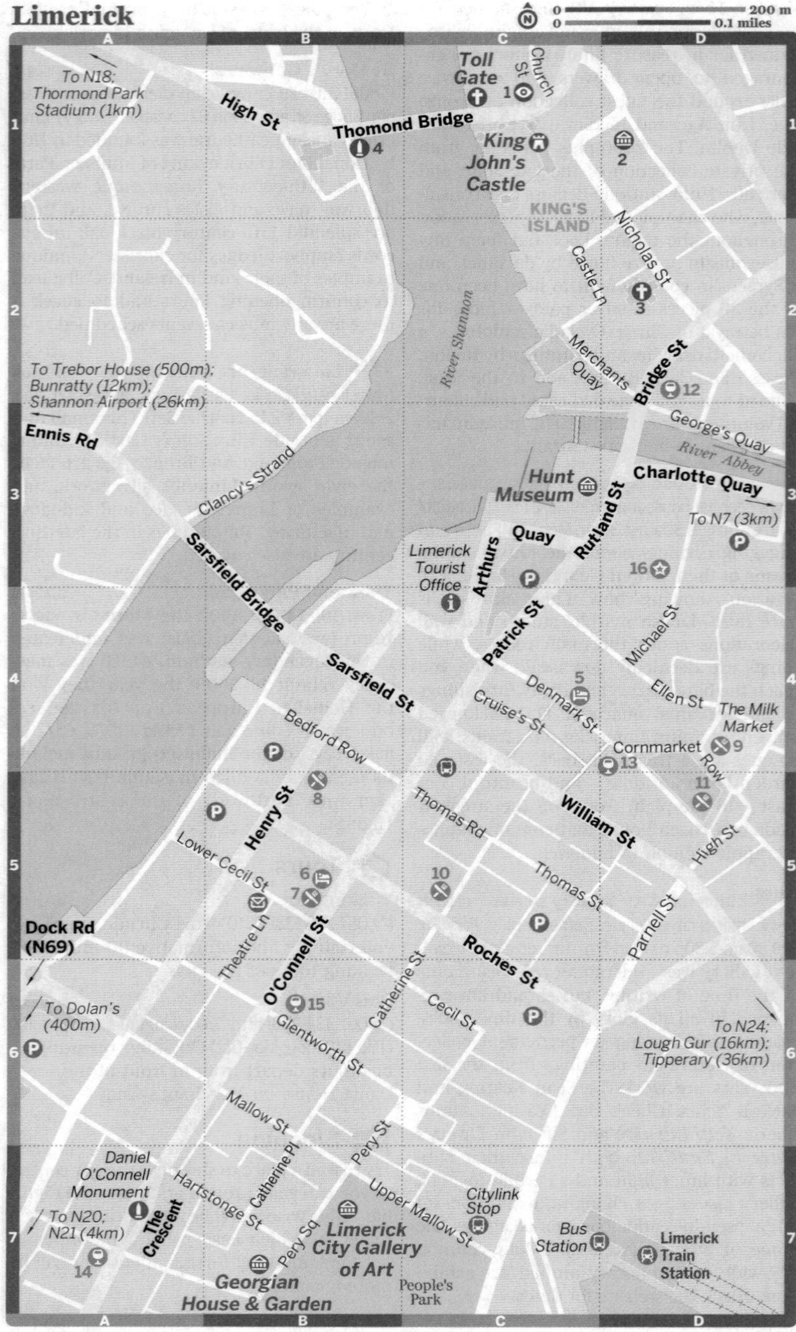

0
200 m
0
0.1 miles
To N18; Thormond Park Stadium (1km)
High St
Thomond Bridge
Toll Gate
Church St
King John's Castle
KING'S ISLAND
Nicholas St
Castle Ln
River Shannon
Merchants Quay
Bridge St
George's Quay
River Abbey
To Trebor House (500m); Bunratty (12km); Shannon Airport (26km)
Ennis Rd
Clancy's Strand
Hunt Museum
Charlotte Quay
Rutland St
To N7 (3km)
Arthurs Quay
Limerick Tourist Office
Sarsfield Bridge
Patrick St
Michael St
Sarsfield St
Denmark St
Cruise's St
Ellen St
The Milk Market
Bedford Row
Cornmarket Row
Henry St
Thomas Rd
William St
High St
Lower Cecil St
Thomas St
Parnell St
Dock Rd (N69)
Theatre Ln
O'Connell St
Catherine St
Roches St
To Dolan's (400m)
Cecil St
Glentworth St
To N24; Lough Gur (16km); Tipperary (36km)
Mallow St
Pery St
Catherine Pl
Daniel O'Connell Monument
Hartstonge St
Upper Mallow St
Citylink Stop
To N20; N21 (4km)
The Crescent
Pery Sq
Limerick City Gallery of Art
Bus Station
Limerick Train Station
Georgian House & Garden
People's Park

Limerick

Top Sights

Georgian House & Garden....B7
Hunt Museum....C3
King John's Castle....C1
Limerick City Gallery of Art....B7
Toll Gate....C1

Sights

1 Bishop's Palace....C1
2 Limerick City Museum....D1
3 St Mary's Cathedral....D2
4 Treaty Stone....B1

Sleeping

5 Boutique Hotel....C4
6 George Boutique Hotel....B5
Savoy....(see 8)

Eating

7 Chocolat....B5
8 Market Square Brasserie....B5
9 Milk Market....D4
10 Sage Cafe....C5
11 Wild Onion....D5

Drinking

12 Locke Bar....D2
13 Nancy Blake's....D4
14 South's....A7
15 White House Pub....B6

Entertainment

16 Trinity Rooms....D3

Alexandra Tce on O'Connell Ave (which runs south from O'Connell St) has several midrange B&Bs. Ennis Rd, leading northwest towards Shannon, also has a selection, although most are at least 1km from the centre.

TOP CHOICE **The Boutique Hotel** HOTEL €€
(061-315 320; www.theboutique.ie; Denmark St; s €49-59, d €59-69;) Rotating works of original art by Limerick artist Claire De Lacy, a fish tank in the lobby, a glassed-in breakfast room on the first-floor balcony and red-and-white-striped decor set this groovy little hotel apart from the pack. Its location near pedestrianised laneways minimises traffic, but it can still get noisy on weekends and during events when the city's hopping, with a popular pub downstairs. Still, it's fantastic value for money.

George Boutique Hotel HOTEL €€
(061-460 400; www.thegeorgeboutiquehotel.com; O'Connell St; s/d from €74/128; P) Designed like something out of a Sunday supplement – all warm and luxurious with gadgets including iPod docks – this sleek place has an atrium lobby and small terrace above the busy streets of the city centre.

The Savoy HOTEL €€
(061-448 700; www.savoylimerick.com; Henry St; d from €99; P) This classy five-star hotel does everything right: staff are professional, rooms have super-comfy king-size beds and a turn-down service, and its spa specialises in Thai massages. It's enticed Limerick's best restaurant, Market Square Brasserie (p325) from its former town house premises to right inside the hotel.

Trebor House B&B €€
(061-454 632; www.treborhouse.com; Ennis Rd; d €64-70; May-Sep; P) The McSweeneys offer a warm welcome in this classic suburban town house (check out the pebble-dash exterior), a 10-minute walk from the city centre. The five rooms have a pastel charm.

Courtbrack Accommodation B&B €
(061-302 500; www.courtbrackaccom.com; Courtbrack Ave; s/d €30/52; May-Aug; P) Student digs during semester, summertime tourist rates at this spiffy red-hued place include continental breakfast. Spotless facilities include a kitchen, laundry and common area with wi-fi. It's 400m southwest of the city centre, just south of Dock Rd (the N69).

Eating

At weekends especially, be sure to book for the better places. George's Quay has some continental flair and tables along the water.

Market Square Brasserie IRISH €€€
(061-448 700; www.savoylimerick.com; Henry St; 6-course menu €35; dinner Tue-Sat) Now at home inside the Savoy Hotel (p325), chef Liam Murrell ingeniously prepares and artfully presents local produce. The likes of game terrine with foie gras, pear and blueberry chutney and lime jam, almond- and caper-crusted halibut, and caramelised popcorn parfait appear on the everchanging menu. Service is smooth, the wine list long and the cheese selection sensational.

RICHARD CUMMINS/LONELY PLANET IMAGES ©

1. Wilds of Tipperary (p340)
Flowers on hillside in the Vee valley near Clogheen.

2. Rock of Cashel, County Tipperary (p335)
This ancient fortress was the seat of kings and churchmen for more than a thousand years.

3. Lough Gur, County Limerick (p330)
Surrounding the lake are dozens of intriguing archaeological sites, including this wedge tomb.

4. Goat, County Tipperary
Goats were first brought to Ireland over 4000 years ago and are still kept for their milk, meat and hides.

STEPHEN SAKS/LONELYPLANETIMAGES ©

Chocolat INTERNATIONAL €€
(☎061-609 709; www.chocolatrestaurant.ie; 109 O'Connell St; mains €12-19.50; ⊙lunch & dinner; 👪) Make that *very* international. This trendy, minimalist place has been packed since its recent opening and no wonder. Food spans the globe – from Thai mango chicken and Singapore noodles to German meatballs and Toulouse sausages, plus plenty of northern, central and southern American classics, including finger-licking ribs. And, of course, there's chocolate, such as Snickers Belgian mousse and white chocolate cheesecake. The inventive, generous cocktails are the best in town, and include a chocolate coffee kiss (Kahlua, Baileys, creme de cacao, Grand Marnier and chocolate syrup).

Sage Cafe CAFE €€
(www.thesagecafe.com; 67-68 Catherine St; dishes €5.50-12; ⊙breakfast & lunch Mon-Sat; 👪) The decor at this licensed cafe says it all: superb taste that doesn't call attention to itself. Breakfast treats and baked goods give way to a line-up of lunch sandwiches, salads such as tiger prawn and cashew nut, and hot plates like lambs liver with apricot stuffing and black pudding potato cake.

Wild Onion CAFE €
(www.wildonioncafe.com; High St; mains €7-10; ⊙breakfast & lunch Tue-Sat) This blue-fronted cafe and bakery is famed for its full-bore American breakfasts (that means no black pudding, but plenty of hash browns, American pork sausages and three-egg omelettes). Hot open sandwiches are the order of the day come lunchtime. No credit cards.

Milk Market MARKET €
(www.milkmarketlimerick.ie; Cornmarket Row) Pick from organic produce and local foods like cheese at the traditional **food market** (⊙8am-4pm Sat) held in Limerick's old market buildings, or browse its produce and craft **shops** (⊙most open Fri-Sun). Other markets are listed on the website.

Drinking & Entertainment

The free *Limerick Event Guide* (LEG; www.eightball.ie) can be found in pubs, eateries and hotels all over town. Most clubs have strict door checks.

TOP CHOICE **Nancy Blake's** PUB
(Upper Denmark St) There's sawdust on the floor and peat on the fire in the cosy front bar of this wonderful old pub. Out back is a vast covered drinking zone that often features live music or televised matches.

White House Pub PUB
(www.whitehousebarlimerick.com; 52 O'Connell St) A classic right in the centre, this corner pub has outdoor seating (under a rare tree) and a good beer list. On some nights it has live acoustic music, on others it helps lead a rebirth of local poetry through readings (www.whitehousepoets.blogspot.com).

Locke Bar PUB
(George's Quay) Picturesque waterside setting, a maze of rooms and bars and great pub grub.

South's PUB
(4 Quinlan St) Frank McCourt's father knocked 'em back here and the *Angela's Ashes* connection is played up, including the toilets named Frank and Angela.

Trinity Rooms NIGHTCLUB
(www.trinityrooms.ie; The Granary, Michael St) Vast club in a 300-year-old waterside building, with hot DJs and a courtyard bar.

Dolan's LIVE MUSIC
(www.dolanspub.com; 3 & 4 Dock Rd) Limerick's best spot for live music promises authentic trad sessions and an unbeatable gig list, as well as cutting-edge stand-ups in two adjoining venues.

University Concert Hall CONCERT HALL
(UCH; ☎061-322 322; www.uch.ie; University of Limerick) Permanent home of the Irish Chamber Orchestra, with regular concerts from visiting acts, plus opera, drama, comedy and dance.

Information

Dangers & Annoyances

Reputation and the unfortunate nickname 'Stab City' aside, central Limerick is not any less safe than other urban Irish areas. Keep alert at night and you should be fine.

Internet Access

Limerick City Library (www.limerickcity.ie/library; The Granary, Michael St; ⊙10am-5.30pm Mon & Tue, to 8pm Wed-Fri, to 1pm Sat)

Medical Services

Both of the following hospitals have accident and emergency departments:

Midwestern Regional Hospital (☎061-482 219; Dooradoyle)

St John's Hospital (☎061-462 222; www.stjohnshospital.ie; St John's Sq)

Money

ATMs are common. The following banks also have bureaux de change.

AIB Bank (106/108 O'Connell St)

Ulster Bank (95 O'Connell St)

Post

Main post office (Lower Cecil St)

Tourist Information

Limerick Tourist Office (☎061-317 522; www.discoverireland.ie/shannon; Arthurs Quay; ⏰9am-5pm Mon-Sat) A large, impressive facility with helpful staff.

ℹ Getting There & Away

Air

Shannon Airport (p353) in County Clare handles domestic and international flights.

Bus

Bus Éireann (☎061-313 333; www.buseireann.ie; Parnell St) services operate from the bus and train stations near the city centre. There are regular buses to Cork (€13.90, 1¾ hours), Tralee (€15.75, two hours) and Dublin (€9.90, 3½ hours), as well as to Galway, Killarney, Rosslare, Ennis, Shannon, Derry and most other centres. You can also get off in Limerick at the bus stop on O'Connell St.

Citylink (☎1890 280 808; www.citylink.ie) has up to seven buses a day to Galway (€14, 1½ hours) and Cork (€14, two hours). Buses stop on Upper Mallow St.

JJ Kavanagh & Sons (☎0818 333 222; www.jjkavanagh.ie) has 11 buses daily to Dublin (€11) and Dublin Airport (€20). Buses stop outside Limerick's tourist office.

Train

Irish Rail (www.irishrail.ie) has regular trains from **Limerick Railway Station** (☎061-315 555; Parnell St) including eight trains daily to Ennis (€9.50, 40 minutes), hourly services to Dublin Heuston (€30, 2½ hours), and six services to Galway (€28.50, two hours). Other routes, including Cork, Tralee, Tipperary, Cahir and Waterford, involve changing at **Limerick Junction**, 20km southeast of Limerick.

ℹ Getting Around

Regular **Bus Éireann** (€5.75) and **JJ Kavanagh & Sons** (€5) buses connect Limerick's bus and train station with Shannon Airport. A taxi from the city centre to the airport costs around €35 to €45. The airport is 26km northwest of Limerick, about 30 minutes by car.

Taxis can be found outside of the tourist office, at the bus and train stations, and in Thomas St, or try **Swift Taxis** (☎061-313 131).

Hire bikes at **Emerald Alpine** (☎061-416 983; www.irelandrentabike.com; Roches St; per day/week €20/80). The company will also retrieve or deliver a bike from anywhere in Ireland for €25.

Around Limerick City

Close to the city there's a clutch of outstanding historic sites that reward a day trip by car or a couple of days by bike.

FRANK MCCOURT

No one has been as closely linked to Limerick in recent years as Frank McCourt (1930–2009). His autobiographical novel *Angela's Ashes* was a surprise publishing sensation in 1996, bringing him fame and honours (including the Pulitzer Prize).

Although he was born in New York City, McCourt's immigrant family returned to Limerick four years later, unable to survive in America. His childhood was filled with the kinds of deprivations that were all too common at the time: his father was a drunk who later vanished, three of his six siblings died in childhood and at age 13 he dropped out of school to earn money to help his family survive.

At age 19, McCourt returned to New York and later worked for three decades as a high school teacher. Among the subjects he taught was writing. From the 1970s he dabbled in writing and theatre with his brother Malachy. He started *Angela's Ashes* only after retiring from teaching in 1987. Its early sales success was thanks to a bevy of enthusiastic critics, but in Limerick the reaction was mixed, with many decrying the negative portrait it painted of the city.

Today McCourt's legacy in Limerick is celebrated. There's an exhibit about the Limerick of the book at the Georgian House & Garden (p323), and you can visit one of the pubs mentioned in the book, South's (p328). Limerick City's tourist office has information about sights related to the book.

WORTH A TRIP

LIMERICK CITY TO TARBERT VIA THE SCENIC N69

The narrow, peaceful N69 road follows the Shannon Estuary west from Limerick for 58km to Tarbert in northern County Kerry. You'll enjoy some great views of the broadening estuary and seemingly endless rolling green hills laced with stone walls. You'll also discover a number of tiny heritage museums and gardens (most usually only open in the high season, approximately June to September).

Hidden just off the N69, a highlight of the route is the village of **Askeaton**, with evocative ruins including the mid-1300s Desmond Castle, a 1389-built Franciscan friary, and St Mary's Church of Ireland and Knights Templar Tower, built around 1829, as well as the 1740-built Hellfire Gentlemen's club. Restoration of the ruins started in 2007 and is expected to continue until 2017. The town's **tourist office** (☎061-392 149; askeatontouristoffice@gmail.com; the Square; ⏱9am-5pm Mon-Sat) has details of ruins that you can freely wander (depending on restoration works) and can arrange free **guided tours** lasting about one hour led by passionate local historians.

At **Foynes** is another of the route's highlights, the fascinating **Foynes Flying Boat Museum** (www.flyingboatmuseum.com; adult/child €9/5; ⏱9am-5pm Apr-Oct). From 1939 to 1945 this was the landing place for the flying boats that linked North America with the British Isles. Big Pan Am clippers – there's a replica here – would set down in the estuary and refuel.

LOUGH GUR

The area around this horseshoe-shaped lake has dozens of intriguing archaeological sites. **Grange Stone Circle**, known as the Lios, is a superb 4000-year-old circular enclosure made up of 113 embanked upright stones. It is the largest prehistoric circle of its kind in Ireland. There's roadside parking and access to the site is free. From Limerick, take the N24 road south towards Waterford and follow the signs onto the R512 for 16km to the stone circle.

Around 1km further south along the R512, at Holycross garage and post office, a left turn takes you towards Lough Gur, past a ruined 15th-century **church**, and a **wedge tomb** on the other side of the road.

Another 2km leads to a car park by Lough Gur and the thatched replica of a Neolithic hut containing the **Lough Gur Stone Age Centre** (www.shannonheritage.com; adult/child €5/3; ⏱10am-5pm early May-Sep). The centre has a good exhibit on prehistoric Irish farms (meaning pre-potato era) and a small museum displaying Neolithic artefacts and a replica of the Lough Gur shield that's now in the National Museum in Dublin. Other displays detail emigration from the area, which included a number of future American mobsters.

Short walks along the lake's edge lead to burial mounds, standing stones, ancient enclosures and other points of interest. Admission to these sites is free. The whole area is ideal for picnics.

KILMALLOCK

POP 1400

Ireland's third-largest town during the Middle Ages (after Dublin and Kilkenny) still has a smattering of medieval buildings that merit a visit.

Kilmallock developed around a 7th-century abbey and from the 14th to the 17th centuries was the seat of the Earls of Desmond. The village lies beside the River Lubach, 26km south of Limerick and a world away from the city's urban racket.

Coming into Kilmallock from Limerick, the first thing you'll see (to your left) is a **medieval stone mansion** – one of 30 or so that housed the town's prosperous merchants and landowners. Further along, the street dodges around the four-storey **King's Castle**, a 15th-century tower house with a ground-floor archway through which the pavement now runs.

FREE **Kilmallock Museum** (Sheares St; ⏱11am-3pm) Across the road from the castle, a lane leads down to this tiny museum, which houses a random collection of historical artefacts and, more fun, a model of the town in 1597 so you can get an idea of what you missed (besides the smells, diseases etc). The museum is the base for the **history trail** around town.

Beyond the museum and across the River Lubach are the moody and extensive ruins of a 13th-century **Dominican priory**, which boasts a splendid five-light window in the choir.

Returning to the main street, head back towards Limerick city, then turn left into Orr St, which runs down to the 13th-century **Collegiate Church**. It has a round tower dating probably to an earlier, pre-Norman monastery on the site.

Further south along the main street, turn left (on foot, the road is one-way against you) into Wolfe Tone St. On the right, just before the bridge, you'll see a plaque marking the house where the Irish poet Aindrias Mac Craith died in 1795. Across the road, one of the pretty, single-storey cottages (the fifth one from the bridge) preserves a 19th-century interior. Obtain the key from next door.

Off the other side of the main street, in Emmet St, is **Blossom Gate**, the one surviving gate of the original medieval town wall.

The excellent **Friars' Gate Theatre & Arts Centre** (☎063-98727; www.friarsgate.ie; Main St) hosts art exhibitions and has a fine little theatre in which it stages plays and music events, and has tourist information about the village.

Two Bus Éireann buses run Monday to Saturday from Limerick to Kilmallock (€8.82, one hour).

Adare & Around

POP 1150

Often dubbed 'Ireland's prettiest village', Adare centres on its clutch of perfectly preserved thatched cottages built by the 19th-century English landlord, the Earl of Dunraven, for workers constructing Adare Manor. Today, the cottages house craft shops and some of the county's finest restaurants, with prestigious golf courses nearby.

Unsurprisingly, tourists are drawn to the postcard-perfect village, set 16km southwest of Limerick on the River Maigue, by the busload. This makes the roads even more clogged (the busy N21 is the village's main street). It's also a popular romantic getaway for many Irish visitors at weekends, when you're best booking accommodation and restaurants in advance, but when you'll also find Adare at its most vibrant.

Sights & Activities

To zoom through the picturesque countryside surrounding Adare in a classic sports car, see p333.

Adare Heritage Centre MUSEUM

(☎061-396 666; www.adareheritagecentre.ie; Main St; admission free; ⌚9am-6pm summer, 9.30am-5pm winter) In the middle of the village, exhibits at Adare's heritage centre explain the history and the medieval context of the village's buildings in an entertaining way. Try picking up the longbow (have you had your spinach today?). Quality Irish crafts are on sale, there's also a busy cafe.

Adare Castle CASTLE

(tours adult/family €6/15; ⌚tour hourly 10am-5pm Jun-Sep) Dating back to around 1200, this picturesque feudal ruin saw rough usage until it was finally wrecked for good by Cromwell's troops in 1657. By then it had already lost its strategic importance. Restoration work is ongoing; look for the ruined great hall with its early 13th-century windows.

Book tours through the Heritage Centre. When tours aren't on, you can view the castle from the busy main road, or more peacefully from the riverside footpath or the grounds of the Augustinian priory.

Religious Houses HISTORIC SITES

Before the Tudor dissolution of the monasteries (1536–39), Adare had three flourishing religious houses, the remains of which can still be seen. In the village itself, next to the heritage centre, the dramatic tower and southern wall of the **Church of the Holy Trinity** date from the 13th-century Trinitarian priory that was restored by the first Earl of Dunraven. Holy Trinity is now a Catholic church. There's a restored 14th-century **dovecote** down the side-turning next to the church.

The ruins of a **Franciscan friary**, founded by the Earl of Kildare in 1464, stand in the middle of Adare Manor golf course beside the River Maigue. Public access is assured, but let them know at the clubhouse that you intend to visit. A track leads away from the clubhouse car park for about 400m – watch out for flying golf balls. There's a handsome tower and a fine sedilia (row of seats for priests) in the southern wall of the chancel.

North of the village, on the N21 and close to the bridge over the River Maigue, is the Church of Ireland parish church, once the **Augustinian priory**, founded in 1315. It was also known as the Black Abbey. The interior of the church is agreeably cavernous, but the real joy is the atmospheric little cloister.

A pleasant, signposted **riverside path**, with wayside seats, starts from just north of the priory gates. Look for a narrow access gap and head off alongside the river. After about 250m, turn left along the road to reach the centre of Adare.

Adare Manor Golf Club GOLF
(www.adaremanorgolfclub.com; 18 holes €95-125) Adare is a big hit with golfers; centrally located courses include the spectacularly set Adare Manor Golf Club.

Sleeping

Sleeping options range from camping to a palatial castle hotel.

TOP CHOICE **Adare Manor** HOTEL €€€
(061-605 200; www.adaremanor.com; Main St; d €290-390; P @) The Earl of Dunraven's magnificent estate is now an imposing yet wonderfully intimate castle hotel. Individually decorated rooms have autumnal tones and antique furniture; dining options, also open to nonguests, include its superb **Oak Room Restaurant** (mains €21-34.50; dinner) and **high tea** (veg/non-veg €18/26.50; 2-5pm) served on tiered plates in the stately drawing room. Guests get reduced rates at the Adare Manor Golf Club (p332).

Dunraven Arms INN €€€
(061-396 633; www.dunravenhotel.com; Main St; s/d from €135/155; @) This jewel of an inn, built in 1792, sits discreetly behind hedged gardens. All 86 rooms have a high standard of traditional luxury, with antiques and high thread count linens. Its **restaurant** (mains €16.50-25; dinner) has an ambitious menu (pan-seared duck with lavender risotto, warm white chocolate cake with cara melised banana), but its **bar menu** (mains €13-14.50; lunch & dinner) is a worthy, more affordable alternative.

Berkeley Lodge B&B €€
(061-396 857; www.adare.org; Station Rd; d €70; P) One of several modern B&Bs on this road, close to the village, this six-room house has in-room TVs, great breakfasts and welcomes early arrivals from Shannon Airport. It's a three-minute walk to the centre and very kid friendly.

Fitzgerald's Woodlands House Hotel HOTEL €€€
(061-605 100; www.woodlands-hotel.ie; Knockanes; d €58-154; P) Just over 1km southeast of Adare, Fitzgerald's Woodlands House is a gorgeous country retreat with high-class amenities, including super-soft goose down-topped mattresses. Little guests are offered nutritious kids menus; there's also a kids club, arcade games for teenagers and a babysitting service. Grown-ups can luxuriate at the onsite spa.

Adare Village Inn INN €
(087 251 7102; www.adarevillageinn.com; Main St; s/d €45/60;) Excellent-value rooms are cosy and come with a fruit basket. The inn is located in the dead centre of town, near the crossroads and village hall.

Adare Camping & Caravan Park CAMPGROUND €
(061-395 376; www.adarecamping.com; Adare; campsites per tent/caravan from €11/22; P) This sheltered, uncrowded site is about 4km south of Adare off the N21 and R519. Percolate your travel-weary bones in the hot tub.

Eating

Adare has some exceptional places to eat.

TOP CHOICE **Wild Geese** IRISH €€
(061-396 451; www.thewild-geese.com; Main St; mains €21-24.50; lunch Sun, dinner Tue-Sat) In a town where upmarket competition is downright fierce, this inviting cottage restaurant keeps the standard consistently high. The ever-changing menu celebrates the best of southwest Ireland's produce, from scallops to sumptuous racks of lamb. The service is genial, preparations are imaginative and the bread basket divine.

The White Sage IRISH €€
(061-396 004; www.whitesagerestaurant.com; Main St; mains €20-29.50; dinner Tue-Sat;) Local, often organic, suppliers have star billing on the menu of this lovely little restaurant, housed in a cottage on the main street. Vegetarian options are limited but inspired, such as cider-infused pear salad and a shallot and goats cheese *tarte tatin*.

Blue Door IRISH €€
(061-396 481; www.bluedooradare.com; Main St; mains €19-26; lunch & dinner;) Gourmet salads, open-faced sandwiches and lasagnes appear at lunch at this cottage restaurant in

WORTH A TRIP

BALLINGARRY

The attractive village of Ballingarry (Baile an Gharraí, meaning 'town of the gardens'), 13km southwest of Adare on the R519, is home to one of County Limerick's hidden dining gems.

The Mustard Seed at Eco Lodge (☎069-68508; www.mustardseed.ie; 4-course menu €64; s/d €100/150; ⏱restaurant dinner daily, restaurant & accommodation closed mid-Jan–mid-Feb; P 📶) Produce picked fresh from this mustard-coloured 19th-century former convent's orchards and kitchen gardens are incorporated in its stunning four-course dinners. The menu changes with the seasons, but might include butternut squash, artichoke and pistachio salad with balsamic truffle dressing, followed by pineapple- and vodka-seared duck with vegetable gratin, and Greek yoghurt meringue. To avoid having to move too far afterwards, book in to one of the lodge's elegant, country-style rooms (some with four-poster beds).

the village centre, while dinner ups the ante with creative twists on local seafood and meat, like beechwood-smoked duck and cod in chardonnay sauce.

Good Room Cafe CAFE €
(☎061-396 218; Main St; dishes €5-10; ⏱breakfast & lunch; 👪) Inventive soups, salads, sandwiches, baked goods and homemade jams at this (very) good room are more contemporary than you'd expect from the cutesy thatched-cottage location. Arrive early before their famous scones sell out.

Drinking

Aunty Lena's PUB
(Main St; 📶) Deceptively large local favourite.

Seán Collins PUB
(Killarney Rd) Adare's most traditional pub.

Bill Chawke Lounge Bar PUB
(Main St) Regular trad music and singalongs.

ℹ Information

The website www.adarevillage.com is a handy source of info.

AIB Bank (☎061-396 544) Near the tourist office; has an ATM and bureau de change.

Tourist office (☎061-396 255; Adare Heritage Centre, www.discoverireland.com/shannon; Main St; ⏱9am-6pm mid-May–mid-Sep, reduced hours rest of year)

Getting There & Around

Hourly Bus Éireann services link Limerick with Adare (€4.50, 25 minutes). Many continue on to Tralee (€15.30, 1¾ hours). Others serve Killarney (€15.30, 1¾ hours).

Spin around Adare in style in a classic Jaguar, Ferrari, MG or Triumph from **Heritage Sports Cars** (☎069-63770; www.heritagesportscars.com), which has free delivery and collection in Adare.

COUNTY TIPPERARY

Landlocked Tipperary boasts the sort of fertile soil that farmers dream of. There's still an upper-crust gloss to traditions here. Local fox hunts are in full legal cry during the winter season and the villages can look like something out of the English shires. The central area of the county is low-lying, but rolling hills spill over from adjoining counties.

Walking and cycling opportunities abound, especially in the Glen of Aherlow near Tipperary town. But the real crowd-pleasers are the iconic Rock of Cashel and Cahir Castle. In between, you'll find bucolic charm along pretty much any country road you choose.

Tipperary Town

POP 4600

Tipperary (Tiobrad Árann) has a storied name, largely due to the WWI song. And indeed, you may find it a long road to Tipperary as the N24 and a web of regional roads converge on the centre and traffic often moves at the same speed as the armies at the Somme. 'Tipp town' itself has few pretensions and there's no need to detour here.

Inside the **Excel Heritage Centre** (Mitchell St), you'll find the **tourist information point** (☎062-80520; ⏱10am-5pm Mon-Sat, 2-5.30pm Sun). It's reached via St Michael's St, a side street leading 200m off the northern side of Main St. Also here is a small gallery, **cafe** (dishes €5-6.50), cinema, a good genealogy

TRACING YOUR ANCESTORS

Genealogical centres in counties Limerick and Tipperary can help trace your ancestors; contact the centres in advance to arrange a consultation.

» **Limerick Genealogy** (☎061-496 542; www.limerickgenealogy.com; Lissanalta House, Dooradoyle Rd, Dooradoyle)

» **Tipperary North Genealogy Centre** (☎067-33850; www.tipperarynorth.ie/genealogy; the Governor's House, Kickham St, Nenagh)

» **Tipperary South Genealogy Centre** (☎062-61122; www.comhaltas.ie; Brú Borí Heritage Centre, Cashel)

» **Tipperary Family History Research** (☎062-80552; www.tfhr.org; Excel Heritage Centre, Mitchell St, Tipperary town)

centre (p334) and **internet access** (€1 per 15min).

Midway along Main St, there's a **statue of Charles J Kickham** (1828-82), a local novelist (author of *Knocknagow*, a novel about rural life) and Young Irelander. He spent four years in London's Pentonville Prison in the 1860s for treason.

In honour of the local patriot, traditional pub **Kickham House** (www.kickhamhouse.com; Main St; mains €8-11; ⏰lunch) has carvery lunches that include smoked haddock and cod pie.

Tipperary Racecourse (☎062-51357; www.tipperary races.ie; Limerick Rd) is one of Ireland's leading tracks. It's 3km out of town and has regular meetings during the year; see the local press for details. The course is within walking distance of Limerick Junction station.

Danny Ryan Music (www.dannyryanmusic.ie; 20 Bank Pl) has a superb selection of musical instruments.

Most buses stop on Abbey St beside the river. **Bus Éireann** (www.buseireann.ie) runs up to eight buses daily on the Limerick (€7.20, 40 minutes) to Waterford route via Cahir and Clonmel.

To reach the **train station**, head south along Bridge St. Tipperary is on the Waterford–Limerick Junction line. There are two daily services to Cahir (25 minutes), Clonmel, Carrick-on-Suir, Waterford and Rosslare Harbour, and multiple connections to Cork, Kerry and Dublin from **Limerick Junction** (☎062-51406), barely 3km from Tipperary station along the Limerick road.

Springhouse Bicycle Hire (☎062-31329; www.springhouse.eu.com; Kilshane; rental day/week €20/80; 📶) has bikes, can offer cycling advice for the region and will pick up and drop off bikes at the bus and train stations. It has a small **B&B** (d €90; P📶). Springhouse is on the N24, 4.5km southeast of Tipperary.

Glen of Aherlow & Galtee Mountains

South of Tipperary are the shapely Slievenamuck Hills and Galtee Mountains, separated by the broad, chequered valley of the Glen of Aherlow. A 25km **scenic drive** through the Glen is signposted from Tipperary town. At the eastern end of the Glen, between Tipperary and Cahir, the village of Bansha (An Bháinseach) marks the start of a 20km trip west to Galbally, an easy bike ride or scenic drive along the R663 that takes in the best of the county's landscapes.

Renowned for its **walking**, the terrain through the region ranges from the lush riverbanks of the Aherlow to pine forests in the hills and windswept, rocky grasslands that seem to stretch on forever. For spectacular views, head 1.6km north of Newtown on the R664 to its popular **lookout** and historic **statue of Christ**.

The R663 from Bansha and the R664 south from Tipperary converge at Newtown at the **Coach Road Inn**, a fine old pub that's popular with walkers. Hidden around the back of the pub, the enthusiastically staffed Glen of Aherlow **tourist office** (☎062-56331; www.aherlow.com; ⏰9.30am-5pm Mon-Fri year-round plus 10am-4pm Sat Jun-Aug) is an excellent source of information on the area, including numerous **walking festivals**.

There's a good range of rural accommodation – much of it catering to walkers.

TOP CHOICE **Aherlow House Hotel** (☎062-56153; www.aherlow house.ie; Newtown; s/d/lodge from €99/120/175; P@📶👪) Up a pine-forested track from the R663, a 1928 hunting lodge has been turned into a luxurious woodland retreat with 29 rooms with king-size beds and 15 contemporary countrified self-catering lodges (minimum two-night stay). There's a flowing **bar** (bar food €11-16; ⌚lunch & dinner), a fine **restaurant** (mains €20-30; ⌚dinner), and glorious mountain views from the terrace.

Against a great backdrop of the Galtees 10km west from Bansha, excellent facilities at **Ballinacourty House Camping Park & B&B** (☎062-56559; www.ballinacourtyhse.com; Glen of Aherlow; campsites €23, s/d €51.50/70; P) include a beautiful garden, a much-loved local **restaurant** (four-course menu €20-30; ⌚lunch Sun, dinner Wed-Sat), a tennis court and minigolf.

The friendly owners of **Homeleigh Farmhouse** (☎062-56228; www.homeleighfarmhouse.com; Newtown; s/d €54/80; dinner €28; P), on a working farm just west of Newtown and the Coach Rd Inn, are founts of walking info. The modern house has five comfortable rooms with private bathrooms; book ahead to enjoy a three-course home-cooked meal after walking up an appetite.

The frequent Bus Éireann link between Tipperary town (€2.60, 20 minutes) and Waterford stops in Bansha. From here it's a walk or bike ride into the hills. See p333 for bike rental information, otherwise a rental car will enable you to explore far and wide between walks.

Cashel

POP 2500

It's no wonder that Cashel (Caiseal Mumhan) is popular with visitors (the Queen included it on her historic visit in 2011). The iconic Rock of Cashel and the clutch of historical religious buildings that crown its breezy summit seem like a magical extension of the rocky landscape itself, and although tourism has been hard-hit by the economic crisis, Cashel maintains a certain charm as a smallish market town.

Cashel is awash in accommodation, but decent places to eat are thinner on the ground.

Sights

The tourist office rents iPods (€20 refundable deposit) for an audioguided tour of the town.

Rock of Cashel HISTORIC SITE

(www.heritageireland.com; adult/child €6/2; ⌚9am-6.15pm Jun-Sep, to 4.45pm Oct-May) The **Rock of Cashel** is one of Ireland's most spectacular archaeological sites. The 'Rock' is a prominent green hill, banded with limestone outcrops. It rises from a grassy plain on the edge of the town and bristles with ancient fortifications – the word 'cashel' is an anglicised version of the Irish word *caiseal*, meaning 'fortress'. Sturdy walls circle an enclosure that contains a complete round tower, a 13th century Gothic cathedral and the finest 12th-century Romanesque chapel in Ireland. For more than 1000 years the Rock of Cashel was a symbol of power and the seat of kings and churchmen who ruled over the region. In the 4th century the Rock of Cashel was chosen as a base by the Eóghanachta clan from Wales, who went on to conquer much of Munster and become kings of the region. For some 400 years it rivalled Tara (p539) as a centre of power in Ireland. The clan was associated with St Patrick, hence the Rock's alternative name of St Patrick's Rock.

In the 10th century, the Eóghanachta lost possession of the rock to the O'Brien (or Dál gCais) tribe under Brian Ború's leadership. In 1101, King Muircheartach O'Brien presented the Rock to the Church, a move designed to curry favour with the powerful bishops and to end secular rivalry over possession of the Rock with the Eóghanachta, by now known as the MacCarthys. Numerous buildings must have occupied the Rock over the years, but it is the ecclesiastical relics that have survived even the depredations of the Cromwellian army in 1647.

It's a five-minute stroll from the town centre to the Rock. You can take some pretty paths including the Bishop's Walk, which ends in the gardens of the Cashel Palace Hotel. Sheep grudgingly allow you to pass. There are a couple of parking spaces for visitors with disabilities at the top of the approach road to the ticket office. The Rock is a major draw for coach parties for most of the year and is extremely busy during July and August: the sweeping views allow you to see a tour bus approaching from any dir ection like a raiding party. The scaffolding moves from place to place each year as part of the never-ending struggle to keep the Rock caulked.

There are reasonable photo opportunities for framing the Rock on the road into town from the Dublin Rd roundabout or the little roads just west of the centre. The best vantage points for photos, however, are from inside the ruins of Hore Abbey (p336).

Call ahead for details of guided tours.

Hall of the Vicars Choral

The entrance to the Rock of Cashel is through this 15th-century building, once home to the male choristers who sang in the cathedral. It houses the ticket office. The exhibits in the adjoining undercroft include some very rare silverware, Bronze Age axes and St Patrick's Cross – an impressive, although eroded, 12th-century crutched cross with a crucifixion scene on one face and animals on the other. A replica stands outside in the castle courtyard. The kitchen and dining hall upstairs contain some period furniture, tapestries and paintings beneath a fine carved-oak roof and gallery. A 20-minute audiovisual presentation on the Rock's history runs every half hour. Showings are in English, French, German and Italian.

Cathedral

This 13th-century Gothic structure overshadows the other ruins. Entry is through a small porch facing the Hall of the Vicars Choral. The cathedral's western location is formed by the **Archbishop's Residence**, a 15th-century, four-storey castle that had its great hall built over the nave. Soaring above the centre of the cathedral is a huge square tower with a turret on the southwestern corner.

Scattered throughout are monuments, panels from 16th-century altar tombs and coats of arms. If you have binoculars, look for the numerous stone heads on capitals and corbels high above the ground.

Round Tower

On the northeastern corner of the cathedral is an 11th- or 12th-century round tower, the earliest building on the Rock of Cashel. It's 28m tall and the doorway is 3.5m above the ground – perhaps for structural rather than defensive reasons.

Cormac's Chapel

If the Rock of Cashel boasted only Cormac's Chapel, it would still be an outstanding place. This compelling building dates from 1127 and the medieval integrity of its trans-European architecture survives. It was probably the first Romanesque church in Ireland. The style of the square towers that flank it to either side may reflect Germanic influences, but there are haunting similarities in its steep stone roof to the 'boat-hull' shape of older Irish buildings, such as the Gallarus Oratory in County Kerry (p309) and the beehive huts of the Dingle Peninsula (p308).

The true Romanesque splendour is in the detail of the exquisite doorway arches, the grand chancel arch and ribbed barrel vault, and the outstanding carved vignettes that include a trefoil-tailed grotesque and a Norman-helmeted centaur firing an arrow at a rampaging lion. The chapel's interior is tantalisingly dark, but linger for a while and your eyes will adjust. Inside the main door, on the left, is the sarcophagus said to house King Cormac, dating from between 1125 and 1150. Frescoes once covered the walls, but only vestiges of these survive. The southern tower leads to a stone-roofed vault and a croft above the nave (no access).

Hore Abbey HISTORIC SITE

Cashel throws in another bonus for the heritage lover. This is the formidable ruin of 13th-century Hore Abbey (also known as Hoare Abbey or St Mary's). Originally Benedictine and settled by monks from Glastonbury in England at the end of the 12th century, it later became a Cistercian house. Enjoyably gloomy, it was gifted to the order by a 13th-century archbishop who expelled the Benedictine monks after dreaming that they planned to murder him.

The abbey is just under 1km north of the Rock in flat farmland.

Brú Ború HERITAGE CENTRE

(☎062-61122; www.comhaltas.ie/locations/detail/bru_boru; admission €3; ⏲9am-5pm, hrs can vary) The privately run heritage and cultural centre is next to the car park below the Rock of Cashel, and offers an absorbing insight into Irish traditional music, dance and song. The centre's main attraction, the **Sounds of History** exhibition, relates the story of Ireland and its music through imaginative audio displays; various other musical events take place in summer.

Cashel Folk Village MUSEUM

(☎062-62525; Dominic St; adult/child €5/2; ⏲9.30am-5.30pm, hrs can vary) An engaging exhibition of old buildings, shopfronts and memorabilia from around the town. It's a bit slipshod in a heart-warming way.

FREE **Cashel Heritage Town Centre Museum** MUSEUM

(www.casheltc.ie; Town Hall, Main St; ⏲9.30am-5.30pm mid-Mar–Oct, closed Sat & Sun Nov–

mid-Mar) Located in the town hall next to the tourist office; displays include a scale model of Cashel in the 1640s.

Bolton Library MUSEUM
(John St; admission €2; by appointment, book at tourist office) A forbidding 1836 stone building houses a splendid 18th-century collection of books, maps and manuscripts from the dawn of printing onwards. There are works by writers from Chaucer to Swift.

Sleeping

The sweet spot for Cashel accommodation is right in the middle of town, an easy walk to the Rock.

TOP CHOICE **Cashel Palace Hotel** HOTEL €€€
(062-62707; www.cashel-palace.ie; Main St; s/d from €95/176; P@) Built in 1732 for a Protestant archbishop, this handsome red-brick, late-Queen Anne house is a local landmark. Fully restored, it has 23 antique-furnished rooms in the gracious main building or quaint mews, with luxuries like trouser presses (as if you wouldn't have someone else attend to that). Some rooms have soaking tubs you'll leave only after you're totally prunified. The **bar** (bar food €10-16; lunch & dinner) is the place to talk about your upcoming hunt before dining at the vaulted-ceilinged **Bishops Buttery Restaurant** (2-/3-course menus from €22/25; lunch & dinner).

Cashel Town B&B B&B €€
(062-62330; www.cashelbandb.com; 5 John St; d from €60; P@) Fresh produce from nearby farmers markets is cooked up for breakfast at this homey B&B, which is part of the Slow Food movement (even the porridge is organic). Within the 1808-built Georgian townhouse are seven comfortable rooms and a cosy guest lounge with a toasty open fire and a piano. It's run by the same folk as the Cashel Holiday Hostel.

Cashel Lodge & Camping Park HOSTEL €€
(062-61003; www.cashel-lodge.com; Dundrum Rd; campsites per person from €8, dm/s/d €20/40/65; P) In a converted two-century-old stone coach house northwest of town on the R505 (follow the signs for Dundrum), this first-class IHH hostel is friendly, relaxing and well equipped, with a bare stone and wood interior and terrific views of the Rock and Hore Abbey.

Hill House B&B €€
(062-61277; www.hillhousecashel.com; Palmers hill; s/d €65/90; P@) With magnificent views across to the Rock, this 1710-built Georgian charmer could easily be called Amazing View House. Set back in gardens, the house is about 400m uphill from Main St. Rooms have a traditional style and come with four-poster beds.

Cashel Holiday Hostel HOSTEL €
(062-62330; www.cashelhostel.com; 6 John St; dm/s/d from €16/30/45;) A friendly and central budget option. In a vividly coloured three-storey Georgian terrace just off Main St, this hostel has 52 beds in four- to eight-bed rooms, as well as singles and doubles. It also has a kitchen, laundry, library and bike storage. Musicians can 'perform for their bed' (which is to say the hostel can set up gigs and source instruments).

Ashmore House B&B €€
(062-61286; www.ashmorehouse.com; John St; s €40-50, d €70-80; P) You're treated like part of the family at this Georgian town house, which has five big, high-ceilinged guestrooms filled with antiques. It's located on a quiet street just off Main St.

Ladyswell House B&B €€
(062-62985; www.ladyswellhouse.com; Ladyswell St; s/d €65/90;) Barely a five-minute walk to the Abbey, look for the vivid yellow door at this five-room B&B. Rooms are spotless and some bathrooms have skylights. Breakfast includes homemade jams, stewed fruit, brown bread and scones.

Eating

Apart from the Rock, Cashel is best-known in Ireland and beyond for award-winning Cashel Blue farmhouse cheese, Ireland's first-ever blue cheese. Although it's still handmade locally (and only locally), it's surprisingly hard to find in shops and restaurant menus in town.

Main St has the greatest concentration of eateries, including the Bishops Buttery Restaurant (p337).

TOP CHOICE **Cafe Hans** CAFE €€
(062-63660; Dominic St; mains €13-19; noon-5pm Tue-Sat;) Competition for the 32 seats is fierce at this gourmet cafe run by the same family as Chez Hans next door. There's a fantastic selection of salads, open sandwiches (including succulent prawns with tangy

Marie Rose sauce) and filling fish, shellfish, lamb and vegetarian dishes, with a discerning wine selection and mouthwatering desserts like homemade caramel ice cream with butterscotch sauce. Arrive before or after the lunchtime rush or plan on queuing.

Chez Hans IRISH €€
(☎062-61177; www.chezhans.net; Dominic St; mains €26-39; ⏱dinner Tue-Sat) Since 1968 this former church has been a place of worship for foodies from all over Ireland and beyond. Still as fresh and inventive as ever, the restaurant gives its blessing to all manner of Irish foods, including lobster, aged beef and quail.

Kearney's Castle Hotel IRISH €€
(☎062-61044; Main St; mains €14-25; ⏱lunch & dinner) Although it looks like a grand old castle (part of the building does comprise a medieval fortified tower), inside it's dungeon-dark and modernised, but there's a good range of meat, fish and poultry dishes.

Bake House CAFE €
(7 Main St; dishes €5-7; ⏱breakfast & lunch) Don't miss the hot pies (served with salad) at this busy spot.

Drinking

Davern's PUB
(20 Main St) Old, old pub popular for a good chat.

Ryan's PUB
(Ladyswell St) Congenial place with a large beer garden that really is a garden.

Mikey Ryan's PUB
(76 Main St) Local gathering spot.

Information

Banks and ATMs are in the centre.

Tourist office (☎062-62511; www.cashel.ie; Town Hall, Main St; ⏱9.30am-5.30pm mid-Mar-Oct, closed Sat & Sun Nov–mid-Mar) Helpful office with reams of info on the area.

Getting There & Away

Bus Éireann (www.buseireann.ie) runs eight buses daily between Cashel and Cork (€11.70, 1½ hours) via Cahir (€4.50, 20 minutes, six to eight daily). The bus stop for Cork is outside the Bake House on Main St. The Dublin stop (€11.70, three hours, six daily) is opposite.

Ring a Link (☎1890 424 141; www.ringalink.ie), a not-for-profit service for rural residents that's also available to tourists, has a service to Tipperary (€3, 50 minutes).

Around Cashel

The atmospheric – and, at dusk, delightfully creepy – ruins of **Athassel Priory** sit in the shallow and verdant River Suir Valley, 7km southwest of Cashel. The original buildings date from 1205, and Athassel was once one of the richest and most important monasteries in Ireland. What survives is substantial: the gatehouse and portcullis gateway, the cloister and stretches of walled enclosure, as well as some medieval tomb effigies. To get here, take the N74 to the village of **Golden**, then head 2km south along the narrow road signed Athassel Abbey. Roadside parking is limited and very tight. The Priory is reached across often-muddy fields. The welter of back lanes is good for cycling.

Cahir

POP 2850

At the eastern tip of the Galtee Mountains 15km south of Cashel, Cahir (An Cathair; pronounced 'care') is a compact and attractive town that encircles its namesake castle, which does a good job of looking like every castle you ever tried building at the beach, with towers, a moat and battlements. Walking paths follow the banks of the **River Suir** – you can easily spend a couple of hours wandering about.

Sights

Cahir Castle HISTORIC SITE
(www.heritageireland.ie; Castle St; adult/child €3/1; ⏱9am-6.30pm mid-Jun–Aug, 9.30am-5.30pm mid-Mar–mid-Jun & Sep–mid-Oct, 9.30am-4.30pm mid-Oct–mid-Mar) Cahir's awesome castle is feudal fantasy in a big way, with a river-island site with moat, rocky foundations, massive walls, turrets and towers, defences and dungeons. Founded by Conor O'Brien in 1142. this castle is one of Ireland's largest. It was passed to the Butler family in 1375. In 1599 it lost the arms race of its day when the Earl of Essex used cannons to shatter the walls, an event explained with a huge model.

The castle was surrendered to Cromwell in 1650 without a struggle; its future usefulness may have discouraged the usual Cromwellian 'deconstruction' – it is largely intact and still formidable. It was restored in the 1840s and again in the 1960s when it came under state ownership.

WORTH A TRIP

FAMINE WARHOUSE

Famine Warhouse (www.heritageireland.ie; admission free; 2.30-5.30pm Wed-Sun Apr-Sep, 2-4pm Sat & Sun Oct-Mar) A relic of one of Ireland's darkest chapters, the Famine Warhouse sits seemingly benignly today amid typical farmland near Ballingarry. During the 1848 rebellion, rebels led by William Smith O'Brien besieged police who had barricaded themselves inside and taken children hostage. Things did not go well and this incident marked the effective end of the rebellion. Besides exhibits about the incident, there are also displays detailing the famine and the mass exodus of Irish emigrants to America.

The warhouse is 30km northeast of Cashel on the R691 about midway to Kilkenny. Be careful navigating as County Tipperary has two Ballingarrys; the wrong one is over by Roscrea.

A 15-minute audiovisual presentation puts Cahir in context with other Irish castles. The buildings within the castle are sparsely furnished, although there are good displays. The real rewards come from simply wandering through this remarkable survivor of Ireland's medieval past. There are frequent guided tours; several good printed guides are for sale at the entrance.

Swiss Cottage HISTORIC BUILDING
(www.heritageireland.ie; Cahir Park; adult/child €3/1; 10am-6pm Apr-late Oct) A pleasant riverside path from behind the town car park meanders 2km south to Cahir Park and the thatched Swiss Cottage, surrounded by roses, lavender and honeysuckle. Built in 1810 as a retreat for Richard Butler, 12th Baron Caher, and his wife, it was designed by London architect John Nash, creator of the Royal Pavilion at Brighton and London's Regent's Park. The cottage-orné style emerged during the late 18th and early 19th centuries in England in response to the prevailing taste for the picturesque. Thatched roofs, natural wood and carved weatherboarding were characteristics and most examples were built as ornamental features on estates.

A lavish example of Regency Picturesque, the cottage is a more of a sizeable house and has extensive facilities. The 30-minute (compulsory) guided tours are thoroughly enjoyable, although you may have to wait for one in the busier summer months.

Sleeping & Eating

Apple Caravan & Camping Park CAMPGROUND €
(052-744 1459; www.theapplefarm.com; Moorstown, Cahir; campsite per person from €6.50; May-Sep;) Set on a farm of apple orchards on the N24 between Cahir (6km) and Clonmel (9km) this quiet and spacious campsite has free use of a tennis court and racquets, and spring water from its own well. Even if you're not staying here, it's worth dropping by its **farm shop** selling its apples, jams and juices.

Tinsley House B&B €
(052-744 1947; www.tinsleyhouse.com; The Square; d from €55; Apr-Sep;) This mannered house has a great location, four period-furnished rooms and a roof garden. The owner, Liam Roche, is an expert on local history and can recommend walks and other activities.

Cahir House Hotel HOTEL €€
(052-744 3000; www.cahirhousehotel.ie; The Square; s €60, d €90-100;) On a prominent corner of the central Square, this landmark hotel has elegant rooms, a beauty salon offering treatments from reflexology and massages through to fake tans, and a long menu of **bar food** (mains €9-13; lunch & dinner).

Lazy Bean Cafe CAFE €
(The Square; dishes €4-7; breakfast & lunch;) Busy, breezy little cafe dishing out tasty sandwiches, salads, soups and wraps.

Farmers Market MARKET €
(Craft Yard; 9am-1pm Sat) Cahir's farmers market attracts the region's best food vendors.

Shopping

Cahir Craft Granary CRAFTS
(www.craftgranary.com; Church St; 10am-5pm Mon-Fri, 9am-5pm Sat year-round plus 1-5pm Sun Jul-Aug & Dec) Hundreds of locals toiled away in a notorious linen mill during the 19th century. Almost 200 years later, the once ominous stone building has been reborn as

the Cahir Craft Granary, with local artists creating and selling works including pottery, carvings, paintings and jewellery. It's just north of the Square, past the post office.

Information

AIB Bank (Castle St) Has an ATM and bureau de change.

Post office (Church St) North of The Square.

Tourist office (052-744 1453; www.discovireland.ie/tipperary; Main St; 9.30am-5pm Mon-Sat Easter-Oct)

Getting There & Away

Bus

Cahir is a hub for several Bus Éireann routes, including Dublin–Cork, Limerick–Waterford, Galway–Waterford, Kilkenny–Cork and Cork–Athlone. There are eight buses per day Monday to Saturday (six buses on Sunday) to Cashel (€4.50, 20 minutes). Buses stop in the car park beside the tourist office.

Train

From Monday to Saturday, the Limerick Junction–Waterford train stops three times daily in each direction.

Mitchelstown Caves

While the Galtee Mountains are mainly sandstone, a narrow band of limestone along their southern side has given rise to the **Mitchelstown Caves** (www.mitchelstowncave.com; Burncourt; adult/child €7/2; 10am-5.30pm Apr-Oct, shorter hours rest of year). Superior to Kilkenny's Dunmore Cave and yet less developed for tourists, these caves are among the most extensive in the country with nearly 3km of passages and spectacular chambers full of textbook formations with names such as the Pipe Organ, Tower of Babel, House of Commons and Eagle's Wing. Tours take about 30 minutes. Year-round, the cave temperature remains a constant 12°C, making it feel warm in winter and chilly in summer.

The caves are near Burncourt, 16km southwest of Cahir and signposted on the N8 to Mitchelstown (Baile Mhistéala).

Mountain Lodge Hostel (052-746 7277; www.anoige.ie/hostels/mountain-lodge; Burncourt; dm €15; Apr-Sep; P) Housed in a former shooting lodge north of the N8 Mitchelstown–Cahir road, this 24-bed An Óige hostel is 6km north of the caves, and a handy base for walking in the Galtee Mountains. It's electricity-free, lit by gas and heated by wood stoves. Check-in is from 5pm.

Frequent **Bus Éireann** (062-51555) buses on several cross-country routes drop off at the Mountain Lodge Hostel gate.

Clonmel

POP 16,000

On the wide River Suir, Clonmel (Cluain Meala; 'Meadows of Honey') is Tipperary's largest and busiest town.

Laurence Sterne (1713–68), author of *A Sentimental Journey* and *Tristram Shandy,* was a native of the town. However, the commercial cheerleader for Clonmel was Italian-born Charles Bianconi (1786–1875), who, at the precocious age of 16, was sent to Ireland by his father in an attempt to break his liaison with a woman. Bianconi later channelled all his frustrated passion into setting up a coach service between Clonmel and Cahir; his company quickly grew to become a nationwide passenger and mail carrier. For putting Clonmel on the map, Bianconi was twice elected mayor.

Clonmel's centre sits on the northern bank of the river. Set back from the quays and running parallel to the river, the main street runs east–west, starting off as Parnell St and becoming Mitchell St and O'Connell St before passing under West Gate, where it changes to Irishtown and Abbey Rd (there's a handy map on a signboard near St Mary's Church). Running north from this long thoroughfare is

WALK: TIPPERARY HERITAGE TRAIL

Extending a distance of 55km from a place called the Vee in the south to Cashel in the north, the **Tipperary Heritage Trail** takes in some beautiful river valleys and ruins. The 30km north from Cahir to Cashel is the best segment, featuring the verdant lands around the River Suir and passes close to highlights such as Athassel Priory. The best stretches around Golden are off roads. Expect to see a fair amount of wildlife as the paths and very minor roads follow the waters and pass through woodlands. Ordnance Survey Discovery series maps 66 and 74 cover the route.

Gladstone St, which has a number of hotels and pubs.

The East Munster Way (p343) passes through Clonmel.

Sights

Turning south down Bridge St, crossing the river and following the road around brings you to Lady Blessington's Bath, a picturesque stretch of the river that's perfect for picnicking.

FREE South Tipperary County Museum MUSEUM
(www.southtippcoco.ie; Mick Delahunty Sq; ⏲10am-5pm Tue-Sat) Informative displays on the history of County Tipperary from Neolithic times to the present are covered at this well-put-together museum, which also hosts changing exhibitions.

Near the museum, look for the life-size **Frank Patterson Statue**, which portrays the son of Clonmel and Ireland's 'Golden Tenor' in full-throated glory. If only it had sound. Among his long list of accomplishments was performing 'Danny Boy' in the Coen Brothers 1990 film *Miller's Crossing*.

FREE Main Guard HISTORIC BUILDING
(☎052-612 7484; www.heritageireland.ie; Sarsfield St; ⏲9.30am-6pm Easter-Sep, hrs can vary) At the junction of Mitchell and Sarsfield Sts is the beautifully restored Main Guard, a Butler courthouse dating from 1675 and based on a design by Christopher Wren. The columned porticos are once again open (after renovations) and exhibits include the ubiquitous model of Clonmel as a walled 17th-century town.

County Courthouse HISTORIC BUILDING
(Nelson St) Sou7th of Parnell St you'll spot the refurbished County Courthouse, designed by Richard Morrison in 1802. It was here that the Young Irelanders of 1848, including Thomas Francis Meagher, were tried and sentenced to transportation to Australia.

Franciscan Friary HISTORIC BUILDING
(Mitchell St) West along Mitchell St (past the town hall with its statue commemorating the 1798 Rising) and south down Abbey St is the Franciscan friary. Inside, near the door, is a 1533 Butler tomb depicting a knight and his lady. There's some fine modern stained glass, especially in St Anthony's Chapel to the north.

Sleeping & Eating

Several B&Bs cluster on Marlfield Rd, due west of the centre.

Hotel Minella HOTEL €€€
(☎052-612 2388; www.hotelminella.ie; Coleville Rd; d €120-180, ste €250-300; P@) Refined yet unpretentious, this family-run luxury hotel sits amid extensive grounds on the south bank of the River Suir, 2km east of the centre. The 90 rooms are divided between an 1863 mansion and a new wing. The latter has almost every kind of convenience, including two suites with their own hot outdoor tubs on private terraces overlooking the river.

Befani's RESTAURANT, B&B €€
(☎052-617 7893; www.befani.com; 6 Sarsfield St; s/d €40/70, mains €15-28.50; ⏲restaurant breakfast, lunch & dinner; @) Between the Main Guard and the Suir, Befani's brings the Mediterranean to Clonmel. Throughout the day there's a tapas menu – be sure to try the Tunisian crab parcels. Its guestrooms aren't huge, but they're attractively fitted out in the sunny colours of the Med.

Catalpa ITALIAN €€
(☎052-612 6821; 5 Sarsfield St; mains €16-26; ⏲lunch Wed-Fri, dinner Tue-Sun) Accomplished Italian cooking at what many locals consider to be Clonmel's best restaurant ranges from classic antipasti platters and pizzas to mains like veal escalopes with Parma ham and mozzarella in sage and marsala sauce.

Niamh's CAFE, DELI €
(1 Mitchell St; mains €10-11.50; ⏲breakfast & lunch Mon-Sat) This smart deli and cafe has a wide range of appealing lunch options (gourmet burgers, pan-fried pork and lasagnes, plus creative sandwiches). Eat in the cafe or take your order away and head to the banks of the Suir.

Drinking & Entertainment

Sean Tierney PUB
(13 O'Connell St) Wander the warren of rooms and floors of this narrow old pub until you find a spot that's just right. The ground-level bar is always alive with craic.

Phil Carroll PUB
(Parnell St) Near Nelson St, this diminutive place is Clonmel's most atmospheric old boozer.

South Tipperary Arts Centre ARTS CENTRE
(☎052-612 7877; www.southtipparts.com; Nelson St) Has an excellent program of art exhibitions, plays and music.

Information

AIB Bank (O'Connell St) Has an ATM and bureau de change.

Circles Internet (www.circles.ie; 16 Market St; per hr €5.70; ⏰11am-11pm)

Post office (Emmet St)

Tourist office (☎052-612 2960; St Mary's Church, Mary St; ⏰9.30am-1pm & 2-4.30pm Mon-Fri) Set in the church grounds.

Getting There & Away

Bus

Bus Éireann (www.buseireann.ie) has buses to Cahir (€4.86, 30 minutes, eight daily), Cork (€15.75, two hours, three daily), Kilkenny (€8.10, one hour, 12 daily), Waterford (€6.30, one hour, eight daily) and a number of other places. Buses stop at the train station.

Train

The **train station** (☎052-612 1982) is on Prior Park Rd past the Oakville Shopping Centre. From Monday to Saturday, the Limerick Junction –Waterford train stops three times daily in each direction.

Around Clonmel

Directly south of Clonmel, over the border in County Waterford, are the Comeragh Mountains. There's a scenic route south to Ballymacarbry and the Nire Valley. For more details, see p197.

Fethard

POP 1400

Fethard (Fiodh Ard) is a quiet, quaint little village that doesn't have any tourism ambitions, despite the impressive medieval ruins scattered about its compact, linear centre. Located 14km north of Clonmel on the River Clashawley, it has a good slice of its old walls still intact. Driving north on the R689 you cross a small ridge and see Fethard in the emerald valley below, looking much as it would have to travellers centuries ago. Its wide main street testifies to its historic role as an important market town.

Sights

Holy Trinity Church CHURCH
(Main St) Fethard's Holy Trinity Church and churchyard lie within a captivating time warp. The church is right off Main St and is reached through a cast-iron gateway. Get the keys from the XL Stop & Shop (aka Whyte's) on Main St, 50m west of the gate.

The main part of the building dates from the 13th century, but its ancient walls have been blighted with mortar for weatherproofing. The handsome west tower was added later and has had its sturdy stonework uncovered. It looks more like a fortified tower house and has savage-looking finials on its corner turrets. The interior of the church has an aisled nave and a chancel of typical medieval style, but is sparsely furnished. A ruined chapel and sacristy adjoin the south end of the church. It's the context of the entire churchyard that's the real winner. Old gravestones descend in ranks to a refurbished stretch of medieval wall complete with a guard tower and a parapet, from where you can look down on the gentle River Clashawley between its horse-trod banks.

Close to the church in Main St is the 17th-century **town hall**, with coats of arms mounted on the facade.

Other Medieval Sights HISTORIC SITES
Fethard's main concentration of medieval remains (some of which have been incorporated into later buildings) are just south of the church at the end of Watergate St. Beside Castle Inn are the ruins of several fortified 17th-century **tower houses**. Just under the archway to the river bank and Watergate Bridge is a fine **sheila-na-gig** (a sexually explicit medieval depiction of a woman) embedded in the wall to your left. You can stroll along the river bank, provided the resident geese are feeling friendly. From here, the backs of the Abbey St houses, although much added to and knocked about in places, once again display the pleasing irregularities of typical medieval building style.

East along Abbey St is the 14th-century **Augustinian friary**, now a Catholic church, with medieval stained glass and another in-your-face **sheila-na-gig** in its east wall.

Eating & Drinking

TOP CHOICE **McCarthy's** PUB €€
(http://mccarthyshotel.net; Main St; mains €13-22; ⏰breakfast Mon-Sat, lunch daily, dinner Wed-Sun) A classic that deserves national acclaim and

WALK: EAST MUNSTER WAY

This 70km walk travels through forest and open moorland, along small country roads and a river towpath. It's clearly laid out with black markers bearing yellow arrows and could be managed in three days, starting at Carrick-on-Suir (p343) in County Tipperary and finishing at Clogheen.

The first day takes you to Clonmel following the old towpath on the Suir for significant portions of the route. At Kilsheelan Bridge, you leave the river to Harney's Crossroads, then wander through Gurteen Wood and the Comeraghs to Sir Thomas Bridge where you rejoin the river.

On the second day the way first leads south into the hills and then descends to Newcastle and the river once more. The third day sees a lot of very atmospheric walking along the quiet River Tar to Clogheen.

Ordnance Survey Discovery series maps 74 and 75 cover the route; information is available at www.southeastireland.com.

preservation, McCarthy's proclaims itself as pub, restaurant and undertaker – and not necessarily in that order. This timeless joint has closely spaced wooden booths and tables amid a thicket of treasures dating back to 1840, and the locals are only too happy to chat. And yes, it is an efficient set-up for wakes.

Getting There & Away

There's no public transport to Fethard but it makes a pleasant cycle from Cashel (p335), 15km to the west.

Carrick-on-Suir

POP 5700

The unassuming market town of Carrick-on-Suir (Carraig na Siúire), 20km east of Clonmel, boasted twice its present population during the late-medieval period, when it was a centre of the brewing and wool industries.

Carrick-on-Suir was once the property of the Butlers, the Earls of Ormond, who built **Ormond Castle** (www.heritageireland.ie; Castle St; admission free; 10am-6pm Easter-Sep), also spelt Ormonde Castle, on the banks of the river in the 14th century. Anne Boleyn, the second of Henry VIII's wives, may have been born here, though other castles also claim this worthy distinction, possibly hoping to boost their own sales of knick-knacks cele brating the beheaded. The Elizabethan mansion next to the castle was built by the 10th Earl of Ormond, Black Tom Butler, in long-term anticipation of a visit by his cousin, Queen Elizabeth I, who rather thoughtlessly never turned up. Some rooms in this Dúchas-owned edifice have fine 16th-century stuccowork, especially the Long Gallery with its depictions of Elizabeth and the Butler coat of arms.

From Carrick-on-Suir, the East Munster Way (p343) winds west to Clonmel before heading south into Waterford.

Dominating the centre of town, the **Carraig Hotel** (051-641 455; www.carraighotel.com; Main St; s/d €60/79;) is one of those classic Irish hotels of an indefinable age that has spread over a few buildings and sprawls from room to room. Its public areas are done up in timeless wood; the 24 rooms are surprisingly modern. Steaks are a speciality at its **restaurant** (mains €15.50-26, bar food €7.50-15; breakfast & lunch daily, dinner Thu-Sun).

Farmers Market (10am-2pm Fri) Carrick-on-Suir's farmers market is held next to the **tourist office** (051-640 200; www.carrickonsuir.ie; 10am-5pm Mon-Fri May-Sep, to 4pm Tue-Fri Oct-Apr), reached by a narrow laneway off Main St.

Bus Éireann (051-879 000; www.buseireann.ie) has numerous services including to Cahir and Clonmel (€6.30, 25 minutes) up to nine times daily. Buses stop at Greenside, the park beside the N24 road.

The **train station** is north of Greenside, off Cregg Rd. From Monday to Saturday, the Limerick Junction–Waterford train stops three times daily in each direction.

Roscrea

POP 5600

Roscrea owes its beginnings to a 5th-century monk, St Cronan, who set up a way station for the travelling poor. Most of the historical structures are on or near the main street, Castle St.

Roscrea Castle, a 13th-century stone edifice right in the town centre, was started in 1213 and is remarkably intact. There are two fortified stone towers, surrounded by walls. Look closely and you can see where the original drawbridge was installed. Inside the courtyard stands **Damer House**, the Queen Anne-style residence of the Damer family. Built in the early 18th century, it no doubt had few problems with burglars owing to its location.

Inside you'll find the **Roscrea Heritage Centre** (www.heritageireland.ie; Castle St; adult/concession €4/2; ⏲10am-6pm Easter-Sep), which contains some interesting exhibits, including one on the medieval monasteries of the midlands and another on early 20th-century farming life. There's a peaceful walled garden by the house.

Up to 12 **Bus Éireann** buses stop at Roscrea between Dublin (€9.90, 2½ hours) and Limerick (€6.75, 1½ hours). Three buses daily serve Cashel (€10.26, 1¼ hours).

Nenagh & Around

The pretty town of Nenagh was a garrison town in the 19th century and before that, the site of a dominant castle. You can see evidence of both just north of the centre on O'Rahilly St; look for the tall steeple of St Mary's of the Rosary church. **Nenagh Castle** looks like the prototype for the rook in chess and is surrounded by cawing crows. The tower dates from the 13th century and has impossibly thick walls.

Nearby, the civic centre is an imposing complex of dark-stone buildings from the 19th century, including an old **gaol**. Next door stands the 1840 **Round House**, a pretty stone building that holds the **Nenagh Heritage Centre** (☎067-31610; www.nenagh.ie; Kickham St; ⏲9am-5pm Mon-Sat, noon-5pm Sun), where you can get tourist info.

It's worth planning your visit around lunchtime to catch Nenagh's excellent delis and cafes.

Country Choice (☎067-32596; 25 Kenyon St; dishes €4.50-11; ⏲Mon-Sat) is a place of pilgrimage for lovers of really great Irish artisan foods. Inside the lavender-painted shop, sample the beautiful lunch menu in the cafe or just have a coffee, and be sure to browse the extensive deli area with homemade preserves, farmhouse cheeses and myriad other treats.

Cinnamon Alley Cafe (Hanly's Pl; mains €11; ⏲breakfast & lunch Tue-Sat) is a stylish little spot hidden down a narrow lane.

McQuaids Traditional Music Shop (38 Pearse St) is crammed with trad instruments and music.

Nenagh is the gateway to the eastern shore of **Lough Derg**, a popular boating and fishing area. There are plenty of visiting boats in summer and you can swim, fish or rent a sailing boat. Enquire at **Shannon Sailing** (☎067-24499; www.shannonsailing.com).

An interesting, scenic lakeside drive from Nenagh is the 24km R494 that winds around to Killaloe and Ballina (p357).

Frequent **Bus Éireann** services include Limerick city (€6.75, 40 minutes).

County Clare

POPULATION 117,000 / AREA 3147 SQ KM

Includes »

Best Places to Eat

- » Crotty's (p361)
- » Naughton's Bar (p363)
- » Morrissey's (p365)
- » Vaughan's Anchor Inn (p368)

Best Places to Stay

- » Rowan Tree Hostel (p347)
- » Cullinan's Guesthouse (p372)
- » Sheedy's Country House Hotel & Restaurant (p375)
- » Gregan's Castle Hotel (p380)

Why Go?

Clare combines the stunning natural beauty of its long and meandering coastline with unique windswept landscapes and dollops of Irish culture.

Rugged nature and the timeless ocean meet on the county's coast. The Atlantic relentlessly pounds year-round, eroding the rocks into fantastic landscapes, and forming sheer cliffs like those at the iconic Cliffs of Moher and strange little islands like those near Loop Head. There are even stretches of beach where surfers flock to the (chilly) waves. The Burren, an ancient region of tortured stone and alien vistas, stretches down to the coast and right out to the Aran Islands.

But if the land is hard, Clare's soul is not: traditional Irish culture and music flourish. And it's not just a show for tourists, either. In little villages like Miltown Malbay, Ennistymon, Doolin and Kilfenora you'll find pubs with year-round sessions of trad music.

When to Go

County Clare's pubs hum to the beats of trad sessions year-round, so even in winter you'll find the craic (good times) – often warmed in the countryside by a turf fire. And while the unsettled seas of winter have a drama that will fill your days with moody idylls, the county literally shines during the more temperate months when long walks along the spectacular soaring cliffs of the coast and the desolate rocks of the Burren don't require full foul weather gear.

County Clare Highlights

1. Swoon to the music in the traditional pubs of **Miltown Malbay** (p365)
2. Lose yourself on the vast sweep of powdery sandy beach at **White Strand** (p365)
3. Delight in the amazing drives, walks and improbable offshore rocky outcrops of **Loop Head** (p363)
4. Find lost dolmens and abandoned abbeys among the rocky expanse of the Burren at **Carron** (p378)
5. Become part of the scene in the artful, tuneful town of **Ennistymon** (p367)
6. Go pub-hopping in musical **Ennis** (p347), where you can find nightly trad sessions on street after street
7. Catch a late-afternoon boat from **Doolin** (p371) to see the soaring **Cliffs of Moher** (p368) in all their radiant glory

ENNIS & AROUND

Ennis

POP 19,000

Ennis (Inis) is the busy commercial centre of Clare. It lies on the banks of the smallish River Fergus, which runs east, then south into the Shannon Estuary.

It's the place to stay if you want a bit of urban flair; from Ennis, you can reach any part of Clare in under two hours. Short on sights, the town's strengths are its food, lodging and traditional entertainment. The town centre, with its narrow, pedestrian-friendly streets, is good for shopping.

History

The town's medieval origins are indicated by its irregular, narrow streets. Its most important historical site is Ennis Friary, founded in the 13th century by the O'Briens, kings of Thomond, who also built a castle here in the 13th century. Much of the wooden town was destroyed by fire in 1249 and again in 1306, when it was razed by one of the O'Briens.

Sights

TOP CHOICE Ennis Friary CHURCH

(Abbey St; adult/child €2/1; 9.30am-6.30pm May-Sep) Just north of the Square is Ennis Friary. It was founded by Donnchadh Cairbreach O'Brien, king of Thomond, sometime between 1240 and 1249 and is a mix of structures dating between the 14th and 19th centuries. A new roof finally replaced one destroyed a mere 200 years ago. Although it pales against the ruins found elsewhere in Clare, it does have a graceful five-section window dating from the late 13th century, and a McMahon tomb (1460) with alabaster panels depicting scenes from the Passion.

TOP CHOICE Clare Museum MUSEUM

(Arthur's Row; admission free; 9.30am-1pm & 2-5.30pm Tue-Sat) Sharing the same building as the tourist office is this diverting little museum. The 'Riches of Clare' exhibition tells the story of Clare from 8000 years ago to the present day using original artefacts grouped into four themes: earth, power, faith and water. It also recounts the development of the submarine by Clare-born JP Holland, who's good for at least two of the themes.

Monuments & Sculptures MONUMENTS

The town centre, the **Square**, features a **Daniel O'Connell monument**. His election to the British parliament by a huge majority in 1828 forced Britain to lift its bar on Catholic MPs and led to the Act of Catholic Emancipation a year later. The 'Great Liberator' stands on an extremely high column, so far above the rest of us you would hardly know he was there.

Eamon de Valera was the parliamentary representative for Clare from 1917 to 1959; a **bronze statue** of him stands near Ennis courthouse.

Numerous **modern sculptures** can be found scattered around the town centre. Works include the *Weathered Woman* on Old Barrack St, which is both interesting and provides a handy place to sit. Get the *Ennis Sculpture Trail* map from the tourist office.

Tours

Ennis Walking Tours WALKING TOUR

(087 648 3714; www.enniswalkingtours.com; tour €8; 11am Wed & Sun May-Oct) The best way to explore Ennis is on foot and the best way to appreciate it is with an expert. This company offers excellent walks that leave from in front of the tourist office.

Festivals & Events

Fleadh Nua TRADITIONAL FESTIVAL

(www.fleadhnua.com) A lively traditional music festival held in late May, with singing, dancing and workshops.

Ennis Trad Festival MUSIC FESTIVAL

(www.ennistradfestival.com) Traditional music is performed in venues across town for one week in November.

Sleeping

Ennis has a great variety of places to stay. There are modest B&Bs on most of the main roads into town, some an easy walk to the centre. Many people drive here straight from Shannon Airport, which is less than 30 minutes to the south.

TOP CHOICE Rowan Tree Hostel HOSTEL €

(065-686 8687; www.rowantreehostel.ie; Harmony Row; dm/s/d from €16/35/55; @) This new hostel is beautifully housed in an 18th-century gentleman's club right on the swift-flowing River Fergus. Some of the bright and airy rooms have fab balconies overlooking

Ennis

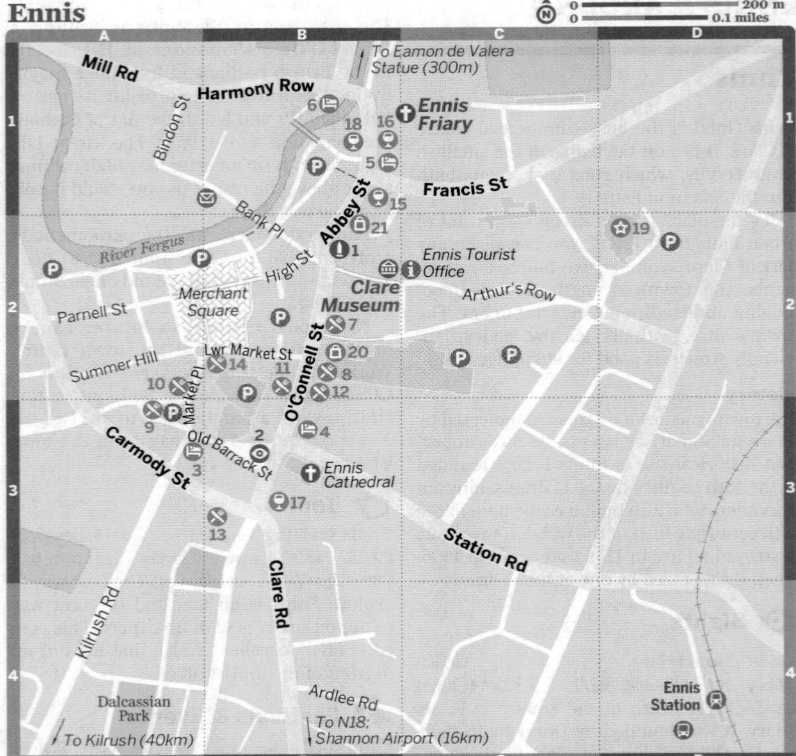

the water. The 150 beds are spread over rooms for one to 14, some with private bathroom. Common areas are superb and there is a lauded cafe/bar.

TOP CHOICE Old Ground Hotel HOTEL €€
(☎065-682 8127; www.flynnhotels.com; O'Connell St; s/d from €90/140; P@) The lobby at this local institution is always a scene: old friends sprawl on the sofas, deals are cut at the tables and ladies from the neighbouring church's altar society exchange gossip over tea. Parts of this rambling landmark date back to the 1800s. The 83 rooms vary greatly in size and decor – don't hesitate to inspect a few. On balmy days, retire to tables on the lawn.

Newpark House INN €€
(☎065-682 1233; www.newparkhouse.com; s/d from €60/100; Apr-Oct; P@) A vine-covered country house dating from 1650, Newpark is 2km north of Ennis. The six rooms have a mix of furnishings old and new; garden views are a fine thing first thing in the morning. To get here, go along Tulla Rd to Scarriff road (R352) and turn right at the Roselevan Arms.

Banner Lodge INN €€
(☎065-682 4224; www.bannerlodge.com; Market St; s/d from €45/80;) You can't really get more central than this, and at great value. Some of the eight rooms are pretty tight, but given the location it is a fair trade-off. The decor in the 2nd-storey inn is dominated by the bold blue carpet and a scattering of antiques. Service is minimal.

Queens Hotel HOTEL €€
(☎065-682 8963; www.irishcourthotels.com; Abbey St; s/d from €50/65; P@) This corner hotel is perfect for those seeking an anonymous stay right in the centre. The 48 modern rooms are standard-hotel in design, with

Ennis

Top Sights
- Clare Museum B2
- Ennis Friary C1

Sights
- 1 Daniel O'Connell Monument B2
- 2 Weathered Woman Statue B3

Sleeping
- 3 Banner Lodge A3
- 4 Old Ground Hotel B3
- 5 Queens Hotel B1
- 6 Rowan Tree Hostel B1

Eating
- 7 Brogan's B2
- 8 Dunnes Stores B2
- 9 Ennis Farmers Market A3
- 10 Food Heaven A2
- Poet's Corner Bar .... (see 4)
- 11 Puccino's B2
- Rowan Tree Cafe/Bar .... (see 6)
- 12 Town Hall Cafe B2
- 13 Tulsi B3
- 14 Zest B2

Drinking
- Brogan's .... (see 7)
- 15 Cíaran's Bar B1
- 16 Cruise's Pub B1
- 17 John O'Dea B3
- Poet's Corner Bar .... (see 4)
- 18 Yolo B1

Entertainment
- 19 Glór D2

Shopping
- 20 Custy's Music Shop B2
- 21 Ennis Bookshop B2

a timeless red and beige motif. Beware of club noise on weekend nights.

Aín Karem HOTEL €€
(☎065-682 0024; ainkaremennis@eircom.net; 7 Tulla Rd; s/d from €45/70; P) Northeast of the centre, this modern two-storey house is pleasantly furnished and rooms are standard size. The neighbourhood has several other B&Bs; it's a 10-minute walk to the centre.

Sycamore House B&B €€
(☎065-682 1343; smsfitz@gofree.indigo.ie; Tulla Rd; s/d from €45/70; P) Right across from Aín Karem, there are four modest rooms in this B&B in a modern, unassuming, typical one-storey Irish house. It's clean and friendly – what more do you want?

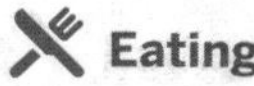

Eating

Ennis has a good mix of restaurants, cafes and bars that serve food. Foodies throng the **Ennis farmers market** (Upper Market St car park; ⌚8am-2pm Fri), which lures some of Clare's best producers.

TOP CHOICE Zest BAKERY, CAFE €
(Market Pl; meals €5-10; ⌚8am-6pm Mon-Sat) A much-welcomed addition to Ennis' fresh food scene, Zest combines a deli, bakery, shop and cafe. Excellent prepared foods from the region are offered along with salads, soups and much more. It's ideal for a coffee or lunch.

Rowan Tree Cafe/Bar MEDITERRANEAN €€
(Harmony Row; mains €7-20; ⌚food 11am-9pm, bar open to late) On the ground floor of Ennis' new hostel, there's nothing low-rent about the excellent Med-accented fare served here. The gorgeous main dining room has a wondrous old wooden floor from the 18th cen tury while tables outside have river views. The foods are locally and organically sourced.

Town Hall Cafe IRISH €€€
(☎065-682 8127; O'Connell St; lunch €6-14, dinner €20-35; ⌚10am-5pm & 6-9.30pm) Adjacent to, and affiliated with, the Old Ground Hotel, this excellent bistro is in the stylishly resurrected old town hall. High ceilings allow large artwork, while the spare settings don't compete with the food on the ever-changing modern Irish menu. Look for local ingredients, especially seafood, taking front and centre stage.

Food Heaven CAFE €
(21 Market St; meals €7-10; ⌚8.30am-6.30pm Mon-Sat) One of several fine choices in the Market St area, this small cafe/deli lives up to its ethereal name with creative and fresh fare. Sandwiches come on renowned brown bread, while soups and salads change daily. Hot specials are just that. Be ready to queue at lunch.

Brogan's PUB €€
(24 O'Connell St; meals €8-20; ⌚10am-10pm) The peas at this popular old pub are always well cooked, and the supply of spuds never-ending. Standards like roasts get top billing along with steaks and an imposing

beer-battered cod. The seafood chowder is loaded with smoked fish.

Poet's Corner Bar IRISH €€
(Old Ground Hotel, O'Connell St; meals €6-14; ⌚12.30-9pm) This famous old bar has a deserved reputation for its traditional dishes, especially the oh-so-fresh fish and chips. Excellent service.

Tulsi INDIAN €€
(Carmody St; meals €10-20; ⌚5-11pm Mon-Sat, 1-4pm Sun) Indian cuisine is excellent at this most accommodating of restaurants. The staff are gracious, constantly serving the large dining room with a mannered feel. Classics such as tandoori chicken are two cuts above the norm.

Puccino's CAFE €
(41 O'Connell St; snacks €2-6; ⌚8am-6pm Mon-Sat) This tiny nook on the main drag has a full coffee bar and blends up fresh fruit smoothies and juices that may help digest that lump of black pudding from breakfast.

Dunnes Stores SUPERMARKET €
(Ennis Town Centre Mall; ⌚7am-8pm) Enormous store that has everything from prepared foods to groceries.

Drinking & Entertainment

As the capital of a renowned music county, Ennis bursts with pubs featuring trad music. In fact, this is the best reason to stay here. Where's best changes often; stroll the streets pub-hopping to find what's on any given night.

Pubs

TOP CHOICE **Cíaran's Bar** PUB
(Francis St) Slip into this small place by day and you can be just another geezer pondering a pint. At night there's usually trad music. Bet you wish you had a copy of the Guinness mural out front!

Brogan's PUB
(24 O'Connell St) On the corner of Cooke's Lane, Brogan's sees a fine bunch of musicians rattling even the stone floors from about 9pm Monday to Thursday, plus even more nights in summer. It's a big pub that rambles from one room to another.

Cruise's Pub PUB
(Abbey St) This friendly bar has a long side courtyard that's perfect for enjoying a fresh-air pint in the shadow of the old friary. There are trad music sessions most nights from 9.30pm.

Poet's Corner Bar PUB
(Old Ground Hotel, O'Connell St) The old hotel pub often has massive trad sessions on Fridays.

John O'Dea PUB
(66 O'Connell St) Unchanged since at least the 1950s, this plain-tile-fronted pub is a hideout for local musicians serious about their trad sessions. Gets some of Clare's best.

Yolo BAR
(Abbey St) Trendy bar/club with a small patio sheltered by shrubs where you can text your crew to come join you. The edgy, moody interior is the place to try some exotic cocktail with an improbable name.

Live Venues

Cois na hAbhna LIVE MUSIC
(☎065-682 0996; www.coisnahabhna.ie; Gort Rd) This pilgrimage point for traditional music and culture is housed in a custom-built pentagonal hall 1.5km north of town along the N18. It has frequent performances and a full range of classes in dance and music. The archive is a resource centre and a library of Irish traditional music, song, dance and folklore relating mainly to County Clare; books and recordings are on sale.

Glór THEATRE
(www.glor.ie; Friar's Walk) Clare's cultural centre is in a striking modern building. Art, traditional music, theatre, dance, photography and film are some of the programs offered.

Shopping

Ennis has the best shopping in the county. On Saturday morning, there is a market at Market Pl. For the best selection of shops, head to O'Connell and Abbey Sts.

Custy's Music Shop MUSIC STORE
(☎065-682 1727; www.custysmusic.com; Cook's Lane, off O'Connell St) A must stop for Irish music, instruments like fiddles, other musical items and general info about the local scene. Has a shop on the web as well.

Ennis Bookshop BOOKSTORE
(13 Abbey St) Excellent independent shop for maps and books of local interest.

Information

Cassidy's Pharmacy (10 O'Connell St; ⏲8am-6pm)

Linkserve (4A Lower Market St; per hr €2; ⏲10.30am-9pm) Head upstairs for surfing and internet calling. Laptop connections.

Post office (Bank Pl) Northwest of the Square.

Tourist office (☎065-682 8366; www.visitennis.ie; Arthur's Row; ⏲9.30am-1pm & 2-5.30pm Tue-Sat, longer hours in summer) Very helpful and efficient. Can book accommodation for a €4 fee; lots of shamrock-embellished gifts.

Getting There & Away

The N18 bypass east of the city lets traffic between Limerick and Galway whiz right past, although trips to the coast still take you through the centre.

Bus

Bus Éireann (☎065-682 4177; www.buseireann.ie) services operate from the bus station beside the train station.

Buses run from Ennis to Cork (€15, three hours, nine daily); Doolin (€12, 1½ hours, two daily) via Corofin, Ennistymon, Lahinch and Liscannor; Galway (€9, 1½ hours, hourly) via Gort; Limerick (€9, 40 minutes, hourly) via Bunratty; and Shannon Airport (€7, 50 minutes, hourly).

To reach Dublin (€19), connect through Limerick.

Train

Irish Rail (www.irishrail.ie) trains from **Ennis station** (☎065-684 0444) serve Limerick (€9, 40 minutes, 10 daily), where you can connect to trains to places further afield like Dublin. The line to Galway (€12, 75 minutes, six daily) is now open and features good Burren scenery.

Getting Around

Most people get their rental cars at Shannon Airport (p353). Parking is fairly good in Ennis. There's a big car park behind the tourist office in Friar's Walk and one alongside the river just off Abbey St.

Burren Taxis (☎065-682 3456) Also, taxi stands are at the train station and the Square.

Tierney's Cycles & Fishing (☎086 803 0369; 17 Abbey St; ⏲9am-6pm Mon-Sat) Has well-maintained mountain bikes costing €20/80 per day/week, including helmet, lock and repair kit. Staff will recommend routes where trucks are less likely to squash you.

Around Ennis

North of Ennis is the early Christian site of Dysert O'Dea; to the southeast are several fine castles. Note that much of the county can be enjoyed as a day trip from Ennis.

Local and express buses cover most areas around Ennis, but their frequency varies; many buses run only May to September (some only July and August) and on certain days. Before making plans confirm times and destinations with Bus Éireann at the Ennis bus station.

DYSERT O'DEA

You can feel the past as you navigate the narrow tracks with grass in the middle to **Dysert O'Dea** (Map p370; ⏲site always open), where St Tola founded a monastery in the 8th century. The church and high cross, the White Cross of St Tola, date from the 12th or 13th century. The cross depicts Daniel in the lion's den on one side and a crucified Christ above a bishop carved in relief on the other. Look for carvings of animal and human heads in a semicircle on the southern doorway of the Romanesque church. There are also the remains of a 12m-high round tower.

In 1318 the O'Briens, who were kings of Thomond, and the Norman de Clares of Bunratty fought a pitched battle nearby, which the O'Briens won, thus postponing the Anglo-Norman conquest of Clare for some two centuries. The 15th-century O'Dea Castle nearby houses the **Clare Archaeology Centre** (www.dysertcastle.com; adult/child €4/2.50; ⏲10am-6pm May-Sep). A 3km history trail around the castle passes some two-dozen ancient monuments – from ring forts and high crosses to a prehistoric cooking site. A further 5km walk along a medieval road takes you to another stone fort.

East of Dysert O'Dea, you can wander along a lovely river in **Dromore Wood** (Map p370; www.heritageireland.ie; Ruan; admission free; ⏲visitor centre 10am-5pm Jun–mid-Sep). This Dúchas nature reserve encompasses some 400 hectares as well as the ruins of the 17th-century O'Brien Castle, two ring forts and the site of Kilakee church.

Getting There & Away

Dysert O'Dea is 1.7km off the Corofin road (R476), 11km north of Ennis. Dromore Wood is 8km east of Dysert, off the N18.

FINDING TRADITIONAL MUSIC IN COUNTY CLARE

From atmospheric small pubs in tiny villages where non-instrument-playing patrons are a minority to rollicking urban boozers in Ennis, Clare is one of Ireland's best counties for traditional music. Eschewing any modern influences from rock or even polkas (as is heard elsewhere), Clare's musicians stick resolutely to the jigs and reels of old, often with little vocal accompaniment.

Although you can find pubs with trad sessions at least one night a week in almost every town and village, the following are our picks for where to start.

» **Doolin** A much-hyped collection of pubs with nightly trad music sessions. However, tourist crowds can erase any sense of intimacy or even enjoyment.

» **Ennis** You can bounce from one music-filled pub to another on most nights, especially in the summer. Musicians from around the county come here to show off and there are good venues for serious trad pursuits.

» **Ennistymon** A low-key farming village inland from Doolin with a couple of ancient pubs that attract superb local talent.

» **Kilfenora** Small village with a big musical heritage on show at the great local pub Vaughan's.

» **Miltown Malbay** This tiny village hosts the annual Willie Clancy Irish Music Festival, one of Ireland's best music festivals. The talented locals can be heard performing through the year in several old pubs.

Bus Éireann (☎065-682 4177) generally runs one bus daily from Ennis which stops along the R476.

QUIN

POP 460

Quin (Chuinche), a tiny village 10km southeast of Ennis, was the site of the Great Clare Find of 1854 – the most important discovery of prehistoric gold in Ireland. Greed and need beat out any good deeds, and only a few of the several hundred torcs, gorgets and other pieces, discovered by labourers working on the Limerick-Ennis railway, made it to the National Museum in Dublin; most were sold and melted down.

Sights

Quin Abbey CHURCH

(⏲site always open) The Franciscan friary was founded in 1433 using part of the walls of an older de Clare castle built in 1280. Despite many periods of persecution, Franciscan monks lived here until the 19th century. The splendidly named Fireballs MacNamara, a notorious duellist and member of the region's ruling family, is buried here. An elegant belfry rises above the main body of the abbey, and you can climb the narrow spiral staircase to look down on the fine cloister and surrounding countryside.

Beside the friary is the 13th-century Gothic **Church of St Finghin**. Numerous cafes and pubs line the quiet streets near the ruins.

KNAPPOGUE CASTLE

About 3km southeast of Quin is **Knappogue Castle & Walled Garden** (www.shannonheritage.com; adult/child €6/3.50; ⏲10am-4.30pm May-Aug). It was built in 1467 by the MacNamaras, who held sway over a large part of Clare from the 5th to the mid-15th century and like early fast-food franchisers littered the region with 42 castles. Knappogue's walls are intact, and it has a fine collection of period furniture and fireplaces. The formal gardens have been restored.

When Oliver Cromwell came to Ireland in 1649, he used Knappogue as a base, which is one of the reasons it was spared destruction. The MacNamara family regained the castle after the Restoration in 1660, and since then windows and other features have been added to make it more 'liveable'.

Knappogue also hosts touristy **medieval banquets** (adult/child €45/24; ⏲6.30pm May-Oct).

CRAGGAUNOWEN

For more ancient Irish heritage tarted up for the masses, visit **Craggaunowen** (www.shannonheritage.com; adult/child €9/5.50; ⏲10am-5pm mid-Apr–Aug). Around 6km southeast of Quin, the complex includes recreated ancient farms, dwellings such as a *crannóg* (artificial island) and a 5th-century ring fort, plus real artefacts including a 2000-year-old oak road. Craggaunowen Castle is a small, well-preserved MacNamara fortified house. With lots of animals like snot-nosed boars, this is a good place for kids who like dirty critters.

Nearby Cullaun Lake is a popular boating and picnic spot, and there are forest trails nearby.

EASTERN & SOUTHEASTERN CLARE

Away from the Atlantic coast and the rugged Burren, Clare rolls gently eastward through low-lying green countryside given emphasis by the occasional range of smooth hills. The county's eastern boundary is the River Shannon and the long, noodle-like inland waterway of Lough Derg, which stretches 48km from Portumna in County Galway to just south of Killaloe. Lakeside villages such as Mountshannon seem in a different world from the rugged, evocative west of Clare, but this is an intimate countryside of water, woods and panoramic views. Southeastern Clare, where the Shannon swells into its broad estuary, is a plain landscape dotted with farms and small villages.

This part of Clare, along with portions of County Limerick, is marketed by Shannon Heritage, which has an excellent website – www.shannonheritage.com – for info.

Shannon Airport

Ireland's second-largest airport used to be a vital fuelling stop for piston-engine planes lacking the range to make it between the North American and European mainlands. Today Shannon (Sionainn) is a low-stress gateway to the region. It's an ideal entry point for the western counties.

About 3km from the airport, **Shannon town**, built to serve airport workers, has the feel of one of those old planned Soviet industrial cities – albeit with more reliable hot water. Don't linger.

Sleeping & Eating

There's B&B accommodation 3km from the airport in Shannon town but Ennis, Limerick and much prettier towns can be reached in 30 minutes. The airport terminal has an often-crowded restaurant. Bring food for your trip from the cafes of Ennis.

Park Inn Shannon Airport HOTEL €€
(061-471 122; www.parkinns.com; r from €80; P @) Wake up in one of the 114 generic hotel rooms here and you could be anywhere, which is the idea as the terminal is just across the car park. This is an option if you have an early flight and want to lose the rental car.

Information

Shannon Town Centre, an enclosed shopping mall off the N19, has banks, basic stores and fast food.

The **airport** (www.shannonairport.com;) has many facilities, including a nice, free observation area for those stuck waiting. Almost everything, including ATMs and currency exchange, is on one level.

Aer Rianta (061-712 000) Provides airport and flight information.

Tourist office (www.shannonregiontourism.ie; 7am-4pm) Near the arrivals area, has regional info, plus guidebooks, maps and oodles of souvenirs for sale.

Getting There & Around

Air

There are nonstop services across the Atlantic to the US; travellers can enjoy the great convenience of pre-clearance for US customs and immigration before they leave Ireland, so there's no waiting in queues once you arrive on the other side of the pond.

Airlines with direct flights to/from Shannon:

Aer Lingus (www.aerlingus.ie) Dublin, Boston, New York JFK, Paris and London Heathrow.

Delta (www.delta.com) New York JFK.

Ryanair (www.ryanair.com) London Stansted and Gatwick, Glasgow and numerous secondary and obscure European airports.

United (www.continental.com) Newark.

Bus

Bus Éireann (www.buseireann.ie) Buy tickets from a machine or the driver. Destinations served by direct buses include Cork (€16, 2½ hours, hourly), Ennis (€7, 50 minutes, hourly), Galway (€15, 1¾ hours, hourly) and Limerick (€7, 30 to 55 minutes, two per hour). Some frequencies are reduced on Sundays.

Car

Virtually every major car rental firm has a desk at the airport.

Taxi

A taxi to the centre of Limerick or Ennis costs about €35 if booked at the taxi desk near arrivals. You may pay more at the outside rank. The taxi desk opens with first flights.

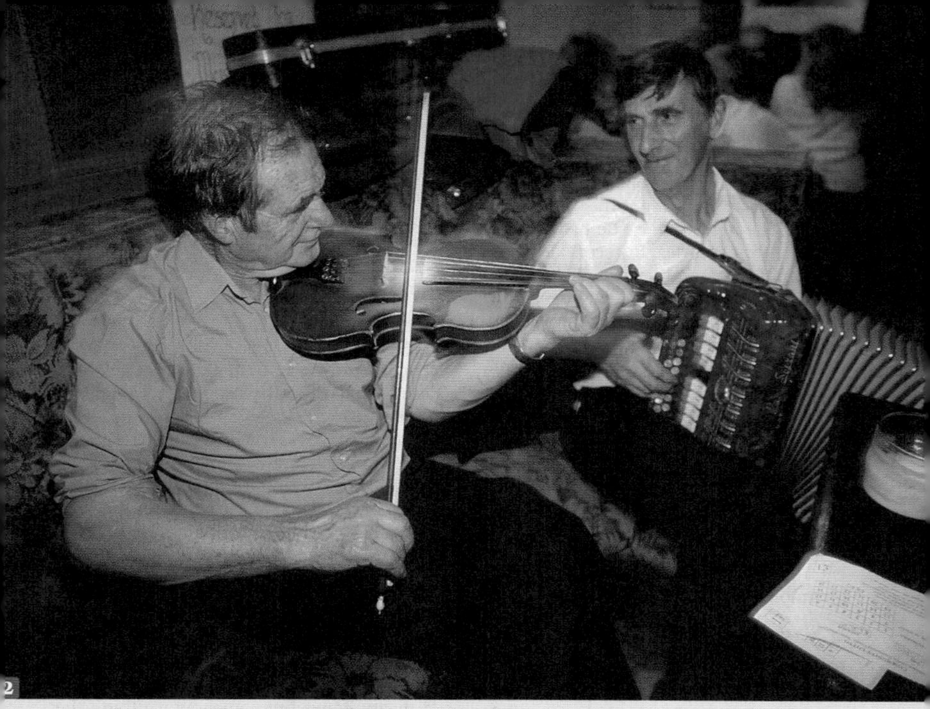

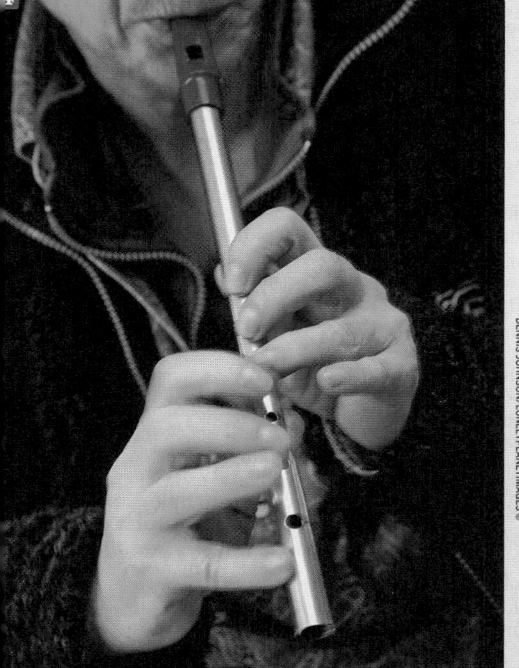

1. Cliffs of Moher, the Burren (p368)
One of the most popular sights in Ireland, these entirely vertical cliffs rise to a height of 203m.

2. Traditional Music (p352)
Musicians playing in a pub in Doolin. Clare is one of Ireland's best counties for traditional music.

3. Cliffs of Moher, the Burren (p368)
A round tower on a headland at the Cliffs of Moher.

4. Tin Whistle
The tin whistle is one of the main instruments used in Ireland's traditional music.

DENNIS JOHNSON/LONELYPLANETIMAGES ©

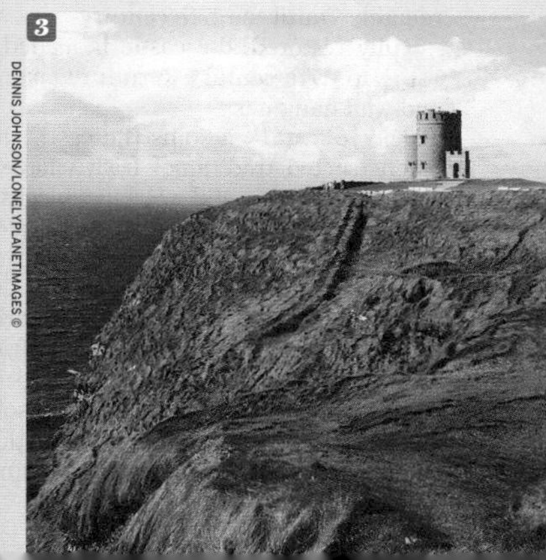

Bunratty

Conveniently located beside the N18 motorway and with plenty of bus-sized parking, Bunratty (Bun Raite) – home to government schemes for hawking tourism hard – draws more tourists than any other place in the region. The namesake castle has stood over the area for centuries. In recent decades it's been spiffed up and surrounded by attractions. A theme park recreates a clichéd Irish village of old (where's the horseshit, lash and disease we ask?) and each year more and more shops crowd the access roads – many selling authentic Irish goods just out of the container from China. There are some rather pricey dining options.

Groups lay siege to Bunratty from April to October. With all the hoopla, it's easy to overlook the actual village, which is at the back of the theme park. It is a pretty place and has numerous leafy spots to stay and eat. It's good if you want something close to Shannon Airport, only 5km west.

Sights & Activities

Bunratty Castle & Folk Park CASTLE
(www.shannonheritage.com; joint-entry ticket to castle & folk park adult/child €16/9; castle 9am-4pm year-round, folk park 9am-6pm Jun-Aug, 9am-5.30pm Sep-May, last admission 45min before closing) Square and hulking Bunratty Castle is only the latest of several constructions to occupy its location beside the River Ratty. Vikings founded a settlement here in the 10th century, and other occupants included the Norman Thomas de Clare in the 1270s. The present structure was put up in the early 1400s by the energetic MacNamara family, falling shortly thereafter to the O'Briens, kings of Thomond, in whose possession it remained until the 17th century.

Fully restored, the castle is loaded with 14th- to 17th-century furniture, paintings and wall hangings.

The **folk park** adjoins the castle. It is a reconstructed traditional Irish village with cottages, a forge and working blacksmith, weavers, post office, pub and small cafe.

A few of the buildings were brought here from elsewhere, but most are recreations. In peak season, employees in period garb can be found explaining the more family-friendly aspects of the late 19th century (there are no workhouses, trigger-happy English soldiers etc). There's a pervading theme-park artificiality (without the rides); you'll find far more surviving authenticity of rural village Ireland in a place like Ennistymon than you will here.

You can get separate entrance tickets to the park when the castle is closed; all prices are slightly reduced in the low season. A gift shop guarding the entrance has an especially garish selection of green schlock including a 'Top of the Morning' alarm clock. (A sign inside the park reads 'Exit to Car Park through shop'.)

Traditional Irish Night
(061-360 788; adult/child €40/24; 7-9.30pm Apr-Oct) Traditional Irish nights are held in a corn barn in the folk park. Lots of red-haired (real or fake, it's clearly a big help in securing employment) servers dish up trad music, dancing, Irish stew, apple pie and soda bread. There's nontraditional wine as well, which may put you in the mood for the singalong. Book online or by phone.

Medieval Banquet
(061-360 788; adult/child €50/24; 5.30pm & 8.45pm) If you skip the high-jinks in the corn barn, you may opt for a medieval banquet, replete with harp-playing maidens, court jesters and food with a medieval motif (lots of meaty items, but somehow we think the real stuff would empty the place right out). It's all washed down with mead – a kind of honey wine. The banquets are very popular with groups, so it's advisable for independent travellers to book well ahead.

The banquets at Knappogue Castle (p352) and Dunguaire Castle (in Galway; p422) are similar but more sedate.

Sleeping

Bunratty has a few hotels and dozens of B&Bs. A big map by the park entrance shows locations; most are away from the castle, park and shop scrum. All are good choices if you have early flights out of Shannon Airport.

Briar Lodge B&B €€
(061-363 388; www.briarlodge.com; Hill Rd; s/d from €50/75; mid-Mar–mid-Oct; P) On a quiet cul-de-sac 1.6km from the castle, this traditionally styled house makes for a good refuge. All five rooms have little extras like curling irons (for that grand banquet entrance!) and some have huge king-size beds.

Cahergal Farmhouse B&B €€
(061-368 358; www.cahergal.com; Newmarket-on-Fergus; s/d from €60/90; P@) Wake up to

the gentle, distant cluck of a chicken at this luxurious B&B on a working farm midway between Bunratty and the airport. Rooms are posh, with king-size beds and bucolic views. The food is farm-hearty with famous baked treats.

 Eating & Drinking

Most of the food choices are as traditional as the theme park.

Durty Nelly's PUB **€€**
(Bunratty House Mews; pub meals €6-15, restaurant mains from €20) Thronging with tourists all summer long, Nelly's manages to provide some charm amid the hubbub, right across from the castle. Meals are better than you'd expect, although the pub is more enjoyable than the restaurant upstairs. There are trad sessions many nights.

Mac's Bar PUB
(MacNamara's; Bunratty Folk Park) This engaging place is actually part of the folk park village. It has traditional music many evenings from June to September, and at weekends the rest of the year. Ignore it during the day, but after the park closes (you can still get in) it starts to feel real.

 Getting There & Away

Bunratty is on the busy **Bus Éireann** (061-313 333) Limerick–Shannon Airport route. Service to both is at least hourly and trips take less than 30 minutes and cost under €5. There are at least five direct buses daily to Ennis (€7, 30 minutes). Buses stop outside the Fitzpatrick Bunratty Shamrock Hotel near the castle.

Killaloe & Ballina

POP 1700

Facing each other across a narrow channel, Killaloe and Ballina are really one destination, even if they have different personalities (and counties). A fine 1770 13-arch one-lane bridge spans the river, linking the pair. You can walk it in five minutes or drive it in about 20 (a Byzantine system of lights controls traffic).

Killaloe (Cill Da Lúa) is picturesque Clare at its finest. It lies on the western banks of lower Loch Deirgeirt, the southern extension of Lough Derg, where the lough narrows at one of the principal crossings of the River Shannon. The village lies snugly against the Slieve Bernagh Hills that rise abruptly to the west. The Arra Mountains create a fine balance to the east and all of Lough Derg is at hand. The village is also on the 180km East Clare Way.

Not as quaint as Killaloe, Ballina is in County Tipperary and has some of the better pubs and restaurants. It lies at the end of a scenic drive from Nenagh along Lough Derg on the R494.

Sights & Activities

The tiny, charming centre of Killaloe is focused on its tiny, charming (and walkable) waterfront. In Ballina, Main St is the focus; it's up the hill from the water.

Killaloe Cathedral CHURCH
(St Flannan's Cathedral; Limerick Rd) The present church dates from the early 13th century and was built by the O'Brien family on top of a 6th-century church. Inside, ornate carvings decorate the Romanesque southern doorway, next to which is the shaft of a stone cross, known as Thorgrim's Stone. It dates from the early Christian period and is unusual in that it bears both the old Scandinavian runic and Irish Ogham scripts. In the cathedral grounds is St Flannan's Oratory, of 12th-century Romanesque design.

Brian Ború Heritage Centre MUSEUM
(www.shannonheritage.com; Lock House, Killaloe; adult/child €3.35/1.75; 10am-5pm May–mid-Sep) Named for the local boy who made good as the king who, according to the political spinmeisters of his time, both unified Ireland and freed it from the Viking scourge. The centre does much to celebrate the legends and has good displays about the nautical heritage of this patchwork of lakes and rivers.

TJ's Angling Centre FISHING
(061-376 009; Main St, Ballina) You can rent fishing tackle for €15 per day and catch your limit in free advice. It also organises fishing trips, although you can hook trout and pike right here in town.

 Tours

Spirit of Killaloe BOAT TOUR
(086 814 0559; Bridge St, Killaloe; adult/child €10/6; 2.30pm May-Sep) Offers hour-long cruises of the waters.

Sleeping

B&Bs abound in the area, especially on the roads along Lough Derg. Book ahead in summer.

TOP CHOICE **Kincora House** B&B €€
(☎061-376 149; www.kincorahouse.com; Church St, Killaloe; s/d from €45/76; P) Set in a town house that's centuries old, this B&B is right in the heart of Killaloe. Four traditional-style rooms have a simple, older feel and could belong to a favoured aunt.

Lakeside Hotel HOTEL €€
(☎061-376 122; www.lakesidehotel.ie; Ballina; s/d from €80/100; P@🛜🏊) With sweeping views of the bridge and its 13 arches, this gentrified waterfront hotel has several attractive public areas and good grounds for strolling. The 43 rooms vary greatly, and prices work in direct ratio to view. All, however, let you use the way-fun 40m water slide.

Lantern House B&B €€
(☎061-923 034; www.lanternhouse.com; Scarriff Rd, Ogonnelloe; s/d from €50/80) About 10km north of Killaloe, and in a hillside location overlooking a sweep of Lough Derg, this glass-fronted house is beautifully encircled by gardens of heather. Some of the six rooms have killer views of sinuous Lough Derg, others not. At times, you can book evening meals.

Arkansas B&B B&B €€
(☎061-376 485; www.arknsas.net; Main St, Ballina; s/d from €40/65; 🛜) There are four basic rooms at this well-run B&B only 300m from the bridge. And the name? The lovely owner says she once saw a fishing trawler named Arkansas and liked the sound of it.

Eating & Drinking

The twin towns hold their excellent **farmers market** (⏲9am-4pm Sun) on the islet off the bridge on the Killaloe side.

Wooden Spoon CAFE €
(Convent Hill; meals €6-12; ⏲9am-7pm Tue-Sat) In a narrow passage just up from the waterfront, this cafe and bakery offers up Med-flavoured fair so flavourful that on balmy days you might think you're near the Riviera. Local chef-done-good Laura Kilkenny also has trad faves such as fresh soda bread, all made with local ingredients and mostly sourced locally.

River Run IRISH €€
(☎061-376 805; www.riverruncafe.com; Main St, Ballina; mains €10-25; ⏲noon-9pm Tue-Sat, noon-3pm Sun) Small, smart and stylish, this blue-fronted bistro has food as creative as the local art for sale on the walls. The selections are kept minimal, but always include good seafood, meat and veggie options. The more casual lunch menu is served until closing.

Gooser's Bar & Eating House SEAFOOD €€€
(www.goosers.ie; Main St, Ballina; dinner mains €10-28; ⏲meals 12.30-10pm) Only the masses of fun-seekers on busy weekends diminish the Gooser's experience. This is a hugely popular thatched pub, noted for its big selection of fish. Sailors make mirth and plough into the hefty seafood platter in the restaurant or go for pub fare at tables outside.

Molly's Bar & Restaurant IRISH €€
(Ballina; meals €8-24; ⏲food served noon-10pm) Guarding the east flank of the bridge, this riverside pub has an alluring rooftop deck that puts you high above the coagulated traffic as well as waterside picnic tables. It offers Irish standards such as bacon and cabbage, plus pub classics like pizza and burgers. Weekend nights there's a festival of live music and DJs.

Liam O'Riains PUB
(Main St, Ballina) At this grizzled, stone-faced old veteran, you're greeted by a cow-eyed, 12kg pike mounted on a wall near the entrance – he's an ugly mother. Everything else here, however, is lovely. Candles glow softly and windows overlook the river below.

Information

The AIB bank at the bottom of Church St in Killaloe has an ATM. There are toilets on the Killaloe side in the car park.

Tourist office (☎061-376 866; Brian Ború Heritage Centre; ⏲10am-6pm May-Oct) On a tiny island off the bridge on the Killaloe side and shares space with the heritage centre. For local info online, try www.killaloe.ie and www.discoverkillaloe.com.

Getting There & Away

There's parking on both sides of the river and that's just what you'll want to do as soon as you arrive. Pretty as it is, the bridge is really a traffic nightmare, so park and walk.

There are four **Bus Éireann** (☎061-313 333) services a day Monday to Saturday from Limerick to Killaloe (€7, 45 minutes). The bus stop is outside the cathedral.

Killaloe to Mountshannon

The journey north to Mountshannon along **Lough Derg** weaves along placid waters shaped like the long dribble left by an overfilled pint of Guinness carried from bar to table. From Killaloe take the R463 to Tuamgraney, then turn east on the R352. There are good viewpoints of the water and Holy Island plus picnic spots.

About 2km north of Killaloe, **Beal Ború** is an earthen mound or fort said to have been Kincora, the fabled palace of the famous Irish king Brian Ború, who, besides lending his name to bad Irish bars the world over, took on the Vikings at the Battle of Clontarf in 1014. Traces of Bronze Age settlement have been found. With its commanding view over Lough Derg, this was obviously a site of strategic importance (and if you see a big splash out in the lough it could be a cousin of the record 32.6kg pike that was caught here).

About 4.5km north of Killaloe is Cragliath Hill, which has another fort, **Grianan-laghna**, named after Brian Ború's great-grandfather, King Lachtna.

Tuamgraney, at the junction of the road to Mountshannon (R352), has an interesting old church, **St Cronan's**, which has parts dating to the 10th century. Inside, a small museum, the **East Clare Heritage Centre** (www.eastclareheritage.com; adult/child €3/1.50; ⏲10am-3pm Mon-Fri), has a passel of artefacts old and not so old of life in the region. Check out the record salmon caught in 1914. The surrounding moody parish **cemetery** also offers a fascinating look into Irish genealogy.

Barely 2km north of Tuamgraney, **Scarriff** is a no-nonsense farm town with an interesting old central commercial triangle.

Mountshannon & Around

POP 350

More than just a 'Tidy Town' award-winning village, Mountshannon (Baile Uí Bheoláin) is good for an agreeable pause on the southwestern shores of Lough Derg. It was founded in 1742 by an enlightened landlord to house a largely Protestant community of flax workers.

The harbour is host to a fair number of fishing boats, and visiting yachts and cruisers in summer. It is the main centre for trips to Holy Island, one of Clare's finest early Christian settlements.

Activities

There's some great fishing around Mountshannon, mainly for brown trout, pike, perch and bream. Ask at your lodging about boat hire and equipment.

Lakeside Holiday Park BOATING
(www.lakesideireland.com; motor boat per day from €40; ⏲May-Oct) Besides lakeside camping, this private park rents out a range of watercraft including kayaks and rowboats. The placid waters of Lough Derg are ideal for a day exploring the shore.

Sleeping & Eating

Hawthorn Lodge B&B €€
(☎061-927 120; www.mountshannon-clare.com; s/d from €50/70; 📶) Just 1km from the tidy

---

DON'T MISS

HOLY ISLAND

Lying 2km offshore from Mountshannon, **Holy Island** (Inis Cealtra) is the site of a **monastic settlement** thought to have been founded by St Cáimín in the 7th century. On the island you will see a **round tower** that is more than 27m tall. Even with the top floor missing, it remains a landmark seen from two counties. You'll also find four old chapels, a hermit's cell and some early Christian gravestones dating from the 7th to 13th centuries. One of the chapels has an elegant Romanesque arch and, inside, an Old Irish inscription that translates as 'Pray for Tornog, who made this cross'.

The Vikings treated this monastery roughly in the 9th century, but under the crowd-pleasing protection of Brian Ború and others, it flourished. During the 17th century as many as 15,000 people would make Easter pilgrimages here.

At Mountshannon Harbour in summer, you may find boats willing to take you over to the island or at least sail around it. **Gerard Madden** (☎086 874 9710, 061-921 615; gerardmmadden@eircom.net; adult/child €10/5; ⏲Apr-Oct) is a noted local historian who leads two-hour tours of the island.

joy that is Mountshannon, this equally tidy country cottage is a modern and relaxed retreat. Set your electric blanket on high and you may never emerge into the chilly albeit fresh morning air.

Mountshannon Hotel HOTEL €€
(061-927 162; www.mountshannon-hotel.ie; Main St; s/d from €50/90; Mar-Oct) A low-key inn in the equally low-key centre of town. The 14 rooms are timeless in a nebulous place between 1950 and 1980. The pub is perfect for a relaxed pint and fish stories. The food is of the chicken Kiev and lasagne school (mains €10 to €20).

Sunrise B&B B&B €€
(061-927 343; www.sunrisebandb.com; Mountshannon; s/d from €55/80;) The breakfast room at this rural B&B just 300m from the village is worthy of an architecture award. Windows literally wrap around the circular room, and a soaring wood ceiling with skylights brings in cheer even on the dullest of days. The four bedrooms are not as dramatic, but are comfy with their warm comforters.

Lakeside Holiday Park CAMPGROUND €
(061-927 225; www.lakesideireland.com; campsites €18; May-Oct) This spacious park has a fine lakeside location with 35 campsites and a few holiday trailers (from €110 per two nights). It hires out boats and kayaks. From Mountshannon, head north along the Portumna road (R352) for 2km and take the first turn-off on the right.

Bourke's the Galley CAFE €
(Main St, Mountshannon; snacks €2-10; 9am-5pm) The sign at this sparkling cafe across from the church reads: Be warm, be welcome, be at home. Of course, home never had such cupcakes. Attached to a deli, Bourke's offers rich coffees, alluring baked goods and fresh light meals you can enjoy on a small terrace.

An Cupán Caifé MODERN IRISH €€€
(061-927 275; Main St; mains €18-28; 6-9.30pm Wed-Sun, plus Sun 1-3pm) This cottagelike restaurant has a Continental atmosphere and a daily menu of steaks and fish. Presentation is slightly formal and the specials are a draw. A three-course Sunday lunch is €20. The wine list is the best in the area.

Getting There & Away

Your own car or bike (or swimming) are your best ways to reach Mountshannon.

North to Galway

North of Mountshannon, the R352 follows Lough Derg to Portumna in County Galway. It's just one of several not-quite-two-lane country roads that weave through the fertile landscapes under arching trees. Another is the R461 from Scarriff, which heads right to the heart of the Burren.

SOUTHWESTERN & WESTERN CLARE

One look at the map and you can see that Loop Head on Clare's southwestern tip is giving the finger to the Atlantic. OK, it's a stubby finger, but still it's emblematic of the never-ceasing titanic struggle between land and sea along this stretch of Irish coast.

The soaring cliffs south of the beach resort of Kilkee to Loop Head are both striking and underappreciated by many visitors. Most save their energies for the much-visited Cliffs of Moher. Marching in geologic lockstep, the formations are undeniably stunning, although in summer you will be marching in lockstep with hordes of other visitors. Escape the crowds at the equally stunning cliffs near Loop Head.

South of the cliffs to Kilkee are the low-key beach towns of Lahinch, Miltown Malbay and Doonbeg. No part of this coast is remotely tropical, but there's a stark windblown beauty that stretches to the horizon. Many a hapless survivor of the Spanish Armada washed ashore here 400 years ago. Tales of their progeny still spice local gossip.

Your best days here may be spent on the smallest roads you can find. Make your own discoveries, whether it's a stretch of lonely beach or something more settled, like the charming heritage town of Ennistymon.

Getting There & Around

BOAT

Shannon Ferry Limited (065-905 3124; www.shannonferries.com; one way/return bicycle & foot passengers €5/7, motorcycles €9/14, cars €18/28; at least hourly 9am-9pm Jun-Aug, 9am-7pm Sep-May) runs a ferry that takes 20 minutes between Tarbert in County Kerry and Killimer in County Clare. It's a real time-saver over detouring through Limerick, and puts you close to the Dingle Peninsula.

BUS

You can usually count on a **Bus Éireann** (www.buseireann.ie) service or two linking all the main towns in the region each day. From Limerick routes run along the Shannon to Kilrush and Kilkee, as well as up through Corofin, Ennistymon, Lahinch, Liscannor and on to the Cliffs of Moher and Doolin. Buses from Ennis follow the same pattern. On the coast between Lahinch and Kilkee services average twice daily in summer. A few other nondaily routes are geared to schoolkids.

Kilrush

POP 2700

Kilrush (Cill Rois) is a small, atmospheric town that overlooks the Shannon Estuary and the hills of Kerry to the south. It has the western coast's biggest **marina** (www.kilrushcreekmarina.ie) at Kilrush Creek, and offers various opportunities to experience the bottlenose dolphins living in the Shannon.

Sights & Activities

St Senan's Catholic church (Toler St) contains eight detailed examples of stained glass by well-known early 20th-century artist Harry Clarke. The main street, **Frances St**, runs directly to the harbour. It is more than 30m wide, reflecting Kilrush's origins as a port and market town in the 19th century when there was much coming and going between land and sea. Look for the **Maid of Eireann monument** at the top of Frances St, which still shows damage caused by departing English troops in 1921.

Vandeleur Walled Garden GARDEN
(www.vandeleurwalledgarden.ie; adult/child €5/2; ⌚10am-6pm Apr-Oct, to 5pm Nov-Mar) This remarkable 'lost' garden was the private domain of the wealthy Vandeleur family – merchants and landowners who engaged in harsh evictions and forced emigration of local people in the 19th century (a current resident said of the Vandeleur: 'That lot fled at liberation'). The gardens lie within a large walled area just east of the centre and have been redesigned and planted with colourful tropical and rare plants. Woodland trails wind around the area, and there's also a cafe.

Shannon Dolphin & Wildlife Centre NATURE CENTRE
(www.shannondolphins.ie; Merchants Quay; ⌚10am-4pm May-Sep) A research facility monitoring the 100 or so dolphins swimming out in the Shannon. Look for the mural of the dolphin on the front of the building, which houses exhibits on the playful cetaceans.

Kilrush Shannon Dolphin Trail TOURING ROUTE
This 4km route ends 3km south of Kilrush at Aylevarro Point, where signs have dolphin info and where you can often see Flipper's progeny frolicking offshore.

Tours

Dolphin Discovery BOAT TOUR
(☎065-905 1327; www.discoverdolphins.ie; Kilrush Creek Marina; adult/child €22/10; ⌚Apr-Oct) Two-hour boat rides on the Shannon offer plenty of dolphin-spotting. Trips depart depending on weather and demand.

Sleeping & Eating

B&Bs are about as common here as dolphins in the Shannon. The local **farmers market** (⌚9am-2pm Thu) is held on the main square.

TOP CHOICE **Crotty's** HOTEL €€
(☎065-905 2470; www.crottyspubkilrush.com; Market Sq; s/d from €45/70; wifi) Brimming with character, Crotty's has an old-fashioned high bar, intricately tiled floors and a series of snugs decked out with traditional furnishings. You can enjoy music many nights in summer. Food is served daily (meals €6 to €16) and includes high-end versions of pub fare. Upstairs are five small, traditionally decorated rooms.

Katie O'Connor's Holiday Hostel HOSTEL €
(☎065-905 1133; katieoconnors@eircom.net; Frances St; dm/d from €15/40; ⌚mid-Mar–Oct; wifi) This fine old main-street house dates from the 18th century, and was one of the town houses of the Vandeleur family. There are 30 beds in two rooms at this delightfully funky IHH-affiliated hostel.

Quayside Restaurant IRISH €€
(17 Frances St; meals €5-12; ⌚9am-5pm Mon-Fri) Local gossip is dissected each morning amid the smells of fresh coffee and the wondrous baked treats emerging form the oven. Tables overlook the townside bustle or boats moored out back.

Information

Tourist info (☎065-905 1577; Frances St) At Katie O'Connor's Holiday Hostel. It's usually open when the hostel is open.

WORTH A TRIP

SCATTERY ISLAND

This uninhabited, windswept, treeless island, 3km southwest of Kilrush in the estuary, was the site of a Christian settlement founded by St Senan in the 6th century. Its 36m-high **round tower** is one of the tallest and best preserved in Ireland, and the entrance is at ground level instead of the usual position high above the foundation. The remains of five **medieval churches** include a 9th-century cathedral. This is a moody and evocative place to wander about. It's past also includes chapters sheltering remnants of the Spanish Armada and time as an English fort.

An exhibition on the history and wildlife of the Heritage Service–administered island is housed in the **Scattery Island Visitor Centre** (www.heritageireland.ie; admission free; ⏲10am-6pm Jun-Sep).

Scattery Island Ferries (☎065-905 1327; www.discoverdolphins.ie; Kilrush Creek Marina; adult/child €12/7; ⏲Jun-Sep) runs boats from Kilrush to the island. There's no strict timetable as the trips are subject to tidal and weather conditions; visits usually last about one hour. You can buy tickets at the small kiosk at the marina.

Getting There & Around

Bus Éireann has one or two buses daily to Limerick (1¾ hours), Ennis (one hour) and Kilkee (15 minutes). Fares average €7.

Gleeson's Cycles (☎065-905 1127; Henry St; per day/week from €20/80) Hire bikes here.

Kilkee

POP 1300

Kilkee's wide beach has the kind of white, powdery sand that's made the Caribbean, well, the Caribbean. Granted the waters are chilly and the winds often brisk, but in summer the strand is thronged with day-trippers and holidaymakers. The sweeping semicircular bay has high cliffs on the north end and weathered rocks to the south. The waters are very tidal, with wide open sandy expanses replaced by pounding waves in just a few hours.

Kilkee (Cill Chaoi) first became popular in Victorian times when rich Limerick families built seaside retreats here. Today, it is well supplied with guesthouses, amusement arcades and takeaways, although good taste – mostly – prevails.

Sights & Activities

Many visitors come for the fine sheltered **beach** and the **Pollock Holes**, natural swimming pools in the Duggerna Rocks. The area offers myriad excellent walks. **St George's Head**, to the north, has good cliff walks and scenery, while south of the bay, the **Duggerna Rocks** form an unusual natural amphitheatre. Further south is a huge **sea cave**. These sights can be reached by driving to Kilkee's West End area and following the coastal path.

Kilkee is a well-known **diving** centre as the dramatic rocks of the shore cliffs continue right below the waves. Experience and local knowledge or guidance are strongly advised. Right at the tip of the Duggerna Rocks is the small inlet of Myles Creek, out from which lies excellent underwater scenery.

Oceanlife Ireland DIVING
(☎065-905 6707; www.oceanlife.ie; St George's Head, Kilkee) By the harbour. Has tanks and other equipment for hire and runs a range of courses.

West Clare Railway HISTORIC SITE
(☎065-905 1284; www.westclarerailway.ie; adult/child €6/3; ⏲10am-6pm May-Sep) A 2km vestige of this historic line survives near Moyasta on the Kilkee Rd (N67) 6km northwest of Kilrush. Run by volunteers, the beautifully restored steam-powered trains shuttle back and forth over the open land.

Sleeping

Kilkee has plenty of guesthouses and B&Bs, though during the high season rates can soar and you may have a problem finding a vacancy.

TOP CHOICE **Lynch's B&B** B&B €
(☎065-905 6420; www.lynchskilkee.com; O'Connell St; s/d from €35/60; 📶) Everything is shipshape in this perfectly located B&B in the centre. Guest rooms have hardwood floors and bedspreads with designs that will bring a smile to aunties everywhere. It's as quiet as the surf at low tide and the breakfast is vast.

Halpin's Townhouse HOTEL €€
(☎065-905 6032; www.halpinsprivatehotels.com; Erin St; s/d from €100/140; ⏰mid-Mar–mid-Nov; @📶) A smart Georgian town house has morphed into a plush 12-room hotel. Close to the centre, it eschews the salt-stained furnishings of many a beach-town place for a minimalist look. Guests enjoy the basement bar with its good wine list.

Strand Guest House INN €€
(☎065-905 6177; www.thestrandkilkee.com; The Strand; s/d from €55/80; 📶) Right across from the water, this six-room guesthouse has been given a bit of a polish, although everything is still as low-key as the town itself. The rooms are simply decorated. Some have great views, as does the inviting bistro/bar, which has picnic tables outside for a little salt-spray in your stout.

Stella Maris Hotel HOTEL €€
(☎065-905 6455; www.stellamarishotel.com; O'Connell St; s/d from €70/120; @) There are 20 unassuming rooms in the year-round choice for lodging in Kilkee. Some on the top floor have views of the surf, some have high-speed internet and some have king-size beds. The hotel is right in the centre and serves good food.

Green Acres Caravan & Camping Park CAMPGROUND €
(☎065-905 7011; Doonaha, Kilkee; campsites €20-24; ⏰Apr-Sep) Beside the Shannon, 6km south of Kilkee on the R487, this is a small, open and peaceful park with 40 sites. Weekly trailer rentals start at €250.

Eating & Drinking

In summer Kilkee's ranks of eateries swell with several that win plaudits with the summering genteel. The small **farmers market** (⏰10am-2pm Sun) is on the large parking area near the bus stop.

TOP CHOICE **Naughton's Bar** SEAFOOD €€
(46 O'Curry St; meals €10-25; ⏰kitchen 5-9.30pm) The terrace alone is enough to make Naughton's a mandatory stop, but the food is even better. Fresh local produce and seafood combine for some mighty fine pub meals at this very atmospheric family-run pub which dates to the 1870s.

Pantry CAFE €
(O'Curry St; meals €6-12; ⏰8am-6pm Apr-Oct) With a Euro-sleek look, this bakery/deli/cafe is filled with surprises and fresh treasures. The scones are plainly the best in Clare and pretty much everything else you order from the seemingly simple menu will have you saying, 'That's the best…I ever had'.

Stella Maris IRISH €€
(O'Connell St; meals €10-25; ⏰noon-9pm) This popular hotel has a good menu of local seafood and steaks on offer through the day. Enjoy quality ocean salmon and shellfish or one of many specials in the bright and simple dining room or in the usually crowded pub.

Murphy Blacks IRISH €€
(☎065-905 6854; The Square; mains €16-25; ⏰5-9.30pm Wed-Sun Apr-Oct) How do you ensure that you're getting the best fish? Go to a place owned by an ex-fisherman. This deservedly popular dinner spot is booked up solid night after night for its carefully crafted dishes. Tables outside are a summer-night treat.

Greyhound Bar PUB
(Main St) Fishers, divers, musicians and locals looking for fun gather at this old bar which is known by the delightful nickname 'the Skinny Dog'. There's good music many nights.

Information

Tourist office (O'Connell St; ⏰9.30am-5pm Jun-Aug) Near the seafront.

Getting There & Away

Bus Éireann has one to two buses daily to Kilkee from Limerick (€11, two hours) and Ennis (€13, 1¼ hours). Both routes pass through Kilrush.

Kilkee to Loop Head

While others are dodging sweater vendors at the Cliffs of Moher, discriminating travellers are coming here for coastal views that in many ways are more dramatic (see the boxed text, p364).

The land from Kilkee south to Loop Head has subtle undulations that suddenly end in dramatic cliffs falling off into the Atlantic. It's a windswept place with timeless striations of old stone walls. You can see literally for miles and there is a rewarding sense of escape from the mainstream. It's good cycling country and offers coastal walks – which is just as well as there's no public transport.

CARRIGAHOLT

POP 150

On 15 September 1588, seven tattered ships of the Spanish Armada took shelter off Carrigaholt (Carraig an Chabaltaigh), a tiny village inside the mouth of the Shannon Estuary. One, probably the *Anunciada*, was torched and abandoned, sinking somewhere out in the estuary. Today, timeless Carrigaholt has one of the simplest and cutest main streets you'll find. The substantial remains of a 15th-century McMahon castle with a square keep overlook the water.

Activities

Dolphinwatch BOAT TOUR
(☎065-905 8156; www.dolphinwatch.ie; Carrigaholt; adult/child €24/12) To view resident bottle nose dolphins (there are more than 100 in the Shannon Estuary), head for Dolphinwatch, next to the post office. It runs two-hour trips in the estuary from April to October, weather permitting. Ask about Loop Head sunset cruises. For more on these broguish relatives of Flipper, see the dolphin sites in and around Kilrush.

Eating & Drinking

TOP CHOICE **Long Dock** PUB, SEAFOOD €€
(West St; meals €6-24; food served 11am-9pm) An atmospheric pub-restaurant combo. Stone walls and floors and a welcoming fire are only the start. Fresh fish is the thing here; you'll see the purveyors out working in the estuary or even drinking at the bar. Nab a table outdoors on a summer night.

Morrissey's Village Pub PUB
(West St) Like Carrigaholt itself, Morrissey's hasn't changed much in a long time and is all the better for it. Get your feet ready for music and dancing many nights through the year.

KILBAHA

POP 50

The land at this minute waterfront village is as barren as the soul of the 19th-century landlord who burned down the local church so his workers wouldn't waste productive hours praying. Even today the scars are felt. Gazing at the ruins of the landlord's house far up the hillside, a local says: 'Yeah, we got rid of him', as if the events of 150 years ago were yesterday.

You can learn more about this story and other aspects of local life from a unique modern-day **scroll**, an open-air sculpture that relates the area's history.

The **Lighthouse Inn** (☎065-905 8358; www.thelighthouseinn.ie; s/d from €40/70; wifi) is a mirthful place right on the water, with 11 basic rooms. The gregarious pub serves sandwiches and the like through the year and more complex seafood dinners (from €14) in summer. Trad sessions some nights are a bonus.

LOOP HEAD

On a clear day, Loop Head (Ceann Léime), Clare's southernmost point, has magnificent views south to the Dingle Peninsula crowned by Mt Brandon (951m), and north to the Aran Islands and Galway Bay. There are bracing walks in the area and a long hiking trail runs along the cliffs to Kilkee. A working **lighthouse** (complete with Fresnel lens) is the punctuation on the point.

The often deserted wilds of the head are perfect for a little DIY fun. **Loop Head Adventures** (☎065-905 8875; loopheadsports@eircom.net; May-Oct) rents gear and gives advice for cycling (bikes €15 per day), fishing (rods and gear €15 per day) and snorkelling (drysuits and gear €35 per day). It's located a short distance from the lighthouse.

DON'T MISS

CLARE'S OTHER CLIFFS

For the jaw-dropping moment of your trip, check out the drama of the soaring cliffs west of Kilkee. On the R487, the Loop Head Rd, look for signs that read 'Scenic Loop' (an understatement). A narrow track curves along the coast for 10km until it reaches the west side of Kilkee. Along the way you will be struck by one stunning vista of soaring coastal cliffs after another. Some have holes blasted through by the surf, others have been separated from land and now stand out in the ocean as lonely sentinels. One utterly isolated basalt tower even has an old house perched on top – how in the world did that get there and who built it? Plan on puttering along, stopping for walks and pausing for passing cows.

Kilkee to Ennistymon

North of Kilkee, the land flattens, with vistas that sweep across pastures and dunes. The N67 runs inland for some 32km until it reaches Quilty. Take the occasional lane to the west and search out unfrequented places such as **White Strand**, north of Doonbeg. **Ballard Bay** is 8km west of Doonbeg, where an old telegraph tower looks over some fine cliffs. **Donegal Point** has the remains of a promontory fort. There's good fishing all along the coast, and safe beaches at Seafield, Lough Donnell and Quilty. Off the coast of Quilty, look for **Mutton Island**, a barren expanse sporting an ancient tower.

DOONBEG

POP 600

Doonbeg (An Dún Beag) is a tiny seaside village about halfway between Kilkee and Quilty. Another Spanish Armada ship, the *San Esteban,* was wrecked on 20 September 1588 near the mouth of the River Doonbeg. The survivors were later executed at Spanish Point. Note the surviving wee little 16th-century **castle tower** next to the graceful seven-arch stone bridge over the river.

White Strand (Trá Ban) is a quiet beach, 2km long and backed by dunes. It's north of town and hard to miss, as it's now been surrounded by the Doonbeg Golf Club. From the public car park, you follow a break in the dunes to a perfect sweep of sand.

Doonbeg also has some decent **surfing** for those who want to get away from the crowds in Lahinch. For golf, the economic collapse means that the **Doonbeg Golf Club** (www.doonbeglodge.com; greens fees from €140) has lost a load of its previous snoot. The championship course is laid out amid the bare, rolling dunes.

Sleeping & Eating

For campers there are often spots on the side roads around Doonbeg that make a good pitch, with glorious sunsets as a bonus. The town has two popular pubs, one trad, one mod.

TOP CHOICE **Morrissey's** INN €€

(☎065-905 5304; www.morrisseysdoonbeg.com; Main St; s/d €70/100; ⏲Mar-Oct; @) Under its fourth-generation owner, this old pub has been transformed into a stylish coastal haven. The six rooms feature king-size beds, flat-screen TVs and large soaking tubs. The pub's **restaurant** (mains €12 to €22) is renowned for its casual but enticing seafood, from fish and chips to succulent local crab claws. Outside there's a terrace overlooking the river, while inside colours reminiscent of a box of good bonbons mingle with stark white walls.

Lodge at Doonbeg HOTEL €€€

(☎065-905 5600; www.doonbeglodge.com; r from €200; P) Built in the style of a vaguely British manor house of indeterminate vintage, this golf resort is actually quite modern and has a range of luxurious rooms, suites and cottages. It sits in grand isolation amid the links and right behind the dunes backing White Strand, one of Clare's finest beaches. Service is unstuffy and public spaces feel intimate.

MILTOWN MALBAY

POP 1600

Like Kilkee, Miltown Malbay was a resort favoured by well-to-do Victorians, though the town isn't actually on the sea: the beach is 2km south at **Spanish Point**. To the north of the Point, there are beautiful **walks** amid the low cliffs, coves and isolated beaches.

A classically friendly place in the chatty Irish way, Miltown Malbay has a thriving music scene. Every year it hosts the Willie Clancy Irish Music Festival (see the boxed text, p366), one of Ireland's great trad music events.

Sleeping & Eating

An Gleann B&B B&B €€

(☎065-708 4281; www.angleann.net; Ennis Rd; s/d from €35/70; P) Possibly the friendliest welcome in town is at this B&B off the R474 about 1km from the centre. The five rooms are basic and comfy and owner Mary Hughes is a delight. Cyclists are catered for.

Old Bake House SEAFOOD €

(Main St; meals €6-15; ⏲noon-9pm) In a region of great seafood chowder, some of the best is at the Old Bake House which serves Irish classics in humble surrounds.

Baker's Café BAKERY €

(Main St; meals €4; ⏲7am-7pm Mon-Sat) Nearby to the Old Bake House, has excellent baked goods and creates enormous sandwiches – perfect for seaside picnics.

Drinking

O'Friel's Bar (Lynch's; ☎065-708 4275; The Square) is one of a couple of genuine old-style places with occasional trad sessions. The other is the dapper **Hillery's** (Main St).

CLARE'S BEST MUSIC FESTIVAL

Half the population of Miltown Malbay seems to be part of the annual **Willie Clancy Irish Music Festival** (☎065-708 4148; www.oac.ie), a tribute to a native son and one of Ireland's greatest pipers. The eight-day festival usually begins in the first or second week in July, when impromptu sessions occur day and night, the pubs are packed and Guinness is consumed by the barrel. Workshops and classes underpin the event; don't be surprised to attend a recital with 40 noted fiddlers. Asked how such a huge affair has happened for almost four decades, a local who teaches fiddle said: 'No one knows, it just does.'

Information

For local information, drop by the cheery **An Ghiolla Finn Gift Shop** (Main St; ⏲10.30am-6pm Mon-Sat). The website, www.visitmiltownmalbay.ie is also useful.

Getting There & Away

Bus Éireann service is paltry. Expect one or two buses daily north and south along the coast and inland to Ennis.

LAHINCH

POP 650

Surf's up, dude! This scruffy old holiday town is now one of the centres of Ireland's hot surfing scene. Schools and stores dedicated to riding the waves cluster here, like surfers waiting for the perfect set.

Lahinch (Leacht Uí Chonchubhair) has always owed its living to beach-seeking tourists. The town sits on protected Liscannor Bay and has a fine beach. Free-spending mobs descend in summer, many wielding golf clubs for play at the famous, traditional-style **Lahinch Golf Club** (☎065-708 1003; www.lahinchgolf.com; greens fees from €100). It dates from 1892 when it was laid out amid the dunes by Scottish soldiers.

Sleeping & Eating

The tourist office has good links to local B&Bs. Waterfront cafes and pubs let you enjoy the action on the waves.

TOP CHOICE **West Coast Lodge** HOSTEL, INN €

(☎065-708 2000; www.lahinchaccommodation.com; Station Rd; dm from €18, r from €50; P@) Flashpackers will cheer this stylish and downright plush hostel and inn in the heart of Lahinch. Power showers, fine cotton sheets and down duvets are just some of the touches found throughout the seven- to 12-bed dorms and private rooms. Check out the surf from the roof deck; rent a bike to go exploring.

Atlantic Hotel HOTEL €€

(☎065-708 1049; www.atlantichotel.ie; s/d from €40/70; @) There's still a pleasant air of bygone times in the reception rooms and bars at this town-centre classic with 14 well-appointed rooms. The restaurant offers fine seafood choices (mains from €15) and the pub is the perfect spot for nursing a pint.

Barrtra Seafood Restaurant SEAFOOD €€

(☎065-708 1280; www.barrtra.com; Miltown Malbay Rd; mains €16-28; ⏲Apr-Sep) The 'Seafood Symphony' menu item says it all at this rural repose 3.5km south of Lahinch. Enjoy views over pastures to the sea from this lovely country cottage, surrounded by pretty kitchen gardens. The cooking eschews flash and lets the inherent tastiness of the food shine.

Drinking

Kenny's PUB

(Main St) The place to hear music, new and trad, after a day on the waves. On Tuesday nights don't miss the White Horse sessions, which attract local talent of all kinds.

Shopping

Lahinch Bookshop BOOKSTORE

(Main St) The best source for hiking maps outside Ennis.

Information

The *only* reliable ATM in the region is outside the tourist office.

Lahinch Fáilte (☎065-708 2082; www.lahinchfailte.com; The Dell; ⏲9am-8pm Jun-Aug, 10am-5pm Sep-May) Tourist office off the northern end of Main St and part of a gift shop.

Getting There & Away

Bus Éireann runs one or two buses daily through Lahinch on the Doolin–Ennis/Limerick routes and one or two daily south along the coast to Doonbeg in summer.

Ennistymon

POP 900

Ennistymon (Inis Díomáin) is a timeless country village located just 4km inland from Lahinch, but worlds away in terms of atmosphere. People go about their business (which involves a lot of cheerful chatting) barely noticing the characterful buildings lining Main St. And behind this facade there's a surprise: the roaring **Cascades**, the stepped falls of the River Inagh. After heavy rain they surge, beer-brown and foaming, and you risk getting drenched on windy days in the flying drizzle. You'll find them through an arch by Byrne's hotel.

Sights & Activities

Courthouse Studios & Gallery ART GALLERY
(Parliament St; noon-4pm Tue-Sat) Besides excellent pubs and good sleeping options, Ennistymon has a healthy arts scene. These studios are in an impressively renovated 1800 building with ever-changing exhibitions by local and international artists.

Ennistymon Horse Market MARKET
On the first Monday of each month is one of Clare's great spectacles: the horse market literally takes over the town's streets as people from around the region come to buy and sell donkeys, mares, thoroughbreds and even a few plain old nags.

Sleeping & Eating

The local **farmers market** (10am-2pm Sat) spreads its fertile wealth on Market Sq.

Falls Hotel HOTEL €€
(065-707 1004; www.fallshotel.ie; s/d from €80/120; P@) This handsome and sprawling Georgian house, built on the ruins of an O'Brien castle, has 140 modern rooms and a large, enclosed pool. Fittings throughout are heavy and traditional. The view of the Cascades from the entrance steps is breathtaking, and there are walks around the 20 hectares of wooded gardens. Welsh poet Dylan Thomas once lived here and there's a bar named after him.

Byrne's IRISH/SEAFOOD/INN €€
(065-707 1080; www.byrnes-ennistymon.ie; Main St; r €70-120; P) The Cascades are just out back at this historic guesthouse and restaurant. When the air is not heavy with mist, you can enjoy a drink at a back-terrace table. The menu is substantial, with plenty of seafood specials (mains €15 to €25). Six large and comfortable rooms await up the creaky heritage stairs.

Drinking

Eugene's PUB
(Main St) Not to be missed, Eugene's is a classic pub that defines craic. Intimate, cosy and has a trademark collection of visiting cards covering its walls, alongside photographs of

SURF'S UP!

Like swells after a storm, Clare's surfing scene keeps getting bigger. Lahinch is the centre for a roiling surf scene: on weekends the breaks in front of the town fill with hundreds of surfers. Thick wetsuits dry on railings and scores of people watch the action from the town's beach and pubs.

Conditions are excellent for much of the year, with the bay's cliffs funnelling regular and reliable sets. And as the waters fill in Lahinch, the action is moving to other spots along the coast, like Doonbeg and Fanore.

Surf shops are proliferating. You can rent gear and get lessons from about €40 per two-hour session; board and wetsuit rentals are about €15 per day. Outfits in Lahinch include:

Ben's Surf Clinic (086 844 8622; www.benssurfclinic.com) Offers lessons plus rents out boards and wetsuits (essential!).

Lahinch Surf School (087 960 9667; www.lahinchsurfschool.com; Main St) Champion surfer John McCarthy offers lessons and various multi-day packages.

Lahinch Surf Shop (065-708 1108; www.lahinchsurfshop.com; Old Promenade) Sells gear from a dramatic surfside location.

Ocean Scene Surf School (065-708 1108; www.oceanscene.ie; Church St) Gives lessons plus has a good live surf-cam on the website.

THE ATM HUNT

It's easy to get caught out cashless in western Clare. Many of the small towns such as Liscannor, Doolin, Lisdoonvarna and Kilfenora have no ATMs. There's one at the **Supervalu** (Church St) in Ennistymon but it is often out of order. The sole ATM in Lahinch is the most reliable.

famous writers and musicians. The inspiring collection of whiskey (Irish) and whisky (Scottish) will have you smoothly debating their relative merits.

Cooley's House PUB
(☎065-707 1712; Main St) Another great old pub, but with music most nights in summer and on Wednesday (trad night) in winter.

Nagle's PUB
(Church St) A trad pub and an undertakers in one. Just the spot for wakes or your last earthly pint.

Getting There & Away

Bus Éireann runs one or two buses daily through Ennistymon on the Doolin–Ennis/Limerick routes and one or two daily south along the coast via Lahinch to Doonbeg in summer. Buses stop in front of Aherne's on Church St.

Liscannor & Around

POP 350

This small seaside village overlooks Liscannor Bay, where the road (R478) heads north to the Cliffs of Moher and Doolin. Liscannor (Lios Ceannúir) has given its name to a type of local stone – slatelike and with a rippled surface – that is used for floors, walls and even roofs.

Sleeping & Eating

TOP CHOICE **Vaughan's Anchor Inn** B&B, SEAFOOD €€
(☎065-708 1548; www.vaughans.ie; Main St; s/d from €50/70; mains €12-25; ⊙kitchen noon-9.30pm) Noted for its excellent seafood (yes to the scallops and halibut), Vaughan's packs 'em in – and out. When it rains, you can settle in the pub by a peat fire, when it shines (sometimes 15 minutes later) you can take in the air at a picnic table. Newly renovated – and compact – rooms offer sleepy refuge.

Moher Lodge Farmhouse B&B €€
(☎065-708 1269; www.cliffsofmoher-ireland.com; s/d €50/70; ⊙Apr-Oct; P) This big bungalow is in a great position overlooking the owner's open farmlands and the sea. The four rooms are welcoming after a day rambling (there's much to ramble to). It's 3km northwest of Liscannor, 1.6km from the Cliffs of Moher.

Drinking

Joseph McHugh's Bar PUB
(Main St) Next to Vaughan's, lots of courtyard tables and regular trad sessions make this old pub a winner.

Getting There & Away

Bus Éireann runs one to three buses daily through Liscannor on the Doolin–Ennis/Limerick routes.

Hag's Head

Forming the southern end of the Cliffs of Moher, Hag's Head is a dramatic place from which to view the cliffs.

There's a huge sea arch at the tip of Hag's Head and another arch visible to the north. The signal tower on the head was erected in case Napoleon tried to attack on the western coast of Ireland. The tower is built on the site of an ancient promontory fort called Mothair, which has given its name to the famous cliffs to the north. A **walking trail** links the head with the cliffs and Liscannor.

Cliffs of Moher

Star of a million tourist brochures, the Cliffs of Moher (Aillte an Mothair, or Ailltreacha Mothair) are one of the most popular sights in Ireland. But like many an ageing star, you have to look beyond the famous facade to appreciate the inherent attributes behind the postcard image.

The entirely vertical cliffs rise to a height of 203m, their edge falling away abruptly into the constantly churning sea. A series of heads, the dark limestone seems to march in a rigid formation that amazes, no matter how many times you look.

Such appeal comes at a price: mobs. This is check-off tourism big time and busloads come and go constantly in summer. A vast visitor centre handles the hordes. Set back into the side of a hill, it's impressively unimpressive – it blends right in. As part of the development, however, the main walkways and viewing areas along the cliffs have been surrounded by a 1.5m-high wall. It's lovely stone, but it's also way too high and set too far back from the edge. The entire reason for coming here (the view – unless you're a bus-spotter) is obscured.

But, like so many oversubscribed natural wonders, there's relief and joy if you're willing to walk for 10 minutes. Past the end of the 'Moher Wall' south, there's still a **trail** along the cliffs to Hag's Head – few venture this far. There's also a path heading north, but you're discouraged from it, so use your common sense. With binoculars you can spot the more than 30 species of **birds** – including darling little puffins – that make their homes among the fissure-filled cliff faces. On a clear day you'll channel Barbra Streisand as you can see forever; the Aran Islands stand etched on the waters of Galway Bay, and beyond lie the hills of Connemara in western Galway.

The roads leading to the cliffs pass through refreshingly undeveloped lands, the rolling hills giving no hint of the dramatic vistas just over the edge.

For uncommon views of the cliffs and wildlife you might consider a **cruise**. The boat operators in Doolin (p374) offer popular tours of the cliffs.

Information

Visitor centre (Map p370; www.cliffsofmoher.ie; admission to site adult/child €6/free; ⏲9am-9.30pm Jul & Aug, 9am-7pm May, Jun & Sep, 9am-6pm Mar, Apr & Oct, 9.15am-5pm Nov-Feb) Actually, revealingly, it's called the 'Cliffs of Moher Visitor Experience', and has glitzy exhibitions about the cliffs and the environment called the 'Atlantic Edge'. Staff lead tours outside and answer questions.

Vendors of 'authentic' sweaters and other tat have stalls near the large free parking area. The basement cafe seems designed to urge you up to the views at the pricier restaurant.

Getting There & Away

Bus Éireann runs one to three buses daily past the cliffs on the Doolin-Ennis/Galway routes. Waits between buses may exceed your ability to enjoy the spectacle so you might combine a bus with a walk. Numerous private tour operators run tours to the cliffs from Galway and the region.

The Doolin area is 6km away. If walking, stick to the minor road right near the cliffs that runs for the final half. Liscannor is under 2km along a path that is part of the marked Burren Way hiking trail (see p370).

THE BURREN

The Burren region is rocky and windswept, an apt metaphor for the hardscrabble lives of those who've eked out an existence here. Stretching across northern Clare, from the Atlantic coast to Kinvara in County Galway, it's a unique striated limestone landscape that was shaped beneath ancient seas, then forced high and dry by a great geological cataclysm. In the Burren, land and sea seem to merge into one vast, moody, rocky and at times fearsome space beneath huge skies and accented with ancient burial chambers and medieval ruins.

This is not the green Ireland of postcards. But there are wildflowers in spring, giving the Burren brilliant, if ephemeral, colour amid the arid beauty. There are also intriguing villages to enjoy. These include the music hub of Doolin on the west coast, Kilfenora inland and Ballyvaughan in the north, on the shores of Galway Bay.

History

Despite its apparent harshness, the Burren supported quite large numbers of people in ancient times, and has more than 2500 historic sites. Chief among them is the 5000-year-old Poulnabrone Dolmen, part of a Neolithic/Bronze Age tomb, and one of Ireland's iconic ancient monuments (see the boxed text, p378).

Around 70 such tombs are in evidence today. Many are wedge-shaped graves, stone boxes tapering both in height and width, and about the size of a large double bed. The dead were placed inside, and the whole structure covered in earth and stones. Gleninsheen, south of Aillwee Caves, is a good example.

Ring forts dot the Burren in prodigious numbers. There are almost 500, including Iron Age stone forts such as Cahercommaun near Carron.

In later times, many castles in the area were built by the region's ruling families, including Leamanegh Castle near Kilfenora. Today, a dwindling band of family farms ekes out a living through hardy crops and cattle.

Flora & Fauna

Soil may be scarce on the Burren, but the small amount that gathers in the cracks is well drained and rich in nutrients. This, together with the mild Atlantic climate, supports an

The Burren

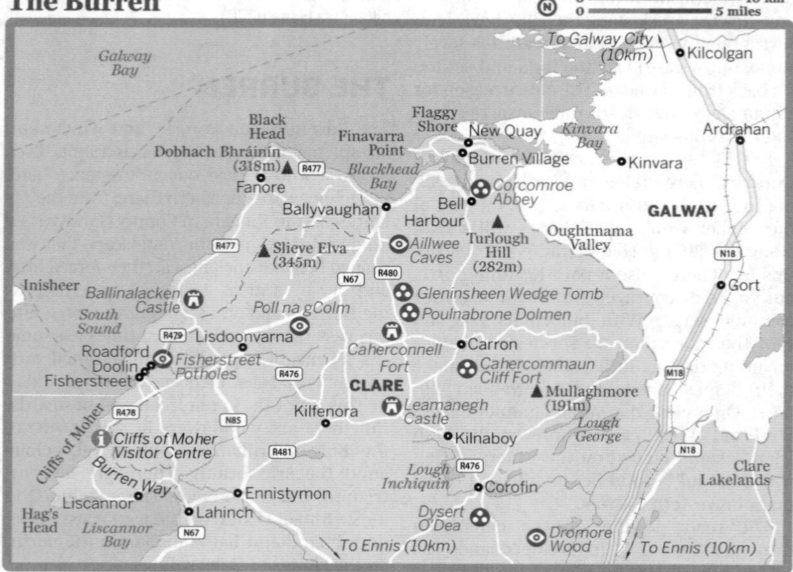

extraordinary mix of Mediterranean, Arctic and alpine plants. Of Ireland's native wildflowers, 75% are found here, including 24 species of beautiful orchids, the creamy-white burnet rose, the little starry flowers of mossy saxifrage and the magenta-coloured bloody cranesbill.

The Burren is a stronghold of Ireland's most elusive mammal, the weasel-like pine marten. It's rarely seen, although there are certainly some living in the Caher Valley. Badgers, foxes and even stoats are common throughout the region. Otters and seals haunt the shores around Bell Harbour, New Quay and Finavarra Point.

Walking

The Burren is a walkers paradise. The bizarre, beautiful landscape, numerous trails and many ancient sites are best explored on foot. 'Green roads' are the old highways of the Burren, crossing hills and valleys to some of the remotest corners of the region. Many of these unpaved ways were built during the Famine as part of relief work, while some date back possibly thousands of years. They're now used mostly by hikers and the occasional farmer. Some are signposted.

The **Burren Way** is a 123km network of marked hiking routes throughout the region.

Guided nature, history, archaeology and wilderness walks are great ways to appreciate the Burren. Typically the cost of the walks averages €15 and there are many options, including individual trips. Recommended guides (call to confirm times, walk locations and to book):

Burren Guided Walks & Hikes (☎065-707 6100, 087 244 6807; www.burrenguidedwalks.com) Longtime guide Mary Howard leads groups on a variety of itineraries.

Burren Hill Walks (☎065-707 7168) 'Gentle' walks visit historic sites while enjoying geologic and floral oddities.

Burren Wild Tours (☎087 877 9565; www.burrenwalks.com) John Connolly offers a broad range of walks and packages.

Heart of Burren Walks (☎065-682 7707; www.heartofburrenwalks.com) Local Burren author Tony Kirby leads walks and archaeology hikes.

ℹ Information

BOOKS & MAPS

There is a wealth of literature about the Burren, and it's best to trawl the bookshops of Ennis and local visitor centres for publications such as Charles Nelson's *Wild Plants of the Burren and the Aran Islands*. The *Burren Journey* books by George Cunningham are excellent for local lore. *The Burren and the Aran Islands: A Walking Guide* by Tony Kirby is an excellent, up-to-date resource.

The Tír Eolas series of foldout maps, *A Rambler's Guide & Map*, shows antiquities and other points of interest. The booklet *The Burren Way* has good walking routes. Ordnance Survey Discovery series maps 51 and 57 cover most of the area.

VISITOR INFORMATION

The Burren Centre in Kilfenora is an excellent resource.

Burren Ecotourism Network (www.burrenecotourism.com) A vast compilation of all things related to Burren tourism.

Burren National Park (www.burrennationalpark.ie) Portions of the Burren in the southeast have been designated a national park, although it has yet to develop visitor facilities; the website has good info on the natural landscape.

Burrenbeo Trust (www.burrenbeo.com; Main St, Kinvara, County Galway) A nonprofit dedicated to promoting the natural beauty of the Burren and increasing awareness. Its website is a tremendous source of info.

Getting There & Away

A few **Bus Éireann** (www.buseireann.ie) buses pass through the Burren. The main routes include one from Limerick and Ennis to Corofin, Ennistymon, Lahinch, Liscannor, the Cliffs of Moher, Doolin and Lisdoonvarna; another connects Galway with Ballyvaughan, Lisdoonvarna and Doolin. Usually there are one to three buses daily, with the most in summer.

Getting Around

By car you can cover a fair amount of the Burren in a day and have a chance to explore some of the many unnamed back roads. Bikes are an excellent means of getting off the main roads; ask about rentals at your accommodation. Finally, walking is a superb way to appreciate the area's subtle beauty and dramatic landscapes.

Doolin

POP 250

Doolin gets plenty of press and chatter as a centre of Irish traditional music, owing to a trio of pubs that have sessions through the year. It's also known for its setting – 6km north of the Cliffs of Moher and down near the ever-unsettled sea, the land is windblown, with huge rocks exposed by the long-vanished top soil.

Given all its attributes, you might be surprised when you realise that Doolin as it's known barely exists. Rather, when you arrive you might be forgiven for exclaiming, 'There's no there here!' For what's called Doolin is really three infinitesimally small neighbouring villages. **Fisherstreet** is right on the water, **Doolin** itself is about 1km east on the little River Aille and **Roadford** is another 1km east. None has more than a handful of buildings, which results in a scattered appearance, without a centre.

ROCK LEGENDS

The geology of the Burren (*Boireann* is the Irish term for 'rocky country') is the result of immense drama and excitement in ancient times that produced the moonlike landscape we see today. Follow the deep rivulets in the stone and you'll see that the barren Aran Islands just offshore are all part of the same formations.

Some 350 million years ago, this entire 560-sq-km area was the bottom of a warm and shallow sea. The remains of coral and shells fell to the seabed, and coastal rivers dumped sand and silt on top of these lime deposits. Time and pressure turned the lower layers to limestone and the upper ones to shale and sandstone.

Massive shifts in the earth's crust some 270 million years ago buckled the edges of Europe and forced the former seabed above sea level. At the same time the stone sheets were bent and fractured to form the long, deep cracks so characteristic of the Burren today.

During numerous ice ages, glaciers scoured the hills, rounding the edges and sometimes polishing the rock to a shiny finish, and dumping a thin layer of rock and soil in the cracks. Huge boulders were carried by the ice, incongruous aliens on a sea of flat rock.

Large areas of the Burren, about 40,000 hectares in all, have been designated as Special Areas of Conservation. Visitors are also asked to resist the temptation to erect 'sham' replicas of dolmens and other monuments, however small, including *Spinal Tap* Stonehenge size.

Still, the area is hugely popular with tourists, especially music-seeking Americans. There are scores of excellent-value hostels and B&Bs widely spread about the rough landscape. It's also a place to get boats to the Aran Islands offshore.

Sights

Tiny **Fisherstreet** is a charmer; you can enjoy dramatic surf vistas at the harbour, some 1.5km further along the coast.

Coming from the Cliffs of Moher, take a small, sinuous road off the R478 and follow it down to Fisherstreet past the stark ruins of a **castle**. Look for signs banning buses and pointing to the Sea View House B&B at the turn from the R478. Boat tours of the Cliffs of Moher are popular.

Activities

One of the most enjoyable ways to pass your time in Doolin is by walking the windswept country. Tracks and paths radiate in all directions; the Cliffs of Moher are 6km southwest.

Caves CAVING

The Doolin area is popular with cavers. The **Fisherstreet Potholes** are nearby, and **Poll na gColm**, 5km northeast of Lisdoonvarna, is Ireland's longest cave, with more than 12km of mapped passageways; see www.cavingireland.org for more details. A little over 1km north of Roadford you'll find **Doolin Cave** (www.doolincave.ie; adult/child €15/8; ⏲10am-5pm mid-Feb–Dec), which boasts an enormous stalactite that looks like a giant squid. The main entrance is at the Fisherstreet Potholes; tour times vary by season.

The rocks to the north of Doolin Harbour are honeycombed with an unusual system of undersea caves called the **Green Holes of Doolin**. They're the longest known undersea caves in temperate waters. Nondivers can look (with care) into Hell, a large gash in the rocks, north of the harbour and about 50m from the sea. The gash is about 6m wide, and the heaving water at the bottom leads to a maze of submarine passages.

The unguided caves mentioned here require experience and full equipment.

Festivals & Events

Micho Russell Festival MUSIC FESTIVAL

(www.doolin-tourism.com) On the last weekend in February, celebrates the work of a legendary Doolin musician and attracts top trad talent.

Sleeping

During the time of Irish overoptimism, there was a building boom of tourist accommodation in the Doolin area. Many newish places are inconveniently far from the music pubs. All the places listed below are reasonably central. From hostels to posh family-run B&Bs, Doolin has terrific accommodation options.

TOP CHOICE **Cullinan's Guesthouse** INN €€

(☎065-707 4183; www.cullinansdoolin.com; Doolin; s €40-60, d €60-90; P 📶) The eight rooms here are all of a high standard, with power showers and comfortable fittings. Right on the Aille (two rooms have balconies), it has a lovely back terrace for enjoying the views. The restaurant is one of the village's best. The owner is well-known local musician James Cullinan.

Sea View House INN €€

(☎065-707 4826; www.ireland-doolin.com; Fisherstreet; r €60-120; P 📶) On high ground right above Fisherstreet village, this big house and its terrace have sweeping ocean views. The common lounge has a telescope for enjoying the vantage point. The rooms have solid mahogany furnishings and DVD players (there's a library).

Aille River Hostel HOSTEL €

(☎065-707 4260; www.ailleriverhosteldoolin.ie; Roadford; dm €17-25, d from €50; ⏲mid-Mar–Dec; P @ 📶) In a picturesque spot by the river in the upper village, this converted 17th-century farmhouse is a great choice. There are turf fires, hot showers and a free laundry. This award-winning IHH hostel has 30 beds, campsites from €16 and bike rentals.

Dounroman House B&B €€

(☎065-707 4774; www.doolinbedandbreakfast.com; Doolin; s/d from €50/75; P 📶) Near the main Doolin crossroads, this two-storey B&B has views over the rough, grassy country side. The rooms are large; some are good for families. Besides the usual trad Irish breakfast, you can opt for locally smoked salmon or potato waffles.

Paddy's Doolin Hostel HOSTEL €

(☎065-707 4421; www.doolinhostel.com; Fisherstreet; dm from €17, d from €50; P 📶) A modern, IHH-affiliated hostel close to the bus stop. There are 90 beds in four- and eight-bed rooms; private rooms with bathrooms are also available. The charms of Fisherstreet are steps away.

Rainbow Hostel HOSTEL €

(☎065-707 4415; www.rainbowhostel.net; Roadford; dm €15-20, d from €40; P📶) Many a friendship has started in the cosy lounge here. IHH-affiliated, this hostel has 30 beds and is in an old farmhouse by the road. It rents bikes (€7 per day).

Toomullin House INN €€

(☎065-707 4723; www.toomullindoolin.com; Doolin; s/d from €55/75; P📶) This whitewashed old stone cottage has jaunty blue trim and is located a short walk from the pubs. The four rooms sleep up to three and they are furnished with the locally ubiquitous simple pine furniture. The hosts are happy to give detailed advice on seeing the local sights.

O'Connors Guesthouse INN €€

(☎065-707 4498; www.oconnorsdoolin.com; Doolin; s/d from €50/70; ⏲Feb-Oct; P📶) On a bend in the Aille, this working farm has 10 rooms of varying sizes in a rather plush farmhouse. Fresh-baked breads in the morning may put you in the mood to clean the barn (not possible actually). Commune with cattle instead. There are also campsites (€20).

Dubhlinn House B&B €€

(☎065-707 4770; www.dubhlinnhouse.com; Doolin; s/d from €50/70; P📶) This gleaming white B&B has good views down towards the water. The three rooms are simply decorated, while the breakfasts are pleasingly lavish; American urbanites will recognise and appreciate the bagel BLT.

Doolin Activity Lodge INN €€

(☎065-707 4888; www.doolinlodge.com; Fisherstreet; s/d from €45/70; P@📶) This impressive purpose-built guesthouse occupies a large compound; the solid stone buildings are quite attractive. There are 14 nicely furnished rooms, some with skylights for watching the rain blow past, as well as self-catering apartments.

Nagles Doolin Caravan & Camping Park CAMPGROUND €

(☎065-707 4458; www.doolincamping.com; campsites from €17; ⏲Apr-Sep; 📶) Let the nearby pounding surf lull you to sleep at this grassy expanse near the harbour. The 60 sites are open to the elements, so pin those pegs down.

Atlantic View B&B B&B €€

(☎065-707 4189; www.doolinferries.com; Doolin Point; s/d from €50/80; P) The perfect spot for guests who want their ocean up close and personal. This modern 12-room lodge is built right near the water, not far from the harbour. Fisherstreet is a five-minute walk.

Eating

All three of the trad music pubs serve Irish classics such as bacon and cabbage and seafood chowder through the day and until about 9pm.

Cullinan's MODERN IRISH €€€

(☎065-707 4183; www.cullinansdoolin.com; Doolin; mains €20-28; ⏲6-9pm Thu-Sat, Mon & Tue Apr-Oct) Attached to the guesthouse of the same name, this excellent and rather posh restaurant offers delicious seafood as well as meat and poultry dishes. The short menu changes depending on what's fresh, but is always creative. Bold combinations are favoured and there's a long wine list.

Doolin Cafe CAFE €€

(Roadford; mains €7-24; ⏲noon-3pm & 6-10pm) The cottage is small, but the flavours are big at this much-loved bistro. Salads, soups and sandwiches are the deal at lunch, while at night there's a range of meats and seafood with fusion preparations.

Drinking & Entertainment

Doolin's rep is largely based on music. A lot of musicians live in the area, and they have a symbiotic relationship with the tourists: each desires the other and each year things grow a little larger. But given the heavy concentration of visitors it's inevitable that standards don't always hold up to those in some of the less-trampled villages in Clare. In summer, the antics of the tourists (joining in with musicians uninvited, trying to sing, ceaselessly demanding 'When Irish Eyes are Smiling' and 'Danny Boy', sending blurry cell-phone snaps worldwide etc) can be entertaining or aggravating depending on your mood.

Doolin's three main music pubs (others are recent interlopers) are listed here in order of their importance to the music scene.

TOP CHOICE **McGann's** PUB

(Roadford) McGann's has all the classic touches of a full-on Irish music pub; the action often spills out onto the street. The food here is the best of the trio. Inside you'll find locals playing darts in its warren of small rooms, some with turf fires. There's a small outside covered area.

O'Connor's PUB

(Fisherstreet) Right on the water, this sprawling favourite packs them in and has a rollicking atmosphere when the music and drinking are in full swing. It easily gets the most crowded and has the highest tourist quotient; on some summer nights you won't squeeze inside and trying to eat is like playing the fiddle for the first time.

MacDiarmada's PUB

(Roadford) Also known as McDermott's, this simple red-and-white old pub can be the rowdy favourite of locals. When the fiddles get going, it can seem like a scene out of a John Ford movie. The inside is pretty basic, as is the menu of sandwiches and roasts. McGann's is a one-minute walk.

Shopping

Magnetic Music MUSIC STORE

(Fisherstreet) All things related to trad music can be found here including CDs by many local musicians.

Information

There are few services. The closest reliable ATM is in Lahinch.

Doolin Internet Cafe (per 30min €3; ⏲8am-7pm; wi-fi) In the Doolin Activity Lodge; also does laundry.

Tourism website (www.doolin-tourism.com)

Getting There & Away

Boat

Doolin is one of two ferry departure points to the Aran Islands (p351) from April to October. Various ferry companies offer numerous departures in season. It takes around half an hour to cover the 8km to Inisheer, the closest of the three islands and the best choice for a day trip from Doolin. A boat to Inishmór takes at least 1½ hours with an Inisheer stop. Ferries to Inishmaan are infrequent. Sailings are often cancelled due to high seas or tides which make the small dock inaccessible. There's much local debate about building a new harbour.

Rates vary as prices are very competitive, with each boat trying to undercut the others. Inisheer should cost about €20 to €25 return. Each boat has an office at Doolin Pier at the harbour but booking in advance on the web can net discounts. Call and confirm times. Most of the boats also offer various Cliffs of Moher tours, which are best done late in the afternoon when the light is from the west.

Cliffs of Moher Cruises (☎065-707 5949; www.mohercruises.com; Doolin Pier; ⏲Apr-Oct) Offers combined Aran Islands trips with Cliffs of Moher cruises on the *Jack B*.

Doolin Ferries (☎065-707 4455, 065-707 4466; www.doolinferries.com; Doolin Pier) Offers sailings to the islands and the cliffs on the Happy Hooker.

O'Brien Line (☎065-707 5555; www.obrienline.com) Usually has the most sailings to the Arans; also offers cliff cruises and combo tickets.

Bus

Bus Éireann runs one to two buses daily to Doolin from Ennis (€12, 1½ hours) and Limerick (€15, 2½ hours) via Corofin, Lahinch and the Cliffs of Moher. Buses also go to Galway (€14, 1½ hours, one or two daily) via Ballyvaughan.

In the summer, various backpacker shuttles often serve Doolin from Galway and other points in Clare. These are amply marketed in hostels.

Getting Around

Most of the hostels and many of the B&Bs rent bikes from €10 per day, as does **Village Crafts** (Fisherstreet).

Lisdoonvarna

POP 950

Lisdoonvarna (Lios Dún Bhearna), often just called 'Lisdoon', is well known for its mineral springs. For centuries people have been visiting the local spa to swallow its waters. Posh in the Victorian era, the town is now a much more plebeian and friendly place. Away from the coast, it's not overrun like Doolin and is a good base for exploring the Burren.

Sights & Activities

Spa Well LANDMARK

At the southern end of town is a spa well, with a sulphur spring, a Victorian pumphouse and an agreeable, wooded setting. The iron, sulphur, magnesium and iodine in the water are supposed to be good for rheumatic and glandular complaints. Closer to the centre, you can drink the water, even if it's not exactly a vintage wine-tasting experience. Look for a trail beside the Roadside Tavern that runs 400m down to two **wells** by the river. One is high in sulphur, the other iron. Mix and match for a cocktail of minerals.

Burren Smokehouse SMOKEHOUSE

(☎065-707 4432; www.burrensmokehouse.ie; Kincora Rd; ⏲10am-5pm Apr-May, 9am-6pm Jun-Oct, shorter hours in winter) You can learn about the

DON'T MISS

LISDOONVARNA MATCHMAKING FESTIVAL

Lisdoonvarna was once a centre for *basadóiri* (matchmakers) who, for a fee, would fix up a person with a spouse. Most of the (mainly male) hopefuls would hit town in September, feet shuffling, cap in hand, after the hay was in. Today, the tradition continues at the much-hyped and ever-expanding **Lisdoonvarna Matchmaking Festival** (www.matchmakerireland.com), held throughout September and early October. Irish and even foreign singles plus those who just enjoy a jolly good time revel in daftness, drinking, merry making, music and much, much dancing. Older, more sedate courtships are recalled by the **statue** on the pub-surrounded Main Sq.

ancient Irish art of oak-smoking salmon from a video (available in six languages) at the Burren Smokehouse. Tasty smoked salmon and other fishies in a myriad of forms are offered for free tasting – perhaps you'll even buy some? Good coffee and tea are sold along with other deli-type foods suitable for picnics. Tourist information is also available. The smokehouse is at the edge of Lisdoonvarna on the Kincora road (N67).

Sleeping & Eating

Book during September's Matchmaking Festival; B&Bs are like mushrooms after the rain.

TOP CHOICE **Sheedy's Country House Hotel & Restaurant** INN €€
(☎065-707 4026; www.sheedys.com; Sulphur Hill; r €70-140; ⊙Apr-Sep; P 📶) Take a leek from the kitchen garden – that's just one of the playful bits of fun you can have at this posh yet relaxed 11-room guesthouse just outside of town. A long porch has comfy chairs for pondering the many gardens or just taking a snooze. Food is excellent. The bar has a huge range of whiskey.

Wild Honey Inn INN €€
(☎065-707 4300; www.wildhoneyinn.com; Kincora Rd; s/d from €40/80; P 📶) In a beautiful old roadside mansion on the edge of town, Wild Honey has 14 stylish rooms which are the perfect weekend getaway (or hideout for that impromptu honeymoon during matchmaking season?). The pub has a delectable menu of Irish classics made with local seafood, meats and produce. In summer there's a lovely garden with tables.

Sleepzone HOSTEL €
(☎065-707 7168; www.sleepzone.ie; Doolin Rd; dm €20-25, s/d €50/70; P @ 📶) Housed in a formerly posh hotel, this 124-bed hostel has an unusual grace. The grounds reflect its past and there are all the usual facilities and free continental breakfasts.

Roadside Tavern PUB €
(Kincora Rd; meals €6-12) Down by the river, this pub is pure craic. Third-generation owner Peter Curtin knows every story worth telling. There are trad sessions daily in summer and during the weekends in winter. Imbibing musicians can be found here anytime. The trad fun extends to the kitchen, which turns out creamy seafood chowders etc. Anything with smoked fish is good as they also run the nearby Burren Smokehouse.

Information

The closest reliable ATM is in Lahinch, worth remembering if you're planning some pricey wooing.

Getting There & Around

Bus Éireann runs one to three buses daily to Doolin via Lisdoonvarna from Ennis, and to Limerick via Corofin, Lahinch and the Cliffs of Moher. Buses also go to Galway via Ballyvaughan and Black Head.

Kilfenora

POP 360

Underappreciated Kilfenora (Cill Fhionnúrach) lies on the southern fringe of the Burren, 8km (a five-minute drive) southeast of Lisdoonvarna. It's a small place, with a diminutive 12th-century cathedral. High crosses adorn the churchyard, and low polychromatic buildings surround the compact centre.

The town has a strong music tradition that rivals that of Doolin, but without the crowds. The **Kilfenora Céili Band** (www.kilfenoraceiliband.com) is a celebrated community that's been playing for 100 years. Its traditional

THE IMMORTAL FATHER TED

Father Ted, the enduring British TV comedy, is set around the high jinks of three Irish priests living on the fictional Craggy Island. Most of the locations used in the show are around Kilfenora and Ennistymon (Eugene's pub was used as a location and the cast drank here). The lonely *Father Ted* house is in Kilnaboy.

Inspired by the great success of Inismór's Tedfest (see the boxed text, p404), the good people of Kilfenora and Ennistymon have organised their own **Father Ted Festival** (www.frtedfestival.com; May) with costume parties, contests, tours and more.

music features fiddles, banjos, squeezeboxes and more.

About 6km east of town on the road to Corofin, look for the towering remains of Leamanegh Castle, an old stone manor house.

Sights

Burren Centre MUSEUM
(065-708 8030; www.theburrencentre.ie; Main St; adult/child €6/5; 9am-5pm mid-Mar–mid-Oct) The centre has a series of entertaining and informative displays on many aspects of the Burren past and present. Stone-age mannequins look on the verge of frostbite. There's a cafe and a very large shop that sells local products.

Cathedral CHURCH
The 11th-century cathedral at Kilfenora was once an important place of pilgrimage. St Fachan (or Fachtna) founded the monastery here in the 6th century, and it later became the seat of Kilfenora diocese, the smallest in the country. Loop around the more recent protestant church and you can enter the oldest part of the ruins, which have a stoic charm. The chancel has two primitive carved figures on top of two tombs.

High Crosses HISTORIC SITE
Kilfenora is best known for its high crosses, three in the glass-covered cathedral ruins and a large one from the 12th century in a field about 100m to the west. Most interesting is the 800-year-old **Doorty Cross**. It lay broken in two until the 1950s, when it was re-erected. A panel in the ruins does an excellent job of explaining the carvings that adorn the crosses.

Sleeping & Eating

Kilfenora has two top-notch pubs.

Kilfenora Hostel HOSTEL €
(065-708 8908; www.kilfenorahostel.com; Main St; dm €20-24, d €52-60; P@) Affiliated with Vaughan's Pub next door, this guesthouse has 46 beds in nine rooms. There's a laundry and a big kitchen. Weary travellers in the lounge may feel they've fallen into the hand of God.

Murphy's B&B B&B €€
(065-708 8040; lika@eircom.net; Main St; s/d from €45/70; mid-Feb–Nov) Right on the main street, Mrs Mary Murphy runs a fine little B&B with the kind of simple rooms you could call your own. She has two more houses nearby.

TOP CHOICE **Vaughan's Pub** PUB €€
(www.vaughanspub.ie; Main St; meals €9-15; kitchen 10am-9pm) Seafood, traditional foods and local produce feature on the Vaughan's appealing menu. The pub has a big reputation in Irish music circles. There's music in the bar every night during the summer and on many nights the rest of the year. The adjacent barn is the scene of terrific set-dancing sessions on Thursday and Sunday nights. Have a pint under the big tree out front.

Linnane's PUB €
(065-708 8157; Main St; meals €5-12; kitchen noon-8pm) Irish standards like smoked salmon and more are fully honoured here. Peat fires warm the almost bare interior; nary a frill in sight. There's trad music many nights in summer.

Getting There & Away

Kilfenora has a nondaily bus service.

Corofin & Around

POP 420

Corofin (Cora Finne), also spelt Corrofin, is a traditional village on the southern fringes of the Burren. It's low-key and a classic place to sample the rhythms of Clare life. The surrounding area features a number of turloughs (small lakes) and several O'Brien castles, including two on the shores of nearby Lough Inchiquin.

About 4km northwest of Corofin, on the road to Leamanegh Castle and Kilfenora (R476), look for the small town of **Kilnaboy**. The ruined church here is well worth seeking out for the sheila-na-gig (carved female figure with exaggerated genitalia) over the doorway.

Sights

Clare Heritage Centre MUSEUM
(www.clareroots.com; Church St; adult/concession €4/2; ⌚9.30am-5.30pm Apr-Oct) Corofin is home to the interesting Clare Heritage Centre, housed in an old church and with a display covering the horrors of the Great Famine. More than 250,000 people lived in Clare before the Famine; even today the county's population is only about 106,000 – a drop of almost 60%. The **Clare Genealogical Centre** (☎065-683 7955; ⌚9am-5.30pm Mon-Fri), in a separate building nearby, has facilities for people researching their Clare ancestry.

Sleeping & Eating

TOP CHOICE **Inchiquin Inn** IRISH €
(☎065-683 7713, 065-683 7594; www.annecampbell.ie; Main St; lunch €6-12; ⌚kitchen 9am-6pm) Townsfolk follow the horses at this oh-so-local pub with a great kitchen. The seafood chowder and bacon and cabbage are some of the best you'll find. The former is thick, tangy and redolent with smoked fish. There's trad music some summer nights. An annual stone-throwing championship out back in June is a huge local party. Hostel beds upstairs are €15 per person.

Lakefield Lodge B&B €€
(☎065-683 7675; www.lakefieldlodgebandb.com; Ennis Rd; s/d from €45/70; ⌚Mar-Oct; P Wi-Fi) A well-run place near the southern edge of the village. There are four comfy rooms in a pleasant bungalow surrounded by gardens and well-placed for Burren hikes.

Fergus View B&B €€
(☎065-683 7606; www.fergusview.com; s/d from €45/70; ⌚Apr-Oct; @ Wi-Fi) The name exactly describes the scene: the River Fergus flows right past. A lovely home with six rooms, its breakfasts have achieved fame for being fresh – often organic – and creative. It's 3km north of Corofin on the R476.

Corofin Hostel & Camping Park HOSTEL/CAMPGROUND €
(☎065-683 7683; www.corofincamping.com; Main St; campsites €20, dm/s/d €16/25/40; ⌚Apr-Sep) Campsites out back have nice open spaces, and inside there are 30 beds. The large common room at this IHH-affiliated hostel right in town has a pool table.

Getting There & Away

Bus Éireann has an infrequent service some weekdays between Corofin and Ennis.

Central Burren

Several roads dotted with sights cross the heart of the Burren. The scenery along the R480 as it passes through the region is harsh but inspiring, highlighting the barren Burren at its best. Amazing prehistoric stone structures can be found throughout this area.

South from Ballyvaughan the R480 branches off the N67 at the sign for Aillwee Caves, passing Gleninsheen Wedge Tomb and the amazing Poulnabrone Dolmen before reaching the Leamanegh Castle ruins, where it joins the R476, which runs southeast to Corofin. At any point along here, try a small road – especially those to the east – for an escape into otherworldly solitude.

The N67 to Lisdoonvarna is marked by sweeping views of the stark Burren landscape. It was originally a famine relief road built in the 1800s.

GLENINSHEEN WEDGE TOMB

One of Ireland's most famous prehistoric grave sites, Gleninsheen lies beside the R480 just south of Aillwee Caves near Ballyvaughan. It's thought to date from 4000 to 5000 years ago. A magnificent gold torc (a crescent of beaten gold that hung round the neck) found here and dating from around 700 BC is now on display at the National Museum in Dublin. Note: the access gate to the tomb is sometimes locked, and signage is poor.

CAHERCONNELL FORT

For a look at a well-preserved *caher* (walled fort) of the late Iron Age-Early Christian period, stop at **Caherconnell Fort** (www.burrenforts.ie; adult/child €6/4; ⌚10am-6pm Jul & Aug, 10am-5pm Mar-Jun, Sep & Oct), a privately run heritage attraction that's more serious than sideshow. Exhibits detail how the evolution of these defensive settlements may have reflected territorialism and competition for land among a growing, settling population. The drystone walling of the fort is in excellent condition. The top-notch visitor centre also has information on many other monuments in the area. It's about 1km south of Poulnabrone Dolman on the R480.

CARRON & AROUND

The tiny village of Carron (Carran on some maps, An Carn in Gaelic), a few kilometres east of the R480, is a wonderfully remote spot. Vistas of the rocky Burren stretch in all directions from Carron's elevated position.

Sights & Activities

Burren Perfumery & Floral Centre PERFUMERY
(www.burrenperfumery.com; Carron; 9am-7pm Jul-Aug, 10am-5pm Sep-Jun) This sweet-smelling stop is a creative treasure. It uses wildflowers of the Burren to produce its scents, and is the only handicraft perfumery in Ireland. There's a free audiovisual presentation on the flora of the Burren, which has a surprising diversity. One example: the many fragrant orchids that grow among the rocks. The centre has an organic cafe, and native and herb gardens. Look for perfumery signs at the T-junction near Carron church. Note that tour buses aren't welcome.

Carron Polje LANDMARK
Below Carron lies Carron Polje, one of the finest turloughs in Ireland. Polje is a Serbo-Croatian term used universally for these shallow depressions that flood in winter and dry out in summer, when the lush grass that flourishes on the surface is used for grazing.

Stretching south from Carron almost to Kilnaboy are some of the Burren's bleakest stretches. Non-native boulders deposited during ice ages litter the stark landscape. Take any narrow track you find, and every so often you'll see an ancient **dolmen**.

Cahercommaun HISTORIC BUILDING
About 3km south of Carron and perched on the edge of an inland cliff is the great stone fort of Cahercommaun. It was inhabited in the 8th and 9th centuries AD by people who hunted deer and grew a small amount of grain. The remains of a souterrain (underground passage) lead from the fort to the outer cliff face. To get there, go south from Carron and take a left turn for Kilnaboy. After 1.5km a path on the left leads up to the fort. Look for a good info board at the start of the path.

Sleeping & Eating

TOP CHOICE **Clare's Rock Hostel** HOSTEL €
(065-708 9129; www.claresrock.com; Carron; dm/s/d €18/30/44; May-Sep; P@) An imposing building of grey exposed stone. It has 30 beds, big spacious rooms and excellent facilities. Guests can hire bikes or cavort with the trolls on the outdoor garden-gnome chessboard.

Cassidy's PUB €
(www.cassidyspub.com; Carron; bar mains €6-12; daily May-Sep, Sat & Sun Oct-Apr) Cassidy's serves up a good range of pub dishes, several with witty names reflecting the establishment's previous incarnation as a British Royal Irish Constabulary (RIC) station, and then as a *garda* (police) barracks. Enjoy trad

DON'T MISS

POULNABRONE DOLMEN

What would a Burren brochure designer do without it? Also known as the Portal Tomb, Poulnabrone Dolmen is one of Ireland's most photographed ancient monuments. The dolmen (a large slab perched on stone uprights) stands amid a swathe of rocky pavements, surprising even the most jaded traveller with its otherworldly appearance; the capstone weighs 5 tonnes. The site is about 8km south of Aillwee and is visible from the R480. A large free parking area and excellent displays make it visitor friendly.

Poulnabrone was built more than 5000 years ago. It was excavated in 1986, and the remains of 16 people were found, as well as pieces of pottery and jewellery. Radiocarbon dating suggests that they were buried between 3800 and 3200 BC. When the dead were originally entombed here, the whole structure was partially covered in a mound of earth, which has since worn away. It's your guess as to how they built it.

music and dancing some weekends. The views from the terrace are as intoxicating as the drink.

Fanore

POP 150

The scenic R477 hugs the barren coast of Clare as it curves past the Arran Islands into Galway Bay. Fanore (Fan Óir), 5km south of Black Head, is less a village and more a stretch of coast with a shop, a pub and a few houses scattered along the main road. It has a fine sandy beach with an extensive backdrop of dunes. You'll find good parking and there are toilets open in summer.

Activities

Surfers flock here throughout the year.

Aloha Surf School SURFING

(☎087 213 3996; www.surfschool.tv; lessons from €35) offers classes for all ages and abilities plus board and wetsuit rental.

Siopa Fan Óir FISHING

(⊙9am-9pm summer, to 7pm winter) There's a well-stocked shop, just across from O'Donohue's pub where you can buy fishing tackle, walking maps, boogie boards and cheap sand buckets.

Sleeping & Eating

Rocky View Farmhouse INN €€

(☎065-707 6103; www.rockyviewfarmhouse.com; s/d €40/68; P 📶) One of the Fanore area's few accommodation/eating options, Rocky View Farmhouse, is a charming house at the heart of the coastal Burren. Its five open and airy rooms are suited to this especially barren end of the region. Organic food is grown and used in the breakfasts, which are served in a sunny conservatory.

O'Donohue's PUB €

(meals €6-15; ⊙Apr-Oct) In many ways the community centre, O'Donohue's, 4km south of the beach, offers no-nonsense soup, hot dishes and sandwiches along with its genuine local character. Done up in bright blue and white, it looks out over the grey sea.

Vasco MEDITERRANEAN €

(www.vasco.ie; mains €8-16; ⊙9am-10pm Jul & Aug, weekends only other times) This stylish outpost is near the beach in Fanore. You can watch the water from the vast, glassed-in terrace or enjoy lounging inside. The food is Med-accented and you can get picnic supplies for the beach.

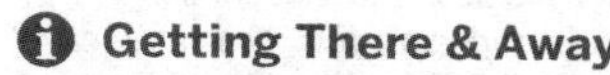

Getting There & Away

Bus Éireann runs one to three buses daily from Galway via Black Head and through Fanore to Lisdoonvarna.

Black Head

Atlantic storms have stripped the land around the unfortunately named Black Head down to bare rock. Grass and the occasional shrub cling to crevices. Standing like sentinels, boulders and the odd cow dot the landscape here, Clare's northwesternmost point.

The main road (R477) curves around the head just above the sea. There's good shore **angling** for pollack, wrasse, mackerel – and sea bass if you're lucky – from the rocky platforms near sea level. These can be fatally dangerous waters, even for those with longstanding local knowledge. Even in apparently calm conditions, watch for sudden surges.

Ballyvaughan & Around

POP 220

Something of a hub for the otherwise dispersed charms of the Burren, Ballyvaughan (Baile Uí Bheacháin) sits between the hard land of the hills and a quiet leafy corner of Galway Bay. It makes an excellent base for visiting the northern reaches of the Burren.

Sights & Activities

About 6km south of Ballyvaughan on the Lisdoonvarna road (N67) is a series of severe bends up **Corkscrew Hill** (180m). The road was built as part of a Great Famine relief scheme in the 1840s. From the top there are spectacular views of the northern Burren and Galway Bay, with Aillwee Mountain and the caves on the right, Cappanawalla Hill on the left, and the partially restored 16th-century Newtown Castle, erstwhile residence of the O'Lochlains, directly below.

Just west of the junction is the **quay**, built in 1829 at a time when boats traded with the Aran Islands and Galway, exporting grain and bacon and bringing in turf – a scarce commodity in the windswept rocks of Burren.

A few metres past the harbour, a signposted track leads to a **seashore bird shelter** offering good views of the tidal shallows.

Aillwee Caves CAVES
(www.aillweecave.ie; combined ticket adult/child €17/10; ⌚10am-5.30pm, to 6.30pm Jul & Aug) Send the kids underground. The main cave here penetrates 600m into the mountain, widening into larger caverns, one with its own waterfall. The caves were carved out by water some two million years ago. Near the entrance are the remains of a brown bear, extinct in Ireland for more than 10,000 years. Often crowded in summer, there's a cafe, and a large raptor exhibit has captive hawks, owls and more. A shop sells locally produced Burren Gold cheese, which is excellent.

Sleeping & Eating

There are several simple B&Bs close to the centre. Ballyvaughan's **farmers market** (⌚10am-2pm Sat) celebrates the huge range of high-quality local produce.

TOP CHOICE **Gregan's Castle Hotel** HOTEL €€€
(☎065-707 7005; www.gregans.ie; s/d from €150/200; P Wi-Fi) This hidden Clare gem is housed in a grand estate dating to the 19th century. The 20 rooms and suites, however, have a plush, stylish feel with just enough modern touches to keep you from feeling you've bedded down in a waxworks. The restaurant specialises in inventive fresh fare sourced locally while the bar is the kind of place to sip something brown and let hours roll away in genteel comfort. The grounds are a fantasy of gardens and when you're not walking in the Burren, there's croquet. The estate is some 6km south of Ballyvaughan on the N67 at Corkscrew Hill.

Hyland's Burren Hotel HOTEL €€
(☎065-707 7037; www.hylandsburren.com; Main St; s/d from €70/90; P) An appealing place, this central hotel has 30 large rooms (a mix of traditional and more spacious modern) and manages to retain a local feel alongside modern hotel shtick. There's a bar and a restaurant. Ask for the hotel's *Walks* leaflet.

Rusheen Lodge INN €€
(☎065-707 7092; www.rusheenlodge.com; Lisdoonvarna Rd; s/d from €70/100; ⌚Feb-Nov; P Wi-Fi) Stylish, imaginative furnishings make this nine-room guesthouse a winner. Enjoy a romp in the colourful gardens. It's about 750m south of the village on the N67.

Oceanville House B&B B&B €€
(☎065-707 7051; www.clareireland.net/oceanville; s/d from €40/65; P Wi-Fi) Near Monk's and the dock, this oceanfront B&B has views across the bay from the dormer windows in its compact upstairs rooms. This is a good spot for walking the village and sampling its pleasures.

Monk's Bar & Restaurant SEAFOOD €€
(Old Pier; mains €10-20; ⌚kitchen noon-8pm) Famed for its excellent seafood, Monk's is a cheerful, spacious and comfortable place. Peat fires warm in winter, while sea breezes cool you at the outdoor tables in summer. The pub is open late and there are trad sessions some nights in high season.

Drinking

TOP CHOICE **Ólólainn** PUB
(Main St) A tiny family-run place on the left as you head out to the pier, Ólólainn (*o-loch-lain*) is the place for a timeless moment or two in old-fashioned snugs. Look for the old whiskey bottles in the window but save all your energy for the amazing selection of rare whiskeys within.

Information

Tourist info desk (www.ballyvaughantourism.com; ⌚9am-6pm daily Mar-Oct, Sat & Sun only Nov-Feb) In a vast gift shop, which does have a small section of local guides and maps.

Getting There & Away

Bus Éireann runs one to three buses daily from Galway through Ballyvaughan and around Black Head to Lisdoonvarna and Doolin.

Northern Burren

Low farmland stretches south from County Galway to the bluff limestone hills of the Burren, which begin west of Kinvara and Doorus in County Galway.

From Oranmore in County Galway to Ballyvaughan, the coastline wriggles along small inlets and peninsulas; some, such as New Quay, are worth a detour. Here, narrow roads traverse low rocky windswept hills dotted with old stone ruins that have yielded to nature.

Inland near Bell Harbour is the largely intact Corcomroe Abbey, while the three ancient churches of **Oughtmama** lie up a quiet side valley. Galway Bay forms the backdrop to some outstanding scenery: bare

DON'T MISS

CORCOMROE ABBEY

Moody and evocative, lonely Corcomroe, a former Cistercian abbey 1.5km inland from Bell Harbour, lies in a small, tranquil valley surrounded by low hills. It is a marvellous building, one of the finest of its kind. The abbey was founded in 1194 by Donal Mór O'Brien. His grandson, Conor na Siudaine O'Brien (died 1267), king of Thomond, is said to occupy the tomb in the northern wall, and there's a crude carving of him below the effigy of a bishop holding a crosier, the pastoral staff that was carried by a bishop or abbot. The surviving vaulting in the presbytery and transepts is very fine and there are some striking Romanesque carvings scattered throughout the abbey, which began a long decline in the 15th century. Often-touching modern graves crowd the ruins.

stone hills shining in the sun, with small hamlets and rich patches of green wherever there's soil.

Buses to/from Galway pass through the area on the N67. Just over the border in Galway, Kinvara makes a good base for this region.

NEW QUAY & THE FLAGGY SHORE

New Quay (Ceibh Nua), on the **Finavarra Peninsula**, is a quiet and rather bucolic break from the rocky rigours of the Burren. It is about 1km off the Kinvara-Ballyvaughan road (N67) and is reached by turning off at Ballyvelaghan Lough 3km north of Bell Harbour.

The **Flaggy Shore**, west of New Quay, is a particularly fine stretch of coastline where limestone terraces step down to the sea. The road hugs the shoreline then curves south past **Lough Muirí**, where you're likely to see a number of wading birds, as well as swans. There are said to be otters in the area. At a T-junction just past the lough, a right turn leads to a rather dingy-looking **Martello tower** on Finavarra Point, a relic of the paranoia over the Napoleonic threat.

Sleeping & Eating

Mount Vernon BOUTIQUE HOTEL €€€
(☎065-707 8126; www.mountvernon.ie; Flaggy Shore; s/d from €120/180; P 📶) Famed Irish impressionist Hugh Lane once called Mount Vernon home until he was lost with the *Lusitania*. Today the rural Georgian lodge is a secluded seaside retreat with five luxurious rooms decorated in period furnishings. Expect to spend your days walking the sinuous shore and staring at the greyclad Burren.

TOP CHOICE **Linnane's Seafood Bar** SEAFOOD €€
(New Quay; meals €9-25; ⏲noon-8pm) This seafood place achieved widespread cachet as a no-nonsense purveyor of fresh seafood sourced from the trap-covered docks behind the restaurant. For centuries this area was famous for its oysters; shellfish are still processed here and you can sometimes buy them from the little works behind the pub.

Shopping

Russell Gallery ART GALLERY
(☎065-707 8185; New Quay; ⏲10am-6pm Mon-Sat, from noon Sun) Specialises in *raku* (Japanese lead-glazed earthenware) work. The airy gallery has a range of other works by Irish artists for sale along with books on the region. It's about 500m west of Linnane's Seafood Bar, at a crossroads.

Wilde & Wooley CLOTHING
(☎065-707 8042; Burren) This is the name for Antoinette Hensey's shop, where she makes custom knitwear from exquisitely dyed wool. The designs are complex and beautiful; a sweater costs upwards of €200. It's nearby to Russell Gallery, just off the N67.

BELL HARBOUR

No more than a crossroads with a growing crop of holiday cottages and a pub, Bell Harbour (Beulaclugga) is about 8km east of Ballyvaughan. There's a pleasant walk along an old green road that begins behind the modern Church of St Patrick, 1km north up the hill from the Y-junction at Bell Harbour, and threads north along Abbey Hill.

Inland from here are the ruins of Corcomroe Abbey, the valley and churches of Oughtmama, and the interior road that takes you through Carron and the the heart of the Burren.

County Galway

POPULATION 250,000 / AREA 3760 SQ KM

Includes »

Best Places to Eat

» Griffin's (p391)

» Cava (p391)

» Mitchell's (p417)

» Moran's Oyster Cottage (p421)

Best Places to Stay

» House Hotel (p389)

» Kilmurvey House (p401)

» Delphi Lodge (p421)

» Dolphin Beach (p416)

Why Go?

County Galway is a problem: its namesake city is such a charmer that you might not manage to tear yourself away to the countryside. Conversely (perversely?), the wild and beautiful Aran Islands and Connemara Peninsula might keep you captive such that you'll never have time for the city. What to do? Both, of course!

Galway city is a swirl of enticing old pubs that hum with trad music sessions throughout the year. More importantly, it has an overlaying vibe of fun and frolic that's addictive.

Offshore, the eroded, sheer swaths of land known as the Aran Islands have a desolate, windswept aura that entrances. Tiny villages cling to the rocks while soft-hearted locals welcome their modern lifeblood: visitors.

In the west, the Connemara Peninsula matches the beauty of the other Atlantic outcrops like Dingle. Tiny roads wander along a coastline studded with islands, surprisingly white beaches and intriguing old villages.

When to Go

Galway City with its excellent restaurants, roaring pubs and student culture is a year-round destination. Elsewhere in more rural parts of the county, you'll be rewarded for visits during the more moderate months. Moody in the depths of winter, the Aran Islands may be unreachable during storms. In scenic Connemara country, many country inns close during December and January and even February. June is a great month across the county as all the seasonal attractions are open but crowds are still low.

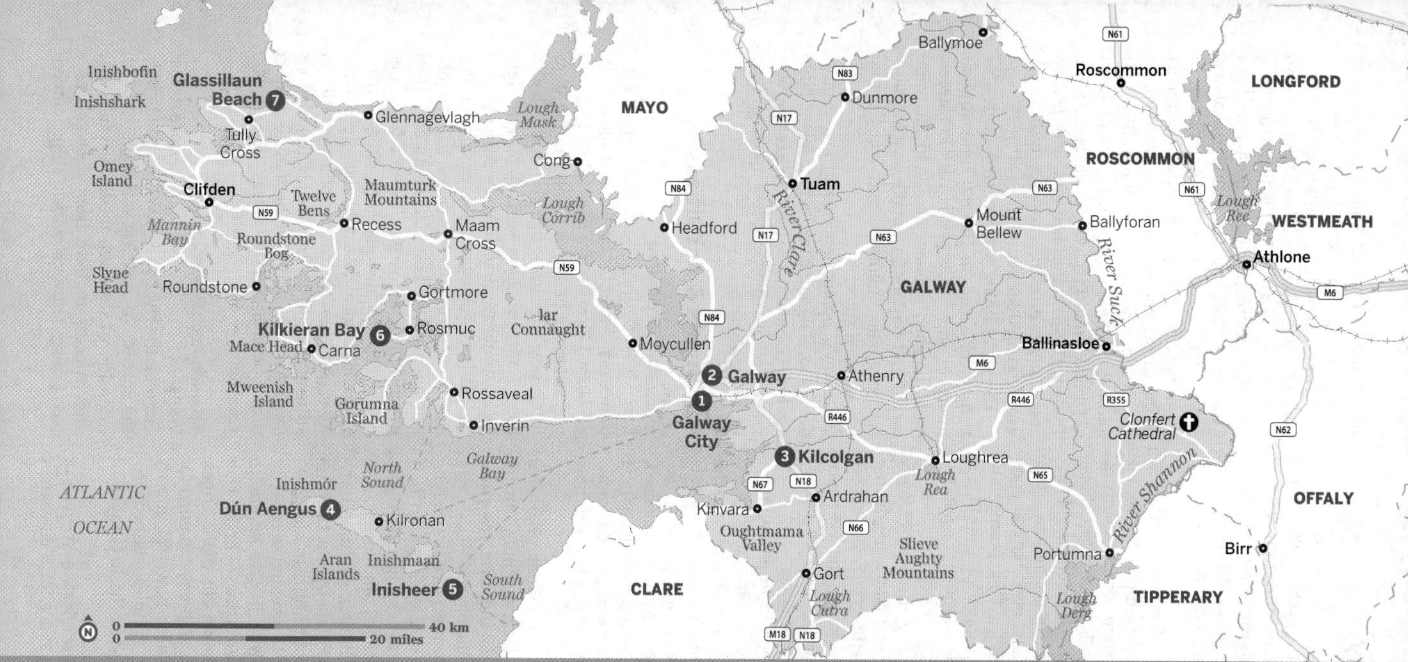

County Galway Highlights

1 Sample **Galway city's** (p393) array of atmospheric pubs and their high-energy trad sessions each week

2 Walk the Prom in **Galway** (p391), absorbing the moods of the bay and gazing out at County Clare and the Aran Islands

3 Enjoy oysters direct from the bay at an iconic oyster restaurant in **Kilcolgan** (p421)

4 Ponder the people who built the enigmatic fort **Dún Aengus** (p400) on Inishmór

5 Visit ancient holy sites and springs, crawl over a famous shipwreck and commune with the rocks on **Inisheer** (p406)

6 Marvel at the range of marine life in **Kilkieran Bay** (p413)

7 Frolic on postcard-perfect **Glassillaun Beach** (p420) on Connemara's north coast, and consider plunging into the inky depths on a scuba adventure

GALWAY CITY

POP 75,000

Arty, bohemian Galway (Gaillimh) is renowned for its pleasures. Brightly painted pubs heave with live music, while cafes offer front-row seats for observing street performers, weekend hen parties run amuck, lovers entwined and more.

Steeped in history, the city nonetheless has a contemporary vibe. Students make up a quarter of its population, and remnants of the medieval town walls lie between shops selling Aran sweaters, handcrafted Claddagh rings, and stacks of secondhand and new books. Bridges arc over the salmon-filled River Corrib, and a long promenade leads to the seaside suburb of Salthill, on Galway Bay, the source of the area's famous oysters.

Galway is a very rainy city, even by Irish standards, and water can play a major role in your visit here, whether you're dodging it from the skies, walking along the bay shore or exploring paths along the river, creeks, canals and gentrifying harbour.

Galway is often referred to as the 'most Irish' of Ireland's cities (and it's the only one where you're likely to hear Irish spoken in the streets, shops and pubs), but some locals lament that these may be the last days of 'old' Galway before it, too, becomes globalised. Still, if you ask a local what they're doing next Tuesday, they will look at you puzzled, knowing that anything can happen between now and then.

Galway's Irish name, Gaillimh, originates from the Irish word *gaill,* meaning 'outsiders' or 'foreigners', and the term resonates throughout the city's history.

From humble beginnings as a tiny fishing village at the mouth of the River Corrib, it grew into an important town when the Anglo-Normans, under Richard de Burgo (also spelled de Burgh or Burke), captured territory from the local O'Flahertys in 1232. Its fortified walls were built from around 1270.

In 1396 Richard II granted a charter transferring power from the de Burgos to 14 merchant families or 'tribes' – hence Galway's enduring nickname: City of the Tribes. (Each of the city's roundabouts is named for one of the tribes.) These powerful, mostly English or Norman families clashed frequently with the leading Irish families of Connemara.

A massive fire in 1473 destroyed much of the town but created space for a new street layout, and many solid stone buildings were erected in the 15th and 16th centuries.

Galway maintained its independent status under the ruling merchant families, who were mostly loyal to the English Crown. Its coastal location encouraged a huge trade in wine, spices, fish and salt with Portugal and Spain, rivalling London in the volume of goods passing through its docks. Its support of the Crown, however, led to its downfall; the city was besieged by Cromwell in 1651 and fell the following year. In 1691 William of Orange's militia added to the destruction. Trade with Spain declined and, with Dublin and Waterford taking most sea traffic, Galway stagnated for centuries.

The early 1900s saw Galway's revival as tourists returned to the city and student numbers grew. In 1934 the cobbled streets and thatched cabins of Claddagh were tarred and flattened to make way for modern, hygienic buildings, and construction has boomed since.

Galway's population has grown rapidly and its local dynamism – helped by the large student population – means that the economic collapse has been less apparent here than elsewhere.

Sights & Activities

TOP CHOICE Hall of the Red Earl — ARCHAEOLOGICAL SITE

(www.galwaycivictrust.ie; Druid Lane; admission free; 9.30am-4.45pm Mon-Fri) Back in the 13th century when the de Burgo family ran the show in Galway, Richard – the Red Earl – had a large hall built as a seat of power. Here locals would come looking for favours or to do a little grovelling as a sign of future fealty. After the 14 tribes took over, the hall fell into ruin and was lost. Lost that is until 1997 when expansion of the city's Custom House uncovered its foundations. Now after 10 years of archaeological research, the site is open for exploration. The custom house is built on stilts overhead, leaving the old foundations open. Artefacts and a plethora of fascinating displays give a sense of Galway life some 900 years ago.

Spanish Arch & Medieval Walls — HISTORIC BUILDING

Framing the river east of Wolfe Tone Bridge, the Spanish Arch (1584) is thought to be an extension of Galway's medieval walls. The arch appears to have been designed as a passageway through which ships entered the city to unload goods, such as wine and brandy from Spain.

Today it reverberates to the beat of bongo drums, and the lawns and riverside form a gathering place for locals and visitors on any sunny day. Many watch kayakers manoeuvre over the minor rapids of the River Corrib.

Although a 1651 drawing of Galway clearly shows its extensive fortifications, depredation by Cromwell and William of Orange and subsequent centuries of neglect saw the walls almost completely disappear. Another surviving portion has been artfully incorporated into the modern shopping mall, **Eyre Square Centre** (Merchants Rd & Eyre Sq), complete with a **tarot-card reader** (☎091-556 826; ⏲by appointment) installed in the basement of a former turret.

Galway City Museum MUSEUM
(Spanish Pde; admission free; ⏲10am-5pm Apr-Oct, closed Mon Nov-Mar) Adjacent to the Spanish Arch, the Galway City Museum is in a glossy, glassy building that reflects the old walls. Exhibits trace aspects of daily life through Galway's history; especially good are the areas dealing with life – smelly and otherwise – during medieval times. Look for the photos of President John F Kennedy's 1963 visit to Galway including one with dew-eyed nuns looking on adoringly. Also check out rotating displays of works by local artists. When the roof deck is open, there are sweeping views out to the bay. The **cafe** is a delightful stop.

Collegiate Church of St Nicholas of Myra CHURCH
(Market St; admission by donation; ⏲9am-5.45pm Mon-Sat, 1-5pm Sun Apr-Sep, 10am-4pm Mon-Sat, 1-5pm Sun Oct-Mar) Crowned by a pyramidal spire, the Collegiate Church of St Nicholas of Myra is Ireland's largest medieval parish church still in use. Dating from 1320, the church has been rebuilt and enlarged over the centuries, though much of the original form has been retained.

Christopher Columbus reputedly worshipped here in 1477. One theory suggests that the story of Columbus' visit to Galway arose from tales of St Brendan's 6th-century voyage to America (see the boxed text, p424). Seafaring has long been associated with the church – St Nicholas, for whom it's named, is the patron saint of sailors.

After Cromwell's victory, the church was used as a stable, and damaged stonework is still visible today. But St Nicholas was relatively fortunate: 14 other Galway churches were razed entirely.

Parts of the church's floor are paved with gravestones from the 16th to 18th centuries; the Lynch Aisle holds the tombs of that illustrious Galway family. A large block tomb in one corner is said to be the grave of James Lynch, a mayor of Galway in the late 15th century, who condemned his son Walter to death for killing a young Spanish visitor. As the tale goes, none of the townsfolk would serve as executioner, so the mayor personally acted as hangman, after which he went into seclusion. Outside on Market St is a stone plaque on the **Lynch Memorial Window**, which relates this legend and claims to be the spot where the gallows stood.

During the day the church is usually all but empty and makes for a welcome escape from Galway's hubbub.

NAVIGATING GALWAY

Galway's compact town centre straddles Europe's shortest river, the Corrib, which connects Lough Corrib to the sea. Most shops and services congregate on the river's eastern bank, while some of the city's best music pubs and restaurants cluster to the west. From this area, known logically as the West Side, a 10-minute waterfront walk leads you out to the beginning of the seaside suburb of Salthill.

Running west from grassy Eyre Sq, the city's pedestrianised shopping mall starts as Williamsgate St, becomes William St and then Shop St, before forking into Mainguard St and High St.

Eyre Square PARK
Galway's central public square is busy in all but the harshest weather. It's a welcome open green space with sculptures and pathways. Its lawns are formally named Kennedy Park in commemoration of JFK's visit to Galway, though you'll rarely, if ever, hear locals refer to it as anything but Eyre Square.

The street running along the southwestern side of the square is pedestrianised and lined with seating, while the eastern side is taken up almost entirely by the Hotel Meyrick (formerly the Great Southern Hotel), an elegant grey limestone pile restored to its Victorian glory. Guarding the upper side of the square, **Browne's Doorway** (1627), a

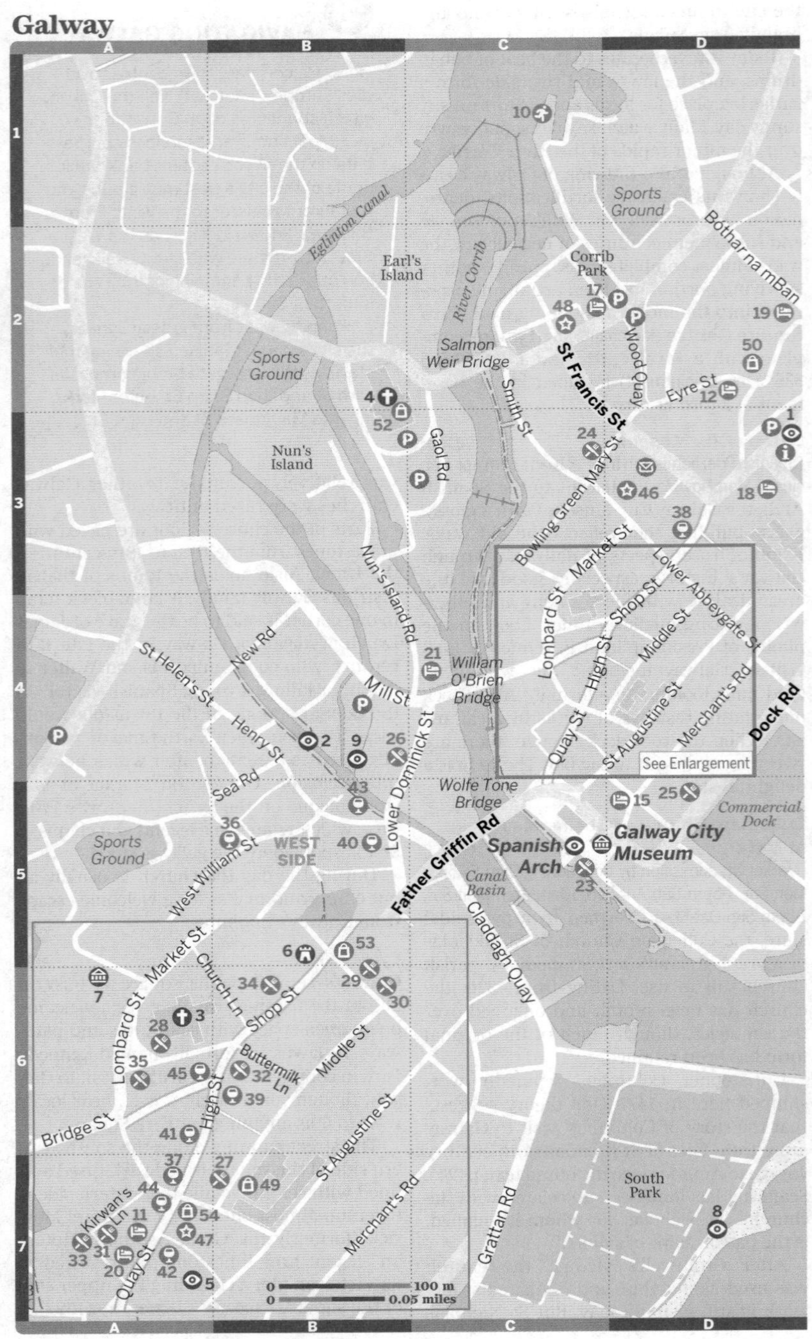

Sports Ground
Bóthar na mBan
Eglinton Canal
Earl's Island
River Corrib
Corrib Park
St Francis St
Wood Quay
Salmon Weir Bridge
Sports Ground
Smith St
Eyre St
Gaol Rd
Nun's Island
Bowling Green
Mary St
Market St
Lower Abbeygate St
Lombard St
Shop St
Middle St
High St
Nun's Island Rd
St Helen's St
New Rd
William O'Brien Bridge
Mill St
Quay St
St Augustine St
Merchant's Rd
Dock Rd
Henry St
Lower Dominick St
See Enlargement
Sea Rd
Wolfe Tone Bridge
Commercial Dock
Sports Ground
West William St
WEST SIDE
Father Griffin Rd
Spanish Arch
Galway City Museum
Canal Basin
Claddagh Quay
Market St
Church Ln
Lombard St
Shop St
Buttermilk Ln
Middle St
Bridge St
High St
St Augustine St
Kirwan's Ln
Merchant's Rd
Quay St
Grattan Rd
South Park
100 m
0.05 miles

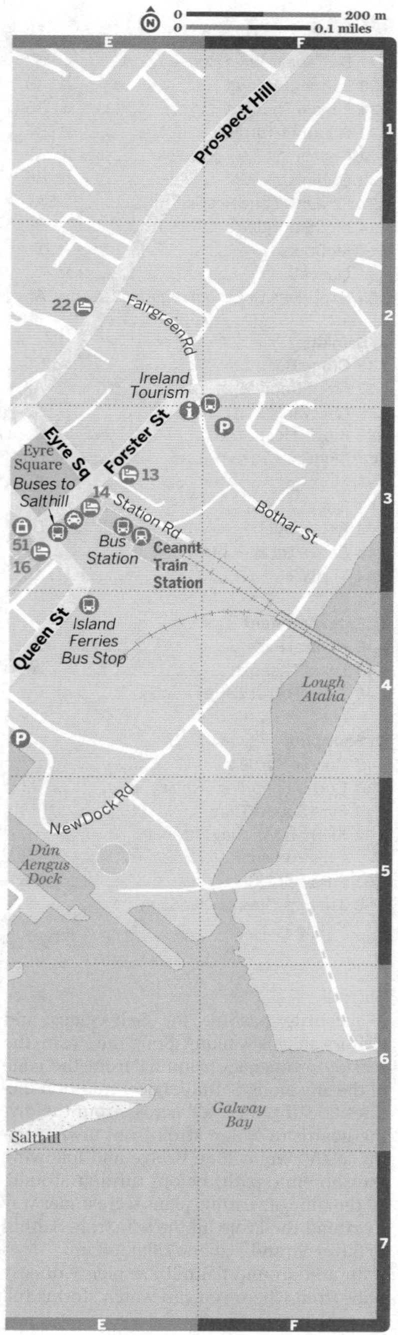

classy, if forlorn, fragment from the home of one of the city's merchant rulers, looks like the remains from a carpet-bombing raid (at least the English can't be blamed for this...).

FREE **Lynch's Castle** HISTORIC BUILDING

(cnr Shop & Upper Abbeygate Sts) Considered the finest town castle in Ireland, the old stone town house Lynch's Castle was built in the 14th century, though much of what you see today dates from around 1600. The Lynch family was the most powerful of the 14 ruling Galway 'tribes', and its members held the position of mayor no fewer than 80 times between 1480 and 1650.

Stonework on the castle's facade includes ghoulish gargoyles and the coats of arms of Henry VII, the Lynches and the Fitzgeralds of Kildare. The castle is now part of AIB Bank and modern-day bankers may wish to shelter behind the thick walls from populist rage.

Salmon Weir LANDMARK

Upstream from Salmon Weir Bridge, which crosses the River Corrib just east of Galway Cathedral, the river cascades down the great weir, one of its final descents before reaching Galway Bay. The weir controls the water levels above it, and when the salmon are running you can often see shoals of them waiting in the clear waters before rushing upriver to spawn.

The salmon and sea-trout seasons usually span February to September, but most fish pass through the weir during May and June.

Galway Cathedral CHURCH

(www.galwaycathedral.org; Gaol Rd; admission by donation; ⏲8am-6pm) Lording over the River Corrib, imposing Galway Cathedral was dedicated by the late Cardinal Richard Cushing of Boston in 1965. The cathedral's unwieldy full name is the Catholic Cathedral of Our Lady Assumed into Heaven and St Nicholas, but its high, curved arches and central dome have a simple, solid elegance even if the greater whole feels rather sterile (although a side chapel with a mosaic of the Resurrection does include a praying JFK in the tableau). The superb acoustics are best appreciated during an **organ recital** (program dates are posted on the website).

From the Spanish Arch, a riverside path runs upriver and across the Salmon Weir Bridge to the cathedral.

Galway

Top Sights
- Galway City Museum ... C5
- Spanish Arch ... C5

Sights
- 1 Browne's Doorway ... D3
- 2 Canal Locks ... B4
- 3 Collegiate Church of St Nicholas of Myra ... A6
- 4 Galway Cathedral ... B2
- 5 Hall of the Red Earl ... A7
- 6 Lynch's Castle ... B5
- 7 Nora Barnacle House ... A6
- 8 Prom ... D7
- 9 Wee Little Stone Bridge ... B4

Activities, Courses & Tours
- 10 Corrib Princess ... C1

Sleeping
- 11 Barnacle's ... A7
- 12 Eyre Square Townhouse ... D2
- 13 Galway City Hostel ... E3
- 14 Hotel Meyrick ... E3
- 15 House Hotel ... D5
- 16 Kinlay House ... E3
- 17 Salmon Weir Hostel ... C2
- 18 Skeffington Arms Hotel ... D3
- 19 Sleepzone ... D2
- 20 Spanish Arch Hotel ... A7
- 21 St Martin's B&B ... C4
- 22 Western Hotel ... E2

Eating
- 23 Ard Bia at Nimmo's ... C5
- 24 Asian Tea House ... C3
- 25 Bar No 8 ... D5
- 26 Cava ... B4
- 27 Da Tang Noodle House ... B7
- 28 Farmers Market ... A6
- 29 Food 4 Thought ... B6
- 30 Gourmet Tart Co ... B6
- 31 Goya's ... A7
- 32 Griffin's ... B6
- 33 Kirwan's Lane Restaurant ... A7
- 34 McCambridge's ... B6
- McDonagh's ... (see 20)
- Quays ... (see 42)
- 35 Sheridans Cheesemongers ... A6

Drinking
- 36 Crane Bar ... B5
- 37 Front Door ... A7
- 38 Garavan's ... D3
- 39 King's Head ... B6
- 40 Monroe's Tavern ... B5
- 41 Murphy's ... A6
- 42 Quays ... A7
- 43 Róisín Dubh ... B5
- 44 Séhán Ua Neáchtain ... A7
- 45 Tig Coílí ... A6

Entertainment
- 46 Central Park ... D3
- 47 Druid Theatre ... A7
- 48 Town Hall Theatre ... C2

Shopping
- 49 Charlie Byrne's ... B7
- 50 Corrib Shopping Centre ... D2
- 51 Eyre Square Centre ... E3
- 52 Kiernan Moloney Musical Instruments ... B3
- 53 P Powell & Sons ... B5
- 54 Thomas Dillon's Claddagh Gold ... A7

Nora Barnacle House HISTORIC BUILDING

(☎091-564 743; 8 Bowling Green; ⊙hours vary) James Joyce's future wife Nora Barnacle (1884–1951) lived here until shortly before they met in Dublin in 1904. It's now a privately owned museum displaying the couple's letters and photographs among period furniture. Looking all of its 100 years and not helped by a grim grey paint job, the house didn't have running water until the 1940s; instead the Barnacle family used a communal pump across the street. Joyce met his future mother-in-law here in 1909; for his part, Joyce's father said after learning Nora's surname: 'She'll stick with him'.

Salthill BEACH

A favourite pastime for Galwegians and visitors alike is walking along the **Prom**, the seaside promenade running from the edge of the city along Salthill. Local tradition dictates 'kicking the wall' across from the diving boards (a 2.5km stroll from town starting at the Wolfe Tone Bridge and following the shoreline path) before turning around. At the time of writing, plans were under way to extend the Prom all the way from Salthill to Silver Strand – about 7.5km all up.

In and around Salthill are plenty of cosy pubs from where you can watch storms roll over the bay.

Tours

If you're short on time, bus tours departing from Galway are a good way to see Connemara, the Burren or the Cliffs of Moher, while boat tours take you to the heart of Lough Corrib. Tours can be booked directly or at the tourist office.

TOP CHOICE Burren Wild Tours NATURE TOUR
(☎087 877 9565; www.burrenwalks.com; adult/student €25/22; ⏲10am) Seasonal bus tours to the Burren and the Cliffs of Moher incorporating an easy 90-minute guided mountain walk. Tours depart from the Coach Station on Bothar St.

Conamara Gaelic Culture Tour CULTURAL TOUR
(☎091-566 566; www.galwaytourcompany.com; 3hr tour €30; ⏲Mar-Oct) Visit tiny farmhouses and learn about Connemara's rich traditions of singing, dancing, storytelling, booze-making and more.

Corrib Princess BOAT TOUR
(☎091-592 447; www.corribprincess.ie; Woodquay; adult/child €15/7; ⏲May-Sep) Two to three 1½-hour cruises on the River Corrib and Lough Corrib per day, departing from Woodquay, just beyond Salmon Weir Bridge.

Lally Tours BUS & WALKING TOUR
(☎091-562 905; www.lallytours.com) Entertaining, informative **bus tours** (adult/child €25/20) of Connemara, or the Burren and the Cliffs of Moher with local guides. Tours depart from the Coach Station on Bothar St; book online for discounts. Two-hour **walking tours** (adult/child €10/8) of Galway depart from the Galway City Museum at 10am.

O'Neachtain Tours BUS TOUR
(☎091-553 188; www.ontours.biz; adult/child from €20/10; ⏲10am) Runs coach tours of Connemara, or the Burren and the Cliffs of Moher. Tours depart from the Coach Station on Bothar St.

Sleeping

You'll find B&Bs lining the major approach roads as well as Salthill, but to take full advantage of Galway's tightly packed attractions, try for a room in the city centre. If you're planning an extended stay, the free *Galway Advertiser* (www.galwayadvertiser.ie) lists rental properties, or try www.daft.ie.

Galway's festivals (boxed text, p395) and easy striking distance from Dublin make it *hugely* popular year-round, especially at weekends. Accommodation often fills far in advance – book ahead!

CITY CENTRE

TOP CHOICE House Hotel HOTEL €€€
(☎091-538 900; www.thehousehotel.ie; Spanish Pde; r €100-200; P 📶) It's a design odyssey at this boutique hotel. Public spaces contrast modern art with trad details and bold accents. The 40 rooms are plush, with beds having elaborately padded headboards (so you don't bonk your, er, well...) and a range of colour schemes. Bathrooms are commodious and ooze comfort.

TOP CHOICE Kinlay House HOSTEL €
(☎091-565 244; www.kinlayhouse.ie; Merchant's Rd; dm €16-30, d €54-70; @ 📶) Easygoing staff, a full range of facilities and a cream-in-the-doughnut location just off Eyre Sq make this a top choice. Spanning two huge, brightly lit floors, Kinlay House belies the dirty powder-blue exterior. Amenities include two self-catering kitchens and two cosy TV lounges. Some rooms have bay views.

TOP CHOICE St Martins B&B B&B €€
(☎091-568 286; 2 Nun's Island Rd; s/d from €50/80; @ 📶) This beautifully kept, renovated older house right on the canal has a flower-filled garden overlooking the William O'Brien Bridge and the River Corrib. The four rooms have all the comforts and the breakfast is a few cuts above the norm (fresh-squeezed OJ!). Owner Mary Sexton wins raves.

GALWAY HOOKERS

Obvious jokes aside, Galway hookers are the iconic small sailing boats that were the basis of local seafaring during the 19th century and part of the 20th century. Small, tough and highly manoeuvrable, these wooden boats are undergoing a resurgence thanks to weekend sailors and hobbyists. The hulls are jet black, due to the pitch used for waterproofing, while the sails flying from the single mast are a distinctive rust colour. Expect to see them all along the Galway coast.

Skeffington Arms Hotel HOTEL €€
(☎091-563 173; www.skeffington.ie; Eyre Sq; r €65-160; @📶) Rooms at the Skeff, overlooking Eyre Sq, eschew the frilly cliché. In fact the only lace you may find in any of the 24 rooms is on your underwear. Pass through the arched traditional entrance into a minimalist haven. Air-con allows early risers to cut out noise from the frolicsome masses roaming the streets on long summer nights.

Salmon Weir Hostel HOSTEL €
(☎091-561 133; www.salmonweirhostel.com; 3 St Vincent's Ave; dm €14-20, d €44-50; @📶) Galway's hippie vibe finds its spiritual home in the Salmon Weir's guitar-strewn lounge room, where informal jam sessions take place most nights. The hostel has a share-house feel, including shared bathrooms for all rooms. There's no breakfast, although coffee and tea are free. The train and bus stations are a five-minute walk.

Galway City Hostel HOSTEL €
(☎091-566 959; www.galwaycityhostel.com; Eyre Sq; dm €12-29, d €40-80; @📶) This cheery spot directly across from the train station is so close you may just wander over barefoot. On balmy days (by Galway standards) you can take your breakfast cereal out onto the balcony. The in-house bar has cheap booze, and reception is open 24/7.

Hotel Meyrick HOTEL €€€
(☎091-564 041; www.hotelmeyrick.ie; Eyre Sq; r €100-250; P@) Known as the Railway Hotel when it opened in 1852, and later as the Great Southern Hotel, this stately showpiece looms large over Eyre Sq. Trad decor is artfully combined with savvy modern touches in its current incarnation. Note the zebra prints on the lobby chairs. Definitely not original equipment: the rooftop hot tub. All 97 guest rooms include bathtubs and high-speed internet.

Eyre Square Townhouse INN €€
(☎091-568 444; www.eyresquaretownhouse.com; 35 Eyre St; r €65-120; 📶) The 11 rooms aren't large but neither is the price at this modest yet well-run inn just off Eyre Sq. Everything has an Ikea feel, which combined with the modern bathrooms makes for a nice stay. The front desk is not continuously staffed.

Spanish Arch Hotel HOTEL €€
(☎091-569 600; www.spanisharchhotel.ie; Quay St; r €60-170; P@) In a sensational spot on the main drag, this 20-room boutique hotel is housed in a 16th-century former Carmelite convent. Its solid-timber bar has a great line-up of live music, so the rooms at the back, while smaller, are best for a quiet night's sleep. Rooms have a coffee-bar palette of creams and browns.

Western Hotel HOTEL €€
(☎091-562 834; www.thewestern.ie; 33 Prospect Hill; r €50-140; P@📶) Three Georgian buildings have been wedded at this central spot just east of Eyre Sq. The 38 rooms are large, modern and comfortable and there's parking in the basement. Good-sized desks await the work-encumbered. The full-on breakfasts are above the always-filling average.

Barnacle's HOSTEL €
(☎091-568 644; www.barnacles.ie; 10 Quay St; dm €10-30, d €47-70; @📶) Very central, this well-run hostel is housed in a medieval building with a modern extension. The kitchen is spacious and there's a warm common room with a big gas fireplace and Playstation (!). Breakfast includes scones and soda bread.

Sleepzone HOSTEL €
(☎091-566 999; www.sleepzone.ie; Bóthar na mBan; dm €15-32, s/d €50/80; @📶) Big (over 200 beds), busy backpacker base has plenty of services, including a pool table and BBQ terrace. Reception is open 24/7.

NEAR THE CENTRE

Among the strips of B&Bs near the centre, College Rd stands out for sheer volume: dozens of choices line the road. You can reach the action after a 10-minute walk along Lough Atalia.

TOP CHOICE **Four Seasons B&B** B&B €€
(☎091-564 078; www.fourseasonsgalway.com; 23 College Rd; s/d from €50/80; P📶) 'If the Ritz is full there's always the Four Seasons.' Of course, this Four Seasons only has seven rooms and the nightly rates will leave you with enough loot for many a pint. One of the best choices on this strip, the Fitzgeralds offer up a large breakfast menu and simple, tidy rooms.

Griffin Lodge B&B €€
(☎091-589 440; www.irishholidays.com/griffin.shtml; 3 Father Griffin Pl; s €45-60, d €55-90; P@) You'll be welcomed like a long-lost friend at this well-kept B&B, which is 500m west of the Spanish Arch. It has eight immaculate rooms in soothing shades of spearmint and moss green.

Dun Aoibhinn Guest House INN €€
(☎091-583 129; www.dunaoibhinnhouse.com; 12 St Mary's Rd; r €45-100; P@⑦) Pronounced doon-*ay*-ven, this restored town house with original leadlight windows and floorboards is less than five minutes' stroll north of West Side's music pubs. Small antique-filled rooms come with flat-screen satellite TVs, laptop safes and fridges, which are filled with the fixings for making your own continental breakfast.

Ballyloughane Caravan & Camping Park CAMPGROUND €
(☎091-755 338; galwcamp@iol.ie; Ballyloughane Beach, Renmore; campsites from €15; ⊙Jun-Aug) This family-run camping ground is clean and secure, and its beachside location affords sweeping views across the bay. It's off the old Dublin Rd (R338), 5km east of the centre.

SALTHILL

St Judes B&B B&B €€
(☎091-521 619; www.st-judes.com; 110 Lower Salthill; r €50-120; P⑦) You may want to hire a butler to accompany you when you stay at this 1920s stone manor house that has the airs of a stately Wayne Manor. The six rooms are much more accommodation for the masses, however. Furnishings are comfy and very, very white. It's located in Salthill, a lovely 20-minute stroll (follow the Prom) from Galway.

Eating

Seafood is Galway's speciality, be it fish and chips, ocean-fresh chowder or salmon cooked to perfection. Galway Bay oysters star on many menus. The city's smorgasbord of eating and drinking options ranges from the market - where farmers in wellington boots unload soil-covered vegetables - to adventurous new restaurants redefining Irish cuisine.

Pedestrianised Quay St is lined with restaurants aimed at the tourist throngs. As one local told us, 'I can remember when all you'd get on Quay St was a hard biscuit, then you'd get run down by a bus.'

Galway's **farmers market** (⊙8am-4pm Sat) fills the streets around St Nicholas Church. It's the region's best and is the place to see the many briny, earthy and dairy delights of the county.

A PERFECT WALK

A fine footpath runs northwest along the Eglington Canal from the Lower Dominick St Bridge. Passing behind several of Galway's better pubs (nod to the smokers who have ducked out back), the path makes a gentle climb. Look to your right for the spot where two creeks enter the canal, a larger one and a very tiny one. Over the small one is a wee little stone bridge that could be the artefact of some leprechaun fantasy or a leftover from a John Ford film. With the water burbling in all directions – and cascading through the canal locks just upstream – it's a spot where the sounds of Galway are literally washed away, leaving you to your own contemplation.

TOP CHOICE **Cava** SPANISH €€
(www.cavarestaurant.ie; 51 Lower Dominick St; meals €10-25; ⊙noon-10pm, later Fri & Sat) The best tapas in Ireland? Possibly yes. Now that no one can afford a trip to Iberia the next best thing is a meal at this superb West Side storefront. From typical fare like roasted potatoes with aioli to more fanciful dishes such as free-range quail with dried figs, the kitchen's efforts never fail to astound.

TOP CHOICE **Griffin's** CAFE, BAKERY €
(www.griffinsbakery.com; Shop St; meals €5-12; ⊙8am-6pm Mon-Sat) A local institution which, although it's been run by the Griffin family since 1876, remains as fresh as a bun hot out of the oven. The small bakery counter is laden with sweet and savoury treats. But the real pleasure lies upstairs in the cafe rooms where you can have fine coffee, tea and choose from sandwiches, hot specials, luscious desserts and much more.

TOP CHOICE **Sheridans Cheesemongers** DELI €€
(14 Churchyard St; ⊙9.30am-6pm Mon-Fri, 9am-6pm Sat) Sheridans Cheesemongers is redolent of the superb local and international cheeses and other deli items within, many with a Med bent. Its real secret, however, is up a narrow flight of stairs. Sample from a huge wine list in an airy and woodsy room while enjoying many of the best items from below (open 2pm to 10pm Tuesday to Friday, noon to 8pm Saturday).

Ard Bia at Nimmo's IRISH €€
(www.ardbia.com; Spanish Arch; cafe dishes €6-12, lunch mains €10-14, dinner mains €16-30; ⏲cafe noon-3pm Wed-Sun, restaurant 6.30-10.30pm Wed-Sat) In Irish, Ard Bia means 'High Food', and that's somewhat apt, given its location in the 18th-century customs house near the Spanish Arch. Local seafood and organic produce feature on the seasonal menu in a setting that defines funky chic. The cafe is a perfect place for a coffee and carrot cake.

McDonagh's SEAFOOD €€
(22 Quay St; fish & chips from €8, restaurant mains €15-25; ⏲cafe & takeaway counter noon-midnight Mon-Sat, 5-11pm Sun, restaurant 5-10pm Mon-Sat) A trip to Galway isn't complete without stopping at McDonagh's. Divided into two parts, with a takeaway counter and a cafe with long communal wooden tables on one side, and a more upmarket restaurant on the other, Galway's best chippy churns out battered cod, plaice, haddock, whiting and salmon nonstop, all accompanied by home-made tartare sauce.

Da Tang Noodle House CHINESE €
(www.datangnoodlehouse.com; 2 Middle St; mains €6-16; ⏲noon-10pm) The cure for every greasy, gloopy sweet & sour yuck you've endured is here at this tidy little noodle house: brilliant fresh fare bursting with flavour. Noodles are the start for soups, stir-fries, sizzling dishes and more. All are made to order and you can get dinner delivered to your hotel room.

Bar No 8 PUB €€
(3 Dock Rd; mains €12-20; ⏲11am-11pm) Bentwood chairs and overstuffed sofas provide comfort in this at once funky and stylish bar overlooking the harbour. Art by patrons is on display. The emphasis on creative pub food places this firmly in the eating category. The fish in the fish and chips is even battered with local Hooker beer.

Kirwan's Lane Restaurant IRISH €€€
(☎091-568 266; Kirwan's Lane; lunch mains €10-18, dinner mains €18-30; ⏲noon-2pm & 6-10pm) Happily hidden on a tiny square within steps of several busy streets, Kirwan's is not only a refuge but also a heaven for those seeking out the best of local cuisine. The menu proudly lists the provenance of the ingredients used in a variety of creative dishes. On sunny days, get a patio table at lunch.

Quays IRISH €€
(Quay St; mains €12-25; ⏲11am-10pm) This sprawling pub does a roaring business downstairs in its restaurant, which has hearty carvery lunches and more ambitious mains at night. The cold seafood platter is simply a symphony of the bounty from Galway Bay. Students on dates and out celebrating get rowdier as the pints and hours pass.

Asian Tea House ASIAN €€
(15 Mary St; mains €15-25; ⏲5-10pm Wed-Mon) This upscale Asian restaurant reflects the owner's years of Eastern travels. Beautiful glazed green tiles set the mood for dishes that range from Malaysia to Vietnam to China. We like the Malaysian sambal chicken,

ADVICE FROM A WRITER

Author Charlie Adley has chronicled Galway life in newspaper columns and much more. An unabashed fan of the place, Adley's heart still had to be won over originally. He came to Galway almost 20 years ago after a life in London, San Francisco and elsewhere. He hasn't looked back.

'The city centre is the perfect size for walking around, chilling out and bumping into people', he says from one of his favourite pubs, Séhán Ua Neáchtain's, where he often has his afternoon office, watching the world go by while a movable feast of friends comes and goes.

Later, after the pub? 'Who knows – Galwegians don't make plans. The perfect Galway day is one that takes its own shape.'

Adley's own perfect day includes 'sitting on a rock on the beach at Salthill; watching the tide turn; looking out at the ocean and trying to spot one of the Aran Islands; just being calm; and appreciating the volatile light and weather, which truly offer a different view across to County Clare every day of the year'.

Visitors looking for the real Galway, he says, need to do the above, plus 'do the pubs and music and you can't go wrong. Galwegians will reach out to you and have a chat; the craic awaits'.

which scores the highest on the hot meter – a rare treat in tongue-sensitive Ireland. Tea choices abound.

Goya's CAFE, DELI €
(www.goyas.ie; 2 Kirwan's Lane; dishes €5-10; ⏲9.30am-6pm Mon-Sat) Cupcake love! Cakes in all sizes are supreme at Goya's, a Galway treasure hidden on a small square. Its cool pale-blue decor, Segafredo coffee and sweet treats make it a perfect spot to take some time out. The deli does a booming lunch trade; enjoy a sandwich at a table outside. The desserts may cause spontaneous eruptions of overloud 'ooohs!'

Food 4 Thought VEGETARIAN €
(Lower Abbeygate St; mains €5-8; ⏲8am-6pm Mon-Sat, 11.30am-4pm Sun;) Besides providing organic and vegetarian sandwiches, savoury scones, and wholesome dishes such as cashew-nut roast, this New Age-y place is great for finding out about energy workshops and yoga classes around town.

McCambridge's DELI, GROCERY €
(www.mccambridges.com; 38/39 Shop St; meals €5-10; ⏲9am-6pm Mon-Sat) This long-running food hall has a superb selection of prepared salads, hot foods and other more exotic treats. Create the perfect picnic or enjoy your selections at the sidewalk tables out front.

Gourmet Tart Co DELI, BAKERY €
(Lower Abbeygate St; mains €5-10; ⏲10am-5pm Mon-Sat) Food porn is an apt description for the stunning array of dishes on offer here in both the deli case and at the bounteous buffet bar. Luscious salads, salmon, beautiful sandwiches and, yes, tarts that give pastry a good name. It's all take out; enjoy your lunch on the grass by the Spanish Arch.

Drinking

Galway's pub selection is second to none, which is why in summer and on weekends they all seem to be thronged. On Saturday nights, the town fills with partiers from the hinterlands, including mad parties of women shedding decades of inhibitions on hen nights. The website **Galway City Pub Guide** (www.galwaycitypubguide.com) is a good resource for this heaving scene.

Most of Galway's pubs have live music at least a couple of nights a week, whether in an informal session or as a headline act. Some swing to tunes every night and you will never be far from a trad session.

TOP CHOICE **Tig Cóilí** PUB
(Mainguard St) Two live *céilidh* (traditional music and dancing sessions) a day draw the crowds to this authentic fire-engine-red pub, just off High St. It's where musicians go to get drunk or drunks go to become musicians…or something like that. A gem.

Séhán Ua Neáchtain PUB
(17 Upper Cross St) Painted a bright cornflower blue, this 19th-century pub, known simply as Neáchtain's (*nock*-tans) or Naughtons, has a wraparound string of tables outside, many shaded by a large tree. It's a place where a polyglot mix of locals plop down and let the world pass them by – or stop and join them for a pint.

Crane Bar PUB
(2 Sea Rd) An atmospheric old pub west of the Corrib, the Crane is the best spot in Galway to catch an informal *céilidh* most nights. Talented bands play its rowdy, good-natured upstairs bar; downstairs at times it seems right out of *The Far Side*.

Róisín Dubh PUB
(www.roisindubh.net; Upper Dominick St) From the rooftop terrace you can see sweeping views of Galway; inside emerging acts play here before they hit the big time. It's *the* place to hear bands.

Murphy's PUB
(9 High St) A complete anomaly among the partying throngs in the centre, Murphy's is a timeless haven where locals still explore the limits of the art of conversation. The sign on the door says it all: 'No hen parties'.

Monroe's Tavern PUB
(Upper Dominick St) Often photographed for its classic, world-weary facade, Monroe's delivers traditional music and ballads, plus it remains the only pub in the city with regular Irish dancing. A pizza joint buried within turns out good pies.

Front Door PUB
(☎091-563 757; High St) Heated balconies and cosy timber booths make this a popular spot for a pint, especially among local women on the 'lap circuit' checking out the male talent.

Garavan's PUB
(☎091-562 537; 46 William St) A genteel old boozer in the city centre that is a place of refuge for those in search of a pint *and* a seat on a busy Saturday night.

HOPPY SALVATION

Irish pubs may be atmospheric places to enjoy a pint and, indeed, many folks fly thousands of miles to sit in a little nook happily quaffing a properly poured creamy Guinness. But once past the stout, things go flat in a hurry. In pub after pub the non-Guinness choices amount to a sad array of bland lagers. What did the Irish ever do to America besides send it some of their finest citizens? In return America has sent the Irish Budweiser, Miller Genuine Draft (MGD) and, horror of horrors, Coors Light. The Dutch haven't done much better by the Emerald Isle, exporting untold hectolitres of Heineken, a beer that inspired a Dutch friend to ask us, 'why do you drink our old man's beer?'

But if the beer situation in much of the country is bleak (whatever happened to Harp?), in Galway there's an alternative to the lame lagers: Hooker. Named for the iconic local fishing boats, this fine, hoppy Irish Pale Ale has won plaudits and, more importantly, a local following.

You can get a Hooker at many Galway pubs including Róisín Dubh, Bar No 8, Tig Cóilí and Monroe's Tavern.

Quays PUB
(☎091-568 347; Quay St) Enormous tavern with endless timber-panelled rooms and passageways, and great vantage points from which to watch live music (ranging from traditional to pop) most nights. Good sidewalk tables.

King's Head PUB
(15 High St) This vast, ancient pub is often too crowded for its own good so come mid-afternoon when you can appreciate preserved details that date back to the 14th century.

☆ Entertainment

Most pubs in Galway have live music at least a couple of nights a week. Róisín Dubh is the best place for bands; Tig Cóilí excels at trad sessions.

Clubs generally get cranking around 11pm and wind down around 2am. Admission prices vary according to the nightly program.

A new film centre may open near the Galway City Museum after construction issues are resolved.

TOP CHOICE **Druid Theatre** THEATRE
(☎091-568 617; www.druidtheatre.com; Chapel Lane) This renowned, long-established and award-winning theatre is famed for staging experimental works by young Irish playwrights, as well as new adaptations of classics. Its home is in one of the oldest parts of Galway, in an old tea warehouse, which was renovated in 2009.

Town Hall Theatre THEATRE
(☎091-569 777; www.tht.ie; Courthouse Sq) The Town Hall Theatre features Broadway and West End shows, and visiting singers.

Central Park NIGHTCLUB
(www.centralparkclub.com; 36 Upper Abbeygate St; cover €6-10; ⏰from 11pm Fri & Sat) With seven bars and a capacity of 1000 people, CPs is a Galway clubbing institution.

Trad on the Prom MUSICAL
(☎001-582 860; www.tradontheprom.com; Salthill Hotel; adult/child from €30/10; ⏰May-Sep) A real show-stopper, this long-running summer musical is a festival of Irish dancing and singing. It's led by Máirín Fahy, a local diva of the fiddle. The glossy production is performed several nights per week in a new venue right on the Salthill promenade. Note that actual ticket prices are carefully camouflaged on the website.

Shopping

Galway has an array of speciality shops dotting its narrow streets, stocking cutting-edge fashion, Irish woollens, outdoor clothing and equipment, local jewellery, books, art and, of course, music. Galway's market is not just about artisan foods. Artists of all sorts plus buskers, bakers and all-around schlock pedlars make it a festive event. At times stalls appear here on days other than Saturday.

Besides the good street shopping, shopping centres include the Eyre Square Centre, with a large Dunne's supermarket, and

Corrib Shopping Centre, a flashy modern place with huge department stores.

TOP CHOICE **Charlie Byrne's** BOOKSTORE
(www.charliebyrne.com; Cornstore, Middle St) A civic treasure with a brilliant collection of new, secondhand and discounted books (many €1) in a succession of rambling rooms. Staff can ferret out that obscure Aran Islands title you were seeking.

P Powell & Sons MUSIC STORE
(powellsmusicshop@eircom.net; William St) You can pick up tin whistles, bodhráns and other instruments here, as well as sheet music. Backpackers note: they stock bongos.

Kiernan Moloney Musical Instruments MUSIC STORE
(www.moloneymusic.com; Old Malt Centre, High St) Fiddles abound at this dealer in fine instruments. If your harp has come unglued, they'll fix it.

Information

Internet Access

A plethora of internet cafes around town charge around €5 per hour. Places open up and close down quickly, but you'll have no problems finding somewhere to log on.

Square Eyes (☎091-500 688; Forster St; ⊙9am-11pm) Internet access upstairs, *Call of Duty* gamer grunts downstairs.

Laundry

Olde Malt Laundrette (☎091-564 990; High St; drop-off service per load €10; ⊙8.30am-6pm Mon-Sat)

Left Luggage

The transport stations are locker free, but there is a central refuge for your bags while you hunt for a room.

Cara Cabs (☎091-563 939; 17 Eyre Sq; ⊙24hr) Taxi office stores bags for €5 per day.

Money

ATMs abound in the city centre.

Post Office

Post office (⊙9am-5.30pm Mon-Sat)

Tourist Information

Ireland Tourism (www.discoverireland.ie; Forster St; ⊙9am-5.45pm daily Easter-Sep, 9am-5.45pm Mon-Sat Oct-Easter) Large, efficient regional information centre that can help arrange local accommodation, and bus tours and ferry trips.

FESTIVALS OF FUN

Galway's packed calendar of festivals turns the city and surrounding communities into what feels like one nonstop party – streets overflow with revellers, and pubs and restaurants often extend their opening hours.

Highlights include:

Cúirt International Festival of Literature (www.galwayartscentre.ie/cuirt) Top-name authors converge on Galway in April for one of Ireland's premier literary festivals, featuring poetry slams, theatrical performances and readings.

Galway Arts Festival (www.galwayartsfestival.ie) A two-week extravaganza of theatre, music, art and comedy in mid-July.

Galway Film Fleadh (www.galwayfilmfleadh.com) One of Ireland's biggest film festivals, held in July around the same time as the arts festival.

Galway Race Week (www.galwayraces.com) Horse races in Ballybrit, 3km east of the city, are the centrepiece of Galway's biggest, most boisterous festival of all. Thursday is a real knees-up: by night the swells have muddy knees on their tuxes and are missing random high heels. The week occurs in late July or early August.

Galway International Oyster Festival (www.galwayoysterfest.com) Oysters are washed down with plenty of pints in the last week in September.

Other regional events of note include:

» Galway hooker boat races, p422

» Yet more oyster festivals, p421

» Bodhrán (hand-held goatskin drum) workshops, p407

» The Aran Islands' rollicking *Father Ted* festival, Tedfest, p404

Galway's Festivals

Galway knows how to party. Major events in its annual calendar draw thousands from across the country, and even the world. Celebrations of culture, food and sport give reasons to visit year-round (p395).

In spring, authors and writers from around the world gather for the Cúirt International Festival of Literature. If this university town already seems literary, wait until you hear readings of prose, verse and poetry streaming out of almost every pub.

As the air warms in summer, the cultural scene heats up for the Galway Arts Festival. The city enjoys performances and exhibits by top drama groups, musicians and bands, comedians, artists and much more. The Galway Film Fleadh, held concurrently, sets screens alight with new and edgy works.

One of the great knees ups, Galway Race Week, draws tens of thousands of punters for a weekend of partying that's a real race to the finish. Whether wearing fine silks, formal wear or casual gear, the race almost seems secondary to the frolic – unless you have wagers, that is.

One of the great joys of autumn is the Galway International Oyster Festival. The oysters are nurtured throughout the year in the shallow tidal waters of Galway Bay. Good for much of the year, the tasty bivalves seem to reach their peak as the days grow short. At celebrations big and small, oysters star across the region.

1

3

Clockwise from top left
1. Galway races finery 2. Horses on the track, Galway races 3. Busy street during the Galway Arts Festival

2
ROAD RUNNER 
CHICKEN BURGERS
HOT & COLD DRINKS
CURRY CHIPS
CHEESE BURGERS
FISH,
HOT - DOGS
BACON ROLLS
BREAKFAST ROLLS

CLADDAGH RINGS

The fishing village of Claddagh once had its own king as well as its own customs and traditions. Now subsumed into the Galway city centre, virtually all remnants of the original village are gone, but Claddagh rings survive as both a timeless reminder and a timeless source of profits.

Popular with people of real or imagined Irish descent everywhere, the rings depict a heart (symbolising love) between two outstretched hands (friendship), topped by a crown (loyalty). Rings are handcrafted at jewellers around Galway, and start from about €20 for a silver band to well over €1000 for a diamond-set blinged-up version worthy of Tony O'Soprano.

Jewellers include Ireland's oldest jewellery shop, **Thomas Dillon's Claddagh Gold** (www.claddaghring.ie; 1 Quay St), which was established in 1750. It has some vintage examples in its small back-room 'museum'.

Tourist information booth (Eyre Sq; ⏲1.30-5.30pm Sat, 9am-12.30pm Sun Oct-Easter, 9am-5.30pm daily Easter-Sep) Dispenses free city maps and local info.

Getting There & Away

Air

Service at tiny **Galway Airport** (GWY; www.galwayairport.com; Carnmore) is limited to **Aer Arran** (www.aerarran.com), which serves Dublin, London Luton, Edinburgh and Manchester.

The closest major airport is **Shannon Airport** (SNN; www.shannonairport.com), served by domestic and international carriers.

Bus

Bus Éireann (www.buseireann.ie) has services to all major cities in the Republic and the North from the **bus station** (☎091-562 000) just off Eyre Sq, near the train station. The one-way fare to Dublin (three to 3¾ hours, hourly) is €15. Other services fan out across the region, including buses to County Clare and Sligo.

Several private bus companies are based at the glossy **coach station** (Bothar St), which is located near the tourist office. They include the following:

Citylink (www.citylink.ie) Offers services to Dublin (2½ to 3¼ hours, hourly), Dublin Airport, Cork, Limerick and Connemara. Departures are frequent and fares are as low as €10.

gobus.ie (www.gobus.ie) Frequent service to Dublin (2½ hours) and Dublin Airport (three hours). Buses have wi-fi.

Train

From the **train station** (☎091-564 222; www.irishrail.ie), just off Eyre Sq, there are up to eight fast, comfortable trains daily to/from Dublin's Heuston Station (one-way from €25, 2¾ hours). Connections with other train routes can be made at Athlone (one hour). The new line to Ennis is open (€12, 75 minutes, six daily).

Getting Around

You'll see pedicab/rickshaws hauling people deep in their cups about the centre on weekend nights. Fares typically are about €5. However, you'll want to give your driver much more if you go for a madcap ride through the pedestrian district. From the **launch point** (William & Ellington Sts), gravity propels the pedicab at breakneck speeds down to Quay St while fellow drunks dive out of the way.

To/From the Airports

Bus service between Galway Airport and Galway is comically useless, with just one bus a day (€3, 15 minutes). A taxi to/from the airport costs about €20, and can be ordered from a bank of free phones at the airport. Some B&Bs and hotels can arrange pick-up.

Bus Éireann (www.buseireann.ie) operates daily services from Shannon Airport to Galway (€15, 1¾ hours, hourly). Citylink and gobus.ie serve Dublin Airport.

Bicycle

Europa Bicycles (☎091-588 830; Hunter's Bldg; ⏲9.30am-6pm Mon-Fri) Hires bikes for €8 to €15 for 24 hours. It's on Earl's Island, opposite Galway Cathedral.

West Ireland Cycling (☎091-588 830; westirelandcycling.com; 11 Upper Dominick St; ⏲9am-6pm Mon-Sat) Rents bikes (from €15 per day) and accessories like child trailers. Also organises bike tours throughout the region.

Bus

You can walk to almost everything in Galway, including out to Salthill, but you'll also find frequent buses departing from Eyre Sq. For Salthill, take bus 1D/1K (€1.60, 15 minutes).

Car

Parking throughout Galway's streets is metered. There are several multistorey and pay-and-display car parks around town.

Galway's unprecedented growth and the resulting lack of infrastructure serving its urban sprawl mean that traffic in and out of the city centre can bank up alarmingly. For a stress-free holiday, leave the roads to commuters at peak hours if possible.

Taxi

Taxi ranks are located on Eyre Sq, on Bridge St and next to the bus-train station. Or try **Abbey Cabs** (☎091-569 469) or **Cara Cabs** (☎091-563 939; 17 Eyre Sq; ⏰24hr).

ARAN ISLANDS

Easily visible from large swaths of coastal Galway and Clare Counties, the Aran Islands sing their own siren song to thousands of travellers each year who find their desolate beauty beguiling. Day-trippers shuttle through in a daze of rocky magnificence, while those who stay longer find places that, in many ways, seem further removed from the Irish mainland than a 40-minute ferry ride or 10-minute flight. Hardy travellers find that low season showcases the islands at their wild, windswept best.

An extension of the limestone escarpment that forms the Burren in Clare, the islands have shallow topsoil scattered with wildflowers, grass for grazing and jagged cliffs pounded by surf. Ancient forts such as Dún Aengus on Inishmór and Dún Chonchúir on Inishmaan are some of the oldest archaeological remains in Ireland.

A web of stone walls (1600km in all) runs across all three islands. They also have a smattering of early *clocháns* (drystone beehive huts from the early Christian period), resembling stone igloos.

Although quite close in appearance as well as proximity, the three Arans have distinct personalities:

Inishmór (Árainn in Irish, meaning 'Big Island') The largest Aran and the most easily accessible from Galway. It is home to one of Ireland's most important and impressive archaeological sites, as well as some lively pubs and restaurants, particularly in the only town, Kilronan. Gets over a thousand or more day-trippers in summer.

Inishmaan (Inis Meáin, 'Middle Island') Often bypassed by the majority of tourist traffic, preserving its age-old traditions and evoking a sense of timelessness. It is a place of great solitude with isolated B&Bs and stark rocky vistas.

Inisheer (Inis Oírr, 'Eastern Island') The smallest island is easily reached from Galway year-round and from Doolin in the summer months. It offers a good combination of ancient sites, interesting walks, trad culture and a bit of life at night.

History

Little is known about the people who built the massive Iron Age stone structures on Inishmór and Inishmaan. Commonly referred to as 'forts', they are believed to have served as pagan religious centres. Folklore holds that they were built by the Firbolgs, a people who invaded Ireland from Europe in prehistoric times.

It is thought that people came to the islands to farm, a major challenge given the rocky terrain. Early islanders augmented their soil by hauling seaweed and sand up from the shore. People also fished the surrounding waters on long *currachs* (rowing boats made of a framework of laths covered with tarred canvas), which remain a symbol of the Aran Islands.

Christianity reached the islands remarkably early, and some of the oldest monastic settlements were founded by St Enda (Éanna) in the 5th century. Enda appears to have been an Irish chief who converted to Christianity and spent some time studying in Rome before seeking out a suitably remote spot for his monastery.

From the 14th century, control of the islands was disputed by two Gaelic families, the O'Briens and the O'Flahertys. The English took over during the reign of Elizabeth I, and in Cromwell's times a garrison was stationed here.

As Galway's importance waned, so did that of the islands, and their isolation meant islanders maintained a traditional lifestyle well into the 20th century. Up to the 1930s, people wore traditional Aran dress: bright red skirts and black shawls for women, baggy woollen trousers and waistcoats with *crios* (colourful belts) for men. The classic heavy cream-coloured Aran sweater, featuring complex patterns, originated and is still hand-knitted on the islands.

Until the last few decades, the islands were, if not centuries from civilisation, then at least a perilous all-day journey in unpredictable seas. Air services began in 1970, changing island life forever, and today fast ferries make a quick (if sometimes still rough) crossing.

ISLAND-HOPPING THE ARANS

It's possible to bounce between the three Aran Islands, allowing you to start at one and return to the mainland from another. However, schedules are geared to return trips to a single island. In order to find ferries between the islands, you'll need to consult with Island Ferries as well as the boats operating from Doolin. There will be at least one connection a day between any two islands, just be prepared for ad hoc schedules. Fares should run €5 to €10.

All three islands now have secondary schools, but as recently as a decade ago, students on the two smaller islands had to move to boarding school in Galway to complete their education, which involved an abrupt switch from speaking Irish to English. Farming has all but died out on the islands and tourism is now the primary source of income; while Irish remains the local tongue, most locals speak English with visitors and converse with each other in Irish.

Information

Although high summer brings throngs of tourists, services on the islands are few. Only Inishmór has a year-round tourist office as well as the only ATM; the majority of places don't accept credit cards (always check ahead). Restaurants, including pubs that serve food, often reduce their opening hours or shut completely during low season.

There are a number of books about the islands, most no more than pretty pictures and florid text. However, the locally published *Guide to the Aran Islands* by Dara O Conaola is a great resource. The official website (www.irelandsislands.com) covers the islands.

Getting There & Away

AIR

All three islands have landing strips. The mainland departure point is Connemara regional airport at Minna, near Inverin (Indreabhán), about 35km west of Galway. **Aer Arann Islands** (☎091-593 034; www.aerarannislands.ie) offers return flights to each of the islands several times daily (hourly in summer) for adult/child/student €45/25/37; the flights take about 10 minutes, and groups of four or more can get group rates. Try for the first or second row for stunning views of the scoured bedrock (best is the seat next to the pilot, avoid rows 3 and 5). If you work out some complex timings, you can visit more than one island in a day. A bus from outside Galway's Kinlay House hostel (p389) to the airport costs €3 each way.

BOAT

Island Ferries (☎091-568 903; www.aranislandferries.com; 37-39 Forster St, Galway; adult/child/student €25/13/20) serves all three islands and also links Inishmaan and Inisheer. Schedules peak in July and August, with several boats a day. The crossing can take up to one hour and is subject to cancellation in high seas. Boats leave from Rossaveal, 40km west of Galway City on the R336. Buses from Galway (€6 return) connect with the sailings; ask when you book.

Ferries to the Arans (primarily Inisheer) also operate from Doolin (p374).

Inishmór

POP 850

Most visitors who venture out to the islands don't make it beyond Inishmór (Árainn) and its main attraction, Dún Aengus, the stunning stone fort perched perilously on the island's towering cliffs. The arid landscape west of Kilronan (Cill Rónáin), Inishmór's main settlement, is dominated by stone walls, boulders, scattered buildings and the odd patch of deep-green grass and potato plants.

Tourism turns the wheels of the island's economy: an armada of tour vans greet each ferry and flight, offering a ride round the sights. As one local said: 'We move 'em through like a conveyor belt.' Happily, you can set your own pace.

The 2010 romantic comedy *Leap Year* starring Amy Adams and Adam Scott was partially filmed on Inishmór. Rather tellingly, it involves a woman bedevilled by travel mishaps.

Inishmór is 14.5km long and 4km at its widest stretch. All boats arrive and depart from Kilronan, on the southeastern side of the island. One principal road runs the length of the island, intersected by small lanes and paths of packed dirt and stone.

Sights

TOP CHOICE **Dún Aengus** HISTORIC SITE

(Dún Aonghasa; www.heritageireland.ie; adult/child €3/1; ⏲10am-6pm) Three spectacular forts stand guard over Inishmór, each believed to be around 2000 years old. Chief among them is Dún Aengus, which has three nonconcentric walls that run right up to sheer drops to the ocean below. It is protected by remarkable *chevaux de frise,* fearsome and densely packed defensive stone spikes that surely helped deter ancient armies from invading the site.

Powerful swells pound the 60m-high cliff face. A complete lack of rails or other modern additions that would spoil this amazing ancient site means that you can not only go right up to the cliff's edge but also potentially fall to your doom below quite easily. When it's uncrowded, you can't help but feel the extraordinary energy that must have been harnessed to build this vast site.

A small visitor centre has displays that put everything in context. A slightly strenuous 900m walkway wanders uphill to the fort, through a rocky landscape lined with hardy plants.

OTHER SIGHTS

Along the road between Kilronan and Dún Aengus you'll find the small, perfectly circular fort **Dún Eochla**.

The ruins of numerous stone churches trace the island's monastic history. The small **Teampall Chiaráin** (Church of St Kieran), with a high cross in the churchyard, is near Kilronan. To the southeast, near Cill Éinne Bay, is the early Christian **Teampall Bheanáin** (Church of St Benen). Near the airstrip are the sunken remains of a church; the spot is said to have been the site of **St Enda's Monastery** in the 5th century, though whatever is visible dates from the 8th century onwards. Past Kilmurvey is the perfect **Clochán na Carraige**, an early Christian stone hut that stands 2.5m tall, and various small early Christian ruins known rather inaccurately as the **Na Seacht dTeampaill** (Seven Churches), comprising a couple of ruined churches, monastic houses and some fragments of a high cross from the 8th or 9th century. To the south of the ruins is **Dún Eoghanachta**, another circular fort.

There's an EU Blue Flag white-sand beach (awarded for cleanliness) at **Kilmurvey**, peacefully situated west of bustling Kilronan. Many sunbathers shed their parkas in summer. In the sheltered little bay of **Port Chorrúch**, up to 50 grey seals sun themselves and feed in the shallows.

Most day-trippers focus on Kilronan and Dún Aengus and jam the roads north of Kilronan. If you're spending the night, bike to sites in the little-visited south such as **Dún Dúchathair**, an ancient fort dramatically perched on a clifftop promontory. Pause at the long and usually empty **beach** south of the airport. You can then visit Dún Aengus after the last ferry has left during the long days of summer.

Sleeping

The tourist office can book rooms for a €4 fee. Advance bookings are advised, particularly in high summer. Many places offer excellent evening meals; those listed under Eating are open to nonguests.

TOP CHOICE **Kilmurvey House** B&B €€
(099-61218; www.kilmurveyhouse.com; Kilmurvey; s/d from €65/110; Apr-Sep) On the path leading to Dún Aengus is this grand 18th-century stone mansion. It's a beautiful setting, and the 12 rooms are well maintained. Hearty meals (dinner €30) incorporate vegetables from the garden, and local fish and meats. You can swim at a pretty beach that's a short walk from the house.

TOP CHOICE **Kilronan Hostel** HOSTEL €
(099-61255; www.kilronanhostel.com; Kilronan; dm €15-20; @) You'll see the pistachio-green Kilronan Hostel perched above Tí Joe Mac's pub even before your ferry docks at the pier, a two-minute walk away. Forty beds are spread across spotless four- and six-bed rooms. A terrace has fine harbour views and eggs in the morning come courtesy of the organically fed chickens out back.

Mainistir House INN, HOSTEL €
(099-61169; www.mainistirhousearan.com; Main istir; dm/s/d €16/40/50; @) Quirky and colourful, this 60-bed guesthouse on the main road north of Kilronan is a fun place for the funky and well-read. A simple breakfast is included in the rates. Dinner is an event.

Man of Aran Cottage B&B €€
(099-61301; www.manofarancottage.com; Kilmurvey; s/d from €55/90; Mar-Oct) Built for the 1930s film of the same name (see the boxed text, p405), this thatched B&B doesn't trade on past glories – its authentic stone-and-wood interiors define charming. The owners are avid organic gardeners (the tomatoes are famous) and their bounty can become your meal (€30).

Ard Mhuiris B&B €€
(099-61333; www.ardmhuiris.com; Kilronan; s/d from €60/80) Less than a five-minute stroll from the centre of town, this very tidy B&B hits the sweet spot of Aran Islands accomo-

Inishmór

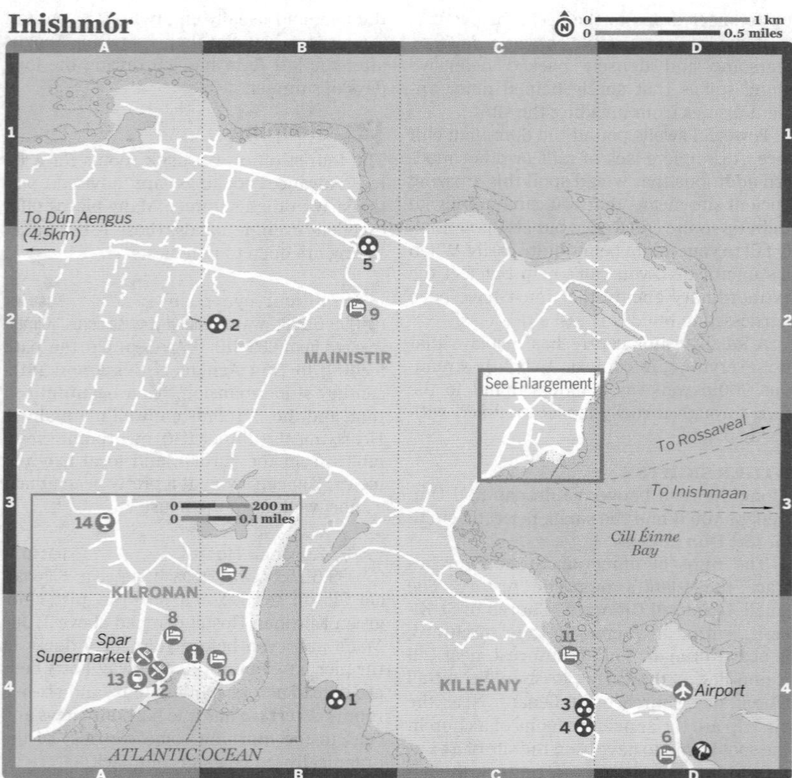

dation: it's quiet, welcoming and has good sea views if you have to curl up in your room on a rainy day.

Ard Einne B&B €€
(☎099-61126; www.ardeinne.com; Killeany; r €90-120) Enjoy broad views of Cill Éinne Bay from this mannered, almost timeless, eight-room guesthouse near various ruins and the airport. It really couldn't be quieter – the surrounds perfect (and the sea views lovely) after a day spent walking. There's a restaurant for guests that features fresh local food.

Pier House Guest House INN €€
(☎099-61417; www.pierhousearan.com; Kilronan; r from €90-120; ⊙Mar-Oct) You won't have time to lose your sea legs in the 100m walk from the ferry to this two-storey house perched on a small rise. The 10 rooms are bright and comfortable.

Tigh Fitz INN €€
(☎099-61213; www.tighfitz.com; Killeany; s/d from €50/80) Near the airport, this jovial pub and guesthouse is a good base if you want to avoid the daytime hubbub of the harbour area. Rooms are simple and, except for some singing from the pub, dead quiet.

Eating

Some of the pubs listed under Drinking offer good bar food.

TOP CHOICE **Mainistir House** VEGETARIAN €€
(☎099-61169; Mainistir; buffet €15; ⊙from 8pm summer, from 7pm winter) Mainistir House cooks up renowned organic, largely vegetarian fare featuring dishes redolent with the tastes of summer – pesto is much in evidence. Nonguests are welcome, but be sure to book.

Inishmór

Sights

1	Dún Dúchathair	B4
2	Dún Eochla	B2
3	St Enda's Monastery	C4
4	Teampall Bheanáin	C4
5	Teampall Chiaráin	B2

Sleeping

6	Ard Einne	D4
7	Ard Mhuiris	B3
8	Kilronan Hostel	A4
9	Mainistir House	B2
10	Pier House Guest House	B4
11	Tigh Fitz	C4

Eating

	Mainistir House	(see 9)
12	O'Malley's@Bayview	A4
	Pier House Guest House	(see 10)

Drinking

13	American Bar	A4
14	Joe Watty's Bar	A3
	Tí Joe Mac's	(see 8)
	Tigh Fitz	(see 11)

O'Malley's@Bayview MODERN IRISH €€
(Kilronan; mains €7-23; 11am-9.30pm Mon-Fri, from 9am Sat & Sun) The terrace here has commanding harbour views. The simple menu belies the talents of the kitchen; choices include fine fish chowder, good burgers and pizza, plus fresh fish at night. Even the garlic bread is good.

Pier House Guest House IRISH €€€
(Kilronan; mains €20-30; noon-10pm) Sitting on the large terrace watching the ferries come and go while grazing your way through a platter of local seafood is one of the island's joys. There's a fireplace inside for when it blows.

Drinking

The pubs have bar food of varying ambition.

Joe Watty's Bar PUB
(Kilronan) This is the best pub in Kilronan, with traditional sessions most nights and rather posh pub food (noon to 8pm) from June to August. Turf fires warm the air on the 50 weeks a year when this is needed.

Tí Joe Mac's PUB
(Kilronan) Informal music sessions, turf fires and a broad terrace with harbour views make Tí Joe Mac's a local favourite. Food is limited to a few sandwiches slapped together between pints.

American Bar PUB
(Kilronan) Two large rooms fill with happy pint quaffers throughout the year. In low season sloshed locals anticipate the next year of tourists (especially the namesakes of the bar). The room on the right as you enter, with its windows and access to the terrace, is the best bet.

Tigh Fitz PUB
(Killeany) Near the airport, this jovial pub has traditional sessions and set dancing every weekend and does excellent bar food (noon to 5pm) from June to August. It's 1.6km from Kilronan (about a 25-minute walk).

Shopping

Glossy shops in Kilronan sell Aran-style sweaters that come with gaudy labels that obfuscate their origins (never the islands, often not Ireland at all). For an authentic hand-knitted version, visit **Mary O'Flaherty** (099-61117; Oat Quarter). Chances are you'll see Mary knitting when you call in. Expect to pay around €100 for the genuine article.

The **tourist office** (Kilronan; 10am-5.45pm May-Sep, 11am-5pm Oct-May) is the place for local books and maps – especially the highly recommended *The Aran Islands* by JM Synge.

Information

Mainistir House (9am-1pm & 5-7pm) Offers public internet access.

Spar supermarket (Kilronan; 9am-6pm Mon-Wed, 9am-7pm Thu-Sat year-round, 10am-5pm Sun Jun-Aug) Has the only ATM in the Arans.

Tourist office (099-61263; Kilronan; 10am-5.45pm May-Sep, 11am-5pm Oct-May) Useful office on the waterfront west of the ferry pier in Kilronan.

Getting Around

The airstrip is 2km southeast of town; a shuttle to Kilronan costs €5 return.

You can bring your own bicycle on the ferry for free. Most places to stay have bicycles for use or rent (universally €10 per day).

Burke Bicycle Hire (087 280 8273) Patrick Burke, near Kilronan Hostel, is an expert on local cycling and can advise on routes that avoid crowds and reach seldom-visited ends of the island.

Aran Cycle Hire Hires out hundreds of sturdy bikes, which it'll deliver to your accommodation anywhere on the island. It's at the pier.

Year-round, numerous **minibuses** (tours €10) greet each ferry and plane. All offer 2½-hour island tours; some of the drivers are such characters (including Thomas O'Toole, ☎087 624 9802) that you'll be laughing too hard to notice the rocky vistas.

To see the island at a gentler pace, **pony traps** (⌚Mar-Nov) with a driver are available for trips between Kilronan and Dún Aengus; the return journey costs between €60 and €100 for up to four people.

Inishmaan

POP 150

The least-visited of the islands, with the smallest population, Inishmaan (Inis Meáin) is a rocky respite. Early Christian monks seeking solitude were drawn to Inishmaan, as was the author JM Synge, who spent five summers here over a century ago (see the boxed text, p405). The island they knew largely survives today: stoic cows and placid sheep, impressive old forts, and warm-hearted locals, who may tell you with a glint in their eye that they had a hard night on the whiskey the previous evening (there are no *gardaí* on the island to enforce last orders at the one pub). Inishmaan's scenery is breathtaking, with a jagged coastline of startling cliffs, empty beaches, and fields where the main crop seems to be stone.

Inishmaan is roughly 5km long by 3km wide. Most of its buildings are spread out along the road that runs east–west across the centre of the island. The principal boat landing is on the eastern side of the island, while the airstrip is in the northeastern corner. Inishmaan's down-to-earth islanders are largely unconcerned with the prospect of attracting tourists' euros, so facilities are few and far between.

Sights

Glorious views of Inishmaan's limestone valleys extend from the elliptical stone fort **Dún Chonchúir**, which is thought to have been built sometime between the 1st and 7th centuries AD.

Teach Synge (☎099-73036; admission €3; ⌚by appointment), a thatched cottage on the road just before you head up to the fort, is where the writer JM Synge spent his summers between 1898 and 1902 researching *The Aran Islands*.

Cill Cheannannach is a rough 8th- or 9th-century church south of the pier. The well-preserved stone fort **Dún Fearbhaigh**, a short distance west, dates from the same era. On a hill, **St Mary's Church** has excellent stained-glass windows from 1939.

In the east of the island, about 500m north of the boat-landing stage is **Trá Leitreach**, a safe, sheltered beach.

Synge's Chair LOOKOUT

At the desolate western edge of the island, Synge's Chair is a lookout at the edge of a sheer limestone cliff with the surf from Gregory's Sound booming below. The cliff ledge is often sheltered from the wind, so do as Synge did and find a comfortable stone seat to take it all in. The formation is two

FATHER TED'S DIVINE INSPIRATION

Devotees of the late 1990s cult British TV series *Father Ted* might recognise Craggy Island – the show's fictional island setting off Ireland's west coast – from its opening sequence showing the *Plassy* shipwreck (p406) on Inisheer. However, apart from this single shot, the sitcom was mostly filmed in London studios, with additional location shots in Counties Clare, Wicklow and Dublin. Alas, the Parochial House and Vaughan's Pub are nowhere to be found here (instead you'll find them around Lisdoonvarna and Kilfenora in County Clare).

This hasn't stopped the Aran Islands from embracing the show as their own. Although there has been some grumbling from its smaller neighbours, Inishmór has seized upon Ted-mania for itself and each year hosts **Tedfest** (www.tedfest.org), a *Father Ted* festival. Held during the purgatory of tourism (late February or March), this three-day carnival of nonsense has been a huge hit.

A popular feature of Tedfest that appeals to locals is the **Craggy Cup** (www.craggycup.com), which pits football teams from various Irish islands against each other. This also provides an excuse for more drinking and, goodness, gambling. Meanwhile, County Clare now has a competing Ted festival – see p376. As he might say: 'Oh feck!'

ARTISTIC ARAN

The Aran Islands have sustained a strong creative streak, partly as a means for entertainment during long periods of isolation and partly, in the words of one local composer, to 'make sure the rest of the country doesn't forget we're here'. Artists and writers from the mainland have similarly long been drawn to the elemental nature of island life.

Dramatist JM Synge (1871–1909) spent a lot of time on the islands. His play *Riders to the Sea* (1905) is set on Inishmaan while his renowned *The Playboy of the Western World* also draws upon his island experiences. His highly readable book *The Aran Islands* (1907) is the classic account of life here and remains in print.

American Robert Flaherty came to the islands in the early 1930s to film *Man of Aran*, a dramatic account of daily life. He was something of a fanatic about the project and got most of the island's people involved in its production. One of the cottages built for the film is today a B&B (Man of Aran Cottage). The film is a classic and is regularly shown in Kilronan on Inishmór.

The map-maker Tim Robinson has written a wonderful two-volume account of his explorations on Aran, called *Stones of Aran: Pilgrimage* and *Stones of Aran: Labyrinthe*.

Local literary talent includes Liam O'Flaherty (1896–1984) from Inishmór. He wrote several harrowing novels, including *Famine*.

minutes' walk from the parking area; you can leg it around the bleak west side of the island from here in an hour.

On the walk out to Synge's Chair, a sign points the way to a **clochán**, hidden behind a house and shed.

Sleeping & Eating

Most B&Bs serve evening meals, usually using organic local foods. Meals generally cost around €20 to €25.

TOP CHOICE An Dún B&B €€
(☎099-73047; www.inismeainaccommodation.com; r €40-100; @) Opposite the entrance to Dún Chonchúir, modern An Dún has a sauna and five comfortable rooms with private bathrooms. The restaurant is open to nonguests and serves lauded local cuisine such as pillowy potatoes (fertilised with seaweed), luscious smoked salmon, and fresh local fish (mains €8 to €25). Rooms are available year-round; the restaurant serves lunch and dinner in summer; there are tables outside.

TOP CHOICE Inis Meáin INN €€€
(☎086 826 6026; www.inismeain.com; r from €250; ⏲Apr-Oct; @) A complete anomaly for the island, where most everything is as basic as a rock – or is a rock – this posh boutique inn has three sumptuous rooms crafted from local materials (rocks). Views seem to go on forever and you can grab a bike and spend your day exploring in blessed isolation. The restaurant serves a changing menu of exquisite dishes made from local foods (dinner mains €15 to €35). Open to nonguests, but book.

Tig Congaile B&B €€
(☎099-73085; bbinismeain@eircom.net; Moore Village; r €45-90) Not far from the pier, Guatemalan-born Vilma Conneely serves guests freshly ground coffee from her native land, but it's her use of local foods that really wins plaudits. Her sea-vegetable soup is famous and best enjoyed – if possible – at a table outside. The dining room is open to nonguests (lunch dishes from €5, dinner from €20; open 10.30am to 9pm). The seven rooms are spacious and have starkly iconic views.

Máire Mulkerrin B&B €
(☎099-73016; s/d from €30/50) Now in her 80s and going strong, Mrs Mulkerrin is a local legend in her skirts and shawls. She keeps a cosy, spick-and-span home, filled with faded family photos, and her stove warms the kitchen all day.

Ard Alainn B&B €
(☎099-73027; s/d with shared bathroom from €30/50; ⏲May-Sep) Signposted just over 2km from the pier, thatched Ard Alainn is a vintage fantasy with fine views out to sea. The five rooms share a bathroom. Breakfasts by hostess Maura Faherty will keep you going all day.

Teach Ósta PUB €€
(mains from €10; ⏲noon-late) The island's perfect pub hums on summer evenings (grab

a table outside for the views) and supplies snacks, sandwiches, soups and seafood platters. Though the pub often keeps going until the wee hours, food service generally stops around 7pm and may not be available in the winter months.

Shopping

Cniotáil Inis Meáin CLOTHING
(☎099-73009) This factory exports fine woollen garments to some of the world's most exclusive shops. You can buy the same sweaters here; call before visiting.

Information

Not far from the pub, a small **shop** (⏰10am-6pm Mon-Fri, 10am-2pm Sat) sells groceries, offers postal services and dispenses advice.

Getting Around

Walking is a fine way to explore the island's sights. A van **tour** (☎099-73993) from the ferry or the airport will cost €20 for a relaxed one or two hours. **Bike rentals** (€10 per day) may be available at the ferry dock, otherwise you can rent one at the shop.

Inisheer

POP 200

Inisheer (Inis Oírr), the smallest of the Aran Islands, has a palpable sense of enchantment, enhanced by the island's deep-rooted mythology, its devotion to traditional culture and ethereal landscapes. Wandering the lanes with their ivy-covered stone walls and making discoveries here and there is the best way to experience the island.

The wheels of change turn very slowly here. Electricity wasn't fully reliable until 1997. Given that there's at best 15cm of topsoil to eke out a living farming, the slow conversion of the economy to tourism has been welcome. Day-trippers from Doolin (as many as 1000 on a balmy summer weekend), 8km across the water, enliven the paths all summer long.

Sights & Activities

Two marked paths offer routes around the island. Set off from the dock on foot, bike or with a driver. A meandering wander covering the main sites will take about four hours on foot. With more time – or days – you can really savour Inisheer.

TOP CHOICE **O'Brien's Castle** HISTORIC BUILDING
A 100m climb to the island's highest point yields dramatic views over clover-covered fields to the beach and harbour. This 15th-century church (Caisleán Uí Bhriain) was built within the remains of a ring fort called Dún Formna, dating from as early as the 1st century AD. You can freely explore the ruins inside and out. Nearby is an 18th-century signal tower.

TOP CHOICE **Tobar Éinne** HISTORIC SITE
Locals still carry out a pilgrimage known as the *Turas* to the Well of Enda, an ever-burbling spring in a remote rocky expanse in the southwest. The ceremony involves, over the course of three consecutive Sundays, picking up seven stones from the ground nearby and walking around the small well seven times, putting one stone down each time, while saying the rosary until an elusive eel appears from the well's watery depths. If, during this ritual, you're lucky enough to see the eel, it's said your tongue will be bestowed with healing powers, enabling you to literally lick wounds.

Teampall Chaoimháin HISTORIC BUILDING
Named for Inisheer's patron saint, who is buried close by, the roofless 10th-century Church of St Kevin and small cemetery perch on a tiny bluff near the Strand. On the eve of St Kevin's 14 June feast day, a mass is held here in the open air at 9pm. Those with ailments sleep here for the night to be healed.

Cill Ghobnait CHURCH
The tiny 8th- or 9th-century Church of St Gobnait is named after Gobnait, who fled here from Clare while trying to escape an enemy who was pursuing her.

Plassy HISTORIC SITE
Dating from 1960, this iconic island sight was a freighter that was thrown up on the rocks in bad weather. Miraculously, all on board were saved; Tigh Ned's pub has a collection of photographs and documents detailing the rescue. An aerial shot of the wreck was used in the opening sequence of the iconic TV series *Father Ted* (see the boxed text, p404).

Áras Éanna ARTS CENTRE
(☎099-75150; www.araseanna.ie) Inisheer's large community arts centre sits out on an exposed stretch of the northern side of the island, a 15-minute walk from the village.

It has visiting artists programs through the summer and various cultural programs and performances.

Festivals & Events

TOP CHOICE Craiceann Inis Oírr International Bodhrán Summer School TRADITIONAL FESTIVAL
(www.craiceann.com) The island reverberates to the thunder of traditional drums for a week in late June. Bodhrán masterclasses, lectures and workshops, are held as well as related events, such as Irish dancing. Craiceann takes its name from the Irish word for 'skin', referring to the goat skin used to make these circular drums, which are held under one arm and played with a wooden beater. The festival – its slogan is 'Lock up your goats!' – features top talent and nightly drumming sessions take place in the pubs.

Sleeping & Eating

Book well in advance during Craiceann week in June. There is camping (with toilets and showers) at the official site by the main beach. There are three pubs, all worth a visit.

TOP CHOICE Fisherman's Cottage & South Aran House B&B €€
(☎099-75073; www.southaran.com; s/d €45/70; ⏰Apr-Oct; 📶) Slow-food enthusiasts run this sprightly B&B and cafe that's a mere five-minute walk from the pier. Lavender grows in profusion at the entrance; follow your nose. Food (lunch and dinner, open to nonguests, mains €12 to €20) celebrates local seafood and organic produce. Rooms are simple yet stylish. Kayaking and fishing are among the activities on offer.

Brú Radharc Na Mara Hostel HOSTEL €
(☎099-75024; radharcnamara@hotmail.com; dm €18-25, d €50; ⏰Mar-Oct) Handily located next to a pub and by the pier, this spotless hostel has ocean views, a large kitchen, a warming fireplace and bikes for hire. The owners also run the adjacent B&B (rooms €50), with basic rooms.

Radharc an Chláir B&B €€
(☎099-75019; bridpoil@eircom.net; r €45-80) This pleasant, modern B&B near O'Brien's Castle has views of the Cliffs of Moher and Galway Bay. Book several weeks ahead, as hostess Brid Poil's home cooking draws many repeat visitors. Guests can arrange evening meals (€20). Some rooms share bathrooms.

WALKING INISHEER'S SHORE

You can circumnavigate Inisheer's 12km shoreline in about five hours and gain a deep understanding of the island that is impossible on a hurried visit to the top sights.

From the Inisheer ferry pier, walk west along the narrow road parallel to the shore and go on straight to the small fishing pier at the northwest corner of the island. Continue along the road with the shingle shore on one side and a dense patchwork of fields, enclosed by the ubiquitous stone walls, on the other. Look for tide pools and grey seals resting in the sun.

About 1km from the acute junction, turn left at the painted sign; about 100m along the paved lane is the **Tobar Éinne**.

Continue southwest as it becomes a rough track. After about 600m, head roughly south across the limestone pavement and strips of grass to the shore. Follow the gently sloping rock platform around the southwestern headland (Ceann na Faochnaí) and walk east to the **lighthouse** near Fardurris Point (two hours from the ferry pier).

Stay with the coast, turning northeast. You'll see the wreck of the **Plassy** in the distance. When necessary, use stiles to cross walls and fences around fields. Note that the grass you see grows on about 5cm of topsoil created by islanders who cleared rocks by hand and then stacked up seaweed over decades.

Head north, following the track, which then becomes a sealed road at the northern end of Lough More. Continue following the road along the northern shore of the island, past the airstrip.

At the airstrip you can diverge for **Teampall Chaoimháin** and **O'Brien's Castle**. Otherwise rest on the lovely sands of the curving **beach** and check out the nearby **Cnoc Rathnaí**, a Bronze Age burial mound (1500 BC), which is remarkably intact considering it was buried under the sand until the 19th century, when it was rediscovered.

Aran Islands Scenery

Blasted by the wind and washed over by waves, the eroded, striated slivers of rock known as the Aran Islands hold a fascination for travellers. Rocky extensions of the Burren in County Clare, they are home to descendants of unimaginably hardy folk who forged their own culture of survival.

Inishmaan

1 Escape the crowds on Inishmaan (p404), the least visited of the Arans. You'll see few others on walks across the dramatic countryside, where every path seems to pass the mysterious remains of past lives and end on a beach trod only by you.

Aran Islands

2 Left to nature, the Arans (p399) would be bare rocks in the Atlantic. But generations of islanders have created green – seaweed and sand gathered and spread by hand over the centuries finally rewards with fertile fields.

Inishmór

3 A thousand day-trippers on a summer weekend come to Inishmór (p400) to see one of Ireland's most impressive ancient wonders. Dún Aengus has been guarding a bluff over the Atlantic for 2000 years.

Inisheer

4 An old castle, ancient churches and a magical spring are just a few of the highlights of Inisheer (p406), the smallest of the Arans. Centuries of history are preserved in rock.

The Plassy Wreck

5 Star of the opening sequence of the comedy classic *Father Ted*, the *Plassy* (p406) was driven ashore on Inisheer by storms in 1963. Its rusting hulk attracts walkers and is the perfect image of the timeless force of the elements.

Clockwise from top left

1. Rocky vistas, Inishmaan 2. Fishing boats at Kilronan pier, Inishmór 3. Local children, Inishmaan

1

3

2

SPOKEN IRISH

One of the most important Gaeltacht (Irish-speaking) areas in Ireland begins around Spiddal in Connemara and stretches along the coast as far as Cashel.

That spoken Irish is enjoying a renaissance around the country (when posh Dublin parents compete to enrol their kids in Irish-language schools, you know something is up) can be credited in no small part to several media outlets based in Connemara and Galway. From this last refuge of the language, Ireland's national Irish-language radio station, Radio na Gaeltachta (www.rte.ie/rnag) and its Irish-language TV station, TG4 (www.tg4.ie), sprang in the 1990s. So, too, has sprouted the Irish-language weekly newspaper *Foinse* (www.foinse.ie).

Tigh Ruairí INN, PUB €€
(Strand House; ☎099-75020; r €50-90; @) Rory Conneely's atmospheric digs host live music sessions in the cosy pub. There are 20 basic rooms, many with views across the waters.

Tigh Ned PUB €
(meals €5-10) Here since 1897, Tigh Ned is a welcoming, unpretentious place, with lively traditional music and inexpensive lunchtime fare. Tables in the garden have harbour views.

Information

In summer a small **kiosk** (⌚10am-6pm Jul-Aug) at the harbour provides tourist information. Like Inishmaan, there's no ATM; bring euros.

Online, www.inisoirr-island.com is a handy resource for planning your trip.

Getting Around

Bikes can be rented from **Rothair Inis Oírr** (per day €10; ⌚May-Sep), which is near the pier and has a good map. Most places to stay also rent bikes to nonguests.

You can take a tour of the island on a **pony trap** (per person per hr €10-15) in summer, or on an atmospheric tractor-drawn, thatched-cottage-style **wagon** (☎086 607 3230). For a great exploration by car, try **Eanna Seoighe** (☎099-75040, 087 284 0767).

CONNEMARA

Think of the best crumble you've ever had, one with a craggy crust that accumulates hollows of perfect flavour. Similarly, the filigreed coast of the Connemara Peninsula is endlessly pleasing, with pockets of sheer delight awaiting discovery.

The name Connemara (Conamara) is Irish for 'Inlets of the Sea' and the coastal roads bear this out as they wind around small bays and coves, some with hidden beaches. A succession of seaside hamlets entice.

Connemara's interior is a kaleidoscope of rusty bogs, lonely valleys and shimmering black lakes. At its heart are the Maumturk Mountains and the pewter-tinged quartzite peaks of the Twelve Bens mountain range, with a network of scenic hiking and biking trails. Everywhere the land is laced by the seemingly endless stone walls you're glad you didn't have to build. It's dazzling at any time of day but especially when the sky and waters sparkle azure, the hills shine green, and bright yellow blooms abound.

Information

Galway's tourist office has a wealth of information on the area. Online, **Connemara Tourism** (www.connemara.ie) and **Go Connemara** (www.goconnemara.com) have region-wide info and links.

Getting There & Around

BUS

Organised tours from Galway (p389) are plentiful and offer a good overview of the region, though ideally you'll want more than one day to absorb the area's charms, plus you'll want the freedom to make your own discoveries.

Bus Éireann (☎091-562 000; www.buseireann.ie) Serves most of Connemara. Services can be sporadic, and many buses operate May to September only, or July and August only. Some drivers will stop in between towns.

Citylink (www.citylink.ie) Has several buses a day linking Galway city with Clifden, with stops in Moycullen, Oughterard, Maam Cross and Recess, and on to Cleggan and Letterfrack. If you're going somewhere between towns, you might be able to arrange a drop-off with the driver.

CAR

Your own wheels are the best way to get off this scenic region's beaten track – though watch out for the narrow roads' stone walls, just waiting to scrape the sides of your car.

Keep an eye out, too, for meandering Connemara sheep – characterised by thick creamy fleece and coal-black faces and legs – which frequently wander onto the road. Even Connemara's flattest stretches of road tend to be bumpy due to the uneven bog beneath the tarmac.

Oughterard & Around

POP 2400

The writer William Makepeace Thackeray sang the praises of the small town of Oughterard (Uachtar Árd), saying, 'A more beautiful village can scarcely be seen'. Even if those charms have faded over the years, it still makes a good gateway to Connemara. And it is one of Ireland's principal angling centres.

Immediately west of Oughterard, the countryside opens up to sweeping panoramas of lakes, mountains and bogs, which get more spectacular the further west you travel.

Sights

If you see tourists wandering around, talking with a drawl and calling people 'pilgrim', it's probably because they are here to relive the iconic film *The Quiet Man;* see the boxed text, p414, for details.

Aughnanure Castle CASTLE

(www.heritageireland.com; adult/child €3/1; ⏲9.30am-6pm early Apr-Sep) Built around 1500, this bleak fortress was home to the 'Fighting O'Flahertys', who controlled the region for hundreds of years after they fought off the Normans. The six-storey tower house stands on a rocky outcrop overlooking Lough Corrib and has been extensively restored. Surrounding the castle are the remains of an unusual double *bawn* (area surrounded by walls outside the main castle, acting as a defence and a place to keep cattle in times of trouble), and underneath the castle the lake washes through a number of natural caverns and caves.

Aughnanure Castle is situated 3km east of Oughterard, off the main Galway road (N59).

Glengowla Mines INDUSTRIAL MUSEUM

(www.glengowlamines.ie; adult/child €8/4; ⏲10am-6pm mid-Mar–mid-Nov) For such ugly work, it's amazing that beautiful materials were extracted from this mine, a 19th-century hole in the ground that yielded all manner of silver, glistening quartz and much more. Visitors learn about the tough lives led here and see some of the beauty left inside. It is 3km west of Oughterard off the N59.

Brigit's Garden GARDEN

(www.galwaygarden.com; Polagh, Roscahill; adult/child €7.50/4.50; ⏲10am-5.30pm Mar-Sep) Can you feel the power of the crystal? Halfway between the villages of Moycullen and Oughterard is Brigit's Garden, a New Age place with lots of lovely plants, yoga classes, Celtic festivals, mythology and a vegetarian cafe.

Sleeping & Eating

Currarevagh House HOTEL €€

(☎091-552 312; www.currarevagh.com; r €80-150; ⏲Mar–mid-Oct; P 📶) You'd be hard-pressed to find a more romantic place than this rambling 19th-century mansion, on vast grounds along Lough Corrib. In fact, you might get your romantic vibes from the inn itself: it was given to the ancestors of the owners as a wedding gift in 1846. Fresh flowers scent the timeless halls and the grounds invite lazy rambles. The food is superlative and features locally caught trout.

Waterfall Lodge INN €€

(☎091-552 168; www.waterfalllodge.net; Glann Rd; s/d €50/80) Decorated in rose-coloured hues and lit by glowing lamps, this double-fronted traditional-style B&B stands amid wooded gardens beside a brook, a lovely 10-minute walk from the village centre. Antiques fill the rooms (try your hand at the old piano).

Canrawer House HOSTEL €

(☎091-552 388; www.oughterardhostel.com; Station Rd; dm €17-20, d €46; ⏲Feb-Oct; P @) Dorms and family rooms are bright and clean, and there's an outdoor patio where you can chat with other guests while enjoying views of the 1-hectare rural site, 1km from the centre of town. If you want to catch the area's wild brown trout for dinner, the owner will show you the way for a fee.

Information

Tourist office (www.oughterardtourism.com; Main St; ⏲9.30am-5.30pm daily summer, Mon-Fri other times) Excellent website.

Getting There & Away

Bus Éireann (www.buseireann.ie) and **Citylink** (www.citylink.ie) have regular buses from Galway to Oughterard.

Lough Corrib

The Republic's biggest lake, Lough Corrib, virtually cuts off western Galway from the rest of the country. Over 48km long and covering some 200 sq km, it encompasses more than 360 islands, including Inchagoill, which has a monastic settlement that can be visited from Oughterard or Cong.

Lough Corrib is world-famous for its salmon, sea trout and brown trout. The highlight of the **fishing** calendar is the mayfly season, when zillions of the small bugs hatch over a few days (usually in May) and drive the fish – and anglers – into a frenzy. Salmon begin running around June. In Oughterard, the owner of **Canrawer House** is a good contact for information and boat hire, as is **Thomas Tuck's Fishing Tackle** (☎091-552 335; Main St, Oughterard; ⏰9am-6.30pm Mon-Sat), an excellent shop teeming with local knowledge.

The largest island on Lough Corrib, **Inchagoill** is a lonely place hiding many ancient remains. Most fascinating is an obelisk called **Lia Luguaedon Mac Menueh** (Stone of Luguaedon, Son of Menueh), which marks a burial site. It stands about 75cm tall, near the Saints' Church, and some people claim that the Latin writing on the stone is the second-oldest Christian inscription in Europe, after those in the catacombs in Rome. **Teampall Phádraig** (St Patrick's Church) is a small oratory of a very early design, with some later additions. The prettiest church is the Romanesque **Teampall na Naoimh** (Saints' Church), probably built in the 9th or 10th century. There are carvings around the arched doorway.

Corrib Cruises (☎092-46029; www.corribcruises.com; adult/child €28/14) sail from Oughterard to Inchagoill and Ashford Castle near Cong.

North of Lough, you can literally go to the dogs near the town of Clonbur. **Joyce**

Connemara

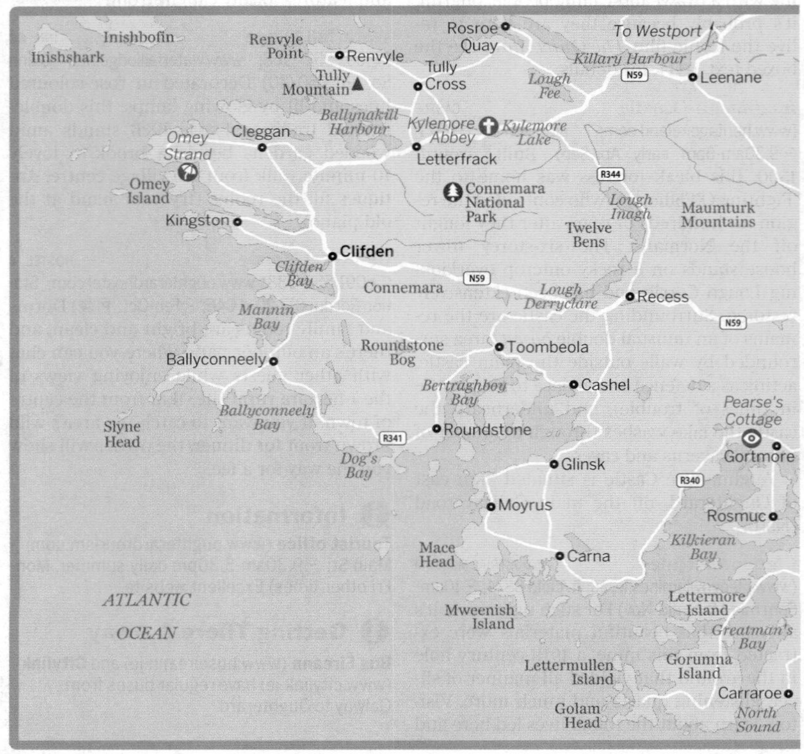

Country Sheepdogs (☎094-954 8853; www.joycecountrysheepdogs.ie; adult/child €7/3; ⊙May-Oct) offers a chance to see the amazing feats performed by working sheep dogs on an actual farm. Book in advance.

Coastal Drive – Galway City to Mace Head

The slow coastal route between Galway and Connemara takes you past pretty seascapes and villages, although the fun doesn't really begin until after Inverin.

Opposite the popular Blue Flag beach **Silver Strand**, 4.8km west of Galway on the R336, are the **Barna Woods**, a dense, deep green forest perfect for rambling and picnicking. Conserved by the Galway County Council, the woods contain the last natural growing oaks in Ireland's west.

Spiddal (An Spidéal) is a refreshingly untouched little village, and the start of the Gaeltacht region. On your right as you approach the village are the **Spiddal Craft & Design Studios** (www.ceardlann.com; ⊙hours vary), where you can watch woodworkers, leatherworkers, sculptors and weavers plying their crafts.

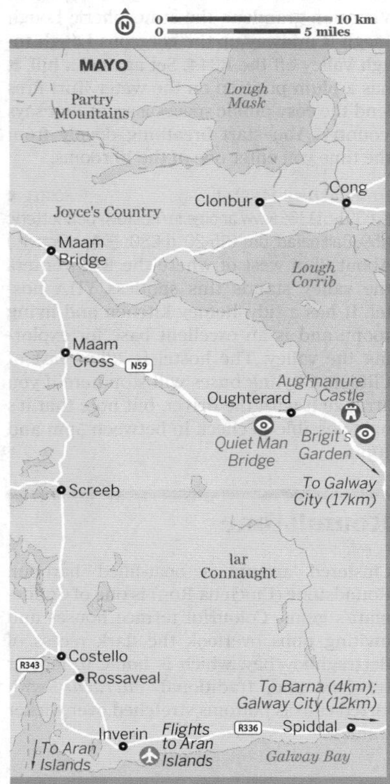

Exceptional traditional music sessions take place at the unassuming **Tigh Hughes** (Spiddal) – it's not uncommon for major musicians to turn up unannounced and join in the craic (fun). Sessions start at around 9pm on Tuesdays. The pub's just adjacent to the main street; turn right at the town centre's little crossroads next to the bank, and it's a couple of doors up on your right. Numerous places to stay line the main road.

West of Spiddal, the scenery becomes more dramatic, with parched fields criss-crossed by low stone walls rolling to a ragged shore. **Carraroe** (An Cheathrú Rua) has fine beaches, including the Coral Strand, which is composed entirely of shell and coral fragments. It's worth wandering the small roads on all sides of **Greatman's Bay** to discover tiny inlets and little coves, often watched over by the genial local donkeys.

Lettermore, **Gorumna** and **Lettermullen** islands are low and bleak, with a handful of farmers eking out an existence from minute, rocky fields. Fish farming is big business.

Near Gortmore, along the R340, is **Patrick Pearse's Cottage** (Teach an Phiarsaigh; www.heritageireland.ie; adult/child €3/1; ⊙10am-6pm Easter & Jun–mid-Sep). Pádraig Pearse (1879–1916) led the Easter Rising with James Connolly in 1916; after the revolt he was executed by the British. Pearse wrote some of his short stories and plays in this small thatched cottage.

The scenic R340 swings south along **Kilkieran Bay**, an intricate and interlinked system of tidal marshes, bogs, swift-flowing streams and elaborate tidal basins. This environmentally protected area contains an amazing diversity of life.

Continuing on, **Carna** is a small fishing village, with pleasant walks out to **Mweenish Island** or north to Moyrus and out to the wild headlands at **Mace Head**.

Sleeping

The following places are worth a stop if you aren't planning to make Roundstone or beyond by nightfall.

BRIDGING THE QUIET MAN

Whenever an American cable TV station needs a ratings boost (and they've already just shown *Gone With the Wind*), they trot out the iconic 1952 film *The Quiet Man*. Starring John Wayne and filmed in lavish colour to capture the crimson locks of his co-star Maureen O'Hara, the film regularly makes the top-10 lists of aging romantic-comedy lovers for its high-energy portrayal of rural Irish life, replete with drinking and fighting, fighting and drinking etc.

Director John Ford returned to his Irish roots and filmed the movie almost entirely on location in Connemara and the little village of Cong, just over the border in County Mayo. One of the most photogenic spots from the film, the eponymous **Quiet Man Bridge**, is just 3km west of Oughterard off the N59. Looking much as it did in the film, the picture-perfect little arched span (whose original name was Leam Bridge) would be a lovely spot even if it hadn't achieved screen immortality. Purists will note, however, that the scene based here had close-ups done on a cheesy set back in Hollywood. That's showbiz.

Hard-core fans will want to buy the superb *The Complete Guide to The Quiet Man* by Des MacHale. It's sold in most tourist offices in the area.

TOP CHOICE **Cashel House Hotel** HOTEL €€

(☎095-31001; www.cashel-house-hotel.com; Cashel; s/d from €90/130; P 📶) At the head of Cashel Bay, this flowered fantasy of a country mansion has 32 period rooms surrounded by 17 hectares of woodland and gardens. It also has a stable of Connemara ponies (riding lessons available), a superb dining room and even a small private beach. Potentates who have graced its sheets include Charles de Gaulle.

Cloch na Scíth INN €€

(☎091-553 364; www.thatchcottage.com; Kellough, Spiddal; r €45-80; P) Set in a story-book garden roamed by ducks and chickens, this century-old thatched cottage has a warm, friendly host, Nancy, who cooks bread in an iron pot over the peat fire (as her grandmother taught her and as she'll teach you).

Lough Inagh Valley

This stark brown landscape beguiles by its very simplicity.

The R344 enters the valley from the south, just west of playfully named Recess. The moody waters of Loughs Derryclare and Inagh reflect the colours of the moment. On the western side is the brooding **Twelve Bens** mountain range. At the north end of the valley, the R344 meets the N59, which loops around Connemara to Leenane.

Towards the northern end of the valley, a track leads west off the road up a blind valley, which is well worth exploring.

Sleeping & Eating

Lough Inagh Lodge INN €€

(☎091-34706; www.loughinaghlodgehotel.ie; s/d from €90/140; dinner €40; P 📶) Steeped in Victorian grandeur, the atmospheric Lough Inagh is midway up the gorgeous Lough Inagh Valley off the R344. Set against a hill, it has a plum position on the water. Turf fires lend the cosy public spaces a scent that says 'country'. You start breathing deeply from the time you enter one of the 13 rooms.

Ben Lettery Hostel HOSTEL €

(☎091-51136; www.anoige.ie/hostels/ben-lettery; N59, Ballinafad; dm €15-20, d €80; ⏱Apr-Oct; P) About 8km west of where the R344 enters the valley stands this spotless YHA hostel. It has a tidy, homey kitchen and living room, and is an excellent base for exploring the valley. The hostel is 13km east of Clifden. Citylink buses will stop here if you arrange it with the driver, but note that it's only possible to check in between 5pm and 10pm.

Roundstone

POP 400

Clustered around a boat-filled harbour, Roundstone (Cloch na Rón) is one of Connemara's gems. Colourful terrace houses and inviting pubs overlook the dark recess of Bertraghboy Bay, which is home to lobster trawlers and traditional *currachs* with tarred canvas bottoms stretched over wicker frames.

Sights & Activities

Wander the short **promenade** for views over the water to ribbons of eroded land.

Roundstone Musical Instruments MUSIC

(www.bodhran.com; Michael Killeen Park; 9am-7pm Jul-Sep, 9.30am-6pm Mon-Sat Oct-Jun) Just south of the village, in the remains of an old Franciscan monastery, is Malachy Kearns' Roundstone Musical Instruments. Kearns is Ireland's only full-time maker of traditional bodhráns. Watch him work and buy a tin whistle, harp or booklet filled with Irish ballads; there's also a small free folk museum and a cafe. Adjacent **craft shops** sell everything from fine pottery to sweaters.

Mt Errisberg WALKING

Looming above the stone pier is Mt Errisberg (298m), the only significant hill along this section of coastline. The pleasant walk from Roundstone to the top takes about two hours. Follow the small road past O'Dowd's pub in the centre of the village. From the summit there are wonderful views across the bay to the distant humps of the Twelve Bens.

Sleeping & Eating

Roundstone House HOTEL €€

(091-35864; www.roundstonehousehotel.com; Main St; s/d from €50/90; Apr-Oct) A dignified presence lining Main St, this sprawling inn has 13 restful rooms with tea kettles and other creature comforts, plus views across the bay. The pub, Vaughan's, has trad sessions some nights in summer and you can enjoy pints and local seafood out on the terrace.

Wits End B&B B&B €

(091-35813; olivercoyne@gmail.com; Main St; s/d from €35/56; Mar-Nov;) Right in the centre of town, this pink palace (well, modest pink house) has rooms looking over the road to the water. It's basic but comfortable and is a mere stumble from the fine pubs.

Anglers Return INN €€

(095-31091; www.anglersreturn.com; Toombeola; s/d from €50/90; P) This gracious lodge defines 'country retreat'. Set among gardens, forests and a stream, the five rooms here have a bucolic charm that is intoxicating from the time you arrive. Decor is a bit frilly, which might put a smile on your face as you chill out. There are no TVs. It's 7km north of Roundstone near the junction of the R341 and R342.

TOP CHOICE **O'Dowd's** SEAFOOD €€

(091-35809; Main St; mains €15-22; restaurant noon-10pm Apr-Sep, noon-3pm & 6-9.30pm Oct-Mar) This well-worn, comfortable old pub hasn't lost any of its authenticity since it starred in the 1997 Hollywood flick *The Matchmaker*. Specialities at its adjoining restaurant include seafood sourced off the old stone dock right across the street.

Roundstone to Clifden

The R341 shadows the coast from Roundstone to Clifden. Beaches along here have such beautiful white sand and turquoise water that, if you added 10°C to the temperature, you could be in Antigua. About 2.5km from Roundstone, look for the turn to **Gurteen Bay** (sometimes spelt Gorteen Bay). After a further 800m there is a turn for **Dog's Bay**. Together, the pair form the two sides of a dog-bone-shaped peninsula lined with idyllic beaches. Park and enjoy a day strolling the grassy heads and frolicking on the hard-packed sand.

Gurteen Beach Caravan & Camping Park (091-35882; www.gurteenbay.com; campsites from €20, caravans from €100; P@) is a peaceful, well-equipped campground in a great spot above the beaches.

At **Ballyconneely** take a detour west off the R341 and visit **Connemara Smokehouse** (www.smokehouse.ie; Bunowen Pier; 9am-1pm & 2-5pm Mon-Fri). You'll learn about how the region's iconic salmon is smoked and get to try some samples.

Clifden & Around

POP 1800

Connemara's 'capital', Clifden (An Clochán), is an appealing Victorian-era country town with an amoeba-shaped oval of streets offering evocative strolls. It presides over the head of the narrow bay where the River Owenglin tumbles into the sea. The surrounding countryside beckons you to walk through woods and above the shoreline.

Though the summer months brighten Clifden's streets, winter gives the town a faded, forgotten charm. In fact it has struggled

WORTH A TRIP

BOGGY DETOUR TO CLIFDEN

Away from the coast, there is an alternative route between Roundstone and Clifden through protected **Roundstone Bog**. The old road is a bumpy ride, passing through eerie, rust-collared desolation. Locals who believe the bog is haunted won't drive this road at night; indeed, the roughness of the road is reason enough to avoid it after dark. In summer, you might see turf being harvested by hand, as blanket bogs cannot be cut mechanically. The road runs west from a junction on the R341 about 4km north of Roundstone. It rejoins the R341 at Ballinaboy.

more than many towns in the region during the economic crisis. The bottom line of course is that visitors are more than welcome.

Sights & Activities

This is pony country and rides along the beaches are popular. You can see the ponies at their swiftest during the annual **Connemara Pony Show** (www.cpbs.ie) held in late August. It draws punters from across western Ireland.

Take the 15-minute stroll down Beach Rd to the **harbour** and look back for the view of Clifden's steeples reflected off the tidal waters.

TOP CHOICE Sky Road SCENIC ROUTE

This 12km route traces a spectacular loop out to the township of Kingston and back to Clifden, taking in some rugged, stunningly beautiful coastal scenery en route. The round trip of about 12km can be easily walked or cycled, but, if you're short on time, you can also drive. Head directly west from Clifden's Market Sq.

Connemara Heritage & History Centre MUSEUM

(www.connemaraheritage.com; Lettershea; adult/child €8/4; ⏲10am-6pm Apr-Oct) Farmer Dan O'Hara lived here until his eviction from the farm and subsequent emigration to New York, where he ended up selling matches on the street. Its present owners have restored the property, turning it into a window onto lost traditional ways, with demonstrations of bog cutting, thatching, sheep shearing and so on. It's possible to stay at the farmhouse in more comfort than Dan ever enjoyed. The homestead is 7km east of Clifden on the N59.

Station House Museum MUSEUM

(Clifden Station House; adult/child €2/free; ⏲10am-5pm Mon-Sat, noon-6pm Sun May-Oct) Located in an old train shed in the upscale hotel development, this small museum is devoted to the story of local ponies and various historic events.

Errislannan Manor PONY RIDES

(☎095-21134; www.connemaraponyriding.com; Ballyconneely Rd) Guides provide lessons and lead treks along the beach and up into the hills on the iconic local ponies. Rates start at €35 per hour and depend on the type and length of ride you want to take. It's 3.5km south of Clifden on the R341.

Sleeping

Numerous attractive choices in the centre allow you to easily partake of Clifden's many charms.

TOP CHOICE Dolphin Beach B&B €€

(☎095-21204; www.dolphinbeachhouse.com; Lower Sky Rd; r €80-180; P 📶) It's hard to find the bones of the 19th-century manor house that forms the basis for this posh B&B set amid some of Connemara's best coastal scenery. Clean lines abound in the bright common areas and in the plush yet relaxed rooms. It's 5km west of Clifden.

Sea Mist House B&B €€

(☎095-21441; www.seamisthouse.com; Market St; r €60-120; 📶) Right in town but opening onto a private fairy-tale garden (which also provides fruit for homemade jam to spread on your freshly baked scones), this beautiful stone house has four immaculate rooms.

Quay House HOTEL €€

(☎095-21369; www.thequayhouse.com; Beach Rd; r €90-180; ⏲mid-Mar–mid-Nov) Down by the harbour, a 10-minute walk from town, this rambling 1820 house has 14 rooms filled with antiques but managing an unfussy style that seems contemporary. Run by an offshoot of the Foyle family of hoteliers, it has pleasures unheard of during past careers as a convent and monastery. Look for influences from celebrities great and small.

Dun Ri Guesthouse INN €€
(☎095-21625; www.dunri.ie; Hulk St; r €45-100; P 📶) Just down the hill from the centre, in a quiet spot near the pony track, this appealing modern inn has 13 spacious rooms. The included breakfast offers many choices; the cheese plate is an excellent change from the norm.

Clifden Station House HOTEL €€
(☎095-21699; www.clifdenstationhouse.com; s/d from €90/120; P @ 📶) Old train sheds just east of the centre have been transformed into boutiques, cafes, a fine pub and this modern hotel. Rooms are spacious, although they suffer slightly from a corporate feel you'd wouldn't expect here at nearly at the end of the earth (or Connemara).

Ben View House B&B €€
(☎095-21256; www.benviewhouse.com; Bridge St; s/d from €45/70) This central 1848 town house has a vintage charm provided by timber beams, polished floorboards and old-fashioned hospitality. The nine rooms are nutty with antiques. It caters to cyclists, with special storage areas and a tolerance for sweat.

Clifden Town Hostel HOSTEL €
(☎095-21076; www.clifdentownhostel.com; Market St; dm €17-22, d from €50) Right in the centre of town, this cheery IHH hostel is set in a cream-coloured house framed by big picture windows. Its sunlit rooms hold 34 beds.

Eating & Drinking

Pubs and restaurants cluster around Clifden's town centre. As elsewhere in these parts, seafood reigns supreme.

TOP CHOICE **Mitchell's** SEAFOOD €€
(☎095-21867; Market St; mains €15-25; ⏲noon-10pm Mar-Oct) Seafood takes centre stage at this elegant spot. From a velvety chowder right through a long list of ever-changing specials, the produce of the surrounding waters is honoured. The wine list does the food justice. Book for dinner. (Lunch specials include sandwiches and casual fare.)

Off the Square MEDITERRANEAN €€
(Main St; mains €10-20; ⏲9am-10pm) Mediterranean flavours make an appearance at this excellent restaurant, which serves meals throughout the day. Casual fare at lunch gives way to superb meals at night. Local meats star; we had a satiny bacon and cabbage special.

Mullarky's Pub PUB
(Main St) Another Foyle family production, this rollicking pub is a riot of local merriment, with live music many nights. Join the fun and you may need to stay in Clifden longer than you thought.

Lowry's Bar PUB €
(Market St; meals €6-10; ⏲10.30am-midnight Sun-Thu, 10.30am-1am Fri & Sat) A time-worn local, Lowry's has traditional pleasures, ranging from the age-old, unadorned look of the place to its *céilidh* sessions, which take place at least a couple of nights a week. The food is 'unpretentious Irish' (eg bangers and mash).

Guy's Bar & Snug PUB €€
(Main St; mains €8-16; ⏲10.30am-11pm) A very well-run pub that combines trad charms with very modern touches. The basic Irish pub chow is quite good, especially dishes made with local seafood.

Information

There are banks with ATMs around Market Sq, as well as a large supermarket.

Clifden Bookshop (Main St) Good for local titles and maps.

Post office (Main St)

Tourist office (www.clifdenchamber.ie; Galway road; ⏲10am-5pm Mon-Sat Easter-Jun & Sep, 10am-5pm daily Jul & Aug) In the Clifden Station House complex.

Getting There & Around

Bus Éireann (www.buseireann.ie) and **Citylink** (www.citylink.ie) have several services daily to Galway along the N59. Fares start at €11 and the trip takes 90 minutes, passing Oughterard on the way.

The compact town centre is easy to cover on foot.

John Mannion & Son (Bridge St) hires out bicycles for €15 per day.

Claddaghduff & Omey Island

Following the filigreed coastline north of Clifden brings you to the tiny village of **Claddaghduff** (An Cladach Dubh), which is signposted off the road to Cleggan. If you turn west here down by the Catholic church, you will come out on **Omey Strand**, and at low tide you can drive or walk across the sand to **Omey Island** (population 20), a low islet of rock, grass, sand and a handful of houses. During summer, horse races are held on Omey Strand.

Cleggan

POP 300

Most visitors ignore Cleggan (An Cloiggean), a small fishing village 16km northwest of Clifden, and hop on the Inishbofin ferry. Big mistake! This classic tiny fishing port exudes charm that starts right at its boat-lined docks.

Oliver's (095-44640; www.oliversbar.com; mains €20-25; 5-9pm) is a locally loved seafood pub. The classic facade is as black as a pint of Guinness. Specials depend on the catch but you can always get the crab claws fried in garlic. Upstairs are six simple B&B rooms (from €60).

Nearby, the **Pier Bar** (Dockside) has a more roguish air although the tables out front under the large trees are just fine.

Citylink (www.citylink.ie) buses continue to Cleggan three times daily from Clifden.

Inishbofin

POP 200

By day sleepy Inishbofin is a haven of tranquillity. You can walk or bike its narrow, deserted lanes, green pastures and sandy beaches, with farm animals and seals for company. But with no *gardaí* on the island to enforce closing times at the pub, by night – you guessed it – Inishbofin has mighty fine craic.

Situated 9km offshore, Inishbofin is compact – 6km long by 3km wide – and its highest point is a mere 86m above sea level. Just off the northern beach is **Lough Bó Finne**, from which the island gets its name; *bó finne* means 'white cow'.

Sights & Activities

St Colman exiled himself to Inishbofin in AD 664, after he fell out with the Church over its adoption of a new calendar. He set up a monastery, supposedly northeast of the harbour, where the more recent ruins of a small 13th-century **church** still stand. Grace O'Malley, the famous pirate queen, used Inishbofin as a base in the 16th century, and Cromwell's forces captured the island in 1652, and used it to inter priests and clerics in harsh conditions.

Inishbofin's pristine waters offer superb **scuba diving** (see the boxed text, p420). Pristine **beaches** and alluring trails encourage exploring.

Heritage Museum MUSEUM
(www.inishbofin.com; admission free; hours vary) Just behind the pier, the small but comprehensive museum gives an overview of the island's history. Displays include the contents of a pre-Famine house, photographs, and traditional farming and fishing equipment.

Festivals & Events

Inishbofin Arts Festival ARTS FESTIVAL
(www.inishbofin.com) The island well and truly wakes up during this May festival which includes accordion workshops, archaeological walks, art exhibitions and concerts by such high-profile Irish bands as the De Dannan.

Sleeping & Eating

You can pitch a tent on most unfenced ground, but not on or near the beaches.

Inishbofin Island Hostel HOSTEL €
(095-45855; www.inishbofin-hostel.ie; camping per person €10, dm €15-18, d €40-50; early Apr-Sep) In an old farmhouse, this snug 38-bed hostel has glassed-in common areas with panoramic views and equally scenic campsites. It's 500m up from the ferry dock.

Doonmore Hotel HOTEL €€
(095-45804; www.doonmorehotel.com; s €50-65, d €80-100; Apr-Sep;) Close to the harbour, Doonmore has comfortable, unpretentious rooms. Lunch (€15) and dinner (€35) in the dining room take advantage of the abundance of locally caught seafood, and the hotel can pack lunches for you to take while exploring the island.

GUIDED WALKS IN CONNEMARA

Maps of the many walking trails in Connemara are sold at bookshops and tourist offices. However, to really appreciate the region's unique geology, natural beauty and ancient history, you may wish to go with a guide.

Connemara Safari (095-21071; www.walkingconnemara.com) runs five-day tours in the region that include meals and accommodation. Tour leaders are experts in fields such as archaeology. Routes include some of the deserted islands off the coast and cost from €700.

Dolphin Hotel & Restaurant INN €€
(☎095-45991; www.dolphinhotel.ie; r €120-140; ⏲Apr-Sep; @) A panoply of beiges dominates the guest rooms at this stylish study in modern minimalism. Solar panels on the roof and an organic kitchen garden lend green cred. Local seafood and vegetarian dishes dominate the menu (mains €15 to €25). There is usually a two-night minimum stay.

Information

Inishbofin's small post office has a grocery shop.

Tourism association (☎095-45861; www.inishbofin.com) Has good info, including detailed online walking guides.

Getting There & Around

Ferries from Cleggan to Inishbofin take 30 to 45 minutes and are run by **Island Discovery** (☎095-45894, 095-45819; www.inishbofinislanddiscovery.com; adult/child return €20/10). In low season there is one ferry a day, rising to three in summer. Dolphins often swim alongside the boats. Confirm ahead, as ferries may be cancelled when seas are rough.

On the island everything is walkable: the island is a mere 3km by 6km.

Kings Bicycle Hire (☎095-45833), at the pier, hires out bicycles for €15 per day.

Letterfrack & Around

POP 200

Founded by Quakers in the mid-19th century, Letterfrack (Leitir Fraic) is ideally situated for exploring Connemara National Park, Renvyle Point and Kylemore Abbey. The village is really a crossroads with a few pubs and B&Bs, but the forested setting and nearby coast are a magnet for outdoors adventure seekers. A 4km walk to the peak of Tully Mountain takes 40 minutes and affords wonderful ocean views.

Sights

TOP CHOICE **Connemara National Park** NATURE RESERVE
(☎095-41054; www.npws.ie, www.heritageireland.ie; admission free; ⏲visitor centre & facilities 9am-5.30pm, park always open) Immediately southeast of Letterfrack, Connemara National Park spans 2000 dramatic hectares of bog, mountain and heath. The visitor centre is in a beautiful setting off a parking area 300m south of the Letterfrack crossroads.

The park encloses a number of the **Twelve Bens**, including Bencullagh, Benbrack and Benbaun. The heart of the park is **Gleann Mór** (Big Glen), through which the River Polladirk flows. There's fine walking up the glen and over the surrounding mountains. There are also short, self-guided walks and, if the Bens look too daunting, you can hike up **Diamond Hill** nearby.

The visitor centre offers an introduction to the park's flora, fauna and geology, and visitors can scrutinise maps and various trails here before heading out into the park. Various types of flora and fauna native to the area are explained, including the Mothra-sized elephant hawkmoth.

Guided nature walks (⏲Jul & Aug) depart from the visitor centre several days a week. They last two to three hours and cover rough, boggy terrain.

Kylemore Abbey HISTORIC BUILDING
(www.kylemoreabbey.com; adult/child €12/free; ⏲9am-7pm summer, 10am-4.30pm winter) A few kilometres east of Letterfrack stands Kylemore Abbey. Magnificently situated on the shores of a lake, this crenulated 19th-century neo-Gothic fantasy was built for a wealthy English businessman, Mitchell Henry, who spent his honeymoon in Connemara. His wife died tragically young.

Admission also covers the abbey's **Victorian walled gardens**. You can stroll around the lake and surrounding woods for free.

Kylemore's tranquillity is shattered in high summer with the arrival of dozens of tour coaches per day, each one followed through the gates by an average of 50 cars (yes, over 2500 cars a day).

Sleeping

Letterfrack Lodge HOSTEL €
(☎095-41222; www.letterfracklodge.com; campsites from €12, dm €18-22, d €40-60; P@) Close to the Letterfrack crossroads, dorms come in a variety of sizes, but all are spacious. Doubles are like a basic B&B. Mike, the owner, is a great source of info on walks of all kinds through the region.

Getting There & Away

Bus Éireann (www.buseireann.ie) and **Citylink** (www.citylink.ie) buses continue to Letterfrack several times daily from Clifden, 15km southwest on the N59.

Leenane & Killary Harbour

The small village of Leenane (also spelled Leenaun) drowses on the shore of dramatic Killary Harbour. Dotted with mussel rafts, the long, narrow harbour is Ireland's only fjord – maybe. Slicing 16km inland and more than 45m deep in the centre, it certainly looks like a fjord, although some scientific studies suggest it may not actually have been glaciated. **Mt Mweelrea** (819m) towers to its north.

Leenane boasts both stage and screen connections. It was the location for *The Field* (1989), a movie with Richard Harris based on John B Keane's poignant play about a tenant farmer's ill-fated plans to pass on a rented piece of land to his son. The village's name made it onto the theatrical map with the success in London and New York of Martin McDonagh's play *The Beauty Queen of Leenane*.

The local **website** (www.leenanevillage.com) is a good source of info.

Sights

Sheep & Wool Centre MUSEUM
(www.sheepandwoolcentre.com; adult/child €5/3; ⏲9.30am-6pm Apr-Oct) After surveying the countryside studded with sheep, you can roam among them here. At the surprisingly compelling little museum you can see spinning and weaving demonstrations, learn about the history of dyeing and see pics of shepherds having their way with sheep. The centre's shop sells locally made handcrafts, as well as topographical walking maps and there is a cafe.

Activities

Killary Cruises BOAT CRUISE
(www.killarycruises.com; adult/child €21/10; ⏲Apr-Oct) From Nancy's Point, about 2km west of Leenane, Killary Cruises offers 1½-hour cruises of Killary Harbour. Dolphins leap around the boat, which passes by a

WORTH A TRIP

CONNEMARA'S NORTH COAST

Although Connemara is a pearl necklace of sights, the north coast is diamond encrusted. Gorgeous beaches compete for your attention with stark, raw mountain vistas and views out to the moody sea.

Eschew the N59 for a series of small roads that follow the twists and turns along the coast for about 15km. Start at **Letterfrack**, where a narrow track leads northwest. Follow various small roads, sticking as close to the water as you can. Watch for sheep. The land here seems to be in the midst of a beautiful dissolution into the sea. You may find yourself on a road that comes to a dead end at a beach. Good! Get out and frolic.

At **Renvyle** you can pause for the night. **Renvyle Beach Caravan & Camping** (☎095-43462; www.renvylebeachcaravanpark.com; Renvyle; campsites €18; ⏲Easter-Sep) has campsites on a grassy expanse with direct access to a sandy beach.

Renvyle House Hotel (☎095-43511; www.renvyle.com; Renvyle; r €100-250; P 📶 🏊) is a luxurious 68-room converted country estate set on 80 hectares. It was once owned by the poet Oliver St John Gogarty (among his better lines: 'If anyone thinks that I amn't divine, He gets no free drinks when I'm making the wine').

Continue east, past a couple of fine country pubs at the tiny crossroads of **Tully Cross**. Stick to the coast and stop often – especially on sunny days to marvel at the rich kaleidoscope of colours: rich cobalt sea, cerulean sky, emerald-green grass, brown hills, slate-grey rocks and white-sand beaches. The beach horse-racing sequences for *The Quiet Man* were shot at **Lettergesh**.

Look for a turn to **Rosroe Quay**, where a truly magnificent crescent of sand awaits at **Glassillaun Beach**. If you're drawn to the beauty of the water, **Scuba Dive West** (☎095-43922; www.scubadivewest.com) is based at Glassillaun Beach, and runs highly recommended courses and dives around the surrounding coastlines and islands. Rates span the gamut.

Continue southeast along the final 5km stretch of road that runs along **Lough Fee**. In spring when the gorse explodes in yellow bloom, the views here are, again, simply breathtaking.

mussel farm and stops at a salmon farm, where you'll see the fish being fed. There are four cruises daily in summer.

Killary Adventure Centre ADVENTURE SPORTS
(☎095-43411; www.killaryadventure.com; ⏲10am-5pm) Canoeing, sea kayaking, sailing, rock climbing, windsurfing and day hikes are but a few of the activities on offer at this adventure centre approximately 3km west of Leenane on the N59. Rates begin at adult/child €48/32.

Aasleagh Waterfall NATURAL FEATURE
There are several excellent walks from Leenane, including one to Aasleagh Water fall (Eas Liath), about 3km away on the northeastern side of Killary Harbour. Also from Leenane, the road runs west for about 2km along the southern shore. Where the highway veers inland, walkers can continue on an old road along the shore to the tiny fishing community of **Rosroe Quay**.

Croagh Patrick Walking Tours WALKING TOUR
(☎098-26090; www.walkingguideireland.com) For guided day and overnight walks in the region, Gerry Greensmyth has a wealth of local expertise.

Sleeping & Eating

Farmers and other locals come for quiet pints and warming Irish coffees at the gentle sweep of traditional pubs near the bridge. Savour a pint and a meal outside at one of the picnic tables or inside amid the dark wood panelling and enormous open fireplaces.

TOP CHOICE **Delphi Lodge** INN €€€
(☎095-42222; www.delphilodge.ie; s/d from €130/200; P@) You'll wish the dreamy views at this gorgeous country estate could follow you into your dreams. Set among truly stunning mountain and lake vistas, this isolated country house has 12 posh bedrooms and a bevy of common areas including a library and billiards room. The cooking is modern Irish, sourced locally. Meals are taken at a vast communal table. Walks, fishing and much more await outside.

Sleepzone Connemara HOSTEL €
(☎095-42929; www.sleepzone.ie; campsites from €12, dm €20-25, s/d €50/70; ⏲Mar-Oct; @) This renovated 19th-century property has over 100 beds in spotless dorms and private rooms. Popular with walkers, its amenities include a bar, barbecue terrace, tennis court and bike hire. Ask about the transport scheme with a Galway-based tour company.

SOUTH OF GALWAY CITY

Take time to smell the oysters on the busy seaside route between Galway City and County Clare. At Kilcolgan, veer east off the N18 and you'll be rewarded with villages like Kinvara, whose charms may play havoc with your schedule – if you have one.

Clarinbridge & Kilcolgan

POP 2100

Some 16km south of Galway, Clarinbridge (Droichead an Chláirin) and Kilcolgan (Cill Cholgáin) are at their busiest during the **Clarinbridge Oyster Festival** (www.clarenbridge.com), held during the second weekend of September. However, the oysters are actually at their best from May through the summer.

Oysters are celebrated year-round at **Paddy Burke's Oyster Inn** (www.paddyburkesgalway.com; Clarinbridge; mains €10-24; ⏲12.30-10pm), a thatched inn by the bridge dishing up heaped servings in a roadside location on the N18.

TOP CHOICE **Moran's Oyster Cottage** (www.moransoystercottage.com; The Weir, Kilcolgan; mains €14-24; ⏲noon-10pm Mon-Sat, 10am-10pm Sun) is a thatched pub and restaurant with a facade as plain as the inside of an oyster shell. Find a seat on the terrace overlooking Dunbulcaun Bay, where the oysters are reared before they arrive on your plate, and you'll think the world's your... It's a well-marked 2km west of the noxious N18, in a quiet cove near Kilcolgan.

Kinvara

POP 400

The small stone harbour of Kinvara (sometimes spelt Kinvarra) sits smugly at the southeastern corner of Galway Bay, which accounts for its Irish name, Cinn Mhara (Head of the Sea). It's a posh little village, the kind of place where all the jeans have creases in them. It makes a good pit stop between Galway and Clare.

See Kinvara's **website** (www.kinvara.com) for details.

Sights

Dunguaire Castle HISTORIC BUILDING

(www.shannonheritage.com; adult/child €6/3.40; ⏲10am-5pm Easter-Sep) The chess-piece-style Dunguaire Castle was erected around 1520 by the O'Hynes clan and is in excellent condition following extensive restoration. It is widely believed that the castle occupies the former site of the 6th-century royal palace of Guaire Aidhne, the king of Connaught. Dunguaire's owners have included Oliver St John Gogarty (1878–1957) – poet, writer, surgeon and Irish Free State senator.

The least authentic way to visit the castle is to attend a **medieval banquet** (☎061-360 788; www.shannonheritage.com; banquet adult/child €50/24; ⏲5.30pm & 8.45pm Easter-Sep). Yuck-filled stage shows and shtick provide diversions while you plough through a big group meal.

Festivals & Events

Cruinniú na mBáid BOAT RACES

Traditional Galway hooker sailing boats race here each year in the Cruinniú na mBáid (Gathering of the Boats) on the second weekend in August.

Fleadh na gCuach MUSIC FESTIVAL

Kinvara's other big date on its annual calendar is the Cuckoo Festival, a traditional music festival in late May that features over 100 musicians performing at upwards of 50 organised sessions. Spin-off events include a parade.

Eating & Drinking

Kinvara has good places to feast on the bounty of its seaside location; a passel of atmospheric pubs only add to the joy. You won't miss at the appropriately named **Fahy's Travellers Inn** (☎091-637 116) and nearby **Connolly's** (☎091-637 131) on the quay.

TOP CHOICE **Keough's** PUB €€

(Main St, Kinvara; mains €8-25; ⏲kitchen 9am-10pm) This friendly local, where you'll often hear Irish spoken, serves up a fresh battered cod; specials are more ambitious and allow the kitchen to show off its considerable talents. Traditional music sessions take place on Mondays and Thursdays, while Saturday nights swing with old-time dancing.

Getting There & Away

Bus Éireann (www.buseireann.ie) links Kinvara with Galway city (30 minutes) and towns in County Clare, such as Doolin, up to three times daily.

EASTERN GALWAY

Lough Corrib separates eastern Galway from the dramatic landscape of Connemara and the county's western coast, and this region is markedly different. This is farm country and there's nary a hint of the geologic drama and cultural excitement that exists in the west of the county. Several diversions provide good reason to exit the M6 to Dublin.

Galway East Tourism (www.galwayeast.com) has regional information.

Getting There & Away

Bus Éireann (www.buseireann.ie) local services connect Galway with Athenry, Ballinasloe and Loughrea.

Athenry

POP 2200

Just 16km east of Galway, Athenry takes its name from a nearby ford (*áth* in Irish) that crosses the River Clare east of the settlement and was the meeting point for three kingdoms, hence Áth an Rí (Ford of the Kings).

The name is synonymous with the stirring song 'The Fields of Athenry', composed by Pete St John in the 1970s, which recounts incarceration resulting from the Famine. Often thought to be adapted from an 1880s ballad (disputed by St John), it's been covered by countless artists, and is sung by passionate crowds at sporting matches, including in adapted forms such as Liverpool Football Club's anthem, 'The Fields of Anfield Road'.

The **website** (www.athenry.net) has info.

Sights

Touted as Ireland's most intact collection of medieval architecture, underrated Athenry boasts a restored **Norman castle** (www.heritageireland.ie; adult/child €3/1; ⏲10am-5pm Easter-Sep), the **Medieval Parish Church of St Mary's**, a **Dominican priory** with superb masonry on its occupational gravestones, and an original **market cross**.

Athenry Arts & Heritage Activity Centre HERITAGE CENTRE
(www.athenryheritagecentre.com; The Square; 1.30-5pm Mon-Fri summer, 11am-4pm Mon-Fri Mar-Oct) The fascinating Athenry Arts & Heritage Activity Centre explores the town's medieval sights and has a fab walking tour map. It organises recreations of medieval life.

Eating

Old Barracks Pantry CAFE €
(Main St; meals €5-10; 9am-6pm) When you're tired of strolling about and catching surprising ancient views, seek restoration here in the upscale cafe-fare and baked goods.

Organic Market MARKET €
(Market Cross; 9am-4pm Fri) The town's organic market is revered.

Loughrea & Around

POP 4000

Named for the little lake at its southern edge, Loughrea (Baile Locha Riach) is a bustling market town 26km southeast of Galway. Loughrea has the shallow remnant of a medieval **moat**, which runs from the lake at Fair Green near the cathedral to the River Loughrea north of town. Since the opening of the M6, the town is less frenetic with traffic and is good for a stroll.

Not to be confused with St Brendan's Church on Church St, which is now a library, **St Brendan's Catholic Cathedral** (Barrack St; 11.30am-1pm & 2-5.30pm Mon-Fri), dating from 1903, is renowned for its Celtic-revival stained-glass windows, furnishings and marble columns.

Near Bullaun, 7km north of Loughrea, is the pillarlike **Turoe Stone**, covered in delicate La La Tène–style relief carvings. It dates from between 300 BC and AD 100. The Turoe Stone wasn't set here originally, but was found at an Iron Age fort a few kilometres away.

On the road east to Ballinasloe, 6.5km from Loughrea, the **Dartfield Horse Museum & Park** (www.dartfield.com; adult/child €10/5; 9am-6pm) allows horse lovers to learn about horse breeding, carriages, the colourful racing industry and the horse's role in Irish history. The pony rides thrill kids and you can book longer riding adventures on horseback.

Gort & Around

POP 3000

If you're a fan of WB Yeats, two sights connected to the great poet near the agricultural town of Gort are a worthwhile detour on your way to or from Galway on the M/N18.

Sights

Central to Gort is **The Square**, with its personable **Christ the King statue** and shop-filled streets radiating out. But most sights are just outside town.

TOP CHOICE **Thoor Ballyle** HISTORIC BUILDING
(Peterswell; adult/child €6/1.50; 9.30am-5pm Mon-Sat May-Sep) This 16th-century Norman tower was the summer home of Yeats from 1922 to 1929 and was the inspiration for one of his best-known works, *The Tower*. In a truly inspired setting by a stream, the tower contains the poet's furnishings. Yeats once wrote 'The sand is running from the upper glass, And when the last grain's through, I shall be lost', a quote which you may well relate to after your last grain falls through while you try to find this place. From Gort take the Loughrea road (N66) for about 3km northeast and look for signs – but these are often misaligned – or just missing. Be prepared to ask.

Coole Park PARK
(www.coolepark.ie; admission free; 10am-5pm) Once home of Lady Augusta Gregory, co-founder of the Abbey Theatre and a patron of Yeats, the house here was demolished by nitwit bureaucrats in 1941. But displays recall its literary legacy and the present-day nature reserve is a beautiful place to stroll. Look for the autograph tree, on which many of Lady Gregory's literary guests carved their initials. It's about 3km north of Gort off the N18.

Kiltartan Gregory Museum MUSEUM
(Kiltartan Cross; 10am-6pm Jun-Aug) Lady Gregory is honoured in full at this small museum close to Coole Park. Housed in an old schoolhouse, it traces the literary patron's life.

TOP CHOICE **Kilmacduagh** HISTORIC SITE
This extensive monastic site is beside a small lake and includes a well-preserved 34m-high round tower, the remains of a small 14th-century cathedral (Teampall Mór MacDuagh), an oratory dedicated to St John the

Baptist, and other little chapels. The original monastery is thought to have been founded by St Colman MacDuagh at the beginning of the 7th century. There are fine views over the Burren from here and you can visit any time. It's about 5km southwest of Gort off the R460.

Eating

Kettle of Fish FISH & CHIPS
(The Square; meals €5-9; ⏲noon-late) The sparkling Kettle of Fish is the sort of joint that reminds you how good expertly prepared fish and chips can be.

Getting There & Away

Until 2013 at the earliest, the M18 from Ennis stops at Gort and tosses drivers onto the less fancy N18. Still, it has extracted traffic from the centre. Most Galway–Ennis buses stop here, as do trains on the new Ennis–Galway railway line.

Ballinasloe

POP 6000

Just off the M6, Ballinasloe (Béal Átha na Sluaighe) is famed for its historic October **horse fair** (www.ballinasloe.com), which dates right back to the high kings of Tara. The fair has an old-time carnival atmosphere, created by the 80,000-plus horse traders and merrymakers who roll into town. They include Ireland's Traveller community, who camp nearby in traditional barrel-topped wagons. To learn more about Traveller culture, the websites of the **Irish Traveller Movement** (www.itmtrav.ie) and **Pavee Point Travellers Centre** (www.paveepoint.ie) are good resources.

Around 6km southwest of town on the R446, **Aughrim** was the site of the bloodiest battle ever fought on Irish soil, which ended in a crucial victory by William of Orange over the Catholic forces of James II. The **Battle of Aughrim Interpretive Centre** (adult/child €5/3; ⏲10am-6pm Tue-Sat, 2-6pm Sun Jun–mid-Sep) helps place it within the context of the War of the Two Kings. Battle sites pepper the surrounding countryside but thickets of signs often leave visitors going in circles when the centre is closed (it has essential directions).

Heading 21km southeast of Ballinasloe brings you to 12th-century **Clonfert Cathedral**. It's on the site of a monastery said to have been founded in AD 563 by St Brendan 'the Navigator', who is believed to be buried here. Although the jury is out on whether St Brendan reached America's shores in a tiny *currach*, there are Old Irish Ogham (the earliest form of writing in Ireland) carvings in West Virginia that date from as early as the 6th century, suggesting an Irish presence in America well before Columbus set foot there.

The marvellous six-arch Romanesque doorway, adorned with surreal human heads, is reason enough to visit. The cathedral is off the R356; you'll need your own car to get here.

Portumna

POP 1900

In the southeast corner of the county, the lakeside town of Portumna is popular for boating and fishing. **Lough Derg Holiday Park** (www.loughderg.net) rents boats for €50/65 half-day/day.

Impressive **Portumna Castle & Gardens** (www.heritageireland.ie; Castle Ave; adult/child €3/1; ⏲9.30am-6pm Apr-Oct) was built in the early 1600s by Richard de Burgo and boasts an elaborate, geometrically laid-out organic garden.

Counties Mayo & Sligo

POPULATION: 195,000 / AREA: 7234 SQ KM

Includes »

Best Places to Eat

- » Source (p449)
- » Pier (p444)
- » Rua (p446)
- » An Port Mór (p435)

Best Places to Stay

- » Delphi Lodge (p430)
- » Newport House (p436)
- » Ice House (p444)
- » Mount Falcon Country House Hotel (p444)
- » Temple House (p453)

Why Go?

Despite their natural wonders and languid charm, the counties Mayo and Sligo remain a well-kept secret offering all of Ireland's wild, romantic beauty but without the crowds. Mayo is the more rugged of the two with scraggy peaks, sheer cliffs, heather-covered moors and beautiful offshore islands where life is dictated by the elements. Sligo is more pastoral and its lush fields, fish-filled lakes and flat-topped mountains inspired William Butler Yeats to compose some of Ireland's most ardent verse. Both counties boast grand stretches of golden sands and legendary breaks that lure the surfing cognoscenti from around the globe. Visit and you'll find all this plus an improbable bounty of prehistoric sites, elegant Georgian towns, little fishing villages and good old-fashioned warm-hearted country hospitality.

When to Go

The weather-beaten shores of Mayo and Sligo can be whipped by brutal winds and rain in winter when only the hardiest tourists and surfers make it here. If you're interested in catching a swell, spring and autumn are your best shot with September and October favoured by those in the know. In summer the region bursts into life with a plethora of festivals and in August you'll get the pick of the crop with the Yeats Festival in Sligo and a variety of small traditional music festivals elsewhere.

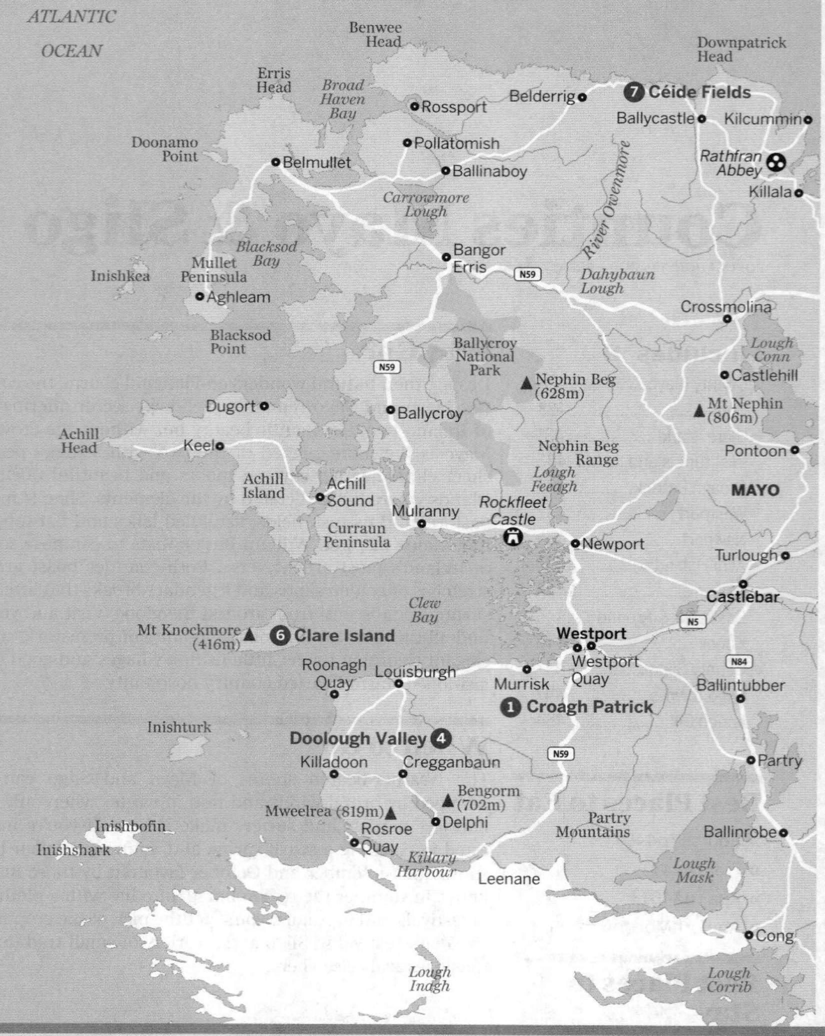

Counties Mayo & Sligo Highlights

1. Follow in St Patrick's footsteps up the conical peak of **Croagh Patrick** (p432)
2. Hit the waves year-round at **Easkey** (p454)
3. Sink into the soft water and coiling seaweed of a **homeopathic bath** at Enniscrone (see boxed text, p455)
4. Walk along the starkly beautiful and poignantly desolate **Doolough Valley** (p430)

5 Make the pilgrimage to the otherworldly **Carrowkeel Megalithic Cemetery** (p453) for panoramic views

6 Go in search of Ireland's pirate queen, Granuaile on craggy **Clare Island** (p431)

7 Marvel at the ancient planning of the world's most extensive Stone Age monument at the **Céide Fields** (p442)

COUNTY MAYO

Mayo's wild beauty and haunting landscapes are reminiscent of Connemara but you'll find far fewer tourists here, which means there are plenty of untapped opportunities for exploration by car, foot, bicycle or horseback. Life here has never been easy and the Potato Famine (1845–51) ravaged the county and prompted mass emigration. Consequently many people with Irish ancestry around the world can trace their roots to this once-plagued land.

Because of its close proximity to Connemara, we've arranged this section going from south to north, starting with the photogenic village of Cong, which can be found just over the border from County Galway.

Cong

POP 150

Sitting on a sliver-thin isthmus between Lough Corrib and Lough Mask, Cong complies with romantic notions of a traditional Irish village. Time appears to have stood still ever since the evergreen classic *The Quiet Man* was filmed here in 1951. As such, the arrival of the morning's first tour bus instantly doubles the number of people strolling the town's tiny streets, but the wooded trails between the lovely old abbey and stately Ashford Castle offer genuine quietude.

Sights

FREE Cong Abbey HISTORIC SITE

(dawn-dusk) An evocative reminder of ecclesiastical times past, the weathered shell of Cong's 12th-century Augustinian abbey is scored by wizened lines from centuries of exposure to the elements. Nevertheless, several finely sculpted features have survived, including a carved doorway, windows and lovely medieval arches (touched up in the 19th century).

Founded in 1120 by Turlough Mór O'Connor, high king of Ireland and king of Connaught, the abbey occupies the site of an earlier 6th-century church. The community once gathered in the chapter house to confess their sins publicly.

From the abbey, moss-encrusted trees guard a path to the river and the diminutive 16th-century **monk's fishing house**, built midway over the river so that the monks could haul their catch straight up through a hole in the floor.

Ashford Castle HISTORIC BUILDING

(094-954 6003; www.ashford.ie; grounds admission €5; 9am-dusk) Just beyond Cong Abbey, the village abruptly ends and the woodlands surrounding Ashford Castle begin. First built in 1228 as the seat of the de Burgo family, owners over the years included the Guinness family (of stout fame). Arthur Guinness turned the castle into a regal hunting and fishing lodge, which it remains today.

The only way to peek into its immaculately restored interior is to stay or dine here. But the surrounding estate – 140 hectares of parkland, covered with forests, streams, bridle paths and a golf course – is open to the public. Heading through the Kinlough Woods gets you away from the golfers and out to the shores of Lough Corrib. You can also walk along the riverbanks to the monk's fishing house.

Quiet Man Museum MUSEUM

(Circular Rd; admission €5; 10am-4pm Mar-Oct) Modelled on Sean Thornton's White O' Mornin' Cottage from the film, the Quiet Man Museum also squeezes in a fascinating regional archaeological and historical exhibition of items from 7000 BC to the 19th century. Film fanatics (or those with a postmodern fascination for the way reality and fiction blur) can take a 75-minute **location tour** (€15; 11am Apr-Sep), which includes museum entry.

Activities

Corrib Cruises BOAT TOUR

(www.corribcruises.com; adult/child €20/10) A range of cruises on Lough Corrib departing from the Ashford Castle pier. A one-hour history cruise leaves daily year-round at 11am; a two-hour island cruise departs at 2.45pm from June to September and visits Inchagoill, an island at the centre of Lough Corrib where there's a 45-minute stop to visit the 5th-century monastic ruins; and a one-hour traditional music cruise departs daily at 6pm from July to September.

Falconry School FALCONRY

(www.falconry.ie) The medieval splendour of Ashford Castle is a fitting setting to learn the ancient art of falconry. The falconry school offers a choice of one-hour (€70) or 90-minute (€105) 'hawk walks' where participants learn about and handle the impressive Harris hawks.

Sleeping

Lisloughrey Lodge HOTEL €€€
(094-954 5400; www.lisloughreylodgehotel.ie; The Quay; r from €160; P@) The lodge, built in the 1820s by Ashford Castle's owners, has been stunningly renovated in bold, contemporary cranberry and blueberry tones, with 50 guest rooms named for wine regions and champagne houses. Kick back in the bar, billiards room, or beanbag-strewn Wii room. Nab a room in the original house for the old world character.

Michaeleen's Manor B&B €€
(094-954 6089; www.congbb.com; Quay Rd, Lisloughrey; s/d €50/65; P) Margaret and Gerry Collins' large, modern home is something of a shrine to *The Quiet Man*. Each of its 12 sparkling rooms is named after a character in the film and decorated with memorabilia and quotations. There's also a sauna, outdoor hot tub, tennis court, and a large fountain replica of the Quiet Man Bridge.

Cong Hostel HOSTEL €
(094-954 6089; www.quietman-cong.com; Quay Rd, Lisloughrey; dm/d €17/52; P@) Well run and welcoming, this An Óige and IHH-affiliated hostel has its own *Quiet Man* screening room showing the film *every* night. Between June and mid-September it also hires bikes (€15 per day) and 18ft boats (€55). You can also choose to camp in the adjacent campground (campsite €20 for two people).

Ashford Castle HOTEL €€€
(094-954 6003; www.ashford.ie; r €350-850; P@) Old world elegance, exquisite rooms and faultless service are on tap at Ashford Castle but if you can't afford to stay you can come for dinner (from €70) at the George V restaurant. Do dress the part though (that's a jacket and tie guys) as it's rather posh around here.

Hazel Grove B&B €
(094-954 6060; www.cong-bnb.com; Drumshiel; s/d from €48/60; P) Warm and friendly Irish hospitality is in store at this simple B&B in a typical family home.

Ryan's Hotel HOTEL €
(094-954 6243; www.ryanshotelcong.ie; Main St; s/d €45/60; P@) Simple, comfortable rooms in the heart of town.

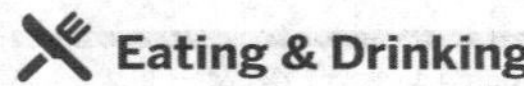

Eating & Drinking

Hungry Monk CAFE €
(Abbey St; mains €6-14; 10am-6pm Mon-Sat, 11am-5pm Sun Apr-Aug, 10am-6pm Wed-Mon Sep-Dec & Mar; @) This cheery little cafe with its bright colours and artfully mismatched furniture is the best lunch spot in town. Locally sourced ingredients make up the fab sandwiches (such as homebaked ham served with mango chutney), soups and salads, the luscious cakes are all homemade and it brews the best coffee in town.

Fennel Seed IRISH €€
(094-954 6004; Ryan's Hotel, Main St; bar food €14-21, mains €15-25; dinner Mon-Sat, 1-7pm Sun) Michael Crowe and Denis Lenihan used to cook at Ashford Castle and have brought their culinary skills to the village, with great success (don't miss their signature 'smoky bake' pie, filled with trout, salmon, mackerel and haddock). Bar food is served in the adjoining Crowe's Nest Pub until 7pm.

Salt IRISH €€€
(094-954 5400; www.lisloughreylodgehotel.ie; The Quay; mains €19-29; dinner nightly May-Sep, Thu-Sun Oct-Apr) Book ahead for Wade Murphy's sophisticated twists on Irish cuisine like seared scallops with black pudding and green pea veloute, followed by seabass with caramelised fennel, and gooseberry souffle with butterscotch and cream. Yum.

Pat Cohan's PUB
(Abbey St) In a bizarre case of life imitating art, this one-time grocery store was disguised in *The Quiet Man* as the fictional Pat Cohan's. But nearly six decades on, *Quiet Man* craziness refuses to die down, and it has now become that pub.

Information

The **tourist office** (094-954 6542; www.congtourism.com; Abbey St; 10am-6pm Mar-Nov) is in the old courthouse building opposite Cong Abbey. There are no banks or ATMS, but you can change money at the post office on Main St, or at the museum.

Getting There & Away

There are three buses to Galway (€10.30, one hour) Monday to Saturday and four to Westport (€9.30, one hour). The bus stops on Main St.

Around Cong

The Cong area is honeycombed with 10 limestone caves, each with a colourful legend or story to its credit.

One of the best is **Pigeon Hole**, in a pine forest about 1.5km west of Cong. It can be reached by road or by the walking track from across the river. Steep, slippery stone steps lead down into the cave, where subterranean water flows in winter. Keep an eye out for the white trout of Cong – a mythical woman who turned into a fish to be with her drowned lover.

Just west of the village is the water-filled **Captain Webb's Hole**. Two centuries ago, a local villain nicknamed Captain Webb for the deformity of his hands and feet, is said to have lured a succession of 12 women here, stripped them and hurled them into the hole's soggy depths to die. His would-be 13th victim however was a canny lass. She asked Webb to look away as she undressed, then promptly pushed him to his own watery grave.

Weathering the elements since the Early Bronze Age, the **Cong Stone Circle** sticks up from a field about 1.5km northeast of Cong, with a further three stone circles directly behind. About 3.5km east of Cong, north off the Cross road (R346), is the overgrown **Ballymacgibbon Cairn**, supposedly the site of the legendary Celtic Battle of Moytura between the invading Dananns and the defending Fir Bolgs.

Turning off at the northern end of the village of Neale, 6km northeast of Cong, you'll find the **Gods of the Neale** stone 200m east of the main road, through an unsigned gateway on the left. This mysterious slab, which is dated 1757, is carved with figures of a human, an animal and a reptile.

Doolough Valley & Around

Desolate Doolough Valley is largely untouched by housing, cut turf or even stone walls. The steep sides of the surrounding mountains simply slide into the steely grey waters of Doo Lough as sheep graze quietly on the hills.

This beautiful scenic route along the R335 from Leenane (County Galway) to Westport is one of Ireland's most poignant spots. It was the site of a tragic Famine walk, which took place in 1849. In icy weather, 400 people died along the road as they walked from Louisburgh to Delphi and back. They'd hoped to receive food and aid from a landlord, but were refused.

Choose a dry day to tackle the road as curtains of rain can greatly diminish the views. If you have time wander down the side roads to the north and west of the valley to reach glorious, often-deserted beaches.

DELPHI

Geographically *just* inside County Mayo, but administratively in County Galway, this swath of mountainous moorland is miles from any significant population, allowing you to set about the serious business of relaxing.

At the southern extent of the Doolough Valley, the area was named by its most famous resident, the second Marquis of Sligo, who was convinced that it resembled the land around Delphi, Greece. If you can spot the resemblance, you've a better imagination than most, but in many ways it's even more striking than its Mediterranean namesake.

Delphi Lodge (☎095-42222; www.delphilodge.ie; s/d from €132/198, cottages per week from €800; P@), a wonderful Georgian mansion built by the Marquis of Sligo, is dwarfed by its mountain backdrop. Blurring the boundaries between private house and country

BOYCOTT BEGINNINGS

It was near the unassuming little village of Neale, near Cong, that the term 'boycott' came into use. In 1880, the Irish Land League, in an effort to press for fair rents and improve the lot of workers, withdrew field hands from the estate of Lord Erne, who owned much of the land in the area. When Lord Erne's land agent, Captain Charles Cunningham Boycott, evicted the striking labourers, the surrounding community began a campaign to ostracise the agent. Not only did farmers refuse to work his land, people in the town refused to talk to him, provide services or sit next to him in church. The incident attracted attention from the London papers, and soon Boycott's name was synonymous with such organised, nonviolent protests. Within a few months, Boycott gave up and left Ireland.

hotel, this place will immediately put you at ease. Beautiful interiors, vast grounds, incredible food (dinner €49), a serious lack of pretension and staff that simply seem to anticipate your needs without ever being overbearing, make it a truly unique place to stay. It's as popular with **fishers** (tuition per half day €125) as it is with those simply aiming to relax. The really keen can have their own catch cooked up and served in the communal dining room.

The multipurpose **Delphi Mountain Resort** (☎095-42208; www.delphimountainresort.com; dm €40, d from €158; P@), built from rough-cut stone and honey-coloured wood, blends seamlessly into its stunning surroundings. You can opt for a day's **surfing**, **kayaking**, **abseiling** or **archery** (€60/45 per day/half-day) followed by a stay in the simple 8-bed dorms or go for a sumptuous suite or loft room and some pampering spa treatments using hand-harvested local seaweed.

LOUISBURGH

POP 314

The northern gateway to the Doolough Valley, the little village of Louisburgh, was founded under curious circumstances in 1795. Based on a simple four-street system known as the Cross, the whole town was designed and built as a living memorial to a relative of the first Marquis of Sligo, Lord Altamont (John Browne): his kinsman was killed at the Battle of Louisburgh in Nova Scotia, 1758.

The **Granuaile Visitor Centre** (☎098-66341; Church St; adult/concession €4/2; ⏰11am-5pm Jun-Sep, 10.30am-2pm Mon-Fri Oct-May), in the library, offers a quick but illuminating glimpse into the life and times of Grace O'Malley (1530–1603) the infamous pirate queen of Connaught.

The safe, sandy beach at Carrowmore just east of the village offers good views of Croagh Patrick and has a lifeguard on duty in summer. There are also some excellent surf beaches in the vicinity. Contact **Surf Mayo** (☎087 621 2508; www.surfmayo.com) for gear rental and lessons.

If you'd like to stay in the area try **Ponderosa** (☎098-66440; Tooreen Rd; s/d €50/70; ⏰Apr-Oct; P) a friendly B&B set in a modern bungalow. For dinner don't miss **Hudson's Pantry** (☎098-23747; Long St; mains €16-24; ⏰dinner Wed-Sun) a simple-looking place that serves an outstanding menu that sees diners coming from miles around. Booking is advisable.

Bus 450 links Westport and Louisburgh (€6.50, 25 minutes, up to three times daily Monday to Saturday) via Murrisk.

KILLADOON

Panoramic ocean views and vast sandy beaches fan out from tiny Killadoon. The empty beaches are idyllic for walking or horse riding – see p434 for riding stables.

Take the narrow coastal road heading south from Louisburgh, or turn west off the R335 at Cregganbaun. Bus 450 from Westport (€8.70) and Louisburgh (€3.40) continues to Killadoon twice daily on Thursdays only. The trip takes about 15 minutes.

Clare Island

POP 130

Clew Bay is dotted with some 365 islands, of which the largest is the mountainous Clare Island, 5km offshore but half a world away. Dominated by rocky **Mt Knockmore** (461m), its varied terrain is terrific for walking and climbing, and swimming can be enjoyed at safe, sandy beaches. The island is also one of the dwindling number of places where you can find choughs (resembling blackbirds but with red beaks).

For more information try www.clareisland.info.

Sights & Activities

The island has the ruins of the Cistercian **Clare Island Abbey** (c 1460) and **Granuaile's Castle**, both associated with the piratical Grace O'Malley. The tower castle was her stronghold, although it was altered considerably when the coastguard took it over in 1831. Grace is said to be buried in the small abbey, which contains a stone inscribed with her family motto: 'Invincible on land and sea'.

The island is a great place to relax, retreat from the world and learn new skills. At **Ballytoughey Loom** (www.clareisland.info/loom) you can take weekend workshops on spinning, weaving and natural dyeing. Nearby **Clare Island Yoga Retreat Centre** (www.yogaretreats.ie) runs yoga retreats and vegetarian cooking courses, and art classes and workshops are held at **Clare Island Art Studio** (www.clareislandfineart.com).

The island is also a popular spot for **diving** with a variety of dive sites and excellent visibility. Contact **Islands West** (www.islandswest.ie) for information.

Sleeping & Eating

O'Grady's B&B €€
(☎098-22991; www.ogradysguesthouse.com; s/d €75/90) You'll find bright, modern rooms with tasteful, neutral colour schemes at this modern B&B near the pier. This place also doubles as the island's only **restaurant** (lunch €5-12, dinner €12-21) and serves an excellent choice of seafood.

Cois Abhainn B&B €€
(☎098-26216; Toremore; s/d €40/70; ⏲May-Oct) For a real 'ends-of-the-earth' feeling, head to the windswept southwestern corner of the island, 5km from the harbour. This cosy B&B has a spectacular location with views of Inishturk Island. Not all rooms have private bathrooms, though prices are the same for all. Evening meals (€20) can be arranged.

Getting There & Around

Ferries depart from Roonagh Quay, 8km west of Louisburgh, around 10 times daily in July and August, twice daily the rest of the year. The trip takes 20 minutes (adult/child return €15/8).

Clare Island Ferries (☎098-23737, 087 241 4653; www.clareislandferry.com)

O'Malley's Ferries (☎098-25045, 086 887 0814; www.omalleyferries.com)

Enquire at the pier for taxis and **bikes** (☎098-25640; per day €10).

Inishturk Island

POP 100

Still further off the beaten track is ruggedly beautiful Inishturk, which lies 12km off Mayo's western coast. It's sparsely populated and little visited, despite the two **sandy beaches** on its eastern side, impressive cliffs, wonderful **flora & fauna**, and a rugged, hilly landscape that's ideal for **walking**. In fact, ambling along the island's maze of country roads is a perfect way to adapt to the pace of life here. The island's website (www.inishturkisland.com) is a good source of information.

If you want to stay, the scenically positioned **Teach Abhainn** (☎098-45510; s/d €40/78; dinner €25; ⏲Apr-Oct), a working farm 1.5km west of the harbour, has mesmerising views, hearty home cooking and comfy rooms.

John Heanue operates a twice-daily **ferry** (☎098-45541, 086 202 9670; adult/child return €25/12.50) from Roonagh Quay, near Louisburgh; the crossing takes 45 minutes. There's also less frequent service to Cleggan in County Galway.

Croagh Patrick

Just 8km southwest of Westport, St Patrick couldn't have picked a better spot for a pilgrimage than this conical mountain (also known as 'the Reek'). On a clear day the tough two-hour climb rewards with stunning views over Clew Bay and its sandy islets.

It was on Croagh Patrick that Ireland's patron saint fasted for 40 days and nights, and where he reputedly banished venomous snakes. Climbing the 765m holy mountain is an act of penance for thousands of pilgrims on the last Sunday of July (Reek Sunday). The truly contrite take the original 40km route from Ballintubber Abbey, Tóchar Phádraig (Patrick's Causeway), and ascend the mountain barefoot.

The trail taken by less contrite folk begins in the village of Murrisk. Opposite the car park is the **National Famine Memorial**, a spine-chilling sculpture of a three-masted ghost ship wreathed in swirling skeletons, commemorating the lives lost on so-called 'coffin ships' employed to help people escape the Famine. The path down past the memorial leads to the scant remains of **Murrisk Abbey**, founded by the O'Malleys in 1547.

For warming turf fires, good food and a convivial atmosphere head for the raspberry-pink-painted pub the **Tavern** (www.tavernmurrisk.com; Murrisk; mains €9-27) which serves great seafood.

Westport

POP 5163

Bright and vibrant even in the depths of winter, Westport is a photogenic Georgian town with tree-lined streets, a riverside mall and a great vibe. With an excellent choice of accommodation, restaurants and pubs renowned for their music, it's an extremely popular spot yet has never sold its soul to tourism. A couple of kilometres west on Clew Bay, the town's harbour, Westport Quay is a picturesque spot for a sundowner.

Westport is Mayo's nightlife hub (though it has clamped down on hen-and-stag revellers), and its central location makes it a convenient and enjoyable base for exploring the county.

THE PIRATE QUEEN

The life of Grace O'Malley (Gráinne Ní Mháille or Granuaile, 1530–1603) reads like an unlikely work of adventure fiction for overactive teenagers. Twice widowed and twice imprisoned for acts of piracy, she was a fearsome presence in the troubled landscape of 16th-century Ireland, when traditional chieftains were locked in battle with the English for control of the country.

Her unorthodox life was the stuff of legend and mythology, hundreds of stories testify to her unequalled courage, skill and dogged determination to protect her clan against virtually anyone else – from rival chieftains to the British army.

Born into a powerful sea-faring family that controlled most of the Mayo coastline and traded internationally, the independent Grace soon decided she should join the family line. Legend has it that while still a child she asked her father if she could join a trip to Spain but was refused on the grounds that seafaring was not for girls. She promptly cut off all her hair, dressed in boys clothing, returned to the ship and announced that she was ready to sail. Her amused family nicknamed her Gráinne Mhaol (pronounced grawn-ya wail; bald Grace), a name which stuck for the rest of her life.

At 15 she was married off to Donal O'Flaherty, a querulous local chieftain, but her astute nature and tactical negotiations ensured that she soon eclipsed her husband in politics and trade. The O'Flahertys were banned from trading in Galway, one of the largest ports in the British Isles, but Grace got around this by waylaying heavily-laden vessels en route to port demanding payment for safe passage. If they refused she simply ordered her men to board and loot to their heart's content. A fearsome commander and terrific sailor, she soon amassed significant wealth.

After her husband's death, Grace settled on Clare Island, though her exploits took her all around the Irish and Scottish coasts. On returning from one trip she stopped off at Howth, then Dublin's busiest port and, as was the custom, sought hospitality at Howth Castle. She was refused entry at the gate and was told the family were at dinner. Incensed, Grace kidnapped the Lord's son and only released him when a promise was made that the castle gates would remain open and an extra place set at every meal for unexpected guests. It is a practice still followed to this day.

By now the only part of Clew Bay not under her control was Rockfleet, so in 1566 Grace married Richard an-Iarrain to gain control of his castle. Under Brehon law marriage was 'for one year certain' and legend has it that when the year was up, Gráinne had established herself firmly in the castle, locked its doors and called out a window 'Richard Burke, I dismiss you'. She effectively ended the marriage but kept the castle. Despite this, Burke and O'Malley remained together until his death 17 years later.

By the 1570s Grace's blatant piracy had come to English attention and many attempts were made to capture her. The new governor of Connaught, Sir Richard Bingham, soon became her arch enemy. Unvanquished, Grace was ordered to London in 1593, whereupon Queen Elizabeth I granted her a pardon and offered her a title: she declined, saying she was already Queen of Connaught.

Grace O'Malley died in her own home in 1603, and is thought to have been buried in the family crypt on Clare Island.

Sights

Westport House HISTORIC BUILDING
(☎098-27766; www.westporthouse.ie; Quay Rd; house & gardens adult/child €12/6.50, house, gardens & Pirate Adventure Park adult/child €24/16.50; ⊙house & gardens 10am-6pm mid-Apr–Aug, to 4pm Mar & Sep) Built in 1730 on the ruins of Grace O'Malley's 16th-century castle, this charming Georgian mansion retains much of its original contents and has some stunning period-styled rooms. The house is set in glorious gardens but the overall effect is marred by its commercial overhaul of recent years. Children will love it however, and the **Pirate Adventure Park**, complete with a swinging pirate ship, a 'pirate's playground' and a rollercoaster-style flume ride through a water channel are big hits.

To reach Westport House, turn right just before Westport Quay.

Westport

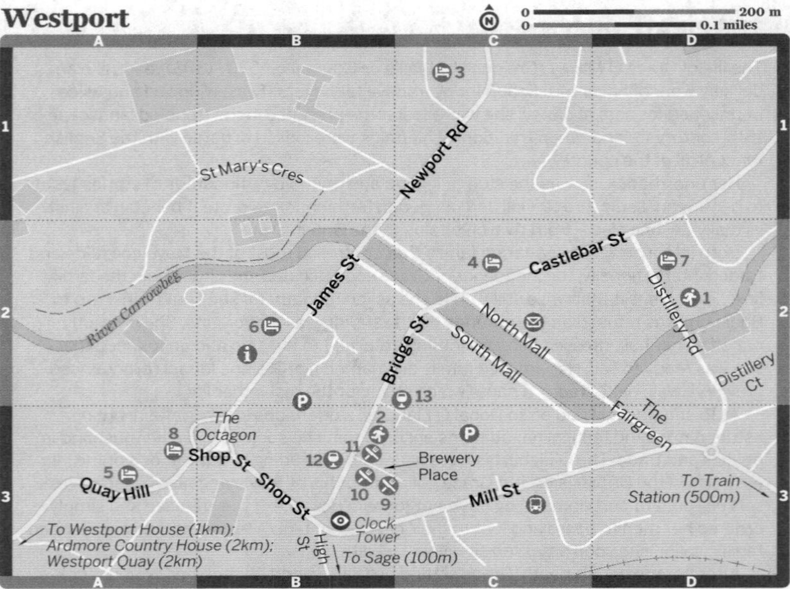

Westport

Activities, Courses & Tours

1 Clew Bay Bike Hire........D2
2 Hewetson........B3

Sleeping

3 Abbeywood Hostel........C1
4 Castlecourt Hotel........C2
5 McCarthy's Lodge........A3
6 Old Mill Holiday Hostel........B2
7 St Anthony's........D2
8 Wyatt Hotel........A3

Eating

9 An Port Mór........B3
10 JJ O'Malleys........B3
11 Sol Rio........B3

Drinking

12 Matt Molloy's........B3
13 Moran's........C2

Clew Bay Heritage Centre MUSEUM
(www.museumsofmayo.com; The Quay; adult/child €3/free; ⏲10am-5pm Mon-Fri Jun-Sep & 3-5pm Sun Jul & Aug) Set in a 19th-century stone building, this museum traces the history, customs and traditions of Westport and Clew Bay. The museum is on The Quay, a couple of kilometres west of town.

Activities

Horse Riding

Beach treks and horse riding on trails overlooking Clew Bay are available from **Carrowholly Stables** (www.carrowholly-stables.com; Carrowholly), 3km north of the town centre off the N59, and **Westport Woods Riding Centre** (www.westportwoodshotel.com) at the hotel of the same name.

Cycling

The area around Westport is great for cycling with gentle coastal routes or more challenging mountain trails within a few kilometres of town. **Clew Bay Bike Hire** (☎098-24818; www.clewbayoutdoors.ie; Distillery Rd; bike hire per day €15; ⏲9am-6pm) can offer advice on routes and trails in the area and has depots along the **Great Western Greenway**, a 54km cycling route between Westport and Achill. With depots in Westport, Newport, Mulranny or Achill, you can start the trail at any point and be picked up on completion. A one way drop off/collection service costs an extra €20.

Fishing

For tackle, camping gear and all-weather clothing, head to **Hewetson** (Bridge St; ⏱10am-5pm Mon-Sat). They also have information about fishing conditions.

Sleeping

Westport is Mayo's major tourist magnet and while there's an abundance of B&Bs and hotels, rooms are in short supply during summer and special events. The tourist office can book rooms for a €4 service fee. Rates drop considerably outside peak periods.

Westport Woods Hotel HOTEL €€
(☎098-25811; www.westportwoodshotel.com; Quay Rd; s/d from €75/110; P@) Hidden behind the stone wall of Westport House, this place prides itself on its green credentials. Rooms are large and spacious but lacking a little soul while service is professional but impressively personalised, for a hotel its size. There's an excellent free children's club, bicycles to borrow, a zip wire, high rope course, a climbing wall and free pick up from the local train station.

Castlecourt Hotel HOTEL €€€
(☎098-55088; www.castlecourthotel.ie; Castlebar St; r from €140; P@) Spacious but cosy rooms that blend contemporary style with classic elegance are on offer at this modern hotel in the town centre. Deluxe rooms have four-poster beds and Jacuzzi baths, there's a luxurious spa, an outdoor rock pool and a decent restaurant on site.

St Anthony's B&B €€
(☎098-28887; www.st-anthonys.com; Distillery Rd; s/d €45/80; P) This genteel B&B sits under cover of a large hedge and thick, twisted vines inhabited by birds' nests. The interior shelters six simple but elegant rooms; two have Jacuzzi-style baths. Call ahead to arrange your arrival time.

Wyatt Hotel HOTEL €€
(☎098-25027; www.wyatthotel.com; The Octagon; r from €129; P) Slap bang in the centre of town, this sunflower-yellow hotel is a local landmark. The rooms are comfortable but rather corporate in style, service is extremely friendly and there's free guest access to the nearby leisure centre.

Old Mill Holiday Hostel HOSTEL €
(☎098-27045; www.oldmillhostel.com; James St; dm €18.50, d €49;) Inside a converted stone mill, this central hostel has 58 beds spread across its well-kept rooms, and inviting communal areas that make for a laid-back social vibe. Rates include free tea, coffee and toast.

Abbeywood Hostel HOSTEL €
(☎098-25496; www.abbeywoodhouse.com; Newport Rd; dm from €20, d €60; ⏱May-Sep; P@) Originally part of a monastery, this orderly hostel hasn't quite lost its institutional aura with stained glass windows in places, polished wood floors and high ceilings. Rates include continental breakfast.

Ardmore Country House HOTEL €€€
(☎098-25994; www.ardmorecountryhouse.com; The Quay; r from €140; ⏱Easter-Oct; P) In a secluded setting overlooking Clew Bay, this lovely guesthouse has 13 luxurious rooms with sleigh beds, richly textured fabrics and a genuinely warm atmosphere.

McCarthy's Lodge B&B €€
(☎098-27050; www.mccarthyslodge.com; Quay Hill; s/d €50/70) Upstairs from a friendly pub, McCarthy's eight rooms are as tidy as the town.

Westport House Caravan & Camping Park CAMPGROUND €
(www.westporthouse.ie; Westport House, Quay Rd; campsites €30; ⏱May-early Sep) Wide-open spaces and proximity to Westport House's funfair-like attractions make this site a hit for families with young children.

Eating

Westport is packed with restaurants and cafes, just wander along Bridge St and the little laneways off it to find a host of options.

An Port Mór SEAFOOD €€
(☎098-26730; www.anportmore.com; 1 Brewery Pl; mains €15-24; ⏱6-10pm Tue-Sun) Hidden down a lane off Bridge St, this wonderful little restaurant packs quite a punch. It's an intimate kind of place with a series of long narrow rooms and a menu that's understandably strong on seafood. Dishes such as Inishturk crab linguine and pan-fried organic Achill sea trout are deceptively simple but just packed with flavour. Book ahead.

Sage ITALIAN €€
(☎098-56700; www.sagewestport.ie; 10 High St; mains €16-23; ⏱dinner Tue-Sun) A wave of warmth hits you as soon as you walk through the door of this stylish Italian restaurant at the top end of town. Smiling staff, the smell of yeast and the bowls of steaming homemade pasta just seem so enticing. The menu lives up to expectations with a good

selection of local fish dishes as well as the generous portions of pasta.

Sol Rio MEDITERRANEAN €€
(☎098-28944; www.solrio.ie; Bridge St; mains lunch €7-14, dinner €13-24; ⊙closed Tue) The extensive menu at this friendly restaurant ranges from pizza and pasta to organic meat and fish. Carefully sourced ingredients and attention to detail mean that dishes are top-notch whether you choose to eat in the simple cafe downstairs or the more stylish restaurant upstairs. Book in advance.

Quay Cottage SEAFOOD €€
(☎098-26412; Harbour; mains €18-25; ⊙dinner mid-Feb–mid-Jan) Serving seafood straight off the boats and steeped in salty-dog charm (including lobster pots hanging from the roof beams), this is the pick of places to eat on Westport's lively harbourfront.

JJ O'Malley's FUSION €€
(☎098-27307; www.jjomalleys.ie; Bridge St; mains €14-25; ⊙dinner) Perennially popular and always buzzing, this feel-good restaurant serves an extensive menu of classic comfort foods from around the globe.

Sheebeen SEAFOOD €€
(☎098-26528; Rosbeg; mains €15-25; ⊙noon-9pm Jun-Aug, Fri dinner, Sat & Sun lunch & dinner Sep-May) This traditional pub serves a fine selection of seafood in relaxed surroundings on the shores of Clew Bay.

Drinking & Entertainment

Westport is thronged with pubs, many of them with live music nightly.

Matt Molloy's PUB
(Bridge St) Matt Malloy, the fife player from the Chieftains, opened this old-school pub years ago and the good times haven't let up. Head to the back room around 9pm and you'll catch live *céilidh* (traditional music and dancing). Or perhaps an old man will simply slide into a chair and croon a few classics.

Moran's PUB
(Bridge St) A preserved holdover from the days when a pub was also a shop, and grocery shopping was an occasion to have a few pints before heading home, having forgotten about the groceries.

Information

Gavin's Video & Internet Cafe (Bridge St; per hr €4; ⊙noon-11pm)

Tourist office (☎098-25711; www.discoverireland.ie/west; James St; ⊙9am-5.45pm Jul & Aug, 9am-5.45pm Mon-Fri, to 4.45pm Sat Mar-Jun & Sep & Oct) Mayo's only official tourist office to open year-round. About half way between the Octagon and the river.

Getting There & Away

BUS Services run to Dublin (€17.10, 4½ hours, two daily), Galway (€14.40, two hours, five daily), Sligo (€16.65, 2½ hours, four Monday to Saturday, two Sunday) and Achill (€12.50, 30 minutes, two daily). Buses depart from Mill St.

TRAIN There are three daily connections to Dublin (€35, 3½ hours).

Newport

POP 590

Newport, a wiggling 12km drive north of Westport, is a picturesque 18th-century village in which there really isn't much to do other than fish in streams, lakes or Clew Bay. The **Bangor Trail** (p440) and **Foxford Trail** end near the town, and the **Great Western Greenway** heads west from here to Achill, 18km away on a traffic-free route along a former rail line. The trains on the Westport-Achill Railway stopped in 1936 but a striking seven-arch viaduct built in 1892 remains and is a popular spot with walkers and cyclists.

If you'd like to stay, head for **Newport House** (☎098-41222; www.newporthouse.ie; Main St; s/d from €148/244; ⊙mid-Mar–Oct; P @) one of Ireland's most romantic country retreats. Strangled by ivy that turns crimson in autumn, this gorgeous Georgian mansion is a stunning place. High ceilings, ornate plaster work, heavy antiques, oil paintings and a grand central staircase give it a memorable old-world elegance and charm. The hotel is famous for its excellent contemporary Irish cuisine and vintage wine list (dinner €62).

Buses between Westport (€3.90) and Achill Island (€8.70) pass through Newport twice daily.

Newport to Achill Island

If you've time, skip the main road from Newport to Achill Island in favour of the longer and narrower but infinitely more scenic **Atlantic Drive**. It's well signposted along the southern edge of the Curraun Peninsula (also spelt Corraun Peninsula).

Alternatively hire a bike and cycle along the Great Western Greenway. Bike hire is available from **Clew Bay Bike Hire** (☎098-24818; www.clewbayoutdoors.ie; bike hire per day €15; ⏲9am-6pm) next to the Newport Hotel car park.

En route look out for signs to **Burrishoole Abbey**, an eerie wind-battered ruin of a Dominican abbey built in 1486 (free entry). Further on, about 5km west of Newport, you'll spot signs for **Rockfleet Castle**. Also known as Carrigahowley, this 15th-century tower (entry is free) is associated with 'pirate queen' Grace O'Malley. She married her second husband, Richard an-Iarrain (impressively nicknamed 'Iron Dick' Burke), to gain control of this castle, and famously fought off an English attack here.

Rising from a narrow isthmus, the hillside village of **Mulranny**, overlooks a wide Blue Flag **beach**. It's a prime vantage point to try counting the 365 or so saucer-sized islands that grace Clew Bay.

Achill Island

POP 960

Ireland's largest offshore island, Achill (An Caol), is connected to the mainland by a short bridge. Despite its accessibility, it has plenty of that far-flung-island feeling: soaring cliffs, rocky headlands, sheltered sandy beaches, broad expanses of blanket bog and rolling mountains. It also has its share of history, having been a frequent refuge during Ireland's numerous rebellions.

Achill is at its most dramatic during winter, when high winds and lashing seas make the island seem downright inhos pitable. The year-round population, though, remains as welcoming as ever. Few visitors choose to appreciate this temperamental side of Achill, preferring its mild summers, when heather, rhododendrons and wildflowers bloom.

A quiet hamlet known as the Valley, whose rugged terrain is dotted with old stone houses, is the island's most traditional quarter, while the village of Keel is the island's main centre of activity.

Sights

The signposted **Atlantic Drive** continues once you cross the bridge as an alternative route to the main roads along the island's southern shore.

THE GREAT WESTERN GHOST TRAIN

A spooky footnote can be added to the Great Western Railway's short-lived history in Achill Sound. Local folklore likes to tell how a 17th-century prophet named Brian Rua O'Cearbhain had a vision that one day 'carts on wheels, blowing smoke and fire' would run here, and that their first and last journeys would carry corpses.

Chillingly, just as work was completed on the rail line to Achill in 1894, tragedy struck when 32 young locals drowned in Clew Bay, and the very first train from Westport to Achill carried the bodies back to their grieving families. The prophecy was completed four decades later when the railway had already ceased to run. Ten migrant workers from Achill were killed in a fire at Kirkintilloch, Scotland in 1937. The railway line was reopened for one last run to bring the bodies back for burial.

Slievemore Deserted Village HISTORIC SITE

The remains of this deserted village at the foot of Slievemore Mountain are slowly but surely being reduced down to rock piles, and are a poignant reminder of the island's past hardships and a lost way of life. Until the mid-19th century, the village was divided between permanent inhabitants and transhumance farmers (known here as 'booleying'), but as the Potato Famine took grip, starvation forced the villagers to the sea and its sources of food. The adjacent graveyard compounds the desolation.

Dooagh HISTORIC SITE

This village is where Don Allum, the first person to row across the Atlantic Ocean in both directions, landed in September 1982 in his 6m-long plywood boat, dubbed the *QE3,* after 77 days at sea. Opposite the memorial, **the Pub** (that's its name) has memorabilia marking the feat.

Activities

Beaches SWIMMING

Some of Achill's scalloped bays are tame enough for swimming. Except in the height of the holiday season, the Blue Flag beaches at **Dooega**, **Keem**, **Dugort** and **Golden Strand** (Dugort's other beach) are often

Achill Island

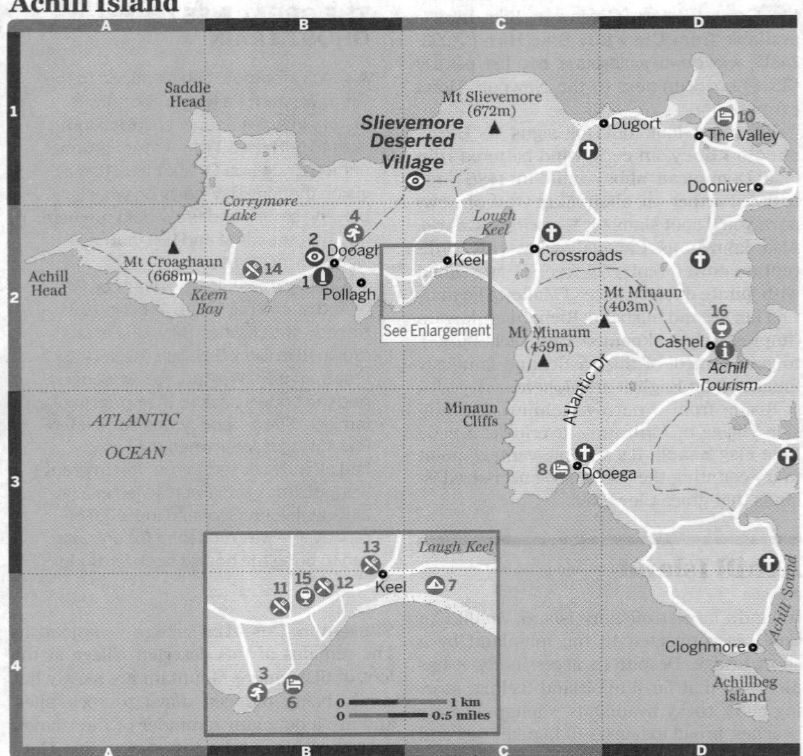

deserted. The beaches at **Dooagh** and **Dooniver** are just as appealing.

Beaches SURFING

The Blue Flag **Keel** beach is one of Ireland's best surfing spots, but there are dangerous rips from its centre to the eastern end (under the Minaun Cliffs). Heed the signs and stick to the western half of the beach. Several companies offer board hire (per day €15) and lessons (per day €40).

Walking WALKING

The island is a wonderful place for walking. **Mt Slievemore** (672m) can be climbed from behind the deserted village for terrific views of Blacksod Bay. A longer climb takes in **Mt Croaghaun** (668m), Achill Head and a walk atop what locals claim are Europe's highest sea cliffs (though Slieve League in County Donegal is thought to be marginally higher).

Achill Tourism (www.achilltourism.com) produces a series of downloadable guides to walks around the island.

Achill Island Scuba Dive Centre DIVING

(☎087 234 9884; www.achilldivecentre.com; Purteen Harbour, Keel) With its clear waters and abundant marine life Achill is a prime diving spot. The dive centre offers training, equipment hire and organised dives.

Calvey's Equestrian Centre HORSE RIDING

(☎087 988 1093; www.calveysofachill.com; Slievemore) Calvey's arrange riding lessons and one- to four-hour treks on Achill's broad beaches and mountain roads.

Ó'Dálaigh PAINTING

(☎098-36137; www.achillpainting.com; Dánlann Yawl Art Gallery, Owenduff) Summertime painting classes are run by Seosamh Ó'Dálaigh who will lead you to a scenic

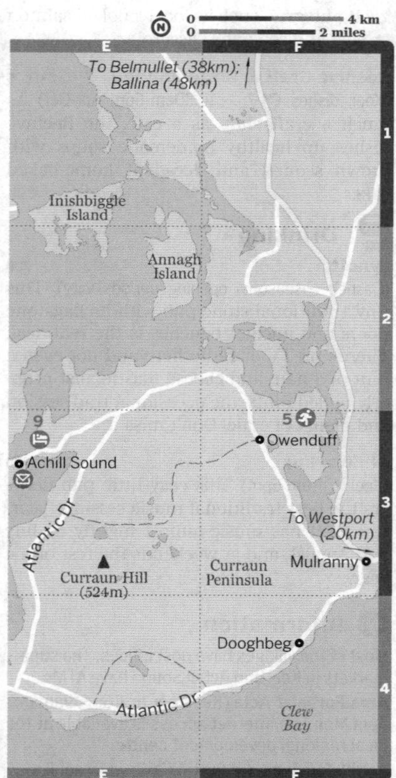

Achill Island

Top Sights

Slievemore Deserted Village C1

Sights

1 Don Allum Memorial B2
2 The Pub B2

Activities, Courses & Tours

3 Achill Island Scuba Dive Centre B4
4 Calvey's Equestrian Centre B2
5 Dánlann Yawl Art Gallery F3

Sleeping

6 Bervie B4
7 Keel Sandybanks Caravan & Camping Park C4
8 Lavelle's Seaside House C3
9 Railway Hostel E3
10 Valley House Hostel D1

Eating

11 Achill Cliff House Hotel Restaurant B4
12 Beehive Craft & Coffee Shop B4
13 Calvey's Restaurant B3
14 Gielty's Clew Bay B2

Drinking

15 Annexe Inn B4
16 Lynott's D2

spot and offer pointers on how to commit it to canvas.

Tony Burke FISHING
(☎098-47257; tmburke@eircom.net; Keel; ⌚Apr-Oct) Organises sea-angling trips, rod and tackle hire.

Festivals

The island hosts several **walking festivals** during the year, usually around St Patrick's Day, the May Day bank holiday and the August bank holiday weekends.

Traditional Irish music resonates for miles in late July during the **Scoil Acla Festival** (www.scoilacla.com), which also has Irish dancing, culture and music workshops.

The **Achill Yawl Festival** takes place between July and September with evening and weekend races of the traditional wooden sailing boats on Achill Sound.

Sleeping

Achill is a great budget destination and there are some decent midrange options, but for top-end luxury you'll need to head to the mainland.

Valley House Hostel HOSTEL €
(☎098-47204; www.valley-house.com; The Valley; campsites per tent €5, plus per person €5, dm €19-21, d €50; P@) Amid unruly gardens, this remote, 42-bed hostel in a creaking old mansion has atmosphere to spare. JM Synge based his play *The Playboy of the Western World* on misadventures here (the staff can tell some great stories!), and the subsequent film *Love and Rage* (1999) was also partially shot here. Bonuses include free scones for breakfast and a cosy licensed pub with patio tables (bar food June to August only).

Bervie B&B €€
(☎098-43114; Keel; s/d €75/110; P) Once a coastguard station, this delightful B&B is a wonderfully friendly place with views over the ocean and direct access onto the beach

from the well-tended garden. The 14 rooms are bright but cosy, with white bedspreads and wooden furniture. There's a great welcome for families and a playroom with a pool table for wet days. Evening meals are available on request (€45).

Lavelles Seaside House B&B €€
(☎098-45116; www.lavellesseasidehouse.com; Dooega; s/d €45/70; P) In the quiet fishing village of Dooega, this 14-room B&B overlooks the ocean and offers a range of comfortable rooms. The five new rooms offer the best deal and decor, ask if one is available. Next door is the local haunt **Mickey's Bar** (mains €8-11) which serves decent seafood in the summer season.

Keel Sandybanks Caravan & Camping Park CAMPGROUND €
(☎098-43211; www.achillcamping.com; Keel; campsites €16; ⏱late-Apr–mid-Sep) This camping ground, an easy stroll from town, overlooks Keel Strand and has a sociable lounge and a laundry room.

Railway Hostel HOSTEL €
(☎098-45187; Achill Sound; campsites per person €6, dm €12; P) Once the island train station, this place is now a basic but social little hostel.

Eating

Calvey's Restaurant IRISH €€
(☎098-43158; www.calveysofachill.com; Keel; lunch mains €8-14, dinner mains €16-28; ⏱lunch & dinner Easter–mid-Sep) As it's attached to its own organic butchery, it's no surprise that the speciality at this award-winning restaurant is meat. Don't miss the rack of organic Achill lamb with its distinct island flavour. There's also a good choice of fish and seafood cooked with seasonal local ingredients.

Achill Cliff House Hotel Restaurant SEAFOOD €€€
(☎098-43400; www.achillcliff.com; Keel; mains €21-26; ⏱lunch Sun, dinner nightly) Locally caught seafood like black sole on the bone with creamy tarragon sauce or herb-crusted baked cod is the order of the day here, but tasty alternatives include ginger and orange roast duckling.

Gielty's Clew Bay PUB €€
(www.gieltys.com; Dooagh; sandwiches €4-7, mains €9-20; ⏱10am-9pm) The building is modern but has a time-honoured atmosphere that's enhanced by open fires and sea views, and good pub grub such as local smoked salmon or beef and red wine casserole.

Beehive Craft & Coffee Shop CAFE €
(Keel; dishes €4-7; ⏱10.30am-6pm Apr-Oct) As much a craft shop as a cafe, the Beehive dishes up healthy homemade soups with brown scones, and decadent home-baked cakes.

Drinking

Lynott's PUB
(Cashel; ⏱seasonal opening periods vary) This tiny, traditional stone pub with its flagstone floors and ancient benches is the real deal. There's no TV or radio here and not even a hint of a ham and cheese toastie, just properly pulled pints, the occasional trad session and plenty of craic. Don't miss it.

Annexe Inn PUB
(Keel; ⏱from 6pm) This cosy little pub delivers the best traditional music sessions year-round. It has music almost nightly in July and August, and at weekends the rest of the year.

Information

Most of the villages have post offices. The supermarkets in Keel and Achill Sound have ATMs.

Áras Forbairt Acla (Keel; per hr €6; ⏱9am-5pm Mon-Fri) Internet access is available at the local regional development centre.

Achill Tourism (☎098-47353; www.achilltourism.com; Cashel; ⏱9am-6pm Mon-Fri Jul & Aug, 10am-4pm Sep-Jun) One of the best sources for information in all Mayo.

Getting There & Around

BUS There's one bus daily to Achill from Westport (€12), with nine stops on the island, including at Dooagh, Keel, Dugort, Cashel and Achill Sound.

BIKE You can hire bikes from Nevin's Newfield Inn in Mulranny.

Bangor Erris

POP 295

This unexceptional little village is the start or end point for the 48km **Bangor Trail**, which connects Bangor and Newport. It's an extraordinary hike that takes walkers through some of the bleakest and most remote countryside in Ireland. Unfortunately, you'll need several 1:50,000 OS maps to cover the trail.

There's one bus daily from Ballina (€11.40, one hour).

Ballycroy National Park

Covering one of Europe's largest expanses of blanket bog, **Ballycroy National Park** (www.ballycroynationalpark.ie; admission free; ⌚visitor centre 10am-5.30pm late-Mar–Oct) was founded in 1998. It is a gorgeously scenic region, where the River Owenduff wends its way through intact bogs.

The park is home to a diverse range of flora and fauna including peregrine falcons, corncrakes and whooper swans. A nature trail with interpretation panels leads from the visitor centre across the bog with great views to the surrounding mountains. If you wish to explore further the **Bangor Trail** crosses the park and leads to some of its most spectacular view points.

Ballycroy is 18km south of Bangor on the N59.

Mullet Peninsula

Dangling some 30km into the Atlantic, this thinly populated Gaeltacht (Irish speaking) peninsula feels more cut off than many islands, and has a similar sense of forsakenness. However, you'll find pristine beaches along its sheltered eastern shore. The main settlement is the functional little town of **Belmullet** (Béal an Mhuirthead).

Sights

The road south from Belmullet loops round the tip of the peninsula to rejoin itself at Aghleam. Near **Blacksod Point** are the remains of an old **church**, and the view across the bay takes in the spot where *La Rata Santa Maria Encoronada*, part of the 1588 Spanish Armada, came in and was later burned by its captain.

The road to Blacksod Point passes the Blue Flag beach of **Elly Bay**, a prime spot for birdwatchers and dolphin-watchers, as well as surfers – contact **UISCE** (☎097-82111; www.uisce.ie) for the local surf low-down. Further south it passes stunning **Mullaghroe Beach**. In the early 20th century, a whaling station operated at nearby Ardelly Point. The weather centre here determined the eventual date for the D-Day Normandy landing.

While here be sure to check out the listings for **Ára Inis Gluiare** (www.arasinisgluaire.ie) a bilingual arts centre in Belmullet. There's usually an interesting selection of exhibitions, workshops, films and performances on offer.

FILLING IN YOUR FAMILY TREE

Many people left Mayo during the Famine years, establishing family roots elsewhere in the world. If your surname is Barrett, Brennan, Burke, Dogherty, Doyle, Duffy, Foy, Gallagher, Harkin, Henry, Joyce, Kelly, Lavelle, McNulty, McNicholas, Moran, Murphy, O'Connor, O'Malley or Walsh, there's a strong chance that your people originally hailed from north Mayo. You can get in touch with your roots at the **Mayo North Family Heritage Centre** (mayo.irishroots.net).

Genealogy services begin with an initial assessment (€95).

Sleeping & Eating

Cheerful cafes ring Belmullet's central roundabout.

Leim Siar B&B €€
(☎097-85004; www.leimsiar.com; Blacksod Point; s/d €48/76; P) Just a short walk from the Blacksod lighthouse, this friendly, purpose-built B&B offers modern comforts and ends-of-the-earth appeal. The rooms are bright and cheery, evening meals are available on request and you can rent bikes to tour the peninsula.

Broadhaven Bay Hotel HOTEL €€
(☎097-20600; www.westernstrandshotel.com; Ballina Rd, Belmullet; s/d €75/120; P@) This large, modern hotel offers extremely comfortable rooms, friendly service and all the services you could expect from a city hotel. However, if you're looking for local character or charm you're in the wrong place.

Information

You'll find all the main services including bank, ATM and post office in Belmullet.

Atlantek Computers (Carter Sq, Belmullet; per half hr €3; ⌚10am-6pm Mon-Sat) Internet access.

Erris tourist office (☎097-81500; www.visiterris.ie; Main St, Belmullet; ⌚9am-5pm Mon-Sat May-Sep, 9am-4pm Mon-Fri Oct-Apr)

PIPELINE PROTEST

The quiet, rural idyll that is Mayo's far-flung northwest has made national headlines in recent years. A David-and-Goliath-like battle continues over the construction of a high-pressure raw gas pipeline between Mayo's offshore Corrib gas field and refinery at Bellanaboy. Shell claims the gas field could provide up to 60% of the country's gas at peak supply.

Fearing the pipeline poses health and safety risks to residents, locals began what has become a tortuous 10 year battle against the proposed route. Protests escalated into violent unrest in 2005 when landowners from Rossport refused to allow Shell workers access to their land despite compulsory purchase orders being in place. A series of arrests were made and the 'Rossport Five' were jailed for 94 days.

Intense media coverage and protests at Shell and Statoil petrol stations across the country followed. One of the Five, Willie Corduff, later won the European category of the Goldman Environmental Prize for grassroots environmental activists.

Revised plans for the pipeline route were submitted to the government in 2009 and with the refinery and offshore pipeline almost complete, the outgoing government approved the planning application in February 2011. Although residents succeeded in getting Shell to agree to reduce the gas pressure and change the route of the pipeline, most are still unhappy with the decision. Meanwhile An Taisce, the heritage protection agency, has made an application for a judicial review of the case claiming that the decision is in breach of EU directives on the conservation of natural habitats. The battle continues.

For the latest on the situation visit www.shelltosea.com or www.corribgaspipeline.ie.

Getting There & Around

There's one daily bus from Ballina to Belmullet (€12.50, 1½ hours), continuing on to Blacksod Point.

Pollatomish

POP 150

Irresistibly remote and pretty, Pollatomish, also spelled Pullathomas, drowses in a serene bay some 16km east of Belmullet, signposted on the road to Ballycastle (R314).

Those who find their way here often extend their stay to stroll on its sandy **beach** or continue on up to **Benwee Head** to take in sensational views.

Kilcommon Lodge Hostel (☎097-84621; www.kilcommonlodge.net; Pollatomish; dm/d €16/40; P@), in a garden setting, is a short stroll from the beach. It's now headed up by the long-time owners' son, Ciarán, an outdoors enthusiast who can organise activities such as surfing, guided walks and rock climbing, as well as Irish-language courses.

Less-energetic travellers can curl up with books and board games by the turf fire in the common room. Breakfast is €6, dinner €16.

McGrath's (www.mcgarthcoaches.com) runs a daily bus service to Ballina.

Ballycastle & Around

POP 250

The superbly sited village of Ballycastle consists of a sole sloping street. Its main draw (apart from breathtaking coastal scenery) is its megalithic tombs – one of the greatest concentrations in Europe.

Sights

CÉIDE FIELDS

A famous wit once described archaeology as being all about 'a series of small walls'. But it's not often that such walls have had experts hopping up and down with such excitement than at Céide Fields, 8km northwest of Ballycastle.

During the 1930s, local man Patrick Caulfield was digging in the bog when he noticed a lot of piled-up stones buried beneath it. About 40 years later, his son Seamus, who had become an archaeologist on the basis of his father's discovery, began extensive exploration of the area. What he, and later others, uncovered was the world's most extensive Stone Age monument, consisting of stone-walled fields, houses and megalithic tombs – about half a million tonnes of stone. Astonishingly, five millennia ago a thriving farming community lived here, growing wheat and barley and grazing sheep and cattle. The award-winning **Interpretive Centre** (☎096-43325; www.heritageireland.ie; R314; adult/child €4/2; ⏰10am-6pm Jun-Sep, 10am-5pm Easter-May & Oct, last tour 1hr prior to closing), in a glass pyramid overlooking the site, gives a fascinating glimpse into these times. However, it's a good idea to take a guided tour of the site itself, or it may seem nothing more than, well, a series of small walls.

Sleeping & Eating

Stella Maris HOTEL €€€

(☎096-43322; www.stellamarisireland.com; Ballycastle; s/d from €125/200; ⏰Easter-Oct; P 📶) This salt-spattered building sits on a lonely stretch of coastline 2.5km west of Bally castle. It was originally a British Coast Guard station, and later a nunnery. Now, upmarket rooms combine antiques and stylish modern furnishings, breakfast includes treats like French toast, and the restaurant is well regarded.

Mary's Cottage Kitchen CAFE €

(Lower Main St, Ballycastle; dishes from €2.50; ⏰10am-3pm Mon-Fri, 10am-2pm Sat) Cosy stone cottages like this are always appealing, and never more so than when they house a bakery that advertises its wares with the aroma of warm apple pie. During the summer tables are set up out back in a leafy garden. Hours can vary.

Getting There & Away

Buses run between Ballycastle and Ballina (€6, 30 minutes) twice a day, Monday to Friday.

Killala & Around

POP 569

The town itself is pretty enough, but Killala is more famous for its namesake bay nearby, and for its role in the French invasion.

Flush with revolutionary fervour and eager to hurt the English in their own backyard, on 22 August 1798 more than 1000 French troops commanded by General Humbert landed at Kilcummin in Killala Bay. It was hoped (or rather promised by Irish patriot Wolfe Tone) that their arrival would inspire the Irish peasantry to revolt against the English.

It's claimed that St Patrick founded Killala, and the Church of Ireland cathedral sits on the site of the first Christian church in Ireland. The 25m round tower still looms over the town's heart; it was struck by lightning in 1800 and the cap was later rebuilt.

Sights

Rathfran Abbey HISTORIC BUILDING

The silence at the remains of this remote Dominican friary, dating from 1274, is broken only by the cawing of crows and the whistling wind. In 1590 the friary was burned by the English, but the resilient monks stayed nearby until the 18th century.

Take the R314 road north out of Killala and, after 5km and crossing the River Cloonaghmore, turn right. After another 2km turn right at the crossroads.

Rosserk Abbey HISTORIC BUILDING

Dipping its toes into the River Rosserk, a tributary of the Moy, this Franciscan abbey dates from the mid-15th century. There's an eye-catching double piscina (perforated stone basin) in the chancel: look for the exquisite carvings of a round tower and several angels. Rosserk was destroyed by Richard Bingham, the English governor of Connaught, in the 16th century.

The abbey is 4km south of Killala off the R314. Look out for the signposts.

Breastagh Ogham Stone MONUMENT

This lichen-covered stone, the height of a basketball player, is etched with an obscure Ogham script but the weathered markings are all but invisible. It's in a field left of the R314, just past the turning for Rathfran Abbey. Cross the ditch where the sign points to the stone.

Lackan Bay BEACH

Lackan Bay beach is a stunning expanse of golden sand. There's good surf here, but you'll need to bring your own equipment. To get here take a right turn off the R314 signposted for Kilcummin. Just after the turn a **sculpture** of a French soldier helping a prostrate Irish peasant marks the place where the first French soldier died on Irish soil.

Getting There & Away

Buses between Ballina (€4.20, 15 minutes) and Ballycastle (€3.90, 15 minutes) stop in Killala twice a day, Monday to Friday.

Ballina

POP 10,409

Mayo's second-largest town, Ballina, is synonymous with salmon. If you're there during fishing season, you'll see droves of green-garbed waders, poles in hand, heading for the River Moy – one of the most prolific rivers in Europe for catching the scaly critters – which pumps right through the heart of town. You'll also spot salmon jumping in the Ridge (salmon pool), with otters and grey seals in pursuit.

During the rest of the year it makes a good regional base thanks to its excellent hotels and good choice of restaurants.

Activities

A list of **fisheries** and permit contacts is available at the tourist office. The season is February to September, but the best fishing is June to August. Information, supplies and licences are available at **Ridge Pool Tackle Shop** (Cathedral Rd). Fly-casting lessons can also be arranged.

Pontoon, near Foxford, is a better base for **trout fishing**, in Loughs Conn and Cullen.

Festivals & Events

One of the best outdoor parties in the country, the week-long **Ballina Salmon Festival** (www.ballinasalmonfestival.ie) takes place in mid July. Festivities include parades, dances, cart racing and more.

Sleeping

Ice House HOTEL €€€
(☎096-23500; www.theicehouse.ie; The Quay; s/d from €130/160; P 📶) This 1800s-built salmon ice store on Ballina's eastern riverbank has been transformed into an ultra-hip hotel. In a nod to the building's origins, there's a handful of 1800s-styled guest rooms with cedar bathtubs, but most have cutting-edge fit-outs (floor-to-ceiling windows, arctic-white moulded furniture). At the water's edge, the vault where boats once unloaded their catch now houses a sleek bar and restaurant, Pier.

Mount Falcon Country House Hotel HOTEL €€€
(☎096-74472; www.mountfalcon.com; Foxford Rd; d from €180; P 📶 🏊) Hidden within 40 hectares between Lough Conn and the River Moy, 5km south of Ballina, this gorgeous 1870s mansion is now a luxury hotel. Rooms in the old house ooze old world grandeur, while those in the modern extension are more contemporary in style. Anglers will be hooked by Mount Falcon's own exclusive fishery along the river.

Red River Lodge B&B €
(☎096-22841; www.redriverlodgebnb.com; The Quay; s/d €40/60; P 📶) Out of town in a tranquil spot overlooking the Moy estuary, this modern B&B has bright rooms with big windows, white linens and silky throws. Breakfast is served in a large conservatory or on the deck overlooking the well-tended garden. The B&B is 5km north of town off the N59.

Eating

Pier IRISH €€€
(☎096-23500; The Quay; dinner mains €24-31; ⊙lunch & dinner) Bathed in light from the giant windows overlooking the river, this chic restaurant at the Ice House is the best table in town. Expect sublime, modern Irish dishes made from artisan produce and immaculately presented.

Gaughan's IRISH €€
(O'Rahilly St; lunch €6-16; ⊙10am-6pm Mon-Sat) Home-cooked staples like old-fashioned roasts, baked gammon and nostalgic desserts are the order of the day at this much-loved Ballina institution. The seafood is top notch but best of all is the authentic charm and convivial atmosphere in this unpretentious former pub. They don't make 'em like this anymore.

Market Kitchen IRISH €€
(www.breananslane.ie; Brennan's Lane; mains €15-25; ⊙dinner) Cosy surroundings and a menu of simple, classic dishes beautifully cooked has the punters coming in droves to this

WORTH A TRIP

NORTH MAYO SCULPTURE TRAIL

Leading artists from eight different countries were commissioned to create this trail of 14 permanent outdoor sculptures reflecting the beauty and wilderness of the northern Mayo countryside. It essentially follows the R314 for 90km from Ballina to Blacksod Point and can be walked.

Tourist offices and bookshops sell the 60-page *North Mayo Sculpture Trail* book detailing each sculpture.

restaurant above Brennan's Pub. Expect posh burgers, seafood pie, pizza and fajitas but not quite as you know them.

Information

Chat'rnet (Bridge St; per hr/day €4/10; ⏲11am-10.30pm Mon-Fri, noon-10pm Sat, 1-10pm Sun) Central internet access.

Post office (O'Rahilly St) On the southern extension of Pearse St.

Tourist office (☎096-70848; Cathedral Rd; ⏲10am-5.30pm Mon-Sat Apr-Oct) Across the River Moy from the centre.

Getting There & Away

BUS The bus station is on Kevin Barry St. Services run to Westport (€11.50, 1½ hours, four daily), Sligo (€13, 1½ hours, five Monday to Saturday, one Sunday) and Dublin (€17, 3¼ hours, seven daily).

TRAIN The train station is on Station Rd at the southern extension of Kevin Barry St. Ballina is on a branch of the main Westport-Dublin line, so you'll have to change at Manulla Junction. Services to Dublin (€35, 3½ hours, three daily) go three times daily.

Castlebar & Around

POP 11,891

Mayo's county town, Castlebar, is a traffic-choked hub for shops and services, but most places of interest for visitors lie outside the town centre.

Castlebar's place in Irish history was cemented in 1798, when General Humbert's outnumbered army of French revolutionary soldiers and Irish peasants pulled off an astonishing victory here. The ignominious cavalry retreat of the British became known as the Castlebar Races.

Sights

FREE National Museum of Country Life MUSEUM

(www.museum.ie; Turlough Park, Turlough; ⏲10am-5pm Tue-Sat, 2-5pm Sun) A celebration of the resourcefulness, ingenuity and self-sufficiency of the Irish people, this extensive museum looks at rural traditions and skills. Set overlooking a lake in the lush grounds of 19th-century Turlough Manor, this stunning purpose-built facility is a branch of the National Museum of Ireland and explores everything from wickerwork to boat building, and herbal cures to traditional clothing. Exhibits concentrate on the period from 1850 to 1950.

WORTH A TRIP

FOXFORD WOOLLEN MILL

Founded by the Sisters of Charity in 1892, the **Foxford Woollen Mill** (www.foxfordwoolenmills.ie; admission free; ⏲10am-6pm Mon-Sat, noon-6pm Sun) was set up to ease post-Famine suffering and provide much-needed work and income for the people of Foxford. The mill was an enormous success and remained open until 1987 by which time its high-quality woven rugs and blankets had an international reputation. At its height it employed 220 skilled craftspeople and its closure was an economic disaster for the area. Local businesspeople managed to salvage the business and it later reopened with the eventual addition of a sparkling new visitor centre. Today you can explore its history through a multimedia tour and visit the working mill. There's a tempting shop selling beautiful contemporary Foxford designs as well as the best of Irish crafts, and an excellent cafe.

Foxford is midway between Ballina and Castlebar.

Follow the signs off the N5, 5km northeast of Castlebar.

Turlough Round Tower HISTORIC BUILDING

With its single lofty window, this impenetrable 9th-century tower calls to mind the fairy tale of Rapunzel. The tower stands on a hilltop by a ruined 18th-century church, a short distance northeast of the National Museum of Country Life.

FREE Ballintubber Abbey HISTORIC BUILDING

(www.ballintubberabbey.ie; Ballintubber; ⏲9am-midnight) The history of this delightful little abbey reads like a collection of far-fetched folk tales. Often referred to as 'the abbey that refused to die', this is the only church in Ireland founded by an Irish king that is still in use. It was set up in 1216 next to the site of an earlier church founded by St Patrick after he came down from Croagh Patrick.

The abbey was burned by Normans, seized by James I and suppressed by Henry VIII. The nave roof was only restored in 1965 after the original was burned down by Cromwell's soldiers in 1653. Mass was outlawed and priests hunted down. Yet worship in the roofless remains continued against all the odds.

Take the N84 south towards Galway and after about 13km turn left at the Emo service station; the abbey is 2km along.

Sleeping & Eating

Breaffy House Hotel HOTEL €€
(☎094-902 2033; www.breaffyhousehotel.com; r from €85; P ≋ ♣) Set in a formidable 19th-century country house set on a vast estate, this large hotel retains some of its period charm but has been much modernised. There are a choice of comfortable rooms (the best are in the main house), a spa and pool and plenty of activities for children.

The hotel is east of Castlebar off the N60.

Rua IRISH €€
(www.caferua.com; Spencer St, Castlebar; mains €7-13; ⊙9am-6pm Mon-Sat; ♣) A gourmet deli downstairs and buzzing cafe upstairs, this place champions artisan, organic produce such as local duck eggs, Sligo pasta, Carrowholly cheese and Ballina smoked sal mon. The artfully mismatched furniture and bright tablecloths give it a cosy, homely feel and the food is equally heart-warming. Rua is open for dinner on the last Friday of the month (three courses €40); don't miss it if you're in town.

Information

Tourist office (☎094-902 1207; Linenhall St, Castlebar; ⊙9.30am-1pm & 2-5.30pm May-Sep) West off the northern end of Main St.

Getting There & Around

BUS Services run to Westport (€4.50, 20 minutes, three daily) and Sligo (€15, 2½ hours, three daily). Services on Sunday are less frequent. Buses stop on Market St.

TRAIN The Westport-Dublin train stops at Castlebar (€35, 3½ hours) three times daily. The station is just out of town on the N84 towards Ballinrobe.

Knock

POP 745

Knock was little more than a downtrodden rural village until 1879, when a divine apparition propelled it to become one of the world's most sacred Catholic shrines. The shrine is now a serious pilgrimage site and dominates the little village.

There's a **tourist office** (☎094-938 8193; ⊙10am-6pm May-Sep) and a cluster of souvenir stalls across from the shrine.

Sights

Knock Marian Shrine HISTORIC SITE
(www.knock-shrine.ie) The Knock shrine encompasses five churches and a museum in the town centre. The story that led to its development goes thus: on the evening of 21 August 1879, in drenching rain, two young Knock women were startled by a vision of Mary, Joseph, St John the Evangelist and sacrificial lamb upon an altar, freeze-framed in dazzling white light against the southern gable of the parish church. They were soon joined by 13 more villagers, all gazing at the heavenly apparition for around two hours as the daylight faded. A Church investigation confirmed it as a bona fide miracle, and a sudden rush of other Vatican-approved miracles followed as the sick and disabled claimed amazing recoveries upon visiting the spot.

Today, people of all Christian denominations and even other faiths pray at the modern **chapel** enclosing a scene of the apparition carved from snow-white marble. A segment of **stone** from the original church mounted on the outside wall (on your right as you're facing the scene of the apparition) has been rubbed smooth by the hands and lips of the faithful. Near the church is the 1970s-built, spiky-topped **Basilica of Our Lady, Queen of Ireland**, which can accommodate over 10,000 worshippers.

Across open grasslands from the basilica, the little **Knock Museum** (adult/child €4/3; ⊙10am-6pm May-Oct, noon-4pm Nov-Apr) follows the story from the first witnesses, through the miraculous cures, the repeated Church investigations and finally to the visit of Pope John Paul II on the event's centenary in 1979.

Getting There & Away

AIR Ireland West Airport Knock (www.irelandwestairport.com), 15km north by the N17, has daily flights to Dublin (Aer Arann) and London Stansted (Ryanair) and less frequent services to a variety of UK airports, Paris and Barcelona. A €10 development fee is payable on departure.

BUS Services run to Westport (€10.50, one hour), Castlebar (€8, 45 minutes) and Dublin (€17, 4½ hours) twice daily (once on Sunday).

COUNTY SLIGO

County Sligo packs as much poetry, myth and folklore into its countryside's lush splendour as any shamrock lover could hope for. It was Sligo that most inspired the Nobel laureate, poet and dramatist William Butler Yeats (1865–1939), who helped cement its pastoral reputation with such verses as 'The Lake Isle of Innisfree', in which he mused about the simple country life. You can still view the lake isle today, along with a cache of prehistoric sites. But it's no complacent backwater: the county town exudes a worldly vitality, and the coast's surf is internationally renowned.

Sligo Town

POP 19,402

Sligo town is in no hurry to shed its cultural traditions but it doesn't sell them out, either. Pedestrian streets lined with inviting shop fronts, stone bridges spanning the River Garavogue, and *céilidh* sessions spilling from pubs contrast with genre-bending contemporary art and glass towers rising from prominent corners of the compact town.

Sights

Sligo Abbey HISTORIC BUILDING

(Abbey St; adult/child €3/1; ⌚10am-6pm Easter–mid-Oct) This handsome abbey was built around 1252 but then burned down in the 15th century and was later rebuilt. Friends in high places saved the abbey from the worst ravages of the Elizabethan era, and rescued the only sculpted altar to survive the Reformation. The doorways reach only a few feet high at the abbey's rear, and the ground around it was swollen by the mass graves from years of famine and war.

The Model ART GALLERY

(www.themodel.ie; The Mall; ⌚11am-5.30pm Wed-Sat, noon-5pm Sun) One of Ireland's leading contemporary arts centres, The Model houses an impressive collection of contemporary Irish art including works by Jack B. Yeats and Louis Le LeBrocquy. Recently expanded to accommodate additional galleries for temporary exhibitions and a permanent performance space and artists' studios, the centre offers an interesting program of experimental theatre, music and film events.

FREE **Sligo County Museum** MUSEUM

(Stephen St; ⌚9.30am-12.30pm & 2-4.45pm Tue-Sat May-Sep, 9.30am-12.30pm Tue-Sat Oct-Apr) The major draw of Sligo's county museum is the Yeats room, which features photographs, letters and newspaper cuttings connected with the poet WB Yeats, as well as drawings by his brother Jack B Yeats, one of Ireland's most important modern artists.

FREE **Yeats Memorial Building** MUSEUM

(www.yeats-sligo.com; ⌚10am-5pm Mon-Fri, tearoom 10am-6pm Mon-Sat) In a pretty setting near Hyde Bridge, you can visit the **WB Yeats Exhibition** which has a video presentation and valuable draft manuscripts; the €2 exhibition catalogue makes a good souvenir of Sligo. The charming **tearoom** has outdoor tables overlooking the river.

Festivals & Events

Sligo knows how to kick up its heels. The tourist office also has details of walking festivals held throughout the year.

ŚO Sligo (www.sosligo.com) A five-day celebration in mid-March of fine food and artisan produce along with cooking competitions, live music and street parties.

Temple House Festival (www.templehousefestival.com) Three-day festival featuring an eclectic line up of music, arts, workshops and woodland crafts. In early June.

Sligo Jazz Festival (www.sligojazzproject.com) Sligo swings in mid-July during this three-day festival.

Yeats International Festival (www.yeats-sligo.com) In late July to mid-August Irish poetry, music and culture are celebrated with three weeks of performances and events around town.

Sligo Live (www.sligolive.ie) Sligo's biggest cultural event is this live music festival in October.

Sleeping

You'll find lots of B&Bs lining Pearse Rd.

Glass House HOTEL €€

(☎071-919 4300; www.theglasshouse.ie; Swan Point; r from €109; P@) You can't miss this futuristic-looking hotel in the centre of town, its sharp glass facade pointing skyward. Inside things are a little more retro with a lurid swirly carpet in the foyer and bedrooms in a choice of psychedelic orange

Sligo Town

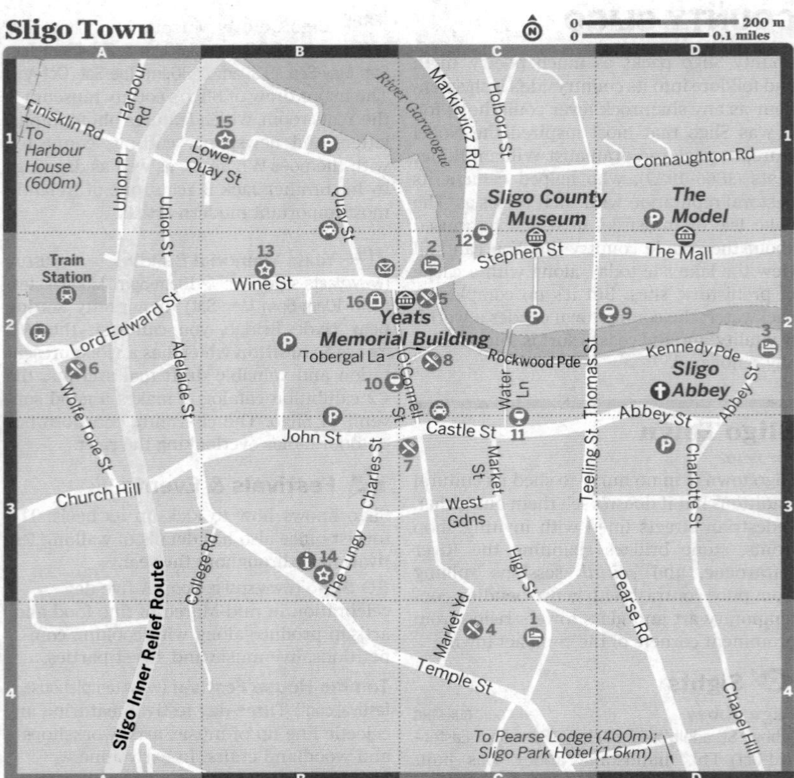

or lime green. It's fun and funky but perhaps trying a little too hard to be cool.

Pearse Lodge B&B €€
(☎071-916 1090; www.pearselodge.com; Pearse Rd; s/d €50/74; P@📶) Welcoming owners Mary and Kieron not only impeccably maintain the six stylish guest rooms at their cosy B&B but are also up on what's happening in town. Mary's breakfast menu includes smoked salmon, French toast with bananas and homemade muesli (and Illy coffee!). A sunny sitting room opens to a beautifully landscaped garden.

Sligo Park Hotel HOTEL €€
(☎071-919 0400; www.sligoparkhotel.com; Pearse Rd; s/d from €89/95; P📶🏊) Set on the edge of town in landscaped gardens with mature trees, this large but tranquil hotel is a local favourite. The pretty, tastefully decorated rooms are bright and modern, there's a pool and spa and excellent service.

Riverside Suites Hotel HOTEL €€
(☎071-914 8080; www.riversidesuiteshotelsligo.com; Millbrook; d from €55, 1-bedroom apt from €60, 2-bedroom apt €129-159; P📶) Giving B&Bs and hostels a run for their money, this modern apart-hotel offers contemporary-styled double rooms and apartments with full kitchen, sleeping up to four adults. It's excellent value but a little soulless.

Harbour House HOSTEL €
(☎071-917 1547; www.harbourhousehostel.com; Finisklin Rd; dm €20, d €44-50; P@📶) Set in an industrial area out of town, this quiet hostel was built in 1870 as a harbour master's house. It has plenty of character but the rooms are a little tired.

An Crúiscin Lan B&B €€
(☎071-916 2857; www.bandbsligo.ie; Connolly St; s/d from 40/60; P📶) The central location is a good selling point for this simple but friendly

Sligo Town

Top Sights

Sligo Abbey D2
Sligo County Museum C2
The Model D2
Yeats Memorial Building C2

Sleeping

1 An Crúiscin Lan C4
2 Glass House C2
3 Riverside Suites Hotel D2

Eating

4 Monmatre C4
5 Ósta C2
6 Silver Apple A2
7 Source C3
8 Tobergal Lane C2

Drinking

9 Furey's D2
10 Hargadons B2
11 Shoot the Crows C3
12 Thomas Connolly C2

Entertainment

13 Clarence Hotel B2
14 Hawk's Well Theatre B3
15 The Factory Performance Space B1

Shopping

16 Michael Quirke B2

B&B. Not all rooms have a private bathroom, those that do cost about €10 more.

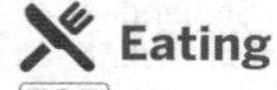

Eating

TOP CHOICE Source IRISH €€
(☎071-914 7605; www.sourcesligo.ie; 1 John St; mains €15-20; ⏰9.30am-5pm Mon, 9.30am-9.30pm Tue-Sun) Three stories of sparkling glass announce Sligo's newest, and most ambitious, culinary project. Source is all about traceability in the food chain and the project champions local suppliers and food-stuffs. Large, arty photos of its favourite fishermen, farmers and cheese producers grace the walls of the ground-floor restaurant with its open kitchen and buzzy atmosphere, while upstairs in the **wine bar** (dishes €4-9; ⏰3-11pm Tue-Sun) things are more sedate with wine from the owners' vineyard in France and plates of Irish-style tapas on offer. The top floor, with its glorious views of Ben Bulben is a **cookery school** offering everything from classes on organic growing to boning and butchery.

Ósta CAFE €
(www.osta.ie; Hyde Bridge, Left Bank; light meals €6.50-10; ⏰8am-7pm Mon-Wed, 8am-8pm Thu-Sat) Ósta is a cafe and a wine bar, and it's well suited to both callings. An array of preserved meats, seafood and Irish farmhouse cheeses accompany its well-chosen wines. It's intimate and well lit, and has a prime quayside location for gazing at the river charging beneath Hyde Bridge.

Tobergal Lane IRISH €€
(☎071-914 6599; www.tobergallanecafe.ie; Tobergal Lane; lunch dishes €6-9, dinner mains €8-18; ⏰10am-10pm) There's a wonderfully warm, relaxed vibe at this arty cafe hidden down a curving laneway. The menu is simple but creatively prepared with specials such as duck confit with puy lentils or baked sea trout with lime and ginger sauce. There's live jazz on Friday nights and Sunday afternoons.

Silver Apple FRENCH €€
(☎071-914 6770; www.silverapple.ie; Lord Edward St; mains €15-23; ⏰5-10pm Mon-Sat, 1-10pm Sun Jul & Aug, 5-10pm Wed-Sun Sep-Jun) The simple entrance to this friendly bistro opposite the bus station belies the quality of food on offer here. It's a cosy kind of place with bare stone walls, retro posters, stained glass and a menu of superb French classics.

Montmartre FRENCH €€
(☎071-916 9901; 1 Market Yard; mains €17-24; ⏰5-11pm Tue-Sat) Tucked away on a quiet back road by the market, this excellent French restaurant is a bit of a local secret. It's an unpretentious place, simply decorated and quietly confident. The menu offers a great choice of seafood but meat lovers and vegetarians are well catered for too. Book ahead.

Drinking

Sligo enjoys some of the best night-time fun in Ireland's northwest, with impromptu sessions striking up at every opportunity.

Hargadons PUB
(4 O'Connell St; www.hargadons.com; lunch mains €8-13, tapas dishes €7-10; ⏰lunch Mon-Sat, tapas 4-8.30pm Thu-Sat) A winning blend of old-world fittings and gastropub style, this pub dating from 1864 is the kind of place you just won't want to leave. Its uneven stone floors, turf fire, antique signage, snug corners and

bowed shelves laden down with ancient bottles give it a wonderful charm. But you'll also get some excellent food (think oysters in a hot chorizo and tabasco sauce or confit of duck leg), live music on Saturday nights and the smoothest of pints.

Thomas Connolly PUB
(Holborn St) Discoloured photos and newspaper clippings, mottled mirrors and ledger books adorn the walls at this old timers' pub. With its simple tongue and groove panelling along the walls, flagstone floors and traditional wood and glass partitions, it has an ancient, down-to-earth atmosphere perfect for slowly sipping a pint and putting the world to rights.

Shoot the Crows PUB
(Castle St) Dark and somewhat dishevelled, this old pub oozes bohemian atmosphere. Early evening draws a good-natured crowd of regulars, and even when the place is packed to the gills it generally has an easygoing vibe. Singalongs and *céilidh* sessions often start up spontaneously.

Furey's PUB
(Bridge St) Old-style bar with superb traditional music most nights, as well as jazz and various open mic opportunities for all comers.

☆ Entertainment

Hawk's Well Theatre THEATRE
(www.hawkswell.com; Temple St) This well-regarded theatre presents concerts, dance and drama.

The Factory Performance Space THEATRE
(www.blueraincoat.com; Lower Quay St) A once-derelict pork abattoir is home to innovative professional theatre company Blue Raincoat, whose program includes original productions.

Clarence Hotel LIVE MUSIC
(Wine St) Sligo's biggest music venue with regular live bands and DJs.

Information

Cafe Online (1 Calry Crt, Stephen St; per hr €3.50; ⊙10am-11pm) Central internet access.

Post office (Wine St)

Tourist office (☎071-916 1201; www.discovereireland.ie/northwest; Temple St; ⊙9am-6pm Mon-Fri, 9am-5pm Sat, 10am-4pm Sun Jun-Aug, 9am-5pm Mon-Fri, 10am-4pm Sat Mar-May & Sep, 9am-5pm Mon-Fri Oct-Feb) Has info on the whole northwest region and stocks an interesting walking tour brochure of Sligo. Located off the beaten track. The office may be moving to O'Connell St in 2012 so check in advance.

Getting There & Away

Air

Sligo Airport (www.sligoairport.com; Strandhill Rd) has direct Aer Arann flights to Dublin twice daily (40 minutes).

Bus

Bus Éireann (☎071-916 0066) leaves from the bus station, situated below the train station on Lord Edward St. Destinations include Ballina (€13, 1½ hours, three daily), Westport (€17, two hours, twice daily) and Dublin (€17, four hours, four daily), as well as Galway and Donegal town. Services are less frequent on Sunday.

Feda O'Donnell (☎074-954 8114; www.feda.ie) operates a service between Crolly (County Donegal) and Galway twice daily (four times on Sunday). Call to confirm departure points.

Train

Trains leave the **station** (☎071-916 9888) for Dublin (€32, four hours, eight daily) via Boyle, Carrick-on-Shannon and Mullingar.

Getting Around

BUS Local buses run to Strandhill and to Rosses Point and sometimes continue to the airport.

TAXI There are taxi stands on Quay St and Grattan St. A taxi to the airport costs about €15.

BIKE Chain Driven Cycles (☎071-912 9008; www.chaindrivencycles; 23 High St; per day/week from €18/54) Offers mountain, hybrid and road bike hire.

Around Sligo Town

ROSSES POINT

POP 872

Rosses Point is a picturesque seaside resort with grassy dunes rolling down to the golden strand. Benbulben, Sligo's most recognisable landmark, arches skywards in the distance. Offshore, the odd **Metal Man** beacon dates from 1821.

Rosses Point has two wonderful **beaches** and one of Ireland's most challenging and renowned golf links, **County Sligo Golf Course** (www.countysligogolfclub.ie), which attracts golfers from all over the world. Fringed by the Atlantic and lying in the shadow of Benbulben, this is possibly Ireland's greatest and most picturesque golf links.

MICHAEL QUIRKE: THE WOODCARVER OF WINE ST

The inconspicuous studio of Michael Quirke, woodcarver, raconteur and local character, is filled with the scents of locally felled timbers and off-cuts of beech stumps. A converted butcher shop, it retains some of the implements of the butcher's trade, including an electric bone saw. Quirke, himself formerly a butcher, began to use his tools for cutting and carving wood in 1968. He divided his time between his twin callings for 20 years, after which he gave up meat, so to speak.

Quirke's art is inspired by Irish mythology, a subject about which he is passionate and knowledgeable, and as he carves he readily chats with the customers and the curious who enter his shop and end up staying for hours. 'Irish mythology, unlike Greek mythology, is alive and constantly changing', he says. 'It's not set in stone, and that's why it's interesting.' He draws unforced connections between Irish myths, music, history, flora, fauna and contemporary events, as well as comparisons in the wider world, such as Australian Aboriginal and Native North American lore.

As he talks and carves, Quirke frequently pulls out a county map, pointing to places that spring from the conversation, leading you on your own magical, mystical tour of the county.

The studio is on Wine St in Sligo town.

If you'd like to stay, aim for **Rosses Point Guesthouse** (☎086 805 1390; www.rossesspointguesthouse.com; dm/d from €18/54; 📶) a sparkly new place in the centre of the village with simple but pristine rooms, a good kitchen and lively atmosphere. The team behind it also run **LSD Kiteboarding** (www.lsdkiteboarding.com) and offer a two-night accommodation and boarding package for €410.

Drop into **Harry's Bar** (on your right as you come into Rosses Point) for a pint and a peek at its historic well, aquarium and maritime bric-a-brac.

Rosses Point is 8km northwest of Sligo on the R291. There are regular buses from Sligo.

CARROWMORE MEGALITHIC CEMETERY

Despite its impressive scale and international importance, **Carrowmore** (www.heritageireland.ie; adult/child €3/1; ⏰10am-6pm mid-Apr–mid-Oct, final admission 5pm; Ⓟ), one of the largest Stone Age cemeteries in Europe, is little visited and largely undervalued. Some 60 monuments including stone circles, passage tombs and dolmens adorn the rolling hills of this haunting site, which is thought to pre-date Newgrange in County Meath by 700 years. Over the centuries, many of the stones have been destroyed, and several remaining stones are on private land.

The delicately balanced dolmens were originally covered with stones and earth, so it requires some effort to picture what this 2.5km-wide area might once have looked like. A large central cairn has been reconstructed to give visitors some insight into the materials and methods used at this time, while an exhibit in the roadside **visitor centre** gives the full low-down on this fascinating site.

To get here, follow the N4 south from Sligo for 5km and follow the signposts.

KNOCKNAREA CAIRN

Sligo's ultimate rock pile, 2km northwest of Carrowmore, **Knocknarea** is popularly believed to be the grave of legendary Queen Maeve (Queen Mab in Welsh and English folk tales). The 40,000 tonnes of stone have never been excavated, despite speculation that a tomb on the scale of the one at Newgrange lies buried below.

The cairn is perched high atop the limestone plateau (328m) and seems to be looking over your shoulder everywhere you dare tread in its ancestral backyard. It's a 45-minute trek to the top, from which a spectacular panoramic view pulls in Benbulben, Rosses Point and the Atlantic Ocean beyond.

Leave Sligo as though for Carrowmore, then follow signs to Knocknarea. Or from Carrowmore, continue down the road, turn right by a church then follow the signposts.

STRANDHILL

POP 1413

The great Atlantic rollers that sweep the shorefront of Strandhill make this long, red-gold **beach** unsafe for swimming. They have, however, made it a surfing mecca. Its handy 24-hour **surfcam** (www.strandhillsurf.eu) brings surfers scurrying whenever the surf's up. Strandhill is 8km west of Sligo along the R292.

Gear hire and lessons can be arranged through **Perfect Day Surf Shop** (www.perfectdaysurfing.com; Shore Rd) and **Strandhill Surf School** (www.strandhillsurf.eu; Beach Front).

Alternatively, take a gentler, warmer dip in the **Voya Seaweed Baths** (see boxed text, p455).

A few kilometres towards Sligo, you can walk – at low tide only! – to **Coney Island**. Its New York namesake was supposedly named by a man from Rosses Point. The island's wishing well is reputed to have been dug by St Patrick (who, if all these tales are to be trusted, led a *very* busy life). Check tide times to avoid getting stranded.

Sleeping

Ocean Wave Lodge B&B €
(071-916 8115; www.oceanwavelodge.com; Top Rd; dm/s/d €20/35/50; P, wi-fi) This large modern house has excellent value, newly decorated rooms. Pale walls and linens contrast with dark wood furniture, cushions and throws in what are fairly minimalist but comfortable rooms. Breakfast is included but there's also a self-catering kitchen and large lounge area for guest use.

Strandhill Lodge & Suites B&B €€
(071-912 2122; www.strandhillodgeandsuites.com; Top Rd; r from €89; P, wi-fi) Brand new and squeaky clean, this excellent guesthouse offers bright, spacious rooms with king size beds, hotel-quality design and trendy neutral styling. There are also three luxurious suites and a self-contained apartment.

Strandhill Lodge & Hostel HOSTEL €
(071-916 8313; www.strandhillaccommodation.com; Shore Rd; dm/s/d €16/20/30; P @ wi-fi) Surfer dudes and dudettes thaw out by the open fire in the common room of this well-run, 34-bed hostel a few paces from the strand. The owners also operate a rather frilly B&B next door and a surf school.

Eating & Drinking

Trá Bán SEAFOOD €€
(071-912 8402; www.trabansligo.ie; Shore Rd; mains €17-27; closed Mon) This justifiably popular spot serves a menu strong on seafood but with a good selection of steak and pasta dishes thrown in. It has a lovely relaxed atmosphere that belies the quality of the food and the chic decor. It's a favourite local haunt so you'd be well advised to book in advance.

Bella Vista IRISH €€
(071-912 2222; Shore Rd; bar mains €12-17; bistro mains €16-26; meals 10am-10pm; wi-fi, child-friendly) Lively Bella Vista serves pizza, pasta and classic pub favourites in its bar, while the more formal bistro serves a modern version of traditional Irish meat and veg, as well as gourmet pizzas.

Venue PUB €€
(Top Rd; mains €12-23) Seafood, fajitas and steaks are part of the decent international menu at this whitewashed pub. Year-round, you'll catch live music every Thursday, Friday and Saturday in its front bar.

Getting There & Away

Strandhill is situated 8km due west of Sligo off the R292 airport road. Buses run from Sligo regularly.

DEER PARK COURT CAIRN

A 10-minute walk from a nearby car park leads through pine-scented forest to this enigmatic court tomb (also called Magheraghanrush). Dating from around 3000 BC, the crumbling structure is comparable to a crude human form, with a large bellylike central court and several protruding burial chambers positioned as though the head and legs.

Take the N16 east from Sligo and turn onto the R286 for Parke's Castle. Almost immediately, turn left at the Y-junction onto a minor road for Manorhamilton. Continue for 3km to the car park, then follow the trail for 50m before veering right up a small hill.

South of Sligo Town

RIVERSTOWN

The endearing **Sligo Folk Park** (071-916 5001; www.sligofolkpark.com; Millview House, Riverstown; adult/child €6/4; 9.30am-5.30pm Mon-Sat, 12-5pm Sun Easter-Oct) revolves around a lovingly restored 19th-century cottage. Humble thatched structures complement this centrepiece, along with scattered farm tools and an exhibit that honours the old country life.

The three-day **James Morrison Traditional Music Festival** (www.morrison.ie) in August includes fun informal seminars on how to sing *sean-nós* ('old-style' songs) or perform traditional Irish reels on instruments such as the button accordion and the fiddle.

Another fine reason to come here is to attend a course on permaculture, bee-keeping

DETOUR: LADIES BRAE

For a DIY adventure well off the beaten track, follow the narrow back roads between Ballymote and Aughris Head. This scenic drive takes you across the Ox Mountains and past the impossibly pretty Ladies Brae where you'll get a panoramic view over the Sligo coastline. You'll also find secluded picnic tables and some superb walks that link with the 78km waymarked **Sligo Way** (www.walkireland.ie).

or even solar panel building at the green-roofed **Gyreum** (071-916 5994; www.gyreum.com; Corlisheen, Riverstown; dm €17-21, d €50-54; P), a pudding-shaped building hidden by the surrounding hills. You can also give your own sermon on a Sunday morning, volunteer to help out or stay in the simple rooms.

For a little more luxury however, head for **Coopershill House** (071-916 5108; www.coopershill.com; Riverstown; s/d from €144/218; Apr-Oct; P) an idyllic Georgian retreat in an estate alive with wildflowers, birdsong and deer. Most of the eight bedrooms have lovely canopy beds as well as original antiques and oil paintings.

Riverstown is 2km east of the N4 at Drumfin. Buses run from Sligo to Riverstown (€4.20, 45 minutes) twice on Thursdays and Fridays.

CARROWKEEL MEGALITHIC CEMETERY

With a God's-eye view of the county from high in the Bricklieve Mountains, it's little wonder this hilltop site was sacred in prehistoric times. The windswept location is simultaneously eerie and uplifting, it's undeveloped nature and spectacular setting giving it an instantly momentous atmosphere. Dotted with around 14 cairns, dolmens and the scattered remnants of other graves, the site dates from the late Stone Age (3000 to 2000 BC).

Climbing up from the car park the first tomb you'll reach is Cairn G. Above its entrance is a roofbox aligned with the midsummer sunset which illuminates the inner chamber. The only other such roofbox known in Ireland is that at Newgrange in County Meath. Everywhere you look across the surrounding hills you'll see evidence of early life here including about 140 stone circles, all that remain of the foundations of a large village thought to have been inhabited by the builders of the tombs.

West off the N4 road, Carrowkeel is closer to Boyle than Sligo town. From the latter, turn right in Castlebaldwin, then left at the fork; it's 2km uphill from the gateway. You can take an Athlone bus from Sligo and ask to be dropped off at Castlebaldwin.

BALLYMOTE & AROUND

POP 1229

This pretty little town merits a visit if only to see the immense ivy-covered shell of **Ballymote Castle**. It was from this early 14th-century castle, fronted by formidable drum towers, that O'Donnell marched to disaster at the Battle of Kinsale in 1601. It's on the Tubbercurry road (R296), opposite the train station in Ballymote.

Eagles soar straight over your head at the new volunteer-run research centre **Eagles Flying** (www.eaglesflying.com; Ballymote; adult/child €9/5.50; 10.30am-12.30pm & 2.30-4.30pm, flying demonstrations 11am & 3pm Apr-Oct). Scientists answer questions about these birds of prey during demonstrations; there's also an on-site minizoo with ducks, donkeys and other cute critters.

Around 6km south of Ballymote at Kesh, the **Caves of Kesh** (sometimes spelt Keash) are rich with mythology and are believed to extend for miles (some say as far as Roscommon). Human remains have been found here, as well as those of cave bears, reindeer, Arctic lemmings and Irish elk.

Just under 10km southwest of Kesh, at the main crossroads of the village of Gurteen (also spelt Gorteen), the **Coleman Irish Music Centre** (www.colemanirishmusic.com; 10am-5pm Mon-Sat) has multimedia music exhibits and hosts workshops and performances. You can add to your music collection or pick up your own instruments and sheet music at the on-site shop.

Temple House (071-918 3329; www.templehouse.ie; Ballymote; s/d from €110/170; Apr-Nov; P) , set in 400 hectares of woodlands, overlooks the ruins of a 13th-century Knights Templar castle and a crystalline lake that you can explore by rowboat. The Georgian mansion has been in the same family since the 1600s, and has six shabby-chic period guest rooms (with sparkling new bathrooms), dusty natural-history collections and decapitated hunting trophies. Dinner costs €45. It's signposted 500m south of the small village of Ballinacarrow (also spelt Ballynacarrow), close to the N17.

The train from Sligo to Dublin stops at Ballymote (€7.20, 20 minutes) eight times daily Monday to Saturday, six on Sunday.

AUGHRIS HEAD

An invigorating 5km **walk** traces the cliffs around remote Aughris Head, where **dolphins** and **seals** can often be seen swimming into the bay. Birdwatchers should look out for kittiwakes, fulmars, guillemots, shags, storm petrels and curlews along the way.

In a stupendous setting on the lovely beach by the cliff walk, the **Beach Bar** (www.thebeachbarsligo.com; mains €10-19; food served 1-8pm daily summer, weekends only winter) is tucked inside a 17th-century thatched cottage, with cracking traditional music sessions and superb seafood including creamy chowder and poached salmon. The owners also operate the B&B **Aughris House** (071-917 6465; tent/van sites €10/20, s/d €30/60; P) next door, with seven comfy rooms and adjacent campsites.

EASKEY & ENNISCRONE

The town of Easkey seems blissfully unaware that it's one of Europe's best year-round surfing destinations. Pub conversations revolve around hurling and Gaelic football, and the road to the beach isn't even signposted (turn off next to the childcare centre). Facilities are few; most surfers camp (free) around the castle ruins by the sea. If you're planning on hitting the waves, information and advice are available from **Easkey Surfing & Information Centre** (Irish Surfing Association; 096-49428; www.isasurf.ie).

Some 14km south at Enniscrone, a stunning beach known as the Hollow stretches for 5km. Surf lessons and board hire are available from Enniscrone-based **Seventh Wave Surf School** (087 971 6389; www.surfsligo.com). The town is also famous for its traditional seaweed baths (see boxed text, p455) which are some of the best and most atmospheric in the country.

Enniscrone enjoys wonderful sunsets and it's worth considering an overnight here. For accommodation try **Seasons Lodge** (096-37122; www.seasonslodge.ie; Enniscrone; s/d €65/110; P), a purpose-built guesthouse with bright, spacious rooms each with a queen size and single bed. Calm, neutral colour schemes and lots of thoughtful extras make it a wonderful place to stay.

Alternatively, **Ceol na Mara** (096-36351; www.ceol-na-mara.com; Enniscrone; s/d €50/80; P) with its simple, crisp rooms and private path to the beach is a good option.

Buses run four times daily (once on Sunday) from Sligo to Easkey (€10.20, one hour) and Enniscrone (€11.50, 1½ hours) from where they continue on to Ballina.

Lough Gill

The mirrorlike 'Lake of Brightness', Lough Gill is home to as many legends as fish. One that can be tested easily is the story that a silver bell from the abbey in Sligo was thrown into the lough and only those free from sin can hear it pealing. (We didn't hear it…)

The lake, southeast of Sligo town, is an easy day trip from anywhere in the county. Two magical swaths of woodland – **Hazelwood** and **Slish Wood** – have loop trails; there are good views of Innisfree Island from the latter.

You can take a **cruise** on the lake from atmospheric Parke's Castle (see p523).

Getting There & Away

The Sligo-Dromahair bus runs along the northern shore of the lake and stops at Slish Wood. By car and bicycle, leave Sligo east via the Mall past the hospital, and turn right off the N16 onto the R286, which leads to the northern shore of Lough Gill. The southern route is less interesting until you reach Dooney Rock.

DOONEY ROCK

Immortalised by Yeats in *The Fiddler of Dooney,* this huge fissured limestone knoll bulges awkwardly upward by the lough's southern shore. There's a great lake view from the top.

Leave Sligo south on the N4 and turn left at the sign to Lough Gill. Another left at the T-junction brings you onto the R287 towards Dooney car park.

INNISFREE ISLAND

This pint-sized island lies tantalisingly close to the lough's southeastern shore, but alas, can't be accessed. Still, it's visible from the shore. Its air of tranquillity so moved Yeats that he famously wrote *The Lake Isle of Innisfree:*

MERMAID DREAMS

Ireland's only native spa therapy is the stuff of mermaid (or merman) fantasies. Part of Irish homeopathy for centuries, steaming your pores open then submerging yourself in a seaweed bath is said to help rheumatism and arthritis, thyroid imbalances, even hangovers. Certainly it leaves your skin feeling baby-soft: seaweed's silky oils contain a massive concentration of iodine, a key presence in most moisturising creams.

Seaweed baths are prevalent along the west coast but two places stand out. **Kilcullen's Seaweed Baths** (☎091-36238; www.kilcullenseaweedbaths.com; Enniscrone; s/tw bath €25/40; ⏲10am-8pm Jun-Sep, noon-8pm Mon-Fri & 10am-8pm Sat & Sun Oct-May) is the most traditional and has buckets of character. Set within a grand Edwardian structure, it seems perfectly fitting to sit with your head exposed and your body ensconced in an individual cedar steam cabinet before plunging into one of the original gigantic porcelain baths filled with amber water and cavorting seaweed.

For an altogether more modern setting, try **Voya Seaweed Baths** (☎071-916 8686; www.celticseaweedbaths.com; Shore Rd, Strandhill; s/tw bath €25/50; ⏲noon-8pm Mon & Tue, 11am-8pm Wed-Fri, 10am-8pm Sat & Sun), which has a beachfront location but somehow just isn't quite as much fun.

If too much relaxation is barely enough, both establishments also offer the chance to indulge in various other seaweed treatments, including body wraps and massages.

I will arise and go now, and go to Innisfree,
And a small cabin build there, of clay and wattles made;
Nine bean rows will I have there, a hive for the honey bee,
And live alone in the bee-loud glade.

Continue east from Dooney Rock and turn left at the crossroads. After 3km turn left again for another 3km. A small road leads down to the lake.

North of Sligo Town

DRUMCLIFF & BENBULBEN

Visible right along Sligo's northern coast, Benbulben (525m), often written Ben Bulben, resembles a table covered by a pleated cloth: its limestone plateau is uncommonly flat, and its near-vertical sides are scored by earthen ribs. Walking here can be dangerous for the uninitiated – the **Sligo Mountaineering Club** (www.sligomountaineeringclub.org) has advice.

Benbulben's beauty was not lost on WB Yeats. Before the poet died in Menton, France in 1939, he had requested: 'If I die here, bury me up there on the mountain, and then after a year or so, dig me up and bring me privately to Sligo'. His wishes weren't honoured until 1948, when his body was interred in the churchyard at Drumcliff, where his great-grandfather had been rector.

Yeats' grave is next to the doorway of the Protestant church, and his youthful bride Georgie Hyde-Lee is buried alongside. Almost three decades her senior, Yeats was 52 when they married. The poet's epitaph is from his poem *Under Ben Bulben:*

Cast a cold eye
On life, on death.
Horseman, pass by!

Visiting the grave is somewhat disturbed by traffic noise along the N15 that no doubt has Yeats rolling over.

In the 6th century, St Colmcille chose the same location for a monastery. You can still see the stumpy remains of the **round tower**, which was struck by lightning in 1936, on the main road nearby. Also in the churchyard is an extraordinary 11th-century **high cross**, etched with intricate biblical scenes.

There's a small **cafe and crafts shop** (⏲9am-6pm) beside the church.

Historic **Lissadell House**, west of Drumcliff off the N15 just past Yeats Tavern, was recently restored to its former glory by its private owners but a bitter argument over rights of way through the estate has forced its closure. Check with the tourist office in Sligo town for updates.

Sleeping & Eating

Yeats Lodge B&B €€
(☎071-917 3787; www.yeatslodge.com; Drumcliff; s/d €48/66; P 📶 ♿) Friendly owners, large,

Yeats' Country

County Sligo's (p447) lush rolling hills, ancient monuments and simple country life captivated and inspired Nobel laureate, poet and dramatist William Butler Yeats (1865–1939) from an early age. Despite living almost all his life abroad, Yeats returned here frequently, enamoured by the glittering lakes, the looming hulk of Benbulben (p455) and the idyllic pastoral setting. On his death Yeats asked to be buried here in what he regarded as 'the country of the heart'.

Sligo is littered with prehistoric monuments and has a rich tradition of myth and folklore, all of which influenced Yeats and his work. You can follow in his footsteps and tour the locations that inspired him, from the waterfall in Glencar (p458) referred to in *The Stolen Child*, to picturesque Innisfree Island (p455) and rugged Dooney Rock (p454).

Yeats' great legacy is celebrated with three weeks of Irish poetry, music and literature during the Yeats International Festival held in Sligo each year, while photographs, letters, draft manuscripts and his personal effects can be seen at the Sligo County Museum and Yeats Memorial Building both in the county town (p447).

Jack B Yeats, William's brother and one of Ireland's most important modern artists, also drew inspiration from Sligo's bucolic countryside, and landscapes remained one of his favoured themes throughout his lifetime.

Clockwise from top left

1. Rowan Gillespie's statue of WB Yeats, Sligo Town
2. Round tower, Drumcliff **3.** Glencar waterfall, County Leitrim **4.** Sunset on the banks of the River Moy

2

3

ISTOCK ©

modern rooms and a tranquil atmosphere make this B&B worth seeking out. There's plenty of space in the guest rooms and the common areas, tasteful rustic decor and lovely views of the surrounding countryside.

Willsborough House B&B **€€**
(☎071-917 3526; www.drumcliffebedandbreakfast.com; Cullaghbeg, Drumcliff; s/d €48/66; P 📶 👪) This modern dormer bungalow has pretty, spacious rooms with pine floors and furniture and a homely atmosphere. It's in a quiet location with lovely views of Benbulben and extremely friendly hosts.

To get here turn right off the N15, 500m past Yeats Tavern.

Henry's Bar & Restaurant IRISH **€€**
(☎071-917 3985; www.henrysrestaurant.ie; Cashelgarran; mains €10-25; ⊙food served 10am-9.30pm Mon-Sat, noon-5pm & 6-9.30pm Sun; 👪) Since it opened in 2008, this sprawling modern expanse of timber and glass has been a winner with families for its easygoing attitude and solid Irish menu with kid-friendly options.

Yeats Tavern SEAFOOD **€€**
(☎071-916 3117; www.yeatstavernrestaurant.com; N15, Drumcliff; mains €14-26; ⊙meals noon-9.30pm) This smart, contemporary pub/restaurant is popular for a pint or Irish coffee, but especially for its seafood, which includes local Drumcliff Bay mussels and Lissadell clams. It's about 300m north of Yeats' grave.

Getting There & Away

Buses run from Sligo to Drumcliff (€3.50, 10 minutes, 10 Monday to Saturday, seven Sunday) and stop at the post office.

LOUGH GLENCAR

Straddling counties Sligo and Leitrim, this picturesque lake is famed for **fishing** as well as its beautiful **waterfall**, and was referred to by Yeats in *The Stolen Child*. The surrounding countryside is best enjoyed by walking east and taking the steep trail north to the valley.

From Drumcliff it's less than 5km to the lake's western shores. There's one bus Monday to Friday, two on Saturday from Sligo (€3.50, 15 minutes).

STREEDAGH & GRANGE

From the village of Grange, signs point towards Streedagh Beach, a grand crescent of sand that saw some 1100 sailors perish when three ships from the Spanish Armada were wrecked nearby. Views extend from the beach to the cliffs at Slieve League in Co Donegal. Locals regularly swim here, even in winter.

Note that horse riding is not allowed on the beach. However, a variety of guided riding opportunities are available at **Island View Riding Stables** (☎071-916 6156; www.islandviewridingstables.com; Grange; adult/child per hr €25/18).

Buses run from Sligo to Grange (€4.50, 10 minutes, 10 Monday to Saturday, seven Sunday) and stop at Rooney's newsagent.

DETOUR: INISHMURRAY ISLAND

It takes some effort to arrange a visit to Inishmurray, an island that was abandoned in 1948, leaving behind early Christian remains and fascinating pagan relics. There are three well-preserved churches, beehive cells and open-air altars. The old monastery, surrounded by a thickset oval wall, was founded in the early 6th century by St Molaise.

The pagan relics were also assembled by Inishmurray monks. There's a collection of cursing stones: those who wanted to lay a curse did the Stations of the Cross in reverse, turning the stones as they went. There were also separate burial grounds for men and women, and a strong belief that if a body was placed in the wrong ground it would move itself during the night.

Only 6km separates Inishmurray from the mainland, but there's no regular boat service, and the lack of a harbour makes landing subject to the weather. Enthusiastic historian Joe McGowan runs excursions from Mullaghmore aboard the **MV Excalibur** (☎071-914 2738; www.sligoheritage.com) from Easter to August for €35 return per person. Trips can also be arranged aboard **MV Celtic Dawn** (☎071-916 6124; tlomax@eircom.net), a popular vessel for sea angling trips.

MULLAGHMORE

The sweeping arc of dark-golden sand and the safe shallow waters make the pretty fishing village of Mullaghmore a popular family destination. It was a favoured holiday spot of Lord Mountbatten, who was killed here when the IRA rigged his boat with explosives in 1979.

Take time to cycle or drive the scenic road looping around Mullaghmore Head, where wide shafts of rock slice into the Atlantic surf. En route you'll pass **Classiebawn Castle** (closed to the public), a neo-Gothic turreted pile built for Lord Palmerston in 1856 and later home to the ill-fated Lord Mountbatten.

Mullaghmore Head is becoming known as one of Ireland's premier **big wave surf** spots with swells of up to 17m allowing for Hawaiian-style adventure. The country's first big wave tow-in surfing competition was held off Mullaghmore Head in 2011.

Mullaghmore's clear waters, rocky outcrops and coves are also ideal for diving, contact **Offshore Watersports** (☎071-919 4769, 087 610 0111; www.offshore.ie; The Pier) about dive trips and gear rental.

If you're lucky you'll get magnificent views from a room at the **Pier Head Hotel** (☎071-916 6171; www.pierheadhotel.ie; Mullaghmore; s/d €50/89; P ; closed late Dec) by the harbour. The rooms are clean and crisp, if a little austere, there's a tiny gym, a panoramic rooftop terrace with hot tub, and decent food in the **bar** (mains from €10 to €21).

The nearest bus stop is 4km away in Cliffony on the N15.

CREEVYKEEL GOORT CAIRN

Shaped like a lobster's claw, this prehistoric **court tomb** (admission free; dawn-dusk) encloses several burial chambers. The structure was originally built around 2500 BC, with several more chambers added later. Once in the unroofed oval court, smaller visitors can duck under the stone-shielded entrance to reach the site's core.

The tomb is north of Cliffony on the N15. Buses run from Sligo to Cliffony (€5.50, 15 minutes, 10 Monday to Saturday, seven Sunday) and stop at Ena's Pub.

County Donegal

POPULATION: 161,000 / AREA: 3001 SQ KM

Includes »

Best Places to Eat

» Castle Murray (p472)
» Mill Restaurant (p485)
» Cove (p485)
» Olde Glen Bar & Restaurant (p489)
» Beach House (p493)

Best Places to Stay

» Frewin House (p491)
» Lough Eske Castle (p465)
» Carnaween House (p477)
» Rathmullan House (p490)
» Glen House (p494)

Why Go?

'Up here it's different', the saying goes, and it's true. County Donegal is the wild child of Ireland. Even before the twins of history and politics conspired to isolate it, Donegal was a place like no other on the island. It's a county of extremes; at times bleak and desolate and beaten by brutal weather, yet in turn a land of unspoilt splendour where stark mountains and sweeping beaches bask in glorious sunshine. The rugged interior with its gorgeous mountain passes and shimmering lakes is only marginally outdone by the long and labyrinthine coastline with its precipitous cliffs, windswept peninsulas and vast expanses of golden sand. The landscape here easily rivals anything Connemara or Kerry has to offer but Donegal sees only a fraction of their visitors. Proudly different and fiercely independent, one-third of the county is official Gaeltacht territory, where Irish is still the lingua franca.

When to Go

Donegal's character is forged by its impetuous weather. In winter the howling winds and sheeting rain can feel Arctic, and storms arrive unannounced. In summer the weather isn't much more reliable but the clouds regularly break into brilliant sunshine that transforms brooding blues and greys into sparkling green. At this time of year you'll also get the pick of traditional music, storytelling and dance festivals that spring up across the county. The beach-side hotels and restaurants come out of hibernation and the surfers hit the waves.

Getting There & Away

Donegal Airport (www.donegalairport.ie) has flights to/from Dublin (50 minutes, two daily) and to Glasgow Prestwick (50 minutes, three per week). It's in the townland (an ancient unit of local government) of Carrick Finn (Charraig Fhion), about 3km northwest of Annagry along the northwestern coast. There's no public transport to the airport, but there are car-rental desks in the terminal.

The **City of Derry Airport** (www.cityofderryairport.com) is just beyond the county's eastern border, in Northern Ireland.

Getting Around

Donegal is not served by train. The bus is your main transport option if you don't have your own car.

In addition to **Bus Éireann** (www.buseireann.ie), private bus company **Lough Swilly** (in Letterkenny 074-912 2863, in Derry 028-7126 2017; www.loughswillybusco.com) traverses the county. Coaches operated by **Feda O'Donnell** (074-954 8114; www.feda.ie) serve the western half of the county from Bundoran to Crolly. Timetables change seasonally, however, so check the website for the latest information.

When driving, road signs in the Gaeltacht communities are in Irish only – although we use English transliterations, their Irish names are included in brackets.

DONEGAL TOWN

POP 2339

Pretty Donegal town occupies a strategic spot at the mouth of Donegal Bay. With a backdrop of the Blue Stack Mountains, a handsome and well-preserved castle, friendly locals and a good choice of places to eat and stay, it makes an excellent base for exploring the wild coastline nearby. On the banks of the River Eske, Donegal town was a stamping ground of the O'Donnells, the great chieftains who ruled the northwest from the 15th to 17th centuries. Today, despite being the county's namesake, it's neither its largest (Letterkenny), nor the county town (the even smaller town of Lifford).

Sights & Activities

Donegal Castle HISTORIC BUILDING

(www.heritageireland.ie; Castle St; adult/child €4/2; 10am-6pm Easter–mid-Sep, 9.30am-4.30pm Thu-Mon mid-Sep–Easter) Guarding a picturesque bend of the River Eske, Donegal Castle remains an imperious monument to both Irish and English might. Built by the O'Donnells in 1474, it served as the seat of their formidable power until 1607, when the English decided to be rid of pesky Irish chieftains once and for all. Rory O'Donnell was no pushover, though, torching his own castle before fleeing to France in the infamous Flight of the Earls. Their defeat paved the way for the Plantation of Ulster by thousands of newly arrived Scots and English Protestants, creating the divisions that still afflict the island to this day.

The castle was rebuilt in 1623 by Sir Basil Brooke, along with the adjacent three-storey Jacobean house. Further restoration in the 1990s has made it a wonderfully atmospheric place to visit, with rooms furnished with French tapestries and Persian rugs. There are guided tours every hour.

Diamond Obelisk MONUMENT

In 1474 Red Hugh O'Donnell and his wife, Nuala O'Brien, founded Donegal's Franciscan friary by the shore south of town. It was accidentally blown up in 1601 by Rory O'Donnell while laying siege to an English garrison, and little remains. Four of its friars, fearing that the arrival of the English meant the end of Celtic culture, chronicled the whole of known Celtic history and mythology from 40 years before the Flood to AD 1618 in *The Annals of the Four Masters* – still one of the most important sources of early Irish history. The obelisk (1937), in the Diamond, commemorates the work, copies of which are displayed in the National Library in Dublin.

Donegal Bay Waterbus BOAT TRIPS

(www.donegalbaywaterbus.com; Donegal Pier; adult/child €15/5; Easter-Oct) The most enjoyable way to explore the highlights of Donegal Bay is to take a 1¼-hour boat tour taking in everything from historic sites to seal-inhabited coves, admiring an island manor and a ruined castle along the way. The tour runs up to three times daily.

Sleeping

Good B&Bs and mediocre hotels are plentiful around Donegal town; for high-end luxury head out to nearby Lough Eske.

Ard na Breatha B&B €€

(074-972 2288; www.ardnabreatha.com; Drumrooske Middle; s/d from €70/110; Feb-Oct; P) In an elevated setting 1.5km north of town, this boutique guesthouse on a working farm has tasteful rooms with pine furniture and

County Donegal Highlights

1. Watching the sun set from the top of Europe's highest sea cliffs, **Slieve League** (p473)
2. Hiking to the **Glen Gesh Pass** for mountain and valley views (p475)
3. Touring flamboyant **Glenveagh Castle** (p488) and beautiful Glenveagh National Park
4. Strolling along the windswept beach at **Tramore** (p484)
5. Sipping a quiet pint in **Molly's Bar** (p485)
6. Taking in the views at the spectacular **Poisoned Glen** (p480)
7. Learning to surf on the white sand beach at **Rossnowlagh** (p467)
8. Collecting semiprecious stones from the raised beaches at **Malin Head** (p497)
9. Exploring the stash of international artworks in **Glebe House** (p489)

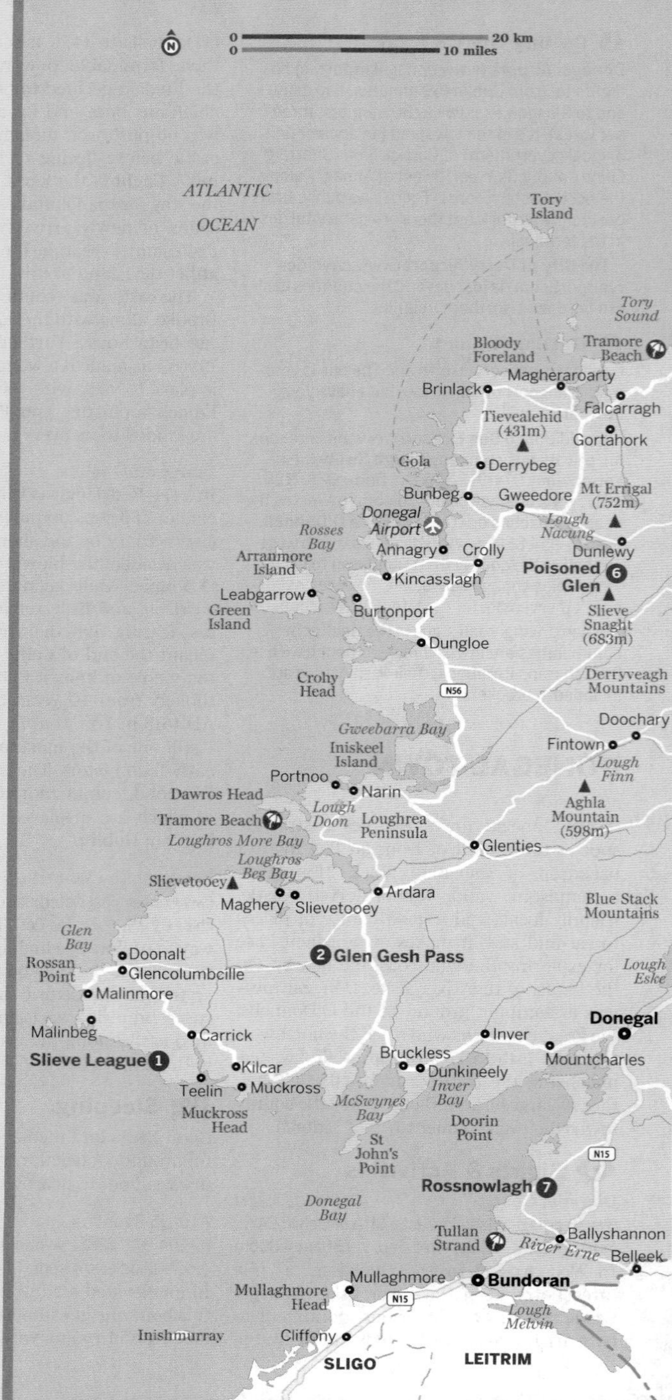

Inishtrahull Sound
Malin Head 8
Ballyhillin
Glengad Head
Pollan Bay
Tullagh Bay
Trawbreaga Bay
Culdaff Bay
Culdaff
Tremore Bay
Kinnagoe Bay
Fanad Head
Dunaff Head
Dunaff
Ballyliffin
Clonmany
Carndonagh
Shrove
Lough Swilly
Lenan Head
Gleneely
Horn Head
Rosguill Peninsula
Slieve Snaght (615m)
Glentogher
Greencastle
Sheep Haven Bay
Portsalon
Dunree
Inishowen Peninsula
Moville
5
Downings
Rosnakill
4 Dunfanaghy
Carrigart
Knockalla Fort
River Crana
Port-na-Blagh
Ards Forest Park
Carrowkeel
Buncrana
Quigley's Point
Fanad Peninsula
Lough Foyle
Creeslough
Muckish Mountain (670m)
Fahan
Milford
Rathmullan
City of Derry Airport
Burnfoot
Muff
Limavady
Inch Island
Inch
Rathmelton
Bridge End
Burt
A2
Kilmacrennan
Glenveagh National Park
Derry
3 Glenveagh Castle
N56
Lough Gartan
9 Glebe House
N13
DERRY
Churchill
Letterkenny
River Foyle
E16-6
Newmills
Claudy
A5
DONEGAL
N13
Raphoe
River Finn
River Deele
Lifford
Strabane
Finn Valley
Stranorlar
Castlefin
Ballybofey
N15
Newtownstewart
TYRONE
A5
Lough Derg
Omagh
Station Island
N32
Pettigo
A5
Lower Lough Erne
Ballygawley
A2
Augher
FERMANAGH
A4
MONAGHAN

wrought-iron beds. It's an incredibly warm and welcoming place, with a full bar and **restaurant** (three-course dinner €38). Food is organic and from the farm or its neighbours where possible. Dinner is available at least Friday to Sunday by reservation.

Cove Lodge B&B €€
(☎074-972 2302; www.thecovelodgebandb.com; Drumgowan; s/d €45/60; P 📶) You'll find subtle floral patterns and rustic charm in the four ground-floor rooms of this tranquil B&B. Located just out of town in a rural setting, it's a taste of Irish country living with all its renowned warmth and friendliness intact. Cove Lodge is 5km south of town on the R267.

Donegal Town Independent Hostel HOSTEL €
(☎074-972 2805; www.donegaltownhostel.com; Killybegs Rd, Doonan; dm €16, d without/with bathroom €38/42; P @ 📶) Run by an energetic couple, rooms at this IHH hostel 1.2km northwest of town off the Killybegs Rd (N56) have quirky murals – from technicolour landscapes to glow-in-the-dark night skies – and some have water views.

Mill Park Hotel HOTEL €€
(☎074-972 2880; www.millparkhotel.com; The Mullins; s/d from €94/118; P @ 📶) A modern hotel with corporate styling in the bedrooms and more rustic but contemporary public areas, this is a decent but characterless option in need of a little attention to detail.

Central Hotel HOTEL €€
(☎074-972 1027; www.centralhoteldonegal.com; The Diamond; s/d from €65/90; P) The Central offers decent but dated rooms, regular live music in the bar, and a leisure centre with pool and gym.

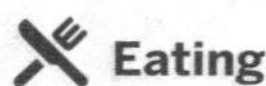

Eating

Aroma CAFE €
(Donegal Craft Village; dishes €5-13; ⏲9.30am-5.30pm Mon-Sat) Hidden in the far corner of Donegal's craft village, this small cafe has a big reputation for fine food. Along with the excellent coffee and luscious cakes, the blackboard specials feature seasonal local produce whipped up into tantalising soups, salads and wholesome hot dishes. There's seating outside for extra space on fine days.

Old Castle Bar SEAFOOD €€
(☎074-972 1262; www.oldecastlebar.com; Castle St; bar mains €10-11, restaurant €17-29; ⏲bar noon-8pm) This old-world boozer just off the Diamond serves upmarket pub classics such as venison pie, Donegal bay oysters, Irish stew, seafood platters and good old bacon and cabbage. The restaurant opens at weekends and serves excellent seafood and steaks.

Harbour Restaurant SEAFOOD €€
(☎074-972 1702; www.theharbour.ie; Quay St; mains €10-26; ⏲5-10pm Mon-Sat, 4-10pm Sun) You'll be surprised by the extensive menu at this popular local haunt, with its nautical theme, bare stone walls and plush furnishings. As well known for its pizza as its seafood, you'll find something for everyone at this friendly, down-to-earth spot.

La Bella Donna ITALIAN €€
(☎074-972 5790; Bridge St; mains €14-25; ⏲dinner Tue-Sat) Pizza, pasta and sizzling steaks in rich sauces pull in the punters at this lively, modern restaurant. It gets very busy at weekends so you'd be advised to book in advance.

Blueberry Tearoom CAFE €
(Castle St; mains €9-12; ⏲9am-7pm Mon-Sat) A perennial local favourite, this cosy cafe serves up simple, honest food in hearty portions. Expect soup, toasties, quiche, panini, sticky cakes of all descriptions and a warm, friendly atmosphere.

Drinking

Reel Inn PUB
(Bridge St) The best craic (fun) in town is invariably found at this old-school pub. Its owner plays the button-box accordion, and his pals join him in traditional music sessions most nights.

McCafferty's PUB
(The Diamond) Sit by the fire, sip what many believe to be the best pint of Guinness in town and just soak up the atmosphere at this cosy, unassuming pub.

Shopping

Donegal Craft Village HANDICRAFTS
(Ballyshannon Rd; ⏲9am-6pm Tue-Sat, 11am-6pm Sun) You won't find any canned leprechauns or Guinness T-shirts here. Instead, this little huddle of craft studios showcases pottery, ironwork, hand-woven fabrics, jewellery and more. It's signposted 1.5km south of town.

Magee's CLOTHING
(www.mageedonegal.com; The Diamond) One room of this small department store is devoted to Donegal tweed, which has been produced here since 1866.

WALK: BLUE STACK MOUNTAINS

If you're not satisfied with admiring the Blue Stack Mountains from a distance, you can take a rewarding, though difficult, trek along a circuitous 18km path through wild and rugged terrain. A complete circuit takes about seven hours, and entails summiting several peaks. The highest, at 674m, is Blue Stack, from which the views of southern Donegal are spectacular. Alternatively, you can walk the short (though steep) distance to Eas Doonan waterfall, which drops some 30m. This walk can be done in about one hour. Note that in wet weather the trail can be boggy.

The trail head is easy to find, though it sounds complicated. Off the N15 from Donegal town, look for the signs for Lough Eske. There are three turnoffs, all leading to Lough Eske Dr. Follow the road anticlockwise towards the northern end of the lake, where the road hairpins twice. Off the second hairpin, take the small road leading to Edergole, where you'll find a walker sign and space to park your car.

It would be wise to equip yourself with the Ordnance Survey Ireland 1:50,000 map No 11 covering this territory. **Mountain Views** (www.mountainviews.ie) is a useful resource and Donegal's tourist office has stacks of information for walkers.

The **Bluestack Centre** (☎074-973 5564; www.donegalbluestacks.com; Drimarone; dm/f €17/50; P), a hostel and community centre with squeaky-clean rooms, makes a handy jumping-off point for hikers. It's often left unmanned, so call ahead. Follow the signposts 8km northwest of Donegal town.

Information

Blueberry Cybercafe (Castle St; per hr €4; ⏲9am-7pm Mon-Sat) Internet cafe above the Blueberry Tearoom. Check in at the counter downstairs.

Post office (Tirchonaill St) North of the Diamond.

Tourist office (☎074-972 1148; donegal@failteireland.ie; Quay St; ⏲9am-6pm Mon-Sat, noon-4pm Sun Jul-Aug, 9am-1pm & 2-5pm Mon-Sat Sep-Jun) In the 'Discover Ireland' building by the waterfront.

Getting There & Away

Bus Éireann (☎074-913 1008; www.buseireann.ie) services connect Donegal with Sligo (€12.50, one hour, six daily), Galway (€18.90, four hours, four daily), Killybegs (€6.90, 35 minutes, three daily), Derry (€14.30, 1½ hours, seven Monday to Saturday, six Sunday) and Dublin (€17.60, 4½ hours, nine daily). The bus stop is on the western side of the Diamond.

Feda O'Donnell (☎074-954 8114; www.fedaodonnell.com) buses run to Galway (€20, four hours, twice daily, three on Friday and Sunday) via Bundoran and Sligo. Call to confirm departure point. Minimum fare within Donegal is €7; buses to Galway cost €20.

Getting Around

The **Bike Shop** (☎074-972 2515; Waterloo Pl; per day €10) rents bikes and has information on cycling in the area. Opening hours vary.

AROUND DONEGAL TOWN

Lough Eske

Almost surrounded by the Blue Stack Mountains, tranquil Lough Eske is a scenic spot perfect for walking, cycling or fishing. Lough Eske translates as 'Lake of the Fish' and is a popular angling centre. The season runs from May to September and there's a purpose-built angling centre on the shore where you can buy permits and hire boats.

There is no public transport to the lake.

Sleeping & Eating

Lough Eske Castle HOTEL €€€
(☎074-972 5100; www.solislougheskecastle.com; d €185-410; ⏲closed Sun-Wed Nov-Mar; P@🛜🏊) Set in vast grounds, this imposing 19th-century castle was all but razed by fire in 1939 but has been painstakingly rebuilt and restored and is now the epitome of elegant country living. Most of the complex including the minimalist rooms, decadent spa and smart **restaurant** (mains €19-36) is spanking new but exudes a sense of classic sophistication mixed with impeccable contemporary style.

Arches Country House B&B €€
(☎074-972 2029; www.archescountryhse.com; Lough Eske; s/d €50/70; P🛜) A modern

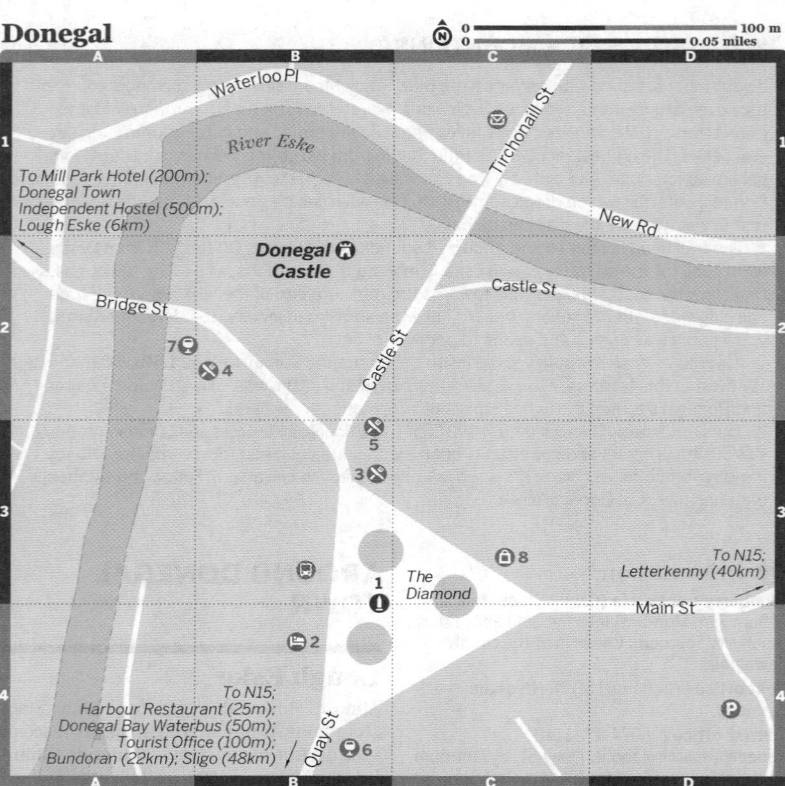

Donegal

Top Sights
Donegal Castle B2

Sights
1 Diamond Obelisk B3

Sleeping
2 Central Hotel B4

Eating
3 Blueberry Tearoom B3
4 La Bella Donna B2
5 Olde Castle Bar B3

Drinking
6 McCafferty's B4
7 Reel Inn A2

Shopping
8 Magee's C3

dormer bungalow in a tranquil spot overlooking the lake, this welcoming B&B is a bucolic getaway, yet just five minutes' drive from Donegal town. The rooms here are beautifully decorated with a blend of country house charm and contemporary style, while owner Noreen is a fount of local knowledge and an extremely gracious host.

Harvey's Point Country Hotel HOTEL €€€
(074-972 2208; www.harveyspoint.com; Harvey's Point; r €150-320; closed Sun-Wed Nov-Christmas & early Jan-Mar; P @) At the water's edge, this elegant retreat is privately owned and run, and it's evident in the pride taken by staff – from the kindly concierge through to the chefs at the excellent French **restaurant** (four-course dinner €59). Rooms range from large to enormous and are decked out in autumnal colours.

Rossnowlagh

POP 50

Rossnowlagh's spectacular 3km-long Blue Flag beach is a wide, sandy stretch of heaven that attracts families, surfers, kite-surfers and walkers throughout the year. The gentle rollers are great for learning to surf or honing your skills, and Ireland's largest and longest-running surfing competition, the **Rossnowlagh Intercounty Surf Contest**, is held here in late October. It's popularly known as the most sociable event in Ireland's surfing calendar.

Sights & Activities

FREE **Franciscan Friary** NOTABLE BUILDING
(10am-8pm Mon-Sat) Hidden deep in a forest at the southern end of the beach, this modern friary is set in beautiful, tranquil gardens which are open to the public. There's also a small museum and a wonderful signed walk, The Way of the Cross, which meanders up a hillside smothered with rhododendrons for spectacular views.

Fin McCool Surf School SURFING
(071-985 9020; www.finmccoolsurfschool.com; gear rental per 3hr €29, 2hr lesson incl gear rental €35; 10am-7pm Easter-Oct, 10am-7pm Sat & Sun mid-Mar–Easter & Nov-Christmas) Tuition, gear rental and accommodation are available at this friendly surf lodge run by Pro Tour surf judge Neil Britton with the help of his extended family, most of whom have competed on the international circuit. The three- and four-bed dorms cost €20 per night, doubles €50.

Sleeping & Eating

Smugglers Creek B&B €€
(071-985 2367; www.smugglerscreekinn.com; s/d €45/80; daily Apr-Sep, Thu-Sun Oct-Mar; P) This combined pub/restaurant/guesthouse perches on the hillside above the bay. It's justifiably popular for its excellent food (mains €13 to €25) and sweeping views (room 4 has the best vantage point and a balcony into the bargain). There's live music on summer weekends.

Sandhouse Hotel HOTEL €€€
(071-985 1777; www.sandhouse-hotel.ie; d €140-300; Feb-Nov; P @) Once an extravagant 19th-century fishing lodge, this beachside hotel has been modernised and lost much of its character. The views are still spectacular and the rooms are comfortable.

Gaslight Restaurant IRISH €€
(071-985 1141; www.gaslight-rossnowlagh.com; mains €11-25) Set on the cliff top, Gaslight offers an extensive menu of well-cooked comfort food and spectacular views over the bay. The owners also run the **Ard na Mara** (071-985 1141; www.ardnamara-rossnowlagh.com; s/d €50/70; P) guesthouse with its bright, sunny rooms.

Getting There & Away

Rossnowlagh is 17km southwest of Donegal town, and isn't served by public transport.

Bundoran

POP 1964

Blinking amusement arcades, hurdy-gurdy fairground rides and fast-food diners are Bundoran's stock-in-trade. But Donegal's best-known seaside resort also has superb surf, and attracts a mixed crowd of young families, OAPs and beach dudes. Outside summer, the carnival atmosphere abates and the town can be quite desolate.

Activities

Surfing

Bundoran has two main surf spots: 'the Peak', an imposing reef break directly in front of the town, which should only be attempted by experienced surfers, and the less formidable beach break at Tullan Strand, just north of the town centre. In spring Bundoran hosts the annual **Bundoran Surfing Championships** (www.isasurf.ie).

The town has three surf schools, each of which rents gear and has its own basic hostel-style accommodation. A three-hour lesson costs about €35, gear rental €20 per day and accommodation €20 for a dorm room or €50 for a double. All offer deals on surf and accommodation packages.

Bundoran Surf Co SURFING
(071-984 1968; www.bundoransurfco.com; Main St)

Donegal Adventure Centre SURFING
(071-984 2418; www.donegaladventurecentre.net; Bayview Ave) Youth-oriented place that also offers kayaking and gorge walking.

Turf n Surf SURFING
(071-984 1091; www.turfnsurf.ie; Bayview Tce) Also runs hill-walking tours and sea-kayaking trips.

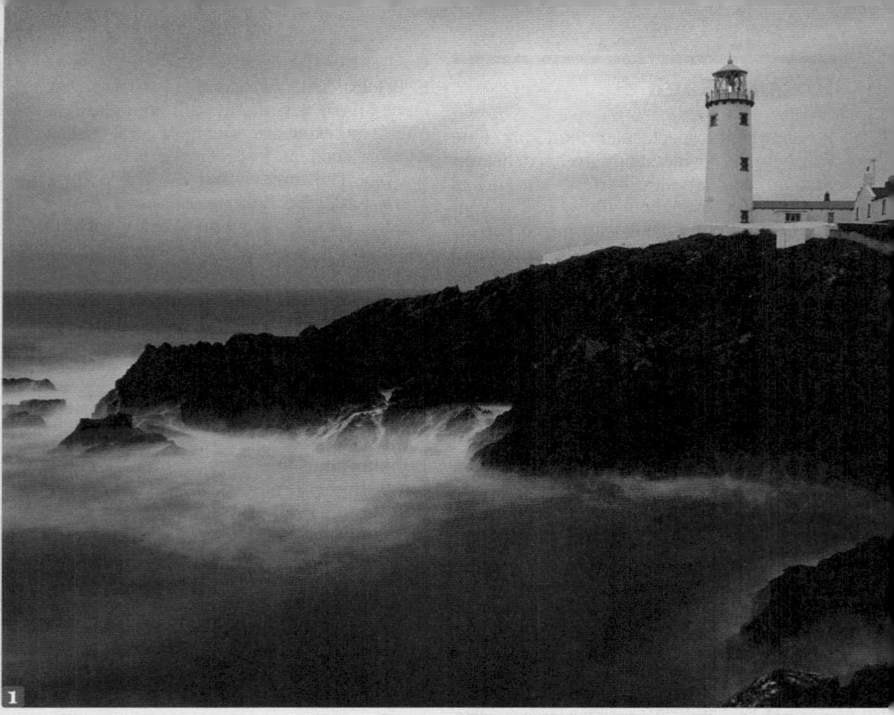

1

5

4

1. Fanad Head, County Donegal (p490)
Lighthouse overlooking the Atlantic on the rocky tip of Fanad Head, the second-most northerly point in Donegal.

2. Teelin, County Donegal (p473)
Southwestern Donegal boasts some of the country's finest scenery and best walking.

3. Blue Stack Mountains (p465)
A lone sheep in the Blue Stack Mountains; the highest peak, at 674m, offers spectacular views.

4. Tramore Beach (p477)
Donegal's wild and rugged coastline is littered with broad sweeps of pristine sands and secluded coves.

5. Horses, County Donegal
Explore the beautiful beaches and surrounding countryside on horseback.

ON BOARD

When local hotelier Mrs Britton bought a surfboard off some visiting surfers in the 1960s, she thought it might make an interesting diversion for her guests. Instead, it became an obsession for her whole family. A pioneer of big wave tow-in surfing in Ireland and a judge on the International Pro Surfing Tour from 1997 to 2004, her grandson Neil Britton has surfed all over the world and is a bit of a legend on the Irish surf scene.

Neil began surfing 20 years ago on Rossnowlagh Beach in County Donegal and now owns and runs the Fin McCool Surf School and Lodge overlooking the strand where it all started.

'Ireland is a surfer's paradise,' says Neil. 'Its location on the edge of the Atlantic Ocean and the unique geology of large stretches of its coastline mean that there are beaches ideal for beginners, high-performance breaks for the competent surfer and massive big wave spots for the very brave (or crazy!).'

For Neil, the jewels in Ireland's surfing crown are located in Ireland's northwest. 'One of my favourite places is Mullaghmore in Sligo, one of Ireland's premier big-wave spots. It's an expert's-only wave, breaking over a shallow, left-hand reef and produces huge, heavy tubes.'

In nearby Bundoran, County Donegal (site of the 2011 European Championship in October), Neil recommends 'the Peak', an excellent intermediate fun wave. 'It's a long V-shaped reef, which can be surfed on winds from south to northeast but is best with west to northwest swells. And for beginners there are plenty of idyllic beginner beaches like Rossnowlagh where I've put down roots. Whichever beach you end up at, you can find yourself sharing a wave with some of our native dolphins and porpoises. A magical surfing experience indeed.'

All along Ireland's south, west and north coasts you'll find surfers out enjoying the water, with major surf centres at Tramore, County Waterford; Garretstown, County Cork; Brandon Bay, County Kerry; Lahinch, County Clare; Easkey and Strandhill in County Sligo; Bundoran and Rossnowlagh in County Donegal; and Portrush in County Antrim. Most of these towns have a developed surf scene with plenty of surf shops, schools and hostels.

Although you can surf year-round in Ireland, Neil advises that conditions are at their best in autumn and spring. 'Surfing in Ireland can be a frustrating experience for a dedicated surfer as although lack of swell is rarely a problem, conditions can lead to weeks of dreaded onshore winds. With a little bit of exploration though, you'll easily find a sheltered bay with better surf.'

Water temperatures in Ireland vary from about 10°C (50°F) in the winter to a balmy 17°C (62°F) in summer. A good 3/2 wetsuit is fine from May to October, but during the winter you'll need a good 5/3 with boots and add on a pair of gloves and hoods if you're planning to be out between December and March.

By and large, Irish surfers are a welcoming bunch and are happy to see foreigners in the water as long as they are respectful and follow the basic etiquette rules of surfing. The famous spots do get crowded, especially during the summer and at weekends, but it's still possible to find a little peak to yourself if you look off the beaten path.

Magic Seaweed (www.magicseaweed.com) has a very good forecast and report service for the major breaks in the country and can prove an invaluable tool for the uninitiated travelling surfer. For a full list of approved surf schools, check out the **Irish Surfing Association** (www.isasurf.ie).

Horse Riding

Donegal Equestrian Centre HORSE RIDING
(☎071-984 1977; www.donegalequestriancentre.com; Finner Rd) The family-run Donegal Equestrian Centre, 1km north of the town, offers rides over the dunes and along the beach (two-hour ride per adult/child €55/45) and lessons for all levels (from €40). Reserve ahead.

Water Activities

Waterworld SWIMMING
(www.waterworldbundoran.com; adult/under 8yr €10/8.50; ⊗noon-6pm Sat & Sun mid-Apr–May

& Sep, 10am-7pm daily Jun-Aug & school holidays) Bundoran's Blue Flag beach isn't safe for swimming, so the place to do it is Waterworld on the waterfront, with wave pools and water slides.

Aquamara SWIMMING
(☎071-984 1173; baths from €22.50; ⏰from 11am Sat & Sun mid-Apr–May & Sep, daily Jun-Aug) On the Waterworld premises, Aquamara provides a decidedly more sedate form of bathing in its seaweed baths.

Sleeping

Burdoran has a great choice of hostels – nonsurfers are welcome at the three surf school lodges – and a glut of soulless, midrange hotels.

Homefield Hostel HOSTEL €
(☎071-982 9357; www.homefieldbackpackers.com; Bayview Ave; dm/d €20/50; P@) Once Viscount Enniskillen's holiday pad, this 260-year-old building later served as an altogether more restrained convent. It's now closer to its original purpose, housing a 60-bed rock-themed hostel, with vinyl records on the walls and a piano.

Glenhaven B&B €€
(☎071-984 1768; www.glenhavenbundoran.com; Tullan Strand Rd; s/d €50/70; P@) A warm welcome and spotless rooms await at this family-friendly B&B just a short walk from the bright lights and nightlife of central Bundoran. The rooms are decked out in contemporary style, the bathrooms are spark ling and the owners very obliging.

Eating & Drinking

Gastronomy isn't Bundoran's strong suit, but there are a couple of stand-out places.

La Sabbia ITALIAN €€
(☎071-984 2253; Bayview Ave; mains €13-25; ⏰dinner nightly Jun-Sep, Thu-Sun Oct-May) This colourful cottage decorated with striking contemporary art has tables spilling out onto the front porch and attracts a lively, upbeat crowd. It's run by a Milanese chef, whose hometown specials include delicious risottos as well as crispy pizzas, and pasta dishes like porcini-filled ravioli.

Maddens Ould Bridge Bar IRISH €€
(☎071-984 2050; www.maddensbridgebar.com; Main St; mains €10-22) At the western end of town, this surfers' hang-out has a decent menu of classic pub grub with a choice of seafood specials thrown in. There's a traditional session on Thursdays (more in summer) and fantastic craic.

Information

Bundoran centres on one long main street just back from the beach. You'll find the banks and post office here.

Tourist office (☎071-984 1350; bundoran@irelandnorthwest.ie; The Bridge, Main St; ⏰Jun-Sep) Glass-paned kiosk opposite the Holyrood Hotel.

Getting There & Around

Bus Éireann buses stop twice on Main St, outside the Phoenix Tavern, and the Celtic Bar. A direct service from Sligo (€8.90, 30 minutes) continues on to Donegal (€6.90, 30 minutes) nine times daily Monday to Saturday, seven on Sunday, and there's a service to Galway (€18.90, 3½ hours, three Monday to Saturday, two Sunday).

You can rent bikes at the **Bike Stop** (☎085 248 8317; East End; per half day/day/week €10/15/60; ⏰8.30am-6pm Mon-Sat, noon-4pm Sun).

SOUTHWESTERN DONEGAL

Mountcharles to Bruckless

Donegal's scenery-o-meter starts to crank up when you reach the coast, just west of Donegal town, and steadily intensifies as you head north. Apart from a scattering of pubs and cafes, there are few places to eat (especially in winter), so stock up before leaving Donegal town or Killybegs.

Getting There & Away

The Donegal to Killybegs bus stops in Mountcharles, Dunkineely and Bruckless six times daily Monday to Saturday, twice on Sunday.

MOUNTCHARLES

POP 497

The hillside village of Mountcharles is the first settlement along the coastal road (N56) west of Donegal town. About 2km south of the village is a safe, sandy **beach**. The shiny-green **pump** at the top of this hillside village was once the backdrop for stories of fairies, ghosts, historic battles and mythological encounters. It was at this point that native poet and *seanachaí* (storyteller) Séamus MacManus practised the ancient art in the 1940s and '50s.

Behind century-old stone walls, the contemporary garden design of **Salthill Gardens** (☎074-973 5387; www.donegalgardens.com; admission €5; ⏲2-6pm Mon-Thu & Sun May-Sep, Sat May-Jul) bursts with perennials, vege tables and shrubs. It's 2km southwest of the village.

DUNKINEELY

POP 363

From dozy little Dunkineely, a minor road runs down the improbably thin finger of land poking into the sea at **St John's Point**. There's a beach with a little bit of sand and sweeping coastal views, and the waters around the point are great for diving.

Overlooking the scanty ruins of the 15th-century McSwyne's Castle, **Castle Murray** (☎074-973 7022; www.castlemurray.com; St John's Point; s/d €65/110; P 📶) is a small hotel with 10 individually decorated guestrooms. Best known for its fabulous French **restaurant** (four-course lunch/dinner €32/45), it's a wonderfully remote and romantic spot with sea views and great walking on the doorstep. Call ahead to check opening times in low season.

BRUCKLESS

POP 180

Bruckless scatters about 2km west of Dunkineely. You can saddle up at **Deane's Equestrian Centre** (☎074-973 7160; www.deanesequestrian.ie; Darney, Bruckless; ⏲10am-4pm Tue-Sun), which offers five-minute pony rides for children (€5), lessons (from €19/16 per adult/child for 30 minutes) and treks (from €35/30 per adult/child for one hour). You'll need to book ahead.

The luxury, ivy-clad, Georgian B&B **Bruckless House** (☎074-973 7071; www.bruckless.com; s/d €60/100; ⏲May-Sep; P) sprawls over 7 hectares of gardens sloping down to the shore. Fronted by a traditional cobbled farmyard, it's home to a stud farm for Connemara ponies. The interior is furnished with antique oriental influences.

KILLYBEGS

POP 1280

The salty scent of fish hauled from the ocean and the sound of cawing seagulls welcome you to Ireland's largest fishing port, Killybegs. A charming working town, Killybegs' oddly angled streets collide at its diamond, a block from the pier.

Sights & Activities

The best beach in the area is at secluded **Fintragh Bay**, about 3km west of town.

Maritime & Heritage Centre MUSEUM
(www.visitkillybegs.com; Fintra Rd; admission €4; ⏲10am-6pm Mon-Fri, plus 1-5pm Sat Jul-Aug) This heritage centre provides a good overview of the town's history, and is set in the factory of Donegal Carpets, whose carpets adorn the White House and Buckingham Palace. You can sometimes see its hand-knotting loom (the world's longest of its kind) at work. The fun wheelhouse simulator lets you 'steer' a fishing trawler into the harbour. There's a good cafe/craft shop on-site.

Killybegs Angling Charters FISHING CHARTERS
(www.killybegsangling.com; Blackrock Pier) If you're interested in taking to the water to catch pollack, ling, brill or turbot, Brian McGilloway has 30 years' experience in charter angling. Boat hire costs €450 while gear rental is from €10 per day.

Tour Donegal GUIDED TOURS
(☎086 262 7722; www.tourdonegal.com) Archaeologist and guide Derek Vial offers an insight into the region's history with guided trips to Stone Age tombs, Iron Age forts, the Slieve League sea cliffs, secluded beaches and hidden fishing villages. Tours cost €30 per hour for one to two people plus €5 per hour for extra people.

Sleeping & Eating

Ritz HOSTEL €
(☎074-973 1309; www.theritz-killybegs.com; Chapel Brae; dm/d/f €20/50/60; P @ 📶) The name might be ironic, but this superbly run 38-bed IHO hostel in the town centre has ritzy facilities including an enormous kitchen with an island workbench and dishwasher, colourful rooms with private bathroom and TVs, and a laundry. Continental breakfast is included.

Drumbeagh House B&B €€
(☎074-973 1307; www.killybegsbnb.biz.ly; Conlin Rd; d €70; P @) Accommodating hosts with plenty of local knowledge and the time to share it make this small B&B a great find. The cosy rooms are tastefully decorated in neutral colours and the locally smoked salmon for breakfast is worth the trip alone.

Tara Hotel HOTEL €€
(☎074-974 1700; www.tarahotel.ie; Main St; s/d from €65/80; @ P) This friendly, modern hotel overlooking the harbour has comfortable,

minimalist rooms, a decent bar and a small gym with jacuzzi, sauna and steam room.

22 Main Street SEAFOOD €€
(☎074-973 2876; www.22mainstreet.com; Main St; mains €12.50-25; ⊙dinner) Recently revamped, this Mediterranean-style bistro offers excellent seafood fresh off the trawlers. It's the town's top restaurant and serves a tempting menu with some nonfish dishes but little for vegetarians.

Information

There are no banking facilities or ATMs west of Killybegs, so stock up on cash here.

Harbour Store (The Harbour) Sells rods, reels and tackle.

Killybegs Information Centre (☎074-973 2346; www.killybegs.ie; Quay St; ⊙9.30am-5.30pm Mon-Fri) In a cabin near the harbour.

Getting There & Away

Buses from Donegal (€6.90, 30 minutes) run six times daily Monday to Saturday, twice on Sunday. Bus 490 heads west to Kilcar (€3.90, 20 minutes) and Glencolumbcille (€6.90, 45 minutes) three times daily Monday to Saturday and once on Sunday.

Kilcar, Carrick & Around

POP 260

Kilcar (Cill Chártha) and its more attractive neighbour Carrick (An Charraig) make good bases for exploring the breathtaking coastline of southwestern Donegal, especially the stunning sea cliffs at Slieve League.

This is fantastic walking country, particularly if you don't mind hoofing up and down a few hills. Kilcar Tourism has some pointers for walking the Kilcar Way; ask at the **Áislann Chill Chartha** (☎074-973 8376; Main St, Kilcar; ⊙9am-10pm Mon-Fri, 2-6pm Sat), a community centre that provides information for tourists. Just outside Kilcar is a small, sandy beach.

Local information is available at the excellent cultural centre, the **Tí Linn Centre** (☎074-973 9077; www.sliabhleague.com; Teelin, Carrick; ⊙10.30am-5.30pm daily Easter-Sep, Fri-Tue Feb-Easter & Oct-Nov), which also has an artisan cafe, and art and craft gallery. The centre also runs one- and three-day archaeology and hill-walking courses.

Sights

Slieve League SEA CLIFFS
The Cliffs of Moher get more publicity, but the sea cliffs at Slieve League are higher. In fact, these spectacular polychrome cliffs are thought to be the highest in Europe, plunging some 600m to the sea. Looking down, you'll see two rocks nicknamed the 'school desk and chair' by locals for reasons that are immediately obvious. From the lower car park, there's a path skirting up around the near-vertical rock face to the aptly named **One Man's Pass**. You can now also drive all the way to the top, where there's a car park. Be aware that mist and rain can roll in unexpectedly and rapidly, making conditions treacherous. The cliffs are particularly scenic at sunset when the waves crash dramatically far below and the ocean reflects the last rays of the day.

The cliffs are, if possible, even more impressive when viewed from the ocean below. Sightseeing boat trips along the Slieve League cliffs can be arranged by contacting **Nuala Star Teelin** (☎074-973 9365; www.sliabhleagueboattrips.com; ⊙Apr-Oct). Prices are €20 to €25 per person, depending on numbers, with reductions for children. The 12-seater boat departs from the Teelin pier approximately every two hours (weather permitting). Sea angling and diving trips can also be arranged.

FREE **Studio Donegal** WOOLLEN MILL
(www.studiodonegal.ie; Glebe Mill, Kilcar; ⊙9am-5.30pm Mon-Fri, plus 9.30am-5pm Sat May-Oct) Beside Kilcar's community centre tweeds are spun and loomed by hand at Studio Donegal. Visitors are often invited upstairs to see spinners and weavers in action.

Activities

Three walks starting in Kilcar are collectively known as the **Kilcar Way**. From Teelin (Tí Linn), experienced walkers can spend a day walking north via Bunglass and the cliff top to Malinbeg, near Glencolumbcille. It shouldn't be attempted in windy conditions or if bad weather is likely to impede visibility.

Sleeping & Eating

Derrylahan Hostel HOSTEL €
(☎074-973 8079; www.homepage.eircom.net/~derrylahan; Derrylahan, Kilcar; campsites per person €8, dm/d €18/50; P) On a working farm, this rustic, well-run IHH hostel has comfortable rooms with private bathroom as well as a 20-person bunk house and plenty of scenic spots to pitch a tent. Bike rental (€20) can be organised if you book

ahead. Located 3km west of the village on the coast road. Pick-ups can be arranged.

Inishduff House B&B €€
(☎074-973 8542; www.inishduffhouse.com; Largy; s/d €50/85; P 📶) On the main road between Killybegs and Kilcar, this modern B&B has large, comfortable rooms, an incredibly warm welcome and wonderful sea views.

Kitty Kelly's MEDITERRANEAN €€
(☎074-973 1925; Kilcar Rd; 3-course dinner €40; ⏰dinner May-Sep) Dining at this restaurant in a 200-year-old, plum-coloured farmhouse feels more like attending an intimate dinner party. The menu is a gourmet take on traditional Irish favourites like rich stew and creamy trifle. It's on the coast road, 5km west of Killybegs. Opening hours vary annually; bookings are essential.

Blue Haven HOTEL €€
(☎074-973 8090; www.bluehaven.ie; Kilcar-Killybegs Rd; mains €13-26) Blue Haven's modern restaurant has giant windows overlooking the bay and an extensive, if predictable, menu of classic dishes. The sunset views are stunning.

Getting There & Away

Bus 490 runs from Donegal through Killybegs to Kilcar (€3.90) and on to Carrick (€5.40), Glencolumbcille (€7.60) three times daily Monday to Saturday and once on Sunday.

Glencolumbcille & Around

POP 255

'There's nothing feckin' here!', endearingly blunt locals forewarn visitors to Glencolumbcille (Gleann Cholm Cille). But, with some stunning walks fanning out from the three-pub village, scalloped beaches, an excellent Irish language and culture centre, and a fine little folk museum, chances are you'll disagree.

Approaching Glencolumbcille via the Glen Gesh Pass does, however, reinforce just how cut off this starkly beautiful coastal haven is from the rest of the world. You drive past miles and miles of hills and bogs before the ocean appears, followed by a narrow, green valley and the small Gaeltacht village within it.

This spot has been inhabited since 3000 BC and you'll find plenty of Stone Age remains throughout the collection of tiny settlements. It's believed that the 6th-century St Colmcille (Columba) founded a monastery here (hence the name, meaning 'Glen of Columba's Church'), and incorporated Stone Age standing stones called *turas* (after the Irish word for a pilgrimage, or journey) into Christian usage by inscribing them with a cross. At midnight on Colmcille's Feast Day (9 June), penitents begin a walkabout of the *turas* and the remains of Colmcille's church before attending Mass at 3am in the local church.

Sights

Father McDyer's Folk Village HISTORIC SITE
(www.glenfolkvillage.com; Doonalt; adult/child €3/2; ⏰10am-6pm Mon-Sat, noon-6pm Sun Easter-Sep) A museum with a mission, this folk centre was established by the forward-thinking Father James McDyer in 1967 to freeze-frame traditional folk life for posterity. It's housed in a huddle of replicated thatched cottages of the 18th and 19th centuries, with genuine period fittings. The *shebeen* (illicit drinking place) sells unusual local wines (made from ingredients such as seaweed and fuchsias) alongside marmalade and whiskey truffles. Admission includes a tour. It's 3km west of the village, by the beach.

Activities

Beaches

There are two sandy beaches with brisk waves in **Doonalt**, immediately west of the village. At **Malinbeg**, a sheltered bay bitten out of low cliffs and filled with firm red-tinged sand, descending 60 steps brings you to another gorgeous little beach just down the coast road.

Walking

A couple of signed loop walks will get you off into the blustery wilds beyond the town. The **Tower Loop** (10km, two to three hours) takes you up over some stunning coastal cliffs, while the more arduous **Drum Loop** (13km, three to four hours) heads into the hills, northeast of the town. Both walks start and finish at Colmcille's church.

Glencolumbcille's **walking centre** (☎074-973 0302; www.ionadsuil.ie; ⏰by arrangement), next door to the fire station, offers information and can arrange guided walks.

Courses

Oideas Gael CULTURAL ACTIVITIES
(www.oideas-gael.com; ⏰mid-Mar–Oct) The cultural centre at the Foras Cultúir Uladh

(Ulster Cultural Foundation), 1km west of the village centre, offers a range of 'cultural activity holidays' – adult courses in Irish language and traditional culture, including dancing, painting and musical instruments. The centre also leads hill-walking programs in the Donegal highlands. Three-day courses cost from €100. Accommodation can be arranged – you'll have a choice of homestay or self-catering, with prices of around €80 for a three-night stay.

Sleeping & Eating

The area has some excellent budget accommodation but places to eat are limited.

Glencolumbcille Hill Walkers Centre HOSTEL €
(☎074-973 0302; www.ionadsuil.ie; d €50; Glencolunmbcille; P) Overlooking sheep-filled paddocks, this smart place has immaculate rooms with private bathroom. Breakfast isn't included but there's an enormous self-catering kitchen. The owners live off-site, so call ahead.

Dooey Hostel HOSTEL €€
(☎074-973 0130; campsites per person €8.50, dm/d €15/30; ⊙Feb–mid-Sep; P) Built into a hillside with a corridor carved out of the plant-strewn rockface and jaw-dropping views of the ocean and hills below, this IHO hostel has character in spades. Facilities are rustic, but clean and comfortable. If you're driving, turn beside the Glenhead Tavern for 1.5km; walkers can take a short cut beside the Folk Village. No credit cards.

Malinbeg Hostel HOSTEL €
(☎074-973 0006; www.malinbeghostel.com; Malinbeg, Glencolumbcille; dm/s/d €14/20/30; ⊙closed Dec–mid-Jan; P) Flung out on a remote stretch of coast, the contemporary Malinbeg Hostel sports spotless rooms (some with private bathroom) and scores big for its proximity to the beach and to the grocery store handily situated across the road.

An Chistin CAFE €€
(Glencolumbcille; mains €10-22; ⊙9am-9.30pm Easter-Oct) Attached to the Oideas Gael cultural centre, this cafe/restaurant serves up surprisingly gourmet fare to a soundtrack of mellow jazz.

Shopping

Glencolumbcille Woollen Mill CLOTHING
(www.rossanknitwear-glenwoolmill.com; Malinmore; ⊙10am-8pm Mar-Oct, to 5.50pm Nov-Feb) This is a great place to stock up on Donegal tweed jackets, caps and ties, and lambs wool scarves and shawls. You can sometimes see weavers in action. It's about 5km southwest of Glencolumbcille, in Malinmore.

John Molloy's CLOTHING
(www.johnmolloy.com; Glencolumbcille) This Ardara manufacturer's Glencolumbcille fac tory outlet sells a wide range of woollies made from natural yarns.

Getting There & Away

Bus 490 leaves for Killybegs (€6.90, 45 minutes) three times daily Monday to Saturday and once on Sunday.

Maghery & the Glen Gesh Pass

POP 640

On the northern edge of the peninsula, tiny Maghery has a picturesque waterfront. If you follow the strand westward, you'll get to a rocky promontory full of caves. During Cromwell's 17th-century destruction, 100 villagers sought refuge here but all except one were discovered and massacred.

About 1.5km east of Maghery is the enchanting **Assarancagh Waterfall**, beyond which is the beginning of a 10km marked trail to the **Glen Gesh Pass** (Glean Géis, meaning 'Glen of the Swans'). It's almost alpine in appearance; cascading mountains and lush valleys are dotted with isolated farmhouses and small lakes. If you're driving or cycling, you can get to the pass directly from Glencolumbcille by following the road signs for Ardara.

Ardara

POP 564

The heart of Donegal's traditional knitwear and tweed industry, the heritage town of Ardara is a pretty gateway to the switchbacks of Glen Gesh Pass. You can visit the weavers at work and see the region's most traditional crafts in action.

Ardara springs to life in late April or early May for the **Cup of Tae Festival** (www.cupoftaefestival.com), a celebration of traditional music, dance and storytelling, particularly featuring the Donegal style of fiddle playing. The festival takes its name from a local musician, John 'the tae' Gallagher. Its small scale makes it a very friendly event.

Sights

Ardara Heritage Centre MUSEUM
(☎074-954 1704; Main St; adult/child €3/1.20; ⏱10am-6pm Mon-Sat, 2-6pm Sun Easter-Sep) Set in the old town courthouse, this centre traces the story of Donegal tweed from sheep shearing to dye production and weaving. A weaver is present to demonstrate how a loom works and explain the stitches used in traditional garments.

Sleeping & Eating

Gort na Móna B&B €€
(☎074-953 7777; www.gortnamonabandb.com; Donegal Rd, Cronkeerin; s/d €50/70; P 📶) Huge but cosy and colourful rooms with orthopaedic mattresses, knotty pine furniture and silky throws make this a real home from home. With excellent home baking and preserves for breakfast, mountain views and a pristine beach on the doorstep, you won't want to leave. Gort na Móna is 2km south of town on the N56.

Bayview Country House B&B €€
(☎074-954 1145; www.bayviewcountryhouse.com; Portnoo Rd; s/d €45/70; ⏱Apr–mid-Oct; P 📶) Just out of town and overlooking the bay, this purpose-built B&B has spacious rooms with pretty floral bedspreads, spotless bathrooms and great views. There's a wood fire, homemade bread and scones, and a genuinely warm welcome for visitors.

Green Gate B&B €€
(☎074-954 1546; www.thegreengate.eu; Ardvally, Ardara; s/d €70/90; ⏱Mar-Nov; P) Follow the mysterious pictorial signs well off the beaten track up a series of steep dirt tracks and you'll eventually find Green Gate, a place you'll either love or hate but will stay with you forever. The traditional thatched cottages here are rustic in the extreme but the views are breathtaking and the host a gregarious eccentric. Phone bookings essential; no credit cards.

Nancy's Bar IRISH €
(Front St; mains €6.50-12.50) This old-world pub-restaurant successfully makes its guests feel as though they're sitting in Nancy's living room. It serves superb seafood and chowder with hearty wheaten bread and is also the best place in town for a social pint or two.

Sheila's Coffee and Cream CAFE €
(Ardara Heritage Centre, Main St; dishes €5-9; ⏱9am-5.50pm Mon-Sat) Attached to the heritage centre, this little cafe is a local favourite and serves a good selection of hot dishes such as fish cakes and lasagne as well as a luscious collection of desserts.

Drinking

Many of the town's pubs offer regular traditional music sessions; just stroll down the main drag until you hear the good cheer pouring out the door.

Corner House PUB
(The Diamond) A good spot to listen to an Irish music session (Friday and Saturday year-round; nightly from June to September), it's the type of place where someone will spontaneously break out into song and, if the mood is right, the rest of the pub will join in.

Shopping

Signs in the town centre point you to the town's knitwear producers.

Eddie Doherty (www.handwoventweed.com; Front St)

DON'T MISS

DONEGAL'S BEST BEACHES

Donegal's wild and rugged coastline is littered with broad sweeps of pristine sands and secluded coves. Here are some of our favourites.

» **Tramore** Hike through the dunes from Dunfanaghy and you'll be rewarded with pristine sands on this secluded stretch of coast (p484).

» **Carrick Finn** A gorgeous sweep of undeveloped sand near Donegal Airport (p478).

» **Portnoo** A wishbone-shaped sheltered cove backed by undulating hills (p477).

» **Portsalon** An idyllic stretch of sand lapped by turquoise water (p490).

» **Culdaff** A long stretch of golden sand, popular with families (p497).

» **Rossnowlagh** A sweeping white-sand beach ideal for learning to surf (p467).

John Molloy's (www.johnmolloy.com)

Kennedy's (Front St)

Triona Design (www.trionadesign.com; Main St)

Information

On the Diamond, the Ulster Bank has an ATM; the post office is nearby on Main St.

Tourist information (074-954 1704; www.ardara.ie; Ardara Heritage Centre; Main St; 10am-6pm Mon-Sat, 2-6pm Sun Easter-Sep)

Getting There & Around

Bus 492 from Killybegs (€3.40, 25 minutes) stops outside the Heritage Centre in Ardara en route to Glenties (€2.50, 10 minutes) four times daily Monday to Saturday, twice on Sunday.

Don Byrne (074-954 1658; West End) rents bikes for €15/60 per day/week.

Loughrea Peninsula

The outer reaches of beautiful Loughrea Peninsula, north of Ardara, glisten with tiny lakes cupped by undulating hills and the wishbone-shaped Blue Flag beach by the twin settlements of **Narin** and **Portnoo**. The beach's sandy tip points towards **Inis-keel Island**, which you can walk out to at low tide. St Connell, a cousin of St Colmcille, founded a monastery here in the 6th century. Hardly any trace remains, but the island is studded with early-medieval Christian remains.

Another adventurous diversion is to track down **Lough Doon**, 3km south of Narin, in the centre of which sits the 2000-year-old **Doon Fort**, a fortified oval settlement that's remarkably well preserved. To reach the fort, you need to hire a rowing boat (around €10) from an adjacent farm. Pick a day that's not too windy.

If the fort whets your appetite for archaeology, the **Dolmen Ecocentre** (www.dolmencentre.com; Kilclooney, Portnoo; 9am-5pm Mon-Fri) can point you towards several other prehistoric sites, including a tortoiselike passage tomb a short walk up a track left of the church.

Also on the peninsula, hemmed in by grassy dunes, is **Tramore Beach**. In 1588 part of the Spanish Armada ran aground here. The survivors temporarily occupied O'Boyle's Island in Kiltoorish Lake, but then marched to Killybegs, where they set sail again in the *Girona*. The *Girona* met a similar fate that year in Northern Ireland, with the loss of over a thousand crew members (see p656).

If you'd like to stay in the area, **Carnaween House** (074-954 5122; www.carnaweenhouse.com; Narin; s/d €55/110; P) is an unexpected gem of a place with brilliant white bedrooms in luxury beach house style. Subtle touches of colour and a minimalist eye mean they are crisp and calm yet strangely cosy. The **restaurant** (mains €14-21; dinner Thu-Sun Jun-Aug, dinner Fri & Sat, lunch Sun Sep-May) serves an excellent selection of seafood and classic Irish dishes brought bang up to date. Book ahead and arrive early to bag the front window and sunset views.

Glenties

POP 811

At the foot of two valleys with a southern backdrop laid on by the Blue Stack Mountains, the proud 'Tidy Town' of Glenties (Na Gleannta) is a good spot for **fishing** and has some cracking **walks** in the surrounding countryside.

Glenties is linked with playwright Brian Friel, whose play (and subsequent film), *Dancing at Lughnasa,* is set in the town.

On the main street there's a Bank of Ireland, with an ATM and bureau de change, and a post office.

If you'd like to stay, **Brennan's B&B** (074-955 1235; www.brennansbnb.com; Main St; s/d €45/70; P) offers a warm welcome and comfy rooms.

Bus 492 from Donegal stops off in Glenties on the way to Dungloe (€8.20, 45 minutes) twice daily.

NORTHWESTERN DONEGAL

Few places in Ireland are more savagely beautiful than northwestern Donegal. Humans have largely been unable to tame the wild and breathtakingly spectacular landscape. The rocky Gaeltacht area between Dungloe and Crolly is known as the Rosses (Na Rossa), and is scattered with shimmering lakes and clean, sandy beaches. Further northwest, between Bunbeg and Dunfanaghy, the scenery is softer but no less stunning. Offshore, the islands of Arranmore and Tory are fascinating to those eager for a glimpse of a more traditional way of life.

WORTH A TRIP

THE BLACK PIG

When the first spluttering steam engine arrived in Donegal in 1895, the locals dubbed the monstrous, billowing creature the Black Pig. The railways gave Donegal's isolated communities a new lease of life and a much-needed connection to the rest of the country. Over 300km of narrow-gauge tracks crossed the county in the railways' heyday but after WWII business declined and the railway closed to passengers in June 1947, and to freight in 1952.

Today the county's only operational railway is the **Fintown Railway** (www.antraen.com; Fintown; adult/child €8/5; ⏲11am-5pm Mon-Sat, 1-5pm Sun Jun-Sep), a charming little tourist train that runs over Easter and during the summer months. Lovingly restored to its original condition, the red-and-white 1940s diesel railcar runs along a rebuilt 5km section of the former County Donegal Railway track along picturesque Lough Finn. The return trip, which includes commentary, takes around 40 minutes.

Fintown is on the R250, 20km northeast of Glenties.

Dungloe

POP 1068

The hub of the Rosses, Dungloe (An Clochán Liath) is a busy little town with ample services for anyone passing through this spectacular locale.

Immortalised in a hit pop song, 'Mary from Dungloe', in the late '60s, the town celebrates with the 10-day **Mary from Dungloe Festival** in late July/early August.

There's a small **tourist office** (☎074-952 1297; www.dungloe.info; Chapel Rd; ⏲Jun-Sep) in Ionad Teampall Chróine, a community building housed in an old church.

Fishing for salmon and trout in the River Dungloe and Lough Dungloe is popular and you can get tackle and permits from **Bonner's** (Main St).

The nearest good beach is 6km southwest of town at **Maghery Bay**.

For accommodation, your best bet is **Radharc an Oileain** (☎074-952 1093; www.dungloebedandbreakfast.com; Quay rd; s/d €45/70; ⏲Apr-Nov; Ⓟ@), a beautiful family-run B&B overlooking the bay.

Getting There & Away

Bus 492 runs from Donegal (€13.50, 1½ hours) to Dungloe, via Killybegs (€11.80, one hour), Ardara (€8.90, 50 minutes) and Glenties (€8.20, 45 minutes) twice daily.

Burtonport & Kincasslagh

POP 345

This pocket-sized port is the embarkation point for Arranmore Island, which looks near enough to wade to. Burtonport (Ailt an Chorráin) has attracted some famously off-the-wall characters over the years. In the 1970s the Atlantis commune was established here, and practised a primal therapy that earned it the nickname 'the Screamers'. Eventually it relocated to the Colombian jungle. Later, the three Silver Sisters chose Burtonport to live out their Victorian lifestyle, complete with Victorian dress. The village seems perfectly ordinary today, though it is pretty.

For fishing and diving trips, contact **Inishfree Charters** (☎074-955 1533; www.inish.ie). Alternatively, you can check in at the cabins by the pier.

Head north of Burtonport on the coast road to reach the picturesque village of **Kincasslagh** and the stunning Blue Flag beach at **Carrick Finn**. This sweeping stretch of sand is backed by mountains and is wonderfully undeveloped, despite being close to Donegal Airport.

Cosy **Limekiln House** (☎074-954 8521; www.limekilnhouse.com; Carrick Finn, Kincasslagh; d with/without bathroom €70/60; Ⓟ) makes a great overnight stop, with comfortable rooms, tempting home baking and a warm welcome. Two of the four rooms have a private bathroom.

You can't miss the giant fibreglass lobster clinging to the wall of the **Lobster Pot** (☎074-954 2012; www.lobsterpot.ie; Main St; bar food €9-22, dinner mains €16-25; ⏲bar food noon-6pm, dinner daily) in Burtonport. Serving up a great selection of seafood, this pub and restaurant is adorned with football jerseys and packed when big game matches are shown on the large TV.

There is currently no public transport to Burtonport.

Arranmore Island

POP 528

Framed by dramatic cliff faces, cavernous sea caves and clear sandy beaches, Arranmore (Árainn Mhór) lies just 5km from the mainland. Measuring just 9km by 5km, the tiny island has been inhabited since the early Iron Age (800 BC), and a prehistoric triangular fort can be seen on the southern side. The west and north are wild and rugged, with few houses to disturb the sense of isolation. The **Arranmore Way** walking path circles the island (allow three to four hours). Off the southwestern tip is **Green Island**, a bird sanctuary for corncrakes, snipes and a variety of seabirds; you can see it from Arranmore (but not visit). Irish is the main language spoken on Arranmore Island, although most inhabitants are bilingual.

The island's pubs put on turf fires and traditional music sessions, and some stay open 24 hours a day to sate thirsty fishermen.

Sleeping & Eating

Arranmore makes an easy day trip but several homes offer B&B accommodation. Try **Claire's** (☎074-952 0042; www.clairesbandb.wordpress.com; Leabgarrow; s/d €40/60; wi-fi) by the ferry terminal for simple but pretty rooms.

Getting There & Around

The **Arranmore Ferry** (☎074-952 0532; www.arranmoreferry.com; return adult/child/car & driver €15/7/30) links Burtonport with Leabgarrow. The journey takes 20 minutes, operates year-round and has up to nine ferries daily in summer.

The same route is covered by **Arranmore Fast Ferry** (☎087 317 1810; www.arranmorefastferry.com), with a fast, passenger-only ferry (€15 return, five minutes, two to three daily) and a car-ferry service (passenger/car and driver €15/30 return, 20 minutes).

Once on the island, you can save your legs by taking a **taxi** (☎086 331 7885).

Gweedore & Around

POP 1390

The Gaeltacht district of Gweedore (Gaoth Dobhair) is a loose assembly of small towns in the shadow of Mt Errigal. It's a good jumping-off point for trips to Tory Island and Glenveagh National Park, but the coast, dotted with white sandy beaches, has been overrun by holiday homes. Consequently, Derrybeg (Doirí Beaga) and Bunbeg (Bun Beag) virtually run into each other along the R257. A few kilometres east, on the R258, a few hotels are scattered along the roadside – and that's pretty much Gweedore.

Away from the coast, dozens of small fishing lakes break up the bleak but spectacularly beautiful landscape. If you're driving, the N56 heading east out of Gweedore is particularly scenic.

On the main road in Bunbeg you'll find banks and an ATM, while Derrybeg has a post office.

Activities

The most beautiful walking trail to be found in the area is the **Tullagobegley Walk** (Siúlóid Tullagobegley), a historical trample over **Tievealehid** (Taobh an Leithid; 431m), which was used for centuries by locals carrying corpses to the 13th-century graveyard in Falcarragh. The 5½-hour walk begins at Lough Nacung (Loch na Cuinge), just east of Gweedore off the N56. The path takes you past some 19th-century silver mines to Keeldrum, a small townland on the outskirts of Gortahork, before finishing up at the Tullagobegley graveyard in Falcarragh.

Unfortunately, the walk is not waymarked so an OS Sheet 1 of the area is invaluable.

Sleeping & Eating

Bunbeg Lodge B&B €€
(☎087 416 7372; www.bunbeglodge.ie; s/d €40/70; P, family) Excellent B&B accommodation is available at this new guesthouse owned by the Flanagan family. Spacious, modern rooms with deep blue and gold feature wallpaper, white linens and sparkling bathrooms make it a top choice. Breakfasts are hearty and the hosts very knowledgeable about the local area.

Sleepy Hollows Campsite CAMPGROUND €
(☎074-954 8272; www.sleepyhollows.ie; Meenaleck, Crolly; campsites per adult/child €10/5; P) The 12 grassy tent sites at this friendly, family-run campground are in secluded woods, thoughtfully removed from the five caravan sites. Due to its diminutive size, bookings are essential. Take the airport turn-off from the village of Crolly and follow the signs 200m past Leo's Tavern.

An Chúirt HOTEL €€
(☎074-953 2900; www.gweedorecourthotel.com; Gweedore; s/d from €70/150; P, wi-fi, pool, family) The

rooms at this large hotel vary enormously, from those with dated floral patterns to deluxe four-poster rooms with oodles of space, heavy brocade curtains and jacuzzi baths. There's an excellent indoor play area for children, a spa, pool and decent, if predictable, offerings in the **restaurant** (mains €14-25).

☆ Entertainment

Leo's Tavern PUB

(☎074-954 8143; www.leostavern.com; Meenaleck, Crolly) You never know who'll drop by for one of the legendary singalongs at Leo's Tavern. It's owned by Leo and Baba Brennan, parents of Enya and her siblings Máire, Ciaran and Pól (the core of the group Clannad), and now run by younger son Bartley. The pub glitters with gold, silver and platinum discs and various other mementos of the successful kids. There's live music nightly in summer and regular sessions throughout the winter. The **restaurant** (mains €13-20) is one of the best spots around for honest Irish pub grub. If you're in the area, don't miss it. To get here from Crolly, take the R259 1km towards the airport, and look for the signs for Leo's.

Getting There & Away

Feda O'Donnell (☎074-954 8114; www.feda.ie) runs a service twice daily (three Friday and Sunday) from Gweedore to Letterkenny (€7, 1½ hours), Donegal (€10, 2¼ hours), Sligo (€12, 3¼ hours) and Galway (€20, 5½ hours).

Ferries depart from Bunbeg for Tory Island (see p482).

Dunlewey & Around

POP 700

Blink and chances are you've missed the tiny hamlet of Dunlewy (Dún Lúiche) beside Lough Dunlewy. You won't miss the spectacular scenery, however, or pinnacle-shaped Mt Errigal, whose bare face towers over the surrounding area. Plan enough time to get out of your car and do some walking here, as it's a magical spot.

Activities

Dunlewey Lakeside Centre ACTIVITY CENTRE

(Ionad Cois Locha; ☎074-953 1699; www.dunleweycentre.com; Dunlewy; admission house & grounds or boat trip adult/child/family €5.95/3.95/14, combined ticket €10/7/15; ⏲10.30am-6pm Mon-Sat, 11am-6pm Sun Easter-Oct) This hugely enjoyable activity centre is a great place if you're travelling with the family in tow. Adults will be intrigued by the 30-minute tour of the thatched cottage that once belonged to local weaver Manus Ferry, who earned world renown for his tweeds (he died in 1975), while kids will adore the petting zoo. But the real highlight, for all ages, is an entertaining boat trip on the lake with a storyteller who vividly brings to life local history, geology and ghoulish folklore. Traditional music concerts (€8) take place on Tuesdays in July and August; you can also catch concerts on some Sunday afternoons in the concert venue. There's a good cafe with a turf fire and craft shop.

Mt Errigal WALKING

The looming presence of Mt Errigal (752m) seemingly dares walkers to attempt the tough but beautiful climb to its pyramid-shaped peak. If you're keen to take on the challenge, pay close attention to the weather. It's a dangerous climb on misty or wet days, when the mountain is shrouded in cloud and visibility is minimal.

There are two paths to the summit: the easier route, which covers 5km and takes around two hours; and the more difficult 3.3km walk along the northwestern ridge, which involves scrambling over scree for about 2½ hours. Details of both routes are available at the Dunlewey Lakeside Centre.

Poisoned Glen WALKING

Legend has it that the stunning ice-carved rock face of the Poisoned Glen got its sinister name when the ancient one-eyed giant king of Tory, Balor, was killed here by his exiled grandson, Lughaidh, whereupon the poison from his eye split the rock and poisoned the glen. The less interesting truth, however, lies in a cartographic gaffe. Locals were inspired to name it An Gleann Neamhe (the Heavenly Glen), but when an English cartographer mapped the area, he carelessly marked it An Gleann Neimhe – the Poisoned Glen.

The R251 has several viewpoints overlooking the glen. It's possible to walk through it, although the ground is rough and boggy. From the lakeside centre a return walk along the glen is 12km and takes two to three hours. Watch out for the green lady – the resident ghost!

Sleeping

Errigal Hostel HOSTEL €

(☎074-953 1180; www.errigalyouthhostel.com; Dunlewey; dm/d €20/52; P) At the base of Mt Errigal, this gleaming 60-bed An Óige hostel has state-of-the-art facilities including a stainless-steel self-catering kitchen, a large laundry room for your muddy climbing gear, light-filled common areas, and pristine dorms and private rooms. Green initiatives include wood-pellet heating. There's a petrol station that also sells groceries next door.

Glen Heights B&B €€
(074-956 0844; www.glenheightsbb.com; Dunlewey; s with/without bathroom €50/45, d €70/66; Easter-Oct; P) Your breakfast may well go cold on the plate right in front of you at this B&B as you'll find it difficult to take your eyes off the breathtaking views of Dunlewey Lake, Mount Errigal and the Poisoned Glen from its conservatory. The rooms are simple but cosy, the bathrooms pristine and the Donegal charm in full swing.

Bloody Foreland

Named for the crimson colour of the rocks at sunset, Bloody Foreland (Cnoc Fola) is a spectacular stretch of coast…or at least it was until holiday homes mushroomed across the horizon. Still, the coast road north and south of here remains wonderfully remote and ideal for cycling. Experienced surfers will find plenty of challenging waves, but you'll need to bring your own gear.

Tory Island

POP 170

Swept by sea winds and stung by salt spray, the remote crag of Tory Island (Oileán Thóraí) has taken its fair share of batterings. With nothing to shield it from savage Atlantic squalls, it's a tribute to the hardiness of Tory Islanders that the island has been inhabited for over 4500 years. Although it's only 11km north of the mainland, the rough sea has long consolidated the island's staunch independence.

So it's no surprise that Tory is one of the last places in Ireland to hold onto traditional Irish culture instead of simply paying lip service to it. The island has its own dialect of Irish and even has an elected 'king', and over the decades its inhabitants had a reputation for distilling and smuggling contraband *poitín* (a peaty whiskey). However, the island is perhaps best known for its 'naive' (or outsider) artists, many of whom have attracted the attention of international collectors.

In 1974, after an eight-week storm that lashed the island mercilessly, the government made plans to evacuate Tory permanently. Father Diarmuid Ó Peícín came to the rescue, spearheading an international campaign to raise funds, create a proper ferry service, establish an electrical supply and more. The demise of the fishing industry has brought its own share of problems, but the community still doggedly perseveres.

The island has just one pebbly beach and two recognisable villages: West Town (An Baile Thiar), containing most of the island's facilities, and East Town (An Baile Thoir). Its eastern end is dominated by jagged quartzite crags like colossal keys, while the southwest slopes down to wave-washed bedrock.

Information is available from the **Tory Island Co-op** (Comharchumann Thoraí Teo; 074-913 5502; www.oileanthorai.com; 9am-5pm Mon-Fri) near the pier, next to the playground. You can also get information at the new craft shop at the top of the pier.

Sights & Activities

Cottages mingle with ancient ecclesiastical treasures in West Town. St Colmcille is said to have founded a monastery here in the 6th century, and reminders of the early Church are scattered throughout the town. One example is the 12th-century **Tau Cross**, an odd, T-shaped cruciform that suggests the possibility of seafaring exchanges with early Coptic Christians from Egypt. The cross greets passengers disembarking from the ferry. Also nearby is a 6th- or 7th-century **round tower**, with a circumference of nearly 16m and a round-headed doorway high above the ground.

The island is a wondrous place for **birdwatching** – over 100 species of seabird inhabit the island, and among the cliffs in the northeast you can see colonies of puffins (around 1400 are thought to inhabit the island).

Sleeping & Eating

To make the most of your visit, plan an overnight stay and experience the island once the day trippers have left. Book accommodation in advance though, as beds can be hard to find in midsummer.

Teach Bhillie B&B €
(074-916 5145; West Town; dm/s & d €35/50) From the ferry, walk 300m left to find this newly renovated B&B with bright, cheery

TORY ISLAND 'NAIVE' ART

Tory Island's distinctive school of painters came about in the 1950s when the English painter Derrick Hill began to spend much of his time on the island, producing many paintings. The islanders often watched him as he worked. As the story goes, one of the islanders approached Hill and said, 'I can do that.' He was James Dixon, a self-taught painter who used boat paint and made his own brushes with donkey hairs. Hill was impressed with the 'painterly' quality of Dixon's work and the two formed a lasting friendship. Other islanders were soon inspired to follow suit, forging unique folksy, expressive styles portraying rugged island scenes. Among them were Patsy Dan Rodgers, now elected 'king' of Tory. The islanders' work has been exhibited in Chicago, New York, Belfast, London and Paris, and fetches impressive prices at auctions. You can often see it at the island's **Dixon Gallery** (West Town), and the Glebe House gallery (p489) on the mainland.

accommodation. Spotless rooms are enlivened with bright splashes of colour, and you'll find the legendary Tory welcome in full force.

Hotel Tory HOTEL **€€**
(☎074-913 5920; West Town; s/d €60/80; ⊙Easter-Oct) The island's only hotel is a fairly rustic place with 14 simple but comfortable bedrooms. The bar here is a hotbed of late-night music, dancing and craic, so be prepared to join in.

Caife an Chreagain IRISH **€€**
(West Town; mains €10-15; ⊙10am-10.30pm Easter-Sep) If that sea air has given you an appetite, head for Mary's welcoming cafe/restaurant, offering great value for money. Outside the summer months (June to August), opening times can vary depending on the weather (and, by extension, the ferries).

☆ Entertainment

Club Sóisialta Thórai COMMUNITY CENTRE
(Tory Social Club; West Town) The island's social life revolves around this merry spot, which along with the hotel has the island's only other pub. Opening times vary; it usually gets going from around 8pm but don't expect the real craic to start until much, much later.

ℹ Getting There & Around

Bring waterproofs for the trip – it can be a wild ride. **Donegal Coastal Cruises** (Turasmara Teo; ☎074-953 1320; wwww.toryislandferry.com) runs boats to Tory (adult/child/student return €26/13/20) from Bunbeg (1½ hours) and Magheraroarty (35 minutes). Sailing times vary according to weather and tides. Check forecasts as it's not uncommon for travellers to be stranded on the island in bad weather.

Magheraroarty is reached by turning off the N56 at the western end of Gortahork near Falcarragh; the road is signposted Coastal Route/Bloody Foreland.

Bike hire can be arranged with **Rothair ar Cíos** (☎074-916 5614; West Town).

Falcarragh & Gortahork

POP 842

You'll find more tourist amenities up the road in Dunfanaghy, but the small workaday towns of Falcarragh (An Fál Carrach) and neighbouring Gortahork (Gort an Choirce) afford an opportunity to experience life in the Gaeltacht region, and there's a good beach nearby.

The 19th-century police barracks now house **Falcarragh Visitors Centre** (An tSean Bheairic; ☎074-918 0888; www.falcarraghvisitorcentre.com; ⊙10am-5pm Mon-Fri, 11am-5pm Sat), which has tourist information and a cafe. The Bank of Ireland at the eastern end of Main St has an ATM, and the post office is at Main St's western end in Falcarragh.

◉ Sights & Activities

It's 4km to the windswept **beach**; follow the signs marked *Trá* from Falcarragh's Main St. The beach is superb for walking, but currents make swimming unsafe.

The grey bulk of **Muckish Mountain** (670m) dominates the coast between Dunfanaghy and the Bloody Foreland. Ascents from either the north or south are steep but relatively straightforward; the easiest is from southeast of Falcarragh by the inland road through Muckish Gap. Sweeping views to Malin Head and Tory Island unfurl from the summit.

Sleeping & Eating

Óstán Loch Altan HOTEL €€

(☎074-913 5267; www.ostanlochaltan.com; Gortahork; s/d €45/90; P 📶) Gortahork's main landmark is this large cream-coloured hotel on the main street. Some of its 39 neutral-toned rooms with satin-quilted fabrics have sea views. It's one of the few places to stay along this stretch of coast that's open all year. Quality **bar food** (€9-19.50) is served from noon to 9pm year-round, while its **restaurant** (mains €21-29.50) opens for lunch and dinner from June to September.

Cuan Na Mara B&B €€

(☎074-913 5327; crisscannon@hotmail.com; Ballyness, Falcarragh; s with/without bathroom €49/47, d €66/62; ⏲Jun-Sep; P 📶) Overlooking Ballyness Bay and Tory island, this dormer bungalow has four cosy guestrooms. It's about 2km from the centre of Falcarragh – take the turn-off signposted *Trá*.

Maggie Dan's ITALIAN €

(☎074-916 5022; www.maggiedans.ie; An Phanc, Gortahork; pizzas around €10; ⏲dinner) A little bit of bohemia in the countryside, this excellent pizzeria facing the Market Sq hosts occasional theatre performances.

Drinking & Entertainment

Teach Ruairí PUB

(www.donegalpub.com; Baltoney, Gortahork) Fronted by red wagon wheels and red shutters, this authentic-as-it-gets pub is tucked 2km west of Gortahork. It is signposted off the Gweedore road and has regular live acoustic music. Decent pub grub is served on weekday evenings and all day at weekends.

Lóistín Na Seamróige PUB

(Shamrock Lodge; Main St, Falcarragh) Owner Margaret grew up on these premises and her pub is the town's living room, especially on Friday mornings when a market sets up outside the front door, and during July and August when there's traditional music.

Getting There & Away

Feda O'Donnell (☎074-954 8114) buses from Crolly stop on Main St, Falcarragh (€7, twice daily Monday to Saturday, three daily Friday and Sunday). From Falcarragh, buses continue to Letterkenny (€7, one hour) and Galway (€20, 5¼ hours).

John McGinley (☎074-913 5201; www.johnmcginley.com) buses from Annagry stop at Gortahork and Falcarragh two to four times daily en route to Letterkenny (€7, one hour) and Dublin (€20, five hours).

Dunfanaghy & Around

POP 316

Clustered around the waterfront, Dunfanaghy's small, attractive town centre has a surprisingly wide range of accommodation and some of the finest dining options in the county's northwest. Glistening beaches, dramatic coastal cliffs, mountain trails and forests are all within a few kilometres.

There are no ATMs in town but the **post office** (Main St) has a bureau de change.

Sights

Ards Forest Park NATURE RESERVE

(☎074-912 1139; www.coillteoutdoors.ie; parking €5; ⏲10am-9pm Apr-Sep, 10am-4.30pm Oct-Mar) Anyone looking to stretch their legs will love this forested park, which is criss-crossed by marked nature trails varying in length from 2km to 13km. It covers the northern shore of the Ards Peninsula and some of the best walks lead to its clean beaches. The woodlands are home to several native species, including ash, birch and sessile oak. Introduced species, both broadleaf and conifer, also proliferate, and you may even encounter foxes, hedgehogs and otters. In 1930 the southern part of the peninsula was taken over by Capuchin monks; the grounds of their friary are open to the public. It's 5km southeast of Dunfanaghy off the N56; daily closing times are posted at the entrance.

Horn Head SCENIC DRIVE

The towering headland of Horn Head has some of Donegal's most spectacular coastal scenery and plenty of birdlife. Its dramatic quartzite cliffs, covered with bog and heather, rear over 180m high, and the view from their tops is heart-pounding.

The road circles the headland; the best approach by bike or car is in a clockwise direction from the Falcarragh end of Dunfanaghy. On a fine day, you'll encounter tremendous views of Tory, Inishbofin, Inishdooey and tiny Inishbeg islands to the west; Sheep Haven Bay and the Rosguill Peninsula to the east; Malin Head to the northeast; and the coast of Scotland beyond. Take care in bad weather as the route can be perilous.

Dunfanaghy Workhouse HISTORIC BUILDING
(www.dunfanaghyworkhouse.ie; Main St; adult/child €4.50/2; ⏲9.30am-5.30pm daily Jul & Aug, 9.30am-4pm Mon-Sat Mar-Jun & Sep) This grim building was the local workhouse, built to keep and employ the destitute. Conditions were excessively harsh. Men, women, children and the sick were segregated and their lives were dominated by gruelling work. It was soon inundated with starving people as the Famine took grip. Two years after it opened in 1845, it accommodated some 600 people – double the number originally planned.

The workhouse, west of the centre, is now a **heritage centre**, which tells the powerful tale of 'Wee Hannah' and her passage through the institution, and also hosts various temporary exhibitions and workshops. On some mornings the place is overrun with busloads of school children.

Doe Castle HISTORIC BUILDING
(Caisléan na dTuath; Creeslough; ⏲10am-6pm) Although the interior of the early 16th-century Doe Castle isn't open to the public, you can wander through the grounds. The castle was the stronghold of the Scottish MacSweeney family until it fell into English hands in the 17th century. The castle is picturesquely sited on a low promontory with water on three sides, and a moat hewn out of the rock on the landward side. The best view is from the Carrigart–Creeslough road. It's signposted 16km from Dunfanaghy on the Carrigart road.

Beaches BEACHES
The wide, sandy and virtually empty **Killahoey Beach** leads right into the heart of Dunfanaghy village. **Marble Hill Beach**, about 3km east of town in Port-na-Blagh, is more secluded but usually crammed in summer. Reaching Dunfanaghy's loveliest spot, **Tramore Beach**, requires hiking 20 minutes through the grassy dunes immediately south of the village.

Activities

Walking

For an exhilarating hike, take the road from Dunfanaghy towards Horn Head until the bridge. After crossing, go through the gate on your left and stroll along the track until you reach the dunes. A well-beaten path will lead you to the magnificent **Tramore Beach**. Turn left and follow it to the end, where you can find a way up onto a path leading north to **Pollaguill Bay**. Continue to the cairn at the end of the bay and follow the coastline for a stupendous view of the 20m **Marble Arch**, carved out by the pounding sea.

A shorter walk begins at Marble Hill Beach in Port-na-Blagh. Take the path on the left side of the beach past the cottage and work your way about 500m through the brush and along the top of the cliff until you reach **Harry's Hole**, a small crevice in the cliff that is popular with daredevil kids, who dive 10m into the water below.

When it's not shrouded in the cloud and mist that locals call *smir,* hulking **Muckish Mountain** (670m) makes a good climb. You can reach it via the village of Creeslough, 11km south of Dunfanaghy on the N56, home to an extraordinary modern church, resembling a half-dissolved sugar cube that mirrors the mountain's shape. Turn right about 2km northwest of Creeslough and continue for about 6km, where a rough track begins the ascent.

Golf

Dunfanaghy Golf Club GOLF
(www.dunfanaghygolfclub.com; green fees weekdays/weekends €30/40) This stunning waterside 18-hole links course is just outside the village on the Port-na-Blagh road.

TOP FIVE SCENIC DRIVES

Practically any stretch of road qualifies as a scenic drive in this rugged county, but the following are especially captivating. So captivating, in fact, that you'll need to take care to keep your eyes on the road, too.

» The coast highway from Dunfanaghy to Gweedore

» The 100-mile loop of isolated Inishowen Peninsula

» The vertiginous heights of Horn Head

» The lingering arc through stunning Glenveagh National Park

» The snaking switchbacks traversing Glen Gesh Pass

Horse Riding

Dunfanaghy Stables HORSE RIDING
(☎074-910 0980; www.dunfanaghystables.com; Main St; adult/child per hr €30/25) Exploring the expansive beaches and surrounding countryside on horseback can be arranged here. Hours vary seasonally.

Sea Angling

The area round Horn Head is well known for its excellent sea angling.

Richard Bowyer FISHING TRIPS
(☎074-913 6640; www.hornheadseasafaris.com; Port-na-Blagh) Organises sea-angling trips from the small pier in Port-na-Blagh between Easter and September.

Surfing, Windsurfing & Kayaking

Jaws Watersports WATER SPORTS
(☎086 173 5109; www.jawswatersports.ie; Main St) Offers surfing, sailing and windsurfing lessons (€40), stand-up paddle boarding (€30), rents gear (€20 per half-day), kayak rental (from €25 per half-day) and runs kayaking trips (€35).

Narosa Life WATER SPORTS
(☎086 883 1090; www.narosalife.com; 2hr surf lesson per adult/child €35/25) Offers surf lessons, yoga and fitness classes, as well as guided walks of Muckish Mountain and Horn Head.

Sleeping

Corcreggan Mill HOSTEL €
(☎074-913 6409; www.corcreggan.com; Corcreggan Mill, Dunfanaghy; campsites per person €8, dm/s/d €17/40/55; P@) Spotless dorms, most with private bathroom, and private rooms are tucked into cosy corners of this lovingly restored former mill house. An organic vegetable garden provides the ingredients for soups and stews (€5 to €10) served in the evening, and you can add a continental/full breakfast for €5/7. Look for signs on the roadside and in the car park reading 'Mill House'.

Whins B&B €€
(☎074-913 6481; www.thewhins.com; s/d €50/74; P) The colourful, individually decorated rooms at the Whins have patchwork quilts, quality furniture and a real sense of character. A wide choice of superb breakfasts is served upstairs in a room overlooking Horn Head. The B&B is about 750m south of the village opposite the golf course.

Arnold's Hotel HOTEL €€
(☎074-913 6208; www.arnoldshotel.com; Main St; s/d €70/100; ⊙Apr-Oct; P@) Open since 1922, this family-run hotel has comfortable but rather corporate rooms. The friendly staff with their suggestions for local activities, helpful attitude and warm welcome more than make up for this though. The bar serves up some decent classic Irish dishes (mains €9 to €23).

Eating

Mill Restaurant & Guesthouse IRISH €€€
(☎074-913 6985; www.themillrestaurant.com; Figart, Dunfanaghy; 3-course menu €43.50; s/d €70/100; ⊙dinner Tue-Sun mid-Mar–mid-Dec; P) An exquisite country setting and perfectly composed meals make dining here a treat. Set in an old flax mill that was for many years the home of renowned watercolour artist Frank Eggington, it also has six high-class guestrooms. The mill is just south of the town on the Falcarragh road. Book in advance.

Cove IRISH €€
(☎074-913 6300; Rockhill, Port-na-Blagh; dinner mains €17.50-24.50; ⊙lunch Sun, dinner Tue-Sun, closed Jan–mid-Mar) Owners Siobhan Sweeney and Peter Byrne are perfectionists who tend to every detail in Cove's art-filled dining room and on your plate. The seafood-skewed cuisine is inventive and deceptively simple with subtle Asian influences. After dinner, retire to the elegant lounge upstairs. It's on the main road in Port-na-Blagh. Book ahead.

Muck 'n' Muffins CAFE €
(Main Sq; sandwiches & snacks €3.50-9.50; ⊙9.30am-5pm Mon-Sat, 11am-5pm Sun, to 9pm Jul & Aug;) A 19th-century rough-stone grain store now houses this waterfront cafe and craft shop. Even on rainy winter days, it's packed with locals tucking into healthy sandwiches, quiches and hot specials, tempting cakes and, of course, muffins.

Drinking

Molly's Bar PUB
(Main St) Be sure to at least peek inside the cherry-red Molly's Bar, a wonderfully old-fashioned pub with proper snugs. It also hosts regular live music (traditional, jazz, blues and more) and events including quiz nights.

Getting There & Away

Feda O'Donnell (www.feda.ie) buses from Crolly (€7, 40 minutes) to Galway (€20, five hours) stop in Dunfanaghy square twice daily Monday to Saturday and three times on Friday and Sunday.

John McGinley (www.johnmcginley.com) buses stop in Dunfanaghy two to four times daily en route to Letterkenny (€7, one hour) and Dublin (€20, five hours).

The **Lough Swilly** (www.loughswillybusco.com) bus from Dungloe stops in Dunfanaghy once daily Monday to Friday en route to Letterkenny (€7, one hour) and Derry (€11.40, two hours).

EASTERN DONEGAL

Letterkenny

POP 17,586

Ruined by the excesses of the Celtic Tiger era, Letterkenny is a market town run amok. Mindless development has resulted in numerous faceless retail parks lining the roads, traffic problems and a complete lack of soul. However, as Donegal's largest town, it's buzzing with students and young professionals, and there's a good choice of restaurants and accommodation. Attractions for visitors are few but if you're using public transport the town is hard to avoid.

Sights

Dominating the town's hillside profile, the enormous Gothic-style **St Eunan's Cathedral** (1901) thrusts skyward on Sentry Hill Rd (take Church Lane up from Main St) and contains much intricate Celtic carving.

Letterkenny's 19th-century workhouse, built to provide Famine relief, now houses the free **Donegal County Museum** (074-912 4613; High Rd; 10am-12.30pm & 1-4.30pm Mon-Fri, 1-4.30pm Sat). Temporary exhibits feature on the ground floor. Upstairs, the permanent collection is worth a peek for its 8000-strong artefacts from prehistoric times on.

Festivals & Events

Earagail Arts Festival ARTS

(www.eaf.ie) Theatre performances, concerts and art exhibits lure culture buffs to this diverse festival held over two weeks in early to mid-July.

Sleeping

Castle Grove HOTEL €€

(074-915 1118; www.castlegrove.com; s/d €65/100; P) Set on an enormous estate that rolls down to the estuary, this Georgian manor, filled with fragrant fresh flowers, manages to be at once grand, yet warm and personal. Its 15 rooms are well worn but elegantly arranged with antiques, and the **restaurant** (Sunday lunch €22.50, dinner menu €45) is a local favourite. From Letterkenny, head 5km along the road to Rathmelton and turn right just before the Silver Tassie hotel.

Station House HOTEL €€

(074-912 3100; www.stationhouseletterkenny.com; Lower Main St; s/d €79/99; P@) Conveniently located in the centre of town, this large, modern hotel has 81 minimalist rooms with rich red bedspreads, low lighting and glass-panelled bathrooms. Everything is immaculately kept, the staff are incredibly helpful and the **Depot cafe/bar** (mains €13 to €25) serves a good choice of classic dishes.

Town View B&B €€

(074-912 1570; www.townviewhouse.com; Leck Rd; s/d €49/70; P@) This family-run guesthouse offers three tastefully decorated downstairs rooms. White linens with a splash of colour, quality furniture and shining bathrooms make it a popular choice, and that's before you get to the impressive array of breakfast dishes and the extremely amicable owners.

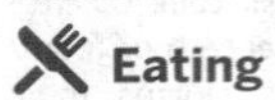

Eating

Lemon Tree IRISH €€

(074-912 5788; www.thelemontreerestaurant.com; 39 Lower Main St; mains €14-22; lunch Sun, dinner daily) With its tiled frontage and dated sign, this place doesn't look too hot from the outside but one taste of the food and you'll be glad you made it in the door. White linens, pale walls and painted wood panelling give it a bright, convivial atmosphere, and the innovative menu offers an excellent choice of fresh seafood, poultry and meat dishes blending French flair with country Irish classics. Everything from the breads to pastries is made on-site.

Yellow Pepper IRISH €€

(074-912 4133; www.yellowpepperrestaurant.com; 36 Lower Main St; lunch mains €8-18, dinner mains €14-22; lunch & dinner) Set in a 19th-century former shirt factory with stone walls, copper light fittings and original hardwood floors, this cosy restaurant is a local favourite. The menu is heavy on fish but also offers plenty for meat lovers and vegetarians. Dishes are exquisitely prepared and beautifully presented. Book ahead.

Beetroot IRISH **€€**
(☎074-912 9759; www.thebeetroot.com; 41 Port Rd; mains €13-22; ⊙lunch Mon-Fri, dinner Wed-Sun) Beetroot's bright wallpaper, bare wood tables and sleek banquettes are a chic backdrop for its slightly dated menu. The food is good but not creative, with dishes such as breaded brie, chicken escalope and Thai curry.

Drinking

McGinley's PUB
(Main St) The best spot in town to catch some live music, this old-style pub with an open fire has trad sessions on Wednesday nights, and live bands Thursday to Saturday. You'll generally find an older crowd downstairs and more livelier action upstairs.

Cottage Bar PUB
(49 Upper Main St) Watch your head! All sorts of bric-a-brac hangs precariously from the ceiling of Letterkenny's most atmospheric pub. It's popular with a young student crowd at weekends but is a good spot for a quiet mid-week pint.

☆ Entertainment

An Grianán Theatre THEATRE
(☎074-912 0777; www.angrianan.com; Port Rd) An Grianán Theatre is both a community theatre and major arts venue for the northwest, presenting national and international drama, comedy and music. It also has a good **cafe** and **bar**.

Regional Cultural Centre THEATRE
(☎074-912 9186; www.donegalculture.com; Port Rd) In a stunning glass-and-aluminium structure, Letterkenny's cultural centre mounts performances, fine arts and multimedia exhibits, and film screenings.

Voodoo NIGHTCLUB
(www.voodoolk.com; 21 Lower Main St) This vast club is the centre of Letterkenny's nightlife. Check the website for events.

Information

You'll find banks and the post office on Letterkenny's elongated Main St. Check out www.letterkenny.ie for useful info on the town and surrounds.

LK Online (Station roundabout; per hr €3; ⊙10.30am-10.30pm) Internet cafe.

Tourist office (☎074-912 1160; www.discovererireland.ie; Neil Blaney Rd; ⊙9am-5.30pm Mon-Sat Jun-Aug, 9.15am-5pm Mon-Fri Sep-May) Large, efficient office situated 1km southeast of town at the end of Port Rd.

Getting There & Away

Letterkenny is a major bus hub for northwestern Ireland. The bus station is by the roundabout at the junction of Ramelton Rd and Port Rd.

Bus Éireann (www.buseireann.ie) express bus 32 runs to Dublin (€17.80, four hours) nine times daily via Omagh (€11.50, one hour) and Monaghan (€14.40, 1¾ hours).

The Derry (€8.50, 35 minutes) to Galway bus 64 stops at Letterkenny four times daily before continuing to Donegal (€8.80, 45 minutes), Bundoran (€13, 1¼ hours), Sligo (€13, two hours) and Galway (€19, five hours).

John McGinley (www.johnmcginley.com) buses run two to five times daily from Annagry to Dublin (€20, 3¾ hours) through Letterkenny and Monaghan.

Lough Swilly (www.loughswillybusco.com) has one daily service Monday to Friday from Derry (€6.60, one hour) to Dungloe (€20, two hours), via Letterkenny and Dunfanaghy.

Feda O'Donnell (www.feda.ie) runs a bus from Crolly (€7, 1½ hours) to Galway (€20, four hours) twice daily via Letterkenny, Donegal, Bundoran and Sligo. Buses stop on the road outside the bus station.

Getting Around

Taxis can be ordered from **Letterkenny Taxis** (☎074-912 7400). There are taxi stands on Main St opposite the square, and opposite the bus station.

Glenveagh National Park

Lakes shimmer like dew in the mountainous valley of **Glenveagh National Park** (Páirc Náisiúnta Ghleann Bheatha; www.glenveaghnationalpark.ie; ⊙10am-6pm mid-Mar–Oct, 9am-5pm Nov–mid-Mar). Alternating between great knuckles of rock, green-gold swaths of bog and scatterings of oak and birch forest, the 16,500 sq km protected area is magnificent walking country. Its wealth of wildlife includes the golden eagle, which was hunted to extinction here in the 19th century but was reintroduced in 2000.

Such serenity came at a heavy price. The land was once farmed by 244 tenants, who were forcibly evicted by landowner John

George Adair in the winter of 1861 following what he called a 'conspiracy', but really because their presence obstructed his vision for the valley. Adair put the final touches on his paradise by building the spectacular lakeside Glenveagh Castle (1870–73), while his wife, Adelia, introduced the park's definitive red deer and rhododendrons.

If anything, things got even more surreal after the Adairs' deaths. The castle was briefly occupied by the IRA in 1922. Then in 1929 the property was acquired by Kingsley Porter, professor of art at Harvard University, who mysteriously disappeared in 1933 (presumed drowned, but rumoured to have been spotted in Paris afterwards). Six years later the estate was bought by his former student, Henry McIlhenny, once described by Andy Warhol as 'the only person in Philadelphia with glamour'. In 1975, McIlhenny sold the whole kit and caboodle to the Irish government.

The park features nature trails along lakes and through woods and blanket bog, as well as a viewing point that's a short walk behind the castle. You'll get free maps and information on self-guided walks at the visitor centre. Excellent themed **ranger-led walks** (☎074-913 7090; adult/child €5/free) are held regularly between April and October but must be booked in advance.

The **Glenveagh Visitor Centre** has a 20-minute audiovisual display on the ecology of the park and the infamous Adair. The **cafe** (Easter & Jun-Sep) serves hot food and snacks, and the reception sells the necessary midge repellent, as vital in summer as walking boots and waterproofs are in winter. Camping is not allowed.

Glenveagh Castle HISTORIC BUILDING
(adult/child €5/2) This delightfully showy castle was modelled in miniature on Scotland's Balmoral Castle. Henry McIlhenny made it a characterful home with liberal reminders of his passion for hunting deer. In fact you'll be hard pressed to find a single room without a representation – or taxidermied remains – of a stag.

Access is by guided tour only. Tours last 30 minutes and take in a series of flamboyantly decorated rooms that remain as if McIlhenny has just stepped out. The most eye-catching, including the tartan-and-antler-covered music room and the pink candy-striped room demanded by Greta Garbo whenever she stayed here, are in the round tower.

The exotic **gardens** are similarly spectacular, boasting a host of terraces, an Italian garden, a walled kitchen garden and the Belgian Walk, built by Belgian soldiers who stayed here during WWI. Their cultured charm is in marked contrast to the wildly beautiful landscape that enfolds the area.

The last guided tours of the castle leave about 45 minutes before closing time. Cars are not allowed beyond the visitor centre. You can walk the scenic 3.6km route to the castle or take the **shuttle bus** (adult single/return €3/2, child return €2; every 15 min).

Lough Gartan

The patriarch of Irish monasticism, St Colmcille (or Columba), was born in a lovely setting near the glassy Lough Gartan, and some isolated stone structures and crosses remain from his lifetime. The lake is 17km northwest of Letterkenny. It's beautiful driving country, but there's no public transport.

Sights & Activities

Colmcille Heritage Centre HISTORIC SITE
(www.colmcilleheritagecentre.ie; Gartan; adult/concession €3/2; 10.30am-5pm Mon-Sat, 1-5pm Sun May-Sep) Colmcille's Hall of Fame is this comprehensive heritage centre on the shore of Lough Gartan, with a lavish display on the production of illuminated manuscripts.

Colmcille's mother, on the run from pagans, supposedly haemorrhaged during childbirth and her blood is believed to have changed the colour of the surrounding Gartan Clay to pure white. Ever since, the clay has been regarded as a lucky charm. Ask nicely and the staff may produce some from under the counter.

On the way to the heritage centre you'll also see signs to the stone pile that once was Colmcille's **abbey**. Further down the road, on a hillside overrun by bleating sheep, is the saint's **birthplace**, marked by a hefty cross. Beside it is an intriguing prehistoric tomb strewn with greening copper coins that's popularly known as the Flagstone of Loneliness, on which Colmcille supposedly slept. Some believe the chunky slab cures homesickness.

To reach the heritage centre, leave Letterkenny on the R250 road to Glenties and Ardara. After a few kilometres, turn right on the R251 to Churchill village and follow the signs. Alternatively, from Kilmacrennan on the N56, turn west and look for signs.

Glebe House HISTORIC BUILDING
(www.heritageireland.ie; Churchill; adult/child €3/1; ⏰11am-6.30pm daily Easter, Jul & Aug, Sat-Thu Jun & Sep) The English painter Derrick Hill bought this historic house in 1953, providing him with a mainland base close to his beloved Tory Island. Before Hill arrived, the house served as a rectory and then a hotel. The 1828-built mansion is sumptuously decorated with an evident love of all things exotic, but its real appeal is Hill's astonishing art collection. In addition to paintings by Hill and Tory Island's 'naive' artists (see the boxed text, p482) are works by Picasso, Landseer, Hokusai, Jack B Yeats and Kokoschka. The woodland gardens are also wonderful. A guided tour of the house takes about 45 minutes.

Gartan Outdoor Education Centre ADVENTURE SPORTS
(www.gartan.com; Gartan, Churchill) Courses including rock climbing, sea kayaking, sailing, surfing, windsurfing, hill climbing and more are offered for both adults and children at this adventure centre. It's located on a 35-hectare estate 18km northwest of Letterkenny on the shores of Lough Gartan.

Doon Well & Rock of Doon

In centuries past, wells were commonly believed to cure afflictions. Judging by the shimmering rosaries, multicoloured rags and trinkets bejewelling nearby bushes, many still believe this to be true of the cupboard-like Doon Well.

A sign points to the overgrown Rock of Doon, which has some far-reaching views. This is where the O'Donnell kings were crowned – presumably so they could get a squiz at what they were inheriting.

Take the signposted turn-off from the N56 just north of Kilmacrennan. The well and rock are about 1.5km north of the village.

NORTHEASTERN DONEGAL

Rosguill Peninsula

The best way to appreciate Rosguill's rugged splendour is by driving, cycling or even walking the 15km **Atlantic Drive**. It's signposted to your left as you come into the sprawling village of **Carrigart** (Carraig Airt) from the south. There are plenty of thirst-quenching pubs in the village, and a pretty, secluded beach at **Trá na Rossan**. On no account should you swim in Mulroy Bay or the surrounding areas, as it's unsafe. Perhaps this is why the summer crowds don't linger here. Most prefer to travel 4km northward to **Downings** (often written as Downies), where the beach is spectacular, though it's much more built-up and lined with rows of static caravans.

Activities

Rosapenna Golf Club GOLF
(www.rosapenna.ie; Downings; green fees €50) Designed by St Andrew's Old Tom Morris in 1891 and remodelled by Harry Vardon in 1906, the scenery at this renowned golf club is as spectacular as the layout, which can challenge even the lowest handicapper.

Mevagh Dive Centre DIVING
(☎074-915 4708; www.mevaghdiving.com; Carrigart; boat dive €30) Donegal's only dive centre offers courses, rents gear (€40 per half-day) and has excellent accommodation (doubles €70) in its purpose-built B&B. Stay-and-dive packages including two nights' B&B and four boat dives cost €175.

Sleeping & Eating

Olde Glen Bar & Restaurant PUB
(Glen, Carrigart; mains €18-24; ⏰dinner Tue-Sat late May–mid-Sep, Fri-Sun Easter-late May, Sat & Sun mid-Sep–Easter) Authentic down to its original 1700s uneven stone floor, this treasure of a traditional pub in the tiny hamlet of Glen serves a sensational pint. Out the back, its small farmhouse-style restaurant serves outstanding blackboard specials. It doesn't take reservations and is popular with locals – turn up by 5.30pm to get a table for the 6pm seating, or by 7pm for a table at the 8pm seating. By the time you leave, you'll feel like a local yourself.

Trá na Rosann Hostel HOSTEL €
(☎074-915 5374; www.anoige.ie; Downings; dm €16; ⏰late May-Aug; Ⓟ) Knockout views envelop this heritage-listed former hunting lodge, now an An Óige hostel. Designed by Sir Edwin Lutyens, this is an atmospheric spot with a colourful history. The trade-off for its tranquil setting is that it's 8km east of Downings and there's no public transport. Note that reception is generally closed from 10am to 5pm.

Beach Hotel HOTEL €€
(Óstán na Trá; ☎074-915 5303; www.beachhotel.ie; Downings; s/d €60/100; P) This large family-run hotel is bright and modern with spacious rooms in calming neutral tones. Many have ocean views, though the beachside caravan park destroys the effect somewhat. Everything is cooked to order in the **restaurant** (mains €12-26; ⊙6-10pm Thu-Tue Ju n-Aug, Sat Sep-May) and **bar food** (mains €9-14) is available throughout the day.

Downings Bay Hotel HOTEL €€
(☎074-915 5586; www.downingsbayhotel.com; Downings; s/d from €50/100; P) Just footsteps from the strand, rooms at thi s spacious, if slightly austere, hotel have subtle checked and striped fabrics. There's an adjacent nightclub, a couple of bars (bar food €9.50 to €19.50) and a decent restaurant, the **Haven** (mains €15-22).

Getting There & Around

A local bus connects Carrigart and Downings (contact Patrick Gallagher, ☎074-913 7037), but you really need your own transport for this area.

Fanad Peninsula

The second-most northerly point in Donegal, Fanad Head thrusts out into the Atlantic to the east of Rosguill. The peninsula curls around the watery expanses of Mulroy Bay to the west, and Lough Swilly to the east, the latter trimmed by high cliffs and sandy beaches. Most travellers stick to the peninsula's eastern flank, visiting the beautiful beach and excellent golf course at Portsalon, and the quiet heritage towns of Rathmelton and Rathmullan. Accommodation is relatively limited, so book ahead in summer.

PORTSALON & FANAD HEAD

Once named the second most beautiful beach in the world by British newspaper the *Observer,* the tawny-coloured Blue Flag **beach** in Ballymastocker Bay, which is safe for swimming, is the principal draw of tiny Portsalon (Port an tSalainn). For golfers, however, the main attraction is the marvellously scenic **Portsalon Golf Club** (☎074-915 9459; www.portsalongolfclub.com; Portsalon; green fees weekdays/weekends €40/50).

It's another 8km to the lighthouse on the rocky tip of Fanad Head, the best part of which is the scenic drive there. Following the rollercoaster road that hugs the cliffs back to Rathmullan, you'll pass the early 19th-century **Knockalla Fort**, built to warn off any approaching French ships.

The peninsula has some crankin' surf – for lessons contact **Adventure One Surf School** (☎074-915 0262; www.adventureone.net; Ballyheirnan Bay, Fanad). Two-hour lessons, which include gear rental, cost €30.

The **Lough Swilly** (☎074-912 2863) bus leaves Letterkenny once daily Monday to Friday for Milford (€4.60, one hour) and Rosnakil.

RATHMULLAN

POP 520

The refined little port of Rathmullan has a tranquillity that belies the momentous events that took place here from the 16th to 18th centuries. In 1587 Hugh O'Donnell, the 15-year-old heir to the powerful O'Donnell clan, was tricked into boarding a ship here and taken to Dublin as a prisoner. He escaped four years later on Christmas Eve and, after unsuccessful attempts at revenge, died in Spain, aged only 30. In 1607, despairing of fighting the English, Hugh O'Neill, the Earl of Tyrone, and Rory O'Donnell, the Earl of Tyrconnell, boarded a ship in Rathmullan harbour and left Ireland for good. This decisive act, known as the Flight of the Earls, marked the effective end of Gaelic Ireland and the rule of Irish chieftains. Large-scale confiscation of their estates took place, preparing for the Plantation of Ulster with settlers from Britain. Also in Rathmullan, Wolfe Tone, leader of the 1798 Rising, was captured.

This picturesque Carmelite **Rathmullan Friary** is so entangled in vines that it would probably crumble should they be cleared away. It was founded around 1508 by the MacSweeneys, and was still used in 1595 when an English commander, George Bingham, raided the place and took off with the communion plate and priestly vestments. Bishop Knox then renovated the friary in 1618 in order to use it as his own residence.

Sprawled over wooded gardens on the shores of Lough Swilly, the **Rathmullan House** (☎074-915 8188; www.rathmullanhouse.com; s/d from €80/220; P@) hotel might be large and luxurious but the welcome from the family owners is so warm that you feel like you're staying with friends. The original house dates from the 1780s, but extensions are sympathetic and stylish. Higher-priced rooms have claw-foot baths and some open to balconies or terraces. There's a tennis court, two genteel bars, and a glass-paned restaurant, the **Weeping Elm** (menus €45-55; dinner Thu-Sun), utilising organic produce from the property's walled gardens.

It's worth heading out of town to find the modern **Glenalla Lodge** (074-915 8750; www.glenallalodge.com; Ray; s/d €40/70; P) B&B with its four spacious guestrooms. Decked out with tasteful wooden furniture, crisp bedspreads and contemporary rustic style, and with the helpful knowledge of a local historian on tap, it's an excellent spot. Glenalla Lodge is 8km north of Rathmullan on the R247.

Set right on the edge of Lough Swilly, the new **Water's Edge** (074-915 8182; www.thewatersedge.ie; mains €9-23; P) restaurant has giant windows overlooking the waterfront. With glorious views and a menu of steaks, pastas and other classics, it's a good place to stop. There are also 10 tranquil, spacious **rooms** (s/d €60/120) decorated with pale tones and uncluttered style. The restaurant is just south of Rathmullan on the R247.

The **Lough Swilly** (074-912 2863) bus from Letterkenny runs to Rathmullan (€4.40, 45 minutes) once on Saturday, en route to Milford.

RATHMELTON

POP 1088

The first community you come to if you're approaching the peninsula from the east is Rathmelton (sometimes called Ramelton), a picture-perfect spot with rows of Georgian houses and rough-walled stone warehouses curving along the River Lennon.

Apart from walking the colourful, picturesque streets there's not much to do here. The ruined **Tullyaughnish Church**, on the hill, is worth a visit because of the Romanesque carvings in the eastern wall, which were taken from a far older church on nearby Aughnish Island, on the River Lennon. Coming from Letterkenny, turn right at the river and follow it round for about 400m.

For accommodation, those prone to romantic daydreaming need look no further than **Frewin House** (074-915 1246; www.frewinhouse.com; s €75-100, d €130-180, cottage per week €550; closed Christmas; P). This fine Victorian rectory in secluded grounds would make every weepy heroine's dreams come true. The four exquisite rooms here combine all the character you would expect from a charming period house – antique furniture, well-worn books and open fires – with a definite sense of contemporary style. The bedrooms are pretty but uncluttered, dinner (€45 to €50) is served communally and by candlelight, and the gardens just beg to be walked with a book and a parasol. It doesn't get much better than this.

The warm welcome and homemade scones on arrival at **Ardeen House** (074-915 1243; www.ardeenhouse.com; s/d €45/90), a lovely B&B overlooking the river, make you feel as if you've just arrived home. The bedrooms are beautifully decorated, breakfasts are a feast and like many past guests you'll leave planning a return trip.

Just over the bridge, about 100m from downtown, the **Bridge Bar** (074-915 1119; Bridgend; mains €19-26; dinner) is one of those lovely old country pubs you came to Ireland for. Its cosy 1st-floor restaurant has good seafood dishes, such as roasted swordfish. There's live music downstairs every Saturday and on Wednesdays in summer.

Lough Swilly (074-912 2863) buses connect Rathmelton with Letterkenny once daily from Monday to Friday and twice on Saturday (€2.75, 30 minutes).

Inishowen Peninsula

The Inishowen Peninsula reaches just far enough into the Atlantic to qualify as the northernmost point on the island of Ireland: Malin Head. It is remote, rugged, desolate and sparsely populated, making it a special and quiet sort of place. Ancient sites and ruined castles abound, as do traditional thatched cottages that aren't yet demoted to storage sheds.

Surrounded by vast estuarine areas and open seas, the Inishowen Peninsula naturally attracts a lot of birdlife. The variety is tremendous, with well over 200 species passing through or residing permanently on the peninsula. Inishowen regularly receives well-travelled visitors from Iceland, Greenland and North America. Irregular Atlantic winds mean rare and exotic species also blow in from time to time. Twitchers should check out *Finding Birds in Ireland*, by Eric Dempsey and Michael O'Clery, or visit www.birdsireland.com.

For information on everything else, visit www.visitinishowen.com.

Buncrana

POP 3411

On the tame side of the peninsula, Buncrana is a busy but appealing town with its fair share of pubs and a 5km sandy beach on the shores of Lough Swilly. You'll find all the local services you'll need here before heading into the wilds further north.

John Newton, the composer of *Amazing Grace,* was inspired to write his legendary song after his ship the *Greyhound* took refuge in the calm waters of Lough Swilly during a severe storm in 1748. He and his crew were welcomed in Buncrana after their near-death experience and his spiritual journey from slave trader to antislavery campaigner had its beginnings here. He went on to become a prolific hymn writer and later mentored William Wilberforce in his fight against slavery. For more information on the story, visit www.amazinggrace.ie.

Sights

O'Doherty's Keep HISTORIC BUILDING

At the northern end of the seafront, the early 18th-century, six-arched Castle Bridge leads to this tower house built by the O'Dohertys, the local chiefs, in 1430. It was burned by the English and then rebuilt for their own use.

Buncrana Castle HISTORIC BUILDING

At the side of the keep is the manor-like Buncrana Castle, built in 1718 by John Vaughan, who also constructed the bridge. Wolfe Tone was imprisoned here following the unsuccessful French invasion in 1798.

Ned's Point Fort HISTORIC BUILDING

Walking 500m further from the keep (turn left and stick to the shoreline) brings you to Ned's Point Fort (1812), built by the British and now under siege from graffiti artists.

Inishowen Peninsula

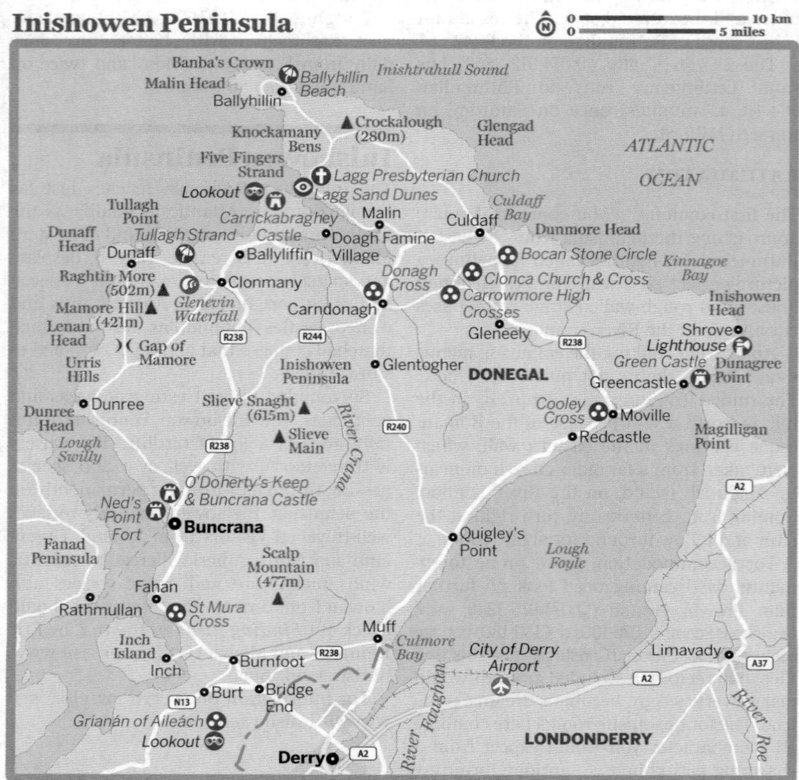

Sleeping & Eating

Westbrook House B&B €€
(☎074-936 1067; www.westbrookhouse.ie; Westbrook Rd; s/d €40/70; P 📶) A handsome Georgian house set in beautiful gardens, Westbrook offers old-world hospitality and charm by the bucket load. Chandeliers, antique furniture and cut glass give it a refined sophistication but the little trinkets and subtle florals make it very much a lived-in and loved home.

Caldra B&B €€
(☎074-936 3703; www.caldrabandb.com; Lisnakelly; s/d €50/80; P 📶 👪) This large, modern B&B has four spacious rooms ideal for families. Expect impressive fireplaces and gilt mirrors in the common areas but more tranquil contemporary style in the guest rooms. The garden and patio overlook Lough Swilly and the mountains.

Tullyarvan Mill HOSTEL €
(☎074-936 1613; www.tullyarvanmill.com; Carndonagh Rd; dm/d €14/42; P) This excellent purpose-built hostel was recently attached to the historic Tullyarvan Mill. Set amid riverside gardens, it also hosts regular cultural events and art exhibits. Head north out of town on the R238 and follow the signs.

Beach House SEAFOOD €€
(☎074-936 1050; www.thebeachhouse.ie; The Pier, Swilly Rd; lunch mains €6.50-17.50, dinner mains €16-26; ⏲daily Jun-Aug, dinner Wed-Sun, lunch Sat & Sun Sep-Dec & Feb-May; 👪) With plate-glass windows facing the lough, this aptly named cafe/restaurant projects an elegant simplicity. Although the menu is also intrinsically simple, the quality and preparation are a cut above: 'surf and turf', for example, comes with fillet steak, crab claws, langoustines and creamy bisque.

Entertainment

Atlantic Bar PUB
(Upper Main St) Dating from 1792, this spearmint-and-moss-green drinking hole is Buncrana's oldest and most atmospheric pub.

O'Flaherty's PUB
(Main St) A central hub for locals and visitors, this old-world pub is a friendly spot and has live traditional music every Wednesday night.

Information

Tourist office (☎074-936 2600; www.visitinishowen.com; Railway Rd; ⏲9.30am-5.30pm Mon-Sat Easter-Aug, to 5pm Sep-Easter)

Getting There & Around

From Buncrana, **Lough Swilly** (www.loughswillybusco.com) buses run seven times daily Monday to Friday, eight times daily on Saturday and four times on Sunday to Derry (€5.30, 1½ hours) and once daily Monday to Saturday to Carndonagh (€5.40, 45 minutes) via Clonmany (€4.40, 25 minutes) and Ballyliffin (€5, 30 minutes).

South of Buncrana

FAHAN

A monastery was founded in Fahan by St Colmcille in the 6th century. Among its ruins is the beautifully carved, 7th-century **St Mura Cross** in the graveyard beside the church. Each face is decorated with a cross, in intricate Celtic weave, and the barely discernible Greek inscription is the only one known in Ireland from this early Christian period.

INCH ISLAND

Few tourists make it to residential Inch Island, accessible from the mainland by a causeway, but it's worth a detour for its birdlife (especially swans), two small beaches and remains of an old fort. **Lenamore Stables** (☎074-938 4022; www.lenamorestables.com), on the mainland in Muff, can set you up for hacking in the area.

Grianán of Aileách FORT
(⏲10am-6pm; P) This amphitheatre-like stone **fort** encircles the top of Grianán Hill like a halo and offers eye-popping views of the surrounding loughs. On clear days you can see as far as Derry. Its mini-arena can resemble a circus whenever a tour bus rolls up and spills its load inside the 4m-thick walls.

The fort may have existed at least 2000 years ago, but it's thought that the site itself goes back to pre-Celtic times as a temple to the god Dagda. Between the 5th and 12th centuries it was the seat of the O'Neills, before being demolished by Murtogh O'Brien, king of Munster. Most of what you see now is a reconstruction built between 1874 and 1878.

The fort is 18km south of Buncrana near Burt, signposted off the N13. The merry-go-round-shaped **Burt Church** at the foot of the hill was modelled on the fort by Derry architect Liam McCormack and built in 1967.

Buncrana to Clonmany

There are two routes from Clonmany to Buncrana: the scenic coastal road via the Gap of Mamore and Dunree Head, and the speedier inland road (R238). The **Gap of Mamore** (elevation 262m) descends dramatically between Mamore Hill and Croagh carragh on its way to Dunree, where the **Fort Dunree military museum** (www.dunree.pro.ie; adult/child €6/4; ⏲10.30am-6pm Mon-Sat, 1-6pm Sun Jun-Sep, 10.30am-4.30pm Mon-Fri, 1-6pm Sat & Sun Oct-May) sits on a rocky outcrop in a 19th-century fort. It's a beautiful spot. If the guns don't impress you, the scenery and birdlife will.

Clonmany & Ballyliffin

POP 700

These two quaint villages and their surrounds have plenty to occupy visitors for a day or two. Both have post offices but no banks.

About 1km north of Ballyliffin is the lovely, sandy expanse of **Pollan Strand**, but the crashing breakers make it unsafe for swimming. A walk north along the dunes brings you to **Doagh Island** (now part of the mainland), where the matchbox ruin of 16th-century **Carrickabraghey Castle** is continually battered by the ocean. Also here is the enthusiastically thrown-together **Doagh Famine Village** (☎074-938 1901; www.doaghfaminevillage.com; Doagh Island; adult/child €7/5; ⏲10am-5pm Easter-late Sep), set in a reconstructed village of thatched cottages. Call ahead to book its tour, packed with entertaining titbits about a disappearing way of life, and insightful comparisons with famine-stricken countries today.

The other beach is at **Tullagh Strand**. Although swimming's possible, the current can be strong and it isn't recommended when the tide's going out.

An 800m trail leads to the cascading 10m **Glenevin Waterfall**, with benches and picnic tables, and some fantastic walking into the mountainous landscape beyond. From Clonmany, follow the road signed to Tullagh Bay, cross the river and bear right at an intersection. Butler's Bridge and the waterfall car park are about 1km further on.

With two championship courses, **Ballyliffin Golf Club** (www.ballyliffingolfclub.com; Ballyliffin; green fees €60-70) is among the best places to play a round of golf in Donegal. The scenery is so beautiful that it can distract even the most focused golfer. Its above-average restaurant, the **Links** (lunch & dinner mains €9.50-20), overlooks the fairways.

Sleeping & Eating

TOP CHOICE **Glen House** B&B €€

(☎074-937 6745; www.glenhouse.ie; Straid, Clonmany; s/d €60/90; P wi-fi family) Despite the grand surroundings and luxurious rooms, you'll find neither the pretension nor the high prices of many country house hotels at this gem of a guesthouse. The welcome couldn't be friendlier or more professional, the rooms are a lesson in restrained sophistication and the setting is incredibly tranquil. The walking trail to Glenevin Waterfall starts next door to the **tearoom** (⏲10am-6pm daily Jun-Aug, Sat & Sun Sep-May), which opens to a timber deck. From September to May there's a minimum two-night stay.

Ballyliffin Lodge HOTEL €€

(☎074-937 8200; www.ballyliffinlodge.com; s/d from €90/150; P wi-fi pool) This elegant 40-room hotel has ultraspacious autumn-hued rooms with heavy fabrics and plenty of scatter cushions. Superior rooms have sublime ocean views. You can treat yourself at the state-of-the-art spa, golf course, sophisticated **Holly Tree Restaurant** (four-course dinner €50) or laid-back **Mamie Pat's** (bar food €10-21).

Getting There & Away

Lough Swilly (☎074-912 2863) buses run once daily Monday to Saturday, between Clonmany and Carndonagh (€2.50, 20 minutes).

Carndonagh

POP 1923

Carndonagh, surrounded by hills on three sides, is a busy commercial centre serving the local farming community. It's not a choice locale in these parts, but convenient for gathering information and provisions.

The locally run **Inishowen tourism office** (☎074-937 4933; www.visitinishowen.com; Malin Rd; ⏲9.30am-5pm Mon-Fri, plus 11am-

WALK: GLENEVIN WATERFALL & RAGHTIN MORE

For tremendous panoramas, you can combine a visit to picturesque Glenevin Waterfall with a steady climb to the wild quartzite summit of Raghtin More (502m). Allow four hours for this 11km route.

From the waterfall, there are two options. Either locate a faint path that climbs steeply out of the eastern side of the gorge, around 10m back from the waterfall. Clamber up the steep peaty slope and cross a 50m section of heather to join a track. Alternatively, if the slope seems too steep for your liking, retrace your route downstream and take the first right at a junction of paths. This path climbs more gently over a lower part of the gorge wall, and will lead you to the same track.

Wherever you join the track, turn right and follow it as it climbs gradually southwest. Firm ground soon gives way to marshy terrain, and at times the track is more like a corridor of reeds and spongy mosses. The western edge of the track generally offers the firmest ground. Continue past a fenced area and climb until you are roughly level with the summit of Raghtin More, to the west. Leave the track here and head west, descending slightly to cross a stream before commencing the climb up the heather-clad slopes beyond.

Arc around to the northwest as you climb, aiming for the col between Raghtin More and Crockmain. Views over Mamore Gap and the Urris Hills become more extensive as you gain height. Heather begins to give way to jumbles of sharp quartzite as you near the wide summit plateau (2½ hours from the start). A high ring of rocks makes for a prominent summit cairn, although the views are better from the trig point, which is 50m to the west. From here, the sweeping panorama embraces Malin Head to the northeast, the Urris Hills to the southwest and a maze of coastal inlets backed by the profiles of north Donegal's mountains beyond.

Descend relatively steep ground northeast from the summit to the col between Raghtin More and Raghtin Beg. The summit of Raghtin Beg (418m) is a short distance to the north and can be readily visited for more good views, especially across the sandy beach at Tullagh Bay. Return to the col and begin to descend through short heather, heading for the fenced area beside the track that you passed on the outward journey. Cross the stream in front of the enclosure, turn left at the track, and follow this back to the car park at the start of the walk.

3pm Sat Jun-Aug) is very helpful. There are banks and an ATM on the Diamond; the post office is in the shopping centre halfway down Bridge St towards the Donagh Cross.

Sights

Once an important ecclesiastical centre, Carndonagh has several early-Christian stone monuments. The delightful 7th-century **Donagh Cross** stands under a shelter by an Anglican church at the Ballyliffin end of town. It's carved with a darling short-bodied, big-eyed figure of Jesus, smiling impishly. Flanking the cross are two small pillars, one showing a man, possibly Goliath, with a sword and shield, the other, David and his harp. In the graveyard there's a pillar with a carved marigold on a stem and nearby a crucifixion scene.

Sleeping & Eating

Ashdale House B&B €€

(074-937 4017; www.ashdalehouse.net; s/d €50/70; Mar-Nov; P) There's an extremely warm welcome for visitors at Carndonagh's best B&B, which is set in a lemon-yellow country house on a working farm. The bright, spacious rooms have pale linens and contemporary style, there are chickens, sheep and donkeys to be fed, and the views of the surrounding countryside are lovely. It's 1.5km out of town on the road towards Malin.

Simpson's PUB €€

(Bridge St; mains €10-21; meals 12.30-9.30pm Mon-Sat, noon-9pm Sun) The old-world charm, buzzing atmosphere and excellent seafood make Simpson's a great stop any time of day. The menu also includes solid surf, turf and international dishes, all of which are made fresh on the premises. The four-course Sunday lunch is only €15.

Butterbean MEDITERRANEAN €€
(074-937 3693; Gaelic Park; mains €9-21; closed Mon;) Carndonagh's new restaurant is a welcome addition to the town and serves a wide selection of dishes, from pasta and seafood to burgers and curries. Although set in modern, minimalist surroundings, it's a down-to-earth place with great ambition.

Getting There & Away

A **Lough Swilly** (074-912 2863) bus leaves Buncrana for Carndonagh (€5.40, 45 minutes) once daily from Monday to Saturday.

Malin Head

Even if you've already seen Ireland's southernmost point and its westernmost point, you'll still be impressed when you clap your eyes on Malin Head, the island's northern extent. The head's rocky, weather-battered slopes feel like they're being dragged unwillingly into the sea. It's great for wandering on foot, absorbing the stark natural setting and pondering deep subjects as the wind tries to blow the clothes off your back. Bring cash with you, as there are no ATMs here.

On the northernmost tip, called **Banba's Crown**, stands a cumbersome cliff-top **tower** that was built in 1805 by the British admiralty and later used as a Lloyds signal station. Around it are unattractive concrete huts that were used by the Irish army in WWII as lookout posts. To the west from the fort-side car park, a path leads to **Hell's Hole**, a chasm where the incoming waters crash against the rocky formations. To the east a longer headland walk leads to the **Wee House of Malin**, a hermit's cave in the cliff face.

Several endangered bird species thrive here, and this is one of the few places in Ireland where you can still hear the call of the endangered corncrake in summer. Other birds to look out for are choughs, snow buntings and puffins.

The Plantation village of **Malin**, on Trawbreaga Bay, 14km southeast of Malin Head, has a pretty movie-set quality. Walkers can head out from the tidy village green on a circular route that takes in **Knockamany Bens**, a local hill with terrific views, as well as **Lagg Presbyterian Church** (3km northwest from Malin), the oldest church still in use on the peninsula. The massive sand dunes at **Five Fingers Strand**, another 1km beyond the church, are a dog's dream.

Sleeping & Eating

Village B&B B&B €€
(074-937 0763; www.malinvillagebandb.com; The Green; s/d €45/70) Sitting right in the centre of the village, this lovely B&B has a choice of cosy rooms, some traditional with antique furniture and brocade armchairs, others more contemporary with white linen and pretty floral patterns. Although you'll get a hearty breakfast here, guests also have use of a kitchen and utility room so you can cook a meal or catch up on some laundry.

Sandrock Holiday Hostel HOSTEL €
(074-937 0289; www.sandrockhostel.com; Port Ronan Pier, Malin Head; dm €12, linen €1.50;) The cinematically changing view from this IHH hostel – above a rocky bay on the western side of the headland – will take your breath away. Seafood can sometimes be bought straight off the boats out front. Inside you'll find 20 beds in two cosy dorms, musical instruments and laundry facilities. Bike rental (per day €10) is also available for nonguests, though you'll have to leave a deposit.

Malin Hotel HOTEL €€
(074-937 0606; www.malinhotel.ie; The Green; s/d from €70/100;) From the village green you'll first spot the old pub, but look beyond it and you'll also see a modern, boxlike hotel behind. Designer wall papers adorn the lavish rooms, and the **pub-restaurant** (mains €9.50-22) serves up good Irish standards.

Drinking

McClean's PUB
(Malin) Easily spotted by the petrol pumps out front, this treasure of an old-time pub has the best craic in Malin and often has live music.

Getting There & Around

The best way to approach Malin Head is by the R238/242 from Carndonagh, rather than up the eastern side from Culdaff.

Lough Swilly (074-912 2863) operates a bus once daily Monday to Saturday between Buncrana and Carndonagh (€7.40, 50 minutes).

Northwest Busways (074-938 2619) runs a bus from Carndonagh to Malin Head once a day Monday to Saturday.

Culdaff & Around

POP 155

Sheep vastly outnumber people around the secluded, resort village of Culdaff on the main Moville–Carndonagh road (R238).

Sheep now also wander the remains of the **Clonca church & cross**. Inside is an intricately carved tombstone sporting a sword and hurling-stick motif. The carved lintel over the door is thought to come from an earlier church. Outside, the remains of the cross show the miracle of the loaves and fishes on the eastern face. Look for the turn-off to Culdaff, on the right if coming from Moville, on the left after about 6km if coming from Carndonagh. The Clonca church and cross are 1.5km on the right behind some farm buildings.

A necklace of around 30 prehistoric stones, called the **Bocan Stone Circle**, embroiders a farmer's field east of Clonca church. From Clonca, continue along the road until you reach a T-junction with a modern church facing you. Turn right here and after about 500m turn left (no sign). The Bocan Stone Circle is inside the first heather-covered field on the left.

The plain stumpy-armed **Carrowmore High Crosses** are all that remain of an ancient monastic site straddling a small lane. One is basically a decorated slab showing Christ and an angel, while the other is a taller, unadorned cross.

From Bocan Stone Circle and Clonca church, retrace the route back to the main Carndonagh–Moville road and turn left, then almost immediately right.

Culdaff has a Blue Flag **beach** that's great for swimming and windsurfing. From Bunagee Pier, sea angling and diving are popular.

McGrory's of Culdaff (☎074-937 9104; www.mcgrorys.ie; bar food €9-20, restaurant mains €14-22; ⏲bar food 12.30-8pm, dinner Tue-Sun, lunch Sun; P) is a raspberry-red village landmark. It has 17 spiffy rooms (single/double from €59/89) decorated with a contemporary eye. Before sleeping, however, head downstairs to catch live music in Mac's Backroom, which books international singer-songwriters and traditional music. McGrory's classic Irish cuisine is the best for miles around.

Inishowen Head

A right turn outside Greencastle leads to Shrove; a sign indicating Inishowen Head is 1km along this road. It's possible to drive or cycle part of the way, but it's also an easy walk to the headland, from where you can see (on a clear day) the Antrim coast as far as the Giant's Causeway. A more demanding walk continues on to the sandy beach of **Kinnagoe Bay**.

Greencastle

POP 530

Seals bob their heads hopefully in the busy little fishing port of Greencastle. The 1305-built Green Castle was a supply base for English armies in Scotland, and for this reason was attacked by Robert Bruce in the 1320s. The castle's vine-netted hulk survives.

An eccentric collection of artefacts can be found at the **Inishowen Maritime Museum & Planetarium** (www.inishowenmaritime.com; museum adult/child €5/3, museum & planetarium €10/6; ⏲9.30am-5.30pm Mon-Sat, noon-5.30pm Sun Easter-Oct), in a former coastguard station next to the harbour. The most fascinating exhibits are from the sunken wrecks of Lough Foyle, including a pair of perfectly preserved military-issue boxer shorts salvaged by marine archaeologists from a ditched WWII bomber. The demise of the Spanish Armada

WASHED-UP TREASURES

Beachcombers will find more than empty shells along the Inishowen Peninsula. The area is renowned for its postglacial strandlines, and its raised beaches continue to rise from the ice age. As a result, the beaches are littered with semiprecious stones: cornelian, agate, jasper and more. Good hunting grounds are the beaches along the northern coast of Malin Head, near Banba's Crown and Ballyhillin.

The stones make unique souvenirs, and you can buy these local treasures artfully polished and made into pendants, bracelets, earrings, brooches, candleholders and other quirky and beautiful items at the workshop of jeweller and craftsperson Petra Watzka at **Malin Pebbles** (www.malinpebbles.com) in Greencastle.

and the departure from these waters of Irish immigrants are two of the museum's more compelling themes. Take care if visiting on a day when local children are testing their homemade rockets out front.

Kealy's Seafood Bar (074-938 1010; The Harbour; lunch mains €8-14.50, dinner mains €16-50; lunch Sat & Sun, dinner Wed-Sun) offers catches so fresh you almost have to fight the harbourside seals for it. The unpretentious nautical-style polished timber decor belies the restaurant's numerous culinary awards. It's a splendid spot for a humble bowl of chowder or a lobster extravaganza.

Local semiprecious stones (see the boxed text, p497) are transformed into jewellery and unusual gifts at **Malin Pebbles** (www.malinpebbles.com; Church Brae), 100m uphill from the ferry.

Lough Swilly (074-912 2863) has two buses Monday to Friday (one on Saturday) from Derry, passing through Greencastle (€7.90, one hour).

Lough Foyle Ferry (074-938 1901; www.loughfoyleferry.com) has a car-ferry service to Magilligan from outside the museum, saving you a 78km drive. Single fares per car/motorcycle/adult/child for the 10-minute crossing cost €12/7.50/2.20/1. It runs every hour on the hour from Greencastle, and at quarter past the hour from Magilligan. The first ferry is at 9am from Greencastle; the last ferry departs Greencastle at 6pm in winter, 8pm in summer. Timetables are posted on the website.

Moville & Around

POP 1427

Essentially a couple of roads beside a harbour, Moville is an elegant spot with old, well-kept buildings. It can be sleepy, but on holiday weekends tourists flood the town. Moville was a busy port during the 19th and early 20th centuries, when thousands of emigrants set sail for America from here.

Main St has several banks with ATMs and the post office.

Sights & Activities

By the gate of the Cooley gravehouse is an unusual 3m-high **cross**. Note the ringhole in its head – through it, the hands of negotiating parties are said to have clasped to seal an agreement. In the graveyard is the **Skull House**, which is associated with St Finian. He lived in a monastery here that was founded by St Patrick and survived into the 12th century. Approaching Moville from the south, look out for a turning on the left for Cooley. The graveyard is just over 1km up this road on the right.

The **coastal walkway** from Moville to Greencastle takes in the stretch of coast where the emigrant steamers used to moor, and also affords some rewarding **birdwatching** opportunities. There's **fishing** off the pier for mackerel, mullet and coalfish.

Festivals & Events

Summer sees a slew of music-oriented festivals, such the **Bob Dylan Festival** and the **Beatles Festival**, both held in July. Check www.visitinishowen.com for details.

Sleeping & Eating

Moville Holiday Hostel HOSTEL €
(074-938 2378; www.movilleholidayhostel.com; Malin Rd; campsites per person €10, dm/d €15/40; P) A private, unpaved road leads off the highway just west of town to a grove of trees and this secluded 20-bed hostel. It's in a nook-and-cranny-filled 18th-century farmhouse beside a river, with some gorgeous spots to pitch a tent. The owner is a fount of info on the area's rich history and folklore. Cash only.

Washington House B&B €€
(074-938 5574; www.washintonhousebandb.com; Ballyrattan, Redcastle; s/d from €50/80; mid-Apr–Sep; P) The five spacious rooms of this new B&B all have queen- or king-size beds and pristine bathrooms. There are wonderful views of Lough Foyle from the patio. The B&B is 5km south of Moville.

Carlton Redcastle Hotel HOTEL €€
(074-938 5555; www.carltonredcastle.ie; s/d from €84/120; P) The peninsula's flashiest luxury resort is along the lough, just south of Moville. Yes, it's part of a chain, but rooms are comfortable and classy, and there's a fine **restaurant** (mains €17-26) overlooking the estuary, plus a decadent spa.

Rosato's ITALIAN €€
(Malin Rd; mains €9-12) This lively pub is the best spot in town for food. It has a good range of pizzas and pasta dishes, and live music on Saturday nights.

Getting There & Away

Lough Swilly (074-912 2863) runs two buses Monday to Friday and one on Saturday to Moville (€6.60, 45 minutes) from Derry.

The Midlands

POPULATION 378,000 / AREA 10,782 SQ KM

Includes »

Best Places to Eat

» Wineport Lodge (p526)

» Glasson Village Restaurant (p526)

» Cottage (p522)

» Left Bank Bistro (p526)

» Oarsman (p522)

Best Places to Stay

» Ballyfin House (p502)

» Castlecoote House (p518)

» Preston House (p501)

» Roundwood House (p502)

» Lough Key House (p517)

Why Go?

Rarely explored by those on their first visit to Ireland and wonderfully free of tour buses and souvenir stalls, the Midlands is brimming with verdant pastoral landscapes, stately homes, archaeological remains and sleepy towns where the locals are genuinely glad to see you. Although the region may not have the scenic drama or sophisticated cities of coastal Ireland, getting lost along its twisting back roads is an unhurried pleasure and you're almost guaranteed to happen upon a local village shop/pub/undertaker's/garage/post office and find it little changed in decades. The Midlands is dominated by the River Shannon, which meanders through fields and forests, drawing boaters and fishers in hordes. Plush hotels and gourmet restaurants have sprung up along its banks, making it a wonderfully scenic and surprisingly cosmopolitan way to travel. If you're in search of a genuine slice of rural Irish life, this area makes the perfect retreat.

When to Go

The Midlands looks its finest in late spring when the fields, hedges and trees glow a lush, radiant green, but the place really comes to life in the summer when you'll find fairs, festivals and special events in towns across the region. It's also the season for cruising the Shannon, the weather is generally better, the days longer and the riverside pubs and restaurants really get into gear. In September, watch out for the Electric Picnic, one of Ireland's best-loved and most eclectic musical festivals.

The Midlands Highlights

1. Slow down a gear and discover the rolling landscapes along the **Shannon–Erne Waterway** (p519)

2. Contemplate the lost land of saints and scholars at Ireland's finest monastic site, **Clonmacnoise** (p509)

3. Nurse a quiet pint in **Morrissey's**, one of Ireland's most atmospheric pubs (p502)

4. Roam the tree-lined streets and explore the castle grounds in elegant **Birr** (p505)

5. Learn about Ireland's greatest disaster at the harrowing Famine Museum at **Strokestown Park House** (p514)

6. Explore the Iron Age oak trackway unearthed at **Corlea** (p524)

7. Wander the corridors and gardens of magnificent **Belvedere House** (p527) and marvel at its spiteful history

COUNTY LAOIS

Little-visited Laois (pronounced leash) is often overlooked as drivers zoom past to sexier sites in the south and west. Away from the main roads, though, is a real hidden corner of Ireland, where historic towns and the unspoiled Slieve Bloom Mountains squeeze in between a patchwork of rivers and walkways.

For all you need to know about Laois, check out www.laoistourism.ie and download the excellent *Laois Heritage Trail* booklet, which does a good job of tying together the county's history. Hard copies are also available at local tourist offices. The handsome heritage town of Abbeyleix makes a much better base than the busy but workaday county town of Portlaoise.

Abbeyleix

POP 1570

Abbeyleix (abbey-*leeks*) is a pretty heritage town with a Georgian market house, graceful terraced housing and a wide leafy main street. The town grew up around a 12th-century Cistercian monastery, but problems with frequent flooding led local 18th-century landowner Viscount de Vesci to level the village and create a new, planned estate town in the present location. During the Famine, de Vesci proved a kinder landlord than many, and the fountain obelisk in the square was erected as a thank you from his tenants.

The town's Georgian character remains intact but, despite the opening of a new bypass, traffic is still heavy. Abbeyleix makes a good base for exploring Laois, with its wonderful food and accommodation options and a chance to sip a pint in one of Ireland's most atmospheric pubs.

Sights

Unfortunately for visitors, de Vesci's magnificent mansion, Abbeyleix House, is in private ownership and is not open to the public. Designed by James Wyatt in 1773, it's an elegant mansion set in roaming parklands 2km southwest of town. It's worth taking a look at the elegant Market House in the town centre, though. Built in 1836, it was recently restored and now houses a library and exhibition space.

Heritage House MUSEUM
(www.abbeyleixheritage.com; adult/child €3/2.50; 9am-5pm Mon-Fri year-round & 1-5pm Sat & Sun May-Sep; P) This museum in an old school building at the northern end of Main St details the town's colourful history. One room looks at the town's carpet-making legacy – the Turkish-influenced carpets once made here were chosen to grace the floors of the *Titanic* – while another showcases the Mulhall Collection, a fascinating selection of memorabilia from the Morrissey family who ran the town's renowned shop and pub from 1775 to 2004. The centre also has a variety of tourist information and a great playground next door.

FREE **Heywood Gardens** GARDEN
(www.heritageireland.ie; 8.30am-9pm May-Aug, to 7pm Apr & Sep, to 5.30pm Oct-Mar; P) Southeast of town, these lavish gardens were landscaped by Edwin Lutyens and Gertrude Jekyll and were completed in 1912. The centrepiece is a sunken garden, where circular terraces lead down to an oval pool with a magnificent fountain.

The gardens are 7km southeast of Abbeyleix, off the R432 to Ballinakill, in the grounds of Heywood Community School.

Abbey Sense Gardens GARDEN
(Dove House, Main St; admission by donation; 9am-4pm Mon-Fri year-round & 2-6pm Sat & Sun Jun-Sep; P) Garden lovers should also make their way to this sensory playground set in the walled gardens of a Brigidine convent. The vibrant planting, wind chimes, humming stone and fragrant blooms aim to stimulate all the senses and are the first of their kind in Ireland.

Sleeping & Eating

Preston House B&B €€
(057-873 1432; www.prestonhouse.ie; Main St; d €85;) A restored Georgian town house on the main street, the grand rooms here are decked out in period style, with dark elegant furniture, big, comfy beds and lashings of charm. With just six guest rooms on offer service is friendly and personal and you'll leave feeling more like a family friend than a paying guest.

Sandymount House B&B €€
(057-873 1063; www.abbeyleix.info; Oldtown; s/d €45/80; P@) Once the home of the de Vesci estate manager, this lovely old country house has been beautifully restored to seamlessly blend modern style with period features. A grand sweeping staircase, marble fireplaces and mature gardens give it an elegant charm, while the spacious rooms are

GETTING AROUND LAOIS

Although the county town of Portlaoise does not merit a visit in itself, it's a useful transport hub. Direct trains run from Portlaoise to Dublin (€22.20, one hour, 14 daily); Cork (€29 to €44, two hours, seven daily) and Limerick (€28.50, 1½ hours, nine daily).

Bus Éireann runs frequent buses on three main routes from Portlaoise: to Cork (€11.70, three hours, six daily) via Abbeyleix, Cashel and Cahir; to Dublin (€9.90, 1½ hours, 12 daily) via Kildare city; and along the N7 to Limerick (€9.90, 2¼ hours, 12 daily) via Mount rath, Borris-in-Ossory and Roscrea.

equipped with flat-screen TVs and individually designed bathrooms. Sandymount House is 2km from Abbeyleix down the R433 towards Rathdowney.

Farran House Farm Hostel HOSTEL €
(☎057-873 4032; www.farmhostel.com; dm €20; P) In a beautifully restored limestone grain loft on a working family farm, this quirky independent hostel has 45 beds in rooms with a bathroom and up to five bunks. When you call, ask for directions and about the possibility of meals, as the hostel is well secluded, about 6km west of Abbeyleix.

McEvoy's FUSION €€
(www.macsabbeyleix.ie; Main St; mains €10-22; ⏲5-10pm Wed-Sat, 1-9pm Sun) Run by the folks from nearby Castle Durrow, this classy wine bar and steak house offers a good choice of international dishes such as Cajun salmon and Thai curries as well as its excellent grills. The ingredients are locally sourced, the interior all tasteful neutrals and as you would expect, the food is cooked to perfection.

Bramleys CAFE €
(www.bramleys.ie; Main St; dishes €5-9.50; ⏲10am-5pm Tue-Sat) You'll find a wonderful selection of soups, salads, hot dishes and tempting desserts at this coffee shop in an upmarket interiors store. It's another top-notch offering from the Castle Durrow team with veg coming from the castle gardens, communal tables weighed down with papers and magazines and some lovely outside seating for sunny days.

Cafe Odhráan CAFE €
(Main St; dishes €4-8; ⏲9.30am-5.30pm Tue-Sat) Small and cosy, with a warm, friendly atmosphere, this simple little place serves up a tempting selection of salads, quiches, crostini, panini and wraps, as well as homemade cakes and scones. Ingredients are locally sourced and include such delicacies as Ballacolla blue brie and Mossfield goat's cheese.

Drinking

TOP CHOICE **Morrissey's** PUB
(Main St) This half-pub, half-shop is one of those increasingly rare places that has withstood the onslaught of modernisation. Ancient biscuit tins, jars of sweets, boxes of tea and a hodgepodge of oddities line the shelves above the pew seats and pot-belly stove. It's a wonderful place to soak up the atmosphere while you cradle a pint at the sloping counter.

Getting There & Away

BUS There are six buses each way daily between Abbeyleix and Dublin (€13, 1¾ hours) and Cork (€13, 2¾ hours). Services run via Portlaoise, Cashel and Cahir.

Durrow

POP 820

Another planned estate village, Durrow's neat rows of houses, pubs and cafes surround a manicured green. On the western side stands the imposing gateway to the 18th-century **Castle Durrow** (☎057-873 6555; www.castledurrow.com; d from €200; P), one of Ireland's top country-house hotels. The rooms here vary from opulent suites with four-poster beds and heavy brocades to more intimate oriental-style rooms. Even if you can't stay overnight, it's worth popping in for a coffee on the terrace overlooking the vast grounds. The excellent **restaurant** (4-course set menu €45; ⏲Wed-Sun) is supplied by the castle's organic kitchen garden.

Durrow is 10km south of Abbeyleix and is accessible by bus (€3.40, 10 minutes, six buses daily in each direction).

Slieve Bloom Mountains

One of the best reasons for visiting Laois is to explore the Slieve Bloom Mountains. Although not as spectacular as some Irish ranges, their sudden rise from a great plain and the absence of visitors make them highly attractive. You'll get a real sense of being away from it all as you tread the deserted blanket bogs, moorland, pine forests and isolated valleys.

For leisurely walking, **Glenbarrow**, southwest of Rosenallis, has an interesting trail by the cascading River Barrow. Other spots to check out are **Glendine Park**, near the Glendine Gap, and the **Cut mountain pass**.

For something more challenging, you could try the **Slieve Bloom Way**, a 77km signposted trail that does a complete circuit of the mountains, taking in most major points of interest. The recommended starting point is the car park at Glenbarrow, 5km from Rosenallis, from where the trail follows tracks, forest firebreaks and old roads around the mountains. The trail's highest point is at Glendine Gap (460m).

You can walk alone or join a guided walk organised by the **Slieve Bloom Walking Club** (☎086 278 9147; www.slievebloom.ie; per person €5; ⌚Sun May-Nov). The website has lots of information on a variety of walks in the mountains and is a good place for initial planning.

There's a good selection of B&Bs in the area but for something more special head for **Roundwood House** (☎057-873 2120; www.roundwoodhouse.com; Slieve Blooms Rd; s/d €80/130; ⌚Feb-Dec; P📶👪), a lush country estate, family home and hotel, where you'll feel like you're a family friend rather than a paying guest. Set in secluded woods, the rooms in this beautiful 17th-century Palladian villa are all elegantly decorated, but have a definite lived-in feel. Children will love all the outdoor space and the friendly dogs, and the communal dinner (€50 per person) is a chance to meet the amiable owners and enjoy a country treat of local foods. Try to get a room in the main house for the best atmosphere and value.

Alternatively, if you're suitably loaded, try **Ballyfin House** (www.ballyfin.com; d from €950), an opulent Regency mansion with lavish interiors. The painstaking eight-year restoration has taken longer than the original build and with 17th-century Flemish tapestries, a Roman sarcophagus bath, secret doorways, a 'whispering room' and a promise that every need shall be catered for, this is Ireland's most exclusive accommodation option. Unfortunately for mere mortals neither the house nor grounds are open to non-residents.

Although there is no public transport across the Slieve Blooms, buses do stop in the nearby towns of Mountrath and Rosenallis.

Mountmellick

POP 2880

A quiet Georgian town lcoated on the River Owenass, Mountmellick was renowned for its linen production in the 19th century and owes much of its history to its Quaker settlers.

A 4km looped and signed **heritage trail**, beginning in the square, leads you on a walking tour of the most important landmarks. For an insight into the town's Quaker and industrial heritage, visit **Mountmellick Museum** (Irishtown; adult/child €5/2; ⌚9am-1pm & 2-5pm Mon-Fri), where you can also see a display of superbly subtle Mountmellick embroidery. Various linens and quilts still being made by locals are on sale here.

Mountmellick is on the N80, 10km north of Portlaoise.

WORTH A TRIP

POVERTY'S LAST STOP AT DONAGHMORE

The farm village of Donaghmore is home to a grim survivor of the Famine. The **Donaghmore Workhouse** (☎086-829 6685; www.donaghmoremuseum.com; adult/child €5/3; ⌚11am-5pm Mon-Fri year-round, plus 2-5pm Sat & Sun Jun-Sep) opened as a last resort for the destitute in 1853. Conditions were intentionally grim, the idea being that if things were especially bad, the poor wouldn't stick around. Overcrowding was rife, families were separated, meals (no more than a bowl of gruel) were taken in silence, toilets were crude and bedding was limited. The loss of dignity that came with entering the workhouse was a tragic reality for many. It was a horrible time, recorded in a chilling fashion at this small museum. The workhouse is just off the R435, 20km west of Durrow.

WORTH A TRIP

ELECTRIC PICNIC

Ireland's answer to Glastonbury, though on a much smaller scale, the annual **Electric Picnic** (www.electricpicnic.ie; 3-day pass €240) is an open-air arts and music festival held over three days in early September. Known for its eclectic line-up, quality services and more mature attitude, it's attracted the likes of Björk, Sigur Rós, Franz Ferdinand, Massive Attack and the Sex Pistols over the years. Apart from the music you'll find a Body & Soul arena, comedy and cinema tents and a silent disco. Tickets are usually sold out months in advance. The festival takes place in the grounds of Stradbally Hall, 10km southeast of Portlaoise.

Portarlington

POP 6010

Portarlington grew up under the influence of French Huguenot and German settlers and has some fine, but neglected, 18th-century buildings along French and Patrick Sts. The 1851 **St Paul's Church** (admission free; ⏲7am-7pm), on the site of the original 17th-century French church, was built for the Huguenots, some of whose tombstones stand in a corner of the churchyard. Portarlington is about 18km northeast of Portlaoise.

About 4km east of town are the impressive ivy-covered ruins of 13th-century **Lea Castle** on the banks of the River Barrow, once the stronghold of Maurice Fitzgerald, second Baron of Offaly. The castle consists of a fairly intact towered keep with two outer walls and a twin-towered gatehouse. Access is through a farmyard, 500m to the north off the main Monasterevin road (R420).

Emo Court

The unusual, green-domed **Emo Court** (www.heritageireland.ie; Emo; adult/child €3/1, grounds free; ⏲10am-6pm Easter-Sep, last admission 5pm, grounds open daylight hr year-round) is an impressive house, designed in 1790 by James Gandon, architect of Dublin's Custom House. It was originally the country seat of the first Earl of Portarlington. After many years as a Jesuit noviciate, the house, with its elaborate central rotunda, was impressively restored.

The extensive grounds, littered with Greek statues, contain over 1000 different trees, including huge sequoias, and shrubs from all over the world. Enjoy a picnic or a long walk through the woodlands to Emo Lake.

Emo is about 13km northeast of Portlaoise, just off the R422, 2km west of the M7.

Rock of Dunamaise

The **Rock of Dunamaise** (admission free; ⏲daylight hr; P) is an arresting sight: a craggy limestone outcrop rising dramatically out of the flat plains. The rock offered early settlers a superb natural defensive position with sweeping views across the surrounding countryside. It was first fortified in the Bronze Age and was recorded on Ptolemy's map of AD 140.

Over the centuries that followed, successive waves of Viking, Norman, Irish and English invaders fought over its occupation and control. The ruins you see today are those of a castle built in the 13th century. It was extensively remodelled in the 15th century and finally destroyed by Cromwell's henchmen in 1650.

You'll need some imagination to envisage the site as it once was, but the views from the summit are breathtaking on a clear day. If you're lucky, you'll be able to see Timahoe round tower to the south, the Slieve Blooms to the west and the Wicklow Mountains to the east.

The rock is situated 6km east of Portlaoise along the Stradbally road (N80).

Timahoe

POP 500

Tiny Timahoe casts a real charm, even if the village is nothing more than a handful of houses fronting a grassy triangle. Screened by a babbling stream and seemingly straight out of a fairy tale, is a tilting 30m-tall, 12th-century **round tower**. The tower, with its unusual carved Romanesque doorway high up on the side, is part of an ancient site that includes the ruins of a 15th-century church. The entire place has a certain magical quality, enhanced by a dearth of visitors.

Timahoe is 13km southeast of Portlaoise on the R426.

COUNTY OFFALY

Apart from the magnificent ecclesiastical city of Clonmacnoise, the green and watery county of Offaly doesn't feature on many tourists' itineraries, though it deserves far greater attention. Steeped in history with numerous castles to visit and the wonderfully atmospheric town of Birr to enjoy, Offaly also offers vast swathes of bog recognised internationally for their plant and animal life, and prime fishing and water sports on the River Shannon and the Grand Canal.

Access www.offaly.ie and www.discoverireland.ie/offaly for more information.

Birr

POP 4100

Feel-good Birr is one of the most attractive towns in the Midlands, with elegant pastel Georgian buildings lining its streets, a magnificent old castle, an excellent choice of accommodation and spirited nightlife with great live music. Despite its appeal, Birr remains off the beaten track and you can enjoy its delights without jostling with the crowds.

In mid-August, the town celebrates its rich history during **Birr Vintage Week and Arts Festival** (www.birrvintageweek.com), with street parades, theatre, music, exhibitions, workshops, guided walks and a traditional fair.

GRAND & ROYAL CANALS

After much debate about linking Dublin to the Shannon by water, work began on the Grand Canal in 1757. The project was beset by problems from the start and encountered huge difficulties and delays. In the meantime, commercial rivals hatched a plan for the competing Royal Canal. The two canals revolutionised transport in Ireland in the early 19th century, but their heyday was short lived, as they were soon superseded by the railways. Today the canals are popular for cruising and fishing, and make wonderfully gentle territory for walking and cycling, with plenty of pretty villages along their banks. With the restoration of the final section of the Royal Canal it is now possible to complete a triangular route from Dublin along the Royal Canal or the Grand Canal to the Shannon and back.

Waterways Ireland (www.waterwaysireland.org) and the **Inland Waterways Association of Ireland** (www.iwai.ie) have a wealth of information on the canals.

Grand Canal

The Grand Canal threads its way from Dublin through Tullamore to join the River Shannon at Shannonbridge, a total of 131km in all. The canal passes through relatively unpopulated countryside, with bogs, picturesque villages and 43 finely crafted locks lining the journey. Near the village of Sallins in County Kildare, the graceful seven-arched **Leinster Aqueduct** carries the canal across the River Liffey. From nearby Robertstown, a 45km spur turns south to join the River Barrow at the pretty town of Athy.

For detailed information on the section of the canal between Robertstown and Lullymore, see p159.

Royal Canal

The 145km Royal Canal follows Kildare's northern border, flowing over a massive **aqueduct** near Leixlip, before it joins the River Shannon at Clondra (or Cloondara) in County Longford. The canal has become a popular amenity for thousands of residents along the north Kildare commuter belt and both the canal and the towpaths are open all the way to the Shannon.

Barges & Boats

You can hire narrow boats at several locations along the canals. Two-/six-berth boats cost from €1090/1935 per week in July and August.

» **Barrowline Cruisers** (www.barrowline.ie; Vicarstown, Co Laois)

» **Canalways** (www.canalways.ie; Rathangan, Co Kildare)

» **Royal Canal Cruisers** (www.royalcanalcruisers.com; Castleknock, Co Dublin)

History

Birr started life as a 6th-century monastic site founded by St Brendan. By 1208 the town had acquired an Anglo-Norman castle, home of the O'Carroll clan who reigned over the surrounding territory.

During the Plantation of 1620, the castle and estate were given to Sir Laurence Parsons. He changed the town's fate by carefully laying out streets, establishing a glass factory and issuing a decree that anyone who 'cast dunge rubbidge filth or sweepings in the forestreet' would be fined four pennies. He also banned barmaids, sentencing any woman caught serving beer to the stocks. The castle has remained in the family for 14 generations, and the present earl and his wife still live on the estate.

Sights

Birr Castle Demesne CASTLE

(www.birrcastle.com; adult/child €9/5; ⏲9am-6pm mid-Mar–Oct, 10am-4pm Nov–mid-Mar) It's easy to spend half a day exploring the attractions and gardens of Birr Castle Demesne. The castle is a private home, however, and cannot be visited. Most of the present building dates from around 1620, with alterations made in the early 19th century.

The 50-hectare castle grounds are famous for their magnificent **gardens** set around a large artificial lake. They hold over 1000 species of plants from all over the world; something always seems to be in bloom. Look for one of the world's tallest box hedges, planted in the 1780s and now standing 12m high, and the romantic Hornbeam cloister.

The Parsons were a remarkable family of pioneering Irish scientists, and their work is documented in the **historic science centre**. Exhibits include the massive **telescope** built by William Parsons in 1845. The 'leviathan of Parsonstown', as it was known, was the largest telescope in the world for 75 years and attracted a wide variety of scientists and astronomers. (It was used to make innumerable discoveries, including the spiral galaxies, and to map the moon's surface.) After the death of William's son, the telescope, unloved and untended, slowly fell to bits. Restoration is currently underway.

Other Buildings & Monuments

Birr has no shortage of first-class Georgian houses; just stroll down tree-lined **Oxmantown Mall** or **John's Mall**, to see some of the best examples.

The tourist office hands out a walking map that details the most important landmarks, including the megalithic **Seffin Stone** (said to be the ancient marker for *Umbilicus Hiberniae* – the Navel of Ireland – used to mark the centre of the country) and **St Brendan's Old Churchyard**, reputedly the site of the saint's 6th-century settlement.

Activities

A beautiful leafy **riverside walk** runs east along the River Camcor from Oxmantown Bridge to Elmgrove Bridge.

If you're feeling more energetic, **Birr Outdoor Education Centre** (www.birroec.ie; Roscrea Rd) offers hill walking and rock climbing in the nearby Slieve Blooms, as well as canoeing and kayaking on local rivers.

Birr Equestrian Centre (www.birrequestrian.ie; Kingsborough House; treks per hr €35), 3km outside Birr on the Clareen road, runs hour-long treks in the surrounding farmland and half-day treks in the Slieve Bloom Mountains.

Sleeping

Brendan House B&B €€

(☎057-912 1818; www.tinjugstudio.com; Brendan St; s/d €55/85) Gloriously eccentric and packed to the gills with knick-knacks, books, rugs, art and antiques, this Georgian town house is a bohemian delight. The three rooms share a bathroom, but the four-poster beds, period charm and artistic style of the place more than make up for this. The owners also run an artists' studio and gallery, offer evening meals on request and can arrange guided mountain walks, castle tours and holistic treatments.

Walcot B&B €€

(☎057-912 1247; www.walcotbedandbreakfast.com; Oxmantown Mall; s/d €60/90; P 👪) This utterly charming Georgian house is set in large gardens in the centre of town. The spacious rooms vary considerably but are decorated in immaculate period style with cast iron, half tester or sleigh beds, antique furniture and heavy curtains. Communal areas are even grander and should make you feel quite regal.

Maltings Guesthouse B&B €€

(☎057-912 1345; www.themaltingsbirr.com; Castle St; s/d from €45/80; P 👪) Based in an 1810 malt storehouse once used by Guinness, this place has a serene location right by the castle and the River Camcor. The 13 simple rooms are spotless, service is friendly and there's a popular restaurant downstairs.

Eating

Riverbank IRISH €€
(☎057-912 1528; riverbankrest@msn.com; Rivers town; mains €14.50-18.50; ⌚closed Mon) This deep-red place set on the banks of the Little Brosna River is well worth the short trip from town for its superb but honest food and friendly atmosphere. There's always a good choice of fish and seafood as well as steaks, grills and traditional favourites on offer. Riverbank is 1.5km south of Birr on the N52.

Thatch FUSION €€€
(☎057-912 0682; www.thethatchcrinkill.com; Crinkill; mains €22-29; ⌚closed Mon; 👪) A traditional thatched Irish pub, just 2km southeast of Birr off the N62, this 200-year-old inn is a great place to sip a pint or enjoy a hearty meal. It's a hugely popular spot for Sunday lunch, when local families gather in force for the simply prepared meats and seafood. Bar food is also available; book in advance.

Emma's Cafe & Deli CAFE €
(31 Main St; meals €5-8; ⌚9.30am-6pm Mon-Sat year-round, 12.30-5.30pm Sun Jun-Aug; 👪) Laid-back and bursting with good food, Emma's is a popular local haunt, serving an interesting range of ciabatta, panini, salads and cakes. There are books and games for children and plenty of tempting deli options for picnics.

Drinking

Chestnut PUB
(Green St) Easily the most appealing pub in the centre, the Chestnut dates to 1823, but has recently been refurbished. The current incarnation mixes dark furniture with a continental cafe style.

Craughwell's PUB
(Castle St) Stop for a snootful at Craughwell's, renowned for its rollicking traditional session on Friday night and impromptu sing-along sessions on Saturday.

☆ Entertainment

Besides the places listed above, you'll find many more humble boozers about Birr.

Melba's Nite Club NIGHTCLUB
(Emmet Sq; ⌚Fri-Sun) In the basement of Dooly's Hotel, this popular club gives a fine insight into the potato-and-stout-fuelled mating habits of rural Ireland.

Birr Theatre & Arts Centre ARTS CENTRE
(www.birrtheatre.com; Oxmantown Hall) A vibrant place with a regular line-up of films, local drama, well-known musicians and more.

Information

The post office is in the northeastern corner of Emmet Sq.

TOURIST INFORMATION Mid-Ireland Tourism (☎057-912 0923; www.midirelandtourism.ie; Brendan St; ⌚9.30am-1pm & 2-5.30pm Mon-Fri) Useful when the tourist office is closed.

Tourist office (☎057-912 0110; Civic Offices, Wilmer Rd; ⌚9.30am-1pm & 2-5.30pm Mon-Sat mid-May–mid-Sep) Good local and regional information.

INTERNET RESOURCES Destination Birr (www.destinationbirr.ie)

Getting There & Away

BUS All buses depart from Emmet Sq. Services run to Dublin (€16, 3½ hours, one daily) via Tullamore, Athlone (€9.80, one hour, four daily Monday to Saturday, two Sunday) and Limerick (€16.50, 1¼ hours, four daily Monday to Saturday, two Sunday).

Kinnitty

POP 340

Kinnitty is a quaint little village that makes a good base for exploring the Slieve Bloom Mountains to the east. Driving out of Kinnitty, the roads across the mountains to Mountrath and Mountmellick, both in County Laois, are particularly scenic.

Look out for the bizarre 10m-high **stone pyramid** in the village graveyard behind the Church of Ireland. In the 1830s, Richard Bernard commissioned this scale replica of the Cheops pyramid in Egypt for the family crypt.

The shaft of the 9th-century **Kinnitty High Cross** was nabbed by Kinnitty Castle in the 19th century and is now displayed on the hotel's terrace. Adam and Eve and the Crucifixion are clearly visible on either face.

Kinnitty Castle (☎057-913 7318; www.kinnittycastlehotel.com; s/d from €95/130), one of Ireland's most renowned mansions, is set on a vast estate and is a former O'Carroll residence rebuilt in neo-Gothic style in the 19th century. A victim of the economic recession, the castle is owned and administered by its bankers but continues to operate as a luxury hotel and wedding venue. Rooms are

WORTH A TRIP

GHOSTS AT LEAP CASTLE

Ireland's most haunted castle, **Leap Castle** (☎086 771 1034; www.leapcastle.net; admission €6; ⏰by arrangement) originally kept guard over a crucial route between Munster and Leinster. The castle was the scene of many dreadful deeds and has quaint features like dank dungeons and a 'Bloody Chapel'. It's famous for its eerie apparitions – the most renowned inhabitant is the 'smelly ghost', a spirit that leaves a horrible stench behind after sightings.

Renovations are ongoing, but you can visit. It lies about 12km southeast of Birr between Kinnitty and Roscrea (in Tipperary) off the R421.

suitably grand and atmospheric. The castle is 3km southeast of town off the R440.

Alternatively try **Ardmore House** (☎057-913 7009; www.kinnitty.com; The Walk; s/d from €55/82; P), a lovely Victorian farmhouse with plenty of old-world charm. The rooms have brass beds, subtle floral patterns, antique furniture and views of the nearby mountains. Turf fires and homemade brown bread complete the cosy, rustic atmosphere. The owners also organise walking tours in the nearby Slieve Bloom Mountains.

Banagher & Around

POP 1640

Sleepy Banagher bursts into life in the summer months when the busy marina is awash with boaters. For the rest of the year, it's a pleasant backwater with pastel-fronted houses marching down the long main street to the banks of the River Shannon where there are some impressive fortifications. Perhaps Banagher's greatest claim to fame, however, is that it was the location for Charlotte Brontë's honeymoon.

Sights

Situated at a crossing point over the River Shannon, Banagher was a place of enormous strategic importance during turbulent times. The hefty fortifications by the bridge include **Cromwell's Castle**, built in the 1650s and modified during the Napoleonic Wars, **Fort Eliza** (a five-sided gun battery whose guardhouse, moat and retaining walls can still be seen), a **military barracks** and **Martello tower**.

St Paul's Church at the far end of Main St contains a resplendent stained-glass window, originally intended for Westminster Abbey.

Activities

Boating

Banagher Marina is a good place to rent cruisers for a trip along the Shannon or the Royal Canal. High season prices for two-/12-berth boats start at about €999/3600. Try **Carrick Craft** (www.cruise-ireland.com) or **Silverline Cruisers** (www.silverlinecruisers.com) for more information.

You can also rent canoes at the marina.

Walking

Head 3km south of Banagher to Lusmagh (just off the R439) to take a tranquil walk down to picturesque **Victoria Lock**, where the Shannon splits into two channels. Cross the lock and walk north along the west bank of the river for 2km to reach 15th-century **Meelick Church**, one of the oldest churches still in use in Ireland. You can also reach Meelick by road. It's about 8km south of Banagher, along tiny tracks on the County Galway side of the border.

Sleeping & Eating

Charlotte's Way B&B €€
(☎057-915 3864; www.charlottesway.com; The Hill; s/d €40/70; P) This tastefully restored former rectory offers four comfy good-value rooms. Breakfasts star eggs fresh from the hens outside. A honeymooning Charlotte Brontë was a frequent visitor and, after her death, her husband Arthur lived here as the rector.

Brosna Lodge Hotel HOTEL €€
(☎057-915 1350; www.brosnalodge.com; Main St; s/d from €50/100; P) This family-run hotel in the centre of town has 14 spacious but rather soulless rooms. The restaurant (mains €14 to €16) serves pretty good food, considering the lack of competition, and you can get bar snacks in the pub.

Flynns Bar & Restaurant IRISH €€
(Main St; mains €9-20) Popular with locals for its grills, steak and pasta, this local bar also has a restaurant at the back serving a decent selection of reliable, if predictable, dishes.

Drinking

JJ Houghs PUB

(Main St) Rivalling the river as Banagher's most appealing feature, Hough's is a 250-year-old vine-clad pub renowned for its music sessions. You'll find someone playing here most nights in summer and at weekends in winter. If there's no live music, you can entertain yourself by poring over the artefact-covered walls or counting stars in the pleasant beer garden.

Getting There & Away

Kearns Transport (www.kearnstransport.com) links Banagher to Birr (€2, 15 minutes), Tullamore (€3, 45 minutes) and Dublin (€10, 2¾ hours) once daily at 8.35am Monday to Saturday and at 6.35pm on Sunday.

Shannonbridge

POP 230

Perfectly picturesque, Shannonbridge gets its name from a narrow 16-span, 18th-century bridge that crosses the river into County Roscommon. It's a small, sleepy village with just one main street and two pubs.

You can't miss the massive 19th-century **fortifications** on the western bank, where heavy artillery was installed to bombard Napoleon in case he was cheeky enough to try to invade by river. The fort has been reincarnated as the **Old Fort Restaurant** (090-967 4973; www.theoldfortrestaurant.com; mains €21.50-29.50; 5-9.30pm Wed-Sat, 12.30-2.30pm Sun), which serves posh nosh in suitably grand surroundings. On a summer evening, a table outside offers beautiful river views.

Don't miss the opportunity to visit **Killeens Village Tavern** (Main St), an old-world pub and shop that is renowned for its warm welcome and lively traditional music. The ceiling of the bar is plastered with old business cards left by customers over the years. There's a music session almost nightly in summer and at weekends during the rest of the year. Traditional pub grub is also available.

Clonmacnoise

Gloriously placed overlooking the River Shannon, **Clonmacnoise** (www.heritageireland.ie; adult/child €6/2; 9am-7pm mid-May–mid-Sep, 10am-5.30pm mid-Sep–mid-May, last admission 45min before closing; P) is one of Ireland's most important ancient monastic cities. The site is enclosed in a walled field and contains numerous early churches, high crosses, round towers and graves in astonishingly good condition. The surrounding marshy area is known as the **Shannon Callows**, home to many wild plants and one of the last refuges of the seriously endangered corncrake (a pastel-coloured relative of the coot).

WORTH A TRIP

SHANNON HARBOUR & AROUND

Just 1km east of where the Grand Canal joins the River Shannon, sleepy Shannon Harbour is a tiny but picturesque town that was once a thriving trading centre. A purpose-built village constructed to serve the waterways, it was home to over 1000 people in its heyday. Along with cargo boats, passenger barges ran from here, many of which took poor locals on their first leg of a long journey to North America or Australia.

Today the waterways are again teeming with boats and walking paths stretching in all directions, making Shannon Harbour an interesting stop for walkers, fishers, boaters and birders.

The village is about 10km northeast of Banagher off the R356. Nearby, 16th-century **Clonony Castle** (087 761 4034; www.clononycastle.ie; admission by donation; by appointment May-Dec), a fortified tower house, is enclosed by a castellated wall. Tales that Henry VIII's second wife, Anne Boleyn, was born here are unlikely to be true, but her cousins Elizabeth and Mary Boleyn are buried beside the ruins. Restoration of the first two floors of the castle is complete and the owner is happy to welcome visitors.

Not far from the castle, the **Rectory** (090-645 7293; www.therectory.ie; Deerpark; s/d €47.50/75; P) is a really lovely old house set in mature gardens. The tranquil guest rooms are lovingly decorated in neutral tones, with crisp white linens and a touch of period style. Deerpark is off the R357, 1.5km from Clonony Castle.

History

Roughly translated, Clonmacnoise (Cluain Mhic Nóis) means 'Meadow of the Sons of Nós'. The marshy land in the area would have been impassable for early traders, who instead chose to travel by water or on eskers (raised ridges formed by glaciers). When St Ciarán founded a monastery here in AD 548, it was the most important crossroads in the country, the intersection of the north–south River Shannon, and the east–west Esker Riada (Highway of the Kings).

The giant ecclesiastical city had a humble beginning and Ciarán died just seven months after building his first church. Over the years, however, Clonmacnoise grew to become an unrivalled bastion of Irish religion, literature and art and attracted a large lay population. Between the 7th and 12th centuries, monks from all over Europe came to study and pray here, helping to earn Ireland the title of the 'land of saints and scholars'. Even the high kings of Connaught and Tara were brought here for burial.

Most of what you can see today dates from the 10th to 12th centuries. The monks would have lived in small huts scattered in and around the monastery, which would probably have been surrounded by a ditch or rampart of earth.

The site was burned and pillaged on numerous occasions by both the Vikings and the Irish. After the 12th century it fell into decline, and by the 15th century it was home only to an impoverished bishop. In 1552 the English garrison from Athlone reduced the site to a ruin: it was reported at the time that 'not a bell, large or small, or an image, or an altar, or a book, or a gem, or even glass in a window, was left which was not carried away'.

Among the treasures that survived the continued onslaughts are the crosier of the abbots of Clonmacnoise in the National Museum in Dublin, and the 12th-century *Leabhar na hUidhre* (The Book of the Dun Cow), now in the Royal Irish Academy in Dublin.

Sights

Museum MUSEUM

Three connected conical huts near the entrance, which now house the museum, echo the design of early monastic dwellings. The centre's 20-minute audiovisual show is an excellent introduction to the site.

The exhibition area contains the original high crosses (replicas have been put in their former locations outside), and various artefacts uncovered during excavation, including silver pins, beaded glass and an Ogham stone. It also contains the largest collection

GRAZING YOUR WAY ALONG THE SHANNON

Cruising along the Shannon is a wonderful way to see some hidden corners of Ireland. It attracts a leisurely crowd of boaters keen to relax, enjoy the views and eat well. Gastropubs and gourmet restaurants have popped up all along the river banks, making a cruise along the Shannon a tempting way to sample the spoils of the lush Midlands pastures. Try Athlone and Carrick-on-Shannon for a great choice of fine-dining options or venture further afield to try some of the following:

Glasson Village Restaurant (p526; 090-648 5001; michaelrosebrooks@gmail.com; Glasson, Co Westmeath; mains €20-30; closed dinner Sun;) Pioneering gourmet restaurant with an informal atmosphere, specialising in seafood.

Keenans (043-332 6052; www.keenans.ie; Tarmonbarry, Co Roscommon; mains €15-29; closed dinner Sun) Spacious, modern restaurant with high ceilings, river views and wholesome, unpretentious food.

Old Fort Restaurant (p509; 090-967 4973; www.theoldfortrestaurant.com; Shannonbridge, Co Roscommon; mains €21.50-29.50; 5-9.30pm Wed-Sat, 12.30-2.30pm Sun) Posh nosh in the grand surroundings of a massive bridgehead, built as defence against Napoleon.

Purple Onion (043-335 9919; www.purpleonion.ie; Tarmonbarry, Co Roscommon; mains €14-24; dinner Tue-Sun, lunch Sun) Popular old-world pub with great service and solid food.

Wineport Lodge (p526; 090-643 9010; www.wineport.ie; Glasson, Co Westmeath; mains €24-33) A deservedly popular fine-dining spot, serving an ambitious international menu.

Clonmacnoise

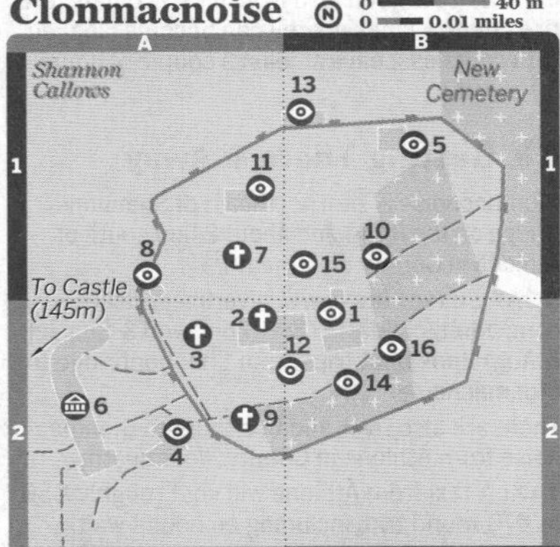

of early Christian grave slabs in Europe. Many are in remarkable condition, with inscriptions clearly visible, often starting with *oroit do* or *ar* (a prayer for).

There's a real sense of drama as you descend to the foot of the imposing sandstone **Cross of the Scriptures**, one of Ireland's finest. It's very distinctive, with unique upward-tilting arms and richly decorated panels depicting the Crucifixion, the Last Judgement, the arrest of Jesus, and Christ in the tomb.

Only the shaft of the **North Cross**, which dates from around AD 800, remains. It is adorned by lions, convoluted spirals and a single figure, thought to be the Celtic god Cernunnos (or Cernenus), who sits in a Buddha-like position. The richly decorated **South Cross** has mostly abstract carvings – swirls, spirals and fretwork – and, on the western face, the Crucifixion plus a few odd cavorting creatures.

Cathedral CHURCH

The biggest building at Clonmacnoise, the cathedral was originally built in AD 909, but was significantly altered and remodelled over the centuries. Its most interesting feature is the intricate 15th-century Gothic doorway with carvings of Sts Francis, Patrick and Dominic. A whisper carries from one side of the door to the other, and this feature was supposedly used by lepers to confess their sins without infecting the priests.

The last high kings of Tara – Turlough Mór O'Connor (died 1156) and his son Ruairí (Rory; died 1198) – are said to be buried near the altar.

Clonmacnoise

Sights

1 Bullaun B2
2 Cathedral A2
3 Cross of the Scriptures (King Flann's Cross) A2
4 Entrance A2
5 Mass Shelter B1
6 Museum A2
7 North Cross A1
8 O'Rourke's Tower A1
9 South Cross A2
10 Temple Ciaran B1
11 Temple Conner A1
12 Temple Doolin B2
13 Temple Finghin & Tower B1
14 Temple Hurpan B2
15 Temple Kelly B1
16 Temple Melaghlin B2

Temples CHURCH

The small churches are called temples, a derivation of the Irish word *teampall* (church). The little, roofed church is **Temple Connor**, still used by Church of Ireland parishioners on the last Sunday of the summer months. Walking towards the cathedral, you'll pass the scant foundations of **Temple Kelly** (1167) before reaching tiny **Temple Ciarán**, reputed to be the burial place of St Ciarán, the site's founder.

The floor level in Temple Ciarán is lower than outside because local farmers have been taking clay from the church for centuries to protect their crops and cattle. The floor has been covered in slabs, but handfuls of clay are still removed from outside the church in the early spring.

Near the temple's southwestern corner is a *bullaun* (ancient grinding stone), supposedly used for making medicines for the monastery's hospital. Today the rainwater that collects in it is said to cure warts.

Continuing round the compound you come to the 12th-century **Temple Melaghlin**, with its attractive windows, and the twin structures of **Temple Hurpan** and **Temple Doolin**.

Round Towers HISTORIC BUILDING

Overlooking the River Shannon is the 20m-high **O'Rourke's Tower**. Lightning blasted the top off the tower in 1135, but the remaining structure was used for another 400 years.

Temple Finghin and its round tower are on the northern boundary of the site, also overlooking the Shannon. The building dates from around 1160 and has some fine Romanesque carvings. The herringbone-patterned tower roof is the only one in Ireland that has never been altered. Most round towers became shelters when the monasteries were attacked, but this one was probably just used as a bell tower since the doorway is at ground level.

Other Remains HISTORIC BUILDINGS
Beyond the site's boundary wall, about 500m east through the modern graveyard, is the secluded **Nun's Church**. From here the main site, including the towers, is not visible. The church has wonderful Romanesque arches with minute carvings; one has been interpreted as Ireland's earliest sheila-na-gig, in an acrobatic pose with feet tucked behind the ears.

To the west of the site, on the ridge near the car park, is a motte with the oddly shaped ruins of a 13th-century **castle**, built by John de Grey, bishop of Norwich, to watch over the Shannon.

Sleeping & Eating

Kajon House B&B €€
(☎090-967 4191; www.kajonhouse.ie; Creevagh; d from €70; ⊙Mar-Oct; P) If you want to stay near the ruins, this is your best option, just 1.5km from the ruins on the road signposted to Tullamore. It's an incredibly friendly place with cosy rooms, a spacious yard with a picnic table and evening meals on offer. You can even have pancakes for breakfast.

Shopping

Core Craft Centre CRAFT CENTRE
(www.corecrafteddesign.com; Old School House, Ballinahown; ⊙10am-6pm Mon-Fri, 11am-6pm Sat) On your way to Clonmacnoise, it's worth stopping here in Ballinahown, to browse the range of contemporary craftwork, bog oak sculpture and pottery on offer. There's an excellent range of items on display and prices are more reasonable than in city craft shops. Ballinahown is on the N62, about 10km from Clonmacnoise.

Information

There's an excellent on-site museum and cafe, and there's a regional **tourist office** (☎090-967 4134; ⊙10am-5.45pm mid-Mar–Oct) near the entrance. If you want to avoid summer crowds, it's a good idea to visit early or late; the tiny country lanes nearby can become clogged with coaches. Leave at least a couple of hours for a visit.

Getting There & Away

Clonmacnoise is 7km northeast of Shannonbridge on the R444 and about 24km south of Athlone in County Westmeath.

BOAT Silver Line (www.silverlinecruisers.com; adult/child €12/8; ⊙2pm Wed & Sun Jul & Aug) Runs boat trips from Shannonbridge to Clonmacnoise.

There are also river and bus tours to Clonmacnoise from Athlone in County Westmeath.

TAXI A taxi from Athlone will cost roughly €50 to €70 round trip, including an hour's wait.

Tullamore

POP 10,900

Tullamore, Offaly's county town, is a bustling but workaday place with a pleasant setting on the Grand Canal. The town is most famous for Tullamore Dew whiskey, although production has long since moved to County Tipperary. You can still visit the old distillery and have a dram of the amber liquid.

Sights

Tullamore Dew Heritage Centre INDUSTRIAL MUSEUM
(www.tullamore-dew.org; Bury Quay; adult/child €6/3.50; ⊙9am-6pm Mon-Sat & noon-5pm Sun May-Sep, 10am-5pm Mon-Sat & noon-5pm Sun Oct-Apr) Located in a 19th-century canalside warehouse, the heritage centre mixes intriguing local history with booze propaganda. Fortunately, the emphasis is on the former and engaging exhibits show the role of the Grand Canal in the town's development. At the end of the tour you'll get to sample what is supposedly the easiest of Irish whiskeys to drink.

Charleville Castle HISTORIC BUILDING
(☎057-932 3040; www.charlevillecastle.ie; guided tours €30, minimum 4 adults; ⊙tours noon-5pm Jun-Aug, by appointment Sep-Apr & mornings Jun-Aug) Spires, turrets, clinging ivy and creaking trees combine to give this hulking structure a haunted feel. Charleville Castle was the family seat of the Burys, who commissioned the design in 1798 from Francis Johnston, one of Ireland's most famous architects. The interior is spectacular, with stunning ceilings, one of the most striking Gothic-revival

TOP 10 TRADITIONAL MIDLANDS PUBS

These charming old-world pubs range from popular tourist haunts to undiscovered gems in little-visited backwaters where nothing has changed in decades.

Morrissey's (p502; Abbeyleix, County Laois) Half-pub, half-shop, Morrissey's is a local institution, complete with a pot-belly stove, sloping counter and shelves decked out with a clutter of curios.

Gunnings (Rathconrath, County Westmeath) Utterly unchanged and unadorned, Gunnings, on the R392 between Ballymahon and Mullingar, is kitted out with ancient stools, cracked lino and yellowing cereal packets; it doesn't get much more authentic than this.

JJ Houghs (p509; Banagher, County Offaly) A 250-year-old pub hung with vines and plastered with knick-knacks, this place is famed for its traditional music.

MJ Henry (Cootehall, County Roscommon) An unadulterated grocery store and pub, Henry's, off the N4 between Boyle and Carrick-on-Shannon, is full of character and little changed since the '70s.

Magans (Killashee, County Longford) Delightful old bar, grocery and hardware store in a tiny village well off the beaten track, on the N63 between Lanesborough and Longford.

Killeens Village Tavern (p509; Shannonbridge, County Offaly) Run by a family of music lovers, this bustling place is well known for its lively traditional sessions and warm welcome.

Mary Lynch's (Coralstown, County Westmeath) An unassuming old-fashioned pub off the N4 between Mullingar and Kinnegad, Lynch's is a perfect place for a pint overlooking the Grand Canal.

Sean's Bar (p526; Athlone, County Westmeath) Ancient pub with log fires, sawdust-strewn floors, a rickety piano and a riverside beer garden.

Coffeey's (Lecarrow, County Roscommon) The centre of the village community and renowned for its craic, Coffeey's, on the N61 between Roscommon and Athlone, is all about the people.

Village Inn (Coolrain, County Laois) This thatched old-style pub at the foot of the Slieve Bloom Mountains, off the N7 between Mountrath and Borris-in-Ossory, is renowned for its traditional music and set dancing.

galleries in Ireland and a kitchen block built to resemble a country church.

Admission is by 35-minute tour only. If you'd like to help restore this pile, you can join groups of international volunteers; contact the castle for details. The entrance is off the N52, south of Tullamore. Frustration ensues if you go too far and reach Blue Ball, a village with hairy traffic.

Sleeping & Eating

Ask at the tourist office for a list of local B&Bs.

Annaharvey Farm B&B €€

(☎057-934 3544; www.annaharveyfarm.ie; Aharney; s/d from €55/90; P 👪) This tranquil equestrian centre and guesthouse is a great place to enjoy a bit of country life and genuine hospitality. The rooms are all tastefully decorated in contemporary neutrals, and there's a choice of family rooms and horse riding on your doorstep. The farm is 6km southeast of Tullamore on the R420.

Sea Dew B&B €€

(☎057-935 2054; www.seadewguesthouse.com; Clonminch Rd; s/d from €45/70; P @ 👪) A purpose-built guesthouse just five minutes' walk from the town centre, this welcoming place has 12 spacious but cosy rooms. There's a lovely outdoor deck in the mature gardens and a play area for children. The guesthouse is just south of the town centre, off the N80.

Sirocco's ITALIAN €€

(☎057-935 2839; Patrick St; mains €12-25; ⊙lunch Thu, Fri & Sun, dinner Mon-Sat; 👪) Serving a good selection of fresh pasta and pizza, as well as meat, chicken and fish dishes, this simple little Italian bistro is a local favourite. Booking ahead is advised.

WORTH A TRIP

LOUGH BOORA

Much of County Offaly's once extensive bogs were stripped of peat for electricity generation during the 20th century. One area, **Lough Boora** (www.loughbooraparklands.com), is now the focus of a scheme to restore its environment. Located 5km west of Blue Ball off the R357, there are over 50km of trails across the area with excellent birdwatching, rare flora, a mesolithic site and a series of impressive environmental **sculptures** (www.sculptureintheparklands.com) to explore.

Information

Tourist office (057-935 2617; tullamoredhc@eircom.net; Bury Quay; 9am-6pm Mon-Sat & noon-5pm Sun May-Sep, 10am-5pm Mon-Sat & noon-5pm Sun Oct-Apr) In the Tullamore Dew Heritage Centre.

Getting There & Away

BUS There are buses to Dublin (€14.40, 2½ hours, five weekdays, three Saturday and Sunday) and Waterford (€18.90, 3¼ hours, two daily) via Portlaoise, Carlow and Kilkenny. Buses stop at the train station.

TRAIN There are trains east to Dublin (€19, 1¼ hours, 12 daily) and west to Galway (€15, 1½ hours, eight daily), as well as Westport and Sligo. The station is on the southwest edge of the centre on Cormac St.

Durrow Abbey

Founded by St Colmcille (also known as St Columba) in the 6th century, Durrow Abbey is most famous for producing the illustrated *Book of Durrow*. The 7th-century text is the earliest of the great manuscripts to have survived – a remarkable feat considering it was recovered from a farm where it was dipped in the cattle's drinking water to cure illnesses. It can be seen at Trinity College, Dublin.

The site contains five early-Christian gravestones and Durrow's splendid 10th-century **high cross**, whose complex, high relief carvings depict the sacrifice of Isaac, the Last Judgement and the Crucifixion; it was possibly created by the same stonemason who carved the Cross of the Scriptures at Clonmacnoise. A laborious process of restoration is underway and some areas may be closed to visitors.

The path north past the church leads to **St Colmcille's Well**, a place of pilgrimage marked by a small cairn.

Durrow Abbey is 7km north of Tullamore down a long lane west off the N52.

COUNTY ROSCOMMON

Studded with over 5000 megalithic tombs, ring forts and mounds, and home to a couple of excellent museums, Roscommon is a haven for history buffs. Add to the mix a couple of well-preserved mansions and some wonderful monastic ruins and it's hard to understand why the county sees so few visitors. Beyond the romance of times past, Roscommon has plenty of rolling countryside littered with lakes and cleaved by the Rivers Shannon and Suck – attributes much appreciated by visiting anglers.

Strokestown & Around

POP 780

Strokestown's main street is a grand tree-lined avenue that remains a testament to the lofty aspirations of one of the local landed gentry who wished it to be Europe's widest. It's a striking feature in what is a now a sleepy town most notable for its historic estate and famine museum.

Over the May Day Bank Holiday weekend, the town bursts into life during the **International Poetry Festival** (www.strokestownpoetry.org).

Sights

Strokestown Park House & Famine Museum HISTORIC BUILDING
(www.strokestownpark.ie; admission house, museum & gardens €12, house or museum or gardens €8; 10.30am-5.30pm) At the end of Strokestown's main avenue, three Gothic arches lead to Strokestown Park House.

The original 12,000-hectare estate was granted by King Charles II to Nicholas Mahon for his support in the English Civil War. Nicholas' grandson Thomas commissioned Richard Cassels to build him a Palladian mansion in the early 18th century. Over the centuries, the estate decreased in size along with the family's fortunes. When it was eventually sold in 1979, it had been whittled down to 120 hectares. The estate was bought as a complete lot, so virtually all of its remaining contents are intact.

Admission to the house is by a 45-minute **guided tour**, taking in a galleried kitchen with state-of-the-art clockwork machinery, and a child's bedroom complete with 19th-century toys and fun-house mirrors.

The **walled garden** contains the longest herbaceous border in Ireland and Britain, which blooms in a rainbow of colours in summer.

In direct and deliberate contrast to the splendour of the house and its grounds is the harrowing **Strokestown Famine Museum**, which sheds light on the devastating 1840s potato blight. There's a huge amount of information to take in, with long panels of text that require some concentration, but you'll emerge with an unblinking insight into the starvation of the poor, and the ignorance, callousness and cruelty of those who were in a position to help. Strokestown landlord Major Denis Mahon ruthlessly evicted starving peasants who couldn't pay their rent, chartering boats to transport them away from Ireland. Almost 600 of these 1000 emigrants died on the overcrowded 'coffin ships'. Perhaps unsurprisingly, Mahon was assassinated by some of his tenants in 1847. The museum also opens visitors' eyes to present-day famine around the world. Allow at least half a day to see the house, museum and gardens.

Cruachan Aí Visitor Centre HISTORIC SITE
(www.rathcroghan.ie; Tulsk; adult/child €5/3; ⏲9am-5pm Mon-Sat) Anyone with an interest in Celtic mythology will be enthralled by the area around the village of Tulsk, which contains 60 ancient national monuments including standing stones, barrows, cairns and fortresses, making it the most important Celtic royal site in Europe.

The landscape and its sacred structures have lain largely undisturbed for the past 3000 years. It's hard to grasp just how significant the site is, as archaeological digs are continuing, but it has already been established that the site is bigger and older than Tara in County Meath and was at one time a major seat of Irish power. The site is currently being considered for Unesco World Heritage status.

The visitor centre has audiovisual displays and informative panels and maps that explain the significance of the sites, and can let you know the current status of access to the (privately owned) monuments.

According to the legend of Táin Bó Cúailnge (Cattle Raid of Cooley), Queen Maeve (Medbh) had her palace at Cruachan. The Oweynagat Cave (Cave of the Cats), believed to be the entrance to the Celtic otherworld, is also nearby. If you dare to enter, look closely at the stones by the entrance where you'll find the 1911 graffiti of Ireland's first president, Douglas Hyde.

Tulsk is 10km west of Strokestown on the N5. Bus Éireann's frequent Dublin to Westport route stops right outside the visitor centre.

Boyle & Around

POP 1600

A quiet town at the foot of the Curlew Mountains, Boyle is a scenic and worthwhile stop, home to beautiful Boyle Abbey, a 4000-year-old dolmen, the hands-on King House Interpretive Centre, and an island-scattered forest park.

If you're here at the end of July, you can catch the lively **Boyle Arts Festival** (www.boylearts.com), which features music, theatre, storytelling and contemporary Irish art exhibitions.

History

The history of Boyle is the history of the King family. In 1603 Staffordshire-born John King was granted land in Roscommon with the aim of 'reducing the Irish to obedience'. Over the next 150 years, through canny marriages and cold-blooded conquests, his descendants made their name and fortune, becoming one of the largest landowning families in Ireland. The town of Boyle grew around their estate.

King House was built in 1730, and in 1780 the family moved to the grander Rockingham House, built in what is now Lough Key Forest Park. Unfortunately, the house was destroyed by fire in 1957.

Actress Maureen O'Sullivan (Mia Farrow's mother) was born in a house on Main St opposite the Bank of Ireland in 1911.

Sights

FREE **King House Interpretive Centre** HISTORIC BUILDING
(www.kinghouse.ie; Main St; ⏲11am-4pm Tue-Sat Apr-Sep) After the King family moved to Lough Key, the imposing Georgian mansion King House became a military barracks for the fearsome Connaught Rangers. The

county council bought the property in 1987, and spent several years and €3.8 million turning it into the inspired King House Interpretive Centre.

Sinister-looking dummies from various eras tell the turbulent history of the Connaught kings, the town of Boyle and the King family, including a grim tale of tenant eviction during the Famine. Kids can try on replica ancient Irish cloaks, brooches and leather shoes, write with a quill, play a regimental drum and build a vaulted ceiling from specially designed blocks.

The mansion's sheltered walled courtyard hosts an **organic market** (⌚10am-2pm Sat) selling a fantastic array of organic meat, fish, vegetables, cheeses, chutneys and breads, as well as hot soups to warm you up.

Boyle Abbey HISTORIC BUILDING
(www.heritageireland.ie; adult/child/family €3/1/8; ⌚10am-6pm Easter-late Oct, last admission 45 min before closing) Gracing the River Boyle is the finely preserved (and reputedly haunted) Boyle Abbey. Founded in 1161 by monks from Mellifont in County Louth, the abbey captures the transition from Romanesque to Gothic style, best seen in the nave, where a set of arches in each style face each other. Unusually for a Cistercian building, figures and carved animals decorate the capitals to the west. After the Dissolution of the Monasteries, the abbey was occupied by the military and became Boyle Castle; the stone chimney on the southern side of the abbey, which was once the refectory, dates from that period.

Guided 40-minute tours of the abbey are available on the hour until 5pm.

Lough Key Forest Park HISTORIC PARK
(www.loughkey.ie; forest admission free, parking €4; ⌚10am-6pm Apr-Aug, 10am-5pm Fri-Sun Sep-Mar) Sprinkled with small islands, Lough Key Forest Park has long been popular for its picturesque ruins, including a 12th-century abbey on tiny Trinity Island and a 19th-century castle on Castle Island. It's also a time-honoured favourite with families for its wishing chair, bog gardens, fairy bridge and viewing tower. There are plenty of marked walking trails through the park.

The 350-hectare park was once part of the Rockingham estate, owned by the King family from the 17th century until 1957. Rockingham House, designed by John Nash, was destroyed by a fire in the same year; all that remains are some stables, outbuildings and eerie tunnels leading to the lake – built to hide the servants from view.

The park recently received a boost with the addition of a **visitor centre**, and the **Lough Key Experience** (adult/child €7.50/5), incorporating a panoramic, 250m-long treetop canopy walk, which rises 7m above the woodland floor and offers superb lake views. Other attractions include the **Boda Borg Challenge** (€13, minimum 3 people) – a series of rooms filled with activities and puzzles (great for sudden bursts of rain); and an outdoor **adventure playground** (adult/child free/€5).

In July and August, **Lough Key Boats** (www.loughkeyboats.com) provides waterskiing lessons, hourly commentated boat trips, rowing-boat hire and fishing advice (record-breaking pike have been caught here).

Lough Key is 4km east of Boyle on the N4. The Bus Éireann Sligo to Dublin route has frequent services from Boyle to Lough Key.

FREE **Drumanone Dolmen** MONUMENT
This astonishing portal dolmen, one of the largest in Ireland, measures 4.5m by 3.3m and was constructed before 2000 BC. It can be tricky to find: follow Patrick St and then the R294 out of town for 5km, until you pass under a railway arch. A sign indicates the path across the railway line. Take care crossing as trains are frequent.

FREE **Douglas Hyde Interpretive Centre** MUSEUM
(☎094-987 0016; dogara@roscommoncoco.ie; Frenchpark; ⌚11am-5pm Mon-Fri 2-6pm Sat & Sun Jul & Aug or by appointment) The life of Roscommon native Dr Douglas Hyde (1860–1949), poet, writer and first president of Ireland, is celebrated at the Douglas Hyde Interpretive Centre. Outside the political arena, Hyde co-founded the Gaelic League in 1893 and spent a lifetime gathering Gaelic poems and folklore that might otherwise have been lost forever.

The centre is housed in the former Protestant church at Frenchpark, 12km southwest of Boyle on the R361. Call ahead to make sure it's open.

Arigna Mining Experience HISTORIC SITE
(www.arignaminingexperience.ie; adult/child €10/6; ⌚10am-5pm) Ireland's first and last coal mine (1600s to 1990) is remembered at the Arigna Mining Experience, set in the hills above Lough Allen. The highlight is the 40-minute

underground tour, which takes you 400m down to the coal face. Tours are led by ex-miners who really bring home the gruelling working conditions and dangers of their job. Wear sturdy shoes as it can be wet and muddy underfoot.

Activities

Covering 118km of north Roscommon, east Sligo and mid-Leitrim, the **Arigna Miners Way & Historical Trail** is a series of well-signposted tracks and hill passes covering the routes taken by miners on their way to work. A guidebook with detailed maps is available from local tourist offices.

Sleeping

Boyle is blessed with a clutch of great B&Bs to choose from.

Lough Key House B&B €€
(☎071-966 2161; www.loughkeyhouse.com; Rockingham; s/d from €50/85; P@) This beautifully restored Georgian country house is a wonderfully atmospheric place to stay, with three guest rooms, each individually decorated with period furniture and tasteful, elegant style. Eggs for breakfast come from the owner's hens, there are bikes to borrow and, if you arrive by bus, you can get picked up from town. Lough Key House is 5km east of town on the N4.

Forest Park House B&B €€
(☎071-966 2227; www.bed-and-breakfast-boyle.com; Rockingham; s/d €45/80; P) Slightly out of town near the entrance to Forest Park, this purpose-built guesthouse has spacious modern rooms with pine woodwork and crisp white linens. The B&B is 4km east of town on the N4.

Cesh Corran B&B €€
(☎071-966 2265; www.marycooney.com; Abbey Tce; s/d €55/80; P) Overlooking the abbey ruins, this immaculately kept place has bright, simple rooms and a very warm welcome. There's a garden, wholesome breakfasts and even a separate bait fridge for anglers.

Lough Key Caravan & Camping Park CAMPGROUND €
(www.loughkey.ie; campsites per person €12; Apr-Aug) Right inside the picturesque Lough Key Forest Park, excellent facilities at this campground include a recreation room, a laundry and a children's play area.

Eating

Boyle has the usual array of Chinese and fast-food restaurants, but not a lot of choice apart from that. Carrick-on-Shannon is a much better place to eat out.

Moving Stairs MEDITERRANEAN €€
(The Crescent; mains €14-18; 5-10pm Wed-Sun) The best spot to eat in town, this pub-restaurant serves a good selection of steaks, chicken dishes and a decent Moroccan lamb tagine. It's also the liveliest place in town in the evenings with regular live music.

Stone House Cafe CAFE €
(Bridge St; lunch €5-8; 10am-6pm Mon-Sat) This little building on the river was once the gate lodge to the private mansion Frybrook House. The cafe serves a selection of soups, sandwiches, panini and cakes, which you can enjoy as the water rushes by.

Drinking & Entertainment

Wynne's Bar PUB
(Main St) This quaint old bar in the centre of town is famous for its traditional music sessions on Friday nights. Come early if you want a seat.

Information

Úna Bhán Tourism Cooperative (☎071-966 3033; www.unabhan.net; 9am-6pm daily May-Aug, 9am-5pm Mon-Fri Sep-Apr) A local cooperative in the grounds of King House.

Getting There & Away

BUS Coaches between Dublin (€17.10, 3½ hours) and Sligo (€10.26, 45 minutes) stop off at Boyle en route. There are six buses daily Monday to Saturday, five on Sunday. Buses pull up near King House.

TRAIN Trains leave eight times daily to Sligo (€14.70, half an hour) and Dublin (€27.50, 2½ hours) via Mullingar. The station is on Elphin St.

Roscommon Town

POP 5020

The county town of Roscommon is very much a place of local business and commerce, but it has a small, stately centre, some significant abbey and castle ruins and a couple of really lovely accommodation options that make it well worth a stop. Unfortunately, mindless planners have allowed developers to line the town's ring road with faceless retail developments.

Sights

Roscommon's central square is dominated by its former courthouse (now the Bank of Ireland). Opposite, the facade of the **old jail** survives. Ask any local about the grim tale of Lady Betty, its infamous hang woman.

Roscommon Castle HISTORIC BUILDING
(dawn-dusk) The impressive ruins of the town's Norman castle stand alone in a field to the north of town, beautifully framed by the landscaped lawns and small lake of the new town park. Built in 1269, the castle was almost immediately destroyed by Irish forces, and its turbulent history continued until the final surrender to Cromwell in 1652. The massive walls and round bastions are a reminder of how significant this fortress once was.

Roscommon County Museum MUSEUM
(The Square; adult/child €2/1; 10am-3pm Mon-Fri Jun–mid-Sep) Set in a former Presbyterian church, this museum contains some interesting pieces, including an inscribed 9th-century slab from St Coman's monastery and a superb medieval sheila-na-gig. The unusual Star of David window supposedly represents the Trinity.

Dominican Priory HISTORIC BUILDING
(dawn-dusk) At the southern end of town, off Circular Rd, the remains of a 13th-century priory are almost hidden behind a primary school. The priory merits a quick visit for its unusual 15th-century carving of eight *gallóglí* ('gallowglasses', who were mercenary soldiers). Wielding seven swords and an axe, they protect an earlier effigy of the priory's founder, Felim O'Connor, set in the north wall.

La Téne Stone MONUMENT
A rare Iron Age spiral-inscribed stone can be seen on private land in Castle strange, 7km southwest of town on the R366.

Activities

Pick up a brochure and map at the tourist office detailing the **Suck Valley Way**, a 75km walking trail along the River Suck, for some pleasant strolls along the river bank. It's a popular spot with anglers for its abundance of rudd, tench, pike and perch.

Sleeping & Eating

TOP CHOICE **Castlecoote House** BOUTIQUE HOTEL €€
(090-666 3794; www.castlecootehouse.com; Castlecoote; s/d from €99/158; P) This beautifully restored Georgian mansion has five impossibly romantic rooms with antique furnishings and views over the orchard, ruined castle or river. Expect marble fireplaces, four-poster beds, chandeliers and croquet on the lawn. The house is about 8km southwest of Roscommon. Take the R366 signposted to Fuerty and follow it to Castlecoote. As you go over the bridge into the village, the double gates of Castlecoote House are on your right.

Gleeson's B&B €€
(090-662 6954; www.gleesonstownhouse.com; The Square; s/d from €65/80, cafe mains €8-13, restaurant mains €14-20; cafe 8am-6pm, restaurant noon-3pm & 6.30-9.15pm; P@) There's a wonderfully warm welcome at this listed 19th-century town house, set back from the square in its own courtyard full of fairy lights. Rooms are decorated in bright Mediterranean colours and exude a cosy, country-house feel. There's a cafe downstairs, as well as the popular Manse restaurant which serves solid but rather staid fare.

Jacksons IRISH €€
(090-663 4140; www.jacksons.ie; The Square; s/d €50/80, lunch mains €5-13, dinner mains €16-20; closed dinner Mon & Tue) The top spot to eat in town, this modern restaurant is run by an award-winning chef keen to make the most of seasonal local produce. The menu features local meat, fish and game in interesting combinations. Upstairs there are 10 big, modern rooms with warm wood furniture and plenty of light.

Information

Tourist office (090-662 6342; www.visitroscommon.com; The Square; 10am-1pm & 2-5pm Mon-Sat Jun-Aug) In the County Museum next to the post office. You can pick up a map of the town and heritage trail here.

Easons (090-662 5049; The Square; 9am-7pm) Internet access is available upstairs for €3 per hour.

Getting There & Away

BUS Express services between Westport (€14.40, 2¼ hours) and Dublin (€17.10, three hours) via Athlone stop in Roscommon three times daily (twice on Sunday). Buses stop on the Mart Rd.

TRAIN Roscommon train station is in Abbeytown, just south of the town centre; there are four trains daily on the line from Dublin (€27, two hours) to Westport (€15 to €26, 1½ hours).

COUNTY LEITRIM

The delights of the unassuming county of Leitrim are a well-kept secret, and it seems the locals like it that way. The untamed landscape and authentic rural charm are genuinely cherished by those who call it home and there's a reluctance to let anyone or anything spoilt it. Despite this, there's an enormous welcome for visitors – just don't bank on being let in on secrets about favourite fishing spots or watering holes until you've been here at least a generation.

Leitrim was ravaged by the famine in the 19th century and spent subsequent generations struggling with mass emigration and unemployment, but today it has become a beloved hideout for artists, writers and musicians as well as a huge boating centre.

The county is split almost in two by Lough Allen, and the mighty River Shannon remains the area's biggest draw. Carrick-on-Shannon, the county town, is a lively centre that makes a great base for exploring the region by water or by road.

Carrick-on-Shannon

POP 3170

Carrick-on-Shannon is a charming town with a riverside location and a thriving community. Since the completion of the Shannon–Erne Waterway, the marina here has become incredibly busy. The town is a hugely popular weekend destination with a good choice of accommodation and restaurants and a great music and arts scene. Plan your visit in advance, especially in summer.

During the 17th and most of the 18th centuries Carrick was a Protestant enclave, and the local residents' wealth can still be seen in the graceful buildings around the town. Catholics were permitted to live in the area known as the 'Liberty' on the Roscommon side of the river.

Sights

Carrick has some wonderful examples of early 19th-century architecture on St George's Terrace including **Hatley Manor**, home of the St George family, and the **Old Courthouse**. Nearby is the refurbished **Market Yard**.

Costello Chapel CHURCH
(Bridge St; ⏲10am-4.30pm Easter-Sep) This diminutive place measures just 5m by 3.6m making it Europe's smallest chapel. It was built in 1877 by Edward Costello, distraught at the early death of his wife Mary. Both husband and wife now rest within the grey limestone interior lit by a single stained-glass window. Their embalmed bodies were placed in lead coffins, which sit on either side of the door under slabs of glass. If the door is locked, ask at St George's Heritage Centre for the key.

St George's Heritage Centre MUSEUM
(St Mary's Close; admission €5; ⏲11am-4pm Wed-Fri) Set in a restored church, this heritage centre looks at the history and landscape of Leitrim from old Gaelic traditions through to Planter times. A tour of the centre also takes in a short walk through the town describing the history of its heritage buildings and a visit to the old Famine workhouse, which remains a bleak memorial to harder times.

Activities

Boat Rental

Carrick is the Shannon–Erne Waterway's boat-hire capital, with several companies based at the marina. The canal's 16 locks are fully automated, you don't need a licence, and you're given full instructions on handling your boat before you set off. Make sure you pick up a chart of the waterway (available from bookshops and boat-hire companies), showing the depths and locations of locks. High-season prices start at around €1000 per week for a two-berth cruiser. Try **Carrick Craft** (www.carrickcraft.com) or **Emerald Star** (www.emeraldstar.ie) for more information.

Cruises

You can take a one-hour cruise on the Shannon on **Moon River** (www.moon-river.net; The Quay), a 110-seater vessel. There are one or two sailings per day (€15) between mid-March and October, increasing to four sailings during July and August; check the information board on the quay for details.

Angling

Carrick-on-Shannon Angling Club
(☎071-962 0313; Ashleigh House) The best place for information on fishing.

The Shannon–Erne Waterway

Ireland's two main river systems, the Shannon and the Erne, meander gracefully between the lush green fields, watery meadows and untamed pastures of the Midlands. En route they feed and carve the land and attract families, boaters and fishers all summer long.

The two rivers were linked in the 1800s as part of a much-needed drainage scheme for the poor soil in the area but their connection was short-lived. It was not until 1994, when a far-sighted restoration project created a symbolic link between Northern Ireland and the Republic, that the combined river system became navigable once again.

Running the length of the Shannon and on through northwestern County Cavan to the southern shore of Upper Lough Erne, the Shannon–Erne Waterway (p523) creates an amazing 750km network of rivers, lakes and artificial navigations. Plush hotels, gourmet restaurants and lively traditional pubs line its banks, making it a surprisingly cosmopolitan, as well as a wonderfully scenic, way to travel.

1

PHOTOLIBRARY ©

3

RICHARD CUMMINS/LONELY PLANET IMAGES ©

TOP STOPS

» **Carrick-on-Shannon** (p519), a charming riverside town with a lively music and arts scene

» **Glasson** (p526), an estate village best known for its outstanding restaurants

» **Athlone** (p524), a vibrant town and Midlands hub

» **Clonmacnoise** (p509), a magnificent ecclesiastical city dating from the 6th century

» **Shannonbridge** (p509), a sleepy village with a cracking traditional pub

» **Banagher** (p508), a popular boating centre with formidable riverside fortifications

Clockwise from top left

1. River Shannon, Limerick City **2.** Fishing from a houseboat, Leitrim **3.** Bastion St, Athlone

2

HOLGER LEUE/LONELY PLANET IMAGES ©

Regatta

Carrick Rowing Club (www.carrickrowingclub.com) Runs an annual regatta on the first Sunday in August, which draws a big crowd.

Sleeping

Carrick has a good choice of accommodation, with plenty of B&Bs and a selection of large, rather characterless hotels.

For extra romance and old-world elegance, there are two luxury castle hotels within a few miles of Carrick. Check their websites for special offers.

Hollywell B&B €€
(071-962 1124; hollywell@esatbiz.com; Liberty Hill; s/d from €65/100; mid-Feb–mid-Nov;) This beautiful ivy-covered Georgian country house, on the Roscommon side of the river, has spacious, restful bedrooms with huge beds. The two superior rooms each have a generous sitting area, with splendid views of the Shannon and its ever-changing light. Hollywell's hosts are full of local knowledge and put on superb breakfasts. The antique furnishings and proximity to the water mean the house isn't suitable for children.

Ciúin House B&B €€
(071-967 1488; www.ciuinhouse.com; Hartley; s/d €55/90;) On the edge of town but within walking distance of the main street, this lovely purpose-built guesthouse has 15 spacious rooms with simple but stylish furnishings. Orthopaedic beds, Jacuzzi baths and crisp linens make it feel more like a hotel than a B&B. To get here, follow Main St to its end, veering left onto Leitrim Rd and left again at the fork for Hartley.

Caldra House B&B €€
(071-962 3040; www.caldrahouse.ie; Caldragh; s/d €45/78;) This creeper-clad Georgian house offers exceptional value, with four period-style rooms decorated with antiques and subtle floral patterns. Set in mature gardens overlooking the Arigna Mountains, it's a very tranquil spot, 3km from town. Follow the R280 north out of town, turning left after 2km, then right at the T-junction.

Lough Rynn Castle HOTEL €€
(071-963 2700; www.loughrynn.ie; Mohill, Co Leitrim; r from €130) A 19th-century pile set on 300 acres on the shores of Lough Rynn, about 10km east of Carrick.

Kilronan Castle HOTEL €€€
(071-961 8000; www.kilronancastle.ie; Ballyfarnon, Co Roscommon; r from €160) An imposing castle overlooking Lough Meelagh, about 10km northwest of Carrick.

Eating

The Cottage IRISH €€
(071-9625933; http://cottagerestaurant.ie; Jamestown; mains €16-26; lunch Sun, dinner Wed-Sun;) Set in a small white-washed cottage overlooking a weir, this humble-looking place belies the quality of food on offer inside. The menu offers a limited but tantalising choice of dishes created using vegetables from the restaurant's own polytunnel, meats from local suppliers and artisan cheeses. The chef/proprietor's Asian roots are evident in dishes such as the duck confit in Asian pastry with spiced orange, pickled cabbage and sweet and sour cucumber or the grilled rump of lamb with cumin spiced sweet potato, lamb samosas and coriander yogurt. It's well worth the trip 5km south east of Carrick to Jamestown, just off the N4.

Oarsman FUSION €€€
(071-962 1733; www.theoarsman.com; Bridge St; lunch mains €6-13, dinner €19-25; lunch Tue-Sat, dinner Thu-Sat) It may look like a pub from the outside, but the Oarsman is best known for its food. Championing local and organic produce, it serves restaurant-quality food in relaxed, informal surroundings. The menu ranges from traditional Irish with a contemporary twist to Asian-inspired dishes. Snacks and bar food are served between lunch and dinner, and they pull a good pint, too.

Victoria Hall Restaurant ASIAN €€
(071-962 0320; www.victoriahall.ie; Victoria Hall, Quay Rd; lunch mains €9-11, dinner €17-24;) The locals' favourite for food, this graceful old parochial hall has had a thoroughly modern makeover and now has a stylish minimalist interior, with a lovely 1st-floor dining area. The open kitchen churns out excellent Asian- and European-inspired dishes, with bento boxes (€15.50) and boxty (a traditional potato pancake) wraps with Thai fillings (€11), the speciality at lunch.

Vittos ITALIAN €€€
(www.vittosrestaurant.com; Market Yard; mains €14-25; Tue-Sat;) In a wood-beamed barn, this family-friendly restaurant has an extensive menu of classic Italian and more traditional Irish dishes, including great pastas

SHANNON–ERNE WATERWAY

Ireland's two main river systems, the Shannon and the Erne, were linked in the mid-1800s as part of a much-needed drainage scheme for the poor soil in the area. The canal was never a success, however, and had already begun to deteriorate by the 1870s. In 1994 a far-sighted renovation project created a symbolic link between Northern Ireland and the Republic when the canal was reopened as the Shannon–Erne Waterway. It creates an amazing 750km network of rivers, lakes and artificial navigations. The waterway runs from the River Shannon beside the village of Leitrim, 4km north of Carrick-on-Shannon, through northwestern County Cavan to the southern shore of Upper Lough Erne, just over the Northern Ireland border in County Fermanagh.

and pizzas and some less-inspired grills. Service is fast and friendly and the atmosphere is warm and cosy.

Drinking

Flynn's Corner House PUB
(cnr Main & Bridge Sts) This authentic old-world pub serves a good pint of Guinness and has live music on Friday nights. Savour it before it's modernised.

Cryan's PUB
(Bridge St) A traditional little pub with few frills, this is another good bet for traditional music sessions on Saturday and Sunday nights.

Anderson's Thatch Pub PUB
(www.andersonspub.com; Elphin Rd) This traditional thatched pub is worth a trip for its live music sessions (Wednesday, Friday and Saturday), old-world atmosphere and country charm. Take the R368 south from town for about 4km.

☆ Entertainment

Dock Arts Centre THEATRE
(www.thedock.ie; St George's Tce; ⏲10am-6pm Mon-Sat) Set in the grand surroundings of the 19th-century former courthouse, this place hosts performances, exhibitions and workshops. Also here is the **Leitrim Design House** (www.leitrimdesignhouse.ie), which features the work of local artists, designers and craftspeople.

ℹ Information

Gartlan's Internet Cafe (Bridge St; per hr €3; ⏲9.30am-7pm Mon-Fri, 10am-6pm Sat)

Post office (St George's Tce)

Tourist office (☎071-962 3274; www.leitrimtourism.com; Old Barrel Store, The Quay; ⏲9.30am-5pm Easter-Sep) Has a walking-tour booklet, which takes in Carrick's places of interest.

ℹ Getting There & Away

BUS The Dublin (€17.10, three hours) to Sligo (€11.70, one hour) coach service stops in Carrick six times in each direction Monday to Saturday (five Sunday). The bus stop is outside Coffey's Pastry Case on Bridge St.

TRAIN Carrick has eight trains daily to Dublin (€27.50, 2¼ hours) and Sligo (€15, 55 minutes). The station is a 15-minute walk, over on the Roscommon side of the river. Turn right across the bridge, then left at the petrol station onto Station Rd.

North Leitrim

North of Carrick-on-Shannon, the Leitrim landscape comes into its own, its ruffled hills, steel-grey lakes and isolated cottages exuding a genuine rural charm. You'll also find a clutch of attractions in this seemingly forgotten part of the country that are easily accessible on a day trip from Sligo.

If you fancy taking to the hills on foot, the **Leitrim Way** walking trail begins in Drumshanbo and ends in Manorhamilton, a distance of 48km.

Sights & Activities

Parke's Castle HISTORIC BUILDING
(www.heritageireland.ie; Fivemile Bourne; adult/child €3/1; ⏲10am-6pm mid-Apr-Sep) The tranquil surrounds of Parke's Castle, with swans drifting by on Lough Gill and neat grass cloaking the old moat, belie the fact that its early Plantation architecture was created out of an unwelcome English landlord's insecurity and fear.

The thoroughly restored, three-storey castle forms part of one of the five sides of the bawn, which also has three rounded turrets at its corners. Join one of the entertaining guided tours after viewing the 20-minute video. Last admission is at 5.15pm.

You can take a 1½-hour cruise on Lough Gill from the castle. Trips aboard the **Rose of Innisfree** (www.roseofinnisfree.com; adult/child €15/7.50; ⏲11am, 12.30pm, 1.30pm, 3.30pm & 4.30pm Easter-Oct) offer live recitals of Yeats' poetry accompanying music. The company runs a bus from Sligo to the castle. Call for departure times and location.

The castle is 11km east of Sligo town on the R286.

Ard Nahoo HEALTH FARM
(☎071-913 4939; www.ardnahoo.com; Mullagh, Dromahair; 4-bed cabin weekend/week €300/450) Cleanse the mind and spirit and get back to basics at Ard Nahoo, a rustic eco-retreat where you can rent a self-catering eco-lodge, join a yoga retreat or detox program, take a course in alternative living or natural healthcare, or simply sign up for some pampering in the spa. Facilities are simple but comfortable and are designed to relieve you of the stress of city living.

Rossinver Organic Centre ORGANIC CENTRE
(www.theorganiccentre.ie; Rossinver; adult/child €5/free; ⏲10am-5pm Feb-Nov) All things good and wholesome come together at the Rossinver Organic Centre, which aims to promote organic horticulture and sustainable living at its beautiful grounds in north Leitrim. You can simply come and tour the beautiful display gardens, or take a course in anything from organic growing to sustainable design, cheese-making, willow sculpture, bread baking or silk painting. The **cafe** (⏲11am-4pm Sat & Sun) serves wonderful vegetarian fare baked with ingredients from the garden.

COUNTY LONGFORD

A solidly agrarian region, County Longford is a quiet place of low hills and pastoral scenes. It has few tourist sights but is a haven for anglers who come for the superb fishing around Lough Ree and Lanesborough.

Longford suffered massive emigration during the Famine of the 1840s and 1850s and it has never really recovered. Many Longford emigrants went to Argentina, where one of their descendants, Edel Miro O'Farrell, became president in 1914.

Longford's eponymous county town is a decidedly workaday place, but there's a friendly **tourist office** (☎043-334 2577; www.longfordtourism.ie; Market Sq; ⏲9am-5.30pm Mon-Sat May-Sep) and plenty of places to eat.

The county's main attraction is the magnificent **Corlea Trackway** (www.heritageireland.ie; Keenagh; admission free; ⏲10am-6pm mid-Apr–Sep), an Iron Age bog road that was built in 148 BC. An 18m stretch of the historic track has now been preserved in a humidified hall at the visitor centre, where you can join a 45-minute tour that details the bog's unique flora and fauna, and fills you in on how the track was discovered, and methods used to preserve it. Wear a windproof jacket as the bog land can be blowy. The centre is 15km south of Longford on the Ballymahon road (R397).

Longford is also home to one of the three biggest portal dolmens in Ireland. The **Aughnacliffe dolmen** has an improbably balanced top stone and is thought to be around 5000 years old. Aughnacliffe is 18km north of Longford town off the R198.

There are hourly buses from Longford town to Dublin (€15, two hours) and Sligo (€13, 1½ hours, six daily Monday to Saturday, five Sunday). Buses stop outside Longford train station off New St.

There are trains almost hourly to Dublin (€34, one hour and 40 minutes) and Sligo (€26, 1½ hours).

COUNTY WESTMEATH

Characterised by lakes and pastures grazed by beef cattle, Westmeath has a wealth of attractions, ranging from a wonderful whiskey distillery and the miraculous Fore Valley, to the country's oldest pub in the confident county town, Athlone. The rivers and lakes attract a steady stream of visitors and a host of gourmet restaurants and fine accommodation options have sprung up in recent years to cater for the discerning crowds.

Athlone

POP 14,350

Set on the banks of the Shannon, the thriving town of Athlone is a magnet for river traffic and is a solid manufacturing base for international companies. It's one of Ireland's most vibrant towns, with a mix of stylish modern developments, big shopping centres and small winding streets, home to independent businesses.

The Shannon splits this former garrison town in two, with most businesses and services sitting on its eastern bank. In the shadow of Athlone Castle, the western bank is an enchanting jumble of twisting streets, colourfully painted houses, historic pubs, antique shops and old book binders, as well as some outstanding restaurants.

Sights & Activities

Athlone Castle HISTORIC BUILDING
(www.athloneudc.ie) The ancient river ford at Athlone was an important crossroads on the Shannon and was the cause of many squabbles over the centuries. By 1210, the Normans had asserted their power and built a castle here. In 1690 the Jacobite town survived a siege by Protestant forces, but it fell a year later – under a devastating bombardment of 12,000 cannonballs – to William of Orange's troops. The castle was soon remodelled and further major alterations took place over the following centuries.

At the time of writing the imposing and well-preserved castle and its visitor centre were closed for refurbishment. Both should reopen in summer 2012.

Dún na Sí Heritage Centre HISTORIC SITE
(090-6481183; Knockdomney; adult/child €3.50/1.50; 9.30am-4.30pm Mon-Thu, to 3.30pm Fri) This folk park 16km east of Athlone just off the M6 near Moate, features a recreated ring fort, portal dolmen, lime kiln, mass rock, farmhouse and forge. There's also a genealogy centre to help trace your roots, a céili on the first Friday of the month year-round and a traditional session with music, song, dance and storytelling at 9pm on Fridays in summer.

Tours

Midland Tours BUS TOURS
(www.midlandtours.com; Ballinahown; tours €20) This company offers a range of half-day tours to Clonmacnoise, the Fore Valley, Birr Castle, Tullamore Heritage Centre and Locke's Distillery, and Strokestown Park House and Famine Museum.

Viking Tours RIVER CRUISES
(086 262 1136; www.vikingtoursireland.ie; 7 St Mary's Pl; adult/child €10/5; May-Sep) Cruise along the Shannon aboard a replica Viking longship, complete with costumed staff and dress-up clothes, including helmets, swords and shields. Head north to Lough Ree or south to Clonmacnoise. A round trip to Clonmacnoise allows a 90-minute stop at the ruins. Call for schedules.

Sleeping

Athlone has a glut of corporate hotels in the centre of town; the following places have more character.

Bastion B&B B&B €€
(090-649 4954; www.thebastion.net; 2 Bastion St; s/d from €45/65;) In a converted draper's shop, this funky B&B's white-on-white interiors are a canvas for eclectic artwork, cactus collections and Indian wall hangings. The five rooms (three with private bathrooms) are crisp and clean, with neatly folded fluffy towels, and there's an arty lounge–breakfast room, where you can kick-start your day with cereal, fruit, ground coffee, fresh bread and a cheeseboard.

Coosan Cottage Eco Guesthouse B&B €€
(090-647 3468; www.ecoguesthouse.com; Coosan Point Rd; s/d €40/80; P) This beautiful, ecofriendly cottage was a labour of love for its owners, blending traditional style with modern thinking. Triple-glazed windows, a wood pellet burner and a heat recovery system are just some of its green credentials. For visitors, though, it's the tranquil surroundings and great breakfasts that will stick in the mind. The cottage is 2.5km from the town centre.

Eating

You'll be spoilt for choice when it comes to dining in Athlone, which has established itself as the culinary capital of the Midlands. Scout around the western bank's backstreets and you'll unearth some gems.

Kin Khao THAI €€
(090-649 8805; www.kinkhaothai.ie; Abbey Lane; mains €17-19; 12.30-2.30pm Wed-Fri, 5.30-10.30pm Mon-Sat, 1.30-10.30pm Sun) What is possibly the best Thai restaurant in Ireland is tucked away near the Dean Crowe Theatre and is renowned for its extensive menu of authentic dishes. All the chefs and staff are Thai (with the exception of one half of the husband-and-wife team who run the place) and you'd be advised to book ahead if you want to join the band of loyal Kin Khao devotees.

Left Bank Bistro MEDITERRANEAN €€
(☎090-649 4446; www.leftbankbistro.com; Fry Pl; lunch mains €9-15, dinner mains €18-27; ⊙closed Sun & Mon) With airy, whitewashed interiors, shelves of gourmet goods, and a menu combining superior Irish ingredients with Mediterranean and Asian influences, this sophisticated deli-bistro attracts those in the know. Lunch features bowls of steaming pasta, big salads and chunky open sandwiches, while dinner dishes up beautifully grilled meat and fish and some extraordinary desserts.

Olive Grove FUSION €€
(☎090-647 6946; www.theolivegrove.ie; Custume Pier; lunch mains €8-12, dinner mains €15-21; ⊙noon-4pm & 5.30-10pm Tue-Sun) This slick waterside restaurant gets rave reviews from happy punters keen on the stylish design and creative menus. The food is good but at times fussy; think pan-fried black pudding with blue cheese and cider sorbet or duck confit with colcannon and pear, orange and date chutney.

Drinking & Entertainment

Sean's Bar PUB
(13 Main St) Age certainly hasn't wearied Sean's Bar. Dating way back to AD 900, Sean's stakes its claim as Ireland's oldest pub. Its log fires, uneven floors (to help flood waters run back down to the river), sawdust, rickety piano and curios collected over the years attest to the theory. The riverside beer garden has live music most nights in summer; to really see things in full swing, turn up at about 5.30pm on a Saturday.

Dean Crowe Theatre THEATRE
(www.deancrowetheatre.com; Chapel St) This refurbished theatre has wonderful acoustics and runs a broad program of theatrical and musical events year-round.

Information

The website www.athlone.ie is a good source of information.

Netcafe (1 Paynes Lane; per hr €3.50; ⊙11am-10pm Mon-Fri, 11am-9pm Sat, noon-9pm Sun)

Post office (Barrack St) Beside the cathedral.

Tourist office (☎090-649 4630; Civic Centre, Church St; ⊙9.30am-1pm & 2-5.15pm Mon-Fri May-Sep)

Getting There & Around

Athlone's bus and train stations are side by side on Southern Station Rd.

BUS There are half-hourly buses to Dublin (€10.80, two hours) and Galway (€10.80, 1½ hours); two daily to Westport (€14.40, three hours) and Mullingar (€10.30, one hour).

TRAIN There are hourly trains to Dublin (€22, 1¾ hours); four daily to Westport (€22, two hours) and nine to Galway (€17.90, 1 hour).

Lough Ree & Around

Many of the 50-plus islands within Lough Ree were once inhabited by monks and their ecclesiastical treasures, drawing Vikings like moths to a flame. These days, the visitors are less bloodthirsty, with sailing, trout fishing and birdwatching the most popular pastimes. Migratory birds that nest here include swans, plovers and curlews.

Poet, playwright and novelist Oliver Goldsmith (1728–74), author of *The Vicar of Wakefield,* is closely associated with the area running alongside the eastern shore of Lough Ree. Known as **Goldsmith Country**, the region is beautifully captured in his writings.

Situated 8km northeast of Athlone on the N55, the little village of **Glasson** was described by Goldsmith as the 'loveliest village of the plain' and is worth a stop for its outstanding restaurants and lively pubs. The **Glasson Village Restaurant** (☎090-648 5001; michaelrosebrooks@gmail.com; mains €20-30; ⊙closed dinner Sun; 👪) is a wonderfully informal place serving excellent food. Nearby is the **Fatted Calf** (☎090-648 5208; www.thefattecalf.ie; Pearsonsbrook; mains €14-22; ⊙closed Mon; 👪), a gastropub serving ambitious dishes, while slightly out of town is the upmarket **Wineport Lodge** (☎090-643 9010; www.wineport.ie; mains €24-33), which has a reputation for the finest modern Irish cuisine.

Getting There & Away

BUS Route 466 from Athlone to Longford stops in Glasson twice daily Monday to Saturday.

Kilbeggan & Around

Little Kilbeggan has two big claims to fame: a restored distillery-turned-museum and Ireland's only National Hunt racecourse.

Whiskey buffs and industrial technology enthusiasts will get a kick out of **Locke's Distillery** (www.lockesdistillerymuseum.ie; Kilbeggan; adult/child €7/free; ⊙9am-6pm Apr-Oct, 10am-4pm Nov-Mar). Established in 1757, this whiskey producer is believed to have been the

THROW AWAY YOUR GUIDEBOOK

Whether you're on the water or travelling by road, there's a host of interesting small towns and villages along and around the Shannon and the Royal and Grand Canals that make wonderfully tranquil stops. Most are rarely visited by touring motorists but are brimming with history, picturesque views and fine pubs.

In Leitrim you'll find **Ballinamore**, a lively spot on the Shannon–Erne Waterway, and **Drumshanbo**, a wonderfully traditional town with an interesting visitor centre. Nearby **Keadue** is a pretty spot that hosts the O'Carolan International Harp Festival, while just to the south is **Keshcarrigan**, home to a collapsed dolmen and some unusual St Patrick's Day festivities. Further west, **Cootehall**, on the River Boyle, has a fine restaurant and a lovely old-world pub. Nearby **Knockvicar** has a riverfront restaurant at its busy marina. Heading south, **Drumsna** is a lovely traditional country village, while nearby **Dromod** is well known for its excellent fishing. **Tarmonbarry** is another good stop, with a good choice of interesting restaurants and pubs, a swish hotel and a lively vibe. Nearby **Clondra**, where the Shannon meets the Royal Canal, is a stunning little place with lovely walks and **Keenagh**, further along the canal, is a sleepy but quaint little town. Finally stop at **Abbeyshrule** to find the ruins of a Cistercian abbey and an interesting viaduct.

oldest licensed pot still in the world before it ceased operation two centuries later. Today you can marvel at hulking machinery, visit a cooper's room and warehouse, and listen to the creaks and groans of the working mill wheel. Guided tours last 50 minutes, finishing off with a whiskey tasting.

Punters from all over the country attend the old-time evening meetings at the **Kilbeggan Races** (www.kilbegganraces.com; ⏱approximately fortnightly May-Sep). The town is transformed on race nights into a buzzing equine centre, where the thrill of the chase is matched by the craic in the pubs.

About 6.5km west of Kilbeggan is **Temple House & Health Spa** (☎057-933 5118; www.templespa.ie; s/d from €95/130, 2/3-course dinner €28/32; ⏱restaurant lunch Wed-Sun, dinner Wed-Sat; P@). The 250-year-old house is set on 40 hectares of grounds on the site of an ancient monastery. Rooms are blissfully tranquil with a mix of period charm and modern style and, although there are plenty of healthy options on the restaurant menu, it's a fine dining experience with locally sourced, organic ingredients topping the bill. Both the restaurant and the day spa are open to non-residents.

Mullingar & Around

POP 8940

A prosperous regional town, Mullingar hums with the activity of locals going about their daily lives. Nearby there are fish-filled lakes and a fantastical mansion with an odious history.

James Joyce visited the town in his youth and it appears in both *Ulysses* and *Finnegans Wake*. Restored sections of the Royal Canal extend in either direction from Mullingar.

Sights

Belvedere House & Gardens HISTORIC BUILDING

(www.belvedere-house.ie; adult/child €8.75/4.75; ⏱house 9.30am-8pm May-Aug, 9.30am-4.30pm Sep-Apr) Don't miss magnificent Belvedere House, an immense 18th-century hunting lodge set in 65 hectares of gardens overlooking Lough Ennell. More than a few skeletons have come out of Belvedere's closets: the first earl, Lord Belfield, accused his wife and younger brother Arthur of adultery. She was placed under house arrest here for 30 years, and Arthur was jailed in London for the rest of his life. Meanwhile, the earl lived a life of decadence and debauchery. On his death, his wife emerged dressed in the fashion of three decades earlier, still protesting her innocence.

Lord Belfield also found time to fall out with his other brother, George, who built a home nearby. Ireland's largest folly, a ready-made 'ruin' called the **Jealous Wall**, was commissioned by the earl so he wouldn't have to look at George's mansion.

Designed by Richard Cassels, Belvedere House contains some delicate rococo plasterwork in the upper rooms. The gardens, with their Victorian glasshouses and lakeshore setting, make for wonderful walking on a sunny day.

Belvedere House is 5.5km south of Mullingar on the N52 to Tullamore.

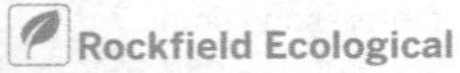

Rockfield Ecological Estate NATURE RESERVE

(☎043-667 6024; imelda.mdaly@gmail.com; Rathaspic, Rathowen; adult/child €10/5; ⊙by appointment) This secluded organic farm is set around a beautiful Georgian house and runs crafts courses and arts events as well as farm tours. To get here head north 24km of Mullingar along the N4 to Rathowen from where the farm is signposted.

FREE **Cathedral of Christ the King** CHURCH

(www.mullingarparish.com; ⊙7.30am-8pm) Mullingar's most obvious landmark is this immense church, built just before WWII. It has large mosaics of St Anne and St Patrick by Russian artist Boris Anrep, as well as a small ecclesiastical museum.

Activities

Trout fishing is popular in the lakes around Mullingar. The fishing season runs from 1 March or 1 May (depending on the lake) to 12 October. Contact the tourist office or the **Shannon Regional Fisheries Board** (www.shannon-fishery-board.ie) for further information.

If you fancy some horse riding, try the **Mullingar Equestrian Centre** (www.mullingarequestrian.com; Athlone Rd).

You can kayak on Lough Ennell from the **Lilliput Adventure Centre** (www.lilliputadventure.com; Jonathan Swift Park). The centre also organises land-based activities such as gorge walking and abseiling courses.

Sleeping & Eating

There are few B&Bs in the centre, but you'll find plenty on the approach roads from Dublin and Sligo.

Novara House B&B €€

(☎044-933 5209; www.novarahouse.com; Dublin Rd; s/d from €50/80; P) This incredibly friendly B&B is just five minutes' walk from the town centre. Set in a modern bungalow, the rooms are simple but spotless with pine furniture and neutral colour schemes but it's the amiable hosts and their warm welcome, homemade scones and cups of tea that will make for a most memorable stay.

Annebrook House Hotel HOTEL €€

(☎044-935 3300; www.annebrook.ie; Pearse St; s/d from €55/100; P) Right in the town centre, the hub of this modern hotel is a lovely 19th-century house with strong connections to local author Maria Edgeworth. Accommodation is in a new annexe, where modern rooms in neutral colours are extremely comfortable but lack soul.

Ilia FUSION €€

(☎044-934 5947; www.ilia.ie; 37 Dominick St; mains €16-27; ⊙dinner Tue-Sun, lunch Sun) Be sure to book in advance for one of Mullingar's most popular haunts. This cosy but clean-cut restaurant serves up a winning array of gourmet comfort food. Think slow roast pork belly, chicken with puy lentils and roast peppers or pumpkin and sage risotto, all cooked with attention and flair. You'll be back for more.

Oscar's MEDITERRANEAN €€

(☎044-934 4909; 21 Oliver Plunkett St; mains €15-25; ⊙lunch Sun, dinner daily) This perennially popular spot is the place to go for wholesome comfort food in a lively atmosphere. Bright colours, a menu that skirts the Mediterranean (think pastas, pizzas and French-inspired meat and poultry) and a decent wine list make it a good evening option.

Drinking & Entertainment

You'll find traditional Irish music in many of the town's pubs; ask at the tourist office for details.

Yukon Bar PUB

(11 Dominick St) A lively pub with a resident fortune teller, this place has a great atmosphere and regular live music. Depending on the day of the week you'll find a range of soul, blues and rock music on offer.

Mullingar Arts Centre THEATRE

(www.mullingarartscentre.ie; County Hall, Lower Mount St) The centre runs a regular program of music, comedy, drama and art exhibitions. In summer there are family-friendly traditional music sessions every weekend.

Information

Post office (Dominick St)

Tourist office (☎044-934 8650; Market Sq; ⊙9.30am-1pm & 2-5pm Mon-Sat)

Getting There & Away

BUS Services run to Dublin (€12.90, 1½ hours, six Monday to Saturday, five Sunday) and

Athlone (€10.30, one hour, two Monday to Saturday, one Sunday).

TRAIN There are 11 direct services to Dublin (€21.50, one hour, 11 Monday to Friday, seven Saturday, five Sunday) and Sligo (€34, two hours, eight Monday to Saturday, six Sunday).

North of Mullingar

The area north of Mullingar is riddled with lakes, the most famous of which is **Lough Derravaragh**, an 8km-long lake associated with the legend of the children of Lír, who were turned into swans here by their jealous stepmother. Each winter the legend is recalled by thousands of snow-white migratory swans that flock here from as far away as Russia and Siberia.

In addition to the lakes and rolling landscapes you'll find plenty of historical interest around the unassuming town of Castlepollard and sleepy Crookedwood.

Sights

Fore Valley HISTORIC SITE

Near the shores of Lough Lene, the emerald-green Fore Valley is a superb place to explore by bicycle or on foot. In AD 630, St Fechin founded a monastery just outside the village of Fore. There's nothing left of this early settlement, but three later buildings in the valley are closely associated with 'seven wonders' said to have occurred here. It's a highly atmospheric place, even in the dead of winter, with sweeping views across a gentle valley.

The oldest of the three buildings is **St Fechin's Church**, containing an early-13th-century chancel and baptismal font. Over the Cyclopean entrance is a huge lintel stone carved with a Greek cross and thought to weigh about 2.5 tonnes. It's said to have been put into place by St Fechin's devotions – the wonder of the stone raised by prayer.

A path runs from the church to the attractive little **anchorite cell** – the anchorite in a stone – which dates back to the 15th century and was lived in by a succession of hermits. The Seven Wonders pub in the village holds the key.

On the other side of the road near the car park is **St Fechin's Well**, filled with water that will not boil. Cynics should beware of testing this claim, as it's said that if you try it, doom will come to your family. Nearby is a branch from the tree that will not burn; the coins pressed into it are a more contemporary superstition.

Further over the plain are the extensive remains of a **13th-century Benedictine priory**, the Monastery of the Quaking Scraw, miraculous because it was built on what once was a bog. In the following century it was turned into a fortification, hence the loophole windows and castlelike square towers. The western tower is in a dangerous state – keep clear.

The last two wonders are the mill without a race and the water that flows uphill. The mill site is marked, and legend has it that St Fechin caused water to flow uphill, towards the mill, by throwing his crosier against a rock near Lough Lene, about 1.5km away.

The **Fore Abbey Coffee Shop** (☎044-966 1780; foreabbeycoffeeshop@gmail.com; ⏰10am-6pm Sat & Sun Oct-Jun, 10am-6pm daily Jun-Aug), on the edge of Fore village, acts as a tourist information office and screens a 20-minute video about the wonders. Guided tours of Fore can be arranged by contacting the coffee shop in advance.

Tullynally Castle Gardens GARDEN

(☎044-966 1159; www.tullynallycastle.com; Castlepollard; gardens adult/child €6/3; ⏰1-6pm Thu-Sun May-Aug) The imposing Gothic revival Tullynally Castle is the seat of the Pakenham family and although closed to visitors, its 12 hectares of gardens and parkland are a wonderful place to roam. Ornamental lakes, a Chinese and a Tibetan garden, and a wonderful stretch of 200-year-old yews are some of the highlights.

The castle is 2km northwest of Castlepollard.

FREE **Multyfarnham Franciscan Friary** CHURCH

(⏰dawn-dusk) Hidden inside a 19th-century church are the remains of the original 15th-century friary that stood here. Outside, look for the unusual Stations of the Cross set beside a stream. The friary is about 3km west of Crookedwood.

FREE **St Munna's Church** CHURCH

Built in a lovely location on the site of a 7th-century church founded by St Munna, this fortified 15th-century church has a barrel-vaulted roof and crenellated battlements. You'll find a weathered sheila-na-gig above a window on the northern side. The church is 2km east of Crookedwood.

Sleeping & Eating

Mornington House B&B €€

(☎044-937 2191; www.mornington.ie; Multyfarnham; s/d from €85/130; ⊙closed Nov-Mar; P) For a little bit of old-world luxury, you could stay at this tranquil guesthouse set in a lovely Victorian home surrounded by mature gardens. The whole house is furnished with period charm. Antique furniture, log fires, brass beds and subtle florals give it a pleasingly lived-in atmosphere. Dinner (€45) can be booked in advance and features fruit and veg from the walled garden.

Hotel Castlepollard HOTEL €€

(☎044-966 1194; www.hotelcastlepolalrd.ie; Castlepollard; s/d €58/80) Overlooking the triangular village green and the town hall, this cosy, country hotel has decent if predictable rooms and a restaurant (mains from €14) serving reliable fare. The hotel bar has live music every weekend.

Getting There & Away

Castlepollard is about 20km north of Mullingar on the R394. Bus 447 runs from Mullingar to Crookedwood (20 minutes) and Castlepollard (30 minutes) at 1.30pm on Thursdays – otherwise you're on your own.

Counties Meath, Louth, Cavan & Monaghan

POPULATION: 440,000 / AREA: 6387 SQ KM

Includes »

Best Places to Eat

» MacNean House & Restaurant (p563)

» Eastern Seaboard Bar & Grill (p550)

» Coastguard Seafoods (p556)

» Olde Post Inn (p561)

» An Tromán (p545)

Best Places to Stay

» D Hotel (p550)

» Ghan House (p558)

» Ross Castle (p562)

» Hilton Park (p566)

» Farnham Estate (p560)

Why Go?

The fertile fields of Counties Meath and Louth attracted Ireland's first settlers, making it the birthplace of Irish civilisation. Although the counties are now part of Dublin's commuter belt, their legacy endures at the mystical tombs at Brú na Bóinne and Loughcrew – both of which predate the Egyptian pyramids – and at Tara, gateway to the otherworld and seat of the high kings of Ireland. Following St Patrick's arrival, the faithful built abbeys, high crosses and round towers to protect their treasured manuscripts. Magnificent ruins throughout Meath and Louth still whisper tales of a time when Ireland was known as the Land of Saints and Scholars.

By contrast, the emerald hills and fish-filled lakes of Counties Monaghan and Cavan offer a far quieter pace. Outdoor activities abound in this little-visited corner of Ireland: boats cruise the Shannon–Erne Waterway, while walking trails take in the wild scenery and expansive views of the Cuilcagh Mountains.

When to Go

Many of Meath, Louth, Cavan and Monaghan's most famous sights have reduced hours or are closed altogether in the chilly low-season months (at least November to March). But once the daffodils appear and new leaves emerge on the trees, the area bursts into life. Tiny villages teem with visitors during dozens of festivals throughout the region in late spring, summer and early autumn. Festival highlights include several in Drogheda, such as its famous Samba Festival, and Carlingford's lively Oyster Festival.

Counties Meath, Louth, Cavan & Monaghan Highlights

1. Exploring the prehistoric remains at the ancient burial sites of **Brú na Bóinne** (p534), especially the dramatic dome of Newgrange
2. Soaking up the water views, slurping oysters and listening to live music in the medieval village of **Carlingford** (p557)
3. Rambling among the evocative ruins and mighty castle of the unassuming town of **Trim** (p542)
4. Following in the footsteps of poet and author Patrick Kavanagh on the quiet roads of **Inniskeen** (p567)
5. Shunning the crowds and setting out for the hilltop tombs of the **Loughcrew Cairns** (p546)
6. Discovering the secrets of the massive earthworks, passage graves and 'stone of destiny' at **Tara** (p539)
7. Checking out the art, architecture and bustling pubs of **Drogheda** (p547)
8. Reeling in fish from the lakes of **County Cavan** (p559)

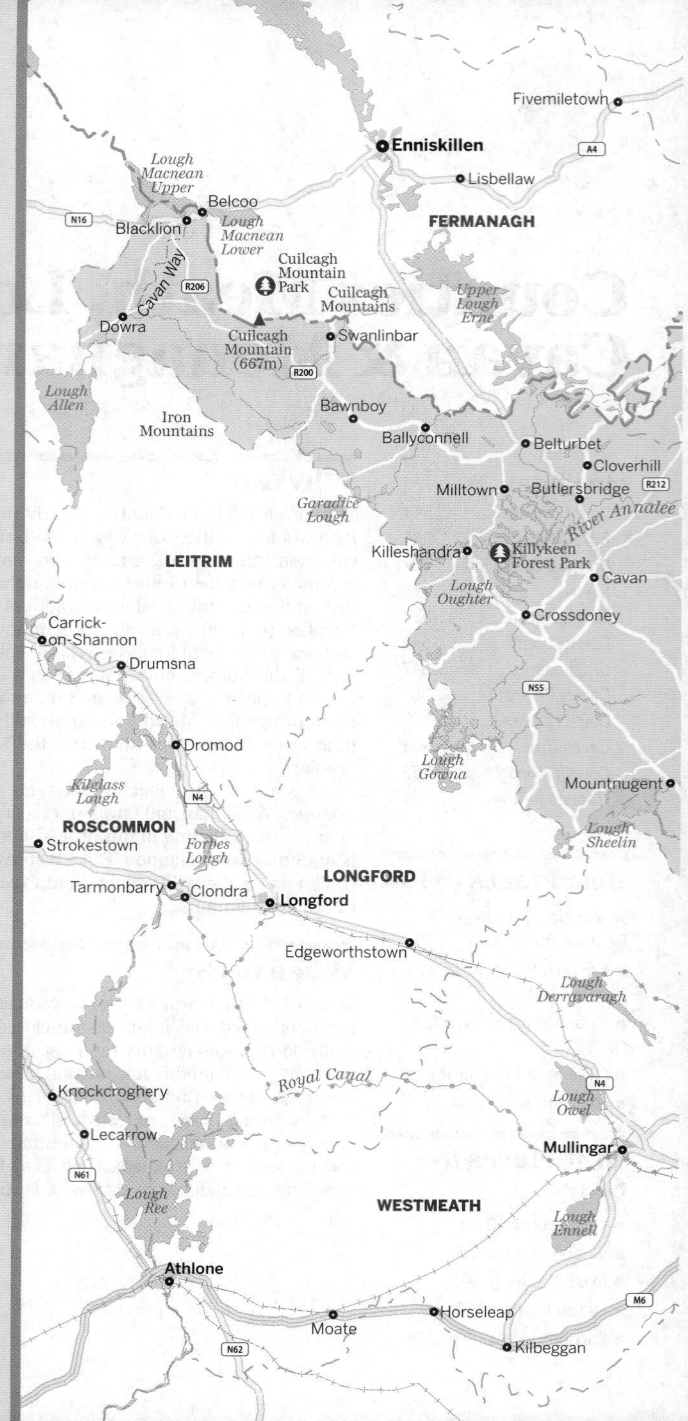

0 20 km
0 10 miles
Augher
Aughnacloy
TYRONE
Ulster Canal
Armagh
Newry Canal
Dromore
Banbridge
Loughbrickland
DOWN
Glaslough
N2
Markethill
ARMAGH
Monaghan
Rossmore Forest Park
Ulster Canal
N54
Clones
Newbliss
MONAGHAN
Newry
Scotshouse
Ballybay
Castleblayney
Meigh
Warrenpoint
Rostrevor
Flagstaff Viewpoint
Crossmaglen
Forkhill
R173
Slieve Foye (587m)
N1
Carlingford Lough
Cootehill
Lough Egish
River Annagh
Shantonagh
N53
Carlingford
Dundalk
Cooley Peninsula
Inniskeen
County Cavan
Lough Sillan
Shercock
Carrickmacross
Ballagan Point
Dundalk Bay
CAVAN
River Glyde
Bailieborough
Dún an Rí Forest Park
Kingscourt
N2
M1
Castlebellingham
Annagassan
River Dee
Ardee
River Dee
Dunany Point
Ballyjamesduff
LOUTH
R166
Dunleer
Virginia
Lough Ramor
Clogher Head
N3
Clogherhead
Monasterboice
Collon
Oldcastle
Beaulieu House
Termonfeckin
R154
R195
Loughcrew Gardens
Mellifont Abbey
Battle of Boyne Site
Baltray
Irish Sea
Loughcrew Cairns
Crossakeel
Kells
Brú na Bóinne
Mornington
Drogheda
White Lake
Loughcrew Hills
Slane
Donore
N1
Dunmoe Castle
River Boyne
Laytown
MEATH
Ardmulchan House
Duleek
Sonairte National Ecology Centre
N52
Lough Lene
Navan
N51
Athlumney Castle
Athboy
M1
Balbriggan
Delvin
Rathcairn
Bective Abbey
Tara
N2
Skyrne
N1
Hill of Tara
River Deel
N3
Trim
DUBLIN
Dunsany Castle
Ratoath
Laracor
Dunshaughlin
Ashbourne
M1
N4
Fairyhouse Racecourse
Summerhill
Royal Canal
Coralstown
Swords
Kinnegad
Black Bull
Dublin Airport
M4
River Boyne
Dunboyne
M50
N1
OFFALY
KILDARE
M4
Dublin
M7

COUNTY MEATH

Meath's rich soil, laid down during the last ice age, attracted settlers as early as 8000 BC. They worked their way up the banks of the River Boyne, transforming the landscape from forest to farmland. One of the five provinces of ancient Ireland, Meath, 'the Middle Kingdom', was at the centre of Irish politics for centuries.

Today, Meath's fertile land and plentiful water supply make it an important centre of agriculture. Its proximity to Dublin brought about unchecked growth for the county's towns during the Celtic Tiger's peak: Navan, Slane and Kells are blighted with soulless housing estates and the resulting traffic can be hellish.

For visitors, though, there are numerous attractions here, including many tangible reminders of Meath's history: the extraordinary necropolis at Brú na Bóinne and smaller passage graves in the Loughcrew Hills, the Hill of Tara – the seat of power for Irish high kings, until the arrival of St Patrick in the 5th century – and the massive castle in Trim chief among them. You'll find loads of info at www.meathtourism.ie.

Brú Na Bóinne

The vast Neolithic necropolis known as Brú na Bóinne (the Boyne Palace) is one of the most extraordinary sites in Europe and shouldn't be missed. A thousand years older than Stonehenge, it's a powerful and evocative testament to the mind-boggling achievements of prehistoric humans.

The complex was built to house the remains of those who were at the top of the social heap and its tombs were the largest

VISITING BRÚ NA BÓINNE

In an effort to protect the tombs and preserve the mystical atmosphere around them, all visits to Brú na Bóinne start at the **Brú na Bóinne Visitor Centre** (041-988 0300; www.heritageireland.ie; Donore; adult/child visitor centre €3/2, visitor centre, Newgrange & Knowth €11/6; 9am-7pm Jun–mid-Sep, 9am-6.30pm May & mid-end Sep, 9.30am-5.30pm Oct & Feb, 9am-5pm Nov-Jan), from where a bus will take you to the tombs. Built in a spiral design echoing Newgrange, the centre houses an extraordinary series of interactive exhibits on prehistoric Ireland and its passage tombs, and has regional tourism info, an excellent cafe and a book and souvenir shop. Upstairs, a glassed-in observation mezzanine looks out over Newgrange.

Allow plenty of time to visit Brú na Bóinne. Plan on an hour's visit for the interpretive centre alone, two hours if you wish to include a trip to Newgrange or Knowth, and half a day to see all three in one go (Dowth is not open to tourists).

In summer, particularly at weekends, and during school holidays, Brú na Bóinne gets very crowded, and you will not be guaranteed a visit to either of the passage tombs. There are only 750 tour slots and on peak days over 2000 people can show up. Tickets are sold on a first-come, first-served basis (no advance booking) so the best advice is to arrive early in the morning or visit midweek and be prepared to wait.

Importantly, if you turn up at either Newgrange or Knowth first, you'll be sent to the visitor centre. Tours depart from a bus stop that you reach by walking across a strikingly designed bridge over the River Boyne. The buses take just a few minutes to reach the sites. Technically you can walk the 4km to either site from the visitor centre, but you're discouraged from doing so as you might get mowed down on the very narrow lanes by the tour bus you've chosen not to take.

Tours are primarily outdoors with no shelter – bring raingear, just in case.

The visitor centre is on the south side of the river. It's 2km west of Donore and 6km east of Slane, where bridges cross the river from the N51. (Ignore your GPS, which will normally direct you to the monuments rather than the visitor centre, and be sure to follow the signs for Newgrange and/or the Brú na Bóinne visitor centre, rather than Newgrange Farm.)

There are a few eating and sleeping options in the immediate area, but Drogheda, 9km northeast, makes an ideal base, with plenty of accommodation. The village of Slane is also close by, 10km northwest.

artificial structures in Ireland until the construction of the Anglo-Norman castles 4000 years later. The area consists of many different sites; the three principal ones are Newgrange, Knowth and Dowth.

Over the centuries the tombs decayed, were covered by grass and trees, and were plundered by everybody from Vikings to Victorian treasure hunters, whose carved initials can be seen on the great stones of Newgrange. The countryside around the tombs is littered with countless other ancient tumuli (burial mounds) and standing stones.

Sights

Newgrange HISTORIC SITE

(adult/child incl visitor centre €6/3) Even from afar, you know that Newgrange is something special. Its white round stone walls topped by a grass dome look otherworldly, and just the size is impressive: 80m in diameter and 13m high. But underneath it gets even better. Here lies the finest Stone Age passage tomb in Ireland, and one of the most remarkable prehistoric sites in Europe. It dates from around 3200 BC, predating the pyramids by some six centuries.

No one is quite sure of its original purpose. It could have been a burial place for kings or a centre for ritual – although the tomb's precise alignment with the sun at the time of the **winter solstice** also suggests it was designed to act as a calendar.

The name derives from 'New Granary' (the tomb did in fact serve as a repository for wheat and grain at one stage), although a more popular belief is that it comes from the Irish for 'Cave of Gráinne', a reference to a popular Celtic myth. *The Pursuit of Diarmuid and Gráinne* tells of the illicit love between the woman betrothed to Fionn McCumhaill (or Finn McCool), leader of the Fianna, and Diarmuid, one of his most trusted lieutenants. When Diarmuid was fatally wounded, his body was brought to Newgrange by the god Aengus in a vain attempt to save him, and the despairing Gráinne followed him into the cave, where she remained long after he died. This suspiciously Arthurian tale (sub in Lancelot and Guinevere for Diarmuid and Gráinne) is undoubtedly a myth, but it's still a pretty good story. Newgrange also plays another role in Celtic mythology as the site where the hero Cúchulainn was conceived.

Over time, Newgrange, like Dowth and Knowth, deteriorated and was at one stage even used as a quarry. The site was extensively restored in 1962 and again in 1975.

A superbly carved kerbstone with double and triple spirals guards the tomb's main entrance, but the area has been reconstructed so that tourists don't have to clamber in over it. Above the entrance is a slit, or roof box, which lets light in. Another beautifully decorated kerbstone stands at the exact opposite side of the mound. Some experts say that a ring of standing stones encircled the mound, forming a great circle about 100m in diameter, but only 12 of these stones remain, with traces of others below ground level.

Holding the whole structure together are the 97 boulders of the kerb ring, designed to stop the mound from collapsing outwards. Eleven of these are decorated with motifs similar to those on the main entrance stone, although only three have extensive carvings.

The white quartzite that decorates the tomb was originally obtained from Wicklow, 70km to the south – in an age before horse and wheel, it was transported by sea and then up the River Boyne – and there is also some granite from the Mourne Mountains in Northern Ireland. Over 200,000 tonnes of earth and stone also went into the mound.

You can walk down the narrow 19m passage, lined with 43 stone uprights (some of them engraved), which leads into the tomb chamber about one-third of the way into the colossal mound. The chamber has three recesses, and in these are large basin stones that held cremated human bones. As well as the remains, the basins would have held funeral offerings of beads and pendants, but these were stolen long before the archaeologists arrived.

Above, the massive stones support a 6m-high corbel-vaulted roof. A complex drainage system means that not a drop of water has penetrated the interior in 40 centuries.

Knowth HISTORIC SITE

(adult/child incl visitor centre €5/3, incl visitor centre & Newgrange €11/6; ⏲Easter-Oct) Northwest of Newgrange, the burial mound of Knowth was built around the same time and seems set to surpass its better-known neighbour in both its size and the importance of the discoveries made here. It has the greatest collection of passage-grave art ever uncovered in Western Europe, and has been under excavation since 1962.

NEWGRANGE WINTER SOLSTICE

At 8.20am on the winter solstice (between 18 and 23 December), the rising sun's rays shine through the roof box above the entrance, creep slowly down the long passage and illuminate the tomb chamber for 17 minutes. There is little doubt that this is one of the country's most memorable, even mystical, experiences.

There's a simulated winter sunrise for every group taken into the mound. To be in with a chance of witnessing the real thing on one of six mornings around the solstice, enter the free lottery that's drawn in late September or early October. Fill out the form at the Brú na Bóinne visitor centre or enter online (www.heritageireland.ie).

The excavations soon cleared a passage leading to the central chamber, which at 34m is much longer than the one at Newgrange. In 1968 a 40m passage was unearthed on the opposite side of the mound. Although the chambers are separate, they're close enough for archaeologists to hear each other at work. Also in the mound are the remains of six early-Christian souterrains (underground chambers) built into the side. Some 300 carved slabs and 17 satellite graves surround the main mound.

Human activity at Knowth continued for thousands of years after its construction, which accounts for the site's complexity. The Beaker folk, so called because they buried their dead with drinking vessels, occupied the site in the Bronze Age (c 1800 BC), as did the Celts in the Iron Age (c 500 BC). Remnants of bronze and iron workings from these periods have been discovered. Around AD 800 to 900, it was turned into a *ráth* (earthen ring fort), a stronghold of the very powerful O'Neill clan. In 965 it was the seat of Cormac MacMaelmithic, later Ireland's high king for nine years, and in the 12th century the Normans built a motte and bailey (a raised mound with a walled keep) here. The site was finally abandoned in about 1400.

Further excavations are likely to continue for the next decade at least, so you may see archaeologists at work when you visit.

Dowth HISTORIC SITE

The circular mound at Dowth is similar in size to Newgrange – about 63m in diameter – but is slightly taller at 14m high. It has suffered badly at the hands of everyone from road builders and treasure hunters to amateur archaeologists, who scooped out the centre of the tumulus in the 19th century. For a time, Dowth even had a tearoom ignobly perched on its summit. Relatively untouched by modern archaeologists, Dowth shows what Newgrange and Knowth looked like for most of their history. Because it's unsafe, Dowth is closed to visitors, though the mound can be viewed from the road between Newgrange and Drogheda. Excavations began in 1998 and will continue for years to come.

Dowth has two entrance passages leading to separate chambers (both sealed), and a 24m early-Christian underground passage at either end, which connect with the western passage. This 8m-long passage leads into a small cruciform chamber, in which a recess acts as an entrance to an additional series of small compartments, a feature unique to Dowth. To the southwest is the entrance to a shorter passage and smaller chamber.

North of the tumulus are the ruins of **Dowth Castle** and **Dowth House**.

Tours

Brú na Bóinne is one of the most popular tourist attractions in Ireland, and there are oodles of organised tours. Most depart from Dublin.

Mary Gibbons Tours HISTORIC TOURS

(☎01-283 9973; www.newgrangetours.com; tour €35) Tours depart from numerous Dublin hotels, beginning at 9.30am Monday to Friday, 7.50am Saturday and Sunday, and take in the whole of the Boyne Valley including Newgrange and the Hill of Tara. The expert guides offer a fascinating insight into Celtic and pre-Celtic life in Ireland, and you'll get access to Newgrange even on days when all visiting slots are filled. Highly recommended. Pay cash on the bus (no credit cards).

Over the Top Tours HISTORIC TOURS

(☎1800 424 252; www.overthetoptours.com; return ticket €17) One or two trips daily from central Dublin.

Sleeping & Eating

Rossnaree B&B €€
(☎041-982 0975; www.rossnaree.ie; Newgrange; d €100-120; ⊙Apr-Dec; P 🛜) At a sharp corner on the narrow road between Donore and Slane is this magnificent Italianate country house overlooking the River Boyne and surrounded by a working farm. The four bedrooms are luxuriously furnished. Groups of four or more can arrange dinner in advance. The events related in the tale 'Fionn and the Salmon of Knowledge' are said to have taken place on this very spot.

Newgrange Lodge HOSTEL, INN €
(☎041-988 2478; www.newgrangelodge.com; dm €19.50-21, d €70; P @ 🛜) Just east of the Brú na Bóinne visitor centre, you'll find this converted farmhouse with a choice of cosy rooms varying from dorms with four to 10 beds, to hotel-standard rooms. All have private bathrooms. Reception is open 24 hours, and there's a self-catering kitchen, two outdoor patios and a barbecue area. Rates include continental breakfast (with scones!).

Brú na Bóinne Visitor Centre Cafe CAFE €
(dishes €4.50-12; ⊙breakfast & lunch; 👪) On the lower level of the Brú na Bóinne visitor centre, this surprisingly good cafe's extensive vegetarian options include nut and lentil loaf, and eggplant and zucchini cake, plus plenty of other treats like salmon and leek tart and beef lasagne.

Getting There & Away

Bus Éireann (☎041-983 5023; www.buseireann.ie) has a service linking the Brú na Bóinne visitor centre with Drogheda's bus station (one way/return €3.40/6.20, 20 minutes, two daily Monday to Saturday), with connections to Dublin.

Battle of Boyne Site

More than 60,000 soldiers of the armies of King James II and King William III fought on this patch of farmland on the border of Counties Meath and Louth in 1690. In the end, William prevailed and James sailed off to France.

Today, the **battle site** (www.battleoftheboyne.ie; adult/child €4/2; ⊙10am-6pm May-Sep, 9.30am-5.30pm Mar & Apr, 9am-5pm Oct-Feb) is part of the Oldbridge Estate farm. At the visitor centre you can watch a short show about the battle, see original and replica weaponry of the time and explore a laser battlefield model. Self-guided walks through the parkland and battle site allow ample time to ponder the events that saw Protestant interests remain in Ireland. Costumed re-enactments take place in summer.

The battle site is 3km north of Donore, signposted off the N51. From Drogheda, it's 3.5km west along Rathmullan Rd (follow the river).

Laytown

Most famous as the site for the only official beach-run horse race in Europe, Laytown is a sleepy seaside village for most of the year. In late August or early September, though, bookies, punters and jockeys descend in force. The **Laytown Races** (www.meath.ie) have been held here for over 140 years; for one day, Laytown's 3km of golden sand are transformed into a racecourse, attracting a diverse crowd of locals, celebrities and die-hard racing fans.

Just outside Laytown on the road to Julianstown is **Sonairte** (☎041-982 7572; http://sonairte.ie; the Ninch, Laytown; adult/child €3/1; ⊙10.30am-5pm Wed-Sun), the National Ecology Centre. Dedicated to promoting ecological

FIONN & THE SALMON OF KNOWLEDGE

One of the best-known stories in the Fenian Cycle tells of the Salmon of Knowledge, a fish that, once consumed, would bestow enormous wisdom on the eater, including the gift of foresight. An old Druid, Finegas, struggled for seven years to catch the salmon, but only managed to land the elusive fish at a time when a young Fionn McCumhaill was at his camp receiving tuition. As befits the inevitable tragedy of these stories, Finegas set the fish to cook and left Fionn to turn it over the fire, ordering him not to eat so much as the smallest bite. But as Fionn turned the spit, a drop of hot oil from the fish landed on his thumb, which he quickly put in his mouth to soothe. Finegas returned, saw what had happened and knew that it was too late; he bade Fionn eat the rest of the fish and so it was that Fionn acquired wisdom and foresight.

awareness, the centre is a wonderful place to learn about sustainable living and organic horticulture. You can take a guided tour of the organic gardens and 200-year-old orchard, follow the nature trail or river walk, or take a course in anything from beekeeping to foraging for wild food and organic gardening. There's a shop and organic cafe on-site, and a **farmers market** sets up from 10.30am to 4pm. The centre is five minutes' walk from Laytown train station.

Trains between Dublin's Connolly Station and Laytown run every half-hour (€12, 50 minutes).

Slane

POP 1099

Slane's 18th-century stone houses and cottages slink down a steep hill to the River Boyne, which glides beneath a narrow bridge. A planned estate village, Slane grew up around the enormous castle after which it was named. At the main crossroads four identical houses face each other: local lore has it that they were built for four sisters who had taken an intense dislike to one another and kept a beady-eyed watch from their individual residences. Slane Castle's massive grey gate is southwest of the town centre.

Slane is 15km west of Drogheda and just 6km west of Brú na Bóinne, at the junction of the N2 and N51.

Sights

Slane Castle CASTLE

(www.slanecastle.ie) Still the private residence of Henry Conyngham, Earl of Mountcharles, Slane Castle is best known in Ireland as the setting for massive outdoor **rock concerts**, such as Kings of Leon in 2011. U2's 1984 album *The Unforgettable Fire* was recorded here (though the castle featured on the album cover is in Moydrum in County Westmeath) and the band have returned to play several occasions in the castle grounds.

Built in 1785 in the Gothic-revival style by James Wyatt, the building was later altered by Francis Johnson for George IV's visits to Lady Conyngham. She was allegedly his mistress, and it's said the road between Dublin and Slane was built especially straight and smooth to speed up the randy king's journeys. In 1991 the castle was gutted by a fire, whereupon it was discovered that the earl was underinsured. A major fundraising drive – of which the summer concerts were a part – led to a painstaking restoration.

Guided tours (adult/child €7/5; ⏲noon-5pm Sun-Thu Jun-Aug) include the neo-Gothic Ballroom, completed in 1821, and the Kings Room, where the monarch stayed while visiting his mistress.

Distilled by the nearby Cooley Distillery, Slane Castle Irish Whiskey was specially created for the Conyngham family, and is for sale at the castle. You can taste it and other Irish whiskeys by booking on a **whiskey-tasting tour** (☎041-982 4080; incl castle tour €12).

The castle is 1km west of the town centre along the Navan road.

Hill of Slane HISTORIC SITE

About 1km north of the village is the Hill of Slane, a fairly plain-looking mound that stands out only for its association with a thick slice of Celto-Christian mythology. According to legend, St Patrick lit a paschal (Easter) fire here in 433 to proclaim Christianity throughout the land. Patrick's fire infuriated Laoghaire, the pagan high king of Ireland, who had expressly ordered that no fire be lit within sight of the Hill of Tara. He was restrained by his far-sighted druids, who warned that 'the man who had kindled the flame would surpass kings and princes'. Laoghaire went to meet Patrick, and all but one of the king's attendants – a man called Erc – greeted Patrick with scorn.

Here the story *really* gets far-fetched. During the meeting, Patrick killed one of the king's guards and summoned an earthquake to subdue the rest. After his Herculean efforts, Patrick calmed down a little and plucked a shamrock from the ground, using its three leaves to explain the paradox of the Holy Trinity – the union of the Father, the Son and the Holy Spirit in one. Laoghaire wasn't convinced, but he agreed to let Patrick continue his missionary work. Patrick's success that day – apart from keeping his own life, starting an earthquake and giving Ireland one of its enduring national symbols – was good old Erc, who was baptised and later became the first bishop of Slane. To this day, the local parish priest lights a fire here on Holy Saturday.

The Hill of Slane originally had a church associated with St Erc and, later, a round tower and monastery, but only an outline of the foundations remains. Later a motte and bailey were constructed, which are still visible on the western side of the hill. You can also see the remains of a ruined church and tower that were once part of an early-16th-century Franciscan friary. On a clear day, from the top of the tower, which is always open, you can see the Hill of Tara and the Boyne Valley, as well as (it's said) seven Irish counties.

Ledwidge Museum MUSEUM
(041-982 4544; www.francisledwidge.com; Janesville; adult/child €3/1; 10am-1pm & 2-5.30pm) Simple yet moving, the Ledwidge Museum is located in a quaint cottage that was the birthplace of poet Francis Ledwidge (1891–1917). He died on the battlefield at Ypres, having survived Gallipoli and Serbia. A keen political activist, Ledwidge was thwarted in his efforts to set up a branch of the Gaelic League in the area, but found an outlet in verse.

The museum provides an insight into Ledwidge's life and works, and the cottage itself is an evocative example of how farm labourers lived in the 19th century. It is about 1.5km east of Slane on the Drogheda road (N51). Opening hours can be erratic – call ahead.

Sleeping & Eating

Slane Farm Hostel HOSTEL €
(041-982 4390; www.slanefarm hostel.ie; Harlinstown House, Navan Rd; camp sites per person €8, dm/s/d/self-catering terraced cottage €18/25/50/70; P@) These former stables, built by the Marquis of Conyngham in the 18th century, have been converted into a wonderful hostel that's part of a working dairy farm. Common areas include a games room and kitchen, with free-range eggs and a vegie plot for guests to use. Free bikes are available. It's 2.5km west of Slane.

Old Post Office BISTRO €€
(041-982 4090; www.theoldpostoffice.ie; Main St; mains €10-28; breakfast & lunch daily, dinner Tue-Sat) This former post office is a tastefully restored restaurant with simple, honest homemade food, and four bright, contemporary B&B guestrooms (doubles €70).

Georges Patisserie BAKERY €
(www.georgespatisserie.com; Chapel St; Tue-Sat) Artisan breads and scones from this French patisserie are good for making sandwiches or a quick pick-me-up; sadly, the spectacular confections in the window are by prior order only.

Drinking & Entertainment

Boyles PUB
(www.boylesofslane.com; Main St) The owner of this pub with a fire-engine-red front, musician Andrew Cassidy, hosts a knock-out line-up of live gigs and trad sessions.

Information

Slane has no tourist office; info is available at www.slanetourism.com.

Getting There & Away

Bus Éireann has four to six buses daily to Drogheda (€4.20, 35 minutes), Dublin (€13.50, one hour) and Navan (€3.90, 20 minutes).

Navan & Around

POP 3710

You won't want to waste too much time in the working town of Navan, Meath's main hub and the crossroads of the busy Dublin road (N3) and the Drogheda–Westmeath road (N51). If you do stop here, Trimgate St is lined with restaurants and pubs.

There are a few sights around the town, however. The impressive and relatively intact **Athlumney Castle** (Kentstown Rd, Athlumney) was built by the Dowdall family in the 16th century, with additions made 100 years later. After King James' defeat at the Battle of the Boyne, Sir Lancelot Dowdall set fire to the castle to ensure that James' conqueror, William of Orange, would never shelter in his home or confiscate it. He watched the blaze from the opposite bank of the river before leaving for France and then Italy. As you enter the estate, take a right towards the Loreto Convent, where you can pick up the keys to the castle. It's about 2km southeast of Navan.

Pleasant **walks** around Navan include the towpath along the old River Boyne canal towards Slane and Drogheda. On the southern bank, you can go as far as Stackallen and the Boyne bridge (about 7km), passing the impressive red-brick **Ardmulchan House** (closed to the public) and, on the opposite bank, the ruins of 16th-century **Dunmoe Castle**.

Tara

The **Hill of Tara** is Ireland's most sacred stretch of turf, an entrance to the underworld, occupying a place at the heart of Irish history, legend and folklore. It was the home of the mystical druids, the priest-rulers of ancient Ireland, who practised their particular form of Celtic paganism under the watchful gaze of the all-powerful goddess Maeve (Medbh). Later it was the ceremonial capital of the high kings – 142 of them in all – who ruled until the arrival of Christianity in the 6th century. It is also one of the most important ancient sites in Europe, with a Stone Age passage tomb and prehistoric burial mounds that date back up to 5000 years.

Although little remains other than humps and mounds of earth on the hill, its historic and folkloristic significance is immense. History and preservation have run headlong into the demands of sprawl and convenience in the Tara Valley, however. A battle between government and campaigners over contentious road construction has been raging for years and work had to be halted on the first day of digging in 2007 when an ancient site that could rival Stonehenge was uncovered. Despite pleas from eminent historians and archaeologists around the world, the controversy continues. For an update on the current situation, visit www.tarawatch.org.

History

The Celts believed that Tara was the sacred dwelling place of the gods and the gateway to the otherworld. The passage grave was thought to be the final resting place of the Tuatha dé Danann, the mythical fairyfolk – they were real enough, but instead of pixies and brownies, they were earlier Stone Age arrivals on the island.

As the Celtic political landscape began to evolve, the druids' power was usurped by warlike chieftains who took kingly titles; there was no sense of a united Ireland, so at any given time there were countless *rí tuaithe* (regional kings) controlling many small areas. The king who ruled Tara, though, was generally considered the big shot, the high king, even though his direct rule didn't extend too far beyond the provincial border. The most lauded of all the high kings was Cormac MacArt, who ruled during the 3rd century.

The most important event in Tara's calendar was the three-day harvest *feis* (festival) that took place at Samhain, a precursor to modern Halloween. During the festival, the high king pulled out all the stops: grievances would be heard, laws passed and disputes settled amid an orgy of eating, drinking and partying.

When the early Christians hit town in the 5th century, they targeted Tara straight away. Although the legend has it that Patrick lit the paschal fire on the Hill of Slane, some people believe it took place on Tara's sacred hump. The arrival of Christianity marked the beginning of the end for Celtic pagan civilisation, and the high kings began to desert Tara, though the kings of Leinster continued to be based here until the 11th century.

In August 1843, Tara saw one of the greatest crowds ever to gather in Ireland. Daniel O'Connell, 'Liberator' and leader of the opposition to union with Great Britain, held one of his monster rallies at Tara, and up to 750,000 people came to hear him speak.

Sights

Rath of the Synods HISTORIC SITE

The names applied to Tara's various humps and mounds were adopted from ancient texts, and mythology and religion intertwine with the historical facts. The Protestant church grounds and graveyard spill onto the remains of the Rath of the Synods, a triple-ringed fort where some of St Patrick's early synods (meetings) supposedly took place. Excavations of the enclosure suggest that it was used between AD 200 and 400 for burials, rituals and living quarters. Originally the ring fort would have contained wooden houses surrounded by timber palisades.

Excavations have uncovered Roman glass, shards of pottery and seals, showing links with the Roman Empire even though the Romans never extended their power to Ireland.

Royal Enclosure HISTORIC SITE

To the south of the church, the Royal Enclosure is a large, oval Iron Age hill fort, 315m in diameter and surrounded by a bank and ditch cut through solid rock under the soil. Inside the Royal Enclosure are several smaller sites.

The **Mound of the Hostages**, a bump in the northern corner of the enclosure, is the most ancient known part of Tara and the most visible of its remains. Supposedly a prison cell for hostages of the 3rd-century king Cormac MacArt, it is in fact a small Stone Age passage grave dating from around 1800 BC that was later used by Bronze Age people. The passage contains some carved stonework, but is closed to the public.

The mound produced a treasure trove of artefacts, including some ancient Mediterranean beads of amber and faience (glazed pottery). More than 35 Bronze Age burials were found here, as well as a mass of cremated remains from the Stone Age.

Although two other earthworks inside the enclosure, **Cormac's House** and the **Royal Seat**, look similar, the Royal Seat is a ring fort with a house site in the centre, while Cormac's House is a barrow (burial mound) in the side of the circular bank. Cormac's House commands the best views of the surrounding lowlands of the Boyne and Blackwater Valleys.

Atop Cormac's House is the phallic **Stone of Destiny**, originally located near the Mound of the Hostages, which represents the joining of the gods of the earth and the heavens. It's said to be the inauguration stone of the high kings, although alternative sources suggest that the actual coronation stone was the Stone of Scone, which was removed to Edinburgh, Scotland, and used to crown British kings. The would-be king stood on top of the Stone of Destiny and, if the stone let out three roars, he was crowned. The mass grave of 37 men who died in a skirmish on Tara during the 1798 Rising is next to the stone.

Enclosure of King Laoghaire HISTORIC SITE
South of the Royal Enclosure is this large but worn ring fort where the king, a contemporary of St Patrick, is supposedly buried standing upright and dressed in his armour.

Banquet Hall HISTORIC SITE
North of the churchyard is Tara's most unusual feature, a rectangular earthwork measuring 230m by 27m along a north–south axis. Tradition holds that it was built to cater for thousands of guests during feasts. Much of this information comes from the 12th-century *Book of Leinster* and the *Yellow Book of Lecan,* which even includes drawings of the hall.

Opinions vary as to the site's real purpose. Its orientation suggests that it was a sunken entrance to Tara, leading directly to the Royal Enclosure. More recent research, however, has uncovered graves within the compound, and it's possible that the banks are in fact the burial sites of some of the kings of Tara.

Gráinne's Fort HISTORIC SITE
Gráinne was the daughter of King Cormac. Betrothed to Fionn McCumhaill (Finn McCool), she eloped with Diarmuid, one of the king's warriors, on her wedding night, becoming the subject of the epic *The Pursuit of Diarmuid and Gráinne.* Gráinne's Fort and the northern and southern **Sloping Trenches** off to the northwest are burial mounds.

Eating

McGuires Coffee Shop CAFE €
(dishes €4-6; breakfast & lunch;) If a walk on the hill has worked up an appetite, this cafe-souvenir shop at the base can restore you with snacks like apple and cinnamon pancakes or waffles with toffee sauce.

Information

Entrance to Tara is free and the site itself is always open. There are good explanatory panels by the entrance. Unfortunately, many people let their dogs roam free on the hill – watch your step!

Old Tara Book Shop (Tue, Thu, Sat & Sun) At the base of the hill, this tiny, jumbled second-hand bookshop is run by Michael Slavin, who has authored an informative little book about the site, *The Tara Walk* (€3).

Tara Visitor Centre (046-902 5903; www.heritageireland.ie; adult/child €3/1; 10am-6pm Jun–mid-Sep) A former Protestant church (with a window by artist Evie Hone) is home to Tara's visitor centre, screening a 20-minute audiovisual presentation about the site.

Getting There & Away

Tara is 10km southeast of Navan, off the Dublin–Cavan road (N3). It's poorly signposted – count on asking for directions.

Bus Éireann (01-836 6111) services linking Dublin and Navan pass within 1km of the site (€11.40, 40 minutes, hourly Monday to Saturday and four times on Sunday). Ask the driver to drop you off at the Tara Cross, where you take a left turn off the main road.

Dunsany Castle

See how the other 1% lives at **Dunsany Castle** (046-902 5198; www.dunsany.com; Dunsany; adult/child/under 9yr €20/10/free; by appointment), the residence of the lords of Dunsany and one of the oldest continually inhabited buildings in Ireland. Construction started on the castle in the 12th century, with major alterations taking place in the 18th and 19th centuries.

Today the castle houses an impressive private art collection and many other treasures related to important figures in Irish history, such as Oliver Plunkett and Patrick Sarsfield, leader of the Irish Jacobite forces at the siege of Limerick in 1691. A guided tour takes almost two hours and offers a fascinating insight into the family history as well as that of the castle. It remains a family home, and maintenance and restoration are ongoing, so opening hours vary and different rooms are open to visitors at different times – call for details.

You can also buy **Dunsany Home Collection** home wares here: locally made table linen and accessories, as well as various articles designed by Lord Dunsany himself.

The castle is about 5km south of Tara on the Dunshaughlin–Kilmessan road.

Trim

POP 1375

Dominated by its mighty castle and atmospheric ruins, the quiet town of Trim was an important settlement in medieval times. Five city gates surrounded a busy jumble of streets, and as many as seven monasteries were established in the immediate area.

It's hard to imagine nowadays, but a measure of Trim's importance was that Elizabeth I considered building Trinity College here. One student who did go to school here – at least for a short time – was Dublin-born Arthur Wellesley, the Duke of Wellington, who studied in Talbot Castle and St Mary's Abbey.

Today, Trim's history is everywhere, with ruins scattered about the town and streets still lined with tiny old workers cottages.

Sights

Trim Castle CASTLE

(King John's Castle; www.heritageireland.ie; adult/child €4/2; ⏲10am-6pm Easter-Sep, 9.30am-5.30pm Oct, 9.30am-5.50pm Sat & Sun Feb-Easter, 9am-5pm Sat & Sun Nov-Jan) This remarkably preserved edifice was Ireland's largest Anglo-Norman fortification and is proof of Trim's medieval importance. Hugh de Lacy founded Trim Castle in 1173, but Rory O'Connor, said to have been the last high king of Ireland, destroyed this motte and bailey within a year. The building you see today was begun around 1200 and has hardly been modified since.

Throughout Anglo-Norman times the castle occupied a strategic position on the western edge of the Pale, the area where the Anglo-Normans ruled supreme; beyond Trim was the volatile country where Irish chieftains and lords fought with their Norman rivals and vied for position, power and terrain. By the 16th century, the castle had begun to fall into decline and in 1649, when the town was taken by Cromwellian forces, it was severely damaged.

In 1996 the castle briefly returned to its former glory as a location for Mel Gibson's *Braveheart*, in which it served as a 'castle double' for the castle at York.

The castle's grassy two-hectare enclosure is dominated by a massive stone keep, 25m tall and mounted on a Norman motte. Inside are three levels, the lowest divided by a central wall. Just outside the central keep are the remains of an earlier wall.

The principal outer-curtain wall, some 500m long and for the most part still standing, dates from around 1250 and includes eight towers and a gatehouse. It also has a number of sally gates from which defenders could exit to confront the enemy. The finest stretch of the outer wall runs from the River Boyne through Dublin Gate to Castle St. Within the northern corner was a church and, facing the river, the Royal Mint, which produced Irish coinage (called 'Patricks' and 'Irelands') into the 15th century.

St Patrick's Cathedral Church CHURCH

(Lornan St) That huge steeple you see belongs to St Patrick's Cathedral Church, parts of which date to the 15th century. Bishops were enthroned here from 1536 but it wasn't given cathedral status until 1955.

Talbot Castle & St Mary's Abbey HISTORIC SITES

Across the River Boyne from the castle are the ruins of the 12th-century Augustinian **St Mary's Abbey**, rebuilt after a fire in 1368 and once home to a wooden statue of Our Lady of Trim, which was revered by the faithful for its miraculous powers.

In 1415 part of the abbey was converted into a fine manor house by Sir John Talbot, then viceroy of Ireland; it came to be known as **Talbot Castle**. The Talbot coat of arms can be seen on the northern wall. Talbot went to war in France where, in 1429, he was defeated at Orleans by Joan of Arc. He was taken prisoner, released and went on fighting the French until 1453. He became known as 'the scourge of France' and even got a mention in Shakespeare's *Henry VI*: 'Is this the Talbot so much feared abroad/That with his name the mothers still their babes?'

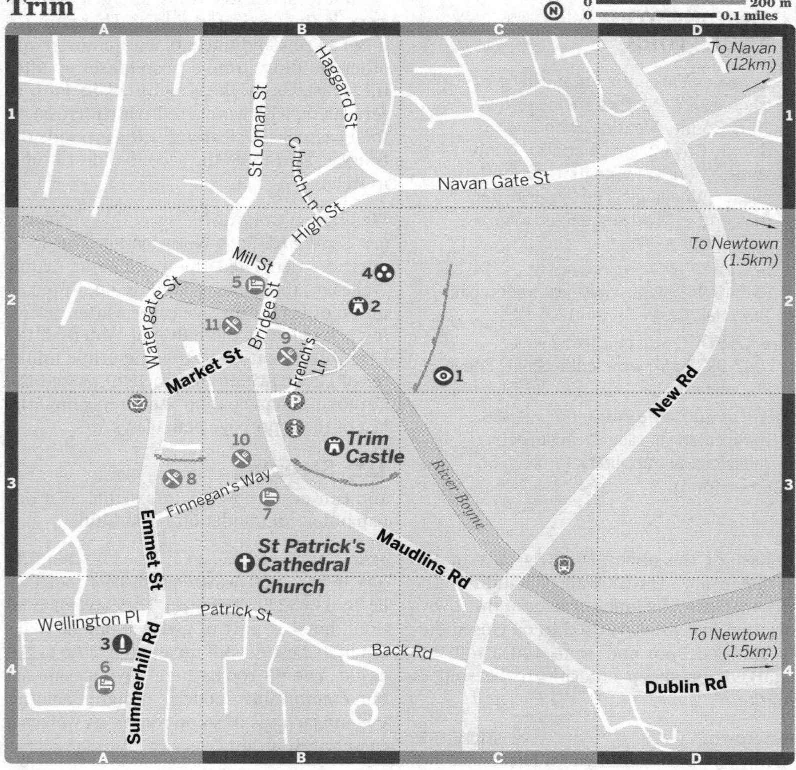

In 1649 Cromwell's soldiers invaded Trim and set fire to the abbey's revered statue, a rather poignant slap in the face of Catholic belief. Just in case the locals didn't get the symbolism of the gesture, the soldiers destroyed the remaining parts of the abbey as well.

In the early 18th century, Talbot Castle was owned by Esther 'Stella' Johnson, the mistress of Jonathan Swift. He later bought the property from her and lived there for a year. Swift was rector of Laracor, 3km southeast of Trim, from around 1700 until his death in 1745. From 1713 he was also – and more significantly – dean of St Patrick's Cathedral in Dublin.

Just northwest of the abbey building is the 40m **Yellow Steeple**, once the bell tower of the abbey, dating from 1368 but damaged by Cromwell's soldiers. It takes its name from the colour of the stonework at dusk.

Trim

Top Sights

St Patrick's Cathedral Church B3
Trim Castle B3

Sights

1 Sheep Gate C2
St Mary's Abbey .... (see 2)
2 Talbot Castle B2
3 Wellington Column A4
4 Yellow Steeple B2

Sleeping

5 Bridge House Tourist Hostel B2
6 Castle Arch Hotel A4
7 Trim Castle Hotel B3

Eating

8 An Tromán A3
9 Franzini O'Brien's B2
10 La Scala B3
11 Wau Asian B2

TRACING YOUR ANCESTORS

Genealogical centres that can help trace your ancestors are located in Trim, County Meath; Cavan Town, County Cavan; and Dundalk, County Louth. (County Monaghan currently has no genealogical centre.) Contact the centres in advance to arrange a consultation.

» **Meath Heritage Centre** (☎046-943 6633; www.meathroots.com; Town Hall, Castle St, Trim)

» **Louth County Library** (042-933 5457; www.louthcoco.ie; Roden Pl, Dundalk)

» **Cavan Genealogy** (☎049-436 1094; cavangenealogy@eircom.net; Johnston Central Library, Farnham St, Cavan town)

East of the abbey ruins is part of the 14th-century town wall, including the **Sheep Gate**, the lone survivor of the town's original five gates. It used to be closed daily between 9pm and 4am, and a toll was charged for sheep entering to be sold at market.

Newtown HISTORIC SITES

About 1.5km east of town on Lackanash Rd, Newtown Cemetery contains an interesting group of ruins. The former **Parish Church of Newtown Clonbun** contains the late 16th-century tomb of Sir Luke Dillon, Chief Baron of the Exchequer during the reign of Elizabeth I, and his wife Lady Jane Bathe. The effigies are known locally as the Jealous Man and Woman, perhaps because of the sword lying between them. Rainwater that collects between the two figures is claimed to cure warts. Apparently you place a pin in the puddle and then jab the wart; when the pin becomes covered in rust, warts will vanish. Some say you should leave a pin on the statue as payment for the cure.

The other ruins here are the **Cathedral of Sts Peter and Paul** and the 18th-century **Newtown Abbey**. The cathedral was founded in 1206 and burned down two centuries later. Although parts of the cathedral wall were flattened by a storm in 1839, it throws a superb echo back to **Echo Gate** across the river.

Southeast of these ruins, and just over the river, is the **Crutched Friary**. There are ruins of a keep, and traces of a watchtower and other buildings from a hospital set up after the Crusades by the Knights of St John of Jerusalem, who wore a red crutch (cross) on their cassocks. **St Peter's Bridge**, beside the friary, is said to be the second-oldest bridge in Ireland.

Wellington Column MONUMENT

(cnr Summerhill Rd & Wellington Pl) The local burghers dedicated this column to Arthur Wellesley, the Duke of Wellington, in recognition of his impressive career: after defeating Napoleon at the Battle of Waterloo, the Iron Duke went on to become prime minister of Great Britain and in 1829 passed the Catholic Emancipation Act, repealing the last of the repressive penal laws.

Sleeping

You can easily cover Trim's sights as a day trip but accommodation is plentiful.

Trim Castle Hotel HOTEL €€

(☎046-948 3000; www.trimcastlehotel.com; Castle St; d €65-130; P@🛜👪) This stylish boutique hotel is part of a development that's doing its best to spiff up an area close to the castle. The 68 rooms here have a compact but comfortable modern design; facilities include jacuzzis in some rooms, as well as a carvery restaurant.

Crannmór House B&B €€

(☎046-943 1635; www.crannmor.com; Dunderry Rd; d €76; P🛜) Rolling farmland and paddocks surround this vine-covered old house about 2km along the road to Dunderry. Bright rooms and traditional hospitality are on offer, and if you're interested in angling, the owner is an experienced *ghillie* (fishing guide).

Castle Arch Hotel HOTEL €€

(☎046-943 1516; www.castlearchhotel.com; Summerhill Rd; d from €99; P@🛜👪) The 22 rooms at this modern business-class hotel have a posh, heavy-drapery design accented with vintage touches. Very friendly service and a great deal at the price.

Bridge House Tourist Hostel HOSTEL €

(☎046-943 1848; bridgehousehostel@gmail.com; Bridge St; dm/d €20/40; P🛜) Quirky old house right on the river with basic four-bed dorm rooms and a couple of doubles. Contact in advance to confirm your arrival time.

Eating

An Tromán CAFE €

(http://artisanfoodstoretrim.webs.com; Market St; dishes €4.50-7; breakfast & lunch Mon-Sat) Crammed with gourmet goodies, this fabulous deli is perfect for picking up the makings of a picnic. If it's not picnic weather, you can order daily specials like a bowl of soup and tuna and sweet corn sandwich, or chicken and mushroom pie and a meringue nest with fruit and fresh cream.

La Scala ITALIAN €€

(046-948 3236; Finnegan's Way; mains €10.50-23.50; 5-10pm Mon-Thu, 1-10pm Fri-Sun;) Contemporary La Scala serves timeless, classic Italian food: porcini mushroom and truffle risotto, *frittura mista* with sea bass, tiger prawns and squid, and chicken breast with ham and mozzarella, as well as a wide range of pastas.

Franzini O'Brien's INTERNATIONAL €€

(046-943 1002; French's Lane; mains €14-25; lunch Sun, dinner daily;) Buzzing local favourite, with a casual atmosphere and an eclectic menu spanning nachos to teriyaki chicken with noodles, and duck wontons.

Wau Asian ASIAN €€

(046-948 3873; Bridge St; mains €8-15.50; lunch Thu, Fri & Sun, dinner daily) Extensive Chinese, Malaysian, Indonesian and Thai dishes. Afterwards, pop into the Sally Rodgers pub below.

Drinking & Entertainment

Marcy Regan's PUB

(Lackanash Rd, Newtown; Thu-Tue) This small, traditional pub beside St Peter's Bridge claims to be Ireland's second oldest. It's a no-frills kind of place just steeped in old-world atmosphere. There's often a trad music session on Friday nights.

Sally Rogers PUB

(046-943 8926; Bridge St) Pop in here (below Wau Asian) for a drink overlooking the river.

Information

Bank of Ireland (Market St) Exchanges money and has an ATM.

Post office (cnr Emmet & Market Sts)

Tourist office (046-943 7227; Castle St; 9.30am-5.30pm Mon-Sat) Has a handy tourist trail map, a cafe and a genealogical centre.

Getting There & Around

Bus Éireann runs a bus at least once an hour between Dublin and Trim (€9.27, 70 minutes). Buses stop on New Rd just beyond the bridge.

Around Trim

There are a couple of evocative Anglo-Norman remains in the area around Trim. **Bective Abbey** was founded in 1147 and was the first Cistercian offspring of magnificent Mellifont Abbey in Louth. The abbey at Bective was much changed in the following years and the remains seen today are 13th- and 15th-century additions, consisting of the chapter house, church, ambulatory and cloister. In 1543, after the Dissolution of the Monasteries, the abbey was used as a fortified house and the tower was built. Bective is 7.5km northeast of Trim on the way to Navan.

Some 12km northwest of Trim, on the road to Athboy, is **Rathcairn**, the smallest Gaeltacht (Irish-speaking) district in Ireland. Rathcairn's population is descended from a group of Connemara Irish speakers who were settled on an estate here as part of a social experiment in the 1930s.

Kells

POP 2257

Kells is best known for the magnificent illuminated manuscript that bears its name, and which so many visitors queue to see on their visit to Trinity College in Dublin. Although the great book wasn't created here, it was stashed in Kells, one of the leading monasteries in the country, from the end of the 9th century until 1541, when it was removed by the Church.

The town has been hard hit by the demise of the Celtic Tiger, including the closure of its heritage centre (though it's hoped the centre may reopen in the coming years – check with the tourist office for updates). However, remnants of the once great monastic site include some interesting high crosses and a thousand -year-old round tower.

On older maps you may see Kells labelled as Ceanannus Mór or just Ceanannus, once its official name; locally it is always known as Kells.

Sights

Market Cross MONUMENT

(Headfort Pl) Until 1996 the Market Cross had stood for centuries in Cross St, at the heart of the town centre. Besides inviting the pious admiration of the faithful, the cross was used as a gallows in the aftermath of the 1798 revolt; the British garrison hanged rebels from the crosspiece, one on each arm so the cross wouldn't fall over. But what a thousand years of foul weather and the sacrilegious British couldn't do, a careless bus driver did in 1996 and with one bad turn the cross was toppled. It was eventually repaired and re-erected.

Round Tower & High Crosses HISTORIC SITES

The Protestant church of **St Columba** (grounds 10am-1pm & 2-5pm Mon-Sat, church Jun-Aug), west of the town centre, has a 30m-high 10th-century round tower on the southern side. It's without its conical roof, but it's known to date back at least as far as 1076, when the high king of Tara was murdered in its confined apartments.

Inside the churchyard are four 9th-century high crosses in various states of repair. The **West Cross**, at the far end of the compound from the entrance, is the stump of a decorated shaft, which has scenes of the baptism of Jesus, the Fall of Adam and Eve, and the Judgement of Solomon on the eastern face, and Noah's ark on the western face. All that is left of the **North Cross** is the bowl-shaped base stone.

Near the tower is the best preserved of the crosses, the **Cross of Patrick and Columba**, with its semi-legible inscription, *Patrici et Columbae Crux,* on the eastern face of the base.

The other surviving cross is the unfinished **East Cross**, with a carving of the Crucifixion and a group of four figures on the right arm.

FREE **St Colmcille's House** HISTORIC SITE

(10am-5pm Sat & Sun Jun-Sep) From the churchyard exit on Church St, St Colmcille's House is left up the hill, among the row of houses on the right side of Church Lane. This squat, solid structure is a survivor from the old monastic settlement. Its name is a misnomer, as it was built in the 10th century and St Colmcille was alive in the 6th century. Experts have suggested that it was used as a scriptorium, a place where monks illuminated books.

The site is usually locked except during the summer months, but ask at the tourist office about the keys or phone **Mrs Carpenter** (046-924 1778; 1 Lower Church View) for access.

Sleeping & Eating

Teltown House B&B B&B €€

(046-902 3239; www.teltownhouse.webs.com; Teltown; d €90; P) This lovingly restored old stone farmhouse is full of character and history, with period-style rooms and an incredibly warm welcome. The farm was the location of the Irish equivalent of the Olympic games 2000 years ago, and 2000 years before *that,* rock art was carved on stones that still stand next to the B&B. Teltown House is midway between Kells and Navan, 6km southeast of Kells, east of the N3 at the Silver Tankard pub.

Headfort Arms Hotel HOTEL €€

(046-924 0063; www.headfortarms.ie; John St; s/d from €69/89; P@) Family run and right in the town centre, the Headfort Arms has 45 comfortable rooms with classic styling and mod cons including flat-screen TVs, orthopaedic mattresses and laptop safes. Rooms in the charming old building have the most character; there's a small spa for indulgent treatments. The hotel's dining options include the independently run **Vanilla Pod** (mains €17-25; lunch Sun, dinner daily) bistro, serving dishes like warm goat's cheese salad with fennel and orange.

Information

Tourist office (046-924 7840; Headfort Pl; 9.30am-1pm & 2-5pm Mon-Fri) Screens a free 13-minute audiovisual presentation.

Getting There & Away

Bus Éireann (01-836 6111) has services from Kells to Dublin (€11.43, 90 minutes, hourly) via Navan. There are also buses to Cavan (€10.53, 45 minutes, hourly).

Loughcrew Cairns

With all the hoopla over Brú na Bóinne, the amazing Stone Age passage graves strewn about the Loughcrew Hills are often overlooked. There are 30-odd tombs here but they're hard to reach and relatively few people ever bother, which means you can enjoy this moody and evocative place in peace.

It's well worth making the effort to get to the three hills, Carnbane East (194m), Carnbane West (206m) and Patrickstown

(279m) – although the last has been so ruined by 19th-century builders that there's little to see other than splendid views of the surrounding countryside.

Like Brú na Bóinne, the graves were all built around 3000 BC, but unlike their better-known and better-excavated peers, the Loughcrew tombs were used at least until 750 BC. As at Newgrange, larger stones in some of the graves are decorated with spiral patterns. Some of the graves look like large piles of stones, while others are less obvious, their cairn having been removed. Archaeologists have unearthed bone fragments and ashes, stone balls and beads.

The cairns are west of Kells, along the R154, near Oldcastle.

CARNBANE EAST

Carnbane East has a cluster of sites. **Cairn T** (049-854 1240; www.heritageireland.ie; admission free; 10am-6pm Jun-Aug; P) is the biggest at about 35m in diameter, with numerous carved stones. One of its outlying kerbstones is called the Hag's Chair, and is covered in gouged holes, circles and other markings. You need the gate key to enter the passageway and a torch to see anything in detail. It takes about half an hour to climb Carnbane East from the car park.

In summer, access to Cairn T is controlled by **Heritage Ireland** (www.heritageireland.ie), which provides guides. But locals are passionate about the place and at any time of the year you can arrange for guides who will not only show you Cairn T but take you to some of the other cairns as well. Enquire at Kells' tourist office, or pick up the key from the cafe at Loughcrew Gardens.

CARNBANE WEST

From the car park, it takes about an hour to reach the summit of Carnbane West, where Cairn D and L, both some 60m in diameter, are located. They're in poor condition, though you can enter the passage and chamber of Cairn L, where there are numerous carved stones and a curved basin stone in which human ashes were placed.

Cairn L is administered by **Heritage Ireland** (www.heritageireland.ie), which gives out the key only to those with an authentic research interest.

LOUGHCREW GARDENS

A labour of love, **Loughcrew Gardens** (049-854 1060; www.loughcrew.com; adult/child €6/3; noon-6pm Mar-Oct) incorporates 2.5 hectares of lawns, terraces and herbaceous borders along with a lime avenue, yew walk, canal and parterre. There's also a medieval moat, tower house and St Oliver Plunkett's family church, as well as a cafe with wi-fi in a log-built lodge.

Every summer (usually in July), the gardens play host to the **Loughcrew Opera** (tickets from €79), where guests are encouraged to dress in period costume and bring a picnic.

Loughcrew Gardens are northwest of Kells, along the R154, near Oldcastle.

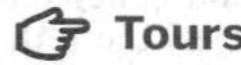

Tours

Beyond the Blarney HISTORIC TOURS
(087 151 1511; www.beyondtheblarney.ie)
Knowledgeable Oldcastle-based outfit offering day tours (from €60) and workshops such as Loughcrew Cairns art (from €40).

COUNTY LOUTH

The Wee County, as it's dubbed, prospered greatly during the Celtic Tiger era thanks to its proximity to Dublin, leading to a welcome increase in activities, restaurants and nightlife (along with commuter congestion).

In the 5th and 6th centuries, Louth was at the centre of ecclesiastical Ireland, with wealthy religious communities at the monastery at Monasterboice and the Cistercian abbey at Mellifont. The 12th-century Norman invaders were responsible for the development of Dundalk and the two towns on opposite banks of the Boyne that united in 1412 to become what is now Drogheda.

Today Drogheda is Louth's most appealing town, a bustling place steeped in history that makes a good base for visiting Brú na Bóinne, just over the border in County Meath. It's a quick trip to the picturesque Cooley Peninsula to enjoy the mountainous landscape and the delightful medieval village of Carlingford.

Louth can easily be covered as a day trip from Dublin, but you'll get more from your visit by spending some time exploring the county.

Drogheda

POP 28,973

Just 48km north of Dublin, Drogheda is a historic fortified town straddling the River Boyne. A clutch of fine old buildings, a handsome cathedral and a riveting museum give it plenty of cultural interest, while its atmospheric old pubs, fine restaurants, numerous sleeping options and good transport links make it an excellent base for exploring the world-class attractions that surround it.

This bend in the fertile Boyne Valley has been a desirable location right back to 910, when the Danes built a fortified settlement here. In the 12th century, the Normans added a bridge and expanded the two settlements on either side of the river. They also built a large defensive motte and bailey on the southern side at Millmount. By the 15th century, Drogheda was one of Ireland's four largest walled towns.

The 17th century brought devastation, however, when Drogheda was the scene of Cromwell's most notorious Irish slaughter in 1649. Things went from bad to worse in 1690, when the town backed the wrong horse at the Battle of the Boyne and surrendered the day after the defeat of James II.

During the Celtic Tiger years, the city became a cheaper alternative for Dublin commuters, triggering new developments along the riverfront. Today, Drogheda remains a thriving multicultural regional hub.

Sights

St Peter's Roman Catholic Church — CHURCH

(West St) Displayed in a glittering brass-and-glass case in the north transept, the shrivelled **head of St Oliver Plunkett** (1629–81) is this church's main draw (the rest of the martyr was separated at his hanging in 1681). Actually it's two churches in one: the first, designed by Francis Johnston in classical style and built in 1791; and the newer addition, built in the Gothic style visible today.

St Laurence's Gate — HISTORIC SITE

Astride the eastwards extension of the town's main street is St Laurence's Gate, the finest surviving portion of the city walls. This imposing pile of stone is not in fact a gate but instead a barbican, a fortified structure used to defend the gate, which was further behind it.

Dating from the 13th century, the structure was named after St Laurence's Priory, which once stood outside the gate; no traces of it now remain. The barbican consists of two lofty towers, a connecting curtain wall and the entrance to the portcullis. When the town walls were completed in the 13th century, they ran for 3km around the town, enclosing 52 hectares.

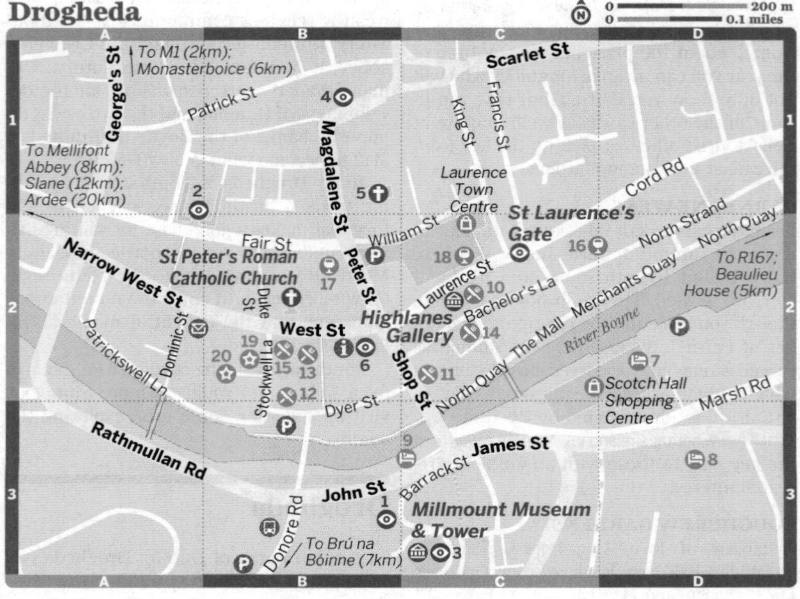

Highlanes Gallery ART GALLERY
(www.highlanes.ie; Laurence St; admission by donation; ⏲10.30am-5pm Mon-Sat) This impressive gallery is set in a beautifully converted 19th-century monastery. As well as a good permanent collection of paintings, there are regular temporary exhibitions. Attached is a shop featuring high-quality Louth craftwork, and a chic cafe, Andersons.

Millmount Museum & Tower MUSEUM
Across the river from town, in a village-like enclave amid a sea of dull suburbia, is Millmount, an artificial hill overlooking the town. The mound may have been a prehistoric burial ground along the lines of Newgrange, but it has never been excavated. Legend has it that it is the burial place of Amergin, a warrior-poet who arrived in Ireland from Spain around 1500 BC.

Drogheda

Top Sights

	Highlanes Gallery	C2
	Millmount Museum & Tower	C3
	St Laurence's Gate	C2
	St Peter's Roman Catholic Church	B2

Sights

1	Butter Gate	B3
2	Courthouse	A1
3	Governor's House	C3
4	Magdalene Tower	B1
5	St Peter's Church of Ireland	B1
6	Tholsel	B2

Sleeping

7	D Hotel	D2
8	Green Door Hostel	D3
9	Salthouse	C3

Eating

10	Andersons	C2
11	Bella Atina	C2
12	D'vine	B2
13	Kierans Deli	B2
14	Stockwell Artisan Foods Café	C2
15	Stockwell Artisan Foods Deli	B2

Drinking

16	C Ní Cairbre	C2
17	Clarke & Sons	B2
18	Peter Matthews	C2

Entertainment

19	Drogheda Arts Centre	B2
20	Earth	B2

The Normans constructed a motte-and-bailey fort on top of this convenient command post overlooking the bridge. It was followed by a castle, which in turn was replaced by a **Martello tower** (adult/child €3/2) in 1808. The tower played a dramatic role in the 1922 Civil War, when it was Drogheda's chief defensive feature and suffered heavy shelling from Free State forces. It has recently been restored and offers great views over the town below.

It was at Millmount that the defenders of Drogheda, led by the governor Sir Arthur Ashton, made their last stand before surrendering to Cromwell. Later, an 18th-century English barracks was built round the base, and today the buildings house craft shops, museums and a restaurant.

A section of the army barracks is now used as the **Millmount Museum** (☎041-983 3097; www.millmount.net; adult/child museum €3.50/2.50, museum & tower €5.50/3; ⏲9.30am-5.30pm Mon-Sat, 2-5pm Sun), which has interesting displays about the town and its history. Exhibits include three wonderful late 18th-century guild banners, perhaps the last in the country. There's also a room devoted to Cromwell's brutal siege of Drogheda and the Battle of the Boyne. The pretty cobbled basement is full of gadgets and kitchen utensils from bygone times, including a cast-iron pressure cooker and an early model of a sofa bed. Across the courtyard, the **Governor's House** opens for temporary exhibitions.

You can drive up to the hilltop or climb Pitcher Hill via the steps from St Mary's Bridge.

The 13th-century **Butter Gate**, just northwest of Millmount, is the only surviving genuine town gate in Drogheda. This tower, with its arched passageway, predates the remains of St Laurence's Gate by about a century.

Other Structures HISTORIC SITES
Right in the centre of town is the 1770-built **Tholsel** (cnr West & Shop Sts), an 18th-century limestone town hall, now occupied by the tourist office.

Heading northwest from here is the restored 19th-century former **courthouse** (Fair St), home to the sword and mace presented to the town council by William of Orange after the Battle of the Boyne.

To the north is **St Peter's Church of Ireland** (William St), not to be confused with St Peter's Roman Catholic Church. This is the church whose spire was burned by Cromwell's men, resulting in the death of 100 people seeking sanctuary inside. Today's church (1748) is the second replacement of the original destroyed by Cromwell. It stands in an attractive close approached through lovely wrought-iron gates. Note the old 'Blue School' (for the education of freemen's sons) of 1844 on one side.

Head up Magdalene St from the church to see the 14th-century **Magdalene Tower**, the bell tower of a Dominican friary founded in 1224. It was here that England's King Richard II, accompanied by a great army, accepted the submission of the Gaelic chiefs with suitable ceremony in 1395. Peace lasted only a few months, however, and Richard's return to Ireland led to his overthrow in 1399. Treasonous connections with the Gaelic Irish also led to the Earl of Desmond's demise; he was beheaded here in 1468.

Keep making your way uphill from here to see the rather charming and more recent **Church of Our Lady of Lourdes** off Hardmans Gardens.

Finally, you can't help but admire the 1855 **Boyne Viaduct** carrying trains over the river east of the centre. Each of the 18 beautiful stone arches has a 20m span; erecting the piers bankrupted one company.

Festivals & Events

Drogheda Arts Festival ARTS
(www.droghedaartsfestival.ie) Theatre, music, film, poetry, visual arts and workshops such as silk painting take place over the May Day weekend in early May.

Drogheda Samba Festival MUSIC
(www.droghedasamba.com) Latin and African beats resonate across Drogheda during the last weekend of June.

Drogheda Food Festival FOOD
(www.drogheda.ie) A huge farmers market, world beer trail and racing waiters and bar staff are among the highlights of Drogheda's foodie fest in mid-August.

Sleeping

Drogheda has plenty of high-standard accommodation to choose from.

TOP CHOICE **D Hotel** HOTEL €€
(041-987 7700; www.thed.ie; Scotch Hall, Marsh Rd; d €69-109; P @ wi-fi family) Slick, hip and unexpected, this is Drogheda's top dog when it comes to accommodation. Minimalist rooms are bathed in light and decked out with designer furniture and cool gadgets. There's a stylish bar and restaurant, a mini gym and fantastic views of the city. The hotel is popular with hen and stag parties, so beware of pounding music on weekends.

Windsor Lodge B&B €€
(041-984 1966; www.barwindsorlodge.com; The Court, North Rd; s/d €40/70; P wi-fi family) This large purpose-built guesthouse has a good choice of modern, spacious rooms with country-style decor and new bathrooms. There's a lovely conservatory, a large lounge and a relaxing outdoor seating area.

Green Door Hostel HOSTEL €
(041-983 4422; www.greendoorireland.com; 13 Dublin Rd; dm €15-20, d with/without bathroom €55/40; @ wi-fi) Set in a grand mid-18th-century Georgian house near the train station, this cheerful hostel has a variety of dorm room sizes and private rooms, the pick of which have their own TVs and kitchenettes.

Orley House B&B €
(041-983 6019; www.orleyhouse.com; Bryanstown, Dublin Rd; d €70; P @ wi-fi family) This spick-and-span B&B about 2km out of town has large comfortable rooms and a warm welcome. It's a well-run place with excellent service, and a hearty breakfast served in a sun-filled conservatory.

Salthouse B&B €€
(041-983 4426; 46 John St; d from €40) This Aussie-owned guesthouse is a good bet, with simple but clean rooms with pine furniture and white linens. It's above its namesake **restaurant** (mains €15-26; breakfast, lunch & dinner), which has a popular bar (with regular live music) and an underutilised terrace overlooking the river.

Eating

TOP CHOICE **Eastern Seaboard Bar & Grill** IRISH €€
(041-980 2570; www.easternseaboard.ie; 1 Bryanstown Centre, Dublin Rd; mains €10.50-33; lunch & dinner; wi-fi family) Build it and they will come... Despite its unpromising location in a business park near the train station, this stylised, contemporary space has been packed since opening, with switched-on staff and quirky details like a backlit decanter collection and metallic fish sculptures. Stunning food like pig's cheek terrine with apple slaw, smoked mackerel pâté, and coffee jelly and vanilla

ice cream is served continuously from lunchtime on. Or you could just drop by for frothy German beers on tap.

Stockwell Artisan Foods Café CAFE €
(www.stockwellartisanfoods.ie; 1 Mayoralty St; mains €9; breakfast & lunch Mon-Sat) The exposed red-brick walls and wooden furniture add to the warmth of this place serving healthy, wholesome wraps, salads, soups and hot dishes. Pick up goodies to go at Stockwell's **deli** (1 Stockwell St; mains €9; breakfast & lunch Mon-Sat), which has a cramped cafe.

Andersons CAFE €
(Highlanes Gallery, Laurence St; mains €6-10; 10.30am-5pm Mon-Sat;) Located in the Highlanes Gallery, this split-level cafe serves a stylish range of bruschetta, bagels and gourmet sandwiches, including open prawn or smoked salmon on multigrain. It also offers baguettes with French brie, as well as cheese, seafood and Mediterranean platters and a great Moroccan salad.

Bella Atina ITALIAN €€
(041-984 4878; 32 Shop St; mains €10-12; dinner Mon-Sat;) In new premises up a flight of stairs from Shop St, the old-school menu at this Italian restaurant features classic pizzas, pastas, and meat and fish dishes. The *penne alla vodka* is a treat.

D'vine MEDITERRANEAN €€
(041-980 0440; Dyer St; mains €14-22; noon-late Wed-Mon) With a cosy interior and sunny courtyard, this wine bar and bistro has a great selection of Mediterranean starting platters, and fish and meat-based mains like pan-fried sea bass and braised lamb shanks, plus a long wine list.

Kierans Deli DELI €
(041-983 8728; 15 West St; Mon-Sat) Renowned deli with a superb selection of picnic options and a hot-food counter for lunch on the run.

Drinking & Entertainment

Drogheda has dozens of bars and pubs, many with live music. Check the event guide at www.drogheda.ie for listings.

C Ní Cairbre PUB
(Carberry's; North Strand) A national treasure, this tiny pub has been owned by the same family since 1880. Old newspaper clippings and long-faded artwork cover most surfaces and it's a great place to catch some traditional music. You might find a session going on any night of the week but especially Tuesday nights and Sunday afternoons.

Peter Matthews PUB
(McPhail's; Laurence St) One of Drogheda's top spots for live music, McPhail's (as it's always called, no matter what the sign says) is popular with a younger crowd and features everything from heavy-metal cover bands to trad sessions. There's a traditional bar at the front and a beer garden out the back.

Clarke & Sons PUB
(Peter St) This wonderful old boozer is right out of a time capsule. Clarke's unrestored wooden interior features snugs and leaded-glass doors that read Open Bar. It attracts an arty crowd and is gay friendly.

Earth NIGHTCLUB
(www.westcourt.ie; Stockwell Lane; Thu-Sun) At the Westcourt Hotel, Drogheda's biggest nightclub attracts a fairly young crowd and can be a bit of a cattle mart, but the music ranges from club classics to hip hop, house and techno, and there's a great beer garden.

Drogheda Arts Centre ARTS CENTRE
(041-983 3946; www.droichead.com; Narrow West St) Drama, music, comedy, film and visual art take to the stage at Drogheda's lively arts centre, which runs regular hands-on workshops such as collage making.

Information

Post office (West St)

Drogheda Library (Stockwell Lane; 10am-8pm Tue & Thu, to 5pm Wed, Fri & Sat) Internet access.

Tourist office (041-987 2843; www.drogheda.ie; West St; 9.30am-5.30pm Mon-Fri, plus 10am-5pm Sat Easter-Sep) Loads of info and super-helpful staff.

Getting There & Away

Bus

Drogheda is on the main M1 Dublin–Belfast route. The bus station is just south of the river on the corner of Rathmullan Rd and Donore Rd. This is one of the busiest bus routes in the country. **Bus Éireann** (041-983 5023) regularly serves Drogheda from Dublin (€6, one hour, one to four hourly). Drogheda to Dundalk is another busy route (€5, 30 minutes, hourly), as is the Brú na Bóinne visitor centre.

Matthews (042-937 8188; http://matthews.ie) has a popular hourly or better service to Dublin (€7) and Dundalk (€7).

Train

The **train station** (☎041-983 8749) is just south of the river and east of the town centre, off Dublin Rd. Drogheda is on the main Belfast–Dublin line (Dublin €15, 35 minutes; Belfast €20, 1½ hours). There are six express trains (and many slower ones) each way, with five on Sunday.

Getting Around

Drogheda is excellent for walking, and many of the surrounding region's interesting sites are within easy cycling distance.

Quay Cycles (☎041-983 4526; 11A North Quay; per day from €15; ⊙May-Oct) Rents bikes.

Around Drogheda

A number of historic sites and attractions lie close to Drogheda, but you'll still need your own transport.

Beaulieu House, Gardens & Car Museum HISTORIC SITE

(☎041-983 8557; www.beaulieu.ie; admission house €8, garden €6, museum €6, combined ticket €20; ⊙11am-5pm Mon-Fri May–mid-Sep, plus 1-5pm Sat & Sun Jul & Aug) Before Andrea Palladio and the ubiquitous Georgian style that changed Irish architecture in the early decades of the 18th century, there was the Anglo-Dutch style, a simpler, less ornate look that is equally handsome. Beaulieu House is a particularly good example and – apparently – the first unfortified mansion to be built in Ireland. It was built between 1660 and 1666 on lands confiscated from Oliver Plunkett's family by Cromwell, and given to the marshal of the army in Ireland, Sir Henry Tichbourne. The red-brick mansion, with its distinctive steep roof and tall chimneys, has been owned by the same family ever since.

The interiors are stunning and house a superb art collection ranging from lesser Dutch masters to 20th-century Irish painters. There's also a wonderfully elegant garden and a classic car museum.

It's about 5km northeast of Drogheda on the Baltray road.

Old Mellifont Abbey HISTORIC SITE

(☎041-982 6459; www.heritageireland.ie; Tullyallen; adult/child €3/1; ⊙visitor centre 10am-6pm Easter-Sep; P) In its Anglo-Norman prime, this abbey was the Cistercians' first and most magnificent centre in the country. Although the ruins are highly evocative and well worth exploring, they still don't do real justice to the site's former splendour.

In the mid-12th century, Irish monastic orders had grown a little too fond of the good life and were not averse to a bit of corruption. In 1142 Malachy, bishop of Down (later canonised for his troubles), was at the end of his tether; he invited a group of hard-core monks from Clairvaux in France to set up shop in a remote location, where they would act as a sobering influence on the local clergy. The Irish monks didn't quite get on with their French guests, and the latter soon left for home. Still, the construction of Mellifont – named for the Latin *mellifons* (honey fountain) – continued, and within 10 years, nine more Cistercian monasteries were established. Mellifont was eventually the mother house for 21 lesser monasteries; at one point as many as 400 monks lived here.

Mellifont not only brought fresh ideas to the Irish religious scene, it also heralded a new style of architecture. For the first time in Ireland, monasteries were built with the formal layout and structure that was being used on the Continent. Only fragments of the original settlement remain, but the plan of the extensive monastery can easily be traced.

Mellifont's most recognisable building, and one of the finest pieces of Cistercian architecture in Ireland, is the lavabo, an octagonal washing house for the monks. It was built in the early 13th century and used lead pipes to bring water from the river. A number of other buildings would have surrounded this main part of the abbey.

After the Dissolution of the Monasteries, a fortified Tudor manor house was built on the site in 1556 by Edward Moore, using materials scavenged from the demolition of many of the buildings.

In 1603, this house was the scene of a poignant and crucial turning point in Irish history. After the disastrous Battle of Kinsale, the vanquished Hugh O'Neill, last of the great Irish chieftains, was given shelter here by Sir Garret Moore until he surrendered to the English lord deputy Mountjoy. After his surrender, O'Neill was pardoned but, despairing of his position, fled to the Continent in 1607 with other old-Irish leaders in the Flight of the Earls. In 1727 the site was abandoned altogether.

The visitor centre describes monastic life in detail. The ruins themselves are always

CROMWELL'S DROGHEDA INVASION

Lauded as England's first democrat and protector of the people, Oliver Cromwell (1599–1658) was an Irish nightmare. Cromwell hated the Irish. To him, they were treacherous infidels, a dirty race of papists who had sided with Charles I during the Civil War. So when 'God's own Englishman' landed his 12,000 troops at Dublin in August 1649, he immediately set out for Drogheda, a strategic fort town and bastion of royalist support.

When Cromwell arrived at the walls of Drogheda, he was met by 2300 men led by Sir Arthur Aston, who boasted that 'he who could take Drogheda could take hell'. After Aston refused to surrender, Cromwell let fly with heavy artillery and after two days the walls were breached. Hell, it seems, was next.

In order to set a terrifying example to any other town that might resist his armies, Cromwell taught the defenders a brutal lesson. Over a period of hours, an estimated 3000 people were massacred, mostly royalist soldiers but also priests, women and children. Aston was bludgeoned to death with his own (wooden) leg. Of the survivors, many were captured and sold into slavery in the Caribbean.

Cromwell defended his action as God's righteous punishment of treacherous Catholics, and was quick to point out that he had never ordered the killing of noncombatants: it was the 17th century's version of 'collateral damage'.

open and there's good picnicking next to the rushing stream. The abbey is about 1.5km off the main Drogheda–Collon road (R168). A back road connects Mellifont with Monasterboice.

Monasterboice HISTORIC SITE

(admission free; ⏲sunrise-sunset; P) Crowing ravens lend an eerie atmosphere to **Monasterboice**, an intriguing monastic site containing a cemetery, two ancient church ruins, one of the finest and tallest round towers in Ireland, and two of the best high crosses.

Down a leafy lane in sweeping farmland, the original monastic settlement here is said to have been founded in the 5th or 6th century by St Buithe, a follower of St Patrick, although the site probably had pre-Christian significance. St Buithe's name somehow got converted to Boyne, and the river is named after him. An invading Viking force took over the settlement in 968, only to be comprehensively expelled by Donal, the Irish high king of Tara, who killed at least 300 of the Vikings in the process.

The high crosses of Monasterboice are superb examples of Celtic art. The crosses had an important didactic use, bringing the gospels alive for the uneducated, and they were probably brightly painted originally, although all traces of colour have long disappeared.

The cross near the entrance is known as **Muirdach's Cross**, named after a 10th-century abbot. The western face relates more to the New Testament, and from the bottom depicts the arrest of Christ, Doubting Thomas, Christ giving a key to St Peter, the Crucifixion, and Moses praying with Aaron and Hur. The cross is capped by a representation of a gabled-roof church.

The **West Cross** is near the round tower and stands 6.5m high, making it one of the tallest high crosses in Ireland. It's much more weathered, especially at the base, and only a dozen or so of its 50 panels are still legible. The more distinguishable ones on the eastern face include David killing a lion and a bear. The western face shows the Resurrection.

A third, simpler cross in the northeastern corner of the compound is believed to have been smashed by Cromwell's forces and has only a few straightforward carvings. This cross makes a great evening silhouette photo, with the round tower in the background.

The **round tower**, minus its cap, is over 30m tall, and stands in a corner of the complex. Records suggest the tower interior went up in flames in 1097, destroying many valuable manuscripts and other treasures. It's closed to the public.

Come early or late in the day to avoid the crowds. It's just off the M1 motorway, about 8km north of Drogheda. The site can be reached directly from Mellifont via a winding route along narrow country roads.

1

2

1. Trim Castle, County Meath (p542)
Proof of Trim's medieval importance, this castle was Ireland's largest Anglo-Norman fortification.

2. Newgrange, County Meath (p535)
Ireland's finest Stone Age passage tomb dates from around 3200 BC, six centuries earlier than the Pyramids.

3. High Cross, County Louth (p553)
A superb example of Celtic art, this high cross at Monasterboice features carvings depicting the gospels.

4. River Boyne, County Meath
Bridge over the River Boyne, near Drogheda.

Dundalk

POP 29,037

An industrial hub, Dundalk is all business and always has been. Although there's not a lot for visitors here, it's a pleasant enough place with a couple of interesting sites.

In the Middle Ages, Dundalk was at the northern limits of the English-controlled Pale, and with partition in 1921 it once again became a border town, this time providing a quick escape from the 'bandit country' of South Armagh.

The **tourist office** (042-933 5484; www.discoverireland/eastcoast; Jocelyn St; 9.30am-1pm & 2-5.15pm Tue-Fri) is next to the museum on Jocelyn St.

Sights

County Museum Dundalk MUSEUM

(www.dundalkmuseum.ie; Jocelyn St; adult/child €3.80/1.25; 10am-5pm Tue-Sat) Different floors in this worthwhile museum are dedicated to the town's early history and archaeology, and to the Norman period. One floor deals with the growth of industry in the area, from the 1750s up to the 1960s – including the cult classic Heinkel Bubble Car.

St Patrick's Cathedral CHURCH

The richly decorated 19th-century St Patrick's Cathedral was modelled on King's College Chapel in Cambridge, England.

Courthouse NOTABLE BUILDING

(cnr Crowe & Clanbrassil Sts) The courthouse is a fine neo-Gothic building with large Doric pillars designed by Richard Morrison. In the front square is the stone **Maid of Éireann**, commemorating the 1798 Rising.

Eating

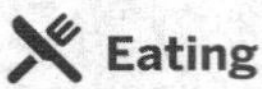

McAteers the Food House CAFE €

(www.mcateersthefoodhouse.com; 14 Clanbrassil St; mains €10-17; breakfast & lunch) Locally sourced organic produce is at the heart of this Aladdin's cave of a deli. If the tantalising goods on display fire up your appetite, its on-site cafe-restaurant cooks up pancakes with bacon and free-range eggs, homemade granola, open-faced sandwiches with Annagassan smoked salmon, and heartier meals such as char-grilled lamb with rosemary jus.

WORTH A TRIP

DROGHEDA TO DUNDALK VIA THE COAST ROAD

Most people just zip north along the M1 motorway but if you want to meander along the coast and see a little of rural Ireland, opt for the R166 from Drogheda north along the coast.

The picturesque little village of **Termonfeckin** was, until 1656, the seat and castle of the primate of Armagh. The 15th-century **castle** (admission free; 10am-6pm), or tower house, is tiny and worth a five-minute stop.

About 2km further north is the busy seaside and fishing centre of **Clogherhead**, with a good, shallow Blue Flag beach at Lurganboy. Squint to ignore the caravan parks and take in the lovely views of the Cooley and Mourne Mountains instead.

A further 14km north, the teensy village of Annagassan absolutely merits a stop for scrumptious picnic goods. At **Coastguard Seafoods** (086 855 8609; Harbour Rd; by appointment), fisherman Terry Butterly oak-smokes quite possibly the finest salmon in Ireland and sells it direct to the public, along with seafood, including live lobsters, for astonishingly cheap prices. You can just turn up, but it's best to call to make sure someone's about to avoid missing out.

For bread to go with the salmon, head to the centre of the village to **O'Neills Bakery** (042-937 2253; until 1pm), a cavernous the five-generations-old bakery with vast ovens (one over a century old), where you can buy still-warm breads, cakes and buns. It appears closed to the public but knock on the door around the side of the building and one of the bakers will let you in. On a chilly day, the inviting aroma of baking bread means you mightn't want to leave.

The 33km route comes to an end in **Castlebellingham**. The village grew up around an 18th-century crenulated mansion, and generations of mud farmers served the landlord within. From here you can continue 12km north to Dundalk along the suburban R132 or join the M1.

Getting There & Around

Bus Éireann (☎042-933 4075; Long Walk) runs an almost hourly service to Dublin (€7.20, 1½ hours). The bus station is near the courthouse.

Clarke Train Station (☎042-933 5521; Carrickmacross Rd) is 900m west of the bus station. It has express trains to Dublin (€15 to €21.50, one hour, seven Monday to Saturday, five Sunday) and Belfast (€19, one hour, eight Monday to Saturday, five Sunday), as well as many slower services.

Cooley Peninsula

Isolated and remote, the Cooley Peninsula has an arresting beauty with forested slopes and sun-dappled, multihued hills rising out of the dark waters of Carlingford Lough. Sweeping views lead the eyes across the water to Northern Ireland's Mourne Mountains, while tiny country lanes wind their way down to deserted stony beaches.

The medieval village of Carlingford is an ideal base. From here, you can continue along the coast road past the pretty village of Omeath to Newry in Northern Ireland. En route, it's worth the short detour to the Flagstaff Viewpoint for a spectacular panorama of the lough and surrounding counties.

CARLINGFORD

POP 623

Someone apparently forgot to tell Carlingford about the Celtic Tiger's demise. Amid the medieval ruins and whitewashed houses, this vibrant little village buzzes with great pubs, chic restaurants and upmarket boutiques, spirited festivals and gorgeous views of the mountains and across Carlingford Lough to Northern Ireland.

As one of the loveliest spots on the coast, Carlingford can be crowded during summer, especially at weekends; book accommodation *well* ahead.

Sights

Holy Trinity Heritage Centre HERITAGE CENTRE

(☎042-937 3454; www.carlingfordheritagecentre.com; Churchyard Lane; adult/concession €3/1.50; ⏰10am-12.30pm & 2-4pm Mon-Fri) Carlingford's heritage centre is in the former Holy Trinity Church. A mural shows what the village looked like in its heyday, and a short video describes the village history and explains what has been done to give it new life in recent years after villagers got together to revive a dying community.

King John's Castle CASTLE

Carlingford was first settled by the Vikings, and in the Middle Ages became an English stronghold under the protection of the castle, which was built on a pinnacle in the 11th to 12th centuries to control the entrance to the lough. On the western side, the entrance gateway was built to allow only one horse and rider through at a time. King John spent a couple of days here in 1210 en route to a battle with Hugh de Lacy at Carrickfergus Castle in Antrim.

Ask at the tourist office about free tours during **Heritage Week** (www.heritageweek.ie) in late August.

Other Sights HISTORIC SITES

Near the tourist office is **Taafe's Castle**, an imposing 16th-century tower house that stood on the waterfront until the land in front was reclaimed to build a short-lived train line. Today it's the storeroom of the attached pub; the best views are from the pub's courtyard.

Carlingford is the birthplace of Thomas D'Arcy McGee (1825–68), one of Canada's founding fathers. A **bust** commemorating him stands opposite Taafe's Castle.

The **Mint**, near the square, is of a similar age and has some interesting Celtic-inspired carvings around the windows. Although Edward IV is thought to have granted a charter to a mint in 1467, no coins were produced here. Near the Mint is the **Tholsel**, the only surviving gate to the original town.

West of the village centre are the remains of a **Dominican friary**, built around 1305 and used as a storehouse by oyster fishermen after 1539.

Activities

For information on angling tours, ask at the tourist office or check online at www.carlingford.ie.

Táin Trail WALKING

Carlingford is the starting point for the 40km Táin Trail, which makes a circuit of the Cooley Peninsula through the Cooley Mountains. The route is a mixture of surfaced roads, forest tracks and green paths. The tourist office has trail info.

Cooley Birdwatching Trail BIRDWATCHING

Much of the Cooley Peninsula is protected and is home to various species of birds including godwits, red-breasted mergansers, buzzards, tits and various finches. Ask at the tourist office for information on the trail.

WORTH A TRIP

FLAGSTAFF VIEWPOINT

Travelling along the Cooley Peninsula from Carlingford to Newry in Northern Ireland, a quick 3km detour rewards you with swooping views of Carlingford Lough, framed by rugged, forested mountains, green fields and glittering blue Irish Sea beyond.

Flagstaff Viewpoint lies *just* over the border in County Armagh. Heading northwest along the coast road (the R173), follow the signs to your left onto Ferryhill Rd, then turn right up to the viewpoint's car park. The quickest way to reach Newry from here is to retrace your steps and rejoin the R173.

Carlingford Adventure Centre OUTDOOR ACTIVITIES
(☎042-937 3100; www.carlingfordadventure.com; Tholsel St) Runs a wide range of activities including sailing, kayaking, windsurfing, rock climbing and archery.

Festivals & Events

Almost every weekend during the warmer months, Carlingford goes event crazy: there are summer schools, medieval festivals, leprechaun hunts, food festivals and anything that'll lure folks in off the M1.

Carlingford Oyster Festival FOOD
(www.carlingford.ie) This mid-August festival celebrates Carlingford's famous oysters with an oyster treasure hunt, fishing competition, music, food markets and a regatta on Carlingford Lough.

Sleeping

TOP CHOICE **Ghan House** INN €€€
(☎042-937 3682; www.ghanhouse.com; Main Rd; d from €105; P@☎) Set in flower-filled gardens, this 18th-century Georgian house has 12 guestrooms, each exquisitely decorated with period antiques and original artworks. Book one of the four rooms in the main house for character and old-world charm – the annexe just doesn't have the same appeal. There's a superb restaurant on-site and a **cookery school** (cooking/wine-tasting courses from €95/35) that attracts top guest chefs and offers an impressive programme of events.

Belvedere House B&B €€
(☎042-938 3828; www.belvederehouse.ie; Newry St; d €90; ☎) An excellent deal, rooms at this lovely B&B are modern but cosy with antique pine furniture, subtle lighting and pretty colour schemes. Guests have access to leisure facilities at the local Four Seasons hotel and breakfast is served in the downstairs Bay Tree restaurant.

McKevitt's Village Hotel HOTEL €€
(☎042-937 3116; www.mckevittshotel.com; Market Sq; s €85-95, d €120-140; P☎) With 17 rooms kitted out in light creams and whites, this hotel is a bit old school, but you get more for your money than at some of Carlingford's pricier options. Kippers are among the breakfast choices cooked to order.

Carlingford Adventure Centre HOSTEL €
(☎042-937 3100; www.carlingfordadventure.com; Tholsel St; dm/s/d €20/25/50) Popular with school groups, this activity centre's accommodation is generally quieter outside term time. Dorms are simple and the welcome isn't as warm as a regular hostel, but it's clean and there are some doubles with private bathrooms.

Eating & Drinking

TOP CHOICE **PJ O'Hares** PUB
(www.pjoharescarlingford.com; Newry St; mains €9.50-19.50; ⊙lunch & dinner) On a sunny Sunday afternoon, there's no better place in Carlingford than the beer garden of this wonderful stone-floor pub; in chilly weather, head for the blazing fire. Main courses include beef and Guinness pie, but you can easily fill up on sublime tapas-style starters such as pan-fried crab claws in garlic butter, tangy chicken wings and, of course, Carlingford oysters. Live music plays regularly (try to catch rockin' local duo the Nooks).

Ghan House IRISH €€€
(☎042-937 3682; www.ghanhouse.com; Main Rd; mains €24-32; ⊙lunch Sun, dinner Mon-Sat) Guests staying at Ghan House receive a discount at its restaurant, which is renowned for its classic food incorporating its own breads, stocks, ice creams and sauces, and herbs and vegetables from its garden. Twice a year, it hosts Georgian banquet nights complete with sword fighting.

Magee's Bistro SEAFOOD €€
(☎042-937 3751; www.mageesbistro.com; Tholsel St; mains €17.50-32; ⏰dinner) The word 'bistro' doesn't do justice to this outstanding seafood restaurant, which has a long, *long* list of fresh catches with creative interpretations, such as cod and salmon parcels in mustard cream sauce.

Kingfisher FUSION €€
(☎042-937 3716; www.kingfisherbistro.com; Dundalk St; mains €17-26; ⏰lunch & dinner) Set in a beautifully restored grain store, the Kingfisher serves up a short but sound menu of modern Irish food with international twists. Go for Thai spiced pork with sticky rice and sweet Asian salad, duck confit or spiced Cajun chicken with sour cream. It's all extremely good.

Bay Tree IRISH €€
(☎042-938 3828; www.belvederehouse.ie; Newry St; mains €18-24; ⏰lunch Sun, dinner daily, closed Mon & Tue winter) Lovely little place at Belvedere House B&B, serving simple, stylish food made from seasonal local ingredients.

Food for Thought DELI, CAFE €
(Dundalk St; dishes €4.50-12; ⏰breakfast & lunch) A rainbow of jams and chutneys lines the walls of this deli-cafe. Croquettes, quiches and fish cakes are among the tasty treats to eat in or take away, with great daily specials too.

Oystercatcher Bistro SEAFOOD €€
(☎042-937 3922; www.theoystercatcher.com; Market Sq; mains €13.50-22; ⏰dinner Wed-Sun) Specialities of these white-tableclothed premises include Capalana (North African–spiced seafood and meat) and cola-marinated pork ribs.

Information

Tourist office (☎042-937 3033; www.carlingford.ie; ⏰10am-5pm) In a former train station next to the bus stop on the waterfront.

Getting There & Around

Bus Éireann (☎042-933 4075) has services to Drogheda (€12.15) and Dublin (€15.30).

There's great cycling around the Cooley Peninsula. Rent wheels and pick up maps of cycling routes at **On Your Bike** (☎087 239 7467; per day/week €20/60). Bikes can be delivered to your accommodation or the tourist office.

COUNTY CAVAN

Cavan is paradise for boaters, anglers, walkers, cyclists and artists. Known as the 'Lake Country', there's supposedly a lake for every day of the year, and the county is famed for its course fishing. Between the steely grey waters is a gentle landscape of meandering streams, bogs and drumlins. Cavan has some spectacular walking trails through the wild Cuilcagh Mountains, which are the source of the 300km River Shannon. The county's quiet, rural charm is best appreciated from the water, especially the tranquil Shannon–Erne Waterway.

The area has an intricate history. Magh Sleacht, a plain near the border village of Ballyconnell, was an important Druidic centre in the 5th century when St Patrick was busy converting the pagan Irish to Christianity, and the area is still littered with tombs, standing stones and stone circles from this time. The Gaelic O'Reilly clan ruled until the 16th century, when they joined the other Ulster lords to fight the Nine Years' War (1594–1603) against the English and were defeated. As part of the Ulster Plantation, Cavan was divided among English and Scottish settlers. In the 1640s, taking advantage of England's troubles, Owen Roe O'Neill led a rebellion against the settlers. O'Neill died in 1649 of suspected poisoning in Clough Oughter Castle near Cavan. After the War of Independence in 1922, the Ulster counties of Cavan, Monaghan and Donegal were incorporated into the Republic.

Cavan's lakes create a tangled knot of narrow, twisting roads – take your time and enjoy the views that appear unexpectedly around each bend.

Activities

FISHING

Cavan's exceptional lake fishing reels in anglers, especially to the county's southern and western borders. It's primarily coarse fishing, but there's also some game angling for brown trout in Lough Sheelin. Most lakes are well signposted, and the types of fish available are marked.

For more information, contact **Cavan Tourism** (☎049-433 1942; www.cavantourism.com) or **Inland Fisheries Ireland** (☎071-985 1435; www.fisheriesireland.ie).

You can also pick up anglers guides from tourist offices.

WALKING

The highlight for many walkers in the region is the Cavan Way, a 26km trail between the hamlets of Blacklion and Dowra through the Cuilcagh Mountains. Heading south from Blacklion, it takes you through an area known locally as the Burren and its ancient burial site Magh Sleacht, which is dotted with prehistoric monuments – court cairns, ring forts and tombs – and was one of the last strongholds of Druidism. It continues past the Shannon Pot, the source of Ireland's longest river, then by road to Dowra, passing over the Black Pigs Dyke, an ancient fortification that once divided Ireland in two.

From Blacklion it's mainly hill walking; from Shannon Pot to Dowra it's mainly road. The highest point on the walk is Giant's Grave (260m). You'll need OS map No 26 and the *Cavan Way* map guide. Maps are on display in Blacklion and Dowra. Detailed route information (including downloadable PDF maps) is available online at www.cavantourism.com. The route can be boggy, so take spare socks!

At Blacklion you can pick up the Ulster Way and at Dowra you can join the Leitrim Way, which runs between Manorhamilton and Drumshanbo.

Cavan Town

POP 3934

Cavan's county town is a solidly workaday place with some handsome Georgian houses and a famous crystal showroom.

Sights

FREE Cavan Crystal Showroom CRYSTAL SHOWROOM

(www.cavancrystaldesign.com; Dublin Rd; 10am-6pm Mon-Sat, noon-5pm Sun) The town's crystal is displayed at this showroom 2km southeast of the town centre on the N3. It also sells a wide variety of local crafts.

Bell Tower HISTORIC SITE

All that remains of the 13th-century Franciscan friary the town grew up around is an ancient bell tower, next to the grave of 17th-century rebel leader Owen Roe O'Neill in Abbey St's cemetery.

Sleeping & Eating

The tourist office can help with accommodation. If you like your spice, the town has a high concentration of Asian eateries, including four Chinese joints.

TOP CHOICE Farnham Estate HOTEL €€€

(049-437 7700; www.farnhamestate.ie; Cavan; d from €130;) Set in misty woodlands, this sprawling 16th-century estate is part of the Radisson group. The luxurious rooms blend contemporary style with period features and character, and there's a garden-view restaurant, a stunning indoor/outdoor infinity swimming pool and a spa (also open to nonguests) with a thermal suite and gym. The estate is 3km west of town on the R198.

Oak Room IRISH €€

(049-437 1414; www.theoakroom.ie; 62 Main St; mains €15-22.50; dinner Tue-Sun;) The Oak Room's decor is minimalist with hardwood floors and eclectic art on the walls, but the menu is ambitious: baked breadcrumbed brie with cranberry and apple compote, followed by roasted prawn salad with mango and lime salsa, or crispy Silverhill duck.

McMahons Cafe Bar CAFE €

(Main St; dishes €5.80-12; 10.30am-late Mon-Fri, 11am-late Sat, 3pm-late Sun) A hip establishment that could hold its own in Dublin, by day McMahons is a funky cafe whipping up squeezed-on-the-spot juices and fresh-filled bagels. At night, its cavernous tiered bar puts on regular live bands, cutting-edge DJs, steaming pizzas and a wicked cocktail list.

Chapter One CAFE €

(www.chapteronecafe.ie; 24 Main St; dishes €5-8.25; breakfast & lunch Mon-Sat;) Heaving at lunchtime when locals descend to dine on the huge range of filled bagels, soups, nachos and specials such as quesadillas, this friendly, informal place is one of the town's most popular cafes.

Cavan Farmers Market MARKET €

(Town Hall St; 10am-1pm Fri) Held in the Town Hall St public car park.

Information

Tourist office (049-433 1942; www.cavantourism.com; Farnham St; 9.45am-1.30pm & 2-5pm Mon-Fri) Above the library.

Getting There & Around

Buses arrive at and depart from the small **bus station** (049-433 1353; Farnham St). There are 10 services daily to Dublin (€12.15, two hours), four daily to Donegal (€15.75, two hours) and three daily (one on Sunday) to Belfast

(€10.53, three hours). There are also various services to small towns throughout the county.

Around Cavan Town

LOUGH OUGHTER & KILLYKEEN FOREST PARK

Rod-wielding anglers congregate at Lough Oughter, which splatters across the map like spilt liquid. Coarse fishing aside, the wildlife-rich lough is also idyllic for naturalists, walkers and anyone wanting to vanish into a landscape of shimmering waters and cathedrallike aisles of trees. It's best accessed via Killykeen Forest Park (049-433 2541; www.coillteout doors.ie; admission free; 9am-9pm), 12km northwest of Cavan, where various nature trails (from 1.5km to 5.8km) lead you through the woods and along the shore. Keep an eye out for stoats, badgers, foxes, grey squirrels and hedgehogs, as well as some amazing birdlife.

Many of the low overgrown islands in the lake were *crannógs* (fortified, artificial islands). The most spectacular is home to Clough Oughter Castle, a 13th-century circular tower perched on a tiny speck of land. It was used as a lonely prison, then as a stronghold by rebel leader Owen Roe O'Neill, who was (probably) poisoned there in 1649, before it was destroyed by Cromwell's army in 1653. Although the castle lies out of reach over the water, it's worth getting near for the view: go on foot via the forest trails, or get a closer look by car by turning left out of the Killykeen park exit and following the narrow road running north from the village of Garthrattan.

BUTLERSBRIDGE

Heading 7km north from Cavan along the N3 you'll pass the pretty village of Butlersbridge. Set on the banks of the River Annalee, Butlersbridge is a good place for a riverside picnic.

Alternatively, pop into the Derragarra Inn (mains €9; lunch & dinner), an ivy-covered pub with a wood-beamed interior, fabulous riverside deck and timeless bar food (roast beef with Yorkshire pudding, breaded cod, Irish stew).

CLOVERHILL

Just 4km north of Butlersbridge on the N54, the lovely little village of Cloverhill is best known for its award-winning restaurant, the Olde Post Inn (047-55555; www.theoldepostinn.com; d €100, 5-course dinner €56; lunch Sun, dinner Tue-Sun; P). The charming red-brick-and-stone restaurant serves outstanding modern Irish cuisine based on traditional ingredients such as suckling pig, salmon, pigeon and lamb, but there's also a vegetarian menu, and a bargain early-bird menu some days. In the former post master's residence, the six guestrooms are small but tasteful, with elegant colour schemes.

BELTURBET

POP 1395

In a prime position on the Shannon–Erne Waterway, this charming, old-fashioned village, 16km northwest of Cavan, is an angler's favourite. It's also a busy base for cruise boats, and a good starting point for a cycling trip along the canal and river system.

You can hire a boat from Emerald Star (049-952 2933; www.emeraldstar.ie; per week from €1352.50; Apr-Oct) to cruise between Belturbet and Belleek and back. Bike hire and route advice are available at Fitz Hire (049-952 2866; fitzpatrickhire@eircom.net; Belturbet Business Park, Creeney; per day €15).

The beautifully restored Belturbet Railway Station (049-952 2074; www.belturbet-station.com; Railway Rd; admission by donation; by appointment) houses a visitor centre exploring the history of rail travel in the area. Trains used the station from 1885 until 1959, after which it languished for 40 years. Call in advance if you'd like to visit.

The cosiest accommodation in town is the welcoming, cherry-coloured Church View Guest House (049-952 2358; www.churchviewguesthouse.com; 8 Church St; s/d €40/70; P). Its cold store room makes it especially popular with anglers – book ahead.

Amigo's Ristorante (049-952 4089; Main St; mains €17-22; dinner) cooks up a long list of pizzas and an even longer range of pastas, plus classic Italian meat and fish dishes.

Local suppliers for the small but stellar Belturbet Farmers Market (4-6pm Fri) include prize-winning Corleggy hard pasteurised goat's cheese. Contact cheesemaker Silke Cropp at Corleggy (049-952 2930) to enquire about cheese-making courses.

Fronted by a photogenic sign of a kicking ass (ie donkey), the Mad Ass Bar (Main St) merits a stop for a pint.

Dublin–Donegal Bus Éireann (049-433 1353) services stop outside the post office.

BALLY WHO?

All over Ireland you'll see the town prefix 'Bally' (and variations thereof, such as Ballyna and Ballina). The ubiquitous term originates from the Irish phrase 'Baile na'. It's often mistranslated as 'town', but there were very few towns in Ireland when the names came about. A closer approximation is 'place of'; hence Ballyjamesduff, for example, means Place of James Duff (or James Duff's place). Dublin's Irish name is Baile Átha Cliath (Place of the Hurdle Ford). If it was anglicised, it too would be a Bally, spelt something like 'Ballycleeagh'.

Other common place names include Carrick (or Carrig), meaning 'rock' in Irish, and Dun, from the Irish *dún* (meaning 'fort').

Southern Cavan

BALLYJAMESDUFF & AROUND

POP 1690

A sleepy market town, Ballyjamesduff was the one-time home of the Earl of Fife, James Duff, an early Plantation landlord. His descendant, Sir James Duff, commanded English troops during the suppression of the 1798 Rebellion.

These days the town is best known as the home of the **Cavan County Museum** (☎049-854 4070; www.cavanmuseum.ie; Virginia Rd; adult/child €3/1.50; ⏲10am-5pm Tue-Sat, plus 2-6pm Sun Jun-Oct), located inside a superbly preserved former convent. Highlights of the impressive collection include a huge array of 18th-, 19th- and 20th-century costumes and folk items, and relics from the Stone, Bronze, Iron and Middle Ages, including the Celtic Killycluggin stone and the three-faced Corleck Head, as well as a 1000-year-old boat excavated from Lough Errill. There's also a large feature on Irish sports.

The area's other main attraction is **Lough Sheelin**, which is famous for its trout fishing. May and June are the best months for anglers, but it's a scenic place for horse riding, walking or boating year-round.

TOP CHOICE **Ross Castle** (☎086 824 2200; www.ross-castle.com; Mountnugent; d €110; P) At Mountnugent, 9km south of Ballyjamesduff, this 1590-built castle was partially destroyed by Cromwell but rebuilt by the Nugent family. Today it's an atmospheric B&B that's not for the fainthearted – the steps get steeper and narrow the higher you climb into its tower, one of its guestrooms has no bathroom door (the bathroom is squished into an alcove), and it's haunted (by the castle builder's daughter, who the owners swear leaves lights shimmering and turns taps on and off). But if that doesn't deter you, it's an unforgettable experience. Call ahead to confirm your arrival time.

Nearby, on the lakeshore, spacious rooms at tranquil **Ross House** (☎049-854 0218; www.ross-house.com; Mountnugent; d/apt €60/80; P) have their own fireplaces and/or conservatories. The hosts organise horse riding (from €18 per hour), horse-riding lessons (from €20 per hour) and boat hire (from €25 per day).

There are no buses to Ballyjamesduff; the closest bus stop is in Virginia.

Eastern Cavan

Many settlements in the county's east, such as the handsome town of **Virginia**, were laid out as 17th-century Plantation estates. While in the area, it's worth stopping at **Kingscourt** to visit **St Mary's Catholic Church**, with its superb 1940s stained-glass windows made by artist Evie Hone.

Just northeast of Kingscourt is the 225-hectare **Dún an Rí Forest Park** (☎042-966 7320; www.coillteoutdoors.ie; cars €5; ⏲9am-9pm). There are colour-coded forest walks (all under 4km long), with picnic places and a wishing well. Look out for mink and otters along the river.

Bordering the forest, the 19th-century **Cabra Castle** (☎042-966 7030; www.cabracastle.com; s/d/cottage from €95/150/110; P wi-fi) is now a deluxe hotel decked out in plush period furnishings. Most rooms are in its courtyard area; there are also self-catering cottages. The lobby and some guestrooms have wi-fi. It's 3km out of Kingscourt on the Carrickmacross road.

Northwestern Cavan

Set against the dramatic backdrop of the Cuilcagh Mountains, the remote northwestern edges of Cavan are some of its most scenic. There's little in the way of public transport in the area but the express Donegal–Dublin buses pass through Ballyconnell and Bawnboy four times daily. The Westport–Belfast bus stops in Blacklion; contact **Bus Éireann** (☎049-433 1353) in Cavan for schedules.

BALLYCONNELL

POP 747

The pretty canal-side village of Ballyconnell is a popular angling centre and a bustling place in summer with visitors making their way along the Shannon–Erne Waterway, which wends its way through town.

In a converted farmhouse, the simple little **Sandville House** (☎049-952 6297; http://homepage.eircom.net/~sandville; dm €20, d from €40; P) is Cavan's only hostel. Rooms have two to 10 beds and there's a meditation room as well as a kitchen. The hostel is 3.5km southeast of the village (signposted off the N87). The Dublin to Donegal bus stops on request at the Slieve Russell Hotel, from where you can prearrange to be picked up. Call ahead as it's often closed for private retreats.

For relaxation of a more luxurious kind, the **Slieve Russell Hotel** (☎049-952 6444; www.slieverussell.ie; Cranaghan; d from €119; P@), 2km southeast of town, has marble columns, fountains, restaurants, bars, and 18- and nine-hole golf courses, with golf lessons available from PGA pros (per hour €45). Its 222 rooms are elegantly furnished; spa treatments include flotation tanks, a herbal sauna and a salt grotto.

BLACKLION & AROUND

POP 174

Traversed by the Cavan Way (p560), the area between Blacklion and Dowra is littered with prehistoric monuments, including the remains of a *cashel* (stone-walled circular fort) and the ruins of several sweathouses, used mostly in the 19th century.

Dedicated foodies make the pilgrimage here to one of the country's finest restaurants, **MacNean House & Restaurant** (☎071-985 3022; www.macneanrestaurant.com; Main St; d €140-200, dinner menus €70-85, with paired wines €125, Sunday lunch €39; ⊙lunch Sun, dinner Wed-Sun; P). Make a reservation before you book your flight to Ireland – the wait for a table at award-winning TV chef Neven Maguire's exceptional restaurant can be several months. Maguire grew up in this gorgeous house and the food here is a celebration of local and seasonal produce. Feast on intricate creations like crab ravioli with Thai broth, foie gras with plum and cream parfait, and caramelised and smoked pork belly; a vegetarian menu is available for €50. Guestrooms, including a brand-new wing, are beautifully decorated and filled with natural light.

Westport–Belfast buses stop in front of Maguire's pub.

CUILCAGH MOUNTAIN PARK

The border between the Republic and Northern Ireland runs along the ridge of Cuilcagh Mountain, the distinctive table-top summit of Cuilcagh Mountain Park, the world's first cross-border Geopark. Its lower slopes are important protected peatland habitats, while the upper slopes have dramatic sweeping cliffs. The visitor centre and the park's biggest attraction, the Marble Arch Caves (p685), lie a short hop over the border from Blacklion, in County Fermanagh.

COUNTY MONAGHAN

Monaghan's quiet, undulating landscape is littered with lakes and tiny rounded hills resembling bubbles in badly pasted wallpaper. Known as drumlins, the bumps are the result of debris left by retreating glaciers during the last ice age. The county's steely

JAMPA LING BUDDHIST CENTRE

On a quest for enlightenment, or just seeking some time out? **Jampa Ling Buddhist Centre** (☎049-952 3448; www.jampaling.org; Owendoon House, Bawnboy; dm/s self-catering €18/23, incl meals €32/39), in a beautiful country setting, is peace on earth. Jampa Ling, meaning 'Place of Infinite Loving Kindness', offers courses, retreats and workshops (€25 to €40, per weekend €215) on Buddhist teachings, gardening, meditation, tai chi, yoga, and medicinal and culinary herbs. You don't have to take part in a course to stay here, but accommodation may not be available if there is an event taking place. All meals, which are included in the day courses and for overnight guests, are vegetarian (and delicious!).

From Ballyconnell, follow the signs to Bawnboy. In the village, turn left at the petrol station and follow the small road for 3km. Continue past the lake and a series of bends; you'll see the centre's stone gates a further 250m ahead on your right.

grey lakes attract plenty of anglers, but few others make it here, making it a tranquil place to roam.

Unlike much of the province, Monaghan was largely left alone during the Ulster Plantation. After the Cromwellian wars, though, local chieftains were forced to sell their land for a fraction of its true value, or have it seized and redistributed to Cromwell's soldiers.

In the early 19th century, lace making became an important facet of the local economy, providing work and income for women. Clones and Carrickmacross were the two main centres of the industry and you can still see the fine needlework on display in both towns.

More recently, Monaghan has been made famous by poet Patrick Kavanagh (1905–67), who was born in Inniskeen. The village's literary resource centre offers an evocative insight into his life and work.

Monaghan Town

POP 6221

It may be the county town, but Monaghan's residents live their lives utterly unaffected by tourism. It's a pleasant place to wander the streets admiring the elegant 18th- and 19th-century limestone buildings.

Monaghan is squashed between two small lakes, Peter's Lake to the north and Convent Lake in the southwest. Its principal streets form a rough arc, broken up by the town's three main squares. From east to west these are Church Sq, the Diamond (the Ulster name for a town square) and Old Cross Sq, all of which are prone to traffic congestion.

Sights & Activities

FREE Monaghan County Museum & Gallery MUSEUM
(www.monaghan.ie; 1-2 Hill St; 11am-5pm Mon-Fri, noon-5pm Sat) Over 70,000 artefacts from the Stone Age to modern times are housed at this excellent regional museum. Its crowning glory is the 14th-century **Cross of Clogher**, an oaken altar cross encased in decorative bronze panels. Other impressive finds include the Lisdrumturk and Altartate Cauldrons, medieval *crannóg* artefacts, and some frightening knuckle-dusters and cudgels relating to the border with the North.

Other Sights HISTORIC SITES
In Church Sq, the hefty obelisk the Dawson Monument (1857) commemorates Colonel Dawson's unfortunate demise in the Crimean War. Overlooking it is the Gothic St Patrick's Church and a stately Doric courthouse (1829). Heading west you'll find the Rossmore Memorial (c 1875), an over-the-top Victorian drinking fountain that dominates the Diamond. The town also has a number of buildings with gently rounded corners, an unusual architectural feature in Ireland.

Just out of the centre of town on the Dublin road is another piece of Victorian whimsy, the mock-14th-century St Macartan's Catholic Cathedral (1861), topped by a teetering 77m-high, needle-sharp spire.

Venture Sports FISHING
(047-81495; venturesports@eircom.net; 71 Glaslough St) Fine fishing abounds in the area; contact Venture Sports for permits, tackle and local knowledge.

Festivals & Events

Féile Oriel MUSIC
(www.feileoriel.com) Traditional music festival over the May bank holiday weekend in early May.

Harvest Blues Festival MUSIC
(www.harvestblues.com) Fabulous blues festival featuring local and international acts in early September.

Sleeping & Eating

If you're after something grander than the town's B&Bs and business hotels, Castle Leslie is 11km northeast (see boxed text).

Ashleigh House B&B €€
(047-81227; www.ashleighhousemonaghan.com; 37 Dublin St; d €70;) Right in the centre of town, this lovely 10-room B&B has been recently refurbished and offers spick-and-span, great-value rooms. All rooms have private bathrooms and are tastefully decorated with countrified printed fabrics; there's a small garden area.

Andy's Bar & Restaurant BISTRO €€
(047-82277; www.andysmonaghan.com; 12 Market St; mains €16-26; restaurant dinner Fri-Sun, bar food dinner Tue-Fri, lunch & dinner Sat & Sun) A longstanding local favourite, this Victorian bar and old-school restaurant still proudly serves the likes of deep-fried brie, prawn

WORTH A TRIP

CASTLE LESLIE

The ancestral home of the Leslie family, **Castle Leslie** (☎047-88100; www.castleleslie.com; Glaslough; d €160-480; P 📶) is a Victorian pile with all the faded grandeur of a well-loved home. The family (who trace their ancestors back to Attila the Hun) acquired the castle in 1665 and its kooky history makes it an entertaining detour for both guests and nonguests.

Each of the 20 guestrooms in the main house has a story: the Red Room, used by WB Yeats, contains the first bath plumbed in Ireland, while in Uncle Norman's Room, guests claim to have been levitated in the Gothic four-poster bed. The Hunting Lodge has a further 30 rooms, with decor ranging from rich traditional drapery to more minimalist contemporary style. Public areas have wi-fi.

Dining options include the open-plan **Snaffles Brasserie** (mains €21.50-29.50) and snug **Conor's Bar** (mains €13-24.50). You can enjoy pampering treatments at the Victorian spa, horse riding (from €35 per hour) or attend its cookery school (call for upcoming courses).

The castle is 11km northeast of Monaghan town along the R185.

cocktails and pavlova, as well as fillet steak on breaded potato croutons with Andy's own pâté.

Drinking & Entertainment

Sherry's PUB

(24 Dublin St) Entering Sherry's, one of Monaghan's oldest bars, is like stepping back into a spinster's parlour from the 1950s. The old tiled floor, beauty board and dusty memorabilia probably haven't been touched in decades.

Squealing Pig PUB, NIGHTCLUB

(www.thesquealingpig.ie; The Diamond; mains €13-27; ⊙lunch Mon-Sat, dinner daily) One of the town's liveliest spots, with a young, fun vibe, solid comfort food (steaks, burgers and battered cod), three bars and a pumping nightclub.

Market House ARTS CENTRE

(☎047-38162; www.monaghan.ie; Market St) This restored 18th-century market hall turned arts venue hosts exhibitions, concerts and drama productions.

Information

Tourist office (☎047-81122, 047-73718; www.monaghantourism.com; Clones Rd; ⊙10am-5pm Mon-Fri)

Getting There & Around

From the **bus station** (☎047-82377; North Rd), there are numerous daily intercity services within the Republic and into the North, including 10 buses daily to Dublin (€12.15, two hours). There are also frequent daily local services to Carrickmacross.

Rossmore Forest Park

Crumbling remains of the Rossmore family's 19th-century castle, including its entrance stairway, buttresses and the family's pet cemetery, can be seen at **Rossmore Forest Park** (☎047-433 1046; www.coillteoutdoors.ie; cars €5; ⊙9am-9pm), where rhododendrons and azaleas blaze with colour in early summer. Along with forest walks and pleasant picnic areas, the park contains several giant redwoods, a fine yew avenue and Iron Age tombs. It's 3km southwest of Monaghan on the Newbliss road (R189).

Clones & Around

POP 1517

Once the site of an important 6th-century monastery that later became an Augustinian abbey, Clones' main sights are ecclesiastical. There's a well-preserved 10th-century **high cross** on the Diamond, decorated with drama-charged biblical stories such as Daniel in the lion's den.

Along with the remains of the **abbey** founded by St Tiernach on Abbey St, there's a truncated 22m-high **round tower**, which dates from the early 9th century, in the cemetery south of town. Nearby is the supposed burial place of Tiernach himself, a chunky 9th-century **sarcophagus** with worn animal-head carvings.

More recently, Clones found fame as a lace-making centre. To learn about the history of Clones lace, see it on display or purchase samples, visit the **Ulster Canal Stores** (☎047-52125; www.cloneslace.com; Cara St); hours vary, so call ahead to make sure it's open.

For a small town, Clones has produced its fair share of famous names. It's the hometown of both heavyweight Kevin McBride, whose defeat of Mike Tyson in 2005 was so crushing that it prompted Tyson's immediate retirement, and featherweight boxer Barry McGuigan, who won the world championship in 1985. Clones-born writer Patrick McCabe set his dark novel *The Butcher Boy* in the town, and in 1997 Neil Jordan filmed the twisted tale here.

Clones upholds its literary traditions when heavyweight poets and authors discuss or read their work at the 'no-brow' **Flat Lake Literary and Arts Festival** (www.theflatlakefestival.com) in early June, which combines high art with popular culture. Top-notch comedy, film, theatre and an art auction also feature in the impressive line-up.

The festival takes place 5km south of Clones along the R212 towards Scotshouse, at what is easily the best place to stay in the area.

Hilton Park (☎047-56007; www.hiltonpark.ie; d €196-270, gate house per week €495; ⏱Apr-Sep; P) is a spellbinding country-house retreat that has been in the same family since 1734. It's a magnificent place with stunning views of the 240-hectare estate. Its six spacious guestrooms are bathed in light and decorated with original furniture, free-standing baths and four-poster or half-tester beds. Top-class cuisine, much of it produced in the estate's organic gardens, is served in regal surroundings (dinner €55, by prior arrangement). Rates include breakfast and high tea on arrival. You can also come for kitchen gardening or art courses.

Bus Éireann (☎047-82377) runs a service from Clones to Monaghan (€4.86, 30 minutes, five buses Monday to Saturday, one Sunday), with connections on to Carrickmacross, Slane and Dublin.

Ulsterbus (☎048-9066 6630; www.translink.co.uk/Ulsterbus) has one direct service per day between Clones and Belfast (€13.20, 2¼ hours, Monday to Friday).

Carrickmacross & Around

POP 1973

Carrickmacross was first settled by early English and Scottish Planters, and its broad main street is dotted with some elegant Georgian houses. It's most famous as the home of delicate Carrickmacross lace, an industry revived in 1871 by the St Louis nuns. The town is a peaceful spot to wander and a great base for anglers.

Father Ted fans may know Carrickmacross as the birthplace of Ardal O'Hanlon, aka Father Dougal McGuire in the TV series. O'Hanlon's first novel *The Talk of the Town* was set in 'Castlecock', a thinly veiled version of the town.

Sights & Activities

Carrickmacross Lace Gallery LACE GALLERY
(☎042-966 2506; www.carrickmacrosslace.ie; Market Sq; ⏱9.30am-4.30pm Mon, to 5.30pm Tue-Fri) In the town's former cattle yards, a local co-operative runs this tiny but fascinating lace gallery, where you can see lace-making demonstrations and check out exquisite designs. Unlike Clones' crocheted lace, designs here are appliquéd on organza using thick thread and close stitches. Excess organza is cut away and the work is embellished with a variety of point stitches, guipure, pops and the lace's distinctive loop edge. Most famously, Carrickmacross lace graced the sleeves of Princess Diana's wedding dress. Carrickmacross' lace makers can take commissions.

St Joseph's Catholic Church CHURCH
(O'Neill St) Craftsmanship also shines at St Joseph's Catholic Church, with 10 windows designed by Harry Clarke, Ireland's most renowned stained-glass artist.

Eastern Regional Fisheries FISHING
Fantastic fishing around Carrickmacross includes Loughs Capragh, Spring, Monalty and Fea. Contact details for guides, boat hire and tackle are listed on www.monaghantourism.com.

Sleeping & Eating

Carrickmacross has some 20 pubs – around one for every 200 residents! – so you won't go hungry, much less thirsty.

Shirley Arms HOTEL €€
(☎042-967 3100; www.shirleyarmshotel.ie; Main St; d from €120; P@) The Shirley Arms is a sleek modern hotel with spacious rooms and decent food slap bang in the centre of town.

White linens, walnut floors and modern bathrooms make the rooms contemporary but rather corporate in style; cable broadband is available. The open-plan bar and lounge make an informal setting for some excellent **bar food** (€13.50-28). The more formal **Whites Restaurant** (mains €19.50-29; ⏲lunch Sun, dinner daily) is pricey.

Information

Carrickmacross has no tourist office, but the tourism section of the town's website, www.carrickmacross.ie, has visitor information.

Getting There & Away

Bus Éireann (☎01-836 6111) services connect with Dublin (€12.15, 1¾ hours, five daily). There are also several private operators on the route. The bus stop is outside O'Hanlon's shop on Main St.

Inniskeen

POP 292

Acclaimed poet Patrick Kavanagh (1904–67) was born in the village of Inniskeen, 10km northeast of Carrickmacross.

Kavanagh's long work *The Great Hunger* (1942) blasted away the earlier clichés of Anglo-Irish verse and revealed Ireland's poor farming communities as half-starved, 'broken-backed' and sexually repressed. His best-known poem, *On Raglan Road* (1946), was an ode to his unrequited love. It doubled as the lyrics for the traditional Irish air 'The Dawning of the Day', which has been performed by Van Morrison, Mark Knopfler, Billy Bragg, Sinéad O'Connor and countless others.

The **Patrick Kavanagh Rural and Literary Resource Centre** (☎042-937 8560; www.patrickkavanaghcountry.com; adult/student/under 12yr €5/3/free; ⏲11am-4.30pm Tue-Fri) is housed in the old parish church where Kavanagh was baptised. The staff have a passion for the poet's life and work that is contagious, and the centre hosts annual events including a **Writers' Weekend** in late July/early August.

Information on **guided literary tours** around town is posted on the resource centre's website. You can walk or drive around the sites in and around the village and the picturesque surrounding countryside (5.6km in all).

Inniskeen is on the Bus Éireann route between Cavan and Dundalk via Carrickmacross, with four services Monday to Saturday.

Belfast

POPULATION 277,000 / AREA 115 SQ KM

Includes »

Best Places to Eat

» Barking Dog (p595)
» Shu (p595)
» Mourne Seafood Bar (p593)
» Molly's Yard (p595)
» Deane's Restaurant (p593)

Best Places to Stay

» Old Rectory (p590)
» Malmaison Hotel (p590)
» Tara Lodge (p591)
» Ten Square (p590)
» Vagabonds (p592)

Why Go?

Once lumped with Beirut, Baghdad and Bosnia as one the four 'Bs' for travellers to avoid, Belfast has pulled off a remarkable transformation from bombs-and-bullets pariah to a hip hotels-and-hedonism party town. The city's skyline is in a constant state of flux as redevelopment continues apace. The old shipyards are giving way to the luxury waterfront apartments of the Titanic Quarter. Victoria Sq, Europe's biggest urban regeneration project, has added a massive city-centre shopping mall to a list of city tourist attractions that includes Victorian architecture, a glittering waterfront lined with modern art, foot-stomping music in packed-out pubs and the UK's second-biggest arts festival.

It might seem strange to celebrate a ship that is famous for sinking on its maiden voyage, but it's somehow fitting that Belfast should mark the centenary of the *Titanic's* creation in 2012, as it builds new pride and optimism out of the wreckage of past disaster.

When to Go

April can be a great time to visit Belfast, when spring flowers in the parks and the annual Titanic – Made in Belfast festival is held. August brings good weather for walking and cycling, along with celebrations of Irish music and dance in West Belfast. October can start to get chilly, but the Festival at Queen's, the UK's second largest arts festival (after Edinburgh), warms things up.

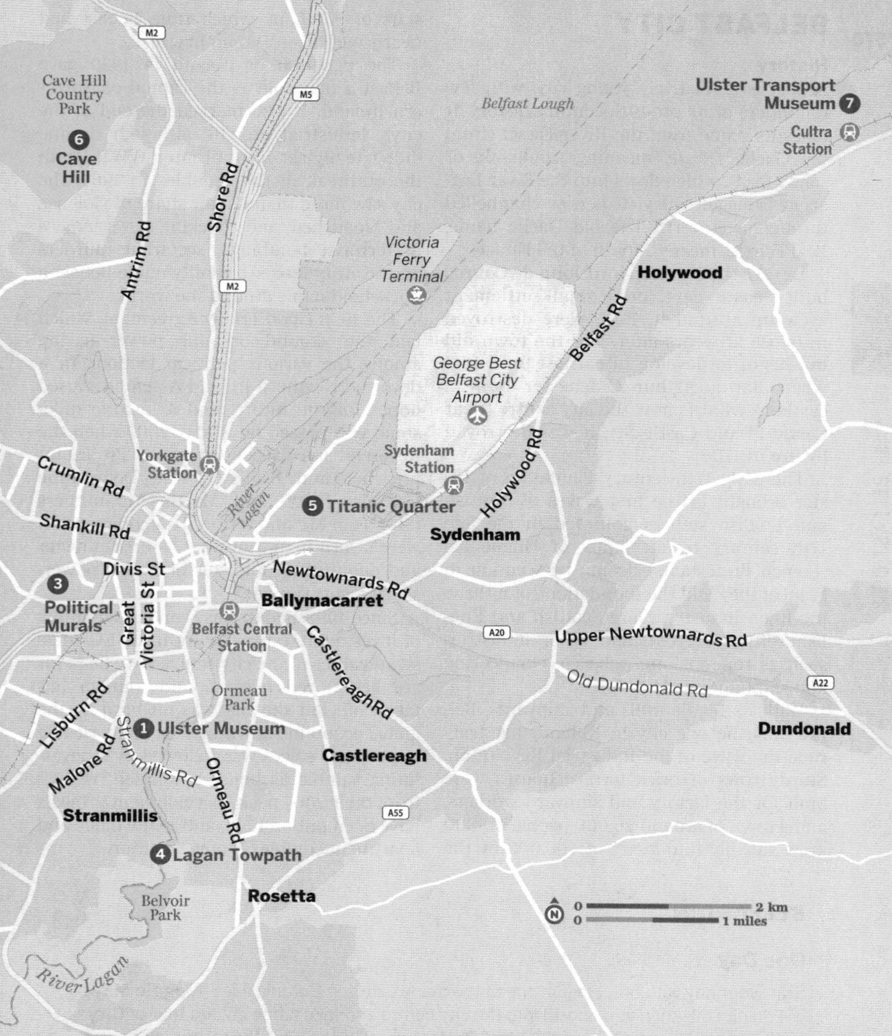

Belfast Highlights

❶ Discover prehistoric treasures, an ancient Egyptian mummy and sunken Armada gold at the revamped **Ulster Museum** (p579)

❷ Sup on a Guinness or three in some of Belfast's beautiful **Victorian pubs**

❸ Ruminate on the powerful **political murals** in West Belfast (p584)

❹ Hire a bike and take a spin along the **Lagan Towpath** (p577) to the former linen town of Lisburn

❺ Learn about the shipyards that gave birth to the *Titanic* in Belfast's **Titanic Quarter** (p578)

❻ Enjoy a panoramic view over the city from the top of **Cave Hill** (p585)

❼ Check out the iconic DeLorean DMC at the **Ulster Transport Museum** (p581)

BELFAST CITY

History

Belfast is a relatively young city, with few reminders of its pre-19th-century history. It takes its name from the River Farset (from the Gaelic *feirste,* meaning sandbank, or sandy ford), which flows into the River Lagan at Donegall Quay (it is now channelled through a culvert). The old Gaelic name, Béal Feirste, means 'Mouth of the Farset'.

In 1177, the Norman lord John de Courcy built a castle here, and a small settlement grew up around it. Both were destroyed in battle 20 years later, and the town did not begin to develop in earnest until 1611 when Baron Arthur Chichester built a castle in what is now the city centre (near Castle Pl and Castle St); it was destroyed by fire in 1708.

The early 17th-century Plantation of Ulster brought in the first waves of Scottish and English settlers, followed in the late 17th century by an influx of Huguenots (French Protestants) fleeing persecution in France; they laid the foundations of a thriving linen industry. More Scottish and English settlers arrived, and other industries such as rope-making, tobacco, engineering and shipbuilding developed.

With its textile mills and shipyards, Belfast was the one city in Ireland that truly rode the wave of the Industrial Revolution. Sturdy rows of brick terrace houses were built for the factory and shipyard workers, and a town of around 20,000 people in 1800 grew steadily into a city of 400,000 by the start of WWI, by which time Belfast had nearly overtaken Dublin in size.

The partition of Ireland in 1920 gave Belfast a new role as the capital of Northern Ireland. It also marked the end of the city's industrial growth, although decline didn't really set in until after WWII. With the outbreak of the Troubles in 1969, the city saw more than its fair share of violence and bloodshed, and shocking news images of terrorist bombings, sectarian murders and security forces' brutality made Belfast a household name around the world.

The 1998 Good Friday Agreement, which laid the groundwork for power-sharing among the various political factions in a devolved Northern Ireland Assembly, raised hopes for the future, and a historic milestone was passed on 8 May 2007 when the Reverend Ian Paisley (firebrand Protestant preacher and leader of the Democratic Unionist Party) and Martin McGuinness (Sinn Féin MP and former IRA commander) were sworn in at Stormont as first minister and deputy first minister of a new power-sharing government.

Since 1998 Belfast has seen a huge influx of investment, especially from the EU. Massive swathes of the city centre have been (or are being) redeveloped, and tourism has taken off. But the city was hit hard by the global economic downturn – a meteoric rise in property prices was followed by a devastating tumble as house prices fell by 40% from their 2007 peak. Development projects have been put on hold, and many office and apartment complexes now sit empty.

BELFAST IN...

One Day

Start your day with breakfast in one of the many cafes on Botanic Ave – **Maggie May's** will do nicely – then stroll north into the city centre and take a free guided tour of **City Hall**. Take a black taxi tour of the **West Belfast murals**, then ask the taxi driver to drop you off at the **John Hewitt Bar & Restaurant** for lunch. Catch a 2pm **Titanic Tour** boat trip around the harbour, then walk across the **Lagan Weir** to visit the **Titanic Quarter**. Round off the day with dinner at **Deane's Restaurant** or **Ginger**.

Two Days

On your second day, take a look at **Queen's University**, explore the fascinating exhibits in the **Ulster Museum** and stroll through the **Botanic Gardens**, then walk south along the river for lunch at **Cutters Wharf**. In the afternoon either continue walking south along the **Lagan Towpath** to Shaw's Bridge and catch a bus back to town, or go for a hike up **Cave Hill**. Have dinner at **Shu** or the **Barking Dog**, then spend the evening crawling traditional pubs such as the **Crown Liquor Saloon**, **Kelly's Cellars** and the **Duke of York**.

RED HAND OF ULSTER

According to legend, the chief of a raiding party – O'Neills or O'Donnells, take your pick – approaching the coast by boat, decided to fire up his troops by decreeing that Ulster would belong to the first man to lay his right hand upon it. As they neared land one particularly competitive chap cut off his own right hand and lobbed it to the shore, thus claiming Ulster as his own. The O'Neill clan later adopted the Red Hand as their emblem and it went on to become the symbol of the Irish province of Ulster.

You'll see the Red Hand of Ulster in many places: on the official Northern Irish flag, in the Ulster coat of arms, above the entrance to the Linen Hall Library on Donegall Sq, and laid out in red flowers in the garden of Mount Stewart House and Gardens in County Down. It also appears in many political murals in the badges of Loyalist terrorist groups, and as a clenched red fist in the badge of the Ulster Volunteer Force (UVF).

Sights

CITY CENTRE

FREE City Hall HISTORIC BUILDING

(Map p572; www.belfastcity.gov.uk; Donegall Sq; guided tours 11am, 2pm & 3pm Mon-Fri, 2pm & 3pm Sat) The Industrial Revolution transformed Belfast in the 19th century, and its rapid rise to muck-and-brass prosperity is manifested in the extravagance of City Hall. Built in classical Renaissance style in fine, white Portland stone, it was completed in 1906 and paid for from the profits of the gas supply company.

The hall is fronted by a statue of a rather dour 'we are not amused' Queen Victoria. The bronze figures on either side of her symbolise the textile and shipbuilding industries, while the child at the back represents education. At the northeastern corner of the grounds is a statue of Sir Edward Harland, the Yorkshire-born marine engineer who founded the Harland & Wolff shipyards and who served as mayor of Belfast from 1885 to 1886. To his south stands a memorial to the victims of the Titanic.

The highlights of the free, 45-minute **guided tour** of City Hall include the sumptuous, wedding-cake Italian marble and colourful stained glass of the entrance hall and rotunda; an opportunity to sit on the mayor's throne in the council chamber; and the idiosyncratic portraits of past lord mayors – each lord mayor is allowed to choose his or her own artist, and the variations in personal style are intriguing.

The **Bobbin Coffee Shop** (9am-4.30pm Mon-Fri, 9am-4pm Sat), in the southeast corner of City Hall, houses an exhibition of photographic portraits of 68 of Belfast's most famous citizens, from footballer George Best and musician Van Morrison to broadcaster Gloria Hunniford and president of Ireland Mary McAleese.

FREE Linen Hall Library HISTORIC BUILDING

(Map p572; www.linenhall.com; 17 Donegall Sq N; 9.30am-5.30pm Mon-Fri, 9.30am-4pm Sat; wi-fi) Opposite City Hall is the Linen Hall Library. Established in 1788 to 'improve the mind and excite a spirit of general inquiry', the library was moved from its original home in the White Linen Hall (the site is now occupied by City Hall) to the present building a century later. Thomas Russell, the first librarian, was a founding member of the United Irishmen and a close friend of Wolfe Tone – a reminder that this movement for independence from Britain had its origins in Belfast. Russell was hanged in 1803 after Robert Emmet's abortive rebellion.

The library houses some 260,000 books, more than half of which are part of its important Irish and local-studies collection. The political collection consists of pretty much everything that has been written about Northern Irish politics since 1966. The library also has a small **coffee shop** (10am-4pm Mon-Fri, 10am-3.30pm Sat). The visitors' entrance is on Fountain St, around the corner from the main door.

FREE Crown Liquor Saloon HISTORIC BUILDING

(Map p572; www.crownbar.com; 46 Great Victoria St; 11.30am-11pm Mon-Sat, 12.30-10pm Sun) There are not too many historical monuments that you can enjoy while savouring a pint of beer, but the National Trust's Crown Liquor Saloon is one of them. Belfast's most famous bar was refurbished by Patrick Flanagan in the late 19th century and displays Victorian decorative flamboyance at its best (he was looking to pull in a posh clientele from the

Central Belfast

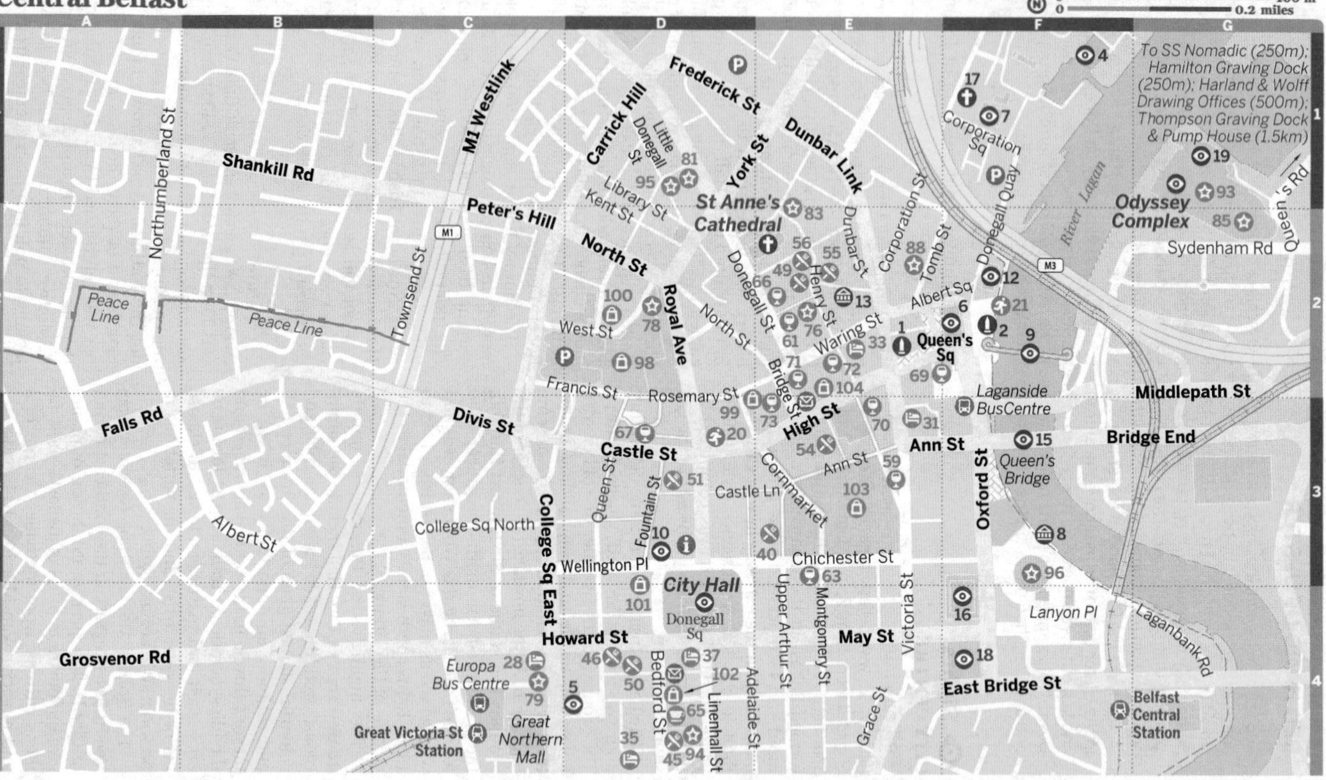

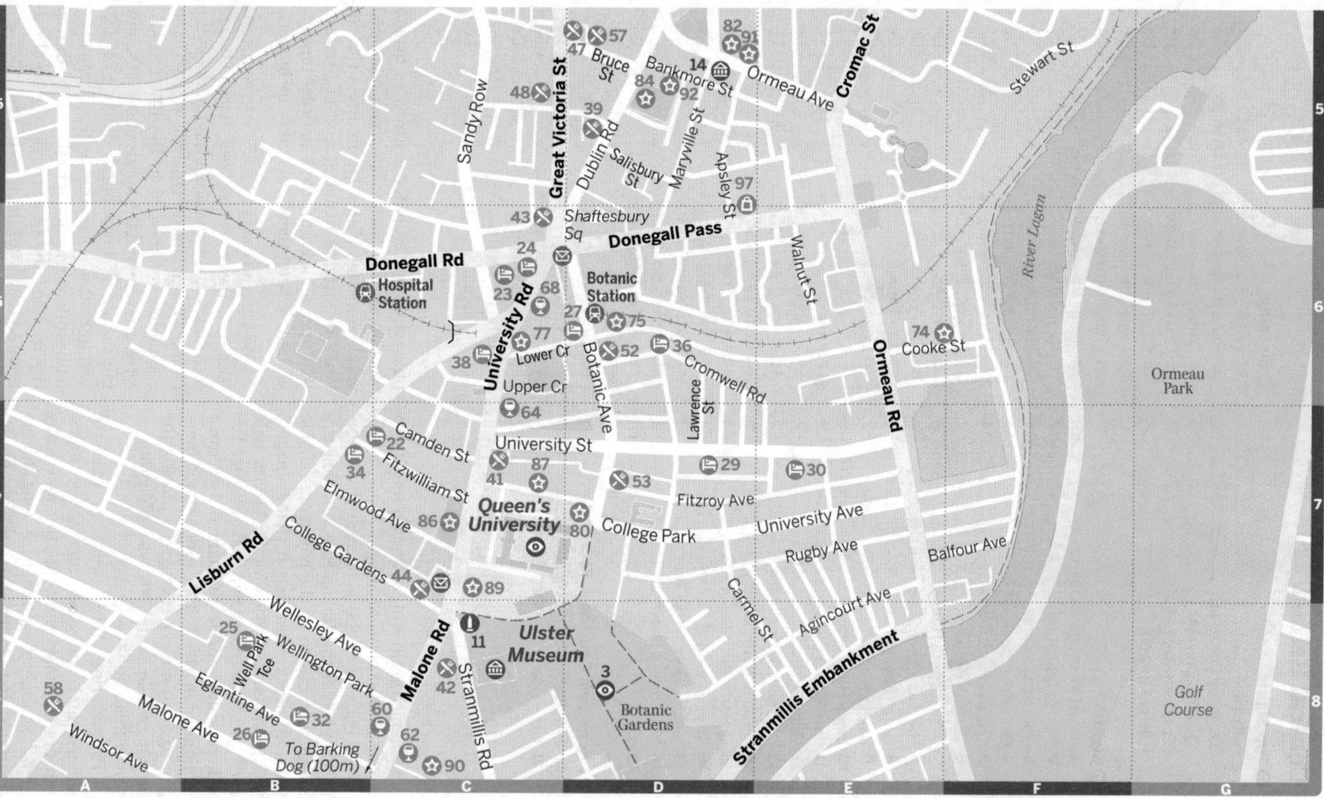
Stewart St
Cromac St
Ormeau Ave
Bankmore St
Bruce St
Great Victoria St
Sandy Row
Dublin Rd
Salisbury St
Maryville St
Apsley St
Shaftesbury Sq
Donegall Pass
Donegall Rd
Hospital Station
Botanic Station
Walnut St
River Lagan
Ormeau Park
Cooke St
Ormeau Rd
University Rd
Lower Cr
Upper Cr
Botanic Ave
Cromwell Rd
Lawrence St
Camden St
University St
Fitzwilliam St
Elmwood Ave
Queen's University
Fitzroy Ave
College Park
University Ave
Rugby Ave
Balfour Ave
Lisburn Rd
College Gardens
Carmel St
Agincourt Ave
Wellesley Ave
Well Park Tce
Wellington Park
Ulster Museum
Malone Rd
Stranmillis Rd
Botanic Gardens
Stranmillis Embankment
Golf Course
Eglantine Ave
Malone Ave
Windsor Ave
To Barking Dog (100m)

Central Belfast

new-fangled train station and Grand Opera House across the street).

The exterior (1885) is decorated with ornate and colourful Italian tiles, and boasts a mosaic of a crown on the pavement outside the entrance. Legend has it that Flanagan, a Catholic, argued with his Protestant wife over what the pub's name should be. His wife prevailed and it was named the Crown in honour of the British monarchy. Flanagan took his sneaky revenge by placing the crown mosaic underfoot where customers would tread on it every day.

The interior (1898) sports a mass of stained and cut glass, marble, ceramics, mirrors and mahogany, all atmospherically lit by genuine gas mantles. A long, highly decorated bar dominates one side of the pub, while on the other is a row of ornate wooden snugs. The snugs come equipped with gunmetal plates (from the Crimean War) for striking matches, and bell-pushes that once allowed drinkers to order top-ups without leaving their seats (alas, no longer).

Grand Opera House HISTORIC BUILDING

(Map p572; www.goh.co.uk; Great Victoria St) One of Belfast's great Victorian landmarks is the Grand Opera House. Opened in 1895, and completely refurbished in the 1970s, it suffered grievously at the hands of the IRA, having sustained severe bomb damage in 1991 and 1993. It was said that as the Europa Hotel next door was home to the media during the Troubles, the IRA brought the bombs to them so they wouldn't have to leave the bar.

The interior has been restored to its original, over-the-top Victorian pomp, with swirling wood and plasterwork, fancy giltwork in abundance and carved elephant heads framing the private boxes in the auditorium.

FREE **Ormeau Baths Gallery** ART GALLERY
(Map p572; www.ormeaubaths.co.uk; 18A Ormeau Ave; ⏲10am-5pm Tue-Sat) Housed in a converted 19th-century public bathhouse, the Ormeau Baths Gallery is Northern Ireland's principal exhibition space for contemporary visual art. The gallery stages changing exhibitions of work by Irish and international artists, and has hosted controversial showings of works by Gilbert and George, and Jake and Dinos Chapman. The gallery is a few blocks south of Donegall Sq.

The Entries HISTORIC SITE
(Map p572) The narrow alleyways running off High St and Ann St, known as the Entries, were once bustling commercial and residential thoroughfares; **Pottinger's Entry**, for example, had 34 houses in 1822.

Joy's Entry is named after Francis Joy, who founded the *Belfast News Letter* in 1737, the first daily newspaper in the British Isles (it's still in business). One of his grandsons, Henry Joy McCracken, was executed for supporting the 1798 United Irishmen revolt.

The United Irishmen were founded in 1791 by Wolfe Tone in Peggy Barclay's tavern in **Crown Entry**, and used to meet in the historic Kelly's Cellars (1720; p596) on Bank St, off Royal Ave.

White's Tavern (1630; p596), on **Wine Cellar Entry**, is the oldest tavern in the city and is still a popular lunchtime meeting spot.

CATHEDRAL QUARTER

The district north of the city centre around St Anne's Cathedral, bounded roughly by Donegall, Waring, Dunbar and York Sts, has been promoted as Belfast's Left Bank, a bohemian district of restored red-brick warehouses and cobbled lanes, lined with artists studios, design offices, and stylish bars and restaurants. It's home to the **Cathedral Quarter Arts Festival**.

FREE St Anne's Cathedral CHURCH

(Map p572; www.belfastcathedral.org; Donegall St; donations accepted; ⌚10am-4pm Mon-Fri) Built in imposing Hiberno-Romanesque style, St Anne's Cathedral was started in 1899 but did not reach its final form until 1981. As you enter you'll see that the black-and-white marble floor is laid out in a maze pattern – the black route leads to a dead end, the white to the sanctuary and salvation. The 10 pillars of the nave are topped by carvings symbolising aspects of Belfast life; look out for the Freemasons' pillar (the central one on the right, or south, side). In the south aisle is the **tomb of Unionist hero Sir Edward Carson** (1854–1935). The stunning mosaic of *The Creation* in the baptistry contains 150,000 pieces of coloured glass; it and the mosaic above the west door are the result of seven years' work by sisters Gertrude and Margaret Martin.

Oh Yeah Music Centre MUSEUM

(Map p572; www.belfastmusic.org; 15-21 Gordon St; admission free; ⌚noon-3pm Mon-Fri, noon-5pm Sat) A charitable organisation that provides rehearsal space for young musicians in a converted whiskey warehouse, the Oh Yeah Music Centre is also home to a museum of Northern Ireland's musical history from folk music to Snow Patrol, with exhibits that range from shamrock-shaped records and electric guitars to historic gig posters, ticket stubs and stage clothing donated by famous bands.

LAGANSIDE & LANYON PLACE

The ambitious **Laganside project** (www.laganside.com) to redevelop and regenerate the centre of Belfast saw the building of the Waterfront Hall, British Telecom's Riverside Tower and the Belfast Hilton in the 1990s. Projects completed since then include the Lanyon Quay office development next to the Waterfront Hall and the restoration of listed buildings such as McHugh's bar on Queen's Sq, the ornate Victorian warehouses now housing the Malmaison Hotel on Victoria St and the Albert Memorial Clock Tower. There are also 30 public artworks set along the waterfront – ask for a **Laganside Art Trail** leaflet at the Belfast Welcome Centre.

The latest stage of the project is the 28-storey **Obel** (Map p572), Belfast's tallest building, which dominates the waterfront at Donegall Quay. Lagan Boat Company (p587) offers special tours that include a trip to the top of the 85m-tall building to take in the views.

A few blocks to the south is the new £320 million shopping mall, **Victoria Square** (Map p572; www.victoriasquare.com; btwn Ann & Chichester St; ⌚9.30am-6pm Mon-Tue, to 9pm Wed-Fri, 9am-6pm Sat, 1-6pm Sun), whose centrepiece is a soaring atrium topped by a vast glass dome with yet another airy viewing platform.

FREE Harbour Commissioner's Office HISTORIC BUILDING

(Map p572; Donegall Quay; ⌚limited opening times) Near the ferry terminal on Donegall Quay is the Italianate Harbour Commissioner's Office (1854). The striking marble and stained-glass interior features art and sculpture inspired by Belfast's maritime history. The captain's table that was built for the *Titanic* survives here – completed behind schedule, it never made it on board. Guided tours of the office are available during the Belfast Maritime Festival in early June. It's also open on European Heritage Open Days, which take place over a weekend in September or October (see the Events section on www.doeni.gov.uk).

FREE Sinclair Seamen's Church CHURCH

(Map p572; Corporation Sq; ⌚2-4pm Wed), This church was built by Charles Lanyon in 1857–58 and was intended to meet the spiritual needs of visiting sailors. Part church, part maritime museum, it has a pulpit in the shape of a ship's prow (complete with red-and-green port and starboard lights), a brass ship's wheel and binnacle (used as a baptismal font) salvaged from a WWI wreck and, hanging on the wall behind the wheel, the ship's bell from HMS *Hood* (the pre-WWI predecessor of the more famous WWII warship of the same name).

Clarendon Dock HISTORIC SITE

(Map p572) North of the Harbour Commissioner's Office is the restored Clarendon Dock. Leading off it are the **dry docks** where Belfast's shipbuilding industry was born – No 1 Dry Dock (1796–1800) is Ireland's oldest and remained in use until the 1960s; No 2 (1826) is still used occasionally. Between the two sits the pretty little **Clarendon Building**, now home to the offices of the Laganside Corporation.

Custom House HISTORIC BUILDING

(Map p572; Custom House Sq) South along the river is the elegant Custom House, built by Lanyon in Italianate style between 1854 and 1857; the writer Anthony Trollope once worked in the post office here. On the waterfront side, the pediment carries sculpted portrayals of Britannia, Neptune and Mercury. The Custom House **steps** were once Belfast's equivalent of London's Speakers' Corner, a tradition memorialised in a bronze statue preaching to an invisible crowd.

Looking across the River Lagan from the Custom House, East Belfast is dominated by the huge yellow cranes of the Harland and Wolff shipyards. The modern Queen Elizabeth Bridge crosses the Lagan just to the south, but immediately south again is **Queen's Bridge** (1843), with its ornate lamps; this was Sir Charles Lanyon's first important contribution to Belfast's cityscape.

Albert Memorial Clock Tower LANDMARK

(Map p572; Queen's Sq) At the east end of High St is Belfast's very own leaning tower. Erected in 1867 in honour of Queen Victoria's dear departed husband, it is not as dramatically out of kilter as the more famously tilted tower in Pisa, but does, nevertheless, lean noticeably to the south – as the locals say, 'Old Albert not only has the time, he also has the inclination.' Restoration work has stabilised its foundations and left its Scrabo sandstone masonry sparkling white.

Lagan Weir LANDMARK

(Map p572) Across the street from the Custom House is **Bigfish** (1999), the most prominent of the many modern artworks that grace the riverbank between Clarendon Dock and Ormeau Bridge. The giant ceramic salmon – a symbol of the regeneration of the River Lagan – is covered with tiles depicting the history of Belfast.

It sits beside Lagan Weir, the first stage of the Laganside Project, completed in 1994. Years of neglect and industrial decline had turned the River Lagan, the original lifeblood of the city, into an open sewer flanked by smelly, unsightly mudflats. The weir, along with a program of dredging and aeration, has improved the water quality so much that salmon, eels and sea trout migrate up the river once again.

For details of the boat tours that depart from here, see p587.

Lanyon Place LANDMARK

(Map p572) A five-minute walk south from the Lagan Weir leads to Lanyon Pl, the Laganside Project's flagship site, dominated by the 2235-seat **Waterfront Hall** (p598). Across Oxford St lie the neoclassical **Royal Courts of Justice** (1933), bombed by the

WALK: LAGAN TOWPATH

Part of Belfast's **Laganside redevelopment project** was the restoration of the towpath along the west bank of the River Lagan. You can now walk or cycle for 20km along the winding riverbank from central Belfast to Lisburn. The cafe in Lisburn's **Island Arts Centre** (www.islandartscentre.com) makes a good target.

A shorter walk along the towpath (10km) starts from **Shaw's Bridge** (Map p586) on the southern edge of the city and heads back towards the city centre. Take bus 8A or 8B from Donegall Sq E to the stop just before the Malone roundabout (where Malone Rd becomes Upper Malone Rd). Bear left at the roundabout (signposted Outer Ring A55) and you'll reach the River Lagan at Shaw's Bridge.

Turn left and follow towpath downstream on the left bank of the river (waymarked with red '9' signs), passing a restored lock-keeper's cottage and canalside cafe at lock number 3. The most attractive part of the walk is **Lagan Meadows** (Map p586), a tree-fringed loop in the river to the right of the path and a good place for a picnic on a summer's day. Further along, **Cutters Wharf** is also a great place for a lunch break. From the pub it's more pleasant walking to **Lagan Weir** in the city centre. Alternatively, make the walk from the city to Shaw's Bridge and catch the bus back.

TITANIC BELFAST

Perhaps the most famous vessel ever launched, RMS *Titanic* was built in Belfast's Harland & Wolff shipyard for the White Star Line. When her keel was laid in 1909 Belfast was at the height of its fame as a shipbuilding powerhouse, and the *Titanic* was promoted by White Star as the world's biggest and most luxurious ocean liner. Ironically, it was also claimed to be 'unsinkable'.

She was launched from H&W's slipway No 3 on 31 May 1911, and spent almost a year being fitted out in the nearby Thompson Graving Dock before leaving Belfast for her maiden voyage on 2 April 1912. In one of the most notorious nautical disasters of all time, she hit an iceberg in the North Atlantic on 14 April 1912, and sank in the early hours of the following day. Of the 2228 passengers and crew on board, only 705 survived; there were only enough lifeboats for 1178 people.

At the time of research an 'iconic visitor attraction' called Titanic Belfast was under construction on the site of the slipways where *Titanic* and her sister ship *Olympic* were built. A dramatic example of modern architecture resembling four giant ships' prows, it was scheduled for completion in time for the centenary of the *Titanic*'s maiden voyage in April 2012; features include a 'Titanic Experience' exhibition and an 'immersive theatre' screening films of the underwater exploration of the wreck.

The **Titanic Stories** (www.the-titanic.com) website contains a wealth of information on the ship and her passengers, and lists all Titanic-related museums and memorials throughout Ireland and the rest of the world.

IRA in 1990 but now emerging from behind the massive security screens that once concealed them.

Lagan Legacy MUSEUM
(Map p572; www.laganlegacy.com; Lanyon Quay; adult/child £4/3; ⏲10am-4pm) Housed in a barge moored on the River Lagan, this museum tells the story of Belfast's maritime and industrial history, bringing together old photographs, original drawings and documents, ship models and artefacts, and video and audio recordings of interviews with retired engineers, designers and shipyard workers.

FREE **St George's Market** MARKET
(Map p572; cnr Oxford & May Sts; ⏲6am-2pm Fri, 9am-3pm Sat, 10am-4pm Sun) South of the courts is this elegant Victorian covered market, built in 1896 for the sale of fruit, butter, eggs and poultry; it's the oldest continually operating market in Ireland. Restored in 1999, it now hosts a variety market on Friday, selling fresh flowers, fruit, vegetables, meat and fish, plus general household and second-hand goods, and the City Food and Garden Market on Saturday, which often has live music. The Sunday market combines food, antiques and local arts and crafts. There's also a two-day Christmas Fair and Market in early December.

TITANIC QUARTER

Belfast's former shipbuilding yards – the birthplace of RMS *Titanic* – stretch along the east side of the River Lagan, dominated by the towering yellow cranes known as **Samson and Goliath** (dating from the 1970s). The area is currently undergoing a £1 billion regeneration project known as **Titanic Quarter** (www.titanicquarter.com), which plans to transform the long-derelict docklands over the next 15 to 20 years.

Queen's Rd strikes northeast from the Odyssey Complex into the heart of the Titanic Quarter, a massive redevelopment area that is part industrial wasteland, part building site and part high-tech business park. Not much remains from the time when the *Titanic* was built, but what does has been restored, and the challenging modern outline of Titanic Belfast now forms the centrepiece of the district. A series of **information boards** along Queen's Rd describe items and areas of interest.

SS Nomadic HISTORIC SHIP
(www.nomadicbelfast.com; Queens Rd) The **Hamilton Graving Dock** (off map p572), just northeast of the Odyssey Complex, is now the permanent berth of SS *Nomadic* – the only surviving vessel of the White Star Line (the shipping company that owned the *Titanic*). In 2006 she was rescued from the breaker's yard and brought to Belfast. The little

steamship once served as a tender ferrying 1st- and 2nd-class passengers between Cherbourg Harbour and the giant Olympic Class ocean liners (which were too big to dock at the French port); on 10 April 1912 she delivered 142 1st-class passengers to the ill-fated *Titanic*. She was still undergoing restoration work at the time of research, but should be open to the public by April 2012.

Harland & Wolff Drawing Offices HISTORIC BUILDING
(off map p572; Queen's Rd; ⊙open to guided tours only) Just long the road from the *Nomadic* are the original Harland & Wolff drawing offices, where the designs for the *Titanic* were first drawn up; you can see inside only as part of a guided tour such as Titanic Tours (p589). Behind the building, where the new Titanic Belfast attraction now sits (though best seen from a boat tour on the river), are the two massive **slipways** where the *Titanic* and her sister ship *Olympic* were built and launched.

FREE **Thompson Pump House & Graving Dock** HISTORIC SITE
(off map p572; Queens Rd; www.titanicsdock.com; admission to visitor centre free, guided tour; ⊙visitor centre 10.30am-4pm) At the far end of Queens Rd is the most impressive monument to the days of the great liners – the vast Thompson Graving Dock where the *Titanic* was fitted out. Its huge size gives you some idea of the scale of the ship, which could only just fit into it.

Beside the dock is the Thompson Pump House, which has an exhibition on Belfast shipbuilding (there's a cafe, too). **Guided tours** (adult/child £6/4; ⊙hourly 11am-3pm) include a viewing of original film footage from the shipyards, and a visit to the inner workings of the pump house and dry dock.

In the dock on the far side of the pump house, naval-history buffs can ogle **HMS Caroline**, a WWI Royal Navy cruiser built in 1914, now serving as a Royal Naval Reserve training ship (not open to the public).

Odyssey Complex LANDMARK
(Map p572; Sydenham Rd) The Odyssey Complex is a huge sporting and entertainment centre on the eastern side of the river across from Clarendon Dock. The complex features a hands-on science centre, W5; a 10,000-seater sports arena (home to the Belfast Giants ice-hockey team); a multiplex cinema with an IMAX screen; a video-games centre; and a dozen restaurants, cafes and bars.

The Odyssey Complex is a five-minute walk across Lagan Weir from the city centre. Metro bus 26 from Donegall Sq W to Holywood stops outside the complex (5 minutes, hourly Monday to Friday only).

W5 SCIENCE CENTRE
(Map p572; www.w5online.co.uk; Odyssey Complex, Sydenham Rd; adult/child £7.70/5.70, 2 adults & 2 children £23; ⊙10am-5pm Mon-Fri, 10am-6pm Sat, noon-6pm Sun, last admission 1hr before closing; 👪) Also known as whowhatwherewhenwhy, and open during school terms only, W5 is an interactive science centre aimed at children of all ages. Kids can compose their own tunes by biffing the 'air harp' with a foam rubber bat, try to beat a lie detector, create cloud rings and tornadoes, and design and build their own robots and racing cars.

SOUTH BELFAST (QUEEN'S QUARTER)

The Golden Mile – the 1.5km stretch of Great Victoria St and Shaftesbury Sq that links the city centre to the university district – was once the focus for much of Belfast's nightlife. These days, with the regeneration of the city centre, it's more tarnished brass than gold, but it still has several decent pubs and eateries. Some of the Golden Mile's former glow has moved to Lisburn Rd, which is lined with trendy boutiques, cafes and wine bars.

Metro buses 8A, 8B and 8C run from Donegall Sq E along Bradbury Pl and University Rd to Queen's University.

TOP CHOICE **Ulster Museum** MUSEUM
(Map p572; www.nmni.com/um; Stranmillis Rd; admission free; ⊙10am-5pm Tue-Sun; 👪) Recently reopened after a major revamp, the Ulster Museum is now one of the North's don't-miss attractions. You could spend several hours browsing the beautifully designed displays, but if you're pressed for time don't miss the Armada Room; Takabuti, a 2500-year-old Egyptian mummy; the Bann Disc; and the Snapshot of an Ancient Sea Floor.

On the ground floor, a potted history of **the Troubles** leads up to the first-floor History Zone where the **Armada Room** houses a display of artefacts and jewellery recovered from the 1588 wreck of the *Girona* (p656) and other Spanish Armada vessels. Among its many treasures is a 16th-century ruby-encrusted golden salamander, bronze cannons, and personal belongings of the officers and crew, including pipes, combs and buttons.

On the same floor is the **Early Peoples gallery**, a spectacular collection of prehistoric stone and bronze artefacts that help provide a cultural context for Ireland's many archaeological sites. The exhibits are beautifully displayed – the **Malone Hoard**, a clutch of 16 polished, Neolithic stone axes discovered only a few kilometres from the museum, looks more like a modern sculpture than a museum exhibit, while the **Bann Disc** is a superb example of Celtic design dating from the Iron Age.

The centrepiece of the **Egyptian Room** is the mummy of Princess Takabuti. She was unwrapped in Belfast in 1835, the first mummy ever to be displayed outside Egypt; more recently, her bleached hair has led the locals to dub her 'Belfast's oldest bleached blonde'.

The **Nature Zone** on the second floor covers geological time, evolution and natural history, with interactive exhibits that will keep the children busy for an hour or two. Highlights include the **Snapshot of an Ancient Sea Floor**, a fossilised portion of 200-million-year-old seabed with jumbled ammonite shells and petrified driftwood; the **Sea Around Us gallery**; and preserved specimens that include a Mexican red-knee tarantula, and the now-extinct Tasmanian tiger.

The top floors are given over to **Irish and European art**, most notably the works of Belfast-born Sir John Lavery (1856–1941), who became one of the most fashionable and expensive portraitists of Victorian London. More modern paintings include Edward McGuire's 1974 portrait of poet Seamus Heaney.

Queen's University UNIVERSITY
(Map p572; University Rd) If you think that Charles Lanyon's **Queen's College** (1849), a Tudor Revival building in red brick and honey-coloured sandstone, has something of an Oxbridge air about it, that may be because he based the design of the central tower on the 15th-century Founder's Tower at Oxford's Magdalen College. Northern Ireland's most prestigious university was founded by Queen Victoria in 1845, one of three Queen's colleges (the others, still around but no longer called Queen's colleges, are in Cork and Galway) created to provide a nondenominational alternative to the Anglican Church's Trinity College in Dublin. In 1908, the college became the Queen's University of Belfast, and today its campus spreads across some 250 buildings. Queen's has around 25,000 students and enjoys a strong reputation in medicine, engineering and law.

Just inside the main entrance is the **Queen's Welcome Centre** (www.queensevents.com; University Rd; admission free; ⏲9.30am-4.30pm Mon-Sat, 10am-1pm Sun) with exhibitions and a souvenir shop. **Guided tours** (£5 per person) are available with advance booking, or you can pick up a leaflet that describes a self-guided tour.

FREE **Botanic Gardens** GARDENS
(Map p572; Stranmillis Rd; ⏲7.30am-sunset) The green oasis of Belfast's Botanic Gardens is a short stroll away from the university. Just inside the Stranmillis Rd gate is a statue of Belfast-born William Thomson, **Lord Kelvin**, who helped lay the foundation of modern physics and who invented the Kelvin scale which measures temperatures from absolute zero (-273°C or 0°K).

The gardens' centrepiece is Charles Lanyon's beautiful **Palm House** (admission free; ⏲11am-noon & 1-4.45pm Apr-Sep, 10am-noon & 1-3.45pm Oct-Mar), built in 1839 and completed in 1852, with its birdcage dome, a masterpiece in cast-iron and curvilinear glass. Nearby is the unique **Tropical Ravine** (admission free; ⏲same as Palm House), a huge red-brick greenhouse designed by the garden's curator Charles McKimm and completed in 1889. Inside, a raised walkway overlooks a jungle of tropical ferns, orchids, lilies and banana plants growing in a sunken glen.

WEST BELFAST (GAELTACHT QUARTER)

Northwest of Donegall Sq, Divis St leads across the Westlink Motorway to Falls Rd and West Belfast (Gaeltacht Quarter). Though scarred by three decades of civil unrest, the former battleground of West Belfast is one of the most compelling places to visit in Northern Ireland. Recent history hangs heavy in the air, but there is a noticeable spirit of optimism and hope for the future.

The main attractions are the powerful murals that chart the history of the conflict, as well as the political passions of the moment and, for visitors from mainland Britain, there is a grim fascination to be found in wandering through the former 'war zone' in their own backyard.

West Belfast grew up around the linen mills that propelled the city into late-19th-century prosperity. It was an area of low-cost, working-class housing, and even in the Victorian era was divided along religious lines. The advent of the Troubles in 1968 solidified the sectarian divide, and since 1970 the ironically named 'Peace Line' has separated the Loyalist and Protestant Shankill district from the Republican and Catholic Falls district.

Despite its past reputation, the area is safe to visit. The best way to see West Belfast is on a **black taxi tour** (p587). The cabs visit the more spectacular murals as well as the Peace Line (where you can write a message on the wall) and other significant sites, while the drivers provide a colourful commentary on the history of the area.

There's nothing to stop you visiting under your own steam, either walking (see our West Belfast Walking Tour, p588) or using the shared black taxis that travel along the Falls and Shankill Rds. Alternatively, buses 10A to 10F from Queen St will take you along the Falls Rd; buses 11A to 11D from Wellington Pl go along Shankill Rd.

You can also pick up a range of free leaflets at the Belfast Welcome Centre that describe walking tours around the Falls and Shankill districts.

FALLS ROAD

Although the signs of past conflict are inescapable, the Falls today is an unexpectedly lively, colourful and optimistic place. Local people are friendly and welcoming, and community ventures such as Conway Mill, the Cultúrlann centre and black taxi tours have seen tourist numbers increase dramatically.

FREE Cultúrlann McAdam Ó Fiaich CULTURAL CENTRE

(Map p586; www.culturlann.ie; 216 Falls Rd; 9am-9pm Mon-Fri, 10am-6pm Sat; wi-fi) The focus for community activity is this Irish language and cultural centre, housed in a red-brick, former Presbyterian church. It's a cosy and welcoming place with a tourist information desk, a shop selling a wide selection of books on Ireland, Irish-language material, crafts, and Irish music CDs, and a good cafe-restaurant, Caifé Feirste. The centre also has an art gallery and a theatre that stages music, drama and poetry events.

Conway Mill ARTS CENTRE

(Map p586; www.conwaymill.org; 5-7 Conway St; 10am-5pm Mon-Fri, 10am- 3pm Sat) Conway Mill is a restored 19th-century flax mill that now houses around 20 artists' studios, an exhibition on the mill's history, an education centre and work spaces for local enterprises. It also houses the **Irish Republican History Museum** (10am-2pm Tue-Sat), a collection of artefacts, newspaper articles, photos and archives relating to the Republican struggle from 1798 to the Troubles.

SHANKILL ROAD

Although the Protestant Shankill district (from the Irish *sean chill,* meaning 'old church') has received less media and tourist attention than the Falls, it also contains many interesting murals. The people here are just as friendly, but the Shankill has far fewer tourists than the Falls. Loyalist communities seem to have more difficulty in presenting their side of the story than the Republicans, who have a far more polished approach to public relations.

To reach Shankill Rd on foot, set off north from City Hall along Donegall Pl and Royal Ave, then turn left on North St and continue straight on across the Westlink Motorway.

OUTSIDE THE CENTRE

Ulster Folk & Transport Museum MUSEUM

(Map p586; www.nmni.com/uftm; Cultra, Holywood; adult/child £6.50/4, combined ticket to both museums £8/4.50; 10am-5pm Tue-Sun Mar-Sep, 10am-4pm Tue-Fri & 11am-4pm Sat & Sun Oct-Feb) Really two museums in one, and lying on either side of the A2 road to Bangor, just north of Holywood, the Ulster Folk & Transport Museum is one of Northern Ireland's finest.

Ulster Folk Museum

Farmhouses, forges, churches and mills, and a complete village have been reconstructed here, with human and animal extras combining to give a powerful impression of Irish life over the past few hundred years. From industrial times, there are red-brick terraces from 19th-century Belfast and Dromore. In summer, thatching and ploughing are demonstrated and there are characters dressed in period costume.

Ulster Transport Museum

The Transport Museum is a sort of automotive zoo, with displays of captive steam locomotives, rolling stock, motorcycles, trams, buses and cars. The highlight of the car collection is the stainless steel–clad prototype of the ill-fated **DeLorean DMC**, made in Belfast in 1981. The car was a commercial disaster but achieved everlasting fame in the *Back to the Future* films.

Most popular is the **RMS Titanic display**, which includes the original design drawings for the *Olympic* and the *Titanic,* photographs

Belfast Murals

Since the start of the Troubles, the gable ends of Belfast's housing estates have been used as informal canvases, painted with colourful murals that serve as territorial markers, political statements and defiant symbols of Loyalist or Nationalist identity (p584).

Solidarity Wall

1 Another popular theme for murals in Republican areas is support for other nationalist and republican movements around the world, including Palestine, the Basque Country and Latin America, notably on the stretch of Falls Rd known as Solidarity Wall (p588).

Nonpolitical Murals

2 Since the advent of the peace process there has been a concerted effort to replace aggressively partisan murals with ones that celebrate nonpolitical subjects, such as footballer George Best, novelist CS Lewis, and the Harland & Wolff shipyards.

King Billy

3 The most iconic of Protestant murals is the image of King Billy (William of Orange), whose victory over the Catholic King James at the Battle of the Boyne in 1690 is still celebrated annually with 12th July parades.

Hunger Strike

4 Many Nationalist murals in West Belfast commemorate the Hunger Strike of 1981, when 10 Republican prisoners starved themselves to death. Most prominent is the image of Bobby Sands, who was elected as a local MP shortly before his death.

Clockwise from top left

1. Murals along Falls Rd **2.** *Titanic* wall mural on Newtownards Rd **3.** King Billy (William of Orange)

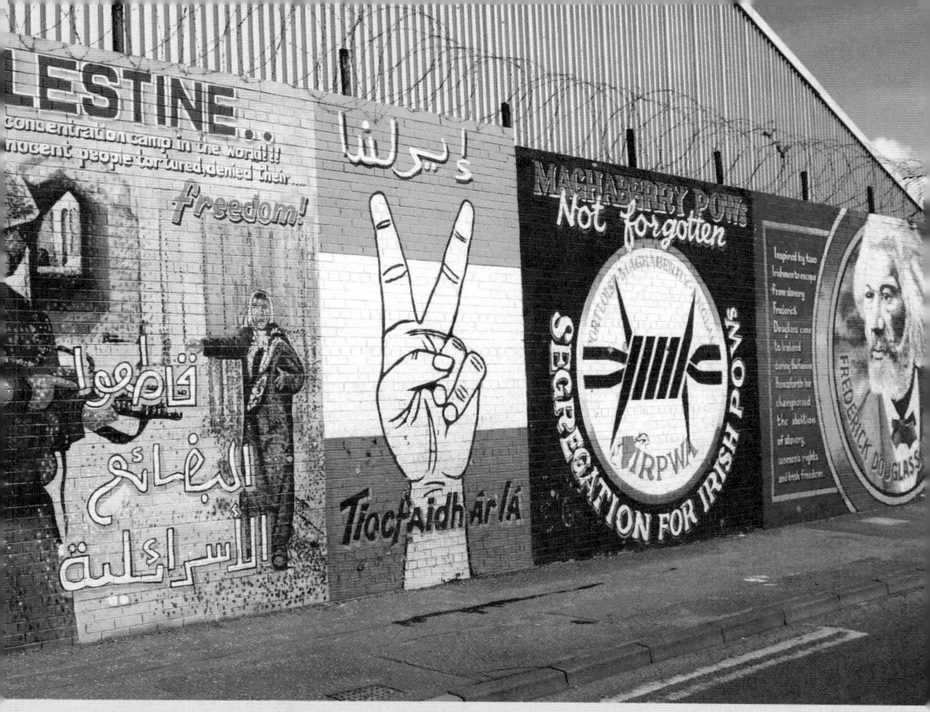
LESTINE
concentration camp in the world!!
nocent people tortured, denied their....
freedom!
Tiocfaidh Ár Lá
MAGHABERRY POWS
Not forgotten
SEGREGATION FOR IRISH POWS
IRPWA
Inspired by two Irishmen to escape from slavery Frederick Douglass came to Ireland during the famine. Henceforth he championed the abolition of slavery, women's rights and Irish freedom.
FREDERICK DOUGLASS

2

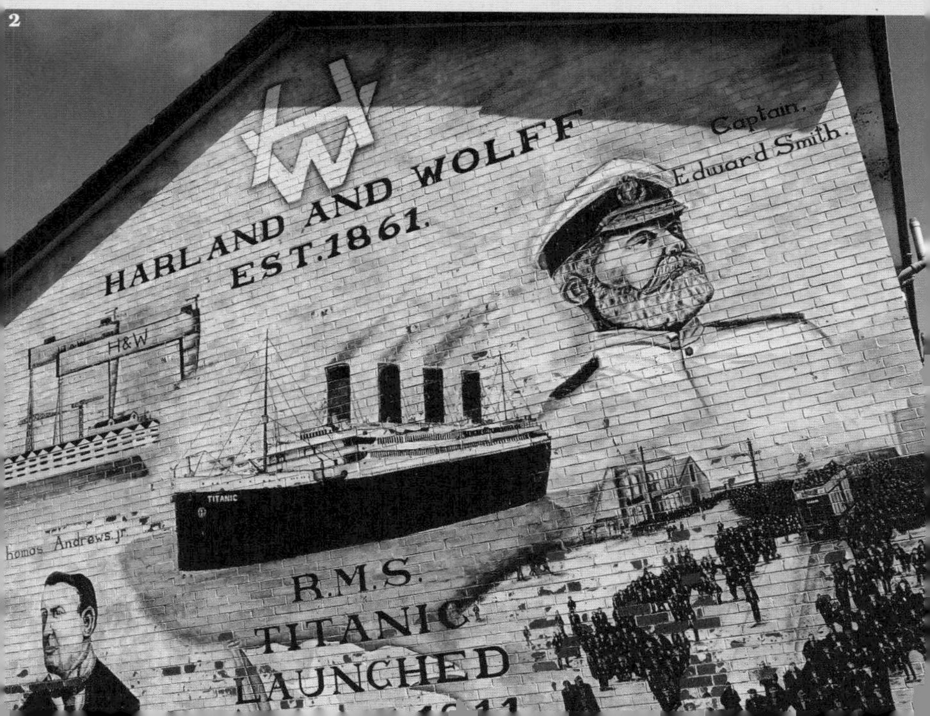
HARLAND AND WOLFF
EST.1861.
Captain.
Edward Smith.
H&W
TITANIC
homas Andrews.jr
R.M.S.
TITANIC
LAUNCHED

MURALS OF BELFAST

Belfast's tradition of political murals is a century old, dating from 1908 when images of King Billy (William III, Protestant victor over the Catholic James II at the Battle of the Boyne in 1690) were painted by Unionists protesting against home rule for Ireland. The tradition was revived in the late 1970s as the Troubles wore on, with murals used to mark out sectarian territory, make political points, commemorate historical events and glorify terrorist groups. As the 'voice of the community' the murals were rarely permanent, but changed to reflect the issues of the day.

Republican Murals

The first Republican murals appeared in 1981, when the hunger strike by Republican prisoners – demanding recognition as political prisoners – at the Maze Prison saw the emergence of dozens of murals of support. In later years, Republican muralists broadened their scope to cover wider political issues, Irish legends and historical events. After the Good Friday Agreement of 1998, the murals came to demand police reform and the protection of nationalists from sectarian attacks.

Common images seen in Republican murals include the phoenix rising from the flames (symbolising Ireland reborn from the flames of the 1916 Easter Rising), the face of hunger-striker Bobby Sands, and scenes and figures from Irish mythology. Common slogans include 'Free Ireland', the Irish Gaelic '*Éirí Amach na Cásca* 1916' (The Easter Rising of 1916) and '*Tiocfaidh Ár Lá*' (Our Day Will Come).

The main areas for Republican murals are Falls Rd, Beechmount Ave, Donegall Rd, Shaw's Rd and the Ballymurphy district in West Belfast; New Lodge Rd in North Belfast; and Ormeau Rd in South Belfast.

Loyalist Murals

Loyalist murals have traditionally been more militaristic and defiant in tone than the Republican murals, which are often artistic and rich in symbolic imagery. The Loyalist battle cry of 'No Surrender!' is everywhere, along with red, white and blue painted kerbstones, paramilitary insignia and images of King Billy, usually shown on a prancing white horse.

You will also see the Red Hand of Ulster, sometimes shown as a clenched fist (the symbol of the Ulster Freedom Fighters, UFF), and references to the WWI Battle of the Somme in 1916 in which many Ulster soldiers died; it is seen as a symbol of Ulster's loyalty to the British crown, in contrast to the Republican Easter Rising of 1916. Common mottoes include '*Quis Separabit*' (Who Shall Divide Us?), the motto of the Ulster Defence Association (UDA); and the defiant 'We will maintain our faith and our nationality'.

Murals Today

In recent years there has been a lot of debate about what to do with Belfast's murals. Some see them as an ugly and unpleasant reminder of a violent past, while others claim they are a vital part of Northern Ireland's history. There's no doubt they have become an important tourist attraction, but there is now a move to replace the more aggressive and militaristic images with murals dedicated to local heroes and famous figures such as footballer George Best and *Narnia* novelist CS Lewis.

There are also some off-beat and amusing artworks, including one that has been baffling passers-by for years. A gable-end on Balfour Ave, off Ormeau Rd, asks the question 'How can quantum gravity help explain the origin of the universe?' It was part of an art installation in 2001, one of 10 questions selected by scientists as the most important unsolved problems in physics. Perhaps it has survived so long as it reflects the still unsolved – and, to outsiders, equally baffling – problem of Northern Ireland's sectarian divide.

If you want to find out more about Northern Ireland's murals, look out for the books *Drawing Support* (three volumes) by Bill Rolston, *The People's Gallery* by the Bogside Artists and the website of the **Mural Directory** (www.cain.ulst.ac.uk/murals).

of the ship's construction and reports of its sinking. At the time of research a new exhibition was being constructed in time for the *Titanic* centenary in April 2012.

Buses to Bangor stop nearby. Cultra Station on the Belfast to Bangor train line is within a 10-minute walk.

FREE Cave Hill Country Park PARK

(Map p586; Antrim Rd; ⌚7.30am-dusk) The best way to get a feel for Belfast's natural setting is to view it from above. In the absence of a private aircraft, head for Cave Hill (368m), which looms over the city's northern fringes. The view from its summit takes in the whole sprawl of the city, the docks and the creeping fingers of urbanisation along the shores of Belfast Lough. Also, the rounded forms of the Mourne Mountains can be seen far away to the south, and on a clear day you can even spot Scotland lurking on the horizon.

The hill was originally called Ben Madigan, after the 9th-century Ulster king, Matudhain. Its distinctive, craggy profile, seen from the south, has been known to locals for two centuries as 'Napoleon's Nose' – it supposedly bears some resemblance to Bonaparte's shnoz, but you might take some convincing. On the summit is an Iron Age earthwork known as **McArt's Fort** where members of the United Irishmen, including Wolfe Tone, looked down over the city in 1795 and pledged to fight for Irish independence. The path leading to the summit from the zoo or castle car park passes beneath the caves that give the hill its name.

Cave Hill Country Park spreads across the hill's eastern slopes, with several waymarked walks and an adventure playground for kids aged three to 14 years. To get here, take buses 1A to 1G from Donegall Sq W to Belfast Castle or Belfast Zoo.

FREE Belfast Castle CASTLE

(Map p586; www.belfastcastle.co.uk; Antrim Rd; ⌚9am-10pm Mon-Sat, 9am-5.30pm Sun) Built in 1870 for the third Marquess of Donegall, in the Scottish Baronial style made fashionable by Queen Victoria's then recently built Balmoral, the multi-turreted pomp of Belfast Castle commands the southeastern slopes of Cave Hill. It was presented to the City of Belfast in 1934.

Extensive renovation between 1978 and 1988 has left the interior comfortably modern rather than intriguingly antique, and the castle is now a popular venue for wedding receptions. Upstairs is the **Cave Hill Visitor Centre** with a few displays on the folklore, history, archaeology and natural history of the park. Downstairs is the **Cellar Restaurant** and a small **antiques shop** (⌚noon-9pm Tue-Fri, noon-10pm Sat, noon-5pm Sun & Mon).

Legend has it that the castle's residents will experience good fortune only as long as a white cat lives there, a tale commemorated in the beautiful formal gardens by nine portrayals of cats in mosaic, painting, sculpture and garden furniture – a good game for the kids is getting them to find all nine.

Belfast Zoo ZOO

(Map p586; www.belfastzoo.co.uk; Antrim Rd; adult/child £8.90/4.70, under 4s, over 60s & visitors with disabilities free; ⌚10am-7pm Apr-Sep, 10am-4pm Oct-Mar, last admission 2hr/90min before closing in summer/winter) Belfast Zoo is one of the most appealing zoos in Britain and Ireland, with spacious enclosures set on an attractive, sloping site; the sea lion and penguin pool with its underwater viewing is particularly good. Some of the more unusual animals include tamarins, Malaysian sun bears and red pandas, but the biggest attractions are the ultra-cute meerkats, the colony of ring-tailed lemurs and the 28-strong herd of Rothschild's giraffe.

FREE Malone House HISTORIC BUILDING

(Map p586; www.malonehouse.co.uk; Upper Malone Rd; ⌚9am-5pm Mon-Sat, noon-4.30pm Sun) Malone House is a late-Georgian mansion in the grounds of Barnett Demesne. Built in the 1820s for local merchant William Legge, the house is now used mainly for social functions and conferences, with art exhibitions staged in the **Higgin Gallery**. The surrounding gardens are planted with azaleas and rhododendrons, with paths leading down to the Lagan Towpath.

The house is about 5km south of the centre; take bus 8A or 8B to Dub Lane, Upper Malone Rd.

FREE Giant's Ring HISTORIC SITE

(Map p586; Ballynahatty Rd; ⌚24hr) This huge prehistoric earthwork, nearly 200m in diameter, is a circular Neolithic ritual complex with a dolmen (known as the Druid's Altar) in the centre. Prehistoric rings were commonly believed to be the home of fairies and consequently treated with respect, but this

Around Central Belfast

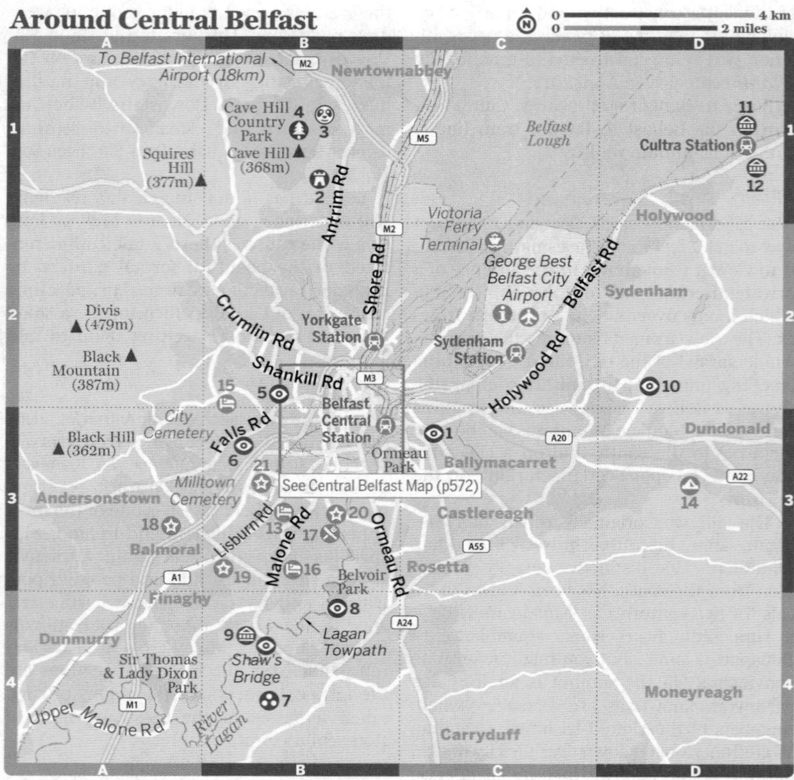

one was commandeered in the 19th century as a racetrack, the 4m-high embankment serving as a natural grandstand. The site is 6.5km south of Belfast city centre, off Milltown Rd near Shaw's Bridge.

FREE **Stormont** NOTABLE BUILDING

(Map p586; Upper Newtonards Rd; grounds 7.30am-dusk, buildings 9am-4pm Mon-Fri) The dazzling white neoclassical facade of the **Parliament Buildings** at Stormont is one of Belfast's most iconic buildings; in the North, 'Stormont' carries the same connotation as 'Westminster' does in Britain and 'Washington' in the USA – the seat of power. For 40 years, from its completion in 1932 until the introduction of direct rule in 1972, it was the seat of the parliament of Northern Ireland. More recently, on 8 May 2007, it returned to the forefront of Irish politics when Ian Paisley and Martin McGuinness – who had been the best of enemies for decades – laughed and smiled as they were sworn in as first minister and deputy first minister, respectively.

The building occupies a dramatic position at the end of a gently rising, 1.5km avenue and is fronted by a defiant statue of the arch-Unionist Sir Edward Carson. Tours of Parliament Buildings are not available to the general public, but you can visit the **Public Gallery** (from noon Mon, from 10.30am Tue) and are free to walk around the extensive grounds, or you can take a virtual tour at www.niassembly.gov.uk/visiting.htm. Nearby, 19th-century **Stormont Castle** is, like Hillsborough in County Down, an official residence of the Secretary of State for Northern Ireland.

Stormont is 8km east of the city centre, off Upper Newtonards Rd. Take bus 20A from Donegall Sq W.

Around Central Belfast

Sights

1 Aunt Sandra's Candy Factory............C3
2 Belfast Castle............B1
3 Belfast Zoo............B1
4 Cave Hill Country Park............B1
5 Conway Mill............B2
6 Cultúrlann McAdam Ó Fiaich............B3
7 Giant's Ring............B4
8 Lagan Meadows............B4
9 Malone House............B4
10 Stormont............D2
11 Transport Museum............D1
12 Ulster Folk Museum............D1

Activities, Courses & Tours

Pirates Adventure Golf............(see 14)

Sleeping

13 All Seasons B&B............B3
14 Dundonald Touring Caravan Park............D3
15 Farset International............B2
16 Old Rectory............B3

Eating

Caifé Feirste............(see 6)
17 Cutters Wharf............B3

Entertainment

18 Casement Park............A3
19 King's Hall............B3
20 Lyric Theatre............B3
21 Windsor Park............B3

Tours

You can find full details of organised tours at the Belfast Welcome Centre. If you want to hire a personal guide, call the Welcome Centre or contact the **Northern Ireland Tourist Guide Association** (www.bluebadgeireland.com; half-/full-day tours £75/140).

Belfast iTours (belfastitours.com) offers nine self-guided video tours of the city that you can download to your smartphone or MP4 player; alternatively you can hire a preloaded MP4 player (£9 for 24 hours) from the Belfast Welcome Centre.

Belfast Bike Tours SIGHTSEEING
(07812 114235; www.belfastbiketours.com; per person £15; 10.30am & 2pm Tue, Thu & Sat Apr-Sep, 10.30am only Tue, Thu & Sat Oct-Mar) These 2½-hour guided tours depart from outside Queen's University, and take you on a leisurely spin along the Lagan Valley to the Giant's Ring and back again. Bikes provided; book in advance.

Lagan Boat Company HISTORY
(Map p572; 9033 0844; www.laganboatcompany.com; adult/child £10/8; 12.30pm, 2pm & 3.30pm daily Apr-Sep, 12.30 & 2pm daily Oct, 12.30 & 2pm Sat & Sun Nov-Mar) The excellent **Titanic Tour** explores the derelict docklands downstream of the weir, taking in the slipways where the liners *Titanic* and *Olympic* were launched and the huge dry dock where they could fit with just nine inches to spare; departs from Donegall Quay near the *Bigfish* sculpture. The **Obel Tour** (£20/18) combines a Titanic boat tour with a trip to the top of the Obel, Ireland's tallest building.

Belfast City Sightseeing SIGHTSEEING
(Map p572; 9032 1321; www.belfastcitysightseeing.com; adult/child £12.50/6; twice hourly 10am-4.30pm) Runs 1¼-hour open-top bus tours that take in City Hall, the Albert Clock, the Titanic Quarter, the Botanic Gardens, and the Falls Rd and Shankill Rd murals in West Belfast. Departs from Castle Pl; hop-on hop-off tickets valid for 48 hours.

Belfast Splash Tours SIGHTSEEING
(9077 0990; www.belfastsplashtours.com; adult/child £12.50/8; 6 daily) Offers one-hour city tours in amphibious buses, part on the road, part on the river (upstream of Lagan Weir); departs from Castle Pl in the city centre.

Taxi Tours

Black taxi tours of West Belfast's murals – known locally as the 'bombs and bullets' or 'doom and gloom' tours – are offered by a large number of taxi companies and local cabbies. These can vary in quality and content, but in general they're an intimate and entertaining way to see the sights and can be customised to suit your own interests. There are also historical taxi tours of the city centre. For a one-hour tour expect to pay from £25 to £30 total for one or two people, and £8 to £10 per person for three to six. Call and they will pick you up from anywhere in the city centre.

The following are recommended:

Harpers Taxi Tours (07711 757178; www.harperstaxitours.co.nr)

Official Black Taxi Tours (9064 2264, toll-free 0800 052 3914; www.belfasttours.com)

Original Belfast Black Taxi Tours (07751 565359; taxitours@live.co.uk)

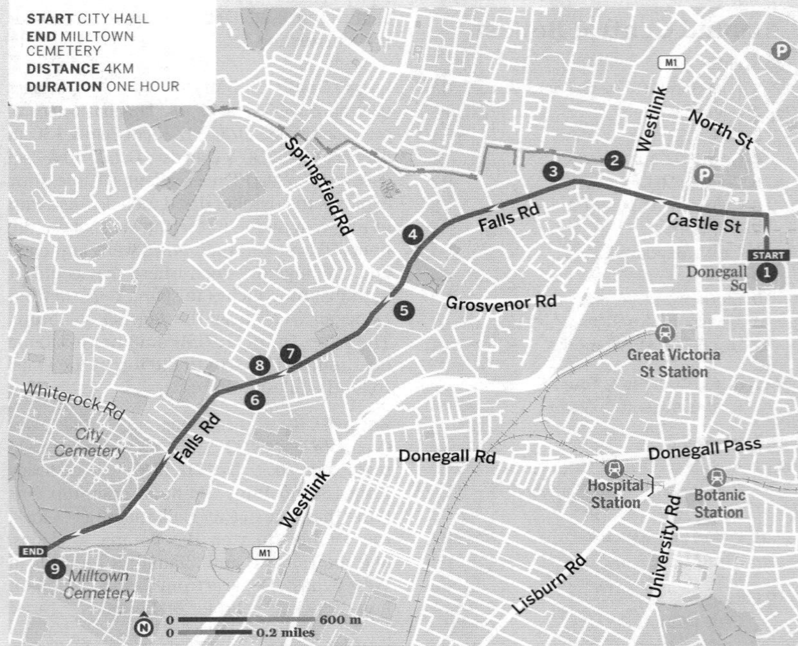

Walking Tour

Republican West Belfast

Starting from 1 **City Hall**, go north along Donegall Pl and turn left on Castle St. Keep straight ahead along Divis St and cross the Westlink dual carriageway. Look along Townsend St, the first street on the right, and you'll see the steel gates that mark the beginning of the so-called 2 **Peace Line**, the 6m-high wall that has divided the Protestant and Catholic communities of West Belfast for almost 40 years. Begun in 1970 as a 'temporary measure', it has outlasted the Berlin Wall and zigzags for some 4km from the Westlink to the lower slopes of Black Mountain.

Next, you'll pass the 3 **Solidarity Wall**, a collection of murals expressing Republican sympathies with, among others, the Palestinians, the Kurds, the Catalonians and the Basques. On the corner of Falls Rd and Sevastopol St is the red-brick 4 **Sinn Féin headquarters**, with its famous mural of a smiling Bobby Sands, the hunger striker who was elected MP for West Belfast just a few weeks before he died in 1981.

Just beyond the 5 **Royal Victoria Hospital** – which in the 1970s and '80s developed a well-earned reputation for expertise in the treatment of gunshot wounds – is the 6 **Cultúrlann McAdam Ó Fiaich** (Irish cultural centre). At Islandbawn St on the right, the 7 **Plastic Bullet Mural** commemorates the 17 people, including eight children, who were killed by plastic baton rounds (now banned) fired by the security services between 1972 and 1989. Two streets on, on the right, is 8 **Beechmount Ave**. Look at the street name – a hand-painted sign reads 'RPG Avenue'. 'RPG' stands for 'rocket-propelled grenade'; the street earned its nickname because it offered a line of sight for IRA rocket attacks on the security forces base in nearby Springfield Rd.

Eventually you reach 9 **Milltown Cemetery** where the 1981 hunger strikers are buried. The Republican plot is halfway along the southern wall – from the entrance head straight on until you reach a crossroads. Turn right and keep straight on to the end of the path.

Walking Tours

Belfast Pub Tours PUB CULTURE
(☎9268 3665; www.belfastpubtours.com; per person £6; ⏲7pm Thu & 4pm Sat May-Oct) A two-hour tour (not including drinks) taking in six of the city's historic pubs, departing from the Crown Dining Rooms, above the Crown Liquor Saloon on Great Victoria St.

Blackstaff Way HISTORY
(☎9029 2631; www.belfast-city-walking-tours.co.uk; per person £6; ⏲11am Sat) A fascinating 1½-hour historical tour through the city along the route of the Blackstaff River, which was channelled underground in 1881. Departs from the Belfast Welcome Centre.

Historic Belfast Walk HISTORY
(☎9024 6609; per person £6; ⏲2pm Wed & Fri-Sun) A 1½-hour tour that explores the architecture and history of the Victorian city centre and Laganside. Departs from the Belfast Welcome Centre.

Titanic Tours HISTORY
(☎9065 9971; 07852 716655; www.titanictours-belfast.co.uk; adult/child £30/15; ⏲on demand) A two-hour luxury tour led by the great-granddaughter of one of the *Titanic*'s crew, visiting various *Titanic*-related sites, for groups of two to five people; includes pick-up and drop-off at your accommodation.

Festivals & Events

Belfast City Council (www.belfastcity.gov.uk/events) organises a wide range of events throughout the year, covering everything from the St Patrick's Day parade to the Lord Mayor's Show. It has a useful online events calendar, as does the **Belfast Welcome Centre** (www.gotobelfast.com/whats_on.aspx).

Féile an Earraigh MUSIC
(www.feilebelfast.com) This four-day festival of traditional Irish and Celtic music, held in February, attracts artists from all over Ireland, Europe and America.

St Patrick's Day CULTURE
(www.belfastcity.gov.uk/events) A celebration of Ireland's patron saint marked by various community festivals and culminating in a grand city-centre parade on 17 March.

Belfast Film Festival FILM
(www.belfastfilmfestival.org) Two-week celebration of Irish and international film held in early April.

Titanic Made In Belfast Festival MARITIME
(www.belfastcity.gov.uk/titanic) Week-long celebration held in early/mid April of the world's most famous ship, and the city that built her, with special exhibitions, tours, lectures and film screenings.

Festival of Fools STREET THEATRE
(www.foolsfestival.com) This five-day festival of street entertainment in late April/early May has events concentrated in Cathedral Quarter and city centre.

Belfast Marathon RUNNING
(www.belfastcitymarathon.com) Avid runners from across the globe come to compete in the marathon on the first Monday in May; it's also a people's event, with a walk and fun run as well.

Cathedral Quarter Arts Festival ARTS
([www.cqaf.com) Twelve days in early May of drama, music, poetry, street theatre and art exhibitions in and around the Cathedral Quarter.

Belfast Maritime Festival MARITIME
(www.belfastcity.gov.uk/maritimefestival) A three-day festival at the beginning of June centred on Queen's Quay and Clarendon Dock, with sailing ships, street entertainment, a seafood festival and live music.

CityDance DANCE
(www.crescentarts.org) Free one-day midsummer dance festival in June, based at the Crescent Arts Centre.

Belfast Pride GAY
(www.belfastpride.com) Ireland's largest celebration of gay, lesbian, bisexual and transgender culture, culminating in a huge city-centre parade; takes place over a week in late July.

Féile An Phobail CULTURE
(www.feilebelfast.com) Said to be the largest community festival in Ireland, the Féile takes place in West Belfast over 10 days in early August. Events include an opening carnival parade, street parties, theatre performances, concerts and historical tours of the City and Milltown cemeteries.

Belfast Festival at Queen's ARTS
(www.belfastfestival.com) The UK's second-largest arts festival held in and around Queen's University over two weeks in late October.

Christmas Festivities CULTURE
(www.belfastcity.gov.uk/events) There's a range of events from late November to 31 December, including carol singing, lamplight processions and a street carnival.

Sleeping

From backpacker hostels to boutique hotels, the range of places to stay in Belfast gets wider every year. The traditional accommodation scene – red-brick B&Bs in the leafy suburbs of South Belfast and city-centre business hotels – is lent a splash of colour in the form of stylish hotel–restaurant–nightclub combos or boutique hotels set in refurbished historic buildings.

Most of Belfast's budget and midrange accommodation is south of the centre, in the university district around Botanic Ave, University Rd and Malone Rd. This area is also crammed with good-value restaurants and pubs, and is mostly within a 20-minute walk of City Hall.

Book ahead in summer or during busy festival periods. The Belfast Welcome Centre will make reservations for a fee of £2. You can also book accommodation through the **Lonely Planet website** (http://hotels.lonelyplanet.com).

CITY CENTRE

TOP CHOICE **Malmaison Hotel** HOTEL ££
(Map p572; ☎9022 0200; www.malmaison-belfast.com; 34-38 Victoria St; r from £95, ste from £325; @ 📶) Housed in a pair of beautifully restored Italianate warehouses (originally built for rival firms in the 1850s), the Malmaison is a luxurious haven of king-size beds, deep leather sofas and roll-top baths big enough for two, all done up in a decadent decor of black, red, dark chocolate and cream. The massive, rock-star Samson suite has a giant bed (almost 3m long), a huge bathtub and, wait for it…a billiard table, with purple baize.

Ten Square HOTEL £££
(Map p572; ☎9024 1001; www.tensquare.co.uk; 10 Donegall Sq S; r from £139; @ 📶) A former bank building to the south of City Hall that has been given a designer feng-shui makeover, Ten Square is an opulent, Shanghai-inspired boutique hotel with friendly and attentive service. Magazines such as *Cosmopolitan* and *Conde Nast Traveller* drool over the dark lacquered wood, low-slung futon-style beds and sumptuous linen, and the list of former guests includes Bono and Brad Pitt.

Fitzwilliam Hotel HOTEL £££
(Map p572; ☎9044 2080; www.fitzwilliamhotelbelfast.com; 1-3 Great Victoria St; r from £115; @ 📶) A new hotel in a truly central location, the Fitzwilliam pushes all the right style buttons with its use of designer fabrics, cool colours and mood lighting. Bedrooms have crisp linen sheets, fluffy bathrobes and powerful showers, and the staff are unstintingly helpful. The restaurant, Menu by Kevin Thornton, is excellent too.

Park Inn HOTEL ££
(Map p572; ☎9067 7710; www.belfast.parkinn.co.uk; 4 Clarence St W; r from £69; 📶 👪) This modern hotel boasts a bright and breezy atmosphere, with slick styling and splashes of bold primary colours. It has a top location, too – only five minutes from City Hall and close to loads of good pubs and restaurants – and is excellent value. There are eight wheelchair-accessible rooms, and family rooms can be arranged.

Merchant Hotel HOTEL £££
(Map p572; ☎9023 4888; www.themerchanthotel.com; 35-39 Waring St; r/ste from £140/200; P @ 📶) Belfast's most flamboyant Victorian building (the old Ulster Bank head office) has been converted into the city's most flamboyant boutique hotel, a fabulous fusion of contemporary styling and old-fashioned elegance.

SOUTH BELFAST

To get to places on or near Botanic Ave, take bus 7A or 7B from Howard St. For places on or near University and Malone Rds, take bus 8A or 8B, and for places on or near Lisburn Rd, take bus 9A or 9B; both depart from Donegall Sq E, and from the bus stop on Great Victoria St across from the Europa BusCentre.

TOP CHOICE **Old Rectory** B&B ££
(Map p586; ☎9066 7882; www.anoldrectory.co.uk; 148 Malone Rd; s/d £53/84; P @ 📶) A lovely Victorian villa with lots of original stained glass, this former rectory has five spacious bedrooms, a comfortable drawing room with leather sofa, and fancy breakfasts (wild boar sausages, scrambled eggs with smoked salmon, freshly squeezed OJ). It's a 10-minute bus ride from the centre – the inconspicuous driveway is on the left, just past Deramore Park South. No credit cards.

BELFAST FOR CHILDREN

W5 is the city's biggest draw for kids – it's hard to drag them away once they get started with the hands-on exhibits. The Odyssey Complex houses other attractions including a video-games arcade, a ten-pin bowling rink and an IMAX cinema. **Belfast Zoo** is a perennial favourite, and the **Ulster Museum** also has plenty of exhibits and special events designed for children of all ages.

For outdoor fun, head for the **Botanic Gardens** or the adventure playground in **Cave Hill Country Park**. Or you can try crazy golf with a difference at **Pirates Adventure Golf** (www.piratesadventuregolf.com; Dundonald Touring Caravan Park, 111A Dundonald Rd; adult/child £6/4; ⏲11am-9pm), a landscaped, 36-hole course decked out with waterfalls, fountains and a giant pirate ship.

Sweeties may not be at the top of parents' shopping lists these days, but you might be prepared to make an exception for **Aunt Sandra's Candy Factory** (www.auntsandras.com; 60 Castlereagh Rd; tours adult/child £4/3; ⏲9.30am-5pm Mon-Fri, 10am-4.30pm Sat). This 1950s-style shop sells handmade fudge, candy, chocolates, toffee apples and other traditional sweets, and you can take a tour of the workshop before buying the goods.

Outside of town, but near enough for a day trip, is the **Ulster Folk & Transport Museums** and, in County Down, the **Ark Open Farm** (p614); both are hugely popular with kids.

The free bimonthly *Whatabout?* booklet (available from the Belfast Welcome Centre) has a 'Family Fun' section, which lists events and attractions of interest to travellers with children. If you're in town in late March, look out for the **Belfast Children's Festival** (www.belfastchildrensfestival.com), which is packed with cultural and educational events.

Tara Lodge B&B ££
(Map p572; ☎9059 0900; www.taralodge.com; 36 Cromwell Rd; s/d £70/85; P@wifi) This B&B is a cut above your average South Belfast B&B, and feels more like a boutique hotel with its stylish, minimalist decor; friendly, efficient staff; delicious breakfasts; and 24 bright and cheerful rooms. It's in a great location, on a quiet side street just a few paces from the buzz of Botanic Ave.

All Seasons B&B B&B ££
(Map p586; ☎9068 2814; www.allseasonsbelfast.com; 356 Lisburn Rd; s/d/f £35/55/65; P wifi) Away from the centre, but right in the heart of trendy Lisburn Rd, All Seasons is a red-brick villa with bright, colourful bedrooms, modern bathrooms, a stylish little breakfast room and a comfortable lounge. Take bus 9A or 9B from the city centre; a taxi will cost around £7. The house is between Cranmore Ave and Cranmore Gardens, 150m past the big police station.

Camera Guest House B&B ££
(Map p572; ☎9066 0026; www.cameraguesthouse.com; 44 Wellington Park; s/d £48/68; wifi family) A cosy, welcoming Victorian B&B with an open fire in the drawing room, the Camera is set in yet another of South Belfast's peaceful, tree-lined terraced streets. The friendly young couple who own the place manage to create a family-friendly atmosphere, and are a fount of knowledge on what to see and do in town.

Malone Lodge Hotel HOTEL ££
(Map p572; ☎9038 8060; www.malonelodge.com; 60 Eglantine Ave; s/d/apt from £75/85/100; P wifi) The centrepiece of a tree-lined Victorian terrace, the modern Malone Lodge has pulled in many plaudits for its large, luxurious rooms with elegant gold and navy decor, good food and pleasant, helpful staff. It also offers five-star self-catering apartments (one- and two-bedroom).

Benedicts HOTEL ££
(Map p572; ☎9059 1999; www.benedictshotel.co.uk; 7-21 Bradbury Pl; s/d from £70/80; @wifi) Set bang in the middle of the Golden Mile, Benedicts is a modern, style-conscious hotel at the heart of South Belfast's nightlife. The rooms, complete with Egyptian cotton sheets and feather-bedded mattresses, are above a huge Gothic bar and restaurant (where you also have breakfast), so don't expect peace and quiet till after 1am.

Crescent Town House HOTEL ££
(Map p572; ☎9032 3349; www.crescenttownhouse.com; 13 Lower Cres; s/d/tr from £75/85/110; @wifi)

NORTHERN IRISH ROOTS?

If you're hoping to track down your Ulster family history, the Public Record Office of Northern Ireland, **PRONI** (☎028 9053 4800; www.proni.gov.uk; 2 Titanic Blvd; ⏲9am-4.45pm Mon-Fri), has opened a fancy new headquarters in Belfast's Titanic Quarter. Admission is free, but a charge is made for copies of documents. Check the website for details of how to register and search the records.

Another stylish boutique hotel with a perfect location, the Crescent is an elegant Victorian town house transformed into a den of designer chic, with its finger on the pulse of the city's party zone. Rooms have silky, Ralph Lauren–style decor and luxury bathrooms with Molton Brown toiletries and walk-in rain-head showers.

Kate's B&B B&B £
(Map p572; ☎9028 2091; katesbb127@hotmail.com; 127 University St; per person £25) Kate's is a homey kind of place, from the window boxes bursting with colourful flowers to the cute dining room crammed with bric-a-brac and a couple of resident cats. The bedrooms are basic but comfortable, and the showers are a bit cramped, but at this price – and only a few minutes' walk from Botanic Ave – we're not complaining.

Vagabonds HOSTEL £
(Map p572; ☎9023 3017; www.vagabondsbelfast.com; 9 University Rd; dm £13-16, tw or d £40; @🛜) Comfy bunks, lockable luggage baskets, private shower cubicles and a relaxed atmosphere are what you get at one of Belfast's newest hostels, run by a couple of experienced travellers. Conveniently located close to both Queen's and the city centre.

City Backpacker HOSTEL £
(Map p572;☎9066 0030; www.ibackpacker.co.uk; 53-55 Malone Ave; dm £14, d £40; @🛜) Leafy South Belfast sprouts another new hostel, stylishly decked out with shiny IKEA-style kit. It's squeezed into a three-storey terrace house on a quiet suburban avenue, so can be a bit cramped when busy; off-season, you can often have a room to yourself.

Arnie's Backpackers HOSTEL £
(Map p572; ☎9024 2867; www.arniesbackpackers.co.uk; 63 Fitzwilliam St; dm £10-14; @🛜) This long-established hostel is set in a quiet terraced house in the university area. A bit on the small side, but coal fires and a friendly crowd make it more cosy than cramped.

Global Village Backpackers HOSTEL £
(Map p572; ☎9031 3533; globalvillagebelfast.com; 87 University St; dm £13-15, d £40; @🛜) This is a brand-new place close to Queen's University, boasting a beer garden, a barbecue and a games room.

Paddy's Palace Belfast HOSTEL £
(Map p572; ☎9033 3367; www.paddyspalace.com; 68 Lisburn Rd; dm £10-15, d £45; P@🛜) Paddy's is beginning to show its age – it could do with a deep clean – but is still good value with friendly staff who are happy to point you to the best local pubs.

Belfast International Youth Hostel HOSTEL £
(Map p572; ☎9031 5435; www.hini.org.uk; 22-32 Donegall Rd; dm £11-16, s £22-32, tw £29-42; P@🛜) Belfast's modern Hostelling International (HI) hostel is conveniently located just off Shaftesbury Sq, so it can be a bit noisy at night when the pubs and clubs empty. The hostel has a kitchen, a laundry, a cafe and free linen; rates are slightly higher on Friday and Saturday nights. Take bus 9A or 9B from Donegall Sq East or Great Victoria St (across from the Europa BusCentre) to Bradbury Pl.

OUTSIDE THE CENTRE

Farset International HOSTEL £
(Map p586; ☎9089 9833; www.farsetinternational.co.uk; 446 Springfield Rd; s/d £34/48; P🛜) This community-run complex in West Belfast is best described as a posh hostel, set in grounds overlooking a small lake, offering 38 rooms with private bathroom and TV. Rates include breakfast, and in the evening you can eat in the restaurant or use the self-catering kitchen.

Dundonald Touring Caravan Park CAMPSITE £
(Map p586; ☎9080 9129; www.theicebowl.com; 111 Old Dundonald Rd, Dundonald; tent/caravan sites £15/23; ⏲mid-Mar–Oct) This small site (22 sites) in a park next to the Dundonald Icebowl is the nearest camping ground to Belfast, 7km east of the city centre and south of the A20 road to Newtownards.

Eating

In recent years, Belfast's restaurant scene has been totally transformed by a wave of new restaurants whose standards compare with the best eating places in Europe.

CITY CENTRE

The main shopping area north of Donegall Sq becomes a silent maze of deserted streets and steel shutters after 7pm, but during the day the many pubs, cafes and restaurants do a roaring trade. In the evening, the liveliest part of the city centre stretches south of Donegall Sq to Shaftesbury Sq.

TOP CHOICE Ginger BISTRO £££
(Map p572; ☎9024 4421; www.gingerbistro.com; 7-8 Hope St; mains £17-22; ⏰noon-3pm Tue-Sat & 5-9pm Mon-Sat) Ginger is one of those places you could walk right past without noticing, but if you do you'll be missing out. It's a cosy and informal little bistro with an unassuming exterior, serving food that is anything but ordinary – the flame-haired owner/chef (hence the name) really knows what he's doing, sourcing top-quality Irish produce and turning out exquisite dishes such as such as scallops with crisp black pudding and chorizo butter. The lunch and pre-theatre (5pm to 6.45pm Monday to Friday) menu offers main courses for £8 to £12.

Cayenne IRISH £££
(Map p572; ☎9033 1532; www.cayenne-restaurant.co.uk; 7 Ascot House, Shaftesbury Sq; mains £18-25, 2-course lunch £12.50; ⏰noon-2.15pm Mon-Fri, to 4pm Sun, 5-11pm Wed-Mon) Behind an anonymous frosted-glass facade lurks this funky, award-winning restaurant operated by celebrity chef Paul Rankin. Grey and black walls lit with the glowing orange-red of the eponymous pepper provide an aura of sophistication. The menu concentrates on Irish produce prepared with an Asian or Mediterranean twist; the set three-course dinner menu (£23 or £28) is good value.

Mourne Seafood Bar SEAFOOD ££
(Map p572; ☎9024 8544; www.mourneseafood.com; 34-36 Bank St; mains £10-17; ⏰noon-5pm Mon, to 9.30pm Tue-Thu, noon-4pm & 5-10.30pm Fri & Sat, 1-6pm Sun) This informal, publike place, all red brick and dark wood with old oil lamps dangling from the ceiling, is tucked behind a fishmonger's shop, so the seafood is as fresh as it gets. On the menu are oysters served *au naturel* or Rockefeller, meltingly sweet scallops, lobster, langoustines, gurnard and sea bass. Hugely popular, so best book ahead, especially on Sunday.

James St South FRENCH, IRISH ££
(Map p572; ☎9043 4310; www.jamesstreetsouth.co.uk; 21 James St S; 2-/3-course lunch £15/17, dinner mains £17-23; ⏰noon-2.45pm & 5.45-10.45pm Mon-Sat, 5.30-9pm Sun) A starkly beautiful white dining room with crisp white table linen creates a perfect stage for the presentation of some of Belfast's finest food – the French-inspired menu offers dishes such as Lough Neagh trout with cockle vinaigrette and quail's egg, while the service is relaxed yet highly professional.

Rhubarb Fresh Food Cafe CAFE £
(Map p572; www.rhubarb-belfast.co.uk; 2 Little Victoria St; mains lunch £6-8; ⏰8am-4pm Mon-Tue, 8am-10pm Wed-Sat) Tucked away in a quiet corner, Rhubarb is a great place for tasty, freshly prepared food that's a cut above your usual cafe fare, from breakfasts, such as French toast, omelettes and Ulster fry, to hot lunches, such as homemade lasagne. The dinner menu (mains £13 to £18) takes things up a notch, with dishes like slow-roast lamb shank with rosemary potatoes.

La Boca ARGENTINIAN ££
(Map p572; www.labocabelfast.com; 6 Fountain St; mains £7-13; ⏰10.30am-8pm Tue, to 9pm Wed-Thu, 10.30am-10pm Fri & Sat; 📶) Named for the dockside district in Buenos Aires, this lively, high-ceilinged bistro is decked out with Latin American flags and local art, and has an Argentine-themed menu that includes grilled steak with *chimichurri* (a sauce of oil, garlic, herbs and spices), ribs marinated in red wine, and braised Patagonian lamb.

Gingeroot INDIAN ££
(Map p572; www.gingeroot.com; 73-75 Great Victoria St; mains £8-12; ⏰noon-3pm & 5.30-11.30pm Mon-Sat, 5.30-10.30pm Sun) A bright, modern restaurant that serves fresh and flavourful Indian dishes – the *jeera* (cumin) chicken is particularly tasty – Gingeroot offers an exceptionally good-value two-course lunch, available noon to 3pm Monday to Saturday (£6.50).

Deane's Restaurant FRENCH, IRISH £££
(Map p572; ☎9033 1134; www.michaeldeane.co.uk; 34-40 Howard St; mains lunch £10-15, dinner £17-24; ⏰noon-3pm & 5.30-10pm Mon-Sat) Despite losing its Michelin star in 2011, the flagship of chef Michael Deane's restaurant fleet is still one of

Northern Ireland's top restaurants. A simple, seasonal menu takes the best of Irish and British produce – beef, game, lamb, seafood – and gives it the gourmet treatment. Typical dishes include 28-day aged sirloin with Cafe de Paris sauce, and fillet of organic salmon with watercress purée and crispy crab cake.

Menu by Kevin Thornton FRENCH/IRISH £££
(Map p572; ☎9044 2130; www.fitzwilliamhotelbelfast.com; Fitzwilliam Hotel, 1-3 Great Victoria St; mains £16-28; ⏲lunch & dinner) The decor in the first-floor restaurant at the Fitzwilliam Hotel is a bit 'boutique overload', with tables and floors of polished oak, white linen and lampshades, a black wall, and strikingly tall, slender-backed chairs in bright cerise. But the food is superb, with the freshest Irish produce given the French gourmet treatment. Two-course lunch £11.

Great Room FRENCH £££
(Map p572; ☎9023 4888; www.themerchanthotel.com; Merchant Hotel, 35-39 Waring St; mains £20-29; ⏲7am-11pm) Set in the former banking hall of the Ulster Bank head office, the Great Room is a jaw-dropping extravaganza of gilded stucco, red plush, white marble cherubs and a vast crystal chandelier glittering beneath a glass dome. The menu matches the decor: decadent but delicious, a French-influenced catalogue of political incorrectness laced with foie gras and truffles. A set three-course dinner menu (£27) is available from 6.30pm to 10pm Monday to Thursday (£23 from 5.30 to 6.30pm).

Deane's Deli Bistro BISTRO ££
(Map p572; www.michaeldeane.co.uk; 44 Bedford St; mains £11-19; ⏲noon-3pm & 5-9pm Mon & Tue, to 10pm Wed-Fri, noon-10pm Sat) Enjoy top-notch nosh at this relaxed and informal bistro, with gourmet burgers and posh fish and chips on the menu.

Avoca Cafe CAFE £
(Map p572; 41 Arthur St; mains £5-12; ⏲9.30am-5pm Mon-Fri, 9am-5pm Sat, 12.30-5pm Sun) You'll find healthy rolls, wraps, salads and sandwiches to sit in or take away here, as well as hot lunch specials such as grilled chicken with Mediterranean vegetables.

Archana INDIAN £
(Map p572; www.archana.co.uk; 53 Dublin Rd; mains £7-10; ⏲noon-2pm & 5pm-midnight Mon-Sat, 5-11pm Sun) Cosy and unpretentious, Archana has a good range of vegetarian dishes. The *thali* – a platter of three curries – is good value at £17/11 for the meat/vegie version.

Morning Star PUB £
(Map p572; www.themorningstarbar.com; 17 Pottinger's Entry; mains £5-15; ⏲food noon-9pm Mon-Sat) Morning Star is famed for its all-you-can-eat lunch buffet (£6; served noon to 4pm).

CATHEDRAL QUARTER & AROUND

John Hewitt Bar & Restaurant PUB £
(Map p572; www.thejohnhewitt.com; 51 Donegall St; mains £7-9; ⏲food served noon-3pm Mon-Sat) Named for the Belfast poet and socialist, this is a modern pub with a traditional atmosphere and a well-earned reputation for excellent food. The menu changes weekly, but includes inventive dishes such as pork and black pepper sausages with buttery mash and red wine gravy, and butterbean and vegetable fritters. It's also a great place for a drink.

No 27 IRISH ££
(Map p572; ☎9031 2884; www.no27.co.uk; 27 Talbot St; mains £15-22; ⏲noon-3pm Mon-Fri & 6-10pm Tue-Sat) One of the Cathedral Quarter's most stylish restaurants, No 27 is a cool confection of red-brick and white pillars scattered with locally produced art (most of it for sale). As much thought has gone into the food as the decor, with carefully crafted dishes such as trout with fennel purée and fennel and grapefruit salad.

Hill Street Brasserie FUSION ££
(Map p572; ☎9058 6868; www.hillstbrasserie.com; 38 Hill St; mains lunch £8-10, dinner £10-20; ⏲noon-2.30pm Mon-Sat & 5-11pm Tue-Sun) In keeping with the design studios and art galleries that throng the nearby streets, this little brasserie is desperately trendy, from the slate-and-wood floor to the aubergine-and-olive colour scheme. The lunch menu is a bargain, offering a choice of homemade burger, meze platter and beer-battered fish and chips.

Nick's Warehouse BISTRO ££
(Map p572; www.nickswarehouse.co.uk; 35-39 Hill St; mains £12-22; ⏲food served noon-3pm & 6-10pm Tue-Sat) A Cathedral Quarter pioneer (opened in 1989), Nick's is an enormous red-brick and blond-wood wine bar and restaurant, buzzing with happy drinkers and diners. The seasonal menu is strong on local produce, and the wine list is intriguing.

SOUTH BELFAST

TOP CHOICE Barking Dog — BISTRO ££

(off map p572; ☎9066 1885; www.barkingdogbelfast.com; 33-35 Malone Rd; mains £10-19; ⏲noon-3.30pm & 5.30-10pm Mon-Sat, to 11pm Fri & Sat, noon-9pm Sun) Chunky hardwood, bare brick, candlelight and quirky design create the atmosphere of a stylishly restored farmhouse, and the menu completes the feeling of cosiness and comfort with simple but sensational dishes such as seared scallops on endive *tarte tatin* and a burger of meltingly tender beef shin wrapped in caramelised onion and horseradish cream. Superb service, too.

Molly's Yard — IRISH ££

(Map p572; ☎9032 2600; www.mollysyard.co.uk; 1 College Green Mews; bistro mains £7-10; restaurant £15-21; ⏲noon-9pm Mon-Thu, to 9.30pm Fri & Sat) A restored Victorian stables courtyard is the setting for this quirky restaurant, with a cosy bar-bistro on the ground floor, outdoor tables in the yard and a rustic dining room (open from 6pm) in the airy roof space upstairs. The menu is seasonal and sticks to half a dozen each of starters and mains. It also has its own microbrewery.

Shu — FRENCH, IRISH ££

(Map p572; ☎9038 1655; www.shu-restaurant.com; 253 Lisburn Rd; mains £15-20; ⏲noon-2.30pm & 6-9pm Mon-Fri, 7-9.30pm Sat) If you want to know who to blame for all those copycat designer restaurants with the dark-wood-and-chocolate-brown-leather decor, then look no further. Lording it over the hipper-than-thou Lisburn Rd since 2000, Shu is the granddaddy of Belfast chic, a stylish restaurant that is still winning awards for its food. The French-influenced menu includes duck confit with date and Earl Grey tea purée, and slow-cooked lamb loin with aubergine caviar.

Beatrice Kennedy — IRISH ££

(Map p572; ☎9020 2290; www.beatricekennedy.co.uk; 44 University Rd; mains £17-20; ⏲5-10.15pm Tue-Sat, 12.30-2.30pm & 5-8.15pm Sun; ☑) Organic veg and locally sourced meats are a staple at this perennial Queen's Quarter favourite (it's where students take their visiting parents for dinner). Recently revamped, the dining room retains its Victorian elegance and period style, while the menu adds a modern twist to traditional Irish seafood, lamb and beef. There's a separate vegetarian menu, with dishes such as butternut squash risotto with rocket pesto and parmesan. From 5pm to 7pm you can get a two-course dinner for £15.

Maggie May's — CAFE £

(Map p572; www.maggiemaysbelfast.co.uk; 50 Botanic Ave; mains £3-7; ⏲8am-10.30pm Mon-Sat, 10am-10.30pm Sun) This is a classic little cafe with cosy wooden booths, colourful murals of old Belfast, and a host of hungover students wolfing down huge Ulster fries at lunchtime. The all-day breakfast menu runs from tea and toast to eggy bread and maple syrup, while lunch can be soup and a sarnie or steak-and-Guinness pie; puddings include Dime Bar and sticky toffee. BYOB.

Café Conor — CAFE-BISTRO ££

(Map p572; www.cafeconor.com; 11A Stranmillis Rd; mains £9-12; ⏲9am-11pm) Set in the glass-roofed former studio of William Conor, a Belfast artist, this is a laid-back bistro with a light and airy dining area dominated by a portrait of Conor himself. The menu offers a range of pastas, salads, burgers and stir-fries, along with favourites such as fish and chips with mushy peas. The breakfast menu, which includes waffles with bacon and maple syrup, is served till 5pm.

Deane's at Queen's — BISTRO ££

(Map p572; www.michaeldeane.co.uk; 1 College Gardens; mains £12-20; ⏲noon-3pm Mon-Sat, 5.30-9pm Mon & Tue, 5.30-10pm Wed-Sat, 1-4pm Sun) A chilled-out bar and grill from Belfast's top chef, Michael Deane, this place focuses on what could be described as good-value, gourmet pub grub: salt and chilli squid, crisp pork belly with creamed celeriac, and smoked haddock and leek fishcake with curried coleslaw.

OUTSIDE THE CENTRE

Caifé Feirste — CAFE £

(Map p586; www.culturlann.ie; Cultúrlann McAdam Ó Fiaich, 216 Falls Rd, West Belfast; mains £5-8; ⏲9am-6pm Mon, to 9pm Tue-Sat, to 4pm Sun) If you're exploring West Belfast, drop into the cafe in this Irish-language and arts centre for some good home-cooked food – the menu includes stews, soups, pizzas, cakes, scones and fresh pastries.

Cutters Wharf — GRILL ££

(Map p586; www.cuttersrivergrill.com; 4 Lockview Rd, Stranmillis; mains £9-20; ⏲food served noon-9pm) One of the few bar-restaurants in Belfast with a waterside setting, Cutters Wharf has a terrace overlooking the River Lagan

TOP FIVE TRADITIONAL PUBS

» Bittle's Bar (p596)
» Crown Liquor Saloon (p596)
» Duke of York (p597)
» Kelly's Cellars (p596)
» White's Tavern (p596)

where you can enjoy an al fresco drink, and a smart upstairs restaurant serving steaks, burgers and seafood.

Drinking

Belfast's pub scene is lively and friendly, with the older traditional pubs complemented – and increasingly threatened – by a rising tide of stylish designer bars.

Standard opening hours are 11am or 11.30am to midnight or 1am Monday to Saturday, and 12.30pm to 11pm or midnight Sunday; some pubs remain closed all day Sunday, or don't open till 4pm or 6pm.

Although the situation has improved in recent years, getting past the bouncers on the door can be a problem – the huge number of security staff employed in the city means that polite, well-trained door staff are a rarity. Some of the flashier bars have a dress code – usually no sneakers, no jeans, no baseball caps (so that the security cameras can get a clear shot of your face) and definitely no football colours. A few even specify 'No political tattoos'.

CITY CENTRE

Crown Liquor Saloon PUB

(Map p572; www.crownbar.com; 46 Great Victoria St) Belfast's most famous bar has a wonderfully ornate Victorian interior. Despite being a tourist attraction, it still fills up with crowds of locals at lunchtime and in the early evening.

Garrick Bar PUB

(Map p572; www.thegarrickbar.com; 29 Chichester St) Established in 1870 but recently refurbished, the Garrick hangs on to a traditional atmosphere with acres of dark wood panelling, tiled floors, a pillared bar and old brass oil lamps. There are snug booths with buttoned leather benches, and a real coal fire in each room. Traditional music sessions in the front bar at 9.30pm on Wednesday, 5pm Friday and 4pm Sunday.

White's Tavern PUB

(Map p572; www.whitestavern.co.uk; 1-4 Wine Cellar Entry) Established in 1630 but rebuilt in 1790, White's claims to be Belfast's oldest tavern (unlike a pub, a tavern provided food and lodging). Downstairs is a traditional Irish bar with an open peat fire and live trad music Friday to Sunday; upstairs is like your granny's living room, stuffed with old armchairs and sofas, and hosting DJs and covers bands at the weekends.

Kelly's Cellars PUB

(Map p572; 1 Bank St) Kelly's is Belfast's oldest pub (1720) – as opposed to tavern; see White's Tavern – and was a meeting place for Henry Joy McCracken and the United Irishmen when they were planning the 1798 Rising. The story goes that McCracken hid behind the bar when British soldiers came for him. A bit rough around the edges (a description that could apply to some of the regulars too), it remains resolutely old-fashioned, but pulls in a broad cross-section of Belfast society and is a good bet for impromptu traditional music sessions.

Bittle's Bar PUB

(Map p572; 103 Victoria St) A cramped and staunchly traditional bar that occupies Belfast's only 'flat iron' building, Bittle's is a 19th-century triangular red-brick building decorated with gilded shamrocks. The wedge-shaped interior is covered in paintings of Ireland's literary heroes by local artist Joe O'Kane. Pride of place on the back wall is a large canvas depicting Yeats, Joyce, Behan and Beckett at the bar with glasses of Guinness, and Wilde pulling the pints on the other side.

Harlem Cafe CAFE-BAR

(Map p572; 34-36 Bedford St) Cool of vibe and quirky of decor, with eclectic art, framed photos of NYC and glass-topped tables full of seashells and starfish, the Harlem is a great place for lounging over coffee with the Sunday papers, or a glass of wine after hitting the shops. Full food menu from breakfast to brunch to pre-theatre dinner.

CATHEDRAL QUARTER & AROUND

TOP CHOICE **John Hewitt Bar & Restaurant** PUB

(Map p572; www.thejohnhewitt.com; 51 Donegall St) Named for the Belfast poet and socialist, the John Hewitt is one of those treasured bars that has no TV and no gaming machines;

the only noise here is the murmur of conversation. As well as Guinness, the bar serves Hilden real ales from nearby Lisburn, plus Hoegaarden and Erdinger wheat beers. There are regular sessions of folk, jazz and bluegrass from 9pm most nights.

Northern Whig BAR

(Map p572; www.thenorthernwhig.com; 2 Bridge St) A stylish, modern bar set in an elegant Georgian printing works, the Northern Whig's airy interior is dominated by three huge Socialist-Realist statues rescued from Prague in the early 1990s. Its relaxing sofas and armchairs encourage serious afternoon loafing, though the pace hots up considerably after 5pm on Friday and Saturday when the stag- and hen-party crowd starts knocking back the vodka tonics and alcopops.

Duke of York PUB

(Map p572; 11 Commercial Ct) Hidden away down an alley in the heart of the city's former newspaper district, the snug, traditional Duke was a hang-out for print workers and journalists and still pulls in a few hacks. One claim to fame is that the Sinn Féin leader, Gerry Adams, worked behind the bar here during his student days back in 1971.

Spaniard BAR

(Map p572; www.thespaniardbar.com; 3 Skipper St) Forget 'style': this narrow, crowded bar, which looks as if it's been squeezed into someone's flat, has more atmosphere in one battered sofa than most 'style bars' have in their shiny entirety. Friendly staff, good beer, an eclectic crowd and cool tunes played at a volume that still allows you to talk: bliss.

Muriel's Bar BAR

(Map p572; 12-14 Church Lane) Hats meet harlotry (ask who Muriel was) in this delightfully snug and welcoming wee bar with a retro-chic decor of old sofas and armchairs, heavy fabrics in shades of olive and dark red, gilt-framed mirrors and a cast-iron fireplace. Gin is Muriel's favourite tipple, and there's a range of exotic brands to mix with your tonic. The food menu is pretty good, too.

McHugh's Bar and Restaurant PUB

(Map p572; www.mchughsbar.com; 29-31 Queen's Sq) This restored pub has a traditional feel with its old wooden booths and benches, and pours a superb pint of Guinness. It also boasts a decent restaurant serving steaks, seafood and stir-fries nonstop from noon till 10pm.

SOUTH BELFAST

Eglantine PUB

(Map p572; www.egbar.co.uk; 32 Malone Rd) The 'Eg' is a local institution, and widely reckoned to be the best of Belfast's student pubs. It serves good beer and good food, and there are DJs spinning most nights. Wicked Wednesday pulls in the crowds with an electric rodeo bull, bouncy boxing, sumo-wrestler suits and other fun; Tuesday is the big music-and-entertainment quiz night. Expect to see a few stag and hen parties stagger through at weekends.

Botanic Inn PUB

(Map p572; www.thebotanicinn.com; 23-27 Malone Rd) The 'Bot' is the second pillar of Malone Rd's unholy trinity of student pubs, along with the 'Eg' and the 'Welly Park' (Wellington Park). The latter has sadly been renovated into airport-departure-lounge anonymity, but the Bot is still a wild place, with dancing in the upstairs Top of the Bot club Wednesday to Saturday (people queue down the street to get in), live acoustic music in the Back Bar on Monday and Wednesday, and big-screen sport when there's a match on.

Molly's Yard RESTAURANT-BAR

(Map p572; 1 College Green Mews; ⏲closed Sun) This atmospheric restaurant–bar was home to Northern Ireland's first microbrewery, but demand was so great that production moved to Lisburn's Hilden Brewery. Molly's three varieties of real ale – Belfast Blonde (a continental-style lager), Molly's Chocolate Stout and Headless Dog, a dark amber ale with a refreshingly hoppy flavour – are still brewed to the same recipe and available on tap here.

Lavery's BAR

(Map p572; www.laverysbelfast.com; 14 Bradbury Pl) Managed by the same family since 1918, Lavery's is a vast, multilevel, packed-to-the-gills boozing emporium, crammed with drinkers young and old, from students to tourists, businessmen to bikers. The Public Bar has live acoustic music from local musicians on Monday and Tuesday, and a retro disco Wednesday to Saturday, while the bohemian Back Bar boasts a classic jukebox.

☆ Entertainment

The Belfast Welcome Centre issues *Whatabout?*, a free bimonthly guide to Belfast events, with pub, club and restaurant listings. The Thursday issue of the *Belfast Telegraph* has an Entertainment section with club, gig and cinema listings, as does the Scene section in Friday's *Irish News*.

Good places to check out the latest in live music and club nights include the **Good Vibes record shop** (Map p572; www.goodvibes-belfast.com; 13 Winetavern St; 10am-5pm Mon-Sat), and the **Oh Yeah Music Centre** (Map p572; www.belfastmusic.org; 15-21 Gordon St; ⏲noon-3pm Mon-Fri, noon-5pm Sat). The following are also useful:

ArtsListings (www.culturenorthernireland.org) A free monthly that covers the arts scene throughout the whole of Northern Ireland.

Belfast Music (www.belfastmusic.org) Online gig listings.

Big List (www.thebiglist.co.uk) A weekly freesheet, published on Wednesday, that covers pubs, clubs and music events all over Northern Ireland, although the emphasis is heavily on Belfast.

Clubbing

Club hours are generally 9pm to 3am, with no admittance after 1am; bouncers can be really picky about who they let in, especially if you're under 21.

QUB Student Union CLUB
(Map p572; www.qubsu-ents.com; Mandela Hall, Queen's Students Union, University Rd) The student union has various bars and music venues hosting club nights, live bands and stand-up comedy. The monthly **Shine** (www.shine.net, admission £22, 1st Sat of month) is one of the city's best club nights with resident and guest DJs pumping out harder and heavier dance music than most of Belfast's other clubs.

Stiff Kitten CLUB
(Map p572; www.thestiffkitten.com; Bankmore Sq, Dublin Rd; admission £3-10; ⏲11am-1am Mon-Wed, to 2am Thu, to 2.30am Fri, to 3am Sat, to midnight Sun) If the student union is too grungy a venue for your tastes, head for the Stiff Kitten, a stylish bar and club under the same management as Shine. Same serious attitude to the music, but it's distinctly glitzier, appealing to an over-25 crowd.

Rain CLUB
(Map p572; www.rainnightclub.co.uk; 10-14 Tomb St; admission £5-10 Sun-Fri/Sat; ⏲9pm-3am) Set in a converted red-brick warehouse, Rain is an opulent and glamorous mainstream nightclub with DJs pumping out commercial music for a mixed, over-21s crowd.

Gay & Lesbian Venues

Belfast's gay and lesbian scene is concentrated in the Cathedral Quarter. For information on what's happening, check out www.gaybelfast.net. As well as the listings below, other gay-friendly pubs include Muriel's Bar, the John Hewitt and the Spaniard.

Kremlin CLUB
(Map p572; www.kremlin-belfast.com; 96 Donegall St; ⏲9pm-2.30am Tue, 9pm-3am Thu-Sun) Gay-owned and operated, the Soviet kitsch-themed Kremlin is the heart and soul of Northern Ireland's gay scene. A statue of Lenin guides you into Tsar, the pre-club bar, from where the Long Bar leads into the main clubbing zone, Red Square. There's something going on seven nights a week – Revolution (admission £5 to £7) on Saturdays is the flagship event, with DJs mixing up dance, house, pop and commercial till 3am.

Dubarrys Bar BAR
(Map p572; 10-14 Gresham St) One of Belfast's newer gay venues, Dubarrys is aimed at a slightly older, more sophisticated crowd who are looking for designer decor, cool tunes and conversation, rather than flashing lights and banging dance music.

Union Street BAR
(Map p572; www.unionstreetpub.com; 8-14 Union St) A stylish modern bar with retro decor and lots of bare brick and dark wood – check out the Belfast sinks in the loo – Union Street pulls in a mixed gay and straight crowd with nightly cabaret and karaoke, and a tempting food menu.

Live Music

Pubs with regular live sessions of traditional Irish music include the Botanic Inn, the Garrick Bar, White's Tavern, the John Hewitt and Kelly's Cellars.

For jazz and blues, head for the John Hewitt, McHugh's, the Crescent Arts Centre or the **Kitchen Bar** (Map p572; www.thekitchenbar.com; 38 Victoria Sq).

Waterfront Hall CONCERTS
(Map p572; www.waterfront.co.uk; 2 Lanyon Pl) The impressive 2235-seat Waterfront is Belfast's flagship concert venue, hosting local, national and international performers from pop stars to symphony orchestras.

Ulster Hall CONCERTS
(Map p572; www.ulsterhall.co.uk; Bedford St) Ulster Hall (built in 1862) is a popular venue for a range of events including rock concerts,

lunchtime organ recitals, boxing bouts and performances by the **Ulster Orchestra** (www.ulsterorchestra.com).

Odyssey Arena CONCERTS
(Map p572; www.odysseyarena.com; 2 Queen's Quay) The home stadium of the Belfast Giants ice-hockey team is also the venue for big entertainment events such as rock and pop concerts and stage shows.

King's Hall CONCERTS
(Map p586; www.kingshall.co.uk; Lisburn Rd) Northern Ireland's biggest exhibition and conference centre hosts a range of music shows, trade fairs and sporting events. It's accessible by any bus along Lisburn Rd or by train to Balmoral Station.

Belfast Empire LIVE MUSIC
(Map p572; www.thebelfastempire.com; 42 Botanic Ave; admission live bands £5-20) A converted late-Victorian church with three floors of entertainment, the Empire is a legendary live-music venue. The regular Thursday-night Gifted session showcases the best of new talent, both local and UK-wide, while Saturday is either big-name bands or tribute bands.

Limelight LIVE MUSIC
(Map p572; www.cdcleisure.net; 17-19 Ormeau Ave) This combined pub and club, along with next-door venue the Spring & Airbrake (under the same management), is one of the city's top venues for live rock and indie music, having hosted bands such as Oasis, Franz Ferdinand, the Manic Street Preachers and the Kaiser Chiefs. It's also home to alternative club night **Helter Skelter** (admission £5; ⏲from 10.30pm Sat) and Belfast's biggest student night, **Shag** (admission £4, ⏲from 10pm Tue).

School of Music CLASSICAL MUSIC
(www.music.qub.ac.uk) Queens University's School of Music stages free lunchtime recitals on Thursday and regular evening concerts in the beautiful, hammer beam-roofed **Harty Room** (Map p572; School of Music, University Sq), and at the **Sonic Arts Research Centre** (Map p572; Cloreen Park), with occasional performances in the larger **Sir William Whitla Hall** (Map p572; University Rd). Download a *Music at Queen's* program from the website.

Comedy

There's no dedicated comedy club in the city, but there are regular comedy nights at various venues including **Spring & Airbrake** (Map p572; Ormeau Ave), **Black Box** (Map p572; www.blackboxbelfast.com; 18-22 Hill St) and **QUB Student Union** (Map p572; www.qubsu-ents.com; Mandela Hall, Queen's Students Union, University Rd) .

DON'T MISS

GETTING INTO IRISH CULTURE

An Droichead (The Bridge; Map p572; www.androichead.com; 20 Cooke St; tickets £5-15), based in South Belfast, is a centre dedicated to Irish language, music and culture. It offers courses in Irish Gaelic, stages traditional dance and *céilidh* workshops, hosts art exhibitions and also serves as a live-music venue. It's a great place to hear live Irish folk music, not only big names from around the country, but also up-and-coming local talent. Check the website, or pick up a flyer from the Belfast Welcome Centre.

Opera & Theatre

Lyric Theatre THEATRE
(Map p586; www.lyrictheatre.co.uk; 55 Ridgeway St) The old Lyric Theatre, where Hollywood star Liam Neeson first trod the boards (he is now a patron), has been demolished; a stunning new theatre has been built on the same site, and opened to great dramatic and architectural acclaim in May 2011.

Black Box ARTS CENTRE
(Map p572; www.blackboxbelfast.com; 18-22 Hill St) Describing itself as a 'home for live music, theatre, literature, comedy, film, visual art, live art, circus, cabaret and all points in between', Black Box is an intimate venue in the heart of the Cathedral Quarter.

Metropolitan Arts Centre ARTS CENTRE
(Map p572; www.buildingthemac.com; St Anne's Sq) A new, early 2012, development in the Cathedral Quarter, the MAC houses two theatres, three art galleries, and a cafe-bar.

Crescent Arts Centre MUSIC & DANCE
(Map p572; www.crescentarts.org; 2-4 University Rd) The Crescent hosts a range of concerts, plays, workshops, readings and dance classes. The Crescent is also the headquarters of the **Belfast Book Festival**, and a dance festival, **City Dance**, both held in June.

Grand Opera House OPERA
(Map p572; www.goh.co.uk; 2-4 Great Victoria St; ⌚box office 8.30am-9pm Mon-Fri, to 6pm Sat) This grand old venue plays host to a mixture of opera, popular musicals and comedy shows. The box office is across the street on the corner of Howard St.

Cinemas

Queen's Film Theatre CINEMA
(Map p572; www.queensfilmtheatre.com; 20 University Sq) A two-screen art-house cinema close to the university, and a major venue for the Belfast Film Festival.

Movie House CINEMA
(Map p572; www.moviehouse.co.uk; 14 Dublin Rd) A convenient city-centre 10-screen multiplex.

Storm Cinemas CINEMA
(Map p572; www.odysseycinemas.co.uk; Odyssey Pavilion) Belfast's biggest multiplex, with 12 screens and stadium seats throughout. It's part of the Odyssey Complex.

Sport

Rugby, football (soccer), Gaelic football and hockey are played through the winter; cricket and hurling through the summer.

Windsor Park FOOTBALL (SOCCER)
(Map p586; off Lisburn Rd) International soccer matches take place here, south of the centre; the aging stadium is slated for a £28m makeover. For details of Northern Ireland international matches, see www.irishfa.com.

Casement Park GAELIC FOOTBALL
(Map p586; www.antrimgaa.net; Andersonstown Rd) In West Belfast; you can see Gaelic football and hurling here.

Odyssey Arena ICE HOCKEY
(Map p572; www.odysseyarena.com; 2 Queen's Quay) The Belfast Giants ice-hockey team draws big crowds to the arena at the Odyssey Complex; the season is September to March. The arena also hosts indoor sporting events including tennis and athletics.

Shopping

For general shopping you'll find all the usual high-street chains and department stores in the compact central shopping area north of City Hall. The main shopping malls are **Victoria Square** (Map p572; www.victoriasquare.com; btwn Ann & Chichester St; ⌚9.30am-6pm Mon-Tue, to 9pm Wed-Fri, 9am-6pm Sat, 1-6pm Sun) and the **Castle Court Centre** (Map p572; Royal Ave). There's late-night shopping till 9pm on Thursdays (Wednesday to Friday at Victoria Square).

Other shopping districts include the ultra-hip **Lisburn Rd** (from Eglantine Ave out to Balmoral Ave) – a long strip of red-brick and mock-Tudor facades lined with fashion boutiques, interior-design shops, art galleries, delicatessens, espresso bars, wine bars and chic restaurants – and the unexpected concentration of designer fashion shops (about a dozen of them) on **Bloomfield Ave** off Newtonards Rd in East Belfast.

Items particular to Northern Ireland that you may like to look out for include fine Belleek china, linen (antique and new) and Tyrone crystal. A good place to shop for Irish crafts and traditional Irish music is **Cultúrlann McAdam Ó Fiaich** (Map p586; www.culturlann.ie; 216 Falls Rd; ⌚9am-5.30pm Mon-Fri, from 10am Sat).

Wicker Man JEWELLERY/SOUVENIRS
(Map p572; www.thewickerman.co.uk; 44-46 High St; ⌚9am-5.30pm Mon-Wed & Fri, to 9pm Thu, to 5.30pm Sat, 1-5.30pm Sun) This shop sells a wide range of contemporary Irish crafts and gifts, including silver jewellery, glassware and knitwear.

Fresh Garbage CLOTHING/JEWELLERY
(Map p572; 24 Rosemary St; ⌚10.30am-5.30pm Mon-Wed, Fri & Sat, to 8pm Thu) Easily recognised by the glumfest of Goths hovering outside the door, this place has been around for more than 20 years but remains a cult favourite for hippie and Goth clothes, band T-shirts and Celtic jewellery.

Steensons JEWELLERY
(Map p572; www.thesteensons.com; Bedford House, Bedford St; 10am-5.30pm Mon-Sat, to 7pm Thu) Showroom selling a range of stylish, contemporary, handmade jewellery in silver, gold and platinum, from a workshop in Glenarm, County Antrim.

Archives Antique Centre ANTIQUES
(Map p572; www.archivesantiquecentre.co.uk; 88 Donegall Pass; ⌚10.30am-5.30pm Mon-Sat) This is a warren of curios and collectables spread over three floors, with Irish silver, brass, pub memorabilia, militaria, books and light fittings.

Matchetts Music MUSIC STORE
(Map p572; 6 Wellington Pl; ⌚9am-5.30pm Mon-Sat) Stocks a range of acoustic instruments, from guitars and mandolins to penny whistles and bodhráns (hand-held goatskin

drums), as well as books of lyrics and guitar chords for traditional Irish songs.

Good Vibes MUSIC STORE
(Map p572; www.goodvibesbelfast.com; 13 Winetavern St; 10am-5pm Mon-Sat) Owned by music producer Terry Hooley (who released *Teenage Kicks* by the Undertones on his Good Vibrations label back in 1978), this is Belfast's best alternative record shop and a source of tickets and info on the latest gigs.

Information

Dangers & Annoyances

Even at the height of the Troubles, Belfast wasn't a particularly dangerous city for tourists, and today you're less at risk from crime here than you are in London. It's best, however, to avoid the so-called 'interface areas' – near the peace lines in West Belfast, Crumlin Rd and the Short Strand (just east of Queen's Bridge) – after dark; if in doubt about any area, ask at your hotel or hostel.

At the time of research dissident republican groups had launched a bombing campaign aimed at police and military targets. Security alerts usually have no effect on visiting tourists (other than roads being closed), but be aware of the potential danger. You can follow the Police Service of Northern Ireland (PSNI) on Twitter (@policeserviceni) and receive immediate notification of any alerts.

One irritating legacy of the Troubles is the absence of left-luggage facilities at bus and train stations. You will also notice a more obvious security presence than elsewhere in the UK and Ireland, in the form of armoured police Land Rovers, fortified police stations and security doors on some shops (mostly outside the city centre), where you have to press the buzzer to be allowed in. There are doormen on many city-centre shops and pubs.

If you want to take photos of fortified police stations, army posts or other military or quasi-military paraphernalia, get permission first, just to be on the safe side. In the Protestant and Catholic strongholds of West Belfast it's best not to photograph people without permission; always ask first and be prepared to accept a refusal. Taking pictures of the murals is not a problem.

Emergency

For national emergency phone numbers, see Need to Know .

Rape Crisis & Sexual Abuse Centre (9032 9002; www.rapecrisisni.com; 10am-midnight)

Victim Support (0845 30 30 900; www.victimsupport.org)

Internet Access

You can use British Telecom's blue, internet-enabled phone boxes around Donegall Sq and at Central Station for 10p per 90 seconds (£1 minimum for up to 15 minutes).

Belfast Welcome Centre (Map p572; www.gotobelfast.com; 47 Donegall Pl; per 20 min £1; 9am-7pm Mon-Sat, 11am-4pm Sun Jun-Sep, 9am-5.30pm Mon-Sat, 11am-4pm Sun Oct-May)

Ground@Waterstones (44-46 Fountain St; per 20min £1; 9am-6pm Mon-Wed, Fri & Sat, to 9pm Thu, 1-5.30pm Sun;) Three computers in the bookshop cafe; free wi-fi – ask at the counter for password.

Linen Hall Library (cnr Fountain St & Donegall Sq; per 30min £1.50; 9.30am-5.30pm Mon-Fri, to 4.30pm Sat;) One computer on each floor; ask at desk before using. Wi-fi £3 for up to three hours (ask for log-in details).

Mega-Bite (Great Northern Mall, Great Victoria St; per 15min £1; 8.30am-8pm Mon-Fri, from 10am Sat, from 11am Sun)

Left Luggage

Because of security concerns, there are no left-luggage facilities at Belfast's airports, train stations and bus stations. However, most hotels and hostels allow guests to leave their bags for the day, and the Belfast Welcome Centre also offers a daytime left-luggage service (£4.50 per item).

Medical Services

For advice on medical and dental emergencies, call **NHS Direct** (0845 4647; 24hr).

Accident and emergency services are available at these hospitals:

City Hospital (9032 9241; 51 Lisburn Rd)

Mater Hospital (9074 1211; 45-51 Crumlin Rd) Near the junction of Antrim Rd and Clifton St.

Royal Victoria Hospital (9024 0503; 274 Grosvenor Rd) West of the city centre.

Ulster Hospital (9048 4511; Upper Newtownards Rd, Dundonald) Near Stormont.

Post

Post office Main post office (Map p572; 12-16 Bridge St; 9am-5.30pm Mon-Sat); Bedford St (Map p572; 16-22 Bedford St); Botanic Gardens (Map p572; cnr University Rd & College Gardens, South Belfast); Shaftesbury Sq (Map p572; 1-5 Botanic Ave)

Tourist Information

Belfast Welcome Centre (Map p572; 9024 6609; www.gotobelfast.com; 47 Donegall Pl; 9am-7pm Mon-Sat & 11am-4pm Sun Jun-Sep, 9am-5.30pm Mon-Sat & 11am-4pm Sun Oct-May) Provides information about the whole of Northern Ireland, and books accommoda tion anywhere in Ireland and Britain. Services

GETTING AROUND

Visitor Pass

The Belfast Visitor Pass (per one/two/three days £6.50/10.50/14) allows unlimited travel on bus and train services in Belfast and around; it can be purchased at airports, main train and bus stations, the Metro kiosk on Donegall Sq, and the Belfast Welcome Centre.

Smartlink Travel Card

If you plan on using city buses a lot, it's worth buying a **Smartlink Travel Card** (available from the Metro kiosk, the Belfast Welcome Centre, and the Europa and Laganside BusCentres). The card costs an initial fee of £1.50, plus £10.50 per 10 journeys – you can get it topped up as you want. Or you can get seven days' unlimited travel for £16. When you board the bus, you simply place the card on top of the ticket machine, and it automatically issues a ticket.

include left luggage (not overnight), currency exchange and internet access.

Cultúrlann McAdam Ó Fiaich (Map p586; ☎9096 4188; 216 Falls Rd; ⏰9.30am-5.30pm Mon-Fri) This cultural centre in West Belfast has a tourist information desk.

Fáilte Ireland (Map p572; Irish Tourist Board; ☎9031 2345; 47 Donegall Pl) In the Belfast Welcome Centre, can book accommodation in the Republic of Ireland.

Tourist information desks George Best Belfast City Airport (Map p586; ☎9093 5372; ⏰8am-7pm Mon-Sat, to 5pm Sun); Belfast International Airport (☎9448 4677; ⏰7.30am-7pm Mon-Sat, 8am-5pm Sun)

Getting There & Away

Air

Belfast International airport (BFS; www.belfastairport.com) Located 30km northwest of the city; flights from Galway, UK, Europe and New York.

George Best Belfast City Airport (Map p586; BHD; www.belfastcityairport.com; Airport Rd) Situated 6km northeast of the city centre; flights from the UK, Cork and Paris.

Boat

Stena Line (☎08705 707070; www.stenaline.co.uk) Car ferries between Belfast and Liverpool in England and Stranraer in Scotland dock at Victoria Terminal 5km north of the city centre; take the M2 motorway north and turn right at junction No 1.

Steam Packet Company (Map p586; ☎08722 992 992; www.steam-packet.com) Car ferries between Belfast and Douglas on the Isle of Man (two or three a week, April to September only) dock at Albert Quay, 2km north of the city centre.

Other car ferries to and from Scotland and England dock at Larne, 37km north of Belfast. For more information on ferry routes and prices, see p734.

Bus

There are **information desks** (⏰7.45am-6.30pm Mon-Fri, 8am-6pm Sat) at both of Belfast's bus stations, where you can pick up regional bus timetables. Contact **Translink** (☎9066 6630; www.translink.co.uk) for timetable and fares information.

National Express (☎0870 580 8080; www.nationalexpress.com) runs a daily coach service between Belfast and London (£45 one way, 14 hours) via the Stranraer ferry, Dumfries, Carlisle, Preston, Manchester and Birmingham. The ticket office is in the Europa BusCentre.

Europa BusCentre (Map p572; ☎9066 6630) Belfast's main bus station is behind the Europa Hotel and next door to Great Victoria St train station; it's reached via the Great Northern Mall beside the hotel. It's the main terminus for buses to Derry, Dublin and destinations in the west and south of Northern Ireland.

Laganside BusCentre (Map p572; ☎9066 6630; Oxford St) This smaller bus station, near the river, is mainly for buses to County Antrim, eastern County Down and the Cookstown area.

Train

For information on train fares and timetables, contact **Translink** (☎9066 6630; www.translink.co.uk). The **NIR Travel Shop** (☎9023 0671; Great Victoria St Station; ⏰9am-5pm Mon-Fri, to 12.30pm Sat) books train tickets, ferries and holiday packages.

Belfast Central Station (Map p572; East Bridge St) East of the city centre; trains run to Dublin and all destinations in Northern Ireland. If you arrive by train at Central Station, your rail ticket entitles you to a free bus ride into the city centre.

Great Victoria St Station (Map p572; Great Northern Mall) Next to the Europa BusCentre; has trains for Portadown, Lisburn, Bangor, Larne Harbour and Derry.

Getting Around

Belfast possesses that rare but wonderful thing – an integrated public-transport system, with buses linking both airports to the central train and bus stations.

To/From the Airports

Belfast International Airport Airport Express 300 bus runs to the Europa BusCentre (one way/return £7/10, 30 minutes) every 10 or 15 minutes between 7am and 8pm, every 30 minutes from 8pm to 11pm, and hourly through the night; a return ticket is valid for one month. A taxi costs about £25.

George Best Belfast City Airport Airport Express 600 bus runs to the Europa BusCentre (one way/return £2/3, 15 minutes) every 15 or 20 minutes between 6am and 10pm. A return ticket is valid for one month. The taxi fare to the city centre is about £7.

For details of the Airporter bus linking both airports to Derry, see p648.

To/From the Ferry Terminals

There is no public transport to the Stena Line and Steam Packet Company ferry terminals. Trains to the ferry terminal at Larne Harbour depart from Great Victoria St Station.

Bicycle

The National Cycle Network route 9 runs through central Belfast, mostly following the western bank of the River Lagan and the north shore of Belfast Lough.

McConvey Cycles (☎9033 0322; www.rentabikebelfast.com; 183 Ormeau Rd; ⏰9am-6pm Mon-Sat, to 8pm Thu) Hires bikes for around £15 a day, or £60 a week.

Bus

Metro (☎9066 6630; www.translink.co.uk) operates the bus network in Belfast. Most city bus services depart from various stops on and around Donegall Sq, at City Hall. You can pick up a free bus map (and buy tickets) from the **Metro kiosk** (⏰8am-5.30pm Mon-Fri) at the northwest corner of the square.

An increasing number of buses are low-floor, 'kneeling' buses with space for one wheelchair. Buy your ticket from the driver (change given); fares range from £1.40 to £2 depending on distance. The driver can also sell you a **Metro Day Ticket** (£3.50), giving you unlimited bus travel within the City Zone all day Monday to Saturday. Cheaper versions allow travel any time after 10am Monday to Saturday (£2.90), or all day Sunday (£2.90).

LEAVING BELFAST

Buses

DESTINATION	PRICE	DURATION (HOURS)	FREQUENCY
Armagh	£8	1¼	hourly Mon-Fri,6 Sat, 4 Sun
Ballycastle	£9	2	3 daily Mon-Fri,2 Sat
Bangor	£3	¾	half-hourly Mon-Sat, 8 Sun
Derry	£10	1¾	half-hourly Mon-Sat, 11 Sun
Downpatrick	£5	1	at least hourly Mon-Sat, 6 Sun
Dublin	£13	3	hourly
Enniskillen	£10	2¼	hourly Mon-Sat, 2 Sun
Newcastle	£7	1¼	hourly Mon-Sat, 8 Sun

Trains

DESTINATION	PRICE	DURATION (HOURS)	FREQUENCY
Bangor	£5	½	half-hourly Mon-Sat, hourly Sun
Dublin	£28	8	8 Mon-Sat, 5 Sun
Larne Harbour	£6	1	hourly
Newry	£10	¾	8 Mon-Sat, 5 Sun
Portrush	£11	1¾	7 or 8 Mon-Sat, four Sun

Car & Motorcycle

A car can be more of a hindrance than a help in Belfast, as parking is restricted in the city centre. For on-street parking between 8am and 6pm Monday to Saturday, you'll need to buy a ticket from a machine. For longer periods, head for one of the many multistorey car parks that are dotted around the city centre.

Dooley Car Rentals (☎0800 0778 774; www.dooleycarrentals.com; Airport Rd, Belfast International Airport, Aldergrove) This Ireland-wide agency is reliable and offers good rates – around £130 a week for a compact car, with no extra charge for driving cross-border to the Republic. You pay an extra £55 up front for a full tank of petrol, but if you return the car with an almost empty tank they're cheaper than the big names.

The major car-hire agencies in Belfast:

Avis (www.avis.co.uk) City (☎0870 608 6374; 69-71 Great Victoria St); Belfast International Airport (☎0844 544 6012); George Best Belfast City Airport (☎0844 544 6028)

Budget (www.budget-ireland.co.uk) City (☎9023 0700; 96-102 Great Victoria St); Belfast International Airport (☎9442 3332); George Best Belfast City Airport (☎9045 1111)

Europcar (www.europcar.co.uk) Belfast International Airport (☎9442 2285); George Best Belfast City Airport (☎9073 9400)

Hertz (www.hertz.co.uk) Belfast International Airport (☎9442 2533); George Best Belfast City Airport (☎9073 2451)

Taxi

Fona Cab (☎9033 3333; www.fonacab.com)

Value Cabs (☎9080 9080; www.valuecabs.co.uk)

AROUND BELFAST

The southwestern fringes of Belfast extend as far as **Lisburn** (Lios na gCearrbhach), 12km southwest of the city centre. Like Belfast, Lisburn grew rich on the proceeds of the linen industry in the 18th and 19th centuries. This history is celebrated in the excellent **Irish Linen Centre & Lisburn Museum** (Market Sq; admission free; ⏲9.30am-5pm Mon-Sat), housed in the fine 17th-century Market House.

The museum on the ground floor has displays on the cultural and historic heritage of the region, while upstairs the award-winning 'Flax to Fabric' exhibition details the fascinating history of the linen industry in Northern Ireland – on the eve of WWI, Ulster was the largest linen-producing region in the world, employing some 75,000 people.

There are plenty of audiovisual and hands-on exhibits – you can watch weavers working on Jacquard looms and even try your hand at spinning flax.

Lisburn Tourist Information Centre (☎9266 0038; Lisburn Sq; ⏲9.30am-5pm Mon-Sat) is on the town's main square. Buses 523, 530 and 532 from Belfast's Upper Queen St go to Lisburn (£2.60, 40 minutes, half-hourly Monday to Friday, hourly Saturday and Sunday), or catch the train (£3.60, 30 minutes, at least half-hourly Monday to Saturday, hourly Sunday) from either Belfast Central or Great Victoria St Stations.

Counties Down & Armagh

POPULATION: 652,000 / AREA: 3702 SQ KM

Includes »

Best Places to Eat

» Jeffers by the Marina (p610)

» Plough Inn (p607)

» Restaurant 23 (p626)

» Uluru Bistro (p632)

» Mourne Seafood Bar (p623)

Best Places to Stay

» Anna's House (p615)

» Fortwilliam Country House (p607)

» Hebron House (p609)

» Dufferin Coaching Inn (p615)

» Cuan (p620)

Why Go?

From the hilltop viewpoint of Scrabo Tower, near Newtownards, the treasures of County Down lie scattered all around you. The sparkling, island-fringed waters of Strangford Lough stretch to the south, with the bird-haunted mudflats of Castle Espie and Nendrum's ancient monastery on one shore, and the picturesque Ards Peninsula on the other. On a clear day you can see the Mourne Mountains in the distance, their velvet curves sweeping down to the sea. Nearby are Downpatrick and Lecale, the old stamping grounds of Ireland's patron saint.

Down's neighbour County Armagh is largely rural, from the low, rugged hills of the south to the lush apple orchards and strawberry fields of the north, with Ireland's ecclesiastical capital, the neat little city of Armagh, in the middle. South Armagh is a peaceful backwater, where you can wander back and forth across the border with the Republic without even noticing.

When to Go

May brings white clouds of apple blossom to County Armagh's orchards, a season celebrated by the Apple Blossom Fair in the early part of the month. Summertime generally has the best weather for hiking and cycling, and August sees the International Walking Festival in the Mourne Mountains. Spring and autumn are both good for birdwatching, but keen birders have a big X on their calendars in October, when tens of thousands of overwintering brent geese begin to arrive at Castle Espie on Strangford Lough.

Counties Down & Armagh Highlights

1. Hike along ancient smugglers' trails among the granite peaks of the **Mourne Mountains** (p623)
2. Test the menus at top-notch restaurants in **Hillsborough** (p607), **Warrenpoint** (p626) and **Bangor** (p608)
3. Explore the stately halls and exquisite gardens of **Mount Stewart House** (p613)
4. Watch vast flocks of geese, ducks and waders at **Castle Espie** (p614)
5. Get off the beaten track on the back roads of **South Armagh** (p627)
6. Follow in the footsteps of Ireland's patron saint in and around **Downpatrick** (p618)
7. Learn the rules of the esoteric Irish sport of road bowling in **Armagh City** (p629)

COUNTY DOWN

Central County Down

Rich farmland spreads to the south of Belfast, with only the rough moorland of Slieve Croob, southwest of Ballynahinch, breaking the flatness of the terrain. The attractive town of Hillsborough lies on the main A1 road from Belfast to Newry.

HILLSBOROUGH

POP 2400

Hillsborough is a name familiar to British ears, as it is the official residence of the Secretary of State for Northern Ireland. Hillsborough Castle is also used to entertain visiting heads of state (US presidents George W Bush and Bill Clinton have both enjoyed its hospitality). This is the Queen's official residence when she is in Northern Ireland.

The elegant little town of Hillsborough (Cromghlinn) was founded in the 1640s by Colonel Arthur Hill, who built a fort here to quell Irish insurgents. Fine Georgian architecture rings the square and lines Main St.

Sights

Hillsborough Castle CASTLE

(www.nio.gov.uk; Main St; guided tour adult/child/family £6/3.50/15, grounds only £3/2/9; ⏲10.30am-4pm Sat May, Jun & Aug) The town's main attraction is this rambling, two-storey late-Georgian mansion built in 1797 for Wills Hill, the first Marquess of Downshire, and extensively remodelled in the 1830s and '40s. The guided tour takes in the state drawing room and dining rooms, and the Lady Grey Room where UK prime minister Tony Blair and US president George W Bush had talks on Iraq in 2003.

FREE **Hillsborough Courthouse** HISTORIC BUILDING

(The Square; ⏲9am-5.30pm Mon-Sat, plus 2-6pm Sun Jul & Aug) A fine old Georgian building, the courthouse exhibits various displays describing the working of the courts in the 18th and 19th centuries.

FREE **St Malachy's Parish Church** CHURCH

(Main St; ⏲9am-5.30pm Mon-Sat) St Malachy's is one of Ireland's most splendid 18th-century churches, with twin towers at the ends of the transepts and a graceful spire at the western end. A tree-lined avenue leads to the church from a statue of Arthur Hill, fourth Marquess of Downshire, at the bottom of Main St.

FREE **Hillsborough Fort** HISTORIC BUILDING

(Main St; ⏲10am-7pm Tue-Sat, 2-7pm Sun Apr-Sep, 10am-4pm Tue-Sat, 2-4pm Sun Oct-Mar) Close to the church, Hillsborough Fort was built as an artillery fort by Colonel Hill in 1650 and remodelled as a Gothic-style tower house in 1758.

Festivals & Events

Each year in late August/early September, around 10,000 people – plus 6000 oysters from Dundrum Bay – converge on Hillsborough for a three-day **Oyster Festival** (www.hillsboroughoysterfestival.com), a celebration of local food, drink and general good fun, which includes an international oyster-eating competition.

Sleeping & Eating

Hillsborough is a bit of a culinary hot spot, with several excellent restaurants. These are popular places, so book a table at weekends to avoid disappointment.

TOP CHOICE **Fortwilliam Country House** B&B ££

(☎9268 2255; www.fortwilliamcountryhouse.com; 210 Ballynahinch Rd; s/d £50/70; P@) The Fortwilliam offers B&B in four luxurious rooms stuffed with period furniture – our favourite is the Victorian room, with its rose wallpaper, huge antique mahogany wardrobe and view over the garden. Your host's hospitality knows no bounds, and breakfast includes fresh eggs from the chickens in the yard, with the smell of home-baked wheaten bread wafting from the Aga. Book well in advance.

TOP CHOICE **Plough Inn** BISTRO ££

(☎9268 2985; www.theploughhillsborough.co.uk; 3 The Square; bar mains £6-12, restaurant £13-23; ⏲bar food noon-2.30pm, restaurant 6-9.30pm) This fine old pub, with its maze of dark wood-panelled nooks and crannies, has been offering 'beer and banter' since 1758. It serves gourmet bar lunches – how about tempura of pheasant and wild duck with sesame, ginger and Asian leaves? – and also offers fine dining in the restaurant around the back, where stone walls, low ceilings and a roaring fireplace make a cosy setting for a menu ranging from wood pigeon to rack of lamb.

Hillside Bar & Restaurant FRENCH, IRISH ££
(☎9268 2765; www.hillsidehillsborough.co.uk; 21 Main St; bar meals £9-11, restaurant mains £17-26; ⌚bar meals noon-2.30pm & 4.30-9pm, restaurant 6-9.30pm Fri & Sat) This is a homely pub serving real ale (and mulled wine beside the fireplace in winter), with live jazz Sunday evenings and a dinky wee beer garden in a cobbled courtyard out the back. The upstairs restaurant offers formal dining, with crisp white table linen and sparkling crystal, and a menu offering French/Irish cuisine.

Information

Tourist office (☎9268 9717; tic.hillsborough@lisburn.gov.uk; The Square; ⌚9am-5.30pm Mon-Sat, plus 2-6pm Sun Jul & Aug) In the Georgian courthouse in the centre of the village.

Getting There & Away

Goldline Express bus 238 from Belfast's Europa BusCentre to Newry stops at Hillsborough (£3, 25 minutes, at least hourly Monday to Saturday, eight Sunday).

SAINTFIELD & AROUND

POP 3000

Saintfield is a pretty and prosperous little town, and a popular weekend destination for visitors from Belfast who come to browse its dozen or so antique shops and tearooms.

Rowallane Garden (www.ntni.org.uk; Crossgar Rd, Saintfield; adult/child £5.70/2.80; ⌚10am-8pm May-Aug, to 6pm Mar, Apr, Sep & Oct, to 4pm Nov-Feb), 2km south of Saintfield, is renowned for its spectacular spring displays of rhododendrons and azaleas, which thrive behind a windbreak of Australian laurels, hollies, pines and beech trees. The walled gardens feature rare primulas, blue Himalayan poppies, plantain lilies, roses, magnolias and delicate autumn crocuses.

For lunch, try the **March Hare** (2 Fairview; mains £3-6; ⌚9am-5.30pm Mon-Sat) at the west end of the main street, a cosy cottage tearoom serving hearty, homemade soups, sandwiches and cakes.

Saintfield is 16km south of Belfast, and is a stop on the Goldline Express bus 215 service from Belfast to Downpatrick.

LEGANANNY DOLMEN

Ulster's most famous Stone Age monument is a strangely elegant tripod dolmen (tomb chamber), that looks as if a giant's hand has placed the capstone delicately atop the three slim uprights. Its elevated position on the western slopes of Slieve Croob (532m) gives it an impressive view to the Mourne Mountains.

Legananny is a challenge to find without the aid of a 1:50,000-scale map. Heading south from Ballynahinch along the B7 to Rathfriland, go through the hamlets of Dromara and Finnis, then look out for a minor road on the left (signposted Legananny Dolmen). Continue for a further 3km, through a crossroads, and look for another road on the left (a signpost is there, but it's difficult to spot). Continue over the hill for 2km, then turn left again at a farm. There's a parking place 50m along, and the dolmen is 50m uphill on the adjacent farm track.

Belfast to Bangor

The coastal region stretching east from Belfast to Bangor and beyond is commuter territory for the capital, and home to many of the North's wealthiest citizens – it's known locally as the 'Gold Coast'. The attractive **North Down Coastal Path** follows the shore from Holywood train station to Bangor Marina (15km), and continues east to Orlock Point.

For information on the Ulster Folk and Transport museums, see p581.

Bangor

POP 76,800

Bangor is to Belfast what Brighton is to London – a Victorian seaside resort that has enjoyed a renaissance as an out-of-town base for city commuters. The Belfast–Bangor train line was built in the late 19th century to connect the capital with the then flourishing resort. The opening of a huge marina and the ongoing redevelopment of the seafront have boosted Bangor's fortunes – it's widely regarded as the most desirable address in Northern Ireland – though the kitsch tradition of British seaside towns survives in the Pickie Family Fun Park.

The bus and train stations are together on Abbey St, at the uphill end of Main St. At the bottom of Main St is the marina, with B&Bs clustered to the east and west on Queen's Pde and Seacliff Rd. Bangor has both a Main St and a High St, which converge on Bridge St at the marina.

WORTH A TRIP

CRAWFORDSBURN

The pretty little conservation village of Crawfordsburn lies just over 3km west of Bangor on the B20. The picturesque **Old Inn** (☎9185 3255; www.theoldinn.com; 15 Main St; r £120-160; P@☎) here was once a resting place on the coach route between Belfast and Donaghadee (formerly the main ferry port for mainland Britain). As a result, it has been patronised by many famous names, including the young Peter the Great (tsar of Russia), Dick Turpin (highwayman), former US president George HW Bush, and a veritable roll call of literary figures, including Swift, Tennyson, Thackeray, Dickens, Trollope and CS Lewis.

Established in 1614, the Old Inn claims to be Ireland's oldest hotel, with the original thatched cottage (now the bar) flanked by 18th-century additions. The atmosphere is cosy and welcoming, with log fires, low ceilings and wood panelling, and there's a lovely garden terrace at the back. The rooms, dressed up with Arts and Crafts–style wall paper and mahogany woodwork, have bags of character, and the inn's lavishly decorated **Lewis Restaurant** (mains £15-19, 4-course lunch Sun £20; ⏰7-9.30pm Mon-Sat, noon-3pm Sun) is one of Northern Ireland's best.

Sights & Activities

FREE North Down Heritage Centre HERITAGE CENTRE
(Castle Park Ave; ⏰10am-4.30pm Tue-Sat, 2-4.30pm Sun, plus 10am-4.30pm Mon Jul & Aug) Housed in the converted laundry, stables and stores of Bangor Castle, this centre displays, among other historical curiosities, a facsimile of *The Antiphonary of Bangor,* a small 7th-century prayer book and the oldest surviving Irish manuscript (the original is housed in Milan's Ambrosian Library). There's also an interesting section on the life of William Percy French (1854–1920), the famous entertainer and songwriter (Bangor is also home to the Percy French Society; www.percyfrench.org). The centre is in Castle Park, west of the train and bus stations.

Blue Aquarius CRUISE
(☎07510 006000; www.bangorboat.com; adult/child from £6/3; ⏰departures from 2pm Jul & Aug, Sat & Sun Apr-Jun & Sep) *Blue Aquarius* offers pleasure cruises around Bangor Bay, departing from the marina pontoon next to the Pickie Family Fun Park. In July and August there are family-friendly **fishing trips** (per adult/child incl tackle & bait £17/12) departing at 9.30am and 7pm daily from the Eisenhower Pier (the right-hand side of the harbour, looking out to sea).

Pickie Family Fun Park AMUSEMENT PARK
(Marine Gardens; per ride £1.50; ⏰10am-10pm Easter-Sep, to sunset Sat & Sun Oct-Easter) Apart from strolling along the seafront, Bangor's main attraction is this old-fashioned seaside entertainment complex that's famous for its swan-shaped pedal boats, complete with kids adventure playground, karts and miniature steam train.

FREE Cockle Row Cottages MUSEUM
(Groomsport; ⏰11.30am-5.30pm Jun-Aug) The fishing village of Groomsport, on the eastern edge of town, has a picturesque harbour overlooked by Cockle Row Cottages, one of which has been restored as a typical fisherman's home of 1910.

Ballyholme Bay BEACH
To the east of the town centre, Ballyholme Bay has a long sandy beach and wide green spaces for the kids to run around in.

Sleeping

TOP CHOICE Hebron House B&B ££
(☎9146 3126; www.hebron-house.com; 68 Princetown Rd; s/d £45/65; P@☎) Breakfast around the communal dining table is a highlight at the Hebron, where landlady Ilona gets inventive with organic produce, dishing up oat-crusted potato cakes with your bacon and eggs, or adding Bushmills whiskey and clotted cream to your porridge. The three bedrooms combine traditional Victorian fittings with elegant modern decor, and there are plush towels, bathrobes and Molton Brown toiletries in the stylish bathrooms.

Cairn Bay Lodge B&B ££
(☎9146 7636; www.cairnbaylodge.com; 278 Seacliff Rd; s/d from £45/80; P☎) This lovely seaside villa overlooking Ballyholme Bay, 1km east of the town centre, oozes Edwardian elegance with its oak-panelled lounge and dining room. There are three bedrooms with

private bathrooms that blend antique charm with contemporary style, plus beautiful gardens, gourmet breakfasts and sea views.

Clandeboye Lodge Hotel HOTEL £££
(☎9185 2500; www.clandeboyelodge.com; 10 Estate Rd, Clandeboye; s/d from £85/100; P@) Looking a little like a modern red-brick church set amid landscaped gardens on the southwest edge of town, the Clandeboye offers informal luxury – big bedrooms, polished granite bathrooms, fluffy bathrobes, Champagne and chocolates – plus a log fire in winter and a drinks terrace in summer.

Ennislare House B&B ££
(☎9127 0858; www.ennislarehouse.com; 7-9 Princetown Rd; s/d £35/65; P) Set in a lovely Victorian town house just 300m north of the train station, the Ennislare has big, bright rooms, stylish decor and a friendly owner who can't do enough to make you feel welcome.

Eating

TOP CHOICE **Jeffers by the Marina** IRISH ££
(☎9185 9555; www.jeffersbythemarina.com; 7 Gray's Hill; mains £12-18; ⏲10.30am-10pm Tue-Sat, 10am-8pm Sun) This chic little cafe-restaurant is immediately likeable, with its laid-back jazzy tunes, cool art, granite table tops and view of the marina. It serves coffee, cakes and snacks all day and also has a fresh and interesting dinner menu that features local organic produce – from Strangford Lough oysters to the signature Irish beef, slow cooked for five hours.

Boat House FRENCH, IRISH ££
(☎9146 9253; www.theboathouseni.co.uk; 2-/3-course lunch £18/22, dinner mains £15-20; ⏲lunch & dinner Wed-Sat, 1-8pm Sun) The Boat House is a cosy little nook of stone, brick and designer decor, tucked into the former Harbour Master's office across the street from the tourist office. The menu features local seafood, lamb and game, deftly prepared with a light Gallic touch.

Coyle's Bistro BISTRO ££
(☎9127 0362; 44 High St; mains £15-20; ⏲5-9pm Tue-Sat, to 8pm Sun) Despite being upstairs from a busy bar, this place is surprisingly intimate and inviting, with wood panelling, mirrored walls and subdued lighting, and a varied menu that ranges from ox cheeks braised in red wine to Moroccan lamb stew. The two-course set menu for two (available 5pm to 7pm) includes a bottle of wine and costs £30.

Rioja MEDITERRANEAN ££
(☎9147 0774; www.riojabangor.co.uk; 119 High St; 2-course dinner £16 Wed-Thu, £20 Fri & Sat; ⏲5-9pm Wed-Sat, noon-2pm Fri) Rioja is a relaxed Mediterranean bistro with terracotta tiles and candle-lit tables, offering a range of Iberian, French and Italian dishes including *cataplana,* a Portuguese seafood casserole. Although it's licensed, you can bring your own wine if you want to (corkage £3); the early bird menu (5pm to 7pm Tuesday to Friday) offers any main course for £10.50.

Red Berry Coffee House CAFE £
(2-4 Main St; mains £3-6; ⏲9am-10pm Mon-Sat, 1-9pm Sun) A chilled-out fairtrade coffee shop that serves big breakfasts (including a stack of pancakes with bacon and maple syrup) till 11.30am, and deli sandwiches and salads thereafter.

Entertainment

Jenny Watts PUB
(41 High St) A traditional pub with a beer garden out back, Jenny's pulls in a mixed-age crowd, offering live music three nights a week, cool tunes (in the upstairs lounge) on Friday and Saturday, and jazz and blues Sunday lunchtime and evening. It also serves good pub grub, and kids are welcome at meal times.

Café Ceol NIGHTCLUB
(www.mintbangor.com; 17-21 High St; admission free-£5; ⏲7pm-1am Thu-Mon) Bangor's biggest and busiest nightclub has a sleek cocktail bar, an intimate lounge and a stylish club venue, **Mint**, which features hip hop and R&B on Thursday, resident DJ on Friday, and commercial dance, house, funk and R&B on Saturday.

Information

Tourist office (☎9127 0069; www.northdowntourism.com; 34 Quay St; ⏲9am-5pm Mon, Tue, Thu & Fri, 10am-5pm Wed & Sat, 1-5pm Sun May-Aug, shorter hr & closed Sun Sep-Apr) Housed in a tower built in 1637 as a fortified customs post.

Bangor Library (80 Hamilton Rd; ⏲9am-9pm Mon-Wed, to 10pm Thu, to 5pm Fri & Sat) Internet access costs £1.50 for 30 minutes.

Getting There & Away

Bus

Ulsterbus services 1 and 2 run from Belfast's Laganside BusCentre to Bangor (£3, 55 minutes, half-hourly Monday to Saturday, eight Sunday). From Bangor, bus 3 goes to Donaghadee (25 minutes, hourly Monday to Saturday, four Sunday) and bus 6 goes to Newtownards (20 minutes, half-hourly Monday to Saturday, seven Sunday).

Train

A regular train service runs from Belfast's Great Victoria St and Central stations to Bangor (£5, 30 minutes, half-hourly Monday to Saturday, hourly Sunday).

Ards Peninsula

The low-lying Ards Peninsula (An Aird) is the finger of land that encloses Strangford Lough, pinching against the thumb of the Lecale Peninsula at the Portaferry Narrows. The northern half of the peninsula has some of Ireland's most fertile farmland, with large expanses of wheat and barley, while the south is a landscape of neat fields, white cottages and narrow, winding roads. The eastern coast has some good sandy beaches.

DONAGHADEE

POP 6500

Donaghadee (Domhnach Daoi) was the main ferry port for Scotland until 1874, when the 34km sea crossing to Portpatrick was superseded by the Stranraer–Larne route. Now it's a pleasant harbour town that's fast becoming part of Belfast's commuter belt.

The town is home to **Grace Neill's**, which dates from 1611 and claims to be Ireland's oldest pub. Among its 17th-century guests was Peter the Great, tsar of Russia, who stopped in for lunch in 1697 on his grand tour of Europe. In the early 19th century, John Keats found the place 'charming and clean' but was 'treated to ridicule, scorn and violent abuse by the local people who objected to my mode of dress and thought I was some strange foreigner'.

In July and August, **MV The Brothers** (☎9188 3403; www.nelsonsboats.co.uk) runs boat trips to Copeland Island (adult/child £5/3, departs 2pm daily, weather permitting), which was abandoned to the seabirds at the turn of the 20th century. There are also sea-angling trips (£10 per person, departures at 10am and 7pm), with all tackle and bait provided.

TOP FIVE ROMANTIC HIDEAWAYS IN NORTHERN IRELAND

- » Bushmills Inn (p657)
- » Galgorm Resort & Spa (p669)
- » Malmaison Hotel (p590)
- » Westville Hotel (p675)
- » Old Inn (p609)

Sleeping & Eating

Pier 36 B&B ££

(☎9188 4466; www.pier36.co.uk; 36 The Parade; s/d £50/70) An excellent pub with comfortable B&B rooms upstairs and a red-brick and terracotta-tiled **restaurant** (lunch mains £9-13, dinner £15-27; ⌚12.30-2.30pm & 5-9.30pm Wed-Sun) at the back, dominated by a yellow Rayburn stove that turns out home-baked bread and the daily roast. The hearty menu includes soups, stews, sausage and champ (a Northern Irish dish of potatoes mashed with spring onions), mussels and other seafood, steaks and a good range of vegie dishes.

TOP CHOICE **Grace Neill's** IRISH ££

(☎9188 4595; www.graceneills.com; 33 High St; 2-/3-course lunch £14/18, dinner mains £15-25; ⌚noon-3pm & 5.30-9pm Mon-Fri, noon-9.30pm Sat, 12.30-8pm Sun) At the back of Ireland's oldest pub is one of the North's best modern bistros, its sea-green, khaki and red-brick walls decked with arty photos of old Donaghadee. The lunch menu could be described as upmarket comfort food, from smoked haddock with poached egg and mustard *velouté* to grilled steak *béarnaise,* while the dinner menu takes the same great ingredients and adds a gourmet twist.

PORTAFERRY

POP 3300

Portaferry (Port an Pheire), a neat huddle of streets around a medieval tower house, enjoys an attractive setting, looking across the turbulent Narrows to a matching tower house in Strangford. A renowned marine biology station on the waterfront uses the lough as an outdoor laboratory, and you can investigate the local marine life yourself at the nearby Exploris aquarium.

Sights & Activities

Exploris AQUARIUM

(www.exploris.org.uk; Castle St; adult/child £7/4.50; ⌚10am-6pm Mon-Fri, 11am-6pm Sat, noon-6pm Sun Apr-Aug, shorter hr Sep-Mar) Next to the tourist office is this outstanding state-of-the-art aquarium, with displays of marine life from Strangford Lough and the Irish Sea. Touch tanks allow visitors to stroke and hold rays, starfish, sea anemones and other sea creatures. Exploris also has a seal sanctuary, where orphaned, sick and injured seals are nursed back to health before being released into the wild.

FREE Portaferry Castle CASTLE

(Castle St; ⏲10am-5pm Mon-Sat, 2-6pm Sun Easter-Aug) Portaferry's castle is a small 16th-century tower house beside the tourist information centre, which, together with the tower house in Strangford, used to control sea traffic through the Narrows.

Local Walks WALKING

Walk up to **Windmill Hill** above the town, topped by an old windmill tower, for a good view over the Narrows to Strangford. The Vikings named this stretch of water Strangfjörthr, meaning 'powerful fjord', because when the tide turns, as it does four times a day, 400,000 tonnes of water per minute churn through the gap at speeds of up to eight knots (15km/h). You get some idea of the tide's remarkable strength when you see the ferry being whipped sideways by the current.

Portaferry hit the headlines in 2008 when **SeaGen** – the world's first commercial-scale tidal energy turbine, built at Belfast's Harland & Wolff shipyard – was installed in the Narrows. The generator is clearly visible, squatting in the channel just south of town like a stumpy red and black lighthouse. The business end is underwater, where two giant turbine blades spin in the tidal currents, generating around 1.2 megawatts of electricity for 18 to 20 hours a day.

There are pleasant walks on the minor roads along shore, north for 2.5km to Ballyhenry Island (accessible at low tide), and south for 6km to the National Trust nature reserve at **Ballyquintin Point**, both good for birdwatching, seal spotting or just admiring the views of the Mourne Mountains.

Des Rogers BOAT TRIP

(☎4272 8297; desmondrogers@netscapeonline.co.uk; per half-/full day around £75/150) Fishing and birdwatching trips from May to September, as well as pleasure cruises on the lough. Book in advance.

John Murray BOAT TRIP

(☎4272 8414; per half-/full day around £75/150) Also organises fishing and birdwatching trips from May to September, along with pleasure cruises. Book in advance.

Sleeping & Eating

Portaferry Hotel HOTEL ££

(☎4272 8231; www.portaferryhotel.com; 10 The Strand; s/d £65/110; P@) Converted from a row of 18th-century terrace houses, this charming seafront hotel has an elegant, Georgian look to its rooms – ask for one with a sea view (£10 extra) – and has a good, family-friendly **restaurant** (bar meals £6-12, mains £10-20) with a French-influenced menu.

Fiddler's Green B&B ££

(☎4272 8393; www.fiddlersgreenportaferry.com; 10-12 Church St; s/d £45/65; P) This popular pub and restaurant provides B&B in four comfortable rooms – one has a four-poster bed (per night £75) – neatly decorated with pine furniture and paintings, and serves up a stonking cooked breakfast. The pub has traditional music sessions every Friday, Saturday and Sunday night.

Adair's B&B B&B £

(☎4272 8412; 22 The Square; s/d £23/44, family per person £22) Mrs Adair's friendly and good-value B&B is an anonymous-looking house right on the main square (there's no sign outside; look for No 22), with three spacious rooms – a single (shared bathroom), a twin (with private bathroom) and a family room (with private bathroom; for up to four people).

Barholm HOSTEL £

(☎4272 9598; www.barholmportaferry.co.uk; 11 The Strand; dm/s/d from £16/21/50; P) Barholm offers year-round B&B and hostel-style accommodation in a Victorian villa in a superb seafront location opposite the ferry slipway. There's a spacious kitchen, laundry facilities and a big, sunny conservatory that doubles as a tearoom. It's popular with groups, so be sure to book ahead.

Information

Tourist office (☎4272 9882; tourism-portaferry@ards-council.gov.uk; Castle St; ⏲10am-5pm Mon-Sat, 2-6pm Sun Easter-Aug) In a restored stable near the tower house.

Getting There & Away

A **car ferry** (one-way car & driver £5.80, motorcyclists £3.50, car passengers & pedestrians £1) between Portaferry and Strangford sails every half-hour between 7.30am and 10.30pm Monday to Friday, 8am to 11pm Saturday and 9.30am to 10.30pm on Sunday. Journey time is about 10 minutes.

LORD CASTLEREAGH

As you wander around Mount Stewart, spare a thought for Robert Stewart, Lord Castlereagh (1769–1822), who spent his childhood here. Despite going down in history as one of Britain's most accomplished foreign secretaries, during his lifetime he was enormously unpopular with the public, who saw him as the spokesman for a violently repressive government. He was savagely attacked in print by liberal reformers, including Daniel O'Connell – who denounced him as 'the assassin of his country' – and the poets Percy Bysshe Shelley and Lord Byron. The latter's notorious *Epitaph for Lord Castlereagh* could hardly be bettered for withering contempt:

> Posterity will ne'er survey
> A nobler scene than this:
> Here lie the bones of Castlereagh;
> Stop, traveller, and piss!

As Chief Secretary for Ireland in the government of William Pitt, Castlereagh was responsible for quelling the 1798 Rising and for passing the 1801 Act of Union. Later he served as foreign secretary during the Napoleonic Wars, and represented Britain at the Congress of Vienna in 1815. Political success did not bring happiness, however; while still in office, Castlereagh succumbed to paranoia and depression and committed suicide by slitting his own throat with a letter knife.

Ulsterbus services 9 and 10 travel from Belfast to Portaferry (£6, 1¼ hours, six daily Monday to Saturday, two Sunday) via Newtownards, Mount Stewart and Greyabbey. More frequent services begin from Newtownards (some buses go via Carrowdore and don't stop at Mount Stewart and Greyabbey; check first).

GREYABBEY

POP 1000

The village of Greyabbey is home to the splendid ruins of **Grey Abbey** (Church Rd; admission free; ⌚10am-5pm Easter-Sep, noon-4pm Sun only Oct-Easter). The Cistercian abbey was founded in 1193 by Affreca, wife of the Norman aristocrat John de Courcy (the builder of Carrickfergus Castle), in thanks for surviving a stormy sea crossing from the Isle of Man. The small visitor centre explains Cistercian life with paintings and panels.

The abbey church, which remained in use as late as the 18th century, was the first in Ireland to be built in the Gothic style. At the east end is a carved tomb, possibly depicting Affreca; the effigy in the north transept may be her husband. The grounds, overlooked by 18th-century Rosemount House, are awash with trees and flowers on spreading lawns, making this an ideal picnic spot.

Hoops Courtyard, off Main St in the village centre, has a cluster of 18 little shops selling antiques and collectables; opening times vary, but all are open on Wednesday, Friday and Saturday afternoons.

Hoops Coffee Shop (Hoops Courtyard, Main St; mains £4-6; ⌚10am-5pm Jul & Aug, Tue-Sat Sep-Jun) is a traditional tearoom with outdoor tables in the courtyard in fine weather, serving good lunches and wicked cream teas.

MOUNT STEWART

The magnificent 18th-century **Mount Stewart House & Gardens** (www.ntni.org.uk; adult/child £7/3.50; ⌚house noon-6pm mid-Mar–Oct) is one of Northern Ireland's grandest stately homes. It was built for the Marquess of Londonderry and is decorated with lavish plasterwork, marble nudes and priceless artworks.

Lady Mairi Vane-Tempest-Stewart (born 1920) – daughter of the seventh marquess – lived and entertained guests in part of the house until her death in November 2009; she gifted the house to the National Trust in 1977. The family is related by marriage to the Goldsmiths via Annabel (born 1934), daughter of the eighth marquess, after whom the famous London nightclub was named. The house's treasures include the chairs used at the Congress of Vienna in 1815 (embroidery added in 1918–22), and a painting of the racehorse Hambletonian by George Stubbs, one of the most important paintings in Ireland.

Much of the landscaping of the beautiful **gardens** (⏲10am-6pm mid-Mar–Oct) was supervised in the early 20th century by Lady Edith, wife of the seventh marquess, for the benefit of her children – the **Dodo Terrace** at the front of the house is populated with unusual creatures from history (dinosaurs and dodos) and myth (griffins and mermaids), accompanied by giant frogs and duck-billed platypuses. The 18th-century **Temple of the Winds** (⏲2-5pm Sun mid-Mar–Oct) is a folly in the classical Greek style built on a high point above the lough.

Mount Stewart is on the A20, 3km northwest of Greyabbey and 8km southeast of Newtownards. Buses from Belfast and Newtownards to Portaferry stop at the gate. The ground floor of the house and most of the gardens are wheelchair accessible. Last admission is one hour before closing time.

Newtownards & Around

POP 27,800

Founded in the 17th century on the site of the 6th-century Movilla monastery, Newtownards (Baile Nua na hArda) today is a busy but unexceptional commercial centre.

The **tourist office** (☎91826846; tourism@ards-council.gov.uk; 31 Regent St; ⏲9.15am-5pm Mon-Fri, 9.30am-5pm Sat) is next to the bus station.

Scrabo Country Park PARK

Newtownards is overlooked by the prominent landmark of Scrabo Hill, located 2km southwest of town. It was once the site of extensive prehistoric earthworks, which were largely removed during construction of the 41m **1857 Memorial Tower** (admission free; ⏲10am-6pm Easter-Sep, noon-4pm Sun only Oct-Easter), built in honour of the third Marquess of Londonderry. Inside there's an audiovisual display on the tower's history and a 122-step climb to the superb viewpoint at the top – on a clear day you can see Scotland, the Isle of Man and even Snowdon in Wales. The disused sandstone quarries nearby provided material for many famous buildings, including Belfast's Albert Memorial Clock Tower.

Somme Heritage Centre HERITAGE CENTRE

(www.irishsoldier.org; 233 Bangor Rd; adult/child £5/4; ⏲10am-5pm Mon-Fri, noon-5pm Sat & Sun Jul & Aug, 10am-4pm Mon-Thu, noon-4pm Sat Apr-Jun & Sep, shorter hr Oct-Mar) Thise grimly fascinating centre vividly illustrates the horrors of the WWI Somme campaign of 1916 from the perspective of men of the 10th (Irish), 16th (Irish) and 36th (Ulster) divisions. It's a high-tech show with short films and reconstructions of the trenches, but there's nothing celebratory about the exhibits, which are intended as a memorial to the men and women who died. A photographic display commemorates the suffragette movement and the part that women played in WWI.

The centre is 3km north of Newtownards on the A21 towards Bangor. Bus 6 from Bangor to Newtownards passes the entrance every half-hour or so.

Ark Open Farm FARM

(www.thearkopenfarm.co.uk; 296 Bangor Rd; adult/3-16yr/under 3yr £4.80/4/free; ⏲10am-6pm Mon-Sat, 2-6pm Sun Apr-Oct, to 5pm Nov-Mar). Opposite the Somme Heritage Centre, on the other side of the dual carriageway, the Ark Open Farm is hugely popular with families, the farm has displays of rare breeds of sheep, cattle, poultry, llamas and donkeys. Kids get to stroke and handfeed the lambs, piglets and ducklings.

Strangford Lough

Almost landlocked, Strangford Lough (Loch Cuan; www.strangfordlough.org) is connected to the open sea by a 700m-wide strait (the Narrows) at Portaferry. Its western shore is fringed by humpbacked islands – half-drowned mounds of boulder clay (called drumlins) left behind by ice sheets at the end of the last ice age. On the eastern shore, the drumlins have been broken down by the waves into heaps of boulders that form shallow tidal reefs (known locally as 'pladdies').

Large colonies of grey seals frequent the lough, especially at the southern tip of the Ards Peninsula where the exit channel opens out into the sea. Birds abound on the shores and tidal mudflats, including brent geese wintering from Arctic Canada, eider ducks and many species of wader. Strangford Lough oysters are a local delicacy.

Sights & Activities

Castle Espie Wildfowl & Wetlands Centre NATURE RESERVE

(www.wwt.org.uk; Ballydrain Rd, Comber; adult/child £6.50/3.20; ⏲10am-5.30pm Jul & Aug, to 5pm Mar-Jun, Sep & Oct, shorter hr Nov-Feb) The Castle Espie reserve is a haven for huge flocks of geese, ducks and swans – around 30,000 light-bellied brent geese (75% of the world's population) spend the winter here – and is a paradise for fledgling ornithologists.

The new visitor centre is a showcase for sustainable development, and the landscaped grounds are dotted with hides for observing waders and waterfowl, as well as the centre's important collection of duck and goose species from all over the world. The best times to visit are in May and June, when the grounds are overrun with goslings, ducklings and cygnets, and October, when the vast flocks of brent geese begin to arrive from Arctic Canada.

The centre is about 2km southeast of Comber, off the Downpatrick road (A22).

FREE **Nendrum Monastic Site** HISTORIC SITE
(Lisbane; ⏲24hr) The Celtic monastic community of Nendrum was built in the 5th century under the guidance of St Mochaoi (St Mahee). It is much older than the Norman monastery at Greyabbey on the opposite shore and couldn't be more different. The scant remains provide a clear outline of its early plan, with the foundations of a number of churches, a round tower, beehive cells and other buildings, as well as three concentric stone ramparts and a monks' cemetery, all in a wonderful island setting. A particularly interesting relic is the stone sundial that has been reconstructed using some of the original pieces. The minor road to Mahee Island from the lough's western shore crosses a causeway to Reagh Island and then a bridge guarded by the ruined tower of 15th-century Mahee Castle.

The small visitor centre (admission free; ⏲10am-5pm Easter-Sep, noon-4pm Sun only Oct-Easter) screens an excellent video comparing Nendrum with Grey Abbey, and there's some interesting material about the concept of time and how we measure it, presented in a child-friendly fashion.

The site is signposted from Lisbane on the A20, 5km south of Comber.

Sleeping & Eating

TOP CHOICE **Anna's House B&B** B&B ££
(☎9754 1566; www.annashouse.com; Tullynagee, 35 Lisbarnett Rd, Lisbane; s/d from £60/90; P 📶) Just west of Lisbane, Anna's is a spacious, ecofriendly country house set in a superb garden with views over a lake from a stunning glass-walled extension. The hospitality is second to none, the food is almost all organic and the bread is home baked, with a breakfast menu that ranges from an Ulster fry or smoked salmon omelette to fresh fruit salad (special diets catered for).

Old Schoolhouse Inn B&B ££
(☎9754 1182; www.theoldschoolhouseinn.com; Ballydrain Rd, Comber; s/d £55/80; P) Just south of Castle Espie on the road to Nendrum, the characterful Old Schoolhouse has seven luxurious, modern rooms, each named for a former US president. The former classroom, now swathed in shades of deep claret and decorated with old musical instruments, houses an award-winning restaurant (3-course dinner £24; ⏲7-10pm) serving local produce cooked in French country-kitchen style.

Old Post Office Tearoom CAFE £
(191 Killinchy Rd, Lisbane; mains £4-7; ⏲9.30am-5pm Mon-Sat) The thatched cottage that once housed the village post office has been lovingly converted into a tearoom and art gallery, with walls of cream plaster and bare stone, pine furniture and a wood-burning stove. It serves great coffee and home-baked scones, plus lunch specials such as lasagne and lovely fresh salads.

Killyleagh

POP 2200

Killyleagh (Cill O Laoch) is a former fishing village dominated by the impressive castle (closed to the public) of the Hamilton family. Built originally by John de Courcy in the 12th century, the Scottish-baronial-style reconstruction of 1850 sits on the original Norman motte and bailey. Outside the gatehouse, a plaque commemorates Sir Hans Sloane, the naturalist, born in Killyleagh in 1660, whose collection was the basis for the founding of the British Museum (London's Sloane Square is named after him). The parish church houses the tombs of members of the Blackwood family (marquesses of Dufferin), who married into the Hamiltons in the 18th century.

In September the Magnus Barelegs Viking Festival (www.killyleagh.org/boatrace) features processions, craft fairs, live music and a Viking boat race on nearby Strangford Lough.

Sleeping & Eating

TOP CHOICE **Dufferin Coaching Inn** B&B ££
(☎4482 1134; www.dufferincoachinginn.com; 35 High St; s/d from £45/65; P 📶) The comfortable

Counties Down & Armagh: Walking & Wildlife

Strangford Lough and the Mourne Mountains have long served as a weekend escape for the people of Belfast, with tranquil coastlines and rugged uplands offering superb wildlife-watching opportunities, challenging hiking routes and glorious scenery.

Mountains of Mourne

1 Celebrated in song and story, the Mountains of Mourne (p623) sweep down to the sea near the holiday resort of Newcastle. These shapely granite hills provide some of the finest hill walking and rock climbing in the North.

Castle Espie Wildfowl & Wetlands Centre

2 Castle Espie Wildfowl & Wetlands Centre (p614) not only protects the wetlands environment that the geese and other migratory birds depend on, but also has its own colourful collection of duck and goose species from around the world.

Mourne Wall

3 Built between 1904 and 1922, the 35km-long Mourne Wall (p624) is one of the most impressive features of the Mourne Mountains. Traversing no fewer than 15 of the Mournes' highest summits, it delineates the catchment area of the Silent Valley reservoirs.

Strangford Lough

4 One of the great birdwatching spectacles of Ireland is the autumn arrival of vast flocks of light-bellied brent geese (75% of the world population) at Strangford Lough (p614). Around 30,000 geese overwinter here.

1

3

Clockwise from top left

1. Mourne Mountains 2. Red-breasted goose, Castle Espie
3. Young boy walking next to Mourne wall

2

lounge in this lovely Georgian house, complete with coal-fired stove and free Sunday papers, was once the village bank – the manager's office in the corner now houses a little library. The seven plush rooms have crisp linen and fluffy towels, and some have four-poster beds; unusually, the smallest double has the bath *in* the bedroom, charmingly hidden behind a curtain. The excellent breakfasts include freshly squeezed orange juice, good coffee and scrambled eggs with smoked salmon.

Killyleagh Castle Towers SELF-CATERING ££
(☎4482 8261; gatehouses@killyleagh.plus.com; High St; apt per week £335-450; P) If you've ever fancied staying in a castle, Killyleagh's three gatehouse towers (complete with spiral staircases and roof terraces) are available for weekly rental, including use of the castle gardens, swimming pool and tennis court. The two smaller towers sleep two or four and the largest sleeps five.

Dufferin Arms PUB ££
(www.dufferinarms.co.uk; 35 High St; bar meals £7-10, dinner mains £10-15; ⏲bar meals noon-3pm & 5-8.30pm Mon-Thu, noon-5pm Fri & Sat, noon-8pm Sun) This comfortably old-fashioned pub (and the larger Stables Bar downstairs) serves decent pub grub, while the cosy, candlelit **Kitchen Restaurant** (⏲5pm-9.30pm Fri & Sat) offers a more intimate atmosphere. Bands play on Friday and Saturday nights from 9pm, with folk and bluegrass sessions on Saturday afternoons from 4pm.

Getting There & Away

Ulsterbus service 11 runs from Belfast to Killyleagh (£4, one hour, 10 daily Monday to Friday, five Saturday, two Sunday) via Comber. Bus 14 continues from Killyleagh to Downpatrick (£3, 20 minutes, 10 daily Monday to Friday, five Saturday).

Downpatrick

POP 10,300

St Patrick's mission to spread Christianity to Ireland began and ended in Downpatrick. Ireland's patron saint is associated with numerous places in this corner of Down – he made his first convert at nearby Saul, and is buried at Down Cathedral – and, on St Patrick's Day (17 March), the town is crammed with crowds of pilgrims and revellers.

Downpatrick – now County Down's administrative centre – was settled long before the saint's arrival. His first church here was constructed inside the earthwork *dún* (fort) of Rath Celtchair, still visible to the southwest of the cathedral. The place later became known as Dún Pádraig (Patrick's Fort), anglicised to Downpatrick in the 17th century.

In 1176 the Norman John de Courcy is said to have brought the relics of St Colmcille and St Brigid to Downpatrick to rest with the remains of St Patrick, hence the local saying, 'In Down, three saints one grave do fill, Patrick, Brigid and Colmcille'. Later the town declined along with the cathedral until the 17th and 18th centuries, when the Southwell family developed the old town centre you see today. The best of its Georgian architecture is centred on English St and the Mall, which lead up to the cathedral, but the rest of the town is a bit bedraggled and looking a little down at heel.

Sights

The **Mall** is the most attractive street in Downpatrick, with some lovely 18th-century architecture including Soundwell School, built in 1733, and a courthouse with a finely decorated pediment.

Saint Patrick Centre HERITAGE CENTRE
(www.saintpatrickcentre.com; 53A Market St; adult/child £4.95/2.55; ⏲9am-5pm Mon-Sat, plus 1-5pm Sun Jul-Aug, 9am-7pm St Patrick's Day) This heritage centre houses a multimedia exhibition called **Ego Patricius**, charting the life and legacy of Ireland's patron saint. Occasionally filled with parties of school kids, the exhibition uses audio and video presentations to tell St Patrick's story, often in his own words (taken from his *Confession*, written in Latin around the year 450, which begins with the words *'Ego Patricius'*, meaning 'I am Patrick'). At the end is a spectacular widescreen film that takes the audience on a swooping, low-level helicopter ride over the landscapes of Ireland.

FREE **Down Cathedral** CATHEDRAL
(www.downcathedral.org; The Mall; ⏲9.30am-4.30pm Mon-Sat, 2-5pm Sun) According to legend, St Patrick died in Saul, where angels told his followers to place his body on a cart drawn by two untamed oxen, and that wherever the oxen halted was where the saint should be buried. They supposedly stopped at the church on the hill of Down, now the site of the Church of Ireland's Down Cathedral.

The cathedral is testimony to 1600 years of building and rebuilding. Viking attacks wiped away all trace of the earliest churches, and the subsequent Norman cathedral and monasteries were destroyed by Scottish raiders in 1316. The rubble was used in a 15th-century church finished in 1512, but after the Dissolution of the Monasteries it was razed to the ground in 1541. Today's building dates largely from the 18th and 19th centuries, with a completely new interior installed in the 1980s.

In the churchyard immediately south of the cathedral is a slab of Mourne granite with the inscription 'Patric', placed there by the Belfast Naturalists' Field Club in 1900, marking the traditional site of **St Patrick's grave**.

To reach the cathedral, take the path to the left of the Saint Patrick Centre, uphill through the landscaped grounds.

FREE **Down County Museum** MUSEUM
(www.downcountymuseum.com; The Mall; ⏲10am-5pm Mon-Fri, 1-5pm Sat & Sun) Downhill from the cathedral is Down County Museum, housed in the town's restored 18th-century jail. In a former cell block at the back are models of some of the prisoners once incarcerated there, and details of their sad stories. Displays cover the story of the Norman conquest of Down, but the biggest exhibit of all is outside – a short signposted trail leads to the **Mound of Down**, a good example of a Norman motte and bailey.

Sleeping & Eating

Denvir's Hotel & Pub B&B ££
(☎4461 2012; www.denvirshotel.com; 14 English St; s/d £40/70;) Recently given a stylish new makeover, Denvir's is an old coaching inn dating back to 1642. It offers B&B in six idiosyncratic rooms with polished floorboards, Georgian windows and period fireplaces. Good food is served in the snug bar and rustic **restaurant** (mains £9-15, 2 courses Mon-Thu £11; ⏲noon-9pm), which has an enormous, 17th-century stone fireplace.

Ardpatrick Country House B&B ££
(☎4483 9434; www.ardpatrickcountryhouse.org; 108 Ballydugan Rd; s/d £33/56; P@) You'll get a warm welcome and a hearty breakfast at this luxurious, modern villa, set in open countryside about 4km southwest of the town centre on the A25. All three rooms are neat as a pin, and all have private bathrooms.

Mill at Ballydugan HOTEL ££
(☎4461 3654; www.ballyduganmill.com; Drumcullen Rd, Ballydugan; s/d/f £60/80/90; P) This huge, eight-storey, 18th-century mill building overlooking Ballydugan Lake has been restored as a hotel and restaurant (restaurant opening hours vary, so ring before visiting), housing 11 atmospheric rooms with lots of exposed stone and timber, and an attractive stone-floored lobby with a huge, roaring fire. It's 3km southwest of Downpatrick, off the A25.

GUITAR MAKER TO THE GREATS

Belfast-born George Lowden has been creating guitars in Northern Ireland since the 1970s, and his hand-built instruments have gained a worldwide reputation for excellence – satisfied Lowden owners include Eric Clapton, Van Morrison, Richard Thompson, Mark Knopfler and the Edge. If you're interested in buying one, you can organise a tour of the workshop at **Lowden Guitars** (www.georgelowden.com; 34 Down Business Park, Belfast Rd, Downpatrick; ⏲Mon-Fri). However, be prepared to shell out upwards of £2600.

Information

Tourist office (☎4461 2233; www.visitdownpatrick.com; 53A Market St; ⏲9.30am-6pm Mon-Sat & 2-6pm Sun Jul & Aug, 10am-5pm Mon-Sat Sep-Jun) In the Saint Patrick Centre, just north of the bus station.

Getting There & Away

Downpatrick is 32km southeast of Belfast. Buses 15, 15A and 515 depart from the Europa BusCentre in Belfast for Downpatrick (£5, one hour, at least hourly Monday to Saturday, six Sunday). There's also the Goldline Express bus 215 (50 minutes, hourly Monday to Saturday).

Goldline Express bus 240 runs from Downpatrick to Newry (£5, 1¼ hours, six daily Monday to Saturday, two Sunday) via Dundrum, Newcastle, Castlewellan and Hilltown.

Around Downpatrick

According to popular tradition, the young St Patrick was kidnapped from Britain by Irish pirates and spent six years as a slave tending sheep (possibly on Slemish, p670). His faith grew in captivity and he prayed daily, eventually escaping back home to his family.

After religious training, St Patrick returned to Ireland to spread the faith and is said to have landed on the shores of Strangford Lough near Saul, northeast of Downpatrick. He preached his first sermon in a nearby barn, and eventually retired to Saul after some 30 years of evangelising.

SAUL

On landing near this spot in 432, St Patrick made his first convert: Díchú, the local chieftain, gave the holy man a sheep barn (*sabhal* in Gaelic, pronounced sawl) in which to preach. West of Saul village is the supposed site of the *sabhal,* with a replica 10th-century **church and round tower** built in 1932 to mark the 1500th anniversary of his arrival.

East of the village is the small hill of **Slieve Patrick** (120m), with stations of the cross along the path to the top and a massive 10m-high statue of St Patrick, also dating from 1932, on the summit. The hill is the object of a popular pilgrimage on St Patrick's Day.

Saul is 3km northeast of Downpatrick off the A2 Strangford road.

STRUELL WELLS

These supposedly curative spring waters are traditionally associated with St Patrick – it is said he scourged himself here, spending 'a great part of the night, stark naked and singing psalms' immersed in what is now the **Drinking Well**.

He must have been a hardy soul – the well-preserved but chilly 17th-century **bathhouses** here look more likely to induce ill health than cure it! The site has been venerated for centuries, although the buildings are all post-1600.

Between the bathhouses and the ruined chapel stands the **Eye Well**, whose waters are said to cure eye ailments.

The wells are in a scenic, secluded glen 2km east of Downpatrick. Take the B1 road towards Ardglass, and turn left after passing the hospital.

Lecale Peninsula

The low-lying Lecale Peninsula is situated east of Downpatrick, isolated by the sea and Strangford Lough to the north, south and east, and the marshes of the Quoile and Blackstaff Rivers to the west. In Irish it's called Leath Chathail (lay-ca-*hal*), meaning 'the territory of Cathal' (an 8th-century prince), and is a region of fertile farmland that is fringed by fishing harbours, rocky bluffs and sandy beaches.

Lecale is a place of pilgrimage for **Van Morrison** fans – Coney Island, immortalised in his song of the same name, is between Ardglass and Killough in the south of the peninsula.

STRANGFORD

POP 550

The picturesque fishing village of Strangford (Baile Loch Cuan) is dominated by **Strangford Castle** (Castle St), a 16th-century tower house that faces its counterpart across the Narrows in Portaferry; it's closed to the public. At the end of Castle St is a footpath called the **Squeeze Gut**, which leads over the hill behind the village, with a fine view of the lough, before looping back to Strangford via tree-lined Dufferin Ave (1.5km), or continuing around the shoreline to Castle Ward Estate (4.5km).

Strangford is located 16km northeast of Downpatrick. See p612 for details of the car ferry between Strangford and Portaferry.

Sleeping & Eating

TOP CHOICE Cuan B&B ££

(☎4488 1222; www.thecuan.com; The Square; s/d £60/90; P) You can't miss the Cuan's green facade, just around the corner from the ferry slip, or the warm welcome from Peter and Caroline, the husband and wife team who run the place. The atmospheric, wood-panelled **restaurant** (mains £11-20; noon-9pm Mon-Thu, to 9.30pm Fri & Sat, to 8.30pm Sun) here is the main attraction, serving giant portions of local seafood, lamb and beef, but there are also nine neat, comfortable and well-equipped rooms if you want to stay the night.

CASTLE WARD ESTATE

Castle Ward enjoys a superb setting overlooking the bay to the west of Strangford, but it has something of a split personality. The house was built in the 1760s for Lord and Lady Bangor – Bernard Ward and his wife, Anne – who were a bit of an odd couple.

Their widely differing tastes in architecture resulted in an eccentric country residence – and a subsequent divorce. Bernard favoured the neoclassical style seen in the front facade and the main staircase, while Anne leant towards the Strawberry Hill Gothic of the rear facade, which reaches a peak in the incredible fan vaulting of her Gothic boudoir.

The house is now part of the **Castle Ward Estate** (www.ntni.org.uk; Park Rd; adult/child grounds & wildlife centre £6/2.70, house tour £4/2; ⏲house 11am-5pm Easter-Oct, grounds 10am-8pm Apr-Sep, to 4pm Oct-Mar). While in the grounds you can visit a Victorian laundry museum, the Strangford Lough Wildlife Centre, Old Castle Ward (a fine 16th-century Plantation tower) and Castle Audley (a 15th-century tower house), and explore a range of walking and cycling trails.

Newcastle

POP 7500

The Victorian seaside resort of Newcastle (An Caisleán Nua) has been given a multi-million-pound makeover and sports a snazzy modern **promenade**, stretching for more than a kilometre along the seafront, complete with modern sculptures and an elegant footbridge over the River Shimna. The facelift makes the most of Newcastle's superb setting on a 5km strand of golden sand at the foot of the Mourne Mountains, and there are hopes that it will transform the town's fortunes from fading bucket-and-spade resort to outdoor activities capital and gateway to the proposed Mourne National Park.

The town is a good base for exploring Murlough National Nature Reserve and the Mourne Mountains – accessible from here on foot, by car or by public transport. Golfers from around the globe flock to the Royal County Down golf course, voted the 'best in the world outside the US' by the magazine *Planet Golf* in 2007.

If you're driving, be aware that the town can be a major traffic bottleneck on summer weekends.

Sights & Activities

The little harbour at the south end of town once served the 'stone boats' that exported Mourne granite from the quarries of Slieve Donard. Newcastle's main attraction is the **beach**, which stretches 5km northeast to the nature reserve.

FREE **Murlough National Nature Reserve** NATURE RESERVE
(car park May-Sep £3.50; ⏲24hr) Footpaths and boardwalks meander among the grassy dunes, with great views back towards the Mournes.

Royal County Down Golf Course GOLF
(www.royalcountydown.org; green fees weekday/weekend £165/180) Stretching north of town is the Royal County Down Golf Course, whose challenging Championship Links – venue for the 2007 Walker Cup – is full of blind tee shots and monster rough, and is regularly voted one of the world's top 10 golf courses. It's open to visitors on Monday, Tuesday, Thursday, Friday and Sunday.

Granite Trail WALKING
Beginning across the road from the harbour, the Granite Trail is a waymarked footpath that leads up a disused funicular railway line that once carried granite blocks to the harbour. The view from the top is worth the steep, 200m climb.

Tropicana SWIMMING
(Central Promenade; adult/child £3.50/3; ⏲11am-7pm Mon & Wed-Fri, 11am-5pm Tue & Sat, 1-5.30pm Sun Jul & Aug) A family entertainment centre with outdoor heated fun pools, giant water slides and paddling pools for toddlers.

Rock Pool SWIMMING
(South Promenade; adult/child £1.80/1.50; ⏲10am-6pm Mon-Sat, 2-6pm Sun Jul & Aug) At the south end of the seafront, this outdoor seawater swimming pool dates from the 1930s.

Soak SPA
(www.soakseaweedbaths.co.uk; 5A South Promenade; 1hr session £25; ⏲11.30am-8pm Thu-Mon Sep-Jun, daily Jul & Aug) If it's too cold for outdoor bathing, you can simmer away in a hot seaweed bath at nearby Soak.

Sleeping

TOP CHOICE **Briers Country House** B&B ££
(☎4372 4347; www.thebriers.co.uk; 39 Middle Tollymore Rd; s/d from £43/65; P) A peaceful farmhouse B&B with a country setting and views of the Mournes, Briers is just 1.5km northwest of the town centre (signposted off the road between Newcastle and Bryansford). Huge breakfasts – vegetarian if you like – are served with a view over the garden, and evening meals are available by prior arrangement.

WALK: SLIEVE DONARD

You can hike to the summit of Slieve Donard (the highest hill in Northern Ireland at 835m) from various starting points in and around Newcastle, but it's a stiff climb, and you shouldn't attempt it without proper walking boots, waterproofs and a map and compass.

On a good day the view from the top extends to the hills of Donegal, the Wicklow Mountains, the coast of Scotland, the Isle of Man and even the hills of Snowdonia in Wales. Two cairns near the summit were long believed to have been cells of St Donard, who retreated here to pray in early Christian times.

The shortest route to the top is via the River Glen from Newcastle. Begin at Donard Park car park, at the edge of town, 1km south of the bus station. At the far end of the car park, turn right through the gate and head into the woods, with the river on your left. A gravel path leads up the River Glen valley to the saddle between Slieve Donard and Slieve Commedagh. From here, turn left and follow the Mourne Wall to the summit. Return by the same route (round trip 9km, allow at least three hours).

Beach House B&B ££
(4372 2345; beachhouse22@tiscali.co.uk; 22 Downs Rd; s/d £50/90; P) Enjoy a sea view with your breakfast at the Beach House, an elegant Victorian B&B with three rooms (all with private bathroom) and a balcony (open to all guests) overlooking the beach.

Tollymore Forest Park CAMPGROUND £
(4372 2428; 176 Tullybranigan Rd; tent/caravan sites £12/15.50) Many of Newcastle's 'camping sites' are for caravans only; the nearest place where you can pitch a tent is amid the attractive scenery of Tollymore Forest Park, in the foothills of the Mourne Mountains, 3km northwest of the town centre. You can hike here (along Bryansford Ave and Bryansford Rd) in 45 minutes.

Harbour House Inn B&B ££
(4372 3445; www.harbourhouseinn.co.uk; 4 South Promenade; s/d from £50/70; P) The Harbour House is a family-friendly pub and restaurant with four plain but serviceable rooms upstairs that are clean and comfortable. It's next to the old harbour, almost 2km south of the bus station, a perfect base for climbing Slieve Donard.

Newcastle Youth Hostel HOSTEL £
(4372 2133; www.hini.org.uk; 30 Downs Rd; dm £14; daily Mar-Oct, Fri & Sat nights only Nov & 1-22 Dec, closed 23 Dec-Feb) This hostel is only a few minutes' walk from the bus station, housed in an attractive 19th-century villa with sea views. It has 37 beds, mostly in six-bed dorms, plus facilities such as a kitchen, laundry and TV room.

Slieve Donard Resort & Spa HOTEL £££
(4372 1066; www.hastingshotels.com; Downs Rd; s/d from £125/160; P) Established in 1897, the Slieve Donard is a magnificent Victorian red-brick pile overlooking the beach, equipped with several restaurants and a luxurious spa. This is where golf legends Tom Watson, Jack Nicklaus and Tiger Woods stay when they're in town.

Eating

TOP CHOICE **Vanilla** IRISH ££
(4372 2268; www.vanillarestaurant.co.uk; 67 Main St; 2-course lunch £13, dinner mains £12-20; noon-3.30pm Thu-Tue, 5-8.30pm Sun-Tue & Thu, 6-9.30pm Fri & Sat) Newcastle-born chef Darren Ireland has introduced a dash of verve and enthusiasm to the local dining scene with this sharply styled bistro, and a menu that shamelessly promotes Irish produce in dishes such as flaky pastry seafood tart with mustard, cheddar and roast onions, and Irish ribeye steak with mushroom and smoked bacon croquettes. Two-course meal for £12.50 Sunday to Thursday.

Maud's CAFE £
(106 Main St; mains £3-7; 9am-9.30pm;) Maud's is a bright, modern cafe with picture windows framing a stunning view across the river to the Mournes. It serves breakfast, good coffee, a range of tempting scones and sticky buns, plus salads, crêpes, pizzas and pastas; there's a kids menu, too.

Sea Salt BISTRO £
(51 Central Promenade; mains £4-7; 10am-5pm Mon-Fri, 9am-5pm Sat & Sun, 7-9pm Fri & Sat) Both delicatessen and bistro, Sea Salt serves

everything from a morning cappuccino to a lunchtime seafood platter, with an evening menu that ranges from Spanish tapas to themed menus from around the world.

Strand Restaurant & Bakery CAFE £
(53-55 Central Promenade; mains £5-9; ⏲8.30am-11pm Jun-Aug, 9am-6pm Sep-May) The Strand has been around since 1930, and dishes up great homemade ice cream and cakes, as well as serving all-day breakfast (£2 to £5), lunch and dinner in its traditional, seaside, chips-with-everything restaurant.

Information

There is **public wi-fi** (per day/week £2.50/5) all along the promenade; buy prepay cards from the BonBon shop between the tourist office and the bridge.

Tourist office (☎4372 2222; newcastle.tic@downdc.gov.uk; 10-14 Central Promenade; ⏲9.30am-7pm Mon-Sat, 1-7pm Sun Jul & Aug, 10am-5pm Mon-Sat, 2-6pm Sun Sep-Jun) Sells local-interest books and maps, and a range of traditional and contemporary crafts.

Getting There & Around

Ulsterbus 20 runs to Newcastle from Belfast's Europa BusCentre (£7, 1¼ hours, at least hourly Monday to Saturday, eight Sunday) via Dundrum. Bus 37 continues along the coast road from Newcastle to Annalong and Kilkeel (£4, 35 minutes, hourly Monday to Saturday, eight Sunday).

Goldline Express bus 240 takes the inland route from Newry to Newcastle (£5, 50 minutes, six daily Monday to Saturday, two Sunday) via Hilltown and continues on to Downpatrick. You can also get to Newry along the coast road, changing buses at Kilkeel.

Bike rental costs around £15/80 per day/week:

Mourne Cycle Tours (☎4372 4348; www.mournecycletours.com; 13 Spelga Ave) Can deliver bikes to your accommodation.

Ross Cycles (☎4377 8029; 44 Clarkhill Rd, Castlewellan; ⏲9.30am-6pm Mon-Sat, 2-5pm Sun)

Around Newcastle

TOLLYMORE FOREST PARK

This scenic **forest park** (Bryansford; car/pedestrian £4/2; ⏲10am-dusk), 3km west of Newcastle, has lengthy walks along the River Shimna and across the northern slopes of the Mournes. The park is littered with Victorian follies, including **Clanbrassil Barn**, which looks more like a church, and grottoes, caves and stepping stones. An electronic kiosk at the car park provides information on the flora, fauna and history of the park.

CASTLEWELLAN

A less rugged outdoor experience is offered by **Castlewellan Forest Park** (Main St, Castlewellan; car/pedestrian £4/2; ⏲10am-dusk), with gentle walks around the castle grounds and **trout fishing** (3-day permit £8.50) in its lovely lake.

In July Castlewellan village is the focus of the **Celtic Fusion Festival** (www.celticfusion.co.uk), a 10-day celebration of Celtic music, art, drama and dance at venues around County Down, including Castlewellan, Newcastle and Downpatrick.

DUNDRUM

Second only to Carrickfergus as Northern Ireland's finest Norman fortress, **Dundrum Castle** (Dundrum; admission free; ⏲10am-5pm daily Easter-Oct, noon-4pm Sun only Nov-Easter) was founded in 1177 by John de Courcy of Carrickfergus. The castle overlooks the sheltered waters of Dundrum Bay, famous for its oysters and mussels.

Set in a wood-panelled Victorian house with local art brightening the walls, **Mourne Seafood Bar** (☎4375 1377; www.mourneseafood.com; 10 Main St; mains £9-16; ⏲12.30-9.30pm, closed Mon & Tue Nov-Mar) is a friendly and informal fishmonger-cum-restaurant. As well as a choice of local oysters served five different ways, the menu includes seafood chowder, crab, langoustines and daily fish specials, all sourced locally.

Dundrum is 5km north of Newcastle. Bus 17 from Newcastle to Downpatrick stops in Dundrum (£2, 12 minutes, eight daily Monday to Friday, four Saturday, two Sunday).

Mourne Mountains

The humpbacked granite hills of the Mourne Mountains dominate the horizon as you head south from Belfast towards Newcastle. This is one of the most beautiful corners of Northern Ireland, with a distinctive landscape of yellow gorse, grey granite and whitewashed cottages, the lower slopes of the hills latticed with a neat patchwork of drystone walls cobbled together from huge, rounded granite boulders.

The hills were made famous in a popular song penned by Irish songwriter William Percy French in 1896, whose chorus, 'Where the Mountains of Mourne sweep down to the sea', captures perfectly their scenic blend of ocean, sky and hillside. For the last decade a debate has rumbled on about the possible creation of Mourne National Park, with tourism and environmental lobbies for the project, and farmers and developers against; at the time of research, no decision had yet been taken.

The Mournes offer some of the best **hill walking** and **rock climbing** in the North. Specialist guidebooks include *The Mournes: Walks* by Paddy Dillon and *A Rock-Climbing Guide to the Mourne Mountains* by Robert Bankhead. You'll also need an Ordnance Survey map, either the 1:50,000 Discoverer Series (Sheet No 29: *The Mournes*), or the 1:25,000 Activity Series *(The Mournes)*. You can buy maps at the tourist office in Newcastle.

History

The crescent of low-lying land on the southern side of the mountains is known as the Kingdom of Mourne. Cut off for centuries by its difficult approaches (the main overland route passed north of the hills), it developed a distinctive landscape and culture. Until the coast road was built in the early 19th century, the only access was on foot or by sea.

Smuggling provided a source of income in the 18th century. Boats carrying French spirits would land at night and packhorses would carry the casks through the hills to the inland road, avoiding the excise men at Newcastle. The Brandy Pad, a former smugglers' path from Bloody Bridge to Tollymore, is a popular walking route today.

Sights

Silent Valley Reservoir NATURE RESERVE

(car/motorcycle £4.50/2, plus per adult/child £1.60/0.60; 10am-6.30pm Apr-Oct, to 4pm Nov-Mar) At the heart of the Mournes is the beautiful Silent Valley Reservoir, where the River Kilkeel was dammed in 1933. There are scenic, waymarked walks around the grounds, a **coffee shop** (11am-5.30pm Sat & Sun Apr-Sep) and an interesting exhibition on the building of the dam. From the car park, a shuttle bus (adult/child return £1.40/1) will take you another 4km up the valley to the Crom Dam. It runs daily in July and August, weekends only in May, June and September.

Mourne Wall LANDMARK

The dry-stone Mourne Wall was built between 1904 and 1922 to keep livestock out of the catchment area of the Kilkeel and Annalong Rivers, which were to be dammed to provide a water supply for Belfast. (Poor geological conditions meant the Annalong could not be dammed, and its waters were diverted to the Silent Valley Reservoir via a 3.6km-long tunnel beneath Slieve Binnian.)

WALK: THE BRANDY PAD

The Brandy Pad is an ancient smugglers' trail across the Mourne Mountains, used in the 18th century to carry brandy, wine, tobacco and coffee to Hilltown, thereby avoiding the excise officer at Newcastle.

The trail begins at the car park at Bloody Bridge on the A2 coast road, 5km south of Newcastle (any bus to Kilkeel will drop you there). From here, the path leads up the valley of the River Bloody Bridge, past old granite workings, to the Mourne Wall at the saddle south of Slieve Donard (3.5km).

On the far side of the wall, a wide path contours north (to your right) across the lower slopes of Slieve Donard, then continues traversing west below the Castles, a huddle of weathered granite pinnacles. Beyond the peaty col beneath Slieve Commedagh, the path descends slightly into the valley of the River Kilkeel (or Silent Valley) and continues traversing with Ben Crom reservoir down to your left to reach Hare's Gap and a reunion with the Mourne Wall.

Go through the gap in the wall and descend to the northwest, steeply at first, then more easily on a broad and stony trail known as the Trassey Track, which leads down to a minor road and the Trassey Bridge car park near Meelmore Lodge (12km from Bloody Bridge; allow three to five hours).

From here you can return to Newcastle on foot through Tollymore Forest Park, along the trail that begins immediately above the car park (8km; allow two to three hours), or in summer you can catch the **Mourne Rambler** (Jul-Aug) bus from either the car park or Meelmore Lodge.

The spectacular wall, 2m high, 1m thick and over 35km long, marches across the summits of 15 of the surrounding peaks including the highest, Slieve Donard (853m).

Activities

Life Adventure Centre OUTDOOR ACTIVITIES
(☎4377 0714; www.onegreatadventure.com; Grange Courtyard, Castlewellan Forest Park) If you fancy a shot at hill walking, rock climbing, canoeing or a range of other outdoor activities, this centre offers one-day, have-a-go sessions for individuals, couples and families (around £60 to £100 per person), as well as Sunday-afternoon taster sessions. It also rents canoes for £30/45 per half-day/day.

Hotrock ROCK CLIMBING
(☎4372 5354; www.hotrockwall.com; Tollymore National Outdoor Centre; adult/child £4.50/2.50; ⏲10am-5pm Mon, to 10pm Tue-Fri, to 6pm Sat & Sun) If the weather is wet, you can still go rock climbing at this indoor climbing wall; you can hire rock boots and harness for £3.50. The entrance is on the B180, 2km west of the Tollymore Forest Park exit gate.

Surfin' Dirt ADVENTURE SPORTS
(☎07739 210119; www.surfindirt.co.uk; Tullyree Rd, Bryansford; ⏲10am-6pm Tue-Sun Jul & Aug, 11am-6pm Sat & Sun Apr-Jun & Sep-Nov) A three-hour beginner's session, including board, safety gear and instruction, at this mountain-boarding track costs £17.50. It's off the B180, 3km west of Bryansford village.

Mount Pleasant HORSE RIDING
(☎4377 8651; www.mountpleasantcentre.com; Bannonstown Rd, Castlewellan; per hr £12-15) More sedate outdoor activities are offered by this horse-riding and pony-trekking centre, which caters for both experienced riders and beginners, and offers various guided treks into the park. Short rides, beach rides and pony trekking can also be arranged.

Mourne Cycle Tours CYCLING
(☎4372 4348; www.mournecycletours.com; 13 Spelga Ave, Newcastle) Provides mountain- and touring-bike hire (from £10/15/80 per half-day/day/week) and can arrange self-guided tours and family cycling weekends, including accommodation.

Festivals & Events

The Mournes are the venue for various hiking festivals, including the **Mourne International Walking Festival** (www.mournewalking.co.uk) in late June, and the **Down District Walking Festival** in early August.

Sleeping

Meelmore Lodge HOSTEL £
(☎4372 6657; www.meelmorelodge.co.uk; 52 Trassey Rd, Bryansford; campsites per adult/child £5/2.50, dm/tw £22/58; P) Set on the northern slopes of the Mournes, 5km west of Bryansford village, Meelmore has hostel accommodation with a cosy lounge and kitchen, a campsite (campervans £15, but no electrical hook-ups) and a good coffee shop.

Cnocnafeola Centre HOSTEL £
(☎4176 5859; www.mournehostel.com; Bog Rd, Atticall; dm/tw/f £20/55/80; P@) This modern, purpose-built hostel is in the village of Atticall, 6km north of Kilkeel, off the B27 Hilltown road, and 3km west of the entrance to Silent Valley. As well as a self-catering kitchen, there's a restaurant that serves breakfast, lunch and dinner.

Getting There & Away

In July and August only, the Ulsterbus 405 **Mourne Rambler** service runs a circular route from Newcastle, calling at a dozen stops around the Mournes, including Bryansford (8 minutes), Meelmore (17 minutes), Silent Valley (40 minutes), Carrick Little (45 minutes) and Bloody Bridge (one hour). There are six buses daily – the first leaves at 9.30am, the last at 5pm; a £5.50 all-day ticket allows you to get on and off as many times as you like.

Bus 34A (July and August only) runs from Newcastle to the Silent Valley car park (45 minutes, two daily), calling at Donard Park (five minutes) and Bloody Bridge (10 minutes).

Mournes Coast Road

The scenic drive south along the A2 coast road from Newcastle to Newry is the most memorable journey in Down. Annalong, Kilkeel and Rostrevor offer convenient stopping points from which you can detour into the mountains.

ANNALONG

The harbour at the fishing village of Annalong (Áth na Long) desperately wants to be picturesque, with an early 19th-century **Corn Mill** (☎4376 8736; Marine Park; adult/child £2.10/1.20) overlooking the river mouth on one side; call to check opening times. The effect is spoiled a bit by graffiti and ugly buildings on the other side.

The **Harbour Inn** (www.harbourinnannalong.co.uk; 6 Harbour Dr; bar mains £6-10, restaurant £12-22; meals 12.30-2.30pm, 5-8pm Sun-Fri, 12.30-9pm Sat;) has an attractive lounge bar with sofas arranged along picture windows beside the harbour, and an upstairs restaurant with a great view of the Mournes.

ROSTREVOR

Rostrevor (Caislean Ruairi) is a pretty Victorian seaside resort famed for its lively pubs. Each year in late July, folk musicians converge on the village for the **Fiddler's Green International Festival** (www.fiddlersgreenfestival.co.uk).

Most of the town's other noted pubs also have regular live music on offer. The best ones to eat in are the **Kilbroney** (31 Church St) and the **Celtic Fjord** (8 Mary St).

To the east is **Kilbroney Forest Park** (Shore Rd; admission free; 9am-10pm Jun-Aug, to 5pm Sep-May). From the car park at the top of the forest drive, a 10-minute hike leads up to a superb view over the lough to Carlingford Mountain, as well as to the **Cloughmore Stone**, a 30-tonne granite boulder inscribed with Victorian-era graffiti.

WARRENPOINT

POP 7000

Warrenpoint (An Pointe) is a Victorian resort at the head of Carlingford Lough, its seaside appeal somewhat diminished by the large industrial harbour at the west end of town. Its broad streets, main square and renovated prom are pleasant enough though, and it has better sleeping and eating options than either Newry or Rostrevor, including a couple of excellent restaurants.

About 2km northwest of the town centre is **Narrow Water Castle** (admission free; 10am-6pm Fri Jul & Aug), a fine Elizabethan tower house built in 1568 to command the entrance to the River Newry.

Sleeping & Eating

Whistledown Hotel HOTEL ££

(4175 4174; www.thewhistledownhotel.com; 6 Seaview; s/d £80/120;) This former guesthouse on the waterfront has been given a boutique-style makeover, with scarlet and pistachio crushed-velvet, bathrooms with triple shower heads and large flat-screen TVs. It also has a stylish bar and **bistro** (mains £10-20; noon-10pm).

TOP CHOICE **Restaurant 23** IRISH ££

(4175 3222; 13 Seaview; mains lunch £8-10, dinner £14-23; lunch & dinner) Set in the Balmoral Hotel on Warrenpoint's waterfront, this innovative restaurant has garnered a Michelin Bib Gourmand and helped turn this corner of County Down into a foodie destination with dishes such as roast scallops with crisp smoked pork and artichoke salad, and sautéed lambs liver with new season asparagus. From Wednesday to Friday there's a three-course set menu for £15.

Information

Tourist office (4175 2256; Church St; 9am-1pm & 2-5pm Mon-Fri, plus Sat & Sun Jun-Sep) In the town hall.

Getting There & Away

Bus 39 runs between Newry and Warrenpoint (£2, 20 minutes, at least hourly Monday to Saturday, 10 on Sunday), with some services continuing on to Kilkeel (one hour).

Newry

POP 22,975

Newry has long been a frontier town, guarding the land route from Dublin to Ulster through the 'Gap of the North', the pass between Slieve Gullion and the Carlingford hills, still followed by the main Dublin–Belfast road and railway. Its name derives from a yew tree (An tIúr) supposedly planted here by St Patrick.

The opening of the Newry Canal in 1742, linking the town with the River Bann at Portadown, made Newry a busy trading port, exporting coal from Coalisland on Lough Neagh, as well as linen and butter from the surrounding area.

Newry today is a major shopping centre, with a busy market on Thursday and Saturday; it's invaded at weekends by shoppers from the South taking advantage of the euro exchange rate and the relative bargains available across the border.

Sights

FREE **Newry and Mourne Museum** MUSEUM

(www.bagenalscastle.com; Bagenal's Castle, Castle St; 10am-4.30pm Mon-Sat, 1-4.30pm Sun) With exhibits on the Newry Canal and local archaeology, culture and folklore, the museum is housed in Bagenal's Castle, the town's oldest surviving building. Recently rediscovered, having been incorporated into more recent buildings, the 16th-century tower house was built for Nicholas Bagenal, grand marshal of the English army in Ireland. The castle also houses the tourist office.

Canals LANDMARK

The **Newry Canal** runs parallel to the river through the town centre, and is a focus for the city's redevelopment. A cycle path runs 30km north to Portadown, following the route of the canal.

Newry Ship Canal runs 6km south towards Carlingford Lough, where the Victoria Lock has been restored to working order as part of a long-term project to reopen the whole canal to leisure traffic. Designed by Sir John Rennie, the civil engineer who designed Waterloo, Southwark and London bridges in London, the ship canal allowed large, sea-going vessels to reach Albert Basin in the centre of Newry.

Sleeping

Marymount B&B ££

(☎3026 1099; patricia.ohare2@btinternet.com; Windsor Ave; s/d £35/60; P) A modern bungalow in a quiet location up a hill off the A1 Belfast road, Marymount is only a 10-minute walk from the town centre. Only one of the three bedrooms comes with a private bathroom.

Canal Court Hotel HOTEL £££

(☎3025 1234; www.canalcourthotel.com; Merchants Quay; s/d from £80/140; P@) You can't miss this huge yellow building opposite the bus station. Although it's a modern hotel, it affects a deliberately old-fashioned atmosphere, with leather sofas dotted around the vast wood-panelled lobby and a restaurant that veers dangerously close to chintzy.

Eating & Drinking

Copper IRISH ££

(☎3026 7772; www.copperrestaurant.co.uk; 9 Monaghan St; mains £9-22; noon-3pm Tue-Sat, 5-9.30pm Tue-Thu, 5-10.30pm Fri & Sat, noon-8.30pm Sun) Recently relocated from Warrenpoint, Copper is an elegant, white-linen-tablecloth kind of restaurant that serves meat sourced from local farms and fish bought from the quayside at Kilkeel, with simplicity and integrity. There's a separate vegetarian menu with inventive dishes such as roast squash grating with confit tomatoes.

Café Krem CAFE £

(14 Hill St; mains £3-5; 8.30am-6pm Mon-Sat;) A friendly, community atmosphere and the best coffee in town make Café Krem stand out from the crowd. There's also wicked hot chocolate, tasty soups, sandwiches, pasta and panini, and a couple of big, soft sofas to sink into.

Brass Monkey PUB ££

(1-4 Sandy St; mains £8-16; bar meals noon-9pm Mon-Sat, 12.30-8.30pm Sun) Newry's most popular pub, with Victorian brass, brick and timber decor, serves good bar meals ranging from lasagne and burgers to seafood and steaks. At weekends you can get a full Irish fried breakfast for £5 (9am till noon).

Information

Tourist office (☎3031 3170; newrytic@newryandmourne.gov.uk; Bagenal's Castle, Castle St; 9am-5pm Mon-Fri, plus 10am-4pm Sat Apr-Sep, closed 1-2pm Oct-Mar)

Getting There & Away

Bus

Newry BusCentre is on the Mall, opposite the Canal Court Hotel. Goldline Express bus 238 runs regularly to Newry from Belfast's Europa BusCentre (£8, 1¼ hours, at least hourly Monday to Saturday, eight Sunday) via Hillsborough and Banbridge.

Bus 44 runs from Newry to Armagh (£5, 1¼ hours, twice daily Monday to Saturday), and Goldline Express bus 295 goes from Newry to Enniskillen (£9, 2¾ hours, twice daily Monday to Saturday, July and August only) via Armagh and Monaghan. Bus 39 departs for Warrenpoint (20 minutes, at least hourly Monday to Saturday, 10 on Sunday) and Rostrevor (30 minutes).

Train

The train station is 2.5km northwest of the centre, on the A25; bus 341 (free for train passengers) goes there hourly from the bus station. Newry is a stop on the train service between Dublin (£19, 1¼ hours, eight daily) and Belfast (£10, 50 minutes, eight daily).

COUNTY ARMAGH

South Armagh

Rural and staunchly Republican, South Armagh is known to its inhabitants as 'God's Country'. But to the British soldiers stationed there in the 1970s it had another, more sinister nickname – 'Bandit Country'. With the Republic only a few miles away, South Armagh was a favourite area for IRA cross-border attacks and bombings. For more than 30 years, British soldiers on foot patrol in village streets and the constant clatter of army helicopters were a part of everyday life.

The peace process has probably had more visible effect here than anywhere else in Northern Ireland. As part of the UK government's 'normalisation process', the army pulled out in 2007 – the hilltop watchtowers have been removed (their former location marked here and there by a defiant Irish tricolour) and the huge barracks at Bessbrook Mill and Crossmaglen have been closed down.

Hopefully, a part of Ireland that was once notorious for its violence will again be known for its historic sites, enchanting rural scenery and traditional music.

BESSBROOK

POP 3150

Bessbrook (An Sruthán) was founded in the mid-19th century by Quaker linen manufacturer John Grubb Richardson as a 'model village' to house the workers at his flax mill. Rows of pretty terraced houses made from local granite line the two main squares, Charlemont and College, each with a green in the middle, and are complemented by a town hall, school, bathhouse and dispensary. It is said that Bessbrook was the inspiration for Bournville (near Birmingham in England), the model village built by the Cadbury family for their chocolate factory.

At the centre of the village is the massive **Bessbrook Mill**. Requisitioned by the British Army in 1970, it served as a military base for more than 30 years – the helipad here was reputedly the busiest in Europe – until the troops moved out in 2007. Planning permission has been granted to convert the mill building into a residential complex.

Just south of Bessbrook is **Derrymore House** (www.ntnni.org.uk; house tour £3.70; ⏲gardens 10am-6pm May-Sep, to 4pm Oct-Apr), an elegant thatched cottage built in 1776 for Isaac Corry, the Irish MP for Newry for 30 years; the Act of Union was drafted in the drawing room here in 1800. The house is only open on a handful of days each year – call or check the website – but the surrounding parkland, laid out by John Sutherland (1745–1826), one of the most celebrated disciples of English landscape gardener Capability Brown, offers scenic trails with views to the Ring of Gullion.

Bessbrook is 5km northwest of Newry. Bus 41 runs from Newry to Bessbrook (15 minutes, hourly Monday to Saturday), while buses 42 (to Crossmaglen) and 44 (to Armagh) pass the entrance to Derrymore House on the A25 Camlough road.

RING OF GULLION

The Ring of Gullion is a magical region steeped in Celtic legend, centred on Slieve Gullion (Sliabh gCuilinn; 576m), where the Celtic warrior Cúchulainn is said to have taken his name after killing the dog *(cú)* belonging to the smith Culainn. The 'ring' is a necklace of rugged hills strung between Newry and Forkhill, 15km to the southwest, encircling the central whaleback ridge of Slieve Gullion. This unusual concentric formation is a geological structure known as a ring dyke.

Killevy Churches — HISTORIC SITE

(admission free; ⏲24hr) Surrounded by beech trees, these ruined, conjoined **churches** were constructed on the site of a 5th-century nunnery that was founded by St Moninna. The eastern church dates from the 15th century, and shares a gable wall with the 12th-century western one. The west door, with a massive lintel and granite jambs, may be 200 years older still. At the side of the churchyard, a footpath leads uphill to a white cross that marks St Moninna's holy well.

The churches are 6km south of Camlough, on a minor road to Meigh. Look out for a crossroads with a sign pointing west to the churches and east to Bernish Rock Viewpoint.

Slieve Gullion Forest Park — PARK

(admission free; ⏲8am-dusk) A 13km scenic drive through this **forest park** provides picturesque views over the surrounding hills. From the parking and picnic area at the top of the drive, you can hike to the summit of Slieve Gullion, the highest point in County Armagh, topped by two early Bronze Age cairns and a tiny lake (1.5km round trip). The park entrance is 10km southwest of Newry on the B113 road to Forkhill.

CROSSMAGLEN

POP 1600

Crossmaglen (Crois Mhic Lionnáin), arranged around one of Ireland's biggest market squares, is a strongly Republican village just 4km inside the border. At the height of the Troubles, the barracks at 'Cross' (or 'XMG', as it was known) was the most feared posting in the British Army.

Now the army has gone, and for today's visitors Crossmaglen is a friendly place with a reputation for Gaelic football (Crossmaglen Rangers were the All-Ireland Club Champions in 2011, and Ulster champions in 2010 and 2011), horse breeding and lively pubs known for their excellent music sessions.

You can get tourist information at **RoSA** (☎3086 8900; 25-26 O'Fiaich Sq; ⏰9am-5pm Mon-Fri).

Murtagh's Bar (☎3086 1378; aidanmurtagh@hotmail.com; 13 North St; s/d £30/50) offers good craic, traditional music, bar meals and B&B, while the modern **Cross Square Hotel** (☎3086 0505; www.crosssquarehotel.com; 4-5 O'Fiaich Sq; s/d £45/70, mains £7-12; ⏰meals 9am-9pm) serves bar meals all day and an à la carte menu at lunch and dinner. There's live music on Friday, Saturday and Sunday nights.

Bus 42 runs from Newry to Crossmaglen (£4, 50 minutes, five daily Monday to Friday, four Saturday) via Camlough and Mullaghbane.

Armagh City

POP 14,600

The little cathedral city of Armagh (Ard Macha) has been an important religious centre since the 5th century, and remains the ecclesiastical capital of Ireland, the seat of both the Anglican and Roman Catholic archbishops of Armagh, and Primates of All Ireland. Their two cathedrals, both named for St Patrick, stare each other out from their respective hilltops.

Despite having a number of attractive Georgian buildings, the town has a bit of a dreary, rundown feel to it, with gap sites, wasteland and boarded-up windows spoiling the streetscape, but it's still worth a visit for the fascinating Armagh Public Library and nearby Navan Fort.

History

When St Patrick began his mission to spread Christianity throughout Ireland, he chose a site close to Emain Macha (Navan Fort), the nerve centre of pagan Ulster, for his power base. In 445 he built Ireland's first stone church on a hill nearby (now home to the Church of Ireland cathedral), and later decreed that Armagh should have preeminence over all the churches in Ireland.

By the 8th century Armagh was one of Europe's best-known centres of religion, learning and craftwork. The city was divided into three districts (called *trians*), centred around English, Scottish and Irish streets. Armagh's fame was its undoing, however, as the Vikings plundered the city 10 times between 831 and 1013.

The city gained a new prosperity from the linen trade in the 18th century, a period whose legacy includes a Royal School, an astronomical observatory, a renowned public library and a fine crop of Georgian architecture.

Armagh is associated with some prominent historical figures. James Ussher (1580–1655), Archbishop of Armagh, was an avid scholar who is best known for pinning down the day of the Creation to Sunday 23 October 4004 BC by adding up the generations quoted in the Bible, a date that was accepted as fact until the late 19th century. His extensive library became the nucleus of the great library at Trinity College, Dublin. Jonathan Swift (1667–1745), Dean of St Patrick's Cathedral in Dublin, and author of *Gulliver's Travels,* was a frequent visitor to Armagh, while the architect Francis Johnston (1760–1829), responsible for many of Dublin's finest Georgian streetscapes, was born in the city.

Sights

FREE **Armagh Public Library** MUSEUM

(www.armaghrobinsonlibrary.org; 43 Abbey St; guided tour £2; ⏰10am-1pm & 2-4pm Mon-Fri) The Greek inscription above the main entrance to Armagh Public Library, founded in 1771 by Archbishop Robinson, means 'the medicine shop of the soul'. Step inside and you'd swear that the archbishop had just swept out of the door, leaving you to browse among his personal collection of 17th- and 18th-century books, maps and engravings.

The library's most prized possession is a first edition of *Gulliver's Travels,* published in 1726 and annotated by none other than Swift himself. It was stolen in an armed robbery in 1999, but was recovered, undamaged, in Dublin 20 months later.

Other treasures of the library include Sir Walter Raleigh's 1614 *History of the World,* the *Claims of the Innocents* (pleas to Oliver Cromwell) and a large collection of engravings by Hogarth and others.

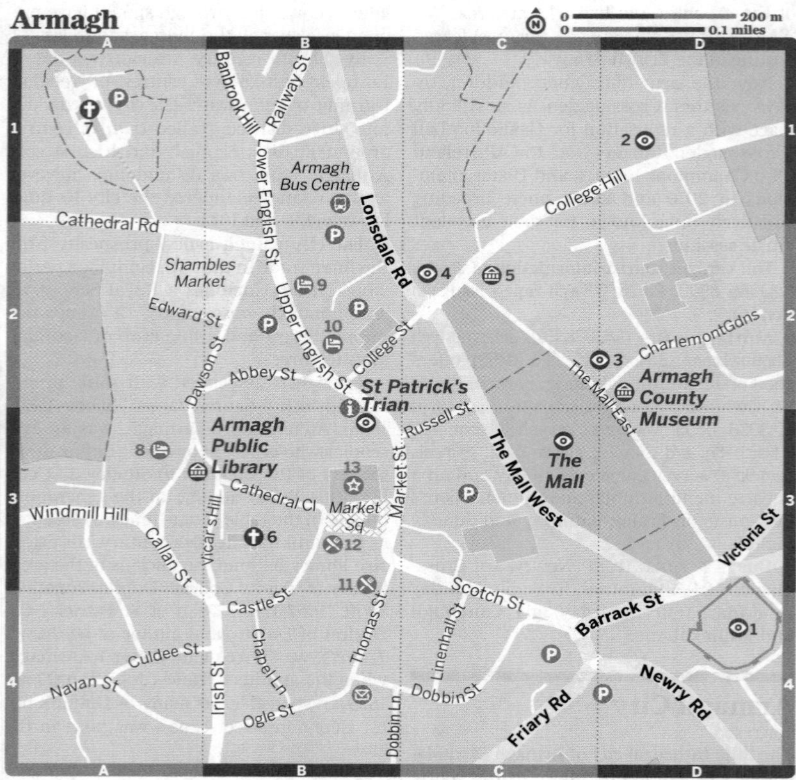

The Mall PARK

The Mall, to the east of the town centre, was a venue for horse racing, cock fighting and bull baiting until the 18th century, when Archbishop Robinson decided that it was all a tad vulgar for a city of learning, and transformed it into an elegant Georgian park.

At its northern end stands **Armagh Courthouse**, rebuilt after being destroyed by a huge IRA bomb blast in 1993. It originally dates from 1809, designed by local man Francis Johnston, who later became one of Ireland's most famous architects. At the southern end, directly opposite the courthouse, is the forbidding **Armagh Gaol**. Built in 1780 to the design of Thomas Cooley, it remained in use until 1988; there are plans to redevelop it into a hotel, shopping mall and heritage centre.

The east side of the park is lined with handsome Georgian terraces including **Charlemont Place**, another creation of Francis Johnston.

FREE **Armagh County Museum** MUSEUM

(www.armaghcountymuseum.org.uk; The Mall East; ⏲10am-5pm Mon-Fri, 10am-1pm & 2-5pm Sat) The city museum displays prehistoric axe heads, items found in bogs, corn dollies and straw-boy outfits, and military costumes and equipment. Don't miss the gruesome cast-iron skull that once graced the top of the Armagh gallows.

FREE **Royal Irish Fusiliers Museum** MUSEUM

(The Mall East; ⏲10am-12.30pm & 1.30-4pm Mon-Fri) Near the county museum, the Royal Irish Fusiliers Museum tells the story of the 'Eagle Takers', the first regiment to capture one of Bonaparte's imperial eagle standards in 1811.

Armagh

St Patrick's Trian HERITAGE CENTRE

(40 Upper English St; adult/child £5/3.25; ⏲10am-5pm Mon-Sat, 2-5pm Sun) The old Presbyterian church behind the tourist office has been turned into a heritage centre and visitor complex known as St Patrick's Trian. There are three exhibitions: the **Armagh Story** explores the history of Armagh from pagan prehistory to the present day; **Patrick's Testament** takes an interactive look at the ancient *Book of Armagh;* and for the kids there's the **Land of Lilliput**, where Gulliver's adventures in Lilliput are recounted by a gigantic model of Jonathan Swift's famous creation.

St Patrick's Church of Ireland Cathedral CATHEDRAL

(www.stpatricks-cathedral.org; Cathedral Close; admission by donation; ⏲9am-5pm Apr-Oct, to 4pm Nov-Mar) The city's Anglican cathedral occupies the site of St Patrick's original stone church. The present cathedral's ground plan is 13th century but the building itself is a Gothic restoration dating from 1834 to 1840. A stone slab on the exterior wall of the north transept marks the **burial place of Brian Ború**, the high king of Ireland, who died near Dublin during the last great battle against the Vikings in 1014.

Within the church are the remains of an 11th-century **Celtic Cross** that once stood nearby, and the **Tandragee Idol**, a curious granite figure dating back to the Iron Age. In the south aisle is a **memorial to Archbishop Richard Robinson** (1709–94), who founded Armagh's observatory and public library. Guided tours, which should be arranged in advance, cost £3 per person.

St Patrick's Roman Catholic Cathedral CATHEDRAL

(www.armagharchdiocese.org; Cathedral Rd; admission by donation; ⏲9am-6pm Mon-Fri, to 8pm Sat, 8am-6.30pm Sun) The other St Patrick's Cathedral was built between 1838 and 1873 in Gothic Revival style, with huge twin towers dominating the approach up flight after flight of steps. Inside it seems almost Byzantine, with every piece of wall and ceiling covered in brilliantly coloured mosaics. The sanctuary was modernised in 1981 and has a very distinctive tabernacle holder and crucifix that seem out of place among the mosaics and statues of the rest of the church. Mass is said at 10am Monday to Friday, and at 9am, 11am and 5.30pm on Sunday.

Armagh Planetarium PLANETARIUM

(www.armaghplanet.com; College Hill; admission to exhibition area per person £2, shows adult/child £6/5; ⏲10am-5pm Mon-Sat) The Armagh Observatory was founded by Archbishop Robinson in 1790 and is still Ireland's leading astronomical research institute. Aimed mainly at educating young people, the nearby Armagh Planetarium has an interactive exhibition on space exploration, and a digital theatre that screens a range of spectacular half-hour shows on its domed ceiling (check website for show times).

Festivals & Events

Apple Blossom Fair FOOD & DRINK

(www.armaghbramley.com) Held on the first Saturday in May at Loughgall Manor Estate (10km northeast of Armagh) in the heart of orchard country. Orchard tours, farmers market, cookery demonstrations and stalls selling all kinds of apple-based products.

Road Bowling SPORT

(www.irishroadbowling.ie) You may be lucky enough to catch a road bowling match, a traditional Irish game now played mostly in Armagh and Cork. Contestants hurl small metal bowls weighing approximately 800g along quiet country lanes to see who can make it to the finishing line with the least number of throws. Games usually take place on Sunday afternoons in summer, with the Ulster Finals held at Armagh in late June. Ask for details at the tourist information centre.

Sleeping

De Averell House B&B ££

(☎3751 1213; www.deaverellhouse.net; 47 Upper English St; s/d/f £45/75/100; P) A converted Georgian town house with five spacious rooms and a self-catering apartment, the De Averell is run by a friendly landlord who can't do enough to help. Rooms at the front can be noisy; the twin at the back is the quietest.

Charlemont Arms Hotel HOTEL ££

(☎3752 2028; www.charlemontarmshotel.com; 57-65 Lower English St; s/d £55/90; P) This hotel dates from the 19th century and has been renovated in charming period decor – oak-panelled dining room, Victorian fireplaces and flagstone-floored cellar restaurant. The bedrooms, in contrast, are modern and stylish.

Armagh City Hostel HOSTEL £

(☎3751 1800; www.hini.org.uk; 39 Abbey St; dm/tw £18/38; daily Mar-Oct, Fri & Sat only Nov-Feb, closed 23 Dec-2 Jan; P) This modern, purpose-built hostel near the Church of Ireland cathedral is more like a small hotel – there are six comfortable twin rooms with private bathrooms, TV and tea-and-coffee facilities, as well as 12 small dorms, a well-equipped kitchen, laundry, lounge and reading room.

Hillview Lodge B&B ££

(☎3752 2000; www.hillviewlodge.com; 33 Newtownhamilton Rd; s/d £38/58; P) Hillview, 1.5km south of Armagh, is a welcoming, family-run guesthouse with a self-contained block containing six appealing rooms with great countryside views. And there's a driving range next door if you feel like improving your golf swing.

Eating

TOP CHOICE **Uluru Bistro** FUSION ££

(☎3751 8051; www.ulurubistro.co.uk; 16-18 Market St; mains lunch £7, dinner £15-20; noon-3pm Tue-Sat, 5-10.30pm Tue-Sun) The Aussie chef at Uluru brings a bit of antipodean flair to Armagh, with a fusion menu that ranges from salt 'n' chilli tempura prawns to chargrilled medallions of marinated kangaroo with sweet-potato chips, plus Irish steak, seafood and venison dishes.

Footlights Bar & Bistro CAFE £

(Market Place Theatre, Market Sq; mains £7-13; cafe 10am-5pm Mon-Sat, dinner 5-9pm Wed-Sat) This stylish little place is a chilled-out haven of coffee- and cream-coloured sofas and chairs in the theatre lobby, with a familiar menu of comfort food such as beef burgers, chicken Caesar salad and duck spring rolls.

Café Papa CAFE £

(15 Thomas St; mains £3-8; 9am-5.30pm Mon-Sat, 6-9pm Fri & Sat) This deli-cum-cafe serves good coffee, cakes, home-baked bread and gourmet sandwiches. It also does bistro dinners on Friday and Saturday evenings when you can bring your own wine.

Entertainment

Market Place Theatre & Arts Centre THEATRE

(www.marketplacearmagh.com; Market St; box office 9.30am-4.30pm Mon-Sat) Armagh's main cultural venue hosts a 400-seat theatre, exhibition galleries and the Footlights Bar & Bistro, which has live bands on Saturday nights.

Armagh Omniplex CINEMA

(www.omniplex.ie; Market St) Four-screen cinema next door to the arts centre.

Information

Armagh City Library (Market St; 9.30am-5.30pm Mon, Wed & Fri, to 8pm Tue & Thu, to 5pm Sat) Internet access for £1.50 per 30 minutes.

Tourist office (☎3752 1800; www.visitarmagh.com; 40 Upper English St; 9am-5pm Mon-Sat, 2-5pm Sun, from noon Sun Jul & Aug) Part of the St Patrick's Trian complex.

Getting There & Away

Goldline Express bus 251 runs from Belfast's Europa BusCentre (£8, one to 1½ hours, hourly Monday to Friday, six Saturday, four Sunday) to Armagh. Bus 44 runs from Armagh

WORTH A TRIP

OXFORD ISLAND

Oxford Island National Nature Reserve protects a range of habitats – woodland, wildflower meadows, reedy shoreline and shallow lake margins – on the southern edge of Lough Neagh. It's criss-crossed with walking trails, information boards and birdwatching hides.

The **Lough Neagh Discovery Centre** (www.oxfordisland.com; Oxford Island, Lurgan; admission free; ⏲10am-1pm & 2-4pm Mon-Sat), set in the middle of a reed-fringed pond inhabited by waterfowl, has a tourist information desk, a museum and a great little cafe with lake-shore views.

One-hour **boat trips** (adult/child £5/2.50; ⏲1.30-5pm Sat & Sun Apr-Oct) on the lough depart from nearby Kinnego Marina, aboard the 12-seater cabin cruiser *Master McGra*.

Oxford Island is just north of Lurgan, signposted from Junction 10 on the M1 motorway.

to Newry (£5, 1¼ hours, twice daily Monday to Saturday), and Goldline Express 295 runs to Enniskillen (£7, two hours, twice daily Monday to Saturday, July and August only) via Monaghan.

Armagh is a stop on the once-daily bus 278 from Coleraine to Monaghan (change here for Dublin) and the once-daily bus 270 from Belfast to Galway.

Around Armagh City

NAVAN FORT

Perched atop a drumlin a little over 3km west of Armagh is Navan Fort (Emain Macha), the most important archaeological site in Ulster. It was probably a prehistoric provincial capital and ritual site, on a par with Tara in County Meath. The site is linked in legend with the tales of Cúchulainn and named as capital of Ulster and the seat of the legendary Knights of the Red Branch.

It was an important centre from around 1150 BC until the coming of Christianity; the discovery of the skull of a Barbary ape on the site indicates trading links with North Africa. The main circular earthwork enclosure is no less than 240m in diameter, and encloses a smaller circular structure and an Iron Age burial mound. The circular structure has intrigued archaeologists – it appears to be some sort of temple, whose roof was supported by concentric rows of wooden posts, and whose interior was filled with a vast pile of stones. Stranger still, the whole thing was set on fire soon after its construction around 95 BC, possibly for ritual purposes.

The nearby **Navan Centre** (www.navan.com; 81 Killylea Rd, Armagh; adult/child £6/4; ⏲10am-7pm Apr-Sep, to 4pm Oct-Mar) has exhibitions placing the fort in its historical context, and a recreation of an Iron Age settlement.

You can walk to the site from Armagh (45 minutes), or you can take bus 73 to Navan village (10 minutes, 10 daily Monday to Friday).

LOUGH NEAGH

Lough Neagh (pronounced 'nay') is the largest freshwater lake in all of Britain and Ireland, big enough to swallow the city of Birmingham (West Midlands, UK, or Alabama, USA – either one would fit). Though vast (around 32km long and 16km wide), the lough is relatively shallow – never more than 9m deep – and is an important habitat for waterfowl. Its waters are home to the pollan, a freshwater herring found only in Ireland, and the dollaghan, a subspecies of trout unique to Lough Neagh. Connected to the sea by the River Bann, the lough has been an important waterway and food source since prehistoric times, and still has an eel fishery that employs around 200 people.

The main points of access to the lough include Antrim Town (p669) on the eastern shore, Oxford Island (p633) in the south and Ardboe (p688) in the west.

The **Loughshore Trail** (www.loughshoretrail.com) is a 180km cycle route that encircles the lough. For most of its length it follows quiet country roads set back from the shore; the best sections for actually seeing the lough itself are west of Oxford Island and south from Antrim town.

Counties Derry & Antrim

POPULATION: 532,000 / AREA: 4918 SQ KM

Includes »

Best Places to Eat

- » Halo Pantry & Grill (p645)
- » Lime Tree (p649)
- » Preference Brasserie (p652)
- » 55 Degrees North (p656)
- » Bushmills Inn (p657)

Best Places to Stay

- » Merchant's House (p644)
- » Downhill Hostel (p650)
- » Clarmont (p653)
- » Whitepark House (p659)
- » Villa Farmhouse (p664)

Why Go?

The north coast of Northern Ireland, from Carrickfergus to Coleraine, is like a giant geology classroom. Here the patient workmanship of the ocean has laid bare the black basalt and white chalk that underlie much of County Antrim, and dissected the rocks into a scenic extravaganza of sea stacks, pinnacles, cliffs and caves. Tourists flock to the surreal geological centrepiece of the Giant's Causeway, its popularity challenged only by the test-your-nerve tightrope of the Carrick-a-Rede rope bridge nearby.

To the west, County Derry's chief attraction is the historic city of Derry, nestled in a broad sweep of the River Foyle. It is the only surviving walled city in Ireland, and a walk around the city walls is one of the highlights of a visit to Northern Ireland. Derry's other draws include the powerful political murals in the Bogside district and the lively music scene in its many pubs.

When to Go

May is the best month for walking the Causeway Coast, as you'll avoid the summer crowds at the Giant's Causeway and enjoy a colourful sprinkling of spring flowers to boot. June and July see the peak of the seabird nesting season – an ideal time to visit the RSPB reserve on Rathlin Island – and also bring the best weather for lounging on the local beaches. The traditional festivities of the Ould Lammas Fair at Ballycastle take place on the last Monday and Tuesday of August.

COUNTY DERRY

Derry/Londonderry

POP 83,700

Northern Ireland's second city comes as a pleasant surprise to many visitors. Derry may not be the prettiest of cities, and it certainly lags behind Belfast in terms of investment and redevelopment, but it has a great riverside setting, several fascinating historical sights and a determined air of can-do optimism that has made it the powerhouse of the North's cultural revival.

In preparation for Derry's year in the limelight as **UK City of Culture 2013** (www.cityofculture2013.com), the city centre was given a makeover and an elegant new footbridge – the **Peace Bridge** – was built across the River Foyle. Confirmed events at the time of writing include a Cultural Olympiad in the run-up to the London Olympics in 2012, and the hosting of the Turner Prize in 2013.

There's lots of history to absorb here, from the Siege of Derry to the Battle of the Bogside – a stroll around the 17th-century city walls is a must, as is a tour of the Bogside murals – and the city's lively pubs are home to a burgeoning live-music scene. But perhaps the biggest attraction is the people themselves: warm, witty and welcoming.

History

The defining moment of Derry's history was the Siege of Derry in 1688–89, an event whose echoes reverberate to this day. King James I granted the city a royal charter in 1613, and gave the London livery companies (trade guilds) the task of fortifying Derry and planting the county of Coleraine (soon to be renamed County Londonderry) with Protestant settlers.

In Britain, the Glorious Revolution of 1688 saw the Catholic King James II ousted in favour of the Protestant Dutch prince, William of Orange. Derry was the only garrison in Ireland that was not held by forces loyal to King James, and so, in December 1688, Catholic forces led by the Earl of Antrim arrived on the east bank of the River Foyle, ready to seize the city. They sent emissaries to discuss terms of surrender, but in the meantime troops were being ferried across the river in preparation for an assault. On seeing this, 13 apprentice boys barred the city gates with a cry of 'There'll be no surrender!'

And so, on 7 December 1688, the Siege of Derry began. For 105 days the Protestant citizens of Derry withstood bombardment, disease and starvation (the condition of the besieging forces was not much better). By the time a relief ship burst through and broke the siege, an estimated half of the city's inhabitants had died. In the 20th century the Siege of Derry became a symbol of Ulster Protestants' resistance to rule by a Catholic Irish Republic, and 'No surrender!' remains a Loyalist battle-cry to this day.

In the 19th century Derry was one of the main ports of emigration to the USA, a fact commemorated by the sculptures of an emigrant family standing in Waterloo Pl. It also played a vital role in the transatlantic trade in linen shirts. Even now, Derry still supplies the US president with 12 free shirts every year.

Sights

WALLED CITY

Derry's walled city is Ireland's earliest example of town planning. It is thought to have been modelled on the French Renaissance town of Vitry-le-François, designed in 1545 by Italian engineer Hieronimo Marino; both are based on the grid plan of a Roman military camp, with two main streets at right angles to each other, and four city gates, one at either end of each street.

Completed in 1619, Derry's **city walls** (www.derryswalls.com) are 8m high and 9m thick, with a circumference of about 1.5km, and are the only city walls in Ireland to survive almost intact. The four original gates (Shipquay, Ferryquay, Bishop's and Butcher's) were rebuilt in the 18th and 19th centuries, when three new gates (New, Magazine and Castle) were added. Derry's nickname, the Maiden City, derives from the fact that the walls have never been breached by an invader.

The walls were built under the supervision of the Honourable The Irish Society, an organisation created in 1613 by King James and the London livery companies to fund and oversee the fortification of Derry and the plantation of the surrounding county with Protestant settlers. The society still exists today (though now its activities are mainly charitable) and it still owns Derry's city walls.

Counties Derry & Antrim Highlights

1. Discovering ancient walls, modern murals and foot-stomping music in the historic city of **Derry** (p635)

2. Surfing or body-boarding among the Atlantic breakers at beaches around **Portrush** (p653)

3. Enjoying a 16.5km hike along the spectacular **Causeway Coast** from Carrick-a-Rede to the Giant's Causeway (p662)

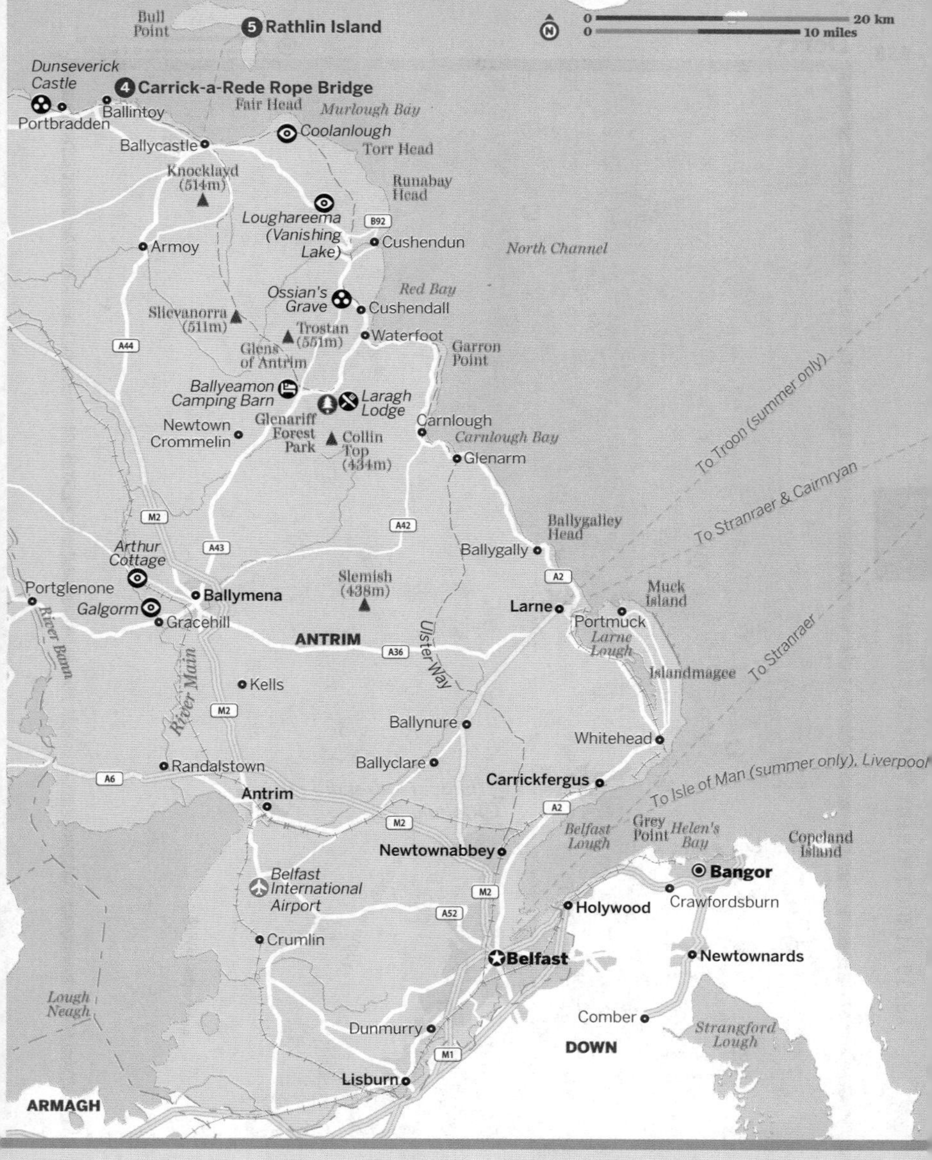

4 Testing your nerve as you wobble across the slender, swaying **Carrick-a-Rede Rope Bridge** (p659)

5 Spotting seabirds and seals at the remote western end of **Rathlin Island** (p663)

6 Learning the secrets of Irish whiskey-making on a tour of the **Old Bushmills Distillery** (p657)

7 Soaking up the spectacular coastal views from the photogenic **Mussenden Temple** (p650) at Downhill

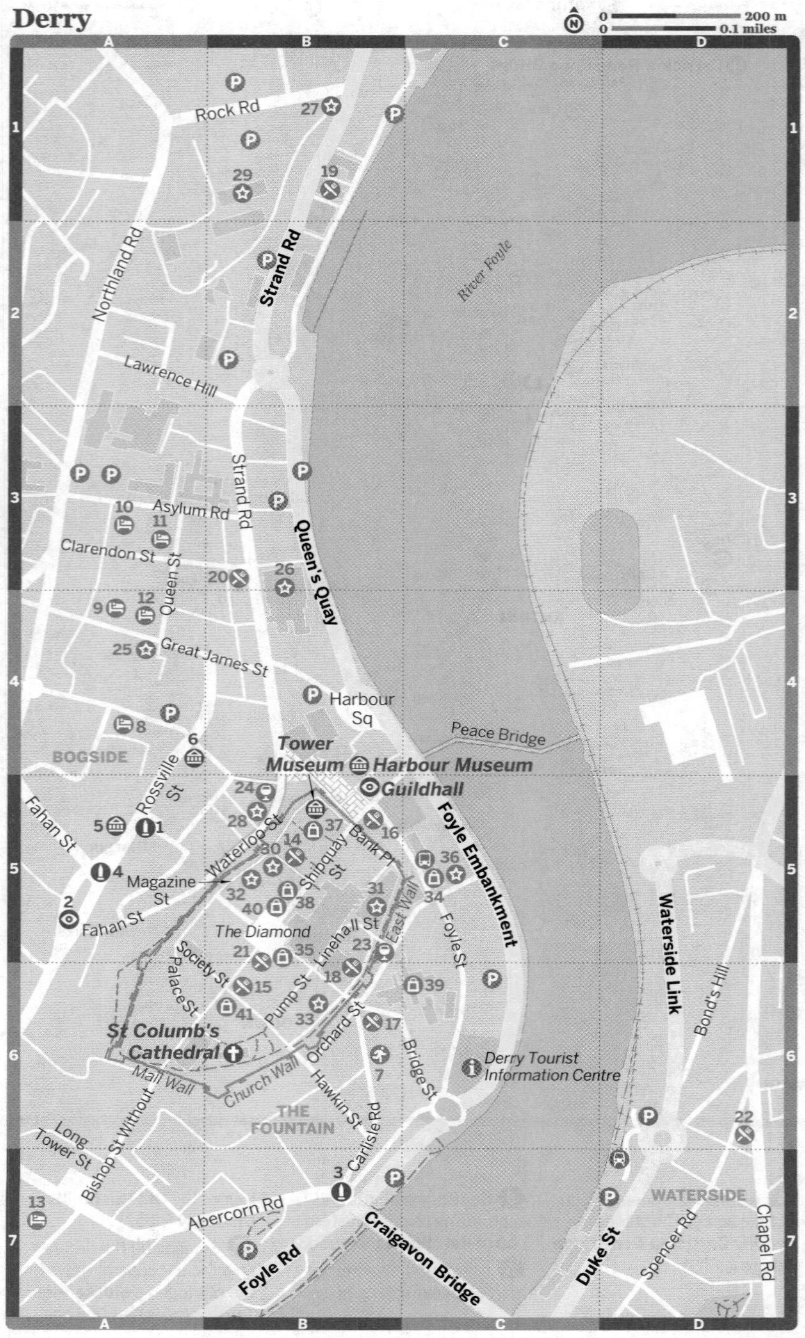
0 200 m
0 0.1 miles
Rock Rd
Strand Rd
Northland Rd
River Foyle
Lawrence Hill
Asylum Rd
Clarendon St
Queen St
Queen's Quay
Great James St
Harbour Sq
Peace Bridge
BOGSIDE
Tower Museum
Harbour Museum
Guildhall
Rossville St
Fahan St
Waterloo St
Bank Pl
Shipquay St
Magazine St
Foyle Embankment
East Wall
Foyle St
The Diamond
Lineahall St
Society St
Palace St
Pump St
Orchard St
St Columb's Cathedral
Mall Wall
Church Wall
Hawkin St
Bridge St
Derry Tourist Information Centre
THE FOUNTAIN
Carlisle Rd
Bishop St Without
Long Tower St
Abercorn Rd
Foyle Rd
Craigavon Bridge
Duke St
Waterside Link
Bond's Hill
WATERSIDE
Spencer Rd
Chapel Rd

Derry

Top Sights

	Guildhall	B5
	Harbour Museum	B4
	St Columb's Cathedral	B6
	Tower Museum	B5

Sights

1	Bloody Sunday Memorial	A5
	Bogside Artists Studio	(see 6)
2	Free Derry Corner	A5
3	Hands Across the Divide Monument	B7
4	Hunger Strikers' Memorial	A5
5	Museum of Free Derry	A5
6	People's Gallery & Studio	A4

Activities, Courses & Tours

7	City Tours	B6

Sleeping

8	Abbey B&B	A4
9	Derry City Independent Hostel	A4
10	Derry Palace Hostel	A3
11	Merchant's House	A3
12	Saddler's House	A4
13	Sunbeam House	A7

Eating

14	Boston Tea Party	B5
15	Café Artisan	B6
16	Café del Mondo	B5
	Encore Brasserie	(see 31)
17	Fitzroy's	B6
18	Halo Pantry & Grill	B6
19	Mange 2	B1
20	Sandwich Co	B3
21	Sandwich Co	B5
22	Spice	D6

Drinking

23	Badgers Bar	B5
24	Peadar O'Donnell's	B5

Entertainment

25	Cultúrlann Uí Chanáin	A4
26	Derry Omniplex	B3
27	Earth@Café Roc	B1
28	Gweedore Bar	B5
29	Magee College	B1
30	Mason's Bar	B5
31	Millennium Forum	B5
32	Nerve Centre	B5
33	Playhouse	B6
34	Sandino's Cafe-Bar	C5

Shopping

35	Austins	B5
36	Cool Discs Music	C5
37	Craft Village	B5
38	Donegal Shop	B5
39	Foyleside Shopping Centre	C6
40	McGilloway Gallery	B5
41	Whatnot	B6

Tower Museum MUSEUM

(Union Hall Pl; adult/child £4.20/2.65; ⌚10am-5pm Tue-Sat, plus 11am-3pm Sun Jul & Aug) Inside the Magazine Gate is this award-winning museum, housed in a replica 16th-century tower house. Head straight to the 5th floor for a view from the top of the tower, then work your way down through the excellent **Armada Shipwreck** exhibition, which tells the story of *La Trinidad Valenciera* – a ship of the Spanish Armada that was wrecked at Kinnagoe Bay in Donegal in 1588. It was discovered by the City of Derry Sub-Aqua Club in 1971 and excavated by marine archaeologists. On display are bronze guns, pewter tableware and personal items – a wooden comb, an olive jar, a shoe sole – recovered from the site, including a 2.5-tonne siege gun bearing the arms of Phillip II of Spain showing him as king of England.

The museum's other exhibition is the **Story of Derry**, where well-thought-out exhibits and audiovisuals lead you through city's history from the founding of the monastery of St Colmcille (Columba) in the 6th century to the Battle of the Bogside in the late 1960s. Allow a good two hours to do the museum justice.

FREE **St Columb's Cathedral** CATHEDRAL

(www.stcolumbscathedral.org; London St; admission free but donation appreciated; ⌚9am-5pm Mon-Sat year-round) Built between 1628 and 1633 from the same grey-green schist as the city walls, this was the first post-Reformation church to be erected in Britain and Ireland, and is Derry's oldest surviving building. It underwent a major restoration in 2010–11.

In the **porch** (under the spire, by the St Columb's Court entrance) you can see the original foundation stone of 1633 that records the cathedral's completion, inscribed:

> If stones could speake
> Then London's prayse
> Should sounde who
> Built this church and
> Cittie from the grounde.

The smaller stone inset, inscribed '*In Templo Verus Deus Est Vereo Colendus*' (The True God is in His Temple and is to be truly worshipped), comes from the original church built here in 1164 and dedicated to the city's patron saint, Colmcille.

Also in the porch is a hollow mortar shell fired into the churchyard during the Great Siege of 1688–89; inside the shell were the terms of surrender. The neighbouring **chapter house** contains more historical artefacts, including paintings, old photos and the four huge padlocks used to secure the city gates in the 17th century.

The **nave**, built in a squat, solid style known as Planter's Gothic, shares the austerity of many Church of Ireland cathedrals, with thick walls, small windows and an open-timbered roof (from 1823) resting on corbels depicting the heads of past bishops and deans. The bishop's throne, at the far end of the nave, is an 18th-century mahogany chair in ornate, Chinese Chippendale style.

The **chancel** and the stained-glass east window depicting the Ascension date from 1887. The flags on either side of the window were captured from the French during the Great Siege; although the yellow silk has been renewed several times since, the poles and gold wirework are original.

OUTSIDE THE WALLS

FREE Guildhall NOTABLE BUILDING

(Guildhall Sq; ⌚9am-5pm Mon-Fri) Standing just outside the city walls opposite the Tower Museum, the neo-Gothic Guildhall was originally built in 1890, then rebuilt after a fire in 1908. As the seat of the old Londonderry Corporation, which institutionalised the policy of discriminating against Catholics over housing and jobs, it incurred the wrath of Nationalists and was bombed twice by the Irish Republican Army (IRA) in 1972. From 2000 to 2005 it was the seat of the Bloody Sunday Inquiry. The Guildhall is noted for its fine stained-glass windows, presented by the London Livery companies. Guided tours are available in July and August.

FREE Harbour Museum MUSEUM

(Harbour Sq; ⌚10am-1pm & 2-5pm Mon-Fri) The small, old-fashioned Harbour Museum, with models of ships, a replica of a *currach* (an early sailing boat of the type that carried St Colmcille to Iona) and the bosomy figurehead of the *Minnehaha,* is housed in the old Harbour Commissioner's Building next to the Guildhall.

Hands Across the Divide MONUMENT

As you enter the city across Craigavon Bridge, the first thing you see is the Hands Across the Divide monument. This striking bronze sculpture of two men reaching out to each other symbolises the spirit of reconciliation and hope for the future; it was unveiled in 1992, 20 years after Bloody Sunday.

BOGSIDE

The Bogside district, to the west of the walled city, developed in the 19th and early 20th centuries as a working-class, predominantly Catholic, residential area. By the 1960s its serried ranks of small, terrace houses had become an overcrowded ghetto of poverty and unemployment, a focus for the emerging civil rights movement and a hotbed of Nationalist discontent.

In August 1969 the three-day 'Battle of the Bogside' – a running street battle between local youths and the Royal Ulster Constabulary (RUC) – prompted the UK government to send British troops into Northern Ireland. The residents of the Bogside and neighbouring Brandywell districts – 33,000 of them – declared themselves independent of the civil authorities, and barricaded the streets to keep the security forces out. 'Free Derry', as it was known, was a no-go area for the police and army, its streets patrolled by IRA volunteers. In January of 1972 the area around Rossville St witnessed the horrific events of Bloody Sunday. 'Free Derry' ended with Operation Motorman on 31 July 1972, when thousands of British troops and armoured cars moved in to occupy the Bogside.

Since then the area has been extensively redeveloped, the old houses and flats demolished and replaced with modern housing, and the population is now down to 8000. All that remains of the old Bogside is **Free Derry Corner** at the intersection of Fahan and Rossville Sts, where the gable end of a house painted with the famous slogan 'You are Now Entering Free Derry' still stands. Nearby is the H-shaped **Hunger Strikers' Memorial** and, a little further

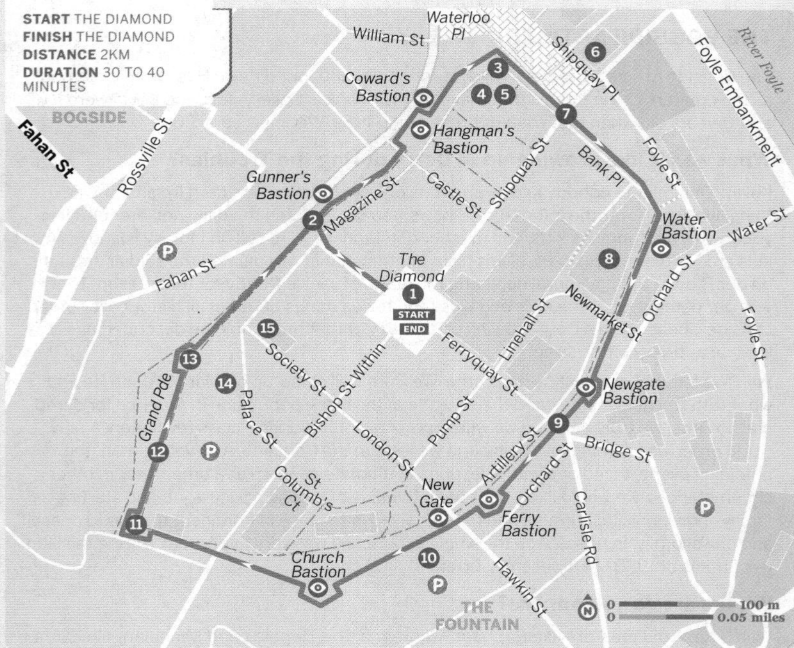

Walking Tour

Derry's Walled City

This walk starts from the Diamond, Derry's central square, dominated by the 1 **war memorial**. Head along Butcher St to 2 **Butcher's Gate** and climb the steps to the top of the city walls.

Stroll downhill to 3 **Magazine Gate**, named for the powder magazine that used to be close by. Inside the walls is the modern 4 **O'Doherty's Tower**, housing the excellent 5 **Tower Museum** (p639); outside the walls stands the red-brick, neo-gothic 6 **Guildhall** (p640).

The River Foyle used to come up to the northeastern wall here. In the middle is the 7 **Shipquay Gate**. The walls turn southwest and climb beside the 8 **Millennium Forum** (p647) to the 9 **Ferryquay Gate**, where the apprentice boys barred the gate at the start of the Great Siege of 1688-89.

The stretch of wall beyond overlooks the 10 **Fountain housing estate**, the last significant Protestant community on the western bank of the Foyle. The round, brick-paved area on the ground outside New Gate is where a 10m-high bonfire is lit on the night before the annual Apprentice Boys' march.

Continue around the southern stretch of wall to the 11 **Double Bastion** at the southwestern corner, home to Roaring Meg, the most famous of the cannons used during the Siege of Derry. The next section of wall is known as the 12 **Grand Parade**, and offers an excellent view of the murals painted by the Bogside Artists (see the boxed text, p643).

An empty plinth on 13 **Royal Bastion** marks the former site of a monument to the Reverend George Walker, joint governor of the city during the Great Siege; it was blown up by the IRA in 1973.

Behind the Royal Bastion is the 1872 Church of Ireland 14 **Chapel of St Augustine**, built on the site of St Colmcille's 6th- century monastery. A little further along is the 15 **Apprentice Boys' Memorial Hall**, with a high mesh fence to protect it from paint bombs hurled from below.

THE BOGSIDE ARTISTS

The Bogside Artists – brothers Will and Tom Kelly, and friend Kevin Hasson – are famous as the creators of the murals that make up the People's Gallery. Tom and Kevin were 10 and 11 years old when the Troubles broke out in 1969, Will in his early 20s.

What was it like growing up in Derry during the Troubles?

Kevin: 'One minute nobody knows about us or Derry or even Northern Ireland; the next thing, we are all over the international news. You could watch the daily riot later on TV in your own front room. As kids, you must understand we were still on fantasy island, as most kids are. Soldiers were, to us, aliens from another planet. We painted the soldier as such on our Bloody Sunday mural depicting the death of Jackie Duddy for that reason. That was our perception at the time and kids tend to see things bereft of all historical or other considerations. All in all, our growing up in Derry at that time could be described as very intense and very bitter-sweet.'

Will: 'We felt that our destiny had come. We were well clued-up on Marxist doctrine and, what with the riots in Paris and the struggle of the black population in America for democratic rights, we truly believed we were part of a global working-class revolution. A new world order was coming into being and we were in the front line. As a young man, the unfolding events faced one with questions of ultimate concern at a time when, in other circumstances, we would likely have been thinking of finding a secure job and starting a family. Individualistic pursuits had to be shelved in the face of imminent threats to oneself and one's family. In retrospect, the whole experience was very hyper-real. During the Hunger Strikes of 1980–81 it became surreal.'

Whose art do you admire?

Will: 'Those old masters like Raphael, Mantegna, the Tiepolos and Michelangelo cannot be equalled when it comes to mural art. Diego Rivera was summoned from Paris 20

north along Rossville St, the **Bloody Sunday Memorial**, a simple granite obelisk that commemorates the 14 civilians who were shot dead by the British Army on 30 January 1972.

People's Gallery Murals MURALS

(Rossville St) The 12 murals that decorate the gable ends of houses along Rossville St, near Free Derry Corner, are popularly referred to as the People's Gallery. They are the work of Tom Kelly, Will Kelly and Kevin Hasson, known as 'the Bogside Artists'. The three men have spent most of their lives in the Bogside, and lived through the worst of the Troubles.

Their murals, mostly painted between 1997 and 2001, commemorate key events in the Troubles, including the Battle of the Bogside, Bloody Sunday, Operation Motorman (the British Army's operation to retake IRA-controlled no-go areas in Derry and Belfast in July 1972) and the 1981 hunger strike. The most powerful images are those painted largely in monochrome, consciously evoking journalistic imagery – *Operation Motorman,* showing a British soldier breaking down a door with a sledgehammer; *Bloody Sunday,* with a group of men led by local priest Father Daly carrying the body of Jackie Duddy (the first fatality on that day); and *Petrol Bomber,* a young boy wearing a gas mask and holding a petrol bomb.

The most moving image is *The Death of Innocence,* which shows the radiant figure of 14-year-old schoolgirl Annette McGavigan, killed in crossfire between the IRA and the British Army on 6 September 1971, the 100th victim of the Troubles. Representing all the children who died in the conflict, she stands against the brooding chaos of a bombed-out building, the roof beams forming a crucifix in the top right-hand corner. At the left, a downward-pointing rifle, broken in the middle, stands for the failure of violence, while the butterfly symbolises resurrection and the hope embodied in the peace process.

The final mural in the sequence, completed in 2004, is the *Peace Mural,* a swirling image of a dove (symbol of peace and of Derry's patron saint, Columba) rising out of years or so *after* the revolution, so we are not as impressed by his work as those who have bought into the myth of Rivera as a contemporary freedom fighter. Incidentally, he did not portray Mexico's history as it was. What he did was offer a Marxist *interpretation* of that history. Not that we compare ourselves to Rivera. His body of work far exceeds our own. But we do recall one lady who came to our studio and told us that she had just returned from Mexico and considered our murals to be better than his! Go figure, as they say.'

Which of the Bogside murals means the most to you?

Tom: '*The Death of Innocence*, for me, is the one that stands out, both the pictorial content of it and the fact that it is a peace and antiwar mural painted long before any of us in Derry thought peace was even possible.'

Kevin: 'Our *Peace Mural* means most to me, as we decided to do that 10 years before we were actually able to get around to realising it. Also, it had a strong community input where both Catholic and Protestant kids worked together to help design it. The dove, in fact, is not just a cliché – it refers to our city's patron saint, St Columba, whose Latin name Columbanus means "dove".'

Will: 'They're like our children – it's unfair to single any one out at the expense of the others. That said, it would be dishonest not to admit that our first-born, *The Petrol Bomber*, is a wee bit special.'

What does Derry being the UK City of Culture 2013 mean for you?

'Where do the Bogside Artists fit in? We don't. We are outside "the loop", not that we were not asked to join. But we figured that we cannot barter our creative freedom for money or anything else. On the contrary, we will be moving into satirical murals – we will be able then to make our views seen. The best is yet to come from the Bogside Artists.'

the blood and sadness of the past towards the sunny yellow hope of a peaceful future.

The murals can be seen online at www.cain.ulst.ac.uk/bogsideartists, and in the book *The People's Gallery*, which is available from the gallery shop and the artists' website.

FREE People's Gallery & Studio ART GALLERY
(www.bogsideartists.com; cnr Rossville St & William St; 9am-6pm) Located on 'Aggro Corner', the street intersection once notorious as the kicking-off point for confrontations between Bogsiders and security forces, the Bogside Artists' gallery provides an exhibition space for local and international artists, and runs art workshops for young people. You can buy prints of the murals, and the Bogside Artists themselves are often in residence – they are happy to sign books and posters, and offer guided tours of the murals.

Museum of Free Derry MUSEUM
(www.museumoffreederry.org; 55-61 Glenfada Park; adult/child £3/2; 9.30am-4.30pm Mon-Fri, plus 1-4pm Sat Apr-Sep, 1-4pm Sun Jul-Sep) Just off Rossville St, this museum chronicles the history of the Bogside, the civil rights movement and the events of Bloody Sunday through photographs, newspaper reports, film clips and the accounts of first-hand witnesses, including some of the original photographs that inspired the murals of the People's Gallery.

 Tours

Bogside Artists Tours ART
(www.bogsideartists.com; People's Gallery & Studio, cnr Rossville & William Sts; per person £5; tours 11am, 2pm & 4pm) Guided walking tours of the famous People's Gallery murals led by the artists themselves. Best to book ahead on the website.

City Tours HISTORY
(7127 1996; www.irishtourguides.com; Carlisle Stores, 11 Carlisle Rd; adult/child £4/2) Runs one-hour Historic Derry walking tours starting from Carlisle Stores at 10am, noon and 2pm year-round. There are also tours of the Bogside and of Derry's murals.

Tours'n'Trails HISTORY
(☎7136 7000; www.toursntrails.co.uk; 44 Foyle St; adult/child £6/4) Offers 1½-hour guided walking tours of the walled city, starting from the tourist office at 11am and 3pm Monday to Saturday from April to October. The price includes admission to St Columb's Cathedral.

Festivals & Events

City of Derry Jazz Festival MUSIC
(www.cityofderryjazzfestival.com) Four days of jazz at various venues; held in early May.

Foyle Days MARITIME
(www.derrycity.gov.uk/foyledays) River-based festival in mid-June, with visiting navy ships, yacht races, boat trips, live music and shore-side street entertainment.

Gasyard Wall Féile IRISH CULTURE
A major cultural festival in August that features live music, street performers, carnival, theatre and Irish-language events.

City of Derry Guitar Festival MUSIC
(www.cityofderryguitarfestival.com) The grounds of University of Ulster host performances and master classes from guitar greats around the world in late August, including classical, acoustic, electric, flamenco and bass.

Halloween Carnival STREET ENTERTAINMENT
(www.derrycity.gov.uk/halloween) Ireland's biggest street party has the entire city dressing up and dancing in the streets from 27 to 31 October.

Foyle Film Festival CINEMA
(www.foylefilmfestival.org) This week-long event in November is the North's biggest film festival.

Sleeping

It's best to book accommodation in advance during festival events.

TOP CHOICE **Merchant's House** B&B ££
(☎7126 9691; www.thesaddlershouse.com; 16 Queen St; s £35-50, d £50-60; @ 📶) Run by the same owners as the Saddler's House, this historic, Georgian-style town house is a gem of a B&B. It has an elegant lounge and dining room with marble fireplaces and antique furniture, TV, coffee-making facilities and even bathrobes in the bedrooms (only one has a private bathroom), and homemade marmalade at breakfast. Call at the Saddler's House first to pick up a key.

Saddler's House B&B ££
(☎7126 9691; www.thesaddlershouse.com; 36 Great James St; s £35-50, d £50-60; @ 📶) Centrally located within a five-minute walk of the walled city, this friendly B&B is set in a lovely Victorian town house. All seven rooms have private bathrooms, and you get to enjoy a huge breakfast in the family kitchen.

Laburnum Lodge B&B ££
(☎7135 4221; www.laburnumlodge.com; 9 Rockfield, Madam's Bank Rd; s/d £40/55; P @ 📶) Readers impressed by the friendly welcome, spacious bedrooms and hearty breakfasts have recommended this suburban villa on a quiet street on the northern edge of town. If you don't have your own transport, the owner can pick you up from the train or bus station.

Sunbeam House B&B ££
(☎7126 3606; sunbeamhouse@hotmail.com; 147 Sunbeam Tce, Bishop St; s/d £35/60; 📶) This attractive red-brick terrace house is a five-minute walk southwest of the walled city. The four cheerfully decorated rooms are a bit on the small side, but there's nothing cramped about the hospitality – or the size of the breakfasts!

Da Vinci's Hotel HOTEL £££
(☎7127 9111; www.davincishotel.com; 15 Culmore Rd; r/ste from £90/150; P @ 📶) This sleek boutique hotel on the west bank of the Foyle is the accommodation of choice for visiting celebrities, businesspeople and politicians, offering spacious, stylish rooms and a hip cocktail bar and restaurant. It's 1.5km north of the city centre.

Derry City Independent Hostel HOSTEL £
(☎7128 0542; www.derry-hostel.co.uk; 44 Great James St; dm £12-15, d from £34; @ 📶) Run by experienced backpackers and decorated with souvenirs from their travels around the world, this small, friendly hostel is set in a Georgian town house, just a short walk northwest of the bus station.

Abbey B&B B&B ££
(☎7127 9000; www.abbeyaccommodation.com; 4 Abbey St; s/d £45/60; @ 📶) There's a warm welcome waiting at this family-run B&B just a short walk from the walled city, on the edge of the Bogside. The six rooms are stylishly decorated and include family rooms able to sleep four.

DERRY/LONDONDERRY

Derry/Londonderry is a town with two names. Nationalists always use Derry, and vandals often deface the 'London' part of the name on road signs. Staunch Unionists insist on Londonderry, which is still the city's (and county's) official name.

The settlement was originally named Doíre Calgaigh (Oak Grove of Calgach), after a pagan warrior-hero; in the 10th century it was renamed Doíre Colmcille (Oak Grove of Columba), in honour of the 6th-century saint who established the first monastic settlement here.

In the following centuries the name was shortened and anglicised to Derrie or Derry. Then in 1613, in recognition of the Corporation of London's role in the 'plantation' of northwest Ulster with Protestant settlers, Derry was granted a royal charter and both town and county were renamed Londonderry. However, people generally continued to call it Derry in everyday speech.

The name remains a touchstone for people's political views. Road signs in Northern Ireland point to Londonderry, those in the Republic point to Derry (or Doíre in Irish), and some tourism industry promotional material covers all bases, using Derry-Londonderry-Doíre.

Arkle House B&B ££
(7127 1157; www.derryhotel.co.uk; 2 Coshquin Rd; s/d £40/60; P @) Located 2km northwest of the city centre, this grand Victorian house is set in private gardens and offers five large, lush bedrooms and a private kitchen for guests to use.

Derry Palace Hostel HOSTEL £
(7130 9051; www.paddyspalace.com; 1 Woodleigh Tce, Asylum Rd; dm/tw from £13/36; P @) Part of the Ireland-wide Paddy's Palace chain, this hostel is central, comfortable and as friendly as they come. There's a sunny garden and a good party atmosphere, and the staff regularly organise nights out at local pubs with traditional music.

Eating

TOP CHOICE **Halo Pantry & Grill** INTERNATIONAL ££
(7127 1567; 5 Market St; mains lunch £6-10, dinner £9-22; Pantry noon-10pm, Grill 5-10pm) Housed over three floors of a converted shirt factory decorated with local art and photography, Halo offers light meals and snacks (including superb homemade lasagne) in the Pantry, and more formal dinners (from steak to seafood) in the upstairs Grill.

Brown's Restaurant IRISH ££
(7134 5180; 1 Bond's Hill, Waterside; mains £13-21; noon-2.30pm Tue-Fri, 5.30-10pm Tue-Sat) From the outside Brown's may not have the most promising location, over the river in Waterside, but step inside and you're in a little art deco enclave of brandy-coloured banquettes and ornate metal light fittings, with the odd Rothko print adorning the walls. The ever-changing menu is a gastronome's delight, making creative use of fresh local produce in dishes such as wood pigeon wrapped in pastry, with creamed shallots, cranberries and red wine sauce.

Encore Brasserie INTERNATIONAL ££
(7137 2492; Millennium Forum, Newmarket St; mains lunch £5, dinner £12-15; noon-3pm Mon-Sat, 5-9pm show nights;) Set in the lobby of the city's main cultural venue, the Encore is a stylish little place with friendly, efficient service and a crowd-pleasing menu of perennial favourites from chicken Caesar salad to herb-crusted salmon.

Café del Mondo CAFE £
(Craft Village, Shipquay St; mains £4-7; 8.30am-6pm Mon-Sat, 10.30am-6pm Sun) A bohemian cafe that serves excellent fairtrade coffee as well as hearty homemade soups, artisan breads and hot lunch specials that use organic, locally sourced produce.

Fitzroy's INTERNATIONAL ££
(2-4 Bridge St; mains lunch £8-9, dinner £11-17; 11am-10pm Mon-Sat, noon-8pm Sun) Informal Fitzroy's does cafe-style burger-and-chips lunches till 5.30pm, and then bistro-style dinners, including Thai chicken curry, homemade fishcakes and Mediterranean vegetable bake.

Mange 2 IRISH, FRENCH ££
(7136 1222; 110-115 Strand Rd; mains £13-23; 12.30-2.30pm Mon-Fri, noon-3.30pm Sun, 5-10pm daily) Set in a shiny, glass-fronted

venue on the riverfront, Mange 2 offers top-quality Irish produce served plain or with an Asian- or French-fusion twist – try slow-braised belly of pork with champ (potatoes mashed with spring onions), buttered cabbage and red onion jus.

Spice INTERNATIONAL ££
(162-164 Spencer Rd, Waterside; mains £10-15, steak £22; ⏲12.30-2.30pm Tue-Fri & Sun, 5.30-10pm Tue-Sat, 5-9pm Sun) If you can't decide what cuisine you fancy, this pleasantly chilled-out eatery offers a range of culinary influences.

Boston Tea Party CAFE £
(15 Craft Village; snacks £2-4; ⏲9am-5.30pm Mon-Sat) Homemade soups, hot lunches, freshly baked cakes, friendly service and the best apple pie in town.

Café Artisan CAFE £
(☎7128 2727; 18-20 Bishop St Within; mains £2-5; ⏲9.30am-5.30pm Mon-Sat; 📶) Delicious homemade soups, deli sandwiches, panini and excellent cappuccinos.

Sandwich Co CAFE £
(sandwiches & salads £3-5; ⏲9am-5pm Mon-Sat) The Diamond (The Diamond); Strand Rd (61 Strand Rd) Good-value, choose-your-own sandwiches and salads.

Drinking

Whatever you do in Derry, don't miss an evening in the city's lively pubs – for the craic rather than the beer, which is nothing to write home about. They're friendly and atmospheric, mostly open until 1am, and are within easy walking distance of each other – there are six within dancing distance along Waterloo St.

Peadar O'Donnell's PUB
(63 Waterloo St) A backpackers' favourite, Peadar's has traditional music sessions every night and often on weekend afternoons as well. It's done up as a typical Irish pub-cum-grocer, down to the shelves of grocery items, shopkeepers scales on the counter and a museum's-worth of old bric-a-brac.

SUNDAY, BLOODY SUNDAY

Tragically echoing Dublin's Bloody Sunday of November 1920, when British security forces shot dead 14 spectators at a Gaelic football match in Croke Park, Derry's Bloody Sunday was a turning point in the history of the Troubles.

On Sunday, 30 January 1972, the Northern Ireland Civil Rights Association organised a peaceful march through Derry in protest against internment without trial, which had been introduced by the British government the previous year. Some 15,000 people marched from Creggan through the Bogside towards the Guildhall, but they were stopped by British Army barricades at the junction of William and Rossville Sts. The main march was diverted along Rossville St to Free Derry Corner, but a small number of youths began hurling stones and insults at the British soldiers.

The exact sequence of events is disputed, but it now seems clear that soldiers of the 1st Battalion the Parachute Regiment opened fire on unarmed civilians. Fourteen people were shot dead, some of them shot in the back; six were aged just 17. Another 14 people were injured, 12 by gunshots and two from being knocked down by armoured personnel carriers. The Catholic population of Derry, who had originally welcomed the British troops as a neutral force protecting them from Protestant violence and persecution, now saw the army as enemy and occupier. The ranks of the Provisional Irish Republican Army (IRA) swelled with a fresh surge of volunteers.

The Widgery Commission, set up in 1972 to investigate the affair, failed to find anyone responsible. None of the soldiers who fired at civilians, nor the officers in charge, were brought to trial or even disciplined; records disappeared and weapons were destroyed.

Long-standing public dissatisfaction with the Widgery investigation led to the massive **Bloody Sunday Inquiry** (www.bloody-sunday-inquiry.org.uk), headed by Lord Saville, which sat from March 2000 till December 2004. The inquiry heard from 900 witnesses, received 2500 witness statements and allegedly cost British taxpayers £400 million; its report was finally published in June 2010.

The events of Bloody Sunday inspired rock band U2's most overtly political song, 'Sunday Bloody Sunday' (1983), and are commemorated in the Museum of Free Derry, the People's Gallery and the Bloody Sunday Monument, all in the Bogside.

Badgers Bar PUB
(16-18 Orchard St) A fine polished-brass and stained-glass Victorian pub crammed with wood-panelled nooks and crannies, Badgers overflows at lunchtime with shoppers enjoying quality pub grub, and offers a quiet haven in the evenings when it attracts a crowd of more mature drinkers.

☆ Entertainment

Clubs & Live Music

Sandino's Cafe LIVE MUSIC
(www.sandinos.com; 1 Water St; live bands £4; ⏲11.30am-1am Mon-Sat, 1pm-midnight Sun) From the posters of Ché to the Free Palestine flag to the fairtrade coffee, this relaxed cafe–bar exudes a liberal, left-wing vibe. There are live bands on Friday nights and occasionally midweek, and DJ sessions on Saturdays. On Sundays there's a traditional Irish music session at 5pm, and live jazz/soul or DJs from 9pm, plus regular theme nights and events.

Mason's Bar LIVE MUSIC
(10 Magazine St; admission free-£12) The city that spawned the Undertones is still turning out raw, rumbustious music; Mason's Friday night sessions are the place to catch the latest offerings from local talent. There's live music from the resident band on Thursdays, and cover bands on Saturdays.

Gweedore Bar LIVE MUSIC
(www.peadars-gweedorebar.com; 59-61 Waterloo St; admission £6-10) Next door to Peadar O'Donnell's and part of the same complex, the Gweedore Bar hosts live rock bands most nights, while the DJ bar upstairs is home to a regular Saturday night disco.

Earth@Café Roc NIGHTCLUB
(129-135 Strand Rd; ⏲Tue, Thu & Sat) Derry's main nightclub and bar complex, close to the university, has reopened after a major refurb, with student nights on Tuesdays and dress-smart parties on Saturdays; search for 'Earth Nite Club Derry' on Facebook.

Concerts, Theatre & Cinema

Playhouse THEATRE
(www.derryplayhouse.co.uk; 5-7 Artillery St; ⏲box office 10am-5pm Mon-Fri) Housed in beautifully restored former school buildings with an award-winning modern extension at the rear, this community arts centre stages music, dance and theatre by local and international performers. It's also home to the **Context Gallery** (⏲11am-5.30pm Tue-Sat), which hosts exhibitions by local artists.

Cultúrlann Uí Chanáin CULTURAL CENTRE
(www.culturlann-doire.ie; 37 Great James St) This brand-new cultural centre devoted to the Irish language stages performances of traditional Irish music, poetry and dance.

Nerve Centre ARTS CENTRE
(www.nerve-centre.org.uk; 7-8 Magazine St) The Nerve Centre was set up in 1990 as a multimedia arts centre to encourage young, local talent in the fields of music and film. The centre has a performance area (live music at weekends), a theatre, a cinema (with an art-house program), a bar and a cafe.

Waterside Theatre THEATRE
(www.watersidetheatre.com; Ebrington Centre, Glendermott Rd) Housed in a former factory 500m east of the River Foyle, stages drama, dance, comedy, children's theatre and live music.

Millennium Forum THEATRE
(www.millenniumforum.co.uk; Newmarket St) Ireland's biggest theatre auditorium is a major venue for dance, drama, concerts, opera and musicals.

Magee College THEATRE
(www.culture.ulster.ac.uk; University of Ulster, Northland Rd) The college hosts a variety of arts, theatre and classical-concert performances throughout the year.

Derry Omniplex CINEMA
(www.omniplex.ie; Quayside Shopping Centre, Strand Rd) This seven-screen multiplex is the place for mainstream movies.

Shopping

An Cló Ceart BOOKS & CRAFTS
(37 Great James St) Housed in the Cultúrlann Uí Chanáin cultural centre, this shop stocks a good range of Irish-language books, traditional music CDs, glasswork, woodwork and jewellery.

Donegal Shop CRAFTS
(8 Shipquay St) A long-established craft shop, the Donegal is crammed with Irish knitwear, Celtic jewellery, Donegal tweeds, Irish linen and souvenirs.

McGilloway Gallery ART
(6 Shipquay St) A commercial gallery that provides a showcase for the best of contemporary Irish art, the McGilloway sells work by local artists and stages around half a dozen exhibitions each year.

Craft Village CRAFTS

(www.derrycraftvillage.com; off Shipquay St) This little courtyard is home to a handful of craft shops selling Derry crystal, hand-woven cloth, ceramics, jewellery and other local craft items. Enter from Shipquay St, Magazine St or Tower Museum.

Whatnot ANTIQUES

(22 Bishop St Within) The Whatnot is an interesting little antique shop crammed with jewellery, militaria, bric-a-brac and collectables.

Cool Discs Music MUSIC STORE

(www.cooldiscsmusic.com; 6/7 Lesley House, Foyle St) One of Northern Ireland's best independent record shops, Cool Discs has a wide selection of music by Irish artists old and new.

Austins DEPARTMENT STORE

(2 The Diamond) The world's oldest independent department store (established 1830), Austins is a good place to shop for Irish linen (it can ship your purchases overseas).

Foyleside Shopping Centre MALL

(Orchard St; 9am-6pm Mon & Tue, to 9pm Wed-Fri, to 7pm Sat, 1-6pm Sun) This huge, four-level mall just outside the eastern city walls contains a Marks & Spencer, Eason bookshop and other high-street chain stores.

Tesco SUPERMARKET

(Quayside Shopping Centre, Strand Rd; 9am-9pm Mon-Thu, 8.30am-9pm Fri, 8.30am-8pm Sat, 1-6pm Sun) Self-caterers can stock up at this big supermarket, just north of the walled city.

Information

Central Library (35 Foyle St; per 30min £1.50; 9.15am-8pm Mon & Thu, to 5.30pm Tue, Wed & Fri, to 5pm Sat) Internet access.

Derry Tourist Information Centre (7126 7284; www.derryvisitor.com; 44 Foyle St; 9am-5pm Mon-Fri, 10am-5pm Sat, plus 10am-4pm Sun Mar-Oct) Covers all of Northern Ireland and the Republic as well as Derry. Sells books and maps, can book accommodation throughout Ireland and has a bureau de change.

Getting There & Away

Air

City of Derry Airport (7181 0784; www.cityofderryairport.com) About 13km east of Derry along the A2 towards Limavady. Direct flights daily to Dublin (Aer Arann), London Stansted, London Luton, Liverpool, Birmingham and Glasgow Prestwick (Ryanair).

Bus

The **bus station** (7126 2261; Foyle St) is just northeast of the walled city.

Airporter (7126 9996; www.airporter.co.uk; Quayside Shopping Centre, Strand Rd) Runs direct from Derry to Belfast International (one way/return £18/28, 1½ hours) and George Best Belfast City (one way/return £18/28, two hours) airports. Every 90 minutes Monday to Friday, every two hours Saturday and Sunday.

Bus Éireann (in Donegal 353-74 912 1309) Bus 64 runs from Derry to Galway (£20, 5¼ hours, three daily, two on Sundays) via Letterkenny, Donegal and Sligo; another four a day terminate at Sligo.

Lough Swilly Bus Company (Bus Station, Foyle St; 7126 2017) Buses to Buncrana, Carndonagh, Dungloe, Letterkenny (£5, 30 to 45 minutes, eight daily Monday to Friday, five on Saturday) and Greencastle (one hour, two daily Monday to Friday, one on Saturday) in County Donegal. There's also a bus from Derry to Malin Head (£6, 1¼ hours) via Carndonagh on Saturdays only.

Maiden City Flyer (bus 212) A fast and frequent service between Derry and Belfast (£11, 1¾ hours, every 30 minutes Monday to Saturday, 11 on Sunday), calling at Dungiven.

Ulsterbus Goldline Express 274 goes from Derry to Dublin (£17.50, four hours, every two hours daily). Other useful Ulsterbus services include the 273 to Omagh (£8, 1¼ hours, hourly Monday to Saturday, six Sunday) and the 234 to Limavady and Coleraine (£6, one hour, five daily Monday to Saturday, two Sunday), continuing to Portstewart and Portrush on weekday evenings.

Train

Derry's train station (always referred to as Londonderry in Northern Ireland timetables) is on the eastern side of the River Foyle; a free Rail Link bus connects with the bus station. There are trains to Belfast (£11, 2¼ hours, seven or eight daily Monday to Saturday, four on Sunday) and Coleraine (£8.20, 45 minutes, seven daily), with connections to Portrush (£10, 1¼ hours).

Getting Around

Bus 143A to Limavady stops at City of Derry airport (30 minutes, seven daily Monday to Friday, three Saturday, one Sunday); otherwise a taxi costs about £13. The **Derry Taxi Association** (7126 0247) and **Foyle Delta Cabs** (7127 9999) operate from the city centre to all areas.

Local buses leave from Foyle St, outside the bus station, leading to the suburbs and sur-

TOP FIVE VIEWPOINTS IN NORTHERN IRELAND

» Binevenagh Lake (p650)
» Fair Head (p665)
» Cuilcagh Mountain (p685)
» Scrabo Hill (p614)
» Slieve Donard (p622)

rounding villages; a day ticket giving unlimited travel on these buses costs £1.70.

You can hire bikes from the Derry Tourist Information Centre. The **Foyle Valley cycle route** runs through Derry, along the west bank of the river.

Limavady & Around

POP 12,000

Enchanted by a folk tune played by a blind fiddler outside her window in 1851, Limavady resident Jane Ross (1810–79) jotted down the melody – then known as 'O'Cahan's Lament', and later as the 'Londonderry Air'. The tune came to be known around the world as 'Danny Boy' – probably the most famous Irish song of all time.

Limavady was granted to Sir Thomas Phillips, the organiser of the Plantation of County Londonderry, by James I in 1612, after the last ruling chief, Sir Donnell Ballagh O'Cahan, was found guilty of rebellion. The town's original Gaelic name is Léim an Mhadaidh, which means 'the Dog's Leap', commemorating one of the O'Cahans' dogs that jumped a gorge across the River Roe to bring warning of an unexpected enemy attack.

Sights & Activities

Today Limavady is a quiet and prosperous small town. There's not much to see except the **blue plaque** on the wall at 51 Main St, opposite the Alexander Arms, commemorating the home of Jane Ross. The town hosts a **jazz and blues festival** (www.limavadyjazzandblues.com) in June.

Roe Valley Country Park PARK

This lovely country park, about 3km south of Limavady, has riverside walks stretching for 5km either side of the River Roe. The area is associated with the O'Cahans, who ruled the valley until the Plantation. The 17th-century settlers saw the flax-growing potential of the damp river valley and the area became an important linen-manufacturing centre.

The **Dogleap Centre** (Roe Valley Country Park, 41 Dogleap Rd; admission free; ⏲10am-5pm Jun-Aug, 1-5pm Sat & Sun Easter-May & Sep) houses a visitor centre and tearoom. Next door is Ulster's first domestic **hydroelectric power station**, opened in 1896; it opens by request at the visitor centre. The nearby **Green Lane Museum** (admission free; ⏲1-4.45pm Sat-Thu Jun-Aug) contains old photographs and relics of the valley's flax industry. The scutch mill, where the flax was pounded, is a 20-minute walk away, along the river, past two watchtowers built to guard the linen when it was spread out in the fields for bleaching.

The River Roe is famous for its sea trout and salmon **fishing** (www.roeangling.com). Day tickets cost £20, and are available from **SJ Mitchell & Co** (☎7772 2128; Central Car Park, Limavady) and the Alexander Arms Hotel. The season runs from the third week in May until 20 October.

The park is signposted off the B192 road between Limavady and Dungiven. Bus 146 from Limavady to Dungiven will drop you at the turn-off; the park is about a 3km walk from the main road.

Eating & Sleeping

Alexander Arms Hotel B&B ££

(☎7776 3443; 34 Main St; s/d from £30/50; P) A long-established hotel and pub dating from 1875, the centrally located Alexander Arms is a friendly, family-run place that offers B&B and serves pub grub and restaurant meals.

TOP CHOICE **Lime Tree** IRISH ££

(☎7776 4300; 60 Catherine St; mains £15-23; ⏲6-9pm Tue-Fri, to 9.30pm Sat) Unfussy decor in shades of burgundy and beige softened by flickering tea-lights makes for a relaxing atmosphere in Limavady's top eatery. The menu promotes local produce – from seafood thermidor made with Donegal fish to fillet steak from award-winning butcher Hunter's of Limavady – and includes vegetarian dishes that are a cut above the usual. There's also an early-bird menu (two/three courses £14.50/17.50) available before 7pm Tuesday to Friday.

Hunter's Bakery & Oven Door Café CAFE £

(5 Market St; mains £3-7; ⏲9am-5.30pm Mon-Sat) If you fancy a quick snack, this homey bakery has a comfy cafeteria at the back, serving good coffee, cakes and light meals. It's a

local institution, patronised by a broad cross-section of the community, with a pleasantly old-fashioned feel.

Information

Tourist office (☎7776 0650; 24 Main St; 9.30am-5pm Mon-Fri, 10am-2pm Sat) In the Roe Valley Arts Centre.

Getting There & Away

Bus 143A runs between Derry and Limavady hourly (four daily on Sunday). There's no direct bus to Belfast from Limavady but connections can be made at Coleraine.

Coastal County Derry

MAGILLIGAN POINT

The huge triangular spit of land that almost closes off the mouth of Lough Foyle is mostly taken up by a military firing range, and is home to a once-notorious prison. Still, it's worth a visit for its vast sandy beaches – **Magilligan Strand** to the west, and the 9km sweep of **Benone Strand** to the northeast, the latter providing a superb venue for kite buggies and mini land yachts. On the point itself, watching over the entrance to Lough Foyle, stands a **Martello tower**, built during the Napoleonic Wars in 1812 to guard against French invasion.

Benone Tourist Complex (☎7775 0555; 59 Benone Ave; campsites £14.50, caravans £18-22; 9am-10pm Jul & Aug, to dusk Apr-Jun & Sep, to 4pm Oct-Mar), adjacent to Benone Strand, is a campsite with outdoor heated pool, a children's pool, tennis courts and a putting green (all open to nonresidents). Note that dogs are not allowed on the beach from May to September.

The **Lough Foyle Ferry** (www.loughfoyleferry.com; car/motorcycle/pedestrian £10/5/2) runs between Magilligan Point and Greencastle in County Donegal year-round. The trip takes 10 minutes and runs hourly from 8am Monday to Friday and 9am Saturday and Sunday, departing on the hour from Greencastle, 15 minutes past from Magilligan. The last ferry is at 9.15pm June to August, 8.15pm May, 7.15pm April and September, and 6.15pm October to March.

DOWNHILL

In 1774 the eccentric Bishop of Derry and fourth Earl of Bristol, Frederick Augustus Hervey, built himself a palatial home, Downhill, on the coast west of Castlerock. It burnt down in 1851, was rebuilt in 1876, and was finally abandoned after WWII. The ruins of the house now stand forlornly on a cliff top.

The original demesne covered some 160 hectares, which is now part of the National Trust's **Downhill Estate** (www.ntni.org.uk; adult/child incl Hezlett House £4.50/2.25, parking £4; temple & facilities 10am-5pm Apr-Sep, grounds dawn-dusk year-round). The beautiful landscaped gardens below the ruins of the house are the work of celebrated gardener Jan Eccles, who became custodian of Downhill at the age of 60 and created the garden over a period of 30 years. She died in 1997 aged 94.

The main attraction here is the little **Mussenden Temple**, built by the bishop to house either his library or his mistress – opinions differ! The randy old clergyman continued an affair with the mistress of Frederick William II of Prussia well into old age.

The main access is from the car parks at the **Lion's Gate** and **Bishop's Gate** on the coast road. A more peaceful alternative is the pleasant, 20-minute walk to the temple from Castlerock village, with fine views west to the beach at Benone and Donegal, and east to Portstewart and the shadowy outlines of the Scottish hills. Begin at the path along the seaward side of the caravan park; halfway there, you have to descend into a steep-sided valley and climb the steps on the far side of the little lake. On the beach below the temple, the bishop used to challenge his own clergy to horseback races, rewarding the winners with lucrative parishes.

On the main road 1km west of the temple, opposite the Downhill Hostel, the scenic **Bishop's Road** climbs steeply up through a ravine and heads over the hills to Limavady. There are spectacular views over Lough Foyle, Donegal and the Sperrin Mountains from the **Gortmore** picnic area, and from the cliff top at **Binevenagh Lake**.

Downhill Hostel (☎7084 9077; www.downhillhostel.com; 12 Mussenden Rd; dm/d £14/50, f from £42 plus per child £5; P @) is a beautifully restored late-19th-century house, tucked beneath the sea cliffs and overlooking the beach, offering very comfortable accommodation in seven-bed dorms, doubles and family rooms. There's a big lounge with an open fire and a view of the sea, and you can hire wetsuits and body boards when the surf's up. You can even paint your own mugs, plates and bowls in the neighbouring pottery. There are no shops in Downhill so bring supplies with you.

Bus 134 between Limavady and Coleraine (20 minutes, nine daily Monday to Friday, six Saturday) stops at Downhill, as does the 234 between Derry and Coleraine.

CASTLEROCK

Castlerock is a small seaside resort with a decent beach. At the turn-off from the main coast road towards Castlerock is the late-17th-century **Hezlett House** (adult/child incl Downhill Estate £4.50/2.25; ⌚10am-5pm Apr-Sep), a thatched cottage noted for its cruck-truss roof gables of stone and turf strengthened with wooden crucks, or crutches. The interior decor is Victorian.

Bus 134 between Limavady and Coleraine (20 minutes, nine daily Monday to Friday, six Saturday) stops at Castlerock, as does the 234 between Derry and Coleraine.

There are nine trains a day from Castlerock to Coleraine (£2.20, 10 minutes) and Derry (£8.20, 35 minutes) Monday to Saturday, and four on Sunday.

Coleraine

POP 25,300

Coleraine (Cúil Raithin), on the banks of the River Bann, is an important transport hub and shopping centre. It was one of the original Plantation towns of County Londonderry, founded in 1613. The University of Ulster was established here in 1968, much to the chagrin of Derry, which had lobbied hard to win it.

Sights & Activities

The tourist office has a *Heritage Trail* leaflet that will guide you around what little remains of the original Plantation town, including **St Patrick's Church**, parts of which date from 1613, and fragments of the town walls.

Causeway Speciality Market MARKET
(⌚9am-2.30pm) On the second Saturday of each month, a market is held in the Diamond. It sells a range of local crafts and organic produce, from hand-turned wooden bowls and homemade candles to farmhouse jam from Ballywalter, County Down, and sheep-milk cheese from County Derry.

FREE **Mountsandel Fort** FORT
(⌚dawn-dusk) Just 1.5km south of the town centre, on the east bank of the river, Mountsandel Fort is a massive and mysterious earthwork that may have been an early-Christian stronghold or a later Anglo-Norman fortification. From the Mountsandel Forest parking area on Mountsandel Rd, a 2.5km circular walk leads high above the River Bann to the fort, where you descend steeply down to the riverbank and return upstream past the Victorian lock and weir at Cutts.

Lady Sandel BOAT TRIPS
(www.banncruise.com; adult/child £8.50/5.50) You can take a 1½-hour river cruise on the *Lady Sandel* from the jetty on Strand Rd (across the river from the town centre) upstream to Macfinn via the lock at Cutts, or downstream to the river mouth. Boats depart at 2pm Saturday and Sunday from Easter to mid-September, plus 3pm Monday to Friday in July and August.

Information

Tourist office (☎7034 4723; info@northcoastni.com; Railway Rd; ⌚9am-5pm Mon-Sat) To get here from the combined train and bus station, turn left along Railway Rd.

Getting There & Away

There are regular trains from Coleraine to Belfast (£10, two hours, seven or eight daily Monday to Saturday, four on Sunday) and Derry (£8.20, 45 minutes, seven or eight daily Monday to Saturday, four on Sunday). A branch line links Coleraine to Portrush (£2.2, 12 minutes, hourly Monday to Saturday, 10 on Sunday).

Portstewart

POP 7800

Ever since Victorian times, when English novelist William Thackeray described it as having an 'air of comfort and neatness', the seaside and golfing resort of Portstewart has cultivated a sedate, upmarket atmosphere that distinguishes it from populist Portrush, 6km further east. However, there's also a sizeable student community from the University of Ulster in Coleraine.

The fantastic beach is the main attraction, along with a couple of world-class golf courses – a combination that created the North's highest property prices and a large demand for holiday homes. However, concerns about overdevelopment were realised when the economic downturn of 2008 hit the North – you'll see no shortage of half-built houses and For Sale signs.

Sights & Activities

The central promenade is dominated by the castellated facade of a Dominican college, looming over the seaside fun and games like a Catholic conscience.

The broad, 2.5km beach of **Portstewart Strand** is a 20-minute walk south of the centre along a coastal path, or a short bus ride along Strand Rd. Parking is allowed on the firm sand, which can accommodate over 1000 cars (open year-round, £5 per car from Easter to October).

Heading in the opposite direction, the **Port Path** is a 10.5km coastal footpath (part of the Causeway Coast Way) that stretches from Portstewart Strand to White Rocks, 3km east of Portrush.

Portstewart is within a few kilometres of three of Northern Ireland's top golf courses: the championship links at **Portstewart Golf Club** (green fees weekday/weekend £80/95), **Royal Portrush** (£135/150) and **Castlerock** (£65/80).

In May the **North West 200 motorcycle race** (www.northwest200.org) is run on a road circuit taking in Portrush, Portstewart and Coleraine – you can see the starting grid painted on the main road on the eastern edge of town. This classic race – Ireland's biggest outdoor sporting event – is one of the last to be run on closed public roads anywhere in Europe, and attracts up to 150,000 spectators; if you're not one of them, it's best to avoid the area on the race weekend.

Sleeping

Don't even think about turning up without a booking during the North West 200 weekend in May.

York HOTEL ££
(☎7083 3594; www.theyorkportstewart.co.uk; 2 Station Rd; s/d £90/120; P 📶) The York brings a bit of boutique chic to Portstewart's mostly staid accommodation scene, with designer rooms in shades of chocolate, cream and cappuccino, red leather chairs, spacious bathrooms with rain-head showers, and big breakfasts served in a glass-lined dining room with stunning views along the coast.

Cromore Halt Inn INN ££
(☎7083 6888; www.cromore.com; 158 Station Rd; s/d £55/80; P 📶) Located about 1km east of the harbour, on the corner of Station and Mill Rds, the motel-style Cromore has a dozen modern, businesslike rooms, along with friendly, helpful staff and a good restaurant.

Cul-Erg B&B B&B ££
(☎7083 6610; www.culerg.co.uk; 9 Hillside, Atlantic Circle; s/d £40/75; P 📶) This family-run B&B is in a modern, flower-bedecked terrace house just a couple of minutes' walk from the promenade. Warm and welcoming, it's set in a quiet cul-de-sac; the rooms at the back have a view of the sea.

Causeway Coast Independent Hostel HOSTEL £
(☎7083 3789; rick@causewaycoasthostel.fsnet.co.uk; 4 Victoria Tce; dm/tw from £12/37; @ 📶) This neat terrace house just northeast of the harbour has spacious four-, six- and eight-bed dorms plus a double room, and good power showers. It has its own kitchen, laundry and welcoming open fire in winter.

Eating & Drinking

TOP CHOICE **Preference Brasserie** EUROPEAN £££
(☎7083 3959; www.preferencebrasserie.co.uk; 81 The Promenade; mains £17-23; ⏲5.30-9.30pm Tue-Sat) This stylish brasserie prides itself on a seasonal menu of fresh local produce served with continental flair – dishes include peppered loin of venison with parsnip and orange purée, and fillet of cod with roast salsify, bacon and vermouth cream sauce.

Morelli's CAFE £
(53 The Promenade; mains £4-8; ⏲9am-11pm, food to 8pm, shorter hr in winter) Morelli's is a local institution, founded by Italian immigrants and famous for its mouth-watering ice cream since 1911. The menu includes breakfast fry-ups, pizza, sandwiches, omelettes, and fish and chips, as well as good coffee and cakes, and there's a great view across the bay to Mussenden Temple, Benone Strand and Donegal.

Anchor Bar & Skippers Restaurant PUB ££
(www.theanchorbar.co.uk; 87-89 The Promenade; mains £8-11; ⏲food noon-9pm) The liveliest of Portstewart's traditional pubs, famed for its Guinness and hugely popular with students from the University of Ulster, the Anchor serves decent pub grub, opens till 1am and has live bands Friday and Saturday. There's also Skippers Restaurant, which serves more sophisticated dishes such as seafood chowder, honey roast duck and vegetable stir-fry.

Getting There & Away

Bus 140 plies between Coleraine and Portstewart (£2.20, 20 to 30 minutes) roughly every half-hour (fewer on Sunday).

COUNTY ANTRIM

Getting There & Around

Translink (9066 6630; www.translink.co.uk) operates several bus services specially designed for tourists visiting the popular Antrim coast and Giant's Causeway areas.

The **Antrim Coaster** (bus 252/256) links Coleraine with Belfast (£10, four hours, two daily Monday to Saturday) via Portstewart, Portrush, Bushmills, the Giant's Causeway, Ballycastle, the Glens of Antrim and Larne, departing Belfast at 9.05am and 3pm. South-bound buses leave Coleraine at 9.35am and 3.40pm. A Sunday service operates from July to September only.

From June to mid-September the **Causeway Rambler** (bus 402) links Bushmills Distillery and Carrick-a-Rede (£5.50, 25 minutes, seven daily) via the Giant's Causeway, White Park Bay and Ballintoy. The ticket allows unlimited travel in both directions for one day.

Portrush

POP 6300

The bustling seaside resort of Portrush (Port Rois) bursts at the seams with holidaymakers in high season and, not surprisingly, many of its attractions are focused unashamedly on good, old-fashioned family fun. However, it is also one of Ireland's top surfing centres and home to the North's hottest nightclub.

Sights & Activities

Curran Strand BEACH

Portrush's main attraction is the beautiful sandy beach of Curran Strand that stretches for 3km to the east of the town, ending at the scenic chalk cliffs of White Rocks. In summer, boats depart regularly for cruises or fishing trips.

FREE **Coastal Zone** AQUARIUM

(8 Bath Rd; 10am-5pm Easter week & Jun-Aug, 10am-5pm Sat & Sun May & Sep) You'll find more activities for kids at the Coastal Zone, including marine-life exhibits, a touch pool, rock-pool rambles and fossil hunts.

Troggs Surf Shop SURFING

(www.troggssurfshop.co.uk; 88 Main St; 10am-6pm) Portrush is the centre of Northern Ireland's surfing scene – the Portrush Open in March is a regular feature on the Irish Surfing Association competition calendar, and the UK Pro Surf Tour held a contest here for the first time in 2007. From April to November the friendly Troggs Surf Shop offers bodyboard/surfboard hire (per day £5/10) and wetsuit hire (per day £7), surf reports and general advice. A two-hour lesson including equipment hire costs £25 per person.

Maddybenny Riding Centre HORSE RIDING

(www.maddybenny.com; Maddybenny Farm, Atlantic Rd; lessons & hacking per hr £12) Beginners are welcome.

Sleeping

Places fill up quickly during summer, so it's advisable to book in advance.

TOP CHOICE **Clarmont** B&B ££

(7082 2397; www.clarmont.com; 10 Landsdowne Cres; per person £35-45) Our favourite among several guesthouses on Landsdowne Cres, the Clarmont has great views and, from polished pine floors to period fireplaces, has a decor that tastefully mixes Victorian and modern styles. Ask for a room with a bay window overlooking the sea.

Albany Lodge Guest House B&B ££

(7082 3492; www.albanylodgeni.co.uk; 2 Eglinton St; s/d from £50/80; P@) This elegant, four-storey Victorian villa has a great location close to the beach, with spectacular views along the coast. The rooms are spacious and welcoming, with pine furniture and warm colours, and the owners are friendly without being in your face. It's worth shelling out a few extra quid for the four-poster suite on the top floor, where you can soak up the view while reclining on your chaise longue.

Portrush Holiday Hostel HOSTEL £

(7082 1288; www.portrushholidayhostel.co.uk; 24 Princess St; dm/d £15/40; @) Just a few minutes' walk from both beach and harbour, this popular hostel is set in a Victorian terrace house, but feels cosy rather than cramped. Staff are friendly and helpful, and facilities include a washing machine, barbecue area and secure storage for bikes.

Counties Derry & Antrim: The Causeway Coast

The north coast of County Antrim from Ballycastle west to Portrush is known as the Causeway Coast, one of the most impressively scenic stretches of coastline in all of Ireland. Whether you drive, cycle or walk its length, it's not to be missed.

Giant's Causeway

1 The grand geological centrepiece of the Antrim Coast is the Giant's Causeway (p658), a spectacular rock formation composed of countless hexagonal basalt columns. A Unesco World Heritage site, it is the North's most popular tourist attraction.

MARTIN MOOS/LONELY PLANET IMAGES ©

Causeway Coast

2 The Causeway Coast (p662) isn't just about the scenery. There are picturesque villages at Ballintoy and Portbradden, historic ruined fortresses at Dunluce and Dunseverick castles, and the chance to savour a dram of Irish whiskey at Bushmills Distillery.

Carrick-a-Rede Rope Bridge

3 Originally rigged and used by local salmon fishermen, the famous Carrick-a-Rede Rope Bridge (p659) is now a popular test of nerve for Causeway Coast visitors, swaying gently 30m above the rocks and the sea.

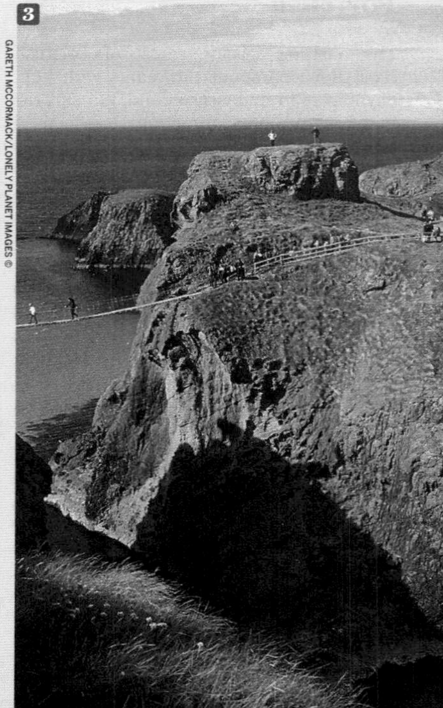
GARETH MCCORMACK/LONELY PLANET IMAGES ©

Antrim Coast

4 Although famous for its dramatic sea-cliff scenery, the Antrim coast also has some excellent sandy beaches. As well as the family-friendly strand at Ballycastle (p660), there's the harder-to-reach but twice-as-beautiful White Park Bay (p662).

Clockwise from top left
1. Stepping stones, Giant's Causeway **2.** Sunset over Giant's Causeway coast **3.** Carrick-a-Rede Rope Bridge

2

Carrick Dhu Caravan Park CAMPGROUND £
(☎7082 3712; 12 Ballyreagh Rd; camp & caravan sites from £18; ⊙Apr-Sep) A small site 1.5km west of Portrush on the A2 towards Portstewart. Facilities include a children's playground and restaurant.

Eating

TOP CHOICE **55 Degrees North** INTERNATIONAL ££
(☎7082 2811; www.55-north.com; 1 Causeway St; mains £10-18; ⊙5-9pm Mon-Fri, 5-9.30pm Sat, 5-8.30pm Sun) One of the north coast's most stylish restaurants, 55 Degrees North boasts a wall of floor-to-ceiling windows allowing diners to soak up a spectacular panorama of sand and sea. The food is excellent, concentrating on clean, simple flavours and unfussy presentation. There's an early-bird menu (three courses £10 to £12) available 5pm to 7pm.

Café 55 CAFE £
(1 Causeway St; mains £5-8; ⊙9am-5pm) Tucked beneath 55 Degrees North, this licensed cafe serves good coffee plus breakfast rolls and pancakes (10am to 11.30am) on an outdoor terrace; it also has daily lunch specials such as fish pie, and an evening menu in summer.

Harbour Bistro BISTRO ££
(☎7082 2430; The Harbour; mains £7-16; ⊙5-10pm Sun-Fri, to 10.30pm Sat) Quality grub – juicy steaks, homemade burgers, spicy chicken, oriental dishes and vegetarian meals – a family-friendly atmosphere (there's a kids menu) and a harbour-side location make the Harbour one of Portrush's most popular eating places.

Coast ITALIAN ££
(The Harbour; mains £6-12; ⊙5-9.30pm Wed-Fri, 4-10.30pm Sat, 3-9.30pm Sun) Another water front place offering stone-baked pizzas, pasta dishes and a range of steak, chicken and fish dishes.

Entertainment

Kelly's Complex CLUB
(www.kellysportrush.co.uk; 1 Bushmills Rd; ⊙Wed & Sat) The North's top clubbing venue regularly features DJs from London and Manchester, and attracts clubbers from as far afield as Belfast and Dublin. Plain and small-looking from the outside, the TARDIS effect takes over as you enter a wonderland of five bars and three dance floors. It's been around since 1996, but **Lush!** (admission £7-12; ⊙9pm-2am Sat) is still one of the best club nights in Ireland.

The complex is on the A2 just east of Portrush, beside the Golf Links Holiday Park.

Getting There & Around

The bus terminal is near the Dunluce Centre. Bus 140 links Portrush with Coleraine (20 minutes) and Portstewart (20 to 30 minutes) every 30 minutes or so.

The train station is just south of the harbour. Portrush is served by trains from Coleraine (£2.20, 12 minutes, hourly Monday to Saturday, 10 on Sunday), where there are connections to Belfast or Derry.

WRECK OF THE GIRONA

The little bay 1km to the northeast of the Giant's Causeway is called Port na Spaniagh – Bay of the Spaniards. It was here, in October 1588, that the *Girona* – a ship of the Spanish Armada – was driven onto the rocks by a storm.

The *Girona* had escaped the famous confrontation with Sir Walter Raleigh's fleet in the English Channel but, along with many other fleeing Spanish ships, had been driven north around Scotland and Ireland by bad weather. Though designed for a crew of 500, when she struck the rocks she was loaded with 1300 people – mostly survivors gathered from other shipwrecks – including the cream of the Spanish aristocracy. Barely a dozen survived.

Somhairle Buidhe (Sorley Boy) MacDonnell (1505–90), the constable of nearby Dunluce Castle, salvaged gold and cannons from the wreck, and used the money to extend and modernise his fortress – cannons from the ship can still be seen on the castle's landward wall. But it was not until 1968 that the wreck site was excavated by a team of archaeological divers. They recovered magnificent treasure of gold, silver and precious stones, as well as everyday sailors' possessions, which are now on display in Belfast's **Ulster Museum** (p579).

For taxis, try **Andy Brown's** (☎7082 2223) or **North West Taxis** (☎7082 4446). A taxi to Kelly's is around £7, and it's £14 to the Giant's Causeway.

Dunluce Castle

Views along the Causeway Coast between Portrush and Portballintrae are dominated by the ruins of **Dunluce Castle** (87 Dunluce Rd; adult/child £4/2; ⏲10am-6pm, last admission 30min before closing), perched atop a dramatic basalt crag. In the 16th and 17th centuries it was the seat of the MacDonnell family (the earls of Antrim from 1620), who built a Renaissance-style manor house within the walls. Part of the castle, including the kitchen, collapsed into the sea in 1639, taking seven servants and that night's dinner with it.

A narrow bridge leads from the mainland courtyard across a dizzying gap to the main part of the fortress. Below, a path leads down from the gatehouse to the Mermaid's Cave beneath the castle crag.

Dunluce is 5km east of Portrush, a one-hour walk away along the coastal path. All the buses that run along the coast stop at Dunluce Castle; see p656.

Bushmills

POP 1350

The small town of Bushmills has long been a place of pilgrimage for connoisseurs of Irish whiskey. A good youth hostel and a restored rail link with the Giant's Causeway have also made it an attractive stop for hikers exploring the Causeway Coast.

Sights & Activities

Old Bushmills Distillery DISTILLERY
(www.bushmills.com; Distillery Rd; adult/child £6/3; ⏲9.15am-5pm Mon-Sat, plus 11am-5pm Sun Jul-Sep, noon-5.30pm Sun Mar-Jun & Oct) Bushmills is the world's oldest legal distillery, having been granted a licence by King James I in 1608. Bushmills whiskey is made with Irish barley and water from St Columb's Rill, a tributary of the River Bush, and matured in oak barrels. During ageing, the alcohol content drops from around 60% to 40%; the spirit lost through evaporation is known, rather sweetly, as 'the angels' share'. After a tour of the distillery you're rewarded with a free sample (or a soft drink), and four lucky volunteers get a whiskey-tasting session to compare Bushmills with other brands.

Giant's Causeway & Bushmills Railway HERITAGE RAILWAY
(www.freewebs.com/giantscausewayrailway; adult/child return £7.50/5.50) Brought from a private line on the shores of Lough Neagh, the narrow-gauge line and locomotives (two steam and one diesel) follow the route of a 19th-century tourist tramway for 3km from Bushmills to below the Giant's Causeway visitor centre. Trains run hourly between 11am and 5.30pm, departing on the hour from the Causeway, on the half-hour from Bushmills, daily in July and August, weekends only from Easter to June and September and October.

Sleeping & Eating

Bushmills Inn Hotel HOTEL £££
(☎2073 3000; www.bushmillsinn.com; 9 Dunluce Rd; s/d from £158/178, ste £298; P@☜) One of Northern Ireland's most atmospheric hotels, the Bushmills is an old coaching inn complete with peat fires, gas lamps and a round tower with a secret library. There are no longer any bedrooms in the old part of the hotel – the luxurious accommodation is in the neighbouring, modern Mill House complex.

Mill Rest Youth Hostel HOSTEL £
(☎2073 1222; www.hini.org.uk; 49 Main St; dm/d £18.50/41; ⏲closed 11am-2pm Jul & Aug, 11am-5pm Mar-Jun, Sep & Oct; @) This modern, purpose-built hostel is just off the Diamond in the centre of town. Accommodation is mostly in four- to six-bed dorms with one twin room with private bathroom. There's also a kitchen, restaurant, laundry and bike shed. The hostel is open daily March to October, Friday and Saturday nights only November to February.

Ballyness Caravan Park & B&B B&B ££
(☎2073 1438; www.ballynesscaravanpark.com; 40 Castlecatt Rd; campervan sites £22, B&B s/d £38/59; ⏲mid-Mar–Oct; @) This ecofriendly caravan park (no tents) is about 1km south of Bushmills town centre on the B66. The farmhouse at the entrance offers B&B accommodation.

TOP CHOICE **Bushmills Inn** IRISH ££
(lunch mains £10-12, dinner mains £15-22; ⏲noon-9.30pm Mon-Sat, 12.30-9pm Sun;) The inn's excellent restaurant, with intimate wooden booths set in the old 17th-century stables,

specialises in fresh Ulster produce and serves everything from sandwiches to full à-la-carte dinners.

Copper Kettle CAFE £
(61 Main St; mains £3-6; ⏲8.30am-5pm Mon-Sat, from 10am Sun) This rustic tearoom serves breakfast fry-ups till 11.30am, and has daily lunch specials as well as good tea, coffee, cakes and scones.

Getting There & Away

See Getting There & Around, p656 for transport information.

Giant's Causeway

When you first see it you'll understand why the ancients believed the causeway was not a natural feature. The vast expanse of regular, closely packed, hexagonal stone columns dipping gently beneath the waves looks for all the world like the handiwork of giants.

This spectacular rock formation – a national nature reserve and Northern Ireland's only Unesco World Heritage Site – is one of Ireland's most impressive and atmospheric landscape features, but it is all too often swamped by visitors – around 750,000 each year. If you can, try to visit midweek or out of season to experience it at its most evocative. Sunset in spring and autumn is the best time for photographs.

Visiting the Giant's Causeway itself is free of charge but the overcrowded, council-run car park charges £6 per car. It's an easy 1km walk from the car park down to the Causeway; minibuses with wheelchair access ply the route every 15 minutes (adult/child £2/1 return). Guided **tours** of the site (June to August only) cost £3.50/2.25 per adult/child.

At the time of research a new visitor centre – described as 'world class' – and parking area were under construction, scheduled to open in summer 2012 (check www.nationaltrust.org.uk/giantscauseway for the latest developments). Until then, limited visitor facilities are provided in the Causeway Hotel.

Sights & Activities

From the car park, it's an easy 10- to 15-minute walk downhill on a tarmac road (wheelchair accessible) to the Giant's Causeway itself. However, a much more interesting approach is to follow the cliff-top path northeast for 2km to the **Chimney Tops** headland, which has an excellent view of the Causeway and the coastline to the west, including Inishowen and Malin Heads.

This pinnacled promontory was bombarded by ships of the Spanish Armada in 1588, who thought it was Dunluce Castle, and the wreck of the Spanish galleon *Girona* (see the boxed text, p656) lies just off the tip of the headland. Return towards the car park and about halfway back descend the **Shepherd's Steps** (signposted) to a lower-level footpath that leads down to the Causeway. Allow 1½ hours for the round trip.

Alternatively, you can visit the Causeway first, then follow the lower coastal path as far as the **Amphitheatre** viewpoint at Port Reostan, passing impressive rock formations such as the **Organ** (a stack of vertical basalt columns resembling organ pipes), and return by climbing the Shepherd's Steps.

You can also follow the cliff-top path east as far as Dunseverick or beyond (see the boxed text, p662).

Sleeping

Causeway Hotel HOTEL ££
(☎2073 1226; www.giants-causeway-hotel.com; 40 Causeway Rd; s/d £60/90; Ⓟ) You can't beat it for location – the National Trust's Causeway Hotel is within a stone's throw of the Causeway, a useful base if you want to explore the coast early or late in the day when the crowds are not around. Rooms 28 to 32 are the best, with outdoor terraces that enjoy sunset views over the Atlantic.

Getting There & Away

Bus 172 from Coleraine and Bushmills to Ballycastle passes the site year round. Also see Getting There & Around, p656.

Giant's Causeway to Ballycastle

Between the Giant's Causeway and Ballycastle lies the most scenic stretch of the Causeway Coast, with sea cliffs of contrasting black basalt and white chalk, rocky islands, picturesque little harbours and broad sweeps of sandy beach. It's best enjoyed on foot, following the 16.5km of waymarked **Causeway Coast Way** between the Carrick-a-Rede car park and the Giant's Causeway, although the main attractions can also be reached by car or bus.

About 8km east of the Giant's Causeway is the meagre ruin of 16th-century **Dunseverick Castle**, spectacularly sited on a grassy

THE MAKING OF THE CAUSEWAY

The story goes that the Irish giant, Finn McCool, built the Causeway so he could cross the sea to fight the Scottish giant Benandonner. Benandonner pursued Finn back across the Causeway, but in turn took fright and fled back to Scotland, ripping up the causeway as he went. All that remains are its ends – the Giant's Causeway in Ireland, and the island of Staffa in Scotland (which has similar rock formations).

The more prosaic scientific explanation is that the causeway rocks were formed 60 million years ago, when a thick layer of molten basaltic lava flowed along a valley in the existing chalk beds. As the lava flow cooled and hardened – from the top and bottom surfaces inward – it contracted, creating a pattern of hexagonal cracks at right angles to the cooling surfaces (think of mud contracting and cracking in a hexagonal pattern as a lake bed dries out). As solidification progressed towards the centre of the flow, the cracks spread down from the top and up from the bottom, until the lava was completely solid. Erosion has cut into the lava flow, and the basalt has split along the contraction cracks, creating the hexagonal columns.

bluff. Another 1.5km on is the tiny seaside hamlet of **Portbradden**, with half a dozen harbourside houses and the tiny, blue-and-white **St Gobban's Church**, said to be the smallest in Ireland. Visible from Portbradden and accessible via the next junction off the A2 is the spectacular **White Park Bay**, with its wide, sweeping sandy beach.

A few kilometres further on is **Ballintoy** (Baile an Tuaighe), another pretty village tumbling down the hillside to a picture-postcard harbour. The restored limekiln on the quayside once made quicklime using stone from the chalk cliffs and coal from Ballymoney.

The main attraction on this stretch of coast is the famous (or notorious, depending on your head for heights) **Carrick-a-Rede Rope Bridge** (www.ntni.org.uk; Ballintoy; adult/child £5.60/2.90; ⏲10am-7pm Jun-Aug, to 6pm Mar-May, Sep & Oct). The 20m-long, 1m-wide bridge of wire rope spans the chasm between the sea cliffs and the little island of Carrick-a-Rede, swaying gently 30m above the rock-strewn water.

The island has sustained a salmon fishery for centuries; fishermen stretch their nets out from the tip of the island to intercept the passage of salmon migrating along the coast to their home rivers. The fishermen put the bridge up every spring as they have done for the last 200 years – though it's not, of course, the original bridge.

Crossing the bridge is perfectly safe, but it can be frightening if you don't have a head for heights, especially if it's breezy (in high winds the bridge is closed). Once on the island there are good views of Rathlin Island and Fair Head to the east. There's a small National Trust information centre and cafe at the car park.

Sleeping & Eating

TOP CHOICE **Whitepark House** B&B ££
(☎2073 1482; www.whiteparkhouse.com; 150 Whitepark Rd, Ballintoy; s/d £75/100; P@Wi-Fi) A beautifully restored 18th-century house overlooking White Park Bay, this B&B has traditional features such as antique furniture and a peat fire complemented by Asian artefacts gathered during the welcoming owners' oriental travels. There are three rooms – ask for one with a sea view.

Sheep Island View Hostel HOSTEL £
(☎2076 9391; www.sheepislandview.com; 42A Main St, Ballintoy; campsites/dm £6/15; P@Wi-Fi) This excellent independent hostel offers dorm beds, basic shared accommodation in the camping barn, or a place to pitch a tent. There's a kitchen and laundry, a village store nearby and a free pick-up service from the Giant's Causeway, Bushmills and Ballycastle. It's on the main coast road near the turn-off to Ballintoy harbour, and makes an ideal overnight stop if you're hiking between Bushmills and Ballycastle.

Whitepark Bay Hostel HOSTEL £
(☎2073 1745; www.hini.org.uk; 157 White Park Rd, Ballintoy; dm/tw £18/42; ⏲Apr-Oct; P@) This modern, purpose-built hostel near the west end of White Park Bay has mostly four-bed dorms, plus twin rooms with TV, all with private bathroom. There is a common room positioned to soak up the view, and the beach is just a few minutes' walk through the dunes.

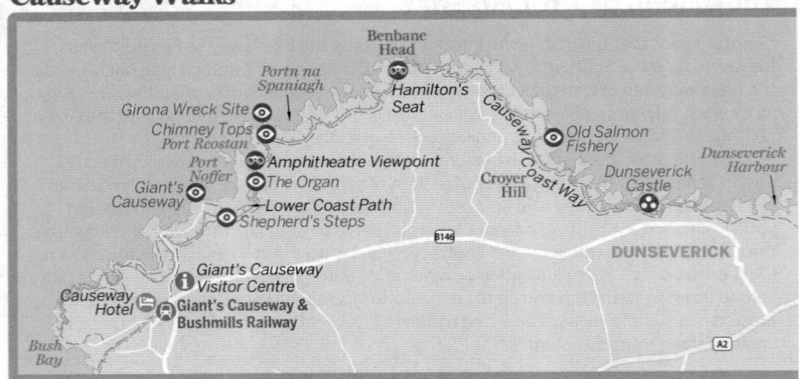

Roark's Kitchen CAFE £

(Ballintoy Harbour; mains £3-6; ⏲11am-7pm Jun-Aug, Sat & Sun only May & Sep) This cute little chalk-built tearoom on the quayside at Ballintoy serves teas, coffees, ice cream, home-baked apple tart and lunch dishes such as Irish stew or chicken and ham pie.

Getting There & Away

Bus 172 between Ballycastle, Bushmills and Coleraine (eight daily Monday to Friday, two on Saturday, three Sunday) is the main, year-round service along this coast, stopping at the Giant's Causeway, Ballintoy and Carrick-a-Rede. Also see Getting There & Around, p656.

Ballycastle

POP 4000

The harbour town and holiday resort of Ballycastle (Baile an Chaisil) marks the eastern end of the Causeway Coast. It's a pretty town with a good bucket-and-spade beach, but apart from that, there's not a lot to see. It's also the port for ferries to Rathlin Island.

Sights & Activities

The town has a family-friendly **promenade**, with a giant sandpit for kids overlooking the marina. A footbridge leads east across the mouth of the River Glenshesk to a good sandy **beach**.

FREE **Ballycastle Museum** MUSEUM

(61A Castle St; ⏲noon-6pm Jul & Aug) The tiny museum in the town's 18th-century court-house has a collection of Irish arts and crafts works.

Marconi Memorial MONUMENT

In the harbour car park, the Marconi Memorial is a plaque at the foot of a rock pinnacle. Guglielmo Marconi's assistants contacted Rathlin Island by radio from Ballycastle in 1898 to prove to Lloyds of London that wireless communication was a viable proposition. The idea was to send notice to London or Liverpool of ships arriving safely after a transatlantic crossing – most vessels on this route would have to pass through the channel north of Rathlin.

Bonamargy Friary HISTORIC SITE

Just east of town are the ruins of Bonamargy Friary, founded in 1485. It's an attractive site to explore, but sadly the vault – which contains the tombs of MacDonnell chieftains, including Sorley Boy MacDonnell of Dunluce Castle – is not open to the public.

Aquasports BOAT TRIPS

(www.aquasports.biz) Offers a range of high-speed boat trips out of Ballycastle harbour, including wildlife tours, cruises along the coast to the Giant's Causeway and tours around Rathlin Island from £25 per person.

Ballycastle Charters FISHING

(☎07751 345791) Three-hour sea-angling trips depart at 11am and 7pm daily except Sunday in summer, and cost £20/15 per adult/child including tackle, bait and lessons.

Festivals & Events

Ballycastle's **Ould Lammas Fair**, held on the last Monday and Tuesday of August, dates back to 1606. Thousands of people descend on the town for the market stalls and fair-

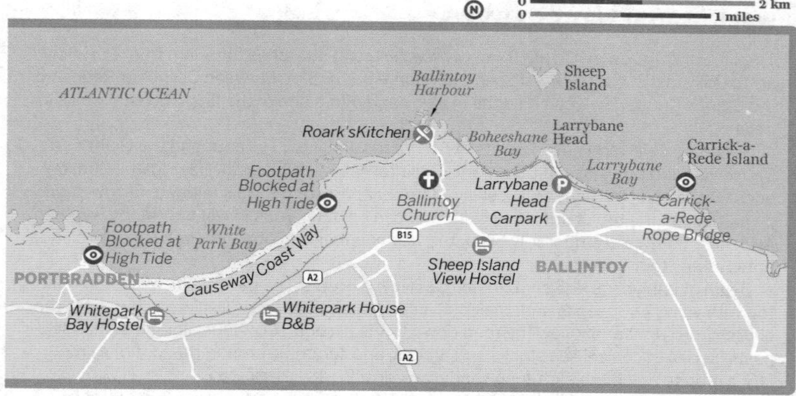

ground rides, and to sample 'yellowman' and dulse. Yellowman is a hard chewy toffee; dulse is dried edible seaweed. The fruit shop on the Diamond often stocks both delicacies.

Sleeping

Glenluce Guesthouse B&B £
(☎2076 2914; www.glenluce.com; 42 Quay Rd; per person £25-40; P 🚻) Recently taken over by an enthusiastic young couple, Glenluce is our favourite among several B&Bs on Quay Rd. It has a luxurious lounge, its own tea shop, and a warm and welcoming family atmosphere. Rooms are spacious and comfortable, if a bit creaky in the floorboard department, and the house is only a few minutes' walk from the beach.

Ballycastle Backpackers HOSTEL £
(☎2076 3612; www.ballycastlebackpackers.net; 4 North St; dm/tw £15/40; P) This is a small and homely hostel set in a terrace house overlooking the harbour, with one six-bed dorm, a family room and a couple of twin and double rooms. There's also a cosy self-catering cottage in the backyard, with two twin rooms with private bathroom (£25 per person per night, also available for rental by the week).

Crockatinney Guest House B&B ££
(☎2076 8801; www.crockatinneyguesthouse.co.uk; 80 Whitepark Rd; s/d £50/65; P) This large, purpose-built guesthouse enjoys a superb location on the coast road 3km west of Ballycastle, with a panoramic view of Rathlin Island, Fair Head and the Scottish coast. All six rooms have private bathrooms – the upstairs rooms have the best views, while the ground floor room is equipped for guests with limited mobility.

Watertop Open Farm CAMPGROUND £
(☎2076 2576; www.watertopfarm.co.uk; 188 Cushendall Rd; campsites per person £5, caravan sites from £18; ⏰Easter-Oct) About 10km east of Ballycastle on the road to Cushendun, child-friendly Watertop is based in a working farm and activity centre, offering pony trekking, sheepshearing and farm tours.

Glenmore Caravan & Camping Park CAMPGROUND £
(☎2076 3584; www.glenmore.biz; 94 White Park Rd; camp/caravan sites from £10/12; ⏰Apr-Oct) Glenmore is a small and peaceful camping ground with its own trout-stocked fishing lough, about 4.5km west of Ballycastle on the B15 road to White Park Bay.

Eating

TOP CHOICE **Cellar Restaurant** IRISH ££
(☎2076 3037; www.thecellarrestaurant.co.uk; 11 The Diamond; mains £10-21; ⏰noon-10pm Mon-Sat, 5-10pm Sun Jun-Aug, 5-10pm Sep-May) This cosy little basement restaurant with intimate wooden booths and a big fireplace is the place to sample Ulster produce – locally caught crab claws grilled with garlic butter, and Carrick-a-Rede salmon are both on the menu, along with Irish beef and lamb, and lobster from Rathlin Island. There are also good vegetarian dishes such as baked peppers stuffed with mushroom and shallot.

WALK: CAUSEWAY COAST WAY

The official **Causeway Coast Way** (www.walkni.com) stretches for 53km from Portstewart to Ballycastle, but the most scenic section – the 16.5km between Carrick-a-Rede and the Giant's Causeway – can be done in a day and offers one of the finest coastal walks in Ireland.

There are cafes and public toilets at Larrybane, Ballintoy Harbour and the Giant's Causeway, and bus stops at Larrybane, Ballintoy village, Whitepark Bay Hostel, Dunseverick Castle and the Giant's Causeway. Note that parts of the walk follow a narrow, muddy path along the top of unfenced cliffs, and can be dangerous in wet and windy weather. Also, high tides can temporarily block the way at either end of White Park Bay; check tide times at any tourist office.

Begin at Larrybane, the car park for **Carrick-a-Rede**. The path starts off along a cliff top with views of Sheep Island, then cuts inland straight towards Ballintoy church. At the church, turn right and follow the road down to the harbour. Continue along the shoreline past a series of conical sea stacks and arches, and scramble around the foot of a limestone crag to reach the 2km-long sandy sweep of **White Park Bay**.

The going here is easiest at low tide, when you can walk on the firm sand. At the far end of the bay (the building with the yellow gable above the dunes is Whitepark Bay Hostel), scramble over rocks and boulders at the bottom of a high limestone cliff for 250m (slippery in places) to **Portbradden**. If you've timed it wrong and the way is blocked by high tide, you can detour up to the hostel and reach Portbradden by walking along the road.

Beyond Portbradden white limestone gives way to black basalt, and the path threads through a natural tunnel in the rocks before weaving around several rocky coves with the high cliffs of Benbane Head visible in the distance. At tiny Dunseverick Harbour you follow a minor road for 200m before descending steps on the right at a waymark. The path then wanders along the grassy foreshore, rounds a headland and crosses a footbridge above a waterfall before reaching the car park at **Dunseverick Castle**.

From here the cliff-top path, narrow in places, climbs steadily, passing an old salmon fishery (the little rusty-roofed cottage on the shore far below). Near **Benbane Head**, the highest and most northerly point on the walk, a wooden bench marks the viewpoint known as Hamilton's Seat (William Hamilton was an 18th-century clergyman and amateur geologist from Derry, who wrote one of the earliest descriptions of the Causeway Coast's geology). Soak up the spectacular panorama of 100m-high sea cliffs, stacks and pinnacles stretching away to the west, before you set off on the final stretch. If you want to visit the causeway itself, descend the **Shepherd's Steps** (signposted), about 1km before the visitor centre and the end of the walk. (Total: 16.5km. Allow five to six hours.)

Thyme & Co CAFE £
(www.thymeandco.co.uk; 5 Quay Rd; mains £6; 8am-4.30pm Tue-Fri, 9.30am-4.30pm Sat, 10.30am-3.30pm Sun;) Thyme is a welcoming cafe with the distinction of a menu that is chock-a-block with homemade dishes prepared using local produce as much as possible – lush salads, shepherd's pie, salmon and egg crumble. Great homebaked scones and excellent coffee, too.

Pantry CAFE £
(41A Castle St; mains £3-5; 9am-5pm Mon-Sat) Housed in a former printer's shop with a lovely original black-and-white mosaic floor, this brisk and cheerful cafe serves a wide range of sandwiches, from pitta to panini and bagels to baguettes, as well as cappuccino and homemade cakes. It's uphill from the Diamond.

Information

There are a couple of banks with ATMs on Ann St, near the Diamond.

Tourist office (2076 2024; tourism@moyle-council.org; 7 Mary St; 9.30am-7pm Mon-Fri, 10am-6pm Sat, 2-6pm Sun Jul & Aug, 9.30am-5pm Mon-Fri Sep-Jun) In the district council building at the east end of town.

Getting There & Away

The bus station is on Station Rd, just east of the Diamond. Ulsterbus Express 217 links Ballycastle with Ballymena, where you change to Goldline Express 218 or 219 for Belfast (£9, two hours, three daily Monday to Friday, two Saturday).

Bus 172 goes along the coast to Coleraine (£4.50, one hour, eight daily Monday to Friday, two on Saturday, three Sunday) via Ballintoy, the Giant's Causeway and Bushmills. Also see Getting There & Around, p656.

Rathlin Island

POP 110

In spring and summer, rugged Rathlin Island (Reachlainn; www.rathlincommunity.org), 6km offshore from Ballycastle, is home to hundreds of seals and thousands of nesting seabirds. An L-shaped island just 6.5km long and 4km wide, Rathlin is famous for the coastal scenery and bird life at **Kebble National Nature Reserve** at its western end.

The island's most illustrious visitor was Scottish hero **Robert the Bruce**, who spent some time here in 1306 while hiding out after being defeated by the English king. Watching a spider's resoluteness in repeatedly trying to spin a web gave him the courage to have another go at the English, whom he subsequently defeated at Bannockburn. The cave where he is said to have stayed is beneath the **East Lighthouse**, at the north-eastern tip of the island.

RSPB West Light Viewpoint (www.rspb.org.uk; admission free; ⏲11am-3pm Apr-Aug) provides stunning views of the neighbouring sea stacks, thick with guillemots, kittiwakes, razorbills and puffins from mid-April to August. During the summer a minibus service runs there from the harbour; public toilets and binocular hire are available.

If you don't have time to visit the Kebble Nature Reserve, the best short walk on the island is through the National Trust's Ballyconagan Nature Reserve to the **Old Coastguard Lookout** on the north coast, with great views along the sea cliffs and across to the Scottish islands of Islay and Jura.

Boathouse Visitor Centre (admission free; ⏲9.30am-5pm May-Sep), south of the harbour, details the history, culture and ecology of the island, and can give advice on walks and wildlife. **Paul Quinn** (☎7032 7960, 07745 566924; www.rathlinwalkingtours.com; per person £4-12) offers guided walking tours of the island.

Sleeping & Eating

The island has a pub, a restaurant and a handful of accommodation options; it is essential to book your accommodation in advance. You can camp for free in the field beside **McCuaig's Bar** (☎2076 3974), just east of the harbour; ask at the bar first. McCuaig's has a cafe and chip shop, and there's a tiny grocery shop a few paces to the west of the ferry berth (turn left as you come off the pier).

Manor House B&B ££
(☎2076 3964; www.rathlinmanorhouse.co.uk; Church Quarter; s/d £42/72) Restored and run by the National Trust, the 18th-century Manor House, on the north side of the harbour, is the island's biggest (12 rooms) and most pleasant place to stay. All rooms have sea views, and evening meals are available by arrangement. The Manor House **restaurant** (mains £12-18, lobster £27; ⏲10.45am-5.30pm Mon, to 11pm Wed-Sun May-Sep) is open to non-residents (booking necessary).

Coolnagrock B&B B&B ££
(☎2076 3983; Coolnagrock; s/d £35/60; ⏲closed Dec) This well-appointed guesthouse is in the eastern part of the island, with great views across the sea to Kintyre. It's a 15-minute walk from the ferry, but you can arrange for the owner to pick you up.

Kinramer Camping Barn HOSTEL £
(☎2076 3948; alison.mcfaul@rspb.org.uk; Kinramer; dm £10) This is a basic bunkhouse located on an organic farm, 5km (a one-hour walk) west from the harbour, where you bring your own food and bedding; it must be booked in advance. You might be able to get a lift there on one of the island minibuses.

Soerneog View Hostel HOSTEL £
(☎2076 3954; www.n-irelandholidays.co.uk/rathlin; Ouig; per person from £12.50; ⏲Apr-Sep) A private house, a 10-minute walk south of the harbour, Soerneog offers basic hostel-style accommodation in one double and two twin rooms.

Getting There & Around

A **ferry** (☎2076 9299; www.rathlinballycastleferry.com) operates daily (adult/child/bicycle return £11.20/5.60/3) from Ballycastle; advance booking is recommended in spring and summer. From April to September there are eight or nine crossings a day, half of which are fast catamaran services (20 minutes), the rest via a slower car ferry (45 minutes); in winter the service is reduced.

Only residents can take their car to Rathlin (except for disabled drivers), but nowhere on the island is more than 6km (about 1½ hours' walk) from the ferry pier. You can hire a bicycle (£8 per day) from Soerneog View Hostel, or take a minibus tour with **McGinn's** (☎2076 3451), which also shuttles visitors between the ferry and Kebble Nature Reserve (£5 return) from April to August.

Glens of Antrim

The northeastern corner of Antrim is a high plateau of black basalt lava overlying beds of white chalk. Along the coast, between Cushendun and Glenarm, the plateau has been dissected by a series of scenic, glacier-gouged valleys known as the Glens of Antrim.

Two waymarked footpaths traverse the region: the **Ulster Way** (p679) sticks close to the sea, passing through all the coastal villages, while the 32km **Moyle Way** runs inland across the high plateau from Glenariff Forest Park to Ballycastle.

TORR HEAD SCENIC ROAD

A few kilometres east of Ballycastle, a minor road signposted 'Scenic Route' branches north off the A2. This alternative route to Cushendun is not for the faint-hearted driver (nor for caravans), as it clings, precarious and narrow, to steep slopes high above the sea. Side roads lead off to the main points of interest – Fair Head, Murlough Bay and Torr Head. On a clear day, there are superb views across the sea to Scotland, from the Mull of Kintyre to the peaks of Arran.

The first turn-off ends at the National Trust car park at Coolanlough, the starting point for a hike to **Fair Head** (see the boxed text). The second turn-off leads steeply down to **Murlough Bay**. From the parking area at the end of this road, you can walk north along the shoreline to some ruined miners' cottages (10 minutes); coal and chalk were once mined in the cliffs above, and burned in a limekiln (south of the car park) to make quicklime.

The third turn-off leads you past some ruined coastguard houses to the rocky headland of **Torr Head**, crowned with a 19th-century coastguard station (abandoned in the 1920s). This is Ireland's closest point to Scotland – the Mull of Kintyre is a mere 19km away across the North Channel. In late spring and summer, a salmon fishery like the one at Carrick-a-Rede operates here, with a net strung out from the headland. The ancient ice house beside the approach road was once used to store the catch.

CUSHENDUN

POP 350

The pretty seaside village of Cushendun is famous for its distinctive Cornish-style cottages, now owned by the National Trust. Built between 1912 and 1925 at the behest of the local landowner, Lord Cushendun, they were designed by Clough Williams-Ellis, the architect of Portmeirion in north Wales. There's a nice sandy **beach**, various short **coastal walks** (outlined on an information board beside the car park), and some impressive **caves** cut into the overhanging conglomerate sea cliffs south of the village (follow the trail around the far end of the holiday apartments south of the river mouth).

Another natural curiosity lies 6km north of the village on the A2 road to Ballycastle – **Loughareema**, also known as the Vanishing Lake. Three streams flow in but none flow out. The lough fills up to a respectable size (400m long and 6m deep) after heavy rain, but then the water gradually drains away through fissures in the underlying limestone, leaving a dry lake bed.

Sleeping

Villa Farmhouse B&B ££

(☎2176 1252; www.thevillafarmhouse.com; 185 Torr Rd; s/d from £35/60; P @) This lovely old whitewashed farmhouse is set on a hillside, 1km north of the village, with great views over the sea and down to Cushendun Bay. The owner is an expert chef and breakfast will be a highlight of your stay – best scrambled eggs in Northern Ireland? Evening meals by arrangement.

Cloneymore House B&B ££

(☎2176 1443; ann.cloneymore@btinternet.com; 103 Knocknacarry Rd; s/d £40/50; P Wi-Fi) A traditional family B&B on the B92 road 500m southwest of Cushendun, Cloneymore has three spacious and spotless rooms named after Irish and Scottish islands – Aran is the biggest. There are wheelchair ramps and a stairlift, and all rooms are equipped for visitors with limited mobility.

Mullarts Apartments SELF-CATERING ££

(☎2176 1221; www.mullartsapartments.co.uk; 114 Tromra Rd; d per weekend/week £140/375; P) An unusual alternative, Mullarts offers three

WALK: FAIR HEAD

From the National Trust car park at Coolanlough, a waymarked path leads north past a small lake dotted with tiny islands, one of which is a *crannóg* (Neolithic island settlement). After 1.5km you arrive at the top of the impressive 180m-high basalt cliffs that mark Fair Head. The cliffs, one of Ireland's most important rock-climbing areas, are split here by a spectacular gully bridged by a fallen rock, known as the Grey Man's Path. The panorama of sea and islands extends from Rathlin Island in the west (to your left), with the Scottish island of Islay to its right, followed by the three pointed hills of Jura, to the dark mass of the Mull of Kintyre and the tiny island of Sanda. To the east is the squat cone of Ailsa Craig with the coast of Ayrshire far beyond.

Turn right and follow the faint trail south along the cliff tops for 1.5km until you reach the upper car park on the Murlough Bay road. From here, another faint path, marked by yellow paint marks, strikes west for 1km back to Coolanlough. (Total: 4km. Allow one to two hours.)

luxury self-catering apartments housed in a converted 19th-century church, 2.5km south of the village. There are two double apartments, and one that can sleep up to six people.

Cushendun Caravan Park CAMPGROUND £
(☎2176 1254; 14 Glendun Rd; camp/caravan sites from £10/18; ⏱Easter-Sep) The local council-run camping ground enjoys a pleasant woodland setting just north of the village and a mere five-minute walk from the beach.

Eating & Drinking

Mary McBride's Pub PUB £
(2 Main St; mains £6-10; ⏱food 12.30-8pm Apr-Sep, to 7pm Oct-Mar) The original bar here (on the left as you go in) is the smallest in Ireland (2.7m by 1.5m) but there's plenty of elbow-bending room in the rest of the pub. The food – standard pub grub – is good and there's Guinness on tap, as well as occasional live music at weekends.

Theresa's Tearoom CAFE £
(1 Main St; mains £4-9; ⏱11am-7pm Easter-Sep, to 6pm Sat & Sun Oct-Easter) The cosy village tearoom beside the bridge offers tea and cakes, sandwiches and salads, and hot lunch dishes such as fish and chips, grilled chicken and vegetable tortilla wraps.

Getting There & Away

Bus 150 runs from Ballymena to Cushendun (one hour, six daily Monday to Friday, four Saturday) via Glenariff Forest Park and Cushendall; Ballymena can be reached by train from Belfast and Derry. The twice-daily **Antrim Coaster** (bus 252/256) links Coleraine with Belfast via the Glens of Antrim and Larne (see p656).

CUSHENDALL

POP 1250

Cushendall is a holiday centre (and traffic bottleneck) at the foot of Glenballyeamon, overlooked by the prominent flat-topped hill of Lurigethan. The beach is small and shingly, though; there are better ones at Waterfoot and Cushendun.

Sights

Curfew Tower HISTORIC BUILDING
The unusual red sandstone Curfew Tower at the central crossroads was built in 1817, based on a building the landowner had seen in China. It was originally a prison 'for the confinement of idlers and rioters'.

Layde Old Church CHURCH
From the car park beside the beach, a coastal path leads 1km north to the picturesque ruins of Layde Old Church, with views across to Ailsa Craig (a prominent conical island also known as 'Paddy's Milestone') and the Scottish coast. Founded by the Franciscans, it was used as a parish church from the early 14th century until 1790. The graveyard contains several grand MacDonnell memorials. Near the gate stands an ancient, weathered ring-cross (with the arms missing), much older than the 19th-century inscription on its shaft.

Ossian's Grave HISTORIC SITE
In Glenaan, 4km northwest of Cushendall, is Ossian's Grave, a Neolithic court tomb romantically, but inaccurately, named after the legendary 3rd-century warrior-poet. The site is signposted off the A2; you can park at the farm and walk up.

WALK: THE GLENARIFF CIRCUIT

This varied 7.5km hike, which ranges from the mossy depths of a waterfall-filled ravine to the edge of the high Antrim Plateau, is one of the best forest-park walks in Northern Ireland. Begin at the Laragh Lodge restaurant, and follow the **boardwalk** (admission £1.50; Easter-Oct) upstream along the Glenariff River to the foaming cascade of Ess-na-Larach, then continue steeply up the zigzags beyond. There's a junction at a wooden bench – the path to the left leads down to the forest park visitor centre (signposted), but go right on the trail heading upstream with the river down to your right.

At the next junction (signposted Hermit's Fall to the right), turn left and follow the path uphill to reach a road, where you turn right. The path now parallels the road for 600m until you reach a sign marked 'Scenic Trail' pointing back the way you came. Go left across the road and, a few metres further on, cross a second road and follow the obvious path up through the forest. You eventually emerge from the trees to get your first open view along Glenariff. Beyond, the path slowly curves around to the right (south; there are more Scenic Trail waymarks, but you are following them in reverse). As you near the head of the next valley (that's the River Inver down below), the path forks near a wooden shelter, the left branch descending steeply; keep right here and continue right to the top of the glen.

The trail then curves left and crosses the three streams that feed the River Inver, then switchbacks up the far side and into thick pine forest, only to emerge into a clearing on a cliff top with a stunning view down Glenariff – the valley floor is slung like a green hammock between steep, black basalt crags. A short distance further on there's a very steep zigzag descent, followed by a level traverse to the left. When you reach a forest road, turn right. After 1km it descends steeply leftwards down to a gate; take the path on the left and cross a footbridge over the river. Turn right, then right again and you'll find yourself back at your starting point. (Total: 7.5km. Allow three to four hours.)

Sleeping & Eating

Village B&B B&B ££
(2177 2366; www.thevillagebandb.com; 18 Mill St; s/d £38/60; Apr-Sep; P) Bang in the middle of town, the Village offers three spotless rooms with private bathrooms and huge hearty breakfasts, and is just across the road from McCollams, the best pub in Cushendall for traditional music.

Cullentra House B&B ££
(2177 1762; www.cullentrahouseireland.com; 16 Cloughs Rd; s/d from £35/50; P) This modern bungalow sits high above the village at the end of Cloughs Rd, offering good views of the craggy Antrim coast. The three rooms are spacious and comfy, and the breakfasts (accompanied by home-baked wheaten bread) are as big as the owners' hospitality.

Cushendall Caravan Park CAMPGROUND £
(2177 1699; 62 Coast Rd; camp/caravan sites £10/18; Easter-Sep) This camping ground overlooks the sea, just over 1km south of the town centre.

Harry's Restaurant BISTRO ££
(2177 2022; 10 Mill St; bar meals £9-10, dinner mains £9-18; 10am-9pm Mon-Sat, noon-9pm Sun) With its cosy lounge-bar atmosphere and friendly welcome, Harry's is a local institution, serving breakfast 10am to noon, pub grub from noon to 6pm – battered cod with mushy peas, burger or Caesar salad, for example – plus an à-la-carte dinner menu in the evenings that ranges from steak to lobster.

Information

Tourist office (2177 1180; 24 Mill St; 10am-1pm & 2-5.30pm Mon-Fri, 10am-1pm Sat Jul-Sep, 10am-1pm Tue-Sat Oct-Jun) Run by the Glens of Antrim Historical Society; also offers internet access.

Getting There & Away

Bus 162 travels from Larne to Cushendall (£7, one hour, three daily Monday to Friday), stopping at Glenarm and Carnlough; there are frequent trains and buses from Belfast to Larne. Bus 150 goes to Cushendun and Glenariff Forest Park.

GLENARIFF

About 2km south of Cushendall is the village of **Waterfoot**, with a 2km-long sandy beach, the best on Antrim's east coast. From here the A43 Ballymena road runs inland along Glenariff, the loveliest of Antrim's glens.

Views of the valley led the writer Thackeray to exclaim that it was a 'Switzerland in miniature', a claim that makes you wonder if he'd ever been to Switzerland!

At the head of the valley is **Glenariff Forest Park** (car/motorcycle/pedestrian £4/2/1.50; ⏲10am-dusk), where the main attraction is **Ess-na-Larach Waterfall**, an 800m walk from the visitor centre. You can also walk to the waterfall from Laragh Lodge, 600m downstream. There are various good walks in the park; the longest is a 10km circular trail.

There's hostel accommodation for hikers at **Ballyeamon Camping Barn** (☎2175 8451; www.ballyeamonbarn.com; 127 Ballyeamon Rd; dm £10; @), 8km southwest of Cushendall on the B14 (1km north of its junction with the A43), close to the Moyle Way and about 1.5km walk from the main entrance to the forest park.

Laragh Lodge (☎2175 8221; 120 Glen Rd; mains £10-15, 4-course Sun lunch £17; ⏲11am-9pm, food noon-9pm) is a restaurant and bar on a side road off the A43, 3km northeast of the main park entrance. A renovated Victorian tourist lodge with assorted bric-a-brac dangling from the rafters, the Laragh dates from 1890 and serves hearty pub-grub-style meals – beef and Guinness pie, fish and chips, sausage and mash (with a couple of vegetarian options) – and offers a traditional roast lunch on Sunday.

You can reach Glenariff Forest Park on Ulsterbus 150 from Cushendun (£4, 30 minutes, six daily Monday to Friday, four Saturday) and Ballymena (£4, 30 minutes).

GLENARM

POP 600

Since 1750 Glenarm (Gleann Arma), the oldest village in the glens, has been the family seat of the MacDonnell family; the present 14th Earl of Antrim lives in **Glenarm Castle** (www.glenarmcastle.com), on a private estate hidden behind the impressive wall that runs along the main road north of the bridge. The castle itself is closed to the public, except for two days in July when a Highland Games competition is held, but you can visit the lovely **walled garden** (adult/child £5/2.50; ⏲10am-5pm Mon-Sat, noon-6pm Sun May-Sep).

The **tourist office** (☎2884 1087; www.glenarmtourism.org.uk; 2 The Bridge; ⏲9.30am-5pm Mon-Fri, 2-6pm Sun) is beside the bridge on the main road. It has internet access for £2 per 30 minutes.

Take a stroll into the old village of neat Georgian houses (off the main road, immediately south of the river). Where the street opens into the broad expanse of Altmore St, look right to see the **Barbican Gate** (1682), the entrance to Glenarm Castle grounds. On the left is **Steensons** (www.thesteensons.com; Toberwine St; ⏲9.30am-5.15pm Mon-Sat), a designer jewellery workshop and visitor centre where you can watch craftspeople at work.

Turn left here and climb steeply up Vennel St, then left again immediately after the last house along the Layde Path to the **viewpoint**, which has a grand view of the village and the coast.

Larne

POP 17,600

As a major port for ferries from Scotland, Larne (Lutharna) is one of Northern Ireland's main points of arrival. However, with its concrete overpasses and the huge chimneys of Ballylumford power station opposite the harbour, poor old Larne is a little lacking in the charm department. After a visit to the excellent tourist information centre, there's no real reason to linger.

Larne Harbour train station is in the ferry terminal. It's a short bus ride or a 15-minute walk from here to the town centre – turn right on Fleet St and right again on Curran Rd, then left on Circular Rd. At the big roundabout, Larne Town train station is to your left, the tourist office is to the right, and the bus station is ahead (beneath the road bridge).

Information

Tourist office (☎2826 0088; larnetourism@btconnect.com; Narrow Gauge Rd; ⏲9am-5pm Mon-Fri, 10am-4pm Sat Easter-Sep, 9am-5pm Mon-Fri Oct-Easter)

Getting There & Away

P&O Irish Sea (www.poirishsea.com) ferries run from Larne to Scotland and England.

Bus 256 provides a direct service between the town centre and Belfast (£4, one hour, hourly Monday to Friday, six Saturday, plus two on Sunday July to September only).

Heading north to the Glens of Antrim, take bus 162 or the *Antrim Coaster* (see p656).

Larne has two train stations, **Larne Town** and **Larne Harbour**. Trains from Larne Town to Belfast Central (£6.20, one hour) depart at least hourly; those from the harbour are timed to connect with ferries.

Carrickfergus

POP 28,000

Northern Ireland's most impressive medieval fortress commands the entrance to Belfast Lough from the rocky promontory of Carrickfergus (Carraig Fhearghais). The old town centre opposite the castle has some attractive 18th-century houses and you can still trace a good part of the 17th-century city walls.

Sights

Carrickfergus Castle CASTLE

(Marine Hwy; adult/child £4/2; ⏲10am-6pm) The central keep of Ireland's first and finest Norman fortress was built by John de Courcy soon after his 1177 invasion of Ulster. The massive walls of the outer ward were completed in 1242, while the red-brick gun ports were added in the 16th century. The keep houses a **museum** and the site is dotted with life-size figures illustrating the castle's history.

The castle overlooks the harbour where **William of Orange** landed on 14 June 1690, on his way to the Battle of the Boyne; a blue plaque on the old harbour wall marks the site where he stepped ashore, and a bronze statue of the man himself stands on the shore nearby.

FREE **Carrickfergus Museum** MUSEUM

(11 Antrim St; ⏲10am-6pm Mon-Sat Apr-Sep, to 5pm Mon-Sat Oct-Mar) The glass-fronted Heritage Plaza on Antrim St houses the local museum, which has a small collection of artefacts relating to the town's history, and a pleasant coffee shop.

FREE **Andrew Jackson Centre** HISTORIC SITE

(Boneybefore) The parents of the seventh US president left Carrickfergus in the second half of the 18th century. His ancestral home was demolished in 1860, but a replica thatched cottage complete with fireside crane and earthen floor now houses this memorial on the coast, 2km north of the castle. It has displays on the life of Jackson, the Jackson family in Ulster and Ulster's connection with the USA, and is open by appointment only; contact the tourist office in advance.

Next door is the **US Rangers Centre**, with a small exhibition on the first US rangers, who were trained during WWII in Carrickfergus before heading for Europe.

Sleeping & Eating

Keep Guesthouse B&B ££

(☎9336 7007; www.thekeepguesthousecarrickfergus.co.uk; 93 Irish Quarter S; s/d from £35/50; 📶) Just across the main road from the marina, and close to the town centre, the Keep has four rooms with attractive, modern decor and original art on the walls; go for the spacious double/family room on the 1st floor if possible.

Dobbin's Inn Hotel HOTEL ££

(☎9335 1905; www.dobbinsinnhotel.co.uk; 6-8 High St; s/d from £45/65; @📶) In the centre of the old town, Dobbin's is a friendly and informal place with 15 small and creaky-floored but comfortable rooms. The building has been around for over three centuries, and has a priest's hole and an original 16th-century fireplace to prove it.

Windrose INTERNATIONAL ££

(☎9335 1164; www.thewindrose.co.uk; Rodgers Quay; mains £9-17; ⏲food noon-9pm) This stylish, modern bar-bistro, with a more formal restaurant upstairs (mains £15 to £25, dinner only), serves a range of dishes from fisherman's pie and mussels to steaks and stir-fries. The outdoor terrace overlooking the forest of yacht masts in the marina is a real sun-trap on a summer afternoon.

Courtyard Coffee House CAFE £

(38 Scottish Quarter; mains £4-6; ⏲9am-4.45pm Mon-Sat) This cafe serves tasty homemade soups and light lunches as well as coffee and cakes, and has a second branch inside Carrickfergus Castle.

Information

Tourist office (☎9335 8049; www.carrickfergus.org; Heritage Plaza, 11 Antrim St; ⏲10am-6pm Mon-Sat Apr-Sep, to 5pm Mon-Sat Oct-Mar; 📶) Has a bureau de change and books accommodation.

Getting There & Away

There's an hourly train service between Carrickfergus and Belfast (£4, 30 minutes).

Inland County Antrim

To the west of the high moorland plateau above the Glens of Antrim, the hills slope down to the agricultural lowlands of Lough Neagh and the broad valley of the River Bann. This region is rarely visited by tourists, who either take the coast road or speed

WORTH A TRIP

GALGORM

About 6km west of Ballymena is the **Galgorm Resort & Spa** (2588 1001; www.galgorm.com; 136 Fenaghy Rd, Galgorm; d/f from £95/135; P@), a 19th-century manor house in a lovely setting on the bank of the River Main. Refurbished by the owners of Belfast's boutique hotel Ten Square, the Galgorm has been redeveloped and extended to create one of Ireland's top country-house hotels.

The rustic atmosphere of the original **Gillie's Bar** (mains lunch £8-18, dinner £12-26; food served noon-10pm), set in the former stables, has been retained, with bare stone walls, huge timber beams, a log fire and cosy sofas, but it has been extended into a spectacular, high-roofed barn with a huge, central free-standing chimney and a monumental staircase framed by crouching sphinxes – all in all, a pretty jaw-dropping setting for some of the fanciest pub grub in Ireland.

through on the way from Belfast to Derry, but there are a few places worth seeking out if you have time to spare.

ANTRIM TOWN

POP 19,800

The town of Antrim (Aontroim) straddles the River Sixmilewater, close to an attractive bay on the shores of Lough Neagh. During the 1798 Rising, the United Irishmen fought a pitched battle along the length of the town's High St.

The **tourist office** (9442 8331; www.antrim.gov.uk; Market Sq; 9am-5pm Mon-Fri, plus 10am-1pm Sat May-Sep) is housed in the beautifully restored **Old Courthouse** (1762), a gem of Georgian architecture. Pick up a free, self-guided heritage trail leaflet.

Beyond the courthouse is the **Barbican Gate** (1818) and a portion of the old castle walls. Pass through the gate and the underpass beyond to reach **Antrim Castle Gardens** (admission free; 9.30am-7pm, or dusk if earlier). The castle burned down many years ago, but the grounds remain as one of the few surviving examples of a 17th-century ornamental garden.

Antrim's 10th-century **Round Tower** (Steeple Rd), on the northeast edge of town, is 28m tall, and one of the finest examples of these monastic towers in all of Ireland. You can explore the site freely, but the tower itself is closed to the public,

Lough Rd leads west from the town centre to **Antrim Lough Shore Park**, where the vast size of Lough Neagh is apparent. There are picnic tables and lakeside walking trails.

The vintage launch **Maid of Antrim** (2582 2159; www.loughneaghcruises.co.uk), built on Scotland's River Clyde in 1963, offers cruises on the lough, departing from Antrim Marina (next to Lough Shore Park) on Sunday afternoons from Easter to October. Booking is essential.

Goldline Express 219 from Belfast to Ballymena stops in Antrim (£4.20, 40 minutes, hourly Monday to Friday, seven on Saturday). There are also frequent trains from Belfast to Antrim (£5.10, 25 minutes, 10 daily Monday to Saturday, five on Sunday) continuing to Derry.

BALLYMENA

POP 29,200

Ballymena (An Baile Meánach) is the home turf of Ian Paisley, the founder of the Free Presbyterian Church and the stridently anti-Nationalist and anti-Catholic Democratic Unionist Party (DUP), who served as First Minister of Northern Ireland until 2008. The town council was the first to be controlled by the DUP in 1977 and voted unanimously to remove all mention of Darwin's theory of evolution from religious education in Ballymena's schools. The town is also the birthplace of the actor Liam Neeson, of *Schindler's List* and *Star Wars* fame.

Sights

FREE **Braid** MUSEUM
(www.thebraid.com; 1-29 Bridge St; 10am-5pm Mon-Fri, to 4pm Sat) Ballymena's new museum is housed in a dramatic modern building that is also home to the town hall, tourist office and arts centre. Interesting exhibitions cover the region's history.

FREE **Ecos Environmental Centre** ECOLOGY CENTRE
(www.ballymena.gov.uk/ecos; Broughshane Rd; 9am-5pm Mon-Fri, noon-5pm Sat & Sun Jun-Aug, 10am-5pm Mon-Fri Easter-Oct) This visitor centre on the eastern edge of town is dedicated to alternative energy sources and sustainable

technology – the centre's waste water is filtered through reed beds and used to irrigate nearby willow coppices, which provide fuel for heating and electricity, supplemented by solar panels. There are lots of hands-on exhibits to keep the kids amused, plus a picnic-and-play area, a pond with ducks to feed, and radio-controlled boats to play with.

Getting There & Away

Goldline Express 219 goes to Ballymena from Belfast (£6, one hour, hourly Monday to Friday, seven Saturday). Bus 128 goes to Carnlough on the coast (£4, one hour, five daily Monday to Friday, one Saturday).

Trains from Belfast run more frequently (£7, 10 daily Monday to Saturday, five on Sunday); Ballymena is on the Derry–Belfast train line.

SLEMISH

The skyline to the east of Ballymena is dominated by the distinctive craggy peak of Slemish (438m). The hill is one of many sites in the North associated with Ireland's patron saint – the young St Patrick is said to have tended goats on its slopes. On St Patrick's Day, thousands of people make a pilgrimage to its summit; the rest of the year it's a pleasant climb, though steep and slippery in wet weather, rewarded with a fine view (allow one hour return from the parking area).

Counties Fermanagh & Tyrone

POPULATION: 230,000/ AREA: 4846 SQ KM

Includes »

Best Places to Eat

» Dollakis (p675)
» Deli on the Green (p689)
» Terrace Restaurant (p676)
» Rectory Bistro (p680)
» Kissin Crust (p678)

Best Places to Stay

» Westville Hotel (p675)
» Cedars Guesthouse (p680)
» Tullylagan Country House (p689)
» Kilmore Quay Club (p678)
» Mullaghmore House (p686)

Why Go?

The ancient landscape of Fermanagh is shaped by ice and water, with rugged hills rising above quilted plains of half-drowned drumlins (rounded hills formed by retreating glaciers) and shimmering, reed-fringed lakes. A glance at the map shows the county is around one-third water – as the locals will tell you, the lakes are in Fermanagh for six months of the year; for the other six, Fermanagh is in the lakes. This watery maze is a natural playground for anglers and canoeists.

County Tyrone – from Tír Eoghain (Land of Owen, a legendary chieftain) – is the homeland of the O'Neill clan, and is dominated by the tweed-tinted moorlands of the Sperrin Mountains, whose southern flanks are dotted with pre historic sites. Apart from the hiking opportunities offered by these heather-clad hills, the county's main attraction is the Ulster American Folk Park, a fascinating outdoor museum celebrating Ulster's historic links with the USA.

When to Go

May marks the start of the mayfly season, the most exciting time for trout fishing on Lough Erne and Lough Melvin, while June is the ideal month for cruising the lakes. If hiking is more to your taste, July is ideal for hillwaking in the Sperrins – you can join a mass pilgrimage to the summit of Mullaghcarn, above Gortin, on Cairn Sunday, the last Sunday in the month. The tail end of summer is enlivened by the Ulster American Folk Park's annual Appalachian and Bluegrass Music Festival.

Counties Fermanagh & Tyrone Highlights

1. Hike over rare blanket bog to the remote summit of **Cuilcagh Mountain** (p685)
2. Ponder the meaning of the strange stone figures on **White Island** (p680) and **Boa Island** (p681)
3. Follow the course of an underground river through the **Marble Arch Caves** (p685)
4. Hire a canoe and explore the reed-fringed backwaters of **Lough Erne** (p684)
5. Learn about the historical links between Ireland and the USA at the **Ulster American Folk Park** (p687)
6. See how the Irish aristocracy enjoyed the high life in the elegant country house of **Florence Court** (p684)
7. Explore the Celtic monastic settlement on **Devenish Island** (p679), and climb to the top of its ancient round tower

COUNTY FERMANAGH

Enniskillen

POP 13,600

Perched amid the web of waterways that link Upper and Lower Lough Erne, Enniskillen (Inis Ceithleann, meaning Ceithleann's Island, after a legendary woman warrior) is an appealing town with a mile-long main street that rides the roller-coaster spine of the island's drumlin. Its attractive waterside setting, bustling with boats in summer, plus a range of lively pubs and restaurants, make Enniskillen a good base for exploring Upper and Lower Lough Erne, Florence Court and the Marble Arch Caves.

Though neither was born here, both Oscar Wilde and Samuel Beckett were pupils at Enniskillen's Portora Royal School (Wilde from 1864 to 1871, Beckett from 1919 to 1923); it was here that Beckett first studied French, a language he would later write in. The town's name is also prominent in the history of the Troubles – on Poppy Day (11 November) in 1987 an IRA bomb killed 11 people during a service at Enniskillen's war memorial.

The main street changes name half a dozen times between the bridges at either end; the prominent clock tower marks the town centre. The other principal street is Wellington Rd, south of and parallel to the main street, where you'll find the bus station, tourist office and car parking. If you're driving, try to avoid rush hour – the bridge at the west end is a traffic bottleneck.

Sights

Enniskillen Castle HISTORIC BUILDING

(www.enniskillencastle.co.uk; Castle Barracks; adult/child €4/3; ⏲2-5pm Mon & 10am-5pm Tue-Fri year-round, also 2-5pm Sat May-Sep & 2-5pm Sun Jul & Aug) Enniskillen Castle, a former stronghold of the 16th-century Maguire chieftains, guards the western end of the town's central island, its twin-turreted **Watergate** looming over passing fleets of cabin cruisers. Within the walls you'll find the **Fermanagh County Museum**, which has displays on the county's history, archaeology, landscape and wildlife. The 15th-century keep contains the **Royal Inniskilling Fusiliers Regimental Museum**, full of guns, uniforms and medals – including eight Victoria Crosses awarded in WWI; it's dedicated to the regiment that was raised at the castle in 1689 to support the army of William I.

Cole's Monument MONUMENT

(admission free; ⏲1.30-3pm mid-Apr–Sep) In Forthill Park, at the eastern end of town, stands Cole's Monument. It commemorates Sir Galbraith Lowry-Cole (1772–1842), who was one of Wellington's generals and the son of the first Earl of Enniskillen. Climb the 108 steps inside the column for a good view of the surrounding area.

Activities

Kingfisher Trail CYCLING

(www.cycleni.com) The Kingfisher Trail is a waymarked, long-distance cycling trail that starts in Enniskillen and wends its way through the back roads of Counties Fermanagh, Leitrim, Cavan and Monaghan. The full route is around 370km long, but a shorter loop, starting and finishing in Enniskillen, and travelling via Kesh, Belleek, Garrison, Belcoo and the village of Florencecourt, is only 115km – easily done in two days with an overnight stay at Belleek. You can get a trail map from the Enniskillen Tourist Information Centre. There's no bicycle hire available in Enniskillen, though; the nearest is in Castle Archdale Country Park (p680).

You can buy **fishing** permits and licences from the tourist information centre, or Home, Field and Stream (p677).

For boat-hire options see p678 and p684. Information on **cruising holidays** on the lakes is at www.fermanaghlakelands.com.

Tours

Blue Badge Tours HISTORY TOURS

(☎6862 1430; breegemccusker@btopenworld.com) Offers guided tours of Enniskillen and the Lough Erne area with local historian Breege McCusker, a registered tourist guide. Special interest tours include prehistoric sites, monastic sites, carved stones and Plantation castles.

Erne Tours BOAT TRIPS

(☎6632 2882; www.ernetoursltd.com; Round 'O' Quay, The Brook; adult/child €10/6; ⏲10.30am, 2.15pm & 4.15pm daily Jul & Aug, 2.15pm & 4.15pm daily Jun, 2.15pm & 4.15pm daily Tue, Sat & Sun May, Sep & Oct) Operates 1¾-hour cruises on Lower Lough Erne aboard the 56-seat waterbus MV *Kestrel,* calling at Devenish Island along the way. It departs from the Round 'O' Quay, just west of the town centre on the A46 to Belleek. There are also **Saturday evening cruises** (adult/child €27/16; ⏲6.30pm May-Sep) that include a three-course dinner at the Killyhevlin Hotel, departing from the hotel jetty.

Enniskillen

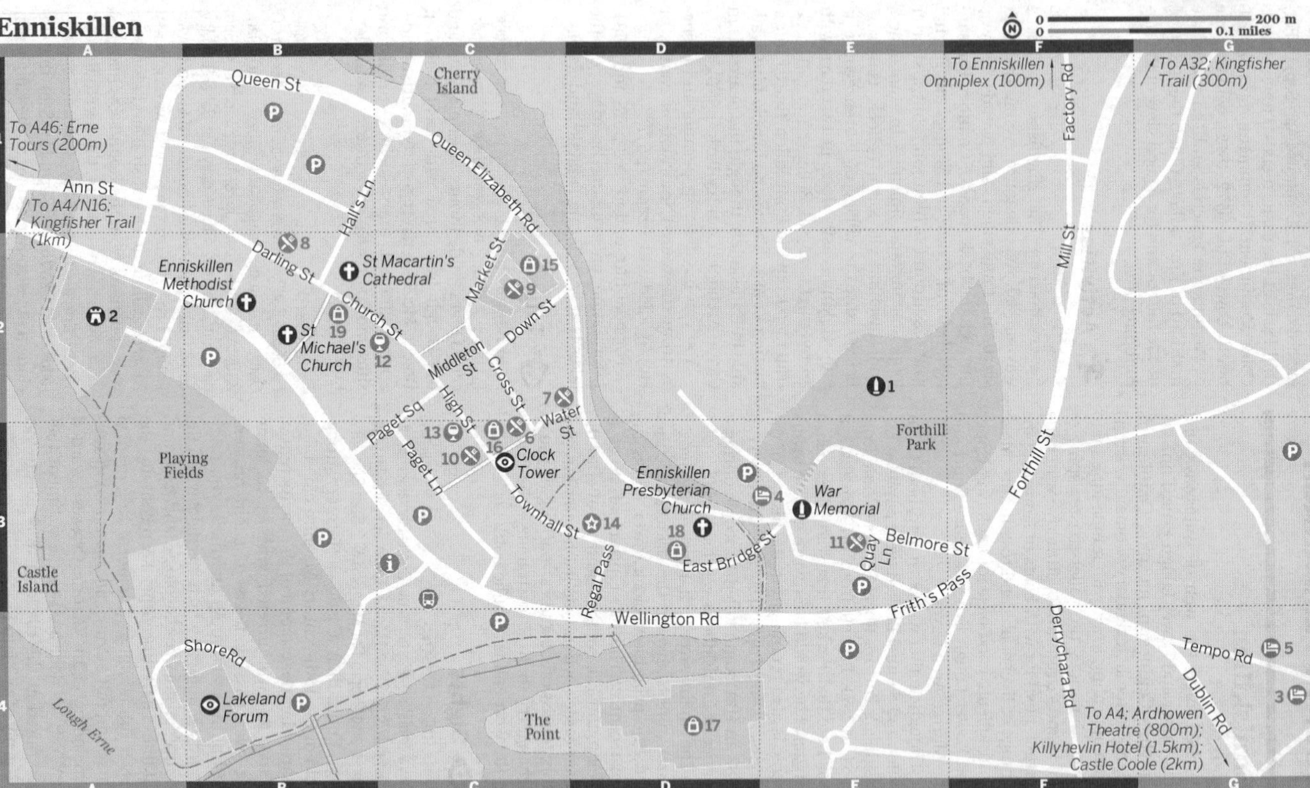

Enniskillen

Sights

Sleeping

Eating

Drinking

Entertainment

Shopping

Sleeping

TOP CHOICE Westville Hotel HOTEL €€

(☎6632 0333; www.westvillehotel.co.uk; 14-20 Tempo Rd; s/d from €80/95; P@📶) The Westville adds a dash of style to Enniskillen's rather staid accommodation scene with designer fabrics, cool colour combinations, good food and welcoming staff. The family suite (from €145) offers great value, sleeping four in two adjoining rooms.

Greenwood Lodge B&B €€

(☎6632 5636; www.greenwoodlodge.co.uk; 17 Killyvilly Ct, Tempo Rd; s/d €40/55; P) The owners of this spacious and modern villa, set on a quiet side street 3km northeast of town off the B80, go out of their way to make you feel welcome. The three homely bedrooms all have private bathrooms, the breakfasts are freshly prepared, and there is secure storage available for bikes.

Belmore Court & Motel HOTEL €€

(☎6632 6633; www.motel.co.uk; Tempo Rd; d from €70, apt from €105; P📶) Housed in an original row of terrace houses linked to a large modern extension, the friendly Belmore offers stylish and spacious 'superior' rooms in the new building (single/double from €65/80) and, in the old, family 'mini-apartments' with self-catering facilities.

Rossole Guesthouse B&B €€

(☎6632 3462; rossoleguesthouse.com; 85 Sligo Rd; s/d from €35/55; P) A modern Georgian-style house with a sunny conservatory overlooking a small lake, the five-room Rossole is an angler's delight – you can fish in the lake, and there's a rowing boat for guests at the bottom of the garden. It's 1km southwest of the town centre on the A4 Sligo road.

Mountview Guesthouse B&B €€

(☎6632 3147; www.mountviewguests.com; 61 Irvinestown Rd; s/d from €50/75; P📶) Indulge in a spot of country-house comfort in this large, ivy-clad Victorian villa set in wooded grounds. There are three bedrooms with private bathrooms, a luxurious lounge and a view over Race Course Lough; it's just a 10-minute (800m) walk north from the town centre.

Bridges Youth Hostel HOSTEL €

(☎6634 0110; www.hini.org.uk; Belmore St; dm/s/tw €18/23/41; P@📶) This modern, purpose-built hostel is in a great location overlooking a river in the centre of town. It has mostly four-bed dorms, each with private bathroom, plus six twin rooms, a kitchen, restaurant, laundry and bike shed. Consult the website for daytime closing hours (when check-in is not available).

Killyhevlin Hotel HOTEL €€€

(☎6632 3481; www.killyhevlin.com; Killyhevlin; s/d €110/160; P@📶) Enniskillen's top hotel is 1.5km south of town on the A4 Maguiresbridge road, in an idyllic setting overlooking Upper Lough Erne. Many of its 43 effortlessly elegant rooms enjoy stunning views over landscaped gardens to the lough.

Eating

TOP CHOICE Dollakis GREEK €€

(☎6634 2616; www.dollakis.co.uk; 2 Cross St; mains lunch €6-9, dinner €14-19; ⏰10am-4pm Tue, 10am-10pm Wed-Sat, 1.30-8.30pm Sun) As well as serving lunch (noon to 4pm), cakes and snacks through the day, this chic little cafe transforms into a Greek-Mediterranean restaurant in the evening. The evening menu includes things such as grilled sea bream stuffed with lemon and herbs, chicken souvlaki and vegetarian moussaka.

Terrace Restaurant IRISH €€
(☎6632 0333; Westville Hotel, 14-20 Tempo Rd; 2-/3-course dinner €30/35; ⊙dinner only) The restaurant at the Westville Hotel combines understated elegance in the dining room with a deft touch in the kitchen – candlelight creates a romantic atmosphere, while delightful dishes such as scallops with pancetta and butternut squash risotto, and roast saddle of rabbit stuffed with black pudding and basil, make for a memorable meal.

Scoffs Wine Bar & Restaurant BISTRO €€
(☎6634 2622; 17 Belmore St; mains €10-19; ⊙5pm-late Mon-Sat, 5-10pm Sun) This busy restaurant has a modern vibe with shades of chocolate-brown and burgundy, dark wood and dim candlelight, and an international menu that includes braised lamb shank with creamy mash and redcurrant and rosemary gravy. The downstairs wine bar offers lighter meals.

Ruby's Coffee & Sandwich Bar CAFE €
(10 High St; snacks €3-5; ⊙9am-5.30pm Mon-Sat) Tucked upstairs in Eason's bookshop is this comfy nook furnished with sofas and armchairs, offering breakfast bagels and croissants, sandwiches and salads, soups and baked potatoes. Free newspapers, too.

Franco's ITALIAN €€
(☎6632 4424; Queen Elizabeth Rd; pizza €10-12, mains €10-27; ⊙noon-11pm) An atmospheric warren of wood-panelled, candlelit nooks set in a former blacksmith's forge, Franco's is always bustling and noisy, and serves a range of Italian, Asian and seafood dishes. Early bird menus (noon to 8pm Monday to Thursday, to 7pm Friday and 5.15pm Saturday) offer two/three courses for €16/20.

Johnston's Jolly Sandwich Bar BAKERY €
(3 Darling St; sandwiches €2-4; ⊙8am-4pm Mon-Fri, 8.30am-4pm Sat) A traditional bakery selling excellent pick-and-mix sandwiches, soup, pies and cakes to take away or eat in.

Rebecca's Place CAFE €
(Buttermarket; snacks €2-5; ⊙9.30am-5.30pm Mon-Sat) A traditional cafe with pine tables and chairs, Rebecca's is set in a craft shop and serves good sandwiches, salads and pastries.

Drinking

TOP CHOICE **Blake's of the Hollow** PUB
(William Blake; 6 Church St) Ulster's best pint of Guinness awaits you in this traditional Victorian pub, almost unchanged since 1887, complete with marble-topped bar, four huge sherry casks, antique silver lamp holders and ancient wood panelling kippered by a century of cigarette smoke. There's traditional music from 9pm on Fridays.

Crowe's Nest BAR
(12 High St) A lively bar with a conservatory and patio out the back for those sunny summer afternoons, the Nest has live music most nights from 9pm in the back bar and traditional music sessions downstairs on Saturday afternoons.

Entertainment

Ardhowen Theatre THEATRE
(www.ardhowentheatre.com; Dublin Rd; ⊙box office 9.30am-4.30pm Mon-Fri, to 7pm before a performance, 11am-1pm, 2-5pm & 6-7pm Sat) The program here includes concerts, local amateur and professional drama and musical productions, pantomimes and films. The theatre is about 2km southeast of the town centre on the A4, in an impressive glass-fronted building overlooking a lake.

Bush Bar NIGHTCLUB
(www.thebushbar.com; 26 Townhall St) The nearest Enniskillen comes to a nightclub, with leather chairs and banquettes in various shades of coffee from dark roast to cafe au lait, a reasonable cocktail menu, and an upstairs lounge that hosts DJs or live bands on Friday and Saturday.

Enniskillen Omniplex CINEMA
(www.omniplex.ie; Factory Rd) A seven-screen cinema, 700m north of the town centre on Race Course Lough.

Shopping

Buttermarket CRAFTS
(Down St) The refurbished buildings in the old marketplace house a variety of craft shops and studios selling paintings, ceramics, jewellery and even fishing flies.

Fermanagh Cottage Industries CRAFTS
(14 East Bridge St) A craft shop selling linen, lace and tweed.

Home, Field & Stream FISHING
(18 Church St) Has a wide range of fishing tackle and also sells fishing licences and permits.

Erneside Shopping Centre SHOPPING MALL
(The Point; ⏲9am-6pm Mon, Tue & Sat, to 9pm Wed-Fri & Sat, 1-6pm Sun) A modern complex of shops, cafes and a supermarket. The Millets store stocks camping and outdoor equipment.

Dolan's Centra FOOD & DRINK
(3 High St; ⏲7.30am-9pm Mon-Sat, 9am-9pm Sun) A handy, late-opening minimarket and post-office counter; also sells Sunday newspapers.

Information

Enniskillen Library (Hall's Lane; ⏲8.30am-5.15pm Mon & Fri, 8.30am-8pm Tue-Thu, 9am-1pm & 2-5pm Sat) Internet access €1.50 per 30 minutes.

Tourist information centre (☎6632 3110; www.fermanagh.gov.uk; Wellington Rd; ⏲9am-5.30pm Mon-Fri, 10am-6pm Sat, 11am-5pm Sun Easter-Sep, shorter hours winter) Books accommodation, changes money, sells fishing licences and provides a postal and fax service.

Getting There & Away

Ulsterbus and Bus Éireann services run to/from Belfast (€10, 2¼ hours, hourly Monday to Saturday, two on Sunday), Omagh (€7, one hour, one daily Monday to Saturday), Dublin (€17, 2½ hours, seven daily Monday to Saturday, four Sunday), Sligo (€12, 1½ hours, five daily Monday to Saturday, two on Sundays) and Donegal (€10, one hour, five daily Monday to Saturday, two on Sundays).

In July and August only, bus 99 goes from Enniskillen to Bundoran (€6, 1¼ hours, four daily Monday to Friday, three Saturday, one on Sunday) via Belleek (45 minutes). Bus 64 goes to Bundoran year-round, twice on Thursdays and once on Sundays.

Around Enniskillen

Sights

Castle Coole HISTORIC BUILDING
(www.ntni.org.uk; Dublin Rd, Enniskillen; adult/child €5/2; ⏲house 11am-5pm daily Jul & Aug, Fri-Wed Jun, Sat, Sun & public holidays mid-Mar–May & Sep, grounds 10am-7pm Mar-Oct, 10am-4pm Nov-Feb) When King George IV visited Ireland in 1821, the second Earl of Belmore had a state bedroom specially prepared at Castle Coole in anticipation of the monarch's visit. The king, however, was more interested in dallying with his mistress at Slane Castle and never turned up. The bedroom, draped in red silk and decorated with paintings depicting *The Rake's Progress* (the earl's sniffy riposte to the king's extramarital shenanigans), is one of the highlights of the one-hour guided tour.

Designed by James Wyatt, this Palladian mansion was built between 1789 and 1795 for Armar Lowry-Corry, the first Earl of Belmore, and is probably the purest expression of late-18th-century neoclassical architecture in Ireland. It is built of silvery-white Portland stone, which was brought in at great expense from southern England – first sent by ship to Ballyshannon, then overland to Lough Erne, by boat again to Enniskillen, and finally by bullock cart for the last 3km.

Building costs of €70,000 nearly bankrupted the first earl, but that didn't stop his son Somerset Lowry-Corry, the second earl, spending another €35,000 on exuberant Regency furnishings and decoration, best seen in the opulent, oval saloon. The eighth Earl of Belmore, John Armar Lowry-Corry, reserves part of the house for his private use, but most of the building is under the care of the National Trust.

The 600 hectares of landscaped **grounds** (adult/child €2.50/1.25) contain a lake that is home to the UK's only nonmigratory colony of greylag geese. It is said that if the geese ever leave, the earls of Belmore will lose Castle Coole.

Castle Coole is on the A4 Dublin road, 2.5km southeast of Enniskillen. You can easily walk there from Enniskillen town centre in 30 minutes – beyond Dunnes Stores, fork left on Tempo Rd and keep straight on along Castlecoole Rd.

Sheelin Irish Lace Museum MUSEUM
(www.irishlacemuseum.com; Bellanaleck; adult/child €4/free; ⏲10am-6pm Mon-Sat Apr-Oct) This museum houses a collection of beautiful Irish lace dating from 1850 to 1900. Lace-making was an important cottage industry in the region both before and after the Famine – prior to WWI there were at least 10 lace schools in County Fermanagh. The museum is just over 6km southwest of Enniskillen.

Upper Lough Erne

About 80km long, Lough Erne is made up of two sections: the Upper Lough to the south of Enniskillen, and the Lower Lough to the north. The two are connected by the River Erne, which begins its journey in County Cavan and meets the sea at Donegal Bay west of Ballyshannon.

Upper Lough Erne is not so much a lake as a watery maze of islands (more than 150 of them), inlets, reedy bays and meandering backwaters. Bird life is abundant, with flocks of whooper swan and goldeneye overwintering here, great crested grebes nesting in the spring, and Ireland's biggest heronry in a 400-year-old oak grove on the island of Inishfendra, just south of Crom Estate.

Lisnaskea is the main town, with shops, pubs, ATMs and a post office.

Sights & Activities

Crom Estate NATURE RESERVE
(Newtownbutler; adult/child €3.25/1; grounds 10am-7pm Jun-Aug, to 6pm mid-Mar–May & Sep-Oct, visitor centre 11am-5pm daily Easter-Sep, Sat & Sun only Oct) Home to the largest area of natural woodland in Northern Ireland, the National Trust's beautiful Crom Estate is a haven for pine martens, rare bats and many species of bird.

You can walk from the visitor centre to the ruins of old **Crom Castle**, with its ancient **walled garden**, abandoned bowling green and gnarled yew trees, and views over the reed-fringed lough to an island folly. There are rowing boats for hire (€6 per hour).

Check the **National Trust website** (www.ntni.org.uk) for details on bat-watching and other wildlife events.

The estate is on the eastern shore of the Upper Lough, 5km west of Newtownbutler.

Knockninny Marina BOATING
(6774 8590; Knockninny House, near Derrylin) Day boats can be hired for fishing or exploring from Knockninny Marina on the west shore of the lough; rates are €50/70 per half-/full-day for a six-seater motor boat with cabin. The marina also rents bikes for €7/12 a half-/full day. It's signposted from the main road just north of Derrylin.

Share Holiday Village OUTDOOR ACTIVITIES
(6772 2122; www.sharevillage.org: Lisnaskea) Guests and day visitors at the Share Holiday Village near Lisnaskea can take part in canoeing, windsurfing, dinghy sailing, archery, orienteering and other activities for €16/13 per adult/child per 2½-hour session.

Inishcruiser BOAT TRIPS
(www.sharevillage.org/inishcruiser; adult/child/family €8/6/22; 2.30pm Sun & public holidays Easter-Sep) The *Inishcruiser* offers 1½- to two-hour cruises on the lough leaving from the Share Holiday Village, 5km southwest of Lisnaskea.

Sleeping & Eating

Kilmore Quay Club B&B
(6772 4369; www.kilmorequayclub.com; Kilmore Quay, Lisnaskea; d from €79; P) A secluded lakeside setting makes for a peaceful night's rest in one of the seven luxurious guest rooms next to the plush, thatch-roofed **Watermill Restaurant** (www.watermillrestaurant.org; mains €18-30; lunch & dinner), where the French-influenced menu leans towards the gourmet end of the spectrum.

Knockninny House B&B €€
(6774 8590; www.knockninnyhouse.com; near Derrylin; s/d from €45/80; P) A Victorian villa built in the 1870s that was Lough Erne's first hotel, Knockninny House enjoys an idyllic lakeside setting, and now offers accommodation in seven country-style bedrooms. There's also a restaurant with an outdoor terrace overlooking the marina, where you can take afternoon tea, and a tiny sandy beach.

Donn Carragh Hotel HOTEL €€
(6772 1206; www.donncarraghhotel.com; Main St, Lisnaskea; s/d from €45/80; P) There's not too much in the way of hotel accommodation around Upper Lough Erne; this pleasant but unexceptional 18-room hotel in the middle of Lisnaskea is the best.

Share Holiday Village CAMPGROUND €
(6772 2122; www.sharevillage.org; Smiths Strand, Lisnaskea; campsites per tent/caravan €11/18; Easter-Sep) Share is a charity that works towards the integration of people with and without disabilities through a range of activities and courses. The holiday village is mostly occupied by groups, but it also has a touring site with space for nine caravans and 24 tents. Booking is strongly recommended. The village is 5km southwest of Lisnaskea, off the B127.

Kissin Crust CAFE €
(125 Main St, Lisnaskea; mains €3-6; 8.30am-5pm Mon-Sat) Very popular with local people, this friendly coffee shop is stacked with home-baked apple pie, lemon meringue pie, quiches and scones, and serves up a lunch

ULSTER WAY

The Ulster Way long-distance walking trail makes a circuit around the six counties of Northern Ireland and Donegal. In total the route covers just over 900km, so walking all of it might take four to five weeks. However, much of the way is on minor roads rather than footpaths, a criticism which has been taken on board by the Northern Ireland Tourist Board (NITB), which has 'relaunched' the Ulster Way and divided it into 'Quality Sections' – good, scenic, off-road walking – separated by Link Sections which can be covered by public transport. Check the **WalkNI website** (www.walkni.com) for details.

Short sections of the Ulster Way that make good day walks include **Cuilcagh Mountain** (boxed text, p685) and the **Causeway Coast Way** (boxed text, p662).

menu of homemade soup, freshly made sandwiches and a hot dish of the day.

Getting There & Away

From Enniskillen, Ulsterbus service 95 runs along the east side of the lough to Lisnaskea (€3, 30 minutes, five daily Monday to Friday, three on Saturdays, plus one on Sundays in July and August only). Bus 58 goes down the west side to Derrylin (€3, 40 minutes, five daily Monday to Friday, two on Saturdays), and continues to Belturbet in County Cavan.

Lower Lough Erne

Lower Lough Erne is a much more open expanse of water than the Upper Lough, with its 90-odd islands clustered mainly in the southern reaches. In early Christian times, when overland travel was difficult, Lough Erne was an important highway between the Donegal coast and inland Leitrim, and there are many ancient religious sites and other antiquities dotted around its shores. In medieval times the lough was part of an important pilgrimage route to Station Island in Lough Derg, County Donegal.

The following sights are described travelling anticlockwise around the lough from Enniskillen.

DEVENISH ISLAND

Devenish Island (from Daimh Inis, meaning Ox Island) is the biggest of several 'holy islands' in Lough Erne. The remains of an **Augustinian monastery**, founded here in the 6th century by St Molaise, include a superb 12th-century **round tower** in near-perfect condition, the ruins of St Molaise's Church and St Mary's Abbey, an unusual 15th-century high cross, and many fascinating old gravestones. Four ladders allow you to climb to the top of the round tower for a cramped view out of the five tiny windows.

A speedboat **ferry** (adult/child return €3/2; ⏲10am, 1pm, 3pm & 5pm daily Apr-Sep) crosses to Devenish Island from Trory Point landing. From Enniskillen, take the A32 towards Irvinestown and after 5km look for the sign on the left, just after a service station and immediately before the junction where the B82 and A32 part company. At the foot of the hill by the lough, turn left for the jetty.

You can also visit as part of a cruise with Erne Tours in Enniskillen.

KILLADEAS

The churchyard at Killadeas, 11km north of Enniskillen on the B82, contains several unusual carved stones. Most famous is the 1m-high **Bishop's Stone**, dating from between the 7th and 9th centuries, which has a Celtic head reminiscent of the White Island figures carved on its narrow western edge, and an engraving of a bishop with bell and crosier on the side. Located nearby is a slab set on edge, with several deep cup-marks – possibly *bullauns* (ancient grinding stones) – on one side, and a cross within a circle on the other. You will also find a broken phallic column and a large, perforated stone.

Sleeping & Eating

Manor House Country Hotel HOTEL €€€
(☎6862 2200; www.manor-house-hotel.com; Killadeas; s/d from €125/140; P Wi-Fi) A grand, 19th-century country house overlooking Lough Erne, the Manor House has had a thorough makeover in neoclassical style, complete with a Greek temple-style lobby, Romanesque pool and Jacuzzis with a view over the lough. The public areas are impressive but the rooms, though luxurious, are a bit on the bland side. The hotel's **Watergate Lounge** (mains €10-18) serves decent pub grub, and has live music at weekends.

CRUISING HOLIDAYS ON LOUGH ERNE

If you fancy exploring Lough Erne as captain of your own motor cruiser, well, you can – and without any previous experience or qualification. Several companies in Fermanagh hire out self-drive, live-aboard cabin cruisers by the week, offering a crash course (not literally, you hope) in boat-handling and navigation at the start of your holiday. Weekly rates in high season (July and August) range from about €820 for a two-berth to €1420 for a four-berth and €1860 for an eight-berth boat. Low- and mid-season rates are around 70% to 90% of the high-season rates.

The main cruiser hire companies in Fermanagh are:

» **Aghinver Boat Company** (☎6863 1400; www.abcboats.com; Lisnarick, Lower Lough Erne)

» **Carrick Craft** (☎3834 4993; www.cruise-ireland.com; Tully Bay, Lower Lough Erne)

» **Carrybridge Boat Company** (☎6638 7034; robert_mclean@btconnect.com; Carrybridge, Lisbellaw, Upper Lough Erne)

» **Corraquill Cruising Holidays** (☎6774 8712; www.corraquill.co.uk; Drumetta, Aghalane, Derrylin, Upper Lough Erne)

» **Manor House Marine** (☎6862 8100; www.manormarine.com; Killadeas, Lower Lough Erne)

CASTLE ARCHDALE COUNTRY PARK

This **park** (Lisnarick; admission free; ⏰9am-7pm Easter-Sep, to 9pm Jul & Aug) has pleasant woodland and lakeshore walks and cycle tracks in the former estate of 18th-century Archdale Manor. The island-filled bay was used in WWII as a base for Catalina flying boats, a history explained in the **visitor centre** (admission free; ⏰10am-5pm daily Jun-Aug, 1-5pm Sat & Sun May & Sep).

You can hire bikes for €4/8/12 per hour/half-/full day, or swap two wheels for four legs – the park offers pony trekking (€15 per hour), as well as short rides (€5 per 15 minutes) for beginners. There are also boats for hire (€55/80 per half-/full day), and you can also rent fishing rods (€5 per day including bait).

The park is 16km northwest of Enniskillen on the B82, near Lisnarick.

Sleeping & Eating

TOP CHOICE Cedars Guesthouse B&B €€
(☎6862 1493; www.cedarsguesthouse.com; Drummal, Castle Archdale; s/d from €45/70; Ⓟ) Set in a former rectory just south of the park entrance, this peaceful 10-room guesthouse goes for a Victorian country-house feel, with rose-patterned bedspreads and antique-style furniture.

Rectory Bistro IRISH €€
(☎6862 1493; mains €11-17; ⏰6-9pm Wed-Sat, 12.30-3pm & 5-9pm Sun) Adjoining the Cedars Guesthouse, this bistro has a welcoming open fireplace, lots of golden pine lit by chunky candles and a sprinkling of Gothic motifs, with a hearty menu that ranges from a fresh crab and smoked salmon pâté to beef and Guinness pie with creamy mashed potato.

Castle Archdale Caravan Park CAMPGROUND €
(☎6862 1333; www.castlearchdale.com; Castle Archdale Country Park; tent sites €20-30, caravan sites €25-30; ⏰Easter-Oct) This attractive, tree-sheltered site is dominated by on-site caravans, but has good facilities, including a shop, launderette, playground and restaurant.

WHITE ISLAND

White Island, in the bay to the north of Castle Archdale Country Park, is the most haunting of Lough Erne's monastic sites. At the eastern tip of the island are the ruins of a small **12th-century church** with a beautiful Romanesque door on its southern side. Inside are six extraordinary **Celtic stone figures**, thought to date from the 9th century, lined up along the wall like miniature Easter Island statues.

This line-up is a modern arrangement; most of the figures were discovered buried in the walls of the church in the 19th century, where the medieval masons had used them as ordinary building stones. The six main figures, all created by the same hand, are flanked on the left by a **sheila-na-gig** (carved female figure with exaggerated genitalia), which is probably contemporary with the church, and flanked on the right by a scowling stone face. The age and interpretation of these figures has been the subject of much debate; it has been suggested that the two central pairs, of equal height, were pillars that once supported a pulpit, and that they represent either saints or aspects of the life of Christ.

A **ferry** (per person €4; ⏲11am-6pm daily Jul & Aug, to 5pm Sat & Sun Apr-Jun & Sep) crosses to the island hourly, on the hour (except for 1pm), from the marina in Castle Archdale Country Park; buy your ticket from the Billieve Boat Hire office. The crossing takes 15 minutes, and allows you around half an hour on the island.

BOA ISLAND

Boa Island, at the northern end of Lower Lough Erne, is connected to the mainland at both ends – the main A47 road runs along its length. Spooky, moss-grown Caldragh graveyard, towards the western end of the island, contains the famous **Janus Stone**. Perhaps 2000 years old, this pagan figure is carved with two grotesque human heads, back to back. Nearby is a smaller figure called the **Lusty Man**, brought here from Lusty More island. Their origin and meaning have been lost to the mists of time.

There's a small sign indicating the graveyard about 1.5km from the bridge at the western tip of the island.

Sleeping & Eating

Lusty Beg Island B&B €€
(☎6863 3300; www.lustybegisland.com; Boa Island, Kesh; s/d €75/115; P @ ✉) This private island retreat, reached by ferry (on demand from 8.30am to 11pm) from a jetty halfway along Boa Island, has self-catering chalets that sleep four to six people (€555 to €855 per week in July and August) but also offers B&B in its rustic 40-room Courtyard Motel. There's a tennis court, nature trail and canoeing on the lough for guests.

Lusty Beg's informal **Island Restaurant** (☎6863 1342; mains €14-18; ⏲1-9pm Jul & Aug) is open to all, and serves everything from burgers and lasagne to beef Wellington and salmon en croute. Booking is necessary; you can summon the ferry from a telephone in the blockhouse on the slipway.

BELLEEK

POP 550

Belleek's (Beal Leice) village street of colourful, flower-bedecked houses slopes up from a bridge across the River Erne, where it flows out of the Lower Lough towards Ballyshannon and the sea. The village is right on the border – the road south across the bridge passes through a finger of the Republic's territory for about 200m before leaving again – and shops accept both pounds sterling and euros.

The imposing Georgian-style building beside the bridge houses the world-famous **Belleek Pottery** (www.belleek.ie; Main St; ⏲9am-6pm Mon-Fri, 10am-6pm Sat, noon-5.30pm Sun Jul-Sep, shorter hours Oct-Jun, closed Sat & Sun Jan-Feb), founded in 1857 to provide local employment in the wake of the Potato Famine. It has been producing fine Parian china ever since, and is especially noted for its delicate basketware. The visitor centre houses a small museum, showroom and restaurant, and there are **guided tours** (adult/child €4/free) of the pottery every half-hour from 9.30am to 12.15pm and 1.45pm to 4pm (till 3pm on Friday) Monday to Friday year-round.

Sleeping & Eating

Hotel Carlton HOTEL €€
(☎6865 8282; www.hotelcarltonbelleek.com; Main St; s/d €70/115; P ☎) Though the rooms are plush and luxurious, the family-friendly Carlton has a welcoming and informal feel to it, and a lovely setting on the banks of the River Erne. There are frequent live music sessions in the hotel's Potters Bar.

Moohan's Fiddlestone B&B €€
(☎6665 8008; www.thefiddlestone.com; 15-17 Main St; s/d €40/65; P) This is a traditional Irish bar and bookies shop offering B&B in five rooms with private bathrooms upstairs. The lively bar downstairs is a popular venue for impromptu music sessions, so don't expect peace and quiet in the evenings.

Thatch Coffee Shop CAFE €
(20 Main St; mains €3-7; ⏲9am-5pm Mon-Sat) This cute little thatched cottage may be Belleek's oldest building (late 18th century), but it serves a thoroughly modern cup of coffee, a delicious smoked-salmon toastie, and excellent homemade cakes and scones.

Black Cat Cove PUB €
(28 Main St; mains €7-10; ⏲noon-9pm) This friendly, family-run pub with antique furniture and an open fire serves good bar meals. It also has music on Tuesday, Wednesday and Thursday nights from May to September.

LOUGH NAVAR FOREST PARK

This **forest park** (admission free; ⏲10am-dusk) lies at the western end of Lower Lough Erne, where the **Cliffs of Magho** – a 250m-high and 9km-long limestone escarpment – rise

1

5

4

1. White Island, County Fermanagh (p680)
Ancient carved stones, thought to date from the 9th century, on White Island, Lower Lough Erne.

2. Boa Island, County Fermanagh (p681)
Boa Island lies at the northern end of Lower Lough Erne and features the spooky Caldragh graveyard.

3. Janus Stone, County Fermanagh (p681)
The 2000-year-old Janus Stone, a pagan figure with two human heads carved back to back, on Boa Island.

4. Magho Viewpoint (p684)
Sunset across Lower Lough Erne from the Cliffs of Magho, one of Ireland's finest panoramas.

5. Cruising Lough Erne (p680)
Children on a houseboat on Lough Erne; cruising holidays are popular on Ireland's waterways.

above a fringe of native woodland on the south shore. An 11km scenic drive through the park leads to the Magho Viewpoint – the panorama from the clifftop here is one of the finest in Ireland, especially before sunset: it looks out over the shimmering expanse of lough and river to the Blue Stack Mountains, the sparkling waters of Donegal Bay and the sea cliffs of Slieve League.

The entrance to Lough Navar Forest Park is on the minor Glennasheevar road between Garrison and Derrygonnelly, 20km southeast of Belleek (take the B52 towards Garrison, and fork left after 2.5km).

Activities

Fishing

The lakes of Fermanagh are renowned for both coarse and game fishing. The Lough Erne trout-fishing season runs from the beginning of March to the end of September. Salmon fishing begins in June and also continues to the end of September. The mayfly season usually lasts a month from the second week in May. There's no closed season for coarse fish.

You'll need both a licence (issued by the Fisheries Conservancy Board) and a permit (from the owner of the fishery); see www.nidirect.gov.uk/angling for details. Licences and permits can be purchased from the tourist information centre and Home, Field & Stream, both in Enniskillen, and from the marina in Castle Archdale Country Park, which also hires out fishing rods. A combined licence and permit for game fishing on Lough Erne costs €8.50/24.50 for three/14 days.

The **Belleek Angling Centre** in the Thatch Coffee Shop in Belleek sells fishing tackle and can arrange boat hire for anglers, and you can get expert instruction in fly-casting from **Michael Shortt** (☎6638 8184; fish.teach@virgin.net; Sydare, Ballinamallard).

Enniskillen's tourist information centre also provides a free guide to angling in Fermanagh and South Tyrone, which has full details of lakes and rivers, fish species, seasons and permit requirements.

Boat Hire

A number of companies hire out day boats at Enniskillen, Killadeas and Castle Archdale Country Park. Rates range from about €10 to €15 per hour for an open rowing boat with outboard motor to €60/90 per half-/full day for a six-seater with cabin and engine. The tourist information centre in Enniskillen has a full list of companies and costs.

Canoeing

The **Lough Erne Canoe Trail** (www.canoeni.com) highlights the attractions along the 50km of lough and river between Belleek and Belturbet. The wide open expanses of the Lower Lough can build up big waves in a strong breeze and are best left to experts, but the sheltered backwaters of the Upper Lough are ideal for beginners and families.

You can pick up a map and guide (€1.50) showing public access points, camping sites and other facilities along the trail from the tourist office in Enniskillen, which also has a list of places where you can hire a canoe.

Watersports

Ultimate Watersports WATER SPORTS
(www.ultimatewatersports.co.uk) Working out of Castle Archdale marina and Lusty Beg island, offers equipment hire and instruction in water-skiing, wakeboarding, jet-skiing, canoeing, dinghy sailing and power-boating.

Getting There & Away

On the eastern side of the lough, Ulsterbus service 194 from Enniskillen to Pettigo via Irvinestown (four or five daily Monday to Saturday) stops near Castle Archdale Country Park (35 minutes) and Kesh (one hour). In July and August only, bus 99 goes from Enniskillen to Belleek (€4, 45 minutes, four daily Monday to Friday, three on Saturday, one on Sunday) along the western shoreline via Blaney and Tully Castle, terminating at Bundoran.

Bus 64 travels from Enniskillen to Belcoo (€2, 25 minutes, seven or eight daily Monday to Friday, three on Saturdays, one on Sundays); the Sunday bus and two of the Thursday buses continue to Garrison, Belleek and Bundoran.

West of Lough Erne

Sights

Florence Court HISTORIC BUILDING
(www.ntni.org; Swanlinbar Rd, Florencecourt; house tour adult/child €5/2, grounds €3.25/1.75; ⏲11am-5pm daily Jul & Aug, Wed-Mon May & Jun, Sat-Thu Sep, Sat & Sun Apr & Oct) Part of the motivation for the first Earl of Belmore to build Castle Coole (near Enniskillen) was to keep up with the Joneses – in the 1770s his aristocratic neighbour William Willoughby Cole, the first Earl of Enniskillen, had overseen the addition of grand Palladian wings to

WALK: CUILCAGH MOUNTAIN VIA THE LEGNABROCKY TRAIL

Rising above Marble Arch and Florence Court, Cuilcagh (*cull*-kay) Mountain (666m) is the highest point in Counties Fermanagh and Cavan, its summit right on the border between Northern Ireland and the Republic.

The mountain is a geological layer cake, with a cave-riddled limestone base, shale and sandstone flanks draped with a shaggy tweed skirt of blanket bog, and a high gritstone plateau ringed by steep, craggy slopes, all part of the **Marble Arch Caves European Geopark** (www.europeangeoparks.org).

Hidden among the sphagnum moss, bog cotton and heather of the blanket bog, you can find the sticky-fingered sundew, an insect-eating plant, while the crags echo to the 'krok-krok-krok' of ravens and the mewing of peregrine falcons. The otherworldly summit plateau is a breeding ground for golden plover and is rich in rare plants such as alpine clubmoss.

The hike to the summit is a 15km round trip (allow five or six hours); the first part is on an easy gravel track, but you'll need good boots to negotiate the boggy ground and steep slopes further on. Start at the Cuilcagh Mountain Park car park, 300m west of the entrance to Marble Arch Caves visitor centre (grid reference 121335; you'll need the Ordnance Survey 1:50,000 Discovery series map, sheet 26). Right next to the car park is the **Monastir sink hole**, a deep depression ringed by limestone cliffs where the River Aghinrawn disappears underground for its journey through the Marble Arch Caves system. (Note that the OS map has wrongly labelled this river the Owenbrean.)

Climb the stile beside the gate and set out along the **Legnabrocky Trail**, a 4WD track that winds through rich green limestone meadows before climbing across the blanket bog on a 'floating' bed of gravel and geotextiles – boardwalks off to one side offer a closer look at bog regeneration areas. The gravel track comes to an end at a gate about 4.5km from the start. From here you follow a line of waymarked wooden posts, squelching your way across spongy bog (don't stray from the route – there are deep bog holes where you can get stuck) before climbing steeply up to the summit ridge, with great views west to the crags above little Lough Atona. The waymarkers come to an end here, so you're on your own for the final kilometre across the plateau, aiming for the prominent cairn on the summit (a map and compass are essential in poor visibility).

The summit cairn is actually a Neolithic burial chamber; about 100m south of the summit you will find two rings of boulders, the foundations of prehistoric huts. On a clear day the view extends from the Blue Stack Mountains of Donegal to Croagh Patrick, and from the Atlantic Ocean to the Irish Sea. Return the way you came.

the beautiful, baroque country house called Florence Court, named after his Cornish grandmother Florence Wrey.

Set in lovely wooded grounds in the shadow of Cuilcagh Mountain, and not to be confused with the nearby, single-worded village of Florencecourt, Florence Court is famous for its rococo plasterwork and antique Irish furniture. The house was badly damaged by fire in 1955 and much of what you see on the one-hour guided tour is the result of meticulous restoration, but the magnificent plaster work on the ceiling of the dining room is original.

In the **grounds** (⏲10am-7pm Mar-Oct, 10am-4pm Nov-Feb) you can explore the walled garden and, on the edge of Cottage Wood, southeast of the house, admire an ancient Irish yew tree. It's said that every Irish yew around the world is descended from this one.

The house is 12km southwest of Enniskillen. Take the A4 Sligo road and fork left onto the A32 to Swanlinbar. Ulsterbus service 192 from Enniskillen to Swanlinbar can drop you at Creamery Cross, about 2km from the house.

Marble Arch Caves CAVES
(☎6634 8855; www.marblearchcaves.net; Marlbank Scenic Loop, Florencecourt; adult/child €8.50/5.50; ⏲10am-5pm Jul & Aug, to 4.30pm Easter-Jun & Sep) To the south of Lower Lough Erne lies a limestone plateau, where Fermanagh's abundant rainwater has carved out a network of subterranean caverns. The largest of these are the **Marble Arch Caves**, first explored by the French caving pioneer

Edouard Martel in 1895, but not opened to the public until 1985.

The 1¼-hour tour of the caves begins with a short boat trip along the peaty, foam-flecked waters of the underground River Cladagh to **Junction Jetty**, where three subterranean streams meet up. You then continue on foot past the Grand Gallery and Pool Chamber, regaled all the time with food-related jokes from your guide. An artificial tunnel leads into the **New Chamber**, from which the route follows the underground River Owenbrean, through the **Moses Walk** (a walled pathway sunk waist-deep into the river) to the **Calcite Cradle**, where the most picturesque formations are to be found. The caves are very popular, so it's wise to phone ahead and book a tour, especially if you're in a group of four or more. (The listed closing time is the starting time of the last tour.)

The caves take their name from a natural **limestone arch** that spans the River Cladagh where it emerges from the caves; you can reach it via a short walk along a signposted footpath from the visitor centre.

Unexpected serious flooding of the caves in the 1990s was found to have been caused by mechanised peat-cutting in the blanket bog on the slopes of Cuilcagh Mountain, whose rivers feed the caves. **Cuilcagh Mountain Park** (www.cuilcaghmountainpark.com) was established to restore and preserve the bog environment, and in 2001 the entire area was designated a Unesco Geopark. The park's geology and ecology are explained in the caves' visitor centre.

The Marble Arch Caves are 16km southwest of Enniskillen, and some 4km from Florence Court (an hour's walk), reached via the A4 Sligo road and the A32.

Loughs Melvin & Macnean

Lough Melvin and Lough Macnean are situated along the border with the Republic, on the B52 road from Belcoo to Belleek. Lough Melvin is famous for its salmon and trout fishing, and is home to two unusual trout species – the sonaghan, with its distinctive black spots, and the crimson-spotted gillaroo – that are unique to the lough, as well as brown trout, ferox trout and char.

Corralea Activity Centre (☎6638 6123; www.activityireland.com; Belcoo), based on Upper Lough Macnean, hires out bicycles (half-/full day €10/15) and two-person canoes (half-/full day €15/20). It also offers instruction in activities such as caving, canoeing, climbing, windsurfing and archery from €22 per day.

The lakeside **Lough Melvin Holiday Centre** (☎6865 8142; www.melvinholidaycentre.com; Garrison; campsites tent/caravan €13/22, dm €22) offers caving, canoeing, walking and fishing holidays, and also has a campsite, dorm accommodation, rooms with private bathrooms and a restaurant and coffee shop.

The **Customs House Country Inn** (☎6638 6285; www.customshouseinn.com; Main St, Belcoo; s/d from €65/90; mains €11-15; P 📶) is a welcoming pub decked out in acres of waxed oak and pine, with a cosy, candlelit restaurant and nine bedrooms with private bathrooms, many with good views of Lough Macnean.

There is also gourmet dining a few hundred metres across the border in Blacklion, County Cavan.

COUNTY TYRONE

Omagh

POP 20,000

Situated at the confluence of the Rivers Camowen and Drumragh, which join to form the River Strule, Omagh is a busy market town that serves as a useful base for exploring the surrounding area by car.

Sadly, for a long time to come, Omagh (An Óghmagh) will be remembered for the devastating 1998 car bomb that killed 29 people and injured 200. Planted by the breakaway group Real IRA, the bomb was the worst single atrocity in the 30-year history of the Troubles. A memorial garden on Drumragh Ave, 200m east of the bus station, remembers the dead.

Sleeping & Eating

Mullaghmore House B&B **€€**
(☎8224 2314; www.mullaghmorehouse.com; Old Mountfield Rd; s/d €42/78; P @ 📶) Offering affordable country-house luxury, this beautifully restored Georgian villa boasts a gleaming mahogany-panelled library, billiards room and marble-lined steam room. The bedrooms have period cast-iron fireplaces and antique furniture, and the owners run courses on antique restoration and traditional crafts. It's 1.5km northeast of the town centre.

Grant's of Omagh INTERNATIONAL €€
(☎8225 0900; 29 George's St; mains €9-20; ⌚4-10pm Mon-Fri, 3-10.30pm Sat, noon-10pm Sun) Grant's – as in US president Ulysses S Grant – bathes in a golden glow of Irish emigrant nostalgia, from the fiddle and bodhrán (hand-held goatskin drum) on the wall above the smoke-blackened fireplace in the front bar to the American-themed restaurant in the back, with a menu that ranges from steak, burgers and lasagne to rack of ribs and Cajun chicken.

Information

The **tourist office** (☎8224 7831; info@omagh.gov.uk; Strule Arts Centre, Town Hall Sq, Bridge St; ⌚10am-5.45pm Mon-Sat) is in the new arts centre, just across the river from the bus station. It has a Town Trail leaflet that guides you around Omagh's remaining historic buildings.

Getting There & Away

The bus station is on Mountjoy Rd, just north of the town centre along Bridge St.

Goldline Express bus 273 goes from Belfast to Omagh (€10, 1¾ hours, hourly Monday to Saturday, six on Sunday) via Dungannon and on to Derry (€8, 1¼ hours). Bus 94 goes to Enniskillen (€7, one hour, six or seven daily Monday to Friday, three on Saturday, one on Sunday) where you can change for Donegal, Bundoran or Sligo. Goldline Express bus 274 runs from Derry to Omagh (€8, one hour, every two hours), and continues to Dublin (€16, three hours) via Monaghan.

Around Omagh

Sights

Ulster American Folk Park HERITAGE PARK
(www.folkpark.com; Mellon Rd; adult/child €6.50/4; ⌚10am-5pm Tue-Sun Mar-Sep, 10am-4pm Tue-Fri, 11am-4pm Sat & Sun Oct-Mar) In the 18th and 19th centuries thousands of Ulster people left their homes to forge a new life across the Atlantic; 200,000 emigrated in the 18th century alone. Their story is told here at one of Ireland's best museums. Last admission is 1½ hours before closing.

The **Exhibition Hall** explains the close connections between Ulster and the USA – the American Declaration of Independence was signed by several Ulstermen – and includes a genuine Calistoga wagon. But the real appeal of the folk park is the **outdoor museum**, where the 'living history' exhibits are split into Old World and New World areas, cleverly linked by passing through a mock-up of an emigrant ship. Original buildings from various parts of Ulster have been dismantled and re-erected here, including a blacksmith's forge, a weaver's thatched cottage, a Presbyterian meeting house and a schoolhouse. In the 'American' section of the park you can visit a genuine 18th-century settler's stone cottage and a log house, both shipped across the Atlantic from Pennsylvania.

Costumed guides and artisans are on hand to explain the arts of spinning, weaving, candle-making and so on, and various events are held throughout the year, including re-enactments of American Civil War battles, a festival of traditional Irish music in May, American Independence Day cele brations in July, and the Appalachian and Bluegrass Music Festival in September. At least half a day is needed to do the place justice.

The park is 8km northwest of Omagh on the A5. Goldline bus 273 from Belfast to Derry (hourly Monday to Saturday, five on Sunday) stops in Omagh, and will stop on request at the park gates.

> **TOP FIVE TRADITIONAL PUBS IN NORTHERN IRELAND**
>
> » Bittle's Bar (p596)
> » Blake's of the Hollow (p676)
> » Grace Neill's (p611)
> » Dufferin Arms (p618)
> » Peadar O'Donnell's (p646)

Sperrin Mountains

When representatives of the London guilds visited Ulster in 1609, the Lord Deputy of Ireland made sure they were kept well away from the Sperrin Mountains (www.sperrinstourism.com), fearing that the sight of these bleak, moorland hills would put them off the idea of planting settlers here. And when it rains there's no denying that the Sperrins can be dismal, but on a sunny spring day, when the russet bogs and yellow gorse stand out against a clear blue sky, they can offer some grand walking. The area is also dotted with thousands of standing stones and prehistoric tombs.

Getting Around

Ulsterbus service 403, the *Sperrin Rambler*, runs twice daily Monday to Saturday between Omagh and Magherafelt, stopping at Gortin, Plumbridge, Cranagh and Draperstown (in County Derry).

GORTIN

The village of Gortin, about 15km north of Omagh, lies at the foot of Mullaghcarn (542m), the southernmost of the Sperrin summits (unfortunately capped by two prominent radio masts). Hundreds of hikers converge for a mass ascent of the hill on **Cairn Sunday** (the last Sunday in July), a revival of an ancient pilgrimage. There are several good walks around the village, and a scenic drive to **Gortin Lakes**, with views north to the main Sperrin ridge.

A few kilometres south of Gortin, towards Omagh, is **Gortin Glen Forest Park** (Gortin Rd; car/pedestrian €3/1; 10am-dusk), whose dense conifer woodland is home to a herd of Japanese sika deer. An 8km scenic drive offers the chance to enjoy the views without breaking into a sweat.

There is hostel accommodation at the **Gortin Accommodation Suite** (8164 8346; www.gortin.net; 62 Main St; dm/f €14/70;), a modern outdoor activity centre in the middle of Gortin village; it also has family rooms with one double and two single beds and private bathrooms.

CREGGAN

About halfway along the A505 between Omagh and Cookstown (20km east of Omagh) is **An Creagán Visitor Centre** (www.an-creagan.com; Creggan; admission free; 11am-6.30pm Apr-Sep, to 4.30pm Oct-Mar), with an exhibition covering the ecology of the surrounding bogs and the archaeology of the region. There's also a restaurant and gift shop.

There are 44 prehistoric monuments within 8km of the centre, including the **Beaghmore Stone Circles**. What this site lacks in stature – the stones are all less than 1m tall – it makes up for in complexity, with seven stone circles (one filled with smaller stones, nicknamed 'dragon's teeth') and a dozen or so alignments and cairns. The stones are signposted about 8km east of Creggan, and 4km north of the A505.

East Tyrone

The market towns of Cookstown and Dungannon are the main settlements in the eastern part of County Tyrone, but the main sights here are in the surrounding countryside.

Sights

Ardboe High Cross HISTORIC SITE

A 6th-century monastic site overlooking Lough Neagh is home to one of Ireland's best-preserved and most elaborately decorated Celtic stone crosses. The 10th-century Ardboe high cross stands 5.5m tall, with 22 carved panels depicting biblical scenes. The western side (facing the road) has New Testament scenes: (from the bottom up) the Adoration of the Magi; the Miracle at Cana; the miracle of the loaves and fishes; Christ's entry into Jerusalem; the arrest (or mocking) of Christ; and, at the intersection of the cross, the Crucifixion.

The more weathered eastern face (towards the lough) shows Old Testament scenes: Adam and Eve; the Sacrifice of Isaac; Daniel in the Lions' Den; the Three Hebrews in the Fiery Furnace. The panels above may show the Last Judgement, and/or Christ in Glory. There are further scenes on the narrow north and south faces of the shaft.

Ardboe is 16km east of Cookstown. Take the B73 through Coagh and ignore the first (white) road sign for Ardboe. Keep straight on until you find the brown sign (on the right) for Ardboe High Cross.

Wellbrook Beetling Mill HISTORIC BUILDING

(www.ntni.org.uk; 20 Wellbrook Rd, Corkhill; adult/child €4.20/2.40; 2-6pm Thu-Tue Jul & Aug, 2-6pm Sat, Sun & public holidays mid-Mar–Jun & Sep) Beetling, the final stage of linen making, involves pounding the cloth with wooden hammers, or beetles, to give it a smooth sheen. Restored to working order by the National Trust, the 18th-century Wellbrook Beetling Mill still has its original machinery, and stages demonstrations of the linen-making process led by guides in period costume. The mill is on a pretty stretch of the River Ballinderry, 7km west of Cookstown, just off the A505 Omagh road.

Donaghmore High Cross HISTORIC SITE

The village of Donaghmore, 8km northwest of Dungannon on the B43 road to Pomeroy, is famed for its 10th-century Celtic high cross. It was cobbled together from two different crosses in the 18th century (note the obvious join halfway up the shaft) and now stands outside the churchyard. The carved biblical scenes are similar to those on the Ardboe cross. The nearby **heritage centre** (Pomeroy Rd; admission free; ⌚9am-5pm Mon-Fri) is based in a converted 19th-century school.

FREE Grant Ancestral Homestead HISTORIC SITE
(Dergina, Ballygawley; ⌚9am-5pm Mon-Sat) Ulysses Simpson Grant (1822–85) led Union forces to victory in the American Civil War and later served as the USA's 18th president for two terms, from 1869 to 1877. His maternal grandfather, John Simpson, emigrated from County Tyrone to Pennsylvania in 1760, but the farm he left behind at Dergina has now been restored in the style of a typical Ulster smallholding, as it would have been during the time of Grant's presidency.

The furnishings in the Grant Ancestral Homestead are not authentic, but the original field plan of the farm survives together with various old farming implements. There's also an exhibition on the American Civil War, a picnic area and children's playground. Confirm opening times by calling the Killymaddy tourist office (☎8776 7259).

The site is 20km west of Dungannon, south of the A4; look out for the signpost 5.5km west of Killymaddy tourist office.

Sleeping & Eating

TOP CHOICE Tullylagan Country House HOTEL €€
(☎8676 5100; www.tullylagan.com; 40b Tullylagan Rd, Cookstown; s/d €65/95; P 🛜 👪) Set amid beautiful riverside gardens 4km south of Cookstown (just off the A29), the ivy-clad Tullylagan goes for the Victorian country manor feel, with shabby-chic sofas, gilt-framed mirrors on deep red walls, and marble-effect bathrooms with period taps. The **restaurant** (two/three courses €19/24; ⌚lunch daily, dinner Mon-Sat) specialises in locally produced seafood, game and beef.

Grange Lodge B&B €€
(☎8778 4212; www.grangelodgecountryhouse.com; 7 Grange Rd, Dungannon; s/d from €60/84; P 🛜) The five-room Grange is a period gem set in its own 8-hectare grounds. Parts of the house, which is packed with antiques, date from 1698, though most are Georgian with Victorian additions. The landlady is an award-winning chef, and the Grange runs cookery courses. A four-course dinner (€36) is available (except Sundays) as long as you book at least 48 hours in advance. It's 5km southeast of Dungannon, signposted off the A29 Moy road.

Avondale B&B B&B €€
(☎8676 4013; www.avondalebb.co.uk; 31 Killycolp Rd, Cookstown; r per person €30; P 🛜) Set in a spacious Edwardian house with a large garden, patio and sun lounge, Avondale offers B&B in two family rooms (one double and one single bed in each), each with private bathroom. It's 3km south of Cookstown, just off the A29 Dungannon road.

TOP CHOICE Deli on the Green BISTRO €€
(☎8775 1775; www.delionthegreen.com; 2 Linen Green, Moygashel; mains lunch €6-9, dinner €10-22; ⌚8.30-11am & noon-3pm Mon-Sat, 5-9.30pm Thu & Fri, 6-9.30pm Sat) Take a break from browsing the designer goodies in the Linen Green shops to relax over a meal in this stylish little bistro. As well as the sandwiches and salads on offer at the deli counter, there are succulent homemade steakburgers and chicken caesar salad, while the breakfast menu includes pancakes with bacon and maple syrup. The evening menu ranges from beer-battered fish and chips to baked hake with chorizo and white bean stew.

Drum Manor Forest Park CAMPGROUND €
(☎8676 2774; Drum Rd, Oaklands; campsites tent & caravan €12.50) A pleasant site 4km west of Cookstown on the A505, with lakes, forest trails, a butterfly farm and an arboretum.

Dungannon Park CAMPGROUND €
(☎8772 8690; dpreception@dungannon.gov.uk; Moy Rd; campsites tent/caravan €10/15; ⌚Mar-Oct) Small (20 pitches) council-run campsite in a quiet, wooded location complete with trout-fishing lake, 2.5km south of Dungannon on the A29 towards Moy and Armagh.

Shopping

Linen Green CLOTHING
(Moygashel; ⌚10am-5pm Mon-Sat) Housed in the former Moygashel Linen Mills, the Linen Green complex includes a range of designer shops and factory outlets, plus a visitor centre with an exhibition covering the history of the local linen industry. It's a good place to shop for bargain men's and women's fashion, shoes, accessories and linen goods or to stop for lunch at the Deli on the Green.

Information

Cookstown tourist office (☎8676 9949; www.cookstown.gov.uk; Burnavon Arts and Cultural Centre, Burn Rd, Cookstown; ⊙9am-5pm Mon-Sat, plus 2-4pm Sun Jul & Aug). Located west of the main street.

Killymaddy tourist office (☎8776 7259; www.flavouroftyrone.com; 190 Ballygawley Rd, Killymaddy; ⊙9am-5pm Mon-Fri, 10am-4pm Sat & Sun) At a caravan site 10km west of Dungannon on the A4 road towards Enniskillen.

Getting There & Away

Bus 210 connects Cookstown with Belfast's Europa BusCentre (€8, 1¾ hours, four daily Saturday, two Sunday to Friday). Bus 261 runs from Belfast's Europa BusCentre to Dungannon (€8, one hour, hourly Monday to Saturday, four on Sundays) and continues to Enniskillen (€8, 1½ hours).

Bus 80 shuttles between Cookstown and Dungannon (€3, 45 minutes, hourly Monday to Friday, eight Saturday). Bus 273 travels from Belfast to Derry via Dungannon (€8, one hour, hourly Monday to Saturday, five on Sundays) and Omagh.

Understand Ireland

Ireland Today

Still Open for Business

In 2011 Ireland went to the polls, elected a brand new government and welcomed both the Queen of England and President Barack Obama, who visited in the space of a frenzied week in May. Ireland finished eighth in the Eurovision Song Contest, which was pretty good given that they'd finished second-last the year before. But one overriding truth overshadowed everything.

Fine Gael are Ireland's largest political party, followed by Labour (Ireland's oldest) and Fianna Fáil, which was the largest party until the 2011 elections.

For the Love of God, Go

In government since 1991, Fianna Fáil had taken credit for the Celtic Tiger but failed to convince the country that the financial meltdown of 2008 was not their fault. They were thrown out of government at the 2011 general election – their worst electoral defeat in history – from 78 seats in the 144-seat Dáil to just 20. Their coalition partners, the Greens, fared even worse: not one of their candidates was elected.

Who's Really in Charge?

The new government is a coalition of centre-right Fine Gael (traditionally Ireland's political bridesmaids) and centre-left Labour, but their policies are hamstrung by the €85 billion bailout given to Ireland by the International Monetary Fund (IMF), the European Union (EU) and European Central Bank (ECB), which has to be repaid at a prohibitively high rate of interest and has resulted in some fairly savage cuts in public spending. In a few short years, Ireland went from being the poster-child for economic success to a terminal patient on financial life support: what happened?

Top Fiction

Dubliners (James Joyce, 1914) A collection of short stories still as poignant and relevant today as when they were written.

The Speckled People (Hugo Hamilton, 2003) Superb memoir of growing up with mixed parentage, told as a novel.

Paddy Clarke Ha Ha Ha (Roddy Doyle, 1993) Wonderful portrait of a 10-year-old boy's trials that was made into a popular film.

The Gathering (Anne Enright, 2007) Powerful account of alcoholism and domestic abuse in an Irish family.

Room (Emma Donoghue, 2010) Inspired by the real-life case of Josef Fritzl, this harrowing, inspirational story of a mother and son's lives as abductees is beautifully told.

belief systems
(% of population)

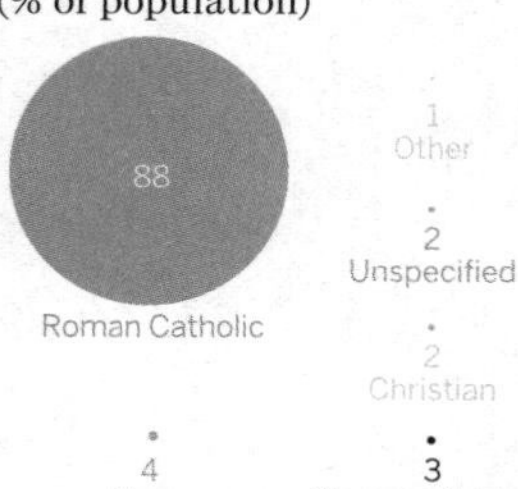

if Ireland were 100 people

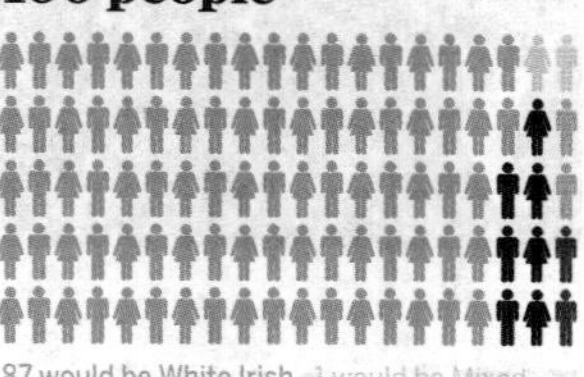

Pop Goes the Bubble

Everyone has a theory as to why it all went south – you'll hear plenty of them on your travels. The facts of the matter are that an unsustainable construction boom saw far too many houses being built and far too many cheap loans given out to both build and buy them. When Lehmann Bros collapsed taking the markets with it, Irish banks' source of cheap credit dried up and their exposure to their debtors was revealed: all six of the main Irish banks risked immediate collapse. Faced with financial Armageddon, the then-minister for finance Brian Lenihan guaranteed all deposits and bondholder investments in the six banks. That guarantee has been the most contentious and divisive decision made in Irish politics since independence. As it stands, Ireland will not be allowed near a money market until at least 2013–14.

In 2011, most opinions were divided between renegotiating the guarantee so as to remove some of the more onerous conditions of it and outright default, arguing that it will force the EU's hand and make them offer Ireland a less stringent deal.

Don't say 'top of the morning' or 'begorrah'. Twenty-first century Ireland will only laugh at such 1950s Hollywood movie expressions. And don't ignore the rounds system. If in a group, buy a round of drinks for the whole table.

Meanwhile, Life Goes On

In economic terms, conditions are tough. Unemployment is up, pay is down and tourism (one of Ireland's most important sources of revenue) fell by roughly 30% between 2008 and 2011. While the old cliché that Ireland is too well used to hard times to let them knock it out of its stride is ridiculously crude and simplistic, there is some truth in it. The Irish – fatalistic and pessimistic to the core – will shrug their shoulders and just get on with their lives. It's not a coincidence that, unlike in Greece, the Irish haven't taken to the streets to protest the restrictive austerity measures that resulted from the banking collapse.

Top Films

Bloody Sunday (Paul Greengrass, 2002) Unmissable account of events in Derry in 1972.

The Dead (John Huston, 1987) Huston brings James Joyce's story to life in his last film, with powerful performances by Donal McCann and Anjelica Huston.

The Magdalene Sisters (Peter Mullan, 2002) The tough story of the brutal treatment of young girls sent to network of infamous industrial schools.

Garage (Lenny Abrahamson, 2007) A tragicomic story of a hapless and lonely garage attendant and his search for friendship and love.

The Crying Game (Neil Jordan, 1992) Race, gender and sexuality explored against the backdrop of the Troubles. Arguably Jordan's finest film.

History

From pre-Celts to Celtic cubs, Ireland's history has been a search for identity, which would have been a little more straightforward if this small island hadn't been of such interest to a host of foreign parties – Celtic tribes, Viking marauders, Norman invaders and the English. Indeed, it is Ireland's fractious relationship with its nearest neighbour that has occupied much of the last thousand years, and it is through the prism of that relationship that a huge part of the Irish identity is reflected – but what emerges isn't nearly as clear-cut as you might expect.

Ireland's tale begins its curving narrative with its earliest arrivals – hunters in the aftermath of the last ice age who crossed a narrow land bridge between Ireland and Britain. Eventually they learnt to farm and, more excitingly for us, work gold – Bronze Age gold work is of an exceptionally high standard (which you can see in Dublin's National Museum, p69).

For a concise, 10-minute read on who the Celts were, see www.ibiblio.org/gaelic/celts.html.

The Celts were the first of the island's invaders, followed by the Vikings in the 9th century and then the Normans, who landed in 1169 to mark the beginning of Ireland's ties with Britain. The Normans consolidated their power by fortifying towns and building castles – lots of them – some of which have survived better than others.

By the 16th century Ireland was looking to cast off the shackles of English rule, but the more they tried, the more England cemented its grip, eventually resulting in a full union in 1801. On the plus side, Dublin was blessed with its rich Georgian heritage, an architectural style still very much in evidence in the capital today.

Ireland – or at least most of it – finally got its independence in 1921, with six counties of Ulster holding firm and remaining loyal to the crown. At the turn of the millennium, Ireland was still a divided country but very much at peace with itself.

You'll find evidence of Ireland's rich history everywhere – in historic

TIMELINE

10,000–8000 BC

After the last ice age ends, humans arrive in Ireland during the mesolithic era, originally crossing a land bridge between Scotland and Ireland. Few archaeological traces remain of this group.

4500 BC

The first Neolithic farmers arrive in Ireland by boat from as far afield as the Iberian peninsula, bringing cattle, sheep and crops, marking the beginnings of a settled agricultural economy.

700–300 BC

Iron technology gradually replaces bronze. The Celtic culture and language arrives, ushering in a thousand years of cultural and political dominance and leaving a legacy still visible today.

sites, monuments, buildings and placenames. We have mentioned some of them in this chapter that you can visit on your travels.

Who the Hell are the Irish?

It took the various Celtic tribes roughly 500 years to settle in Ireland. Beginning in the 8th century BC, the last of the tribes, commonly known as the Gaels (which in the local language came to mean 'foreigner'), came ashore in the 3rd century BC and proceeded to divide the island into five provinces – Leinster, Meath, Connaught, Ulster and Munster (Meath later merged with Leinster) – that were themselves subdivided into territories controlled by as many as one hundred minor kings and chieftains, all of whom nominally paid allegiance to a high king who sat at Tara, in County Meath.

The Celts set about creating the basics of what we now term 'Irish' culture: they devised a sophisticated code of law called the Brehon Law, which remained in use until the early 17th century; and their swirling, mazelike design style, evident on artefacts nearly 2000 years old, is considered the epitome of Irish design. Some excellent ancient Celtic designs survive in the Broighter hoard in the National Museum in Dublin (p69). The Turoe Stone (p423) in County Galway is another fine representative of Celtic artwork.

The Course of Irish History by TW Moody and FX Martin is a hefty volume by two Trinity College professors who trace much of Ireland's history back to its land and its proximity to England.

Getting into the Habit

Although St Patrick (see the boxed text, p696) gets all the credit, between the 3rd and 5th centuries Ireland was Christianised by a host of missionaries, who converted pagan tribes by fusing their local druidic rituals with the new Christian teaching and thereby creating a hybrid known as Celtic or Insular Christianity.

Irish Christian scholars excelled in the study of Latin and Greek philosophy and Christian theology in the monasteries that flourished at, among other places, Clonmacnoise in County Offaly, Glendalough in County Wicklow (see p142) and Lismore in County Waterford. It was the golden age, and the arts of manuscript illumination, metalworking and sculpture flourished, producing such treasures as the *Book of Kells* (p63), ornate jewellery and the many carved stone crosses that dot the 'island of saints and scholars'.

Rape, Pillage & Plunder: A Viking's Day Out

The next group to try their luck were the Vikings, who first showed up in AD 795 and began plundering the prosperous monasteries. In self-defence, the monks built round towers, which served as lookout posts and places of refuge during attacks; you can see surviving examples of these at the likes of Glendalough (see p142).

300 BC–AD 800

Ireland is divided into five provinces, known in Irish as *cúigi* (literally, 'fifth part'): Leinster, Meath, Connaught, Ulster and Munster. Meath later merges with Leinster.

AA WORLD TRAVEL LIBRARY/ALAMY ©

» Statue of St Patrick at Croagh Patrick, overlooking Clew Bay

AD 431–2

Pope Celestine I sends Bishop Palladius to Ireland to minister to those 'already believing in Christ'; St Patrick arrives the following year to continue the mission.

Despite the monks' best efforts, the Vikings had their way, mostly due to superior weaponry but also thanks to elements of the local population, who sided with the marauders for profit or protection. By the 10th century, the Norsemen were well established in Ireland, having founded towns like Wicklow, Waterford, Wexford and their capital Dyfflin, which later became Dublin. The Vikings were defeated at the Battle of Clontarf in 1014 by Brian Ború, king of Munster, but Ború was killed and the Vikings, much like the Celts before them, eventually settled, giving up the rape-rob-and-run policy in favour of integration and assimilation: by intermarrying with the Celtic tribes, they introduced red hair and freckles to the Irish gene pool.

Top Monastic Sites

» **Cashel** County Tipperary

» **Clonmacnoise** County Offaly

» **Glendalough** County Wicklow

The English are Coming!

The '800 years' of English rule in Ireland nominally began with the Norman invasion of 1169, which was really more of an invitation as the barons, led by Richard Fitz Gilbert de Clare, Earl of Pembroke (1130–76; aka Strongbow), had been asked to assist the king of Leinster in a territorial squabble. Two years later, King Henry II of England came ashore with a substantial army and a request from Pope Adrian IV to bring the rebel Christian missionaries to heel.

ST PATRICK

Ireland's patron saint is remembered all around the world on 17 March, when people of all ethnicities drink Guinness and wear green clothing. But behind the hoopla was a real man with a serious mission. For it was Patrick (389–461) who introduced Christianity to Ireland.

The plain truth of it is that he wasn't Irish. This symbol of Irish pride hailed from what is now Wales, which at the time of his birth was under Roman occupation.

Patrick's arrival in Ireland was made possible by Irish raiders who kidnapped him when he was 16, and took him across the channel to work as a slave. He found religion, escaped from captivity and returned to Britain. But he vowed to make it his life's work to make Christians out of the Irish. He was ordained, then appointed Bishop of Ireland. Back he went over the channel.

He based himself in Armagh, where St Patrick's Church of Ireland Cathedral (see p631) stands on the site of his old church. Patrick quickly converted peasants and noblemen in great numbers. Within 30 years, much of Ireland had been baptised and the country was divided into Catholic dioceses and parishes. He also established monasteries throughout Ireland, which would be the foundations of Irish scholarship for many centuries.

So next St Paddy's Day, as you're swilling Guinness and champing down corned beef and cabbage, think of who the man really was.

550–800

The flowering of early monasticism in Ireland. The great monastic teachers begin exporting their knowledge across Europe, ushering in Ireland's 'Golden Age'.

795–841

Vikings plunder Irish monasteries; their raping and pillaging urges sated, they establish settlements throughout the country, including Dublin, and soon turn it into a centre of economic power.

1014

The Battle of Clontarf takes place on Good Friday between the forces of the high king, Brian Ború, and the forces led by the king of Leinster, Máelmorda mac Murchada.

1169

Henry II's Welsh and Norman barons land in Wexford and capture Waterford and Wexford with MacMurrough's help. It is the beginning of an 800-year occupation by Britain.

Despite the king's overall authority, the Anglo-Norman barons carved Ireland up between them and over the next 300 years set about consolidating their feudal power. Once again the effects of assimilation were in play, as the Anglo-Normans and their hirelings became, in the oft-quoted phrase, *Hiberniores Hibernis ipsis* ('more Irish than the Irish themselves'). They dotted the country with castles, but their real legacy is in the cities they built, like magnificent Kilkenny, which today still retains much of its medieval character. The Anglo-Normans may have pledged allegiance to the English king, but in truth they were loyal only to themselves: by the turn of the 16th century, the Crown's direct rule didn't extend any further than a cordon surrounding Dublin known as the Pale. But you can only ignore an English king for so long...

Divorce, Dissolution & Destruction

When Henry VIII declared himself head of the church in England in 1534, following his split with the papacy over his divorce from Catherine of Aragon, the Anglo-Normans cried foul and some took arms against the crown. Worried that an Irish rising would be of help to Spain or France, Henry responded firmly, quashing the rebellion, confiscating the rebels' lands and (as in England) dissolving all Irish monasteries. He then had himself declared King of Ireland.

Elizabeth I continued her father's work by broadening the rule of the crown into Connaught and Munster. This sparked the Nine Years' War (1594–1603) between Elizabeth's forces and an alliance of Irish chieftains led by Hugh O'Neill, Earl of Tyrone. The decisive battle of the conflict took place in Kinsale in 1601, when a Spanish naval force and O'Neill's army were comprehensively routed. O'Neill surrendered in 1603 (but only after Elizabeth's death), and in 1607, he and 90 other Ulster chiefs sailed to Europe, leaving Ireland forever. This was known as the Flight of the Earls, and it left Ulster open to English rule and to the policy of Plantation, which involved confiscating the lands of the flown earls and redistributing them to subjects loyal to the crown. Although the confiscations happened all over the country, they were most thorough in Ulster.

BEYOND THE PALE

The expression 'beyond the Pale' came into use when the Pale was the English-controlled part of Ireland. To the British elite, the rest of Ireland was considered uncivilised.

Bloody Religion

At the outset of the English Civil War in 1641, the Irish threw their support behind Charles I against the very Protestant parliamentarians in the hope that victory for the king would lead to the restoration of Catholic power in Ireland. When Oliver Cromwell and his Roundheads defeated the Royalists and took Charles' head off in 1649, Cromwell then turned his attention to the disloyal Irish. His nine-month campaign was effective and brutal (Drogheda was particularly mistreated, see p553); yet more lands were confiscated – Cromwell's famous utterance that the

1172
King Henry II invades Ireland, forcing the Cambro-Norman warlords and some of the Gaelic Irish kings to accept him as their overlord.

1350–1530
The Anglo-Norman barons establish power bases independent of the English Crown. Over the following two centuries, English control gradually recedes to an area around Dublin known as 'the Pale'.

1366
The English Crown enacts the Statutes of Kilkenny, outlawing intermarriage, the Irish language and other Irish customs to stop the Anglo-Normans from assimilating too much with the Irish. It doesn't work.

1534–41
Henry VIII orders the dissolution of the monasteries and confiscation of church property. In 1541 he arranges for the Irish Parliament to declare him King of Ireland.

Irish could 'go to hell or to Connaught' seems odd given the province's beauty, but there wasn't much arable land out there – and Catholic rights restricted even more.

The Boyne & Penal Laws

Catholic Ireland's next major setback came in 1690. Yet again the Irish had backed the wrong horse, this time supporting James II after his deposition in the Glorious Revolution by the Dutch Protestant King William of Orange (who was married to James' own daughter Mary!). After James had unsuccessfully laid siege to Derry for 105 days (the Loyalist cry of 'No surrender!', in use to this day, dates from the siege), in July he fought William's armies by the banks of the Boyne in County Louth and was roundly defeated.

The final ignominy for Catholic Ireland came in 1695 with the passing of the Penal Laws, known collectively as the 'popery code', which prohibited Catholics from owning land or entering any higher profession. Irish culture, music and education were banned in the hope that Catholicism would be eradicated. Most Catholics continued to worship at secret locations, but some prosperous Irish converted to Protestantism to preserve their careers and wealth. Land was steadily transferred to Protestant owners, and a significant majority of the Catholic population became tenants living in wretched conditions. By the late 18th century, Catholics owned barely 5% of the land.

Cromwell: An Honourable Enemy by Tom Reilly advances the unpopular view that perhaps the destruction of Cromwell's campaign is grossly exaggerated. You're no doubt familiar with the common view; here's the contrary position. (Yes, Reilly is Irish.)

If at First You Don't Succeed...

Beginning towards the end of the 18th century, the main thrust of opposition to Irish inequalities resulting from the Penal Laws came from an unlikely source. A handful of liberal Protestants, versed in the ideologies of the Enlightenment and inspired by the revolutions in France and the newly established United States, began organising direct opposition to the British rule.

The best known was Theobald Wolfe Tone (1763–98), a young Dublin lawyer who led a group called the United Irishmen in their attempts to reform and reduce British power in Ireland (Loyalist Protestants prepared for the possibility of conflict by forming the Protestant Orange Society, later known as the Orange Order). Wolfe Tone attempted to enlist French help in his uprising, but the French failure to land an army of succour in 1796 left the organisation exposed to retribution and the men met their bloody end in the Battle of Vinegar Hill in 1798. Three years later, the British sought to put an end to Irish agitation by passing the Act of Union, but the Nationalist genie was already out of the bottle.

1585

Potatoes from South America are introduced to Ireland, where they eventually become a staple on nearly every table in the country.

OLIVER STREWE/LONELYPLANETIMAGES ©

» Potatoes in County Cork

1594

Hugh O'Neill, Earl of Tyrone, orders lead from England to reroof his castle, but instead uses it for bullets – instigating the start of the Nine Years' War.

1601

The Battle of Kinsale is fought between Elizabeth's armies and the combined rebel forces led by Hugh O'Neill. O'Neill surrenders and the back of the Irish rebellion against the Crown is broken.

Hunger & Heroic Leadership

The 19th century was marked by repeated efforts to wrest some kind of control from Britain. There were the radical Republicans, who advocated use of force to found a secular, egalitarian republic that tried – and failed – in 1848 and 1867. And there were the moderates, who advocated nonviolent and legal action to force the government into concession.

The Great Liberator

Dominating the moderate landscape for nearly three decades was Kerry-born Daniel O'Connell (1775–1847), who tirelessly devoted himself to the cause of Catholic Emancipation. In 1828 he was elected to the British Parliament, but also being a Catholic, he couldn't actually take his seat: to avoid the possibility of an uprising, the government was forced to pass the 1829 Act of Catholic Emancipation, allowing some well-off Catholics voting rights and the right to be elected as MPs.

O'Connell continued to fight for Irish self-determination and became known as a powerful speaker, not only on behalf of Ireland but against all kinds of injustice, including slavery: the abolitionist leader Frederick Douglass was one of his greatest admirers (their relationship was specifically referred to by President Obama during his 2011 visit). O'Connell, known as 'the Liberator,' was adored by the Irish, who turned out in their tens of thousands to hear him speak, but his unwillingness to step outside the law was to prove his undoing: when the government banned one of his rallies from going ahead, O'Connell stood down – ostensibly to avoid the prospect of violence and bloodshed. But Ireland was in the midst of the Potato Famine, and his failure to defy the British was seen as capitulation; he was imprisoned for a time and died a broken man in 1847.

DIASPORA

In 1870, after the Great Famine and ongoing emigration, more than a third of all native-born Irish lived outside Ireland.

The Uncrowned King of Ireland

Charles Stewart Parnell (1846–91) was the other great 19th-century statesman. Like O'Connell, he too was a powerful orator, but the primary focus of his artful attentions was land reform, particularly the reduction of rents and the improvement of working conditions (conveniently referred to as the 'Three Fs': fair rent, free sale and fixity of tenure). Parnell championed the activities of the Land League, who instigated the strategy of 'boycotting' (named after one particularly unpleasant agent called Charles Boycott) tenants, agents and landlords who didn't adhere to the Land League's aims: these people were treated like lepers by the local population. In 1881 they won an important victory with the passing of the Land Act, which granted most of the league's demands.

Parnell's other great struggle was for a limited form of autonomy for Ireland. Despite the nominal support of the Liberal leader William

1607

O'Neill and 90 other Ulster chiefs sail to Europe, leaving Ireland forever. Known as the Flight of the Earls, it leaves Ulster open to English rule and the policy of Plantation.

1641

During the English Civil War, the native Irish and Anglo-Norman Catholics support Charles I against the Protestant parliamentarians in the hope of restoring Catholic power in Ireland.

1649–53

Cromwell lays waste to Ireland after the Irish support Charles I in the English Civil War; this includes the mass slaughter of Catholic Irish and the confiscation of two million hectares of land.

1688–90

Following the deposition of King James II, James' Catholic army fights William's Protestant forces, resulting in William's victory at the Battle of the Boyne, 12 July 1690.

Gladstone, Home Rule bills introduced in 1886 and 1892 were uniformly rejected by Parliament. Like O'Connell before him, Parnell's star plummeted dramatically: in 1890 he was embroiled in a divorce proceeding that scandalised puritanical Ireland. The 'uncrowned king of Ireland' was forced to resign and died less than a year later.

For articles exploring the Irish struggle, check out http://larkspirit.com.

Rebellion Once Again

Ireland's struggle for some kind of autonomy picked up pace in the second decade of the 20th century. The radicalism that had always been at the fringes of Irish Nationalist aspirations was once again beginning to assert itself, partly in response to a hardening of attitudes in Ulster. Mass opposition to any kind of Irish independence had resulted in the formation of the Ulster Volunteer Force (UVF), a Loyalist vigilante group whose 100,000-plus members swore to resist any attempt to impose home rule on Ireland. Nationalists responded by creating the Irish Volunteer Force (IVF) and a showdown seemed inevitable.

THE GREAT FAMINE

As a result of the Great Famine of 1845–51, a staggering three million people died or were forced to emigrate from Ireland. This great tragedy is all the more inconceivable given that the scale of suffering was attributable to selfishness as much as to natural causes. Potatoes were the staple food of a rapidly growing, desperately poor population and, when a blight hit the crops, prices soared. The repressive Penal Laws ensured that farmers, already crippled with high rents, could ill afford the few subsistence potatoes provided. Inevitably, most tenants fell into arrears with little or no concession given by the mostly indifferent landlords and were evicted or sent to the dire conditions of the workhouses.

Shamefully, during this time there were abundant harvests of wheat and dairy produce – the country was producing more than enough grain to feed the entire population and it's said that more cattle were sold abroad than there were people on the island. But while millions of its citizens were starving, Ireland was forced to export its food to Britain and overseas.

The Poor Laws, in place at the height of the Famine, deemed landlords responsible for the maintenance of their poor and encouraged many to 'remove' tenants from their estates by paying their way to America. Many Irish were sent unwittingly to their deaths on board the notoriously scourged 'coffin ships'. British prime minister Sir Robert Peel made well-intentioned but inadequate gestures at famine relief, and some – but far too few – landlords did their best for their tenants.

Mass emigration continued to reduce the population during the next one hundred years and huge numbers of Irish emigrants who found their way abroad, particularly to the USA, carried with them a lasting bitterness.

1695

The Penal Laws (aka the 'popery code') prohibit Catholics from owning a horse, marrying outside their religion, building churches out of anything but wood, and from buying or inheriting property.

1795

Concerned at the attempts of the Society of United Irishmen to secure equal rights for non-Establishment Protestants and Catholics, a group of Protestants create the Orange Institution.

1798

The flogging and killing of potential rebels sparks a rising led by the United Irishmen and their leader, Wolfe Tone. Wolfe Tone is captured and taken to Dublin, where he commits suicide.

1801

The Act of Union unites Ireland politically with Britain. The Irish Parliament votes itself out of existence following a campaign of bribery. Around 100 Members of Parliament move to the House of Commons in London.

Home Rule was finally passed in 1914, but the outbreak of WWI meant that its enactment was shelved for the duration. For most Irish, the suspension was disappointing but hardly unreasonable and the majority of the volunteers enlisted to help fight the Germans.

The Great Hunger by Cecil Woodham-Smith is the classic study of the Great Famine of 1845–51.

The Easter Rising

A few, however, did not heed the call. Two small groups – a section of the Irish Volunteers under Pádraig Pearse and the Irish Citizens' Army led by James Connolly – conspired in a rebellion that took the country by surprise. A depleted Volunteer group marched into Dublin on Easter Monday 1916 and took over a number of key positions in the city, claiming the General Post Office on O'Connell St as its headquarters. From its steps, Pearse read out to passers-by a declaration that Ireland was now a republic and that his band was the provisional government. Less than a week of fighting ensued before the rebels surrendered to the superior British forces. The rebels weren't popular and had to be protected from angry Dubliners as they were marched to jail.

The Easter Rising would probably have had little impact on the Irish situation had the British not made martyrs of the rebel leaders. Of the 77 given death sentences, 15 were executed, including the injured Connolly, who was shot while strapped to a chair. This brought about a sea change in public attitudes, and support for the Republicans rose dramatically.

Neil Jordan's movie *Michael Collins,* starring Liam Neeson as the revolutionary, depicts the Easter Rising, the founding of the Free State and Collins' violent demise.

War with Britain

By the end of WWI, Home Rule was far too little, far too late. In the 1918 general election, the Republicans stood under the banner of Sinn Féin and won a large majority of the Irish seats. Ignoring London's Parliament, where technically they were supposed to sit, the newly elected Sinn Féin deputies – many of them veterans of the 1916 Easter Rising – declared Ireland independent and formed the first Dáil Éireann (Irish assembly or lower house), which sat in Dublin's Mansion House under the leadership of Éamon de Valera (1882–1975). The Irish Volunteers became the Irish Republican Army (IRA) and the Dáil authorised it to wage war on British troops in Ireland.

As wars go, the War of Independence was pretty small fry. It lasted 2½ years and cost around 1200 casualties. But it was a pretty nasty affair, as the IRA fought a guerrilla-style, hit-and-run campaign against the British, whose numbers were swelled by returning veterans of WWI known as Black and Tans (on account of their uniforms, a mix of army khaki and police black), most of whom were so traumatised by their wartime experiences that they were prone to all kinds of brutality.

1828–29
Daniel O'Connell exploits a loophole in the law to win a seat in Parliament but is unable to take it because he is Catholic. The prime minister passes the Catholic Emancipation Act giving limited rights to Catholics.

1845–51
A mould ravages the potato harvest. The British government adopts a laissez-faire attitude, resulting in the deaths of between 500,000 and one million, and the emigration of up to two million others.

1879–82
The Land War, led by the Land League, sees tenant farmers defying their landlords en masse to force the passing of the Land Act in 1881, which allows for fair rent, fixity of tenure and free sale.

1884
The Gaelic Athletic Association (GAA) is founded in Hayes Hotel, Thurles, County Tipperary. Its aim is to promote Gaelic games and culture; today hurling and Gaelic football are immensely popular.

A Kind of Freedom

A truce in July 1921 led to intense negotiations between the two sides. The resulting treaty, signed on 6 December 1921, created the Irish Free State, made up of 26 of 32 Irish counties. The remaining six – all in Ulster – remained part of the UK. The treaty was an imperfect document: not only did it cement the geographic divisions on the island that 50 years later would explode into the Troubles, it caused a split among Nationalists – between those who believed the treaty to be a necessary stepping stone towards full independence, and those who saw it as capitulation to the British and a betrayal of Republican ideals. This division was to determine the course of Irish political affairs for virtually the remainder of the century.

The Irish in America by Michael Coffey takes up the history of the Famine where many histories leave off: the turbulent experiences of Irish immigrants in the USA.

Civil War

The treaty was ratified after a bitter debate and the June 1922 elections resulted in a victory for the pro-Treaty side. But the anti-Treaty forces rallied behind de Valera, who, though president of the Dáil, had not been a member of the treaty negotiating team (affording him, in the eyes of his critics and opponents, maximum deniability should the negotiations go pear-shaped) and objected to some of the treaty's provisions, most notably the oath of allegiance to the English monarch.

Within two weeks of the elections, civil war broke out between comrades who, a year previously, had fought alongside each other. The most prominent casualty of this particularly bitter conflict was Michael Collins (1890–1922), mastermind of the IRA's campaign during the War of Independence and a chief negotiator of the Anglo-Irish Treaty – shot in an ambush in his native Cork (see p252). Collins himself had presaged the bitterness that would result from the treaty: upon signing it, he is said to have declared, 'I tell you, I have signed my own death warrant.'

The events leading up to the Anglo-Irish War and their effect on ordinary people are movingly and powerfully related in JG Farrell's novel *Troubles*, first published in 1970.

The Making of a Republic

The Civil War ground to an exhausted halt in 1923 with the victory of the pro-treaty side, who governed the new state until 1932. Defeated but unbowed, de Valera founded a new party in 1926 called Fianna Fáil (Soldiers of Ireland) and won a majority in the 1932 elections – they would remain in charge until 1948. In the meantime, de Valera created a new constitution in 1937 that did away with the hated oath of allegiance, reaffirmed the special position of the Catholic Church and once again laid claim to the six counties of Northern Ireland. In 1948 Ireland officially left the Commonwealth and became a republic but, as historical irony would have it, it was Fine Gael, as the old pro-treaty party were now known, that declared it – Fianna Fáil had surprisingly lost the election that year. After 800 years, Ireland – or at least a substantial chunk of it – was independent.

1890s

The Gaelic Revival, championed by poet WB Yeats, sees a focused interest in the Irish language and Irish culture, including folklore, sport, music and the arts.

1904

16 June is the day in which all of the events of James Joyce's Ulysses take place – chosen because it was the date Joyce first went out with his wife, Nora.

1916

The Easter Rising: a group of Republicans take Dublin's General Post Office and announce the formation of an Irish republic. After less than a week of fighting, the rebels surrender to the superior British forces.

JOHN SONES/LONELYPLANETIMAGES ©

» Easter Rising 1916 mural

Growing Pains & Roaring Tigers

Unquestionably the most significant figure since independence, Éamon de Valera's contribution to an independent Ireland was immense but, as the 1950s stretched into the 1960s, his vision for the country was mired in a conservative and traditional orthodoxy that was at odds with the reality of a country in desperate economic straits, where chronic unemployment and emigration were but the more visible effects of inadequate policy. De Valera's successor as Taoiseach was Sean Lemass, whose tenure began in 1959 with the dictum 'a rising tide lifts all boats'. By the mid-1960s his economic policies had halved emigration and ushered in a new prosperity that was to be mirrored 30 years later by the Celtic Tiger.

A History of Ireland by Mike Cronin summarises all of Ireland's history in less than 300 pages. It's an easy read, but doesn't offer much in the way of analysis.

Partners in Europe

In 1972 the Republic (along with Northern Ireland) became a member of the European Economic Community (EEC), which brought an increased measure of prosperity thanks to the benefits of the Common Agricultural Policy, which set fixed prices and guaranteed quotas for Irish farming produce. Nevertheless, the broader global depression, provoked by the oil crisis of 1973, forced the country into yet another slump and emigration figures rose again, reaching a peak in the mid-1980s.

From Celtic Tiger...

In the early 1990s, European funds helped kick start economic growth. Huge sums of money were invested in education and physical infrastructure, while the policy of low corporate tax rates coupled with attractive incentives made Ireland very attractive to high-tech businesses looking for a door into EU markets. In less than a decade, Ireland went from being one of the poorest countries in Europe to one of the wealthiest: unemployment fell from 18% to 3.5%, the average industrial wage somersaulted to the top of the European league and the dramatic rise in GDP meant that the country laid claim to an economic model of success that was the envy of the entire world. Ireland became synonymous with the term 'Celtic Tiger'.

...to Rescue Cat

From 2002 the Irish economy was kept buoyant by a gigantic construction boom that was completely out of step with any measure of responsible growth forecasting. The out-of-control international derivatives market flooded Irish banks with cheap money, who lent it freely.

Then Lehmann Bros and the credit crunch happened. The Irish banks nearly went to the wall, but were bailed out at the last minute, and before Ireland could draw breath, the International Monetary Fund (IMF) and

1919–21

Irish War of Independence, aka the Black and Tan War on account of British irregulars wearing mixed police (black) and army (khaki) uniforms, begins in January 1919.

1921

Two years and 1200 casualties later, the war ends in a truce on 11 July 1921 that leads to peace talks. After negotiations in London, the Irish delegation signs the Anglo-Irish Treaty on 6 December.

1921–22

The treaty gives 26 counties of Ireland independence and allows six largely Protestant Ulster counties the choice of opting out. The Irish Free State is founded in 1922.

1922–23

Unwilling to accept the terms of the treaty, forces led by Éamon de Valera take up arms against their former comrades, led by Michael Collins. A brief but bloody civil war ensues, resulting in the death of Collins.

the European Union held the chits of the country's mid-term economic future. Ireland found itself yet again confronting the demons of its past: high unemployment, limited opportunity and massive emigration.

It's (Not So) Grim Up North

For the Cause of Liberty: A Thousand Years of Ireland's Heroes by Terry Golway vividly describes the struggles of Irish nationalism.

Since 8 May 2007, Northern Ireland has been governed in relative harmony by a constituent assembly, currently led by First Minister Peter Robinson of the Democratic Unionist Party (DUP) and Deputy First Minister Martin McGuinness of Sinn Féin (SF). Even if you'd only kept a lazy eye on Irish affairs these last four decades, you'd know that the presence of a one-time Loyalist firebrand like Robinson – who made his career on his vocal enmity towards all forms of Irish nationalism – and an ex-IRA commander like McGuinness in the same cabinet is a minor political miracle.

But it isn't really. It's the painstaking result of a process of dialogue and negotiation that has sought to untie a Gordian knot of historical resentment, mistrust, violence and engrained prejudice that began with the Plantations of Ireland in the 16th century.

Ireland Divided

A History of Ulster by Jonathan Bardon is a serious and far-reaching attempt to come to grips with Northern Ireland's saga.

Following the Anglo-Irish Treaty, a new Northern Ireland Parliament was constituted on 22 June 1922, with James Craig as the first prime minister. His Ulster Unionist Party (UUP) was to rule the new state until 1972, with the minority Catholic population (roughly 40%) stripped of any real power or representative strength by a Parliament that favoured the Unionists through economic subsidy, bias in housing allocations and gerrymandering: Derry's electoral boundaries were redrawn so as to guarantee a Protestant council, even though the city was two-thirds Catholic. The overwhelmingly Protestant Royal Ulster Constabulary (RUC) and their paramilitary force, the B-Specials, made little effort to mask their sectarian bias. To all intents and purposes, Northern Ireland was an apartheid state.

We Shall Overcome

The first challenge to the Unionist hegemony came with the long-dormant IRA's border campaign in the 1950s, but it was quickly quashed and its leaders imprisoned. A decade later, however, the authorities met with a far more defiant foe in the shape of the Civil Rights Movement, founded in 1967 and heavily influenced by its US counterpart as it sought to redress the blatant sectarianism in Derry. In October 1968 a mainly Catholic march in Derry was violently broken up by the RUC amid rumours that the IRA had provided 'security' for the marchers. Nobody knew it at the time, but the Troubles had begun.

1932

After 10 years in the political wilderness, de Valera leads his Fianna Fáil party into government and goes about weakening the ties between the Free State and Britain.

1948

Fianna Fáil loses the 1948 general election to Fine Gael in coalition with the new Republican Clann an Poblachta. The new government declares the Free State to be a republic at last.

1969

Marches by the Northern Ireland Civil Rights Association are disrupted by Loyalist attacks and police action, resulting in rioting, culminating in the Battle of the Bogside. The Troubles begin.

1972

The Republic (and Northern Ireland) become members of the EEC. On Bloody Sunday, 13 civilians are killed by British troops; Westminster suspends the Stormont government and introduces direct rule.

In January 1969 another civil rights movement, called People's Democracy, organised a march from Belfast to Derry. As the marchers neared their destination, they were attacked by a group of Protestants. The police first stood to one side and then swept through the predominantly Catholic Bogside district. Further marches, protests and violence followed, with many Republicans arguing that the police only added to the problem. In August British troops went to Derry and then Belfast to maintain law and order. The British army was initially welcomed in some Catholic quarters, but soon it too came to be seen as a tool of the Protestant majority. Overreaction by the army actually fuelled recruitment into the long-dormant IRA, whose numbers especially increased after Bloody Sunday (30 January 1972), when British troops killed 13 civilians in Derry.

The Troubles

Following Bloody Sunday, the IRA more or less declared war on Britain. While continuing to target people in Northern Ireland, it moved its campaign of bombing to the British mainland, targeting innocents and earning the condemnation of citizens and parties from both sides of the sectarian divide. Meanwhile, Loyalist paramilitaries began a sectarian campaign against Catholics. Passions reached fever pitch in 1981 when Republican prisoners in the North went on a hunger strike, demanding the right to be recognised as political prisoners. Ten of them fasted to death, the best known being an elected MP, Bobby Sands.

The waters were further muddied by an incredible variety of parties splintering into subgroups with different agendas. The IRA had split into 'official' and 'provisional' wings, from which sprang more extreme Republican organisations such as the Irish National Liberation Army (INLA). Myriad Protestant, Loyalist paramilitary organisations sprang up in opposition to the IRA, and violence was typically met with violence.

Overtures of Peace

By the early 1990s, it was clear to Republicans that armed struggle was a bankrupted policy. Northern Ireland was a transformed society – most of the injustices that had sparked the conflict in the late 1960s had long since been rectified and most ordinary citizens were desperate for an end to hostilities. A series of negotiated statements between the Unionists, Nationalists and the British and Irish governments – brokered in part by George Mitchell, Bill Clinton's special envoy to Northern Ireland – eventually resulted in the historic Good Friday Agreement of 1998.

The agreement called for the devolution of legislative power from Westminster (where it had been since 1972) to a new Northern Ireland Assembly, but posturing, disagreement, sectarianism and downright

Books on the Troubles

» *Lost Lives*, David McKittrick

» *Ten Men Dead*, David Beresford

» *The Faithful Tribe: An Intimate Portrait of the Loyal Institutions*, Ruth Dudley Edwards

Many films depict events related to the Troubles, including *Bloody Sunday* (2002), *The Boxer* (1997; starring Daniel Day-Lewis) and *In the Name of the Father* (1994; also starring Day-Lewis).

1973–74

The Sunningdale Agreement results in a new Northern Ireland Assembly. Unionists oppose the agreement and the Ulster Workers' Council calls a strike that paralyses the province and brings an end to the Assembly.

1981

Ten Republican prisoners die from a hunger strike. The first to die, Bobby Sands, had three weeks earlier been elected to Parliament on an Anti-H-Block ticket. Over 100,000 people attend Sands' funeral.

1993

Downing Street Declaration is signed by British prime minister John Major and Irish prime minister Albert Reynolds. It states that Britain has no 'selfish, strategic or economic interest in Northern Ireland'.

Mid-1990s

Low corporate tax, restraint in government spending, transfer payments from the EU and a low-cost labour market result in the 'Celtic Tiger' boom, transforming Ireland into one of Europe's wealthiest countries.

obstinance on both sides made slow work of progress, and the assembly was suspended four times – the last from October 2002 until May 2007.

During this period, the politics of Northern Ireland polarised dramatically, resulting in the falling away of the more moderate UUP and the emergence of the hardline Democratic Unionist Party (DUP), led by Ian Paisley; and, on the Nationalist side, the emergence of the IRA's political wing, Sinn Féin, as the main torch-bearer of Nationalist aspirations, under the leadership of Gerry Adams and Martin McGuinness.

IRA

Brendan O'Brien's popular *Pocket History of the IRA* summarises a lot of complex history in a mere 150 pages, but it's a good introduction.

A New Northern Ireland

Eager to avoid being seen to surrender any ground, the DUP and Sinn Féin dug their heels in on key issues, with the main sticking points being decommissioning of IRA weapons and the identity and composition of the new police force ushered in to replace the RUC. Paisley and the Unionists made increasing demands of the decommissioning bodies (photographic evidence, Unionist witnesses etc) as they refused to accept anything less than an open and complete surrender of the IRA. Sinn Féin refused to join the police board that monitored the affairs of the Police Service of Northern Ireland (PSNI), effectively making no change to their policy of total noncooperation with the security forces.

But the IRA did finally decommission all of its weapons, and Sinn Féin eventually agreed to join the police board. The DUP abandoned its intransigence towards its former Republican enemies and the two sides got down to the business of governing a province whose pressing needs had long since been shunted aside by the dictatorship of sectarianism.

AMERICAN CONNECTIONS

Today more than 40 million Americans have Irish ancestry – a legacy of successive waves of emigration, spurred by events from the Potato Famine of the 1840s to the Depression of the 1930s. Many of the legendary figures of American history, from Davy Crockett to John Steinbeck, and 16 out of the 42 US presidents to date are of Irish descent.

Here's a list of places covered in this guide that have links to past US presidents or deal with the experience of Irish emigrants to the USA:

» Andrew Jackson Centre (p668), County Antrim
» Dunbrody Famine Ship (p178), County Wexford
» Grant Ancestral Homestead (p689), County Tyrone
» Kennedy Homestead (p179), County Wexford
» Queenstown Story Heritage Centre (p235), County Cork
» Ulster American Folk Park (p687), County Tyrone

1994
Sinn Féin leader Gerry Adams announces a 'cessation of violence' on behalf of the IRA on 31 August. In October the Combined Loyalist Military Command also announces a ceasefire.

1998
On 10 April negotiations culminate in the Good Friday Agreement, under which the new Northern Ireland Assembly is given full legislative and executive authority.

1998
The 'Real IRA' detonates a bomb in Omagh, killing 29 people and injuring 200. It is the worst single atrocity in the history of the Troubles, but public outrage and swift action by politicians prevent a Loyalist backlash.

2005
The IRA orders its units not to engage in 'any other activities' apart from assisting 'the development of purely political and democratic programmes through exclusively peaceful means'.

Proof that Northern Ireland had finally achieved some kind of normality came with the 2011 Assembly elections, which returned the DUP and Sinn Féin as the two largest parties, mandating them to keep going.

But old enmities die hard. The murder of a young PSNI officer called Ronan Kerr in April 2011 was a bitter reminder of the province's violent history, but even in tragedy there was a sense that something fundamental had shifted: Kerr was a Catholic member of a police force that has gone to great lengths to disavow its traditionally pro-Protestant bias and his murder was condemned with equal strength by both sides of the divide. Perhaps most tellingly, First Minister Peter Robinson's presence at the funeral was the first time Robinson had ever been to a Catholic requiem mass.

Ireland Since the Famine by FSL Lyons is a standard text for all students of modern Irish history.

2007
The Northern Ireland Assembly resumes after a five-year break when talks between Unionists and Republicans remain in stalemate. They resolve their primary issues.

2008
The Irish banking system is declared virtually bankrupt following the collapse of Lehmann Bros; Ireland is on the brink of economic disaster as the extent of the crisis is revealed.

2010
Ireland receives €85 billion bailout package from the IMF and the EU, which alleviates the banking crisis but leaves the country in strict financial shackles.

2011
Queen Elizabeth II is the first British monarch to visit the Republic of Ireland; the visit is heralded as a resounding affirmation of the close ties between the two nations.

The Irish Way of Life

Being Irish, he had an abiding sense of tragedy, which sustained him through temporary periods of joy.

William Butler Yeats

The Irish Pulse

The Irish are justifiably renowned for their easygoing, affable nature. They're famous for being warm and friendly, which is just another way of saying that the Irish love a bit of a chat, whether it be with friends or strangers. They will entertain you with their humour, alarm you with their willingness to get stuck into a good debate and cut you down with their razor-sharp wit. Slagging – the Irish version of teasing – is an art form, which may seem caustic to unfamiliar ears, but is quickly revealed as an intrinsic element of how the Irish relate to one another. It is commonly assumed that the mettle of friendship is proven by how well you can take a joke rather than by the payment of a cheap compliment.

The Irish aren't big on talking themselves up, preferring their actions to speak for themselves. They also admire the peculiar art of self-deprecation, known locally as *an beál bocht a chur ort,* or 'putting on the poor mouth', the mildly pejorative practice of making out that things are far worse than they really are in order to evoke sympathy or the forbearance of creditors, of vital importance in the days when the majority of the Irish were at the mercy of an unforgiving landlord system. As a result, the Irish also have the trait of begrudgery – although it's something only recognised by them and generally kept within the wider family. It's kind of amusing, though, to note that someone like Bono is subject to more intense criticism in Ireland than anywhere else in the world.

Beneath all of the garrulous sociability and self-deprecating twaddle lurks a dark secret, which is that at heart the Irish are low on self-esteem. They're therefore very suspicious of praise and tend not to believe anything nice that's ever said about them. The Irish wallow in false modesty like a sport.

Nevertheless, the prosperity of the last two decades and the radical lifestyle shifts it entailed have imbued the Irish with a renewed sense of confidence and a conviction that they are deserving of a seat at anyone's table. For the first time, the Irish, particularly the under-30s, have no problem relaying their achievements and successes, in contrast to the older generation who were brought up in the belief that telling anyone they were doing well was unseemly and boastful.

As Ireland adjusts to the new, post-crash economic realities, an interesting gap in perspective has emerged: the younger generation, raised on boundless possibility, have struggled to adjust to circumstances that are oh-so-familiar to their parents, who were brought up in a time when unemployment, emigration and a cap on ambition were basic facts of life.

While Ireland's economic woes may be depressingly familiar to the older generation and forced many of the country's younger people to try their luck elsewhere, this is not the Ireland of yesteryear. The two decades since 1990 have transformed the country immeasurably, with prosperity, modernity and multiculturalism helping shift traditional attitudes and social mores.

Nurse & Curse of the People

This goes some way towards explaining the fractious relationship Ireland has with alcohol. The country regularly tops the list of the world's biggest binge drinkers, and while there is an increasing awareness of, and alarm at, the devastation caused by alcohol to Irish society (especially to young people), drinking remains the country's most popular social pastime, with no sign of letting up; spend a weekend night walking around any town in the country and you'll get a firsthand feel of the influence and effect of the booze.

Some experts put Ireland's binge-drinking antics down to the dramatic rise in the country's economic fortunes, but statistics have long revealed that Ireland has had an unhealthy fondness for 'taking the cure', although the acceptability of public drunkenness is a far more recent phenomenon: the older generation are never done reminding the youngsters that they would *never* have been seen staggering in public.

Lifestyle

The Irish may like to grumble – about work, the weather, the government and those *feckin' eejits* on reality TV shows – but if pressed will tell you that they live in the best country on earth. There's loads *wrong* with the place, but isn't it the same way everywhere else?

Traditional Ireland – of the large family, closely linked to church and community – is quickly disappearing, as the increased urbanisation of Ireland continues to break up the social fabric of community interdependence that was a necessary element of relative poverty. Contemporary Ireland is therefore not altogether different from any other European country, and you have to travel further to the margins of the country – the islands and the isolated rural communities – to find an older version of society.

Multiculturalism

Ireland has long been a pretty homogenous country, but the arrival of thousands of immigrants from all over the world – 10% of the population is foreign-born – has challenged the mores of racial tolerance and integration. To a large extent it has been successful, although if you scratch beneath the surface, racial tensions can be exposed.

The tanking of the economy has exacerbated these tensions and the 'Irish jobs for Irish people' opinion is being opined with greater vehemence and authority – even though they remain very much a minority for now. Irrespectively, the flow of emigrants from Eastern Europe has slowed up dramatically as many believe their prospects to be better at home.

Religion

About 3.7 million residents in the Republic call themselves Roman Catholic, followed by 3% Protestant, 0.5% Muslim and the rest an assortment of other beliefs including none at all. In the North, the breakdown is about 53% Protestant and 44% Catholic (with about 3% other or no religion).

BABY NAMES

Top of the list for most popular baby names in 2011 were Jack and Ava.

The average number of children per family has fallen to 1.4, the lowest in Irish history.

SPIRITUALITY

Most Irish Protestants are members of the Church of Ireland, an offshoot of the Church of England, and the Presbyterian and Methodist churches.

Statistics don't tell the whole story, though, and the influence of the Catholic Church has waned dramatically in the last decade – a complaint during the (as yet unpublished) census of 2011 was that the form didn't allow for an expression of 'non-believer.' Most young people see the Church as irrelevant and out of step with the major social issues of the day including divorce, contraception, abortion, homosexuality and cohabitation. The terrible revelations of widespread abuse of children by parish priests, and the untidy efforts of the Church authorities to sweep the truth under the carpet, have provoked a seething rage among many Irish at the Church's gross insensitivity to the care of its flock, while many older believers feel an acute sense of betrayal that has led them to question a lifetime's devotion to their local parishes. The deep fissures provoked by the revelations were perhaps best expressed by Taoiseach Enda Kenny in 2011 on the back of the publication of a report into abuses in the diocese of Cloyne in County Cork and, for the first time, an explicit accusation against the Vatican itself for attempting to frustrate the inquiry. Speaking in the Dail, Kenny railed against the 'dysfunction, disconnection, elitism… [and] narcissism that dominates the culture of the Vatican to this day.'

According to a poll, 70% of Irish citizens believe in God and 22% believe in some kind of spirit or life-force. Only 4% declared themselves non-believers.

Such vehemence on the part of an Irish premier, which would have been considered unthinkable in years past, resulted in the Vatican withdrawing the papal nuncio – again a gesture that previously would have been unheard of.

And then there's money: increased prosperity means that the Irish have become used to being rewarded in *this* life, and so many have replaced God with Mammon as a focus of worship. But old habits die hard, and Sunday Mass is still a feature of the weekly calendar, especially in rural communities. Oddly enough, the primates of both the Roman Catholic Church (Archbishop Sean Brady) and the Church of Ireland (Archbishop Robert Eames) sit in Armagh, Northern Ireland, the traditional religious capital of St Patrick. The country's religious history clearly overrides its current divisions.

GAY-FRIENDLY IRELAND

The best things that ever happened to gay Ireland were the taming of the dictating church and the enactment of protective legislation against any kind of sexual discrimination. According to Brian Merriman, the Artistic Director of the International Dublin Gay Theatre Festival, the collapse of church authority and the shocking revelations of priestly abuse, coupled with the liberalisation of the divorce law, helped Ireland come to terms with its own sexual and social honesty. So much so that in 2011 the government passed the Civil Partnership Act, which gave same-sex couples rights and responsibilities comparable with civil marriage.

'Ireland is no longer talking about 'them' when referring to anyone who is vaguely unconventional; they're talking about 'us' and that every family has the potential to be different,' he says with great conviction. 'It's not just 'them' who have the gay in the closet. They're everywhere!'

But it's not all good. There is a huge difference still between attitudes in urban and rural Ireland, he says, and while legislation and liberalisation have been very important, there is still a legacy of internalised homophobia.

'Our enemies are no longer as clearly visible, so it's hard to know sometimes who exactly thinks what.'

He believes, however, that gays and lesbians need to be more visible in Irish society, if only to continue the struggle for parity of esteem and respect. The Civil Partnership Act is one important step.

TV

Irish TV is small fry; it always has been. It lacks the funding and the audience available to behemoths like the BBC. But – and this is a huge but – compared to that of most other European countries it is actually quite good. However, the national broadcaster, RTE, gets its fair share of abuse for being narrow-minded, conservative, boring, short-sighted and way behind the times – and that's just for turning down the chance to produce the enormously successful comedy-drama series *Father Ted* (a gentle and hilarious poke at conservative Ireland, which was then commissioned by Britain's Channel 4).

There are four terrestrial TV channels in Ireland. RTE's strengths are its widespread sports coverage and news and current affairs programming – it's thorough, insightful and often hard-hitting. Programs like *Today Tonight* and *Prime Time* are as good as, or better than, anything you'll see elsewhere in the world; the reporting treats the audience like mature, responsible adults who don't need issues dumbed down or simplified. But let's not forget the Angelus, Ireland's very own call to prayer: 18 sombre hits of a church bell heard at 6pm on RTE1 (and at noon on radio). Undoubtedly out of step with a fast-paced and secular society, it is a daily reminder of the state-encouraged piety of not so long ago.

An Irish birthday tradition for kids is 'the bumps', where the celebrants are lifted by their limbs and swung up and down a number of times corresponding to their age plus one.

The purely commercial TV3 has a lightweight programming philosophy, with second-string US fluff to complement its diet of reality TV shows and celebrity nonsense – although its *Nightly News with Vincent Browne* is an intelligent barometer of the day's affairs. The Irish-language station TG4 has the most diverse and challenging output, combining great movies (in English) with an interesting selection of dramas and documentaries *as gaeilge* (in Irish with English subtitles). The main British TV stations – BBC, ITV and Channel 4 – are also available in most Irish homes, through cable.

The big players in the digital TV business are the homegrown NTL and the behemoth that is Sky, who continue to make solid progress in bringing the multichannel revolution into Irish homes.

Radio

The Irish love radio – up to 85% of the population listen in on any given day. The majority tend to stick with RTE, the dominant player with three stations: Radio 1 (88.2-90FM; mostly news and discussion), Radio 2 (90.4-92.2FM; lifestyle and music) and Lyric FM (96-99FM; classical music). In Northern Ireland, the BBC rules supreme, with BBC Radio Ulster flying the local flag in addition to the four main BBC stations.

Females outnumber males in Dublin by 20,000.

Independent competitors to RTE are owned by telecommunications impresario Denis O'Brien and include Today FM (100-102FM; music, chat and news) and the talk radio Newstalk (106-108FM; news, current affairs and lifestyle). The rest of the radio landscape is filled out by the 25 or so local radio stations that represent local issues and tastes: the northwest's Highland Radio – heard in Donegal, Sligo, Tyrone and Fermanagh – is Europe's most successful local radio station, with an 84% market share.

Music

Ireland's literary tradition may have the critics nodding sagely, but it's the country's ability to render music to the ear that will remain with you long after your Irish day is done. There's music for every occasion and every mood, from celebration to sorrow.

Traditional & Folk

Irish music (known in Ireland as traditional music, or just trad) has retained a vibrancy not found in other traditional European forms, which have lost out to the overbearing influence of pop music. Although Irish music has kept many of its traditional aspects, it has itself influenced many forms of music, most notably US country and western – a fusion of Mississippi Delta blues and Irish traditional tunes that, combined with other influences like Gospel, is at the root of rock and roll. Other reasons for trad music's current success include the willingness of its exponents to update the way it's played (in ensembles rather than the customary *céilidh* – traditional music and dance – bands), the habit of pub sessions (introduced by returning migrants) and the economic good times that encouraged the Irish to celebrate their culture rather than trying to replicate international trends. And then, of course, there's *Riverdance,* which made Irish dancing sexy and became a worldwide phenomenon, despite the fact that most aficionados of traditional music are seriously underwhelmed by its musical worth. Good stage show, crap music.

US *Late Show* host David Letterman once described the uillean pipes as 'a sofa hooked up to a stick'.

Traditionally, music was performed as a background to dancing, and while this has been true ever since Celtic times, the many thousands of tunes that fill up the repertoire aren't nearly as ancient as that; most aren't much older than a couple of hundred years. Because much of Irish music is handed down orally and aurally, there are myriad variations in the way a single tune is played, depending on the time and place of its playing. The blind itinerant harpist **Turlough O'Carolan** (1680–1738) wrote more than 200 tunes – it's difficult to know how many versions their repeated learning has spawned.

THE NUTS & BOLTS OF TRADITIONAL MUSIC

Despite popular perception, the harp isn't widely used in traditional music (it *is* the national emblem, but that probably has more to do with the country traditionally being run by people pulling strings). The bodhrán (*bow*-rawn) goat-skin drum is much more prevalent, although it makes for a lousy symbol. The uillean pipes, played by squeezing bellows under the elbow, provide another distinctive sound, although you're not likely to see them in a pub. The fiddle isn't unique to Ireland but it is one of the main instruments in the country's indigenous music, along with the flute, tin whistle, accordion and bouzouki (a version of the mandolin). Music fits into five main categories (jigs, reels, hornpipes, polkas and slow airs), while the old style of singing unaccompanied versions of traditional ballads and airs is called *sean-n ós*.

TRADITIONAL PLAYLIST

- » *The Quiet Glen* (Tommy Peoples)
- » *Paddy Keenan* (Paddy Keenan)
- » *Compendium: The Best of Patrick Street* (Various)
- » *The Chieftains 6: Bonaparte's Retreat* (The Chieftains)
- » *Old Hag You Have Killed Me* (The Bothy Band)

More folksy than traditional, **the Dubliners**, fronted by the distinctive gravel voice and grey beard of Ronnie Drew (1934–2008), made a career out of bawdy drinking songs that got *everybody* singing along. Other popular bands include **the Fureys**, comprising four brothers originally from the travelling community (no, not like the Wilburies) along with guitarist Davey Arthur. And if it's rousing renditions of Irish rebel songs you're after, you can't go past the Wolfe Tones.

Since the 1970s, various bands have tried to blend traditional with more progressive genres, with mixed success. The first band to pull it off was Moving Hearts, led by Christy Moore, who went on to become the greatest Irish folk musician ever (see p163).

Hot Press (www.hotpress.com) is a fortnightly magazine featuring local and international music interviews and listings.

Popular Music

From the 1960s onward, Ireland produced its fair share of great rock musicians, including Van Morrison, Thin Lizzy, Celtic rockers Horslips, punk poppers the Undertones and Belfast's own Stiff Little Fingers (SLF), Ireland's answer to the Clash. And then there was Bob Geldof's Boomtown Rats, who didn't like Mondays or much else either.

But they all paled in comparison to the supernova that is U2, formed in 1976 in North Dublin and as of the late 1980s one of the world's most successful rock bands. Needless to say, their musical output of late has dipped – perhaps it's their other commitments (African debt relief, the Spiderman on Broadway fiasco) – but they remain Ireland's most popular band worldwide by far.

THE VOICE: LUKE KELLY

With a halo of wiry ginger hair and a voice like hardened honey, Luke Kelly (1940–84) was perhaps the greatest Irish folk singer of the 20th century, a performer who used his voice in the manner of the American blues' singers he admired so much, to express the anguish of being 'lonely and afraid in a world they never made' (to quote AE Housman). He was a founding member of the Dubliners, along with Ronnie Drew (1934–2008), Barney McKenna (1939–) and Ciaran Burke (1935–88), but he treated Dublin's most famous folk group as more of a temporary cooperative enterprise. He shared the singing duties with Drew, lending his distinctive voice to classic drinking ditties like *Dirty Old Town* and rousing rebel songs like *A Nation Once Again*, but it was his mastery of the more reflective ballad that made him peerless. His rendition of *On Ragland Road*, from a poem by Patrick Kavanagh that the poet himself insisted he sing, is the most beautiful song about Dublin we've ever heard; but it is his version of Phil Coulter's *Scorn Not His Simplicity* that grants him his place among the immortals. Coulter wrote the song following the birth of a son with Down's Syndrome and even though it became one of Luke's best-loved songs, he had such respect for it that he rarely sang it at the Dubliners' boisterous gigs.

Recommended listening: *Luke Kelly: The Collection*.

BEST IRISH ROCK ALBUMS

» *Loveless* (My Bloody Valentine)
» *Boy* (U2)
» *The End of History* (Fionn Regan)
» *Live & Dangerous* (Thin Lizzy)
» *I Do Not Want What I Haven't Got* (Sinead O'Connor)
» *St Dominic's Preview* (Van Morrison)
» *O* (Damien Rice)
» *Inflammable Material* (Stiff Little Fingers)
» *The Book of Invasion* (Horslips)
» *Becoming a Jackal* (Villagers)

The Contemporary Scene

Irish sensitivity is best expressed through song, and there's no shortage of the feelings-out-front singer-songwriter. The established crop include Paddy Casey, Damien Rice and the excellent Fionn Regan (his single 'Be Good or Be Gone' was a big hit and featured on *Grey's Anatomy*), while Belfast-born Duke Special followed up on the success of *Songs from the Deep Forest* (2007) with two albums in quick succession: *Orchestral Manoeuvres in Belfast* and *I Never Thought This Day Would Come* (both 2008). Oh, and don't forget a certain Glen Hansard, whose band the Frames were a fixture on the scene for nearly two decades, but achieved international fame only when he (and co-singer Markéta Irglová) won the Oscar for Best Song in 2008 for 'Falling Slowly' from the movie *Once;* their success resulted in a new band, The Swell Season, whose album Strict Joy (2009) also did very well.

Other names to look out for are Julie Feeney – her second album *Pages* (2009) is stunning; Cathy Davey (2007's *Tales of Silversleeve* is worth a listen); and Lisa Hannigan, who played for a number of years with Damien Rice before heading out on her own with the superb *Sea Saw* (2009). We're also big fans of the Nick Cave–like Adrian Crowley – *Season of the Sparks* (2009) and *Long Distance Swimmer* (2007) are recommended (the latter won Ireland's most prestigious musical award, the Choice Music Prize, in 2009) – and Villagers, whose 2010 *Becoming a Jackal* is outstanding.

Ireland does its bit for alt-rock with the likes of Fight Like Apes, whose second album *The Body of Christ And The Legs of Tina Turner* (2010) was very well received, while Cast of Cheers, As I Watch You From Afar (ASIWYFA) and the Ambience Affair are all bands looking very promising in 2011.

The live music scene is especially vibrant, with performances in virtually every kind of venue, from an impromptu stage at the back of a pub to a mega-gig in an 80,000 capacity stadium, regularly filling the pages of the 'what's on' guides. But what makes live music so special are the Irish crowds themselves, who engage fully with the performers, lending the whole experience an added quality that has been remarked upon by musicians as diverse as the Rolling Stones to Barbra Streisand.

Literary Ireland

Of all their national traits, characteristics and cultural expressions, it's perhaps the way the Irish speak and write that best distinguishes them. Their love of language and their great oral tradition have contributed to Ireland's legacy of world-renowned writers and storytellers. And all this in a language imposed on them by a foreign invader. The Irish responded to this act of cultural piracy by mastering a magnificent hybrid – English in every respect but flavoured and enriched by the rhythms, pronunciation patterns and grammatical peculiarities of Irish.

The Mythic Cycle

Before there was anything like modern literature there was the Ulaid (Ulster) Cycle – Ireland's version of the Homeric epic – written down from oral tradition between the 8th and 12th centuries. The chief story is the Táin Bó Cúailnge (Cattle Raid of Cooley), about a battle between Queen Maeve of Connaught and Cúchulainn, the principal hero of Irish mythology. Cúchulainn appears in the work of Irish writers right up to the present day, from Samuel Beckett to Frank McCourt.

Modern Literature

From the mythic cycle, zip forward 1000 years, past the genius of Jonathan Swift (1667–1745) and his *Gulliver's Travels;* stopping to acknowledge acclaimed dramatist Oscar Wilde (1854–1900); *Dracula* creator Bram Stoker (1847–1912) – some have claimed that the name of the count may have come from the Irish *droch fhola* (bad blood) – and the literary giant that was James Joyce (1882–1941), whose name and books elicit enormous pride in Ireland.

The majority of Joyce's literary output came when he had left Ireland for the artistic hotbed that was Paris, which was also true for another great experimenter of language and style, Samuel Beckett (1906–89). His work centres on fundamental existential questions about the human condition and the nature of self. He is probably best known for his play *Waiting for Godot,* but his unassailable reputation is based on a series of stark novels and plays.

THE GAELIC REVIVAL

While Home Rule was being debated and shunted, something of a revolution was taking place in Irish arts, literature and identity. The poet William Butler Yeats and his coterie of literary friends (including Lady Gregory, Douglas Hyde, John Millington Synge and George Russell) championed the Anglo-Irish literary revival, unearthing old Celtic tales and writing with fresh enthusiasm about a romantic Ireland of epic battles and warrior queens. For a country that had suffered centuries of invasion and deprivation, these images presented a much more attractive version of history.

Of the dozens of 20th-century Irish authors to have achieved published renown, some names to look out for include playwright and novelist Brendan Behan (1923–64), who wove tragedy, wit and a turbulent life into his best works including *Borstal Boy*, *The Quare Fellow* and *The Hostage*. Inevitably, Behan died young of alcoholism.

Belfast-born CS Lewis (1898–1963) died a year earlier, but he left us *The Chronicles of Narnia*, a series of allegorical children's stories, three of which have been made into films. Other Northern writers have, not surprisingly, featured the Troubles in their work: Bernard McLaverty's *Cal* (also made into a film) and his more recent *The Anatomy School* are both wonderful.

Contemporary Fiction

» The Empty Family (Colm Tóibín)

» Ghost Light (Joseph O'Connor)

» The Forgotten Waltz (Anne Enright)

» Room (Emma Donoghue)

» John The Revelator (Peter Byrne)

Contemporary Scene

"I love James Joyce. Never read him, but he's a true genius." Yes, the stalwarts are still great, but ask your average Irish person who their favourite home-grown writer is and they'll most likely mention someone *who's still alive*.

They might mention Roddy Doyle (1958–), whose mega-successful Barrytown quartet – *The Commitments*, *The Snapper*, *The Van* and *Paddy Clarke, Ha Ha Ha* – have all been made into films. Most recently, he's turned to social and political history with a new trilogy, beginning with *A Star Called Henry* (2000), the story of an IRA hitman called Henry Smart; followed by *Oh, Play That Thing!* (2004) and *The Dead Republic* (2010), both of which follow Henry on his adventures in the US.

Sebastian Barry (1955–) started his career as a poet with *The Water Colorist* (1983), became famous as a playwright, but achieved his greatest success as a novelist. He was shortlisted for the Man Booker Prize twice: in 2005 for his WWI drama *A Long Way Down* and the absolutely compelling *The Secret Scripture* (2008), about a 100-year-old inmate of a mental hospital who decides to write an autobiography. It was the Costa Book of the Year in 2008 and won the prestigious James Tait Black Memorial Prize in 2009.

Anne Enright (1962–) did nab the Booker for *The Gathering* (2007), a zeitgeist tale of alcoholism and abuse – she described it as 'the intellectual equivalent of a Hollywood weepie'. Another Booker Prize winner

LIVING POET'S SOCIETY

Seamus Heaney (1939–) was born in Derry but now lives mostly in Dublin. He is the bard of all Ireland and evokes the spirit and character of the country in his poetry. He won the Nobel Prize for Literature in 1995, and the humble wordsmith compared all the attention to someone mentioning sex in front of their mammy. *Opened Ground – Poems 1966–1996* (1998) is our favourite of his books.

Dubliner Paul Durcan (1944–) is one of the most reliable chroniclers of changing Dublin. He won the prestigious Whitbread Prize for Poetry in 1990 for *'Daddy, Daddy'* and is a funny, engaging, tender and savage writer. Poet, playwright and Kerryman Brendan Kennelly (1936–) is an immensely popular character around town. He lectures at Trinity College and writes a unique brand of poetry that is marked by its playfulness, as well as historical and intellectual impact. Eavan Boland (1944–) is a prolific and much-admired writer, best known for her poetry, who combines Irish politics with outspoken feminism; *In a Time of Violence* (1995) and *The Lost Land* (1998) are two of her most celebrated collections.

To find out more about poetry in Ireland in general, visit the website of the excellent **Poetry Ireland** (www.poetryireland.ie), which showcases the work of new and established poets. For a taste of modern Irish poetry in print, try *Contemporary Irish Poetry*, edited by Fallon and Mahon. *A Rage for Order*, edited by Frank Ormsby, is a vibrant collection of the poetry of the North.

is heavyweight John Banville (1945–), who won it for *The Sea* (2009); we also recommend either *The Book of Evidence* (1989) or the masterful roman-à-clef *The Untouchable* (1998), based loosely on the secret-agent life of art historian Anthony Blunt. Banville's precise and often cold prose divides critics, who consider him either the English language's greatest living stylist or an unreadable intellectual; if you're of the latter inclination then you should check out his immensely enjoyable (and highly readable) crime novels, written under the pseudonym of Benjamin Black: *Christine Falls* (2006), *The Silver Swan* (2007), *The Lemur* (2008) and *Elegy for April* (2010).

Another big hitter is Wexford-born but Dublin-based Colm Tóibin (1955–), who spent four years looking for a publisher for his first novel *The South* (1990) but has gone on to become a hugely successful novelist and scholar. His novels *The Master* (2004) and *Brooklyn* (2009) were both very well received; his latest work, *The Empty Family* (2011), is a collection of short stories. Of the host of younger writers making names for themselves, we recommend the work of Claire Kilroy (1973–), whose three novels – *All Summer* (2003), *Tenderwire* (2006) and *All the Names Have Been Changed* (2009) have established her as a genuine talent.

Like some of their famous antecedents, some Irish novelists have gone abroad to write and find success. Joseph O'Neill (1964–) won the PEN/Faulkner Award for fiction for his post-9/11 novel *Netherland* (2009), while Colum McCann (1965–), who also tackled 9/11 but in a far more allegorical fashion, picked up the National Book Award for *Let the Great World Spin* (2009).

Chick Lit

Authors hate the label and publishers profess to disregard it, but chick lit is big business, and few have mastered it as well as the Irish. Doyenne of them all is Maeve Binchy (1940–) whose mastery of the style has seen her outsell most of the literary greats – her latest in a long line of bestsellers is *Heart And Soul* (2008). Hot on her heels is Marian Keyes (1963–), author of 11 bestsellers that tackle themes like alcoholism and mental health. Her latest book is *The Brightest Star in the Sky* (2009). Former agony aunt Cathy Kelly (she keeps her age a secret) has written 13 novels, each more successful than the last – in 2010 she published two, *The Perfect Holiday* and *Homecoming*.

PS I LOVE YOU

There's no ignoring Cecelia Ahern (1981–), daughter of former Taoiseach Bertie Ahern and author of the staggeringly successful *PS I Love You* (2004), which was made into a terrible film starring Hilary Swank. She's followed up with six similarly saccharine books since.

TOP IRISH READS

» **Angela's Ashes** The Pulitzer Prize–winning novel by Frank McCourt tells the relentlessly bleak autobiographical story of the author's poverty-stricken Limerick childhood in the Depression of the 1930s.

» **Amongst Women** John McGahern's simple, economical piece centres on a west-of-Ireland family in the social aftermath of the War of Independence.

» **Reading in the Dark** Seamus Deane (the Guardian Fiction Prize winner) recounts a young boy's struggles to unravel the truth of his own history growing up during the Troubles of Belfast.

» **The Sea** The Booker Prize–winning novel by John Banville is an engrossing meditation on mortality, grief, death, childhood and memory.

» **Double Drink Story** By Caitlin Thomas (née MacNamara), wife of Welsh poet Dylan Thomas. This is an eloquent, self-deprecating account of their debauched life, their love-hate relationship and the burden of creativity.

» **The Butcher Boy** Patrick McCabe's novel is a brilliant, gruesome, tragicomedy about an orphaned Monaghan boy's descent into madness. It was later made into a successful film by Neil Jordan.

Irish Landscapes

Irish literature, song and painting makes it pretty clear that the landscape exerts a powerful sway on the people who have lived in it. This is especially true for those who have left, for whom the aul' sod is still a land worth pining for, and many visitors still anticipate experiencing this land's subtle influence on perception and mood. Once you've travelled the country, you can't help but agree that the vibrant greenness of gentle hills, the fearsome violence of jagged coasts and the sombre light of so many cloudy days is an integral part of experiencing Ireland.

In 1821 the body of an Iron Age man was found in a bog in Galway with his cape, shoes and beard still intact.

The entire island stretches a mere 486km north to south and 275km east to west, so Ireland's impressive topographical variety may come as a surprise. The countryside does indeed have an abundance of the expected greenery. Grass grows nearly everywhere in Ireland, but there are notable exceptions, particularly around the dramatic coasts.

Cliffs & Stones

Massive rocky outcrops, like the Burren in County Clare, are for the most part inhospitable to grass, and although even there the green stuff does sprout up in enough patches for sheep and goats to graze on, these vast, otherworldly landscapes are mostly grey and bleak. Nearby, the dramatic Cliffs of Moher are a sheer drop into the thundering surf below. Similarly, there is no preparing for the extraordinary hexagonal stone columns of the Giant's Causeway in County Antrim or the rugged drop of County Donegal's Slieve League, Europe's highest sea cliffs. Sand dunes buffer many of the more gentle stretches of coast. Smaller islands dot the shores of Ireland, many of them barren rock piles supporting unique ecosystems – Skellig Michael is a breathtakingly jagged example just off the Kerry coast.

Of the nine counties that originally comprised the province of Ulster, six are now part of Northern Ireland while three are part of the Republic.

The rural farms of the west coast have a rugged, hard-earned look to them, due mostly to the rock that lies so close to the surface. Much of this rock has been dug up to create tillable soil and converted into stone walls that divide tiny paddocks. The Aran Islands stand out for their spectacular networks of stone walls.

Mountains & Forests

The west of Ireland is a bulwark of cliffs, hills and mountains and is the country's most mountainous area. The highest mountains are in the

THE BOG

The boglands, which once covered one-fifth of the island, are more of a whiskey hue than green – that's the brown of heather and sphagnum moss, which cover uncut bogs. Visitors will likely encounter a bog in County Kildare's Bog of Allen or while driving through the western counties – much of the Mayo coast is covered by bog, and huge swaths also cover Donegal.

southwest; the tallest mountain in Ireland is Carrantuohil (1039m) in County Kerry's Macgillycuddy's Reeks.

The Irish frequently lament the loss of their woodlands, much of which were cleared by the British (during the reign of Elizabeth I) to build ships for the Royal Navy. Little of the island's once plentiful oak forests survive today, and much of what you'll see is the result of relatively recent planting. Instead, the countryside largely comprises green fields divided by hedgerows and stone walls. Use of this land is divided between cultivated fields and pasture for cattle and sheep.

Ireland's National Parks

» Burren

» Connemara

» Glenveagh

» Killarney

» Wicklow Mountains

» Ballycroy

Plants

Although Ireland is sparsely wooded, the range of surviving plant species is larger here than in many other European countries, thanks in part to the comparatively late arrival of agriculture.

There are remnants of the original oak forest in Killarney National Park and in southern Wicklow near Shillelagh. Far more common are pine plantations, which are growing steadily. Hedgerows, planted to divide fields and delineate land boundaries throughout Ireland, actually host many of the native plant species that once thrived in the oak forests – it's an intriguing example of nature adapting and reasserting itself. The Burren in County Clare is home to a remarkable mixture of Mediterranean, alpine and arctic species.

The bogs of Ireland are home to a unique flora adapted to wet, acidic, nutrient-poor conditions and whose survival is threatened by the depletion of bogs for energy use. Sphagnum moss is the key bog plant and is joined by other species such as bog rosemary, bog cotton, black-beaked sedge (whose spindly stem grows up to 30cm high) and various types of heather and lichen. Carnivorous plants also thrive, such as the sundew, whose sticky tentacles trap insects, and bladderwort, whose tiny explosive bladders trap aquatic animals in bog pools.

Mammals

Apart from the fox and badger, which tend to shy away from humans and are rarely seen, the wild mammals of Ireland are mostly of the ankle-high 'critter' category, such a rabbits, hedgehogs and shrews. Hikers often spot the Irish hare, or at least glimpse the blazing-fast blur of one running away. Red deer roam the hillsides in many of the wilder parts of the country, particularly the Wicklow Mountains and in Killarney National Park, which holds the country's largest herd.

For most visitors, the most commonly sighted mammals are those inhabiting the sea and waterways. The otter, rarely seen elsewhere in Europe, is thriving in Ireland. Seals are a common sight in rivers and along the shore, as are dolphins, which follow the warm waters of the Gulf Stream towards Ireland. Some colonise the coast of Ireland year-round, frequently swimming into the bays and inlets off the western coast.

The illustrated pocket guide *Animals of Ireland* by Gordon D'Arcy is a handy, inexpensive introduction to Ireland's varied fauna.

ANIMALS OF IRELAND

Birdlife

Many travellers visit Ireland specifically for the birding. Ireland's westerly location on the fringe of Europe makes it an ideal stopover point for birds migrating from North America and the Arctic. In autumn, the southern counties become a temporary home to the American waders (mainly sandpipers and plovers) and warblers. Migrants from Africa, such as shearwaters, petrels and auks, begin to arrive in spring in the southwestern counties.

The reasonably rare corncrake, which migrates from Africa, can be found in the western counties, in Donegal and around the Shannon Callows, and on islands such as Inishbofin in Galway. In late spring and early summer, the rugged coastlines, particularly cliff areas and islands, become a haven for breeding seabirds, mainly gannet, kittiwake, Manx shearwater, fulmar, cormorant and heron. Puffins, resembling penguins with their tuxedo colour scheme, nest in large colonies on coastal cliffs.

The lakes and low-lying wetlands attract large numbers of Arctic and northern European waterfowl and waders such as whooper swans, lapwing, barnacle geese, white-fronted geese and golden plovers. The important Wexford Wildfowl Reserve holds half the world's population of Greenland white-fronted geese, and little tern breed on the beach there, protected by the dunes. Also found during the winter are teal, redshank and curlew. The main migration periods are April to May and September to October.

The magnificent peregrine falcon has been making something of a recovery and can be found nesting on cliffs in Wicklow and elsewhere. In 2001, 46 golden eagle chicks from Scotland were released into Glenveagh National Park in Donegal in an effort to reintroduce the species. So far, the project's success has been down to the efforts of one pair of eagles: after successfully rearing a chick in 2007, they hatched two more in 2009. Some of the eagles have expanded their range well beyond the park – frequent sightings have been reported in Counties Mayo and Antrim.

Irish Birds by David Cabot is a pocket guide describing birds and their habitats, and outlines the best places for serious bird watching.

Environmental Issues

Ireland does not rate among the world's biggest offenders when it comes to polluting the environment, but the country's recent economic growth has led to an increase in industry and consumerism, which in turn generate more pollution and waste. While the population density is among Europe's lowest, the population is rising. The last 10 years have seen the untrammelled expansion of suburban developments around all of Ireland's major towns and cities; the biggest by far is, inevitably, around Dublin, especially in the broadening commuter belt of Counties Meath and Kildare. The collapse of the construction bubble in 2008 has put an end to much of this development, but the rows of semi-detached houses still remain. As more people drive cars and fly in planes, Ireland grows more dependent on nonrenewable sources of energy. The amount of waste has risen substantially since the early 1990s.

Needless to say, concern for the environment is growing and the government has taken some measures to offset the damage that thriving economies can cause. In 2007 the Irish Energy Centre was renamed **Sustainable Energy Ireland** (SEI; www.sei.ie) and charged with promoting and assisting the development of renewable energy resources, including solar, wind, hydropower, geothermal and biomass resources. As it stands, the country is only tapping a fraction of these: in 2009 only 4.9% of the country's energy requirements (heat, electricity and transport) were being met by renewables.

For information on parks, gardens, monuments and inland waterways see www.heritageireland.ie.

The European Renewables Directive has set Ireland a target of sourcing 16% of all energy requirements by 2020, which given the economic constraints put upon the country now seems overly optimistic: the country

NATIONAL NATURE RESERVES

There are 66 state-owned and 10 privately owned National Nature Reserves (NNRs) in the Republic, represented by Dúchas (the government department in charge of parks, monuments and gardens), which are defined as areas of importance for their special flora, fauna or geology. Northern Ireland has over 45 NNRs which are leased or owned by the Department of the Environment. These include the Giant's Causeway and Glenariff in Antrim, and North Strangford Lough in County Down. More information is available from the **Northern Ireland Environment Agency** (www.ni-environment.gov.uk).

just doesn't have the funds to make major infrastructural investments in renewable technology like wind farms or the manufacture of solar panels.

On a more practical level, a number of recycling programs have been very successful, especially the 'plastax' – a €0.24 levy on all plastic bags used within the retail sector, which has seen their use reduced by a whopping 90%.

Look for *Reading the Irish Landscape* by Frank Mitchell and Michael Ryan for info on Ireland's geology, archaeology, urban growth, agriculture and afforestation.

While this is a positive sign, it doesn't really put Ireland at the vanguard of the environmental movement. Polls seem to indicate the Irish are slightly less concerned about the environment than are the citizens of most other European countries, and the country is a long way from meeting its Kyoto Protocol requirement for reduced emissions. The government isn't pushing the environmental agenda much beyond ratifying EU agreements, although it must be said that these have established fairly ambitious goals for reduced air pollution and tighter management of water quality.

The annual number of tourists in Ireland far exceeds the number of residents (by a ratio of about 1.5 to one), so visitors can have a huge impact on the local environment. Tourism is frequently cited as potentially beneficial to the environment – that is, responsible visitor spending can help stimulate ecofriendly sectors of the economy. Ecotourism is not really burgeoning in a formalised way, although an organisation called the **Greenbox** (www.greenbox.ie) has established standards for ecotourism on the island and promotes tour companies that comply to these standards. The rising popularity of outdoor activities such as diving, surfing and fishing create economic incentives for maintaining the cleanliness of Ireland's coasts and inland waters, but increased activity in these environments can be harmful if not managed carefully.

Ireland's comprehensive and efficient bus network makes it easy to avoid the use of a car, and the country is well suited to cycling and walking holidays. Many hotels, guesthouses and hostels tout green credentials, and organic ingredients are frequently promoted on restaurant menus. It's not difficult for visitors to minimise their environmental footprint while in Ireland.

Sporting Ireland

For many Irish, sport is akin to religion. For some it's all about faith through good works such as jogging, cycling and organised team sports. For everybody else, observance is enough, especially from the living room couch or the pub stool, where the mixed fortunes of their favourite teams are followed with elevated hope and vocalised despair.

Gaelic Football & Hurling

Gaelic games are at the core of Irishness; they are enmeshed in the fabric of Irish life and hold a unique place in the heart of its culture. Their resurgence towards the end of the 19th century was entwined with the whole Gaelic revival and the march towards Irish independence. The beating heart of Gaelic sports is the **Gaelic Athletic Association** (GAA; www.gaa.ie), set up in 1884 'for the preservation and cultivation of National pastimes'. The GAA is still responsible for fostering these amateur games. It warms our hearts to see that after all this time – and amid the onslaught of globalisation and the general commercialisation of sport – they are still far and away the most popular sports in Ireland.

Gaelic games are fast, furious and not for the faint-hearted. Challenges are fierce, and contact between players is extremely aggressive. Both sports are county-based games. The dream of every club player is to represent his county, with the hope of perhaps playing in an All-Ireland final in September at Croke Park in Dublin, the climax of a knockout championship that is played first at a provincial and then interprovincial level.

In order to avoid competing (and losing) with the more popular English Premier League, whose season runs from mid-August to mid-May, the League of Ireland runs its season from April to November, the only European league to do so. Northern Ireland's Irish League still follows the British winter timetable.

Football

There is huge support in Ireland for the 'world game', although fans are much more enthusiastic about the likes of Manchester United, Liverpool and the two Glasgow clubs (Rangers and Celtic) than the struggling

RULES OF THE GAMES

Both Gaelic football and hurling are played by two teams of 15 players whose aim is to get the ball through what resembles a rugby goal: two long vertical posts joined by a horizontal bar, below which is a soccer-style goal, protected by a goalkeeper. Goals (below the crossbar) are worth three points, whereas a ball placed over the bar between the posts is worth one point. Scores are shown thus: 1-12, meaning one goal and 12 points, giving a total of 15 points.

Gaelic football is played with a round, soccer-size ball, and players are allowed to kick it or hand-pass it, like Aussie Rules. Hurling, which is considered by far the more beautiful game, is played with a flat stick or bat known as a hurley or *camán*. The small leather ball, called a *slíothar*, is hit or carried on the hurley; handpassing is also allowed. Both games are played over 70 action-filled minutes.

YOU SAY SOCCER, I SAY FOOTBALL

To distinguish it from Gaelic Football, you'll often hear it referred to as 'soccer' – especially in Gaelic strongholds whereby doing so implies scorn on so-called 'garrison sports' – which will allay American confusion but only irritate the Brits. But Irish fans of Association Football (the official name of the sport) will always call it football and the other Gaelic Football or, in Dublin, gah – which is just a pronunciation of the letters GAA (Gaelic Athletic Association).

pros and part-timers who make up the **National League** (www.fai.ie) in the Republic and the **Irish League** (www.irishfa.com) in Northern Ireland. It's just too difficult for domestic teams to compete with the multi millionaire glitz and glamour of the English Premiership, which has always drawn off the cream of Irish talent.

At an international level, the Republic and Northern Ireland field separate teams; in 2009 both were performing adequately, but it was all a far cry from their relative moments of glory – the 1980s for Northern Ireland and 1988 to 2002 for the Republic.

Rugby

Although traditionally the preserve of Ireland's middle classes, rugby captures the mood of the whole island in February and March during the annual Six Nations Championships, because the Irish team is drawn from both sides of the border and is supported by both Nationalists and Unionists. In recognition of this, the Irish national anthem is no longer played at internationals, replaced by the slightly dodgy but thoroughly inoffensive *Ireland's Call*, a song written especially for the purpose – although nobody seemed to mind it in 2009 when Ireland won its first Grand Slam (a clean sweep of victories in one campaign) since 1948.

Rugby is arguably more exciting at a provincial level, where Leinster and Munster have an ongoing rivalry (both have won the Heineken Cup, Europe's premier competition, twice; Leinster most recently in 2009 and 2011) and Ulster are just a step behind them. Rugby isn't big in the west so Connaught aren't very good.

Most counties are good at one Gaelic sport and not the other. Kilkenny, Waterford, Clare and Tipperary are traditionally hurling counties; Kerry, Meath, Mayo and all nine Ulster counties are better at football. Cork, Galway, Offaly, Wexford and Dublin have the privilege of being good at both sports.

Horse Racing & Greyhound Racing

A passion for horse racing is deeply entrenched in Irish life and comes without the snobbery of its English counterpart. If you fancy a flutter on the gee-gees you can watch racing from around Ireland and England on the TV in bookmakers shops every day. No money ever seems to change hands in the betting, however, and every Irish punter will tell you they 'broke even'.

Ireland has a reputation for producing world-class horses for racing and other equestrian events like showjumping, also very popular albeit in a much less egalitarian kind of way. Major annual races include the Irish Grand National (Fairyhouse, April), Irish Derby (the Curragh, June) and Irish Leger (the Curragh, September). For more information on events contact **Horse Racing Ireland** (www.hri.ie).

Traditionally the poor-man's punt, greyhound racing ('the dogs'), has been smartened up in recent years and partly turned into a corporate outing. It offers a cheaper, more accessible and more local alternative to horse racing. There are 20 tracks across the country, administered by the **Irish Greyhound Board** (www.igb.ie).

Road Bowling

The object of this sport is to throw a cast-iron ball weighing approximately 800g along a public road (normally one with little traffic) for a designated distance, usually 1km or 2km, with speed, control and accuracy. The person who does it in the least number of throws is the winner. Participants traditionally bet during the game.

Irish academic Dr Fintan Lane's book *Long Bullets: A History of Road Bowling in Ireland* traces the sport to the 17th century.

The ball is known as a **bowl** or **bullet**. A **shot** is a throw and a **kitter-paw** is a left-handed thrower. If you hear someone talking about their **butt**, they are referring to the throwing mark on the road. **Breaking butt** means someone has stepped over the mark before releasing the ball. **Faugh an Bheallach** is a traditional Irish battle cry and means you should get out of the way. A **sop** is a tuft of grass placed where the bowl should first strike the road and a **score** is a match.

The main centre for road bowling is Cork, which has 200 clubs, and, to a lesser extent, Armagh. Competitions take place throughout the year, attracting considerable crowds. The sport has been taken up in various countries around the world, including the US, UK, Germany and the Netherlands, and a world championship competition has been set up (see www.irishroadbowling.ie). In Ireland the sport is governed by the Irish Road Bowling Association.

Survival Guide

Accommodation

Accommodation options range from bare and basic to pricey and palatial. The spine of the Irish hospitality business is the ubiquitous B&B, but in recent years they have been challenged by a plethora of midrange hotels and guesthouses. Online resources for accommodation include the following:

» **www.daft.ie** Online classified paper for short- and long-term rentals.

» **www.elegant.ie** Specialises in self-catering castles, period houses and unique properties.

» **www.familyhomes.ie** Lists (you guessed it) family-run guesthouses and self-catering properties.

» **www.gulliver.ie** Fáilte Ireland and the Northern Ireland Tourist Board's web-based accommodation reservation system.

» **www.irishlandmark.com** Not-for-profit conservation group that rents self-catering properties of historical and cultural significance, such as castles, gate lodges and lighthouses.

» **www.stayinireland.com** Lists guesthouses and self-catering options.

B&Bs & Guesthouses

Bed and breakfasts are small, family-run houses, farmhouses and period country houses with fewer than five bedrooms. Standards vary enormously, but most have some bedrooms with private bathroom at a cost of roughly €35 to €40 (£20 to £25) per person per night. In luxurious B&Bs, expect to pay €55 (£38) or more per person. Off-season rates – usually October through to March – are usually lower, as are midweek prices often.

Guesthouses are like upmarket B&Bs but bigger – the Irish equivalent of a boutique hotel. Facilities are usually better and sometimes include a restaurant.

Other tips:

» Facilities in B&Bs range from basic (bed, bathroom, kettle) to beatific (whirlpool baths, LCD TVs, wi-fi) as you go up in price.

» Most B&Bs take credit cards but the occasional rural one might not have facilities; check when you book.

» Advance reservations are strongly recommended, especially in peak season (June to September).

» If full, B&B owners may recommend another house in the area (possibly a private house taking occasional guests, not in tourist listings).

Camping, Canals & Caravan Parks

Camping and caravan parks aren't as common in Ireland as they are in Britain or on the continent. Some hostels have camping space for tents and also offer house facilities, which makes them better value than the main camping grounds. At commercial parks the cost is typically somewhere between €12 and €20 (£7 to £10) for a tent and two people. Prices for campsites in this book are for two people unless stated otherwise. Caravan sites cost around €15 to €25 (£11 to £15). Most parks are open only from Easter to the end of September or October.

An alternative to normal caravanning is to hire a horse-drawn caravan with which to wander the countryside. In high season you can hire one for around €800 a week. Search Fáilte Ireland's www.discoverireland.ie for a list of operators, or see www.irishhorsedrawncaravans.com.

Another unhurried and pleasurable way to see the countryside (with slightly less maintenance) is by barge on one of the country's canal systems. As above, contact Fáilte Ireland for a list of rental companies.

Another option is to hire a boat, which you can live aboard while cruising Ireland's inland waterways. One company offering boats for hire on the Shannon-Erne Waterway is **Emerald Star** (☎071-962 0234; www.emeraldstar.ie).

Hostels

The prices quoted in this book for hostel accommodation are for those aged over 18. A dorm bed in high

A 'STANDARD' HOTEL RATE?

There is no such thing. Prices vary according to demand – or have different rates for online, phone or walk-in bookings. B&B rates are more consistent, but virtually every other accommodation will charge wildly different rates depending on the time of year, day, festival schedule and even your ability to do a little negotiating. The following price ranges have been used in our reviews of places to stay. Prices are all based on a double room with private bathroom, in high season.

BUDGET	REPUBLIC	NORTHERN IRELAND
Budget (€/£)	<€60	<£40
Midrange (€€/££)	€60-150	£40-100
Top end (€€€/£££)	>€150	>£100

season generally costs €10 to €25 (£8 to £14). Many hostels now have family and smaller rooms.

The following is a list of the relevant hostel associations:

An Óige (www.anoige.ie) Hostelling International (HI)–associated national organisation with 26 hostels scattered around the Republic.

HINI (www.hini.org.uk) HI-associated organisation with six hostels in Northern Ireland.

Independent Holiday Hostels of Ireland (IHH; www.hostels-ireland.com) Eighty tourist-board approved hostels throughout all of Ireland.

Independent Hostel Owners of Ireland (IHO; www.independenthostelsireland.com) Independent hostelling association.

Hotels

Hotels range from the local pub to medieval castles. In most cases, you'll get a better rate than the one published if you go online or negotiate directly with the hotel, especially out of season. The explosion of bland midrange chain hotels (many Irish-owned) has proved a major challenge to the traditional B&B or guesthouse: they might not have the same personalised service but their rooms are clean and their facilities generally quite good.

House Swapping

House swapping has become a popular and affordable way to visit a country and enjoy a real home away from home. There are several agencies in Ireland that, for an annual fee, facilitate international swaps. The fee pays for access to a website and a book giving house descriptions, photographs and the owner's details. After that, it's up to you to make arrangements. Use of the family car is sometimes included.

Homelink International House Exchange (www.homelink.ie)

Intervac International Holiday Service (www.intervac-homeexchange.com)

Rental Accommodation

Self-catering accommodation is often rented on a weekly basis and usually means an apartment or house where you look after yourself. The rates vary from one region and season to another. **Fáilte Ireland** (www.discoverireland.ie) publishes a guide for registered self-catering accommodation; you can check listings at their website.

Business Hours

Hours in both the Republic and Northern Ireland are roughly the same. Throughout this book we don't list opening and closing hours unless they differ significantly from those listed here:

Banks 10am to 4pm Monday to Friday (to 5pm Thursday)

Offices 9am to 5pm Monday to Friday

Post offices Northern Ireland 9am to 5.30pm Monday to Friday, 9am to 12.30pm Saturday; Republic 9am to 6pm Monday to Friday, 9am to 1pm Saturday. Smaller post offices may close at lunch and one day per week.

Pubs Northern Ireland 11.30am to 11pm Monday to Saturday, 12.30pm to 10pm Sunday. Pubs with late licences open until 1am Monday to Saturday, and midnight Sunday; Republic 10.30am to 11.30pm Monday to Thursday, 10.30am to 12.30am Friday and Saturday, noon to 11pm Sunday (30 minutes 'drinking up' time allowed). Pubs with bar extensions open to 2.30am Thursday to Saturday. All pubs close Christmas Day and Good Friday.

Restaurants Noon to 10.30pm; many close one day of the week.

Shops 9am to 5.30pm or 6pm Monday to Saturday (until 8pm on Thursday & sometimes Friday), noon to 6pm Sunday (in bigger towns only). Shops in rural towns may close at lunch and one day per week.

Tourist offices 9am to 5pm Monday to Friday, 9am to 1pm Saturday. Many extend their hours in summer, and open fewer hours/days or close from October to April.

Climate

Belfast

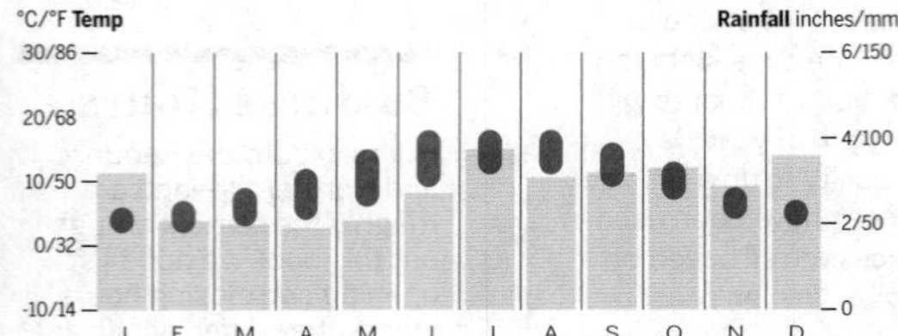

Dublin

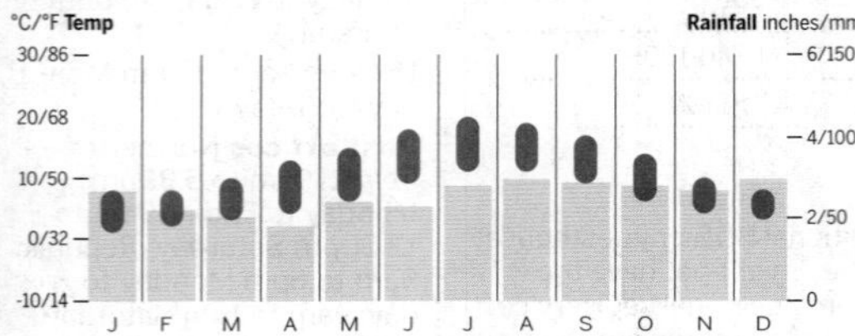

Galway

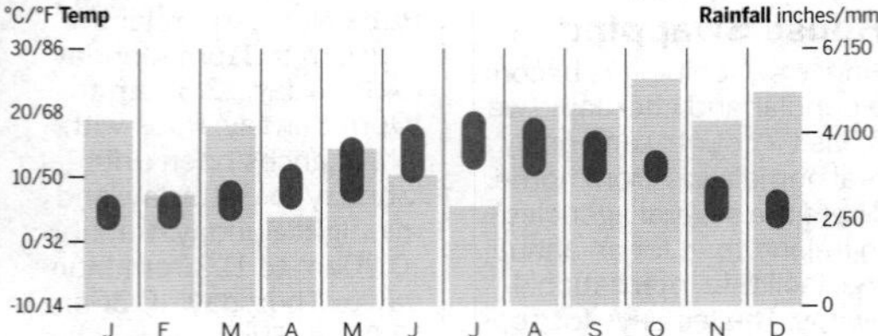

Children

» Children are not allowed in pubs after 7pm.

» Car seats (around €50/£30 per week) are mandatory in hire cars for children aged nine months to four years.

» Baby-changing facilities can be found only in larger cities, and then only in large shopping centres.

For further general information see Lonely Planet's *Travel with Children*. Also check out the following:

www.eumom.ie For pregnant women and parents with young children.

www.babygoes2.com Travel site with family-friendly accommodation worldwide.

Customs Regulations

Both the Republic of Ireland and Northern Ireland have a two-tier customs system: one for goods bought duty-free outside the European Union (EU); the other for goods bought in another EU country where tax and duty is paid. There is technically no limit to the amount of goods transportable within the EU, but customs will use certain guidelines to distinguish personal use from commercial purpose. Allowances are as follows:

Duty free For duty-free goods from outside the EU, limits include 200 cigarettes, 1L of spirits or 2L of wine, 60ml of perfume and 250ml of eau de toilette.

Tax and duty paid Amounts that officially constitute personal use include 3200 cigarettes (or 400 cigarillos, 200 cigars or 3kg of tobacco) and either 10L of spirits, 20L of fortified wine, 60L of sparkling wine, 90L of still wine or 110L of beer.

Cats & Dogs

Cats and dogs from anywhere outside Ireland and the UK are subject to strict quarantine laws. The EU Pet Travel Scheme, whereby animals are fitted with a micro chip, vaccinated against rabies and blood-tested six months *prior* to entry, is in force in the UK and the Republic of Ireland. No preparation or documentation is necessary for the movement of pets directly between the UK and the Republic. Contact the **Department of Agriculture, Food & Rural Development** (☎01-607 2000; www.agriculture.gov.ie) in Dublin for further details.

Electricity

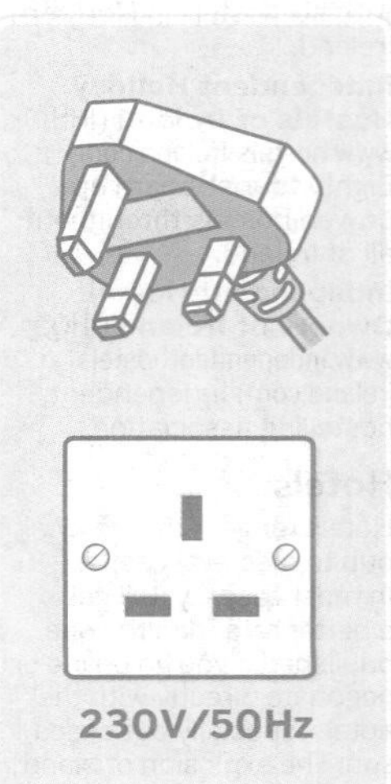

Embassies & Consulates

This is a selection of embassies in Dublin and consular offices in Belfast. For a complete list of embassies, see the website of the **Department of Foreign Affairs** (www.dfa.ie), which also lists Ireland's diplomatic missions overseas.

Australia (☎01-664 5300; www.ireland.embassy.gov.au; 7th fl, Fitzwilton House, Wilton Tce, Dublin 2)

Canada (☎01-234 4000; www.canada.ie; 7-8 Wilton Tce, Dublin 2)

France (☎01-277 5000; www.ambafrance.ie; 36 Ailesbury Rd, Dublin 4)

Germany (embassy ☎01-269 3011; www.dublin.diplo.de; 31 Trimleston Ave, Booterstown, Blackrock, Co Dublin; consulate ☎028-9024 4113; Chamber of Commerce House, 22 Great Victoria St, Belfast)

Italy (☎01-660 1744; www.ambdublin.esteri.it; 63-65 Northumberland Rd, Ballsbridge, Dublin 4)

Netherlands (embassy ☎01-269 3444; www.netherlandsembassy.ie; 160 Merrion Rd, Ballsbridge, Dublin 4; consulate ☎028-9077 9088; c/o All-Route Shipping Ltd, 14-16 West Bank Rd, Belfast)

UK ☎01-205 3700; www.britishembassy.ie; 29 Merrion Rd, Ballsbridge, Dublin 4)

USA (embassy ☎01-668 8777; www.usembassy.ie; 42 Elgin Rd, Ballsbridge, Dublin 4; consulate ☎028-9038 6100; Danesfort House, 223 Stranmillis Rd, Belfast)

Food

Our cafe and restaurant listings appear in order of price, with the cheapest appearing first. We've used the following price ranges: budget (under €10/£10), midrange (€10 to €20/£10 to £20) and top end (above €20/£20). Please note that our hierarchies of favourite places aren't written in stone (as authors, we can crave caviar on a Monday and cod and chips on a Friday).

For explanations of peculiarities of Irish menus and further reading on Irish food and drink, see the At the Irish Table chapter (p41).

Gay & Lesbian Travellers

Ireland is a pretty tolerant place for gays and lesbians. Bigger cities like Dublin, Galway and Cork have a well-established gay scene, as does Belfast and Derry in Northern Ireland. That said, you'll still find pockets of homophobia throughout the island, particularly in smaller towns and rural areas. Resources include the following:

Gaire (www.gaire.com) Message board and info for a host of gay-related issues.

Gay & Lesbian Youth Northern Ireland (www.glyni.org.uk)

Gay Men's Health Project (☎01-660 2189; www.hse.ie) Practical advice on men's health issues.

National Lesbian & Gay Federation (NLGF; ☎01-671 9076; www.nlgf.ie) Publishes the monthly *Gay Community News* (www.gcn.ie).

Northern Ireland Gay Rights Association (Nigra; ☎9066 5257)

Outhouse (☎01-873 4932; www.outhouse.ie; 105 Capel St, Dublin) A gay, lesbian and transgender community centre.

Health

No jabs are required to travel to Ireland. Excellent health care is readily available. For minor, self-limiting illnesses, pharmacists can give valuable advice and sell over-the-counter medication. They can also advise when more specialised help is required and point you in the right direction.

EU citizens equipped with a European Health Insurance Card (EHIC), available from health centres or, in the UK, post offices, will be covered for most medical care – but not non-emergencies or emergency repatriation. While other countries, such as Australia, also have reciprocal agreements with Ireland and Britain, many do not.

In Northern Ireland, everyone receives free emergency treatment at accident and emergency (A&E) departments of state-run NHS hospitals, irrespective of nationality.

Insurance

Insurance is important: it covers you for everything from medical expenses and luggage loss to cancellations or delays in your travel arrangements, depending on your policy.

While EU citizens have most medical care covered with a EHIC card, an additional insurance policy for all other issues is recommended.

Worldwide travel insurance is available at www.lonelyplanet.com/travel_services. You can buy, extend and claim online at any time – even if you're already on the road.

All cars on public roads must be insured. If you are bringing your own vehicle, check that your insurance will cover you in Ireland.

Internet Access

With the advent of 3G and wi-fi networks, internet cafes are increasingly disappearing from Irish towns. The ones that are left generally charge up to €6/£5 per hour.

If you'll be using your laptop or mobile device to get online, most hotels and an increasing number of B&Bs, hostels, bars and restaurants offer wi-fi access, charging anything from nothing to €5/£5 per hour.

Otherwise, most hotels and hostels in larger towns and cities have internet access via a desktop for customer use.

Legal Matters

Illegal drugs are widely available, especially in clubs. The possession of small quantities of marijuana attracts a fine or warning, but harder drugs are treated more seriously. Public drunkenness is illegal but commonplace – the police will usually ignore it unless you're causing trouble.

Contact the following for assistance:

Legal Aid Board (☎066-947 1000; www.legalaidboard.ie) Has a network of local law centres.

Northern Ireland Legal Services Commission (www.nilsc.org.uk)

Maps

Michelin's 1:400,000-scale Ireland map (No 923) is a decent single sheet map, with clear cartography and most of the island's scenic roads marked. The four maps – North, South, East and West – that make up the Ordnance Survey Holiday map series at 1:250,000 scale are useful if you want more detail. Collins also publishes a range of maps covering Ireland.

The Ordnance Survey Discovery series covers the whole island in 89 maps at a scale of 1:50,000.

These are all available at the **National Map Centre** (☎01-476 0471; www.mapcentre.ie; 34 Aungier St, Dublin), through www.osi.ie and many bookshops around Ireland.

Money

The currency in the Republic of Ireland is the euro (€); Northern Ireland uses the pound sterling (£). Although notes issued by Northern Irish banks are legal tender throughout the UK, many businesses outside of Northern Ireland refuse to accept them and you'll have to swap them in British banks.

ATMs

Usually called 'cash machines', ATMs are easy to find in cities and all but the smallest of towns. Watch out for ATMs that have been tampered with; card-reader scams ('skimming') have become a real problem.

Credit & Debit Cards

Visa and MasterCard credit and debit cards are widely accepted in Ireland. American Express is only accepted by the major chains, and very few places accept Diners or JCB. Smaller businesses, like pubs or some B&Bs, prefer debit cards (and will charge a fee for credit cards). Nearly all credit and debit cards use the chip-and-PIN system: if your card isn't PIN enabled you should be able to sign in the usual way, but an increasing number of businesses will not accept your card.

Taxes & Refunds

Non-EU residents can claim Value Added Tax (VAT – a sales tax, 21% of the purchase price of luxury goods except for books, children's clothing or educational items) back on their pur chases so long as the store operates either the Cashback or Taxback refund program (they should display a sticker). You'll get a voucher with your purchase that must be stamped at the *last point of exit* from the EU. If you're travelling on to Britain or mainland Europe from Ireland, hold on to your voucher until you pass through your final customs stop in the EU; it can then be stamped and you can post it back for a refund of duty paid.

VAT in Northern Ireland is 20%; shops participating in the Tax-Free Shopping refund scheme will give you a form or invoice on request to be presented to customs when you leave. After customs have certified the form, it will be returned to the shop for a refund and the cheque sent to you at home.

Tipping

You're not obliged to tip if the service or food was unsatisfactory (even if it's been automatically added to your bill as a 'service charge').

Hotels Only for bellhops who carry luggage, then €1/£1 per bag

Pubs Not expected unless table service is provided, then €1/£1 for a round of drinks

Restaurants 10% for decent service, up to 15% in more expensive places

Taxis 10% or rounded up to the nearest euro/pound

Toilet attendants €0.50/50p

Travellers Cheques

Safer than cash but hardly ever used: travellers cheques have become increasingly rare as credit/debit cards have become the method of choice. They are rarely accepted for purchases so for cash you'll still have to go to a bank or a change bureau.

Photography

The following are some useful tips for taking decent-quality pics in Ireland:

» Natural light can be very dull, so use higher ISO speeds than usual, such as 400 for daylight shots.

» In Northern Ireland, get permission before talking photos of fortified police stations, army posts or other military or quasi-military paraphernalia.

» Don't take photos of people in Protestant or Catholic strongholds of West Belfast without permission; always ask and be prepared to accept a refusal.

Public Holidays

Public holidays can cause road chaos as everyone tries to get somewhere else for the break. It's wise to book accommodation in advance around these times.

The following are public holidays in both the Republic and Northern Ireland:

New Year's Day 1 January

St Patrick's Day 17 March

Easter (Good Friday to Easter Monday inclusive) March/April

May Holiday 1st Monday in May

Christmas Day 25 December

St Stephen's Day (Boxing Day) 26 December

St Patrick's Day and St Stephen's Day holidays are taken on the following Monday when they fall on a weekend. In the Republic, nearly everywhere closes on Good Friday even though it isn't an official public holiday. In the North, most shops open on Good Friday but close the following Tuesday.

Northern Ireland

Spring Bank Holiday Last Monday in May

Orangeman's Day 12 July

August Holiday Last Monday in August

Republic

June Holiday 1st Monday in June

August Holiday 1st Monday in August

October Holiday Last Monday in October

Safe Travel

Ireland is safer than most countries in Europe, but normal precautions should be observed.

Northern Ireland is as safe as anywhere else, but there are areas where the sectarian divide is bitterly pronounced, most notably in parts of Belfast. It's probably best to ensure your visit to Northern Ireland doesn't coincide with the climax of the Orange marching season on 12 July; sectarian passions are usually inflamed and even many Northerners leave the province at this time.

Telephone

In this book, area codes and individual numbers in the Republic are listed together, separated by a hyphen. Area codes in the Republic have three digits and begin with a 0, eg ☎021 for Cork, ☎091 for Galway and ☎061 for Limerick. The only exception is Dublin, which has a two-digit code (☎01). Always use the area code if calling from a mobile phone, but you don't need it if calling from a fixed-line number within the area code.

In Northern Ireland, the area code for all fixed-line numbers is ☎028, but you only need to use it if calling from a mobile phone or from outside Northern Ireland. We haven't included the area code for numbers in the Northern Ireland chapter of this book. To call Northern Ireland from the Republic, use ☎048 instead of ☎028, without the international dialling code.

Other codes:

» ☎1550 or ☎1580 – premium rate

» ☎1890 or ☎1850 – local or shared rate

» ☎0818 – calls at local rate, wherever you're dialling from within the Republic

» ☎1800 – free calls

Free call and lo-call numbers are not accessible from outside the Republic. Other tips:

» Prices are lower during evenings after 6pm and weekends.

» If you can find a public phone that works, local calls in the Republic cost €0.30 for around three minutes (around €0.60 to a mobile), regardless of when you call. From Northern Ireland local calls cost about 40p, or 60p to a mobile, although this varies somewhat.

» Pre-paid phonecards can be purchased at both news agencies and post offices, and work from all payphones for both domestic and international calls.

Directory Enquiries

For directory enquiries, a number of agencies compete for your business.

» In the Republic, dial ☎11811 or ☎11850; for international enquiries it's ☎11818.

» In the North, call ☎118 118, ☎118 192, ☎118 500 or ☎118 811.

» Expect to pay at least €1/£1 from a landline and up to €2/£2 from a mobile phone.

International Calls

To call out from Ireland dial ☎00, then the country code (☎1 for USA, ☎61 Australia etc), the area code (you usually drop the initial zero) then the number. Ireland's international dialling code is ☎353.

Mobile Phone

» Ireland uses the GSM 900/1800 cellular phone system, which is compatible with European and Australian, but not North American or Japanese, phones.

» SMS ('texting') is a national obsession – most people under 25 communic8 mostly by txt (jst w@ wl d en lang l%k lk n d fucha f dis S hw we tlk 2day?)

» Pay-as-you-go mobile phone packages with any of the main providers start at around €40 and usually include a basic handset and credit of around €10.

» SIM-only packages are also available, but make sure your phone is compatible with the local provider.

Time

In winter, Ireland is on Greenwich Mean Time (GMT), also known as Universal Time Coordinated (UTC), the same as Britain. In summer, the clock shifts to GMT plus one hour, so when it's noon in Dublin and London, it's 4am in Los Angeles and Vancouver, 7am in New York and Toronto, 1pm in Paris, 7pm in Singapore, and 9pm in Sydney.

Tourist Information

In both the Republic and the North there's a tourist office in almost every big town; most can offer a variety of services including accommodation and attraction reservations, currency-changing services, map and guidebook sales and free publications.

In the Republic, the tourism purview falls to **Fáilte Ireland** (Republic ✆1850 230 330, the UK 0800 039 7000; www.discoverireland.ie). It also has six regional offices:

Cork & Kerry (✆021-425 5100; Cork Kerry Tourism, Áras Discover, Grand Pde, Cork)

Dublin (✆01-605 7700; www.visitdublin.com; Dublin Tourism Centre, St Andrew's Church, 2 Suffolk St, Dublin)

East Coast & Midlands (✆044-934 8761; East Coast & Midlands Tourism, Dublin Rd, Mullingar) For Kildare, Laois, Longford, Louth, Meath, North Offaly, Westmeath and Wicklow.

Ireland North West & Lakelands (✆071-916 1201; Temple St, Sligo) For Cavan, Donegal, Leitrim, Monaghan and Sligo.

Ireland West (✆091-537 700; Ireland West Tourism, Áras Fáilte, Forster St, Galway) For Galway, Roscommon and Mayo.

Shannon Region (✆061-361 555; Shannon Development, Shannon, Clare) For Clare, Limerick, North Tipperary and South Offaly.

South East (✆051-875 823; South East Tourism, 41 The Quay, Waterford) For Carlow, Kilkenny, South Tipperary, Waterford and Wexford.

In Northern Ireland, it's the **Northern Irish Tourist Board** (NITB; head office ✆028-9023 1221; www.discovernorthernireland.com). Outside Ireland, Fáilte Ireland and the NITB unite under the banner Tourism Ireland. More information about offices around the world can be found at the international website, www.discoverireland.com.

Travellers with Disabilities

All new buildings have wheelchair access, and many hotels have installed lifts, ramps and other facilities. Others, especially B&Bs, have not adapted as successfully so you'll have far less choice. Fáilte Ireland and NITB's accommodation guides indicate which places are wheelchair accessible.

In big cities, most buses have low-floor access and priority space on board, but the number of kneeling buses on regional routes is still relatively small.

Trains are accessible with help. In theory, if you call ahead, an employee of Iarnród Éireann (Irish Rail) will arrange to accompany you to the train. Newer trains have audio and visual information systems for visually impaired and hearing-impaired passengers.

The **Citizens' Information Board** (✆01-605 9000; www.citizensinformationboard.ie) in the Republic and **Disability Action** (✆028-9066 1252; www.disabilityaction.org) in Northern Ireland can give some advice to travellers with disabilities. Travellers to Northern Ireland can also check out the website www.allgohere.com.

Visas

If you're a European Economic Area (EEA) national, you don't need a visa to visit (or work in) either the Republic or Northern Ireland. Citizens of Australia, Canada, New Zealand, South Africa and the US can visit the Republic for up to three months and Northern Ireland for up to six months. They are not allowed to work unless sponsored by an employer.

Full visa requirements for visiting the Republic are available online at www.dfa.ie; for Northern Ireland's visa requirements see www.ukvisas.gov.uk.

To stay longer in the Republic, contact the local *garda* (police) station or the **Garda National Immigration Bureau** (✆01-666 9100; www.garda.ie; 13-14 Burgh Quay, Dublin). To stay longer in Northern Ireland, contact the **Home Office** (UK Border Agency; ✆0870-606 7766; www.ukba.homeoffice.gov.uk).

Volunteering

Volunteering opportunities are limited, but there are projects where you can lend a helping hand. Check out www.volunteeringireland.ie for all relevant information, including how to sign up and where to go.

Women Travellers

Ireland should pose no problems for women travellers. Finding contraception is not the problem it once was, although anyone on the pill should bring adequate supplies.

Rape Crisis Network Ireland (☎1800-77 88 88; www.rcni.ie) In the Republic. Runs a 24-hour helpline.

Rape Crisis & Sexual Abuse Centre (☎028-9032 9002; www.rapecrisisni.com) In Northern Ireland. Operates a 24-hour helpline.

Work

EEA citizens are entitled to work legally in the Republic of Ireland and Northern Ireland. Non-EEA citizens with an Irish parent or grandparent are eligible for dual citizenship (and the right to work), although this procedure can be quite lengthy – enquire at an Irish embassy or consulate in your own country.

Full-time US students aged 18 and over can get a four-month work permit for Ireland, plus insurance and support information, through **Work & Travel Ireland** (☎01-602 1788; www.workandtravelireland.org).

Most Commonwealth citizens with a UK-born parent are entitled to work in the North (and the rest of the UK) through the 'Right of Abode'. Most Commonwealth citizens under 31 are eligible for a Working Holidaymaker Visa – valid for two years, allows you to work for a total of 12 months, and must be obtained in advance. Check with the **UK Border Agency** (www.ukba.homeoffice.gov.uk) for more info.

Transport

GETTING THERE & AWAY

Entering the Country

Dublin is the main point of entry for most visitors. In recent years, the growth of no-frills airlines means more routes and cheaper prices between Ireland and other European countries. If arriving in the Republic of Ireland:

» The overwhelming majority of airlines serving Ireland fly into the capital.

» Dublin is home to two seaports that serve as the main points of sea transport with Britain; ferries from France arrive in the southern port of Rosslare.

» Dublin is also the nation's premier rail hub.

> **FARE GO**
>
> Travel costs throughout this book are for single (one-way) adult fares, unless otherwise stated.

For information on visa requirements, see p732. Flights, tours and rail tickets can be booked online at www.lonelyplanet.com/bookings.

Air

Airports

Ireland's main airports:

Cork (ORK; ☎021-431 3131; www.corkairport.com)

Dublin (DUB; ☎01-814 1111; www.dublinairport.com)

Shannon (SNN; ☎061-712 000; www.shannonairport.com)

Other airports in the Republic with scheduled services from Britain:

Donegal (CFN; ☎074-954 8284; www.donegalairport.ie; Carrickfinn)

Kerry (KIR; ☎066-976 4644; www.kerryairport.ie; Farranfore)

Knock (NOC; ☎094-936 8100; www.irelandwestairport.com)

Waterford (WAT; ☎051-875 589; www.flywaterford.com)

Northern Ireland's airports:

Belfast International (BFS; ☎028-9448 4848; www.belfastairport.com) Flights from Britain, Continental Europe and the USA.

Derry (LDY; ☎028-7181 0784; www.cityofderryairport.com)

George Best Belfast City (BHD; ☎028-9093 9093; www.belfastcityairport.com)

Land

Eurolines (www.eurolines.com) has a thrice-daily coach and ferry service from London's Victoria Station to Dublin Busáras. For information on border crossings, see p736.

Sea

The main ferry routes between Ireland and the UK and mainland Europe:

» Belfast to Liverpool (England; 8½ hours)

» Belfast to Stranraer (Scotland; 1¾ hours)

» Cork to Roscoff (France; 14 hours)

» Dublin to Liverpool (England; fast/slow four/8½ hours)

» Dublin & Dun Laoghaire to Holyhead (Wales; fast/slow 1½/three hours)

» Larne to Cairnryan (Scotland; 1½ hours)

» Larne to Fleetwood (England; six hours)

» Rosslare to Cherbourg & Roscoff (France; 20½ hours)

» Rosslare to Fishguard & Pembroke (Wales; 3½ hours)

Competition from budget airlines has forced ferry operators to discount heavily and offer flexible fares, meaning great bargains at quiet times of the day or year. For example, the popular route across the Irish Sea between Dublin and Holyhead can be had for as little as €10 for a foot passenger and €80 for a car plus up to four passengers.

Main operators include the following:

Brittany Ferries (www.brittany-ferries.com)

Irish Ferries (www.irishferries.com)

Ferry Fast Boat Routes

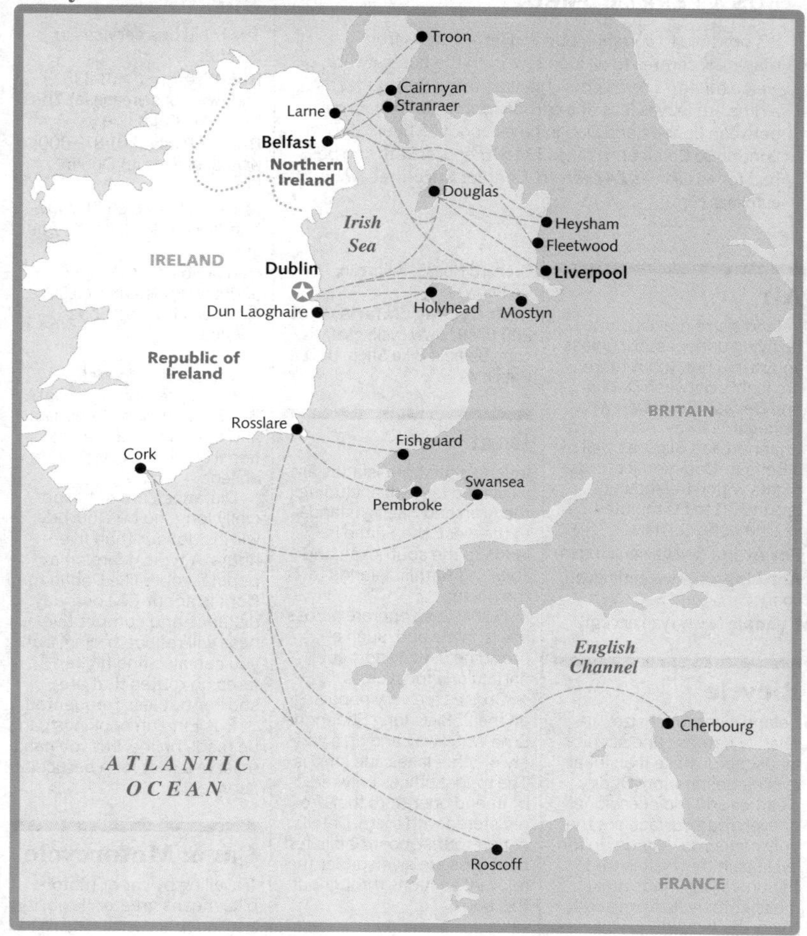

Isle of Man Steam Packet Company/Sea Cat (www.steam-packet.com)

Norfolkline (www.norfolkline.com)

P&O Irish Sea (www.poirishsea.com)

Stena Line (www.stenaline.com)

A very useful online tool is www.ferrybooker.com, a single site covering all sea ferry routes and operators out of the UK (the mainstay of sea travel to Ireland).

GETTING AROUND

The big decision in getting around Ireland is to go by car or use public transportation. Your own car will make the best use of your time and help you reach even the most remote of places via the spidery network of secondary and tertiary roads, but hire and fuel costs can be expensive for budget travellers – while parking hassles and traffic jams in most urban centres affect everyone – so public transport is often the better choice.

The bus network, made up of a mix of public and private operators, is extensive and generally quite competitive – although journey times can be slow. The rail network is quicker but more limited, serving only major towns and cities, and can be quite costly. Both buses and trains get busy during peak times; you'll need to book in advance to be guaranteed a seat.

BUS & FERRY COMBO

It's possible to combine bus and ferry tickets from major UK centres to all Irish towns on the bus network, which mightn't be as convenient as flying on a budget airline but leaves less of a carbon footprint. The journey between London and Dublin takes about 12 hours; the London to Belfast trip takes 13 to 16 hours. Both can be had for as little as £42 return. Contact **Eurolines** (www.eurolines.com).

Air

Ireland's size makes domestic flying unnecessary unless you're in a hurry, but there are flights between Dublin and Belfast, Cork, Derry, Donegal, Galway, Kerry, Shannon and Sligo, as well as a Belfast–Cork service. Most flights within Ireland take around 30 to 50 minutes.

Domestic carriers:

Aer Árann (www.aerarann.com)

Aer Lingus (www.aerlingus.com)

Ryanair (www.ryanair.com)

Bicycle

Ireland's compact size, relative flatness and scenic landscapes make it an ideal cycling destination. Dodgy weather and the occasional uneven road surface are the only concerns. A good tip for cyclists in the west is that the prevailing winds make it easier to cycle from south to north.

Buses will carry bikes, but only if there's room. For trains, bear in mind:

» Intercity trains charge up to €10 per bike.

» Bikes are transported in the passenger compartment.

» Book in advance (www.irishrail.ie), as there's only room for three bikes per service.

Organisations that arrange cycle tours throughout Ireland:

Go Ireland (☎066-976 2094; www.govisitireland.com; Old Orchard House, Killorglin, Co Kerry)

Irish Cycling Safaris (☎01-260 0749; www.cyclingsafaris.com; Belfield Bike Shop, UCD, Dublin 4)

Boat

Ireland's offshore islands are all served by boat, including the Aran and Skellig Islands to the west, the Saltee Islands to the southeast, and Tory and Rathlin Islands to the north.

Ferries also operate across rivers, inlets and loughs, providing useful short cuts, particularly for cyclists.

Cruises are very popular on the 258km-long Shannon–Erne Waterway and on a variety of other lakes and loughs. The tourist offices only recommend operators that are registered with them. Details of non-tourist-board-affiliated boat trips are given under the relevant sections throughout this book.

Border Crossings

Security has been progressively scaled down in Northern Ireland in recent years and all border crossings with the Republic are now open and generally unstaffed. Permanent checkpoints have been removed and ramps levelled. On major routes your only indication that you have crossed the border will be a change in road signs and the colour of number plates and postboxes.

Bus

The main bus services in Ireland:

Bus Éireann (☎01-836 6111; www.buseireann.ie) The Republic's bus line.

Dublin Bus (☎01-872 000; www.dublinbus.ie) Dublin's bus service.

Metro (☎9066 6630; www.translink.co.uk) Belfast's bus service.

Ulsterbus (☎028-9066 6600; www.ulsterbus.co.uk) Northern Ireland's bus service.

Private buses compete – often very favourably – with Bus Éireann in the Republic and also run where the national buses are irregular or absent.

Distances are not especially long: no bus journey will last longer than five hours. A typical fare on a popular route like Dublin to Cork is about €12 one way: distance and competitiveness will reflect pricing, but you can also find higher fares on routes that are shorter but less frequented.

Bus Éireann bookings can be made online, but you can't reserve a seat for a particular service.

Car & Motorcycle

Travelling by car or motorbike means greater flexibility and independence. The road system is extensive, and the constantly growing network of motorways has cut driving times considerably. Downsides include traffic jams, problems with parking in urban centres and the high cost of petrol.

Hire

Compared with many countries (especially the USA), hire rates are expensive in Ireland; you should expect to pay around €250 a week for a small car (unlimited mileage) but rates go up at busy times and drop off in quieter seasons. The main players:

Avis (www.avis.ie)
Budget (www.budget.ie)
Europcar (www.europcar.ie)
Hertz (www.hertz.ie)
Sixt (www.sixt.ie)
Thrifty (www.thrifty.ie)

The major car hire companies have different web pages on their websites for different countries, so the price of a car on the Irish page can differ from the same car's price on the USA or Australia page. You have to surf a lot of sites to get the best deals. **Nova Car Hire** (www.novacarhire.com) acts as an agent for Alamo, Budget, European and National, and offers greatly discounted rates.

Other tips:

» Most cars are manual; automatic cars are available, but they're more expensive to hire.

» If you're travelling from the Republic into Northern Ireland, it's important to be sure that your insurance covers journeys to the North.

» The majority of hire companies won't rent you a car if you're under 23 and haven't had a valid driving licence for at least a year.

» Some companies in the Republic won't rent to you if you're aged 74 or over; there's no upper age limit in the North.

» Motorbikes and mopeds are not available for rent in Ireland.

Parking

All big towns and cities have covered short-stay car parks that are conveniently signposted.

» On-street parking is usually by 'pay and display' tickets available from on-street machines or disc parking (discs, which rotate to display the time you park your car, are available from newsagencies). Costs range from €1.50 to €4.50 per hour; all-day parking in a car park will cost around €24.

» Yellow lines (single or double) along the edge of the road indicate restrictions. Usually you can park on single yellow lines between 7pm and 8am while double yellow lines means no parking at any time. Always look for the nearby sign that spells out when you can and cannot park.

» In Dublin, Cork and Galway, clamping is rigorously enforced: it'll cost you €85 to have the yellow beast removed. In Northern Ireland, the fee is £100 for removal.

Roads & Rules

Motorways (marked by M+number on a blue background) and primary roads (N+number on a green background) are the fastest way to get around and will deliver you quickly from one end of the country to another. Secondary and tertiary roads (marked as R+number) are much more scenic and fun, but they can be very winding and exceedingly narrow – perfect for going slowly and enjoying the views.

» EU licenses are treated like Irish licences.

» Non-EU licences are valid in Ireland for up to 12 months.

» You must carry your driving licence at all times.

» If you plan to bring a car from Europe, it's illegal to drive without at least third-party insurance.

The basic rules of the road:

» Drive on the left; overtake to the right.

» Safety belts must be worn by the driver and all passengers.

» Children aged under 12 aren't allowed to sit in the front passenger seat.

» Motorcyclists and their passengers must wear helmets.

BUS & RAIL PASSES

There are a number of bus- or train-only and bus-and-rail passes worth considering if you plan on doing a lot of travel using public transport:

Emerald Card (Bus & Rail) Eight days' travel out of 15 consecutive days (€218) to 15 days out of 30 (€375) on all national and local services within the Republic and Northern Ireland.

Irish Rambler (Bus) Three days' travel out of eight consecutive days (€53) to 15 days out of 30 (€168) on all Bus Éireann services.

Irish Rover (Bus) Three days' travel out of eight consecutive days (€68) to 15 days out of 30 on all Bus Éireann and Ulster Bus services, as well as local services in Cork, Galway, Limerick, Waterford and Belfast.

Irish Explorer (Bus & Rail) Eight days' travel out of 15 consecutive days (€194) on trains and buses within the Republic.

Irish Explorer (Rail) Five days' travel out of 15 consecutive days (€115.50) on trains in the Republic.

Children aged under 16 pay half-price for all these passes and for all normal tickets. Children aged under three travel for free on public transport. You can buy the above passes at most major train and bus stations in Ireland.

Train Routes

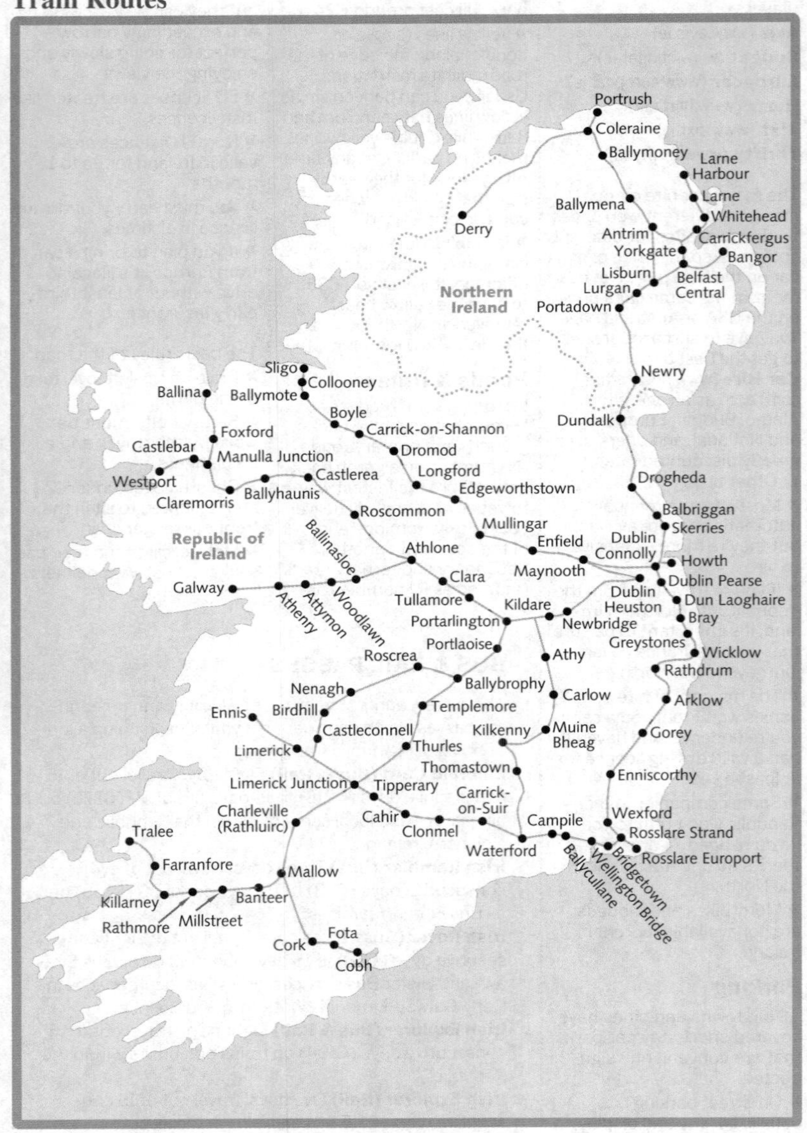

» When entering a roundabout, give way to the right.

» In the Republic, speed-limit and distance signs are in kilometres (although the occasional older white sign shows distances in miles); in the North, speed-limit and distance signs are in miles. Speed limits:

Republic 120km/h on motorways, 100km/h on national roads, 80km/h on regional and local roads, and 50km/h or as signposted in towns.

Northern Ireland 70mph on motorways, 60mph on main roads, 30mph in built-up areas.

Drinking and driving is taken very seriously; in both the Republic and Northern Ireland you're allowed a maximum blood-alcohol level of 80mg/100mL (0.08%) – and campaigners want it reduced to 50mg/100mL.

MOTORING ORGANISATIONS

The two main motoring organisations:

» **Automobile Association** (AA; www.aaireland.ie) Republic (☎in Dublin 01-617 9999, in Cork 021-425 2444, breakdown assistance 1800 667 788); Northern Ireland (☎0870-950 0600, breakdown assistance 0800-667 788)

» **Royal Automobile Club** (RAC; www.rac.ie) Republic (☎1890 483 483); Northern Ireland (☎0800 029 029, breakdown assistance 0800 828 282)

Hitching

Hitching is becoming increasingly less popular in Ireland, even though it's still pretty easy compared to other European countries. Travellers who decide to hitch should understand that they are taking a small but potentially serious risk, and we don't recommend it. If you do plan to travel by thumb, remember it's illegal to hitch on motorways.

Local Transport

Dublin and Belfast have comprehensive local bus networks, as do some other larger towns.

» The Dublin Area Rapid Transport (DART) line runs roughly the length of Dublin's coastline, while the Luas tram system has two popular lines.

» Taxis tend to be expensive. For daytime rates, flagfall is €4.10 and fares start at €1.03 per km after that (night-time rates are a bit higher). More details are available in the relevant sections throughout this book.

Tours

Organised tours are a convenient way of exploring the country's main highlights if your time is limited. Tours can be booked through travel agencies, tourist offices in the major cities, or directly through the tour companies themselves. Some of the most reputable operators:

Bus Éireann (www.buseireann.ie) Runs day tours to various parts of the Republic and the North.

CIE Tours International (www.cietours.ie) Runs four- to 11-day coach tours of the Republic and the North, including accommodation and meals.

Grayline Tours (www.irishcitytours.com) Dublin-based company offering half- and full-day tours of attractions around Dublin as well as the Ring of Kerry.

Paddywagon Tours (www.paddywagontours.com) Activity-filled three- and six-day tours all over Ireland with friendly tour guides. Accommodation is in IHH hostels.

Railtours Ireland (☎01-856 0045; www.railtoursireland.com) For train enthusiasts, organises a series of one- and two-day train trips in association with Iarnród Éireann.

Ulsterbus Tours (www.ulsterbus.co.uk) Runs a large number of day trips throughout the North and the Republic.

Train

Given Ireland's relatively small size, train travel is an expensive luxury. All of the Republic's major towns and cities are on the limited rail network, which is operated by **Iarnród Éireann** (Irish Rail; ☎1850 366 222; www.irishrail.ie) and fans out from Dublin in such a way that connections between destinations not on the same line usually involve an out-of-the-way trip to the capital. There's no north–south route along the western coast, no network in Donegal and no direct connections from Waterford to Cork or Killarney.

Fares are high. A mid-week one-way ticket from Dublin to Cork will cost around €65; the return fare is only marginally more expensive – a feature designed to offer an incentiv for rail travel but making for poor-value one-way fares. The cheapest fares are always online.

Northern Ireland Railways (NIR; ☎028-9089 9411; www.nirailways.co.uk; Belfast Central Station) runs four routes from Belfast: One links with the system in the Republic via Newry to Dublin; the other three go east to Bangor, northeast to Larne and northwest to Derry via Coleraine.

Language

WANT MORE?

For in-depth language information and a witty insight into the quirks of language in Ireland, check out Lonely Planet's *Irish Language & Culture*. You'll find it at **shop .lonelyplanet.com**, or you can buy Lonely Planet's iPhone phrasebooks at the Apple App Store.

Irish (Gaeilge) is the country's official language. In 2003 the government introduced the Official Languages Act, whereby all official documents, street signs and official titles must be either in Irish or in both Irish and English. Despite its official status, Irish is really only spoken in pockets of rural Ireland known as the Gaeltacht, the main ones being Cork *(Corcaigh)*, Donegal *(Dún na nGall)*, Galway *(Gaillimh)*, Kerry *(Ciarraí)* and Mayo *(Maigh Eo)*.

Ask people outside the Gaeltacht if they can speak Irish and nine out of 10 of them will probably reply, *'ah, cupla focal'* (a couple of words), and they generally mean it. Irish is a compulsory subject in schools for those aged six to 15, but Irish classes have traditionally been rather academic and unimaginative, leading many students to resent it as a waste of time. As a result, many adults regret not having a greater grasp of it. In recent times, at long last, a new Irish curriculum has been introduced cutting the hours devoted to the subject but making the lessons more fun, practical and celebratory.

PRONUNCIATION

Irish divides vowels into long (those with an accent) and short (those without) and also disinguishes between broad (**a**, **á**, **o**, **ó**, **u**) and slender (**e**, **é**, **i** and **í**), which can affect the pronunciation of preceding consonants. Other than a few odd-looking clusters, like **mh** and **bhf** (pronounced both as w), consonants are generally pronounced as they are in English.

Irish has three main dialects: Connaught Irish (in Galway and northern Mayo), Munster Irish (in Cork, Kerry and Waterford) and Ulster Irish (in Donegal). The blue pronunciation guidelines given here are an anglicised version of modern standard Irish, which is essentially an amalgam of the three – if you read them as if they were English, you'll be able to get your point across in Gaeilge without even having to think about the specifics of Irish pronunciation or spelling.

BASICS

Hello.	*Dia duit.*	deea gwit
Hello. (reply)	*Dia is Muire duit.*	deeas moyra gwit
Good morning.	*Maidin mhaith.*	mawjin wah
Good night.	*Oíche mhaith.*	eekheh wah
Goodbye.		
(when leaving)	*Slán leat.*	slawn lyat
(when staying)	*Slán agat.*	slawn agut
Yes.	*Tá.*	taw
It is.	*Sea.*	sheh
No.	*Níl.*	neel
It isn't.	*Ní hea.*	nee heh

Signs

Fir	fear	Men
Gardaí	gardee	Police
Leithreas	lehrass	Toilet
Mna	mnaw	Women
Oifig An Phoist	iffig ohn fwisht	Post Office

Thank you (very) much.

Go raibh (míle) maith agat.	goh rev (meela) mah agut

Excuse me.

Gabh mo leithscéal.	gamoh lesh scale

I'm sorry.

Tá brón orm.	taw brohn oruhm

I don't understand.

Ní thuigim.	nee higgim

Do you speak Irish?

An bhfuil Gaeilge agat?	on wil gaylge oguht

What is this?

Cad é seo?	kod ay shoh

What is that?

Cad é sin?	kod ay shin

I'd like to go to ...

Ba mhaith liom dul go dtí ...	baw wah lohm dull go dee ...

I'd like to buy ...

Ba mhaith liom ... a cheannach.	bah wah lohm ... a kyanukh

another/ one more	*ceann eile*	kyawn ella
nice	*go deas*	goh dyass

MAKING CONVERSATION

Welcome.

Ceád míle fáilte. (lit: 100,000 welcomes)	kade meela fawlcha

How are you?

Conas a tá tú?	kunas aw taw too

..., (if you) please.

...más é do thoil é.	... maws ay do hall ay

What's your name?

Cad is ainm duit?	kod is anim dwit

My name is (Sean Frayne).

(Sean Frayne) is ainm dom.	(shawn frain) is anim dohm

DAYS OF THE WEEK

Monday	*Dé Luaín*	day loon
Tuesday	*Dé Máirt*	day maart
Wednesday	*Dé Ceádaoin*	day kaydeen
Thursday	*Déardaoin*	daredeen
Friday	*Dé hAoine*	day heeneh
Saturday	*Dé Sathairn*	day sahern
Sunday	*Dé Domhnaigh*	day downick

CUPLA FOCAL

Here are a few phrases *os Gaeilge* (in Irish) to help you impress the locals:

Tóg é gobogé.
Take it easy.
tohg ay gobogay

Ní féidir é!
Impossible!
nee faydir ay

Ráiméis!
Nonsense!
rawmaysh

Go huafásach!
That's terrible!
guh hoofawsokh

Ní ólfaidh mé go brách arís!
I'm never ever drinking again!
knee ohlhee mey gu brawkh ureeshch

Slainte!
Your health!/Cheers!
slawncha

Táim go maith.
I'm fine.
thawm go mah

Nollaig shona!
Happy Christmas!
nuhlig hona

Cáisc shona!
Happy Easter!
kawshk hona

Go n-éirí an bóthar leat!
Bon voyage!
go nairee on bohhar lat

NUMBERS

1	*haon*	hayin
2	*dó*	doe
3	*trí*	tree
4	*ceathaír*	kahirr
5	*cúig*	kooig
6	*sé*	shay
7	*seacht*	shocked
8	*hocht*	hukt
9	*naoi*	nay
10	*deich*	jeh
11	*haon déag*	hayin jague
12	*dó dhéag*	doe yague
20	*fiche*	feekhe

GLOSSARY

12 July – the day the *Orange Order* marches to celebrate Protestant King William III's victory over the Catholic King James II at the Battle of the Boyne in 1690

An Óige – literally 'the Youth'; Republic of Ireland Youth Hostel Association
An Taisce – National Trust for the Republic of Ireland
Anglo-Norman – Norman, English and Welsh peoples who invaded Ireland in the 12th century
Apprentice Boys – *Loyalist* Loyalist organisation founded in 1814 to commemorate the Great Siege of Derry in August every year
ard – literally 'high'; Irish place name
Ascendancy – refers to the Protestant aristocracy descended from the Anglo-Normans and those who were installed here during the *Plantation*

bailey – outer wall of a castle
bawn – area surrounded by walls outside the main castle, acting as a defence and as a place to keep cattle in times of trouble
beehive hut – see *clochán*
Black & Tans – British recruits to the Royal Irish Constabulary shortly after WWI, noted for their brutality
Blarney Stone – sacred stone perched on top of Blarney Castle; bending over backwards to kiss the stone is said to bestow the gift of gab
bodhrán – hand-held goatskin drum
Bronze Age – earliest metal-using period, around 2500 BC to 300 BC in Ireland; after the Stone Age and before the *Iron Age*
B-Specials – Northern Irish auxiliary police force, disbanded in 1971
bullaun – stone with a depression, probably used as a mortar for grinding medicine or food, often found at monastic sites

caher – circular area enclosed by stone walls
cairn – mound of stones over a prehistoric grave
cashel – stone-walled *ring fort*; see also *ráth*
céilidh – session of traditional music and dancing; also called 'ceili'
Celtic Tiger – nickname of the Irish economy during the growth years from 1990 to about 2002
Celts – *Iron Age* warrior tribes that arrived in Ireland around 300 BC and controlled the country for 1000 years
ceol – music
chancel – eastern end of a church, where the altar is situated, reserved for the clergy and choir
chipper – slang term for fish 'n' chips fast-food restaurant
cill – literally 'church'; Irish place name; also 'kill'
cillín – literally 'little cell'; a hermitage, or sometimes a small, isolated burial ground for unbaptised children and other 'undesirables'
Claddagh ring – ring worn in much of *Connaught* since the mid-18th century, with a crowned heart nestling between two hands; if the heart points towards the hand then the wearer is partnered or married, if towards the fingertip he or she is looking for a mate
clochán – circular stone building, shaped like an old-fashioned beehive, from the early Christian period
Connaught – one of the four ancient provinces of Ireland, made up of Counties Galway, Leitrim, Mayo, Roscommon and Sligo; sometimes spelled 'Connacht'; see also *Leinster, Munster* and *Ulster*
craic – conversation, gossip, fun, good times; also known as 'crack'
crannóg – artificial island made in a lake to provide habitation in a good defensive position
currach – rowing boat made of a framework of laths covered with tarred canvas; also known as 'cúrach'

Dáil – lower house of the parliament of the Republic of Ireland; see also *Oireachtas* and *Seanad*
DART – Dublin Area Rapid Transport train line
demesne – landed property close to a house or castle
diamond – town square
dolmen – tomb chamber or portal tomb made of vertical stones topped by a huge capstone; from around 2000 BC
drumlin – rounded hill formed by retreating glaciers
Dúchas – government department in charge of parks, monuments and gardens in the Republic; formerly known as the Office of Public Works
dún – fort, usually constructed of stone
DUP – Democratic Unionist Party; founded principally by Ian Paisley in 1971 in hard-line opposition to Unionist policies held by the *UUP*

Éire – Irish name for the Republic of Ireland
esker – raised ridge formed by glaciers

Fáilte Ireland – 'Welcome Board'; Irish Tourist Board
Fianna – mythical band of warriors who feature in many tales of ancient Ireland
Fianna Fáil – literally 'Warriors of Ireland'; a major political party in the Republic, originating from the *Sinn Féin* faction opposed to the 1921 treaty with Britain
Fine Gael – literally 'Tribe of the Gael'; a major political party in the Republic, originating from the *Sinn Féin* faction that favoured the 1921 treaty with Britain; formed the first government of independent Ireland
fir – men (singular 'fear'); sign on men's toilets; see also *leithreas* and *mná*

fleadh – festival

GAA – Gaelic Athletic Association; promotes Gaelic football and hurling, among other Irish games

Gaeltacht – Irish-speaking

gallóglí – mercenary soldiers of the 14th to 15th century; anglicised to 'gallowglasses'

garda – Irish Republic police; plural 'gardaí'

ghillie – fishing or hunting guide; also known as 'ghilly'

gort – literally 'field'; Irish place name

hill fort – a hilltop fortified with ramparts and ditches, usually dating from the *Iron Age*

HINI – Hostelling International of Northern Ireland

Hunger, the – colloquial name for the Great Famine of 1845-51

hurling – Irish sport similar to hockey

Iarnród Éireann – Republic of Ireland Railways

INLA – Irish National Liberation Association; formed in 1975 as an *IRA* splinter group; it has maintained a ceasefire since 1998

IRA – Irish Republican Army; the largest Republican paramilitary organisation, founded 80 years ago with the aim to fight for a united Ireland; in 1969 the IRA split into the Official IRA and the Provisional IRA; the Official IRA is no longer active and the PIRA has become the IRA

Iron Age – metal-using period that lasted from the end of the *Bronze Age*, around 300 BC (the arrival of the Celts), to the arrival of Christianity, around the 5th century AD

jarvey – driver of a *jaunting car*

jaunting car – Killarney's traditional horse-drawn transport; see also *jarvey*

knackered – slang for tired or worn out

Leinster – one of the four ancient provinces of Ireland, made up of Counties Carlow, Dublin, Kildare, Kilkenny, Laois, Longford, Louth, Meath, Offaly, West Meath, Wexford and Wicklow; see also *Connaught, Munster* and *Ulster*

leithreas – toilets; see also *mná* and *fir*

leprechaun – mischievous elf or sprite from Irish folklore

lough – lake, or long narrow bay or arm of the sea

Loyalist – person, usually a Northern Irish Protestant, insisting on the continuation of Northern Ireland's links with Britain

Luas – light-rail transit system in Dublin; Irish for 'speed'

marching season – *Orange Order* parades, which take place from Easter and throughout summer to celebrate the victory by Protestant King William III of Orange over Catholic James II in the Battle of the Boyne on 12 July 1690, and the union with Britain

Mesolithic – also known as the Middle Stone Age; time of the first human settlers in Ireland, about 8000 BC to 4000 BC; see also *Neolithic*

midden – refuse heap left by a prehistoric settlement

mná – women; sign on women's toilets; see also *fir* and *leithreas*

motte – early Norman fortification consisting of a raised, flattened mound with a keep on top; when attached to a *bailey* it is known as a motte-and-*bailey* fort, many of which were built in Ireland until the early 13th century

Munster – one of the four ancient provinces of Ireland, made up of Counties Clare, Cork, Kerry, Limerick, Tipperary and Waterford; see also *Connaught, Leinster* and *Ulster*

nationalism – belief in a reunited Ireland

Nationalist – proponent of a united Ireland

Neolithic – also known as the New Stone Age; a period characterised by settled agriculture lasting from around 4000 BC to 2500 BC in Ireland; followed by the *Bronze Age;* see also *Mesolithic*

NIR – Northern Ireland Railways

NITB – Northern Ireland Tourist Board

NNR – National Nature Reserves

North, the – political entity of Northern Ireland, not the northernmost geographic part of Ireland

NUI – National University of Ireland; made up of branches in Dublin, Cork, Galway and Limerick

Ogham stone – a stone etched with Ogham characters, the earliest form of writing in Ireland, with a variety of notched strokes

Oireachtas – Parliament of the Republic of Ireland, consisting of the *Dáil,* the lower house, and the *Seanad,* the upper house

Orange Order – the largest Protestant organisation in Northern Ireland, founded in 1795, with a membership of up to 100,000; name commemorates the victory of King William of Orange in the Battle of the Boyne

óstán – hotel

Palladian – style of architecture developed by Andrea Palladio (1508-80), based on ancient Roman architecture

paramilitaries – armed illegal organisations, either *Loyalist* or *Republican,* usually associated with the use of violence and crime for political and economic gain

partition – division of Ireland in 1921

passage grave – Celtic tomb with a chamber reached by a narrow passage, typically buried in a mound

penal laws – laws passed in the 18th century forbidding Catholics from buying land and holding public office

Plantation – settlement of Protestant immigrants (known as Planters) in Ireland in the 17th century

poitín – illegally brewed whiskey, also spelled 'poteen'

Prod – slang for Northern Irish Protestant

provisionals – Provisional IRA, formed after a break with the official *IRA* (who are now largely inconsequential); named after the provisional government declared in 1916, they have been the main force combating the British army in *the North;* also known as 'provos'

PSNI – Police Service of Northern Ireland

ráth – *ring fort* with earthen banks around a timber wall; see also *cashel*

Real IRA – splinter movement of the *IRA*; opposed to *Sinn Féin's* support of the Good Friday Agreement; responsible for the Omagh bombing in 1998 in which 29 people died; subsequently called a ceasefire but has been responsible for bombs in Britain and other acts of violence

Republic of Ireland – the 26 counties of the South

Republican – supporter of a united Ireland

republicanism – belief in a united Ireland, sometimes referred to as militant nationalism

ring fort – circular habitation area surrounded by banks and ditches, used from the *Bronze Age* right through to the Middle Ages, particularly in the early Christian period

RTE – Radio Telifís Éireann; the national broadcasting service of the Republic of Ireland, with two TV and four radio stations

RUC – Royal Ulster Constabulary, the former name for the armed Police Service of Northern Ireland *(PSNI)*

SDLP – Social Democratic and Labour Party; the largest nationalist party in the Northern Ireland Assembly, instrumental in achieving the Good Friday Agreement; its goal is a united Ireland through nonviolent means; mostly Catholic

Seanad – upper house of the parliament of the Republic of Ireland; see also *Oireachtas* and *Dáil*

shamrock – three-leafed plant said to have been used by St Patrick to illustrate the Holy Trinity

shebeen – from the Irish 'síbín'; illicit drinking place or speakeasy

sheila-na-gig – literally 'Sheila of the teats'; female figure with exaggerated genitalia, carved in stone on the exteriors of some churches and castles; explanations include male clerics warning against the perils of sex to the idea that they represent Celtic war goddesses

Sinn Féin – literally 'We Ourselves'; a *Republican* party with the aim of a united Ireland; seen as the political wing of the *IRA* but it maintains that both organisations are completely separate

slí – hiking trail or way

snug – partitioned-off drinking area in a pub

souterrain – underground chamber usually associated with *ring* and *hill forts;* probably provided a hiding place or escape route in times of trouble and/or storage space for goods

South, the – Republic of Ireland

standing stone – upright stone set in the ground, common across Ireland and dating from a variety of periods; some are burial markers

Taoiseach – Republic of Ireland prime minister

teampall – church

TD – *teachta Dála;* member of the lower house *(Dáil)* of the parliament of the Republic of Ireland

Tinkers – derogatory term used to describe Irish itinerant communities; see also *Travellers*

trá – beach or strand

Travellers – the term used today to describe Ireland's itinerant communities

Treaty – Anglo-Irish Treaty of 1921, which divided Ireland and gave relative independence to the South; cause of the 1922-23 Civil War

tricolour – green, white and orange Irish flag symbolising the hoped-for union of the 'green' Catholic Southern Irish with the 'orange' Protestant Northern Irish

turlough – a small lake that often disappears in dry summers; from the Irish 'turlach'

UDA – Ulster Defence Association; the largest *Loyalist* paramilitary group; it has observed a ceasefire since 1994

uillean pipes – Irish bagpipes with a bellow strapped to the arm; 'uillean' is Irish for 'elbow'

Ulster – one of the four ancient provinces of Ireland; sometimes used to describe the six counties of *the North,* despite the fact that Ulster also includes Counties Cavan, Monaghan and Donegal (all in the Republic); see also *Connaught, Leinster* and *Munster*

Unionist – person who wants to retain Northern Ireland's links with Britain

United Irishmen – organisation founded in 1791 aiming to reduce British power in Ireland; it led a series of unsuccessful risings and invasions

UUP – Ulster Unionist Party; the largest *Unionist* party in Northern Ireland and the majority party in the Assembly; founded in 1905 and led by Unionist hero Edward Carson from 1910 to 1921; from 1921 to 1972 the sole Unionist organisation but is now under threat from the *DUP*

UVF – Ulster Volunteer Force; an illegal *Loyalist* Northern Irish paramilitary organisation

Volunteers – offshoot of the IRB that came to be known as the *IRA*

behind the scenes

SEND US YOUR FEEDBACK

We love to hear from travellers – your comments keep us on our toes and help make our books better. Our well-travelled team reads every word on what you loved or loathed about this book. Although we cannot reply individually to postal submissions, we always guarantee that your feedback goes straight to the appropriate authors, in time for the next edition. Each person who sends us information is thanked in the next edition – and the most useful submissions are rewarded with a free book.

Visit **lonelyplanet.com/contact** to submit your updates and suggestions or to ask for help. Our award-winning website also features inspirational travel stories, news and discussions.

Note: We may edit, reproduce and incorporate your comments in Lonely Planet products such as guidebooks, websites and digital products, so let us know if you don't want your comments reproduced or your name acknowledged. For a copy of our privacy policy visit lonelyplanet.com/privacy.

OUR READERS

Many thanks to the travellers who used the last edition and wrote to us with helpful hints, useful advice and interesting anecdotes:

Eveline Apers, Hilary Benson, Niki Byrne, Sheryl Clough, Rebecca Collett, Alexandre Coninx, James Dara Brady, Vincenza Degni, Chris Drivdahl, Brid Dunne, Beth Elliot, Parzefall Eveline, Alex Farrill, Hans-christian Fath, Jer Foley, Nola Frawley, Soeren Goeckel, Richard Gugelmann, Agnieszka Haremza, Aidan Harney, Kate Hill, Susan Hook, Matthew Howard, Karl Hughes, Theodor Ickler, Linda Jerrom, Miriam Kersten, Séamus Laffan, Patrick Loughman, Carl Maguire, Clare Martin, Trevor Mazzucchelli, Michael McGettrick, Robert McKeown, Norma Midgley, Deborah Murphy, Rita Murphy, Kate O'Brien, Bettina, Joe and Stella O'Connell, Helen O'Sullivan, Michael Phelan, Marie Plisnier, Stella Read, Alana Rosser, Francesco Segoni, Eamonn Stafford, VJ Studley, Teresa Thornhill, Ingrid Thuet, Miguel Viñas, Giovanni Viscardi.

AUTHOR THANKS

Fionn Davenport

Thanks to Glenn, Cat and all at Lonely Planet; to my fellow authors who make me want to visit the places they've written about and to the various tourist authorities, B&B owners, hoteliers and restaurateurs for providing information, sustenance and decent pillows along my travels.

Catherine Le Nevez

Sláinte first and foremost to Julian - I couldn't have done it without you. *Sláinte* too to all the locals, fellow travellers and tourism professionals who provided insights and great craic. A particular shout-out to Micheál in Dingle, Paula in Drogheda, Robert in Cavan and the Killarney crew (you know who you are!). Thanks also to Cliff Wilkinson, Cat Craddock, Glenn van der Knijff, Fionn and the *Ireland* team, and all at Lonely Planet. As ever, *merci encore* to my family.

Etain O'Carroll

Thank you to all the tourist office staff who answered endless questions, in particular Kieran Henderson at Visit Inishowen. Special thanks to Neil Britton for the surfing low down, to Oda, Luan, Sinead, Roisin, Yvonne and Eustelle for all their tips, and to Mark, Osgur and Neven for company on the road. Finally huge thanks to Mrs O for providing a home away from home, putting up with the mess and feeding us all so well.

Ryan Ver Berkmoes

Like a conversation over nothing in particular in an Irish pub, thanks to those who helped me on this book threaten to go on and on and on... But a few: in Galway, Charley Adley was a friend and muse as always (I owe you beers!). Delo Collier demystified the Red Earl and Anna Farrell proved a brilliant seatmate and a bakery specialist. Patrick Burke set the wheels in motion on Inishmor. And Erin did Ardmore and Annah did Murp.

Neil Wilson

Thanks to the Belfast Welcome Centre, to friendly and helpful tourist office staff all over Northern Ireland, and to Tom and Will Kelly and Kevin Hasson (the Bogside Artists).

ACKNOWLEDGMENTS

Climate map data adapted from Peel MC, Finlayson BL & McMahon TA (2007) 'Updated World Map of the Köppen-Geiger Climate Classification', *Hydrology and Earth System Sciences*, 11, 163344.

Illustrations pp66–67, 76–77 and 144–145 by Javier Martinez Zarracina.

Cover photograph: Coastal overview of Classiebawn Castle. Mullaghmore, Gareth McCormack. Image research provided by lonely planetimages.com. Many of the images in this guide are available for licensing from Lonely Planet Images: www.lonelyplanetimages.com.

This Book

This 10th edition of Lonely Planet's Ireland guidebook was researched and written by Fionn Davenport (coordinator), Catherine Le Nevez, Etain O'Carroll, Ryan Ver Berkmoes and Neil Wilson. They also researched and wrote the 9th edition. This guidebook was commissioned in Lonely Planet's Oakland office and produced by the following:

Commissioning Editors Catherine Craddock-Carrillo, Katie O'Connell, Glenn van der Knijff, Clifton Wilkinson

Coordinating Editor Sonya Mithen

Coordinating Cartographer Jennifer Johnston

Coordinating Layout Designer Wendy Wright

Managing Editors Brigitte Ellemor, Tasmin Waby McNaughtan

Managing Cartographer Amanda Sierp

Managing Layout Designer Jane Hart

Assisting Editors Janet Austin, Alice Barker, Kate Daly, Cathryn Game, Paul Harding, Asha Ioculari, Andi Jones, Craig Kilburn, Anne Mulvaney, Fionnuala Twomey, Kate Whitfield, Helen Yeates

Assisting Cartographers Mick Garrett, Karen Grant

Assisting Layout Designers Yvonne Bischofberger, Adrian Blackburn, Carol Jackson

Cover Research Aude Vauconsant

Internal Image Research Rebecca Skinner

Illustrator Javier Martinez Zaracina

Language Content Laura Crawford, Annelies Martens

Thanks to Ryan Evans, Chris Girdler, Trent Paton, Anthony Phelan, Gerard Walker

index

000 Map pages
000 Photo pages

000 Map pages
000 Photo pages

000 Map pages
000 Photo pages

H

000 Map pages
000 Photo pages

000 Map pages
000 Photo pages

000 Map pages
000 Photo pages

T

U

000 Map pages
000 Photo pages

how to use this book

These symbols will help you find the listings you want:

- Sights
- Beaches
- Activities
- Courses
- Tours
- Festivals & Events
- Sleeping
- Eating
- Drinking
- Entertainment
- Shopping
- Information/Transport

These symbols give you the vital information for each listing:

- Telephone Numbers
- Opening Hours
- Parking
- Nonsmoking
- Air-Conditioning
- Internet Access
- Wi-Fi Access
- Swimming Pool
- Vegetarian Selection
- English-Language Menu
- Family-Friendly
- Pet-Friendly
- Bus
- Ferry
- Metro
- Subway
- London Tube
- Tram
- Train

Reviews are organised by author preference.

Look out for these icons:

TOP CHOICE Our author's recommendation

FREE No payment required

A green or sustainable option

Our authors have nominated these places as demonstrating a strong commitment to sustainability – for example by supporting local communities and producers, operating in an environmentally friendly way, or supporting conservation projects.

Map Legend

Sights
- Beach
- Buddhist
- Castle
- Christian
- Hindu
- Islamic
- Jewish
- Monument
- Museum/Gallery
- Ruin
- Winery/Vineyard
- Zoo
- Other Sight

Activities, Courses & Tours
- Diving/Snorkelling
- Canoeing/Kayaking
- Skiing
- Surfing
- Swimming/Pool
- Walking
- Windsurfing
- Other Activity/Course/Tour

Sleeping
- Sleeping
- Camping

Eating
- Eating

Drinking
- Drinking
- Cafe

Entertainment
- Entertainment

Shopping
- Shopping

Information
- Post Office
- Tourist Information

Transport
- Airport
- Border Crossing
- Bus
- Cable Car/Funicular
- Cycling
- Ferry
- Metro
- Monorail
- Parking
- S-Bahn
- Taxi
- Train/Railway
- Tram
- Tube Station
- U-Bahn
- Other Transport

Routes
- Tollway
- Freeway
- Primary
- Secondary
- Tertiary
- Lane
- Unsealed Road
- Plaza/Mall
- Steps
- Tunnel
- Pedestrian Overpass
- Walking Tour
- Walking Tour Detour
- Path

Boundaries
- International
- State/Province
- Disputed
- Regional/Suburb
- Marine Park
- Cliff
- Wall

Population
- Capital (National)
- Capital (State/Province)
- City/Large Town
- Town/Village

Geographic
- Hut/Shelter
- Lighthouse
- Lookout
- Mountain/Volcano
- Oasis
- Park
- Pass
- Picnic Area
- Waterfall

Hydrography
- River/Creek
- Intermittent River
- Swamp/Mangrove
- Reef
- Canal
- Water
- Dry/Salt/Intermittent Lake
- Glacier

Areas
- Beach/Desert
- Cemetery (Christian)
- Cemetery (Other)
- Park/Forest
- Sportsground
- Sight (Building)
- Top Sight (Building)

Ryan Ver Berkmoes

Counties Clare, Galway and Wexford From Galway to Wexford, with plenty of delights in between, Ryan Ver Berkmoes has delighted in the great swath of Ireland. He first visited Galway in 1985 when he remembers a grey place where the locals wandered the muddy tidal flats for fun and frolic. Times have changed! From lost rural pubs to lost memory, he's revelled in a place where his first name brings a smile and his surname brings a 'huh?' Follow him at ryanverberkmoes.com

Read more about Ryan at:
lonelyplanet.com/members/ryanverberkmoes

Neil Wilson

Belfast, Counties Down & Armagh, Derry & Antrim and Fermanagh & Tyrone Neil's first visit to Northern Ireland was in 1994, during the first flush of post-ceasefire optimism, and his interest in the history and politics of the place intensified a few years later when he found out that most of his mum's ancestors were from Ulster. Working on recent editions of the Ireland guidebook has allowed him to witness first hand the progress being made towards a lasting peace, as well as enjoying some excellent hiking and biking in the Ring of Gullion and the Mourne Mountains. Neil is a full-time travel writer based in Edinburgh, Scotland, and has written more than 50 guidebooks for half a dozen publishers.

Read more about Neil at:
lonelyplanet.com/members/neilwilson

OUR STORY

A beat-up old car, a few dollars in the pocket and a sense of adventure. In 1972 that's all Tony and Maureen Wheeler needed for the trip of a lifetime – across Europe and Asia overland to Australia. It took several months, and at the end – broke but inspired – they sat at their kitchen table writing and stapling together their first travel guide, *Across Asia on the Cheap*. Within a week they'd sold 1500 copies. Lonely Planet was born.

Today, Lonely Planet has offices in Melbourne, London and Oakland, with more than 600 staff and writers. We share Tony's belief that 'a great guidebook should do three things: inform, educate and amuse'.

OUR WRITERS

Fionn Davenport

Coordinating author Counties Dublin, Wicklow and Cork Despite its myriad economic problems, Ireland has proven itself to be undaunted, beautiful and just as bloody interesting as it ever was. Fionn suspected as much, but he needed to traipse through his hometown of Dublin and explore the wilds of west Cork to have it confirmed in spades.

Catherine Le Nevez

Counties Kerry, Limerick & Tipperary and Meath, Louth, Cavan & Monaghan Catherine's wanderlust kicked in when she roadtripped across Europe aged four and she's been hitting the road at every opportunity since, completing her Doctorate of Creative Arts in Writing, Masters in Professional Writing, and post-grad qualifications in Editing and Publishing along the way. With Celtic connections including Irish and Breton heritage (and a love of Guinness!), Catherine's travelled throughout every county in the emerald isle, and has covered 20 of them for Lonely Planet, including several editions of this book.

Etain O'Carroll

The Midlands; Counties Mayo & Sligo and Donegal Born and bred in the boggy hinterland of the Irish midlands, Etain made the great escape to become a travel writer and photographer but despite criss-crossing the globe somehow the lure of the old sod never quite went away. She now writes about her homeland for a variety of publications and has worked on several editions of Lonely Planet *Ireland*. Savouring pristine beaches and remote pubs was one of the sheer joys of research for this edition.

Read more about Etain at:
lonelyplanet.com/members/etainocarroll

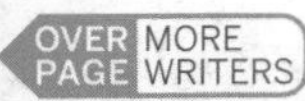

Published by Lonely Planet Publications Pty Ltd
ABN 36 005 607 983
10th edition – Jan 2012
ISBN 978 1 74179 824 1

10 9 8 7 6 5 4 3 2
Printed in China